Mathematics
for GCSE & IGCSE®

Thousands of practice questions and
worked examples covering the new Grade 9-1
GCSE and IGCSE® Maths courses.

Higher Level

Editors:

Rob Harrison, Shaun Harrogate, Paul Jordin, Sarah Oxley, Andy Park, David Ryan, Jonathan Wray

Contributors:

Katharine Brown, Eva Cowlishaw, Alastair Duncombe, Stephen Green, Philip Hale, Phil Harvey,
Judy Hornigold, Claire Jackson, Mark Moody, Charlotte O'Brien, Rosemary Rogers,
Manpreet Sambhi, Neil Saunders, Jan Walker, Kieran Wardell, Jeanette Whiteman

Published by CGP

ISBN: 978 1 78294 437 9

Clipart from Corel®
Printed by Elanders Ltd, Newcastle upon Tyne.

Contents

Geometry and Measures

Throughout the book, the more
challenging questions are marked like this:

Section 1 — Arithmetic, Multiples and Factors

1.1 Calculations

Order of Operations

BODMAS tells you the correct order to carry out mathematical operations.

BRACKETS, **O**THER, **D**IVISION, **M**ULTIPLICATION, **A**DDITION, **S**UBTRACTION

Example 1

Work out: a) $20 - 3 \times 4$ b) $30 \div (15 - 12)$

a) $20 - 3 \times 4 = 20 - 12 = \underline{\mathbf{8}}$

b) $30 \div (15 - 12) = 30 \div 3 = \underline{\mathbf{10}}$

Exercise 1

Answer these questions without using your calculator.

1   Work out the following.

a) $5 + 1 \times 3$	**b)** $11 - 2 \times 5$	**c)** $18 - 10 \div 5$	**d)** $24 \div 4 + 2$
e) $35 \div 5 + 2$	**f)** $36 - 12 \div 4$	**g)** $2 \times (4 + 10)$	**h)** $(7 - 2) \times 3$
i) $4 + (48 \div 8)$	**j)** $56 \div (2 \times 4)$	**k)** $(3 + 2) \times (9 - 4)$	**l)** $(8 - 7) \times (6 + 5)$
m) $2 \times (8 + 4) - 7$	**n)** $5 \times 6 - 8 \div 2$	**o)** $18 \div (9 - 12 \div 4)$	**p)** $100 \div (8 + 3 \times 4)$
q) $7 + (10 - 9 \div 3)$	**r)** $20 - (5 \times 3 + 2)$	**s)** $48 \div 3 - 7 \times 2$	**t)** $36 - (7 + 4 \times 4)$

2   Work out the following.

a) $\dfrac{16}{4 \times (5 - 3)}$	**b)** $\dfrac{8 + 2}{15 \div 3}$	**c)** $\dfrac{4 \times (7 + 5)}{6 + 3 \times 2}$	**d)** $\dfrac{6 + (11 - 8)}{7 - 5}$
e) $\dfrac{12 \div (9 - 5)}{25 \div 5}$	**f)** $\dfrac{8 \times 2 \div 4}{5 - 6 + 7}$	**g)** $\dfrac{3 \times 3}{21 \div (12 - 5)}$	**h)** $\dfrac{36 \div (11 - 2)}{8 - 8 \div 2}$

Negative Numbers

Adding a negative number is the same as subtracting a positive number. So '+' next to '–' means **subtract**.
Subtracting a negative number is the same as adding a positive number. So '–' next to '–' means **add**.

Example 2

Work out: a) $1 - (-4)$ b) $-5 + (-2)$.

a) $1 - (-4) = 1 + 4 = \underline{\mathbf{5}}$

b) $-5 + (-2) = -5 - 2 = \underline{\mathbf{-7}}$

Exercise 2

1   Work out the following without using your calculator.

a) $-4 + 3$	**b)** $-1 - 4$	**c)** $-12 + 15$	**d)** $6 - 17$
e) $4 - (-2)$	**f)** $-6 - (-2)$	**g)** $-5 + (-5)$	**h)** $-5 - (-5)$
i) $-23 - (-35)$	**j)** $48 + (-22)$	**k)** $-27 + (-33)$	**l)** $61 - (-29)$

When you multiply or divide two numbers which have the **same** sign, the answer is **positive**.
When you multiply or divide two numbers which have **opposite** signs, the answer is **negative**.

Example 3

Work out: a) $24 \div (-6)$ b) $(-5) \times (-8)$.

a) $24 \div (-6) = \underline{-4}$ b) $(-5) \times (-8) = \underline{40}$

Exercise 3

Answer these questions without using your calculator.

1 Work out the following.
a) $3 \times (-4)$ b) $(-15) \div (-3)$ c) $12 \div (-4)$ d) $2 \times (-8)$
e) $(-72) \div (-6)$ f) $56 \div (-8)$ g) $(-16) \times (-3)$ h) $(-81) \div (-9)$
i) $(-13) \times (-3)$ j) $7 \times (-6)$ k) $45 \div (-9)$ l) $(-34) \times 2$

2 Work out the following.
a) $[(-3) \times 7] \div (-21)$ b) $[(-24) \div 8] \div 3$ c) $[55 \div (-11)] \times (-9)$ d) $[(-3) \times (-5)] \times (-6)$
e) $[(-63) \div (-9)] \times (-7)$ f) $[35 \div (-7)] \times (-8)$ g) $[(-60) \div 12] \times (-10)$ h) $[(-12) \times 3] \times (-2)$

3 Copy the following calculations and fill in the blanks.
a) $(-3) \times \boxed{} = -6$ b) $(-14) \div \boxed{} = -2$ c) $\boxed{} \times 4 = -16$ d) $\boxed{} \div (-2) = -5$
e) $(-8) \times \boxed{} = -24$ f) $(-18) \div \boxed{} = 3$ g) $\boxed{} \times (-3) = 36$ h) $\boxed{} \div 11 = -7$

Decimals

Example 4

Work out: a) $4.53 + 1.6$ b) $8.5 - 3.07$

1. Set out the sum by lining up the decimal points.
2. Fill in any gaps with 0's.
3. Add or subtract the digits one column at a time.

a)
$$\begin{array}{r} 4.53 \\ + 1.60 \\ \hline 6.13 \end{array}$$

b)
$$\begin{array}{r} 8.\overset{4}{\cancel{5}}\overset{1}{0} \\ - 3.07 \\ \hline 5.43 \end{array}$$

Exercise 4

Answer these questions without using your calculator.

1 Work out the following.
a) $2 + 1.8$ b) $6 - 5.1$ c) $12.74 + 7$ d) $23 - 18.591$
e) $5.1 + 1.8$ f) $6.3 + 5.4$ g) $11.7 - 8.2$ h) $0.8 - 0.03$
i) $10.83 + 7.4$ j) $0.029 + 1.8$ k) $91.7 + 0.492$ l) $6.474 + 0.92$
m) $67.5 - 4.31$ n) $16.3 - 5.16$ o) $9.241 - 2.8$ p) $0.946 - 0.07$

2 Copy the following calculations and fill in the blanks.

a)
$$\begin{array}{r} \boxed{}.6\,\boxed{} \\ + \;0.\boxed{}0 \\ \hline 8.21 \end{array}$$

b)
$$\begin{array}{r} 5.\boxed{}8 \\ + \;\boxed{}.4\,\boxed{} \\ \hline 6.40 \end{array}$$

c)
$$\begin{array}{r} 6.75 \\ + \;\boxed{}.4\,\boxed{} \\ \hline 9.\boxed{}3 \end{array}$$

d)
$$\begin{array}{r} 5.\boxed{}3 \\ - \;2.1\,\boxed{} \\ \hline \boxed{}.31 \end{array}$$

3   Mo travels 2.3 km to the shops, then 4.6 km to town. How far has she travelled in total?

4   Sunita buys a hat for £18.50 and a bag for £31.99. How much does she spend altogether?

5   A block of wood is 4.2 m long. A 2.75 m long piece is cut from it. What length is left?

6   Jay's meal costs £66.49. He uses a £15.25 off voucher. How much does he have left to pay?

Example 5

Work out 0.32 × 0.6

1. Multiply each decimal by a power of 10 to get a whole number multiplication.

2. Multiply the whole numbers.

3. Divide by the product of the powers of 10 you multiplied by in Step 1.

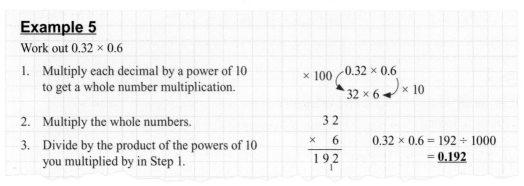

Exercise 5

Answer these questions without using your calculator.

1    $132 \times 238 = 31\,416$. Use this information to work out the following.
   a) 13.2 × 238   **b)** 1.32 × 23.8   **c)** 1.32 × 0.238   **d)** 0.132 × 0.238

2   Work out the following.
   a) 0.92 × 10   **b)** 1.41 × 100   **c)** 72.5 × 1000   **d)** 16.7 × 8
   e) 31.2 × 6   **f)** 68.8 × 3   **g)** 3.1 × 40   **h)** 0.7 × 600
   i) 0.6 × 0.3   **j)** 0.05 × 0.04   **k)** 0.08 × 0.5   **l)** 0.04 × 0.02
   m) 2.1 × 0.6   **n)** 8.1 × 0.5   **o)** 3.6 × 0.3   **p)** 1.6 × 0.04
   q) 0.61 × 0.6   **r)** 5.2 × 0.09   **s)** 6.3 × 2.1   **t)** 1.4 × 2.3
   u) 2.4 × 1.8   **v)** 3.9 × 8.3   **w)** 0.16 × 3.3   **x)** 0.64 × 0.42

3   1 litre is equal to 1.76 pints. What is 5 litres in pints?

4   1 mile is equal to 1.6 km. What is 3.5 miles in km?

5   Petrol costs £1.35 per litre. A car uses 9.2 litres during a journey. How much does this cost?

6   A shop sells apples for £1.18 per kg. How much would it cost to buy 2.5 kg of apples?

Example 6

Work out 0.516 ÷ 0.8

1. Multiply both numbers by 10, so you are dividing by a whole number.

2. Line up the decimal points to set out the calculation, then divide.

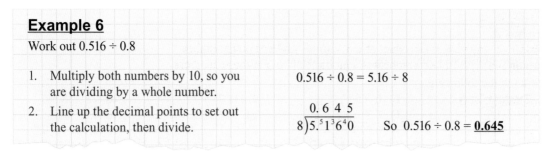

Exercise 6

Answer these questions without using your calculator.

1   Work out the following.
   a) 25.9 ÷ 10   **b)** 8.52 ÷ 4   **c)** 2.14 ÷ 4   **d)** 8.62 ÷ 5
   e) 17.1 ÷ 6   **f)** 0.081 ÷ 9   **g)** 49.35 ÷ 7   **h)** 12.06 ÷ 8

2 Work out the following.

    a) $6.4 \div 0.2$ **b)** $1.56 \div 0.2$ **c)** $0.624 \div 0.3$ **d)** $8.8 \div 0.2$

    e) $3.54 \div 0.4$ **f)** $3.774 \div 0.4$ **g)** $5.75 \div 0.5$ **h)** $0.275 \div 0.5$

    i) $22.56 \div 0.03$ **j)** $16.42 \div 0.02$ **k)** $0.257 \div 0.05$ **l)** $1.08 \div 0.08$

    m) $7.665 \div 0.03$ **n)** $0.039 \div 0.06$ **o)** $7.5 \div 0.05$ **p)** $50.4 \div 0.07$

    q) $0.9 \div 0.03$ **r)** $0.71 \div 0.002$ **s)** $63 \div 0.09$ **t)** $108 \div 0.4$

    u) $1.76 \div 0.008$ **v)** $8.006 \div 0.2$ **w)** $20.16 \div 0.007$ **x)** $1.44 \div 1.2$

3 A school jumble sale raises £412.86. The money is to be split equally between three charities. How much will each charity receive?

4 It costs £35.55 to buy nine identical books. How much does one book cost?

5 A 2.72 m ribbon is cut into equal pieces of length 0.08 m. How many pieces will there be?

6 It costs £6.93 to buy 3.5 kg of pears. How much do pears cost per kg?

Exercise 7 — Mixed Exercise

Answer these questions without using your calculator.

1 At midday the temperature was 6 °C. By midnight, the temperature had decreased by 7 °C. What was the temperature at midnight?

2 Work out: $-4.2 - (1.5 \times -0.3)$

3 Ashkan spends £71.42 at the supermarket. His receipt says that he has saved £11.79 on special offers. How much would he have spent if there had been no special offers?

4 On his first run, Ted sprints 100 m in 15.32 seconds. On his second run, he is 0.47 seconds quicker. How long did he take on his second run?

5 Asha bought 2 CDs each costing £11.95 and 3 CDs each costing £6.59. She paid with a £50 note. How much change did she receive?

6 It costs £31.85 to buy 7 identical DVDs. How much would it cost to buy 3 DVDs?

7 A single pack of salt and vinegar crisps costs 70p. A single pack of cheese and onion crisps costs 65p. A multipack of 3 salt and vinegar and 3 cheese and onion costs £3.19. How much would you save buying a multipack instead of the equivalent amount in individual packs?

1.2 Multiples and Factors

Multiples

A **multiple** of a number is a product of that number and any other number.
A **common multiple** of two numbers is a multiple of both of those numbers.

Example 1

    a) List the multiples of 5 between 23 and 43.

        These are the numbers between 23 and 43   **25, 30, 35, 40**
        that 5 will divide into.

    b) Which of the numbers in the box on the right | 24   7   28   42   35 |
        are common multiples of 2 and 7?

        The multiples of 2 are 24, 28 and 42, while   **28, 42**
        the multiples of 7 are 7, 28, 35 and 42.

Exercise 1

1 List the first five multiples of: **a)** 9 **b)** 13 **c)** 16

2 a) List the multiples of 8 between 10 and 20.
b) List the multiples of 12 between 20 and 100.
c) List the multiples of 14 between 25 and 90.

3 Write down the numbers from the box that are:
a) multiples of 10
b) multiples of 15
c) common multiples of 10 and 15

5	10	15	20	25	30	35
40	45	50	55	60	65	70
75	80	85	90	95	100	105

4 a) List the multiples of 3 between 19 and 35.
b) List the multiples of 4 between 19 and 35.
c) List the common multiples of 3 and 4 between 19 and 35.

5 List all the common multiples of 5 and 6 between 1 and 40.

6 List all the common multiples of 6, 8 and 10 between 1 and 100.

7 List all the common multiples of 9, 12 and 15 between 1 and 100.

8 List the first five common multiples of 3, 6 and 9.

Factors

A number's **factors** divide into it exactly.
A **common factor** of two numbers is a factor of both of those numbers.

Example 2

a) Write down all the factors of: (i) 18 (ii) 16

1. Check if 1, 2, 3... divide into the number.
2. Stop when a factor is repeated.

(i) $18 = 1 \times 18$ $18 = 2 \times 9$ $18 = 3 \times 6$
So the factors of 18 are **1, 2, 3, 6, 9, 18**.

(ii) $16 = 1 \times 16$ $16 = 2 \times 8$ $16 = 4 \times 4$
So the factors of 16 are **1, 2, 4, 8, 16**.

b) Write down the common factors of 18 and 16.

These are the numbers which appear in both lists from part (a).

1, 2

Exercise 2

1 List all the factors of each of the following numbers.

a) 10   **b)** 4   **c)** 13   **d)** 20   **e)** 25
f) 24   **g)** 35   **h)** 32   **i)** 40   **j)** 50
k) 9   **l)** 15   **m)** 36   **n)** 49   **o)** 48

2 a) Which number is a factor of all other numbers?
b) Which two numbers are factors of all even numbers?
c) Which two numbers must be factors of all numbers whose last digit is 5?
d) Which four numbers must be factors of all numbers whose last digit is 0?

3 A baker has 12 identical cakes. In how many different ways can he divide them up into equal packets? List the possibilities.

4 In how many different ways can 100 identical chairs be arranged in rows of equal length? List all the ways the chairs can be arranged.

5 **a)** List all the factors of: **(i)** 15 **(ii)** 21.
 b) Hence list the common factors of 15 and 21.

6 List the common factors of each of the following pairs of numbers.
 a) 15, 20 **b)** 12, 15 **c)** 30, 45 **d)** 50, 90 **e)** 25, 50
 f) 24, 32 **g)** 36, 48 **h)** 64, 80 **i)** 45, 81 **j)** 96, 108

7 List the common factors of each of the following sets of numbers.
 a) 15, 20, 25 **b)** 12, 18, 20 **c)** 30, 45, 50 **d)** 15, 16, 17
 e) 8, 12, 20 **f)** 9, 27, 36 **g)** 24, 48, 96 **h)** 33, 121, 154

1.3 Prime Numbers and Prime Factors

A **prime number** is a number that has no other factors except **itself** and **1**. **1** is **not** a prime number.

Example 1

Which of the numbers in the box on the right are prime?

1. Look for factors of each of the numbers.

2. If there aren't any, it's prime.

$$16 \quad 17 \quad 18 \quad 19 \quad 20$$

$16 = 2 \times 8, \quad 18 = 3 \times 6, \quad 20 = 4 \times 5$

17 has no factors other than 1 and 17.

19 has no factors other than 1 and 19.

So the prime numbers are **17** and **19**.

Exercise 1

1 Consider the following list of numbers: 11, 13, 15, 17, 19
 a) Which number in the list is not prime?
 b) Find two factors greater than 1 that can be multiplied together to give this number.

2 **a)** Which three numbers in the box on the right are not prime?
 b) Find two factors greater than 1 for each of your answers to (a).

$$31 \quad 33 \quad 35 \quad 37 \quad 39$$

3 Write down the prime numbers in this list: 5, 15, 22, 34, 47, 51, 59

4 **a)** Write down all the prime numbers less than 10.
 b) Find all the prime numbers between 20 and 50.

5 **a)** For each of the following, find a factor greater than 1 but less than the number itself.
   (i) 4 **(ii)** 14 **(iii)** 34 **(iv)** 74
 b) Explain why any number with last digit 4 cannot be prime.

6 Without doing any calculations, explain how you can tell that none of the numbers in this list are prime.

$$20 \quad 30 \quad 40 \quad 50 \quad 70 \quad 90 \quad 110 \quad 130$$

Writing a Number as a Product of Prime Factors

Whole numbers which are not prime can be broken down into **prime factors**.

Example 2

Write 12 as the product of prime factors. Give your answer in index form.

Make a factor tree.
1. Find any two factors of 12. Circle any that are prime.
2. Repeat step 1 for any factors which aren't prime.
3. Stop when all the factor tree's branches end in a prime.
4. Give any repeated factors as a power, e.g. $2 \times 2 = 2^2$
   — this is what is meant by index form.

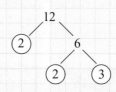

$$12 = 2 \times 2 \times 3 = \underline{2^2 \times 3}$$

Exercise 2

Give your answers to these questions in index form where appropriate.

1 Write each of the following as the product of two prime factors.
   a) 14   b) 33   c) 10   d) 25
   e) 55   f) 15   g) 21   h) 22
   i) 35   j) 39   k) 77   l) 121

2 a) Copy and complete the three factor trees below.

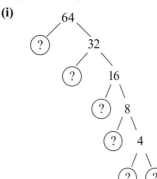 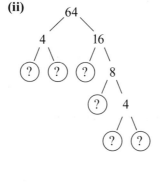 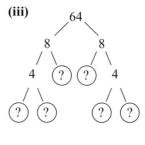

   b) Use each of your factor trees to write down the prime factors of 64. What do you notice?

3 Write each of the following as the product of prime factors.
   a) 6   b) 30   c) 42   d) 66
   e) 70   f) 46   g) 110   h) 78
   i) 190   j) 210   k) 138   l) 255

4 Write each of the following as the product of prime factors.
   a) 8   b) 44   c) 24   d) 16
   e) 48   f) 72   g) 90   h) 18
   i) 50   j) 28   k) 27   l) 60
   m) 98   n) 36   o) 150   p) 132
   q) 168   r) 225   s) 325   t) 1000

5 Square numbers have all their prime factors raised to even powers.
For example, $36 = 2^2 \times 3^2$ and $64 = 2^6$.
  a) Write 75 as a product of prime factors.
  b) What is the smallest number you could multiply 75 by to form a square number?
  Explain your answer.

6 By first writing each of the following as a product of prime factors, find the smallest
integer that you could multiply each number by to give a square number.
  a) 180   **b)** 250   **c)** 416   **d)** 756   **e)** 1215

1.4   LCM and HCF

The **least common multiple (LCM)** of a set of numbers is the smallest of their common multiples.
The **highest common factor (HCF)** of a set of numbers is the largest of their common factors.

Example 1

Find the least common multiple (LCM) of 4, 6 and 8.

1. Find the multiples of 4, 6 and 8.

  Multiples of 4 are: 4, 8, 12, 16, 20, 24, 28...
  Multiples of 6 are: 6, 12, 18, 24, 30, 36...
  Multiples of 8 are: 8, 16, 24, 32, 40, 48...

2. The LCM is the smallest number
  that appears in all three lists.

  So the LCM of 4, 6 and 8 is **24**.

Exercise 1

1 Find the LCM of each of the following pairs of numbers.
  a) 3 and 4   **b)** 3 and 5   **c)** 6 and 8   **d)** 2 and 10
  e) 6 and 7   **f)** 4 and 9   **g)** 10 and 15   **h)** 15 and 20

2 Find the LCM of each of the following sets of numbers.
  a) 3, 6, 8   **b)** 2, 5, 6   **c)** 3, 5, 6
  d) 4, 9, 12   **e)** 5, 7, 10   **f)** 5, 6, 9

3 Laurence and Naima are cycling around a circular course. They leave the start-line at the same time and
need to do 10 laps. It takes Laurence 8 minutes to do one lap and Naima 12 minutes.
  a) After how many minutes does Laurence pass the start-line? Write down all possible answers.
  b) After how many minutes does Naima pass the start-line? Write down all possible answers.
  c) When will they first pass the start-line together?

4 Mike visits Oscar every 4 days, while Narinda visits Oscar every 5 days. If they both visited today, how
many days will it be before they visit on the same day again?

5 A garden centre has between 95 and 205 potted plants. They can be arranged exactly in rows
of 25 and exactly in rows of 30. How many plants are there?

6 There are between 240 and 300 decorated plates hanging on a wall, and the number of plates divides
exactly by both 40 and 70. How many plates are there?

7 Jill divides a pile of sweets into 5 equal piles. Kay then divides the same sweets into 7 equal piles.
What is the smallest number of sweets there could be?

Example 2

Find the highest common factor of 12 and 15.

1. Find the common factors.
2. The HCF is the biggest number that appears in both lists.

The factors of 12 are: ①, 2, ③, 4, 6, 12
The factors of 15 are: ①, ③, 5, 15

So the highest common factor of 12 and 15 is **3**.

Exercise 2

1　**a)** Find the common factors of 12 and 20.
　　b) Hence find the highest common factor (HCF) of 12 and 20.

2　Find the HCF of each of the following pairs of numbers.
　　a) 8 and 12　　　　**b)** 24 and 32　　　　**c)** 18 and 24　　　　**d)** 36 and 60
　　e) 14 and 15　　　　**f)** 12 and 36　　　　**g)** 35 and 42　　　　**h)** 56 and 63

3　Find the HCF of each of the following sets of numbers.
　　a) 6, 8, 16　　　　　　**b)** 12, 15, 18　　　　　　**c)** 24, 30, 36
　　d) 18, 36, 72　　　　　**e)** 36, 48, 60　　　　　**f)** 25, 50, 75

4　Find the largest number that will divide into both 133 and 209.

5　A chef is serving parsnips and carrots onto plates. There are 63 carrots and 91 parsnips to go around.
Each plate must only have either carrots or parsnips — there is no mixing of vegetables.
Each plate must have the same number of vegetables on it.
Each plate must have the greatest possible number of vegetables on it.
　　a) How many plates will contain carrots?
　　b) How many plates will contain parsnips?

6　Kim is dividing counters into equal piles.
She has 207 tangerine counters and 253 gold counters.
Each pile must contain only one of the colours.
What is the least number of piles she can make **in total**?

Example 3

a) Use prime factors to find the HCF of 60 and 72.

1. Write 60 and 72 as products of prime factors.
2. Find the numbers that appear in both lists (including repeats).
3. The HCF is the product of these numbers.

$60 = ② \times ② \times ③ \times 5$

$72 = ② \times ② \times 2 \times ③ \times 3$

Both lists contain $2 \times 2 \times 3$

So HCF $= 2 \times 2 \times 3 = \underline{\mathbf{12}}$

b) Use prime factors to find the LCM of 84 and 98.

1. Write 84 and 98 as products of prime factors, in index form.
2. Find the highest power of each prime factor that appears in either list.
3. The LCM is the product of these numbers.

$84 = ②^2 \times ③ \times 7$

$98 = 2 \times ⑦^2$

So LCM $= 2^2 \times 3 \times 7^2 = \underline{\mathbf{588}}$

Exercise 3

1 a) Write 150 and 250 as products of their prime factors.
   b) Hence find the HCF of 150 and 250.

2 a) Write 120 and 155 as products of their prime factors.
   b) Hence find the HCF of 120 and 155.

3 a) Write 76 and 88 as products of their prime factors.
   b) Hence find the LCM of 76 and 88.

4 a) Write 210 and 700 as products of their prime factors.
   b) Hence find the LCM of 210 and 700.

5 Use prime factors to find **(i)** the HCF and **(ii)** the LCM of each of the following pairs of numbers.
   a) 36 and 48   b) 60 and 75   c) 54 and 96   d) 108 and 144
   e) 200 and 240   f) 168 and 196   g) 210 and 308   h) 150 and 180

6 Use prime factors to find the highest number that will divide into both 93 and 155.

7 Use prime factors to find the lowest number that divides exactly by both 316 and 408.

8 One day, Arran divides his action figures into equal groups of 26.
   The next day, he divides them up into equal groups of 12.
   Use prime factors to find the lowest possible number of action figures he owns.

9 Jess goes swimming once every 21 days. Seamus goes swimming once every 35 days.
   They both went swimming today. Use prime factors to find the number of days it will be
   until they both go swimming on the same day again.

10 Luke changes the ink in his printer every 216 days.
    Alesha changes the ink in her printer every 188 days.
    They both changed the ink in their printers today.
    Use prime factors to find the number of days it will be until they
    each change the ink in their printers on the same day again.

11 a) Write 30, 140 and 210 as products of their prime factors.
    b) Hence find the HCF of 30, 140 and 210.

12 a) Write 121, 280 and 550 as products of their prime factors.
    b) Hence find the LCM of 121, 280 and 550.

13 Use prime factors to find **(i)** the HCF and **(ii)** the LCM of each of the following sets of numbers.
    a) 65, 143 and 231   b) 63, 567 and 1323   c) 175, 245 and 1225   d) 126, 150 and 1029
    e) 104, 338 and 1078   f) 102, 612 and 6545   g) 770, 1540 and 5005   h) 891, 4719 and 2431

14 a) Use prime factors to find a pair of numbers that have HCF = 12 and LCM = 120.
    b) Use prime factors to find a pair of numbers that have HCF = 20 and LCM = 300.

Section 2 — Approximations

2.1 Rounding

Numbers can be approximated (or rounded) to make them easier to work with.
For example, a number like 5468.9 could be rounded:

- to the nearest **whole number** (= 5469)
- to the nearest **ten** (= 5470)
- to the nearest **hundred** (= 5500)
- to the nearest **thousand** (= 5000)

Exercise 1

1. **a)** Round the following to the nearest whole number.

    (i) 9.7   **(ii)** 8.4   **(iii)** 12.2   **(iv)** 45.58   **(v)** 11.04

   b) Round the following to the nearest ten.

    (i) 27   **(ii)** 32   **(iii)** 48.5   **(iv)** 658   **(v)** 187 523

   c) Round the following to the nearest hundred.

    (i) 158   **(ii)** 596   **(iii)** 4714   **(iv)** 2369   **(v)** 12 345

   d) Round the following to the nearest thousand.

    (i) 2536   **(ii)** 8516   **(iii)** 12   **(iv)** 9500   **(v)** 56 985

2. Raj says Italy has an area of 301 225 km². Round this figure to the nearest thousand km².

3. At its closest, Jupiter is about 390 682 810 miles from Earth. Write this distance to the nearest million miles.

Decimal Places

You can also round to different numbers of decimal places.
For example, a number like 8.9471 could be rounded:

- to **one** decimal place (= 8.9)
- to **two** decimal places (= 8.95)
- to **three** decimal places (= 8.947)

Exercise 2

1. Round the following numbers to: **(i)** one decimal place **(ii)** three decimal places.

   a) 2.6893   **b)** 0.0324   **c)** 5.6023   **d)** 0.0425

   e) 6.2571   **f)** 0.35273   **g)** 0.07953   **h)** 0.96734

   i) 0.25471   **j)** 2.43658   **k)** 6.532561   **l)** 0.008723

2. The mass of a field vole is 0.0384 kilograms. Round this mass to two decimal places.

3. The length of a snake is 1.245 metres. Round this length to one decimal place.

Significant Figures

You can also round to different numbers of **significant figures** (s.f.).
The first significant figure is the first **non-zero** digit.

Example 1

a) Round 52 691 to one significant figure.
    The <u>second</u> digit is less than 5, so round down.   a) 5②691 — rounds <u>down</u> to **50 000**

b) Round 6.578 to two significant figures.
    The <u>third</u> digit is more than 5, so round up.   b) 6.5⑦8 — rounds <u>up</u> to **6.6**

c) Round 0.00097151 to three significant figures.
    The <u>fourth</u> significant figure is equal to 5, so round up.   c) 0.000971⑤1 — rounds <u>up</u> to **0.000972**

Exercise 3

1 Round the following numbers to one significant figure.
   a) 476　　　　　b) 31　　　　　c) 7036　　　　　d) 867　　　　　e) 3729
   f) 79 975　　　g) 146 825　　　h) 993　　　　　i) 0.0672　　　j) 0.349
   k) 0.000555　　l) 0.0197　　　m) 0.47892　　　n) 0.000798　　o) 0.11583

2 Round the following numbers to two significant figures.
   a) 741　　　　　b) 6551　　　　c) 7067　　　　　d) 2649　　　　e) 11.806
   f) 674.81　　　g) 136 164　　　h) 974.008　　　i) 0.003753　　j) 0.02644
   k) 0.0001792　l) 0.08735　　　m) 3570.4　　　　n) 0.5635　　　o) 0.0007049

3 Round the following numbers to three significant figures.
   a) 4762　　　　b) 46.874　　　c) 5067　　　　　d) 594.5　　　　e) 35 722
   f) 693 704　　　g) 80.569　　　h) 925 478　　　i) 0.5787　　　j) 0.08521
   k) 0.10653　　　l) 0.00041769　m) 146.83　　　n) 34.726　　　o) 0.0084521

4 The speed of sound is 1236 km/h.
   Round this speed to two significant figures.

5 The diameter of Saturn is 120 536 km.
   Round this diameter to three significant figures.

6 The density of hydrogen gas is 0.0899 kg/m³.
   Round this density to one significant figure.

7 The table shows the mass (in kg) of some mammals. Round each mass to two significant figures.

Mammal	Mass (kg)
Common vole	0.0279
Badger	9.1472
Meerkat	0.7751
Red squirrel	0.1998
Shrew	0.00612
Hare	3.6894

Estimation

Example 2

Estimate the value of $\dfrac{9.7 \times 326}{1.823 \times 5.325}$ by rounding each number to one significant figure.

The symbol '≈' means 'is approximately equal to'.

The actual value is 325.7 (to 4 significant figures), so this is a good approximation.

$$\frac{9.7 \times 326}{1.823 \times 5.325} \approx \frac{10 \times 300}{2 \times 5}$$

$$= \frac{3000}{10} = \underline{300}$$

Exercise 4

1 Estimate each of the following by rounding each number to one significant figure.
   a) 102.2 × 4.2　　　b) 288.7 × 7.8　　　c) 40.73 × 1.06　　　d) 542.04 × 1.88
   e) 306.9 ÷ 6.4　　　f) 3.9 ÷ 5.1　　　　g) 494.27 ÷ 5.05　　　h) 205.52 ÷ 8.44
   i) 361.42 ÷ 78.63　　j) 7.57 × 3.81　　　k) 142.75 × 9.56　　　l) 8.31 ÷ 1.86

2 Each of the following questions is followed by three possible answers.
   Use estimation to decide which answer is correct.
   a) 101 × 52 = (5252, 4606, 6304)　　　　　b) 6.4 × 7.35 = (38.24, 47.04, 55.64)
   c) 22.4 × 49.8 = (1865.32, 1494.72, 1115.52)　d) 0.79 × 1594.3 = (1259.50, 864.80, 679.57)
   e) 12.76 ÷ 4.2 = (1.29, 6.542, 3.04)　　　　f) 588 ÷ 12.4 = (75.78, 47.42, 69.86)
   g) 0.94 ÷ 3.68 = (0.124, 0.901, 0.255)　　　h) 675.89 ÷ 7.074 = (95.55, 85.74, 112.34)

3 Estimate each of the following by rounding each number to one significant figure.
   a) $\dfrac{9.9 \times 285}{18.7 \times 3.2}$　　　b) $\dfrac{64.4 \times 5.6}{17 \times 9.5}$　　　c) $\dfrac{174.3 \times 3.45}{162.8 \times 10.63}$　　　d) $\dfrac{310.33 \times 2.68}{316.39 \times 0.82}$
   e) $\dfrac{13.7 \times 5.2}{12.3 \div 3.9}$　　　f) $\dfrac{432.4 \times 2.75}{233.39 \times 0.81}$　　　g) $\dfrac{173.64 \times 10.6}{64.44 \div 5.58}$　　　h) $\dfrac{176.65 \div 8.84}{564.36 \div 2.78}$

Example 3

Estimate the value of $\sqrt{61}$ to 1 d.p.

1.	Find the closest square number on either side of the number in the question.	61 is between 49 (= 7^2) and 64 (= 8^2).
2.	Decide which it's closest to, then make a sensible estimate of the digit after the decimal point.	61 is much closer to 64, so a sensible estimate is $\sqrt{61} \approx$ **7.8**.

Exercise 5

1 Estimate the following roots to the nearest whole number.

    a) $\sqrt{18}$ **b)** $\sqrt{67}$ **c)** $\sqrt{51}$ **d)** $\sqrt{86}$ **e)** $\sqrt{116}$

2 Estimate the following roots to 1 decimal place.

    a) $\sqrt{11}$ **b)** $\sqrt{30}$ **c)** $\sqrt{20}$ **d)** $\sqrt{37}$ **e)** $\sqrt{45}$

2.2 — Upper and Lower Bounds

Upper and lower bounds show the maximum and minimum actual values that a rounded number can be.

Example 1

A length is given as 12 m, when rounded to the nearest metre. State its upper and lower bounds.

The smallest number that would round up to 12 m is 11.5 m.   Lower bound = **11.5 m**

The largest number that would round down to 12 is 12.49999999... so, by convention, we say that the upper bound is 12.5   Upper bound = **12.5 m**

Exercise 1

1 The following figures have been rounded to the nearest whole number. State their lower and upper bounds.

    a) 10   **b)** 15   **c)** 34   **d)** 26   **e)** 76

    f) 102   **g)** 99   **h)** 999   **i)** 249   **j)** 2500

2 Give the lower and upper bounds of the following measurements.

    a) 645 kg (measured to the nearest kg)   **b)** 255 litres (measured to the nearest litre)

    c) 165 g (measured to the nearest g)   **d)** 800 g (measured to the nearest 100 g)

    e) 155 cm (measured to the nearest cm)   **f)** 130 km (measured to the nearest km)

3 State the lower and upper bounds of the following prices.

    a) £15 (when rounded to the nearest £1)   **b)** £320 (when rounded to the nearest £10)

    c) £76.70 (when rounded to the nearest 10p)   **d)** £600 (to the nearest £50)

Example 2

Find the maximum and minimum perimeter of a rectangular garden measuring 38 m by 20 m to the nearest metre.

1.	The upper bounds of the dimensions of the garden are 38.5 m and 20.5 m so use these to calculate the maximum possible perimeter.	(2 × 38.5) + (2 × 20.5) = 77 + 41 = 118 m Maximum perimeter = **118 m**
2.	The lower bounds of the dimensions of the garden are 37.5 m and 19.5 m so use these to calculate the minimum possible perimeter.	(2 × 37.5) + (2 × 19.5) = 75 + 39 = 114 m Minimum perimeter = **114 m**

Exercise 2

1 Find the maximum and minimum possible perimeter of the following:

   a) A rectangle with sides 5 cm and 6 cm measured to the nearest cm.

   b) A square with sides of 4 m measured to the nearest m.

   c) An equilateral triangle with side length 7 cm measured to the nearest cm.

   d) A parallelogram with sides 8.5 cm and 9.6 cm measured to the nearest mm.

   e) A regular pentagon with sides 12.5 cm measured to the nearest mm.

2 The number of sweets in a jar is 670, to the nearest 10.

   a) What is the maximum possible number of sweets in the jar?

   b) What is the minimum possible number of sweets in the jar?

3 A dressmaker needs to sew a ribbon border onto a rectangular tablecloth. If the tablecloth measures 2.55 m by 3.45 m to the nearest cm, what is the longest length of ribbon that could be needed?

4 Last year Jack was 1.3 m tall, measured to the nearest 10 cm. This year he has grown 5 cm, to the nearest cm. Calculate the tallest height and the shortest height he could actually be this year.

5 A number, when rounded to two decimal places, equals 0.40.
   Write down the smallest possible value of the number.

Example 3

Find the maximum and minimum possible area of a rectangular room that measures 3.8 m by 4.6 m, to the nearest 10 cm. Give your answer to two decimal places.

1. The maximum possible area is 3.85 m × 4.65 m.   3.85 m × 4.65 m = 17.9025 m²
                                                                    = **17.90 m²** (to 2 d.p.)

2. The minimum possible area is 3.75 m × 4.55 m.   3.75 m × 4.55 m = 17.0625 m²
                                                                    = **17.06 m²** (to 2 d.p.)

Exercise 3

1 Mr McGregor wants to build a fence around his garden, leaving a 2 m gap for the gate.
   The garden is a rectangle measuring 12 m by 15 m.
   All measurements are given to the nearest metre.

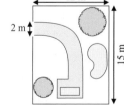

   a) (i) Give the minimum width of the gate.

   (ii) Give the maximum length and width of the garden.

   (iii) Hence find the maximum amount of fencing needed to fence the side of the garden with the gate on it.

   (iv) Calculate the maximum total length of fencing needed to fence the garden.

   b) By finding the maximum width of the gate and the minimum dimensions of the garden, calculate the minimum total length of fencing needed.

2 Ian is fitting skirting board to a room measuring 4.5 m by 3.7 m with a door that is 0.5 m wide. If all measurements are to the nearest 10 cm, calculate the maximum and minimum possible length of skirting board that will be needed.

3 Calculate the maximum and minimum possible volumes for a storage unit that measures 4.00 m by 3.00 m by 1.90 m to the nearest cm.

4 Find the maximum and minimum possible values of the following.

   a) The area of a rectangle with sides given as 5 cm and 6 cm, measured to the nearest cm.

   b) The volume of a cube with sides given as 6 cm, measured to the nearest cm.

   c) The volume of a cuboid with sides given as 3.5 cm, 4.4 cm and 5.6 cm, measured to the nearest mm, rounding your answer to 2 d.p.

5 Michael ran for a measured time of 10 seconds at 6.5 m/s. If his time was measured to the nearest second, calculate the maximum possible distance that he could have run.

6 Kelly ran a 1500 m race in 260 s. The time was measured to the nearest second and the distance to the nearest 10 metres. Calculate the maximum and minimum possible values of her speed in m/s.

7 A snail travels a distance of 5 m in 45 minutes. If the distance is measured to the nearest cm and the time to the nearest minute, what is the maximum possible speed of the snail in cm/s?

8 Max wants to paint a wall that measures 2.1 m by 5.2 m. A tin of paint states that it will cover 3.5 m². If the tin contains exactly 0.5 litres of paint, and all other measurements are correct to 1 d.p., find the maximum volume of paint needed to paint the wall.

Representing Bounds Using Intervals

Bounds can be written as an **interval** or **inequality**.
They can also be used to show the maximum and minimum values of **truncated** numbers.

Example 4
Truncate the following values to 2 d.p.   a) 17.65342   b) 203.0496923
Delete any decimal places after 2 d.p.   a) **17.65**   b) **203.04**

Exercise 4

1 Truncate the following values to 1 decimal place.
   a) 1.354   **b)** 19.133   **c)** 55.73   **d)** 103.67183   **e)** 85.955

2 Truncate the following values to 2 decimal places.
   a) 2738.29109   **b)** 1.24692   **c)** 3.38204   **d)** 17.160   **e)** 100.0984

Example 5
The approximate mass of a rock is 18.4 kg.
Find the interval within which m, the actual mass of the rock, lies if:

a) the mass has been rounded to 1 decimal place.
   The lower bound is 18.35 kg, and the upper bound is 18.45 kg. The actual value must be strictly less than 18.45 kg, or it would round to 18.5 kg.   **18.35 kg $\leq m <$ 18.45 kg**

b) the mass has been truncated to 1 decimal place.
   The lower bound is 18.4 kg, and the upper bound is 18.5 kg. The actual value must be strictly less than 18.5 kg, or it would truncate to 18.5 kg.   **18.4 kg $\leq m <$ 18.5 kg**

Exercise 5

1 Given that the following values have been rounded to 1 d.p., write down an inequality for each to show the range of possible actual values.
   a) $m = 7.6$ **b)** $n = 15.2$ **c)** $p = 37.1$ **d)** $q = 109.9$ **e)** $r = 70.0$

2 Given that the following values have been truncated to 2 d.p., write down an inequality for each to show the range of possible actual values.
   a) $s = 6.57$ **b)** $t = 25.71$ **c)** $u = 33.47$ **d)** $v = 99.99$ **e)** $w = 51.00$

3 Alasdair is canoeing down a river and says that he has travelled 10 km to the nearest 100 m. Write down the interval within which the actual distance in km, d, lies. Give your answer as an inequality.

4 Given that $x = 3.2$ to 1 d.p. and $y = 8.34$ to 2 d.p., find the interval that contains the actual value of $2x + y$. Give your answer as an inequality.

Section 3 — Fractions

3.1 Equivalent Fractions

Equivalent fractions are fractions that are equal in value.

To find an equivalent fraction, multiply or divide the numerator (the top number) and denominator (the bottom number) by the **same thing**.

Example 1

Find the value of b if $\frac{12}{30} = \frac{4}{b}$.

1. Find what you need to divide by to get from one numerator to the other.

2. Divide the denominator by the same number.

$$\overset{\div 3}{\overset{\frown}{\frac{12}{30}}} = \frac{4}{b}$$

$$\underset{\div 3}{\underset{\smile}{\frac{12}{30}}} = \frac{4}{10} \qquad \text{So } \boldsymbol{b = 10}.$$

Exercise 1

Answer Questions 1-2 without using a calculator.

1 Find the values of the letters in the following fractions.

a) $\frac{1}{5} = \frac{a}{10}$

b) $\frac{1}{4} = \frac{b}{12}$

c) $\frac{3}{4} = \frac{c}{16}$

d) $\frac{1}{20} = \frac{d}{60}$

e) $\frac{1}{5} = \frac{5}{e}$

f) $\frac{1}{6} = \frac{3}{f}$

g) $\frac{7}{12} = \frac{35}{g}$

h) $\frac{9}{10} = \frac{81}{h}$

i) $\frac{1}{a} = \frac{5}{15}$

j) $\frac{3}{b} = \frac{12}{20}$

k) $\frac{c}{3} = \frac{10}{15}$

l) $\frac{d}{14} = \frac{9}{42}$

m) $\frac{e}{9} = \frac{15}{27}$

n) $\frac{f}{51} = \frac{9}{17}$

o) $\frac{11}{g} = \frac{55}{80}$

p) $\frac{1}{h} = \frac{11}{121}$

2 Sharon and Dev both take a test. Sharon gets $\frac{4}{6}$ of the questions right and Dev gets $\frac{37}{42}$ of the questions right. Who gets the most questions right?

Simplifying Fractions

Simplifying a fraction means writing an equivalent fraction using the **smallest** possible numbers. This is also known as 'expressing a fraction in its **lowest terms**'.

Example 2

Express $\frac{24}{30}$ as a fraction in its lowest terms.

1. Divide the numerator and denominator by any common factor.

2. Repeat this until the numerator and denominator have no more common factors.

3. 4 and 5 have no common factors, so this fraction is in its lowest terms.

$$\overset{\div 3}{\overset{\frown}{\frac{24}{30}}} = \underset{\div 3}{\underset{\smile}{\frac{8}{10}}}$$

$$\overset{\div 2}{\overset{\frown}{\frac{8}{10}}} = \underset{\div 2}{\underset{\smile}{\frac{4}{5}}}$$

Exercise 2

Answer Questions 1-2 without using a calculator.

1 Write the following fractions in their lowest terms.

a) $\dfrac{9}{45}$
b) $\dfrac{15}{36}$
c) $\dfrac{15}{20}$
d) $\dfrac{12}{15}$
e) $\dfrac{21}{35}$

f) $\dfrac{24}{64}$
g) $\dfrac{72}{162}$
h) $\dfrac{45}{165}$
i) $\dfrac{36}{126}$
j) $\dfrac{70}{182}$

2 Simplify these fractions, then state which fraction is not equivalent to the other two.

a) $\dfrac{6}{18}, \dfrac{5}{20}, \dfrac{9}{27}$
b) $\dfrac{6}{8}, \dfrac{9}{15}, \dfrac{15}{25}$
c) $\dfrac{4}{18}, \dfrac{6}{33}, \dfrac{10}{45}$
d) $\dfrac{18}{24}, \dfrac{60}{80}, \dfrac{24}{40}$

3 Simplify each of these fractions. Use a calculator where necessary.

a) $\dfrac{91}{130}$
b) $\dfrac{175}{230}$
c) $\dfrac{204}{348}$
d) $\dfrac{1029}{3486}$

3.2 Mixed Numbers

A **mixed number** is a whole number combined with a fraction. $\Rightarrow 2\frac{1}{2}$

A fraction where the numerator is bigger than the denominator is an **improper** fraction. $\Rightarrow \frac{5}{2}$

Example 1

Write the mixed number $4\frac{3}{5}$ as an improper fraction.

1. Find the fraction which is equivalent to 4 and which has 5 as the denominator. Remember, $4 = \frac{4}{1}$.

2. Combine the two fractions into one improper fraction.

$$\overset{\times 5}{\frac{4}{1} = \frac{20}{5}}$$
$$\underset{\times 5}{}$$

So $4\frac{3}{5} = \frac{20}{5} + \frac{3}{5} = \frac{23}{5}$

Exercise 1

Answer Questions 1-2 without using the fractions button on your calculator.

1 Find the values of the letters to write the following mixed numbers as improper fractions.

a) $1\frac{1}{3} = \dfrac{a}{3}$
b) $1\frac{2}{7} = \dfrac{b}{7}$
c) $2\frac{1}{2} = \dfrac{c}{2}$
d) $3\frac{4}{7} = \dfrac{d}{7}$

2 Write the following mixed numbers as improper fractions.

a) $1\frac{4}{5}$
b) $1\frac{5}{12}$
c) $2\frac{9}{10}$
d) $5\frac{3}{10}$

e) $4\frac{3}{4}$
f) $9\frac{5}{6}$
g) $12\frac{2}{5}$
h) $15\frac{5}{7}$

i) $6\frac{5}{6}$
j) $3\frac{1}{9}$
k) $10\frac{3}{10}$
l) $7\frac{2}{3}$

Example 2

Write $\frac{13}{5}$ as a mixed number in its simplest terms.

1. Split the numerator into:
    (i) a multiple of the denominator,
    plus (ii) a 'remainder' (since $13 \div 5 = 2$, with <u>remainder 3</u>).

2. Separate the fraction to write it as a mixed number.

$$\frac{13}{5} = \frac{10 + 3}{5}$$
$$= \frac{10}{5} + \frac{3}{5}$$
$$= 2 + \frac{3}{5} = 2\frac{3}{5}$$

Exercise 2

Answer Questions 1-4 without using your calculator.

1 Write the following improper fractions as mixed numbers.

a) $\frac{5}{3}$ b) $\frac{9}{5}$ c) $\frac{17}{10}$ d) $\frac{12}{7}$ e) $\frac{13}{11}$

f) $\frac{9}{4}$ g) $\frac{13}{6}$ h) $\frac{16}{5}$ i) $\frac{20}{9}$ j) $\frac{11}{3}$

2 a) Simplify the improper fraction $\frac{26}{4}$.

   b) Use your answer to write $\frac{26}{4}$ as a mixed number.

3 Write the following improper fractions as mixed numbers in their lowest terms.

a) $\frac{18}{12}$ b) $\frac{10}{4}$ c) $\frac{50}{15}$ d) $\frac{18}{4}$ e) $\frac{24}{18}$

f) $\frac{35}{25}$ g) $\frac{18}{8}$ h) $\frac{51}{12}$ i) $\frac{34}{6}$ j) $\frac{98}{8}$

4 Find the number in each list that is not equivalent to the other two.

a) $\frac{6}{4}$, $\frac{5}{2}$, $1\frac{1}{2}$ b) $2\frac{1}{3}$, $3\frac{1}{2}$, $\frac{7}{3}$ c) $\frac{19}{4}$, $\frac{15}{4}$, $4\frac{3}{4}$ d) $2\frac{2}{3}$, $\frac{11}{3}$, $\frac{16}{6}$

3.3   Ordering Fractions

Putting two or more fractions over a **common denominator** means rewriting them so they all have the same denominator.

If fractions have a common denominator, then you can use their **numerators** to put them in order.

Example 1

Rewrite $\frac{5}{6}$ and $\frac{3}{8}$ so they have a common denominator.

24 is a multiple of both 6 and 8, so use this as the common denominator.

$$\frac{5}{6} = \frac{20}{24} \qquad \frac{3}{8} = \frac{9}{24}$$

These fractions are equivalent to $\frac{20}{24}$ and $\frac{9}{24}$.

Exercise 1

Answer Questions 1-2 without using a calculator.

1 Rewrite the following pairs of fractions so they have a common denominator.

a) $\frac{2}{9}, \frac{1}{3}$

b) $\frac{2}{3}, \frac{3}{4}$

c) $\frac{5}{6}, \frac{1}{7}$

d) $\frac{2}{9}, \frac{1}{2}$

e) $\frac{3}{8}, \frac{4}{5}$

f) $\frac{5}{6}, \frac{7}{12}$

g) $\frac{7}{8}, \frac{3}{10}$

h) $\frac{2}{5}, \frac{4}{9}$

2 Rewrite the following groups of fractions so they have a common denominator.

a) $\frac{3}{4}, \frac{5}{8}, \frac{7}{12}$

b) $\frac{1}{5}, \frac{7}{10}, \frac{9}{20}$

c) $\frac{1}{7}, \frac{4}{21}, \frac{5}{14}$

d) $\frac{1}{2}, \frac{3}{8}, \frac{2}{3}$

e) $\frac{2}{5}, \frac{5}{12}, \frac{11}{30}$

f) $\frac{1}{8}, \frac{7}{20}, \frac{3}{5}$

g) $\frac{2}{3}, \frac{5}{7}, \frac{5}{6}$

h) $\frac{5}{18}, \frac{7}{24}, \frac{11}{30}$

Example 2

Put the fractions $\frac{1}{2}, \frac{3}{8}$, and $\frac{3}{4}$ in order, from smallest to largest.

1. Put the fractions over a common denominator first — in this case, 8.

So the fractions are equivalent to $\frac{4}{8}, \frac{3}{8}$ and $\frac{6}{8}$.

2. Use the numerators to put the fractions in order.

In order, these are: $\frac{3}{8}, \frac{4}{8}, \frac{6}{8}$.

3. Write the ordered fractions in their original form.

So in order, the original fractions are $\frac{3}{8}, \frac{1}{2}, \frac{3}{4}$.

Exercise 2

Answer Questions 1-4 without using a calculator.

1 Write down the larger fraction in each pair below.

a) $\frac{1}{4}, \frac{5}{8}$

b) $\frac{3}{5}, \frac{7}{10}$

c) $\frac{4}{7}, \frac{9}{14}$

d) $\frac{11}{18}, \frac{2}{3}$

e) $\frac{5}{6}, \frac{3}{4}$

f) $\frac{2}{3}, \frac{3}{5}$

g) $\frac{2}{3}, \frac{3}{4}$

h) $\frac{7}{10}, \frac{3}{4}$

In Questions 2-4, put each of the sets of fractions in order, from smallest to largest.

2 a) $\frac{1}{2}, \frac{5}{8}, \frac{7}{16}$

b) $\frac{2}{5}, \frac{3}{10}, \frac{7}{20}$

c) $\frac{3}{4}, \frac{7}{12}, \frac{5}{8}$

d) $\frac{5}{6}, \frac{11}{12}, \frac{19}{24}$

3 a) $\frac{4}{9}, \frac{5}{12}, \frac{2}{3}$

b) $\frac{9}{10}, \frac{11}{12}, \frac{4}{5}$

c) $\frac{1}{4}, \frac{3}{11}, \frac{5}{22}$

d) $\frac{7}{9}, \frac{4}{5}, \frac{13}{15}$

e) $\frac{7}{8}, \frac{5}{6}, \frac{13}{16}$

f) $\frac{3}{15}, \frac{7}{27}, \frac{12}{45}$

g) $\frac{5}{16}, \frac{7}{20}, \frac{9}{25}$

h) $\frac{11}{36}, \frac{4}{15}, \frac{9}{24}$

4 Charlene runs $\frac{7}{8}$ of a mile, while Dave runs $\frac{17}{20}$ of a mile. Who runs further?

3.4 Adding and Subtracting Fractions

You can only add and subtract fractions that have a **common denominator**.

Example 1

A maths exam has 24 questions. $\frac{1}{8}$ of the questions are on number topics, $\frac{1}{3}$ of the questions are on algebra, and the rest are on geometry.

What fraction of the questions are geometry questions?

1. The fractions of number questions, algebra questions and geometry questions must add up to 1.

   Fraction of geometry questions $= 1 - \frac{1}{8} - \frac{1}{3}$

2. Put the fractions over a common denominator.

   $$1 = \frac{24}{24} \qquad \overset{\times 3}{\underset{\times 3}{\frac{1}{8} = \frac{3}{24}}} \qquad \overset{\times 8}{\underset{\times 8}{\frac{1}{3} = \frac{8}{24}}}$$

3. Subtract to find the fraction of geometry questions.

   Fraction of geometry questions $= \dfrac{24}{24} - \dfrac{3}{24} - \dfrac{8}{24} = \dfrac{24 - 3 - 8}{24}$

   $= \dfrac{13}{24}$

Exercise 1

Answer Questions 1-2 without using your calculator.

1 Work out the following. Give your answers in their simplest form.

a) $\frac{2}{3} - \frac{1}{4}$

b) $\frac{2}{3} + \frac{4}{5}$

c) $\frac{5}{6} + \frac{9}{10}$

d) $\frac{3}{7} + \frac{3}{4}$

e) $\frac{6}{11} + \frac{7}{9}$

f) $\frac{8}{9} + \frac{12}{21}$

g) $\frac{3}{5} + \frac{6}{7}$

h) $\frac{15}{16} + \frac{3}{5}$

2 Work out the following. Give your answers in their simplest form.

a) $\frac{1}{9} + \frac{5}{9} + \frac{11}{18}$

b) $1 - \frac{2}{10} - \frac{2}{8}$

c) $\frac{3}{4} + \frac{1}{8} - \frac{7}{16}$

d) $\frac{6}{7} + \frac{1}{14} - \frac{1}{2}$

e) $\frac{1}{4} + \frac{2}{3} + \frac{5}{6}$

f) $\frac{1}{5} + \frac{1}{3} + \frac{3}{15}$

g) $\frac{9}{10} - \frac{5}{6} + \frac{3}{12}$

h) $1\frac{1}{6} + \frac{5}{7} - \frac{1}{3}$

Exercise 2

1 In a school survey, $\frac{1}{2}$ of the pupils said they walk to school. $\frac{1}{5}$ said they catch the bus. The rest arrive by car. What fraction come to school by car?

2 Jake, Frank and Olga are sharing a cake. Jake eats $\frac{2}{7}$ of the cake, Frank eats $\frac{3}{8}$ and Olga eats the rest. What fraction of the cake does Olga eat?

3 $\frac{1}{6}$ of the flowers in a garden are roses, $\frac{3}{24}$ of the flowers are tulips, $\frac{3}{8}$ are daisies and the rest are daffodils. What fraction of the flowers are daffodils?

4 A bag contains a mixture of sweets. $\frac{2}{9}$ of the sweets are white chocolates, $\frac{1}{12}$ of the sweets are milk chocolates, $\frac{1}{5}$ are toffees and the rest are mints. What fraction of the sweets are mints?

Adding and Subtracting Mixed Numbers

To add or subtract mixed numbers, first change them into **improper fractions** with a **common denominator**.

Example 2

Work out $1\frac{1}{3} + 2\frac{5}{6}$.

1. Write the mixed numbers as improper fractions.

   $1 = \frac{3}{3}$, so $1\frac{1}{3} = \frac{3}{3} + \frac{1}{3} = \frac{4}{3}$

   $2 = \frac{12}{6}$, so $2\frac{5}{6} = \frac{12}{6} + \frac{5}{6} = \frac{17}{6}$

2. Rewrite the improper fractions with a common denominator.

   $$\frac{4}{3} \overset{\times 2}{\underset{\times 2}{=}} \frac{8}{6}$$

3. Add the numerators. Give your answer as a mixed number in its simplest form.

   So $1\frac{1}{3} + 2\frac{5}{6} = \frac{8}{6} + \frac{17}{6} = \frac{25}{6} = \frac{24}{6} + \frac{1}{6} = 4\frac{1}{6}$

Exercise 3

Answer Questions 1-3 without using your calculator.

1 Work out the following. Give your answers in their simplest form.

   a) $2\frac{3}{8} - \frac{3}{4}$ **b)** $4\frac{5}{12} - 2\frac{5}{6}$ **c)** $4\frac{3}{14} - 1\frac{6}{7}$ **d)** $7\frac{5}{9} - 1\frac{11}{18}$

2 Work out the following. Give your answers in their simplest form.

   a) $1\frac{3}{5} + \frac{3}{4}$ **b)** $2\frac{5}{8} + \frac{2}{3}$ **c)** $3\frac{1}{5} + 2\frac{3}{7}$ **d)** $1\frac{1}{6} + 4\frac{7}{15}$

   e) $3\frac{3}{4} - \frac{5}{7}$ **f)** $5\frac{2}{5} - 3\frac{7}{9}$ **g)** $2\frac{1}{4} - 1\frac{6}{7}$ **h)** $2\frac{5}{11} + 3\frac{2}{3}$

   i) $5\frac{7}{12} + 3\frac{2}{5}$ **j)** $4\frac{3}{8} - 1\frac{2}{9}$ **k)** $1\frac{4}{7} + 3\frac{5}{9}$ **l)** $5\frac{3}{20} - 1\frac{7}{12}$

3 The table shows the number of pies eaten by three contestants in a pie eating contest. Calculate the total number of pies eaten.

Contestant	1	2	3
No. of pies eaten	$17\frac{7}{8}$	$9\frac{5}{12}$	$40\frac{5}{18}$

3.5 Multiplying and Dividing Fractions

To multiply a whole number by any fraction:
- **multiply** by the **numerator**
- **divide** by the **denominator**

Example 1

Find $\frac{3}{4}$ of 15.

You can replace 'of' with a multiplication sign.

You need to multiply 15 by 3, and then divide by 4.
(Or you can divide by 4, and then multiply by 3.)

$\frac{3}{4} \times 15 = \frac{3 \times 15}{4} = \frac{45}{4}$

$= 11\frac{1}{4}$

Exercise 1

Answer Questions 1-2 without using your calculator.

1 Work out the following. Write your answers as mixed numbers.

a) $48 \times \frac{2}{7}$ **b)** $27 \times \frac{1}{6}$ **c)** $32 \times \frac{2}{3}$ **d)** $34 \times \frac{4}{5}$

e) $80 \times \frac{2}{9}$ **f)** $45 \times \frac{5}{12}$ **g)** $72 \times \frac{3}{11}$ **h)** $62 \times \frac{5}{8}$

2 Find the following.

a) $\frac{3}{4}$ of 28 **b)** $\frac{2}{9}$ of 32 **c)** $\frac{3}{8}$ of 48 **d)** $\frac{5}{12}$ of 60

e) $\frac{5}{6}$ of 24 **f)** $\frac{4}{5}$ of 15 **g)** $\frac{5}{6}$ of 27 **h)** $\frac{7}{12}$ of 98

Multiplying Fractions

To multiply two or more fractions, multiply the numerators and denominators **separately**.
To multiply **mixed numbers**, change them to improper fractions first.

Example 2

Work out $4\frac{1}{2} \times 3\frac{3}{5}$. Give your answer as a mixed number.

1. Write the mixed numbers as improper fractions. $\quad 4\frac{1}{2} = \frac{8}{2} + \frac{1}{2} = \frac{9}{2} \qquad 3\frac{3}{5} = \frac{15}{5} + \frac{3}{5} = \frac{18}{5}$

2. Multiply the two fractions. $\quad$ So $4\frac{1}{2} \times 3\frac{3}{5} = \frac{9}{2} \times \frac{18}{5} = \frac{9 \times 18}{2 \times 5} = \frac{162}{10}$

3. Simplify your answer and write it as a mixed number. $\quad \frac{162}{10} = \frac{81}{5} = \frac{80}{5} + \frac{1}{5} = \mathbf{16\frac{1}{5}}$

Exercise 2

1 Work out the following. Give your answers in their lowest terms.

a) $\frac{3}{5} \times \frac{1}{6}$ **b)** $\frac{5}{6} \times \frac{2}{15}$ **c)** $\frac{5}{12} \times \frac{3}{4}$ **d)** $\frac{6}{7} \times \frac{7}{8}$ **e)** $\frac{7}{10} \times \frac{5}{14}$

2 Work out the following without using your calculator. Give your answers in their lowest terms.

a) $1\frac{5}{6} \times \frac{2}{3}$ **b)** $3\frac{3}{4} \times \frac{2}{5}$ **c)** $2\frac{1}{7} \times \frac{2}{9}$ **d)** $1\frac{11}{12} \times \frac{1}{4}$

e) $4\frac{3}{5} \times \frac{4}{5}$ **f)** $2\frac{4}{9} \times \frac{3}{8}$ **g)** $2\frac{3}{7} \times 3\frac{1}{6}$ **h)** $3\frac{4}{9} \times 1\frac{7}{8}$

Dividing by Fractions

Swapping the numerator and the denominator of a fraction gives you the **reciprocal** of that fraction.
Dividing by a fraction is the same as **multiplying by its reciprocal**.

Example 3

Work out $2\frac{2}{3} \div 1\frac{1}{5}$.

1. Write both numbers as improper fractions. $\quad 2\frac{2}{3} = \frac{6+2}{3} = \frac{8}{3} \qquad 1\frac{1}{5} = \frac{5+1}{5} = \frac{6}{5}$

2. Multiply $\frac{8}{3}$ by the reciprocal of $\frac{6}{5}$.
   Simplify your answer and write it as a mixed number. $\quad \frac{8}{3} \div \frac{6}{5} = \frac{8}{3} \times \frac{5}{6} = \frac{8 \times 5}{3 \times 6} = \frac{40}{18} = \frac{20}{9} = 2\frac{2}{9}$

Exercise 3

Answer Questions 1-3 without using your calculator.

1 Work out the following. Give your answers in their simplest form.

a) $\frac{3}{4} \div \frac{9}{16}$ b) $\frac{5}{7} \div \frac{11}{14}$ c) $\frac{2}{5} \div 3$ d) $\frac{3}{7} \div 6$

2 By first writing them as improper fractions, find the reciprocal of each of the following.

a) $1\frac{11}{12}$ b) $2\frac{3}{4}$ c) $5\frac{2}{3}$ d) $4\frac{2}{7}$

3 By first writing any mixed numbers as improper fractions, work out the following.

a) $2\frac{1}{2} \div \frac{1}{3}$ b) $1\frac{1}{6} \div \frac{1}{4}$ c) $2\frac{3}{7} \div 3$ d) $4\frac{4}{9} \div 6$

e) $\frac{2}{3} \div 3\frac{2}{5}$ f) $\frac{3}{4} \div 4\frac{1}{7}$ g) $\frac{4}{7} \div 3\frac{4}{9}$ h) $\frac{4}{9} \div 6\frac{1}{10}$

i) $1\frac{1}{4} \div 1\frac{1}{5}$ j) $2\frac{2}{3} \div 1\frac{1}{4}$ k) $4\frac{5}{6} \div 2\frac{1}{3}$ l) $3\frac{2}{3} \div 2\frac{1}{10}$

m) $4\frac{3}{4} \div 1\frac{1}{6}$ n) $6\frac{2}{5} \div 2\frac{3}{10}$ o) $5\frac{1}{7} \div 1\frac{4}{5}$ p) $3\frac{3}{10} \div 2\frac{1}{7}$

3.6 Fractions and Decimals

All fractions can be written as either a **terminating** or **recurring** decimal. In a terminating decimal the digits stop. A recurring decimal has a repeating pattern in its digits which goes on forever.

A recurring decimal is shown using a dot above the first and last repeated digits.

For example, $0.111... = 0.\dot{1}$, $0.151515... = 0.\dot{1}\dot{5}$, $0.12341234... = 0.\dot{1}23\dot{4}$.

Converting Fractions to Decimals Using a Calculator

Use a calculator to convert a fraction to a decimal by **dividing** the numerator by the denominator.

Example 1

Use a calculator to convert the following fractions to decimals.

a) $\frac{1}{6}$ This is a 'recurring decimal' — one that repeats forever. The calculator tells you the answer is 0.1666... Show the repeating digit with a dot.

$\frac{1}{6} = 1 \div 6 = 0.1666... = \underline{\mathbf{0.1\dot{6}}}$

b) $\frac{41}{333}$ The answer on your calculator is 0.123123123... Show the repeating pattern by putting dots over the first and last digits of the repeated group.

$\frac{41}{333} = 41 \div 333$
$= 0.123123123... = \underline{\mathbf{0.\dot{1}2\dot{3}}}$

Exercise 1

1 Use a calculator to convert the following fractions into decimals.

a) $\frac{329}{500}$ b) $\frac{97}{128}$ c) $2\frac{1}{8}$ d) $6\frac{7}{20}$

e) $2\frac{37}{100}$ f) $4\frac{719}{1000}$ g) $7\frac{11}{32}$ h) $8\frac{7}{16}$

2 Use a calculator to convert the following fractions to decimals.

a) $\frac{5}{6}$　　　　b) $\frac{4}{9}$　　　　c) $\frac{67}{111}$　　　　d) $\frac{1111}{9000}$

e) $\frac{4}{15}$　　　　f) $\frac{1234}{9999}$　　　　g) $\frac{88}{3}$　　　　h) $\frac{456}{123}$

3 By first writing these fractions as decimals, put each of the following lists in order, from smallest to largest.

a) $\frac{167}{287}, \frac{87}{160}, \frac{196}{360}$　　　　b) $\frac{96}{99}, \frac{16}{17}, \frac{5}{6}$　　　　c) $\frac{963}{650}, \frac{13}{9}, \frac{77}{52}$

Converting Fractions to Decimals Without Using a Calculator

You can use the following to convert fractions with denominators of **10**, **100** or **1000**.

$$\frac{1}{10} = 0.1, \qquad \frac{1}{100} = 0.01, \qquad \frac{1}{1000} = 0.001$$

Example 2

Write $\frac{123}{300}$ as a decimal.

1. Divide top and bottom to find an equivalent fraction with a denominator of 10.

$$\frac{123}{300} \xrightarrow[\div 3]{\div 3} \frac{41}{100}$$

2. Then rewrite as a decimal.

$$\frac{41}{100} = 41 \times \frac{1}{100} = 41 \times 0.01 = \underline{\mathbf{0.41}}$$

Exercise 2

Answer Questions 1-2 without using your calculator.

1 a) Find the value of a if $\frac{13}{20} = \frac{a}{100}$.

b) Use your answer to write the fraction $\frac{13}{20}$ as a decimal.

2 Write the following fractions as decimals.

a) $\frac{46}{100}$　　　b) $\frac{492}{1000}$　　　c) $\frac{9}{30}$　　　d) $\frac{3}{5}$　　　e) $\frac{17}{50}$

f) $\frac{22}{25}$　　　g) $\frac{43}{50}$　　　h) $\frac{96}{300}$　　　i) $\frac{1}{500}$　　　j) $\frac{33}{250}$

k) $\frac{103}{200}$　　　l) $\frac{306}{3000}$　　　m) $\frac{2}{5}$　　　n) $\frac{12}{25}$　　　o) $\frac{333}{500}$

p) $\frac{24}{50}$　　　q) $\frac{180}{2000}$　　　r) $\frac{31}{50}$　　　s) $\frac{7}{20}$　　　t) $\frac{123}{200}$

You can also divide the numerator by the denominator using **pen and paper** (instead of a calculator).

Example 3

Write $\frac{1}{8}$ as a decimal.

You need to work out $1 \div 8$.

1. 8 doesn't go into 1.
2. 8 goes into 10 once, with remainder 2.
3. 8 goes into 20 twice, with remainder 4.
4. 8 goes into 40 exactly 5 times.

$$\begin{array}{r} 0.1\ 2\ 5 \\ 8\overline{)1.^10^20^40} \end{array}$$

So $\frac{1}{8} = \underline{\mathbf{0.125}}$

3 Write the following fractions as decimals without using your calculator.

a) $\frac{1}{50}$ b) $\frac{1}{40}$ c) $\frac{9}{20}$ d) $\frac{1}{16}$ e) $\frac{7}{8}$

f) $\frac{7}{40}$ g) $\frac{1}{125}$ h) $\frac{13}{80}$ i) $\frac{3}{32}$ j) $\frac{21}{32}$

Example 4

Write $\frac{3}{11}$ as a decimal without using a calculator.

1. Work out $3 \div 11$ using a written method.

2. Eventually the digits of the answer start to repeat. The remainders are repeating as well — 3, 8, 3, 8.

3. Mark the first and last digits of the repeating group.

$$\begin{array}{r} 0.\,2\,7\,2\,7\,2 \\ 11\overline{)3.\,{}^30^80^30^80^30} \end{array}$$

So $\frac{3}{11} = 0.\dot{2}\dot{7}$

Exercise 3

Answer Questions 1-2 without using your calculator.

1 Write the following fractions as recurring decimals.

a) $\frac{4}{9}$ b) $\frac{1}{6}$ c) $\frac{1}{11}$ d) $\frac{2}{3}$

e) $\frac{4}{11}$ f) $\frac{7}{15}$ g) $\frac{5}{6}$ h) $\frac{7}{9}$

i) $\frac{11}{30}$ j) $\frac{28}{45}$ k) $\frac{47}{90}$ l) $\frac{27}{110}$

2 a) Write the following fractions as recurring decimals.

(i) $\frac{1}{7}$ (ii) $\frac{2}{7}$ (iii) $\frac{3}{7}$ (iv) $\frac{4}{7}$ (v) $\frac{5}{7}$

b) What do you notice about the repeating pattern?

c) Use your answers to parts **a)** and **b)** to write down the decimal which is equivalent to $\frac{6}{7}$.

Converting Decimals to Fractions

You can quickly convert a **terminating decimal** to a fraction with a denominator of 10, 100, 1000 or another power of 10.

Example 5

Write 0.025 as a fraction without using your calculator.

The final digit is in the 'thousandths' column — so write this as a fraction with denominator 1000.

$$0.025 = \frac{25}{1000} = \frac{1}{40}$$

You can convert a **recurring decimal** into a fraction too.

Example 6

Convert the recurring decimal 0.171717... into a fraction without using your calculator.

1. Call the recurring decimal r.

$r = 0.171717...$

2. The last digit of the repeating sequence is in the **hundredths** column. So multiply r by 100 to get one whole part of the repeating sequence on the left of the decimal point.

$100r = 0.171717... \times 100 = 17.171717...$

3. Subtract your original number, r.

$100r - r = 17.171717... - 0.171717...$

4. Rearrange the equation to find r as a fraction.

$99r = 17$

So $r = \dfrac{17}{99}$

Exercise 4

Answer the questions in this Exercise without using your calculator.

1 Write each of the following decimals as a fraction in its simplest form.

   a) 0.12   **b)** 0.236   **c)** 0.084   **d)** 0.375   **e)** 0.7654321

2 Write each of the following recurring decimals as a fraction in its simplest form.

   a) 0.181818...   **b)** 0.010101...   **c)** 0.207207207...   **d)** 0.72007200...   **e)** 0.142857142857...

3 Write each of the following recurring decimals as a fraction in its simplest form.

   a) $0.\dot{1}$ **b)** $0.3\dot{4}$ **c)** $0.\dot{8}6\dot{3}$ **d)** $0.07\dot{5}$ **e)** $0.8\dot{7}\dot{2}$

3.7 Fractions Problems

Exercise 1

Answer the questions in this Exercise without using your calculator.

1 Use equivalent fractions to write $\frac{3}{4}$, $\frac{2}{3}$, $\frac{5}{6}$ and $\frac{11}{16}$ in order, from smallest to largest.

2 **a)** Convert the fractions $\frac{39}{100}$, $\frac{7}{20}$, $\frac{8}{25}$ and $\frac{3}{10}$ into decimals.

   b) Put the fractions in order, from smallest to largest.

3 Copy the scale on the right, making sure it's divided into 24 parts. Mark the positions of the following fractions on the scale.

   a) $\frac{1}{3}$ **b)** $\frac{5}{8}$ **c)** $\frac{5}{12}$ **d)** $\frac{5}{6}$

Evaluate the expressions in Questions 4-7.

4 **a)** $\frac{5}{7} + \frac{2}{3}$ **b)** $\frac{3}{8} - \frac{2}{9}$ **c)** $\frac{6}{10} + \frac{3}{6}$ **d)** $\frac{2}{5} - \frac{1}{8}$

5 **a)** $\frac{7}{12} \times \frac{6}{11}$ **b)** $\frac{3}{5} \div \frac{7}{15}$ **c)** $\frac{4}{7} \times \frac{6}{8}$ **d)** $\frac{5}{9} \div \frac{15}{24}$

6 **a)** $2\frac{1}{8} + 3\frac{2}{5}$ **b)** $2\frac{3}{10} - 1\frac{7}{8}$ **c)** $3\frac{2}{5} + 4\frac{1}{4}$ **d)** $4\frac{5}{8} - 2\frac{1}{2}$

7 **a)** $1\frac{1}{6} \times 2\frac{1}{3}$ **b)** $3\frac{3}{4} \div 1\frac{1}{2}$ **c)** $3\frac{1}{2} \times 6\frac{7}{8}$ **d)** $5\frac{1}{2} \div 1\frac{1}{4}$

8 A plank of wood is 20 inches long. Three pieces of length $7\frac{3}{4}$ inches, $5\frac{5}{16}$ inches and $2\frac{1}{8}$ inches are cut from the plank. What length of wood is left over?

9 Work out the following.

a) $\frac{1}{4} \times \frac{2}{3} + \frac{5}{12}$

b) $\frac{7}{30} + \frac{2}{3} \times \frac{4}{5}$

c) $\frac{2}{3} \div \frac{5}{6} - \frac{1}{5}$

d) $\frac{15}{16} - \frac{3}{8} \div \frac{1}{3}$

e) $1\frac{1}{2} + \frac{2}{5} \times \frac{3}{4}$

f) $1\frac{1}{2} \times \frac{2}{5} + \frac{3}{4}$

g) $3\frac{3}{4} - 1\frac{1}{6} \div \frac{3}{8}$

h) $3\frac{3}{4} \div 1\frac{1}{6} - \frac{3}{8}$

10 Which of the fractions $\frac{4}{5}$, $\frac{5}{6}$, $\frac{9}{16}$, $\frac{17}{40}$ and $\frac{2}{9}$ are equivalent to recurring decimals?

11 The length of a rectangle is $3\frac{3}{5}$ cm and the width is $1\frac{5}{8}$ cm.

a) Find the rectangle's perimeter.

b) Find the rectangle's area.

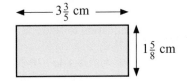

12 Pat's cat eats $\frac{2}{3}$ of a tin of cat food every morning and every evening.

How many tins of cat food will Pat need to buy to feed the cat for a week?

13 It takes Ella $1\frac{1}{4}$ minutes to answer each question on her maths homework.

How many questions can she answer in 20 minutes?

14 Which of the fractions on the right is closest to $\frac{3}{4}$?

$\boxed{\dfrac{11}{15} \quad \dfrac{7}{10} \quad \dfrac{4}{5} \quad \dfrac{5}{6}}$

15 What numbers need to go in the boxes to make the following true?

a) $\frac{2}{5}$ of $100 = \boxed{}$ of 50

b) $\frac{3}{4}$ of $\boxed{} = \frac{2}{3}$ of 90

c) $\frac{1}{4}$ of $64 = \frac{1}{7}$ of $\boxed{}$

16 In Ancient Egypt, fractions were written using sums of unit fractions.
For example, instead of writing $\frac{3}{5}$, Ancient Egyptians would write $\frac{1}{2} + \frac{1}{10}$.

Find the fractions that Ancient Egyptians could have written in the following ways.

a) $\frac{1}{3} + \frac{1}{12}$

b) $\frac{1}{2} + \frac{1}{3} + \frac{1}{7}$

c) $\frac{1}{2} + \frac{1}{5} + \frac{1}{20}$

17 A bag contains a mixture of different coloured counters. $\frac{1}{3}$ of the counters are red, 0.4 of the counters are blue, and the rest are yellow.

a) What fraction of the counters are yellow?

b) If there are 60 counters altogether, work out how many of each colour are in the bag.

18 Show that:

a) $\frac{24}{112}$ is not equivalent to $\frac{3}{8}$.

b) $\frac{1}{5}$ is not one third of $\frac{1}{15}$.

c) $\frac{1}{4}$ is not halfway between $\frac{1}{2}$ and $\frac{1}{5}$.

d) $\frac{8}{9}$ is greater than $0.8\dot{7}$.

19 Put the quantities shown in the boxes below in order, from smallest to largest.

a) $\boxed{\dfrac{8}{16}} \quad \boxed{\dfrac{6}{11}} \quad \boxed{0.5\dot{4}} \quad \boxed{\dfrac{5}{9}}$

b) $\boxed{\dfrac{51}{110}} \quad \boxed{\dfrac{116}{232}} \quad \boxed{0.4\dot{6}} \quad \boxed{\dfrac{8}{15}}$

20 To go on the 'Deathcoaster' ride, you must be at least $1\frac{1}{3}$ m tall. Jess is $1\frac{1}{2}$ m tall. Eric's height is $\frac{8}{9}$ of Jess's height. Xin is $\frac{2}{7}$ m shorter than Jess. Abbas is 1.3 m tall. Which of the friends can go on the ride?

Section 4 — Ratio and Proportion

4.1 Ratios

Simplifying Ratios

Ratios are used to compare quantities. You can **simplify** ratios by dividing the numbers by **common factors**, just like you do with fractions.

Example 1

There are 15 fiction books and 10 non-fiction books on a shelf.
Write down the ratio of fiction books to non-fiction books in its simplest form.

1. Write down the ratio and divide both sides
   by the same number.

2. Stop when you can't divide any further.

$$\div 5 \left(\begin{array}{c} 15 : 10 \\ 3 : 2 \end{array} \right) \div 5$$

The simplest form is **3 : 2**

Exercise 1

1 Write down each of the following ratios in its simplest form.
   a) 2 : 6   **b)** 5 : 15   **c)** 40 : 10   **d)** 4 : 6   **e)** 24 : 6
   f) 20 : 8   **g)** 7 : 28   **h)** 15 : 9   **i)** 16 : 12   **j)** 25 : 3
   k) 48 : 36   **l)** 18 : 72   **m)** 80 : 32   **n)** 150 : 350   **o)** 121 : 33

2 Write down each of the following ratios in its simplest form.
   a) 6 : 2 : 4   **b)** 15 : 12 : 3   **c)** 16 : 24 : 80   **d)** 21 : 49 : 42   **e)** 12 : 32 : 16

3 There are 18 boys in a class of 33 pupils. Find the ratio of boys to girls in its simplest form.

4 Isabel and Sophia share a bag of 42 sweets. Isabel has 16 sweets.
Find the ratio of Sophia's sweets to Isabel's sweets, giving your answer in its simplest form.

Example 2

Write the ratio 1 m : 40 cm in its simplest form.

1. Rewrite the ratio so that the units are the same,
   then remove the units altogether.

2. Simplify as normal.

1 m : 40 cm is the same as 100 cm : 40 cm.

$$\div 20 \left(\begin{array}{c} 100 : 40 \\ 5 : 2 \end{array} \right) \div 20$$

The simplest form is **5 : 2**

Exercise 2

1 Write these ratios in their simplest form.
   a) 10p : £1   **b)** 20 mm : 4 cm   **c)** 10 g : 1 kg   **d)** 2 weeks : 7 days
   e) 40p : £1   **f)** 30 cm : 2 m   **g)** 18 mins : 1 hour   **h)** 6 days : 3 weeks
   i) 1 m : 150 mm   **j)** 6 months : 5 years   **k)** 8 cm : 1.1 m   **l)** 9 g : 0.3 kg
   m) 2.5 hours : 20 mins   **n)** £1.25 : 75p   **o)** 65 m : 1.56 km   **p)** 1.2 kg : 480 g

2 Emma's mass is 54 kg. Her award-winning pumpkin has a mass of 6000 g.
Find the ratio of the pumpkin's mass to Emma's mass. Give your answer in its simplest form.

3 The icing for some cupcakes is made by mixing 1.6 kg of icing sugar with 640 g of butter.
Find the ratio of butter to icing sugar. Give your answer in its simplest form.

Example 3

Nigel makes a smoothie by mixing half a litre of blueberry juice with 100 millilitres
of plain yoghurt. How much yoghurt does he use for every millilitre of juice?

1. Write down the ratio of juice to yoghurt
    and remove the units.

    0.5 l : 100 ml is the same as 500 ml : 100 ml

2. Simplify so that the juice side
    (the left hand side) equals 1.

    $$\div 500 \left(\begin{array}{c} 500:100 \\ 1:0.2 \end{array} \right) \div 500$$

    So he uses **0.2 ml** of yoghurt for 1 ml of juice.

Exercise 3

1 Write down the following ratios in the form $1:n$.

a) 2:6	**b)** 7:35	**c)** 6:24	**d)** 30:120
e) 2:7	**f)** 4:26	**g)** 8:26	**h)** 2:1
i) 10:3	**j)** 6:21	**k)** 8:5	**l)** 5:9

2 Write down each of these ratios in the form $1:n$.

a) 10 mm : 5 cm	**b)** 12p : £6	**c)** 30 mins : 2 hours	**d)** 500 g : 20 kg
e) 90 m : 7.2 km	**f)** 14 cm : 5.6 m	**g)** 50p : £6.25	**h)** 4.5 m : 900 mm

3 Two towns 4.8 km apart are shown on a map 12 cm apart.
Find the ratio of the map distance to the true distance in the form $1:n$.

4 A recipe uses 125 ml of chocolate syrup and 2½ litres of milk.
How much milk does it use for every millilitre of chocolate syrup?

Using Ratios

Example 4

The ratio of men to women in an office is 3:4.
If there are 9 men in the office, how many women are there?

1. Write down the ratio and find what you have to
    multiply the left-hand side by to get 9.

2. Multiply the right-hand side by the same number.

$$\times 3 \left(\begin{array}{c} 3:4 \\ 9:? \end{array} \right. \longrightarrow \left. \begin{array}{c} 3:4 \\ 9:12 \end{array} \right) \times 3$$

So there are **12** women.

Exercise 4

1 A recipe uses sugar and butter in the ratio 2:1. How much butter is needed for 100 g of sugar?

2 A wood has oak and beech trees in the ratio 2:9. 42 of the trees are oak. How many are beech?

3 The ages of a father and son are in the ratio 8:3. If the father is 48, how old is the son?

4 A cardboard cut-out of a footballer is 166 cm tall. The height of the cut-out and the footballer's actual height are in the ratio 5:6. How tall is the footballer?

5 Mai and Sid split their savings in the ratio 7:6. Sid gets £51. How much do they have in total?

6 A fruit punch is made by mixing pineapple juice, orange juice, and lemonade in the ratio 1:3:6. If 500 ml of pineapple juice is used, how much orange juice is needed?

7 Jem orders a pizza with olives, slices of courgette and slices of goat's cheese in the ratio 8:3:4. How many slices of courgette and how many slices of goat's cheese would she get with 24 olives?

8 Mo, Liz and Dee's heights are in the ratio 32:33:37. Mo is 144 cm tall. What is the combined height of the three people?

9 Max, Molly and Maisie are at a bus stop. The number of minutes they have waited can be represented by the ratio 3:7:2. Molly has been waiting for 1 hour and 10 minutes. How long have Max and Maisie been waiting?

10 The ratio of children to adults in a swimming pool must be 5:1 or less. If there are 32 children, how many adults must there be?

11 A TV-show producer is selecting a studio audience. He wants the ratio of under-30s to over-30s to be at least 8:1. If 100 under-30s are selected, find the maximum number of over-30s.

12 A recipe uses 1 aubergine for every 3 people. How many aubergines should you buy for 10 people?

13 Olga is allowed no more than 5 minutes of reality TV for every minute of news programmes she watches. She watches 45 mins of reality TV. What's the least amount of news she should watch?

Ratios and Fractions

Example 5

A box of doughnuts contains jam doughnuts and chocolate doughnuts in the ratio 3:5. What fraction of the doughnuts are chocolate flavoured?

1. Find the total number of 'parts'. | $3 + 5 = 8$ parts altogether.
2. Write the number of parts that are chocolate as a fraction of the total. | 5 of the parts are chocolate. So $\frac{5}{8}$ are chocolate.

Exercise 5

1 A recipe uses white flour and brown flour in the ratio 2:1. What fraction of flour is brown?

2 A tiled floor has blue and white tiles in the ratio 9:4. What fraction of the tiles are blue?

3 The ratio of women to men in a tennis club is 13:7. What fraction of the players are men?

4 In a tournament the numbers of home wins, away wins and draws were in the ratio 7:2:5. What fraction of the games were home wins?

5 Amy's sock drawer has spotty, stripy and plain socks in the ratio 5:1:4. What fraction are stripy?

6 At a music festival there are men, women and children in the ratio 13:17:5. What fraction of the people are children?

7 James eats peaches, pears and pomegranates in the ratio 5:3:2.
a) What fraction of the fruit are peaches?
b) What fraction of the fruit are pears?

8 At a birthday party there are purple, red and blue balloons in the ratio 3:8:11.
a) What fraction of the balloons are blue?
b) What fraction of the balloons are purple?
c) What fraction of the balloons aren't red?

Example 6

$\frac{2}{7}$ of Hannah's DVDs are horror films. The rest are comedies.

Find the ratio of comedies to horror films.

1. Find the number of 'parts' corresponding to each film type.	$\frac{2}{7}$ = 2 parts out of 7 are horror So 7 − 2 = 5 parts are comedies
2. Write this as a ratio.	Ratio of comedies to horror is **5 : 2**

Exercise 6

1. In a bag of red sweets and green sweets, $\frac{1}{3}$ are red. Find the ratio of red to green sweets.

2. Al has watched $\frac{3}{10}$ of the episodes of a TV series. Find the ratio of episodes he's watched to ones he hasn't.

3. $\frac{1}{8}$ of the balls in a bag are red, $\frac{5}{8}$ are blue and the rest are green. Find the ratio of red to blue to green balls.

4. Last season, a rugby team won half of their matches by more than 10 points and a quarter of their matches by less than 10 points. They lost the rest. Find the team's ratio of wins to losses.

5. A cycling challenge has three routes — A, B and C. $\frac{7}{10}$ of the competitors choose route A, $\frac{1}{5}$ choose route B and the rest choose route C. What is the ratio of competitors choosing route A to those choosing route C?

6. During one day at a pizza restaurant, $\frac{3}{8}$ of the pizzas ordered were pepperoni, $\frac{1}{2}$ were cheese and tomato and the rest were spicy chicken. Write down the ratio of pepperoni to cheese and tomato to spicy chicken.

7. A DIY shop sells $\frac{2}{3}$ as many nails as it does screws. Write the ratio of nails to screws in its simplest form.

8. In a bowl of salad there are $\frac{5}{2}$ as many tomatoes as there are lettuce leaves.
   a) Write this as a ratio of tomatoes to lettuce leaves. Give your ratio in its simplest form.
   b) There are 45 tomatoes in the salad bowl. How many lettuce leaves are there?

9. One third of the counters in a box are red, one fifth are white and the rest are beige. Find the ratio of red to beige counters.

4.2   Dividing in a Given Ratio

Ratios can be used to divide an amount into two or more **shares**.
The numbers in the ratio show how many parts of the whole each share gets.

Example 1

Divide £54 in the ratio 4 : 5.

1. Find the total number of parts.	4 + 5 = 9 parts altogether
2. Work out the amount for one part.	9 parts = £54 So 1 part = £54 ÷ 9 = £6
3. Multiply by the number of parts for each share.	£6 × 4 = £24, £6 × 5 = £30 So the shares are **£24** and **£30**.

Exercise 1

1. Divide £48 in the following ratios.
   a) 2 : 1   b) 1 : 3   c) 5 : 1   d) 7 : 5

2. Divide 72 cm in the following ratios.
   a) 2 : 3 : 1   b) 2 : 2 : 5   c) 5 : 3 : 4   d) 7 : 6 : 5

3   Share £150 in these ratios.
   a) $1:4:5$ **b)** $15:5:30$ **c)** $6:7:2$ **d)** $13:11:6$

4   Find the smallest share when each amount below is divided in the given ratio.
   a) £22 in the ratio $5:6$ **b)** 450 g in the ratio $22:28$
   c) 45 kg in the ratio $2:3:4$ **d)** 1800 ml in the ratio $5:6:7$

5   Find the largest share when each amount below is divided in the given ratio.
   a) £30 in the ratio $1:3$ **b)** 36 g in the ratio $3:2$
   c) 150 kg in the ratio $10:7:3$ **d)** 24 000 ml in the ratio $5:7:20$

Example 2

A drink is made using three times as much apple juice as orange juice, and four times as much lemonade as orange juice. How much lemonade is needed to make 5 litres of the drink?

1. Write down the ratios of the amounts of each drink.	apple juice : orange juice : lemonade 3 : 1 : 4
2. Find the total number of 'parts'.	$3 + 1 + 4 = 8$ parts altogether
3. Work out the amount for one 'part'.	8 parts = 5 litres So 1 part = $5 \div 8 = 0.625$ litres
4. Lemonade makes up 4 'parts'.	0.625 litres $\times 4 = \underline{\mathbf{2.5}}$ litres of lemonade.

Exercise 2

1   Share 32 sandwiches in the ratio $3:5$.

2   Kat and Lindsay share 30 cupcakes in the ratio $3:2$. How many do they each get?

3   There are 112 people in an office. The ratio of men to women is $9:5$. How many men and how many women are there?

4   Lauren is 16 and Cara is 14. Their grandad gives them £1200 to share in the ratio of their ages. How much money do they each get?

5   Tangerine paint is made from yellow and red paint in the ratio $4:3$. How much of each colour is needed to make 42 litres of tangerine paint?

6   In a school of 600 pupils, there are seven times as many right-handed pupils as left-handed pupils. How many pupils are right-handed?

7   Daniel puts one-and-a-half times as much money into a business as his partner Elsie.
   They share the profits in that same ratio.
   How much of a £5700 profit does Daniel get?

8   There are 28 passengers on a bus. There are two-and-a-half times as many passengers on the phone as not on the phone. How many passengers are on the phone?

9
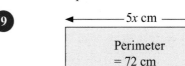

The length and width of a rectangle are in the ratio $5:1$. If the perimeter of the rectangle is 72 cm, calculate the length and the width of the rectangle.

Exercise 3

1   Gemma, Alisha and Omar have a combined height of 490 cm. If their heights are in the ratio $31:32:35$, how tall are they?

2   A quiz team share their £150 prize money in the ratio $2:4:6$. What is the least amount that any team member receives?

3 A box of 48 chocolates contains dark, milk and white chocolates in the ratio $2:7:3$. Jeff doesn't like dark chocolates. How many of the chocolates can he happily eat?

4 Claire owns 20 handbags, which are black, brown and purple in the ratio $5:3:2$. She is choosing a bag and doesn't want it to be brown. How many bags does she have to choose from?

5 A fruit salad has twice as many raspberries as redcurrants, and three times as many strawberries as redcurrants. How much of each fruit is needed to make 450 g of fruit salad?

6 Nicky, Jacinta and Charlie share a bag of 35 sweets so that Nicky gets half as much as Jacinta and Charlie gets half as much as Nicky. How many sweets do each of them get?

7 The angles in a triangle are in the ratio $2:1:3$. Find the sizes of the three angles.

8 The four angles in a quadrilateral are in the ratio $1:5:2:4$. Calculate the sizes of all four angles.

9 A rope is cut into three pieces in the ratio $2:1:4$. The third piece is 22 cm longer than the first piece. What is the length of the second piece?

10 Bri wins £60 000. She keeps half, and shares the other half between three charities in the ratio $3:5:4$. What is the difference between the largest and least amounts that the charities receive?

11 Andrew, Pierre and Susanne, are making tomato sauce. They share out tomatoes in the ratio $2:3:5$. Susanne gets 16 tomatoes fewer than Pierre. How many tomatoes do they have in total?

12 Ali and Max earn £200 one weekend. They share it according to the hours they worked. Ali worked 10 hours and Max worked 6 hours. Ali had help from her brother Tim, so she splits her share with him in the ratio $4:1$. How much do Ali, Max and Tim each get?

13 Dan, Stan and Jan are aged 8, 12 and 16. They get pocket money each week in the ratio of their ages. Dan normally gets £6, but has been naughty, so this week all the money is split between Stan and Jan, in the ratio of their ages, to the nearest penny. How much do they each receive this week?

4.3   More Ratio Problems

Example 1

A shop only sells green and brown garden sheds.
The ratio of green sheds sold to the total number of sheds sold is $5:7$.
What is the ratio of green sheds sold to brown sheds sold?

5 out of every 7 sheds sold are green, so 2 in every 7 are brown. $7 - 5 = 2$
For every 5 green sheds sold, 2 brown sheds are sold.   green : brown = **5 : 2**

Exercise 1

1 A reptile house only contains snakes and lizards. The ratio of snakes to the total number of reptiles is $3:8$.
   a) What fraction of the reptiles are snakes?
   b) What is the ratio of snakes to lizards?

2 A biscuit tin only contains digestives and bourbons. The ratio of digestives to the total number of biscuits is $4:7$. What is the ratio of digestives to bourbons?

3 When Dan makes a cup of tea, the ratio of water to milk is $15:2$. What is the ratio of water to the total amount of liquid in the cup?

4 A rock album is sold as a digital download and on a CD. The ratio of digital downloads to CDs sold is $53:46$. What is the ratio of CDs sold to the total number of albums sold?

Example 2

Ashraf collects coins. He has 45 gold coins, and the ratio of gold coins to silver coins is $9:13$.
If he sells 15 silver coins, what will be the new ratio of gold coins to silver coins?
Give your ratio in its simplest form.

1. Scale up to find the original number of silver coins.

$\times 5 \left(\begin{array}{c} 9:13 \\ 45:65 \end{array} \right) \times 5$

2. Work out the remaining number of silver coins.

$65 - 15 = 50$ silver coins

3. Write out the new ratio and simplify.

$\div 5 \left(\begin{array}{c} 45:50 \\ \mathbf{9:10} \end{array} \right) \div 5$

Exercise 2

For the following questions, give each ratio in its simplest form.

1 In a bakery, the ratio of fruit scones to cheese scones is $3:4$.
 a) Given that there are 24 cheese scones, how many fruit scones are there?
 b) If 6 fruit scones were sold, what would be the new ratio of fruit scones to cheese scones?

2 An aquarium contains fish and crabs. The ratio of fish to crabs is $4:1$. There are 16 fish in the aquarium.
If 2 more crabs were added to the aquarium, what would be the new ratio of fish to crabs?

3 A village has detached houses and terraced houses in the ratio $5:7$. There are 56 terraced houses.
If 12 new detached houses were built, what would be the new ratio of detached houses to terraced houses?

4 At the beginning of the week, a bookshop which sells school books has
48 English books in stock and the ratio of English to Maths books is $2:5$.
At the end of the week, the ratio of English to Maths books is $3:4$.
Given that the shop sold 12 English books during the week, how many Maths books did it sell?

5 A bag contains black and white tokens in a ratio of $3:2$.
8 black tokens and 2 white tokens are added to the bag.
The ratio of black to white tokens is now $2:1$. How many white tokens were in the bag to begin with?

4.4   Proportion

Direct Proportion

If the ratio between two things is always the same, then they're in **direct proportion**.

Example 1

If 8 chocolate bars cost £6, calculate the cost of 10 chocolate bars.

1. Find the cost of one bar.

1 bar costs £6 $\div$ 8 = £0.75

2. Multiply by the new number of bars.

10 bars cost £0.75 $\times$ 10 = **£7.50**

Exercise 1

1 The cost of 8 identical books is £36. What is the cost of 12 of these books?

2 If it takes 1.8 kg of flour to make 3 loaves of bread, how much flour is needed to make 5 loaves?

3 5 litres of water are needed to make 4 jugs of squash. How much water is needed to make 3 jugs of squash?

4 30 m of material costs £21.60. How much would 18 m of this material cost?

5 Convert £7.50 into Japanese yen given that £20 is worth 2620 Japanese yen.

6 If 10 litres of paint costs £45, find the cost of:
   a) 3 litres   **b)** 14 litres   **c)** 13.2 litres

7 Ryan earns £192 for cleaning 12 cars. How much more will he earn if he cleans another 5 cars?

8 Grace buys 11 pens for £12.32 and 6 notepads for £5.88.
   How much would she pay altogether for 8 pens and 5 notepads?

Example 2

Oliver has 30 euros (€) left over from a holiday in France. Assuming the exchange rate
is £1 = €1.14, how many pounds can he exchange his euros for?

1. On a calculator, work out how many pounds €1 is worth.   €1 = £1 ÷ 1.14 = £0.877...

2. Multiply the number on the calculator
    by the number of euros.   €30 = 30 × £0.877... = **£26.32** (to 2 d.p.)

Exercise 2

1 If £1 is worth €1.14, convert the following amounts in euros (€) into pounds.
   a) €10   **b)** €100   **c)** €250

2 1 kg is approximately equal to 2.2 pounds (lbs). Calculate the approximate weight of 8.25 lbs of sugar in kg.

3 If 7 of the same DVDs cost £84, how many DVDs can be bought for £48?

4 If 24 houses can be built by 6 builders in one year, how many builders would it take to build 52 houses in the same amount of time?

5 Use the exchange rate £100 = 1055 Chinese yuan to convert 65 Chinese yuan into pounds.

Exercise 3

1 A bus travels 50 km in 40 minutes. Assuming the bus travels at the same average speed, calculate:
   a) the time it would take to travel 65 km
   b) the distance the bus would travel in 16 minutes

2 A car uses 35 litres of petrol to travel 250 km. Assuming its fuel consumption stays constant, calculate:
   a) how far, to the nearest km, the car can travel on 50 litres of petrol
   b) how many litres of petrol the car would use to travel 400 km

3 A 58 g bar of chocolate contains 11 g of fat.
   a) To the nearest gram, how much fat is this per 100 g?
   b) If my diet only allows me to eat 5 g of fat, how much of the chocolate bar can I eat?
        Give your answer to 1 decimal place.

4 Philip changed £50 into Swiss francs. The exchange rate was £1 = 1.47 Swiss francs.
   a) How many Swiss francs did he get?

   The next week, he changed 30 Swiss francs into pounds with exchange rate £1 = 1.50 Swiss francs.
   b) How many pounds did he get back?

Example 3

Two people can build four identical walls in three days.
At this rate, how many of these walls could ten people build in 3.75 days?

1. First find how many walls 2 people
    can build in 3.75 days.

Keeping the number of people (2) constant:

Can build: 4 walls in 3 days
$4 \div 3 = 1\frac{1}{3}$ walls in 1 day
$3.75 \times 1\frac{1}{3} = 5$ walls in 3.75 days

2. Then find how many walls 10 people
    can build in 3.75 days.

Keeping the number of days (3.75) constant:

2 people can build 5 walls
1 person can build $5 \div 2 = 2.5$ walls
10 people can build $2.5 \times 10 = 25$ walls

Exercise 4

1   It takes three people five minutes to eat six
    hotdogs. At this rate, how many hotdogs
    could five people eat in ten minutes?

2   Ten people can count 850 coins in two minutes.
    At this rate, how many coins could 22 people
    count in five minutes?

3   It takes two people ninety minutes to plant 66
    flower bulbs. At this rate, how many bulbs
    could three people plant in three hours?

4   Two toy makers can make eight toy soldiers in
    two weeks. How many soldiers could seven toy
    makers make in three weeks if they work at the
    same rate?

Inverse Proportion

If one quantity decreases as another increases, then they're **inversely proportional**.

Example 4

Four people take five and a quarter hours to dig a hole.
How long would it take seven people to dig the same sized hole at the same rate?

1. Work out how long 1 person will take — the
    fewer people there are, the longer it will take.

4 people take 5.25 hours
1 person will take $5.25 \times 4 = 21$ hours

2. Divide by the new number of people.

7 people will take $21 \div 7 = \underline{\textbf{3 hours}}$.

Exercise 5

1   It takes three people two hours to paint a wall.
    How long would it take five people to paint the
    same wall at the same rate?

2   It takes four teachers two and a half hours to mark
    a set of test papers. How long would it take six
    teachers to mark the same set of papers at the
    same rate?

3   Four chefs can cook a dish in twenty minutes.
    They hire an extra chef. How long will it take
    the five of them to cook the same dish, if they all
    work at the same rate as the original four?

4   A journey takes two and a quarter hours when
    travelling at an average speed of 30 mph.
    How long would the same journey take when
    travelling at an average speed of 45 mph?

5   It will take five builders sixty-two days to
    complete a particular project.
    a) At this rate, how long would the project take if
        there were only two builders?
    b) If the project needed completing in under forty
        days, what is the minimum number of builders
        that would be required?

Example 5

It takes 5 examiners 4 hours to mark 125 exam papers.
How long would it take 8 examiners to mark 200 papers at the same rate?

1. Split the calculation up into stages by keeping one variable constant each time.	<u>Keeping the number of papers (125) constant</u>: 5 examiners take 4 hours
2. First find how long it will take 8 examiners to mark 125 papers.	1 examiner will take $4 \times 5 = 20$ hours 8 examiners will take $20 \div 8 = 2.5$ hours
3. Then find how long it will take 8 examiners to mark 200 papers.	<u>Keeping the number of people (8) constant</u>: 1 paper will take $2.5 \div 125 = 0.02$ hours 200 papers will take $0.02 \times 200 = $ **4 hours**.

Exercise 6

1 It takes 45 minutes for two people to clean six identical rooms.
   How long would it take five people to clean 20 of the same rooms at the same rate?

2 It takes two electricians nine days to rewire two identical houses.
   How long would it take three electricians to rewire three of the same houses at the same rate?

3 It takes four bakers 144 minutes to bake 72 identical buns.
   How long would it six bakers to bake 96 of these buns?

4 Three people take twenty minutes to shovel snow from two identical driveways.
   At this rate, how long would it take two people to shovel snow from five of the same driveways?

5 Fourteen people can paint 35 identical plates in two hours. At this rate, how many people
   would be needed to paint 60 of the same plates in two and a half hours?

6 It will take twelve workers three weeks to complete four stages of a ten-stage project.
   Each stage of the project takes the same number of man-hours to complete.
   a) At this rate, how long would it take fifteen workers to complete the whole project?
   b) The project needs completing in under four weeks. What is the minimum number of
   workers that would be required, given that they all work at the same rate as the original workers?

4.5   Ratio and Proportion Problems

Exercise 1

1 A builder mixes 10 bags of cement with 25 bags of sand. Write down the ratio of cement to sand:
   a) in its simplest form   **b)** in the form $1:n$ **c)** in the form $n:1$
   d) Write down the ratio of bags of cement to the total number of bags used in its simplest form.

2 On a particular day, the ratio of male to female customers in a shop is $18:45$.
   a) Write down the ratio of male to female customers in its simplest form.
   b) What fraction of the customers are male?

120 mm   35 cm

3 A picture has a width of 120 mm. An enlargement of the picture is
   made with a width of 35 cm.
   a) Write the ratio of the original width to the enlarged width
   in its simplest form.
   b) The enlarged picture has a height of 18 cm.
   What is the height of the original picture, to the nearest millimetre?

4 A farm has sheep, cows and pigs in the ratio $8:1:3$.
   a) What fraction of the animals are pigs?
   b) If there are 16 sheep in the field, how many animals are there altogether?

5 The only ingredients of a particular cereal are raisins, nuts and oats.
   By weight, the ratio of raisins to nuts is $3:1$, and the ratio of oats to raisins is $1:2$.
   a) What fraction of the weight of the cereal is made up of raisins?
   b) How many grams of nuts, to the nearest gram, are needed to make 450 g of the cereal?

6 Luiz, Seth and Fran share £1440 in the ratio $3:5:7$. Fran splits her share with her sister Ali in the ratio $4:1$.
   a) How much does each person end up with?
   b) Find the ratio of the amount that Fran ends up with to the amount that Seth ends up with.
   Give your answer in its simplest form.

7 Jonathan makes orange squash by mixing orange concentrate and water in the ratio $1:10$.
   Caroline mixes the concentrate and water in the ratio $2:15$. Whose squash is stronger?

8 Evie is making wedding invitation cards in three different colours — blue, green and purple.
   She uses the different colours in the ratio $2:7:3$. Evie has made 12 green cards so far and has
   72 more green cards to make. Work out how many purple cards she will need to make.

9 A map has a scale of $1:200\,000$. The real distance between two towns is 60 km.
   How many centimetres apart are the towns on the map?

10 It costs £20 to put 12.5 litres of petrol in my car.
   a) How much will it cost me for a full tank of petrol if the tank holds 60 litres?
   b) How much petrol can I put in my car for £30?

11 Emma changed £500 into rand before going on holiday to South Africa.
   The rate of exchange at the time was £1 = 10.4 rand.
   a) How many rand did she get for her £500?

   Emma spent 4000 rand on holiday. When she got home, she changed her leftover rand into pounds.
   The exchange rate was now £1 = 9.8 rand.
   b) How much money did she get back in pounds?

12 On the right is a recipe for cupcakes.
   a) How much butter would you need to make 10 cupcakes?
   b) How much flour would you need to make 35 cupcakes?
   c) If you only had 1 egg, but plenty of the other ingredients, how many cupcakes would you be able to make?

> **Cupcakes (makes 25)**
>
> Butter, 200 g   Plain flour, 280 g
> Caster sugar, 250 g   Eggs, 4

13 On a normal day, 20 planes depart from an airport to go to Spain and Finland in the ratio $4:1$.
   On one particular day, 2 additional flights went to Spain, and so the of ratio Spanish to Finnish flights was $3:1$.
   How many additional flights departed for Finland on this day?

14 Eight lumberjacks can chop down three identical trees in an hour and a half.
   a) At this rate, how many trees could eight lumberjacks chop down in six hours?
   b) How long would it take eight lumberjacks to chop down eight trees at the same rate?
   c) At this same rate, how many trees could six lumberjacks chop down in an eight hour day?

15 It takes five minutes for seven people to drink 24.5 pints of water.
   At this rate, how long would it take fifteen people to drink 157.5 pints of water?

16 Eight paperboys can deliver the morning newspapers in 20 minutes. One morning, one paperboy is off sick.
   To the nearest second, how long will it take the rest of them to deliver all the newspapers at their usual rate?

17 A carpenter can build a bookshelf in eight days, if working five and a half hours per day.
   At this rate, how long would it take the carpenter to build the bookshelf if he worked eight hours per day?

Section 5 — Percentages

5.1 Percentages

Writing One Number as a Percentage of Another

'Per cent' means 'out of 100'. Writing an amount as a **percentage** means writing it as a number out of 100.

Example 1

Express 15 as a percentage of 50.

1. Write the amount as a fraction.
2. Write an equivalent fraction which is 'out of 100' by multiplying top and bottom by the same number.
3. Write the amount as a percentage.

$$\overset{\times 2}{\frac{15}{50}} = \frac{30}{100} \underset{\times 2}{}$$

So 15 is **30%** of 50.

Exercise 1

Answer Questions 1-5 **without** using your calculator.

1   A chess club has 25 members. 12 of these members are female.
    Express the number of female members of the club as a percentage.

2   There are 300 counters in a bag, 45 of which are green. Express the amount of green counters as a percentage.

3   Write each of the following amounts as a percentage.

   a) 11 out of 25   **b)** 33 out of 50   **c)** 3 out of 20   **d)** 8 out of 10

   e) 100 out of 400   **f)** 890 out of 1000   **g)** 48 out of 32   **h)** 36 out of 60

   i) 63 out of 75   **j)** 200 out of 160   **k)** 14 out of 35   **l)** 54 out of 180

4   Out of 24 pupils in a class, 18 walk to school.

   a) What percentage of the class walk to school?

   b) What percentage of the class do not walk to school?

5   39 out of 65 people in a book club have blonde hair. What percentage do not have blonde hair?

Example 2

Express 333 as a percentage of 360.

1. Write the amount as a fraction.
2. Divide the top number by the bottom number. Use a calculator if necessary.
3. Multiply by 100% to write as a percentage.

$\frac{333}{360}$

$333 \div 360 = 0.925$

$0.925 \times 100\% = 92.5\%$

So 333 is **92.5%** of 360.

Exercise 2

You may use a calculator to answer Questions 1-6.

1   Write each of the following amounts as a percentage.

   a) 15 out of 24   **b)** 221 out of 260   **c)** 661 out of 500   **d)** 328 out of 800

   e) 258 out of 375   **f)** 77 out of 275   **g)** 323 out of 850   **h)** 301 out of 250

2   A school has 875 pupils. 525 are boys. What is this as a percentage?

3   171 out of 180 raffle tickets were sold for a summer fete. What percentage of the tickets were sold?

4 Write each of the following amounts as a percentage.

a) 116.6 out of 212   b) 41.6 out of 128   c) 53.5 out of 428   d) 226.8 out of 210

e) 47.25 out of 126   f) 697.15 out of 382   g) 85.86 out of 265   h) 17.92 out of 512

5 The jackpot for a lottery was £10 250. John won £1896.25. What percentage of the total jackpot did he win?

6 Curtis receives £5.60 pocket money per week from his parents, and £2.40 pocket money per week from his grandparents. What percentage of his total pocket money comes from his grandparents?

Finding a Percentage Without a Calculator

You can find some percentages without a calculator using the following rules.

- **50%** $= \frac{1}{2}$, so find 50% of something by **dividing by 2** (which is the same as multiplying by $\frac{1}{2}$).
- **25%** $= \frac{1}{4}$, so find 25% of something by **dividing by 4** (which is the same as multiplying by $\frac{1}{4}$).
- **10%** $= \frac{1}{10}$, so find 10% of something by **dividing by 10** (which is the same as multiplying by $\frac{1}{10}$).

Example 3
Find 75% of 44.

1. First find 25% by dividing by 4.   25% of 44 = 44 ÷ 4 = 11

2. 75% = 3 × 25%, so multiply by 3.   So 75% of 44 = 3 × 11 = **33**

Exercise 3

Answer Questions 1-3 **without** using your calculator.

1 Find each of the following.

a) 50% of 24   b) 25% of 36   c) 10% of 90   d) 10% of 270

e) 75% of 20   f) 5% of 140   g) 35% of 300   h) 45% of 500

2 Find each of the following.

a) 75% of 12   b) 5% of 260   c) 130% of 90   d) 40% of 150

e) 70% of 110   f) 180% of 70   g) 15% of 220   h) 65% of 120

3 A wooden plank is 9 m long. 55% of the plank is cut off. What length of wood has been cut off?

Finding a Percentage With a Calculator

To find a percentage of an amount, change the percentage into a decimal then **multiply** by the amount.

Example 4
Find 67% of 138.

Change 67% into a decimal then multiply.   67% = 0.67   0.67 × 138 = **92.46**

Exercise 4

You may use a calculator to answer Questions 1-5.

1 Find each of the following.

a) 17% of 200   b) 109% of 11   c) 68% of 320   d) 221% of 370

e) 79% of 615   f) 73% of 801   g) 91% of 769   h) 96% of 911

2   What is 12% of 68 kg?

3   Jeff is on a journey of 385 km. So far, he has completed 31% of his journey. How far has he travelled?

4   Which is larger, 22% of £57 or 46% of £28? By how much?

5   A jug can hold 2.4 litres of water. It is 34% full. How much more water will fit in the jug?

5.2   Percentages, Fractions and Decimals

You can switch between percentages, fractions and decimals in the following ways.

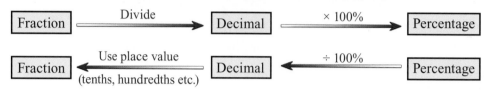

Example 1

Write 24% as: a) a decimal   b) a fraction in its simplest terms.

1.   Divide by 100% to write as a decimal.   a) $24\% \div 100\% = \underline{\textbf{0.24}}$

2.   The final digit of 0.24 (the '4') is in the hundredths column, so write 0.24 as 24 hundredths, and then simplify.   b) $0.24 = \dfrac{24}{100} = \dfrac{\textbf{6}}{\textbf{25}}$

Exercise 1

1   **a)** Find the fraction equivalent to $\dfrac{3}{20}$ which has 100 as the denominator.

   b) Write $\dfrac{3}{20}$ as   **(i)** a percentage   **(ii)** a decimal.

2   **a)** By calculating $5 \div 11$, write $\dfrac{5}{11}$ as a recurring decimal.

   b) Hence write $\dfrac{5}{11}$ as a percentage.

3   Write each of the following percentages as **(i)** a decimal, and **(ii)** a fraction in its simplest terms.
   a) 75%   **b)** 130%   **c)** 40%   **d)** 65%   **e)** 95%
   f) 34%   **g)** 48%   **h)** 205%   **i)** 2%   **j)** 6%

4   Write each of the following fractions as **(i)** a decimal, and **(ii)** a percentage.
   a) $\dfrac{3}{10}$ **b)** $\dfrac{1}{5}$ **c)** $\dfrac{7}{8}$ **d)** $\dfrac{1}{3}$ **e)** $\dfrac{1}{9}$
   f) $\dfrac{2}{15}$ **g)** $\dfrac{7}{11}$ **h)** $\dfrac{1}{6}$ **i)** $\dfrac{7}{16}$ **j)** $\dfrac{7}{9}$

5   Write each of the following decimals as **(i)** a percentage, and **(ii)** a fraction in its simplest terms.
   a) 0.35   **b)** 1.7   **c)** 0.52   **d)** 0.6   **e)** 0.48
   f) 0.72   **g)** 0.4   **h)** 0.01   **i)** 2.68   **j)** 0.14

6   Raj answers 0.86 of the questions in a test correctly. Write this as a percentage.

7   8% of the members of a drama group have green eyes. Write this as a decimal.

8 $\dfrac{3}{5}$ of the pupils in a class are right-handed. What percentage of the class are right-handed?

9   Raphael eats 36% of a cake. Write this percentage as a fraction in its lowest terms.

10   The probability of it raining tomorrow is $\dfrac{17}{25}$. Write this probability as a percentage.

Example 2

Put $\frac{1}{3}$, 33% and 0.3 in order, from smallest to largest.

Write the amounts in the same form.
(Here, I've chosen to write them all as decimals.)

1. Calculate $1 \div 3$ to write $\frac{1}{3}$ as a decimal.

2. Calculate $33\% \div 100\%$ to write 33% as a decimal.

3. Put the decimals in order, from smallest to largest.

4. Rewrite in their original forms.

$$\begin{array}{r} 0.33 \\ 3\overline{)1.^10^00} \end{array} \quad \text{So } \frac{1}{3} = 0.33... = 0.\dot{3}$$

$33\% \div 100\% = 0.33$

$0.3, 0.33, 0.\dot{3}$

$0.3, 33\%, \frac{1}{3}$

Exercise 2

Answer Questions 1-5 **without** using your calculator.

1   For each of the following pairs, write down which is larger.
    a) 0.35, 32%
    b) 0.58, 68%
    c) 0.4, 4%
    d) 0.09, 90%
    e) 0.2, $\frac{21}{100}$
    f) 0.6, $\frac{7}{10}$
    g) 0.7, $\frac{3}{4}$
    h) 0.55, $\frac{3}{5}$

2   Put the numbers in each of the following lists in order, from smallest to largest.
    a) 0.42, 25%, $\frac{2}{5}$
    b) 0.505, 45%, $\frac{1}{2}$
    c) 0.37, 38%, $\frac{3}{8}$
    d) 0.2, 22%, $\frac{2}{9}$
    e) 0.13, 12.5%, $\frac{3}{20}$
    f) 0.25, 23%, $\frac{9}{40}$
    g) 0.4, 2.5%, $\frac{1}{25}$
    h) 0.006, 0.06%, $\frac{3}{50}$

3   Margaret is buying a car. She needs to pay $\frac{2}{5}$ of the total cost as a deposit.
    Her parents give her 35% of the cost of the car to help her buy it. Is this enough to pay the deposit?

4   In a season, Team X won 14 out of the 20 matches they played. Team Y won 60% of their matches.
    Which team had the highest proportion of wins?

5   In a game, the winner is the person who transfers more counters from one box to another.
    Oliver transfers 65% of his counters. Jen transfers $\frac{11}{20}$ of her counters. Who has won?

Example 3

$\frac{1}{4}$ of pupils in a school bring a packed lunch, 65% have school dinners, and the rest go home for lunch.
What percentage of pupils go home for lunch?

1. Write $\frac{1}{4}$ as a percentage by writing it as a fraction out of 100.

2. Find the percentage that don't go home for lunch by adding the percentages for 'packed lunches' and 'school dinners'.

3. Subtract this from 100% to find the percentage who do go home for lunch.

$\frac{1}{4} = \frac{25}{100}$ So $\frac{1}{4} = 25\%$

$25\% + 65\% = 90\%$

$100\% - 90\% = \underline{\textbf{10\%}}$

Exercise 3

Answer Questions 1-7 **without** using your calculator.

1   In a school survey of food preferences, 50% of pupils said they prefer pizza, $\frac{1}{5}$ said they prefer shepherd's pie and the rest said they prefer roast chicken. Find the percentage that prefer roast chicken.

2   In a car park, $\frac{2}{5}$ of the cars are red, 0.12 of the total number are white, 15% are blue, and the rest are black. Find the percentage of cars in the car park that are black.

3   Ainslie is keeping a record of the birds in his garden. Of the birds he has seen this month, $\frac{3}{8}$ were sparrows, 41.5% were blackbirds, and the rest were robins. What percentage were robins?

4 $\frac{3}{4}$ of the people at a concert arrived by train, 5% walked, and the rest came by car. What percentage came by car?

5 Beverley eats 0.3 of a pie, Victoria eats $\frac{1}{10}$, Patrick eats 20%, and Gus eats the rest.
What percentage of the pie does Gus eat?

6 $\frac{1}{4}$ of Hattie's jackets are leather, $\frac{1}{5}$ are denim, 30% are suede, and the rest are corduroy.
Find the percentage of Hattie's jackets that are corduroy.

7 In a school, the ratio of girls to boys is $3:7$. 25% of the girls and 20% of the boys are part of a sports club.
In total what percentage of the school pupils are part of a sports club?

5.3   Percentage Increase and Decrease

To **increase** an amount by a percentage, **calculate** the percentage then **add** it to the original amount.
To **decrease** an amount by a percentage, **subtract** the percentage from the original amount.

Example 1
Increase 450 by 15% without using your calculator.

1. Find 10% and 5% of 450.	10% of 450 = 450 ÷ 10 = 45 5% of 450 = 45 ÷ 2 = 22.5
2. Add these to find 15% of 450.	So 15% of 450 = 45 + 22.5 = 67.5
3. Add this to the original amount.	450 + 67.5 = **517.5**

Exercise 1

Answer Questions 1-5 **without** using your calculator.

1 Increase each of the following amounts by the percentage given.
   a) 90 by 10%   **b)** 60 by 25%   **c)** 80 by 75%   **d)** 270 by 20%
   e) 110 by 60%   **f)** 480 by 115%   **g)** 140 by 45%   **h)** 100 by 185%

2 Decrease each of the following amounts by the percentage given.
   a) 55 by 10%   **b)** 48 by 75%   **c)** 25 by 30%   **d)** 120 by 60%
   e) 125 by 40%   **f)** 11 by 70%   **g)** 150 by 55%   **h)** 520 by 15%

3 A farmer has 380 acres of land. He sells 35% of his land. How much does he have left?

4 A population decreases by 15% from 2400. What is the new population?

5 A TV costs £485, plus 20% VAT. Find the total cost of the TV after the VAT is added.

Example 2
Fabian deposits £150 into an account which pays 5% interest per year.
How much will be in the account after one year?

Find 5% of £150 and add this to £150.	5% = 0.05 0.05 × £150 = £7.50
	£150 + £7.50 = **£157.50**

Exercise 2

You may use a calculator to answer Questions 1-7.

1 Increase each of the following amounts by the percentage given.
   a) 490 by 11%   **b)** 101 by 16%   **c)** 55 by 137%   **d)** 89 by 61%
   e) 139 by 28%   **f)** 426 by 134%   **g)** 854 by 89%   **h)** 761 by 77%

2 Decrease each of the following amounts by the percentage given.
   a) 77 by 8%   **b)** 36 by 21%   **c)** 82 by 13%   **d)** 101 by 43%
   e) 189 by 38%   **f)** 313 by 62%   **g)** 645 by 69%   **h)** 843 by 91%

3   David's height increased by 20% between the ages of 6 and 10. He was 50 inches tall at age 6.
How tall was he at age 10?

4   2 years ago, Alison earned £31 000 per year. Last year, she got a pay rise of 3%.
This year, she got a pay cut of 2%. How much does she now earn per year?

Example 3

A number, x, is decreased by 25% to 63. Find x.

1.   Write 63 as a percentage of x.

2.   Divide 63 by 75% to get the original number.

$63 = 100\% - 25\% = 75\%$ of x

$x = 63 \div 75\% = 63 \div 0.75 = \underline{\textbf{84}}$

5   A fridge costs £200 after a 50% reduction. Calculate the original price of the fridge.

6   Andy buys a top hat that has been reduced in a sale by 35%. If the sale price is £13.00, find the original price.

7   In the past year, the number of frogs living in a pond has increased by 10% to 528, and the number of newts living there has increased by 15% to 621. How many frogs and how many newts lived in the pond a year ago?

Exercise 3

Answer Questions 1-2 **without** using your calculator.

1   Roberto's weekly wage of £400 is decreased by 5%. Mary's weekly wage of £350 is increased by 10%.
Who now earns more? By how much?

2   Gerry puts £5500 into an account that pays 10% interest per year. Raj puts £6000 into an account that pays 5% interest per year. Who has more money in their account after one year? By how much?

You may use a calculator to answer Questions 3-5.

3   University A has 24 500 students. Over the next year, the number of students increases by 2%.
University B has 22 500 students. Over the next year, the number of students increases by 9%. Which University has more students at the end of the year? By how much?

4   The population of Barton is 152 243, and increases by 11% each year. The population of Meristock is 210 059, and decreases by 8% each year. Which town has the larger population after one year? By how much? Give your answer to the nearest whole number.

5   Misha buys a £750 TV on hire purchase. To do this, she pays a deposit and then 24 monthly payments.

   a) Calculate the size of the deposit if it is 35% of the selling price.

   b) Calculate the total cost of the TV bought on hire purchase if the 24 monthly payments each cost £22.55.

   c) How much more does Misha have to pay to buy the TV on hire purchase than if she bought it at its selling price of £750? Express your answer as a percentage of the selling price.

Finding a Percentage Increase or Decrease

To find a percentage increase or decrease:
   (i) calculate the **difference** between the new amount and the original amount,
   (ii) find this as a percentage of the **original** amount.

Example 4

A house price increases from £145 000 to £187 050. Find the percentage increase.

1.   Calculate the difference.

2.   Write as a fraction of the original amount, then divide the top number by the bottom number.

3.   Multiply by 100% to write as a percentage.

$187\ 050 - 145\ 000 = 42\ 050$

$\dfrac{42\ 050}{145\ 000} = 42\ 050 \div 145\ 000 = 0.29$

$0.29 \times 100\% = 29\%$. So it is a **29%** increase.

Exercise 4

Answer Questions 1-7 **without** using your calculator.

1 Find the percentage increase when:
   a) a price of £10 is increased to £12.
   b) a price of £20 is increased to £52.

2 Find the percentage decrease when:
   a) a price of £10 is decreased to £8.
   b) a price of £25 is decreased to £22.

3 The number of people working for a company increases from 45 to 72. Find the percentage increase in the number of people working for the company.

4 The price of a local newspaper increases from 80p to £1. Find the percentage increase.

5 Percy is on a healthy eating plan. His weight drops from 80 kg to 68 kg. Find the percentage decrease in Percy's weight.

6 In an experiment, the mass of a chemical drops from 75 g to 69 g. Find the percentage decrease.

7 In a sale, the price of a toaster is reduced from £50 to £30. Find the percentage reduction

5.4   Compound Percentage Change

Compound Interest

Interest is a percentage of money that is added on to an initial figure over a period of time.
For **compound interest** calculations, the interest earned in each period is **added** to the initial figure.

Example 1

Mr Zupnik invests £600 in a bank account at 5% per annum compound interest.
How much money will he have in the bank after two years?

1. 'Per annum' means 'per year'. Find 5% of £600 to find the first year's interest earned. Add this amount on to the initial amount.

   £600 ÷ 20 = £30
   £600 + £30 = £630

2. Now find 5% of £630 to find the second year's interest:

   £630 ÷ 20 = £31.50

3. Add this on to the first year figure to find the total after two years.

   £630 + £31.50 = **£661.50**

Exercise 1

1 A bank pays 3% per annum compound interest. Calculate how much interest the following accounts will earn.
   a) £250 invested for 1 year.
   b) £45 invested for 3 years.
   c) £100 invested for 2 years.
   d) £1500 invested for 2 years.
   e) £90 invested for 4 years.
   f) £360 invested for 5 years.

2 Josephine invests £3500 in a bank account that pays annual compound interest of 4.5%.
   How much money will she have in the bank   a) after 2 years?   b) after 5 years?

Compound Growth

Compound growth is when a quantity gets larger by a **periodical percentage increase**.

The formula for **compound growth** is: $P_n = P_0 \times (1 + r/100)^n$

P_n = amount after n periods, P_0 = initial amount, n = number of periods, r = percentage rate of growth or decay

Example 2

Calculate the compound interest paid on £500 for 3 years at a rate of 5%.

1. Use the formula for compound growth: $P_n = P_0 \times (1 + r/100)^n$

2. Plug in the numbers... $P_0 = £500, \ r = 5, \ n = 3$

3. Subtract the initial figure from the final value to find the interest paid.

   $P_n = 500 \times (1 + 5/100)^3 = 500 \times 1.157625 = 578.81$

   Interest $= P_n - P_0 = £578.81 - £500.00 = $ **£78.81**

Exercise 2

1   Use the formula for compound growth to calculate the interest earned by the following investments:
   a) £400 for 2 years at an annual rate of 5%.   **b)** £750 for 5 years at an annual rate of 3%.
   c) £50 for 7 years at an annual rate of 5.5%.   **d)** £25 for 12 years at an annual rate of 6%.

2   Use the formula for compound growth to calculate the amount of money you would have if you invested:
   a) £1000 at an annual rate of 4.5% for 5 years.   **b)** £500 at an annual rate of 7.25% for 6 years

3   Calculate how much money you will have
   after 4 years if you invest £680 at 2.5%
   annual compound interest.

4   The population of the UK in 2010 was 62 000 000.
   The population is increasing by 0.6% every year.
   Assuming that this rate of growth continues, how
   many people will reside in the UK by 2025?

5   During 2000 and 2001 a bank paid interest at a
   compound rate of 2% per annum. During 2002,
   2003 and 2004 this rate rose to 3%. Calculate
   the total interest paid over five years if £650 was
   invested at the beginning of the year 2000.

6   In 2010 a group called 'Smiley Faced People'
   decided to spread a little happiness around the
   world. Their numbers increase by 6% every year
   as more and more people decide to join their happy
   band. If the original group had 20 members, how
   many people will be in the group in 2020?

7   Find the value of a bar of gold, initially valued
   at £750, after seven months when gold prices are
   rising at a rate of 0.1% per month.

8   A colony of ants has set up home in Mr Murphy's
   shed. On Monday there were 250 ants.
   If the colony of ants grows at a rate of 5% per day,
   how many ants will there be on Saturday?

9   Mrs Honeybun is expecting twins.
   Every month her waistline increases by 5%.
   If her waist measurement started at 70 cm,
   what is her waistline after nine months?

10 Fiona Feline loves cats almost as much as she
   loves mathematics, and enjoys combining her
   two passions. She wants to make sure that every
   month she increases the number of cats in her
   house by 7%. If she has 100 cats at the beginning
   of January, how many cats will she have at the end
   of June (to the nearest cat)?

Compound Decay

Compound decay is the opposite of compound growth — it's when an amount gets smaller by a particular
percentage over a certain period. When applied to money, compound decay is known as **depreciation**.

The formula for **compound decay** is: $P_n = P_0 \times (1 - r/100)^n$

Example 3

A car was bought for £8000. Its value depreciated by 20% each year.
a) What was the value of the car after 3 years?   b) What was the value of the car after 10 years?

a)   The value when bought is 100%. After   a)   80% of £8000
   one year, this value will have decreased
   by 20%, so will be 80% of the original $= £8000 \times 0.8 = £6400$ (after one year)
   value. Multiply by 0.8 to find 80% of
   the original value. Multiply by 0.8 twice   £6400 × 0.8 = £5120 (after two years)
   more to find the value after three years.
                                                       £5120 × 0.8 = **£4096** (after three years)

b)   The quickest way to calculate this is by   b) $P_n = P_0 \times (1 - r/100)^n$ $P_0 = 8000$, $r = 20$, $n = 10$
   using the formula for compound decay:
                                                       $P_n = 8000 \times (1 - 20/100)^{10}$

                                                       $P_n = 8000 \times 0.8^{10} = 858.99$ (to 2 d.p.), so $P_n =$ **£858.99**

Exercise 3

1 Use the formula for compound decay to answer the following questions.

   a) Find the depreciation on £550 after 3 years at a depreciation rate of 3% per annum.

   b) Find the depreciation on £750 after 6 years at a depreciation rate of 2.5% per annum.

   c) What is the value of a car that cost £10 000 after five years of depreciation at 15%?

   d) What is the value of a car that cost £12 000 after 4 years of depreciation at 25%?

2 Claire the Evil Genius buys a laser for £68 000. It will depreciate at 20% per annum for the first two years and at 15% per annum for the next three years. What is the value of the laser after 5 years?

3 Mr Butterworth is on a diet and is losing weight at a rate of 2% of his total body weight every week. If he weighs 110 kg when he starts his diet, what will his body weight be at the end of 8 weeks?

4 Calculate the depreciation of a house after five years if it was bought for £650 000 and house prices are falling at a rate of 2.5% per annum.

5 Calculate the value of a car after seven years if it was bought for £6000 and depreciation is at a rate of 7.5% per annum.

6 The activity of a radioactive source decreases by 6% every hour. If the initial activity is 1200 Bq, calculate the activity after 10 hours.

7 A farmer buys a combine harvester for £210 000. It will depreciate by 30% for the first year and at 25% per annum for the next four years. What is the value of the combine harvester after 5 years?

8 Find the final value of an investment of £3500 that grows by 0.75% per annum for two years but then depreciates at a rate of 1.25% per annum for the next seven years

9 Find the final value of an investment of £1000 that grows by 5% per annum for the first two years but then depreciates at a rate of 2% per annum for the next three years.

Example 4

How long will it take (to the nearest month) for a motorbike valued at £2500 to depreciate to less than £1150 if depreciation is at a rate of 5% per month?

1. Using the formula for compound decay, you know the values of P_n, P_0 and r, and you want to find the value of n:

$P_n = P_0 \times (1 - r/100)^n$ $P_n = £1100$, $P_0 = £2500$, $r = 5$,

$1100 = 2500 \times (1 - 0.05)^n$
$\quad\quad = 2500 \times 0.95^n$

2. Use trial and improvement to find the value of n.

Try $n = 10$:	$2500 \times 0.95^{10} = 1496.84$	n is too small
Try $n = 20$:	$2500 \times 0.95^{20} = 896.21$	n is too big
Try $n = 15$:	$2500 \times 0.95^{15} = 1158.23$	n is too small
Try $n = 16$:	$2500 \times 0.95^{16} = 1100.32$	correct

$n =$ **16 months** (to the nearest month)

Exercise 4

1 A beehive population is decreasing at a rate of 4.9% per year. If there are initially 500 bees in the hive, how many years will it take for the beehive population to halve?

2 Mr Quasar is visiting Las Vegas and has taken $1000 to gamble in the casino. He is very unlucky and loses money at a rate of 15% a day. After how many days will Mr Quasar have less than $100 left?

3 The number of foxes in an area is falling by 12% per year. If there are 300 foxes then how long will it be before the number has fallen to below 200?

4 There are 500 harmful bacteria in a colony. When the population of harmful bacteria reaches 1000 it becomes unsafe and must be destroyed. If the growth in the number of bacteria is at a rate of 15% per hour, how many hours will it be until the colony must be destroyed?

5.5 Percentages Problems

Exercise 1

Answer the following questions **without** using your calculator.

1 Write each of the following amounts as a percentage.

    a) 13 out of 50   **b)** 27 out of 40   **c)** 72 out of 90   **d)** 12 out of 36

    e) 27 out of 45   **f)** 56 out of 80   **g)** 48 out of 120   **h)** 34 out of 170

2 For each of the following lists, write down which amount is not equal to the others.

    a) $0.25, 40\%, \frac{1}{4}$ **b)** $0.5, 20\%, \frac{1}{2}$ **c)** $0.125, 1.25\%, \frac{1}{8}$ **d)** $0.44, 44\%, \frac{4}{9}$

    e) $0.8, 8\%, \frac{4}{5}$ **f)** $0.615, 40\%, \frac{6}{15}$ **g)** $0.22, 44\%, \frac{22}{50}$ **h)** $0.25, 25\%, \frac{4}{24}$

3 At the Broughton bake sale, 18 of the 30 cakes for sale are Victoria sponge. What percentage of the cakes are not Victoria sponge?

4 Sarah has won 65% of her last 60 badminton games. How many games has she won?

5 There are 55 chocolates in a tin. 33 of the chocolates are milk chocolate. The rest are dark chocolate. What percentage are dark chocolate?

6 A school has 1200 pupils. 50% of the pupils get the bus to school, 20% walk and 5% get to school by bicycle. The remaining pupils are driven to school by their parents. How many pupils is this?

7 A pot of yoghurt normally contains 450 g. A special offer pot contains 35% extra free. How many grams of yoghurt does the special offer pot contain?

8 Write ⅛, 10% and 0.11 in order, from smallest to largest.

9 Jonny eats 60% of a steak and ale pie. Write this percentage as a fraction.

10 A coat normally costs £160, but in a sale, the price was reduced by 35%. Calculate the sale price of the coat.

11 A newborn baby weighs 3.2 kg. His weight increases by 5% over the next fortnight. What does he weigh at the end of the fortnight?

12 House A is valued at £420 000 and House B is valued at £340 000. After 5 years the value of House A has decreased by 15% and the value of House B has increased by 5%. What is the difference in value of the two houses after 5 years?

Exercise 2

You may use a calculator to answer the questions in this exercise.

1 Find each of the following:

    a) 3% of 210   **b)** 41% of 180   **c)** 73% of 467   **d)** 4.5% of 900

    e) 59% of 713   **f)** 82% of 823   **g)** 0.5% of 360   **h)** 0.7% of 860

2 Felicity goes shopping with £120 and spends £49 on brightly coloured trainers. What percentage of her money does she spend on trainers?

3 125 people work in an office. 12% of the office workers are men. How many workers is this?

4 28 of the 59 penguins at a zoo suffer from heatstroke during a particularly hot summer. What percentage of the penguins is this?

5 Paul is knitting a jumper for his Grandma Betty. So far he has knitted 87% of the jumper and used 108 m of wool. How many more metres of wool will he need to finish the jumper?

6 Sandra gets paid £1385 per month. In December she gets a Christmas bonus of £83.10. What percentage of her monthly wage is this bonus?

7 The insurance for a car normally costs £356. With a no-claims discount, the cost is reduced by 27%. What is the reduced cost of the insurance?

8 Kelly and Nasir both had maths tests last week. Kelly scored $\frac{47}{68}$ and Nasir scored $\frac{35}{52}$. Who got the higher percentage score?

9 Write $\frac{2}{33}$, 0.061 and 6% in order, from smallest to largest.

10 Dave loves a bargain and buys a feather boa which has been reduced in price by 70%. If the sale price is £2.85, what was the original price of the boa?

11 Two shops had a sale on a suit that had previously cost £92. Shop A had 70% off the original price, while Shop B had $\frac{7}{8}$ off. Which shop had the lower price, and by how much?

12 A cafe sells 270 ice cream sundaes in April and 464 in May. Find the percentage increase in ice cream sales.

13 Last summer, 385 000 people visited a holiday resort. $\frac{1}{8}$ were German, 0.11 were French and the rest were British.

  a) What percentage were British?

  b) How many British people visited the resort?

14 During a season, the average attendance for a local sports team's matches was 11 350. The following season, the average attendance was 11 123. Find the percentage decrease in attendance figures.

15 A car is bought for £12 950. Three years later, it is sold for £8806. After another three years, it is sold again for £4403.

  a) Find the percentage decrease in the car's price over the first three years.

  b) Find the percentage decrease in the car's price over the next three years.

16 In a sofa store 30% of the sofas are leather. 40% of the leather sofas are black. What percentage of the total number of sofas are made from black leather?

17 Pravin buys a £599 TV on hire purchase with a deposit of 37% and 36 monthly payments of £13.47. Calculate the total cost of the TV.

18 Consider two squares. Square A has side length x, and square B has side length $0.8x$. What is the percentage increase in area if you were to increase the area of square B to the area of square A?

Exercise 3

You may use a calculator to answer the questions in this exercise.

1 Tony deposits £3250 into a savings account that earns 8.5% interest per year. How much will he have at the end of the year?

2 The population of an island is 12 500. Each year, the population increases by 8%.

  a) Find the population of the island after 2 years.

  b) What is the population after 5 years?

3 Murray invests £575 in a bank account that pays annual compound interest of 7.5%. How much money will he have in the bank:

  a) after 3 years?

  b) after 6 years?

4 Ed gets a loan of £30 000 from a bank to set up a butterfly farm. The loan charges 6.8% annual compound interest, and Ed chooses to pay it back in one lump sum after 4 years. How much does he have to pay?

5 Find the final value of an investment of £2500 that earns 0.5% per month for the first six months but then depreciates at a rate of 0.25% per month for the next 9 months.

6 Mr Potter collects books. He has room on his book shelves for 6400 books. Every year he buys one book for every ten that he already owns. He starts with a collection of 4000 books. How many years will it take until he needs to buy new shelves?

7 Between 2000 and 2004, a bank pays interest at an annual compound rate of 2.5%. Between 2005 and 2007 this rate rises to 3.5%. Calculate the value at the end of 2007 of £800 invested at the beginning of 2000.

8 Calculate how long it would take for a car's value to fall below £120, if its initial value is £900 and the depreciation rate is 40% every six months.

9 James has invested his money unwisely. Each year the value of his assets depreciates by 10%. If he started with assets worth £5000, how many years will it take until his assets are valued at less than half their original worth?

10 On a very hot day the water in a glass of squash is evaporating at a rate of 20% per hour. The glass contains 150 ml. How many whole hours will it take to evaporate to below 40 ml?

11 The population of rabbits on a remote island starts at only 18 but explodes to 900, with a monthly population growth of 48%. Calculate how many months it takes to reach this number.

12 Prof. Plague has created a fungus that he thinks will cure the common cold. He needs the number of fungi to increase at a rate of 20% per hour in order to work properly. If he has 20 fungi at 10:00 a.m. and 100 fungi at 7:00 p.m., did he achieve his desired rate of fungus growth?

Section 6 — Expressions

6.1 Simplifying Expressions

An **algebraic expression** involves **variables** — letters that represent numbers. E.g. a $6b$ xyz $a + b$ $x^2 + y^2 + z^2$

(Remember — a is the same as $1a$, and $6b$ is the same as $6 \times b$.)

Expressions **do not** contain an equals sign ($=$).

Collecting Like Terms

A 'term' is a group of numbers or variables combined only by **multiplying** or **dividing**. Terms are separated by plus or minus signs. In the expression $2x + 6$, $2x$ and 6 are terms.

Expressions can sometimes be **simplified** by collecting **like terms**. 'Like terms' contain **exactly the same** combination of letters.

Example 1

Simplify the expression $x + x^2 + yx + 7 + 4x + 2xy - 3$ by collecting like terms.

There are four sets of like terms:
   (i)   terms involving just x
   (ii) terms involving x^2
   (iii) terms involving xy (or yx, which means the same)
   (iv) terms involving just numbers
Collect the different sets together separately.

$$x + x^2 + yx + 7 + 4x + 2xy - 3$$
$$= (x + 4x) + x^2 + (xy + 2xy) + (7 - 3)$$
$$= \mathbf{5x + x^2 + 3xy + 4}$$

Exercise 1

1   Simplify these expressions by collecting like terms.

   a) $c + c + c + d + d$ **b)** $a + b + a - a + b$ **c)** $x + y + x + y + x - y$

   d) $3m + m + 2n$ **e)** $5x + 2y + 3x$ **f)** $3a + 5b + 8a + 2b$

   g) $6p + q + p + 3q$ **h)** $5a - 2a + 5b + 2b$ **i)** $4b + 8c - b - 5c$

2   Simplify these expressions by collecting like terms.

   a) $x + 7 + 4x + y + 5$ **b)** $a + 2b + b - 8 - 5a$ **c)** $5x + 2y + 6 + 4y + 2x - 9$

   d) $13m + 7 + 2n - 8m - 3$ **e)** $5x + 2y + 3x - 2y - 3$ **f)** $13a - 5b + 8a + 12b + 7$

3   Simplify these expressions.

   a) $16p + 4q + 4 - 2p + 3q - 8 - 6q$ **b)** $6a + 9b - 12 + 4b - 2a + 15$

   c) $14b + 8c - b + 3 - 5c - 5b + 4$ **d)** $-3x + 9y + 2z - 2x - 5 + 4y - 8x$

   e) $-5m + 3 - 6n - 4 + 3n - 6m - 2n$ **f)** $8p + 6q + 14 - 6r - 4p - 14r - 2q - 23$

4   Simplify the following expressions by collecting like terms.

   a) $x^2 + 3x + 2 + 2x + 3$ **b)** $x^2 + 4x + 1 + 3x - 3$ **c)** $x^2 + 4x + x^2 + 2x + 4$

   d) $x^2 + 2x^2 + 4x - 3x$ **e)** $p^2 - 5p + 2p^2 + 3p$ **f)** $3p^2 + 6q + p^2 - 4q + 3p^2$

   g) $8 + 6p^2 - 5 + pq + p^2$ **h)** $4p + 5q - pq + p^2 - 7q$ **i)** $6b^2 + 7b + 9 - 4b^2 + 5b - 2$

5   Simplify the following expressions by collecting like terms.

   a) $ab + cd - xy + 3ab - 2cd + 3yx + 2x^2$ **b)** $pq + 3pq + p^2 - 2qp + q^2$

   c) $3ab - 2b + ab + b^2 + 5b$ **d)** $4abc - 3bc + 2ab + b^2 + 5b + 2abc$

Multiplying Variables

Powers work with **letters** in exactly the same way as they work with numbers.

$$a^2 = a \times a$$
$$a^3 = a \times a \times a \qquad a^m \times a^n = a^{m+n}$$

Example 2

Simplify these expressions.   a) $b \times b \times b \times b$ b) $4a \times 5b$ c) $3a \times 6a$

1. If the same letter is multiplied by itself, write it as a power.
2. Multiply numbers and letters separately.

a) $b \times b \times b \times b = \underline{\mathbf{b^4}}$

b) $4a \times 5b = 4 \times 5 \times a \times b = \underline{\mathbf{20ab}}$

c) $3a \times 6a = 3 \times 6 \times a \times a = \underline{\mathbf{18a^2}}$

Exercise 2

1 Simplify the following expressions.

a) $a \times a \times a$
b) $2a \times 3a$
c) $8p \times 2q$
d) $3a \times 7a$
e) $5x \times 3y$
f) $m \times m \times m \times m$
g) $12a \times 4b$
h) $6p \times 8p$

2 Simplify the following expressions.

a) $a \times ab$
b) $4a^2 \times 5a$
c) $2p \times 7q^2$
d) $4ab \times 2ab$
e) $x^2 \times xy$
f) $3i^2 \times 8j^3$
g) $9n^2m \div 3n^2$
h) $9xy \times 7xz$
i) $4st \times 5t$
j) $12a^2 \div 4a$
k) $16p^3q \div 2p^2$
l) $6abc \times 5a^2b^3c^4$

Example 3

Expand the brackets in these expressions.   a) $(3x)^2$ b) $(xy^2)^2$

a) $(3x)^2 = 3x \times 3x = 3 \times 3 \times x \times x = \underline{\mathbf{9x^2}}$

b) $(xy^2)^2 = xy^2 \times xy^2 = x \times x \times y^2 \times y^2 = \underline{\mathbf{x^2y^4}}$

3 Expand the brackets in these expressions.

a) $(2y)^2$
b) $(a^2)^2$
c) $(3c)^3$
d) $(2z^2)^3$
e) $a(2b)^2$
f) $5(q^2)^2$
g) $(xy)^2$
h) $i(jk)^2$

6.2   Expanding Brackets

You can **expand** (or remove) brackets by multiplying everything **inside** the brackets by the letter or number **in front**.

$$a(b + c) = ab + ac$$
$$a(b - c) = ab - ac$$

Example 1

Expand the brackets in these expressions.   a) $3(a + 2)$ b) $8(n - 3m)$

a) $3(a + 2) = (3 \times a) + (3 \times 2) = \underline{\mathbf{3a + 6}}$

b) $8(n - 3m) = (8 \times n) - (8 \times 3m) = \underline{\mathbf{8n - 24m}}$

Exercise 1

1 Expand the brackets in these expressions.

a) $2(a + 5)$
b) $4(b + 3)$
c) $5(d + 7)$
d) $3(p + 4)$
e) $4(x + 8)$
f) $6(5 - r)$
g) $4(b - 4)$
h) $5(3 - y)$
i) $8(y - 5)$
j) $3(x + y)$
k) $9(d - 9)$
l) $4(x + 7)$
m) $3(x + 12)$
n) $12(t - r)$
o) $7(x - y)$
p) $11(4 - b)$

2 Expand the brackets in these expressions.

a) $3(2n - 6m)$ b) $5(4u + 8v)$ c) $7(5n - 6m)$ d) $3(u + 8v)$

e) $4(4x - 7y)$ f) $3(2p - 11q)$ g) $8(2s - 12t)$ h) $6(4x + 5y)$

Example 2

Expand the brackets in these expressions.   a) $m(n + 7)$ b) $a(a - 4)$

a) $m(n + 7) = (m \times n) + (m \times 7) = \underline{\boldsymbol{mn + 7m}}$

b) $a(a - 4) = (a \times a) - (a \times 4) = \underline{\boldsymbol{a^2 - 4a}}$

3 Expand the brackets in these expressions.

a) $x(y + 5)$ b) $p(q + 2)$ c) $a(b + 4)$ d) $m(p + 8)$

e) $x(x - 2)$ f) $p(8 - q)$ g) $x(8 - x)$ h) $a(b - 12)$

i) $a(b + 12)$ j) $x(y + 7)$ k) $p(q + 3)$ l) $x(y + 6)$

m) $p(3q - 8)$ n) $r(5 - s)$ o) $t(14 - t)$ p) $a(2b - 4)$

Example 3

Expand the brackets in the following expressions.   a) $-(q + 4)$ b) $-3(4 - 2a)$

You can think of $-(q + 4)$ as $-1 \times (q + 4)$.
A minus sign outside the brackets reverses
the sign of everything inside the brackets.

a) $-(q + 4) = (-1 \times q) + (-1 \times 4)$
$= (-q) + (-4)$
$= \underline{\boldsymbol{-q - 4}}$

b) $-3(4 - 2a) = (-3 \times 4) - (-3 \times 2a)$
$= (-12) - (-6a)$
$= \underline{\boldsymbol{-12 + 6a}}$

Remember: $-(-6a) = 6a$.

4 Expand the brackets in the following expressions.

a) $-(q + 2)$ b) $-(x + 7)$ c) $-(h + 3)$ d) $-(g + 3)$

e) $-(m + 3)$ f) $-(n - 11)$ g) $-(p + 4)$ h) $-(q - 7)$

i) $-v(v + 4)$ j) $-v(v - 5)$ k) $-x(12 - x)$ l) $-y(4 + y)$

5 Expand the brackets in the following expressions.

a) $-6(5g - 3)$ b) $-7(4v + 8)$ c) $-2(5 + 4m)$ d) $-5(10 - 8v)$

e) $-5(2 + 3n)$ f) $-4z(8 - 2z)$ g) $-2(6b - 3)$ h) $-4y(2y + 6)$

i) $-4p(u - 7)$ j) $-2(12 - v)$ k) $-8(7 - w)$ l) $-5y(5 - x)$

Example 4

Simplify the expression $3(x + 2) - 5(2x + 1)$.
1. Multiply out both sets of brackets.
2. Collect like terms.

$3(x + 2) - 5(2x + 1) = (3x + 6) - (10x + 5)$
$= 3x + 6 - 10x - 5$
$= \underline{\boldsymbol{-7x + 1}}$

Exercise 2

1 Simplify the following expressions.

a) $2(z + 3) + 4(z + 2)$ b) $3(c + 1) + 5(c + 7)$ c) $4(u + 6) + 8(u + 5)$ d) $2(c + 2) + 3(c + 5)$

e) $3(v + 5) + 6(v + 7)$ f) $3(w + 4) + 7(w + 2)$ g) $7(a + 3) + (a + 4)$ h) $2(z - 7) + (z + 5)$

i) $3(x - 3) + (x + 12)$ j) $9(b + 2) + (b - 3)$ k) $8(y + 9) + (y - 3)$ l) $4(10b - 5) + (b - 2)$

2 Simplify the following expressions.

a) $5(p-3)-(p+6)$ b) $2(c-6)-(c+5)$ c) $5(q-3)-(q+1)$

d) $2(j-5)-(j-3)$ e) $5(y-4)-(y-2)$ f) $5(3c-6)-(c-3)$

g) $5(f-3)-(6+f)$ h) $12(d-7)-(9-d)$ i) $11(5x-3)-(x+2)$

3 Simplify the following expressions.

a) $5(2q+5)-2(q-2)$ b) $2(3c-8)-8(c+4)$ c) $4(5q-1)-2(q+2)$

d) $3(a-6)-4(a-1)$ e) $5(4z-3)-3(z-5)$ f) $5(q-2)-3(q-4)$

g) $2(y+15)-11(y-6)$ h) $3(6x-3)+9(x-2)$ i) $10(g-2)-4(g+12)$

4 Simplify the following expressions.

a) $4p(3p+5)-3(p+1)$ b) $6(4m+5)+7m(2m+3)$ c) $4(3k+1)-k(7k+9)$

d) $9b(2b+5)+4b(6b+6)$ e) $4(t+1)-7t(8t-11)$ f) $7h(3h+2)-10h(4h-1)$

g) $8x(3x-4)+12x(x+5)$ h) $8(u-1)-2u(20u+9)$ i) $5b(9b-32)-10b(3b-30)$

When expanding pairs of brackets, multiply each term in the left bracket by each term in the right bracket.

$$(a+b)(c+d) = ac + ad + bc + bd$$

Example 5

Expand the brackets in the following expressions.   a) $(q+4)(p+3)$ b) $3(x-2)^2$

Multiply each term in the left bracket by each term in the right bracket. Write the letters in each term of the answer in alphabetical order.

a) $(q+4)(p+3) = \underline{pq+3q+4p+12}$

Write out $(x-2)^2$ as $(x-2)(x-2)$. Multiply each term in the left bracket by each term in the right bracket. Collect like terms, then multiply the whole lot by 3.

b) $3(x-2)^2 = 3 \times (x-2)(x-2)$
$= 3 \times (x^2 - 2x - 2x + 4)$
$= 3 \times (x^2 - 4x + 4)$
$= \underline{3x^2 - 12x + 12}$

Exercise 3

1 Expand the brackets in the following expressions.

a) $(a+2)(b+3)$ b) $(j+4)(k-5)$ c) $(x-4)(y-1)$ d) $(x+6)(y+2)$

e) $(2+x)(8+y)$ f) $(9-a)(b-3)$ g) $(t-5)(s+3)$ h) $(y+12)(z-3)$

2 Expand the brackets in the following expressions.

a) $2(a+1)(p+6)$ b) $5(x+3)(y-7)$ c) $3(j-2)(k+4)$ d) $8(g+5)(h+9)$

e) $2(w-6)(z-8)$ f) $6(x-5)(y-2)$ g) $9(x+4)(3-y)$ h) $7(a-7)(b-8)$

3 Expand the brackets in the following expressions.

a) $(x+8)(x+3)$ b) $(b+2)(b-4)$ c) $(a-1)(a+2)$ d) $(d+7)(d+6)$

e) $(c+5)(3-c)$ f) $(y-8)(6-y)$ g) $2(x+2)(x+1)$ h) $(z-12)(z+9)$

i) $3(y+2)(3-y)$ j) $4(b-3)(b+2)$ k) $6(x-2)(x-4)$ l) $12(a+9)(a-8)$

4 Expand and simplify the following expressions.

a) $(x+1)^2$ b) $(x+4)^2$ c) $(x+5)^2$ d) $(x-2)^2$

e) $(x-3)^2$ f) $(x-6)^2$ g) $4(x+1)^2$ h) $2(x+5)^2$

i) $3(x-2)^2$ j) $2(x+6)^2$ k) $5(x-3)^2$ l) $2(x-4)^2$

When expanding triple brackets, multiply two brackets together, then multiply the result by the remaining bracket.

$$(a + b)(c + d)(e + f) = (a + b)(ce + cf + de + df)$$
$$= a(ce + cf + de + df) + b(ce + cf + de + df)$$
$$= (ace + acf + ade + adf + bce + bcf + bde + bdf)$$

Example 6

Expand and simplify the following expressions.   a) $(r + 2)(s + 1)(t + 4)$ b) $5(y - 1)^3$

1. Multiply each term in the second bracket by each term in the third bracket.

   a) $(r + 2)(s + 1)(t + 4) = (r + 2)(st + 4s + t + 4)$

2. Multiply the result by each term in the first bracket — simplify if possible.

   $= r(st + 4s + t + 4) + 2(st + 4s + t + 4)$
   $= \underline{rst + 4rs + rt + 4r + 2st + 8s + 2t + 8}$

1. Write out $(y - 1)^3$ as $(y - 1)(y - 1)(y - 1)$.
2. Multiply each term in the second bracket by each term in the third bracket.
3. Collect like terms before multiplying the result by each term in the first bracket.
4. Collect like terms before multiplying the result by 5.

   b) $5(y - 1)^3 = 5 \times (y - 1)(y - 1)(y - 1)$
   $= 5 \times (y - 1)(y^2 - y - y + 1)$
   $= 5 \times [y(y^2 - 2y + 1) - (y^2 - 2y + 1)]$
   $= 5 \times (y^3 - 2y^2 + y - y^2 + 2y - 1)$
   $= 5 \times (y^3 - 3y^2 + 3y - 1)$
   $= \underline{5y^3 - 15y^2 + 15y - 5}$

Exercise 4

1 Expand the brackets in the following expressions.

   a) $(a + 1)(b + 1)(c + 2)$ b) $(d - 2)(e + 3)(f + 2)$ c) $(4 + g)(h + 2)(i - 3)$

   d) $(j - 2)(k - 5)(l + 3)$ e) $(m - 5)(n - 1)(p - 3)$ f) $(2 - q)(r + 4)(s - 6)$

   g) $(3t + 2)(1 + u)(4 + v)$ h) $(2w + 2)(x + 7)(y - 2)$ i) $(-3 + z)(5 - 2a)(b + 3)$

2 Expand and simplify the following expressions.

   a) $(x + 3)(x + 1)(y + 2)$ b) $(p + 4)(p - 2)(q + 1)$ c) $(s + 5)(s - 2)(t - 3)$

   d) $(r - 3)(r - 2)(r - 5)$ e) $(y - 4)(y - 6)(y - 3)$ f) $(3q + 2)(1 + q)(q + 5)$

   g) $(2u + 4)(u - 3)(u + 4)$ h) $(1 - v)(v + 2)(v - 2)$ i) $(1 - 3z)(z + 5)(z - 3)$

3 Expand and simplify the following expressions.

   a) $2(z + 3)(z + 2)(z + 1)$ b) $5(u + 5)(u + 2)(u + 2)$ c) $6(c + 2)(c - 2)(c + 3)$

   d) $3(v + 4)(v - 3)(v - 2)$ e) $4(w - 4)(w - 5)(w - 2)$ f) $-(x - 7)(x + 5)(x + 1)$

   g) $-2(4s + 2)(s - 3)(s - 2)$ h) $-3(2y + 1)(y + 3)(y - 1)$ i) $3(3 - 2q)(3q + 3)(q - 2)$

4 Expand and simplify the following expressions.

   a) $(x + 3)^3$ b) $(x + 2)^3$ c) $(x - 2)^3$ d) $(x + 4)^3$

   e) $(3 - x)^3$ f) $(5 - x)^3$ g) $3(x - 1)^3$ h) $2(x + 5)^3$

   i) $3(2 + 2x)^3$ j) $-(5 - 2x)^3$ k) $-4(3 - 3x)^3$ l) $\frac{1}{4}(2x + 4)^3$

Factorising is the opposite of expanding brackets.
You look for a **common factor** of all the terms in an expression, and 'take it outside' the brackets.
To factorise an expression fully, look for the **highest common factor** of all the terms.

For a lot of these questions, you'll need to remember how to **divide** two powers: $a^m \div a^n = \dfrac{a^m}{a^n} = a^{m-n}$

Example 1

Factorise the expression $12x - 18y$.

1. 6 is the largest common factor of $12x$ and $18y$.
   So 6 goes outside the brackets.

2. Divide each term by the common factor, and write the results inside the brackets: $12x \div 6 = 2x$ and $18y \div 6 = 3y$

$$12x - 18y = 6(\quad - \quad)$$
$$= 6(2x - \quad)$$
$$= \underline{\mathbf{6(2x - 3y)}}$$

Example 2

Factorise $3x^2 + 2x$.

1. x is the only common factor of $3x^2$ and $2x$.
   So x goes outside the brackets.

2. Divide each term by the common factor, and write the results inside the brackets: $3x^2 \div x = 3x$ and $2x \div x = 2$

$$3x^2 + 2x = x(\quad + \quad)$$
$$= x(3x + \quad)$$
$$= \underline{\mathbf{x(3x + 2)}}$$

Exercise 1

1 Factorise the following expressions.

a) $2a + 10$	**b)** $3b + 12$	**c)** $15 + 3y$	**d)** $28 + 7v$
e) $5a + 15b$	**f)** $9c - 12d$	**g)** $3x + 12y$	**h)** $21u - 7v$
i) $4a^2 - 12b$	**j)** $3c + 15d^2$	**k)** $5c^2 - 25f$	**l)** $6x - 12y^2$

2 Simplify the following.

a) $x^2 \div x$	**b)** $2y^2 \div y$	**c)** $8p^2 \div p$	**d)** $35n^2 \div 7n$
e) $10d^2 \div 2d$	**f)** $24m^2 \div 3m$	**g)** $12a^2 \div 2a$	**h)** $22b^2 \div 11b$

3 Factorise the following expressions.

a) $3a^2 + 7a$	**b)** $4b^2 + 19b$	**c)** $2x^2 + 9x$	**d)** $4x^2 - 9x$
e) $21q^2 - 16q$	**f)** $15y - 7y^2$	**g)** $7y + 15y^2$	**h)** $27z^2 + 11z$
i) $10d^3 + 27d$	**j)** $4y^3 - 13y^2$	**k)** $11y^3 + 3y^4$	**l)** $22w - 5w^4$

Example 3

Factorise the expression $15x^2 - 10xy$.

1. 5 <u>and</u> x are common factors of $15x^2$ and $10xy$.
   So $5x$ goes outside the brackets.

2. Divide each term by the common factor, and write the results inside the brackets:
   $15x^2 \div 5x = 3x$ and $10xy \div 5x = 2y$

$$15x^2 - 10xy = 5x(\quad - \quad)$$
$$= 5x(3x - \quad)$$
$$= \underline{\mathbf{5x(3x - 2y)}}$$

4   Factorise the following expressions.

   a) $15a + 10ab$ **b)** $12b + 9bc$ **c)** $16xy - 4y$ **d)** $21x + 3xy$

   e) $14a + 7ab$ **f)** $15c - 12cd$ **g)** $3x - 15xy$ **h)** $24uv + 6v$

5   Factorise the following expressions.

   a) $10p^2 + 15pq$ **b)** $12xy + 8y^2$ **c)** $15ab - 20a^2$ **d)** $12q^2 - 18pq$

   e) $30ab^2 + 25ab$ **f)** $14x^2 - 28xy^2$ **g)** $12xy^2 + 8x^2y$ **h)** $8ab^2 + 10a^2b$

   i) $6a^2 + 9a^2b$ **j)** $12pq - 8p^3$ **k)** $8a^2 + 6a^4b^2$ **l)** $24x^3y - 16x^2$

Exercise 2

1   The expression $4x^3y^2 + 8xy^4$ contains two terms.

   a) What is the highest numerical common factor to both terms?

   b) What is the highest power of y that is common to both terms?

   c) What is the highest power of x that is common to both terms?

   d) Factorise the expression.

2   Factorise the following expressions.

   a) $x^6 + x^4 - x^5$ **b)** $8a^2 + 17a^6$ **c)** $5x^3 - 15x^2$ **d)** $12y^6 + 6y^4$

   e) $24b^2c^3 - 8c$ **f)** $24q^2 - 18q^5$ **g)** $2x^3 - 4x^5$ **h)** $25z^2 + 13z^6$

   i) $12p^2 + 15p^5q^3$ **j)** $9a^4b + 27ab^3$ **k)** $15b^4 - 21a^2 + 18ab$ **l)** $22pq^2 - 11p^3q^3$

   m) $x^2y^3 + x^3y + x^5y + x^2y^6$ **n)** $16x^2y - 8xy^2 + 2x^3y^3$ **o)** $36x^7y^2 + 8x^2y^9$ **p)** $5x^4 + 3x^3y^4 - 25x^3y$

3   Factorise the following expressions.

   a) $13x^2y^2 + 22x^6y^3 + 20x^5y^3$ **b)** $16a^5b^5 - a^4b^5 - ab^3$ **c)** $21p^6q^2 - 14pq^2 + 7p^3q$

   d) $14xy^4 + 13x^5y^3 - 5x^6y^4$ **e)** $7xy^2 + 4y^6 + 17x^5y^2$ **f)** $16c^6d^5 - 14c^3 + 8c^3d^6$

   g) $16a^6b^4 + 8a^4b^2$ **h)** $18jk + 21j^3k^6 - 15j^2k^3$ **i)** $36x^2y^4 - 72x^5y^7 + 18xy^3$

   j) $20a^4b^5 + 4a^3b^4 - 5a^6b^{15}$ **k)** $11x^2y^3 + 11x^3y^2 + 66xy^5$ **l)** $2jk - 9j^4k - 12j^2k^3$

6.4   Factorising — Quadratics

A **quadratic expression** is one of the form $ax^2 + bx + c$ where a, b and c are constants ($a \neq 0$).
You can **factorise** some quadratics.

> ### Example 1
> Factorise: a) $x^2 + 6x + 8$ b) $x^2 + 2x - 15$
>
> 1.   Find two numbers that add up to 6 and multiply to 8:   a) $4 + 2 = 6$ and $4 \times 2 = 8$
>
>   Then $x^2 + 6x + 8 = \underline{\mathbf{(x + 4)(x + 2)}}$
>
> 2.   You can check this by expanding the brackets. $(x + 4)(x + 2) = x^2 + 2x + 4x + 8$
>
> 1.   You need two numbers that multiply to -15, so one   b) $5 + -3 = 2$ and $5 \times -3 = -15$
>   must be positive and the other must be negative.
>
> 2.   They add up to $+2$, so the positive one is bigger.   Then $x^2 + 2x - 15 = \underline{\mathbf{(x + 5)(x - 3)}}$

Exercise 1

1   Factorise each of the following expressions.

   a) $x^2 + 5x + 6$ **b)** $a^2 + 7a + 12$ **c)** $x^2 + 8x + 7$

   d) $z^2 + 8z + 12$ **e)** $x^2 + 5x + 4$ **f)** $v^2 + 6v + 9$

2 Factorise each of the following expressions.

a) $x^2 + 4x + 3$ b) $x^2 - 6x + 8$ c) $x^2 - 7x + 10$

d) $x^2 - 5x + 4$ e) $y^2 + 3y - 10$ f) $x^2 + 2x - 8$

g) $s^2 + 3s - 18$ h) $x^2 - 2x - 15$ i) $t^2 - 4t - 12$

Example 2

Factorise $2x^2 - 5x - 3$.

1. The $2x^2$ must come from multiplying $2x$ by x, so put $2x$ in one bracket and x in the other.

$$2x^2 - 5x - 3 = (2x +/-\ \ )(x +/-\ \ )$$

2. For the other numbers in the brackets, try combinations of numbers that multiply to give -3.

$$(2x + 3)(x - 1) = 2x^2 - 2x + 3x - 3 = 2x^2 + x - 3 \ \ ✗$$

$$(2x + 1)(x - 3) = 2x^2 - 6x + x - 3 = 2x^2 - 5x - 3 \ \ ✓$$

so $2x^2 - 5x - 3 = \underline{(2x + 1)(x - 3)}$

Exercise 2

1 Factorise the following expressions.

a) $2x^2 + 3x + 1$ b) $3x^2 - 16x + 5$ c) $5x^2 - 17x + 6$ d) $2t^2 - 5t - 12$

e) $2x^2 - 13x + 6$ f) $3b^2 - 7b - 6$ g) $5x^2 + 12x - 9$ h) $2x^2 - 3x + 1$

i) $7a^2 + 19a - 6$ j) $11x^2 - 62x - 24$ k) $7z^2 + 38z + 15$ l) $3y^2 - 26y + 16$

Example 3

Factorise $6x^2 - 19x + 10$

1. The $6x^2$ could come from $6x \times x$ **or** from $3x \times 2x$.

2. The second term in the quadratic is negative (–) but the third term is positive (+). This implies that both factors are of the form $(ax - b)$.

3. Try $(6x - 1)(x - 10)$.

$$(6x - 1)(x - 10) = 6x^2 - 60x - x + 10 = 6x^2 - 61x + 10 \ \ ✗$$

4. The $-61x$ tells you that you need to avoid products like $6x \times 10$ which give too large answers. Try $(3x - 2)(2x - 5)$ instead.

$$(3x - 2)(2x - 5) = 6x^2 - 15x - 4x + 10 = 6x^2 - 19x + 10 \ \ ✓$$

So $6x^2 - 19x + 10 = \underline{(3x - 2)(2x - 5)}$

---

2 Factorise the following expressions.

a) $6x^2 + 5x + 1$ b) $6x^2 - 13x + 6$ c) $15x^2 - x - 2$ d) $10x^2 - 19x + 6$

e) $25a^2 + 65a + 36$ f) $12x^2 - 19x + 5$ g) $12u^2 + 6u - 6$ h) $14w^2 + 25w + 9$

Difference of Two Squares

Some quadratic expressions have no middle term, e.g. $x^2 - 49$. These quadratics have factors that are the same, except that one has a **positive** term and one has a **negative** term. For example, $x^2 - 49$ factorises to $(x - 7)(x + 7)$.

More generally: $a^2 - b^2 = (a + b)(a - b)$ This is known as the **difference of two squares**.

Example 4

Factorise $x^2 - 16$

$16 = 4^2$

Difference of two squares says: $x^2 - a^2 = (x + a)(x - a)$.

$x^2 - 16 = x^2 - 4^2$ So, $x^2 - 16 = \underline{(x + 4)(x - 4)}$

Exercise 3

1 Factorise each of the following expressions.

   a) $x^2 - 25$ **b)** $x^2 - 9$ **c)** $x^2 - 36$ **d)** $x^2 - 81$

2 A quadratic expression is of the form $16x^2 - 9$.

   a) Find $\sqrt{16x^2}$

   b) Write the expression $16x^2 - 9$ in the form $a^2 - b^2$.

   c) Hence factorise $16x^2 - 9$.

3 Factorise each of the following expressions.

   a) $4x^2 - 49$ **b)** $x^2 - 64$ **c)** $36x^2 - 4$ **d)** $9x^2 - 100$

   e) $b^2 - 121$ **f)** $16z^2 - 1$ **g)** $25x^2 - 16$ **h)** $27t^2 - 12$

Exercise 4 — Mixed Exercise

1 Factorise each of the following expressions.

   a) $x^2 - 4x - 5$ **b)** $t^2 - 8t + 16$ **c)** $x^2 - 36$ **d)** $y^2 - y - 20$

   e) $x^2 - x - 12$ **f)** $y^2 + 8y + 12$ **g)** $x^2 + 5x - 6$ **h)** $x^2 - 4x - 45$

   i) $s^2 - 10s + 16$ **j)** $x^2 + 12x + 32$ **k)** $b^2 + b - 6$ **l)** $t^2 - 9t + 14$

2 Factorise each of the following expressions.

   a) $16a^2 - 25$ **b)** $b^2 - 7b - 18$ **c)** $100x^2 - 64$ **d)** $y^2 + 19y + 84$

   e) $z^2 - 1$ **f)** $36x^2 - 169$ **g)** $5x^2 - 3x - 2$ **h)** $81t^2 - 121$

   i) $4c^2 - 196$ **j)** $a^2 + 9a - 36$ **k)** $z^2 - 15z + 56$ **l)** $144y^2 - 225$

   m) $2z^2 + 21z + 40$ **n)** $3x^2 - 17x - 28$ **o)** $x^2 - 2x + 1$ **p)** $7t^2 + 6t - 16$

   q) $4y^2 - 2y - 2$ **r)** $6z^2 - 27z + 12$ **s)** $8x^2 + 19x + 6$ **t)** $2x^2 - 13x + 21$

6.5 Algebraic Fractions

Simplifying Algebraic Fractions

Algebraic fractions can be simplified by **factorising** the numerator and/or the denominator, and then cancelling out any **common factors**. For algebraic fractions with **quadratic expressions**, factorise the quadratics **first**, then look for any factors that can be cancelled out.

Example 1

Simplify $\dfrac{3x^2y^4}{21xy^5}$.

1. 3 is a common factor, so it can be cancelled.

2. x is a common factor, so it can be cancelled.

3. y^4 is a common factor, so it can be cancelled.

$$\frac{3x^2y^4}{21xy^5} = \frac{\cancel{3} \times x^2 \times y^4}{\cancel{3} \times 7 \times x \times y^5}$$

$$= \frac{x^{\cancel{2}} \times y^4}{7 \times \cancel{x} \times y^5}$$

$$= \frac{x \times \cancel{y^4}}{7 \times y^{\cancel{5}}}$$

$$= \frac{x}{7 \times y} = \frac{x}{7y}$$

Exercise 1

1 Simplify:

   a) $\dfrac{2x}{x^2}$ **b)** $\dfrac{49x^3}{14x^4}$ **c)** $\dfrac{18xy}{6y^2}$ **d)** $\dfrac{25s^3t}{5s}$ **e)** $\dfrac{26a^2b^3c^4}{52b^5c}$

2 Simplify:

a) $\dfrac{7x}{5x - x^2}$ b) $\dfrac{48t - 6t^2}{8s^2t}$ c) $\dfrac{3cd}{8c + 6c^2}$ d) $\dfrac{2x - 4}{8y}$ e) $\dfrac{12}{4a^2b^3 + 8a^7b^9}$

Example 2

Simplify $\dfrac{x^2 - 16}{x^2 + 8x + 16}$.

1. Factorise the numerator and the denominator.
2. Cancel any common factors.

$$\dfrac{x^2 - 16}{x^2 + 8x + 16} = \dfrac{\cancel{(x + 4)}(x - 4)}{\cancel{(x + 4)}(x + 4)} = \dfrac{x - 4}{x + 4}$$

---

3 Simplify:

a) $\dfrac{4st + 8s^2}{8t^2 + 16st}$ b) $\dfrac{6y + 8}{15y + 20}$ c) $\dfrac{15xz + 15z}{25xyz - 25yz}$ d) $\dfrac{6xy - 6x}{3y - 3}$ e) $\dfrac{3a^2b + 5ab^2}{7ab^3}$

4 Simplify each of the following fractions as far as possible.

a) $\dfrac{2x - 8}{x^2 - 5x + 4}$ b) $\dfrac{6a - 3}{5 - 10a}$ c) $\dfrac{x^2 + 7x + 10}{x^2 + 2x - 15}$

d) $\dfrac{x^2 - 7x + 12}{x^2 - 2x - 8}$ e) $\dfrac{x^2 + 4x}{x^2 + 7x + 12}$ f) $\dfrac{2t^2 + t - 45}{4t^2 - 81}$

Adding and Subtracting Algebraic Fractions

Algebraic fractions should be treated in just the same way as numerical fractions.
This means that to add or subtract them, they need to have a **common denominator**.

Example 3

Express $\dfrac{x - 2}{3} + \dfrac{2x + 3}{4}$ as a single fraction.

1. The fractions are being added,
   so first find a common denominator.
2. Here, the common denominator is $4 \times 3 = 12$.
3. Then convert both fractions into fractions
   with denominator 12, so they can be added.

$$\dfrac{x - 2}{3} + \dfrac{2x + 3}{4}$$
$$= \dfrac{4(x - 2)}{12} + \dfrac{3(2x + 3)}{12}$$
$$= \dfrac{4(x - 2) + 3(2x + 3)}{12}$$
$$= \dfrac{4x - 8 + 6x + 9}{12} = \dfrac{10x + 1}{12}$$

Exercise 2

1 Express each of these as a single fraction, simplified as far as possible.

a) $\dfrac{x}{4} + \dfrac{x}{5}$ b) $\dfrac{x}{2} - \dfrac{x}{3}$ c) $\dfrac{2b}{7} + \dfrac{b}{6}$ d) $\dfrac{5z}{6} - \dfrac{4z}{9}$

2 Express each of these as a single fraction, simplified as far as possible.

a) $\dfrac{x - 2}{5} + \dfrac{x + 1}{3}$ b) $\dfrac{2t + 1}{4} + \dfrac{t - 1}{3}$ c) $\dfrac{3x - 1}{4} + \dfrac{2x + 1}{6}$ d) $\dfrac{c + 2}{c} + \dfrac{c + 1}{2c}$

Example 4

Express $\dfrac{2x-1}{x+1} - \dfrac{3}{x-2}$ as a single fraction.

1. The fractions are being subtracted, so first find a common denominator.

2. To do this, multiply both the numerator and denominator of the left-hand side by $(x-2)$, and the right-hand side by $(x+1)$.

3. Subtract the fractions and expand the brackets.

4. Simplify by collecting like terms.

$$\dfrac{2x-1}{x+1} - \dfrac{3}{x-2}$$

$$= \dfrac{(2x-1)(x-2)}{(x+1)(x-2)} - \dfrac{3(x+1)}{(x+1)(x-2)}$$

$$= \dfrac{(2x-1)(x-2) - 3(x+1)}{(x+1)(x-2)}$$

$$= \dfrac{2x^2 - 5x + 2 - 3x - 3}{(x+1)(x-2)}$$

$$= \dfrac{2x^2 - 8x - 1}{(x+1)(x-2)}$$

3 Express each of these as a single fraction, simplified as far as possible.

a) $\dfrac{2}{x+1} + \dfrac{1}{x-3}$

b) $\dfrac{x-2}{x-1} - \dfrac{x+1}{x+2}$

c) $\dfrac{2a-3}{a+2} + \dfrac{3a+2}{a+3}$

d) $\dfrac{x+2}{3x-2} + \dfrac{x-3}{2x+1}$

e) $\dfrac{s-2}{3s-1} + \dfrac{s+1}{3s+2}$

f) $\dfrac{x-2}{5} + \dfrac{x+1}{3x}$

g) $\dfrac{y+3}{y+1} - \dfrac{y+2}{y+3}$

h) $\dfrac{x-3}{x+2} - \dfrac{2x+1}{x+1}$

i) $\dfrac{2x+3}{x-2} - \dfrac{x-4}{x+3}$

Example 5

Express $\dfrac{x}{x^2+3x+2} + \dfrac{x-1}{x+2}$ as a single fraction.

1. Factorise the terms in each denominator.

2. Here the denominators have a common factor, $(x+2)$.

3. The fractions need to be added, so their denominators need to be the same.
   Multiply both the numerator and the denominator of the right-hand fraction by the same term, $(x+1)$.

4. Add the fractions and simplify the numerator by collecting like terms.

$$\dfrac{x}{x^2+3x+2} + \dfrac{x-1}{x+2}$$

$$= \dfrac{x}{(x+1)(x+2)} + \dfrac{x-1}{x+2}$$

$$= \dfrac{x}{(x+1)(x+2)} + \dfrac{(x-1)(x+1)}{(x+2)(x+1)}$$

$$= \dfrac{x+(x^2+x-x-1)}{(x+1)(x+2)} = \dfrac{x^2+x-1}{(x+1)(x+2)}$$

Exercise 3

1 Express each of the following expressions as a single fraction, simplified as far as possible.

a) $\dfrac{x-2}{(x-3)(x+1)} + \dfrac{5}{(x-3)}$

b) $\dfrac{3x}{(x+1)(x+2)} + \dfrac{1}{x+2}$

c) $\dfrac{1}{(x+4)} - \dfrac{(x-2)}{(x+4)(x+3)}$

2 Express each of the following expressions as a single fraction, simplified as far as possible.

a) $\dfrac{z}{z^2+3z+2} + \dfrac{10}{z+1}$

b) $\dfrac{x-3}{x^2+x-6} + \dfrac{2x}{x-2}$

c) $\dfrac{x-3}{x^2+4x} + \dfrac{3}{x+4}$

d) $\dfrac{a+1}{a^2-2a-3} - \dfrac{a+1}{a^2+4a+3}$

3 Express each of the following expressions as a single fraction, simplified as far as possible.

a) $\dfrac{2t+1}{t^2+3t} - \dfrac{t+2}{t^2+4t+3}$

b) $\dfrac{x}{x^2-9} + \dfrac{x+2}{x^2-5x+6}$

c) $\dfrac{3x}{x^2-4x+3} + \dfrac{x}{x^2-5x+4}$

d) $\dfrac{2y-1}{y^2-3y+2} - \dfrac{y-1}{y^2-5y+6}$

Multiplying and Dividing Algebraic Fractions

Example 6

Express $\dfrac{x-2}{x^2+6x+8} \times \dfrac{2x+4}{x^2+2x-8}$ as a single fraction.

1. Factorise each term as far as possible.
2. Cancel any factor which appears on the top of either fraction and on the bottom of either fraction.
3. Multiply the terms.

$$\dfrac{x-2}{x^2+6x+8} \times \dfrac{2x+4}{x^2+2x-8}$$

$$= \dfrac{\cancel{x-2}}{\cancel{(x+2)}(x+4)} \times \dfrac{2\cancel{(x+2)}}{\cancel{(x-2)}(x+4)}$$

$$= \dfrac{1}{(x+4)} \times \dfrac{2}{(x+4)} = \dfrac{2}{(x+4)^2}$$

Exercise 4

1 Express each of the following as a single fraction, simplified as far as possible.

a) $\dfrac{x}{y} \times \dfrac{3}{x^2}$

b) $\dfrac{2a}{4b^2} \times \dfrac{5b}{a^3}$

c) $\dfrac{t}{2} \times \dfrac{24st}{6t}$

d) $\dfrac{64xy^2}{9y} \times \dfrac{3x^3}{16x^2y}$

2 Express each of the following as a single fraction, simplified as far as possible.

a) $\dfrac{1}{x+4} \times \dfrac{3x}{x+2}$

b) $\dfrac{6a+b}{12} \times \dfrac{3a}{b+1}$

c) $\dfrac{1}{2z+5} \times \dfrac{3z}{z-1}$

d) $\dfrac{t^2+5}{12} \times \dfrac{4t^3}{1-t}$

3 Express each of the following as a single fraction, simplified as far as possible.

a) $\dfrac{x^2-16}{x^2+5x+6} \times \dfrac{x+3}{x+4}$

b) $\dfrac{x^2+4x+3}{x^2+6x+8} \times \dfrac{x+4}{2x+6}$

c) $\dfrac{x^2-3x-4}{x^2+5x+6} \times \dfrac{x^2+4x+4}{x-4}$

d) $\dfrac{z^2+3z-10}{z^2+4z+3} \times \dfrac{z^2+6z+5}{z-2}$

Example 7

Express $\dfrac{3x+6}{x^2-9} \div \dfrac{x+2}{x^2+4x+3}$ as a single fraction.

1. This is a division, so turn the second fraction over and change the sign to a multiplication.
2. Factorise each term as far as possible.
3. Cancel any factor which appears on both the top and the bottom of either fraction.

$$\dfrac{3x+6}{x^2-9} \div \dfrac{x+2}{x^2+4x+3}$$

$$= \dfrac{3x+6}{x^2-9} \times \dfrac{x^2+4x+3}{x+2}$$

$$= \dfrac{3\cancel{(x+2)}}{\cancel{(x+3)}(x-3)} \times \dfrac{(x+1)\cancel{(x+3)}}{\cancel{(x+2)}}$$

$$= \dfrac{3}{(x-3)} \times \dfrac{(x+1)}{1} = \dfrac{3(x+1)}{x-3}$$

4 Express each of the following as a single fraction, simplified as far as possible.

a) $\dfrac{4x}{3y^2} \div \dfrac{2x}{12y^4}$

b) $\dfrac{18a}{6b^2} \div \dfrac{a}{20b}$

c) $\dfrac{3x^3y^5}{4x^5y} \div \dfrac{xy}{28}$

d) $\dfrac{ab^2}{15} \div \dfrac{a^2}{5b}$

5 Express each of the following as a single fraction, simplified as far as possible.

a) $\dfrac{y-2}{3y+2} \div \dfrac{y-2}{4y^4}$

b) $\dfrac{2c+1}{3d^2} \div \dfrac{cd}{18}$

c) $\dfrac{1-x^3y^5}{25x^2} \div \dfrac{y}{5}$

d) $\dfrac{12t^5}{6t+3t^3} \div \dfrac{18t^2}{9t}$

6 Express each of the following as a single fraction, simplified as far as possible.

a) $\dfrac{x^2 - 4x + 3}{x^2 + 9x + 20} \div \dfrac{x^2 - x - 6}{x^2 + 7x + 12}$

b) $\dfrac{x^2 - 4x + 4}{x^2 + 6x + 5} \div \dfrac{2x - 4}{3x + 15}$

c) $\dfrac{y^2 - 5y + 6}{y^2 + y - 20} \div \dfrac{y - 2}{3y - 12}$

d) $\dfrac{x^2 - 4x + 4}{x^2 + 7x + 10} \div \dfrac{x^2 + 3x - 10}{x^2 - x - 6}$

e) $\dfrac{x^2 + 2x + 1}{x^2 - 5x + 4} \div \dfrac{x^2 + 4x + 3}{x^2 - 2x - 8}$

f) $\dfrac{t^2 - 9}{t^2 + 3t + 2} \div \dfrac{t^2 + 6t + 9}{t^2 + 8t + 7}$

6.6   Expressions Problems

Exercise 1

1   Simplify each of the following expressions by collecting like terms.

a) $3x - 2x + 5x - x$

b) $8y + 2y - 5y + 3y$

c) $5a - 3a + 2a - 10a$

d) $3x + 2y - 4x + 5y$

e) $6x + 3y - 2x - y$

f) $8s + 4 + 3t - 2s - 5t + 2$

g) $9p - 5 + 3p + 4q + 3q - 7$

h) $3x^2 + 5x - 7 + 2x^2 - 3x + 4$

i) $4x^2 - x + 6 - 3x^2 + 4x + 5$

2   Expand and then collect like terms in each of the following expressions.

a) $5(x - 2) + 3(x + 1)$

b) $6(x + 3) + 3(x - 4)$

c) $4(a + 3) - 2(a + 2)$

d) $5(p + 2) - 3(p - 4)$

e) $2(2x + 3) - 3(2x + 1)$

f) $5(2x - 1) + 4(3x - 2)$

g) $3(3b - 1) - 5(2b - 3)$

h) $x(x + 3) + 2(x - 1)$

i) $2x(2x + 3) + 3(x - 4)$

3   A triangle has sides of lengths $(x + 2)$ cm, $(3x - 1)$ cm and $(2x + 4)$ cm. Find a simplified expression for the perimeter of the triangle.

4   A rectangle is $(x + 5)$ cm long and $(x - 2)$ cm wide. Find expanded expressions for
a)   the perimeter of the rectangle,
b)   the area of the rectangle.

5   A square has sides $(3x - 2)$ cm long. Find expanded expressions for
a)   the perimeter of the square,
b)   the area of the square.

6   Zeke has 3 gems, each valued at £$(2x + 3)$, and Sharon has 4 gems, each valued at £$(3x - 4)$. Write an expression for the total value of the 7 gems.

7   I travel at $2x$ miles per hour for 3 hours, and then at $(x + 20)$ miles per hour for 2 hours. Write an expression to describe the total distance I travel.

8   Write an expression for the total cost of 3 widgets, each costing $(x - 2)$ pence, and 4 widgets, each costing $(2x + 3)$ pence.

9   A sports ground is a rectangle $(2x + 3)$ m long and $(2x - 5)$ m wide.
a)   Write an expression for the length of a white line painted around the edge of the ground.
b)   Write an expression for the number of square metres of turf that would be needed to re-lay the whole ground.

10   Rufina makes 36 scones to sell. The ingredients cost £x and she sells the scones for y pence each. Write an expression to describe the profit, in pence, that she makes.

11   A swimming pool is $(2x - 3)$ m long, $(x + 2)$ m wide and 2 m deep.
Write an expression for the volume of the pool
a)   in cubic metres.
b)   in litres.

$(x + 2)$ m $(2x - 3)$ m   2 m

12   A music stand is made of 3 strips of metal, each $(x + 20)$ cm long, and 5 strips of metal, each $(2x - 5)$ cm long. Write an expression for the total length of metal required to make the music stand.

13   Expand and simplify each of the following expressions.

a) $(x + 1)(x + 3)$

b) $(s + 2)(s + 5)$

c) $(x - 3)(x + 4)$

d) $(y + 2)(y - 6)$

e) $(x - 4)(x - 5)$

f) $(t - 6)(t + 1)$

14   Expand and simplify each of the following expressions.

a) $(2x + 3)(x - 3)$

b) $(3x + 1)(2x + 5)$

c) $(3t - 2)(2t + 1)$

d) $(2a - 5)(3a - 2)$

e) $(4x + 1)(x + 3)$

f) $(2y - 3)(2y + 1)$

g) $(x + 5)(x - 5)$

h) $(2z - 3)(2z + 3)$

i) $(2x + 1)^2$

j) $(b + 5)^2$

k) $(3x - 2)^2$

l) $(3x + 4)^2$

m) $(x + 1)(x - 2)(x + 3)$

n) $(y - 5)(y - 3)(y + 2)$

o) $-(t - 8)(t - 1)(t + 1)$

p) $3(z + 4)(z - 3)(z + 2)$

Exercise 2

1 Factorise each of the following expressions as far as possible.

a) $4x - 8$ b) $6a + 3$ c) $5t - 10$

d) $3x + 6xy$ e) $6x - 15y + 12$ f) $8a + 12b - 16$

2 Factorise each of the following expressions as far as possible.

a) $15x - 10x^2$ b) $8xy - 12x^2$ c) $y^2 + 4xy$

d) $6xy + 9x^2y^2$ e) $pq^2 - p^2q$ f) $a^2b - 2ab + ab^2$

g) $6c^2d - 9cd^2 + 12c^3$ h) $16x^2 + 12x^2y - 8xy^2$ i) $jk^3 - 2j^2k^2$

3 Factorise each of the following expressions as far as possible.

a) $5x^4y + 25x^2y^6$ b) $4p^7q^3 - 2p^2q^3$ c) $6ab^3 - 4ab^4 + 8ab^2$

d) $9c^2d - 9c^5d^2 + 15c^3$ e) $14x^3 + 7x^2y - 7xy^4$ f) $8j^9k^8 - 6j^5k^4$

4 Factorise each quadratic.

a) $a^2 + 6a + 8$ b) $x^2 + 4x + 3$ c) $z^2 - 5z + 6$ d) $x^2 + 3x - 18$

e) $x^2 - 8x + 15$ f) $x^2 + 9x + 20$ g) $x^2 + 2x - 24$ h) $x^2 - 3x - 10$

5 Factorise each quadratic.

a) $t^2 + 5t - 14$ b) $x^2 + x - 20$ c) $a^2 - 4a - 5$ d) $m^2 + 7m + 10$

e) $x^2 + 4x - 21$ f) $x^2 - 100$ g) $r^2 - 3r - 18$ h) $x^2 - 12x + 27$

6 Factorise each quadratic.

a) $2x^2 + 5x + 2$ b) $3m^2 - 8m + 4$ c) $3x^2 - 5x - 2$ d) $4g^2 + 4g + 1$

e) $6n^2 + 13n + 6$ f) $16k^2 - 9$ g) $5x^2 + 2x - 3$ h) $10z^2 + 11z - 6$

Exercise 3

1 Express each of the following as a single, simplified, algebraic fraction.

a) $\dfrac{a}{4} + \dfrac{a}{8}$ b) $\dfrac{x}{7} - \dfrac{x}{9}$ c) $\dfrac{p}{3} + \dfrac{5p}{6}$

d) $\dfrac{2x}{3} - \dfrac{2x}{7}$ e) $\dfrac{y-1}{2} + \dfrac{y+1}{3}$ f) $\dfrac{3x+1}{4} + \dfrac{x-3}{5}$

g) $\dfrac{t-2}{4} - \dfrac{t+3}{3}$ h) $\dfrac{2}{x+3} + \dfrac{4}{x-1}$ i) $\dfrac{5}{z+2} - \dfrac{3}{z+3}$

2 Simplify the following expressions.

a) $\dfrac{z+2}{z+3} + \dfrac{z+1}{z-2}$ b) $\dfrac{3}{x^2 + 4x + 3} + \dfrac{2}{x^2 + x - 6}$

c) $\dfrac{4}{t^2 + 6t + 9} - \dfrac{3}{t^2 + 3t}$ d) $\dfrac{x}{x^2 - 16} + \dfrac{x-2}{x^2 - 5x + 4}$

e) $\dfrac{3p}{p-2} - \dfrac{2p-4}{p^2}$ f) $\dfrac{x^2 - 4}{3x - 3} \times \dfrac{9}{2x - 4}$

3 Simplify the following expressions.

a) $\dfrac{x^2 - 7x + 12}{x^2 + 3x + 2} \times \dfrac{x+1}{x-3}$ b) $\dfrac{x^2 + x - 12}{x^2 - 4} \times \dfrac{x^2 + 2x}{3x + 12}$

c) $\dfrac{a^2 - 7a + 10}{a^2 + 5a + 6} \times \dfrac{a^2 + 2a - 3}{a^2 - 3a - 10}$ d) $\dfrac{8}{x} \div \dfrac{6}{x^2}$

e) $\dfrac{y-1}{2} \div \dfrac{x+1}{3}$ f) $\dfrac{s^2 + 4s + 3}{s^2 - 16} \div \dfrac{s+1}{s+4}$

g) $\dfrac{b^2 + 5b + 6}{b^2 + 6b + 5} \div \dfrac{2b+6}{3b+3}$ h) $\dfrac{x^2 + 8x + 15}{x^2 + 4x - 12} \div \dfrac{x^2 + 4x + 3}{x^2 + 8x + 12}$

Section 7 — Powers and Roots

7.1 Squares, Cubes and Roots

Squares and **cubes** are written using **powers**, e.g. $4 \times 4 = 4^2$ and $4 \times 4 \times 4 = 4^3$.

The square of **any** number is **positive**.
The cube of a **positive** number is always **positive**, but the cube of a **negative** number is always **negative**.

Example 1

Find: a) 4^2 b) $(-4)^2$ c) $(-4)^3$

$4^2 = 4 \times 4 = \mathbf{\underline{16}}$ $(-4)^2 = -4 \times -4 = \mathbf{\underline{16}}$ $(-4)^3 = -4 \times -4 \times -4 = \mathbf{\underline{-64}}$

Exercise 1

1 Find the square of each of the following numbers, without using a calculator.

    a) 5   **b)** 7   **c)** 100   **d)** 20   **e)** -2

    f) -5 **g)** -11 **h)** -30 **i)** 0.1   **j)** 0.5

2 Find the cube of each of the following numbers, without using a calculator.

    a) 2   **b)** 5   **c)** -10 **d)** 6   **e)** -8

    f) -1 **g)** 9   **h)** 20   **i)** -300 **j)** -0.1

3 Without using a calculator, find:

    a) 3^2 **b)** 3^3 **c)** $(-3)^3$ **d)** $(-3)^2$ **e)** $(-8)^2$

    f) 12^2 **g)** $(-5)^3$ **h)** $-(10^3)$ **i)** $((-2)^2)^3$ **j)** $((-2)^3)^2$

Every positive number has two **square roots**, one positive and one negative.
The symbol $\sqrt{}$ is used for the **positive** square root.
Negative numbers **don't** have square roots.

Every number has exactly one **cube root**. The symbol $\sqrt[3]{}$ is used for cube roots.

Example 2

a) Find both square roots of 16.

   1. $4^2 = 16$, so the positive square root is 4. $\sqrt{16} = \mathbf{\underline{4}}$

   2.   There's also the negative square root. $-\sqrt{16} = \mathbf{\underline{-4}}$

b) Find the cube root of 64.

   $4^3 = 64$, so the cube root is 4. $\sqrt[3]{64} = \mathbf{\underline{4}}$

Exercise 2

1 Without using a calculator, find:

    a) $\sqrt{36}$ **b)** $\sqrt{10\,000}$ **c)** $-\sqrt{16}$ **d)** $\sqrt{81}$

    e) $\sqrt{121}$ **f)** $\sqrt{169}$ **g)** $-\sqrt{144}$ **h)** $\sqrt{400}$

    i) The square roots of 49   **j)** The square roots of 9 000 000

2 Without using a calculator, find:

a) $\sqrt[3]{8}$ b) $\sqrt[3]{27}$ c) $\sqrt[3]{1000}$ d) $\sqrt[3]{-1}$

e) $\sqrt[3]{-125}$ f) $\sqrt[3]{512}$ g) The cube root of 216   h) The cube root of –8

Example 3

Calculate $\sqrt{10^2 - 6^2}$.

The square root and cube root symbols act like brackets. $\sqrt{10^2 - 6^2} = \sqrt{100 - 36}$
Evaluate the expression inside before you find the root. $= \sqrt{64}$
                                                                 $= \underline{\mathbf{8}}$

Exercise 3

1 Without using a calculator, find:

a) $2^3 + 3^2$ b) $5^3 - 10^2$ c) $4^3 + 7^2$ d) $(11 - 6)^3$

e) $\sqrt{3^2 + 7}$ f) $\sqrt{3^2 + 4^2}$ g) $\sqrt{13^2 - 5^2}$ h) $\sqrt[3]{5^2 + 2}$

i) $\sqrt{3^2 + 3^3}$ j) $\sqrt{4 \times (10^2)}$ k) $\sqrt[3]{(3 + 5)^2}$ l) $\sqrt[3]{3^2 \times 2^3 + 12^2}$

2 **Use your calculator** to find the following, giving your answers to 2 decimal places where appropriate.

a) 1.2^2 b) 3.4^2 c) 6.25^2 d) 4.58^2 e) 24.2^2

f) $\sqrt{344}$ g) $\sqrt{89.4}$ h) $\sqrt{(3 + 7)}$ i) $\sqrt{5^2 + 7}$ j) 3.4^3

k) 8.6^3 l) $\sqrt[3]{144}$ m) $\sqrt[3]{38.6}$ n) $\sqrt[3]{38 + 43}$ o) $(3.8 + 4.6)^3$

7.2   Indices and Index Laws

Index notation (or 'powers') can be used to show repeated multiplication of a number or letter.
For example, $2 \times 2 \times 2 = 2^3$. This is read as "2 to the power 3".

Powers have an **index** and a **base**:

base $\Rightarrow 2^3 \Leftarrow$ index

Example 1

a) Rewrite the following using index notation.

(i) $3 \times 3 \times 3 \times 3 \times 3$

$3 \times 3 \times 3 \times 3 \times 3 = \underline{\mathbf{3^5}}$

(ii) $b \times b \times b \times b \times c \times c$

$b \times b \times b \times b \times c \times c = b^4 \times c^2$
$= \underline{\mathbf{b^4 c^2}}$

b) Rewrite 100 000 using powers of 10.

$100\ 000 = 10 \times 10 \times 10 \times 10 \times 10$
$= \underline{\mathbf{10^5}}$

Exercise 1

1 Write the following using index notation.

a) $3 \times 3 \times 3 \times 3 \times 3 \times 3 \times 3$ b) $2 \times 2 \times 2 \times 2 \times 2$ c) $7 \times 7 \times 7 \times 7 \times 7 \times 7 \times 7$

d) $9 \times 9 \times 9 \times 9 \times 9 \times 9 \times 9 \times 9$ e) $12 \times 12 \times 12 \times 12$ f) $17 \times 17 \times 17$

2 Using index notation, simplify the following.

a) $h \times h \times h \times h$

b) $t \times t \times t \times t \times t$

c) $s \times s \times s \times s \times s \times s \times s$

d) $a \times a \times b \times b \times b$

e) $k \times k \times k \times k \times k \times f \times f \times f$

f) $m \times m \times n \times m \times n \times m$

3 Rewrite the following as powers of 10.

a) $10 \times 10 \times 10$

b) 10 million

c) 10 000

d) 100 thousand

e) 100 000 000

Exercise 2

1 Evaluate the following using a calculator.

a) 3^4

b) 2^8

c) 6^5

d) 8^3

e) 4^4

f) 13^5

g) 3^{10}

h) 9^5

i) 3×2^8

j) 8×5^4

k) $8 + 2^5$

l) $150 - 3^4$

m) $2^7 + 10^5$

n) $3^4 \times 2^5$

o) $7^5 + 8^4$

p) $8^7 \div 4^6$

q) $10^4 \times 10^3$

r) $2^4 \times 2^2$

s) $(9^3 + 4)^2$

t) $3^4 \div 5^4$

Example 2

Simplify $\left(\frac{2}{5}\right)^2$.

With powers of fractions, the power is applied to both the top and bottom of the fraction.

$$\left(\frac{2}{5}\right)^2 = \frac{2^2}{5^2} = \frac{4}{25}$$

Exercise 3

1 Write the following as fractions without indices.

a) $\left(\frac{1}{2}\right)^2$

b) $\left(\frac{1}{2}\right)^3$

c) $\left(\frac{1}{4}\right)^2$

d) $\left(\frac{2}{3}\right)^2$

e) $\left(\frac{3}{10}\right)^2$

f) $\left(\frac{3}{2}\right)^3$

g) $\left(\frac{5}{3}\right)^4$

h) $\left(\frac{4}{5}\right)^2$

i) $\left(\frac{4}{3}\right)^3$

j) $\left(\frac{6}{7}\right)^3$

Laws of Indices

Where a, m and n are any numbers or variables:

$$a^m \times a^n = a^{m+n}$$
$$a^m \div a^n = a^{m-n}$$
$$(a^m)^n = a^{m \times n}$$
$$a^1 = a$$
$$a^0 = 1$$

Example 3

Simplify the following, leaving the answers in index form.

a) $3^8 \times 3^5$

This is multiplication, so add the indices.

$$3^8 \times 3^5 = 3^{8+5} = \underline{\mathbf{3^{13}}}$$

b) $10^8 \div 10^5$

This one's division, so subtract the indices.

$$10^8 \div 10^5 = 10^{8-5} = \underline{\mathbf{10^3}}$$

c) $(2^7)^2$

For one power raised to another power, multiply the indices.

$$(2^7)^2 = 2^{7 \times 2} = \underline{\mathbf{2^{14}}}$$

Exercise 4

1 Without using a calculator, simplify the following. Leave your answers in index form.

a) $3^2 \times 3^6$ **b)** $10^7 \div 10^3$ **c)** $a^6 \times a^4$ **d)** $4^7 \times 4^4$ **e)** $(4^3)^3$

f) $6^7 \div 6^4$ **g)** 7×7^6 **h)** $8^6 \div 8^5$ **i)** $(c^5)^4$ **j)** $\dfrac{b^8}{b^5}$

k) $(11^2)^5$ **l)** $2^3 \times 2^{10}$ **m)** $f^{75} \div f^{25}$ **n)** $\dfrac{20^{222}}{20^{210}}$ **o)** $(g^{11})^8$

p) $e^{12} \times e^3$ **q)** $(100^3)^{23}$ **r)** $17^{540} \div 17^{96}$ **s)** $34^{315} \times 34^{49}$ **t)** $(14^7)^d$

2 For each of the following, find the number that should replace the square.

a) $3^3 \times 3^6 = 3^\blacksquare$ **b)** $q^8 \div q^3 = q^\blacksquare$ **c)** $8^\blacksquare \times 8^{10} = 8^{12}$ **d)** $(6^{10})^4 = 6^\blacksquare$

e) $t^5 \times t^4 = t^\blacksquare$ **f)** $(15^6)^\blacksquare = 15^{24}$ **g)** $(9^\blacksquare)^{10} = 9^{30}$ **h)** $r^7 \times r^\blacksquare = r^{13}$

i) $5^\blacksquare \div 5^6 = 5^7$ **j)** $6^5 \times 6^\blacksquare = 6^{12}$ **k)** $10^\blacksquare \div 10^2 = 10^4$ **l)** $12^{14} \div 12^\blacksquare = 12^7$

m) $(p^7)^\blacksquare = p^{49}$ **n)** $13^6 \div 13^\blacksquare = 13$ **o)** $s^9 \times s^\blacksquare = s^{14}$ **p)** $(2^\blacksquare)^5 = 2^{40}$

In Questions 3-4, simplify each expression without using a calculator. Leave your answers in index form.

3 a) $3^2 \times 3^5 \times 3^7$ **b)** $5^4 \times 5 \times 5^8$ **c)** $(p^6)^2 \times p^5$ **d)** $(9^4 \times 9^3)^5$

e) $7^3 \times 7^5 \div 7^6$ **f)** $8^3 \times 8^7 \div 8^9$ **g)** $(12^8 \div 12^4)^3$ **h)** $(q^3)^6 \div q^4$

4 a) $\dfrac{3^4 \times 3^5}{3^6}$ **b)** $\dfrac{r \times r^4}{r^2}$ **c)** $\dfrac{8^5 \times 8^4}{8^2 \times 8^3}$ **d)** $\left(\dfrac{6^3 \times 6^9}{6^7}\right)^3$

e) $\dfrac{s^8 \times s^4}{s^3 \times s^6}$ **f)** $\dfrac{2^5 \times 2^5}{(2^3)^2}$ **g)** $\dfrac{4^4 \times 4^6}{4^8 \times 4}$ **h)** $\dfrac{7 \times 7^8}{7^2 \times 7^3}$

i) $\dfrac{5^5 \times 5^5}{5^8 \div 5^3}$ **j)** $\dfrac{10^8 \div 10^3}{10^4 \div 10^4}$ **k)** $\dfrac{(t^6 \div t^3)^4}{t^9 \div t^4}$ **l)** $\dfrac{(8^5)^7 \div 8^{12}}{8^6 \times 8^{10}}$

5 a) Write: **(i)** 4 as a power of 2   **(ii)** 4^5 as a power of 2   **(iii)** $2^3 \times 4^5$ as a power of 2

     b) Write: **(i)** 9×3^3 as a power of 3   **(ii)** $5 \times 25 \times 125$ as a power of 5   **(iii)** 16×2^6 as a power of 4

     c) Evaluate: **(i)** $2^2 \times 4^2$ **(ii)** $100^2 \times 10^5$ **(iii)** $3^3 \times 2^3$

Negative Indices

Where a and m are any numbers or variables:

$$a^{-m} = \dfrac{1}{a^m}$$

Exercise 5

1 Write the following as fractions.

a) 4^{-1} **b)** 7^{-1} **c)** 2^{-2} **d)** 5^{-3} **e)** 2×3^{-1}

2 Write the following in the form a^{-m}.

a) $\dfrac{1}{5}$ **b)** $\dfrac{1}{11}$ **c)** $\dfrac{1}{3^2}$ **d)** $\dfrac{1}{2^7}$ **e)** $5 \times \dfrac{1}{7^2}$

3 Simplify the following.

a) $\left(\dfrac{1}{2}\right)^{-1}$ **b)** $\left(\dfrac{2}{3}\right)^{-1}$ **c)** $\left(\dfrac{1}{3}\right)^{-2}$ **d)** $\left(\dfrac{5}{2}\right)^{-3}$ **e)** $\left(\dfrac{7}{10}\right)^{-2}$

Example 4

Simplify the following.

a) $y^4 \div \dfrac{1}{y^3}$

    1. Rewrite $\dfrac{1}{y^3}$ using negative indices.

    2. Subtract the indices.

$$y^4 \div \dfrac{1}{y^3} = y^4 \div y^{-3}$$
$$= y^{4-(-3)} = \underline{\mathbf{y^7}}$$

b) $z^8 \times (z^4)^{-2}$

    1. Multiply the indices to simplify $(z^4)^{-2}$.

    2. Now add the indices.

    3. Anything to the power 0 is 1.

$$z^8 \times (z^4)^{-2} = z^8 \times z^{4 \times (-2)} = z^8 \times z^{-8}$$
$$= z^{8+(-8)} = z^0$$
$$= \underline{\mathbf{1}}$$

4 Without using a calculator, simplify the following. Leave your answers in index form.

a) $5^4 \times 5^{-2}$

b) $8^{-10} \times 8^7$

c) $g^6 \div g^{-6}$

d) $(3^2)^{-8}$

e) $(h^{-5})^{-1}$

f) $2^{16} \div \dfrac{1}{2^4}$

g) $17^9 \times \dfrac{1}{17^3}$

h) $\dfrac{1}{7^8} \times 7^{-2}$

i) $\left(\dfrac{1}{p^4}\right)^5$

j) $k^{10} \times k^{-6} \div k^0$

k) $4^{-5} \div 4^{-8} \times 4^{-1}$

l) $\left(\dfrac{l^{-5}}{l^6}\right)^{-3}$

m) $\dfrac{12^5}{12^{-5}} \times \dfrac{1}{12^{-8}}$

n) $\dfrac{6^{-3} \times 6^{10}}{6^4 \times 6^{-5}}$

o) $\dfrac{(3^{-2})^3}{3^8 \times 3^{-8}}$

p) $\dfrac{m^7 \div m^{-3}}{m^{-2} \div m^9}$

q) $\dfrac{7^4}{7^7 \times 7^{-8} \div 7^{-2}}$

r) $\dfrac{n^{-4} \times n}{(n^{-3})^6}$

s) $\left(\dfrac{10^7 \times 10^{-11}}{10^9 \div 10^4}\right)^{-5}$

t) $13^{-4} \div \dfrac{1}{13^{-11}}$

5   a) Write the number 0.01 as:

    (i) a fraction of the form $\dfrac{1}{a}$ **(ii)** a fraction of the form $\dfrac{1}{10^m}$ **(iii)** a power of 10

     b) Rewrite the following as powers of 10.

      (i) 0.1   **(ii)** 0.00000001   **(iii)** 0.0001   **(iv)** 1

Example 5

Evaluate $2^4 \times 5^{-3}$. Give the answer as a fraction.

    1. Turn the negative index into a fraction.

    2. Evaluate the powers.

$$2^4 \times 5^{-3} = 2^4 \times \dfrac{1}{5^3} = \dfrac{2^4}{5^3}$$
$$= \dfrac{16}{125}$$

6 Evaluate the following without using a calculator. Write the answers as fractions.

a) 3^{-1}

b) 3^{-2}

c) $3^2 \times 5^{-2}$

d) $2^{-3} \times 7^1$

e) $\left(\dfrac{1}{2}\right)^{-2} \times \left(\dfrac{1}{3}\right)^2$

f) $6^{-4} \div 6^{-2}$

g) $(-9)^2 \times (-5)^{-3}$

h) $8^{-5} \times 8^3 \times 3^3$

i) $10^{-5} \div 10^6 \times 10^4$

j) $4 \times 3^{-1} \times 4 \div 3^3$

k) $6^2 \times 10^{-5} \div 100^{-1}$

l) $\left(\dfrac{3}{4}\right)^{-1} \div \left(\dfrac{1}{2}\right)^{-3}$

Fractional Indices

Where a and m are any numbers or variables: $\quad a^{\frac{1}{m}} = \sqrt[m]{a}$

Example 6

Find $27^{\frac{2}{3}}$

1. Split up the index using $(a^m)^n = a^{m \times n}$.

2. You could write $\left(27^{\frac{1}{3}}\right)^2$ or $\left(27^2\right)^{\frac{1}{3}}$.
    Pick the one that makes things easiest to work out.

$$27^{\frac{2}{3}} = 27^{\frac{1}{3} \times 2}$$
$$= \left(27^{\frac{1}{3}}\right)^2$$
$$= \left(\sqrt[3]{27}\right)^2$$
$$= 3^2 = \underline{\mathbf{9}}$$

Exercise 6

1 Rewrite the following expressions in the form $\sqrt[m]{a}$ or $\left(\sqrt[m]{a}\right)^n$.

    a) $a^{\frac{1}{5}}$ **b)** $a^{\frac{1}{8}}$ **c)** $a^{\frac{3}{5}}$ **d)** $a^{\frac{2}{5}}$ **e)** $a^{\frac{5}{2}}$

Evaluate the expressions given in Questions 2-3 without using a calculator.

2   **a)** $64^{\frac{1}{2}}$ **b)** $144^{\frac{1}{2}}$ **c)** $64^{\frac{1}{3}}$
      d) $16^{\frac{1}{4}}$ **e)** $1\,000\,000^{\frac{1}{2}}$ **f)** $1\,000\,000^{\frac{1}{6}}$

3   **a)** $125^{\frac{2}{3}}$ **b)** $9^{\frac{3}{2}}$ **c)** $400^{\frac{3}{2}}$
      d) $1000^{\frac{5}{3}}$ **e)** $32^{\frac{3}{5}}$ **f)** $8000^{\frac{4}{3}}$

4 Evaluate the following using a calculator. Give your answers to 2 decimal places where appropriate.

    a) $7^{\frac{1}{2}}$ **b)** $424^{\frac{1}{2}}$ **c)** $0.02^{\frac{1}{2}}$ **d)** $11^{\frac{1}{3}}$ **e)** $200^{\frac{1}{3}}$

    f) $(-12)^{\frac{1}{3}}$ **g)** $912^{\frac{4}{9}}$ **h)** $2.71^{\frac{7}{8}}$ **i)** $-\left(3.33^{\frac{3}{10}}\right)$ **j)** $0.4^{\frac{4}{5}}$

Exercise 7 — Mixed Exercise

1 Simplify the following. Leave your answers in index form.

    a) $7^6 \times 7^9$ **b)** $d^{-4} \div d^6$ **c)** $(4^8)^3$ **d)** $14^2 \times 14^{\frac{1}{2}}$

    e) $(p^2)^{\frac{1}{2}}$ **f)** $9^{-2} \times \sqrt[4]{9}$ **g)** $23^{\frac{1}{3}} \div 23^2$ **h)** $\left(c^{10} \div c^2\right)^{\frac{1}{4}}$

    i) $q^{\frac{1}{4}} \div \sqrt{q}$ **j)** $12^{\frac{2}{3}} \div 12^{-\frac{2}{3}}$ **k)** $(99^4)^{-\frac{1}{3}}$ **l)** $\dfrac{1}{r^{\frac{1}{4}}} \times r^{\frac{3}{2}}$

    m) $21^{-3} \div 21^{-\frac{3}{2}}$ **n)** $2^4 \times \dfrac{1}{\sqrt[3]{2}} \times 2^{-\frac{1}{2}}$ **o)** $\left(\dfrac{s^{\frac{9}{10}}}{s^{\frac{3}{5}}}\right)^{-4}$ **p)** $t \times t^{-\frac{1}{6}} \times t^{-\frac{1}{2}} \div t^{\frac{1}{6}}$

2 Simplify the following.

    a) $(27m)^{\frac{1}{3}}$ **b)** $\left(\dfrac{n^5}{100}\right)^{\frac{3}{2}}$ **c)** $(y^4z^3)^{-\frac{3}{4}}$ **d)** $\left(\dfrac{b^9}{64c^3}\right)^{\frac{2}{3}}$

    e) $\dfrac{s^4}{\sqrt[3]{8s}}$ **f)** $\dfrac{\sqrt{36t^3}}{2t^{-2}}$ **g)** $\sqrt[4]{u^2} \times (2u)^{-2}$ **h)** $\sqrt{\dfrac{v^2 \times 16v^{\frac{1}{2}}}{100v}}$

3 Write the following as powers of 2.

    a) 8 **b)** $\sqrt{2}$ **c)** $8\sqrt{2}$ **d)** $\dfrac{1}{8\sqrt{2}}$

4 Write the following expressions.

    a) $3 \times \sqrt[3]{3}$ as a power of 3   **b)** $16\sqrt{4}$ as a power of 4   **c)** 5 as a power of 25

    d) 2 as a power of 8   **e)** $\dfrac{\sqrt{10}}{1000}$ as a power of 10   **f)** $\dfrac{81}{\sqrt[3]{9}}$ as a power of 3

7.3 Standard Form

In **standard form** (or standard index form), numbers are written like this:

A can be any number between 1 and 10 (but not 10 itself) $\Rightarrow$ $\text{A} \times 10^n$ $\Leftarrow$ n can be any integer

Example 1

Write these numbers in standard form.

a) 360 000

$360\,000 = 3.6 \times 100\,000 = \underline{\mathbf{3.6 \times 10^5}}$

b) 0.000036

$0.000036 = 3.6 \times 0.00001 = \underline{\mathbf{3.6 \times 10^{-5}}}$

Exercise 1

Write the following numbers in standard form.

1   **a)** 250   **b)** 1100   **c)** 330   **d)** 48 000   **e)** 5 900 000
    f) 2 750 000   **g)** 8560   **h)** 7340   **i)** 808 080   **j)** 7450
    k) 2700   **l)** 1 400 140   **m)** 930 078   **n)** 54 000 000 000   **o)** 290 070

2   **a)** 0.0025   **b)** 0.0067   **c)** 0.0303   **d)** 0.00048   **e)** 0.000056
    f) 0.375   **g)** 0.000078   **h)** 0.07070   **i)** 0.00000000021   **j)** 0.0005002

Example 2

Write the following standard form numbers as ordinary numbers.

a) 3.5×10^3

$3.5 \times 10^3 = 3.5 \times 1000 = \underline{\mathbf{3500}}$

b) 4.67×10^{-5}

$4.67 \times 10^{-5} = 4.67 \div 10^5 = 4.67 \div 100\,000 = \underline{\mathbf{0.0000467}}$

Exercise 2

1   Write the following out as ordinary numbers.

    a) 3×10^6 **b)** 4×10^2 **c)** 9.4×10^4 **d)** 8.8×10^5 **e)** 4.09×10^3
    f) 1.989×10^8 **g)** 6.69×10^1 **h)** 7.20×10^0 **i)** 3.56×10^{-6} **j)** 4.23×10^{-2}
    k) 9.45×10^{-4} **l)** 8.88×10^{-5} **m)** 1.9×10^{-8} **n)** 6.69×10^{-1} **o)** 7.05×10^{-6}

Multiplying and Dividing in Standard Form

Example 3

Calculate $(2.4 \times 10^7) \times (5.2 \times 10^3)$. Give your answer in standard form.

1. Rearrange to put the index and non-index parts together.

$2.4 \times 5.2 \times 10^7 \times 10^3$

2. Multiply the non-index parts and add the indices.

$= 12.48 \times 10^{7+3}$

3. This isn't in standard form — 12.48 isn't between 1 and 10. Convert 12.48 to standard form.

$= 12.48 \times 10^{10}$

$= 1.248 \times 10 \times 10^{10}$

4. Add the indices again to get the answer in standard form.

$= \underline{\mathbf{1.248 \times 10^{11}}}$

Exercise 3

1 Convert the following numbers to standard form.

    a) 0.034×10^4 **b)** 0.00567×10^9 **c)** 0.0505×10^3 **d)** 907×10^5

    e) 95.32×10^2 **f)** 0.034×10^{-4} **g)** 0.0505×10^{-3} **h)** 567×10^{-5}

    i) 907×10^{-5} **j)** 26.3×10^{-6} **k)** 845000×10^{-3} **l)** 0.00613×10^{-4}

2 Calculate the following. Give your answers in standard form.

    a) $(3.4 \times 10^7) \times (4.5 \times 10^{-4})$ **b)** $(4.6 \times 10^9) \times (5.5 \times 10^{-4})$ **c)** $(6 \times 10^5) \times (2.37 \times 10^2)$

    d) $(3.4 \times 10^{-4}) \times (2.8 \times 10^2)$ **e)** $(3.4 \times 10^{-5}) \times (8.7 \times 10^5)$ **f)** $(1.2 \times 10^4) \times (5.3 \times 10^6)$

    g) $(7.2 \times 10^{-4}) \times (1.5 \times 10^{-7})$ **h)** $(3.6 \times 10^6) \times (1.2 \times 10^4)$ **i)** $(3.3 \times 10^{-3}) \times (6.6 \times 10^{-6})$

Example 4

Calculate $(9.6 \times 10^7) \div (1.2 \times 10^4)$. Give your answer in standard form.

1. Rewrite as a fraction.
$$\frac{9.6 \times 10^7}{1.2 \times 10^4}$$

2. Separate the index and non-index parts.
$$= \frac{9.6}{1.2} \times \frac{10^7}{10^4}$$

3. Simplify the two fractions.
$$= 8 \times 10^{7-4}$$
$$= \underline{\mathbf{8 \times 10^3}}$$

---

3 Calculate the following. Give your answers in standard form.

    a) $(3.6 \times 10^7) \div (1.2 \times 10^4)$ **b)** $(8.4 \times 10^4) \div (7 \times 10^8)$ **c)** $(1.8 \times 10^{-4}) \div (1.2 \times 10^8)$

    d) $(4.8 \times 10^3) \div (1.2 \times 10^{-2})$ **e)** $(8.1 \times 10^{-1}) \div (0.9 \times 10^{-2})$ **f)** $(13.2 \times 10^5) \div (1.2 \times 10^4)$

Adding and Subtracting in Standard Form

To add or subtract numbers in standard form, the powers of 10 have to be the same.

Example 5

Calculate $(3.7 \times 10^4) + (2.2 \times 10^3)$

1. The powers of 10 don't match.
   Change 2.2×10^3 so that both numbers are multiplied by 10^4.

2. Add the non-index parts.

$$(3.7 \times 10^4) + (2.2 \times 10^3)$$
$$= (3.7 \times 10^4) + (0.22 \times 10^4)$$
$$= (3.7 + 0.22) \times 10^4$$
$$= \underline{\mathbf{3.92 \times 10^4}}$$

Exercise 4

Calculate the following, giving your answers in standard form.

1   **a)** $(5.0 \times 10^3) + (3.0 \times 10^2)$ **b)** $(6.4 \times 10^2) + (8.0 \times 10^1)$ **c)** $(1.8 \times 10^5) + (3.2 \times 10^3)$

    d) $(9.9 \times 10^8) + (5.5 \times 10^6)$ **e)** $(6.2 \times 10^{-2}) + (4.9 \times 10^{-1})$ **f)** $(6.9 \times 10^{-4}) + (3.8 \times 10^{-5})$

    g) $(3.7 \times 10^{-1}) + (1.1 \times 10^0)$ **h)** $(6.5 \times 10^3) + (9.4 \times 10^4)$ **i)** $(5.5 \times 10^7) + (5.5 \times 10^8)$

2   **a)** $(5.2 \times 10^4) - (3.3 \times 10^3)$ **b)** $(7.2 \times 10^{-3}) - (1.5 \times 10^{-4})$ **c)** $(3.6 \times 10^7) - (9.4 \times 10^6)$

    d) $(6.5 \times 10^{-2}) - (3.3 \times 10^2)$ **e)** $(2.8 \times 10^4) - (1.2 \times 10^3)$ **f)** $(8.4 \times 10^2) - (6.3 \times 10^0)$

    g) $(8.4 \times 10^4) - (8.3 \times 10^2)$ **h)** $(28.4 \times 10^{-1}) - (9.3 \times 10^{-2})$ **i)** $(21.7 \times 10^3) - (9.2 \times 10^2)$

Exercise 5 — Mixed Exercise

Give all your answers in this exercise in standard form.

1 Albert measured the length of his favourite hair each day for three days. On the first day it grew 3.92×10^{-4} m, on the second day it grew 3.77×10^{-4} m, and on the third day it grew 4.09×10^{-4} m. By how much in metres did the hair grow in total over the three days?

2 The Hollywood film 'The Return of Dr Arzt' cost 3.45×10^8 to make. It made a total of 8.9×10^7 at the box office. What was the loss made by the film?

3 A scientist has a sample of bacteria containing 6.25×10^{12} cells. If the average mass of each cell is 2.4×10^{-13} g, what is the total mass of the sample in grams?

4 A country has a population of 8.32×10^7 people. There are 5.2×10^4 branches of the supermarket Spendalot in the country. How many people are there per Spendalot store?

5 To 3 significant figures, the mass of the Earth is 5.97×10^{24} kg, and the mass of the Sun is 3.33×10^5 times the mass of the Earth. What is the mass of the Sun in kg? Give your answer to 3 s.f.

6 The regular ant is a rare and possibly fictional species of ant. Every adult regular ant measures exactly 6.5×10^{-3} m in length. How many adult regular ants would fit on a line 325 m long?

7 Earth is approximately 4.54×10^9 years old. Humans are thought to have evolved around 2.5×10^5 years ago. For what percentage of the age of the Earth have humans been present? Give your answer to 3 s.f.

7.4 Surds

A **surd** is a root that you can't write out exactly as a fraction or decimal. E.g. $\sqrt{2} = 1.4142135...$
If a question involving surds asks for an **exact answer**, you have to leave the surds in.

Multiplying and Dividing Surds

Where a and b are any numbers:

$$\sqrt{a} \times \sqrt{b} = \sqrt{a \times b}$$

$$\sqrt{a} \div \sqrt{b} = \frac{\sqrt{a}}{\sqrt{b}} = \sqrt{\frac{a}{b}}$$

These two rules are used to simplify expressions containing surds.
The aim is to make the number under the root as small as possible, or get rid of the root completely.

Example 1

Simplify $\sqrt{72}$.

1. Break 72 down into factors — one of them needs to be a square number.
2. Write as two roots multiplied together.
3. Evaluate $\sqrt{9}$.
4. $\sqrt{8}$ can be broken down further.

$$\begin{aligned}
\sqrt{72} &= \sqrt{8 \times 9} \\
&= \sqrt{8} \times \sqrt{9} \\
&= \sqrt{8} \times 3 \\
&= \sqrt{2} \times \sqrt{4} \times 3 \\
&= \sqrt{2} \times 2 \times 3 \\
&= \mathbf{6\sqrt{2}}
\end{aligned}$$

Exercise 1

1 Simplify:

a) $\sqrt{12}$ b) $\sqrt{20}$ c) $\sqrt{24}$ d) $\sqrt{50}$ e) $\sqrt{27}$

f) $\sqrt{32}$ g) $\sqrt{108}$ h) $\sqrt{300}$ i) $\sqrt{98}$ j) $\sqrt{192}$

Example 2

Find $\sqrt{5} \times \sqrt{15}$. Simplify your answer.

1. Use $\sqrt{a} \times \sqrt{b} = \sqrt{a \times b}$.
2. Now find factors of 75 so you can simplify.

$$\sqrt{5} \times \sqrt{15} = \sqrt{5 \times 15} = \sqrt{75}$$
$$= \sqrt{25 \times 3} = \sqrt{25} \times \sqrt{3}$$
$$= \mathbf{5\sqrt{3}}$$

2 Rewrite the following in the form $a\sqrt{b}$, where a and b are integers. Simplify your answers where possible.

a) $\sqrt{2} \times \sqrt{24}$ b) $\sqrt{3} \times \sqrt{12}$ c) $\sqrt{3} \times \sqrt{24}$ d) $\sqrt{2} \times \sqrt{10}$ e) $\sqrt{3} \times \sqrt{15}$

f) $\sqrt{40} \times \sqrt{2}$ g) $\sqrt{3} \times \sqrt{60}$ h) $\sqrt{7} \times \sqrt{35}$ i) $\sqrt{50} \times \sqrt{10}$ j) $\sqrt{8} \times \sqrt{24}$

Example 3

Find $\sqrt{40} \div \sqrt{10}$.

1. Rewrite as a single root.
2. Do the division.

$$\sqrt{40} \div \sqrt{10} = \sqrt{40 \div 10}$$
$$= \sqrt{4}$$
$$= \mathbf{2}$$

Exercise 2

1 Calculate the exact values of the following. Simplify your answers where possible.

a) $\sqrt{90} \div \sqrt{10}$ b) $\sqrt{72} \div \sqrt{2}$ c) $\sqrt{200} \div \sqrt{8}$ d) $\sqrt{243} \div \sqrt{3}$

e) $\sqrt{294} \div \sqrt{6}$ f) $\sqrt{80} \div \sqrt{10}$ g) $\sqrt{120} \div \sqrt{10}$ h) $\sqrt{180} \div \sqrt{3}$

i) $\sqrt{180} \div \sqrt{9}$ j) $\sqrt{96} \div \sqrt{6}$ k) $\sqrt{3850} \div \sqrt{22}$ l) $\sqrt{2520} \div \sqrt{35}$

Example 4

Simplify $\sqrt{\dfrac{1}{4}}$.

Rewrite as two roots, then evaluate $\sqrt{1}$ and $\sqrt{4}$.

$$\sqrt{\frac{1}{4}} = \frac{\sqrt{1}}{\sqrt{4}} = \frac{1}{2}$$

2 Simplify the following as far as possible.

a) $\sqrt{\dfrac{1}{9}}$ b) $\sqrt{\dfrac{4}{25}}$ c) $\sqrt{\dfrac{81}{36}}$ d) $\sqrt{\dfrac{49}{121}}$ e) $\sqrt{\dfrac{100}{64}}$

f) $\sqrt{\dfrac{18}{200}}$ g) $\sqrt{\dfrac{2}{25}}$ h) $\sqrt{\dfrac{108}{147}}$ i) $\sqrt{\dfrac{27}{64}}$ j) $\sqrt{\dfrac{98}{121}}$

Adding and Subtracting Surds

You can simplify expressions containing surds by collecting like terms.
You might have to simplify individual terms first to make the surd parts match.

Example 5

Simplify $\sqrt{12} + 2\sqrt{27}$.

1. Break 12 and 27 down into factors.

$$\sqrt{12} + 2\sqrt{27} = \sqrt{4 \times 3} + 2\sqrt{9 \times 3}$$
$$= \sqrt{4} \times \sqrt{3} + 2 \times \sqrt{9} \times \sqrt{3}$$
$$= 2\sqrt{3} + 2 \times 3 \times \sqrt{3}$$
$$= 2\sqrt{3} + 6\sqrt{3}$$

2. The surds are the same, so add the non-surd parts.

$$= \underline{\mathbf{8\sqrt{3}}}$$

Exercise 3

1 Simplify the following as far as possible.

a) $2\sqrt{3} + 3\sqrt{3}$ b) $7\sqrt{7} - 3\sqrt{7}$ c) $7\sqrt{5} - 3\sqrt{5}$

d) $2\sqrt{3} + 3\sqrt{7}$ e) $2\sqrt{7} - 3\sqrt{7}$ f) $2\sqrt{32} + 3\sqrt{2}$

g) $2\sqrt{27} - 3\sqrt{3}$ h) $3\sqrt{24} - 3\sqrt{6}$ i) $5\sqrt{7} + 3\sqrt{28}$

j) $2\sqrt{125} - 3\sqrt{80}$ k) $\sqrt{108} + 2\sqrt{300}$ l) $5\sqrt{294} - 3\sqrt{216}$

Multiplying Brackets Using Surds

Multiply out brackets with surds in them in the same way as you multiply out brackets with variables.
Once the brackets are expanded, simplify the surds if possible.

Example 6

Expand and simplify $(1 + \sqrt{3})(2 - \sqrt{8})$.

1. Expand the brackets first.

$$(1 + \sqrt{3})(2 - \sqrt{8})$$
$$= (1 \times 2) + (1 \times -\sqrt{8}) + (\sqrt{3} \times 2) + (\sqrt{3} \times -\sqrt{8})$$
$$= 2 - \sqrt{8} + 2\sqrt{3} - \sqrt{24}$$

2. Simplify the surds.

$$= 2 - \sqrt{4 \times 2} + 2\sqrt{3} - \sqrt{4 \times 6}$$
$$= \underline{\mathbf{2 - 2\sqrt{2} + 2\sqrt{3} - 2\sqrt{6}}}$$

Exercise 4

1 Simplify the following as far as possible.

a) $(1 + \sqrt{2})(2 - \sqrt{2})$ b) $(2 + \sqrt{3})(1 + \sqrt{2})$ c) $(3 - \sqrt{7})(3 - \sqrt{7})$

d) $(5 + \sqrt{3})(3 - \sqrt{3})$ e) $(4 - \sqrt{7})(5 - \sqrt{2})$ f) $(1 + \sqrt{5})(7 + \sqrt{2})$

g) $(3 - 3\sqrt{2})(3 - \sqrt{2})$ h) $(4 + 2\sqrt{5})(2 + \sqrt{2})$ i) $(2 - 3\sqrt{3})(5 - 3\sqrt{2})$

j) $(7 + 2\sqrt{2})(7 - 2\sqrt{2})$ k) $(2 + \sqrt{6})(4 - \sqrt{3})$ l) $(1 - 2\sqrt{10})(6 - \sqrt{15})$

Rationalising the Denominator

'**Rationalising a denominator**' means 'getting rid of surds from the bottom of a fraction'.
For the simplest type, you do this by multiplying the top and bottom of the fraction by a surd.

Example 7

Rationalise the denominator of $\dfrac{5}{2\sqrt{15}}$.

Multiply by $\dfrac{\sqrt{15}}{\sqrt{15}}$ to eliminate $\sqrt{15}$ from the denominator.

$$\frac{5}{2\sqrt{15}} = \frac{5\sqrt{15}}{2 \times \sqrt{15} \times \sqrt{15}}$$

$$= \frac{5\sqrt{15}}{2 \times 15} = \frac{5\sqrt{15}}{30} = \frac{\sqrt{15}}{6}$$

Exercise 5

1   Rationalise the denominators of the following fractions. Simplify your answers as far as possible.

   a) $\dfrac{6}{\sqrt{6}}$ b) $\dfrac{8}{\sqrt{8}}$ c) $\dfrac{5}{\sqrt{5}}$ d) $\dfrac{1}{\sqrt{3}}$ e) $\dfrac{1}{\sqrt{7}}$

   f) $\dfrac{15}{\sqrt{5}}$ g) $\dfrac{9}{\sqrt{3}}$ h) $\dfrac{7}{\sqrt{5}}$ i) $\dfrac{12}{\sqrt{6}}$ j) $\dfrac{8}{\sqrt{2}}$

2   Rationalise the denominators of the following fractions. Simplify your answers as far as possible.

   a) $\dfrac{1}{5\sqrt{5}}$ b) $\dfrac{1}{3\sqrt{3}}$ c) $\dfrac{1}{3\sqrt{7}}$ d) $\dfrac{3}{4\sqrt{8}}$ e) $\dfrac{3}{2\sqrt{5}}$

   f) $\dfrac{2}{7\sqrt{3}}$ g) $\dfrac{5}{2\sqrt{2}}$ h) $\dfrac{1}{6\sqrt{12}}$ i) $\dfrac{10}{7\sqrt{5}}$ j) $\dfrac{5}{9\sqrt{10}}$

If the denominator is the sum or difference of an integer and a surd (e.g. $1 + \sqrt{2}$),
use the difference of two squares to eliminate the surd: $(a + b)(a - b) = a^2 - b^2$

Example 8

Rationalise the denominator of $\dfrac{2 + 2\sqrt{2}}{1 - \sqrt{2}}$.

Multiply top and bottom by $(1 + \sqrt{2})$
to get rid of the surd in the denominator.

$$\frac{2 + 2\sqrt{2}}{1 - \sqrt{2}} = \frac{(2 + 2\sqrt{2})(1 + \sqrt{2})}{(1 - \sqrt{2})(1 + \sqrt{2})}$$

$$= \frac{2 + 2\sqrt{2} + 2\sqrt{2} + 4}{1 + \sqrt{2} - \sqrt{2} - 2}$$

$$= \frac{6 + 4\sqrt{2}}{-1} = -6 - 4\sqrt{2}$$

3   Rationalise the denominators of the following fractions. Simplify your answers as far as possible.

   a) $\dfrac{1}{2 + \sqrt{2}}$ b) $\dfrac{5}{1 - \sqrt{7}}$ c) $\dfrac{3}{4 + \sqrt{2}}$ d) $\dfrac{2}{3 - \sqrt{13}}$ e) $\dfrac{10}{5 + \sqrt{11}}$

   f) $\dfrac{4}{\sqrt{3} + 4}$ g) $\dfrac{2}{1 + 2\sqrt{5}}$ h) $\dfrac{9}{12 - 3\sqrt{17}}$ i) $\dfrac{\sqrt{2}}{2 + 3\sqrt{2}}$ j) $\dfrac{\sqrt{7}}{5 - 2\sqrt{2}}$

4   Rationalise the denominators of the following fractions. Simplify your answers as far as possible.

   a) $\dfrac{1 + \sqrt{2}}{1 - \sqrt{2}}$ b) $\dfrac{2 + \sqrt{3}}{1 - \sqrt{3}}$ c) $\dfrac{1 - \sqrt{5}}{2 - \sqrt{5}}$ d) $\dfrac{3 + \sqrt{5}}{1 - \sqrt{5}}$ e) $\dfrac{4 + 2\sqrt{5}}{2 - \sqrt{2}}$

   f) $\dfrac{1 + 2\sqrt{2}}{1 - 2\sqrt{2}}$ g) $\dfrac{2 + 3\sqrt{3}}{5 + \sqrt{3}}$ h) $\dfrac{7 + 2\sqrt{5}}{6 + 3\sqrt{3}}$ i) $\dfrac{1 + 7\sqrt{2}}{5 - 3\sqrt{8}}$ j) $\dfrac{7 + 8\sqrt{2}}{9 + 5\sqrt{2}}$

5   Show that $\dfrac{1}{1 - \dfrac{1}{\sqrt{2}}}$ can be written as $2 + \sqrt{2}$.

6   Show that $\dfrac{1}{1 + \dfrac{1}{\sqrt{3}}}$ can be written as $\dfrac{3 - \sqrt{3}}{2}$.

Section 8 — Formulas

8.1 Writing Formulas

A **formula** is a set of instructions for working something out.
E.g. $s = 4t + 3$ is a formula for s — it tells you how to find s, given the value of t.

Example 1

The cost (C) of hiring a bike is £5 per hour plus a fixed cost of £25.
Write a formula for the cost of hiring a bike for h hours.

1. Multiply the number of hours (h) by the cost per hour.
2. Add on the fixed cost.

Cost (in £) for h hours $= 5h$

So $\boldsymbol{C = 5h + 25}$

Exercise 1

1 Claudia owns f films. Barry owns twice as many films as Claudia.

   a) How many films does Barry own?

   b) How many films do Claudia and Barry own in total?

   c) How many films would they own in total if they each gave away 3 of their films?

2 I have b flower bulbs. To find the number of flowers that should grow from them (F), multiply the number of bulbs by 3 and then add 5. Write a formula for the number of flowers I can expect.

3 Charlotte has c marbles. Lee has 25 fewer marbles than Charlotte.
   Write a formula for l, the number of marbles that Lee has.

4 Alf has £18 in the bank. He gets a job, and for each hour he works, he is paid £8. Assuming he spends nothing, write a formula for the amount of money (M) Alf will have after he has worked for h hours.

5 The instructions for cooking a goose are to cook for 50 minutes per kg, plus 25 minutes.
   Write a formula to find the time taken (t) to cook a goose weighing n kg.

6 Write a formula for the cost (C) of having t trees cut down if it costs p pounds per tree plus a fixed amount of £25.

7 The cost of hiring crazy golf equipment is a fixed price of £3 plus 8p for every minute of use.
   Write a formula for the cost (C) of hiring the equipment for g minutes of crazy golf.

8 To convert speeds from km/h to mph, divide the speed in km/h by 8, then multiply by 5.

   a) Write a formula to convert km/h (k) to mph (m).

   b) Write a formula to convert mph (m) to km/h (k).

9 To convert temperatures from degrees Fahrenheit to degrees Celsius, subtract 32, then divide by 1.8.

   a) Write a formula to convert degrees Fahrenheit (f) to degrees Celsius (c).

   b) Write a formula to convert degrees Celsius (c) to degrees Fahrenheit (f).

10 A sequence of shapes is made out of matchsticks.
   The first shape in the sequence is made from 4 matchsticks.
   Each subsequent shape in the sequence is made by adding 3 matchsticks to the previous shape.
   Write a formula for the number of matchsticks (M) needed to make the nth shape in the sequence.

8.2 Substituting into a Formula

Example 1

Use the formula $v = u + at$ to find v if $u = 2.6$, $a = -18.3$ and $t = 4.9$.

Replace each letter with its value.

$v = u + at$
$= 2.6 + (-18.3 \times 4.9)$
$= 2.6 + (-89.67)$
$= \underline{\mathbf{-87.07}}$

Exercise 1

1 If $x = 4$ and $y = 3$, find z when:
  a) $z = x + 2$ **b)** $z = y - 1$ **c)** $z = x + y$ **d)** $z = y - x$
  e) $z = 2x$ **f)** $z = 3y$ **g)** $z = 3y - 2$ **h)** $z = 6x - y$

2 If $m = 5$ and $n = 2$, find l when:
  a) $l = mn$ **b)** $l = m^2$ **c)** $l = m - n^2$ **d)** $l = \dfrac{2m}{n}$
  e) $l = m(m - n)$ **f)** $l = n^2 + n$ **g)** $l = \dfrac{n}{m}$ **h)** $l = mn^2$

3 If $a = -4$ and $b = -3$, find c when:
  a) $c = a - 4$ **b)** $c = b + a$ **c)** $c = 4b$ **d)** $c = 6b - a$
  e) $c = b^3$ **f)** $c = -\dfrac{4b}{2a}$ **g)** $c = 5a - b^2$ **h)** $c = 6a^2 - 2ab + 2b^2$

4 If $p = -4.8$ and $q = 3.2$, find r when:
  a) $r = p + 6.7$ **b)** $r = q - p$ **c)** $r = -4q$ **d)** $r = 8.4q - p$
  e) $r = (-q)^3$ **f)** $r = \dfrac{2.1q}{3.5p}$ **g)** $r = -3.2p + q^2$ **h)** $r = 4.1p^2 - 2.8pq$

5 If $r = \frac{3}{4}$ and $s = -\frac{1}{3}$, find q when:
  a) $q = 4r$ **b)** $q = -2s$ **c)** $q = rs$ **d)** $q = \dfrac{s}{r}$
  e) $q = r + s$ **f)** $q = r - s$ **g)** $q = 4r + s$ **h)** $q = 3s + 2r$

In Questions 6-8 give all rounded answers to 2 decimal places.

6 Use the formula $v = u + at$ to find v if:
  a) $u = 3$, $a = 7$ and $t = 5$ **b)** $u = 12$, $a = 17$ and $t = 15$
  c) $u = 2.3$, $a = 4.1$ and $t = 3.4$ **d)** $u = 5.25$, $a = 9.81$ and $t = 4.39$
  e) $u = 3$, $a = -10$ and $t = 5.6$ **f)** $u = -34$, $a = -1.37$ and $t = 63.25$

7 Use the formula $s = ut + \frac{1}{2}at^2$ to find s if:
  a) $u = 7$, $a = 2$ and $t = 4$ **b)** $u = 24$, $a = 11$ and $t = 13$
  c) $u = 3.6$, $a = 5.3$ and $t = 14.2$ **d)** $u = 9.8$, $a = 48.2$ and $t = 15.4$
  e) $u = -11$, $a = -9.81$ and $t = 12.2$ **f)** $u = 66.6$, $a = -1.64$ and $t = 14.2$

8 If $x = 12$, $y = 2.5$ and $z = -0.25$, find w if:
  a) $w = x + 2y - 4z$ **b)** $w = 2x^2 - y + z$ **c)** $w = -3x + y^3 - (2z)^2$ **d)** $w = 0.5x - yz$
  e) $w = -2x^3 + y^2z$ **f)** $w = \dfrac{4z}{y} - x$ **g)** $w = -\dfrac{12}{x} + \dfrac{y}{z}$ **h)** $w = \dfrac{x^2 + 3y - 8z}{2y^2}$

Exercise 2

1 The formula for working out the velocity (v, in metres per second) of a moving object is $v = \frac{d}{t}$, where d is the distance travelled (in metres) and t is the time taken (in seconds). Find the velocity (in metres per second) of each of the following.

   a) a runner who travels 800 metres in 110 seconds

   b) a cheetah that travels 400 metres in 14 seconds

   c) a car that travels 1000 metres in 60 seconds

   d) a plane that travels 640 000 metres in 3600 seconds

   e) a satellite that travels 40 000 000 metres in 5000 seconds

2 Use the formula $c = \frac{5}{9}(f - 32)$ to convert the following temperatures in degrees Fahrenheit (f) to degrees Celsius (c).

   a) 212 °F   **b)** 68 °F   **c)** −40 °F   **d)** 98.6 °F

3 You can convert between two quantities, x and y, using the formula $y = 2x^2 - 8$. Use the formula to convert the following values of x into y-values.

   a) $x = 3$ **b)** $x = 5$ **c)** $x = 9$ **d)** $x = 10$

4 The sum (S) of the numbers $1 + 2 + 3 + ... + n$ is given by the formula $S = \frac{1}{2}n(n + 1)$. Work out the sum for each of the following.

   a) $1 + 2 + 3 + ... + 10$ **b)** $1 + 2 + 3 + ... + 100$ **c)** $1 + 2 + 3 + ... + 1000$

5 The number of seconds taken for a pendulum to swing forwards and then backwards once (T) is given by the formula $T = 2\pi\sqrt{\frac{l}{10}}$, where l is the length of the pendulum in metres.

   Calculate how long it will take a pendulum to swing backwards and forwards once if:

   a) $l = 1$ metre   **b)** $l = 0.5$ metres   **c)** $l = 0.25$ metres   **d)** $l = 16$ metres

6 Find the volumes (V) of the cylinders below, using the formula on the left.

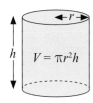

$V = \pi r^2 h$

a)
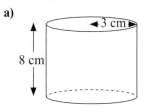
3 cm
8 cm

b)
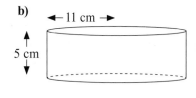
11 cm
5 cm

7 Find the volumes (V) of the cones below, using the formula on the left.

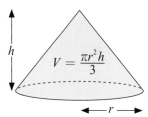

$V = \dfrac{\pi r^2 h}{3}$

a)
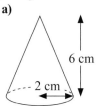
6 cm
2 cm

b)
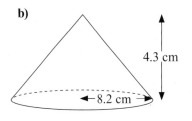
4.3 cm
8.2 cm

8.3 Rearranging Formulas

Making a particular letter the subject of a formula means rearranging the formula so that letter is on its own.

Example 1
Make x the subject of the formula $y = 4 + bx$.

1. You need to get x on its own.	$y = 4 + bx$
2. Subtract 4 from both sides.	$y - 4 = bx$
3. Divide both sides by b and write x on the left-hand side.	$x = \dfrac{y - 4}{b}$

Example 2
Make y the subject of the formula $w = \dfrac{1 - y}{2}$.

1. You need to get y on its own.	$w = \dfrac{1 - y}{2}$
2. Multiply both sides by 2.	$2w = 1 - y$
3. Add y to both sides (so it's positive).	$2w + y = 1$
4. Subtract $2w$ from both sides.	$y = 1 - 2w$

Exercise 1

1 Make x the subject of each of the following formulas.
   a) $y = x + 2$ **b)** $b = x - 5$ **c)** $2z = 3r + x$
   d) $y = 4x$ **e)** $c = 2x + 1$ **f)** $k = 2(1 + 2x)$
   g) $v = \frac{2}{3}x - 2$ **h)** $u = \dfrac{1 + 5x}{2}$ **i)** $y + 1 = \dfrac{x - 1}{3}$

2 Make x the subject of each of the following formulas.
   a) $z = 1 - x$ **b)** $p = 2 - 7x$ **c)** $3r = 1.8 - 4.2x$
   d) $u + 2 = 3 - 2x$ **e)** $t = 1 - \frac{1}{3}x$ **f)** $uv = 3(2 - 3x)$
   g) $y = \dfrac{4 - x}{3}$ **h)** $w = \dfrac{1 - 2x}{5}$ **i)** $z = \dfrac{4(2 - x)}{7}$

3 Consider the formula $w = \dfrac{1}{1 + y}$.
   a) Multiply both sides of the formula by $1 + y$.
   b) Hence make y the subject of the formula.

4 Make y the subject of the following formulas.
   a) $a = \dfrac{1}{y}$ **b)** $w = \dfrac{3}{2y}$ **c)** $2b = \dfrac{1}{1 + y}$
   d) $z + 2 = \dfrac{2}{1 - y}$ **e)** $k = \dfrac{2}{3y} + 1$ **f)** $c = \dfrac{1}{y} + b$
   g) $uv = \dfrac{1}{1 - 2y}$ **h)** $a + b = \dfrac{2}{4 - 3y}$ **i)** $z = 10 - \dfrac{2}{3y}$

5 Consider the formula $2k = 12 - \sqrt{w - 2}$.
   a) Make $\sqrt{w - 2}$ the subject of the formula.
   b) By first squaring both sides of your answer to part (a), make w the subject of the formula.

6   Make w the subject of the following formulas.

a) $a = \sqrt{w}$ b) $x = 1 + \sqrt{w}$ c) $y = \sqrt{w - 2}$

d) $y + 2 = a - \sqrt{w}$ e) $f - 3 = 2\sqrt{w}$ f) $a = \sqrt{1 - 2w}$

g) $j = \sqrt{3 + 4w}$ h) $2 - e = 2\sqrt{1 - 3w}$ i) $\sqrt{a + 2} = \sqrt{a - w}$

7   Consider the formula $t = 1 - 3(z + 1)^2$.

a) Make $(z + 1)^2$ the subject of the formula.

b) By first square rooting both sides of your answer to part (a), make z the subject of the formula.

8   Make z the subject of the following formulas.

a) $x = 1 + z^2$ b) $2t = 3 - z^2$ c) $u = (z + 2)^2$

d) $xy = 1 - 4z^2$ e) $t + 2 = 3(z - 2)^2$ f) $b = 2 + (2z + 3)^2$

g) $g = 4 - (2z + 3)^2$ h) $k = 1 - 6(1 - z)^2$ i) $r = 4 - 2(5 - 3z)^2$

Example 3

Make a the subject of the formula $x(a + 1) = 3(1 - 2a)$.

$$x(a + 1) = 3(1 - 2a)$$

1. Expand the brackets by multiplying. $ax + x = 3 - 6a$

2. Rearrange the formula so all the a's are on one side. $ax + 6a = 3 - x$

3. Factorise the left hand side and rearrange to get a on its own. $a(x + 6) = 3 - x$

$$a = \frac{3 - x}{x + 6}$$

---

9   Make a the subject of the following formulas.

a) $x(a + b) = a - 1$ b) $a = 1 + ab$ c) $x - ab = c - ad$

d) $7(1 - 3a) = 2(a - 2)$ e) $a - 9 = 4(b - a) + 2$ f) $a = 2(3 - 2a) - 3(1 - a)$

g) $c = \dfrac{1 + a}{1 - 2a}$ h) $2e = \dfrac{2 + 3a}{a}$ i) $y = \dfrac{a}{a - b}$

8.4   Formulas Problems

Exercise 1

1   Melanie has half as many sweets as Jane.

a) If Jane has j sweets, write a formula to calculate the number of sweets (m) that Melanie has.

b) Find m when $j = 24$.

2   To book a swimming pool for a party, there is a fixed charge of £30 plus a fee of £1.25 for each person who attends.

a) Write a formula to calculate the hire cost (C) for n people.

b) Calculate C when $n = 32$.

3   The number of matchsticks (m) needed to make h hexagons is given by the formula $m = 5h + 1$.

a) How many matchsticks are needed to make 6 hexagons?

b) Rearrange the formula to make h the subject.

c) How many hexagons can you make with 36 matchsticks?

4   You are given the formula $g = \frac{8}{5}h + 17$.

a) Rearrange the formula to make h the subject.

b) Find h if: **(i)** $g = 66$ **(ii)** $g = 212$ **(iii)** $g = -40$ **(iv)** $g = 81$

5   To hire skates at the park there is a fixed charge of £5, plus a charge of £1.70 for each half-hour.

    a) Write a formula to calculate the cost (C) for h half-hour periods.

    b) Calculate the cost of hiring skates for two and a half hours.

    c) Rearrange your formula to make h the subject.

    d) Asher spends £15.20 on hiring skates. How long was he skating for?

6   The surface area (A) of the shape on the right is
given approximately by the formula $A = 21.5d^2$.

    a) Rearrange the formula to make d the subject.

    b) Find d if $A = 55$ cm². Give your answer to 2 s.f.

7   The time in minutes (T) taken to cook a joint of beef is given by $T = 35w + 25$,
where w is the weight of the joint in kg.

    a) How long would it take to cook a 1.5 kg joint?

    b) Make w the subject of the formula.

    c) What weight of beef needs to be cooked for 207 minutes?

    d) What weight of beef needs to be cooked for 3 hours and 48 minutes?

8   The formula for calculating the cost in pounds (C) of a quarterly gas bill is $C = 0.06n + 7.5$,
where n is the number of units of gas used.

    a) What is the fixed cost per quarter charged by the gas supplier?

    b) What is the cost per unit?

    c) José uses 760 units of gas. How much will he have to pay?

    d) Rearrange the formula to make n the subject.

    e) Tracy's gas bill is £40.50. How many units of gas did she use?

9   For each of the following formulas, **(i)** make x the subject, and **(ii)** find x when $y = -1$.

    a) $-2 + y = \dfrac{3}{4 - x}$
    b) $y = \dfrac{1}{\sqrt{1 - x}}$
    c) $2(1 - x) = y(3 + x)$

    d) $y = \dfrac{2 - 3x}{1 + 2x}$
    e) $y = 8 - \dfrac{1}{\sqrt{x}}$
    f) $2y - 1 = 3\sqrt{2 - x}$

10   Consider the formula $s = \left(\dfrac{u + v}{2}\right)t$. Find the value of:

    a) s when $u = 2.3$, $v = 1.7$ and $t = 4$.

    b) t when $s = 3.3$, $u = 1$ and $v = 2$.

    c) u when $s = 4.5$, $t = 6$ and $v = 7$.

    d) v when $s = 0.5$, $t = 0.25$ and $u = 3$.

11   Consider the formula $v^2 = u^2 + 2as$.

    a) Find the values of v when $u = 2$, $a = 1$ and $s = 4$.

    b) Find the value of a when $s = 2$, $u = 9$ and $v = 11$.

    c) Find the values of u when $a = 3$, $s = 4$ and $v = 7$.

12   Consider the formula $x = \dfrac{1 + \sqrt{y + 3}}{2 - z}$.

    a) Find the value of x when $y = 1$ and $z = -1$.

    b) Find the value of z when $y = 6$ and $x = -2$.

13   Consider the formula $x = \dfrac{2(k + 1)}{(1 - y)^2}$.

    a) Find the value of x when $k = -17$ and $y = 5$.

    b) Find the values of y when $k = -26$ and $x = -2$.

Section 9 — Equations

9.1 Solving Equations

Solving an equation means finding the value of an unknown letter that satisfies the equation.

Example 1

Solve the equation $15 - 2x = 7$.

1. Add $2x$ to both sides — so the coefficient of x is positive.
2. Subtract 7 from both sides.
3. Divide both sides by 2.

$15 - 2x = 7$
$15 = 7 + 2x$
$8 = 2x$
$\underline{x = 4}$

Exercise 1

1 Solve each of the following equations.

a) $x + 9 = 12$
b) $x - 7.3 = 1.6$
c) $15 - x = 14$
d) $12 - x = 9$
e) $9x = 54$
f) $-5x = 50$
g) $60x = -36$
h) $40x = -32$
i) $\dfrac{x}{3} = 2$
j) $\dfrac{x}{2} = 3.2$
k) $-\dfrac{x}{0.2} = 3.2$
l) $\dfrac{2x}{5} = 6$

2 Solve each of the following equations.

a) $8x + 10 = 66$
b) $10x + 15 = 115$
c) $12x + 9 = 105$
d) $15x + 12 = 72$
e) $1.5x - 3 = -24$
f) $1.8x - 8 = -62$
g) $2.6x - 7 = -59$
h) $4.8x - 9 = -57$
i) $12 - 4x = 8$
j) $47 - 9x = 11$
k) $8 - 7x = 22$
l) $17 - 10x = 107$
m) $\dfrac{x}{2} - 1 = 2$
n) $\dfrac{x}{3} + 2 = -3$
o) $-\dfrac{2x}{3} - \dfrac{3}{4} = \dfrac{1}{4}$
p) $-\dfrac{3x}{5} + \dfrac{1}{3} = \dfrac{2}{3}$

Example 2

Solve the equation $8(x + 2) = 36$.

1. Expand the brackets by multiplying.
2. Subtract 16 from both sides.
3. Divide both sides by 8.
4. You could also solve this equation by dividing both sides by 8 first, then finding x as usual.

$8(x + 2) = 36$
$8x + 16 = 36$
$8x = 20$
$\underline{x = 2.5}$

3 Solve each of the following equations.

a) $7(x + 4) = 63$
b) $8(x + 4) = 88$
c) $11(x + 3) = 132$
d) $14(x + 5) = 98$
e) $16(x - 3) = -80$
f) $13(x - 4) = -91$
g) $14(x - 2) = -98$
h) $18(x - 3) = -180$
i) $2.5(x + 4) = 30$
j) $1.5(x + 2) = 12$
k) $3.5(x + 6) = 63$
l) $4.5(x + 3) = 72$
m) $98 = 7(2 - x)$
n) $165 = 15(4 - x)$
o) $315 = 21(6 - x)$
p) $171 = 4.5(8 - x)$

4 a) Multiply both sides of the equation $\dfrac{1}{x-2} = 3$ by $(x-2)$.

  b) Hence solve the equation $\dfrac{1}{x-2} = 3$.

5 Solve each of the following equations.

  a) $\dfrac{1}{x} = 2$ **b)** $\dfrac{2}{x} = 5$ **c)** $\dfrac{12}{x-2} = 4$ **d)** $\dfrac{3}{1-2x} = 2$

Example 3

Solve the equation $4(x+2) = 2(x+6)$.

1. Multiply out the brackets.
2. Rearrange so that all the x terms are on one side.
3. Find x.

$4(x+2) = 2(x+6)$
$4x + 8 = 2x + 12$
$4x - 2x = 12 - 8$
$2x = 4$
$\underline{x = 2}$

Exercise 2

1 Solve each of the following equations.

  a) $6x - 4 = 2x + 16$ **b)** $17x - 2 = 7x + 8$ **c)** $9x - 26 = 5x - 14$

  d) $10x - 5 = 3x + 9$ **e)** $6x - 12 = 51 - 3x$ **f)** $5x - 13 = 87 - 5x$

  g) $4x - 3 = 0.5 - 3x$ **h)** $10x - 18 = 11.4 - 4x$ **i)** $4x + 9 = 6 - x$

2 Solve each of the following equations.

  a) $3(x+2) = x + 14$ **b)** $5(x+3) = 2x + 57$ **c)** $6(x+2) = 3x + 48$

  d) $8(x-8) = 2(x-2)$ **e)** $20(x-2) = 5(x+1)$ **f)** $6(x-3) = 3(x+8)$

  g) $5(x-5) = 2(x-14)$ **h)** $4(x-3) = 2(x-8)$ **i)** $6(x-2) = 3(x+6)$

  j) $7(2x + \frac{1}{7}) = 14(3x - 0.5)$ **k)** $6(x-1) = 4(6.2 - 2x)$ **l)** $-4(x-3) = 8(0.7 - x)$

Example 4

Solve the equation $\dfrac{x-2}{2} = \dfrac{6-x}{6}$.

1. Cross-multiply. This is the same as multiplying both sides by 2 and by 6.

2. Solve for x.

$\dfrac{x-2}{2} = \dfrac{6-x}{6}$

$6(x-2) = 2(6-x)$
$6x - 12 = 12 - 2x$
$8x = 24$
$\underline{x = 3}$

Exercise 3

1 Solve the following equations.

  a) $\dfrac{x}{4} = 1 - x$ **b)** $\dfrac{x}{3} = 8 - x$ **c)** $\dfrac{x}{5} = 11 - 2x$

  d) $\dfrac{x}{3} = 2(x-5)$ **e)** $\dfrac{x}{2} = 4(x-7)$ **f)** $\dfrac{x}{5} = 2(x+9)$

2 Solve the following equations.

a) $\dfrac{x+4}{2} = \dfrac{x+10}{3}$

b) $\dfrac{x+2}{2} = \dfrac{x+4}{6}$

c) $\dfrac{x+3}{4} = \dfrac{x+9}{7}$

d) $\dfrac{x-2}{3} = \dfrac{x+4}{5}$

e) $\dfrac{x-3}{4} = \dfrac{x+2}{8}$

f) $\dfrac{x-6}{5} = \dfrac{x+3}{8}$

g) $\dfrac{x-10}{10} = \dfrac{10-x}{3}$

h) $\dfrac{x-2}{4} = \dfrac{15-2x}{3}$

i) $\dfrac{x-4}{6} = \dfrac{12-3x}{2}$

Exercise 4 — Mixed Exercise

Solve each of the following equations.

1 a) $7x + 1 = 50$ b) $4x + 68 = 144$ c) $8x - 7 = 12.5$ d) $35x - 100 = -415$

2 a) $8(x + 3) = 72$ b) $11(x + 4) = -132$ c) $0.5(2x - 9) = 90$ d) $6(5 - x) = -42$

3 a) $4(x + 5) = x - 6$ b) $3(x - 3) = 6x + 45$ c) $8(x + 9) = x + 1$

   d) $3(x - 10) = 7(x - 4)$ e) $12(2 + x) = 5(x + 3)$ f) $9(x - 2) = 11(x + 5)$

4 a) $\dfrac{x+1}{5} = \dfrac{x+5}{7}$

b) $\dfrac{x+3}{2} = \dfrac{x+2}{3}$

c) $\dfrac{x+12}{3} = \dfrac{x+6}{8}$

d) $\dfrac{x-8}{5} = \dfrac{x+4}{3}$

e) $\dfrac{x-9}{9} = \dfrac{x+1}{4}$

f) $\dfrac{x-11}{6} = \dfrac{x+2}{7}$

9.2   Writing Equations

Example 1

The sum of three consecutive numbers is 63. What are the numbers?

1. Call the first number x, then the other two numbers are $(x + 1)$ and $(x + 2)$. $x + (x + 1) + (x + 2) = 63$

2. Form an equation in x. $3x + 3 = 63$

3. Solve the equation. $3x = 60$

     $x = 20$

So the numbers are **20**, **21** and **22**.

Exercise 1

1 I think of a number. I double it, and then add 3. The result equals 19.
  a) Write the above description in the form of an equation.
  b) Solve your equation to find the number I was thinking of.

2 I think of a number. I divide it by 3, and then subtract 11. The result equals –2.
  What number was I thinking of?

3 The sum of four consecutive numbers is 42. What are the numbers?

4 The sum of three consecutive even numbers is 30. What are the numbers?

5 Anna, Bill and Christie are swapping football stickers. Bill has 3 more stickers than Anna.
  Christie has twice as many stickers as Anna. The three of them have 83 stickers in total.
  How many stickers does each person have?

6 Deb, Eduardo and Fiz are raising money for charity. Eduardo has raised £6 more than Deb. Fiz has raised three times as much as Eduardo. The three of them have raised £106.50 in total. How much did each of them raise?

7 Stacey is three years older than Macy. Tracy is twice as old as Stacey. The three of them have a combined age of 41. How old is each person?

Example 2

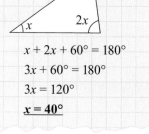

Use the triangle to write an equation involving x.
Solve your equation to find x.

1. The angles in a triangle always add up to 180°.
2. Solve the equation.

$$x + 2x + 60° = 180°$$
$$3x + 60° = 180°$$
$$3x = 120°$$
$$\underline{x = 40°}$$

Exercise 2

1 For each triangle below, **(i)** write an equation involving x, and **(ii)** solve your equation to find x.

a) $3x$, $5x$, $20°$

b) $110°$, $3x$, $4x$

c) $23x$, $7x$, $30x$

d) $3x - 10°$, $10x$, $6x$

e) $2x + 40°$, $3x$, $5x$

f) $3x - 5°$, $5x$, $5x - 10°$

2 A triangle has angles of size x, $2x$ and $(70° - x)$. Find the value of x.

3 For each shape below, **(i)** find the value of x, and **(ii)** find the area of the shape.

a) $4x$ cm
Perimeter = 146 cm
$(x + 8)$ cm

b) $(x + 10)$ cm
Perimeter = 186 cm
$(x + 3)$ cm

4 A rectangle has sides of length $(4 - x)$ cm and $(3x - 2)$ cm. The perimeter of the rectangle is 8.8 cm. Find the rectangle's area.

5 The triangle and rectangle shown below have the same area. Find the perimeter of each shape.

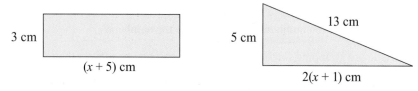

3 cm
$(x + 5)$ cm

5 cm
13 cm
$2(x + 1)$ cm

Iterative methods can be used to find approximate solutions to equations.
They involve repeating calculations until you get close enough to the exact solution.

Example 1

The equation $x^2 + 2x = 17$ has a solution between 3 and 4.
By considering values in this interval, find a solution to
this equation to 1 decimal place.

x	$x^2 + 2x - 17$	
3.0	–2	Negative
3.1	–1.19	Negative
3.2	–0.36	Negative
3.3	0.49	Positive
3.21	–0.2759	Negative
3.22	–0.1916	Negative
3.23	–0.1071	Negative
3.24	–0.0224	Negative
3.25	0.0625	Positive

1. Rearrange the equation into $x^2 + 2x - 17 = 0$
2. Try (in order) the values of x between 3 and 4
   with 1 d.p. until there's a sign change.

   $x = 3.2$ is negative and $x = 3.3$ is positive.
   So x is between 3.2 and 3.3.

3. Try (in order) the values of x between 3.2 and 3.3
   with 2 d.p. until there's a sign change.

   $3.24 < x < 3.25$ and all the values in this interval
   round to 3.2 to 1 d.p. so a solution is $\underline{\mathbf{x = 3.2}}$ (to 1 d.p.).

Example 2

The equation $x^2 + 4x - 6 = 0$ has a solution between 1 and 2.
Use an iterative method to find the solution correct to 1 d.p.

A solution is in the interval $1 \leq x \leq 2$.
Narrow the interval by looking for a change in sign.
Stop when both values round to the same number to 1 d.p.

x	$x^2 + 4x - 6$	
1	–1	Negative
2	6	Positive
1.5	2.25	Positive
1.2	0.24	Positive
1.1	–0.39	Negative
1.15	–0.0775	Negative

$x = 1$ is too small and $x = 2$ is too big.
$x = 1.5$ is too big, so $1 < x < 1.5$.
$x = 1.2$ is too big, so $1 < x < 1.2$.
$x = 1.1$ is too small, so $1.1 < x < 1.2$.
$x = 1.15$ is too small, so $1.15 < x < 1.2$.
So a solution is $\underline{\mathbf{x = 1.2}}$ (to 1 d.p.).

Exercise 1

Use iterative methods to solve all equations in this Exercise.

1 A solution to the equation $x^2 + x - 10 = 0$ lies between 2 and 3.
   a) Evaluate $x^2 + x - 10$ for $x = 2.5$.
   b) Is the solution to $x^2 + x - 10 = 0$ greater than or less than 2.5?
   c) State whether the solution is greater than or less than the following.
      (i) 2.6   **(ii)** 2.7   **(iii)** 2.8
   d) Evaluate $x^2 + x - 10$ for values of x to find the solution to $x^2 + x - 10 = 0$ correct to 1 d.p.

2 A solution to $x^2 + 2x = 30$ lies between 4 and 5. Find the solution correct to 1 d.p.

3 The following equations have solutions between 5 and 6. Find the solutions correct to 1 d.p.
   a) $x^3 + 5x = 175$ b) $x^3 - 3x = 155$

4 The solution to the equation $2^x = 20$ lies between 4 and 5. Find x, correct to 1 decimal place.

5 A solution to $x^2 + x = 35$ lies between 5.4 and 5.5. Find the solution correct to 2 d.p.

6 Find the positive solutions to the following equations. Give your answers correct to 2 d.p.

    a) $x^2 + x = 23$ **b)** $x^2 + 2x = 17$ **c)** $x^2 + 5x = 62$ **d)** $x^2 + 7x = 100$

7 The equation $x^2 + x = 48$ has a solution between 6 and 7.
    Find this solution. Give your solution correct to 3 decimal places.

8 The equation $x^3 + 4x = 21$ has a solution between 2 and 3.
    Find this solution. Give your solution correct to 3 decimal places.

9 The rectangle on the right has an area of 100 cm².

    a) Write down an equation in x.

    b) Use an iterative method to find x,
        correct to 1 decimal place.

    c) Find the lengths of the sides of the rectangle,
        correct to 1 decimal place.

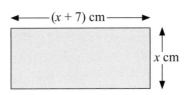

10 A cannonball is fired upwards from the ground.
After x seconds, its height (h) in metres is given by the formula $h = 100x - 5x^2$.
It travels upwards for 10 seconds until it reaches a height of 500 m, then falls back towards the ground.

    a) How many seconds does it take the ball to reach a height of 200 m as it rises?
        Give your answer correct to 1 decimal place.

    b) After how many seconds does the ball first reach a height of 400 metres?
        Give your answer correct to 1 decimal place.

    c) As it falls back down to the ground, it passes a height of 200 metres for a second time.
        Find the number of seconds after being fired that it passes this height.
        Give your answer correct to 1 decimal place.

Recursive Iteration

Recursive iteration is when you put in a starting value, complete the calculation, then put the result back in and repeat until you've got the answer you need. Each iteration gives you a **more accurate** answer.

Example 2

Use the iteration machine below to find a solution to the equation $x^3 + 2x - 7 = 0$ to 1 d.p.
Use the starting value $x_0 = 2$.

| 1. Begin with x_n | → | 2. Find the value of x_{n+1} by using the formula $x_{n+1} = \sqrt[3]{7 - 2x_n}$ | → | 3. If $x_n = x_{n+1}$ rounded to 1 d.p. then stop. If $x_n \neq x_{n+1}$ rounded to 1 d.p. go back to step 1 and repeat using x_{n+1}. |

1. Substitute x_0 into the equation to find x_1. $x_1 = \sqrt[3]{7 - 2(2)}$ $x_1 = 1.44224957...$

2. Put x_1 back into the equation to find x_2. $x_2 = \sqrt[3]{7 - 2(1.44224957...)}$ $x_2 = 1.602535155...$

3. Repeat until two consecutive terms round to the same number to 1 d.p. $x_3 = \sqrt[3]{7 - 2(1.602535155...)}$ $x_3 = 1.559796392...$

    x_2 and x_3 both round to 1.6 to 1 d.p. so a solution is **$x = 1.6$**.

Exercise 2

1 Using the following iteration machine, find a solution to the equation $-2x^2 + 3x + 1 = 0$ to 1 d.p. Use the starting value $x_0 = 1$.

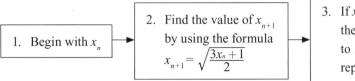

1. Begin with x_n

2. Find the value of x_{n+1} by using the formula
$$x_{n+1} = \sqrt{\frac{3x_n + 1}{2}}$$

3. If $x_n = x_{n+1}$ rounded to 1 d.p. then stop. If $x_n \neq x_{n+1}$ rounded to 1 d.p. go back to step 1 and repeat using x_{n+1}.

2 Use the iteration machine below to find a solution to the equation $x^3 + 4x - 2 = 0$ to 2 d.p. Use the starting value $x_0 = 0$.

1. Begin with x_n

2. Find the value of x_{n+1} by using the formula
$$x_{n+1} = \frac{2x_n^3 + 2}{3x_n^2 + 4}$$

3. If $x_n = x_{n+1}$ rounded to 2 d.p. then stop. If $x_n \neq x_{n+1}$ rounded to 2 d.p. go back to step 1 and repeat using x_{n+1}.

3 Use the iteration formula $x_{n+1} = \dfrac{2x_n^2 + 11}{4x_n}$ to find a solution to $2x^2 = 11$ to 3 d.p. Use the starting value $x_0 = 3$.

4 The equation $2x^3 + 2x - 7 = 0$ has one solution.

a) Show that $2x^3 + 2x - 7 = 0$ can be written as $x = \sqrt[3]{\dfrac{7 - 2x}{2}}$.

b) Using the iteration $x_{n+1} = \sqrt[3]{\dfrac{7 - 2x_n}{2}}$ find the solution to $2x^3 + 2x - 7 = 0$ to 3 d.p. Use $x_0 = 1$ as the starting value.

9.4 Equations Problems

Exercise 1

1 Solve the following equations.

a) $\dfrac{x + 8}{3} = 4$ **b)** $\dfrac{x - 5}{6} = 5$ **c)** $\dfrac{x - 2.5}{7} = 3$ **d)** $\dfrac{x + 6}{5} = 4.2$

e) $9 + 5x = 54$ **f)** $12 - 6x = 84$ **g)** $30 + 7x = 9$ **h)** $13 - 3.5x = 34$

i) $\dfrac{x + 3}{5} = -12$ **j)** $\dfrac{x - 3}{7} = -5$ **k)** $24 - 8x = -16$ **l)** $17 - 12x = 149$

2 Solve the following equations.

a) $72 = 4.5(8 + 2x)$ **b)** $7(x - 3) = 3(x - 6)$ **c)** $6(x - 2) = 4(x - 3)$

d) $12(x + 3) = 6(x + 15)$ **e)** $108 = 6(2 - x)$ **f)** $9x - 144 = 42 + 15x$

g) $5x - 9 = 54 - 8x$ **h)** $12(x - 3) = 4(6 + 2x)$ **i)** $12(4x - 3) = 4(2x + 1)$

3 Solve the following equations.

a) $\dfrac{x - 2}{5} = \dfrac{9 - x}{3}$ **b)** $\dfrac{x - 5}{6} = \dfrac{12 - 3x}{4}$ **c)** $\dfrac{x - 7}{8} = \dfrac{15 - 4x}{6}$

d) $\dfrac{x}{7} = 10 - 3x$ **e)** $\dfrac{3x}{8} = 16 + 3x$ **f)** $\dfrac{2x}{5} = 18 - 2x$

4 I think of a number. I subtract 4, then divide by 5. The result equals 15.

a) Write this information in the form of an equation.

b) Solve the equation to find the number I was thinking of.

5 Find the value of x in each of the following.

a)

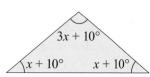

b)

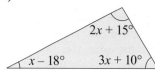

c)

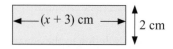

6 The area of this rectangle is 12 cm². Find the rectangle's perimeter.

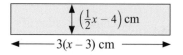

7 The perimeter of this rectangle is 180 cm. Find the rectangle's area to 1 d.p.

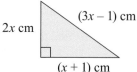

8 Find the positive solutions to the following equations. Give your answers correct to 1 d.p.

a) $x^2 + 3x = 16$

b) $x^2 + 4x = 100$

c) $x^2 - 6x = 130$

d) $x^2 - 3x = 20$

e) $x^4 + 10x = 30$

f) $x^4 + 2x^2 + 5x = 20$

9 The triangle and rectangle shown have the same area. The perimeter of the triangle is 12 cm.

a) Find the value of x.

b) Hence find the area of the triangle.

c) Use an iterative method to find the value of y, correct to 1 decimal place.

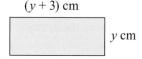

10 A ball is thrown upwards from the ground.
After x seconds, its height (h) in metres is given by the formula $h = 55x - 5x^2$.
It starts to fall back to the ground after 5 seconds.

a) After how many seconds does the ball first reach a height of 105 metres? Give your answer correct to 2 decimal places.

b) Once it starts to fall, after how many seconds does the ball reach a height of 105 metres again? Give your answer correct to 2 decimal places.

11 Lol, Maddie and Norm took part in a javelin competition. Lol threw x m.
The distance that Maddie threw is the square of the distance that Lol threw.
Norm threw 30 m. The total distance of their three throws put together is 128 m.

a) Use the information given to write an equation in x.

b) Use an iterative method to find the distance that each person has thrown, correct to the nearest cm.

12 Using an iterative method, find the value of x in each of the following. Give your answers correct to 1 d.p.

a)

b)

9.5 Identities

An **equation** is a way of showing that two expressions are equal for some particular values of an unknown.
Identities are like equations, but are **always true**, for any value of the unknown.
Identities have the symbol '$\equiv$' instead of '$=$'.

E.g. $x - 1 = 2$ is an equation — it's only true when $x = 3$.
   $x + 1 \equiv 1 + x$ is an identity — it's always true, whatever the value of x is.

Example 1
In which of the following equations could you replace the '$=$' sign with '$\equiv$'?
(i) $6 + 4x = x + 3$ (ii) $x(x - 1) = -(x - x^2)$

1. You can rearrange equation (i) to give $3x = -3$.
    This has only one solution ($x = -1$), so it isn't an identity.
2. If you expand the brackets in (ii) you get $x^2 - x = -x + x^2$.
    Both sides are the same, so (ii) is true for any value of x.

You can replace the '$=$' with '$\equiv$' in equation (ii), but not in equation (i).

Exercise 1

1   For each of the following, state whether or not you could you replace the box with the symbol '$\equiv$'.

   a) $4x \,\square\, 10$
   b) $x^2 + 2x + 1 \,\square\, 0$
   c) $x^2 - 3 \,\square\, 3 - x^2$
   d) $2(x + 1) \,\square\, x - 1$
   e) $3(x + 2) - x \,\square\, 2(x + 3)$
   f) $3(2 - 3x) + 2 \,\square\, 8x$
   g) $x^2 + 2x + 1 \,\square\, (x + 1)^2$
   h) $(x + 2)^2 + 1 \,\square\, x^2 + 4x + 5$
   i) $4(2 - x) \,\square\, 2(4 - 2x)$
   j) $4x^2 - x \,\square\, 2(x^2 - 2x)$

Example 2
Find the value of k if $(x + 2)(x - 3) \equiv x^2 - x + k$

1. Expand the brackets on the left hand side.
2. There's an x^2 and a $-x$ on both sides already.
    To make both sides identical, k must be -6.

$(x + 2)(x - 3) \equiv x^2 - x + k$
$x^2 + 2x - 3x - 6 \equiv x^2 - x + k$
$x^2 - x - 6 \equiv x^2 - x + k$
$\underline{k = -6}$

2   Find the value of a if:

   a) $2(x + 5) \equiv 2x + 1 + a$
   b) $ax + 3 \equiv 5x + 2 - (x - 1)$
   c) $3(x + a) \equiv 12 + 3x$
   d) $4(1 - 2x) \equiv 2(a - 4x)$
   e) $(x + 4)(x - 1) \equiv x^2 + ax - 4$
   f) $(x + 2)^2 \equiv x^2 + 4x + a$
   g) $3(x^2 - 2) \equiv a(6x^2 - 12)$
   h) $3(x - 4)^2 \equiv 3x^2 - 24a(x - 2)$
   i) $4 - x^2 \equiv (a + x)(a - x)$
   j) $(2x - 1)(3 - x) \equiv ax^2 + 7x - 3$

3   Prove that $(x + 5)^2 + 3(x - 1)^2 \equiv 4(x^2 + x + 7)$

4   Prove that $3(x + 2)^2 - (x - 4)^2 \equiv 2(x^2 + 10x - 2)$

Section 10 — Direct and Inverse Proportion

10.1   Direct Proportion

Two quantities are **directly proportional** if they are always in the same ratio.
This can be written as a **proportionality statement**:

e.g. $p \propto l$ which is read as p is proportional to l or p varies directly as l or just p varies as l

You can write this as an equation: $p = kl$ where k is called the **constant of proportionality**.

The graph of a proportional relationship is a **straight line** through the origin.
The **gradient** of the graph is equal to the constant of proportionality.

Example 1

y is directly proportional to x.
Fill in the gaps in the table.

x	3	5	10	12	
y			25		100

1.   Write the proportionality statement and make it into an equation. $y \propto x$, so $y = kx$
2.   The table shows that when $x = 10$, $y = 25$. Use this to find k.

$$25 = k \times 10$$
$$k = 25 \div 10 = 2.5$$
$$\text{So } y = 2.5x$$

3.   Use the equation to complete the table:

x	3	5	10	12	$100 \div 2.5 = \underline{\textbf{40}}$
y	$2.5 \times 3 = \underline{\textbf{7.5}}$	$2.5 \times 5 = \underline{\textbf{12.5}}$	25	$2.5 \times 12 = \underline{\textbf{30}}$	100

Exercise 1

1   In each of the following tables, y is directly proportional to x.
Use this information to fill in the gaps in each table.

a)

x	22	33
y	2	

b)

x	24	
y	18	24

c)

x	7	2	10	21	
y			15		36

d)

x	−4	0		12
y	−14		21	

e)

x		8
y	12	9

f)

x	−27	78		
y		104	272	980

Example 2

m is directly proportional to e. Given that $m = 72$ when $e = 6$,

a)   find the constant of proportionality,

1.   Write the proportionality statement and make it into an equation. $m \propto e$, so $m = ke$
2.   Use the given values to find k. $72 = k \times 6$, so $k = 72 \div 6$

$$\underline{k = 12}$$

b)   calculate the value of e when $m = 37$.

1.   Put the value of k from part a) into the equation $m = ke$. $m = 12e$
2.   Substitute $m = 37$ into the equation and solve for e. $37 = 12e$

$$e = 37 \div 12 = \underline{\textbf{3.08}} \text{ (to 2 d.p.)}$$

2 j is directly proportional to h. When $j = 15$, $h = 5$. What is the value of j when $h = 40$?

3 r varies directly as t. When $r = 9$, $t = 6$. What is the value of r when $t = 7.5$?

4 f is directly proportional to g. When $f = 27$, $g = 378$. What is the value of f when $g = 203$?

5 p is directly proportional to q. When $p = 11$, $q = 3$. What is the value of q when $p = 82.5$?

6 c is directly proportional to d. When $c = 13$, $d = 221$.
    a) What is the value of c when $d = 646$?   **b)** What is the value of d when $c = 22.5$?

7 Given that $b = 142$ when $s = 16$ and that b is directly proportional to s, find the value of:
    a) b when $s = 18$,   **b)** s when $b = 200$.

8 **a)** Which of these graphs show y and x in direct proportion? Explain your answer.

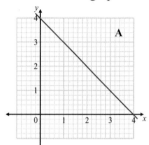 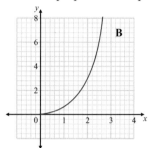 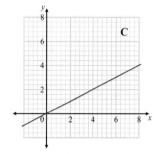

    b) For any graphs which do show direct proportion, what is the constant of proportionality?

Other Types of Direct Proportion

- If a is directly proportional to the square of u then $a \propto u^2$, so $a = ku^2$.
- If a is directly proportional to the cube of u then $a \propto u^3$, so $a = ku^3$.
- If h is directly proportional to the square root of g then $h \propto \sqrt{g}$, so $h = k\sqrt{g}$.

Example 3

p is directly proportional to the square of d. Given that $p = 125$ when $d = 5$,
a) find p when $d = 7$,
    1. Write the proportionality statement and make it into an equation. $p \propto d^2$, so $p = kd^2$
    2. Use the given values to find k. $125 = k \times 5^2 = 25k$,
        so $k = 125 \div 25 = 5$
    3. Substitute $k = 5$ into $p = kd^2$. $p = 5d^2$
    4. Substitute in $d = 7$ and solve for p. $p = 5 \times 7^2 = \underline{\textbf{245}}$
b) find d when $p = 2500$.
    Substitute $p = 2500$ into the equation and solve for d. $2500 = 5d^2$
        $d^2 = 2500 \div 5 = 500$
        $d = \pm\sqrt{500} = \underline{\textbf{±22.36}}$ (to 2 d.p.)

Exercise 2

1 In each of the following cases, y is directly proportional to the square of x.
    a) If $y = 64$ when $x = 2$, find y when $x = 5$.
    b) If $y = 539$ when $x = 7$, find x when $y = 1331$.
    c) If $y = 32$ when $x = 3$, find y when $x = 12.5$.

2 In each of the following cases, p varies directly as the cube of q.
    a) When $p = 81$, $q = 3$. Find p when $q = 5$.
    b) When $p = 1000$, $q = 5$. Find q when $p = 64$.
    c) When $p = -0.24$, $q = -0.2$. Find p when $q = -0.5$.

3 t is directly proportional to the square root of z and $t = 35$ when $z = 100$.

    a) Find t when $z = 625$.

    b) Find z when $t = 6$.

4 y is directly proportional to the cube of x.
Complete the table.

x	2	8	10	
y		256		950

5 y is directly proportional to the square root of x.
Complete the table.

x	1	9	16	
y		84		560

6 y is directly proportional to the square of x.
Complete the table.

x	2	3		4.5
y		76.5	100	

7 f varies directly as the square of g. It is found that $g = 100$ when $f = 200$.

    a) Find f when $g = 61.5$.   **b)** Given that $g > 0$, find the exact value of g when $f = 14$.

8 The time taken for a ball to drop from its maximum height is directly proportional to the square root of the distance fallen. Given that a ball takes 3 seconds to drop 34.1 m, find the time taken for the ball to drop 15 m.

9 The volume of a sphere is directly proportional to the cube of its radius.
The volume of a sphere of radius 12 cm is 2304π cm³.

    a) Find the constant of proportionality in terms of π.
Use this to write an equation for the volume of a sphere in terms of its radius.

    b) Find the volume of a sphere of radius 21 cm, in terms of π.

    c) Find the radius of a sphere of volume 1000 cm³, correct to 1 decimal place.

10.2 Inverse Proportion

If two quantities are **inversely proportional**, the **product** of the two quantities is **constant**.
Inverse proportion can be written as a **proportionality statement**:

    e.g. $y \propto \dfrac{1}{x}$ which is read as either y is inversely proportional to x or y varies inversely as x

As with direct proportion, you can rewrite this as an equation using a constant of proportionality: $y = \dfrac{k}{x}$

Example 1

y is inversely proportional to x.
Fill in the gaps in the table.

x	1	5	10	
y			20	100

1. Write the proportionality statement and make it into an equation.

2. The table shows that when $x = 10$, $y = 20$. Use this to find k.

$y \propto \dfrac{1}{x}$, so $y = \dfrac{k}{x}$

$20 = \dfrac{k}{10}$

$k = 20 \times 10 = 200$

So $y = \dfrac{200}{x}$

3. Use the equation to complete the table:

x	1	5	10	200 ÷ 100 = **2**
y	200 ÷ 1 = **200**	200 ÷ 5 = **40**	20	100

Exercise 1

1 In each of the following tables, y is inversely proportional to x.
Use this information to fill in the gaps in each table.

a)

x	12	
y	15	12

b)

x	11	22
y	4	

c)

x	1	3	6	20	
y			15		270

d)

x		7
y	25.2	9

Example 2

y is inversely proportional to x and $x = 4$ when $y = 15$.

a) Find y when $x = 10$.

    1. Write the proportionality statement and make it into an equation. $y \propto \frac{1}{x}$, so $y = \frac{k}{x}$

    2. Use the given values to find k. $15 = k \div 4$, so $k = 15 \times 4 = 60$

    3. Put $k = 60$ into the equation. $y = \frac{60}{x}$

    4. Substitute $x = 10$ into the equation and solve for y. $y = \frac{60}{x} = \frac{60}{10} = \underline{\mathbf{6}}$

b) Sketch the graph of the relationship.

    An inverse proportion relationship
always gives a hyperbola.
The curve never touches or crosses
the x- or y-axes — both axes are
asymptotes to the curve.

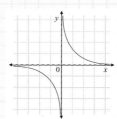

Exercise 2

1 p is inversely proportional to q. When $p = 7$, $q = 4$. What is the value of p when $q = 56$?

2 m varies inversely as n. When $m = 6$, $n = 6$. What is the value of m when $n = 3$?

3 g varies inversely as h. When $g = 4$, $h = 0.2$. What is the value of g when $h = 5$?

4 s is inversely proportional to t. When $s = 5$, $t = 16$. What is the value, to 3 s.f., of t when $s = 48$?

5 e is inversely proportional to f. When $e = 9$, $f = 8$.
   a) What is the value of e, to 3 s.f., when $f = 54$?
   b) What is the value of f, to 3 s.f., when $e = 27$?
   c) Sketch the graph for this relationship.

6   Given that w is inversely proportional to z and $w = 15$ when $z = 4$,
   a) find z when $w = 25$,
   b) explain what happens to z when w is doubled,
   c) explain what happens to w when z is trebled.

Other Types of Inverse Proportion

- If a is inversely proportional to the square of u then $a \propto \frac{1}{u^2}$, so $a = \frac{k}{u^2}$.

- If a is inversely proportional to the cube of u then $a \propto \frac{1}{u^3}$, so $a = \frac{k}{u^3}$.

- If h is inversely proportional to the square root of g then $h \propto \frac{1}{\sqrt{g}}$, so $h = \frac{k}{\sqrt{g}}$.

Example 3

y is inversely proportional to the cube of x, and when $x = 4$, $y = 10$.
Find the value of x when $y = 50$.

    1. Write the proportionality statement and make it into an equation. $y \propto \frac{1}{x^3}$, so $y = \frac{k}{x^3}$.

    2. Use the given values to find k. $10 = k \div 4^3 = k \div 64$
                                             so $k = 10 \times 64 = 640$

    3. Substitute $k = 640$ into $y = \frac{k}{x^3}$. $y = \frac{640}{x^3}$

    4. Substitute $y = 50$ into the equation and solve for x. $50 = \frac{640}{x^3}$

                                                     $x^3 = 640 \div 50 = 12.8$

                                                     $x = \sqrt[3]{12.8} = \underline{\mathbf{2.34}}$ (2 d.p.)

Exercise 3

1 Complete these tables.

   a) y is inversely proportional to the square of x.

x	2	5		0.4
y	8		2	

   b) y is inversely proportional to the square root of x and k is positive.

x		9	100	
y	6	8		$\frac{1}{3}$

   c) y is inversely proportional to the cube of x.

x	2	8		0.4
y		4	10	

2 m is inversely proportional to the square root of t and when $t = 4$, $m = 4$. The constant of proportionality is a positive integer.
   a) Write an equation for m in terms of t.
   b) What is the value of t when $m = 2$.

3 h is inversely proportional to the cube of f. It is known that $h = 12.5$ when $f = 2$. Find the value of h when $f = 5$.

4 a is inversely proportional to the square of c and when $c = 6$, $a = 3$. Find the two possible values of c when $a = 12$.

5 $y \propto \dfrac{1}{x^3}$
   a) Describe in words the proportion relationship between y and x.
   b) If $y = 15$ when $x = 2$, write an equation for y in terms of x.
   c) Find y when $x = 2.5$.
   d) What value of x will make y equal to 100?

6 The air pressure from an electric pump is inversely proportional to the square of the radius of the tube to the pump. A tube with radius 10 mm creates 20 units of air pressure.
   a) How much pressure will a tube of radius 15 mm create?
   b) If an air-bed is to be pumped up using a maximum of 30 units of air pressure, what radius of tube should be used to achieve the quickest fill?

7 b is inversely proportional to the square of c. When $c = 1$, $b = 64$. Find values of b and c such that $b = c$.

8 The quantities u and v are related by the equation $v = \dfrac{k}{u^2}$.
   a) Decide which of the following statements are true and which are false:
     (i) u is proportional to the square of v.   **(ii)** v multiplied by the square of u is equal to a constant.
     (iii) If you double v, you halve u.   **(iv)** If you double u, you divide v by 4.

   b) If $k = 900$ and u and v are both positive integers, find at least 3 sets of possible values for u and v.

10.3   Direct and Inverse Proportion Problems

Exercise 1

1   **a)** Copy and complete the table on the right if:
     (i) y is directly proportional to x,
     (ii) y is inversely proportional to x.

x	2	3	9	
y		8		100

   b) Explain in words the main difference between direct and indirect proportion.

2 p is inversely proportional to the cube of g and when $g = 1.5$, $p = 10$.
   a) Find p when $g = 2.1$.   **b)** Find g when $p = 15$.

3 b varies directly as the square root of d. Given that $b = 5$ when $d = 2.2$, find b when $d = 0.5$.

4 A person's reach with an upstretched arm is roughly proportional to their height. On average, statistics show that a person can reach 1.3 times their height. Write down both a proportionality statement and an equation for this situation. Would you expect a person of height 1.75 m to be able to touch a ceiling 2.5 m high? Show working to justify your answer.

5 Match each of the following statements to one of the tables and one of the sketch graphs below.

    A y is directly proportional to x

    B y is directly proportional to the square of x

    C y is directly proportional to the cube of x

    D y is directly proportional to the square root of x

K

x	1	3
y	10	270

L

x	4	20
y	2	10

M

x	2	5
y	20	125

N

x	4	25
y	4	10

Q 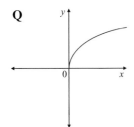   **R** 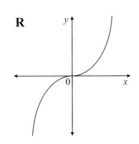   **S** 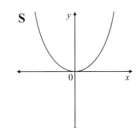   **T**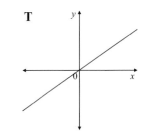

x	−6	−4	−2	2	4	6
y				6		

    a) Copy and complete the table above if:

        (i) y is inversely proportional to x

        (ii) y is inversely proportional to the square of x

        (iii) y is inversely proportional to the cube of x

        (iv) y is inversely proportional to the square root of x

    b) Using your tables, sketch graphs of the 4 types of inverse proportionality.
        Include asymptotes in your sketches where necessary.

7 In the following situations, state what the constant of proportionality represents.
[Hint: set up the proportionality statement and the corresponding equation in each case.]

    a) The time taken for a journey is inversely proportional to the speed travelled.

    b) The amount of VAT paid on an item varies directly as the cost of the item.

    c) The length of a rectangle is indirectly proportional to its width.

    d) The length of an original photograph is directly proportional to the length of an enlargement of the photograph.

    e) The height of a cylinder is inversely proportional to the area of the base of the cylinder.

8 Coulomb's inverse square law states that the force of attraction or repulsion between two point charges is directly proportional to the product of the sizes of the charges and inversely proportional to the square of the distance between them.

This can be written as: $F = k \dfrac{Q_1 \times Q_2}{d^2}$,

where Q_1 and Q_2 represent the sizes of the point charges,
d is the distance between the point charges, and k is a constant.

If the force is found to be 10^6 units when the sizes of two point charges, Q_1 and Q_2, are each equal to 10^{-2} units and the points are 3 metres apart, find the force when these same point charges are 8 metres apart.

Section 11 — Quadratic Equations

11.1 Solving Quadratics by Factorising

If $p \times q = 0$ then either $p = 0$ or $q = 0$. This can be used to solve **quadratic equations** by **factorisation**.
E.g. if you can factorise an equation to give $(x - a)(x - b) = 0$, then either $x - a = 0$ or $x - b = 0$, so $x = a$ or $x = b$.

Example 1

Solve the equation $x^2 - 3x + 2 = 0$.

1. Factorise the left-hand side. $(x - 1)(x - 2) = 0$
2. Put each factor equal to zero. $x - 1 = 0$ or $x - 2 = 0$
3. Solve to find the two possible values for x. $\underline{x = 1}$ or $\underline{x = 2}$

Exercise 1

1 Find the possible values of x for each of the following.

   a) $x(x + 8) = 0$ **b)** $(x - 5)(x - 1) = 0$

   c) $(x + 2)(x + 6) = 0$ **d)** $(x - 9)(x + 7) = 0$

2 a) Factorise the following expressions.

     (i) $x^2 + 6x$ **(ii)** $x^2 + x - 2$ **(iii)** $x^2 - x - 2$

     (iv) $x^2 + 2x - 24$ **(v)** $x^2 + 13x + 36$

   b) Use your answers to part (a) to solve the following equations.

     (i) $x^2 + 6x = 0$ **(ii)** $x^2 + x - 2 = 0$ **(iii)** $x^2 - x - 2 = 0$

     (iv) $x^2 + 2x - 24 = 0$ **(v)** $x^2 + 13x + 36 = 0$

3 Solve the following equations by factorising.

   a) $x^2 - 3x = 0$ **b)** $x^2 + 5x = 0$ **c)** $x^2 - x = 0$

   d) $x^2 + 12x = 0$ **e)** $x^2 + 3x + 2 = 0$ **f)** $x^2 - 3x + 2 = 0$

   g) $x^2 + 4x + 4 = 0$ **h)** $x^2 - 4x + 4 = 0$ **i)** $x^2 + 3x - 4 = 0$

   j) $x^2 - 3x - 4 = 0$ **k)** $x^2 + 5x + 4 = 0$ **l)** $x^2 - 5x + 4 = 0$

   m) $x^2 - 4x - 5 = 0$ **n)** $x^2 - 5x + 6 = 0$ **o)** $x^2 - 7x + 6 = 0$

   p) $x^2 - x - 12 = 0$ **q)** $x^2 + 8x + 12 = 0$ **r)** $x^2 - 2x - 24 = 0$

   s) $x^2 - 15x + 36 = 0$ **t)** $x^2 + 16x - 36 = 0$

Example 2

Solve the equation $8x^2 + 6x - 9 = 0$.

1. Factorise the left-hand side. $(2x + 3)(4x - 3) = 0$
2. Put each factor equal to zero. $2x + 3 = 0$ or $4x - 3 = 0$
3. Find the values of x which make each factor equal zero. $2x = -3$ or $4x = 3$
                                                                               $\underline{x = -1.5}$ or $\underline{x = 0.75}$

Exercise 2

1 Find the possible values of x for each of the following.

   a) $x(2x - 3) = 0$ **b)** $(x - 2)(3x - 1) = 0$

   c) $(3x + 4)(2x + 5) = 0$ **d)** $(4x - 7)(5x + 2) = 0$

2 **a)** Copy and complete the following factorisations.

     (i) $2x^2 + 7x + 5 = (2x + 5)(\quad)$ **(ii)** $3x^2 + 5x + 2 = (3x + \quad)(x + \quad)$

     (iii) $4x^2 + 4x - 15 = (2x - 3)(\quad)$ **(iv)** $4x^2 + 11x + 6 = (4x + \quad)(x + \quad)$

     (v) $6x^2 + 7x - 10 = (6x \quad)(\quad 2)$ **(vi)** $12x^2 - 21x - 6 = 3(\quad + 1)(\quad - 2)$

   b) Use your answers to part (a) to solve the following equations.

     (i) $2x^2 + 7x + 5 = 0$ **(ii)** $3x^2 + 5x + 2 = 0$

     (iii) $4x^2 + 4x - 15 = 0$ **(iv)** $4x^2 + 11x + 6 = 0$

     (v) $6x^2 + 7x - 10 = 0$ **(vi)** $12x^2 - 21x - 6 = 0$

3 Solve the following equations by factorising.

   a) $3x^2 + 5x = 0$ **b)** $2x^2 + x - 3 = 0$ **c)** $3x^2 + 10x + 7 = 0$ **d)** $5x^2 + 3x - 2 = 0$

   e) $3x^2 - 11x + 6 = 0$ **f)** $6x^2 - 11x + 3 = 0$ **g)** $4x^2 + 17x + 4 = 0$ **h)** $4x^2 - 16x + 15 = 0$

   i) $4x^2 + 5x - 21 = 0$ **j)** $6x^2 + x - 22 = 0$ **k)** $10x^2 + 23x + 12 = 0$ **l)** $12x^2 - x - 1 = 0$

   m) $12x^2 + 4x - 5 = 0$ **n)** $9x^2 - 18x + 8 = 0$ **o)** $18x^2 + x - 4 = 0$ **p)** $18x^2 - 29x - 14 = 0$

Example 3

Solve the equation $12x^2 - 8x = 15$.

  1. Rearrange to get zero on one side. $12x^2 - 8x - 15 = 0$

  2. Factorise the left-hand side of the equation. $(2x - 3)(6x + 5) = 0$

  3. Put each factor equal to zero. $2x - 3 = 0$ or $6x + 5 = 0$

  4. Solve for each x. $2x = 3$ or $6x = -5$

$$x = \frac{3}{2} \quad \text{or} \quad x = -\frac{5}{6}$$

Exercise 3

Rearrange the following equations, then solve them by factorising.

1 **a)** $x^2 = x$ **b)** $x^2 + 2x = 3$ **c)** $x^2 - 3x = 10$ **d)** $10x - x^2 = 21$

   e) $x^2 = 6x - 8$ **f)** $x^2 = 4x + 21$ **g)** $8x - x^2 = 12$ **h)** $3x^2 = 6x + 9$

   i) $x^2 + 21x = 11 - x^2$ **j)** $4x^2 + 4x = 3$ **k)** $6x^2 + x = 1$ **l)** $6x^2 = 7x - 2$

   m) $3x^2 = 2 + x$ **n)** $4x^2 + 1 = 4x$ **o)** $6x^2 = 11x + 7$ **p)** $9x^2 + 25 = 30x$

2 **a)** $x(x - 2) = 8$ **b)** $x(x + 2) = 35$ **c)** $x(x - 1) = 72$

   d) $(x + 3)(x + 9) + 9 = 0$ **e)** $(x - 6)(x - 8) + 1 = 0$ **f)** $(x + 3)(x + 1) = 4x + 7$

   g) $(2x + 1)(x - 1) = -16x - 8$ **h)** $(3x + 4)^2 = 7(3x + 4)$ **i)** $(3x - 4)(x - 2) - 5 = 0$

   j) $(3x + 2)(4x + 1) - 3 = 0$ **k)** $2(4x + 1)(x - 1) + 3 = 0$ **l)** $(3x - 2)(3x + 1) = -\frac{1}{2}(21x + 6)$

3 **a)** $x + 1 = \dfrac{6}{x}$ **b)** $x - 2 = \dfrac{4}{x + 1}$ **c)** $x + 2 = \dfrac{28}{x - 1}$

   d) $2x + 1 = \dfrac{10}{4 - x}$ **e)** $3x - 1 = \dfrac{4}{2x + 1}$ **f)** $6x - 1 = \dfrac{4}{4x + 1}$

11.2 Completing the Square

Completing the square of a quadratic expression $x^2 + bx + c$ means writing it in the form $(x + p)^2 + q$.

To complete the square of $x^2 + bx + c$:

1. Write out the bracket $\left(x + \frac{b}{2}\right)^2$.
2. Work out what to add or subtract to get the original expression.

Example 1

a) Write $x^2 + 6x - 5$ in completed square form.

1. $b = 6$, so $\frac{b}{2} = 3$. Expand $(x + 3)^2$. $\qquad$ $(x + 3)^2 = x^2 + 6x + 9$

2. To get $c = -5$ instead of $+9$, subtract 14. $\qquad$ $x^2 + 6x - 5 = x^2 + 6x + 9 - 14$

$$= \underline{\mathbf{(x + 3)^2 - 14}}$$

b) Write $x^2 + 7x + 1$ in completed square form.

1. $b = 7$, so $\frac{b}{2} = \frac{7}{2}$. Leaving this as a fraction, expand $\left(x + \frac{7}{2}\right)^2$. $\qquad$ $\left(x + \frac{7}{2}\right)^2 = x^2 + 7x + \frac{49}{4}$

2. To get $c = +1$ instead of $+\frac{49}{4}$, subtract $\frac{45}{4}$. $\qquad$ $x^2 + 7x + 1 = x^2 + 7x + \frac{49}{4} - \frac{45}{4}$

$$= \underline{\left(x + \frac{7}{2}\right)^2 - \frac{45}{4}}$$

Exercise 1

1 Find the value of c in each of the following equations.

a) $x^2 + 2x + 2 = (x + 1)^2 + c$ $\qquad\qquad$ b) $x^2 + 2x - 9 = (x + 1)^2 + c$

c) $x^2 + 4x + 2 = (x + 2)^2 + c$ $\qquad\qquad$ d) $x^2 - 4x + 7 = (x - 2)^2 + c$

e) $x^2 - 6x + 11 = (x - 3)^2 + c$ $\qquad\qquad$ f) $x^2 - 8x + 3 = (x - 4)^2 + c$

g) $x^2 + 10x + 64 = (x + 5)^2 + c$ $\qquad\qquad$ h) $x^2 + 12x - 24 = (x + 6)^2 + c$

i) $x^2 + 16x + 56 = (x + 8)^2 + c$ $\qquad\qquad$ j) $x^2 + 20x + 500 = (x + 10)^2 + c$

In Questions 2-3, write each expression in completed square form.

2 a) $x^2 + 2x + 6$ $\qquad\qquad$ b) $x^2 - 2x + 4$ $\qquad\qquad$ c) $x^2 - 2x - 10$

d) $x^2 - 4x + 10$ $\qquad\qquad$ e) $x^2 + 4x + 20$ $\qquad\qquad$ f) $x^2 + 6x + 1$

g) $x^2 + 8x + 60$ $\qquad\qquad$ h) $x^2 + 8x + 81$ $\qquad\qquad$ i) $x^2 + 10x - 2$

j) $x^2 - 12x + 100$ $\qquad\qquad$ k) $x^2 + 12x + 44$ $\qquad\qquad$ l) $x^2 + 14x$

m) $x^2 - 14x + 96$ $\qquad\qquad$ n) $x^2 - 20x - 200$ $\qquad\qquad$ o) $x^2 + 20x - 150$

3 a) $x^2 + 3x + 1$ $\qquad\qquad$ b) $x^2 + 3x - 1$ $\qquad\qquad$ c) $x^2 - 3x + 1$

d) $x^2 + 5x + 12$ $\qquad\qquad$ e) $x^2 + 5x + 3$ $\qquad\qquad$ f) $x^2 - 5x + 20$

g) $x^2 + 7x + 10$ $\qquad\qquad$ h) $x^2 - 7x - 1$ $\qquad\qquad$ i) $x^2 - 9x - 10$

j) $x^2 + 11x + 25$ $\qquad\qquad$ k) $x^2 + 19x + 90$ $\qquad\qquad$ l) $x^2 + 13x + 40$

m) $x^2 - 13x - 1$ $\qquad\qquad$ n) $x^2 + 15x - 125$ $\qquad\qquad$ o) $x^2 - 21x + 110$

Solving Quadratics by Completing the Square

You can use completing the square to solve quadratics, including ones that **can't** be factorised.
This method often gives an answer containing a **surd**.
Remember that if the question asks for an **exact answer**, that means you should leave it in surd form.

Example 2

Find the exact solutions to the equation $x^2 - 4x + 1 = 0$ by completing the square.

1. $b = -4$, so $\frac{b}{2} = -2$. Expand $(x - 2)^2$. $(x - 2)^2 = x^2 - 4x + 4$

2. Complete the square. $x^2 - 4x + 1 = (x - 2)^2 - 3$

3. Use the completed square to rewrite
and solve the original equation.

$x^2 - 4x + 1 = 0$
so $(x - 2)^2 - 3 = 0$
$(x - 2)^2 = 3$

4. There's a positive and negative square root. $x - 2 = \pm\sqrt{3}$

5. For the exact solutions, leave in surd form. $\underline{x = 2 - \sqrt{3}}$ or $\underline{x = 2 + \sqrt{3}}$

Exercise 2

1 Find the exact solutions of the following equations by completing the square.

a) $x^2 + 4x + 4 = 0$ b) $x^2 - 6x + 9 = 0$ c) $x^2 - 2x - 4 = 0$ d) $x^2 + 4x + 3 = 0$

e) $x^2 + 6x - 4 = 0$ f) $x^2 + 8x + 4 = 0$ g) $x^2 + 8x + 5 = 0$ h) $x^2 - x - 1 = 0$

i) $x^2 - 5x + 4 = 0$ j) $x^2 - 7x + 9 = 0$ k) $x^2 + 9x + 8 = 0$ l) $x^2 - 11x + 25 = 0$

2 Solve the following equations by completing the square. Give your answers to 2 decimal places.

a) $x^2 + 6x + 4 = 0$ b) $x^2 - 7x + 8 = 0$ c) $x^2 - 2x - 5 = 0$ d) $x^2 + 4x + 1 = 0$

e) $x^2 + 6x - 3 = 0$ f) $x^2 + 8x + 8 = 0$ g) $x^2 - 6x + 2 = 0$ h) $x^2 - x - 10 = 0$

i) $x^2 - 5x + 3 = 0$ j) $x^2 - 7x + 2 = 0$ k) $x^2 + 9x + 10 = 0$ l) $x^2 - 11x + 20 = 0$

Example 3

Solve the equation $2x^2 - 8x + 3 = 0$ by completing the square.
Give your answers to 2 decimal places.

1. Divide by 2 so that the coefficient of x^2 is 1. $x^2 - 4x + \frac{3}{2} = 0$

2. $b = -4$, so $\frac{b}{2} = -2$. Expand $(x - 2)^2$. $(x - 2)^2 = x^2 - 4x + 4$

3. Complete the square. $x^2 - 4x + \frac{3}{2} = (x - 2)^2 - \frac{5}{2}$

4. Use the completed square to rewrite
and solve the original equation.

$x^2 - 4x + \frac{3}{2} = 0$, so $(x - 2)^2 - \frac{5}{2} = 0$

$(x - 2)^2 = \frac{5}{2}$

$x - 2 = \pm\sqrt{\frac{5}{2}}$

$x = 2 - \sqrt{\frac{5}{2}}$ or $x = 2 + \sqrt{\frac{5}{2}}$

$\underline{x = 0.42}$ or $\underline{x = 3.58}$ (to 2 d.p.)

3   Find the exact solutions of the following equations by completing the square.

a) $3x^2 + 2x - 2 = 0$ b) $5x^2 + 2x = 10$ c) $4x^2 - 6x - 1 = 0$ d) $2x^2 = 12x - 5$

e) $2x^2 - 16x - 7 = 0$ f) $4 = 4x^2 + 3x$ g) $3x^2 = 10 - 5x$ h) $10x^2 + 7x - 1 = 0$

4   Solve the following equations by completing the square. Give your answers to 2 decimal places.

a) $2x^2 + 2x - 3 = 0$ b) $3x^2 + 2x - 7 = 0$ c) $4x^2 + 8x = 11$ d) $15 = 12x - 2x^2$

e) $2x^2 - 16x - 19 = 0$ f) $6x^2 = 1 - 3x$ g) $5x^2 + 10x - 11 = 0$ h) $3x^2 + 9x - 7 = 0$

11.3   The Quadratic Formula

The **general form** of a quadratic equation is: $ax^2 + bx + c = 0$

The **formula** for solving this equation is:

$$x = \frac{-b \pm \sqrt{b^2 - 4ac}}{2a}$$

Example 1

Solve the equation $x^2 - 5x + 3 = 0$, giving your answers to 2 decimal places.

1. Write down a, b and c. $a = 1, b = -5, c = 3$

2. Substitute these values into the formula.

$$x = \frac{5 \pm \sqrt{(-5)^2 - 4 \times 1 \times 3}}{2 \times 1}$$

$$= \frac{5 \pm \sqrt{25 - 12}}{2}$$

$$= \frac{5 \pm \sqrt{13}}{2}$$

$$x = \frac{5 - 3.606}{2} \quad \text{or} \quad x = \frac{5 + 3.606}{2}$$

$$\underline{x = 0.70} \quad \text{or} \quad \underline{x = 4.30} \quad \text{(to 2 d.p.)}$$

Exercise 1

1   Use the quadratic formula to solve the following equations. Give your answers to 2 decimal places.

a) $x^2 + 3x + 1 = 0$ b) $x^2 + 2x - 2 = 0$ c) $x^2 - 3x - 3 = 0$ d) $x^2 - 2x - 5 = 0$

e) $5x + x^2 - 4 = 0$ f) $x^2 - 8x + 11 = 0$ g) $x^2 - 6 - 7x = 0$ h) $x^2 + 6x - 2 = 0$

i) $x^2 + 4x - 1 = 0$ j) $x^2 + 5x - 9 = 0$ k) $10 + x^2 + 8x = 0$ l) $x^2 - 7x - 11 = 0$

2   Find the exact solutions to the following equations.

a) $x^2 - 3x + 1 = 0$ b) $x^2 - 2x - 12 = 0$ c) $x^2 - 3x - 8 = 0$ d) $x^2 - 4 - 2x = 0$

e) $x^2 + 5x - 1 = 0$ f) $x^2 - 8x - 5 = 0$ g) $2 - 7x + x^2 = 0$ h) $x^2 + 6x - 5 = 0$

i) $4x + x^2 - 6 = 0$ j) $x^2 - 5x - 3 = 0$ k) $8x + 13 + x^2 = 0$ l) $x^2 + 3 - 7x = 0$

3   Rearrange the following equations and solve them using the quadratic formula. Give your answers to 2 d.p.

a) $x^2 + 3x = 6$ b) $x^2 = 7 + 3x$ c) $x^2 + 1 = 4x$ d) $x^2 - 5x + 11 = 2x + 3$

e) $2x^2 - 7x + 14 = x^2 + 7$ f) $(x + 1)^2 = 12$ g) $x^2 - x + 8 = x + 15$ h) $5x + 12 = (x + 1)(x + 7)$

4 Rearrange the following equations, then use the quadratic formula to find their exact solutions.

a) $x^2 = 1 - 3x$ **b)** $x^2 = 3(x + 3)$ **c)** $(x + 1)(x + 2) = 7x$ **d)** $(x - 8)x = 3 - x$

e) $x(x - 4) = 2(x - 2)$ **f)** $2(x + 5) = (x + 2)^2$ **g)** $(x - 1)^2 = 14$ **h)** $(2x - 1)(x + 2) = x^2 + 9$

Example 2

Show that the equation $2x^2 + 2x + 5 = 0$ has no real solutions.

1. Write down a, b and c.

$a = 2,\ b = 2,\ c = 5$

2. Substitute these values into the formula.

$$x = \frac{-2 \pm \sqrt{2^2 - 4 \times 2 \times 5}}{2 \times 2}$$

$$= \frac{-2 \pm \sqrt{4 - 40}}{4}$$

$$= \frac{-2 \pm \sqrt{-36}}{4}$$

3. You can't go any further, because you can't find $\sqrt{-36}$. There is no real value for $\sqrt{-36}$. So there are no real solutions to the equation $2x^2 + 2x + 5 = 0$.

---

5 Solve the following equations if possible. Give your answers to 2 decimal places.

a) $3x^2 - x - 1 = 0$ **b)** $2x^2 - 2x - 3 = 0$ **c)** $2x^2 + 2x + 3 = 0$ **d)** $2x^2 - 3x - 1 = 0$

e) $2x^2 + x - 5 = 0$ **f)** $3x^2 - x + 5 = 0$ **g)** $4x^2 - 10x - 1 = 0$ **h)** $2x^2 + 3x - 12 = 0$

i) $3x^2 - 4x - 2 = 0$ **j)** $5x^2 - 10x + 4 = 0$ **k)** $3x^2 + 3x - 1 = 0$ **l)** $10x^2 + 4x - 1 = 0$

m) $3x^2 - 5x - 1 = 0$ **n)** $2x^2 - 7x - 3 = 0$ **o)** $2x^2 + 3x + 5 = 0$ **p)** $3x^2 + 9x + 2 = 0$

6 Rearrange the following equations and solve them where possible. Give your answers to 2 decimal places.

a) $8x + 8 = -3x^2$ **b)** $2(x^2 - 1) = x$ **c)** $3x^2 + 7 = 4(x + 1)$

d) $x^2 - 12x + 13 = -x^2 - x$ **e)** $(5x + 1)(x + 1) = 3x - 1$ **f)** $(2x + 1)^2 = 11x - 1$

g) $2(2x - 5)(x + 1) = -11x$ **h)** $(x - 5)^2 = x(1 - 3x)$ **i)** $(2x + 3)(x + 3) = 10x$

7 Find the exact solutions, where possible, of the following equations.

a) $x^2 + 5x = 3$ **b)** $x^2 + 4x = 7$ **c)** $x^2 - 8x = 14$ **d)** $2x^2 + 5x = 13$

e) $x^2 = 3x - 3$ **f)** $x^2 = 7x - 4$ **g)** $2x^2 = 3x - 23$ **h)** $x^2 = 5 - 9x$

i) $3x^2 = 6 - 10x$ **j)** $x = \dfrac{15}{x + 3}$ **k)** $x - 5 = \dfrac{2}{x - 1}$ **l)** $2x + 1 = \dfrac{1}{x - 3}$

m) $3x + 1 = \dfrac{2}{2x - 1}$ **n)** $4x - 1 = \dfrac{7}{x + 1}$ **o)** $3x + 2 = \dfrac{3}{3x - 5}$ **p)** $\dfrac{1}{x - 1} = \dfrac{x + 1}{x + 3}$

q) $\dfrac{x}{2x^2 - 1} = \dfrac{1}{x + 2}$ **r)** $\dfrac{1}{2x - 1} = \dfrac{x}{x^2 + 3}$ **s)** $\dfrac{1}{x + 1} + \dfrac{1}{x + 2} = 1$ **t)** $\dfrac{1}{2x - 1} + \dfrac{1}{x + 3} = 5$

11.4 Quadratic Equations Problems

Exercise 1

1 Solve the following equations where possible, either by factorising, completing the square or using the quadratic formula. Give your answers to 2 decimal places where appropriate.

a) $x^2 - 8x - 20 = 0$

b) $x^2 + x - 20 = 0$

c) $x^2 - 21x + 27 = 0$

d) $x^2 - 18x - 3 = 0$

e) $x^2 - 5x - 50 = 0$

f) $x^2 + 2x - 64 = 0$

g) $x^2 + 2x - 48 = 0$

h) $3x^2 - 4x - 15 = 0$

i) $2x^2 - x - 18 = 0$

j) $6x^2 - 5x - 7 = 0$

k) $8x^2 + 18x - 5 = 0$

l) $5x^2 = x - 7$

m) $(x + 1)(x - 1) - 80 = 0$

n) $(2x + 1)(x - 9) = 2$

o) $(3x + 2)(4x + 1) = 10$

p) $\dfrac{1}{x + 1} = \dfrac{x + 1}{x - 2}$

q) $\dfrac{x}{2x^2 + 1} = \dfrac{1}{x - 2}$

r) $\dfrac{1}{3x + 1} = \dfrac{x}{2x^2 + 3}$

s) $\dfrac{1}{x + 1} + \dfrac{1}{x - 2} = 5$

t) $\dfrac{1}{2x - 1} + \dfrac{1}{5x - 3} = 1$

Example 1

I think of a number, add 2 then square the answer. The result is 16.
What are the possible values of the number I thought of?

1. Choose a variable.

2. Turn the words into an equation: Think of a number and add 2...

3. ...then square the answer. The result is 16.

4. Rearrange and solve the quadratic.

Let x be the unknown number.

$x + 2$

$(x + 2)^2 = 16$

$x^2 + 4x + 4 = 16$

$x^2 + 4x - 12 = 0$

$(x + 6)(x - 2) = 0$

$x + 6 = 0$ or $x - 2 = 0$

$\underline{x = -6}$ or $\underline{x = 2}$

Exercise 2

In each of the following cases, let x be the unknown number.
For each one, set up and solve an equation to find all possible values of x.

1 I think of a number, add one and square the answer. The result is 9.

2 I think of a number, square it and add 3. The result is 147.

3 I think of a number, square it, then subtract the original number. The result is 30.

4 The square of a number plus the original number is 22.

5 25 subtract the square of a number makes 9.

6 I think of a number, square it and add 5 times the original number and the result is 24.

7 A number is doubled, then squared. The result is 36.

8 A number is squared, then doubled and then 4 is subtracted. The result is the original number.

9 I think of a number, add 5, then square the answer. The result is 100.

10 I think of a number, double it and subtract 1 and then square the answer. The result is 64.

Exercise 3

1 Each of the following describes a different rectangle. Find the value of x in each case.

a) Width $= x$ m, length $= (x + 3)$ m, area $= 28$ m^2.

b) Width $= x$ m, length $= (x + 7)$ m, area $= 30$ m^2.

c) Width $= (x - 2)$ m, length $= x$ m, area $= 28$ m^2.

d) Width $= x$ m, length $= (x + 10)$ m, area $= 144$ m^2.

2 A fence is erected adjoining a wall, as shown in the diagram.
The rectangle enclosed by the fence and the wall has width x m,
length y m and area A m^2. The total length of fence used is 20 m.

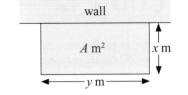

   a) Show that $y = 20 - 2x$.
   b) If $A = 50$, show that $x(20 - 2x) = 50$.
   c) Solve the equation $x(20 - 2x) = 50$.
   Hence find the dimensions of the rectangle if its area is 50 m^2.

Questions 3-5 describe a rectangle bounded on three sides by a fence and on one side by a wall,
as in Question 2. In each case, find all the possible values of the dimensions of the rectangle.
Give your answers to 2 d.p. where appropriate.

3 Total length of fence used = 13 m, area of rectangle = 8 m^2

4 Total length of fence used = 200 m, area of rectangle = 5000 m^2

5 Total length of fence used = 150 m, area of rectangle = 2000 m^2

6 Each of the following describes a different rectangle.
In each case, write out and solve a quadratic equation to find all possible values of x.
   a) Width = x cm, perimeter = 24 cm, area = 32 cm^2.
   b) Width = x cm, perimeter = 30 cm, area = 56 cm^2.
   c) Width = x cm, perimeter = 100 cm, area = 600 cm^2.
   d) Width = x m, perimeter = 17 m, area = 8 m^2.

Example 2

Find the value of x in the triangle shown.

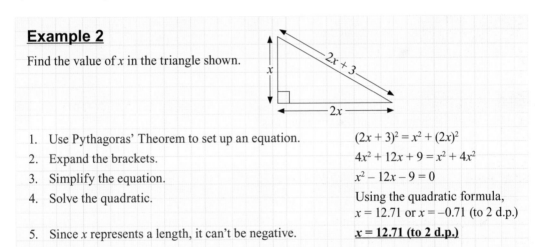

1. Use Pythagoras' Theorem to set up an equation. $(2x + 3)^2 = x^2 + (2x)^2$
2. Expand the brackets. $4x^2 + 12x + 9 = x^2 + 4x^2$
3. Simplify the equation. $x^2 - 12x - 9 = 0$
4. Solve the quadratic.   Using the quadratic formula,
                                                             $x = 12.71$ or $x = -0.71$ (to 2 d.p.)
5. Since x represents a length, it can't be negative.   **$x = 12.71$ (to 2 d.p.)**

Exercise 4

Find the value of x in each of the following triangles. Give your answers to 2 decimal places where appropriate.

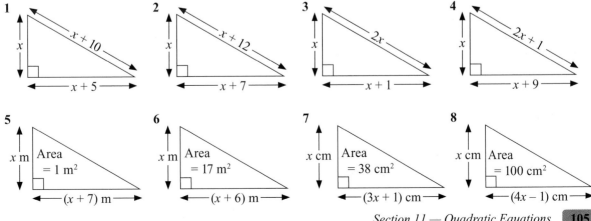

Section 12 — Simultaneous Equations

12.1 Simultaneous Equations

Simultaneous equations have two unknowns, and you will be given two equations.
The solution will be the values of the unknowns that make both equations true.

There are two main algebraic methods for solving simultaneous equations – elimination and substitution.

Example 1

Solve the simultaneous equations: (1) $x + y = 11$
(2) $x - 3y = 7$

Elimination method:

1. Subtract equation (2) from
   equation (1) to eliminate x.

   $$\begin{array}{r} x + y = 11 \\ -(x - 3y) = -7 \\ \hline 4y = 4 \end{array}$$

2. Solve the equation for y. $y = 1$

Substitution method:

1. Rearrange equation (1) to
   get one variable on its own. $x = 11 - y$

2. Substitute $x = 11 - y$ into
   equation (2). Solve for y. $(11 - y) - 3y = 7$
   $11 - 4y = 7$
   $4 = 4y$
   $y = 1$

Now both methods continue in the same way:

3. Put $y = 1$ into one of the original equations and solve for x. $x + 1 = 11$
   $x = 10$

4. Use the other equation to check the answer.   Check: $x - 3y = 10 - 3(1) = 7$
   $x = 10$, $y = 1$

Exercise 1

Solve each of the following pairs of simultaneous equations.

1 **a)** $x + 3y = 13$
   $x - y = 5$

b) $2x - y = 7$
   $4x + y = 23$

c) $x + 2y = 6$
   $x + y = 2$

d) $3x - 2y = 16$
   $2x + 2y = 14$

e) $x - y = 8$
   $x + 2y = -7$

f) $2x + 4y = 16$
   $3x + 4y = 24$

g) $4x - y = -1$
   $4x - 3y = -7$

h) $3x + y = 11$
   $6x - y = -8$

i) $e + 2f = 7$
   $6e + 2f = 10$

j) $3g + h = 5\frac{1}{5}$
   $3g - 2h = -6\frac{4}{5}$

k) $3z - 2u = 57$
   $5z - 2u = 111$

l) $4j - 2i = 8$
   $4j + 7i = -37$

Example 2

Solve the simultaneous equations: (1) $5x - 4y = 23$
(2) $2x + 6y = -25$

Elimination method:

1. Multiply equation (1) by 3 and equation (2) by 2
   to get $+12y$ in one and $-12y$ in the other.

   $$\begin{array}{lr} 3 \times (1): & 15x - 12y = 69 \\ 2 \times (2): & 4x + 12y = -50 \\ \hline & 19x = 19 \end{array}$$

2. Add the resulting equations to eliminate y.

3. Solve the equation for x. $x = 1$

4. Put $x = 1$ into one of the original
   equations and solve for y. $5 - 4y = 23$
   $-4y = 18$
   $y = -4.5$

5. Use the other equation to check the answer.   Check: $2x + 6y = 2(1) + 6(-4.5) = 2 - 27 = -25$
   $x = 1$, $y = -4.5$

2

a) $3x + 2y = 16$
$2x + y = 9$

b) $4x + 3y = 16$
$5x - y = 1$

c) $4x - y = 22$
$3x + 4y = 26$

d) $5x - 3y = 12$
$2x - y = 5$

e) $2x + 3y = 10$
$x - y = 5$

f) $4x - 2y = 8$
$x - 3y = -3$

g) $4x + 2y = 14$
$8x + y = 10$

h) $2x - y = 11$
$-4x - 7y = 5$

i) $8y - 2d = 0$
$5y + 4d = 26\frac{1}{4}$

j) $3e - 5r = 17$
$9e + 2r = -17$

k) $4p + 3m = -\frac{4}{7}$
$7p - 9m = -1$

l) $2c + 4v = 580$
$3c + 2v = 542$

3

a) $3x - 2y = 8$
$5x - 3y = 14$

b) $4p + 3q = 17$
$3p - 4q = 19$

c) $4u + 7v = 15$
$5u - 2v = 8$

d) $5k + 3l = 4$
$3k + 2l = 3$

e) $2c + 6d = 19$
$3c + 8d = 28$

f) $3r - 4s = -22$
$8r + 3s = -4$

g) $3m + 5n = 14$
$7m + 2n = 23$

h) $3e - 5f = 8\frac{1}{2}$
$7e - 3f = 15\frac{1}{2}$

i) $3w + 2z = 2$
$10w - 5z = 5$

j) $2g + 7h = 270$
$-5g + 2h = -324$

k) $5i + 2j = 2.2$
$4i - 3j = -5.6$

l) $3a - 6b = -10$
$11a - 9b = -41$

Example 3

Sue buys 4 dining chairs and 1 table for £142.
Ken buys 6 of the same chairs and 2 of the same tables for £254.
What is the price of one chair? What is the price of one table?

1. Choose some variables.

Let the cost of one chair be £c
and the cost of one table be £t.

2. Write the question as
two simultaneous equations.

(1) $4c + t = 142$
(2) $6c + 2t = 254$

3. Multiply equation (1) by 2 to
give the same coefficients of t.
Subtract equation (2) from equation (1).

$$2 \times (1): \quad 8c + 2t = 284$$
$$-1 \times (2): \quad -6c - 2t = -254$$
$$2c \quad\quad = 30$$

4. Solve the resulting equation for c.

$$c = 15$$

5. Put $c = 15$ into one of the original
equations and solve for t.

$4(15) + t = 142$
$60 + t = 142$
$t = 82$

6. Use the other equation to check the answer.

Check: $6c + 2t = 6(15) + 2(82) = 90 + 164 = 254$

7. Write the answer in terms
of the original question.

The chairs cost £15 each.
The tables cost £82 each.

Exercise 2

1 The sum of two numbers, x and y, is 58, and the difference between them is 22.
Given that x is greater than y, use simultaneous equations to find both numbers.

2 A grandfather with 7 grandchildren bought 4 sherbet dips and 3 Supa-Choc bars for £1.91 last week
and 3 sherbet dips and 4 Supa-Choc bars for £1.73 the week before. Calculate the price of each item.

3 3 kg of organic apples and 2 kg of organic pears cost £19.80, while 2 kg of these apples and 3 kg of
these pears cost £20.70. Work out the price of 1 kg of the apples and the price of 1 kg of the pears.

4 A teacher with a back problem is concerned about the weight of the books she carries home.
She knows that 2 textbooks and 30 exercise books weigh a total of 6.9 kg and that 1 textbook and
20 exercise books weigh a total of 4.2 kg. The doctor has suggested she does not carry over 5 kg at a time.
   a) Calculate the masses of one exercise book and one textbook.
   b) Can she carry 1 textbook and 25 exercise books?
   c) If she needs to carry 2 textbooks, how many exercise books could she carry?

5 Three friends have just finished a computer game. At the end of the game, Zoe, with 7 yellow aliens and 5 blue spiders scored 85 points; James, with 6 yellow aliens and 11 blue spiders scored 93 points. Hal had 8 yellow aliens and 1 blue spider. How many points did Hal score?

6 An interior designer recently spent £1359.55 buying 25 kettles and 20 toasters for a new development. She spent £641.79 on 12 kettles and 9 toasters for a smaller group of new houses. For her current assignment she needs 80 kettles and 56 toasters. If the price of each toaster and each kettle is the same in all three cases, how much should she allow for this cost on her current assignment?

7 The lengths of the sides of an equilateral triangle are $3(x + y)$ cm, $(5x + 2y - 1)$ cm and $5(x + 1)$ cm. Find the side length of the triangle.

12.2 More Simultaneous Equations

If a set of simultaneous equations includes a quadratic, there could be more than one pair of solutions. It's usually easiest to solve simultaneous equations of this type using the substitution method.

Example 1

Solve the simultaneous equations: (1) $x + y = 5$
                                                          (2) $2x^2 + xy = 14$

1.	Rearrange equation (1) to get y on its own.	$y = 5 - x$
2.	Substitute $y = 5 - x$ into $2x^2 + xy = 14$.	$2x^2 + x(5 - x) = 14$
		$x^2 + 5x = 14$
3.	Rearrange to get zero on the right hand side.	$x^2 + 5x - 14 = 0$
4.	Solve the quadratic.	$(x + 7)(x - 2) = 0$
		$x + 7 = 0$ or $x - 2 = 0$
		$x = -7$ or $x = 2$
5.	Use one of the original equations to find a y-value for each x.	If $x = -7$, then $-7 + y = 5$, so $y = 12$.
		If $x = 2$, then $2 + y = 5$, so $y = 3$.
6.	Write the solutions in pairs.	**$x = -7, y = 12$ and $x = 2, y = 3$**

Exercise 1

1 Find the solutions to each of the following pairs of simultaneous equations.

a) $y = x^2 - 4x + 8$
  $y = 2x$

b) $y = x^2 - x - 1$
  $y = 2 - 3x$

c) $y = x^2 - 4x - 28$
  $y = 3x + 2$

d) $y = x^2 + 3x - 2$
  $y = 3 - x$

e) $y = x^2 - 4x + 2$
  $y = 2x - 6$

f) $y = x^2 - 2x - 3$
  $y = 3x + 11$

g) $y = x^2 - x - 5$
  $y = 2x + 5$

h) $y = x^2 - 4x + 8$
  $y = x + 4$

i) $y = 2x^2 + x - 2$
  $y = 8x - 5$

j) $y = 2x^2 + 9x + 30$
  $y = 9 - 8x$

k) $y = 4x^2 - 5x + 2$
  $y = 2x - 1$

l) $y = 7x^2 - 12x - 1$
  $y = 8x + 2$

2 The sketch on the right shows two lines, A and B. The equation of line A is $y = 2x - 2$, and the equation of line B is $5y = 20 - 2x$.

a) What are the coordinates of the point where $x = 1$ on
  (i) line A? **(ii)** line B?

b) How do the graphs of lines A and B show that there is exactly one point where the equations $y = 2x - 2$ and $5y = 20 - 2x$ are both true?

c) Find the coordinates of the point where lines A and B cross.

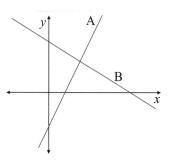

3 The sketch on the right shows the line $2y = x + 3$
and the curve $y = x^2 - 2x - 2$. M and N are the
points where the line cuts the curve.

Find the coordinates of M and N by solving
simultaneous equations.

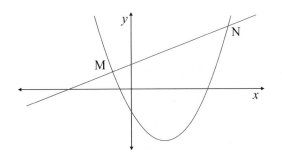

4 Find where the line $y = 4 - 3x$ cuts the curve $y = 6x^2 + 10x - 1$ by solving the equations simultaneously.

5 Use simultaneous equations to find the coordinates where the line $y = 5x$ meets the curve $y = x^2 + 3x + 1$.
What can you say about the line and the curve?

6 Solve these equations simultaneously: $x - 4y = 2$ and $y^2 + xy = 0$

7 Solve these pairs of simultaneous equations.

a) $x + y = 7$
$\quad\ x^2 - xy = 4$

b) $x + y = 5$
$\quad\ x + xy + 2y^2 = 2$

c) $2x + y = 3$
$\quad\ y^2 - x^2 = 0$

d) $x - y = 4$
$\quad\ x^2 + y = 2$

e) $3x + y = 4$
$\quad\ x^2 + 3xy + y^2 = -16$

f) $4y + x = 10$
$\quad\ xy + x = -8$

g) $5 = y - 2x$
$\quad\ 2x^2 - y + 3 = x$

h) $3y^2 = x - 8y$
$\quad\ x + 3y = 4$

i) $3y - x = 2$
$\quad\ y^2 + xy + x = 1$

j) $x - y + 5x^2 = 1$
$\quad\ y + 2x = 1$

k) $4y - x = 2$
$\quad\ x^2 - 3xy = 88$

l) $x + y = 0$
$\quad\ x^3 - 3x^2y + y^2 = 0$

8 In the sketch on the right, the equation of the line is
$3y - 2x = -1$ and the equation of the circle is $x^2 + y^2 = 1$.

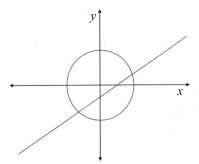

a) Show that at the points where the line
crosses the circle, $13y^2 + 6y - 3 = 0$.

b) Use the quadratic formula to find the exact
values of y when $13y^2 + 6y - 3 = 0$.

c) Find the exact coordinates of the points
where the line crosses the circle.

9 Solve these pairs of simultaneous equations. Give your answers correct to 2 d.p.

a) $2y - 7x = 2$
$\quad\ 3x^2 + 2xy - 6 = 0$

b) $x + y = 3$
$\quad\ x^2 + y^2 = 25$

10 Find the exact coordinates of the points of intersection of the graphs of each of the following pairs of equations.

a) $x = 3y + 4$
$\quad\ x^2 + y^2 = 34$

b) $2x + 2y = 1$
$\quad\ x^2 + y^2 = 1$

c) $\sqrt{5}\,y - x = 6$
$\quad\ x^2 + y^2 = 36$

Section 13 — Inequalities

13.1 Inequalities

Write **inequalities** using the following symbols:
Solving inequalities is very similar to solving
equations. The answer will always be an inequality.

>	**greater than**	≥	**greater than or equal to**
<	**less than**	≤	**less than or equal to**

Example 1

Solve the following inequalities. Show the solutions on a number line.
a) $x + 4 < 8$ b) $1 + 2x \leq 4x - 5$

1. Rearrange as you would with an equation.

2. An empty circle shows that the number is not included.

3. A solid circle shows that the number is included.

a) $x + 4 < 8$
   $x < 8 - 4$
   $\underline{x < 4}$

b) $1 + 2x \leq 4x - 5$
   $1 + 5 \leq 4x - 2x$
   $6 \leq 2x$
   $\underline{3 \leq x}$

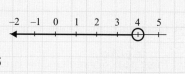

Exercise 1

In Questions 1-3, solve each inequality and show the solution on a number line.

1 **a)** $x + 9 > 14$ **b)** $x + 3 \leq 12$ **c)** $x - 2 \geq 14$ **d)** $x - 7 < 19$
   e) $18 < x + 2$ **f)** $12 \leq x - 4$ **g)** $1 > x - 17$ **h)** $31 \geq x + 30$

2 **a)** $3x \geq 9$ **b)** $5x < 25$ **c)** $2x > 8$ **d)** $7x \leq 21$
   e) $4x < -16$ **f)** $9x > -72$ **g)** $11x \leq 33$ **h)** $2x < 45$

3 **a)** $\frac{x}{2} \geq 3$ **b)** $2 > \frac{x}{5}$ **c)** $\frac{x}{3} < 8$ **d)** $\frac{x}{7} \leq 5$
   e) $-1 > \frac{x}{8}$ **f)** $\frac{x}{6} \leq 0.5$ **g)** $\frac{x}{1.1} \geq 10$ **h)** $\frac{x}{0.2} < -3.2$

Example 2

Solve the inequalities.   a) $-2x < 8$ b) $-\frac{x}{3} \geq -5$

When multiplying or dividing both sides
of an inequality by a negative number,
you need to 'flip' the inequality sign.

a) $-2x < 8$
   $x > 8 \div -2$
   $\underline{x > -4}$

b) $-\frac{x}{3} \geq -5$
   $x \leq -5 \times -3$
   $\underline{x \leq 15}$

In Questions 4-7, solve each inequality.

4 **a)** $-3x \geq 36$ **b)** $-96 \leq -12x$ **c)** $-\frac{x}{3} < -28$ **d)** $11 \leq -\frac{x}{7}$

5 **a)** $4x + 11 < 23$ **b)** $5x + 3 \leq 43$ **c)** $-3x - 7 \geq -1$ **d)** $65 < 7x - 12$
   e) $2x + 16 \geq -8$ **f)** $-5 < -9x - 14$ **g)** $8x - 4.2 < 12.6$ **h)** $-4x + 2.6 \leq 28.6$

6 **a)** $\frac{x + 2}{3} < 1$ **b)** $\frac{x + 4}{5} \geq 2$ **c)** $\frac{x - 8}{2} > 7$ **d)** $\frac{x - 8}{4} \leq 0.5$
   e) $\frac{x}{4} - 2.5 \geq 1$ **f)** $1 < \frac{x + 5.5}{2}$ **g)** $-1 > \frac{x - 3.1}{8}$ **h)** $-\frac{x}{3.2} + 1.3 \leq 5$

7 **a)** $4x + 2 < 2x - 2$ **b)** $3x + 5 \leq 4 + x$ **c)** $3x - 3 \geq -1 + x$ **d)** $6 - x < 7x - 2$

   e) $\frac{x}{2} - 5 \geq 3 - \frac{x}{2}$ **f)** $1 - 2x < \frac{x + 3}{2}$ **g)** $2x + 4 > \frac{2x - 3}{8}$ **h)** $\frac{x}{4} + \frac{3}{2} \leq \frac{1}{4} - x$

Compound Inequalities

A **compound inequality** combines multiple inequalities into one.
For example, $3 < x \leq 9$ means that $3 < x$ **and** $x \leq 9$.

Example 3

Solve the inequality $-4 < 2x + 2 < 6$. Show your solution on a number line.

1. Write down the two separate inequalities. $-4 < 2x + 2$ and $2x + 2 < 6$

2. Solve the inequalities separately.

   ① $-4 < 2x + 2$ ② $2x + 2 < 6$
   $-6 < 2x$ $2x < 4$
   $-3 < x$ $x < 2$

3. Combine the inequalities back into one.

4. Draw the number line.   So $\underline{-3 < x < 2}$

Exercise 2

1 Solve the following inequalities. Show each solution on a number line.

   a) $7 < x + 3 \leq 15$ **b)** $2 \leq x - 4 \leq 12$ **c)** $-1 \leq x + 5 \leq 4$ **d)** $21 \leq x - 16 \leq 44$

In Questions 2-4, solve each of the inequalities given.

2 **a)** $16 < 4x < 28$ **b)** $32 < 2x \leq 42$ **c)** $27 < 4.5x \leq 72$ **d)** $-22.5 \leq 7.5x < 30$

3 **a)** $17 < 6x + 5 < 29$ **b)** $8 < 3x - 4 \leq 26$ **c)** $-42 < 7x + 7 \leq 91$

   d) $-18.8 \leq 10x + 14.2 < -6.8$ **e)** $61.7 < 12x - 6.3 \leq 101.7$ **f)** $-2 < 2x + 3 < 5$

4 **a)** $5.1 \leq -x + 2.5 < 9.7$ **b)** $-5.6 < -x - 6.8 < 12.9$ **c)** $-24 < -8x \leq 40$

   d) $62.72 < -11.2x \leq 94.08$ **e)** $-30 < -7x + 12 \leq 61$ **f)** $-9 < -13x - 9 \leq 17$

13.2   Quadratic Inequalities

An inequality that contains an x^2 term is called a **quadratic inequality**.
You can solve a quadratic inequality by **sketching a graph** of the equivalent quadratic equation.

Example 1

Solve the inequality $x^2 > 4$. Show your solution on a number line.

1. Rearrange to get a quadratic expression, $x^2 - 4$, $x^2 > 4$
   on the left-hand side and 0 on the right-hand side. $x^2 - 4 > 0$

2. Factorise $x^2 - 4$. This tells you that the graph of $(x + 2)(x - 2) > 0$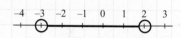
   $y = x^2 - 4$ crosses the x-axis at $x = 2$ and $x = -2$.
   Sketch the graph of $y = x^2 - 4$.

3. The quadratic is greater than zero when the   So $\underline{x < -2}$ and $\underline{x > 2}$
   graph is above the x-axis — in this case, where
   $x < -2$ and $x > 2$.

Example 2

Solve the inequality $x \le 6 - x^2$. Show your solution on a number line.

1. Rearrange the inequality.

2. Factorising gives that the graph crosses the x-axis at $x = 2$ and $x = -3$.

3. The quadratic is less than or equal to zero when the graph is on or below the x-axis — in this case, where $-3 \le x \le 2$.

$x \le 6 - x^2$

$x^2 + x - 6 \le 0$

$(x + 3)(x - 2) \le 0$ ⟶

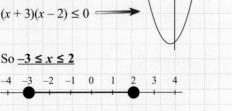

So $-3 \le x \le 2$

Exercise 1

1 Consider the inequality $x^2 > 16$.

   a) Rearrange the inequality into the form $f(x) > 0$, where $f(x)$ is a quadratic expression.

   b) **(i)** Factorise $f(x)$.
      (ii) Write down the x-coordinates of the points where the graph of $y = f(x)$ crosses the x-axis.

   c) Hence solve the inequality $x^2 > 16$.

In Questions 2-4, solve each quadratic inequality and show the solution on a number line.

2 **a)** $x^2 > 16$ **b)** $x^2 \le 9$ **c)** $x^2 > 25$ **d)** $x^2 \ge 36$
   e) $x^2 < 1$ **f)** $x^2 \le 49$ **g)** $x^2 > 64$ **h)** $x^2 < 100$

3 **a)** $x^2 < \dfrac{1}{4}$ **b)** $x^2 \ge \dfrac{1}{25}$ **c)** $x^2 \le \dfrac{1}{121}$ **d)** $x^2 > \dfrac{1}{36}$
   e) $x^2 < \dfrac{4}{9}$ **f)** $x^2 \ge \dfrac{25}{49}$ **g)** $x^2 \le \dfrac{9}{16}$ **h)** $x^2 < \dfrac{16}{169}$

4 **a)** $2x^2 < 18$ **b)** $3x^2 \ge 75$ **c)** $5x^2 < 80$ **d)** $2x^2 \ge 98$

5 Consider the inequality $4x \le 12 - x^2$.

   a) Rearrange the inequality into the form $g(x) \le 0$, where $g(x)$ is a quadratic expression.

   b) **(i)** Factorise $g(x)$.
      (ii) Write down the x-coordinates of the points where the graph of $y = g(x)$ crosses the x-axis.

   c) Hence solve the inequality $4x \le 12 - x^2$.

In Questions 6-8, solve each inequality.

6 **a)** $x^2 + x - 2 < 0$ **b)** $x^2 - x - 2 \le 0$ **c)** $x^2 - 8x + 15 > 0$ **d)** $x^2 + 6x + 5 \le 0$
   e) $x^2 - x - 12 \ge 0$ **f)** $x^2 - 6x - 7 < 0$ **g)** $x^2 - 7x + 12 \le 0$ **h)** $x^2 + 10x + 24 \ge 0$
   i) $x^2 - 6x - 16 < 0$ **j)** $x^2 + 2x - 15 < 0$ **k)** $x^2 - 10x - 11 \le 0$ **l)** $x^2 + 11x + 18 < 0$

7 **a)** $x^2 - 2x > 48$ **b)** $x^2 - 3x \le 10$ **c)** $x^2 + 20 < 9x$ **d)** $x^2 + 18 \le 9x$
   e) $5x \ge 36 - x^2$ **f)** $x^2 < 9x + 22$ **g)** $x^2 < 6x + 27$ **h)** $32 < 12x - x^2$

8 **a)** $x^2 - 4x > 0$ **b)** $x^2 + 3x \le 0$ **c)** $x^2 - 5x < 0$ **d)** $x^2 + 8x \ge 0$
   e) $x^2 > 12x$ **f)** $x^2 \le 2x$ **g)** $x^2 \ge 9x$ **h)** $3x \le -x^2$

13.3 Graphing Inequalities

An inequality can be represented on a **graph**. To do this, turn the inequality into an **equation**, draw its **graph**, and then **shade** the required region.

Example 1

On a graph, shade the region that satisfies the inequality $y \le x + 2$.

1. Draw the line $y = x + 2$. When graphing inequalities, use a solid line for $\le$ or $\ge$ and a dashed line for $<$ or $>$.

2. Find which region to shade by testing the coordinates of any point not on the line and seeing if they satisfy the inequality. E.g. the point (0, 0) satisfies the inequality because $0 \le 0 + 2$, so shade the region which includes (0, 0) — below the line.

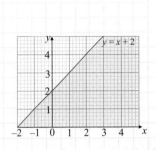

Exercise 1

In Questions 1-3, draw a graph and shade the region that satisfies the inequality.

1 a) $x \le 2$ **b)** $x < -1$ **c)** $x \ge -5$ **d)** $x < 1$
   e) $y > -4$ **f)** $y \ge 4$ **g)** $y < 2$ **h)** $y \le -1$

2 a) $y < x + 1$ **b)** $y > x - 3$ **c)** $y \ge x + 3$ **d)** $y \le 5 - x$
   e) $y \le 2x$ **f)** $y > 2x + 3$ **g)** $y < 3x - 1$ **h)** $y > 2x - 5$

3 a) $y < \dfrac{1}{2}x + 2$ **b)** $y \le \dfrac{1}{2}x - 3$ **c)** $y < \dfrac{x-1}{2}$ **d)** $y > \dfrac{3x+5}{2}$

4 Consider the inequality $2x > 6 - y$.
   a) Rearrange the inequality into the form '$y > ...$'
   b) Hence draw a graph and shade the region that satisfies the inequality $2x > 6 - y$.

5 For each of the following, draw a graph and shade the region that satisfies the inequality.
   a) $x + y \le 5$ **b)** $x + y > 0$ **c)** $y - x > 4$ **d)** $x - y \le 3$
   e) $2x - y \ge 8$ **f)** $x + 2y \ge 4$ **g)** $2x + 3y < 6$ **h)** $3x + 2y \ge 6$
   i) $2x + 5y > 10$ **j)** $5 < -10x - y$ **k)** $x - 2y - 6 \le 0$ **l)** $-y + x + 1 < y - x$

Example 2

On a graph, shade the region that satisfies the inequalities $y < x$, $x < 3$ and $y \ge 4 - x$.

1. Draw the lines $y = x$, $x = 3$ and $y = 4 - x$ on the same graph.

2. The region that satisfies all three inequalities is below $y = x$, to the left of $x = 3$ and on and above $y = 4 - x$.

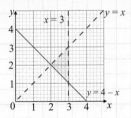

Exercise 2

In Questions 1-7, draw a graph and shade the region that satisfies the inequalities.

1 a) $x > 1$ and $y \le 2$ **b)** $x \le 4$ and $y \le 3$ **c)** $x \ge 0$ and $y > 1$

2 a) $1 < x < 4$ **b)** $-2 < x \le 1$ **c)** $-4 \le x < -1$
   d) $3 < y \le 6$ **e)** $-4 < y < 2$ **f)** $-5 \le y < 0$

3 **a)** $-2 < x < 0$ and $y > 1$
   d) $x < -1$ and $-1 \le y \le 4$

   b) $2 < x \le 6$ and $y \le 5$
   e) $1 \le x < 4$ and $2 < y < 5$

   c) $x \ge 0$ and $-6 < y < -2$
   f) $-2 < x \le 3$ and $2 \le y \le 6$

4 **a)** $y > 1$ and $y < 4 - x$
   d) $x > -4$ and $y \ge x + 3$

   b) $x < 2$ and $x + y \ge 1$
   e) $y \ge 0$ and $x < 6 - y$

   c) $y > -1$ and $y \le x - 2$
   f) $x < 3$ and $3 \le x - y$

5 **a)** $0 < x < 4$ and $y > x$
   d) $-5 \le y \le -1$ and $y < -x$

   b) $1 < x \le 5$ and $y \le 1 + 2x$
   e) $-5 \le x < -2$ and $x + 1 < y$

   c) $-1 < y < 4$ and $x + y > 1$
   f) $-3 < y \le 1$ and $y - 2x \le 6$

6 **a)** $x > -2$, $y < 5$ and $y > x + 4$
   d) $y > x - 2$ and $x + y \le 4$

   b) $x \ge -1$, $y < 4$ and $y < x + 3$
   e) $x + y \ge -4$ and $y \le x + 5$

   c) $x \le 6$, $y > -1$ and $6 < 2x + 2y$
   f) $y \ge x - 3$ and $4 < x + y$

7 **a)** $x > -5$, $y \ge x - 3$ and $x + y < 7$
   c) $y < 6$, $2y > x - 4$ and $5 < x + y$
   e) $y < 2x - 4$, $y > x - 4$ and $x + y \le 8$

   b) $x < 6$, $x + y > -5$ and $y \le 2x + 1$
   d) $y \ge -4$, $y < 2x - 2$ and $x + 2y \le 8$
   f) $y < 3x - 4$, $4y \ge x - 12$ and $x + y \le 6$

Finding Inequalities from Graphs

To find the inequalities represented on a graph, **find the equations** of the
boundary lines and then decide which **inequality sign** to use.

Example 3

Find the inequalities which are represented by the shaded region shown.

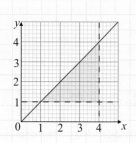

1. The horizontal line is $y = 1$. The shaded region is above this line,
    and the line is dashed. This represents the inequality $y > 1$.

2. The vertical line is $x = 4$. The shaded region is to the left of this
    line, and the line is dashed. This represents the inequality $x < 4$.

3. The diagonal line is $y = x$. The shaded region is below this line,
    and the line is solid. This represents the inequality $y \le x$.

   $\underline{y > 1, x < 4 \text{ and } \underline{y \le x}}$

Exercise 3

1 Write down the inequality represented by the shaded region in each of the following graphs.

a)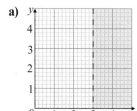

b)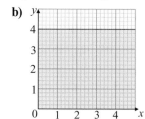

c)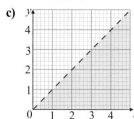

2 By first finding the equation of the line shown, write down the inequality
   represented by the shaded region in each of the following graphs.

a)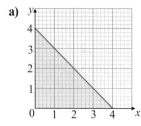

b)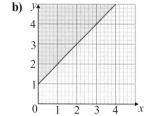

c)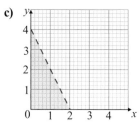

In Questions 3-5, find the inequalities which are represented by the shaded region in each of the graphs.

3 **a)** 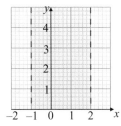 **b)** 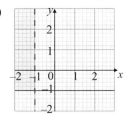 **c)**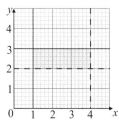

4 **a)** 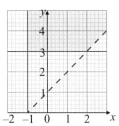 **b)** 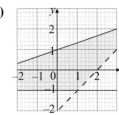 **c)**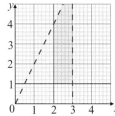

5 **a)** 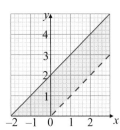 **b)** 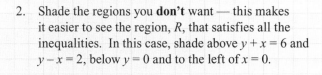 **c)**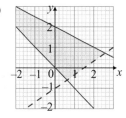

13.4 Linear Programming

Linear programming uses graphs of inequalities to solve problems, usually involving **maximising** or **minimising** a particular quantity. To solve a linear programming problem, represent the region that satisfies the given inequalities on a graph. The **optimal solution** (the maximum or minimum value of your quantity) can then be found at one of the **vertices** of this region.

Example 1

x and y satisfy the inequalities $y + x \leq 6$, $y - x \leq 2$, $x \geq 0$ and $y \geq 0$.
Find the maximum possible value of $2y + x$. For what values of x and y does this occur?

1. Draw the graphs of $y + x = 6$, $y - x = 2$, $x = 0$ and $y = 0$.

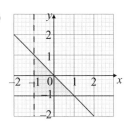

2. Shade the regions you **don't** want — this makes it easier to see the region, R, that satisfies all the inequalities. In this case, shade above $y + x = 6$ and $y - x = 2$, below $y = 0$ and to the left of $x = 0$.

3. Every point in R represents a pair of values which satisfy all the inequalities, but the maximum value of $2y + x$ will occur at one of the vertices of R. Try the coordinates of these points and find the highest value.

(x, y)	$(0, 0)$	$(0, 2)$	$(2, 4)$	$(6, 0)$
$2y + x$	0	4	10	6

So the maximum value of $2y + x$ is **10**, and this occurs when $\underline{x = 2}$ and $\underline{y = 4}$.

Exercise 1

1 x and y satisfy the inequalities $y \leq x + 1$, $y \leq 7 - 2x$, $y \geq 0$ and $x \geq 0$.

   a) Draw the lines $y = x + 1$, $y = 7 - 2x$, $y = 0$ and $x = 0$ on the same graph.

   b) On your graph, shade the regions which do not satisfy the given inequalities.
       Label the unshaded region R.

   c) Find the value of $3x + y$ for each vertex of R.

   d) Hence write down the maximum value of $3x + y$, and the values of x and y for which this occurs.

2 x and y satisfy the inequalities $y + x \leq -2$, $2y - x \leq 2$, $y \geq -2$ and $x \leq -1$.

   a) Represent these inequalities graphically.

   b) Find the maximum value of $x - 2y$, and the values of x and y for which this occurs.

3 x and y satisfy the inequalities $y \leq x$, $2y + x \leq 6$, $y \geq 0$ and $1 \leq x \leq 5$.

   a) Represent these inequalities graphically.

   b) Find the maximum value of $3x + 2y$ and the values of x and y for which this occurs.

   c) Find the minimum value of $2x - 3y$ and the values of x and y for which this occurs.

4 x and y satisfy the inequalities $y \geq x - 1$, $y + x \geq 4$ and $y \leq 5$.
Find the maximum value of the expression $y + 5x$.

Example 2

A shop sells xylophones and yo-yos. The number of yo-yos in stock at the beginning of each week must be at least 3 times as many as the number of xylophones in stock, and the total number of items in stock at the beginning of the week cannot exceed 40. Xylophones are worth £25 and yo-yos are worth £10.

Call the number of xylophones in stock x and the number of yo-yos in stock y.
Find the maximum possible value of items in stock at the beginning of each week, and the number of each item which must be in stock to achieve this value.

1. Use the information given to form inequalities:
    • 'at least 3 times as many yo-yos as
      xylophones' means $y \geq 3x$,
    • 'total number of items in stock cannot
      exceed 40' means $x + y \leq 40$,
    • you can't have a negative number of items
      in stock, so $x \geq 0$ and $y \geq 0$.

$y \geq 3x$, $x + y \leq 40$, $x \geq 0$, $y \geq 0$

2. Represent the inequalities graphically.

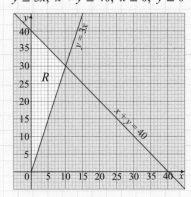

3. Each xylophone is worth £25 and each yo-yo is
    worth £10, so the total value of stock is
    $25x + 10y$. The maximum value will occur at
    one of the vertices of the region R.

(x, y)	$(0, 0)$	$(10, 30)$	$(0, 40)$
$25x + 10y$	0	550	400

So the maximum stock value is **£550**, from having **10 xylophones** and **30 yo-yos**.

Exercise 2

1 Eleanor wants to spend her birthday money on DVDs and CDs. Call the number of DVDs she buys x and the number of CDs she buys y. Write an inequality to represent each of the following.
   a) Eleanor wants to buy at least 1 DVD.
   b) Eleanor wants to buy at least 3 CDs.
   c) DVDs cost £8 each, CDs cost £5 each and Eleanor has £50 to spend.

2 A bakery sells chocolate cake and carrot cake. Call the number of chocolate cakes sold each day x and the number of carrot cakes sold each day y. Assume all the cakes made each day are sold on that day.
   a) Write an inequality to represent each of the following.
      (i) The baker wants to sell at least twice as many carrot cakes as chocolate cakes each day.
      (ii) The baker only has enough flour to make a total of 14 cakes each day.
   b) There are two more inequalities which must be satisfied in this situation.
      Write them down and explain why they must be true.

3 A decorator is buying paint from his supplier — undercoat, which costs £12 per tin, and matt emulsion, which costs £24 per tin. He needs to buy at least 4 tins of undercoat and at least as many tins of matt emulsion as undercoat. He has £216 to spend in total. Let x be the number of tins of undercoat he buys and y be the number of tins of matt emulsion he buys.

   a) Write down 3 inequalities that the decorator must satisfy when buying his paint. Simplify the inequalities if possible.
   b) Represent these inequalities graphically.
   c) Use your graph to list all the possible combinations of paint he can buy.

4 A club has x regular members and y Gold members. Regular membership costs £25 per year and Gold membership costs £75 per year. The club needs to collect at least £1500 in membership fees each year. The club has a maximum of 50 members, and must have at least 15 regular members.
   a) Write down 4 inequalities which the club must satisfy.
   b) Represent these inequalities graphically.
   c) Find the minimum possible number of Gold members.
   d) Find the maximum amount the club can expect to receive in membership fees each year, and the number of regular and Gold members that are needed to achieve this amount.

5 A company makes decorative cups and saucers. It takes 4 hours to make a cup and 2 hours to make a saucer. Each week there are a total of 48 hours allocated to the making of cups and saucers. The company can only make one item at a time, and the number of saucers that the company makes must be no greater than the number of cups they make. Each cup is sold for £14 and each saucer is sold for £11. Let x be the number of cups made and y the number of saucers made.
   a) Write down 4 inequalities which the company must satisfy and represent these inequalities graphically.
   b) What is the maximum number of cups that can be made in one week?
   c) Find the company's maximum possible weekly income, and the number of cups and saucers that need to be made to achieve this.

6 A delivery company is buying x motorbikes and y vans. Motorbikes cost £8000 and vans cost £16 000. They have £80 000 to spend on buying vehicles, and must buy at least 7 vehicles, including at least 1 van. The cost of maintaining a motorbike is £800 per year, and the cost of maintaining a van is £950 per year.
   a) Write down 4 inequalities which the company must satisfy. Represent these inequalities graphically.
   b) List the different possible combinations of motorbikes and vans that are available to the company.
   c) Which is the cheapest combination to maintain, and how much does this maintenance cost per year?

Section 14 — Sequences

14.1 Term to Term Rules

A **sequence** is a list of numbers or shapes which follows a particular **rule**.
Each number or shape in the sequence is called a **term**.

Number Sequences

Arithmetic sequences (or linear sequences) — where the
terms increase or decrease by the **same value** each time.

Geometric sequences (or geometric progressions) — where consecutive terms are
found by **multiplying** or **dividing** by the **same value**, often called the **common ratio**.

Other sequences — e.g. adding a changing number each time or adding together the two previous terms.

Example 1

Consider the sequence 2, 6, 18, 54...

a) Explain the rule for finding the next term in the sequence.

The rule for finding the next term involves multiplication.

$$2 \xrightarrow{\times 3} 6 \xrightarrow{\times 3} 18 \xrightarrow{\times 3} 54...$$

Multiply the previous term by 3.

b) Write down the next three terms in the sequence.

Multiply each term by 3 to get the next term.

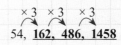

54, **162, 486, 1458**

Exercise 1

1 Write down the first 5 terms of the sequence with:

a) first term = 14; further terms generated by the rule 'multiply the previous term by 4, then subtract 1'.

b) first term = 11; further terms generated by the rule 'multiply the previous term by –2, then add 1'.

2 The first four terms of a sequence are 3, 6, 12, 24.

a) Write down what you multiply each term in the sequence by to find the next term.

b) Write down the next three terms in the sequence.

For Questions 3-4:   **(i)** explain the rule for finding the next term in the sequence.
(ii) find the next three terms in the sequence.

3 **a)** 3, 5, 7, 9...   **b)** 1, 2, 4, 8...   **c)** 4, 12, 36, 108...   **d)** 4, 7, 10, 13...

e) 5, 3, 1, –1...   **f)** 1, 1.5, 2, 2.5...   **g)** 0.01, 0.1, 1, 10...   **h)** 192, 96, 48, 24...

4 **a)** 0, –4, –8, –12...   **b)** 16, 8, 4, 2...   **c)** –2, –6, –18, –54...   **d)** 1, –2, 4, –8...

5 The first four terms of a sequence are 1, 3, 9, 27.

a) Explain the rule for finding the next term in this sequence.

b) Use your rule to find: **(i)** the 5th term   **(ii)** the 7th term   **(iii)** the 9th term

6 Copy the following sequences and fill in the blanks.

a) 7, 13, 19 , 25, ☐, 37   **b)** 9, 5, ☐, –3, –7, –11   **c)** ☐, –4, –16, –64, ☐, –1024

d) –72, ☐, –18, –9, ☐, –2.25   **e)** ☐, 0.8, 3.2, 12.8, ☐, 204.8   **f)** –63, –55, ☐, ☐, ☐, –23

7 The first four terms of a sequence are –5, –2, 1, 4.

    a) Explain the rule for finding the next term in this sequence.

    b) Use your rule to find: **(i)** the 5th term   **(ii)** the 10th term

    c) The 25th term of this sequence is 67. Work out the 54th term of the sequence.

Example 2

Find the next three terms in the sequence 4, 5, 7, 10...

1. Try finding the difference between neighbouring terms.

2. Here, the difference is **increasing by 1** each time.

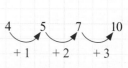

3. Use this to find the next three terms in the sequence.
Start with 10. Then add 4. Then add 5. Then add 6.

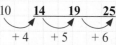

Exercise 2

1 For each sequence below, find: **(i)** the difference between neighbouring terms for the first 5 terms,
                                   (ii) the next three terms in the sequence.

    a) 7, 8, 10, 13, 17...   **b)** 3, 4, 6, 9, 13...   **c)** 5, 7, 11, 17, 25...

    d) 20, 18, 15, 11, 6...   **e)** 3, 5, 9, 15, 23...   **f)** 1, 2, 0, 3, –1...

2 The sequence 1, 1, 2, 3, 5... is known as the Fibonacci sequence. Each term in the sequence is found by adding together the previous two terms. Find the next three terms in the sequence.

3 The first 5 terms of a sequence are 1, 1, 2, 6, 24.

    a) For the first 5 terms, find the number you multiply by each time to get the next term.

    b) Find the next two terms in the sequence.

Example 3

The rule for finding the next term in a sequence is 'multiply the previous term by 3, add on x'.
The 1st term is 2, and the 4th term is 119. Find the value of x.

1. Use the rule to write down an expression
for each term until you reach the 4th term.

    1st term $= 2$

    2nd term $= (3 \times 2) + x = 6 + x$

    3rd term $= 3(6 + x) + x = 18 + 3x + x = 18 + 4x$

    4th term $= 3(18 + 4x) + x = 54 + 12x + x = 54 + 13x$

2. You know that the 4th term is 119, so you
can write down an equation for the 4th term.
Then just solve the equation to find x.

    $54 + 13x = 119$

    $13x = 119 - 54 = 65$

    $x = 65 \div 13 = \underline{\mathbf{5}}$

Exercise 3

1 Find b for each of the sequences described below.

    a) 1st term = 6, 3rd term = 27; rule = multiply the previous term by 2, add b.

    b) 1st term = 1, 4th term = 43; rule = multiply the previous term by 4, subtract b.

    c) 1st term = 180, 4th term = 33; rule = divide the previous term by 2, add b.

    d) 1st term = 3, 4th term = –15; rule = multiply the previous term by –2, add b.

    e) 1st term = 9, 3rd term = –135; rule = multiply the previous term by b, subtract 54.

Example 4

The rule for finding the next term in a sequence is $x_{n+1} = 2x_n + 3$ where $x_0 = 4$.
What is the value of x_4?

1. Substitute x_0 into the formula for x_n to get x_1.

2. Substitute x_1 into the formula for x_n to get x_2.
   Substitute x_2 to get x_3 and then x_3 to get x_4.

$x_1 = 2x_0 + 3 = (2 \times 4) + 3 = 11$

$x_2 = 2x_1 + 3 = (2 \times 11) + 3 = 25$

$x_3 = 2x_2 + 3 = (2 \times 25) + 3 = 53$

$x_4 = 2x_3 + 3 = (2 \times 53) + 3 = \underline{\textbf{109}}$

Exercise 4

1 In each of the following, use the sequence rules and the values of x_0 to find the value of x_5.

a) $x_{n+1} = x_n + 5$ where $x_0 = 3$ b) $x_{n+1} = x_n - 7$ where $x_0 = 20$ c) $x_{n+1} = 3x_n$ where $x_0 = 2$

d) $x_{n+1} = 2x_n + 3$ where $x_0 = 3$ e) $x_{n+1} = \frac{1}{2}x_n + 2$ where $x_0 = 4$ f) $x_{n+1} = \frac{1}{2}x_n + 8$ where $x_0 = 8$

2 A sequence is generated using the rule $x_{n+1} = 2x_n - 6$ where $x_0 = 8$. Find the following:

a) x_3 b) x_5 c) $x_2 + x_4$ d) $x_1 + x_2 - x_3$ e) $x_3(x_5 - x_1)$

Shape Sequences

Example 5

The matchstick shapes on the right form
the first three patterns in a sequence.

a) Draw the fourth and fifth patterns in the sequence.

b) How many matchsticks are needed to make the eighth pattern in the sequence?

1. You have to add 3 matchsticks to add an
    extra square to the previous pattern.

a)

2. There are 16 matchsticks in the 5th pattern.
    So there are $16 + 3 + 3 + 3 = 25$ matchsticks
    in the eighth pattern.

b) **25 matchsticks**

Exercise 5

1 The first three patterns of several sequences are shown below.

For each of the sequences: **(i)** explain the rule for making the next pattern,
                              (ii) draw the fourth and fifth patterns in the sequence,
                              (iii) find the number of matches needed to make the sixth pattern.

a)

b)

c)

2 For each of the sequences below:

    (i) Draw the next three patterns in the sequence.

    (ii) Explain the rule for generating the number of circles in the next pattern.

    (iii) Work out how many circles there are in the 7th pattern.

    (iv) Work out how many circles there are in the 10th pattern.

a)   **b)**

c)   **d)**

14.2 Using the nth Term

You can also work out a term by using its **position** (n) in the sequence.

For example, the 1st term (x_1) has $n = 1$, the 2nd term (x_2) has $n = 2$, the 10th term (x_{10}) has $n = 10$, and so on.

Example 1

The nth term of a sequence is $7n - 1$. Find the first four terms of the sequence.

1. To find the 1st, 2nd, 3rd and 4th terms of the sequence, substitute the values $n = 1$, $n = 2$, $n = 3$ and $n = 4$ into the formula.

    $(7 \times 1) - 1 = 6$

    $(7 \times 2) - 1 = 13$

    $(7 \times 3) - 1 = 20$

    $(7 \times 4) - 1 = 27$

2. Write the terms in order to form the sequence.

    So the first four terms are **6, 13, 20, 27.**

Exercise 1

1 Find the first five terms of a sequence if the nth term is given by:

    a) $n + 5$ **b)** $3n + 2$ **c)** $4n - 2$ **d)** $5n - 1$

    e) $10 - n$ **f)** $3 - 4n$ **g)** $10n - 8$ **h)** $-7 - 3n$

2 Find the first five terms of a sequence if the nth term is given by:

    a) $n^2 + 1$ **b)** $2n^2 + 1$ **c)** $3n^2 - 1$ **d)** $n(n - 1)$

3 The nth term of a sequence is $2n + 20$. Find the value of:

    a) the 5th term   **b)** the 10th term   **c)** the 20th term   **d)** the 100th term

4 The nth term of a sequence is $100 - 3n$. Find the value of:

    a) the 3rd term   **b)** the 10th term   **c)** the 30th term   **d)** the 40th term

5 The nth term of a sequence can be found using the formula $x_n = 35 + 5n$. Find the value of:

    a) x_1 **b)** x_5 **c)** x_{10} **d)** x_{20} **e)** x_{100}

6 Each of the following gives the nth term for a different sequence.

    For each sequence, find: **(i)** the 5th term   **(ii)** the 10th term   **(iii)** the 100th term

    a) $n + 11$ **b)** $2n + 3$ **c)** $6n - 1$ **d)** $4n + 12$

    e) $100 - n$ **f)** $30 - 3n$ **g)** $100n - 8$ **h)** $-20 + 2n$

7 Each of the following rules generates a different sequence.
For each sequence, find: **(i)** x_4 **(ii)** x_{10} **(iii)** x_{20}

  a) $x_n = 8n + 4$ **b)** $x_n = 450 - 5n$ **c)** $x_n = \frac{1}{2}n + 30$ **d)** $x_n = 3n^2$

  e) $x_n = 2n^2 + 8$ **f)** $x_n = n^2 + n$ **g)** $x_n = 5n^3 - 50$ **h)** $x_n = 3n - n^2 + 100$

8 Each of the following gives the nth term for a different sequence.
For each sequence, find: **(i)** the 2nd term   **(ii)** the 5th term   **(iii)** the 20th term

  a) $2n^2$ **b)** $2n^2 + 3$ **c)** $4n^2 - 5$ **d)** $3(n^2 + 2)$

  e) $\frac{1}{2}n^2 + 20$ **f)** $n(n + 1)$ **g)** $400 - n^2$ **h)** $n^3 + 2$

Example 2

The nth term of a sequence is $4n + 5$.

a) Which term has the value 41?
b) Which is the first term in this sequence to have a value greater than 100?

  1. Make the nth term equal to 41.

  2. Solve the equation to find n.

    a) $4n + 5 = 41$
        $4n = 36$
        $n = 9$
     So the **9th term** is 41.

  1. Find the value of n which would give a value of 100.

  2. The first term that will give a value over 100 will be the next whole number value of n.

    b) $4n + 5 = 100$
        $4n = 95$
        $n = 23.75$

     So the first term with a value greater than 100 must be the **24th term**.

     (Check: 23rd term = 97, 24th term = 101 ✔)

Exercise 2

1 **a)** The nth term of a sequence is $7n + 4$. Which term of the sequence has the value 53?
  b) The nth term of a sequence is $5n - 8$. Which term of the sequence has the value 37?
  c) The nth term of a sequence is $4n + 3$. Which term of the sequence has the value 27?
  d) The nth term of a sequence is $2n - 5$. Which term of the sequence has the value 11?

2 The nth term of a sequence is $17 - 2n$.
  a) Which term of the sequence has the value 9?
  b) Which term of the sequence has the value –3?

3 The nth term of a sequence is $50 - 6n$. Find which terms have the following values.
  a) 2   **b)** 26   **c)** –4   **d)** –22

4 The nth term of a sequence is $n^2 - 1$.
  a) Which term of the sequence has the value 8?
  b) Which term of the sequence has the value 99?

5 The nth term of a sequence is $n^2 + 1$. Find which terms have the following values.
  a) 5   **b)** 26   **c)** 50   **d)** 82

6 The nth term of a sequence is $4n - 10$.
Which term in the sequence is the first to have a value greater than 50?

7 The formula for the number of matches in the *n*th pattern of the following 'matchstick sequences' is shown below. For each of the sequences:

    (i) find the number of matches needed to make the 6th pattern,

    (ii) find the number of matches needed to make the 100th pattern.

a)

Number of matches in *n*th pattern = $2n + 1$

b)

Number of matches in *n*th pattern = $4n + 1$

8 The *n*th term in a sequence is $3n - 25$.

    a) Which term in the sequence is the first to have a value greater than 35?

    b) Which term in the sequence is the first to have a value greater than 0?

9 The formula for the number of circles in the *n*th triangle in the sequence shown on the right is $\frac{n(n + 1)}{2}$.

    a) Find the number of circles needed to make the 6th triangle.

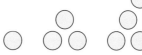

    b) Find the number of circles needed to make the 58th triangle.

    c) Which term in the sequence will be the first term to be made from over 200 circles?

10 a) The *n*th term of a sequence is $-3n + 20$. Which term has the value –25?

    b) The *n*th term of a sequence is $25 - n^2$.

        (i) Which term has the value –39?

        (ii) Which is the last term in the sequence to have a value more than –1?

11 The *n*th term of a sequence is $-n(n + 2)$.

    a) Which term has the value –48?   **b)** Which is the first term to have a value less than –20?

14.3 Finding the nth Term

Arithmetic Sequences

You can find the **nth term** of an arithmetic sequence (linear sequence) if you know the **first term** *a* and the **difference** *d* between the terms. The *n*th term is $a + (n - 1)d$.

Example 1

Find the *n*th term of the sequence 45, 42, 39, 36...

1. Find the values of the first term and the difference between the terms.	45 42 39 36 first term $a = 45$

45   42   39   36

     – 3   – 3   – 3   difference $d = -3$

2. Substitute into the formula: $a + (n - 1)d$. $a + (n - 1)d = 45 + (n - 1) \times -3$

3. Simplify the expression. $= 45 - 3n + 3 = -3n + 48$

4. Write down and check your formula.   So the *n*th term is **$-3n + 48$**.

                                  (Check: 2nd term is $(-3 \times 2) + 48 = 42$ ✔)

Exercise 1

1 Find the formula for the *n*th term of each of the following sequences.
  a) 7, 13, 19, 25...
  b) 3, 10, 17, 24...
  c) 4, 8, 12, 16...
  d) 6, 16, 26, 36...
  e) 5, 10, 15, 20...
  f) 7, 27, 47, 67...
  g) 41, 81, 121, 161...
  h) 3, 11, 19, 27...

2 Find the formula for the *n*th term of each of the following sequences.
  a) −1, 1, 3, 5...
  b) −2, 1, 4, 7...
  c) −9, −5, −1, 3...
  d) −45, −26, −7, 12...

3 For each of the following sequences: **(i)** Find the formula for the *n*th term.
  (ii) Find the value of the 70th term.
  a) 10, 8, 6, 4...
  b) 40, 37, 34, 31...
  c) 70, 60, 50, 40...
  d) 78, 69, 60, 51...
  e) 60, 55, 50, 45...
  f) 100, 92, 84, 76...
  g) 6, 3, 0, −3...
  h) −10, −25, −40, −55...

4 **a)** Find the *n*th term of sequence A, which starts 4, 7, 10, 13...
  b) Find the *n*th term of sequence B, which starts 5, 8, 11, 14...
  c) **(i)** How does each term in sequence B compare with the corresponding term in sequence A?
  (ii) What do you notice about the formulas giving the *n*th term for these two sequences?

5 **a)** Find the *n*th term of the sequence 13, 9, 5, 1...
  b) Use your answer to part **a)** to write down the *n*th term of the sequence 11, 7, 3, −1...

6 In the sequences below, the horizontal and vertical lines between each pair of dots are 1 unit long.
  For each of the following sequences, find **(i)** the number of dots in the *n*th pattern in the sequence.
  (ii) the area of the *n*th pattern in the sequence.
  (iii) the area and number of dots in the 23rd pattern in the sequence.

a)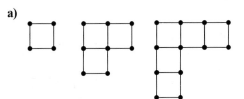

b)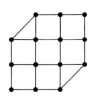

Example 2

A sequence has *n*th term $3n + 2$. Is 37 a term in the sequence?

1. Make an equation by setting the formula for the *n*th term equal to 37. Then solve your equation to find *n*.

$$3n + 2 = 37$$
$$3n = 35$$
$$n = 11.666...$$

2. Since *n* is not a whole number, 37 is not a term in the sequence.

So 37 **is not** a term in the sequence.

Exercise 2

1 Show that 80 is a term in the sequence with *n*th term equal to $3n - 1$.

2 A sequence has *n*th term $21 - 2n$. Show that −1 is a term in this sequence, and write down the corresponding value of *n* to show its position.

3 **a)** Find the *n*th term of the sequence whose first four terms are 12, 18, 24, 30...
  b) Show whether 34 is a term in this sequence. If it is, write down its position.

4 A sequence has *n*th term equal to $17 + 3n$. Determine whether each of the following is a term in this sequence.
  a) 52
  b) 98
  c) 105
  d) 248
  e) 996

5 A sequence starts –5, –1, 3, 7. Determine whether each of the following is a term in this sequence. For those that are, state the corresponding values of *n*.

a) 43 **b)** 71 **c)** 138 **d)** 384 **e)** 879

Example 3

Find the *n*th term of the sequence $\frac{1}{3}, \frac{2}{5}, \frac{3}{7}, \frac{4}{9}$...

1. Find the *n*th term for the numerator and denominator of the fractions separately.

   numerator:

   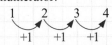

   numerator of *n*th term = *n*

2. The sequence in the numerator is easy to see — the *n*th term is just *n*.

3. Find the sequence in the denominator in the same way as any other arithmetic sequence. Find the first term, *a*, and the common difference, *d*, and substitute them into $a + (n-1)d$.

   denominator:

   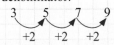

   first term $a = 3$
   difference $d = 2$

   $a + (n-1)d = 3 + (n-1) \times 2$
   $= 3 + 2n - 2 = 2n + 1$

   denominator of *n*th term = $2n + 1$

4. Combine the *n*th terms for the numerator and denominator to find the *n*th term for the sequence.

   *n*th term of the sequence $= \dfrac{n}{2n + 1}$

Exercise 3

1 Find the *n*th term of each of the following sequences.

a) $\frac{1}{2}, \frac{1}{4}, \frac{1}{6}, \frac{1}{8}$...

b) $\frac{1}{3}, \frac{1}{6}, \frac{1}{9}, \frac{1}{12}$...

c) $\frac{5}{2}, \frac{6}{3}, \frac{7}{4}, \frac{8}{5}$...

d) $\frac{1}{5}, \frac{4}{10}, \frac{7}{15}, \frac{10}{20}$...

e) $\frac{5}{4}, \frac{4}{3}, \frac{3}{2}, \frac{2}{1}$...

f) $\frac{5}{9}, \frac{8}{8}, \frac{11}{7}, \frac{14}{6}$...

g) $\frac{16}{3}, \frac{36}{7}, \frac{56}{11}, \frac{76}{15}$...

h) $\frac{1}{30}, \frac{-1}{40}, \frac{-3}{50}, \frac{-5}{60}$...

Example 4

a) Find *a* and *d* for an arithmetic sequence where the 1st term is 11 and the 6th term is 51.

1. You know *a* straight away — it's the 1st term. $a = 11$

2. Write an equation for the 6th term using *n*th term = $a + (n-1)d$.

   When $n = 6$, $a + (n-1)d = 51$
   $11 + (6-1)d = 51$
   $11 + 5d = 51$

3. Solve the equation to find *d*.

   $5d = 51 - 11 = 40$
   $d = 40 \div 5 = 8$

   So **_a = 11_** and **_d = 8_**.

b) Find *a* and *d* for an arithmetic sequence where the 3rd term is 8 and the 4th term is 5.

1. *d* is the difference between the 3rd and 4th terms, because they are consecutive.

   So d = 4th term – 3rd term
   $= 5 - 8 = -3$

2. Write an equation for one of the terms using *n*th term = $a + (n-1)d$.

   When $n = 3$, $a + (n-1)d = 8$
   $a + (3-1) \times -3 = 8$
   $a + 2 \times -3 = 8$

3. Solve the equation to find *a*.

   $a - 6 = 8$
   $a = 8 + 6 = 14$

   So **_a = 14_** and **_d = -3_**.

Example 5

The 2nd term of an arithmetic sequence is 7 and the 5th term is 19.
a) Find the values of a and d.

1. Write equations for the 2nd and 5th terms using nth term $= a + (n-1)d$.

   2nd term: $a + d = 7$
   5th term: $a + 4d = 19$

2. Solve the simultaneous equations. Subtract the 2nd term equation from the 5th term equation to eliminate a.

$$a + 4d = 19$$
$$\underline{-(a + d = 7)}$$
$$3d = 12$$
$$d = 4$$

3. Solve the equation for d.

4. Put $d = 4$ into one of the original equations and solve for a.

$$a + 4 = 7$$
$$a = 3$$

So $\underline{a = 3}$ and $\underline{d = 4}$.

5. Use the other equation to check.

(Check: $a + 4d = 3 + 4 \times 4 = 19$ ✔)

b) Find the nth term of the sequence.

1. Substitute into the formula $a + (n-1)d$.

$$a + (n-1)d = 3 + (n-1) \times 4$$
$$= 3 + 4n - 4$$
$$= 4n - 1$$

2. Simplify the expression.

3. Write down and check your formula.

So the nth term is $\underline{4n - 1}$.

(Check: 2nd term is $(4 \times 2) - 1 = 7$ ✔)

Exercise 4

1 For each of the following arithmetic sequences, find: **(i)** a and d **(ii)** the nth term of the sequence
  a) 1st term $= 3$, 4th term $= 9$ **b)** 1st term $= 9$, 5th term $= 25$
  c) 5th term $= 17$, 6th term $= 21$ **d)** 9th term $= -6$, 10th term $= -7$
  e) 1st term $= -5$, 19th term $= -95$ **f)** 4th term $= -8$, 5th term $= 2$

2 In each of the following arithmetic sequences, you are given two of the terms. For each sequence, find:
  (i) a and d **(ii)** the nth term of the sequence
  a) 3rd term $= 15$, 6th term $= 30$ **b)** 2nd term $= 12$, 5th term $= 33$
  c) 4th term $= 25$, 7th term $= 49$ **d)** 2nd term $= 13$, 6th term $= -7$
  e) 3rd term $= -3$, 6th term $= 24$ **f)** 6th term $= 61$, 9th term $= 97$

3 Given that the second term of an arithmetic sequence is -7 and the fifteenth term is 32, find:
  a) a and d **b)** the nth term of the sequence

4 Given that the third term of an arithmetic sequence is 4 and the twelfth term is 1, find:
  a) a and d **b)** the nth term of the sequence

5 The 61st term of an arithmetic sequence is 546 and the 81st term is 726
  Is 42 a term in this sequence?

Geometric Sequences

The nth term of a **geometric sequence** (or exponential sequence) is given by the formula ar^{n-1} where a is the first value of the sequence and r is the number you multiply each term by to get the next.

Example 6

A sequence begins 2, 10, 50, 250. Find the nth term of the sequence.

The first term of the sequence is 2 and you multiply each term by 5 to get the next term.

$a = 2$
$r = 5$
So the formula for the nth term is $\mathbf{2 \times 5^{n-1}}$

Exercise 5

1 For each of the following sequences, find: **(i)** the next term **(ii)** the nth term
   a) 1, 4, 16, 64...
   b) 1, 2, 4, 8, 16...
   c) 5, 25, 125, 625...
   d) 3, 9, 27, 81...
   e) 2, 6, 18, 54...
   f) $\sqrt{3}$, 3, $3\sqrt{3}$, 9...
   g) 6, 12, 24, 48...
   h) 3, $3\sqrt{2}$, 6, $6\sqrt{2}$, 12...

2 Find the nth term for each of the following sequences: **a)** $\dfrac{5}{2}, \dfrac{15}{14}, \dfrac{45}{98}, \dfrac{135}{686} \cdots$ **b)** $\dfrac{2}{9}, \dfrac{4}{27}, \dfrac{8}{81}, \dfrac{16}{243} \cdots$

Quadratic Sequences

The nth term of a **quadratic sequence** has the form $an^2 + bn + c$ where a, b and c are constants and $a \neq 0$.

Example 7

Find the nth term of the quadratic sequence 1, 8, 19, 34, 53...

1. Find the difference between each pair of terms.

2. Work out the difference between the differences — you should get a constant difference. Here it's +4.

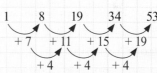

3. Divide the constant difference by 2 to get the coefficient of the n^2 term.

$4 \div 2 = 2$ so the rule contains a $2n^2$ term.

4. For each term in the sequence, subtract the corresponding $2n^2$ term. This will leave a linear sequence.

term:	1	8	19	34	53
$2n^2$:	2	8	18	32	50
term $- 2n^2$:	-1	0	1	2	3

5. Work out the rule for the remaining linear sequence and add it to the $2n^2$ term.

The rule for the linear sequence is $n - 2$.
So the rule for the sequence is $\mathbf{2n^2 + n - 2}$.

Exercise 6

1 For each of the following sequences, find: **(i)** the nth term **(ii)** the 10th term
   a) 1, 5, 11, 19, 29...
   b) 5, 12, 21, 32, 45...
   c) 5, 12, 23, 38, 57...
   d) 7, 20, 39, 64, 95...
   e) 6, 24, 52, 90, 138...
   f) 10, 23, 44, 73, 110...

Cubic Sequences

The nth term of a **cubic sequence** has the form $an^3 + bn^2 + cn + d$ where a, b, c and d are constants and $a \neq 0$.

Example 8

Find the nth term of the cubic sequence 2, 12, 34, 74, 138...

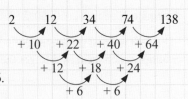

1. Find the difference between each pair of terms.

2. Work out the difference between the differences twice.
   You should be left with a constant difference. Here it's +6.

3. Divide the constant difference by 6 to get the coefficient of the n^3 term.

   $6 \div 6 = 1$ so the rule contains an n^3 term.

4. For each term in the sequence, subtract the corresponding n^3 term. This will leave a linear or quadratic sequence.

term:	2	12	34	74	138
n^3:	1	8	27	64	125
term $- n^3$:	1	4	7	10	13

5. Work out the rule for the remaining sequence and add it to the n^3 term.

   The rule for the remaining sequence is $3n - 2$. So the rule for the sequence is $\boldsymbol{n^3 + 3n - 2}$.

Exercise 7

1. For each of the following sequences, find: **(i)** the nth term   **(ii)** the 8th term
   a) 9, 16, 35, 72, 133...   **b)** 8, 21, 46, 89, 156...   **c)** 3, 20, 63, 144, 275...   **d)** 6, 19, 48, 99, 178...

14.4   Arithmetic Series

An **arithmetic series** is the sum of the terms in an arithmetic sequence.

To find the sum of the first n terms, use the formula: $S_n = \frac{n}{2}[2a + (n-1)d]$.

Example 1

Find the sum of the first n terms of the arithmetic sequence 2, 6, 10, 14, 18, ... , for
a) $n = 5$ b) $n = 100$

1. Find the values of a and d.

   2   6   10   14   18
     +4 +4 +4 +4

   So $a = 2$ and $d = 4$.

2. Substitute the values of n, a and d into the sum to n terms formula.

   a) $n = 5$, so $S_5 = \frac{5}{2}[2 \times 2 + (5-1) \times 4]$

   $= \frac{5}{2}[4 + 4 \times 4]$

   $= \frac{5}{2} \times 20 = \underline{\mathbf{50}}$

   ($n = 5$ is easy to check — $2 + 6 + 10 + 14 + 18 = 50$ ✔)

   b) $n = 100$, so $S_{100} = \frac{100}{2}[2 \times 2 + (100-1) \times 4]$

   $= 50[4 + 99 \times 4]$

   $= 50 \times 400 = \underline{\mathbf{20\,000}}$

Exercise 1

1 Find the sum of the first 20 terms for the following arithmetic sequences with:

    a) first term = 6, common difference = 0   **b)** first term = 4, common difference = 3

    c) first term = –13, common difference = 2   **d)** first term = 23, common difference = –4

2 For the following arithmetic sequences find the sum of the first 5, 10, and 50 terms:

    a) 5, 10, 15, 20, 25, ...   **b)** 3, 7, 11, 15, 19, ...   **c)** –13, –5, 3, 11, 19, ...   **d)** 49, 43, 37, 31, 25, ...

3 The first three patterns of an arithmetic sequence are shown below.

How many matchsticks would you need in total to make the first 75 patterns in the sequence?

Example 2

The 5th term of an arithmetic series is 9 and the 11th term is 27.
Find the sum of the first 30 terms.

   1. Write equations for the 5th and 11th terms using nth term $= a + (n-1)d$.

      5th term: $a + 4d = 9$
      11th term: $a + 10d = 27$

   2. Solve the simultaneous equations. Subtract the 5th term equation from the 11th term equation to eliminate a.

$$
\begin{aligned}
a + 10d &= 27 \\
-(a + 4d) &= 9 \\
\hline
6d &= 18 \\
d &= 3
\end{aligned}
$$

   3. Solve the equation for d.

   4. Put $d = 3$ into one of the original equations and solve for a.

$$
\begin{aligned}
a + 4 \times 3 &= 9 \\
a + 12 &= 9 \\
a &= -3
\end{aligned}
$$

So $a = -3$ and $d = 3$.

   5. Use the other equation to check.

(Check: $a + 10d = -3 + 10 \times 3 = 27$ ✔)

   6. Substitute the values $n = 30$, $a = -3$ and $d = 3$ into the sum to n terms formula.

$$
\begin{aligned}
S_{30} &= \frac{30}{2}[2 \times -3 + (30-1) \times 3] \\
&= 15(-6 + 29 \times 3) \\
&= 15 \times 81 = 1215
\end{aligned}
$$

So the sum of the first 30 terms is **1215**.

Exercise 2

1 The first term of an arithmetic series is 10 and the seventh term is 46. Find the sum of the first 20 terms.

2 The eighth term of an arithmetic series is 3 and the ninth term is –1. Find the sum of the first 12 terms.

3 The fifth term of an arithmetic series is 21 and the eleventh term is 45. Find the sum of the first 25 terms.

4 The third term of an arithmetic series is –5 and the fourteenth term is 17. Find the sum of the first 50 terms.

5 The nth term of an arithmetic series is $-6n + 23$. Find the sum of the first 101 terms.

Section 15 — Straight-Line Graphs

15.1 Straight-Line Graphs

Horizontal and Vertical Lines

All **horizontal** lines have the equation $y = a$ (where a is a number),
since every point on the same horizontal line has the same y-coordinate (a).

All **vertical** lines have the equation $x = b$ (where b is a number), since every
point on the same vertical line has the same x-coordinate (b).

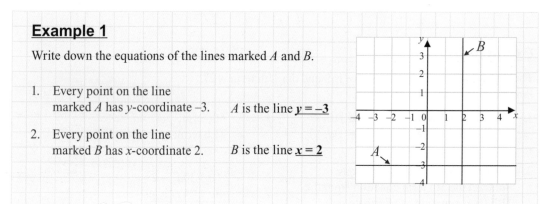

Example 1

Write down the equations of the lines marked A and B.

1. Every point on the line
    marked A has y-coordinate –3. A is the line $\underline{y = -3}$

2. Every point on the line
    marked B has x-coordinate 2. B is the line $\underline{x = 2}$

Exercise 1

1   Write down the equations of each of the lines labelled A to E on the right.

2   **a)** Draw a set of coordinate axes and plot the graphs
    with the following equations.

   (i) $y = 3$ **(ii)** $y = -6$ **(iii)** $y = -1$

   (iv) $x = 2$ **(v)** $x = 4$ **(vi)** $x = -6$

   b) What is the y-coordinate of every point on the x-axis?

   c) Write down the equation of the x-axis.

3   Write down the equation of the y-axis.

4   Write down the equation of each of the following.

   a) The line which is parallel to the x-axis, and which passes through the point (4, 8).

   b) The line which is parallel to the y-axis, and which passes through the point (–2, –6).

   c) The line which is parallel to the line $x = 4$, and which passes through the point (1, 1).

   d) The line which is parallel to the line $y = -5$, and which passes through the point (0, 6).

5   Write down the coordinates of the points where the following pairs of lines intersect.

   a) $x = 8$ and $y = -11$ **b)** $x = -5$ and $y = -13$ **c)** $x = 0.7$ and $y = 80$ **d)** $x = -\frac{6}{11}$ and $y = -500$

Other Straight-Line Graphs

The equation of a straight line which **isn't** horizontal or vertical contains **both x and y**.
There are a few different methods that can be used to draw straight-line graphs — one is shown below.

Example 2

a) Complete the table to show the value of $y = 2x + 1$ for values of x from 0 to 5.

x	0	1	2	3	4	5
y						
Coordinates						

b) Draw the graph of $y = 2x + 1$ for values of x from 0 to 5.

a)

x	0	1	2	3	4	5
y	$2 \times 0 + 1$ $= 1$	$2 \times 1 + 1$ $= 3$	$2 \times 2 + 1$ $= 5$	$2 \times 3 + 1$ $= 7$	$2 \times 4 + 1$ $= 9$	$2 \times 5 + 1$ $= 11$
Coordinates	(0, 1)	(1, 3)	(2, 5)	(3, 7)	(4, 9)	(5, 11)

b)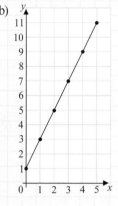

1. Use the equation $y = 2x + 1$ to find the y-value corresponding to each value of x.

2. Use the numbers from the first and second rows to fill in the third row.

3. Plot the coordinates from your table on a grid, and join them up to draw the graph.

Exercise 2

1 a) Copy and complete this table to show the value of $y = 2x$ for values of x from –2 to 2.

x	–2	–1	0	1	2
y					
Coordinates					

b) Draw a set of axes with x-values from –5 to 5 and y-values from –10 to 10.
Plot the coordinates from your table.

c) Join up the points to draw the graph with equation $y = 2x$ for values of x from –2 to 2.

d) Use a ruler to extend your line to show the graph of $y = 2x$ for values of x from –5 to 5.

e) Use your graph to fill in the missing coordinates of these points on the line:

(i) (4, ☐)   (ii) (–3, ☐)   (iii) (☐, –10)

2 a) Copy and complete the table to show the value of $y = 8 - x$ for values of x from 0 to 4.

x	0	1	2	3	4
y					
Coordinates					

b) Draw a set of axes with x-values from –5 to 5 and y-values from 0 to 13.
Plot the coordinates from your table

c) Join up the points to draw the graph of $y = 8 - x$ for values of x from 0 to 4.
Use a ruler to extend your line to show the graph of $y = 8 - x$ for values of x from –5 to 5.

3 For each of the following equations draw a graph for values of x from -5 to 5.

a) $y = x - 3$ b) $y = -4x$ c) $y = \frac{x}{2}$ d) $y = 2x + 5$

e) $y = 4 - x$ f) $y = 8 - 3x$ g) $y = -1 - 2x$ h) $y = \frac{x}{4} + 1$

4 Draw a graph of the following equations for the given range of x-values.

a) $y = x$ for $-4 \le x \le 4$ b) $y = x + 7$ for $-7 \le x \le 0$ c) $y = -2x + 8$ for $0 \le x \le 5$

d) $y = 1.5x$ for $-5 \le x \le 5$ e) $y = 0.5x + 2$ for $-2 \le x \le 4$ f) $y = -2 - 0.5x$ for $-4 \le x \le 4$

15.2   Gradients

The **gradient** of a straight line is a measure of **how steep** it is.

To find the gradient of a line, divide the 'vertical distance' between two points on the line by the 'horizontal distance' between those points.

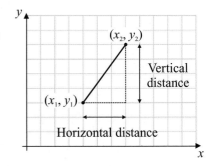

$$\textbf{Gradient} = \frac{\textbf{Vertical distance}}{\textbf{Horizontal distance}} = \frac{y_2 - y_1}{x_2 - x_1}$$

A line sloping upwards from left to right has a **positive gradient**.
A line sloping downwards has a **negative gradient**.

Regardless of the type of graph, the gradient always means '**y-axis units per x-axis units**'.

Example 1

Find the gradient of the line that passes through points $P(-3, 1)$ and $Q(4, 5)$.

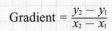

1.   Call the coordinates of P (x_1, y_1), and the coordinates of Q (x_2, y_2).

2.   Use the formula for the gradient.

$$\text{Gradient} = \frac{y_2 - y_1}{x_2 - x_1}$$

3.   The line slopes upwards from left to right. So you should get a positive answer.

$$= \frac{5 - 1}{4 - (-3)}$$

$$= \frac{4}{7}$$

Exercise 1

1 Points $P(x_1, y_1)$ and $Q(x_2, y_2)$ are plotted on this graph.

a) Without doing any calculations, state whether the gradient of the line containing P and Q is positive or negative.

b) Calculate the vertical distance $y_2 - y_1$ between P and Q.

c) Calculate the horizontal distance $x_2 - x_1$ between P and Q.

d) Find the gradient of the line containing P and Q.

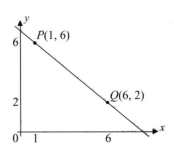

2 Use the points shown to find the gradient of each of the following lines.

a)

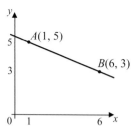

b)

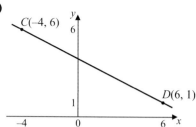

c)

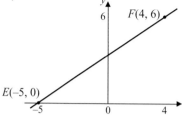

3 For each line shown below: **(i)** Use the axes to find the coordinates of each of the marked points.
                               (ii) Find the gradient of each of the lines.

a)

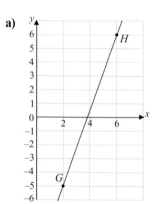

b)

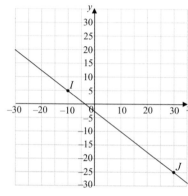

c)

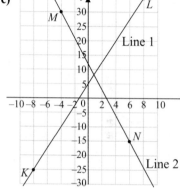

4 a) Plot the points $U(-1, 2)$ and $V(2, 5)$ on a grid.

  b) Find the gradient of the line containing points U and V.

5 a) Find the difference between the y-coordinates of the points $Y(2, 0)$ and $Z(-4, -3)$.

  b) Find the difference between the x-coordinates of Y and Z.

  c) Hence find the gradient of the line containing points Y and Z.

6 Find the gradients of the lines containing the following points.

  a) $A(0, 4)$, $B(2, 10)$

  b) $C(1, 3)$, $D(5, 11)$

  c) $E(-1, 3)$, $F(5, 7)$

  d) $G(-3, -2)$, $H(1, -5)$

  e) $I(5, -2)$, $J(1, 1)$

  f) $K(-4, -3)$, $L(-8, -6)$

7 Find the gradients of lines A-D on the graph below.

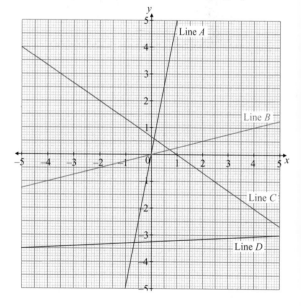

15.3 Equations of Straight-Line Graphs

The equation of a straight line can be written in the form $y = mx + c$. E.g. for $y = 3x + 5$, $m = 3$ and $c = 5$.

When written in this form:
- m is the **gradient** of the line,
- c tells you the **y-intercept** — the point where the line crosses the y-axis.

Example 1

Write down the gradient and coordinates of the y-intercept of $y = 2x + 1$.

The equation is already in the form $y = mx + c$, so you just need to read the values for the gradient and y-intercept from the equation.

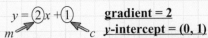

gradient = 2
y-intercept = (0, 1)

Example 2

Find the gradient and coordinates of the y-intercept of $2x + 3y = 12$.

1. Rearrange the equation into the form $y = mx + c$.

2. Write down the values for the gradient and y-intercept.

$$2x + 3y = 12 \quad \searrow -2x$$
$$3y = -2x + 12 \quad \searrow \div 3$$
$$y = \left(-\frac{2}{3}\right)x + 4$$
$$m = -\frac{2}{3}$$

So the **gradient** $= -\frac{2}{3}$, **y-intercept = (0, 4)**

Exercise 1

1 Write down the gradient and the coordinates of the y-intercept for each of the following graphs.

a) $y = 2x - 4$
b) $y = 5x - 11$
c) $y = -3x + 7$
d) $y = 4x$

e) $y = \frac{1}{2}x - 1$
f) $y = -x - \frac{1}{2}$
g) $y = 3 - x$
h) $y = 3$

2 Match the graphs to the correct equation from the box.

$y = x + 2$

$y = \frac{7}{3}x - 1$

$y = -x + 6$

$y = 3x$

$y = -\frac{1}{3}x + 4$

$y = \frac{1}{3}x + 2$

A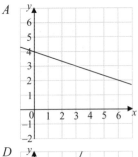

B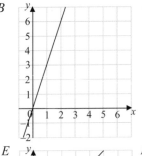

C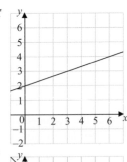

D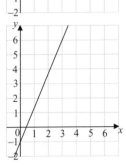

E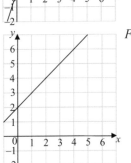

F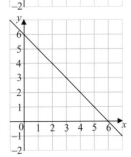

3   Find the gradient and the coordinates of the y-intercept for each of the following graphs.

a) $y = 4 + 2x$

b) $2y = 2x + 6$

c) $3y = 9 - 3x$

d) $y - 5 = 7x$

e) $y + x = 8$

f) $y - 12 = 3x$

g) $x = 6 + 2y$

h) $3x + y = 1$

i) $3y - 6x = 15$

j) $4x = 2y + 5$

k) $9 = 2x + 3y$

l) $4x = 5y - 5$

m) $6x - y = 7$

n) $8x - 2y = 14$

o) $11 = 9x + 2y$

p) $5x + 4y = -3$

q) $y + 2x - 3 = 0$

r) $6x - 3y = 2$

s) $9x = 6 - 3y$

t) $4y - 6x + 8 = 0$

u) $5x - 5y = 2$

v) $6x - 3y + 1 = 0$

w) $\frac{1}{2} = -4x - 2y$

x) $-5x = 6y$

Example 3

Find the equation of the straight line that passes through the points $A(-3, -4)$ and $B(-1, 2)$.

1. Write down the equation for a straight line.

$y = mx + c$, m = gradient and $c = y$-intercept.

2. Find the gradient (m) of the line.

$\text{gradient} = \dfrac{y_2 - y_1}{x_2 - x_1} = \dfrac{2 - (-4)}{-1 - (-3)} = \dfrac{6}{2} = 3$

So the equation of the line must be $y = 3x + c$.

3. Substitute the value for the gradient and the x and y values for one of the points into $y = mx + c$, then solve to find c.

At point B, $x = -1$ and $y = 2$.

$2 = 3 \times (-1) + c$

$2 = -3 + c$

$c = 5$ So the equation of the line is $\underline{\mathbf{y = 3x + 5}}$.

Exercise 2

1   Find the equations of the following lines based on the information given.

a) gradient = 8, passes through $(0, 2)$

b) gradient = -1, passes through $(0, 7)$

c) gradient = 11, passes through $(0, -5)$

d) gradient = -6, passes through $(0, -1)$

e) gradient = 3, passes through $(1, 10)$

f) gradient = $\frac{1}{2}$, passes through $(4, -5)$

g) gradient = -7, passes through $(2, -4)$

h) gradient = 6, passes through $(-1, 2)$

i) gradient = 5, passes through $(-3, -7)$

j) gradient = -4, passes through $(-3, 3)$

2   Find the equations of the lines passing through the following points.

a) $(3, 7)$ and $(5, 11)$

b) $(1, 4)$ and $(3, 14)$

c) $(5, 1)$ and $(2, -5)$

d) $(4, 1)$ and $(-3, -6)$

e) $(-2, 1)$ and $(1, 7)$

f) $(2, 8)$ and $(-1, -1)$

g) $(-3, 2)$ and $(-2, 5)$

h) $(4, 5)$ and $(-6, 0)$

i) $(-7, 8)$ and $(-1, 2)$

j) $(2, -1)$ and $(4, -9)$

k) $(-1, 10)$ and $(-3, 4)$

l) $(3, 4)$ and $(-5, -8)$

3   Find the equations of the lines A to L shown below. Write all your answers in the form $y = mx + c$.

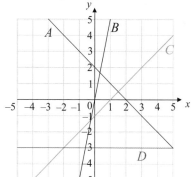 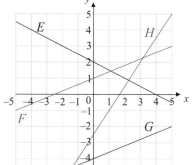 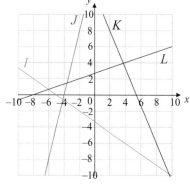

4 Find the equations for the lines
   shown on the graph on the right.
   Give your answers in the form
   $y = mx + c$.

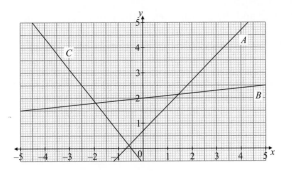

15.4 Parallel and Perpendicular Lines

Parallel Lines

Lines that are **parallel** have the **same gradient**.

Example 1

Which of the following lines is parallel to the line $2x + y = 5$?

a) $y = 3 - 2x$ b) $x + y = 5$ c) $y - 2x = 6$

1. Rearrange the equation
    into the form $y = mx + c$
    to find its gradient.

    $2x + y = 5$
    $y = 5 - 2x$
    $y = -2x + 5$ So the gradient $(m) = -2$.

2. Rearrange the other
    equations in the same way.
    Any that have $m = -2$ will
    be parallel to $2x + y = 5$.

    a) $y = 3 - 2x$ b) $x + y = 5$ c) $y - 2x = 6$

    $y = -2x + 3$ $y = -x + 5$ $y = 2x + 6$

    $m = -2$ $m = -1$ $m = 2$

    So **line a)** is parallel to $2x + y = 5$.

Example 2

Find the equation of line L, which passes through the point $(5, 8)$ and is parallel to $y = 3x + 2$.

1. Find the gradient of the line $y = 3x + 2$.

    Equation of a straight line: $y = mx + c$

    The gradient of $y = 3x + 2$ is 3.

2. The lines are parallel, so line L
    will have the same gradient.

    So the equation of line L must be $y = 3x + c$.

3. Substitute the values for x and y at point $(5, 8)$
    into the equation. Solve to find c and hence
    the equation of line L.

    At $(5, 8)$, $x = 5$ and $y = 8$:
    $8 = 3(5) + c$
    $8 = 15 + c$
    $c = -7$ So the equation of line L is $\underline{\mathbf{y = 3x - 7}}$.

Exercise 1

1 Write down the equations of three lines that are parallel to: **a)** $y = 5x - 1$ **b)** $x + y = 7$

2 Work out which of the following are the equations of lines parallel to: **(i)** $y = 2x - 1$ **(ii)** $2x - 3y = 0$

    a) $y - 2x = 4$ **b)** $2y = 2x + 5$ **c)** $2x - y = 2$

    d) $2x + y + 7 = 0$ **e)** $2x + 6 = 3y$ **f)** $3y + 2x = 2$

    g) $y = 1 + 2x$ **h)** $3y = 3 + 2x$ **i)** $6x - 9y = -2$

3 Which of the lines listed below are parallel to the line shown in the diagram?

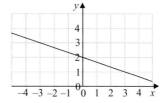

    a) $y + 3x = 2$ **b)** $3y = 7 - x$

    c) $y = 4 - 3x$ **d)** $x - 3y = 8$

    e) $y = 3 - \frac{1}{3}x$ **f)** $6y = -2x$

4 For each of the following, find the equation of the line which is parallel to the given line and passes through the given point. Give your answers in the form $y = mx + c$.

    a) $y = 5x - 7$, $(1, 8)$ **b)** $y = 2x$, $(-1, 5)$ **c)** $y = \frac{1}{2}x + 3$, $(6, -7)$

    d) $y = 4x - 9$, $(7, 13)$ **e)** $y = 8x - 1$, $(-3, -5)$ **f)** $y = x + 17$, $(5, -7)$

    g) $2y = 6x + 3$, $(-3, 4)$ **h)** $y = 7 - 9x$, $(1, -11)$ **i)** $x + y = 4$, $(8, 8)$

    j) $2x + y = 12$, $(-4, 0)$ **k)** $6x - 2y = 15$, $(1, -4)$ **l)** $x + 3y + 1 = 0$, $(-9, 9)$

Perpendicular Lines

If the gradient of a line is m, then the gradient of a perpendicular line is $-\dfrac{1}{m}$.

The product of the gradients of two **perpendicular** lines is **−1**.

$$m \times -\frac{1}{m} = -1$$

Example 3

Find the equation of line B, which is perpendicular to $y = 5x - 2$ and passes through the point $(10, 4)$.

1. Use the gradient of $y = 5x - 2$ to find the gradient of line B.

    The line $y = 5x - 2$ has gradient $m = 5$.

    So the gradient of line B is $-\dfrac{1}{m} = -\dfrac{1}{5}$.

2. Substitute this gradient into the equation for a straight line along with the values for x and y at the point given.

    The equation of line B is $y = -\dfrac{1}{5}x + c$.

    At the point $(10, 4)$, $x = 10$, $y = 4$

    $4 = -\dfrac{1}{5}(10) + c$

    $4 = -2 + c$

3. Solve this equation to find c and hence the equation of line B.

    $c = 6$

    So the equation of line B is $y = -\dfrac{1}{5}x + 6$.

Exercise 2

1 Find the gradient of a line which is perpendicular to a line with gradient:

   a) 6   **b)** –3   **c)** $\frac{1}{2}$ **d)** –1   **e)** $-\frac{1}{4}$ **f)** 12   **g)** –7   **h)** $\frac{2}{3}$

   i) –2   **j)** 1   **k)** 1.5   **l)** 0.3   **m)** –4.5   **n)** $-\frac{4}{3}$ **o)** –1.2   **p)** $3\frac{1}{2}$

2 Write down the equation of any line which is perpendicular to:

   a) $y = 2x + 3$ **b)** $y = -3x + 11$ **c)** $y = 5 - 6x$ **d)** $y = 9x - 1$

   e) $2y = 5x + 1$ **f)** $x + y = 2$ **g)** $2x + 3y = 5$ **h)** $5x - 10y = 4$

3 Match the following equations into pairs of perpendicular lines.

   a) $y = 3x - 6$ **b)** $y = 2x - 3$ **c)** $8 - x = 3y$ **d)** $4x - 6y = 3$

   e) $y + 3x = 2$ **f)** $2y - 3x = 6$ **g)** $x + 2y = 8$ **h)** $4y + 8x = 6$

   i) $8y - 4x = 3$ **j)** $3y - 4 - x = 0$ **k)** $4x + 6y - 3 = 0$ **l)** $2y = 8 - 3x$

4 For each of the following, find the equation of the line which is perpendicular to the given line and passes through the given point. Give your answers in the form $y = mx + c$.

   a) $y = -3x + 1$, $(9, 8)$ **b)** $y = \frac{1}{2}x - 5$, $(3, -4)$ **c)** $y = \frac{1}{4}x - 7$, $(1, -9)$

   d) $y = 6x + 11$, $(18, 1)$ **e)** $y = \frac{4}{3}x + 15$, $(12, -1)$ **f)** $y = 8 - 2.5x$, $(15, 2)$

   g) $x + y = 8$, $(3, 0)$ **h)** $2y = 6x - 1$, $(-6, 1)$ **i)** $3y + 8x = 1$, $(8, 7)$

   j) $x + 2y = 6$, $(1, 9)$ **k)** $x - 5y - 11 = 0$, $(-2, 8)$ **l)** $4x - y = 7$, $(2, 1)$

15.5   Line Segments

Midpoint of a Line Segment

The midpoint of a line segment is **halfway** between the end points.
The midpoint's x- and y-coordinates are the **averages** of the end points' **x- and y-coordinates**.

Example 1

Find the midpoint of the line segment AB.

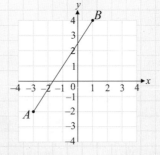

1. Write down the coordinates of the end points A and B. $A(-3, -2)$ and $B(1, 4)$

2. Find the average of the x-coordinates by adding them together and dividing by 2. Find the average of the y-coordinates in the same way.

$$\left(\frac{-3 + 1}{2}, \frac{-2 + 4}{2}\right) = (-1, 1)$$

The midpoint has coordinates **$(-1, 1)$**.

Exercise 1

1 Find the coordinates of the midpoint of the line segment *AB*, where *A* and *B* have coordinates:

a) $A(8, 0)$, $B(4, 6)$ **b)** $A(5, 2)$, $B(3, 0)$ **c)** $A(-2, 3)$, $B(6, 5)$

d) $A(4, -7)$, $B(-2, 1)$ **e)** $A(-3, 0)$, $B(9, -2)$ **f)** $A(-6, -2)$, $B(-4, 6)$

g) $A(-1, 3)$, $B(-1, -7)$ **h)** $A(-2, -8)$, $B(5, -8)$ **i)** $A(0.5, -4)$, $B(-8, 6)$

j) $A(-\frac{1}{2}, 4)$, $B(\frac{1}{2}, -3)$ **k)** $A(2p, q)$, $B(6p, 7q)$ **l)** $A(8p, 2q)$, $B(2p, 14q)$

2 Find the midpoint of each side of the following triangles.

a)

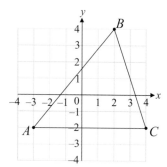

b)

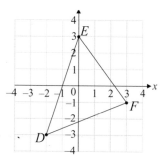

3 Point *A* has the coordinates $A(1, 8)$. The midpoint, *M*, of the line segment *AB* has the coordinates $M(5, 3)$. Find the coordinates of *B*.

4 The coordinates of the endpoint, *C*, and midpoint, *M*, of the line segment *CD* are $C(6, -7)$ and $M(2, -1)$. Find the coordinates of point *D*.

5 Use the diagram below to find the midpoints of the following line segments.

a) *AF*   **b)** *AC*   **c)** *DF*

d) *BE*   **e)** *BF*   **f)** *CE*

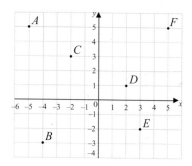

Length of a Line Segment

Example 2

Calculate the length of the line segment *AB*. Give your answer to three significant figures.

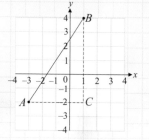

1. Think of the line segment as the hypotenuse of a right-angled triangle *ABC*.

2. Calculate the length of *AC* and *BC*.

3. Calculate the length of *AB* using Pythagoras' theorem.

Length of $AC = 1 - (-3) = 4$

Length of $BC = 4 - (-2) = 6$

$$AB = \sqrt{AC^2 + BC^2}$$

$$AB = \sqrt{4^2 + 6^2}$$

$$AB = \sqrt{52} = \underline{\textbf{7.21}} \text{ (to 3 s.f.)}$$

Exercise 2

In Questions 1-2, give all rounded answers to 3 significant figures.

1 Find the length of the line segments with the following end point coordinates.

a) (5, 9) and (1, 6)

b) (15, 3) and (11, 8)

c) (5, 4) and (4, 1)

d) (3, 7) and (3, 14)

e) (−1, 9) and (9, −3)

f) (9, −4) and (−1, 12)

g) (1, −2) and (8, 2)

h) (−3, 7) and (−2, −3)

i) (−1, −1), (−5, 9)

j) (2, 4) and (−1, −4)

k) (0, −1) and (4, 8)

l) (−2, −1) and (11, 8)

2 Find the length of each side of the shapes below.

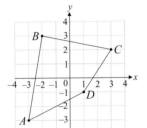

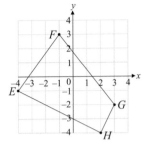

Coordinates and Ratio

Example 3

Points A, B and C lie on a straight line.
Point A has coordinates (−3, 4) and point B has coordinates (3, 1).
Point C lies on line segment AB such that $AC:CB = 1:2$.
Find the coordinates of point C.

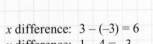

1. Find the difference between the x- and y-coordinates of A and B.

   x difference: $3 - (-3) = 6$
   y difference: $1 - 4 = -3$

2. Use the given ratio to see how far along AB point C is.

   C is $\frac{1}{3}$ of the way along AB, so x: $\frac{1}{3} \times 6 = 2$

                  y: $\frac{1}{3} \times -3 = -1$

3. Add the results to the coordinates of A to get C.

   x-coordinate: $-3 + 2 = -1$
   y-coordinate: $4 + -1 = 3$ **Point C lies at (−1, 3).**

Exercise 3

1 Point C lies on the line segment AB. Find the coordinates of C given that:

a) $A(-6, -4)$ $B(10, 4)$ $AC:CB = 1:1$ **b)** $A(3, -3)$ $B(6, 6)$ $AC:CB = 1:2$

c) $A(-3, 5)$ $B(9, 1)$ $AC:CB = 3:1$ **d)** $A(0, 4)$ $B(10, -1)$ $AC:CB = 2:3$

e) $A(-20, 1)$ $B(8, -13)$ $AC:CB = 3:4$

2 Using the following points, find the specified ratios.

a) Find $AB:BC$ given $A(0, 0)$, $B(2, 2)$ and $C(6, 6)$.

b) Find $DE:EF$ given $D(1, 0)$, $E(-3, 4)$ and $F(-4, 5)$.

c) Find $GH:HI$ given $G(-1, -2)$, $H(5, 2)$ and $I(14, 8)$.

d) Find $JK:KL$ given $J(-6 -2)$, $K(-2, 6)$ and $L(1, 12)$.

e) Find $MN:NO$ given $M(4, -7)$, $N(1, -8.5)$ and $O(-5, -11.5)$.

f) Find $PQ:QR$ given $P(7, 4)$, $Q(3.5, -1)$ and $R(-7, -16)$.

3 Point T lies on the line segment SU. Find the coordinates of U given that:

a) $S(0, 5)$ $T(3, 8)$ $ST:TU = 3:1$ **b)** $S(6, 2)$ $T(12, -4)$ $ST:TU = 3:2$

c) $S(-2, -4)$ $T(18, 11)$ $ST:TU = 5:4$ **d)** $S(-5, 3)$ $T(3, -1)$ $ST:TU = 1:5$

Exercise 4 — Mixed Exercise

1 AB is a line segment joining $A(2, 8)$ and $B(10, -7)$.

   a) Find the midpoint of line segment AB.   **b)** Calculate the length of line segment AB.

2 For each of the line segments shown on the right:

   a) Find the midpoint of the line segment.

   b) Calculate the length of the line segment.
      Give your answer to one decimal place.

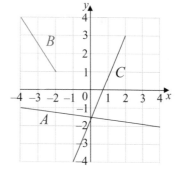

3 Find the length and midpoint of the line segments
with the following end points. Give your answers
to 3 significant figures where appropriate.

   a) $(1, 3)$ and $(5, 7)$ **b)** $(7, 11)$ and $(4, 5)$

   c) $(-2, 8)$ and $(6, 1)$ **d)** $(4, -3)$ and $(-2, 9)$

   e) $(7, -12)$ and $(-5, -2)$ **f)** $(-8, 1)$ and $(-6, -7)$

4 The diagram on the right shows lines AB and CD.
Line CD intersects AB at the midpoint, M, of line AB.

   a) Find the midpoint, M, of line AB.

   b) Given that $CM : MD = 2 : 1$, find the length of the line segment CD.
      Give your answer to one decimal place.

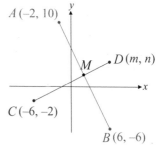

5 Line segment P is the graph of $y = 2x + 3$ for $-2 \leq x \leq 6$.

   a) Find the midpoint of line segment P.

   b) Calculate the length of line segment P.
      Give your answer to three significant figures.

15.6   Straight-Line Graphs Problems

Exercise 1

1 Draw the following lines.

   a) $y = -2x + 5$ **b)** $y = 4x - 7$

   c) $y = -3x + 4$ **d)** $y = -5x + 1$

   e) $x + y = 1$ **f)** $2x + y = 3$

   g) $x = 2y - 5$ **h)** $x = 6 - 3y$

2 Find the gradient of the line joining
the following points.

   a) $(2, 3)$ and $(4, 7)$ **b)** $(1, 2)$ and $(2, 6)$

   c) $(1, 4)$ and $(3, 2)$ **d)** $(1, 6)$ and $(3, 5)$

   e) $(3, 1)$ and $(5, 4)$ **f)** $(6, 4)$ and $(7, 1)$

   g) $(-1, -2)$ and $(2, -4)$ **h)** $(4, -3)$ and $(8, -1)$

   i) $(3, -4)$ and $(-5, -2)$ **j)** $(-1, 8)$ and $(-9, -1)$

3 Match each of the equations with the graphs A-E.

$y = 2x$	$y + x = 0$	$y - x = 0$
	$y = -0.5x$	$2y = x$

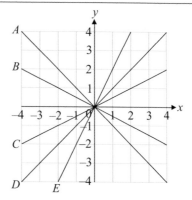

4 a) The line through points $A(-1, 4)$ and $B(2, a)$ has a gradient of 5. Find a.

b) Points $C(2, 7)$ and $D(b, -2)$ lie on a line with a gradient of -3. Find b.

5 Find the gradient and the coordinates of the y-intercept of the following lines.

a) $y = 5x - 9$ **b)** $y = 7x + 3$ **c)** $y = 11 - 2x$ **d)** $y = -8 + 3x$

e) $5x + y = 12$ **f)** $6 = 2x + 3y$ **g)** $x = 4y - 7$ **h)** $2y + 9 = 8x$

6 Match the equations below and the graphs shown on the right.

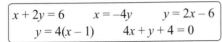

$$x + 2y = 6 \qquad x = -4y \qquad y = 2x - 6$$
$$y = 4(x - 1) \qquad 4x + y + 4 = 0$$

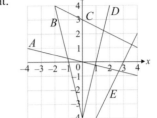

7 Find the equations of the lines through the following pairs of points.

a) $(1, 2)$ and $(0, 6)$ **b)** $(8, 7)$ and $(0, -9)$

c) $(4, 5)$ and $(6, 6)$ **d)** $(5, -8)$ and $(-1, 10)$

e) $(2, -9)$ and $(5, -15)$ **f)** $(2, 0)$ and $(-6, -2)$

8 Decide whether each of the following lines are parallel to the line $y = \frac{1}{2}x + 8$, perpendicular to it, or neither.

a) $y = 3 - 2x$ **b)** $8y - 4x = 5$ **c)** $y - 2x = 4$ **d)** $3x - 6y = 1$

e) $4y + 2x = 8$ **f)** $y = 2(x - 4)$ **g)** $2y = x - 7$ **h)** $y + 2x = 8$

9 Jonah plots three points on the line segment AC at the following coordinates: $A(-6, -2)$, $B(p, q)$, $C(10, 6)$.

a) Given that $AB:BC = 1:3$, find the values of p and q.

b) Calculate the length of the line segment AB. Give your answer to one decimal place.

c) Jonah draws another point, D, on the line segment AC such that $AB:DC = 4:1$. What is the length of the line segment DC?

10 Find the gradient, length and midpoint of each side of the following shapes. Give your answers to 3 s.f. where appropriate.

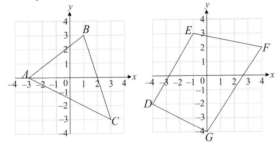

Write all equations in your answers to Questions 12-14 in the form $y = mx + c$.

12 Find the equations of the lines shown on the graph on the right.

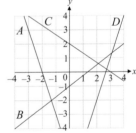

13 Find the equation of the line parallel to the given line that passes through the given point.

a) $y = 3x - 11$, $(5, 9)$ **b)** $y = 10 - 7x$, $(1, 11)$

c) $y + 2 = 9x$, $(2, -16)$ **d)** $x + y = 5$, $(-2, 9)$

e) $3x + 2y = 23$, $(8, 5)$ **f)** $x - 11 = 3y$, $(18, 1)$

11 Find the total perimeter of the following shapes. Give your answers to three significant figures.

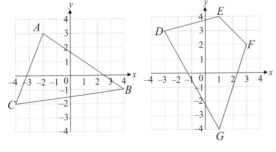

14 Find the equation of the line perpendicular to the given line and passing through the given point.

a) $y = 4x + 1$, $(12, 9)$ **b)** $y = 5 - 2x$, $(14, 8)$

c) $y + 16 = 3x$, $(-6, -1)$ **d)** $x + 3y = 17$, $(-4, 2)$

e) $3x + 2y = 8$, $(9, -1)$ **f)** $x - 3 = 5y$, $(-2, 2)$

Section 16 — Other Types of Graph

16.1 Quadratic Graphs

Quadratic functions always have x^2 as the highest power of x.
The graphs of quadratic functions are always the same shape, called a **parabola**.

If the coefficient of x^2 is **positive**, the parabola is u-shaped.
If the coefficient of x^2 is **negative**, the parabola is n-shaped.

Example 1

Draw the graph of $y = x^2 - 3$.

1. Use a table to find the coordinates of points on the graph.

x	-4	-3	-2	-1	0	1	2	3	4
x^2	16	9	4	1	0	1	4	9	16
$x^2 - 3$	13	6	1	-2	-3	-2	1	6	13

2. Plot the coordinates and join the points with a smooth curve.

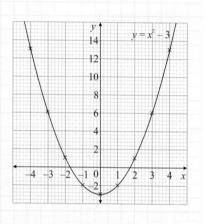

Exercise 1

1 Copy and complete each table and draw graphs for the following quadratic equations.

a) $y = x^2$

x	-4	-3	-2	-1	0	1	2	3	4
x^2		9				1			

b) $y = x^2 + 2$

x	-4	-3	-2	-1	0	1	2	3	4
x^2	16			1			4		
$x^2 + 2$	18			3			6		

c) $y = 2x^2$

x	-4	-3	-2	-1	0	1	2	3	4
x^2		9				1			
$2x^2$		18				2			

d) $y = 6 - x^2$

x	-4	-3	-2	-1	0	1	2	3	4
x^2			4			1		9	
$6 - x^2$			2			5		-3	

2 Draw the graph of $y = x^2 + 5$ for values of x between -4 and 4.
   a) Use your graph to find the value of y when: **(i)** $x = 2.5$ **(ii)** $x = -0.5$
   b) Use your graph to find the values of x when: **(i)** $y = 6.5$ **(ii)** $y = 10$

3 Draw the graph of $y = 2x^2 - 7$ for values of x between -4 and 4.
   a) Use your graph to find the value of y when: **(i)** $x = 1.5$ **(ii)** $x = -3.5$
   b) Use your graph to find the values of x when: **(i)** $y = 5$ **(ii)** $y = 20$

4 Draw the graph of $y = 4 - x^2$ for values of x between -4 and 4.
   Write down the values of x where the graph crosses the x-axis.

5 Draw the graph of $y = 3x^2 - 11$ for values of x between -4 and 4.
   Write down the values of x where the graph crosses the x-axis.

Example 2

Draw the graph of $y = x^2 + 3x - 2$.

1. Add extra rows to the table to make it easier to work out the y-values.

x	-4	-3	-2	-1	0	1	2	3	4
x^2	16	9	4	1	0	1	4	9	16
$+3x$	-12	-9	-6	-3	0	3	6	9	12
-2	-2	-2	-2	-2	-2	-2	-2	-2	-2
$x^2 + 3x - 2$	2	-2	-4	-4	-2	2	8	16	26

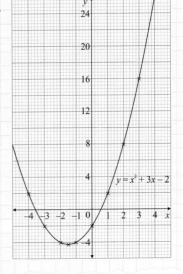

2. The table doesn't tell you the lowest point on the curve, so you need to find one more point before you can draw the graph. Quadratic graphs are always symmetrical, so the x-coordinate of the lowest point curve is halfway between the two lowest points from the table (or any pair of points with the same y-coordinate).

So the lowest point of the graph is halfway between $x = -2$ and $x = -1$, when $x = -1.5$ and $y = (-1.5)^2 + (3 \times -1.5) - 2 = -4.25$.

Exercise 2

1 Copy and complete each table and draw graphs for the following quadratic equations.

   a) $y = x^2 + 2x + 3$

x	-4	-3	-2	-1	0	1	2	3	4
x^2			4					9	
$+2x$			-4					6	
$+3$			3					3	
$x^2 + 2x + 3$			3					18	

   b) $y = x^2 - 4x - 1$

x	-4	-3	-2	-1	0	1	2	3	4
x^2	16					1			
$-4x$	16					-4			
-1	-1					-1			
$x^2 - 4x - 1$	31					-4			

c) $y = 4 + 2x - x^2$

x	-4	-3	-2	-1	0	1	2	3	4
4		4				4			
$+2x$		-6				2			
$-x^2$		-9				-1			
$4 + 2x - x^2$		-11				5			

d) $y = 2x^2 + 3x - 7$

x	-4	-3	-2	-1	0	1	2	3	4
$2x^2$		18						18	
$+3x$		-9						9	
-7		-7						-7	
$2x^2 + 3x - 7$		2						20	

2 Draw the graph of $y = x^2 - 5x + 3$ for values of x between -3 and 6.
   a) Use your graph to find the value of y when: **(i)** $x = -1.5$ **(ii)** $x = 1.5$
   b) Use your graph to find the values of x when: **(i)** $y = 8$ **(ii)** $y = -2$

3 Draw the graph of $y = 11 - 2x^2$ for values of x between -4 and 4.
   a) Use your graph to find the value of y when: **(i)** $x = -2.5$ **(ii)** $x = 1.25$
   b) Use your graph to find the values of x when: **(i)** $y = 0$ **(ii)** $y = 11$

4 **a)** Expand and simplify $(x + 3)(x - 2)$.
   b) Use your answer from **a)** to draw the graph of $y = (x + 3)(x - 2)$.
   c) Write down the coordinates of the points where the graph crosses the x-axis.
   d) What is the connection between your answer to part **c)** and the equation $(x + 3)(x - 2) = 0$?

16.2 Cubic Graphs

Cubic functions have x^3 as the highest power of x.

Cubic graphs all have the same basic shape of a curve with a 'wiggle' in the middle. The curve goes up from the bottom left if the coefficient of x^3 is positive, and down from the top left if it's negative.

Example 1

Draw the graph of $y = x^3 + 3x^2 + 1$.

1. Add extra rows to the table to make it easier
    to work out the y-values.

x	-4	-3	-2	-1	0	1	2
x^3	-64	-27	-8	-1	0	1	8
$+3x^2$	48	27	12	3	0	3	12
$+1$	1	1	1	1	1	1	1
$x^3 + 3x^2 + 1$	-15	1	5	3	1	5	21

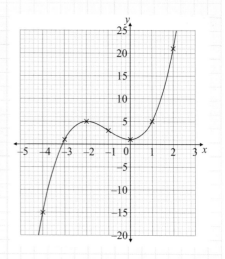

2. Plot the coordinates and join the points
    with a smooth curve.

Exercise 1

1 Copy and complete each table and draw graphs for the following cubic equations.

a) $y = x^3$

x	−3	−2	−1	0	1	2	3
x^3		−8			1		

b) $y = x^3 + 5$

x	−3	−2	−1	0	1	2	3
x^3	−27					8	
$x^3 + 5$	−22					13	

c) $y = x^3 - 3x + 7$

x	−4	−3	−2	−1	0	1	2	3	4
x^3	−64					1			
$-3x$	12					−3			
$+7$	7					7			
$x^3 - 3x + 7$	−45					5			

d) $y = x^3 - 3x^2 - x + 3$

x	−3	−2	−1	0	1	2	3	4
x^3		−8					27	
$-3x^2$		−12					−27	
$-x$		2					−3	
$+3$		3					3	
$x^3 - 3x^2 - x + 3$		−15					0	

e) $y = 2x^3 - 2x^2 - 3x + 5$

x	−3	−2	−1	0	1	2	3
$2x^3$			−2				54
$-2x^2$			−2				−18
$-3x$			3				−9
$+5$			5				5
$2x^3 - 2x^2 - 3x + 5$			4				32

f) $y = 5 - x^3$

x	−3	−2	−1	0	1	2	3
5		5					5
$-x^3$		8					−27
$5 - x^3$		13					−22

g) $y = 3x^3 - 4x^2 + 2x - 8$

x	−3	−2	−1	0	1	2	3
$3x^3$	−81				3		
$-4x^2$	−36				−4		
$+2x$	−6				2		
-8	−8				−8		
$3x^3 - 4x^2 + 2x - 8$	−131				−7		

2 Draw the graph of $y = x^3 + 3$ for values of x between -3 and 3.
Use your graph to estimate the value of y when $x = -2.5$.

3 Draw the graph of $y = x^3 - 6x^2 + 12x - 5$ for values of x between -1 and 5.
Write down the value(s) of x when the graph crosses the x-axis.

4 Draw the graph of $y = x^3 - x^2 - 6x$ for values of x between -3 and 4.
Use your graph to estimate the value of x when: **a)** $y = 10$ **b)** $y = -15$

16.3   Reciprocal Graphs

Reciprocal functions contain a $\frac{1}{f(x)}$ term (where $f(x)$ is a function of x).

Reciprocal functions don't have values for every x — they're said to be **undefined** when the denominator of the $\frac{1}{f(x)}$ term is zero.

Reciprocal graphs have **asymptotes**. An asymptote is a line the graph gets very close to, but never touches.

The graph of $y = \frac{1}{x}$ has asymptotes at $x = 0$ and $y = 0$.

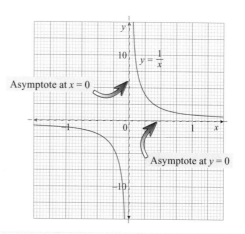

Asymptote at $x = 0$

Asymptote at $y = 0$

Example 1

Find the equations of the asymptotes of the graph of $y = \frac{2}{x} - 2$.
Use your answer to sketch the graph.

1. As the (positive or negative) size of x increases, $\frac{2}{x}$ gets closer to zero, so y gets closer to -2.
    But $\frac{2}{x}$ never actually equals zero, so $y = -2$ is an asymptote.

2. The bottom of the fraction $\frac{2}{x}$ can get close to zero, but can never equal zero.
    So the vertical asymptote is at $x = 0$.

3. Draw a sketch with the same basic shape as $y = \frac{1}{x}$.
    When x is very small, $\frac{2}{x}$ is very large and when x is large, $\frac{2}{x}$ is very small.

The graph of $y = \frac{2}{x} - 2$ has asymptotes at $y = -2$ and $x = 0$.

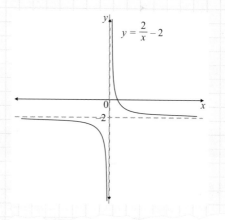

Exercise 1

1 Copy and complete each table and draw graphs for the following reciprocal functions.
Give any rounded numbers to 2 decimal places.

a) $y = \frac{4}{x}$

x	-5	-4	-3	-2	-1	-0.5	-0.1	0.1	0.5	1	2	3	4	5
$\frac{4}{x}$	-0.8			-2					8					

b) $y = \dfrac{1}{x+3}$

x	−6	−5	−4	−3.5	−3.1	−2.9	−2.5	−2	−1	0	2
$x+3$			−1				0.5			3	
$\dfrac{1}{x+3}$			−1				2			0.33	

c) $y = \dfrac{1}{x} + 3$

x	−5	−4	−3	−2	−1	−0.5	−0.1	0.1	0.5	1	2	3	4	5
$\dfrac{1}{x}$			−0.33			−2					0.5			
$+3$			3			3					3			
$\dfrac{1}{x} + 3$			2.67			1					3.5			

d) $y = -\dfrac{1}{x}$

x	−5	−4	−3	−2	−1	−0.5	−0.1	0.1	0.5	1	2	3	4	5
$-\dfrac{1}{x}$		0.25			1							−0.33		

e) $y = 5 - \dfrac{1}{x}$

x	−5	−4	−3	−2	−1	−0.5	−0.1	0.1	0.5	1	2	3	4	5
5		5					5							5
$-\dfrac{1}{x}$		0.25					10							−0.2
$5 - \dfrac{1}{x}$		5.25					15							4.8

2 a) For what value of x is the expression $\dfrac{1}{x-2}$ undefined?

b) What happens to the value of $\dfrac{1}{x-2}$ as x increases?

c) Give the equations of the asymptotes of the graph $y = \dfrac{1}{x-2}$.

3 Find the equations of the asymptotes of each of the following graphs.

a) $y = -\dfrac{6}{x}$

b) $y = \dfrac{1}{x} + 4$

c) $y = \dfrac{1}{x+5}$

d) $y = \dfrac{1}{2x} - 1$

e) $y = \dfrac{1}{3-x} + 10$

f) $y = 8 - \dfrac{4}{5x-2}$

16.4 More Reciprocal Graphs

The graph of $y = \dfrac{1}{x^2}$ is similar to the graph of $y = \dfrac{1}{x}$ but because square numbers are always positive,

$y = \dfrac{1}{x^2}$ has only **positive values**.

The lines $y = 0$ and $x = 0$ are asymptotes of the graph of $y = \dfrac{1}{x^2}$.

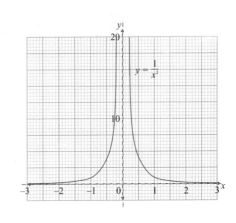

Example 1

Draw the graph of $y = \dfrac{1}{(x+3)^2}$, including asymptotes.

x	-7	-6	-5	-4	-3.5	-2.5	-2	-1	0	1
$\dfrac{1}{(x+3)^2}$	0.06	0.11	0.25	1	4	4	1	0.25	0.11	0.06

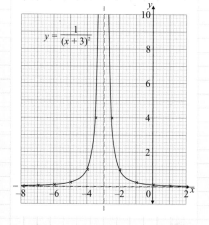

As the size of x increases, $\dfrac{1}{(x+3)^2}$ gets closer to zero,
so $y = 0$ is an asymptote.

$\dfrac{1}{(x+3)^2}$ is undefined when $(x+3)^2 = 0$,
so $x = -3$ is an asymptote.

Exercise 1

1 Copy and complete each table and draw graphs for the following reciprocal functions.
Give any rounded numbers to 2 decimal places.

a) $y = \dfrac{2}{x^2}$

x	-4	-3	-2	-1	-0.5	0.5	1	2	3	4
x^2		9			0.25		1			
$\dfrac{2}{x^2}$		0.22			8		2			

b) $y = \dfrac{1}{(x+1)^2}$

x	-5	-4	-3	-2	-1.5	-0.5	0	1	2	3
$x+1$	-4					0.5				
$(x+1)^2$	16					0.25				
$\dfrac{1}{(x+1)^2}$	0.06					4				

c) $y = \dfrac{1}{(x-2)^2}$

x	-2	-1	0	1	1.5	2.5	3	4	5	6
$x-2$		-3						2		
$(x-2)^2$		9						4		
$\dfrac{1}{(x-2)^2}$		0.11						0.25		

d) $y = \dfrac{1}{x^2} - 5$

x	-4	-3	-2	-1	-0.5	0.5	1	2	3	4
x^2	16						1			16
$\dfrac{1}{x^2}$	0.06						1			0.06
$\dfrac{1}{x^2} - 5$	-4.94						-4			-4.94

e) $y = -\dfrac{1}{x^2}$

x	−4	−3	−2	−1	−0.5	0.5	1	2	3	4
x^2			4			0.25			9	
$-\dfrac{1}{x^2}$			−0.25			−4			−0.11	

f) $y = 4 - \dfrac{1}{x^2}$

x	−4	−3	−2	−1	−0.5	0.5	1	2	3	4
x^2				1						16
$\dfrac{1}{x^2}$				1						0.06
$4 - \dfrac{1}{x^2}$				3						3.94

2 Write down the equations of the asymptotes of the following graphs.
Use your answers to help you sketch the graphs.

a) $y = \dfrac{1}{x^2}$

b) $y = \dfrac{1}{(x-1)^2}$

c) $y = \dfrac{1}{(x+8)^2}$

d) $y = -\dfrac{1}{(x+1)^2}$

e) $y = \dfrac{1}{x^2} + 6$

f) $y = 3 - \dfrac{1}{(x+4)^2}$

16.5   Exponential Graphs

Exponential functions have the form $y = a^x$, where $a > 0$.

When $a > 1$, as x increases,
a^x quickly gets very large.
As x gets more negative,
a^x gets smaller and smaller
but never reaches 0, so the
x-axis is an asymptote.

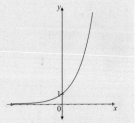

When $a < 1$, as x increases,
a^x gets smaller and smaller
but never reaches 0, so the
x-axis is an asymptote.
As x gets more negative,
a^x quickly gets very large.

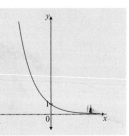

Exercise 1

1 Copy and complete each table and draw graphs for the following exponential functions.
Give any rounded numbers to 2 decimal places.

a) $y = 3^x$

x	−3	−2	−1	0	1	2	3
3^x		0.11					27

b) $y = 0.25^x$

x	−3	−2	−1	0	1	2	3
0.25^x			4			0.06	

c) $y = 4^x + 3$

x	−3	−2	−1	0	1	2	3
4^x	0.02					16	
$+3$	3					3	
$4^x + 3$	3.02					19	

d) $y = 2^{-x}$

x	−3	−2	−1	0	1	2	3
2^{-x}		4		1			

2 For each of the following graphs, write down the equation of the asymptote and the point where each graph crosses the y-axis. Use your answers to help you sketch the graphs.

a) $y = 5^x$

b) $y = 2^x - 1$

c) $y = 10 - 3^x$

d) $y = 0.1^x$

e) $y = 0.5^x + 3$

f) $y = 10^{-x}$

3 £100 is invested in a bank account that pays 5% interest per year.
The amount of money in the account (in pounds) after x years is equal to 100×1.05^x.
Draw a graph of $y = 100 \times 1.05^x$ for values of x from 0 to 10, to show how the amount of money in the account changes over 10 years.

4 The value of a car depreciates at a rate of 20% per year. When the car was new, it cost £6000.
The value of the car in pounds, V, is given by the formula $V = 6000 \times 0.8^t$, where t is the car's age in years.

a) Draw a graph of V to show how the value of the car decreases over 6 years.

b) Use your graph to estimate the value of the car after 3½ years.

16.6   Circle Graphs

The equation of a circle with **radius r** and **centre (a, b)** is $(x - a)^2 + (y - b)^2 = r^2$.

Example 1

Sketch the graphs of the following equations.

a) $x^2 + y^2 = 16$
    1. $a = 0$ and $b = 0$, so the centre of the circle is $(0, 0)$.
    2. $\sqrt{16} = 4$, so the radius of the circle is 4.

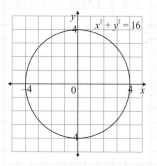

b) $(x - 3)^2 + (y + 2)^2 = 9$
    1. $a = 3$ and $b = -2$, so the centre of the circle is $(3, -2)$.
    2. $\sqrt{9} = 3$, so the radius of the circle is 3.

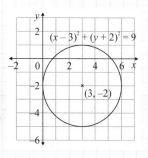

Exercise 1

1 For each of the following equations, give the centre and radius of the circle.

a) $x^2 + y^2 = 25$

b) $x^2 + y^2 = 1$

c) $(x - 1)^2 + (y - 2)^2 = 4$

d) $(x - 5)^2 + (y - 3)^2 = 81$

e) $(x + 2)^2 + (y - 1)^2 = 9$

f) $(x - 2)^2 + (y + 2)^2 = 64$

g) $(x + 1)^2 + (y + 3)^2 = 49$

h) $x^2 + y^2 = 6.25$

i) $x^2 + (y - 5)^2 = 12.25$

2 Write down the equation of each of the following circles.

a)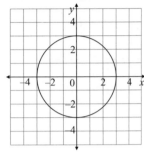

b)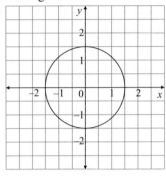

c)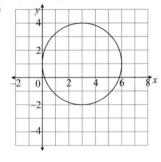

d)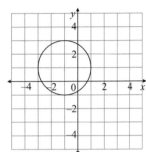

e)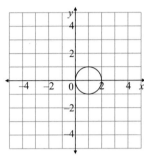

f)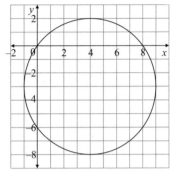

3 a) Draw the graph of $(x-2)^2 + (y-1)^2 = 9$
   b) Use your graph to find: **(i)** the approximate values of y when $x = 3$,
                                   (ii) the approximate values of x when $y = -1$.

4 On the same axes, draw the graphs of $x^2 + (y+2)^2 = 9$ and $y = 2x - 1$.
   Use your graph to find the approximate coordinates of the points of intersection of the two graphs.

5 a) Show that $(x-1)^2 = x^2 - 2x + 1$
   b) Expand and simplify $(y+2)^2$.
   c) Use your answers to **a)** and **b)** to sketch the graph of $x^2 - 2x + y^2 + 4y = 11$

6 A circle with centre (3, 3) and radius 5 is drawn on the same axes as the graph of $(x+1)^2 + (y+2)^2 = 4$.
   Draw the circles and find their approximate points of intersection.

16.7 Trigonometric Graphs

The trigonometric functions **sine**, **cosine** and **tangent** are **periodic** functions — they all have patterns that repeat.

Sine and cosine have similar wave-shaped graphs.

Each function takes values between –1 and 1, and they both repeat every 360°.

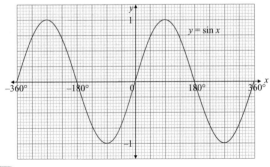

The graph of tangent has a period of 180°. It has asymptotes at −90° and 90°, and it repeats every 180°.

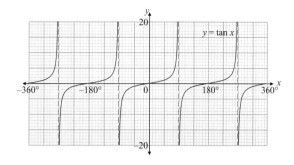

Exercise 1

In Questions 1–6, give all rounded numbers to 2 decimal places.

1 **a)** Copy and complete the table and draw the graph of $y = \cos x$ for values of x between 0° and 360°.

x	0°	30°	45°	60°	90°	120°	135°	150°	180°	210°	225°	240°	270°	300°	315°	330°	360°
$\cos x$	1						−0.71					−0.5				0.87	

b) Use your graph to find, to the nearest degree, the values of x between 0° and 360° when
  (i) $\cos x = 0.4$ **(ii)** $\cos x = -0.75$

2 **a)** Copy and complete the table and draw the graph of $y = 2\sin x$ for values of x between 0° and 360°.

x	0°	30°	45°	60°	90°	120°	135°	150°	180°	210°	225°	240°	270°	300°	315°	330°	360°
$\sin x$		0.5				0.87			0						−0.71		
$2\sin x$		1				1.73			0						−1.41		

b) Use your graph to find, to the nearest degree, the values of x between 0° and 360° when
  (i) $2\sin x = 1.2$ **(ii)** $2\sin x = -0.8$

3 Copy and complete the table and draw the graph of $y = 2 + \cos x$ for values of x between 0° and 360°.

x	0°	30°	45°	60°	90°	120°	135°	150°	180°	210°	225°	240°	270°	300°	315°	330°	360°
$\cos x$		0.87				−0.5			−1			−0.5					
$2 + \cos x$		2.87				1.5			1			1.5					

4 Copy and complete the table and draw the graph of $y = \tan x$ for values of x between 0° and 360°.

x	0°	30°	45°	60°	80°	85°	95°	100°	120°	150°
$\tan x$		0.58						−1.73		

x	180°	210°	240°	260°	265°	275°	280°	300°	330°	360°
$\tan x$			1.73							0

5 **a)** Copy and complete the table and draw the graph of $y = \sin 2x$ for values of x between 0° and 360°.

x	0°	30°	45°	60°	90°	120°	135°	150°	180°	210°	225°	240°	270°	300°	315°	330°	360°
$2x$		60°			180°					420°				600°			
$\sin 2x$		0.87			0					0.87				−0.87			

b) Describe the connection between the graph of $y = \sin 2x$ and the graph of $y = \sin x$.

6 a) Copy and complete the table and draw the graph of $y = \cos(x - 90°)$ for values of x between $0°$ and $360°$.

x	0°	30°	45°	60°	90°	120°	135°	150°	180°	210°	225°	240°	270°	300°	315°	330°	360°
$x - 90°$	-90°	-60°			0°				60°					210°			
$\cos(x - 90°)$	0	0.5			1				0.5					-0.87			

b) What do you notice about the graph of $y = \cos(x - 90°)$?

16.8 Transforming Graphs

The graph of a function can be **transformed** to give a new graph that is
a **translation**, a **stretch** or a **reflection** of the original.

Translations

When a graph is **translated**, the **shape** of the graph **stays the same** but it **moves** on the coordinate grid.

If $y = f(x)$ is the original graph, then

$y = f(x) + a$ is a translation a **units up**

$y = f(x - a)$ is a translation a **units right**

Example 1

The diagram shows the graph of $y = x^2$.

Draw the graph of $y = (x + 4)^2 - 3$.

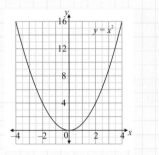

1. $y = (x + 4)^2$ is a translation
   4 units left from $y = x^2$.

2. $y = (x + 4)^2 - 3$ is a translation
   3 units down from $y = (x + 4)^2$.

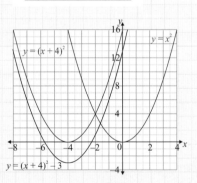

Exercise 1

1 Describe each translation shown by the functions below.

    a) $y = f(x) + 3$ **b)** $y = f(x - 1)$ **c)** $y = f(x + 2)$ **d)** $y = f(x) - 6$

    e) $y = f(x - 7)$ **f)** $y = f(x - 5) + 6$ **g)** $y = f(x + 6) - 4$ **h)** $y = f(x - 3) + 2$

2 Each of these functions is a translation of the function $y = x^2$.
    For each function, describe the translation and sketch the graph.

    a) $y = x^2 + 1$ **b)** $y = x^2 + 5$ **c)** $y = x^2 - 2$ **d)** $y = (x - 4)^2$

    e) $y = (x + 1)^2$ **f)** $y = (x + 3)^2 - 2$ **g)** $y = (x - 2)^2 - 2$ **h)** $y = (x - 5)^2 + 3$

3 Each of these functions is a translation of the function $y = x^3$.
For each function, describe the translation and sketch the graph.

a) $y = (x + 1)^3$ **b)** $y = x^3 + 4$ **c)** $y = x^3 - 5$ **d)** $y = (x - 3)^3 + 2$

e) $y = (x - 5)^3 + 4$ **f)** $y = (x + 2)^3 - 3$ **g)** $y = (x - 4)^3 + 6.5$ **h)** $y = (x + 2.5)^3 - 3$

4 These graphs are translations of the graph $y = x^2$. Find the equation of each graph.

a)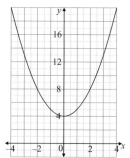

b)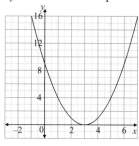

c)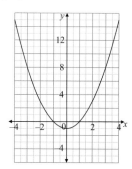

d)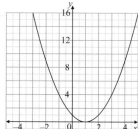

e)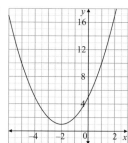

f)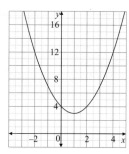

g)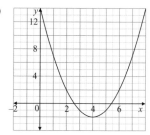

h)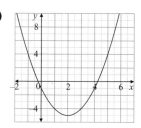

5 Each of the following functions is a translation of
the function $y = \sin x$. For each one, describe the
translation and sketch the graph for $0° \leq x \leq 360°$.

a) $y = (\sin x) + 1$ **b)** $y = (\sin x) - 2$

c) $y = \sin (x + 60°)$ **d)** $y = \sin (x - 90°)$

e) $y = \sin (x + 180°)$ **f)** $y = \sin (x - 360°)$

g) $y = \sin (x - 30°) + 1$ **h)** $y = \sin (x + 90°) + 2$

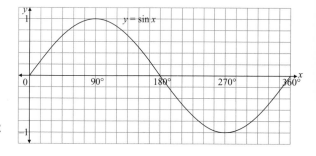

6 For each of the following, give another equation that produces the same graph.

a) $y = \tan x$ **b)** $y = \cos (x + 180°)$ **c)** $y = \sin (x + 45°)$

Reflections

Graphs of functions can be **reflected** in the *x*- or *y*-axis.

> If $y = f(x)$ is the original graph, then $\quad y = -f(x) \quad$ is a reflection in the **x-axis**.
>
> $\quad y = f(-x) \quad$ is a reflection in the **y-axis**.

If a point doesn't change during the transformation it's called an **invariant point**.

Example 2

The diagram shows the graph of $y = \sin(x - 45°)$ for $-180° \leq x \leq 180°$.

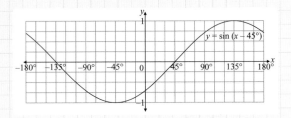

Draw the following graphs.

a) $y = \sin(-x - 45°)$

$\quad y = \sin(-x - 45°)$ is a reflection in the y-axis.

b) $y = -\sin(x - 45°)$

$\quad y = -\sin(x - 45°)$ is a reflection in the x-axis.

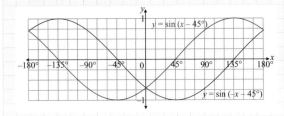 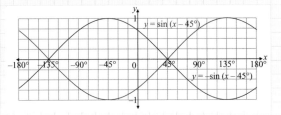

Exercise 2

1 The graph on the right shows the function $y = f(x)$.
The graphs of the following functions are reflections of the graph of $y = f(x)$.
In each case, describe the reflection and sketch the graph.

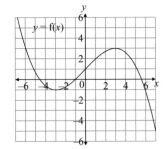

a) $y = f(-x)$

b) $y = -f(x)$

2 Sketch the graphs of each of the following pairs of functions.
Use a single set of axes for each pair of graphs.

a) $y = \sin x, \ y = -\sin x$

b) $y = \cos x, \ y = -\cos x$

c) $y = x^2, \ y = -x^2$

d) $y = \dfrac{1}{x}, \ y = -\dfrac{1}{x}$

e) $y = x - 2, \ y = -x - 2$

f) $y = 2^x, \ y = 2^{-x}$

3 Sketch the graphs of $y = x^3, y = -x^3$ and $y = (-x)^3$.
Explain why two of the graphs are the same.

Stretches

Graphs of functions can be **stretched** in the direction parallel to the *x*-axis or parallel to the *y*-axis.

If $y = f(x)$ is the original graph, then $\qquad$ $y = af(x)$ $\qquad$ is a stretch of **scale factor *a*** in the ***y*-direction**

$\qquad\qquad\qquad\qquad\qquad\qquad\qquad\quad$ $y = f(ax)$ $\qquad$ is a stretch of **scale factor $\frac{1}{a}$** in the ***x*-direction**

If the scale factor of a stretch is **negative**, the graph is **reflected** in the axis before the stretch is applied.

Example 3

The diagram shows the graph of $y = \sin x$ for $-180° \leq x \leq 180°$.

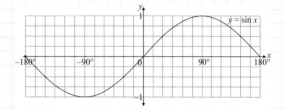

Draw the following graphs.

a) $y = 2\sin x$

$\quad$ $y = 2\sin x$ is a stretch of scale factor 2, parallel to the *y*-axis.

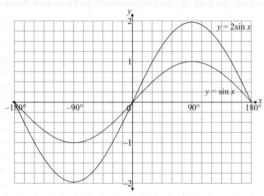

b) $y = \sin 2x$

$\quad$ $y = \sin 2x$ is a stretch of scale factor $\frac{1}{2}$, parallel to the *x*-axis.

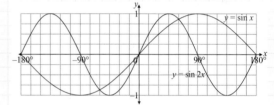

Exercise 3

1 The graph on the right shows the function $y = f(x)$. The graph of each of the following functions is a stretch of the graph of $y = f(x)$. In each case, describe the stretch and sketch the graph.

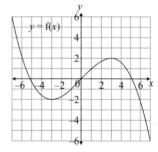

a) $y = f(3x)$ $\qquad\qquad\qquad$ **b)** $y = f(5x)$

c) $y = f(\frac{1}{2}x)$ $\qquad\qquad\quad$ **d)** $y = f(\frac{1}{4}x)$

e) $y = 3f(x)$ $\qquad\qquad\qquad$ **f)** $y = 1.5f(x)$

g) $y = \frac{1}{3}f(x)$ $\qquad\qquad\quad$ **h)** $y = \frac{1}{10}f(x)$

2 These graphs are stretches of the graph $y = \sin x$. Find the equation of each graph.

a)

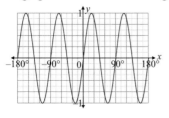

b)

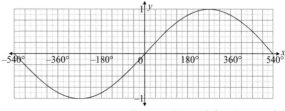

c)

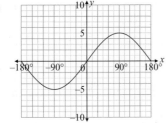

d)

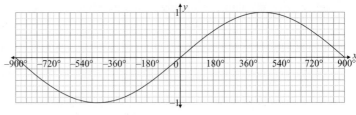

e)

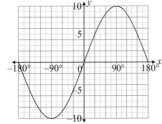

f)

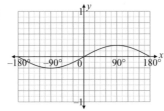

g)

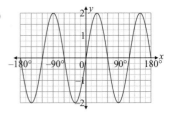

h)

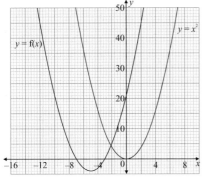

i)

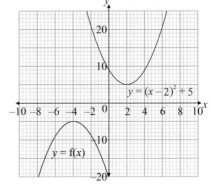

Exercise 4 — Mixed Exercise

1 The graph of $y = (-x - 2)^2$ is obtained by applying a translation then a reflection to the graph of $y = x^2$.

  a) Sketch the graph of $y = x^2$.

  b) Apply a translation to the graph of $y = x^2$ to give the graph of $y = (x - 2)^2$.

  c) Apply a reflection to your graph from part **b)** to give the graph of $y = (-x - 2)^2$.

2 For the following pairs of functions, describe the transformations that transform the graph of the first function to the graph of the second. Sketch each pair of graphs on a single set of axes.

  a) $y = x^2$, $y = -(x - 1)^2$ **b)** $y = x^2$, $y = (-x - 3)^2$

  c) $y = \cos x$, $y = -\cos (x + 90°)$ **d)** $y = \sin x$, $y = \sin (-x) + 1$

3 On each of the following graphs, the curve marked $y = f(x)$ has been obtained by applying the transformations described. In each case, use the equation of the original curve to find $y = f(x)$.

  a) $y = f(x)$ is obtained by applying a translation then another translation to $y = x^2$

  b) $y = f(x)$ is obtained by applying a translation then a reflection in the *x*-axis to $y = (x - 2)^2 + 5$

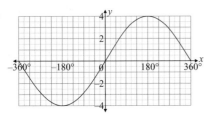

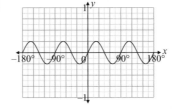

c) $y = f(x)$ is obtained by applying a translation then a stretch to $y = \cos x$

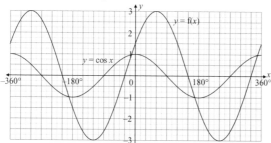

d) $y = f(x)$ is obtained by applying a stretch then another stretch to $y = \sin x$

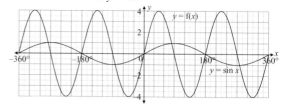

e) $y = f(x)$ is obtained by applying a stretch then a translation to $y = x^2$

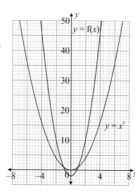

f) $y = f(x)$ is obtained by applying a translation then a stretch to $y = x^2$

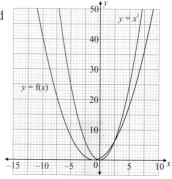

16.9   Graphs Problems

Exercise 1

1 Match each of these equations to one of the graphs below.

(i) $y = x^3$　　　　**(ii)** $y = \dfrac{1}{x^2}$　　　　**(iii)** $y = 2x$　　　　**(iv)** $y = x^2 + 1$

(v) $y = 3 - x^2$　　　**(vi)** $y = \dfrac{1}{x}$　　　**(vii)** $y = 2^x - 1$　　　**(viii)** $x^2 + y^2 = 1$

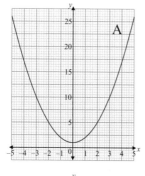

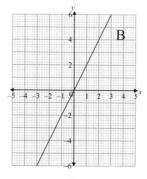

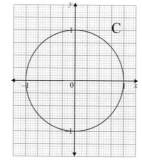

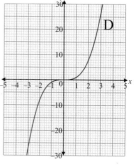

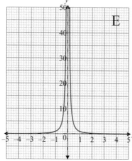

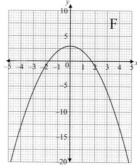

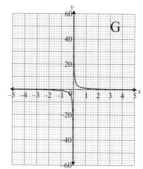

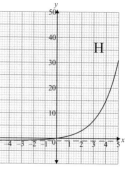

2 Graphs A-F below are transformations of the graph $y = x^2$. Match each graph to its equation.

(i) $y = x^2 - 3$ **(ii)** $y = x^2 + 2$ **(iii)** $y = (x - 1)^2$

(iv) $y = (-x)^2 + 1$ **(v)** $y = -x^2$ **(vi)** $y = (x + 1)^2 - 2$

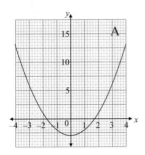
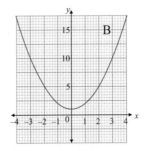
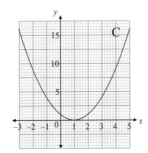

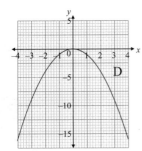
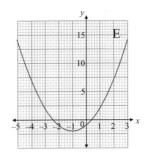
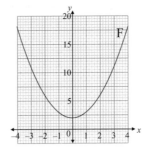

3 The graph of $y = x^2$ has a minimum point at (0, 0).

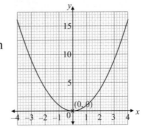

a) (i) The graph of $y = x^2$ is transformed to give the graph of $y = x^2 + 3$.
Describe what this transformation does to the coordinates of each point on the original graph.

    (ii) What are the coordinates of the minimum point of the graph of $y = x^2 + 3$?

b) Write down the coordinates of the minimum point of:
    (i) $y = (x - 1)^2$ **(ii)** $y = (x + 3)^2 - 2$

4 A turning point is a place where the gradient of a graph changes from positive to negative, or from negative to positive.
The graph of $y = f(x)$ shown on the right has two turning points, (0, 4) and (2, 0).

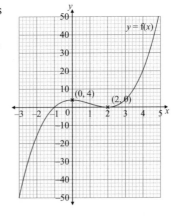

Use the graph of $f(x)$ to sketch the graphs of the following functions. On each graph, mark the coordinates of the two turning points.

a) $f(x) + 2$ **b)** $f(x - 3)$

c) $f(x) - 1$ **d)** $f(x + 2)$

e) $f(-x)$ **f)** $-f(x)$

g) $f(x + 1) - 2$ **h)** $f(x - 2) - 3$

i) $-f(x + 1)$ **j)** $f(-x) - 1$

5 a) Plot the graph of $y = x^2 - x - 1$ for values of x between -2 and 3.

b) Use your graph to find the values of x for which:
    (i) $y = 0$ **(ii)** $y = 3$

6 Even functions are functions with graphs that have the y-axis as a line of symmetry. $y = x^2$ is an example of an even function.

Odd functions are functions with graphs that have rotational symmetry of order 2 about the origin. $y = x^3$ is an example of an odd function.

Sketch the following graphs and say whether the functions are even, odd or neither.

a) $y = x^2 + 5$ **b)** $y = -x^3$ **c)** $y = \sin x$ **d)** $y = (x - 3)^2$

e) $y = \cos x$ **f)** $y = x^3 - 4$ **g)** $y = \tan x$ **h)** $y = \dfrac{1}{x}$

7 a) Draw the graph of $y = \cos x$ for values of x between $-360°$ and $360°$.

b) Use your graph to find the values of x between $-360°$ and $360°$ for which:
    (i) $\cos x = 0.25$ **(ii)** $\cos x = -0.25$

c) If $\cos 50° = 0.643$, use your graph to write down all the values of x between $-360°$ and $360°$ for which:
    (i) $\cos x = 0.643$ **(ii)** $\cos x = -0.643$

8 Susan uses a credit card to buy a computer that costs £500.
The credit card company charges 3% interest per month. If she pays nothing back, the amount in pounds Susan will owe after t months is given by the formula $b = 500 \times (1.03)^t$.

a) Explain what the numbers 500 and 1.03 represent in the formula.

b) Draw a graph to show how this debt will increase during one year if Susan doesn't repay any money.

c) Use your graph to estimate how long the interest on the credit card will take to reach £100.

9 A stone is dropped from the top of a 55 m-high tower. The distance in metres, h, between the stone and the ground after t seconds is given by the formula $h = 55 - 5t^2$.

a) Draw a graph of the height of the stone for values of t between 0 and 5 seconds.

b) Use your graph to estimate, to 3 significant figures, how long it takes the stone to hit the ground.

10 Point P has coordinates $(3, 4)$.

a) Use Pythagoras' theorem to find the distance of P from the origin.

b) Use your answer to **a)** to write the equation of the circle with centre $(0, 0)$ that passes through point P.

c) A second circle has centre $(5, 4)$ and also passes through P. Write down the equation of this circle.

11 a) Expand and simplify $(x + 4)^2 + (y - 1)^2$.

b) Use your answer to sketch the graph of $x^2 + 8x + y^2 - 2y = -13$.

12 Mozzarellium-278 is a radioactive element that has a half-life of approximately 30 minutes. This means that every 30 minutes the amount of mozzarellium-278 in a sample halves. Starting with a 100 g sample of mozzarellium-278, the formula $m = 100 \times (0.5)^{2t}$ gives the mass in grams remaining after t hours.

a) Use the formula to find the mass of mozzarellium-278 left in the sample, to the nearest gram, after:
    (i) 1 hour   **(ii)** 3 hours

b) Draw a graph to show the radioactive decay of the sample of mozzarellium-278.

c) Use your graph to find how long it takes until only 10% of the mozzarellium-278 remains in the sample.

Section 17 — Using Graphs

17.1 Interpreting Real-Life Graphs

You can use graphs to describe real-life situations.

Example 1

The graph shows the temperature of an oven as it heats up.

a) Describe how the temperature of the oven changes during the first 10 minutes shown on the graph.

b) What is the temperature of the oven after 7 minutes?

c) How long does it take for the temperature to reach 190 °C?

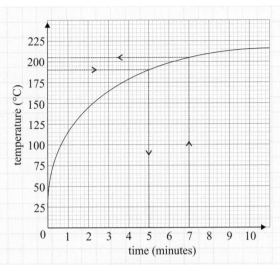

The curve is very steep at first, then begins to level out as the temperature increases.

a) The temperature rises quickly at first, but then rises more slowly as the oven heats up.

b) **205 °C**   c) **5 minutes**

Exercise 1

Use the graph on the right to answer Questions 1–3.

1 a) Convert 38 km/h into miles per hour, to the nearest 1 mph.

   b) (i) Convert 25 mph into km/h.

      (ii) Use your answer to convert 75 mph into km/h.

2 The speed limit on a particular road is 30 mph. A driver travels at 52 km/h. By how many miles per hour is the driver breaking the speed limit?

3 The maximum speed limit in the UK is 70 mph. The maximum speed limit in Spain is 120 km/h. Which country has the greater speed limit, and by how much?

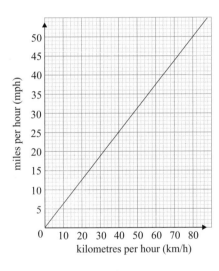

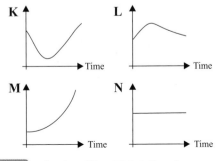

4 Each statement below describes one of the graphs on the left. Match each statement to the correct graph.

   a) The temperature rose quickly, and then fell again gradually.

   b) The number of people who needed hospital treatment stayed at the same level all year.

   c) The cost of gold went up more and more quickly.

   d) The temperature fell overnight, but then climbed quickly again the next morning.

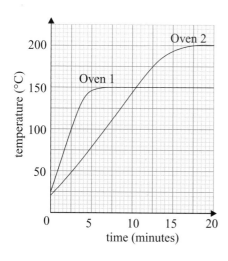

5 The graph on the left shows the temperature in two ovens as they warm up.

   a) Which oven reaches 100 °C more quickly?

   b) Which oven reaches a higher maximum temperature?

   c) How long does it take Oven 2 to reach its maximum temperature?

   d) Calculate the rate at which the temperature of Oven 1 changes in the first 3 minutes after being switched on.

   e) (i) After how many seconds are the two ovens at the same temperature?

      (ii) What temperature do they both reach at this time?

6 The graph shows the depth of water in a harbour between 08:00 and 20:00.

   a) Describe how the depth of water changed over this time period.

   b) At approximately what time was the depth of water the greatest?

   c) What was the minimum depth of water during this period?

   d) At approximately what times was the water 3 m deep?

   e) Mike's boat floats when the depth of the water is 1.6 m or over. Estimate the amount of time that his boat was not floating during this period.

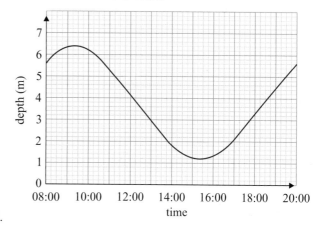

7 A vase that is 30 cm tall is filled using a tap flowing at a steady rate. The graph on the right shows how the depth of water varies in the vase over time.

   a) Describe how the depth of water in the vase changes over time.

   b) How long did it take for the water depth to be half the height of the vase?

   c) Which of the diagrams A-D shown below best matches the shape of the vase?

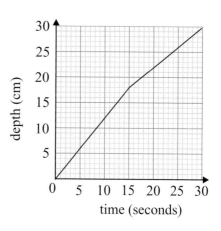

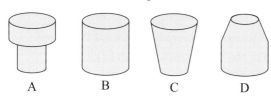

A   B   C   D

17.2 Drawing Real-Life Graphs

You could be asked to sketch or draw a graph representing a real-life situation.

Example 1

A plumber charges customers a standard fee of £40, plus £30 per hour for all work carried out.

a) Draw a graph to show how the plumber's fee varies with the amount of time the job takes.

b) Use the graph to estimate the amount of time a job costing £250 would have taken.

1. Make a table showing the fee for different numbers of hours.
   A 1-hour job will cost £40 + £30 = £70.
   A 2-hour job will cost £40 + (2 × £30) = £100 etc.

a)

Time (hours)	1	2	3	4	5
Fee (£)	70	100	130	160	190

2. Plot the values on a sheet of graph paper and join the points to draw the graph.

   For each extra hour, the fee increases by £30, so this is a straight-line graph.

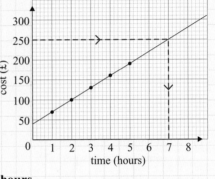

3. Follow the grid across from £250, then read downwards to find the correct time.

b) **7 hours**

Exercise 1

1 The instructions for cooking different weights of chicken are as follows:

   'Cook for 35 mins per kg, plus an extra 25 minutes.'

a) Copy and complete the table below to show the cooking times for different weights of chicken.

Weight (kg)	1	2	3	4	5
Time (minutes)					

b) Use the values from your table to draw a graph showing the cooking times for different weights of chicken.

c) A chicken cooks in 110 minutes. What is the weight of the chicken?

2 Alfred sells high-tech 'stealth fabric' on his market stall.
The cost of the fabric is £80 per metre for the first 3 metres, then £50 per metre after that.

a) Draw a graph showing how the cost of the stealth fabric varies with the amount purchased.

b) Use your graph to find how much it would cost to buy 6.5 metres of stealth fabric.

c) Bruce bought some fabric to make a stealth cape. If he was charged £480, how much fabric did he buy?

3   A farm allows people to pick their own Brussels sprouts.
They charge 60p per kilogram of sprouts picked, plus an admin fee of £2.40 per customer.

   a) Draw a graph showing how the total cost per customer varies with the mass of sprouts picked.

   b) Use your graph to find the cost of picking 4.5 kg of sprouts.

   c) What mass of sprouts did a customer pick if she was charged £6.60?

4   This table shows how the fuel efficiency of a car in miles per gallon
(mpg) varies with the speed of the car in miles per hour (mph).

Speed (mph)	55	60	65	70	75	80
Fuel Efficiency (mpg)	32.3	30.7	28.9	27.0	24.9	22.7

   a) Plot the points from the table on a graph and join them up with a smooth curve.

   b) Use your graph to predict the fuel efficiency of the car when it is travelling at 73 mph.

5   Helena is a baby girl. A health visitor records the weight of Helena every two months.
The measurements are shown in the table below.

Age (months)	0	2	4	6	8	10	12	14	16
Weight (kg)	3.2	4.6	5.9	7.0	7.9	8.7	9.3	9.8	10.2

   a) Draw a graph to show this information.
Join your points with a smooth curve.

   b) Keira is 9 months old and has a weight of 9.1 kg.
Use your graph to estimate how much heavier Keira is than Helena was at the same age.

6   A car is driven along a straight track to test its acceleration.
The distance in metres, d, that the car has travelled after t seconds is given by $d = 2t^2 + t$.

   a) Draw a graph of d against t for $0 \leq t \leq 5$.

   b) Use your graph to find the distance the car will have travelled after 3.5 seconds.

7   The empty conical flask shown is filled from a steadily
running tap. Sketch a graph to show the depth of water
in the flask t seconds after it has started to be filled.

8   The number of cells, N, in a sample after d days is $N = 5000 \times 1.2^d$.

   a) Copy and complete the table to show the number of
cells in the sample for the values of d given.

d	0	1	2	3	4
N					

   b) Draw a graph to show this information.

   c) Use your graph to estimate how many days it takes for there to be 9000 cells in the sample.

9   Five years ago, two crows were put onto a deserted island. The number of crows on the island (C) is given
by the equation $C = 2^{x+1}$, where x is the number of years since the crows were first put onto the island.

   a) Draw a graph to show how the number of crows on the island has changed in the past 5 years.

   b) Estimate how many years it took for there to be 30 crows on the island.

17.3 Solving Simultaneous Equations Graphically

Any point where two graphs **intersect** is a solution to the equations of **both** graphs.

You can solve **simultaneous equations** by plotting the graphs of both equations and finding the point(s) where they intersect.

Example 1

a) Plot the graphs $x + y = 8$ and $y = 2x + 2$.

b) Use your graphs to solve the simultaneous equations $x + y = 8$ and $y = 2x + 2$.

1. Both equations are straight lines — they can be written in the form $y = mx + c$.

   Find three pairs of x- and y-values for each graph and plot them.

a) $x + y = 8$

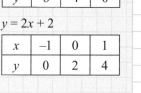

x	0	4	8
y	8	4	0

$y = 2x + 2$

x	–1	0	1
y	0	2	4

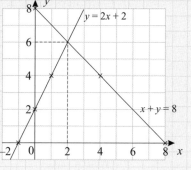

2. Find the x- and y-values of the point where the graphs intersect.

b) The graphs cross at (2, 6), so the solution is **$x = 2$ and $y = 6$**.

Exercise 1

1 The diagram on the right shows the graphs $y = \frac{1}{2}x + 4$ and $y = -\frac{1}{4}x + 7$.

Use the diagram to find the solution to the simultaneous equations $y = \frac{1}{2}x + 4$ and $y = -\frac{1}{4}x + 7$.

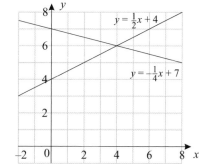

Draw the graphs in Questions 2–4 for $-8 \le x \le 8$ and $-8 \le y \le 8$.

2 a) Draw the graph of $x + y = 5$.

 b) On the same axes, draw the graph of $y = x - 3$.

 c) Use your graphs to solve the simultaneous equations $x + y = 5$ and $y = x - 3$.

3 Solve the following simultaneous equations by drawing graphs.

 a) $x + y = 7$ and $y = x - 3$

 b) $x + y = 8$ and $y = x$

 c) $x + y = 9$ and $y = 2x$

 d) $x + y = 1$ and $y = 2x - 7$

 e) $2x + y = 2$ and $y = x + 5$

 f) $2x + y = -7$ and $y = x + 2$

 g) $x + \frac{1}{2}y = -4$ and $y = 2x$

 h) $y = 2x + 3$ and $y = 4x + 2$

 i) $y = 2x - 5$ and $2x + y = 1$

 j) $y = \frac{1}{4}x$ and $x + 2y = 3$

 k) $y = \frac{1}{2}x$ and $x + 2y = 6$

 l) $y = 2x - 1$ and $y = 4x$

 m) $y = 2x + 8$ and $2x + 3y = 4$

 n) $y = x$ and $4x - 2y = 5$

 o) $y = 2x$ and $y = 4x + 3$

4 a) Draw the graphs of $y = x + 3$ and $y = x - 2$.

 b) Explain how this shows that the simultaneous equations $y = x + 3$ and $y = x - 2$ have no solutions.

Example 2

a) Draw the graphs of $y = \frac{1}{2}x - 1$ and $y = x^2 - 5x - 4$ for $-2 \leq x \leq 7$.

b) Solve the simultaneous equations $y = \frac{1}{2}x - 1$ and $y = x^2 - 5x - 4$.

a) $y = \frac{1}{2}x - 1$

x	-2	0	2
y	-2	-1	0

$y = x^2 - 5x - 4$

x	-2	-1	0	1	2	3	4	5	6	7
y	10	2	-4	-8	-10	-10	-8	-4	2	10

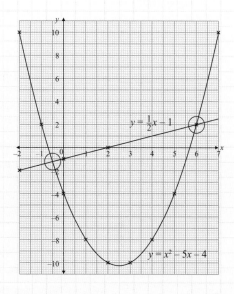

The points where the graphs cross are the solutions to the simultaneous equations. There are two crossing points, so there are two solutions.

b) The graphs intersect at $(6, 2)$ and $(-0.5, -1.25)$.

So the solutions are
$x = 6$ and $y = 2$, and
$x = -0.5$ and $y = -1.25$.

Exercise 2

1   Each of the following diagrams shows the graphs of two simultaneous equations.
Use the graphs to find the solutions to each pair of simultaneous equations.

a)
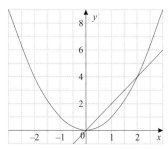

b)
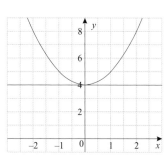

c)
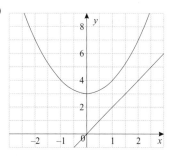

2   For each of the following   **(i)** Draw the graphs for the x-value range given.
   (ii) Use these graphs to solve the pair of simultaneous equations.
   Give your answers correct to 1 decimal place.

a) $y = x - 1$ and $y = x^2 - 3$ $-4 \leq x \leq 4$ **b)** $2x + y = 8$ and $y = x^2$ $-4 \leq x \leq 4$

c) $y = x + 2$ and $y = x^2 + x + 1$ $-4 \leq x \leq 4$ **d)** $x + y = 3$ and $y = x^2 - 3x$ $-3 \leq x \leq 5$

e) $x + y = 1$ and $y = x^2 - 1$ $-4 \leq x \leq 4$ **f)** $y = \frac{1}{2}x$ and $y = x^2 - 3x - 2$ $-3 \leq x \leq 5$

g) $y = x + 6$ and $y = x^2 + 5x + 1$ $-6 \leq x \leq 3$ **h)** $y = \frac{1}{2}x + 1$ and $y = \frac{1}{2}x^2 - 5$ $-6 \leq x \leq 6$

17.4 Solving Quadratic Equations Graphically

You can solve quadratic equations by plotting their graphs.

Example 1

The graph on the right shows
$y = x^2 + 2x - 3$ for $-5 \leq x \leq 3$.

a) Use the graph to solve
   (i) $x^2 + 2x - 3 = 0$ (ii) $x^2 + 2x - 11 = 0$

b) Explain how the graph shows that the
   equation $x^2 + 2x + 3 = 0$ has no solutions.

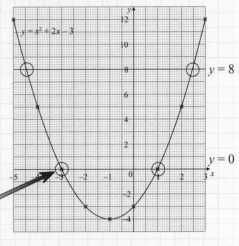

1. For points on the curve, $x^2 + 2x - 3 = 0$ is
   the same as $y = 0$. So the solutions to the
   equation will be the x-values where the
   graph $x^2 + 2x - 3$ cuts $y = 0$ (the x-axis).
   The graph cuts the x-axis twice, so there
   are two solutions.

2. For $x^2 + 2x - 11 = 0$, rearrange the equation to get
   the equation of the graph on the left-hand side.

3. Draw a line at $y = 8$. The solutions are
   the x-values where the graphs cross.

a) (i) **$x = -3$ and $x = 1$**

   (ii) $x^2 + 2x - 11 = 0$
   $x^2 + 2x - 3 = 8$
   $x = 2.5$ and $x = -4.5$ (to 1 d.p.)

b) $x^2 + 2x + 3 = 0$ is equivalent to $x^2 + 2x - 3 = -6$.
   The line $y = -6$ does not cross the graph of
   $y = x^2 + 2x - 3$, so the equation has no solutions.

Exercise 1

1 a) Draw the graph of $y = x^2 + 2x$ for $-5 \leq x \leq 3$.
   b) Use your graph to solve the following equations.
      (i) $x^2 + 2x = 0$ (ii) $x^2 + 2x = 10$ (iii) $x^2 + 2x = 7$

2 a) Draw the graph of $y = x^2 - 3x + 1$ for $-2 \leq x \leq 5$.
   b) Use your graph to solve the following equations.
      (i) $x^2 - 3x + 1 = 0$ (ii) $x^2 - 3x + 1 = 3$ (iii) $x^2 - 3x + 1 = -0.5$

3 a) Rearrange the following equations into the form $x^2 + 4x + a = 0$.
      (i) $x^2 + 4x - 7 = 3$ (ii) $x^2 + 4x - 7 = -4$ (iii) $x^2 + 4x - 7 = -9$
   b) Draw the graph of $y = x^2 + 4x - 7$ for $-7 \leq x \leq 3$.
   c) Use your answers to a) and b) to find the roots of the following equations.
      (i) $x^2 + 4x - 7 = 0$ (ii) $x^2 + 4x - 10 = 0$ (iii) $x^2 + 4x - 3 = 0$ (iv) $x^2 + 4x + 2 = 0$

4 a) Draw the graph of $y = 6 + x - x^2$ for $-4 \leq x \leq 5$.
   b) Use the graph to find the roots of the following equations.
      (i) $5 + x - x^2 = 0$ (ii) $16 + x - x^2 = 0$ (iii) $3 + x - x^2 = 0$ (iv) $10 + x - x^2 = 0$

5 a) Draw the graph of $y = 2x^2 - 3x - 1$ for $-2 \leq x \leq 4$.
   b) Use the graph to solve the following equations.
      (i) $2x^2 - 3x - 1 = 0$ (ii) $2x^2 - 3x - 5 = 0$ (iii) $2x^2 - 3x - 10 = 0$ (iv) $2x^2 - 3x = 0$

Example 2

The equation $y = x^2 + 5x$ is plotted on the graph on the right. By drawing a suitable straight line, use the graph to find the solutions to $x^2 + 6x + 5 = 0$.

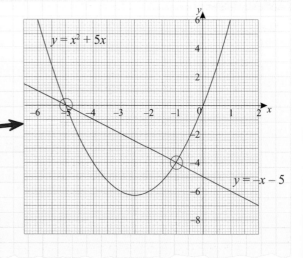

1. Rearrange
    $x^2 + 6x + 5 = 0$ so it
    has $x^2 + 5x$ on one side.

    $x^2 + 6x + 5 = 0$
    $x^2 + 5x = -x - 5$

2. Plot $y = -x - 5$.

3. The solutions to
    $x^2 + 6x + 5 = 0$ are the
    x-coordinates of the
    points where $y = -x - 5$
    and $y = x^2 + 5x$ cross.

    So the solutions to
    $x^2 + 6x + 5 = 0$ are
    $x = -1$ and $x = -5$.

Exercise 2

1   For each of the following:
    (i)   Draw graphs of $y = f(x)$ and $y = g(x)$ on the same axis.
    (ii) Combine the equations by writing $f(x) = g(x)$, then rearrange your
          new equation into the form $ax^2 + bx + c = 0$, where a, b and c are integers.
    (iii) Show that the x-coordinates of the intersection points of the graphs drawn in part **(i)**
          are the solutions to the equation you've written in part **(ii)**.

    a) $f(x) = x + 1$ and $g(x) = x^2 + 3x$, for $-5 \le x \le 2$.
    b) $f(x) = x - 1$ and $g(x) = x^2 - 3x + 1$, for $-2 \le x \le 5$.
    c) $f(x) = -x + 4$ and $g(x) = 6x - x^2$, for $-2 \le x \le 8$.
    d) $f(x) = -x + 2$ and $g(x) = x^2 + 2x - 3$, for $-5 \le x \le 3$.
    e) $f(x) = 2x - 6$ and $g(x) = x^2 - 5x - 4$, for $-2 \le x \le 7$.
    f) $f(x) = x + 4$ and $g(x) = x^2 + 4x - 6$, for $-7 \le x \le 3$.
    g) $f(x) = \frac{1}{2}x - 3$ and $g(x) = 4 + x - x^2$, for $-4 \le x \le 5$.
    h) $f(x) = 2x + 1$ and $g(x) = 2x^2 + x - 4$, for $-3 \le x \le 3$.
    i) $f(x) = 2x^2 - 3x - 2$ and $g(x) = 5 - x$, for $-2 \le x \le 4$.
    j) $f(x) = x + 3$ and $g(x) = 4 - 2x - 2x^2$, for $-4 \le x \le 3$.

2   **a)** Draw the graph of $y = x^2 - 2x$ for $-3 \le x \le 5$.
    b) Rearrange $x^2 - 4x - 1 = 0$ into the form $x^2 - 2x = mx + c$.
    c) By drawing a suitable straight line, use your graph to
        find the solutions to the quadratic equation $x^2 - 4x - 1 = 0$.

3   **a)** Draw the graph of $y = x^2 + 3x - 7$ for $-6 \le x \le 3$.
    b) By drawing a suitable straight line, use your graph to find
        the solutions to the quadratic equation $x^2 - 1 = 0$.

4   **a)** Draw the graph of $y = x^2 + 4x - 9$ for $-7 \le x \le 3$.
    b) Use your graph to find the solutions to the quadratic equation $x^2 + 5x - 11 = 0$.

5   **a)** Draw the graph of $y = x^2 + 2x + 1$ for $-5 \le x \le 3$.
    b) Use your graph to find the solutions to the quadratic equation $x^2 + 3x + 1 = 0$.

6   **a)** Draw the graph of $y = 4x - x^2$ for $-2 \le x \le 5$.
    b) Use your graph to find the solutions to the quadratic equation $5x - x^2 - 5 = 0$.

17.5 Sketching Quadratic Graphs

A **sketch** doesn't have to be completely accurate. Just draw the graph in **roughly** the correct position and label the **important points** — e.g. turning points, y-intercepts and x-intercepts.

Sketching Quadratics using Factorising

Example 1

Sketch the graph of $y = x^2 + x - 6$.
Label the turning point and x-intercepts with their coordinates.

1. Factorise the equation $x^2 + x - 6 = 0$ to find the x-intercepts.
   $x^2 + x - 6 = 0$
   $(x + 3)(x - 2) = 0$
   $x = -3$ and $x = 2$ so the x-intercepts are **(-3, 0)** and **(2, 0)**.

2. Use symmetry to find the turning point — the x-coordinate is halfway between the x-intercepts. Find the y-coordinate by substituting the x-coordinate into the equation.

   x-coordinate $= (2 + -3) \div 2 = -0.5$
   y-coordinate $= (-0.5)^2 + (-0.5) - 6 = -6.25$
   So the turning point has coordinates **(-0.5, -6.25)**.

3. Use this information to sketch the graph — the x^2 term is positive so the graph is U-shaped.

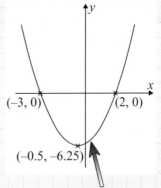

Exercise 1

1 For each of the following equations, find the coordinates of: **(i)** the x-intercepts **(ii)** the turning point
   a) $y = (x - 1)(x + 1)$
   b) $y = (x + 7)(x + 1)$
   c) $y = (x + 10)(x + 6)$

2 Sketch the graphs of these equations. Label the turning points and x-intercepts with their coordinates.
   a) $y = x^2 - 4$
   b) $y = x^2 - 4x - 12$
   c) $y = x^2 + 12x + 32$
   d) $y = x^2 + x - 20$
   e) $y = -x^2 - 2x + 3$
   f) $y = -x^2 - 14x - 49$
   g) $y = 2x^2 + 4x - 16$
   h) $y = 5x^2 - 6x - 8$
   i) $y = -2x^2 - x + 6$

Sketching Quadratics by Completing the Square

Example 2

Sketch the graph of $y = x^2 + 8x - 5$. Label the x-intercepts, y-intercept and turning point.

1. Complete the square, then set $y = 0$ and solve to find the two x-intercepts.
   The completed square form is $y = (x + 4)^2 - 21$.
   Solve $(x + 4)^2 - 21 = 0 \rightarrow x = -4 - \sqrt{21}$ and $x = -4 + \sqrt{21}$
   So the x-intercepts are **$(-4 - \sqrt{21}, 0)$** and **$(-4 + \sqrt{21}, 0)$**.

2. Find the y-intercept by substituting in $x = 0$.
   $y = 0^2 + (8 \times 0) - 5 = -5$ so the y-intercept is **(0, -5)**.

3. The turning point occurs when the brackets of the completed square are equal to 0.
   $(x + 4) = 0$ so $x = -4$ and $y = -21$

4. Sketch and label the graph.

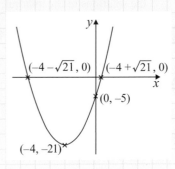

Exercise 2

1 For each of the following equations, find the coordinates of:
   (i) the x-intercepts   **(ii)** the y-intercept   **(iii)** the turning point
   a) $y = (x + 5)^2 - 9$ **b)** $y = (x - 3)^2 - 30$ **c)** $y = (x - 4)^2 - 13$

2 By completing the square, sketch the graphs of the following equations.
   Label the x-intercepts, y-intercepts and turning points where appropriate.
   a) $y = x^2 - 6x - 5$ **b)** $y = x^2 - 4x + 2$ **c)** $y = x^2 + 8x - 6$
   d) $y = x^2 + 2x + 8$ **e)** $y = x^2 - x + 10$ **f)** $y = -x^2 + 10x - 6$

17.6   Gradients of Curves

You can measure the **gradient** at a point on a curve by drawing a **tangent to the curve** at that point.
The gradient of the tangent is equal to the gradient of the curve.

Example 1

The graph of $y = 2x^2 - 5x - 1$ is shown on the right.
Find the gradient of the curve at $x = 2$.

Draw a tangent to the curve
at $x = 2$ and find the gradient
of this line.

$\text{Gradient} = \dfrac{y_2 - y_1}{x_2 - x_1}$

$= \dfrac{6}{2} = \underline{\mathbf{3}}$

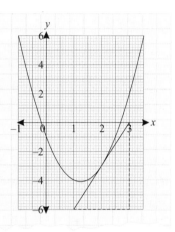

Exercise 1

1 **a)** Draw the graph of $y = x^2$ for $-5 \leq x \leq 5$.
   b) Draw tangents to find the gradient at: **(i)** $x = 4$ **(ii)** $x = -4$
   c) What do you notice about the gradients at these two points?

2 **a)** Draw the graph of $y = 6x - x^2$ for $-2 \leq x \leq 8$.
   b) Write down the gradient of the curve at $x = 3$.

3 **a)** Draw the graph $y = x^2 + 4x$ for $-6 \leq x \leq 2$.
   Find the gradient of the graph at: **(i)** $x = 0$ **(ii)** $x = -5$
   b) Draw the graph $y = x^2 + 3x - 2$ for $-6 \leq x \leq 2$.
   Find the gradient of the graph at: **(i)** $x = 1$ **(ii)** $x = -4$
   c) Draw the graph $y = x^2 + 4x + 5$ for $-6 \leq x \leq 2$.
   Find the gradient of the graph at: **(i)** $x = -3$ **(ii)** $x = 0.5$
   d) Draw the graph $y = 2x^2 + 3x - 2$ for $-4 \leq x \leq 4$.
   Find the gradient of the graph at: **(i)** $x = 0$ **(ii)** $x = 1$ **(iii)** $x = -2.5$

4 **a)** Copy and complete the table on the right for $y = \dfrac{1}{x}$.
   b) Draw the graph of $y = \dfrac{1}{x}$.
   c) Find the gradient of the graph at:
        (i) $x = 2$ **(ii)** $x = 0.2$ **(iii)** $x = 0.6$

x	0.1	0.2	0.5	1	1.5	2	3
y							

5 **a)** Copy and complete the table on the right for $y = \dfrac{1}{x+1}$.

b) Draw the graph of $y = \dfrac{1}{x+1}$.

c) Find the gradient of the graph at:
  (i) $x = -0.4$ **(ii)** $x = 0.5$.

x	−0.9	−0.8	−0.5	0	0.5	1	2
y							

6 **a)** Draw the graph of $y = x^3 - 2x^2 - 8x$ for $-4 \le x \le 3$.

b) Find the gradient of the graph at the points where: **(i)** $x = -3$ **(ii)** $x = 2$

7 **a)** Draw the graph of $y = x^3 + x^2 - 6x$ for $-4 \le x \le 3$.

b) Find the gradient of the graph at: **(i)** $x = -1$ **(ii)** $x = 2$

c) Use your graph to estimate the x-values at which the gradient of the graph is zero.

Tangents to a Circle

Example 2

The graph of $x^2 + y^2 = 25$ is shown on the right.
Find the equation of the tangent at the point $(-3, 4)$.

1. Find the gradient of the radius of the circle at $(-3, 4)$.

   Gradient of radius $= \dfrac{4 - 0}{-3 - 0} = -\dfrac{4}{3}$

2. A tangent and a radius meet at 90° so they
   are perpendicular — if the gradient of the radius
   is m, the gradient of the tangent is $-\dfrac{1}{m}$.

   Gradient of tangent $= -\dfrac{1}{\left(-\frac{4}{3}\right)} = \dfrac{3}{4}$

3. Find the equation of the tangent by substituting $(-3, 4)$ into $y = \dfrac{3}{4}x + c$.

   $4 = \dfrac{3}{4} \times -3 + c$

   $c = 4 + \dfrac{9}{4} = \dfrac{25}{4}$ Equation of the tangent: $y = \dfrac{3}{4}x + \dfrac{25}{4}$

Exercise 2

1 **a)** Sketch the graph of $x^2 + y^2 = 100$.

b) Find the equations of the tangents to the graph at these points:
  (i) $(6, 8)$ **(ii)** $(8, 6)$ **(iii)** $(-8, -6)$ **(iv)** $(-6, 8)$

2 **a)** Sketch the graph of $x^2 + y^2 = 625$.

b) Find the equations of the tangents to the graph at these points:
  (i) $(15, 20)$ **(ii)** $(-7, 24)$ **(iii)** $(-15, -20)$ **(iv)** $(24, -7)$

3 **a)** Find the equation of the tangent to $x^2 + y^2 = 16$ at the point $(-2\sqrt{2}, 2\sqrt{2})$.

b) Find the equation of the tangent to $x^2 + y^2 = 16$ at the point $(2\sqrt{2}, -2\sqrt{2})$.

c) What do you notice about the two tangents from parts **a)** and **b)**?

4 Two tangents are drawn to the circle with equation $x^2 + y^2 = 25$.
The two tangents touch the circle at $(4, 3)$ and $(-4, 3)$.
Find the coordinates where the two tangents intersect.

Section 18 — Functions

18.1 Functions

A **function** is a rule that turns one number (the **input**) into another number (the **output**).

For example, the function $f(x) = x + 3$ is a rule that adds 3 to the input value x.
This function could also be written as $f: x \rightarrow x + 3$.

Example 1

For the function $f(x) = 30 - 2x^2$, find: a) $f(4)$,   b) $f(-2)$

To find $f(4)$, substitute $x = 4$ into $30 - 2x^2$.

a) $f(4) = 30 - 2 \times 4^2$
$= 30 - 2 \times 16$
$= 30 - 32 = \underline{-2}$

Substitute $x = -2$ into $30 - 2x^2$.

b) $f(-2) = 30 - 2 \times (-2)^2$
$= 30 - 2 \times 4$
$= 30 - 8 = \underline{\underline{22}}$

Exercise 1

1   a) $f(x) = x - 5$ Work out: **(i)** $f(11)$ **(ii)** $f(36)$ **(iii)** $f(4)$
    b) $f(x) = 4x$ Work out: **(i)** $f(0)$ **(ii)** $f(7)$ **(iii)** $f(1.5)$
    c) $f(x) = 3x + 4$ Find: **(i)** $f(0)$ **(ii)** $f(1)$ **(iii)** $f(-2)$
    d) $g(x) = 5x - 7$ Calculate: **(i)** $g(3)$ **(ii)** $g(6)$ **(iii)** $g(-1)$
    e) $f(x) = -x$ Write down: **(i)** $f(2)$ **(ii)** $f(17)$ **(iii)** $f(-9)$
    f) $f: x \rightarrow 11 - 2x$ Work out: **(i)** $f(3)$ **(ii)** $f(5.5)$ **(iii)** $f(-5)$

2   a) $g(x) = x^2$ Calculate: **(i)** $g(6)$ **(ii)** $g(-6)$ **(iii)** $g\left(\frac{1}{2}\right)$
    b) $f(x) = x^2 - 4x$ Work out: **(i)** $f(7)$ **(ii)** $f(-3)$ **(iii)** $f(1.5)$
    c) $g: x \rightarrow 20 - 3x^2$ Work out: **(i)** $g(2)$ **(ii)** $g(3)$ **(iii)** $g(-1)$
    d) $h(x) = 2x^2 - x + 4$ Calculate: **(i)** $h(5)$ **(ii)** $h(-2)$ **(iii)** $h(8)$
    e) $f(t) = (4t - 3)^2$ Calculate: **(i)** $f(2)$ **(ii)** $f(0)$ **(iii)** $f(0.75)$

3   a) $g(x) = \dfrac{20}{x}$ Work out: **(i)** $g(10)$ **(ii)** $g(1.25)$ **(iii)** $g(-0.5)$

    b) $g(x) = \sqrt{2x - 1}$ Work out: **(i)** $g(5)$ **(ii)** $g(13)$ **(iii)** $g\left(\frac{5}{8}\right)$

    c) $g: x \rightarrow \dfrac{18}{x^2 + 2}$ Work out: **(i)** $g(0)$ **(ii)** $g(2)$ **(iii)** $g(-4)$

    d) $f(x) = \dfrac{4x - 1}{x + 2}$ Work out: **(i)** $f(0)$ **(ii)** $f(1)$ **(iii)** $f(-3)$

    e) $g(x) = \dfrac{30}{\sqrt{x + 1}}$ Work out: **(i)** $g(3)$ **(ii)** $g(24)$ **(iii)** $g(1.56)$

    f) $h(x) = \sqrt{\dfrac{x}{3x + 1}}$ Work out: **(i)** $h(0)$ **(ii)** $h(1)$ **(iii)** $h(16)$

    g) $f(x) = 8^x - 1$ Work out: **(i)** $f(0)$ **(ii)** $f\left(\frac{1}{3}\right)$ **(iii)** $f\left(-\frac{2}{3}\right)$

    h) $f(t) = 2^{-t} + 5t$ Work out: **(i)** $f(1)$ **(ii)** $f(-3)$ **(iii)** $f(3)$

Example 2

For the function $f(x) = 30 - 2x^2$, find an expression for $f(2t)$.

To find $f(2t)$, replace x with $2t$ and expand.

$$f(2t) = 30 - 2 \times (2t)^2$$
$$= 30 - 2 \times 4t^2$$
$$= \underline{\mathbf{30 - 8t^2}}$$

4 **a)** f: $x \rightarrow 2x + 1$

Find expressions for: **(i)** $f(k)$ **(ii)** $f(2m)$ **(iii)** $f(3w - 1)$

b) $f(x) = 2x^2 + 3x$

Find expressions for: **(i)** $f(u)$ **(ii)** $f(3a)$ **(iii)** $f(t^2)$

c) $f(x) = \dfrac{4x - 1}{x + 4}$

Find expressions for: **(i)** $f(t)$ **(ii)** $f(-x)$ **(iii)** $f(2x)$

d) $f(x) = \sqrt{5x - 1}$

Find expressions for: **(i)** $f(w)$ **(ii)** $f(3x)$ **(iii)** $f(1 - 2x)$

e) $f(x) = 4x^2 - 5x + 1$

Find expressions for: **(i)** $f(h)$ **(ii)** $f(-2x)$ **(iii)** $f\left(\dfrac{1}{x}\right)$

Domain and Range

The **domain** of a function is the set of all the values that can be put into it.
The **range** of a function is the collection of values that 'come out of' the function.
Each value in the domain maps onto a value in the range.

Mapping diagrams show how values in the range correspond to values in the domain.
E.g. Here, the domain of the function $f(x) = 2x$ is {1, 2, 3, 4} and the range is {2, 4, 6, 8}.

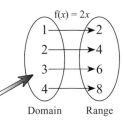

Example 3

The domain of the function $f(x) = x^2 + 1$ is {−1, 0, 1, 2}. Find the range of $f(x)$.

Find all the possible outputs of the function.

$f(-1) = (-1)^2 + 1 = 2$
$f(0) = 0^2 + 1 = 1$
$f(1) = (1)^2 + 1 = 2$
$f(2) = (2)^2 + 1 = 5$

So the range is **{1, 2, 5}**.

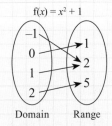

Exercise 2

1 Find the range of each of the following functions.

a) $f(x) = x + 4$ Domain: {1, 2, 3, 4, 5}

b) $f(x) = 3x$ Domain: {−2, −1, 0, 1, 2}

c) f: $x \rightarrow 2x + 5$ Domain: {0, 1, 2, 3, 4, 5}

d) $f(x) = 6x + 1$ Domain: {0, 1, 2, 3}

e) $g(x) = 20 - 3x$ Domain: {−1, 0, 1, 2, 3}

f) $f(x) = x^2$ Domain: {−2, −1, 0, 1, 2}

g) $g(x) = \dfrac{6}{x}$ Domain: {1, 2, 3, 4, 5, 6}

h) $f(t) = 2t^2 - 3t$ Domain: {0, 1, 2, 3, 4}

i) g: $x \rightarrow (2x + 1)^2$ Domain: {−1, 0, 1, 2}

j) $f(x) = \dfrac{30}{x + 1}$ Domain: {0, 2, 4}

Example 4

The domain of the function $f(x) = 3x - 2$ is $1 \le x \le 4$. Find the range of $f(x)$.

For a continuous domain, sketching the graph of the function can help you find the range.

Sketch the graph of $y = 3x - 2$. The marked section of the x-axis represents the domain.

The corresponding part of the y-axis is the range.

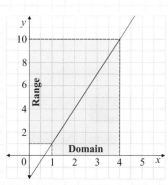

The range of $f(x)$ is $\underline{1 \le f(x) \le 10}$.

In Questions 2-3, find the range of each function.

2
a) $f(x) = x + 2$ Domain: $0 \le x \le 3$
b) $f(x) = x - 1$ Domain: $3 \le x \le 4$

c) $f(x) = 2x$ Domain: $0 \le x \le 2$
d) $f(x) = \frac{x}{4}$ Domain: $-4 < x \le 8$

e) $f(x) = 3x + 4$ Domain: $-1 \le x \le 2$
f) $f(x) = 2x + 5$ Domain: $0 \le x \le 5$

g) $f: x \rightarrow 4x - 3$ Domain: $1 \le x < 4$
h) $f(x) = 5x - 2$ Domain: $-2 < x \le 3$

i) $f(x) = 2x + 7$ Domain: $0 \le x \le 6$
j) $g(x) = 10 - x$ Domain: $1 < x < 7$

k) $g(x) = 12 - x$ Domain: $-2 \le x \le 5$

3
a) $f(x) = 2x^2$ Domain: $2 \le x \le 5$
b) $f: x \rightarrow \sqrt{x}$ Domain: $9 \le x < 64$

c) $f(x) = x^2 - 1$ Domain: $-2 \le x \le 3$
d) $f(x) = 2x^2 + 5$ Domain: $-3 \le x \le 3$

Example 5

a) What values must be excluded from the domain of the function $f(x) = \dfrac{5}{x - 3}$?

  1. You can't divide by zero, so the denominator can't equal zero. x is excluded if $x - 3 = 0$

  2. This is the only restriction on the domain.   The domain must exclude $\underline{x = 3}$.

b) What values must be excluded from the domain of $g(x) = \sqrt{2x - 1}$?

Square roots of negative numbers are not allowed, so x is excluded when the expression inside the square root is less than zero.

x must be excluded from the domain if
$$2x - 1 < 0$$
$$2x < 1$$
$$x < 0.5$$

The domain of $g(x)$ must exclude $\underline{x < 0.5}$.

Exercise 3

1 Find the values which must be excluded from the domain of each of the following functions.

a) $f(x) = -\dfrac{1}{x}$

b) $f(x) = \dfrac{1}{2x + 1}$

c) $f: x \rightarrow \dfrac{3x - 1}{2x + 4}$

d) $f(x) = \dfrac{3}{x^2 - 25}$

e) $g(x) = \sqrt{x}$

f) $g: x \rightarrow \sqrt{x - 1}$

g) $g(x) = \sqrt{3 - 4x}$

h) $g(x) = \sqrt{3 + 10x}$

2 State which, if any, values must be excluded from the domain of each of the following functions.

a) $f(x) = \dfrac{10}{x + 2}$ b) $g(x) = \sqrt{5x - 10}$ c) $f(x) = 2x^2$ d) $f: t \to \dfrac{2}{t^2}$

e) $g: x \to \sqrt{6 - 2x}$ f) $f(x) = \dfrac{1}{x(x - 4)}$ g) $g(x) = \sqrt{7 + \dfrac{x}{3}}$ h) $g(x) = \sqrt{x^2 - 9}$

3 Find the largest possible domain and range of each of the following functions.

a) $f(x) = \dfrac{9}{5x + 3}$ b) $g(x) = 10 - x^2$ c) $f: x \to \sqrt{3x - 15}$ d) $f(x) = \dfrac{1}{x} + 2$

18.2 Composite Functions

If $f(x)$ and $g(x)$ are two functions, then $gf(x)$ is a **composite function**.

$gf(x)$ means 'put x into function f, then put the answer into function g'.
$gf(x)$ is also sometimes written $g(f(x))$.

Example 1

If $f(x) = 3x - 2$ and $g(x) = x^2 + 1$, then:

Calculate the value of $f(3)$,
then use it as the input in g to find $gf(3)$.

Replace x with $g(x)$ in the expression for $f(x)$.

a) Calculate $gf(3)$

$$gf(3) = g(3 \times 3 - 2)$$
$$= g(7) = 7^2 + 1$$
$$= \underline{\textbf{50}}$$

b) Find $fg(x)$

$$fg(x) = f(x^2 + 1)$$
$$= 3(x^2 + 1) - 2$$
$$= 3x^2 + 3 - 2$$
$$= \underline{\textbf{3x}^2 + \textbf{1}}$$

Exercise 1

1 $f(x) = x + 3$, $g(x) = x - 1$ a) Find $g(4)$ b) Use your answer to a) to find $fg(4)$
     c) Find $f(5)$ d) Use your answer to c) to find $gf(5)$

2 $f(x) = 2x$, $g(x) = x + 2$ a) Find $g(1)$ b) Use your answer to a) to find $fg(1)$
     c) Find $f(3)$ d) Use your answer to c) to find $gf(3)$

3

a) $f(x) = x - 5$, $g(x) = 4x$ Find: **(i)** $fg(7)$ **(ii)** $gf(8)$ **(iii)** $gf(x)$

b) $f(x) = 2x - 1$, $g(x) = 3x + 1$ Find: **(i)** $gf(0)$ **(ii)** $fg(2)$ **(iii)** $fg(x)$

c) $f(x) = x + 5$, $g(x) = \dfrac{x}{2}$ Find: **(i)** $fg(8)$ **(ii)** $gf(-1)$ **(iii)** $gf(x)$

d) $f(x) = 9 - x$, $g(x) = 3x$ Find: **(i)** $fg(-2)$ **(ii)** $gf(5)$ **(iii)** $fg(x)$

e) $f(x) = 5x - 4$, $g(x) = \dfrac{x}{4}$ Find: **(i)** $fg(4)$ **(ii)** $gf(4)$ **(iii)** $gf(x)$

f) $f(x) = 2x$, $g(x) = 1 - 3x$ Find: **(i)** $fg(2)$ **(ii)** $gf(-3)$ **(iii)** $fg(x)$

g) $f(x) = 4x + 3$, $g(x) = 5x$ Find: **(i)** $fg(3)$ **(ii)** $ff(2)$ **(iii)** $gf(x)$

h) $f(x) = 2x + 1$, $g(x) = 11 - x$ Find: **(i)** $gf(3)$ **(ii)** $gg(4)$ **(iii)** $fg(x)$

i) $f(x) = \dfrac{1}{x}$, $g(x) = 3x - 7$ Find: **(i)** $fg(3)$ **(ii)** $fg(x)$ **(iii)** $gf(x)$

4 **a)** $f(x) = 10 - x,$ $\quad g(x) = x^2$ Find: **(i)** gf(8) **(ii)** ff(2) **(iii)** gf(x)

b) $f(x) = \sqrt{x},$ $\quad g(x) = 2x + 1$ Find: **(i)** ff(16) **(ii)** fg(40) **(iii)** gf(x)

c) $f(x) = x^2 + 5,$ $\quad g(x) = 3x - 4$ Find: **(i)** gf(−1) **(ii)** gf(x) **(iii)** gg(x)

d) $f(x) = 6 - x,$ $\quad g(x) = 2x^2 - 1$ Find: **(i)** fg(4) **(ii)** fg(x) **(iii)** ff(x)

e) $f(x) = \sqrt{3x + 1},$ $\quad g(x) = 12 - 2x$ Find: **(i)** gf(8) **(ii)** gg(x) **(iii)** fg(x)

Example 2

If $f(x) = x^2$ and $g(x) = 7 - 2x$, find fgf(x).

Find gf(x) first, then use that as the input for f.

$$fgf(x) = fg(x^2)$$
$$= f(7 - 2x^2)$$
$$= \underline{(7 - 2x^2)^2}$$

5 **a)** $f(x) = \dfrac{1}{3x + 2},$ $\quad g(x) = 2x - 5,$ $\quad h(x) = x^2$ Find: **(i)** hgf(−1) **(ii)** fg(x) **(iii)** hf(x)

b) $f(x) = x^3,$ $\quad g(x) = 6 - x,$ $\quad h(x) = 10 - 2x$ Find: **(i)** fgh(4) **(ii)** gh(x) **(iii)** fh(x)

c) $f(x) = 2x + 4,$ $\quad g(x) = \dfrac{1}{3x + 1},$ $\quad h(x) = \sqrt{x}$ Find: **(i)** fh(25) **(ii)** fg(0.5) **(iii)** hgf(x)

d) $f(x) = x^2 + x,$ $\quad g(x) = \dfrac{1}{2x + 3}$ Find: **(i)** ff(3) **(ii)** gf(−1) **(iii)** gf(x)

18.3   Inverse Functions

An **inverse function** reverses the effect of a function. 'The inverse of f(x)' is written **f⁻¹(x)**.

Example 1

Find the inverse of the function $g(x) = \dfrac{7x + 1}{2}$.

1.   Write g(x) out as a function machine.

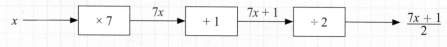

2.   Reverse each step in turn to get the inverse.

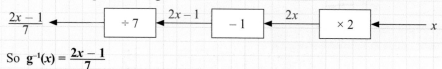

So $g^{-1}(x) = \dfrac{2x - 1}{7}$

Exercise 1

In Questions 1-3, find the inverse of each function.

1 **a)** $f(x) = x + 4$ **b)** $f(x) = x - 3$ **c)** $f(x) = x - 7$ **d)** $f(x) = x + 1$

   e) $f(x) = 8x$ **f)** $g(x) = 2x$ **g)** $g(x) = \dfrac{x}{3}$ **h)** $f(x) = \dfrac{x}{6}$

2 **a)** $f(x) = 4x + 3$ **b)** $f(t) = 2t - 9$ **c)** $g(x) = 3x - 5$ **d)** $f(x) = 8x + 11$

   e) $f(x) = \dfrac{x}{5} - 7$ **f)** $g(x) = \dfrac{x}{8} + 1$ **g)** $f(t) = \dfrac{t - 3}{2}$ **h)** $h(x) = \dfrac{x + 15}{4}$

3 **a)** $f(x) = \dfrac{2x + 6}{5}$ **b)** $g(x) = \dfrac{3x - 1}{4}$ **c)** $f(x) = x^2 - 3$ **d)** $g(x) = (2x + 7)^2$

Example 2

Find the inverse of the function $f(x) = \dfrac{\sqrt{4x-1}}{3}$.

1. Write the equation $y = f(x)$.

   If $y = f(x)$, then $y = \dfrac{\sqrt{4x-1}}{3}$

2. Swap round the x's and y's.

   Let $x = \dfrac{\sqrt{4y-1}}{3}$

3. Rearrange to make y the subject.

   $3x = \sqrt{4y-1}$

   $9x^2 = 4y - 1$

   $9x^2 + 1 = 4y$

   $y = \dfrac{9x^2 + 1}{4}$

4. This is the inverse of $f(x)$.

   $f^{-1}(x) = \dfrac{9x^2 + 1}{4}$

In Questions 4-8, find the inverse of each function.

4 **a)** $f(x) = \dfrac{x}{5} - 8$ **b)** $f(x) = \dfrac{x-6}{4}$ **c)** $f(x) = \dfrac{3x+1}{5}$ **d)** $g(x) = \dfrac{2x}{5} - 7$

5 **a)** $f(x) = 7 - 3x$ **b)** $g(x) = 11 - 4x$ **c)** $f(x) = \dfrac{9-7x}{4}$ **d)** $h(x) = \dfrac{1-6x}{9}$

6 **a)** $f(x) = x^2 - 5$ **b)** $g(x) = 4x^2 + 1$ **c)** $g(x) = (3x-1)^2$ **d)** $h(x) = \dfrac{(1-2x)^2}{5}$

7 **a)** $f(x) = \sqrt{x} - 8$ **b)** $f(x) = 6\sqrt{x} + 1$ **c)** $g(x) = \sqrt{19-2x}$ **d)** $f(x) = 25 - 4\sqrt{x}$

8 **a)** $h(x) = \dfrac{8}{x-1}$ **b)** $f(x) = \dfrac{4}{x} - 7$ **c)** $g(x) = 8 - \dfrac{2}{\sqrt{x}}$ **d)** $f(x) = \sqrt{\dfrac{2}{x-1}}$

9 The inverse of the function $g(x) = \dfrac{1-2x}{3x+5}$ can be found by rearranging the equation $x = \dfrac{1-2y}{3y+5}$.

   a) Show that, if $x = \dfrac{1-2y}{3y+5}$, then $3xy + 2y = 1 - 5x$.

   b) Factorise the expression $3xy + 2y$, and hence find $g^{-1}(x)$.

10 Find the inverse of each of the following functions:

   a) $f(x) = \dfrac{2+3x}{x-2}$ **b)** $g(x) = \dfrac{4x+1}{2x-7}$ **c)** $f(x) = \dfrac{x}{3x+2}$

18.4 Functions Problems

Example 1

Let $f(x) = 4x - 7$ and $g(x) = \dfrac{1}{3x+2}$. Solve the equation $fg(x) = 1$.

1. First find $fg(x)$.

   $fg(x) = f\left(\dfrac{1}{3x+2}\right) = 4\left(\dfrac{1}{3x+2}\right) - 7 = \dfrac{4}{3x+2} - 7$

2. Now let $fg(x) = 1$ and solve for x.

   $\dfrac{4}{3x+2} - 7 = 1$

   $\dfrac{4}{3x+2} = 8$

   $8(3x+2) = 4$

   $24x + 16 = 4$

   $24x = -12$

   $\underline{x = -0.5}$

Exercise 1

1 $f(x) = 5x - 7$ and $g(x) = 2x + 5$
   a) Calculate f(8).
   b) Calculate fg(1).
   c) Solve $f(x) = g(x)$.
   d) Find $g^{-1}(x)$.

2 $f(x) = 4x + 1$ and $g(x) = 2x + 5$
   a) Solve $f(x) = 25$
   b) Find fg(x)
   c) Work out $f^{-1}(x)$

3 $f(x) = 6x + 5$ and $g(x) = \dfrac{x + 3}{2}$
   a) Work out g(11).
   b) Find gf(x).
   c) Work out $g^{-1}(x)$

4 The function $f(x) = 4x - 1$ has domain $0 \le x \le 6$.
   a) Write down the range of function f.
   b) Solve $f(x) = 13$

5 $f(x) = \sqrt{x + 1}$ and $g(x) = 4x$.
   a) What values must be excluded from the domain of f?
   b) Calculate gf(x).
   c) Work out $f^{-1}(x)$.

6 $f(x) = 2x - 3$
   a) Solve $f(x) = 5$.
   b) Find $f^{-1}(x)$.
   c) Solve the equation $f(x) = f^{-1}(x)$
   d) Work out ff(x)

7 $f(x) = 2x - 3$ and $g(x) = 18 - 3x$
   a) Solve $f(x) = g(x)$.
   b) Work out gf(x).
   c) Calculate $g^{-1}(x)$.

8 $f(x) = \dfrac{1}{x} - 5$ and $g(x) = \dfrac{1}{x + 5}$
   a) Calculate g(–3).
   b) Work out fg(x).
      How are functions f and g related?

9 $f(x) = \dfrac{4}{5x - 15}$ and $g(x) = 2\sqrt{x}$
   a) What value of x must be excluded from the domain of f?
   b) Solve $f(x) = 0.2$.
   c) Work out fg(x). What values must be excluded from the domain of fg(x)?

10 $f(x) = 2x^2 + 5$ and $g(x) = 3x - 1$
   a) The domains of functions f and g are the set of all real numbers. What are the corresponding ranges?
   b) Work out gg(4).
   c) Work out $g^{-1}(x)$ and solve $fg^{-1}(x) = 55$.

11 $f(x) = \dfrac{x}{x - 3}$ and $g(x) = x^2 + 3$
   a) Calculate f(5).
   b) Work out $f^{-1}(x)$.
   c) Find fg(x).

12 An object is dropped off the top of a tower.
   The distance, s metres, the object has travelled t seconds after being released is given by the formula $s = f(t)$, where $f(t) = 5t^2$.
   a) Calculate f(4).
   b) Solve the equation $f(t) = 12.8$.

13 The function $f(t) = \dfrac{9t}{5} + 32$ can be used to convert a temperature from degrees Celsius to degrees Fahrenheit.
   a) Find f(20).
   b) Solve the equation $f(t) = 60.8$.
   c) Work out $f^{-1}(t)$.
   d) Explain what your answers to parts a)–c) represent.

14 Jill uses the following formula to estimate the temperature T (in degrees Fahrenheit) at height h (in thousands of feet) above sea level: $T = f(h)$ where $f(h) = 60 - \frac{7}{2}h$.
   a) Calculate f(4).
   b) Find the temperature at a height of 7000 feet above sea level.
   c) Work out $f^{-1}(32)$. Explain what this answer tells you in the context of this question.

Section 19 — Differentiation

19.1 Differentiating Powers of x

The result of **differentiating** $y = x^n$, where n is any number, is $\dfrac{dy}{dx} = nx^{n-1}$

$\dfrac{dy}{dx}$ is also called the **derivative** of y.

Example 1

Differentiate each of the following.

a) $y = x^3$

Multiply by 3, and subtract 1 from the index.

$\dfrac{dy}{dx} = 3 \times x^{3-1} = \underline{\mathbf{3x^2}}$

b) $y = 2x^4$

Differentiate x^4, and multiply by 2.

$\dfrac{dy}{dx} = 2 \times 4 \times x^{4-1} = \underline{\mathbf{8x^3}}$

c) $y = x^2 - 6x + 5$

1. Rewrite the equation as powers of x using $x = x^1$ and $1 = x^0$.

2. Differentiate each term separately.

3. The derivative of x is 1, and the derivative of a constant is 0.

$y = x^2 - 6x^1 + 5x^0$

$\dfrac{dy}{dx} = 2x^{2-1} - 6 \times 1x^{1-1} + 5 \times 0x^{0-1}$

$= 2x^1 - 6x^0 + 0$

$= \underline{\mathbf{2x - 6}}$

Exercise 1

1 Find $\dfrac{dy}{dx}$ for each of the following.

a) $y = x^5$ **b)** $y = x^7$ **c)** $y = x^4$ **d)** $y = x^9$

e) $y = x^3 + x^2 + 2$ **f)** $y = x^6 - x^5 + x^4$ **g)** $y = x^4 + x^2 + 2$ **h)** $y = 3x^4$

i) $y = 8x^3$ **j)** $y = 6x^5$ **k)** $y = 7x^2$ **l)** $y = 4x^6$

m) $y = 3x^2 + 2x + 4$ **n)** $y = 5x^3 - 8x^2 + 3x + 1$ **o)** $y = 7 + 4x - 2x^2$ **p)** $y = 2x^4 + 11x^2 - 5$

q) $y = \frac{1}{3}x^3 - x + 9$ **r)** $y = \frac{3}{5}x^5 - \frac{1}{2}x^2 + 6x$ **s)** $y = \frac{2}{3}x^6 + \frac{5}{2}x^4 - 8x^3$ **t)** $y = \frac{3x^4}{4} - \frac{x^3}{6} + x^2$

Example 2

a) Differentiate $y = \dfrac{3}{x^2} - \dfrac{4}{x} + 2$

1. Rewrite the fractions using negative indices.

2. Differentiate each term separately.

$y = 3x^{-2} - 4x^{-1} + 2$

$\dfrac{dy}{dx} = (3 \times -2x^{-2-1}) - (4 \times -1x^{-1-1}) + 0$

$= -6x^{-3} + 4x^{-2}$

$= -\dfrac{6}{x^3} + \dfrac{4}{x^2}$

b) Differentiate $s = \dfrac{4t^5}{5} - \dfrac{t^3}{6}$

The variables are s and t, so the derivative is $\dfrac{ds}{dt}$, not $\dfrac{dy}{dx}$.

$\dfrac{ds}{dt} = \dfrac{4}{5} \times 5t^{5-1} - \dfrac{1}{6} \times 3t^{3-1}$

$= 4t^4 - \dfrac{1}{2}t^2$

Find the derivative of each of the following equations.

2 a) $y = \dfrac{1}{x^4}$

b) $y = \dfrac{1}{x^3} + \dfrac{1}{x} - x^2$

c) $y = \dfrac{1}{x^2} + \dfrac{8}{x} - 4$

d) $y = \dfrac{4}{x^3} - \dfrac{6}{x^2}$

e) $y = \dfrac{4}{x^2} - 5x^2$

f) $y = 6 - \dfrac{3}{x}$

3 a) $y = x(x + 5)$

b) $y = 3x(x - 4)$

c) $y = x^2(2x - 3)$

d) $y = 2x^3(4x + 1)$

e) $y = (x + 4)(x + 2)$

f) $y = (x - 5)(x + 3)$

g) $y = (x - 4)(x + 4)$

h) $y = (2x + 1)(x + 3)$

i) $y = (3x - 2)(2x + 1)$

j) $y = (x - 2)^2$

k) $y = (2x + 1)^2$

l) $y = \dfrac{1}{x^2}(5 + 3x)$

m) $y = x\left(\dfrac{6}{x^2} - 1\right)$

n) $y = \dfrac{2}{x^3}(3x + 1)$

o) $y = \left(\dfrac{1}{x} + 3\right)\left(\dfrac{2}{x} - 5\right)$

4 a) $a = 15 - 8b - 2b^2$

b) $y = 6t + 5 - 5t^2$

c) $x = 5t^3 + 4t^2 - 2t$

d) $x = \dfrac{2}{3}u^3 + \dfrac{3}{2}u^2 - u + 4$

e) $y = \dfrac{3}{2}z^4 - \dfrac{5}{6}z^3 + \dfrac{7}{2}z^2$

f) $m = \dfrac{n^4 - 2n^3 + n^2}{4}$

g) $r = \dfrac{8 - s^2}{2}$

h) $s = \dfrac{t^2 + 4}{t}$

i) $x = \dfrac{t^3 - 8t^2}{2t}$

19.2 Finding Gradients

The **gradient** of a curve constantly **changes** — and the gradient at any point on a curve equals the gradient of a **tangent** to the curve at that point.

At the point (a, b) on the graph of $y = f(x)$, the gradient is the value of the derivative $\dfrac{dy}{dx}$ when $x = a$.

For this reason, the derivative is sometimes called the **gradient function**.

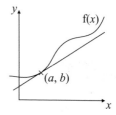

Example 1

A curve has the equation $y = 3x^2 - 5x + 4$.

a) Find the gradient of the curve at the point $(2, 6)$.

   1. Differentiate to find $\dfrac{dy}{dx}$. $\dfrac{dy}{dx} = 6x - 5$

   2. Find the value of $\dfrac{dy}{dx}$ when $x = 2$.   When $x = 2$, $\dfrac{dy}{dx} = 6 \times 2 - 5 = \underline{7}$

b) Find the coordinates of the point on the curve where the gradient is -2.

   1. Solve $\dfrac{dy}{dx} = -2$ to find x when the gradient is -2. $\dfrac{dy}{dx} = -2$ when $6x - 5 = -2$

                                                      $6x = 3$

                                                      $x = 0.5$

   2. Put $x = 0.5$ into the original equation to find the y-coordinate.

                                        $y = 3x^2 - 5x + 4$

                                            $= 3(0.5)^2 - 5 \times 0.5 + 4$

                                            $= 0.75 - 2.5 + 4$

                                            $= 2.25$

           The gradient of the curve is -2 at the point $\underline{\textbf{(0.5, 2.25)}}$.

Example 2

A curve has equation $y = x^2 - \dfrac{16}{x}$.

a) Find the gradient of the tangent to the curve at the point (4, 12).

    1. Differentiate to find $\dfrac{dy}{dx}$.

$$y = x^2 - 16x^{-1}$$
$$\frac{dy}{dx} = 2x^1 - 16 \times -1x^{-2} = 2x + \frac{16}{x^2}$$

    2. Find the value of $\dfrac{dy}{dx}$ when $x = 4$.

When $x = 4$, $\dfrac{dy}{dx} = 2 \times 4 + \dfrac{16}{16} = \mathbf{9}$

b) Find the x-coordinate of the point on the curve where the tangent is horizontal.

If the tangent is horizontal, the gradient must be zero, so solve $\dfrac{dy}{dx} = 0$.

$\dfrac{dy}{dx} = 0$ when $2x + \dfrac{16}{x^2} = 0$

$$2x^3 + 16 = 0$$
$$x^3 = -8$$
$$\underline{x = -2}$$

Exercise 1

1 Find the gradient of the graph of:

a) $y = x^2$ where   **(i)** $x = 5$ **(ii)** $x = -2$

b) $y = 6 - 3x$ where   **(i)** $x = 0$ **(ii)** $x = 2$

c) $y = x^3 - 2x$ where   **(i)** $x = 1$ **(ii)** $x = -1$

d) $y = 2x^2 - 5x + 1$ where   **(i)** $x = 3$ **(ii)** $x = 0.5$

e) $y = 6 - \dfrac{1}{2}x^2$ where   **(i)** $x = 4$ **(ii)** $x = -3$

f) $y = 12 + x - 3x^2$ where   **(i)** $x = -3$ **(ii)** $x = \dfrac{3}{4}$

g) $y = 2x^3 - 4x^2 - 3x + 1$ where   **(i)** $x = -1$ **(ii)** $x = \dfrac{2}{3}$

h) $y = 4x - \dfrac{1}{x^2}$ where   **(i)** $x = 1$ **(ii)** $x = -2$

i) $y = \dfrac{2}{3}x^3 - \dfrac{9}{2}x^2 + x$ where   **(i)** $x = 1$ **(ii)** $x = -2$

j) $y = (2x - 3)(x + 4)$ where   **(i)** $x = -1$ **(ii)** $x = -\dfrac{5}{4}$

2 Find the gradient of the tangent to the graph of:

a) $y = 3x^2 - 7x - 5$ at   **(i)** $(0, -5)$ **(ii)** $(2, -7)$

b) $y = 6 - x - 4x^2$ at   **(i)** $(-1, 3)$ **(ii)** $(2, -12)$

c) $y = x^2(4 - x)$ at   **(i)** $(4, 0)$ **(ii)** $(0, 0)$

d) $y = (x - 2)(x + 3)$ at   **(i)** $(5, 24)$ **(ii)** $(-1, -6)$

e) $y = x - \dfrac{4}{x}$ at   **(i)** $(1, -3)$ **(ii)** $(-2, 0)$

3 a) Find the gradient of the curve $y = x^2 + 7x + 3$ at $x = -3$.
    b) Find the x-coordinate of the point on this curve where the gradient is 15.

4 a) Find the gradient of the curve $y = x^2 + 2x - 7$ at $x = 4$.
    b) Find the x-coordinate of the point on the curve where the gradient is 0.

5 a) Find the gradient of the curve $y = 5 + 3x - x^2$ at $x = 0$.

   b) Find the x-coordinate of the point on this curve where the gradient is 7.

6 a) Find the gradient of the curve $y = x^3 + 2x$ at $x = \frac{1}{2}$.

   b) Find the x-coordinates of the points on this curve where the gradient is 5.

7 a) Find the gradient of the curve $y = x^3 - 4x^2 - 3x + 1$ at $x = 4$.

   b) Find the x-coordinates of the points on this curve where the gradient is 0.

8 a) Find the x-coordinates of the points on the curve $y = \frac{2}{3}x^3 - \frac{7}{2}x^2 + 5x$ where the gradient is 2.

   b) Find the x-coordinates of the points on this curve where the gradient is -1.

9 Find the coordinates of the points on the curve $y = 8 - \frac{16}{x}$ where the gradient is 4.

10 Find the coordinates of the points on the curve $y = \frac{1}{3}x^3 + x^2 - 8x$ where the tangent is horizontal.

11 A curve has equation $y = x^2 - 3x + 1$.

   a) Find the y-coordinate of the point on the curve where $x = 2$.

   b) Find the gradient of the curve at the point where $x = 2$.

   c) Show that the equation of the tangent at the point where $x = 2$ is $y = x - 3$.

12 The equation of a curve is $y = 6 + 5x - x^3$.

   Find the equation of the tangent to the curve at the point with coordinates $(1, 10)$.

19.3 Maximum and Minimum Points

The gradient of a curve is **zero** at **turning points**. A turning point can be either a **maximum** or a **minimum**.

At a **maximum point**, the gradient changes from **positive** to **zero** to **negative**:

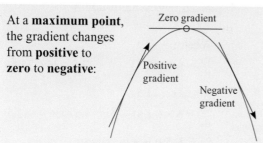

At a **minimum point**, the gradient changes from **negative** to **zero** to **positive**:

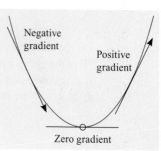

To find the **turning points** of the graph of $y = \mathrm{f}(x)$, solve the equation $\frac{dy}{dx} = 0$.

Example 1

The graph of the equation $y = x^2 - 8x + 3$ has one turning point.
Find the coordinates of the turning point.

1.   Differentiate to find $\frac{dy}{dx}$.

$$\frac{dy}{dx} = 2x - 8$$

2.   Solve $\frac{dy}{dx} = 0$ to get the x-coordinate of the turning point.

$$\frac{dy}{dx} = 0 \quad \text{when} \quad 2x - 8 = 0$$
$$2x = 8$$
$$x = 4$$

3.   Use the original equation to find y when $x = 4$.

So $y = 4^2 - 8 \times 4 + 3$
$y = 16 - 32 + 3$
$y = -13$

The turning point of $y = x^2 - 8x + 3$ is at **$(4, -13)$**.

Exercise 1

1 Find the coordinates of the minimum point of the graphs of each of the following equations.

a) $y = x^2 - 6x + 11$ **b)** $y = x^2 - 2x + 5$ **c)** $y = 2x^2 + 4x + 1$

d) $y = (x - 3)(x + 5)$ **e)** $y = 2x^2 - 12x + 5$ **f)** $y = 3x^2 + 6$

g) $y = 3x^2 + 48x - 2$ **h)** $y = \frac{1}{2}x^2 - 7x + 7$ **i)** $y = 5x^2 + 15x - 3$

2 Find the coordinates of the maximum point of the graphs of each of the following equations.

a) $y = 11 + 8x - 2x^2$ **b)** $y = 5 + 3x - x^2$ **c)** $y = (7 - x)(x - 2)$

d) $y = (3 - x)(x + 8)$ **e)** $y = 9 - 8x - 2x^2$ **f)** $y = 12 + 5x - 5x^2$

g) $y = 4 + 24x - 3x^2$ **h)** $y = 1 - 16x - 4x^2$ **i)** $y = -1 + 2x - 2x^2$

Example 2

The curve $y = 2x^3 - 3x^2 - 36x + 15$ has turning points at $(3, -66)$ and $(-2, 59)$.
Identify whether each of these points is a maximum or a minimum.

1. Differentiate to find $\frac{dy}{dx}$. $\frac{dy}{dx} = 6x^2 - 6x - 36$

2. Find the gradients to the left and right of $(3, -66)$.   When $x = 2.5$,

3. You can use the gradients to sketch
the graph near $(3, -66)$. To the left,
at $x = 2.5$, the graph is decreasing.
To the right, at $x = 3.5$, it's increasing.
So $(3, -66)$ is a minimum.

$x = 2.5$, $x = 3.5$,
negative   positive
gradient   gradient

$(3, -66)$

$\frac{dy}{dx} = 6 \times (2.5)^2 - 6 \times 2.5 - 36 = -13.5$

When $x = 3.5$,

$\frac{dy}{dx} = 6 \times (3.5)^2 - 6 \times 3.5 - 36 = 16.5$

So **(3, –66) is a minimum.**

4. Do the same for $(-2, 59)$.
Here the curve's increasing before
the turning point and decreasing
after it, so it's a maximum.

$(-2, 59)$

$x = -2.5$, $x = -1.5$,
positive   negative
gradient   gradient

When $x = -2.5$,

$\frac{dy}{dx} = 6 \times (-2.5)^2 - 6 \times -2.5 - 36 = 16.5$

When $x = -1.5$,

$\frac{dy}{dx} = 6 \times (-1.5)^2 - 6 \times -1.5 - 36 = -13.5$

So **(–2, 59) is a maximum.**

---

3 **a)** Find $\frac{dy}{dx}$ if $y = x^3 - 3x^2 + 7$.

b) Show that the graph of $y = x^3 - 3x^2 + 7$ has turning points at $(0, 7)$ and $(2, 3)$.

c) For each of the following values of x, find the gradient of the graph of $y = x^3 - 3x^2 + 7$
and describe the shape of the graph at that point.
   (i) $x = -0.5$ **(ii)** $x = 0.5$ **(iii)** $x = 1.5$ **(iv)** $x = 2.5$

d) Using your answers to part (c), explain whether each turning point of
the graph of $y = x^3 - 3x^2 + 7$ is a maximum or a minimum.

4 Find the coordinates of the turning points of each of the following curves,
and identify whether each turning point is a maximum or a minimum.

a) $y = 13 - 2x - x^2$ **b)** $y = x^2 - x + 3$ **c)** $y = 3x(x - 4)$ **d)** $y = 3x^2 - 8x + 2$

5 Find the coordinates of the turning point on the curve $y = \frac{6}{x^2} + 12x$ and identify the type of turning point.

6 Find the coordinates of the turning points of each of the following curves.
Determine the nature of each turning point.

a) $y = 6x^2 - x^3 - 10$

b) $y = x^3 - 6x^2 - 15x + 7$

c) $y = 9x^2 - x^3 - 24x$

d) $y = x^3 - 3x^2 - 9x + 4$

e) $y = 24x - 2x^3 - 7$

f) $y = \frac{1}{3}x^3 + x^2 + \frac{5}{3}$

g) $y = 120x + 3x^2 - 2x^3$

h) $y = 2x^3 + 18x^2 + 48x - 10$

7 Find the coordinates of the turning points on the curve $y = \frac{1}{x^3} - \frac{3}{x}$ and determine their nature.

19.4 Using Differentiation

The derivative $\frac{dy}{dx}$ gives the **rate of change** of y with respect to x, or 'how fast y is changing compared to x'.

Example 1

A water tank used by a garden centre is filled by the rain and emptied as the water is used to water plants.
The volume of water in the tank over a particular week is modelled by the equation $v = 30 + 6t - t^2$,
for $0 \leq t \leq 7$, where v is the volume in litres, and t is the time in days from the start of the week.

a) Find the rate, in litres per day, at which the volume of water is increasing after 2 days.

   1.   Differentiate to find $\frac{dv}{dt}$, the rate of change of v. $\frac{dv}{dt} = 6 - 2t$

   2.   Calculate $\frac{dv}{dt}$ when $t = 2$.   When $t = 2$, $\frac{dv}{dt} = 6 - 2 \times 2 = $ **2 l/day**

b) Find the maximum volume of water in the tank during the week.

   1.   Solve $\frac{dv}{dt} = 0$ to find t at the maximum.   When $\frac{dv}{dt} = 0$,

                                     $6 - 2t = 0$, so $t = 3$

   2.   Find v when $t = 3$.   So $v = 30 + 6 \times 3 - 3^2$

                                          = **39 litres**

Exercise 1

1 The value of shares in a company is modelled by the equation $v = -5t^2 + 30t + 40$, where v is the value in
pence of one share and t is the time in years after the shares were first traded.

a) Find v when $t = 0$.

b) (i)   Solve the equation $-5t^2 + 30t + 40 = 0$.

   (ii) What does the positive solution to
       $-5t^2 + 30t + 40 = 0$ represent?

   (iii) Explain why the negative solution to
       $-5t^2 + 30t + 40 = 0$ doesn't mean anything.

c) The rate of change of the share value is given by $\frac{dv}{dt}$.
Differentiate to find an expression for $\frac{dv}{dt}$.

d) Find t when $\frac{dv}{dt} = 0$.
What was happening to the share value at this point?

e) Copy the axes shown on the right onto graph paper
and draw the graph of $v = -5t^2 + 30t + 40$.

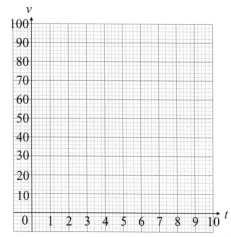

2 An object is thrown up into the air.
Its height (s metres) above the ground after t seconds is given by $s = 2 + 4t - 5t^2$.

a) Work out $\dfrac{\mathrm{d}s}{\mathrm{d}t}$.

b) Find the maximum height the object reaches.

3 The mass, y kg, of a child aged x years old is given by the formula $y = x^3 - 5x^2 + 10x + 3.3$ for $0 \leq x \leq 3$.

a) Work out $\dfrac{\mathrm{d}y}{\mathrm{d}x}$.

b) Find the rate, in kg per year, at which the child's mass is increasing when the child is one year old.

4 The temperature, y °C, of a mug of coffee t minutes after it is made
is given by the equation $y = 0.05t^2 - 4t + 93$ for $0 \leq t \leq 30$.

a) Write down the temperature of the coffee when it is made.

b) At what rate is the temperature decreasing after 10 minutes?

Velocity and Acceleration

Velocity and acceleration are both examples of rates of change.

The **velocity**, v, of an object at time t is
the rate of change of its **displacement**, s:
$$v = \frac{\mathrm{d}s}{\mathrm{d}t}$$

The **acceleration**, a, of an object at time t
is the rate of change of its **velocity**:
$$a = \frac{\mathrm{d}v}{\mathrm{d}t}$$

Example 2

An object travels along a straight line. Its displacement from its starting position
after time t seconds ($t \geq 0$) is s metres. s is given by the formula $s = 5t^2 + 8t - t^3$.

a) Find the velocity of the object after 5 seconds.

1. $v = \dfrac{\mathrm{d}s}{\mathrm{d}t}$ so differentiate the expression for s.

2. Substitute $t = 5$ to find the velocity after 5 seconds.

3. The time is in seconds and the distance in metres,
so the velocity is measured in m/s.

$v = \dfrac{\mathrm{d}s}{\mathrm{d}t} = 10t + 8 - 3t^2$

So when $t = 5$,

$v = 10 \times 5 + 8 - 3 \times 5^2$

$= \underline{-17 \text{ m/s}}$

b) Find the acceleration of the object after 3 seconds.

1. $a = \dfrac{\mathrm{d}v}{\mathrm{d}t}$ so differentiate the expression for v from part a).

2. Substitute $t = 3$ to find the velocity after 3 seconds.

3. The time is in seconds and the velocity in m/s,
so the acceleration is measured in m/s².

$a = \dfrac{\mathrm{d}v}{\mathrm{d}t} = 10 - 6t$

So when $t = 3$,

$a = 10 - 6 \times 3 = \underline{-8 \text{ m/s}^2}$

Exercise 2

1 The displacement (s metres) of a moving object
from its starting point at time t seconds is given by
the equation $s = 10t - t^2$ for $t \geq 0$.

a) Work out $\dfrac{\mathrm{d}s}{\mathrm{d}t}$.

b) Find the velocity at time $t = 2$.

c) Find the time when the velocity is zero.

2 The displacement (s metres) of a moving object
from its starting point at time t seconds is given by
the equation $s = 8t + 3t^2 - t^3$ for $t \geq 0$.

a) Find the displacement at time $t = 1$.

b) Work out $\dfrac{\mathrm{d}s}{\mathrm{d}t}$.

c) Find the velocity at time $t = 2$.

3   An object travels in a straight line.
    Its displacement (s metres) from its starting point at time t seconds is given by $s = 6t^2 - t^3$ for $0 \le t \le 6$.
    a) Find an expression for the velocity of the object at time t.
    b) Show that the object is moving faster at time $t = 2.5$ than at time $t = 3$.
    c) Find the time when the object is at its maximum displacement from the starting point.

4   The displacement (s metres) of an object from a fixed point after t seconds ($t \ge 0$) is given by $s = 6 + 7t - 2t^2$.
    a) Find an expression for the velocity of the object at time t.
    b) Find the velocity of the object at time $t = 1$.
    c) Find the velocity of the object at $t = 4$ seconds.
    d) Find an expression for the acceleration of the object at time t.

Exercise 3 — Mixed Exercise

1   An object is travelling along a straight line.
    Its velocity (v m/s) at time t seconds ($t \ge 0$) is given by the formula $v = 4 + 3t - t^2$.
    a) Find the velocity of the object at time $t = 1$.
    b) Work out $\dfrac{dv}{dt}$.
    c) Find the acceleration of the object at time $t = 1$. Is it speeding up or slowing down at this time?

2   An object is travelling along a straight line.
    Its velocity (v m/s) at time t seconds ($t \ge 0$) is given by the formula $v = 8t - 5t^2$.
    a) Find the velocity of the object at time $t = 0.4$.
    b) Work out $\dfrac{dv}{dt}$.
    c) Find the time when the acceleration of the object is zero.

3   The mass, y kg, of grain harvested from a field when x kg of fertilizer is applied
    is given by the equation $y = -\frac{1}{4}x^2 + 75x + 8000$ for $0 \le x \le 200$.
    a) Work out $\dfrac{dy}{dx}$.
    b) Calculate how much fertilizer should be used in order to harvest the largest possible amount of grain.

4   The velocity (v m/s) of an object moving in a straight line at time t seconds ($t \ge 0$) is given by $v = 4t^2 - 6t + 5$.
    a) Find an expression for the acceleration of the object at time t.
    b) Find the time when the object has its minimum velocity.

5   An object is dropped off the top of a cliff. Its height (s metres) above
    the ground after t seconds ($t \ge 0$) is given by the equation $s = 45 - 5t^2$.
    a) Write down the height of the cliff.
    b) Work out how long it takes for the object to hit the ground.
    c) Work out $\dfrac{ds}{dt}$.
    d) Find the velocity of the object when it hits the ground.

6   An object moves in a straight line. Its velocity (v m/s) after t seconds is given by $v = 2t + \dfrac{8}{t}$ for $t \ge 1$.
    a) Find the velocity of the object after 4 seconds.
    b) Find an expression for the acceleration of the object at time t.

7   An ice cream seller estimates that the profit £P that he makes per day if he sells
    ice creams at £x each is $P = -100x^3 + 150x^2 + 600x - 200$ for $0 \le x \le 4$.
    a) Work out $\dfrac{dP}{dx}$.   b) Calculate the selling price which will give maximum profit.

8   The area, A m^2, of weed on the surface of a pond at time t months is given by $A = 32 - \dfrac{30}{t}$ for $t \ge 1$.
    a) Find the area of pond covered by weed after 2 months.
    b) Find the rate at which the area of weed is increasing after 3 months.

Section 20 — Matrices

20.1 Matrix Addition and Subtraction

An $m \times n$ matrix has m **rows** and n **columns**.
$m \times n$ is the **order** of the matrix.

A **zero matrix** is a matrix where all the entries are 0.

An **identity matrix** is a square matrix where the **leading diagonal** (from top left to bottom right) is filled with 1s, and all the other entries are 0. Identity matrices are usually labelled **I**.

You can add or subtract matrices that have the same number of rows and columns as each other.

$$A = \begin{pmatrix} 1 & 2 \\ 2 & 3 \\ 3 & 4 \end{pmatrix} \quad B = \begin{pmatrix} 1 & 2 & 3 \\ 2 & 5 & 7 \end{pmatrix} \quad C = \begin{pmatrix} 1 & 2 & 3 \\ 2 & 5 & 12 \\ 3 & 8 & 4 \end{pmatrix}$$

3×2 matrix $\qquad 2 \times 3$ matrix $\qquad 3 \times 3$ matrix

$$D = \begin{pmatrix} 0 & 0 & 0 \\ 0 & 0 & 0 \\ 0 & 0 & 0 \end{pmatrix} \qquad I = \begin{pmatrix} 1 & 0 & 0 \\ 0 & 1 & 0 \\ 0 & 0 & 1 \end{pmatrix}$$

3×3 zero matrix $\qquad 3 \times 3$ identity matrix

Example 1

Find $\begin{pmatrix} 6 & 3 \\ 2 & 9 \\ 7 & -1 \end{pmatrix} + \begin{pmatrix} 2 & 8 \\ 11 & 3 \\ 1 & 16 \end{pmatrix}$

Add the numbers in the same place in each matrix. The result goes in that position in the answer.

$\begin{pmatrix} 6 & 3 \\ 2 & 9 \\ 7 & -1 \end{pmatrix} + \begin{pmatrix} 2 & 8 \\ 11 & 3 \\ 1 & 16 \end{pmatrix} = \begin{pmatrix} 6+2 & 3+8 \\ 2+11 & 9+3 \\ 7+1 & -1+16 \end{pmatrix} = \begin{pmatrix} 8 & 11 \\ 13 & 12 \\ 8 & 15 \end{pmatrix}$

Exercise 1

In Questions 1-2, find the resultant matrix for each expression.

1 a) $\begin{pmatrix} 4 & 3 \\ 1 & 2 \end{pmatrix} + \begin{pmatrix} 3 & 2 \\ 8 & 6 \end{pmatrix}$

b) $\begin{pmatrix} 5 & 9 \\ 2 & 0 \end{pmatrix} - \begin{pmatrix} 6 & 3 \\ 3 & 5 \end{pmatrix}$

c) $\begin{pmatrix} 7 & 12 \\ 13 & 19 \end{pmatrix} + \begin{pmatrix} 8 & 10 \\ 12 & 3 \end{pmatrix}$

d) $\begin{pmatrix} 10.8 & 11.3 \\ 12.6 & 13.5 \end{pmatrix} + \begin{pmatrix} 0 & 0 \\ 0 & 0 \end{pmatrix}$

e) $\begin{pmatrix} 14 & 26 \\ 32 & 11 \end{pmatrix} + \begin{pmatrix} 1 & 0 \\ 0 & 1 \end{pmatrix}$

f) $\begin{pmatrix} 6 & -4 \\ 10 & 7 \end{pmatrix} + \begin{pmatrix} -8 & -2 \\ 5 & 1 \end{pmatrix}$

g) $\begin{pmatrix} 25 & 22 \\ -17 & 20 \end{pmatrix} - \begin{pmatrix} -15 & 18 \\ -9 & 16 \end{pmatrix}$

h) $\begin{pmatrix} 49 & 32 \\ 40 & 52 \end{pmatrix} + \begin{pmatrix} 14 & 12 \\ 23 & 17 \end{pmatrix}$

i) $\begin{pmatrix} 31 & 28 \\ 37 & 36 \end{pmatrix} - \begin{pmatrix} 28 & 26 \\ 17 & 19 \end{pmatrix}$

2 a) $\begin{pmatrix} 4 & 7 \\ 9 & 6 \\ 11 & 5 \end{pmatrix} + \begin{pmatrix} 3 & 8 \\ 12 & -3 \\ 2 & 8 \end{pmatrix}$

b) $\begin{pmatrix} -2 & 8 & 14 \\ 9 & -1 & 0 \end{pmatrix} - \begin{pmatrix} 7 & -3 & 8 \\ 6 & 4 & -4 \end{pmatrix}$

c) $\begin{pmatrix} 6 & 17 & 9 \\ 11 & -8 & 10 \\ -2 & 14 & 7 \end{pmatrix} + \begin{pmatrix} 4 & 13 & -4 \\ -1 & -6 & 15 \\ 18 & 3 & -2 \end{pmatrix}$

d) $\begin{pmatrix} 8 & 3 \\ 11 & 9 \end{pmatrix} + \begin{pmatrix} 1 & 7 \\ 2 & 6 \end{pmatrix} + \begin{pmatrix} 5 & 6 \\ -3 & 8 \end{pmatrix}$

3 Find the value of each of the letters in the following equations.

a) $\begin{pmatrix} 4 & a \\ 8 & 12 \end{pmatrix} + \begin{pmatrix} b & 7 \\ 3 & -6 \end{pmatrix} = \begin{pmatrix} 15 & 2 \\ 11 & 6 \end{pmatrix}$

b) $\begin{pmatrix} 1 \\ p \\ -3 \end{pmatrix} + \begin{pmatrix} 5 \\ 7 \\ q \end{pmatrix} = \begin{pmatrix} r \\ 16 \\ -8 \end{pmatrix}$

c) $\begin{pmatrix} 18 & -15 \\ j & 13 \end{pmatrix} - \begin{pmatrix} 10 & k \\ 5 & 6 \end{pmatrix} = \begin{pmatrix} 8 & 3 \\ 12 & m \end{pmatrix}$

d) $\begin{pmatrix} 28 & 16 \\ 19 & 23 \end{pmatrix} + \begin{pmatrix} a & b \\ c & d \end{pmatrix} = \begin{pmatrix} 16 & 32 \\ 24 & 38 \end{pmatrix}$

4 $A = \begin{pmatrix} 1 & 2 \\ 0 & 8 \\ 7 & 2 \end{pmatrix}$ $B = \begin{pmatrix} 0 & -2 & -3 \\ 2 & 1 & 0 \end{pmatrix}$ $C = \begin{pmatrix} 1 & -1 & 3 \\ 6 & 4 & 2 \\ 0 & -8 & -1 \end{pmatrix}$ $D = \begin{pmatrix} 11 & 42 \\ 0 & 19 \\ 21 & 0 \end{pmatrix}$ $E = \begin{pmatrix} -1 & 51 & 43 \\ 16 & -3 & -6 \end{pmatrix}$

Work out the following.

a) $A + D$

b) $B + E$

c) $D - A$

d) $B - E$

e) $E - B$

f) $C + I$

g) $I - C$

h) $A + A + D$

20.2   Matrix Multiplication

Multiplying by a Scalar

To **multiply** a matrix by a **scalar** (number), multiply each entry in the matrix by that number.

Example 1

Find $3\begin{pmatrix} 0 & -1 & 4 \\ 1 & -2 & 5 \end{pmatrix}$

Multiply each number in the matrix by 3.

$$3\begin{pmatrix} 0 & -1 & 4 \\ 1 & -2 & 5 \end{pmatrix} = \begin{pmatrix} 3 \times 0 & 3 \times -1 & 3 \times 4 \\ 3 \times 1 & 3 \times -2 & 3 \times 5 \end{pmatrix} = \begin{pmatrix} 0 & -3 & 12 \\ 3 & -6 & 15 \end{pmatrix}$$

Exercise 1

In Questions 1-3, find the resultant matrix for each expression.

1 a) $2\begin{pmatrix} 3 & 1 \\ 1 & 0 \end{pmatrix}$

b) $8\begin{pmatrix} 7.5 & 6 \\ 12 & 4.2 \end{pmatrix}$

c) $7\begin{pmatrix} -1 & 9 \\ 3 & -2 \end{pmatrix}$

d) $11\begin{pmatrix} -9 & 15 \\ -13 & 18 \end{pmatrix}$

e) $-2\begin{pmatrix} 15 & 30 \\ -19 & 29 \end{pmatrix}$

f) $-\begin{pmatrix} -9 & 32 \\ -13 & -51 \end{pmatrix}$

2 a) $\frac{1}{3}\begin{pmatrix} 3 & 9 \\ 0 & 6 \\ 12 & 0 \end{pmatrix}$

b) $\frac{1}{2}\begin{pmatrix} -10 & 18 & -4 \\ 0 & -12 & 2 \end{pmatrix}$

c) $-\frac{1}{4}\begin{pmatrix} 4 & 0 & 60 \\ 16 & -8 & 44 \\ -2 & 10 & 0 \end{pmatrix}$

3 a) $a\begin{pmatrix} 21 \\ -81 \end{pmatrix}$

b) $-b\begin{pmatrix} -12 & 21 & -48 \\ 0 & -12 & 51 \end{pmatrix}$

c) $\frac{c}{2}(12 \quad -2 \quad 22 \quad -36)$

4 Find the value of each of the letters in the following equations.

a) $3\begin{pmatrix} 4 & a \\ b & c \end{pmatrix} = \begin{pmatrix} 12 & 18 \\ 27 & -6 \end{pmatrix}$

b) $m\begin{pmatrix} -19 \\ 14 \\ -29 \end{pmatrix} = \begin{pmatrix} -114 \\ 84 \\ n \end{pmatrix}$

c) $e\begin{pmatrix} -13 & 8 & f \\ 0 & -21 & g \end{pmatrix} = \begin{pmatrix} 65 & h & -35 \\ 0 & i & 70 \end{pmatrix}$

5 Find the resultant matrix for each of the following expressions.

a) $2\begin{pmatrix} 4 & 0 \\ 1 & 2 \end{pmatrix} + \begin{pmatrix} 3 & 1 \\ 0 & -6 \end{pmatrix}$

b) $3\begin{pmatrix} 4 \\ 6 \\ -2 \end{pmatrix} + 2\begin{pmatrix} -1 \\ 4 \\ 7 \end{pmatrix}$

c) $5\begin{pmatrix} -3 & 1 & 3 \\ 6 & -2 & 4 \end{pmatrix} - 4\begin{pmatrix} 5 & 1 & -5 \\ -2 & -1 & 7 \end{pmatrix}$

6 $\mathbf{A} = \begin{pmatrix} 0 & -2 & -3 \\ 2 & 1 & 0 \end{pmatrix}$ $\mathbf{B} = \begin{pmatrix} 1 & -20 & -30 \\ 5 & 11 & 0 \end{pmatrix}$ $\mathbf{C} = \begin{pmatrix} -45 & -26 & 3 \\ 22 & 0 & -6 \end{pmatrix}$

Work out the following.

a) $-12\mathbf{A}$ b) $\mathbf{A} + 2\mathbf{B}$ c) $3\mathbf{A} - \mathbf{B}$
d) $2\mathbf{C} - 4\mathbf{A}$ e) $11\mathbf{A} + 3\mathbf{B}$ f) $\mathbf{C} - 2\mathbf{B}$

Multiplying Matrices

You can **multiply two matrices** together if the number of columns in the first matrix is equal to the number of rows in the second matrix. Multiplying an $m \times n$ matrix by an $n \times p$ matrix gives an $m \times p$ matrix.

Multiply matrices using the following method:
$$\begin{pmatrix} a & b & c \\ d & e & f \end{pmatrix} \begin{pmatrix} u & x \\ v & y \\ w & z \end{pmatrix} = \begin{pmatrix} au + bv + cw & ax + by + cz \\ du + ev + fw & dx + ey + fz \end{pmatrix}$$

Example 2

$\mathbf{A} = \begin{pmatrix} 2 & 3 \\ 0 & 1 \\ 4 & 5 \end{pmatrix}$, $\mathbf{B} = \begin{pmatrix} 2 & 3 \\ 5 & -1 \end{pmatrix}$. Find $\mathbf{C} = \mathbf{AB}$.

1. Combine the <u>first row</u> of **A** with the <u>first column</u> of **B** to get the entry in the <u>first row</u> and <u>first column</u> of **C**.

$\begin{pmatrix} 2 & 3 \\ 0 & 1 \\ 4 & 5 \end{pmatrix} \begin{pmatrix} 2 & 3 \\ 5 & -1 \end{pmatrix} \rightarrow \begin{pmatrix} (2 \times 2) + (3 \times 5) & \\ & \end{pmatrix}$

2. Combine the <u>first row</u> of **A** with the <u>second column</u> of **B** to get the entry in the <u>first row</u> and <u>second column</u> of **C**.

$\begin{pmatrix} 2 & 3 \\ 0 & 1 \\ 4 & 5 \end{pmatrix} \begin{pmatrix} 2 & 3 \\ 5 & -1 \end{pmatrix} \rightarrow \begin{pmatrix} 19 & (2 \times 3) + (3 \times -1) \\ & \end{pmatrix}$

3. Continue in this way until you have multiplied every row of **A** by every column of **B**.

$\mathbf{C} = \mathbf{AB} = \begin{pmatrix} 19 & 3 \\ (0 \times 2) + (1 \times 5) & (0 \times 3) + (1 \times -1) \\ (4 \times 2) + (5 \times 5) & (4 \times 3) + (5 \times -1) \end{pmatrix}$

$= \begin{pmatrix} 19 & 3 \\ 5 & -1 \\ 33 & 7 \end{pmatrix}$

Exercise 2

1 In each of the following, copy the calculation and fill in the blanks to complete the matrix multiplication.

a) $\begin{pmatrix} 2 & 4 \\ 1 & 3 \end{pmatrix} \begin{pmatrix} 4 & 5 \\ 0 & 1 \end{pmatrix} = \begin{pmatrix} (2 \times 4) + (4 \times \square) & (2 \times \square) + (4 \times 1) \\ (1 \times 4) + (\square \times 0) & (1 \times \square) + (\square \times \square) \end{pmatrix} = \begin{pmatrix} 8 & \square \\ \square & 8 \end{pmatrix}$

b) $\begin{pmatrix} 1 & 0 \\ 2 & 5 \\ 4 & 1 \end{pmatrix} \begin{pmatrix} 3 & 1 & -1 \\ 2 & 0 & -2 \end{pmatrix} = \begin{pmatrix} (1 \times 3) + (0 \times \square) & (1 \times \square) + (\square \times 0) & (\square \times -1) + (0 \times -2) \\ (\square \times 3) + (\square \times 2) & (2 \times \square) + (5 \times \square) & (2 \times -1) + (5 \times \square) \\ (4 \times \square) + (\square \times \square) & (4 \times 1) + (\square \times 0) & (4 \times \square) + (\square \times \square) \end{pmatrix} = \begin{pmatrix} 3 & \square & \square \\ \square & \square & \square \\ \square & \square & \square \end{pmatrix}$

In Questions 2-4, find the resultant matrix for each expression.

2 a) $\begin{pmatrix} 1 & 3 \\ 4 & 2 \end{pmatrix} \begin{pmatrix} a & b \\ c & d \end{pmatrix}$ **b)** $\begin{pmatrix} -1 & 2 \\ 0 & -4 \end{pmatrix} \begin{pmatrix} p & q \\ r & s \end{pmatrix}$ **c)** $\begin{pmatrix} 11 & 13 \\ -12 & 21 \end{pmatrix} \begin{pmatrix} w & x \\ y & z \end{pmatrix}$

3 a) $\begin{pmatrix} 1 & 2 \\ 3 & 0 \end{pmatrix}\begin{pmatrix} 2 & 4 \\ 6 & 7 \end{pmatrix}$

b) $\begin{pmatrix} -1 & 9 \\ 13 & -4 \end{pmatrix}\begin{pmatrix} 11 & 14 \\ -6 & 0 \end{pmatrix}$

c) $\begin{pmatrix} 31 & 12 \\ 22 & 7 \end{pmatrix}\begin{pmatrix} 1 & -4 \\ -16 & -1 \end{pmatrix}$

d) $\begin{pmatrix} 12 & 17 \\ 99 & 26 \end{pmatrix}\begin{pmatrix} 0 & 0 \\ 0 & 0 \end{pmatrix}$

e) $\begin{pmatrix} -5 & 2 \\ -4 & -1 \end{pmatrix}\begin{pmatrix} 1 & 0 \\ 0 & 1 \end{pmatrix}$

f) $\begin{pmatrix} 1 & 0 \\ 0 & 1 \end{pmatrix}\begin{pmatrix} -9 & 8 \\ -5 & 4 \end{pmatrix}$

g) $\begin{pmatrix} 11 & 7 \\ 13 & 6 \end{pmatrix}\begin{pmatrix} -10 & -2 \\ -8 & -4 \end{pmatrix}$

h) $\begin{pmatrix} -25 & -7 \\ -30 & -11 \end{pmatrix}\begin{pmatrix} -15 & -34 \\ -20 & -55 \end{pmatrix}$

i) $\begin{pmatrix} 31 & 18 \\ -32 & -40 \end{pmatrix}\begin{pmatrix} -19 & 48 \\ -65 & 47 \end{pmatrix}$

4 a) $\begin{pmatrix} 2 & 10 \\ 5 & 4 \\ 6 & 3 \end{pmatrix}\begin{pmatrix} 4 & 5 & 6 \\ -1 & 3 & 2 \end{pmatrix}$

b) $\begin{pmatrix} 1 & 13 \\ 0 & 21 \\ -4 & -5 \end{pmatrix}\begin{pmatrix} 12 & 4 & 30 \\ 5 & 1 & -10 \end{pmatrix}$

c) $\begin{pmatrix} 10 & 14 & -3 \\ 6 & 0 & -12 \end{pmatrix}\begin{pmatrix} 5 & 6 \\ 7 & 8 \\ -3 & -1 \end{pmatrix}$

d) $\begin{pmatrix} -11 & 7 & 13 \\ 20 & -6 & 5 \end{pmatrix}\begin{pmatrix} -1 & 7 \\ 8 & 1 \\ -5 & -11 \end{pmatrix}$

e) $\begin{pmatrix} 4 \\ -12 \end{pmatrix}(15 \ \ -9)$

f) $(-10 \ \ 7 \ \ 5)\begin{pmatrix} -12 \\ -1 \\ -9 \end{pmatrix}$

g) $\begin{pmatrix} 19 & -27 & 41 \\ -52 & 36 & 61 \\ 24 & -11 & -16 \end{pmatrix}\begin{pmatrix} 1 & 0 & 0 \\ 0 & 1 & 0 \\ 0 & 0 & 1 \end{pmatrix}$

h) $\begin{pmatrix} 1 & 2 & 1 \\ -5 & 3 & 10 \\ 0 & 1 & -1 \end{pmatrix}\begin{pmatrix} 0 & 3 & -3 \\ 0 & 1 & 2 \\ 0 & -2 & 1 \end{pmatrix}$

i) $\begin{pmatrix} 4 & 0 & 6 \\ 8 & -2 & 11 \\ -3 & 1 & 5 \end{pmatrix}\begin{pmatrix} 5 & -3 & -1 \\ 1 & 4 & 8 \\ 0 & 4 & 9 \end{pmatrix}$

5 For each of the following, find the order of the resultant matrix (you do not have to multiply the matrices).

a) $\begin{pmatrix} 1 & 1 \\ 3 & 0 \end{pmatrix}\begin{pmatrix} 1 & 4 \\ 3 & 5 \end{pmatrix}$

b) $\begin{pmatrix} 1 & 4 & -1 \\ 6 & 1 & -2 \end{pmatrix}\begin{pmatrix} 0 & 6 \\ 17 & 9 \\ -2 & 1 \end{pmatrix}$

c) $\begin{pmatrix} 2 & 1 \\ 5 & 9 \\ 7 & 1 \end{pmatrix}\begin{pmatrix} 41 & 2 & 6 \\ -1 & 3 & 0 \end{pmatrix}$

d) $\begin{pmatrix} 1 & 1 \\ 3 & 0 \end{pmatrix}\begin{pmatrix} 4 & 8 & 9 \\ 1 & 3 & 0 \end{pmatrix}$

e) $\begin{pmatrix} 1 \\ 2 \end{pmatrix}(1 \ \ 3)$

f) $(-1 \ \ 0 \ \ 2)\begin{pmatrix} 2 \\ 3 \\ 0 \end{pmatrix}$

6 $\mathbf{A} = \begin{pmatrix} 1 & -2 \\ 5 & 3 \end{pmatrix}$ $\mathbf{B} = \begin{pmatrix} 0 & 4 \\ 1 & -6 \end{pmatrix}$ $\mathbf{C} = \begin{pmatrix} -2 & 16 \\ 3 & 2 \end{pmatrix}$ $\mathbf{D} = \begin{pmatrix} 4 & -7 & 1 \\ -6 & 3 & -2 \end{pmatrix}$

a) Show that: **(i) BI = B** **(ii) AB = C** **(iii) AC ≠ CA**

b) Find $\mathbf{A}^2$ (where $\mathbf{A}^2 = \mathbf{AA}$).

c) (i) Find **BC**. **(ii)** Find **CA**. **(iii)** Hence show that **(BC)A = B(CA)**.

d) Find **CAB**.

e) Explain why you can't work out **DA**.

f) **D** is multiplied by another matrix, **E**, of order 3 × 5. The result is matrix **F**. What is the order of **F**?

Example 3

Find the values of a, b, c and d if $\begin{pmatrix} a & b \\ c & d \end{pmatrix}\begin{pmatrix} 1 & 2 & 0 \\ 2 & 1 & 2 \end{pmatrix} = \begin{pmatrix} 7 & 5 & 6 \\ 0 & 3 & -2 \end{pmatrix}$.

1. Multiply the matrices to find an expression for the resultant.

$\begin{pmatrix} a & b \\ c & d \end{pmatrix}\begin{pmatrix} 1 & 2 & 0 \\ 2 & 1 & 2 \end{pmatrix} = \begin{pmatrix} a+2b & 2a+b & 2b \\ c+2d & 2c+d & 2d \end{pmatrix}$

2. Put this equal to the result given in the question.

$\begin{pmatrix} a+2b & 2a+b & 2b \\ c+2d & 2c+d & 2d \end{pmatrix} = \begin{pmatrix} 7 & 5 & 6 \\ 0 & 3 & -2 \end{pmatrix}$

3. Put corresponding entries equal to each other and solve to find the unknowns.

$2b = 6$, so $\underline{\mathbf{b = 3}}$

$2d = -2$, so $\underline{\mathbf{d = -1}}$

$a + 2b = 7$, so $\underline{\mathbf{a}} = 7 - 2b = 7 - (2 \times 3) = \underline{\mathbf{1}}$

$c + 2d = 0$, so $\underline{\mathbf{c}} = -2d = -2 \times -1 = \underline{\mathbf{2}}$

7 Find the value of each of the letters in the following equations.

a) $\begin{pmatrix} 4 & a \\ 5 & b \end{pmatrix}\begin{pmatrix} 1 & 2 \\ 0 & 3 \end{pmatrix} = \begin{pmatrix} 4 & 11 \\ 5 & 4 \end{pmatrix}$

b) $(1 \quad -3 \quad 10)\begin{pmatrix} 4 \\ p \\ -2 \end{pmatrix} = (-49)$

c) $\begin{pmatrix} -3 & x & 4 \\ w & -12 & 8 \end{pmatrix}\begin{pmatrix} 1 & -4 \\ 3 & 0 \\ -2 & 11 \end{pmatrix} = \begin{pmatrix} -35 & y \\ -14 & -64 \end{pmatrix}$

d) $\begin{pmatrix} 2 & -1 \\ 5 & 6 \\ 3 & -9 \end{pmatrix}\begin{pmatrix} l & -6 & 9 \\ -5 & m & 7 \end{pmatrix} = \begin{pmatrix} 25 & -20 & 11 \\ 20 & 18 & 87 \\ 75 & -90 & n \end{pmatrix}$

8 Find the values of a, b, c and d in each of the following.

a) $\begin{pmatrix} a & b \\ c & d \end{pmatrix}\begin{pmatrix} 1 & 0 \\ 2 & 3 \end{pmatrix} = \begin{pmatrix} 0 & -3 \\ 10 & 9 \end{pmatrix}$

b) $\begin{pmatrix} a & b \\ c & d \end{pmatrix}\begin{pmatrix} 8 & 0 \\ 1 & 3 \end{pmatrix} = \begin{pmatrix} -13 & 9 \\ -3 & -9 \end{pmatrix}$

c) $\begin{pmatrix} a & b \\ c & d \end{pmatrix}\begin{pmatrix} 4 & 1 & 3 \\ 0 & 2 & 2 \end{pmatrix} = \begin{pmatrix} 12 & 7 & 13 \\ 4 & 11 & 13 \end{pmatrix}$

20.3   Inverse Matrices and Determinants

The Determinant

The **determinant**, $|A|$, of the 2×2 matrix $\mathbf{A} = \begin{pmatrix} a & b \\ c & d \end{pmatrix}$ is given by: $\boxed{|\mathbf{A}| = ad - bc}$

Example 1

Find the determinant of the matrix $\mathbf{A} = \begin{pmatrix} 8 & -1 \\ 5 & 4 \end{pmatrix}$

If $\begin{pmatrix} a & b \\ c & d \end{pmatrix} = \begin{pmatrix} 8 & -1 \\ 5 & 4 \end{pmatrix}$, then $a = 8$,

$b = -1$, $c = 5$ and $d = 4$.

$|\mathbf{A}| = (8 \times 4) - (-1 \times 5) = 32 - (-5)$

$\qquad = \underline{37}$

Exercise 1

1 Find the determinant of each of the following matrices.

a) $\begin{pmatrix} 2 & 1 \\ 3 & 5 \end{pmatrix}$

b) $\begin{pmatrix} 1 & 0 \\ 0 & 1 \end{pmatrix}$

c) $\begin{pmatrix} 0 & 2 \\ 3 & 0 \end{pmatrix}$

d) $\begin{pmatrix} 7 & -4 \\ 6 & 12 \end{pmatrix}$

e) $\begin{pmatrix} -15 & 7 \\ 8 & 4 \end{pmatrix}$

f) $\begin{pmatrix} -21 & -12 \\ 9 & 5 \end{pmatrix}$

g) $\begin{pmatrix} 35 & -11 \\ -13 & 3 \end{pmatrix}$

h) $\begin{pmatrix} -23 & -41 \\ -13 & -15 \end{pmatrix}$

i) $\begin{pmatrix} 1 & b \\ 5 & a \end{pmatrix}$

j) $\begin{pmatrix} -2 & -13 \\ 4 & p \end{pmatrix}$

k) $\begin{pmatrix} k & m \\ n & l \end{pmatrix}$

l) $\begin{pmatrix} p & -1 \\ -1 & p \end{pmatrix}$

m) $\begin{pmatrix} c & 12 \\ c & 5 \end{pmatrix}$

n) $\begin{pmatrix} -f & -g \\ 14 & -4 \end{pmatrix}$

o) $\begin{pmatrix} 2w & x \\ 3y & w \end{pmatrix}$

p) $\begin{pmatrix} s & -t \\ -2 & 2s \end{pmatrix}$

2 By first calculating the resultant matrix for each expression, find the determinant of each of the following.

a) $\begin{pmatrix} 11 & 12 \\ 0 & -2 \end{pmatrix} + \begin{pmatrix} 7 & -3 \\ 0 & 2 \end{pmatrix}$

b) $\begin{pmatrix} 21 & -32 \\ 43 & -41 \end{pmatrix} - \begin{pmatrix} 17 & -12 \\ -11 & 13 \end{pmatrix}$

c) $5\begin{pmatrix} 12 & 5 \\ 10 & -4 \end{pmatrix}$

d) $\frac{1}{2}\begin{pmatrix} 4 & 24 \\ 12 & 8 \end{pmatrix}$

e) $-2\begin{pmatrix} 13 & 8 \\ 7 & -2 \end{pmatrix}$

f) $-\begin{pmatrix} -11 & -20 \\ 3 & 6 \end{pmatrix}$

g) $\begin{pmatrix} 1 & -2 \\ 0 & 4 \end{pmatrix}\begin{pmatrix} -12 & 2 \\ 5 & -7 \end{pmatrix}$

h) $\begin{pmatrix} 7 & -3 \\ 3 & -10 \end{pmatrix}\begin{pmatrix} -2 & -4 \\ -11 & 10 \end{pmatrix}$

i) $\begin{pmatrix} 8 & 1 & -2 \\ 4 & 0 & -11 \end{pmatrix}\begin{pmatrix} -5 & 8 \\ 12 & 7 \\ 6 & -1 \end{pmatrix}$

Inverse Matrices

The **inverse**, $\mathbf{A}^{-1}$, of the matrix $\mathbf{A}$ is the matrix that satisfies $\mathbf{AA}^{-1} = \mathbf{A}^{-1}\mathbf{A} = \mathbf{I}$.

The inverse of the 2 × 2 matrix $\mathbf{A} = \begin{pmatrix} a & b \\ c & d \end{pmatrix}$ is given by: $\mathbf{A}^{-1} = \dfrac{1}{(ad - bc)}\begin{pmatrix} d & -b \\ -c & a \end{pmatrix}$

$\mathbf{A}$ only has an inverse if its **determinant** is **non-zero** — i.e. if $ad - bc \neq 0$.
If its determinant is equal to zero, then a matrix is said to be **singular**.

Example 2

Find the inverse of the matrix $\mathbf{A} = \begin{pmatrix} 4 & 8 \\ 2 & 6 \end{pmatrix}$

1. Find the determinant. $|\mathbf{A}| = (4 \times 6) - (2 \times 8) = 24 - 16 = 8$

2. Use the formula to find the inverse — $\mathbf{A}^{-1} = \dfrac{1}{8}\begin{pmatrix} 6 & -8 \\ -2 & 4 \end{pmatrix}$
   simplify your answer if necessary.

3. You can check your answer by $= \dfrac{1}{4}\begin{pmatrix} 3 & -4 \\ -1 & 2 \end{pmatrix}$
   checking that $\mathbf{AA}^{-1} = \mathbf{I}$.

Exercise 2

1 Show that each of the following matrices is singular.

a) $\begin{pmatrix} 4 & 8 \\ 2 & 4 \end{pmatrix}$

b) $\begin{pmatrix} 1 & -2 \\ 3 & -6 \end{pmatrix}$

c) $\begin{pmatrix} 25 & -5 \\ -15 & 3 \end{pmatrix}$

d) $\begin{pmatrix} -6 & -28 \\ -3 & -14 \end{pmatrix}$

2 Verify that $\begin{pmatrix} 8 & -5 \\ 3 & -2 \end{pmatrix}$ is the inverse of $\begin{pmatrix} 2 & -5 \\ 3 & -8 \end{pmatrix}$.

3 Verify that $-\dfrac{1}{6}\begin{pmatrix} 9 & -8 \\ -12 & 10 \end{pmatrix}$ is the inverse of $\begin{pmatrix} 10 & 8 \\ 12 & 9 \end{pmatrix}$.

4 Find the inverse of each of the following matrices where possible, or show that the matrix is singular.

a) $\begin{pmatrix} 5 & 6 \\ 3 & 4 \end{pmatrix}$

b) $\begin{pmatrix} 5 & 8 \\ 4 & 6 \end{pmatrix}$

c) $\begin{pmatrix} 3 & 10 \\ 2 & 8 \end{pmatrix}$

d) $\begin{pmatrix} 7 & 3 \\ 3 & 2 \end{pmatrix}$

e) $\begin{pmatrix} 6 & 7 \\ 5 & 7 \end{pmatrix}$

f) $\begin{pmatrix} 6 & 3 \\ 8 & 4 \end{pmatrix}$

g) $\begin{pmatrix} 12 & 9 \\ 4 & 3 \end{pmatrix}$

h) $\begin{pmatrix} 14 & 6 \\ 7 & 3 \end{pmatrix}$

i) $\begin{pmatrix} 3 & -2 \\ 2 & 1 \end{pmatrix}$

j) $\begin{pmatrix} 4 & -2 \\ -8 & 4 \end{pmatrix}$

k) $\begin{pmatrix} -4 & 12 \\ -5 & 15 \end{pmatrix}$

l) $\begin{pmatrix} -1 & 13 \\ 2 & 4 \end{pmatrix}$

m) $\begin{pmatrix} -12 & -3 \\ 22 & 4 \end{pmatrix}$

n) $\begin{pmatrix} -14 & 21 \\ -8 & 12 \end{pmatrix}$

o) $\begin{pmatrix} -8 & -21 \\ -7 & -18 \end{pmatrix}$

p) $\begin{pmatrix} -31 & -16 \\ -41 & 17 \end{pmatrix}$

5 For each of the following: **(i)** Find the values of x that make the matrix singular.
                                   (ii) Find the inverse, assuming the matrix is not singular.

a) $\begin{pmatrix} x & 12 \\ 2 & 1 \end{pmatrix}$

b) $\begin{pmatrix} x & 3 \\ x & 4 \end{pmatrix}$

c) $\begin{pmatrix} x & -11 \\ 0 & x \end{pmatrix}$

d) $\begin{pmatrix} 2x & 1 \\ -x & x \end{pmatrix}$

6 By first calculating the resultant matrix for each expression, find the inverse of each of the following.

a) $6\begin{pmatrix} 21 & 15 \\ -12 & -4 \end{pmatrix}$

b) $\begin{pmatrix} 4 & -2 \\ 3 & 4 \end{pmatrix}\begin{pmatrix} -1 & -2 \\ 6 & 8 \end{pmatrix}$

c) $\begin{pmatrix} 0 & -1 \\ -6 & 5 \end{pmatrix}\begin{pmatrix} -21 & 3 \\ 6 & -4 \end{pmatrix}$

7 a) Find X^{-1} if $X = \begin{pmatrix} 26 & -31 \\ -5 & 6 \end{pmatrix}$.

b) Hence show that $XX^{-1} = X^{-1}X$.

8 Given the matrix $Y = \begin{pmatrix} -38 & 53 \\ 5 & -7 \end{pmatrix}$, show that $(Y^{-1})^{-1} = Y$.

9 Given the matrices $P = \begin{pmatrix} -7 & 11 \\ -3 & 4 \end{pmatrix}$ and $Q = \begin{pmatrix} 1 & 0 \\ 5 & -4 \end{pmatrix}$, show that $(PQ)^{-1} = Q^{-1}P^{-1}$.

Using Inverse Matrices

You can use the fact that $AA^{-1} = I$ to **solve equations** that involve matrices.

If $\;AB = X\;$ then $\;B = A^{-1}X\;$ and $\;A = XB^{-1}$

Example 3

Find B if $A = \begin{pmatrix} 3 & -4 \\ 2 & 1 \end{pmatrix}$ and $AB = \begin{pmatrix} -10 & -12 \\ -3 & 3 \end{pmatrix}$

$$\begin{pmatrix} 3 & -4 \\ 2 & 1 \end{pmatrix} B = \begin{pmatrix} -10 & -12 \\ -3 & 3 \end{pmatrix}$$

1. Use the fact that if $AB = X$ then $B = A^{-1}X$ to form an equation for B.

$$B = \begin{pmatrix} 3 & -4 \\ 2 & 1 \end{pmatrix}^{-1} \begin{pmatrix} -10 & -12 \\ -3 & 3 \end{pmatrix}$$

2. Find the inverse of A.

$$\begin{pmatrix} 3 & -4 \\ 2 & 1 \end{pmatrix}^{-1} = \frac{1}{3 - (-8)}\begin{pmatrix} 1 & 4 \\ -2 & 3 \end{pmatrix} = \frac{1}{11}\begin{pmatrix} 1 & 4 \\ -2 & 3 \end{pmatrix}$$

3. Multiply to find B.

$$\text{So } B = \frac{1}{11}\begin{pmatrix} 1 & 4 \\ -2 & 3 \end{pmatrix}\begin{pmatrix} -10 & -12 \\ -3 & 3 \end{pmatrix} = \frac{1}{11}\begin{pmatrix} -22 & 0 \\ 11 & 33 \end{pmatrix}$$

$$B = \begin{pmatrix} -2 & 0 \\ 1 & 3 \end{pmatrix}$$

Exercise 3

1 a) Using the fact that if $AB = X$ then $B = A^{-1}X$, find N if $M = \begin{pmatrix} -5 & 6 \\ -2 & 1 \end{pmatrix}$ and $MN = \begin{pmatrix} 3 & -3 \\ 4 & -11 \end{pmatrix}$.

b) Find Q if $P = \begin{pmatrix} 4 & 11 \\ 1 & 6 \end{pmatrix}$ and $PQ = \begin{pmatrix} -12 & -13 \\ -3 & 0 \end{pmatrix}$.

2 a) Using the fact that if $AB = X$ then $A = XB^{-1}$, find E if $F = \begin{pmatrix} 6 & 1 \\ 0 & -2 \end{pmatrix}$ and $EF = \begin{pmatrix} 12 & -4 \\ -6 & -9 \end{pmatrix}$.

b) Find K if $L = \begin{pmatrix} -3 & -2 \\ -7 & -6 \end{pmatrix}$ and $KL = \begin{pmatrix} 29 & 18 \\ 73 & 50 \end{pmatrix}$.

3 a) Use the fact that $A^{-1}A = I$ to show that if $AB = X$ then $B = A^{-1}X$.

b) Use the fact that $BB^{-1} = I$ to show that if $AB = X$ then $A = XB^{-1}$.

Section 21 — Sets

21.1 Sets

A **set** is a specific group of items or numbers. The items in a set are called **elements** of the set.

> **Set Notation**
>
> A = {...}   A is the set of ...
>
> $x \in$ A x is an element of A
>
> $y \notin$ A y is not an element of A
>
> n(A)   the number of elements in A
>
> $\varnothing$ or {}   the empty set (a set containing no elements)

Exercise 1

1 List the elements of the following sets.

   a) A = {months of the year with fewer than 31 days}

   b) B = {months of the year with fewer than 4 letters in their name}

   c) C = {months of the year with the letter a in their name}

2 List the elements of the following sets.

   a) A = {even numbers between 11 and 25}

   b) B = {prime numbers less than 30}

   c) C = {square numbers less than 200}

   d) D = {factors of 30}

   e) E = {multiples of 7 between 30 and 60}

Some sets are defined using an algebraic expression.
E.g. A = $\{x : x + 2 < 5\}$ is read as 'A is the set of numbers x, such that $x + 2$ is less than 5'.

To be able to list the elements of a set like this, you need to know the **universal set**.
The universal set for a particular set A is a list of possible elements of A.
The symbol for a universal set is ξ.

> ### Example 1
>
> **a)** List the members of A = $\{x : x < 15\}$ if $\xi = \{x : x \text{ is a square number}\}$
>
>   A is the set of numbers x, such that x is less than 15.
> But elements of A must be in the universal set,
> so here A = {square numbers less than 15}   A = {1, 4, 9}
>
> **b)** List the members of A = $\{x : x < 15\}$ if $\xi = \{x : x \text{ is a prime number}\}$
>
>   The definition of A is the same as in part a), but ξ is different.
> A = {prime numbers less than 15}   A = {2, 3, 5, 7, 11 13}
>
> **c)** List the members of A = $\{x : x < 15\}$ if $\xi = \{x : x > 15\}$
>
>   A = {numbers that are both greater than 15 and less than 15}
> No elements of ξ fit the definition of an element of A, so A is empty.   A = $\varnothing$

Exercise 2

1 **a)** If $\xi = \{x : x$ is a positive integer, $x \le 10\}$, list all the elements of:
    (i)   A = $\{x : x$ is odd$\}$
    (ii) B = $\{x : x$ is a factor of 16$\}$
    (iii) C = $\{x : x$ is a square number$\}$
    (iv) D = $\{x : x$ is a factor of 30$\}$

  b) If $\xi = \{x : x$ is an integer, $20 \le x \le 30\}$, list all the elements of:
    (i)   A = $\{x : x$ is odd$\}$
    (ii) B = $\{x : x$ is even$\}$
    (iii) C = $\{x : x$ is prime$\}$
    (iv) D = $\{x : x$ is a multiple of 3$\}$

2 For all the sets in this question, $\xi = \{x : x$ is a positive integer, $x < 30\}$
  A = $\{$prime numbers$\}$ B = $\{$square numbers$\}$ C = $\{$cube numbers$\}$ D = $\{$multiples of 4$\}$
  a) List the members of A, B, C and D.
  b) Find   **(i)** n(A)   **(ii)** n(B)   **(iii)** n(C)   **(iv)** n(D)
  c) Find   **(i)**   n(E) where E = $\{x : x \in$ both A and B$\}$
                 (ii) n(F) where F = $\{x : x \in$ both B and D$\}$
                 (iii) n(G) where G = $\{x : x \in$ B but not D$\}$
                 (iv) n(H) where H = $\{x : x \notin$ A, $x \notin$ B, $x \notin$ C, $x \notin$ D$\}$

3 List the members of A = $\{x : 10 < x < 40\}$ for each of the following universal sets.
  a) $\xi = \{x : x$ is a square number$\}$
  b) $\xi = \{x : x$ is a prime numbers$\}$
  c) $\xi = \{x : x$ is a multiple of both 3 and 5$\}$
  d) $\xi = \{x : x$ is a triangle number$\}$
  e) $\xi = \{x : x$ is an integer $< 15\}$

4 A = $\{1, 2, 3, 4\}$ B = $\{0, 2, 4\}$
  a) List the elements of the following sets.
    (i)   C = $\{x : x \in$ either A or B or both$\}$
    (ii) D = $\{x : x \in$ A but not B$\}$
    (iii) E = $\{x : x = a - b, a \in$ A, $b \in$ B, $x < 1\}$
  b) Each element of the following sets is a pair of coordinates. List the elements of each set.
    (i)   F = $\{(a, b) : a \in$ A, $b \in$ B, $a + b < 5\}$
    (ii) G = $\{(a, b) : a \in$ A, $b \in$ B, $a \times b > 6\}$

21.2 Venn Diagrams

Venn diagrams are used to display sets and to show when they overlap.

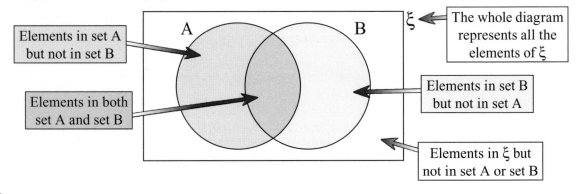

Example 1

Given that ξ = {positive integers less than or equal to 12}, draw a Venn diagram for the sets
A = {$x : x$ is a multiple of 3}   B = {$x : x$ is a factor of 30}

1. Write out sets A and B: A = {3, 6, 9, 12}
                                 B = {1, 2, 3, 5, 6, 10}

2. 3 and 6 are in both sets, so they go in the overlap
    between the circles. The other elements of each set
    go in the circles for A and B, but not in the overlap.

3. The elements of ξ that aren't in either set go outside
    the circles.

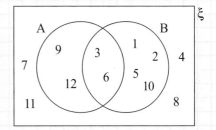

Exercise 1

1 Draw Venn diagrams to show the following sets, where ξ = {$x : x$ is a positive integer, $x \le 10$}.
   a) A = {1, 3, 5}   B = {1, 3, 7}
   b) A = {2, 3, 4, 5}   B = {1, 3, 5, 7, 9}
   c) A = {2, 6, 10}   B = {1, 3, 6, 9}
   d) A = {2, 3, 4, 5, 6}   B = {1, 3, 7}
   e) A = {2, 4, 6, 8, 10}   B = {1, 3, 5, 7, 9}

2 **a)** Draw Venn diagrams to show the following sets, where ξ = {$x : x$ is a positive integer, $x \le 10$}.
       (i)   A = {$x : x$ is odd}   B = {$x : x$ is prime}
       (ii)   A = {$x : x$ is a square number}   B = {$x : x$ is a cube number}
       (iii) A = {$x : x$ is even}   B = {$x : x$ is a multiple of 3}

   b) Draw Venn diagrams to show the following sets, where ξ = {$x : x$ is an integer, $20 \le x \le 30$}.
       (i)   A = {$x : x$ is odd}   B = {$x : x$ is a multiple of 5}
       (ii)   A = {$x : x$ is a multiple of 3}   B = {$x : x$ is a multiple of 4}
       (iii) A = {$x : x$ is even}   B = {$x : x$ is a factor of 100}

3 The Venn diagram on the right represents sets A, B and C.
   a) List the elements of set A.
   b) Which elements are in both set A and set C?
   c) What is the value of n(B)?
   d) List the elements which are in both set A and set B, but not in set C.
   e) Which elements of set C are not also in set B?
   f) List the elements which are neither in set A nor set B.

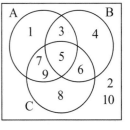

4 Draw Venn diagrams to show the following sets, where ξ = {$x : x$ is a positive integer, $x \le 10$}.
   a) A = {1, 2, 3, 5, 6}   B = {5, 6, 7, 8, 9}   C = {1, 4, 5, 9}
   b) A = {2, 3, 4, 5, 6}   B = {2, 3, 6, 7, 8}   C = {2, 3, 5, 8, 9}
   c) A = {1, 2, 3, 10}   B = {2, 4, 5, 10}   C = {3, 5, 6, 10}
   d) A = {4, 5, 6, 8}   B = {1, 2, 3}   C = {3, 4, 7, 9}

5 Draw Venn diagrams to show the following sets, where ξ = {$x : x$ is an integer, $1 \le x \le 16$}
   a) A = {$x : x$ is a multiple of 2}   B = {3, 6, 10, 11, 12}   C = {4, 8, 9, 10, 11, 12, 15}
   b) A = {$x : x$ is a square number}   B = {$x : x$ is a multiple of 4} C = {$x : x > 8$}
   c) A = {$x : x$ is prime}   B = {$x : x$ is odd}   C = {$x : x < 10$}
   d) A = {$x : x$ is a factor of 32}   B = {$x : x$ is a multiple of 4} C = {$x :$ is a square number}
   e) A = {$x : x$ is odd}   B = {$x : x$ is a multiple of 3} C = {$x : x$ is a multiple of 5}

Solving Problems with Venn Diagrams

Venn diagrams can be labelled with the **number of elements** belonging in each area.
This type of Venn diagram can be used to solve problems involving the numbers of elements in sets.

Example 2

A and B are sets. $n(A) = 24$, $n(B) = 16$ and $n(\xi) = 32$. 4 elements of ξ are neither in A nor B.

a) Draw a Venn diagram to show sets A and B. Label each part of the diagram with
   a number or expression representing the number of elements in that part.

   Call the number of elements in both A and B x.
   Then the number of elements in A only is $n(A) - x = 24 - x$,
   and the number of elements in B only is $n(B) - x = 16 - x$.

   Fill in the diagram with the number of elements in each part.

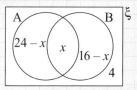

b) Find the number of elements that are in both set A and set B.

   Use $n(\xi) = 32$ to write and solve an equation for x.

   $n(\xi) = (24 - x) + x + (16 - x) + 4 = 32$
   $44 - x = 32$
   $x = 12$
   So **12 elements** are in both A and B.

Exercise 2

1 a) In the Venn diagram,
   $n(\xi) = 40$. Find:

   (i) x,
   (ii) $n(A)$.

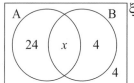

b) If $n(\xi) = 30$, find:

   (i) x,
   (ii) $n(A)$,
   (iii) $n(\text{not } B)$.

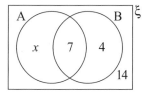

c) If the number of
   elements in A or B
   or both is 40, find:

   (i) x,
   (ii) $n(A)$,
   (iii) $n(\xi)$.

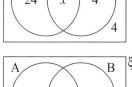

d) In the Venn diagram,
   $n(A) = 50$ and $n(B) = 40$.
   Find:

   (i) x and y,
   (ii) $n(\xi)$,
   (iii) $n(A \text{ or } B \text{ or both})$.

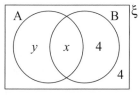

2 In each of the following, A and B are sets.
   In each case, draw a Venn diagram to represent the situation, and use it to answer the questions.

a) Set A contains 26 elements in total.
   18 of the elements of set A are not in set B.
   10 of the elements of set B are not in set A.
   12 elements of ξ are neither in A nor B.

   Find: **(i)** $n(B)$, **(ii)** $n(\xi)$.

b) 9 of the elements of set A are not in set B.
   17 of the elements of set B are not in set A.
   4 elements are in both set A and set B.
   $n(\xi) = 40$

   Find the number of elements of ξ that are:
   (i) not in A,   **(ii)** not in B.

c) 3 elements are in both set A and set B.
   15 elements of ξ are not in A.
   $n(B) = 7$ and $n(\xi) = 25$.

   Find the total number of elements in:
   (i) ξ, but not in A or B,
   (ii) A but not B,
   (iii) set A.

d) 37 of the elements of set B are not in set A.
   If the number of elements that are in both set A
   and set B is x, $n(A) = 34 + x$.
   4 elements of ξ are neither in A nor B.
   $n(\xi) = 88$

   Find the total number of elements in:
   (i) both A and B,   **(ii)** B.

Example 3

In a class of 30 students, 5 study both geography and history,
15 study history but not geography and 6 study neither subject.

a) Draw a Venn diagram to show this information.

The universal set is the whole class.
Call the number who study geography only x, and complete
the Venn diagram with the information from the question.

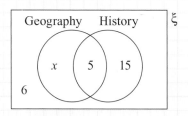

b) Find how many students in total study geography.

$$n(\xi) = 30$$
$$30 = 6 + 5 + 15 + x$$
$$x = 30 - 26 = 4$$

4 students study geography but not history.
So $4 + 5 = $ **9 students** in total study geography.

Exercise 3

For each of Questions 1-8, draw a Venn diagram to represent the situation and use it to answer the question.

1 In a class of pupils, 6 play the guitar and piano, 8 play the guitar only, 4 play the piano only
and 12 play neither instrument. How many pupils are in the class?

2 50 people at a bus stop were asked whether they liked tea or coffee.
16 liked tea only, 18 liked coffee only and two liked neither drink.
How many liked both tea and coffee?

3 36 children were asked about their pets.
8 owned geese only, 12 owned ducks only and 12 owned ducks and geese.
How many owned neither geese nor ducks?

4 Of the 60 members at a sports club, 30 play both hockey and netball,
6 play hockey but not netball and 14 play neither.
How many play netball but not hockey?

5 In a group of friends, 8 like horror movies and 12 like comedies.
These numbers include 6 people who like both genres.
3 like neither type of film. How many are in the group?

6 A company produces 120 different products.
32 of the products are made using grommets but not widgets.
20 of the products are made using widgets but not grommets.
46 of the products require neither widgets nor grommets.
How many products are made using widgets?

7 Of the 55 pupils in a school's year 11, everybody passed at least one of English and maths.
Including those who passed both subjects, 44 passed maths and 50 passed English.
How many passed exactly one of English and maths?

8 100 people are auditioning for a TV talent show. 22 of them can sing, but can't dance.
15 of them can dance but can't sing. The number who can neither dance nor sing is
1 more than the number of people who can both dance and sing.
How many of the auditionees can neither dance nor sing?

21.3 Unions and Intersections

$A \cap B$	$A \cup B$
the **intersection** of A and B	the **union** of A and B
= the set of elements that are in both A **and** B	= the set of elements that are in A **or** B or both

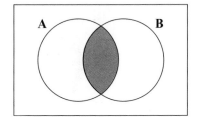

Example 1

For the sets represented on the Venn diagram on the right, list the elements of: a) $A \cap B$ b) $A \cup B$

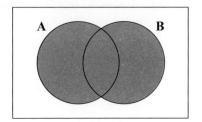

$A \cap B$ means "everything that's in both A and B" — its elements are in the part of the diagram where the circles overlap.

$A \cup B$ means "everything that's in A or B or both"

a) $A \cap B = \{0, 8, 19\}$

b) $A \cup B = \{-7, 0, 1, 5, 8, 15, 19\}$

Exercise 1

1 For each of the following, list the elements of **(i)** $A \cap B$ and **(ii)** $A \cup B$.

a) 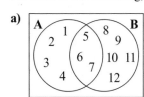 b) c) d)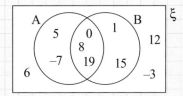

2 Describe each of the following.

   a) $A \cap B$ when A = {blue cars} and B = {four-wheel-drive cars}
   b) $A \cup B$ when A = {boys' names} and B = {girls' names}
   c) $A \cap B$ when A = {towns in France} and B = {seaside towns}
   d) $A \cup B$ when A = {countries in Europe} and B = {countries not in Europe}
   e) $A \cap B$ when A = {right-handed people} and B = {people with fair hair}

3 For each of the following sets of numbers, list the elements of **(i)** $A \cap B$ and **(ii)** $A \cup B$.

   a) A = {even numbers}   B = {positive integers less than 20}
   b) A = {positive even numbers less than 20}   B = {positive odd numbers less than 20}
   c) A = {square numbers less than 70)   B = {cube numbers less than 70}
   d) A = {prime numbers less than 10}   B = {multiples of 3 less than 10}

4 Find $A \cap B$ for each of the following, where the universal set is the set of all real numbers.

   a) $A = \{x : 0 < x < 50\}$ $B = \{x : 30 < x < 100\}$ **b)** $A = \{x : 20 < x \leq 30\}$ $B = \{x: 30 \leq x < 100\}$
   c) $A = \{x : x \leq 100\}$ $B = \{x : x \leq 50\}$ **d)** $A = \{x : x < 50\}$ $B = \{x : x > 60\}$
   e) $A = \{x : x > 20\}$ $B = \{x : x \leq 150\}$

Example 2

Shade, on separate copies of the Venn diagram on the right, the regions representing:

a) $(A \cap B) \cup C$ b) $A \cap (B \cup C)$

a) $(A \cap B) \cup C$ means 'in both A and B, or in C'.
It's represented by $A \cap B$ combined with C.

$A \cap B$:   C: $(A \cap B) \cup C$:

b) $A \cap (B \cup C)$ means 'in A, and in either B or C or both'.
It's represented by the area where A and $B \cup C$ overlap.

A: $B \cup C$: $A \cap (B \cup C)$:

Exercise 2

1 On separate copies of the Venn diagram below, shade each of the following regions.

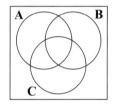

   a) $A \cap B \cap C$
   b) $A \cup B \cup C$
   c) $(A \cup B) \cap C$
   d) $A \cup (B \cap C)$

2 On separate copies of the Venn diagram below, shade each of the following regions.

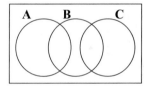

   a) $(A \cap B) \cup C$
   b) $A \cup B \cup C$
   c) $(A \cup B) \cap C$
   d) $A \cup (B \cap C)$

3 For the sets A, B and C shown on the right, find:
   a) $A \cap C$
   b) $A \cap B$
   c) $A \cap B \cap C$
   d) $B \cap C$
   e) $(A \cap C) \cup (B \cap C)$

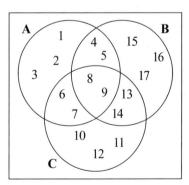

4 For the sets L, M and N shown on the right, find:
   a) $L \cap M$
   b) $L \cup N$
   c) $M \cap N$
   d) $L \cap N$
   e) $(L \cap M) \cup N$

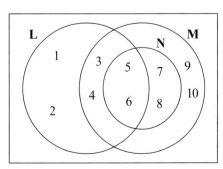

5 On a day in winter, members of a class arrived at school wearing hats (H), scarves (S) and gloves (G).

a) Describe what each of the shaded areas represents.

(i)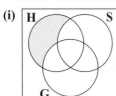

(ii)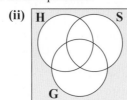

(iii)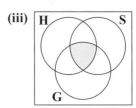

b) Draw diagrams to show the following groups of students.
   (i) Those wearing scarves only.
   (ii) All those wearing gloves.
   (iii) Those wearing exactly two of hat, scarf and gloves.

6 The Venn diagram on the right is labelled with the number of elements in each region. Find:

a) $n(A)$
b) $n(A \cap B)$
c) $n(B \cup C)$
d) $n((A \cup B) \cap C)$
e) $n(A \cup (B \cap C))$

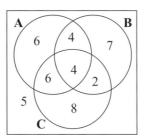

7 a) On separate copies of the Venn diagram on the right, shade the following regions.
   (i) $(A \cup C) \cap B$
   (ii) $(A \cap B) \cup (B \cap C)$

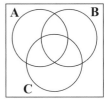

b) What do your diagrams show about $(A \cup C) \cap B$ and $(A \cap B) \cup (B \cap C)$?

c) Use diagrams to show that $A \cup (B \cap C) = (A \cup B) \cap (A \cup C)$.

8 a) Assuming neither A nor B are empty, draw diagrams to show the following:
   (i) $A \cap B = \varnothing$
   (ii) $A \cap B = A$
   (iii) $A \cup B = B$

b) What can you say about A and B if $A \cap B = A \cup B$?

21.4 Complement of a Set

A'

the **complement** of A

= the set of elements of the universal set that are **not** in set A

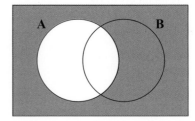

Example 1

For the sets represented on the Venn diagram on the right, list the elements of: a) A'   b) $(A \cup B)'$

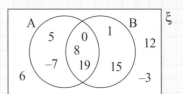

A' means "everything that's not in A".

$(A \cup B)'$ means "everything that's not in $A \cup B$".

a) A' = {−3, 1, 6, 12, 15}

b) $(A \cup B)'$ = {−3, 6, 12}

Exercise 1

1 For each of the following, describe or list the elements of A', the complement of set A.

   a) ξ = {polygons with fewer than 5 sides}   A = {quadrilaterals}

   b) ξ = {months of the year with fewer than 30 days}   A = {February}

   c) ξ = {factors of 18}   A = {multiples of 2}

   d) ξ = {books in a library}   A = {paperback books}

   e) ξ = {cars}   A = {cars with an automatic gearbox}

2 For each of the following, list the elements of B', the complement of set B.

   a) ξ = {1, 2, 3, 4, 5, 6, 7, 8, 9, 10}   B = {even numbers}

   b) ξ = {prime numbers}   B = {odd numbers}

   c) ξ = {$x : x$ is an even number, $0 < x \le 30$}   B = {factors of 100}

   d) ξ = {factors of 120}   B = {$x : x < 20$}

3 A = {multiples of 3} and B = {multiples of 4}, where the universal set is ξ = {$x : x$ is an integer, $1 \le x \le 20$}

   a) List the elements of A ∪ B.   **b)** List the elements of (A ∪ B)'.

4 **a)** Draw diagrams to show the following sets.   **(i)** (A ∩ B)'   **(ii)** A ∩ B'   **(iii)** A ∪ B'

   b) Name the sets shaded in each of the following diagrams.

5 A group of people were asked to try two new biscuits. If J is the set of people who liked the Chocolate Jamborees and F is the set of people who liked the Apricot Fringits, what do the following sets represent?

   a) F'   **b)** (J ∪ F)'   **c)** J' ∪ F

6 For the Venn diagram shown on the right, list the members of the following sets.

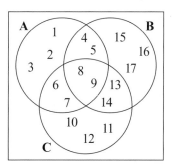

   a) A' ∩ B

   b) (A ∪ B ∪ C)'

   c) (A ∪ B) ∩ C'

   d) A ∩ B' ∩ C

   e) (B ∪ C)'

7 Name the sets shaded in each of the following diagrams.

   a)   **b)** 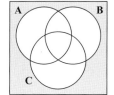   **c)**

8 On copies of the diagram shown, shade the following regions.

a) $A \cap B'$
b) $(A \cup B)'$
c) $(A \cap B') \cup C$
d) $(A \cup B)' \cap C$
e) $(A \cap B') \cup (A' \cap B)$

9

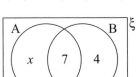

Given that $n(B') = 20$, find:

a) x **b)** $n(A \cup B')$

10

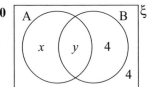

Given that $n(A \cap B)' = 15$ and $n(A) = 12$, find:

a) x **b)** y **c)** $n(A' \cup B')$

Draw Venn diagrams to help solve Questions 11-14.

11 Given that $n(P' \cap Q) = 11$, $n(P \cup Q)' = 7$, $n(Q') = 10$ and $n(\xi) = 25$, find:

a) $n(Q)$ **b)** $n(P')$ **c)** $n(P \cap Q)'$ **d)** $n(P \cup Q')$

12 Given that $n(L \cap M) = 12$, $n(L \cup M)' = 8$, $n(L') = 10$ and $n(M') = 14$, find:

a) $n(L)$ **b)** $n(\xi)$ **c)** $n(L \cap M)'$ **d)** $n(L \cup M')$

13 $\xi = \{x : x$ is an integer, $11 \leq x \leq 24\}$ is the universal set for the sets $A = \{11, 14, 16, 20, 21, 24\}$, $B = \{11, 13, 16, 19, 22, 24\}$ and $C = \{13, 14, 15, 16, 21, 22, 23, 24\}$. List the elements of each of the following.

a) $A' \cap B$ **b)** $A \cap B' \cap C'$ **c)** $B \cap (A' \cup C')$ **d)** $(A \cap B') \cup C$

14 If $A = \{$multiples of 2$\}$, $B = \{$multiples of 5$\}$ and $C = \{$multiples of 3$\}$, where $\xi = \{x : x$ is an integer, $1 \leq x \leq 30\}$, list the elements of:

a) $(A \cap C) \cup B'$ **b)** $A' \cap B' \cap C$ **c)** $(A' \cap C') \cup B$

21.5 Subsets

$$L \subseteq M$$
L is a **subset** of M = all of the elements of set L are also in set M

$$L \subset M$$
L is a **proper subset** of M = L is a subset of M, but is not equal to M

$$N \not\subset M$$
N is **not a proper subset** of M = some elements of N are not in M

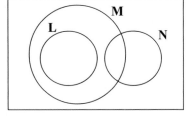

For all sets: 1. The empty set is a subset of any set, i.e. for any set A, $\varnothing \subseteq A$.
                 2. Every set is a subset of itself, i.e. for any set A, $A \subseteq A$.
                 3. For any two sets A and B, if $A \subseteq B$ and $B \subseteq A$, then $A = B$.

Example 1

a) List the subsets of $A = \{x, y\}$

   Remember to include the empty set and set A itself in the list. $\varnothing, \{x\}, \{y\}, \{x, y\}$

b) List the proper subsets of $B = \{1, 2, 3\}$

   Proper subsets of B include the empty set, but not set B itself. $\varnothing, \{1\}, \{2\}, \{3\}, \{1, 2\}, \{1, 3\}, \{2, 3\}$

Exercise 1

1 Copy the following placing $\subset$, $\not\subset$ or $\subseteq$ between the sets to make a correct statement.

   a) {cats} ___ {fish}

   b) {Monday} ___ {days of the week}

   c) {spring, summer, autumn, winter} ___ {seasons of the year}

   d) {Fred, George} ___ {boys' names}

   e) {red, yellow, brown} ___ {colours in a rainbow}

   f) {tennis, squash, football} ___ {racquet sports}

2 Pair together the following sets and subsets writing a correct statement for each pair, e.g. $H \subset A$.

   A = {days of the week}   G = {ball sports}

   B = {Steven, Philip}   H = {Monday, Wednesday}

   C = {rugby, football}   I = {13, 17, 53}

   D = {2, 6, 30}   J = {motorcycle, car, train}

   E = {factors of 30}   K = {boys' names}

   F = {prime numbers}   L = {modes of transport}

3 For the set A = {1, 2, 3, 4}:

   a) How many subsets are there which contain only 1 element?

   b) List the subsets of A with: (i) two elements   (ii) three elements

   c) How many subsets does A have in total?

4 List all the subsets of the following sets.

   a) M = {a, b, c}   b) N = {2, 3, 5, 7}   c) O = {9, S, dormouse, spoon}

5 The diagram shows the relationship between four sets A, B, C and D. Each area of the diagram contains at least one element.

   a) State whether each of the following statements is true or false.

   (i) $C \subset A$ (ii) $D \not\subset B'$ (iii) $(A \cap B) \subset B$

   (iv) $(A \cap B) \subset C$ (v) $B' \subset C'$ (vi) $C \not\subset (A \cup B)$

   (vii) $B \not\subset D'$ (viii) $(C \cup D) \subset A$

   b) Copy the following statements and complete them by placing either $\subset$ or $\not\subset$ in each of the gaps.

   (i) A ___ $(A \cap B)$ (ii) $(B \cap C)$ ___ $(A \cap C)$ (iii) A' ___ B'

   (iv) C ___ $(A \cup C)$ (v) B ___ D'   (vi) A' ___ D'

6 Draw Venn diagrams to show the following situations.

   a) Sets P and Q where   (i) $Q \subset P$ (ii) $P \subset Q'$

   b) Sets W, X and Y where

   (i) $W \subset Y$ and $Y \subset X$ (ii) $W \subset X$, $Y \subset X$ and $W \cap Y = \varnothing$ (iii) $W \subset (X \cap Y)$

7 If A = {$x : 0 \leq x \leq 18$}, B = {$y : y$ is a multiple of 3} and C = {$z : z$ is a factor of 15}, state whether each of the following is true or false.

   a) $B \subset A$ b) $A \subseteq C$ c) $C \subset B$ d) $C \subset A$

   e) {6} $\subseteq$ B   f) $6 \subset B$ g) $(B \cap C) \subset A$ h) $(B \cup C) \subset A$

21.6 Sets Problems

Exercise 1

1 For the sets shown in the diagram:

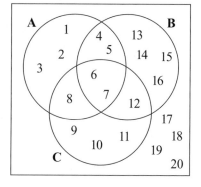

a) State whether each of the following is true or false. For those that are false, change the right hand side of the expression to make a correct statement.

   (i) $n(A) = 7$ **(ii)** $n(A \cap B) = 4$

   (iii) $n(B') = 12$ **(iv)** $12 \in C$

   (v) $20 \in B'$ **(vi)** $C \cap B' = \{9, 10, 11\}$

   (vii) $(B \cup C) \cap A = \{4, 5, 6, 7, 8\}$ **(viii)** $(A \cup B)' \cap A' = \{9, 10, 11\}$

b) List the members of each of the following sets.

   (i) $A \cap C$ **(ii)** $A \cap B$ **(iii)** $A \cap B \cap C$ **(iv)** $(B \cap C)$

   (v) $(A \cap C) \cup (B \cap C)$ **(vi)** $A' \cap C$ **(vii)** $(A \cup B)'$ **(viii)** $(A' \cap C) \cup (B' \cap C)$

2 For each of the following, draw a Venn diagram to show the sets and use it to help answer the questions.

a) $\xi = \{$positive integers less than 20$\}$ $T = \{$multiples of 2$\}$ $F = \{$multiples of 5$\}$

   Find: **(i)** $n(T \cap F)$ **(ii)** $n(T \cup F)'$

b) $\xi = \{$positive integers less than 20$\}$ $T = \{$multiples of 2$\}$ $S = \{$square numbers$\}$

   Find: **(i)** $T \cap S$ **(ii)** $n(T')$

3 $\xi = \{$polygons$\}$, $Q = \{$quadrilaterals$\}$, $T = \{$triangles$\}$, $S = \{$shapes with sides of equal length$\}$

   Describe each of the following: **a)** $T \cap S$ **b)** $T \cap Q$

4 $\xi = \{$positive integers less than or equal to 20$\}$,

   $X = \{x : 10 < x < 20\}$, $Y = \{$prime numbers$\}$, $Z = \{$multiples of 3$\}$

   Find: **a)** $X \cap Y$ **b)** $X' \cap Z$ **c)** $Y \cap Z$ **d)** $X' \cap Z'$ **e)** $n(Y \cap X)$

5 Draw a diagram to show two sets A and B such that $B \subset A$. Add sets C and D to your diagram such that: **(i)** C is a subset of A but not of B, and $C \cap B \neq \emptyset$, and **(ii)** $D \subset B$ and $D \cap C = \emptyset$.

6 Name the sets corresponding to the shaded area in each of the following diagrams.

a) 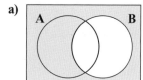   b) 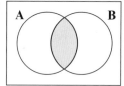   c) 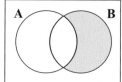   d)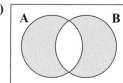

7 On separate copies of the Venn diagram on the right, shade the areas corresponding to the following sets:

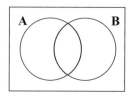

a) $A' \cup B$

b) $(A \cup B)'$

c) $A' \cap B'$

8 Name the sets corresponding to the shaded area in each of the following diagrams.

a)   **b)** 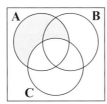 **c)** 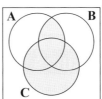 **d)**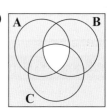

9 On separate copies of the Venn diagram on the right, shade the areas corresponding to the following sets:

a) $A \cap B \cap C'$
b) $A \cap B'$
c) $(A \cap B) \cup (A \cap C)$

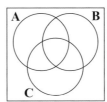

10 50 families were asked about the children they had. 30 of those asked said they had girls in the family while 38 said they had boys. 23 families had both boys and girls.

a) Draw a Venn diagram to represent this.
b) How many families had no children?

11 In a class of 36 students, 28 are taking GCSE Advanced Knitting and 18 are taking GCSE Motorcycle Maintenance. 13 take both subjects.

a) Represent this information on a Venn diagram.
b) How many in the class take neither subject?

12 $A = \{x : x$ is an even number$\}$ $B = \{y : 4 \leq y \leq 27\}$ $C = \{z : z$ is a multiple of 4$\}$

If $\xi = \{$positive integers less than or equal to 30$\}$, state whether each of the following is true or false.

a) $A \subseteq C$ **b)** $C \subseteq A$ **c)** $C \subset B$ **d)** $B \subset C$ **e)** $C \subset (A \cup B)$
f) $C \subset (A \cap B)$ **g)** $(B \cap C) \subset A$ **h)** $(B \cup C) \subset A$ **i)** $(A \cap C) \subset B$ **j)** $(A \cap C) \subset C$

13 A group of 100 people were asked whether they had in their pockets any of three items.

72 had all three of keys, crayons and a magic ring.

Including those with all three items, 74 had both keys and crayons, 80 had both keys and a magic ring and 78 had both crayons and a magic ring.

Of those with exactly one item, 3 had just keys, 5 just crayons and 3 just a magic ring.

a) Show the results of this survey on a Venn diagram.
b) Of those asked, how many had   **(i)** none of the items,   **(ii)** exactly two of the items?

14 100 members of a health spa were asked whether they used the gym, pool or sauna. The replies were as follows:

A total of 52 used the gym, 30 used the pool and 65 used the sauna.
17 used the gym and the pool, 18 used the pool and the sauna, 30 used the gym and the sauna.
15 used all three.

a) Draw a Venn diagram showing this information.
b) Find how many people: **(i)** don't use the gym, the pool or the sauna,
                    (ii) use only one of the gym, pool and sauna,
                    (iii) use at least two out of the gym, pool and sauna.

Section 22 — Angles and 2D Shapes

22.1 Angles and Lines

Angles at a point **on a straight line** add up to **180°**.

$a + b + c = 180°$

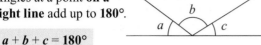

Angles **around a point** add up to **360°**.

$a + b + c + d = 360°$

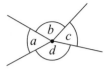

Example 1

Find the size of angle b.

1. Angles around a point add up to 360°. Use this to form an equation in terms of b.

   $b + 2b + 80° + 40° + 90° = 360°$

   $3b + 210° = 360°$

2. Simplify and solve your equation to find b.

   $3b = 360° - 210° = 150°$

   $\boldsymbol{b = 50°}$

Exercise 1

1 Find the missing angles marked with letters. (The angles aren't drawn accurately.)

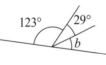
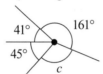
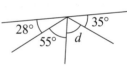

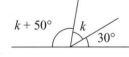

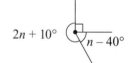

2 Explain why the line *AOB* on the right cannot be a straight line.

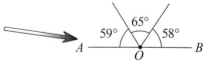

3 Given that $x = 40°$, find the value of m.

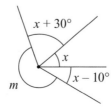

208   *Section 22 — Angles and 2D Shapes*

Vertically Opposite and Alternate Angles

When two straight lines **intersect**, two pairs of **vertically opposite angles** (sometimes just called **opposite angles**) are formed. Vertically opposite angles are equal.

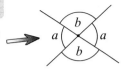

When a straight line crosses two parallel lines, it forms two pairs of **alternate angles** (in a sort of Z-shape). Alternate angles are equal.

Example 2

Find the values of a, b, c and d in the diagram.

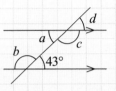

1. a and $43°$ are alternate angles, so they are equal.
2. b and the angle marked $43°$ lie on a straight line, so they add up to $180°$.
3. c and b are alternate angles, so they are equal.
4. a and d are vertically opposite angles, so they are equal.

$\underline{\mathbf{a = 43°}}$
$43° + b = 180°$
$b = 180° - 43° = \underline{\mathbf{137°}}$
$c = b = \underline{\mathbf{137°}}$
$d = a = \underline{\mathbf{43°}}$

Exercise 2

In Questions 1-4, the angles aren't drawn accurately, so don't try to measure them.

1 Find the missing angles marked by letters.

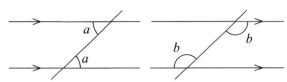

2 Find the missing angles marked by letters.

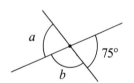
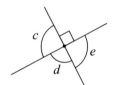
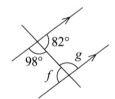
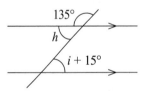

3 The diagram on the right shows two isosceles triangles. Find the missing angles marked by letters.

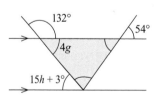

4 Find the missing angles marked by letters.

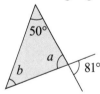

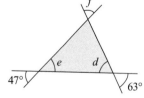
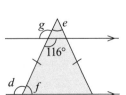
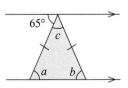
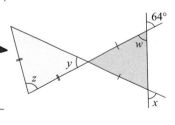

Corresponding Angles and Allied Angles

Corresponding angles formed by parallel lines are equal.

Corresponding angles form a sort of F-shape.

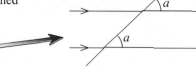

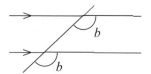

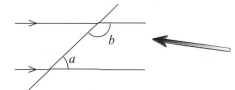

When a straight line crosses two parallel lines to make a kind of C-shape, the interior angles are known as **allied angles** and add up to 180°.

Example 3

Find the values of a, b and c shown in the diagram.

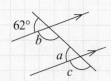

1. a and 62° are corresponding angles, so they are equal.

   $\underline{\underline{a = 62°}}$

2. b and the angle marked 62° lie on a straight line, so they add up to 180°. (Or you could say a and b are allied angles, so they add up to 180°.)

   $62° + b = 180°$
   $b = 180° - 62° = \underline{\underline{118°}}$

3. c and b are corresponding angles, so they're equal.

   $c = b = \underline{\underline{118°}}$

Exercise 3

In Questions 1-3, the angles aren't drawn accurately, so don't try to measure them.

1 Find the missing angles marked by letters.

 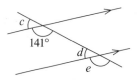 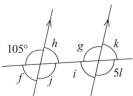 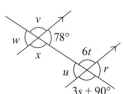

2 Two wooden posts stand vertically on sloped ground. The first post makes an angle of 99° with the downward slope, as shown. Find the angle that the second post makes with the upward slope, labelled y on the diagram.

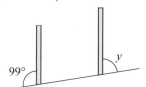

3 Find the missing angles marked by letters.

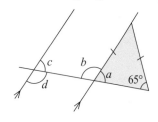 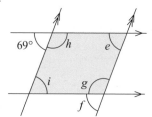 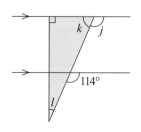

Exercise 4 — Mixed Exercise

In Questions 1-2, the angles aren't drawn accurately, so don't try to measure them.

1 Find the missing angles marked by letters. In each case, give a reason for your answer.

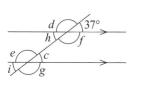

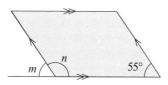

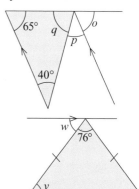

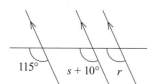

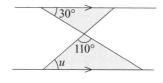

2 The diagram on the right shows some scaffolding. The triangle formed between the two horizontal bars is isosceles.

Find the size of angles *w*, *x*, *y* and *z*, giving a reason for your answer in each case.

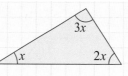

22.2   Triangles

An **isosceles** triangle has 2 equal sides and 2 equal angles.

An **equilateral** triangle has 3 equal sides and 60° angles.

The sides and angles of a **scalene** triangle are all different.

A **right-angled** triangle has 1 right angle.

An **acute-angled** triangle has 3 acute angles.

An **obtuse-angled** triangle has 1 obtuse angle.

The angles in **any** triangle add up to 180°.

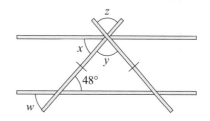

$a + b + c = 180°$

Example 1

Find the value of *x* in the triangle shown.

1. Form an equation in *x*.

2. Solve your equation to find *x*.

$x + 2x + 3x = 180°$

$6x = 180°$

$x = 180° \div 6 = \underline{\mathbf{30°}}$

Exercise 1

In Questions 1-8, the angles aren't drawn accurately, so don't try to measure them.

1 Find the missing angles marked with letters.

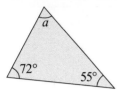 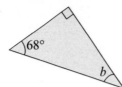 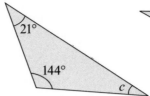 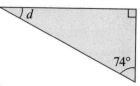

2 Find the missing angles marked with letters.

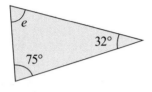 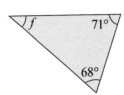 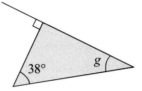 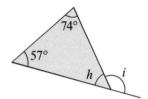

3 Find the values of the letters shown in the following diagrams.

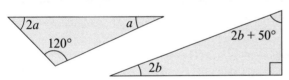

4 Find the values of the letters shown in these diagrams of isosceles triangles.

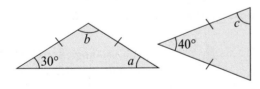 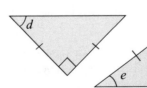 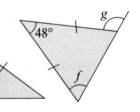

5 **a)** Find the value of *x*.
   b) Find the value of *y*.

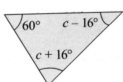

7 Find the values of angles *a*, *b* and *c*.

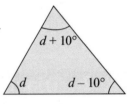

6 **a)** Find the value of *p*.
   b) Find the value of *q*.

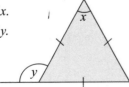

8 Use the properties of parallel lines to prove that the angles inside a triangle equal 180°.

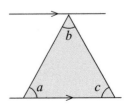

22.3   Quadrilaterals

A **quadrilateral** is a 4-sided shape. The angles in a quadrilateral add up to **360°**.

Example 1

Find the missing angle x in this quadrilateral.

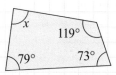

1. The angles in a quadrilateral add up to 360°.
   Use this to write an equation involving x.

   $79° + 73° + 119° + x = 360°$
   $271° + x = 360°$

2. Then solve your equation to find the value of x.

   $x = 360° - 271° = \underline{\mathbf{89°}}$

Exercise 1

1   Find the values of the letters in the following quadrilaterals.
     (They're not drawn accurately, so don't try to measure them.)

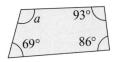 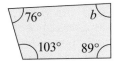   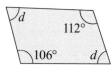 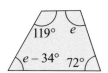

Squares, Rectangles, Parallelograms and Rhombuses

A **square** is a quadrilateral with 4
equal sides and 4 angles of 90°.

A **rectangle** is a quadrilateral with 4 angles of
90° and opposite sides of the same length.

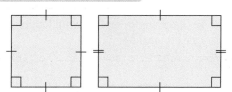

A **parallelogram** is a quadrilateral with 2 pairs of
equal, parallel sides. A **rhombus** is a parallelogram
where all the sides are the same length.

Opposite angles of both shapes are equal.
Neighbouring angles add up to 180°. $a + b = 180°$

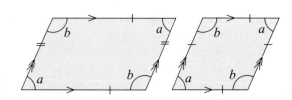

Example 2

Find the size of the angles marked with letters in this rhombus.

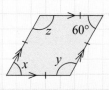

1. Opposite angles in a rhombus are equal, so $x = 60°$.
2. Neighbouring angles in a rhombus add up to 180°.
   Use this fact to find angle y.
3. Opposite angles in a rhombus are equal,
   so z is the same size as y.

$\underline{\mathbf{x = 60°}}$
$60° + y = 180°$
$y = 180° - 60° = \underline{\mathbf{120°}}$

$\underline{\mathbf{z = 120°}}$

2 Calculate the values of the letters in these quadrilaterals.
(They're not drawn accurately, so don't try to measure them.)

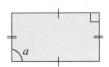 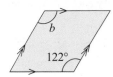 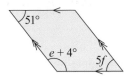

Kites and Trapeziums

A **kite** is a quadrilateral with
2 pairs of equal sides and 1 pair of
equal angles in opposite corners.

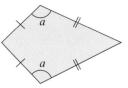

$a + b = 180°$ $c + d = 180°$ $a + b = 180°$

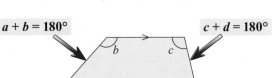   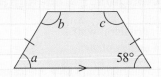

A **trapezium** is a quadrilateral
with 1 pair of parallel sides.

An **isosceles trapezium** is a trapezium
with 2 pairs of equal angles, and 2 sides of
the same length.

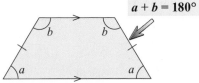

Example 3

Find the size of the angles marked with letters
in this isosceles trapezium.

1. This is an isosceles trapezium, so *a* must equal 58°. $\underline{\textbf{a = 58°}}$

2. Angle *c* and the angle of 58° must add up to 180°. $c + 58° = 180°$
                                                                  $c = 180° - 58° = \underline{\textbf{122°}}$

3. It's an isosceles trapezium, so *b* must equal *c*. $b = \underline{\textbf{122°}}$

3 Find the size of the angles marked by letters in these kites.
(They're not drawn accurately, so don't try to measure them.)

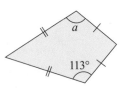 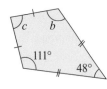 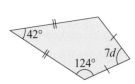 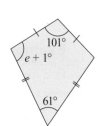

4 Find the size of the angles marked by letters in these trapeziums. (Don't measure them.)

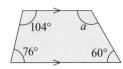 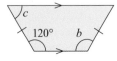 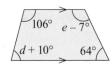 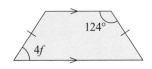

Exercise 2 — Mixed Exercise

1 Write down all the different types of quadrilaterals which satisfy each of the following properties.

   a) 4 equal sides
   b) 4 angles of 90°
   c) 2 pairs of equal sides
   d) 2 pairs of parallel sides
   e) at least 1 pair of parallel sides
   f) exactly 1 pair of parallel sides

2 Find the size of the angles marked by letters in these diagrams. (Don't measure them.)

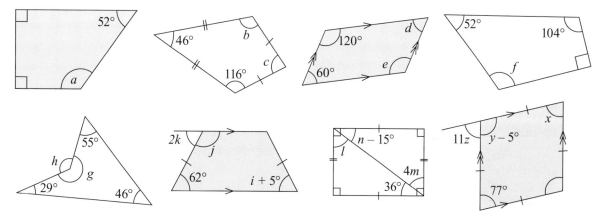

3 A quadrilateral has 40°, 83° and 99° angles. Find the size of the fourth angle.

4 A parallelogram has two angles of 100° each. Find the size of the other two angles.

5 An isosceles trapezium has two angles of 53°. Find the size of the other two angles.

6 A kite has exactly one angle of 50° and exactly one angle of 90°. Find the size of the other two angles.

22.4 Polygons

A **polygon** is a shape whose sides are all straight.

A **regular polygon** has sides of equal length and angles that are all equal.

Polygons have special names depending on the number of sides they have.

pentagon = **5** sides	**oct**agon = **8** sides
hexagon = **6** sides	**non**agon = **9** sides
heptagon = **7** sides	**dec**agon = **10** sides

Interior Angles

The **interior angles** of a polygon are the angles inside each vertex (corner).

The **sum** of a polygon's interior angles (S) and its **number of sides** (n) are related by this formula.

$$S = (n - 2) \times 180°$$

(This formula comes from being able to split up a polygon into triangles.)

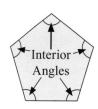

Interior Angles

Example 1

A pentagon has four interior angles of 100°. Find the size of the fifth angle.

1. A pentagon has 5 sides, so substitute $n = 5$ into the equation.

2. Write an equation for the size of the missing angle, x.

3. Solve your equation to find x.

$S = (n - 2) \times 180° = (5 - 2) \times 180° = 540°$

$100° + 100° + 100° + 100° + x = 540°$

$400° + x = 540°$

$x = 540° - 400° = \underline{\mathbf{140°}}$

Exercise 1

1 Find the sum of the interior angles of a polygon with:

   a) 6 sides   **b)** 10 sides   **c)** 12 sides   **d)** 20 sides

2 For each of the following shapes: **(i)** Find the sum of the interior angles.

                                                (ii) Find the size of the missing angle.

a)

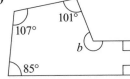

b)

c)

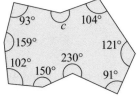

3 Find the size of each of the interior angles in the following shapes.

   a) Regular octagon   **b)** Regular nonagon   **c)** Regular decagon

4 **a)** Four angles of a pentagon are 110°. Find the size of the fifth angle.

   b) Is this a regular pentagon? Give a reason for your answer.

5 Find the number of sides of a regular polygon with interior angles of: **a)** 60°   **b)** 150°

6 Draw a pentagon. By dividing it into triangles, show that the sum of the interior angles of the pentagon is 540°.

Exterior Angles

The **exterior angles** of a polygon are the angles between a side and a line that extends out from one of the neighbouring sides.

The sum of the exterior angles of any polygon is **360°**. $a + b + c + d + e = 360°$

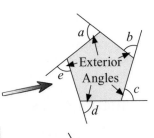

You can use the **exterior angle** to find the corresponding **interior angle** using this formula:

$$\text{Interior angle} = 180° - \text{Exterior angle}$$

In a **regular n-sided polygon**, all the exterior angles are **equal** and their size is given by:

$$\text{Exterior angle} = \frac{360°}{n}$$

Example 2

Find the size of each of the exterior angles of a regular hexagon.

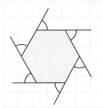

1. A hexagon has 6 sides.

2. The hexagon is regular so put $n = 6$ into the exterior angle formula.

$360° \div 6 = 60°$
So each exterior angle is **60°**.

Exercise 2

1 Find the size of each of the exterior angles of the following polygons.

a) regular octagon   **b)** regular nonagon   **c)** regular heptagon

2 Find the size of the angles marked by letters in these diagrams.

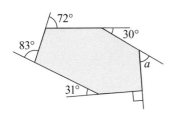

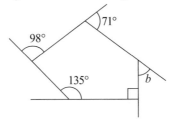

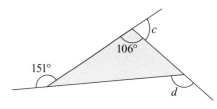

3 Find the size of the unknown exterior angle in a shape whose other exterior angles are:

a) 100°, 68°, 84° and 55°
b) 30°, 68°, 45°, 52°, 75° and 50°
c) 42°, 51°, 60°, 49°, 88° and 35°
d) 19°, 36°, 28°, 57°, 101°, 57° and 22°

Example 3

A regular polygon has exterior angles of 30°.
How many sides does the polygon have?

It's a regular polygon so just put 30° into the exterior angle formula.

$30° = \dfrac{360°}{n}$

$n = 360° \div 30° = 12$

So the regular polygon has **12 sides**.

4 A regular polygon has exterior angles of 45°.

a) How many sides does the polygon have? What is the name of this kind of polygon?
b) Sketch the polygon.
c) What is the size of each of the polygon's interior angles?
d) What is the sum of the polygon's interior angles?

5 The exterior angles of some regular polygons are given below. For each exterior angle, find:

(i) the number of sides the polygon has,
(ii) the size of each of the polygon's interior angles,
(iii) the sum of the polygon's interior angles.

a) 40°   **b)** 120°   **c)** 10°   **d)** 9°   **e)** 6°
f) 5°   **g)** 4°   **h)** 3°   **i)** 4.8°

6 Find the values of the letters in the following diagrams.

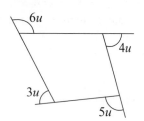

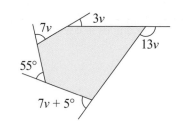

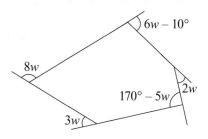

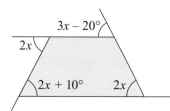

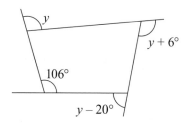

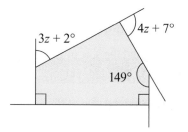

7 Prove that the sum of the exterior angles of this polygon is 360°.

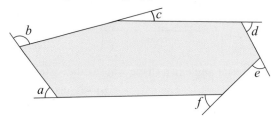

22.5 Symmetry

A **line of symmetry** on a shape is a mirror line.
Each side of the line of symmetry is a **reflection** of the other.

The **order of rotational symmetry** of a shape is the number of positions
you can rotate (turn) the shape into so that it looks exactly the same.

Exercise 1

1 For each of the shapes below, state: **(i)** the number of lines of symmetry,
                                              (ii) the order of rotational symmetry.

a)
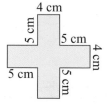

b)
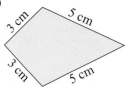

c)
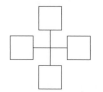

d)

e)

f)
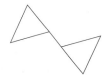

g)   an isosceles
      trapezium

h)   a regular
      decagon

2 Copy the diagram below, then shade two more squares to make a pattern with no lines of symmetry and rotational symmetry of order 2.

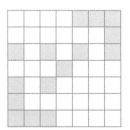

3 Copy the diagram below, then shade four more squares to make a pattern with 4 lines of symmetry and rotational symmetry of order 4.

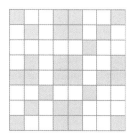

22.6   Angles and 2D Shapes Problems

Exercise 1

For Questions 1-3, find the value of each letter. (The pictures aren't drawn accurately, so don't measure them.)

1

62° u v

y 102° w x 71° 95°

p 62° q

r 108° 85°

2

122° 122° a a

35° b 55°

48° d + 10° c

74° g + 3° 2f e h 40°

3

61° a b

43° c d

e 4f 98°

91° g h 4i

102° k j l + 5°

2m + 7° 58°

½n o p 125°

11r − 3° 4q + 5° 33°

4 Copy and complete the table.

	equilateral triangle	parallelogram	isosceles trapezium	regular nonagon
No. of sides				
Lines of symmetry				
Order of rotational symmetry				
Sum of interior angles				

5 Find the size of the exterior angles of a regular polygon with:

   a) 10 sides   **b)** 12 sides

   c) 15 sides   **d)** 25 sides

6 Are the lines AB and CD parallel to each other? Explain your answer.

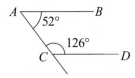

7 **a)** Calculate the sum of the internal angles of a pentagon.

   b) Use your answer to find the size of angle w.

8 Find angle p in the diagram below.

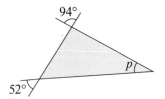

9 Find x, y and z.

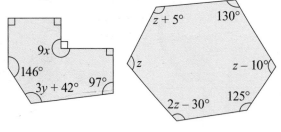

10 The diagram below shows a kite and a square.

   a) Write down the value of a.

   b) Use your answer to find the size of angles b and c.

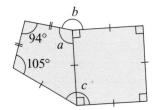

11 **a)** Find x in the diagram below.

     b) Use your answer to find y.

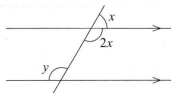

12 Find x and y in the diagram below.

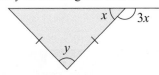

13 The shape below is made up of a regular polygon and a parallelogram. Calculate angle x.

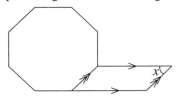

14 Kendra wants to draw a star with 12 equal length sides. She calculates that each of the acute interior angles needs to be 40°. Calculate the size of each reflex interior angle.

15 Prove that $x = 60° - a$ in the diagram on the right.

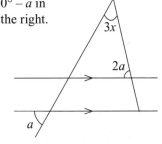

16 Use the angle properties of parallel lines to prove that the interior angles of any trapezium add to 360°.

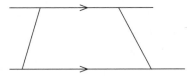

Section 23 — Circle Geometry

Circumference: the distance around the outside of a circle.

Radius: a line from the centre of a circle to the edge.
The circle's centre is the same distance from all points on the edge.

Diameter: a line from one side of a circle to the other through the centre.
The diameter is twice the radius: $d = 2r$

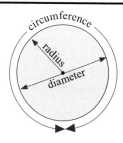

Tangent: a straight line that just touches the circle.

Arc: a part of the circumference.

Chord: a line between two points on the circle.

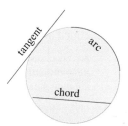

Sector: an area of a circle like a "slice of pie".

Segment: an area of a circle between an arc and a chord.

23.1 Circle Theorems 1

Rule 1 The **angle in a semicircle** is a **right angle**.

Rule 2

A **tangent** to a circle makes a **right angle with the radius** at that point.

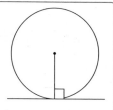

Example 1

a) Find the missing angle x.

By the 'angles in a semicircle' rule, $\angle ABC = 90°$.
So using angles in a triangle,
$x = 180 - 90 - 52 = \underline{\textbf{38°}}$

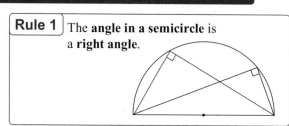

b) Find the missing angle y.

Tangent and radius make an angle of 90°, so $y = 90 - 49 = \underline{\textbf{41°}}$

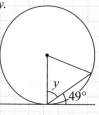

Exercise 1

In Questions 1–8, find the value in degrees of each letter used in the diagrams.

1

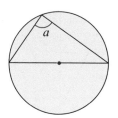

2

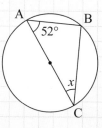

3

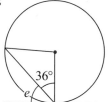

4

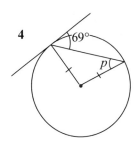

5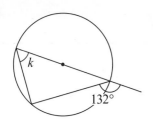

6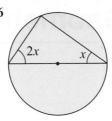

7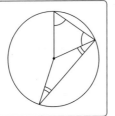

8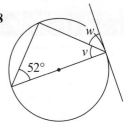

Rule 3

A triangle formed by **two radii** is **isosceles**.

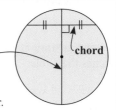

Rule 4

A **diameter bisects** a **chord** at right angles.

So any chord which is a **perpendicular bisector** of another chord must be a diameter.

chord

Example 2

a) Find the missing angle k.

Two sides of the triangle are radii, so it must be isosceles. So both angles at the edge of the circle are the same size. So $k = \frac{1}{2}(180 - 98) = \underline{\mathbf{41°}}$

b) $BD = DE$. Find the missing angle l.

AC is a perpendicular bisector of the chord BE, so it must be a diameter. So using angles in a semicircle, $\angle ABC = 90°$, and $\angle DBC = 90 - 61 = 29°$. $\angle BDC = 90°$, so $l = 180 - 90 - 29 = \underline{\mathbf{61°}}$.

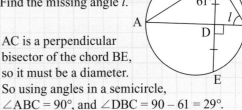

Exercise 2

In Questions 1–4, find the missing angles marked with letters.

1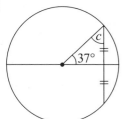

2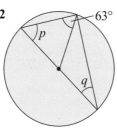

3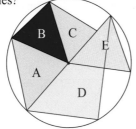

4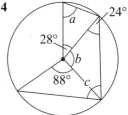

5 Which of triangles A-E can you be certain are isosceles? Explain your answer.

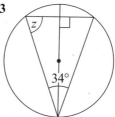

6 Which of angles a-i must be right angles? Explain your answer.

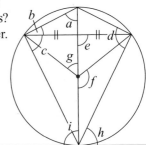

23.2 Circle Theorems 2

Rule 5

The angle subtended **at the centre** of a circle is **double** the angle subtended **at the circumference** by the same arc.

An angle **subtended by an arc** is an angle made where two lines from the ends of the arc meet. The subtended angle is **inside** the shape formed by the arc and the lines.

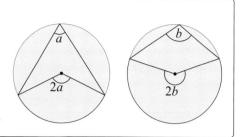

Example 1

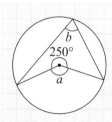

Find the missing angles *a* and *b*.

Angles at a point sum to 360°, so *a* = 360 − 250 = **110°**.

Angle at the centre is double the angle at the edge, so $b = \frac{a}{2} = \frac{110}{2} = $ **55°**.

Exercise 1

In Questions 1–8, calculate the missing angles marked with letters.

1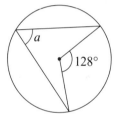

2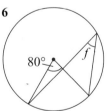

3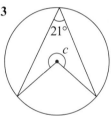

4

5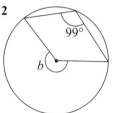

6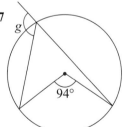

7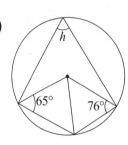

8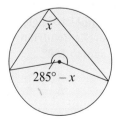

9 Show that ∠AOD = 64°.

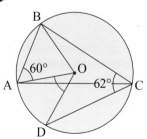

10 Find angle *m*, then use your answer to work out angle *n*.

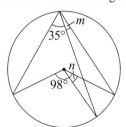

11 Find the size of angle *x*.

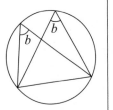
Example 2

Find the missing angles a, b and c.

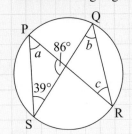

$a = 180 - 86 - 39 = \underline{\mathbf{55°}}$.

a and b are angles in the same segment, so $a = b = \underline{\mathbf{55°}}$.

Similarly, c is in the same segment as $\angle PSQ$, so $c = \angle PSQ = \underline{\mathbf{39°}}$.

Exercise 2

In Questions 1–8, calculate the missing angles marked with letters.

1
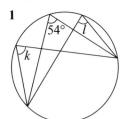

2
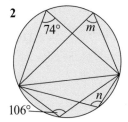

3
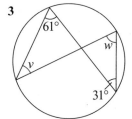

4
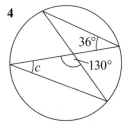

5
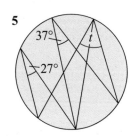

6
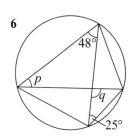

7
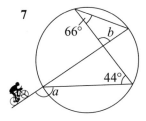

8
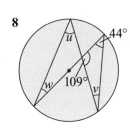

9 Find the size of angles x, y and z.
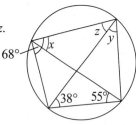

10 Find the size of angles r and s.
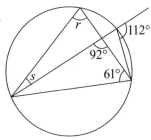

Rule 7

Opposite angles in a **cyclic quadrilateral** sum to **180°**.

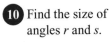

$a + c = 180°$
$b + d = 180°$

A **cyclic quadrilateral** is any quadrilateral which can be drawn with **all four vertices** touching a circle.

Example 3

Find the missing angles x and y.

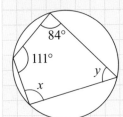

It's a cyclic quadrilateral, so opposite angles add up to 180°.

$x = 180 - 84 = \underline{\mathbf{96°}}$
$y = 180 - 111 = \underline{\mathbf{69°}}$

Exercise 3

Calculate the missing angles marked with letters.

1

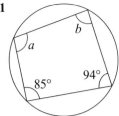

2

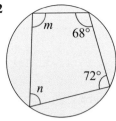

3

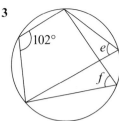

4

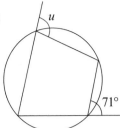

5

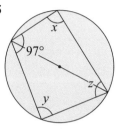

6

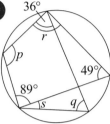

7

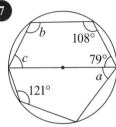

8

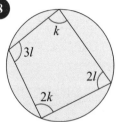

23.3 Circle Theorems 3

Rule 8

Two **tangents** to a circle drawn from a single point outside the circle are the **same length**, and create congruent right-angled triangles.

Two triangles are **congruent** if both are the same size and have the same angles.

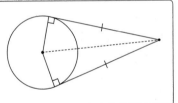

Example 1

Find the size of the missing angle x.

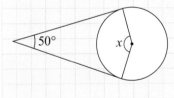

The two longer edges can be extended to form tangents. A tangent meets a radius at a right angle, so the two unmarked angles are right angles.

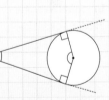

The shape shown is a quadrilateral, so the angles sum to 360°. So x = 360 – 90 – 90 – 50 = **130°**.

Exercise 1

In Questions 1–6, calculate the missing angles marked with letters.

1

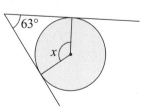

2

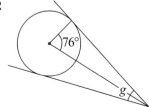

3

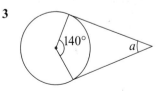

4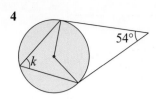
54°
k

5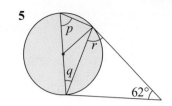
p
r
q
62°

6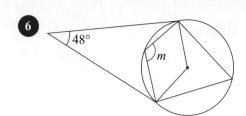
48°
m

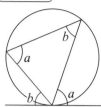

Rule 9 | **The Alternate Segment Theorem:**

The angle between **a tangent and a chord** is equal to the angle subtended from the ends of the chord in the **alternate segment**.

The **alternate segment** to an angle between a tangent and a chord is the segment on the other side of the chord.

b
a
a
b

alternate segment to *b*
b

B
x
C
114°
y
46°
A

Example 2

Find: a) angle *x*   b) angle *y*

a)   *x* is in the alternate segment to the 46° angle, so *x* = **46°**.

b)   ∠ACB is in the alternate segment to *y*, so using angles on a straight line, *y* = ∠ACB = 180 − 114 = **66°**.

Exercise 2

1   According to the alternate segment theorem, which angle in the diagram on the right is

   a) equal to angle *a*?

   b) equal to angle *c*?

In questions 2–9, find the angles marked with letters.

c
b
a
d
e
g
h
f

2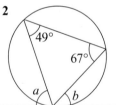
49°
67°
a
b

3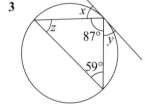
x
z
87°
y
59°

4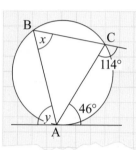
76° 70°
p
q

5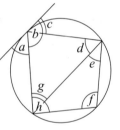
135°
a
b
c

6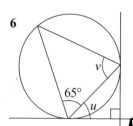
v
65°
u

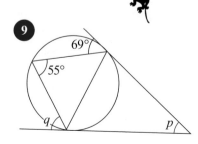

7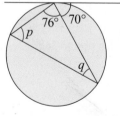
m
n
l
61°
30°

8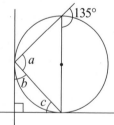
j
94°
i
78°

9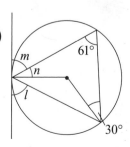
69°
55°
q
p

Rule 10

If two **chords** PQ and RS cross at point T, then **PT × QT = RT × ST**.

This is true whether T is inside or outside of the circle.

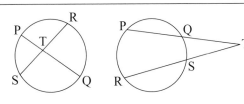

Example 3

a) In the diagram below, AZ = 3 cm, BZ = 5 cm and CZ = 6 cm. Find the length of DZ.

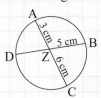

$$AZ \times CZ = BZ \times DZ$$
$$3 \times 6 = 5 \times DZ$$
$$DZ = 18 \div 5 = \textbf{3.6 cm}$$

b) If EF = g m, FY = 2g m, GH = 4 m and HY = 9 m, find the value of g.

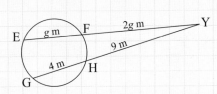

$$EY \times FY = GY \times HY$$
$$(g + 2g) \times 2g = (4 + 9) \times 9$$
$$3g \times 2g = 13 \times 9$$
$$6g^2 = 117$$
$$g^2 = 19.5$$
$$g = \textbf{4.42} \text{ (to 2 d.p.)}$$

Exercise 3

In Questions 1–8, give your answers to 3 significant figures where necessary.

1 Find a if:
IX = 9 mm
JX = 3 mm
KX = 7 mm
LX = a mm

5 Find c if:
AT = $2c$ cm
BT = 7 cm
CT = c cm
DT = 4 cm

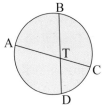

2 Find d if:
ZU = 2.5 m
YU = d m
WU = 2.5 m
XU = 1.8 m

6 Find b if:
EF = 6 mm
FS = 4 mm
GH = b mm
HS = 3 mm

3 WM = 5 cm
WN = 12 cm
WP = 3 cm
WO = j cm

a) Find j.
b) Find PO.

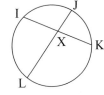

7 Find e if:
LR = 6 cm
KL = e + 10 cm
NR = 12 cm
MN = e + 8 cm

4 Find h if:
QR = h m
RV = 7 m
ST = 9 m
TV = 6.5 m

8 Find f if:
OP = 2 cm
PQ = 4 cm
RQ = f cm
SR = 5 mm

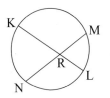

Section 23 — Circle Geometry **227**

Exercise 1

In Questions 1–7, calculate the value of each letter. Explain your reasoning in each case.

1
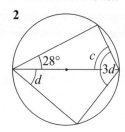

2
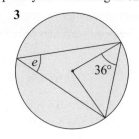

3
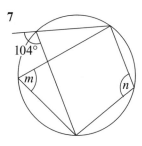

4
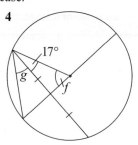

5
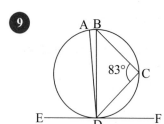

6
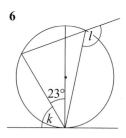

7

8 Show that ∠NMO = 30°.
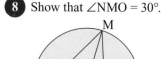

9

a) What is the size of ∠BDE?

b) How does the answer to part a) prove
    that AD is not a diameter of the circle?

10 Joel wants to prove that N is **not** the
centre of the circle shown on the right.
Answer the questions below, explaining
your answer in each case.

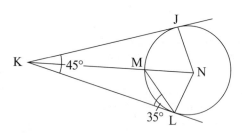

a) If N **were** the centre of the circle, what would the sizes of ∠KLN and ∠MLN be?

b) (i)   If N **were** the centre of the circle, why would MN = LN?
    (ii) If MN = LN, what would the sizes of ∠LMN and ∠MNL be?

c) (i)   If N **were** the centre of the circle, why would that mean triangles KJN and KLN were congruent?
    (ii) If triangles KJN and KLN were congruent, what would the size of ∠JNL be?

Joel says that N **can't be** the centre of the circle, because if it is, then ∠JKL is not 45°.

d) If N **were** the centre of the circle, what would the size of ∠JKL be?

Section 24 — Units, Measuring and Estimating

24.1 Converting Metric Units — Length, Mass and Volume

To convert between units, multiply or divide by the correct **conversion factor**.

Length
1 cm = 10 mm
1 m = 100 cm
1 km = 1000 m

Mass
1 g = 1000 mg
1 kg = 1000 g
1 tonne = 1000 kg

Volume
1 litre (l) = 1000 ml
1 ml = 1 cm^3

Example 1

Find the total of 0.2 tonnes, 31.8 kg and 1700 g. Give your answer in kg.

1. Convert all the masses to kilograms.

    0.2 tonnes = 0.2 × 1000 = 200 kg
    1700 g = 1700 ÷ 1000 = 1.7 kg

2. Add the masses together.

    200 kg + 31.8 kg + 1.7 kg = **233.5 kg**

Exercise 1

1 Convert each measurement into the units given.
  a) 3000 kg into tonnes
  b) 400 mg into g
  c) 123 ml into litres
  d) 51.16 g into kg
  e) 12.6 kg into tonnes
  f) 271.65 cm into m
  g) 150 cm^3 into litres
  h) 1532 g into tonnes
  i) 1005 cm into km
  j) 3023 mg into kg

2 Jack buys 1.2 kg of flour. How many pizzas can he make if each pizza needs 300 g of flour?

3 Hafsa is having a party for 32 guests.
  Her glasses have a capacity of 400 ml each.
  If she wants everyone to have a glass of juice, how many 2 litre bottles of juice should she buy?

4 A go-kart has a 5 litre petrol tank.
  It uses 10 ml of petrol per lap of a 400 m track.

  a) If James fills up the tank, how many laps of the track can he do?

  b) How many km can James travel on each full tank of petrol?

5 Sharon, Leuan and Elsie get into a cable car while skiing. Sharon weighs 55.2 kg, Leuan weighs 78.1 kg and Elsie weighs 65.9 kg. Their skis weigh 10 000 g a pair. The cable car is unsafe when carrying a mass of over half a tonne. Will Sharon, Leuan and Elsie be safe?

6 Milly runs a 1500 m fun run, a 50 m sprint and a 13.2 km race.
  How many km has she run in total?

7 Find the difference in the amounts of liquid held by the two containers shown below.
  Give your answer in cm^3.

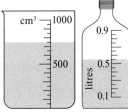

8 A reservoir contains 600 000 litres of water. During a period of heavy rain, the volume of water in the reservoir increases by 750 000 ml every day. The reservoir can only hold 800 000 litres of water. At this rate, how many days will it take for the reservoir to start overflowing?

9 A lasagne recipe requires 0.7 kg of minced beef, 400 g of tomato sauce, 300 g of cheese sauce, 0.2 kg of lasagne sheets and 2500 mg of herbs and spices.

  a) How many kg do these ingredients weigh?

  b) 0.2 kg of ingredients are needed to feed one person. How many people can be fed with this recipe?

24.2 Converting Metric Units — Area and Volume

Area is measured in units squared (e.g. m², cm², mm²).
To convert between different units of area, multiply or divide by the **square** of the 'length' conversion factor.

Volume is measured in units cubed (e.g. m³, cm³, mm³).
To convert between different units of volume, multiply or divide by the **cube** of the 'length' conversion factor.

Example 1

a) Convert an area of 0.06 m² to cm².

1. Work out the conversion factor from cm² to m².   1 m = 100 cm, so 1 m² = 100 × 100 = 10 000 cm²

2. Multiply by the conversion factor.   0.06 m² = 0.06 × 10 000 = **600 cm²**

b) Convert a volume of 382 000 cm³ to m³.

Find and divide by   1 m = 100 cm, so 1 m³ = 100³ cm³ = 1 000 000 cm³
the conversion factor.

So 382 000 cm³ = 382 000 ÷ 1 000 000 = **0.382 m³**

Exercise 1

1   Convert each of these measurements into the units given.

   a) 84 mm² into cm²
   b) 1750 cm² into m²
   c) 29 000 mm² into cm²
   d) 0.001 km³ into m³
   e) 15 cm³ into mm³
   f) 0.2 m³ into cm³
   g) 3 150 000 m² into km²
   h) 8500 mm² into cm²
   i) 1700 cm² into m²
   j) 0.435 km³ into m³
   k) 6.7 km³ into m³
   l) 0.000045 cm³ into mm³

2   Sandeesh wants to carpet two rectangular rooms. One of the rooms measures 1.7 m by 3 m,
   while the other is 670 cm by 420 cm. How many square metres of carpet will she need?

3   A 1 litre bottle of squash says to dilute 25 cm³ of squash with 0.5 litres of water to make one glass.
   a) How many glasses of squash can you get from this bottle?
   b) What is the total volume of one glass of squash in cm³?

4   A swimming pool measures 3 m deep and has a base with area 375 m².
   a) Find the volume of the pool in cm³.
   b) How many litres of water can the pool hold?

5   A brand of coffee powder is sold in cuboid packets with dimensions 20.7 cm by 25.5 cm by 10 cm.
   a) A volume of 0.003 m³ of coffee powder has already been used.
   What volume (in m³) of coffee powder is left?

   b) Find the total surface area of the packet of coffee powder.
   Give your answer in mm².

6   Convert each of these measurements into the units given.

   a) 1.2 m² into mm²
   b) 0.001 km² into cm²
   c) 50 million mm² into m²
   d) 673 000 000 cm² into km²
   e) 0.000005 km² into mm²
   f) 60 500 mm² into m²
   g) 3 million mm³ into km³
   h) 0.0006 m³ into mm³
   i) 999 cm³ into km³
   j) 17 440 mm³ into m³
   k) 19 cm³ into m³
   l) 0.00345 km³ into mm³

24.3 Metric and Imperial Units

To convert between metric and **imperial** units, multiply or divide by the **conversion factors** below. The symbol '$\approx$' means 'approximately equal to'.

Length	**Mass**	**Volume**
1 inch $\approx$ 2.5 cm	1 ounce $\approx$ 28 g	1 pint $\approx$ 0.57 litres
1 foot = 12 inches $\approx$ 30 cm	1 pound = 16 ounces $\approx$ 450 g	1 gallon = 8 pints $\approx$ 4.5 litres
1 yard = 3 feet $\approx$ 90 cm	1 stone = 14 pounds $\approx$ 6400 g	
1 mile $\approx$ 1.6 km	1 kg $\approx$ 2.2 pounds	

Example 1

Convert 6 pounds and 2 ounces into kilograms. Give your answer to two significant figures.

1. Write the whole mass using the same unit.

    1 pound = 16 ounces,
    so 6 pounds and 2 ounces = $(6 \times 16) + 2 = 98$ ounces

2. Convert this into grams first.
    Then convert the result into kg.

    98 ounces $\approx 98 \times 28 = 2744$ g = **2.7 kg** (to 2 s.f.)

Exercise 1

1 Convert each of the following masses into pounds and ounces.
   a) 1904 g   b) 840 g   c) 2688 g   d) 4.90 kg   e) 0.98 kg

2 Convert each of the following into feet and inches.
   a) 2 m   b) 52.5 cm   c) 1.5 km   d) 0.75 m   e) 50 mm

3 State which is the greater amount in each of the following pairs.
   a) 10 feet or 3.5 m   b) 1 stone or 7 kg   c) 10 miles or 12 km   d) 15 pints or 9 litres
   e) 3 pounds or 1.5 kg   f) 5 stone or 31 kg   g) 160 stone or 1 tonne   h) 2 gallons or 10 litres

4 A ride at a theme park states you must be 140 cm or over to ride.
   Maddie is 4 feet 5 inches and Lily is 4 feet 9 inches. Can they both go on the ride?

5 A running track is 400 m. How many laps of the track make one mile?

6 Jamie and Oliver are cooking. They need 1 pound and 12 ounces of meat for their recipe.
   They see 750 g of meat in the supermarket. Will this be enough?

7 A large box of juice holds 3 litres.

   a) How many pint jugs can be filled from the box?

   b) Approximately how many litres of juice will be left in the box?

8 Marion is on holiday in Spain. Her car measures speed in mph but the Spanish road signs are in km/h.
   The speed limit is 90 km/h. What is this in mph? Give your answer to the nearest mph.

Exercise 2

1 Complete each of these calculations. Give each of your answers to two significant figures.
   a) 681 cm + 12.4 yards $\approx$ ◯ m
   b) 16.49 km + 21.5 miles $\approx$ ◯ km
   c) 3 kg + 1 stone + 1.5 kg $\approx$ ◯ kg
   d) 100 cm + 2 yards + 15 feet $\approx$ ◯ cm
   e) 3 l + 4.5 pints + 250 ml $\approx$ ◯ ml
   f) 7 m + 8 inches + 35 mm $\approx$ ◯ cm

2 Jacob's mother asks him to buy 4 pints of milk. The shop only sells milk in 1 litre, 2 litre
   and 4 litre cartons. Which of these amounts is closest to what his mother asked for?

3 Lotte's car travels 55 miles per gallon of petrol.
If her car contains 45 litres of petrol, how many whole miles can she travel?

4 The weights of 10 people getting into a lift are shown below. The lift has a weight limit of 1 tonne.
Will the total weight of the 10 people exceed this limit?

11 stone 4 pounds	10 stone	7 stone 2 pounds	13 stone 1 pound	15 stone 4 pounds
12 stone	8 stone 9 pounds	10 stone 3 pounds	16 stone	11 stone 6 pounds

24.4   Estimating in Real Life

You can **estimate** how big something is by comparing it with something you already know the size of.

Example 1

Estimate the height of this lamp post.

Estimate the height of the man,
then use this to estimate the
height of the lamp post.

Average height of a man ≈ 1.8 m.

The lamp post is roughly twice
the height of the man.

Height of the lamp post ≈ 2 × 1.8 m = **3.6 m**

1.8 m

Example 2

Give a sensible unit for measuring the height of a room.

Most rooms are taller than an average man, but not that
much taller — roughly 2 to 3 metres. So it makes sense to
measure the height of a room in metres (or possibly cm).

A sensible unit is **metres**.

Exercise 1

1 Suggest a sensible metric unit you would use to measure each of the following.

   a) the length of a pencil   **b)** the mass of a tomato   **c)** the length of an ant

   d) the mass of a bus   **e)** the distance from Birmingham to Manchester

2 Estimate each of the following, using sensible metric units.

   a) the height of your bedroom   **b)** the length of a family car   **c)** the height of a football goal

   d) the arm span of an average man   **e)** the diameter of a football   **f)** the volume of a typical bath tub

For Questions 3-4 give your answer in sensible metric units.

3 Estimate the length and height of the bus.

4 Estimate the height and length of this dinosaur by
comparing it with a chicken.

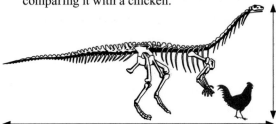

Section 25 — Compound Measures

25.1 Compound Measures

Compound measures are measures that are made up of **two or more other measures**.
For example, **speed** is a compound measure — it is made up of **distance** and **time**.

Speed, Distance and Time

Distance, time and (average) speed are connected by the formula:

$$\text{Speed} = \frac{\text{Distance}}{\text{Time}}$$

Example 1

A car travels 240 km in 45 minutes. What is the average speed of the car in km/h?

1. Convert the time to hours.

2. Substitute the distance and time into the formula.

3. The units of speed are a combination of the units of distance (km) and time (hours).

$45 \text{ mins} = 45 \div 60 = 0.75 \text{ hours}$

$\text{Speed} = \dfrac{\text{Distance}}{\text{Time}}$

$= \dfrac{240}{0.75} = \textbf{320 km/h}$

Exercise 1

1 Find the average speed of the following.
   a) a plane flying 1800 miles in 4.5 hours
   b) a lift travelling 100 m in 80 seconds
   c) a cyclist travelling 34 km in 1.6 hours
   d) an escalator step moving 15 m in 24 seconds

2 Find the average speed of the following in km/h.
   a) a train travelling 30 000 m in 2.5 hours
   b) a river flowing 2.25 km in 45 minutes
   c) a fish swimming 0.5 km in 12 minutes
   d) a balloon rising 700 m in 3 minutes

3 A spacecraft travels 232 900 miles to the moon in 13.7 hours.
Calculate the average speed of the spacecraft.

4 It takes a high speed train 25 minutes to travel 240 km.
Calculate the average speed of the train in kilometres per hour.

5 A bobsleigh covers 1.4 km in 65 seconds. Find its average speed in metres per second.
Give your answer to two significant figures.

6 A tortoise walks 98 cm in 8 minutes. Find the tortoise's average speed in m/s.
Give your answer to one significant figure.

You can rearrange the formula for speed to find distance and time.

$$\text{Distance} = \text{Speed} \times \text{Time}$$

$$\text{Time} = \frac{\text{Distance}}{\text{Speed}}$$

Example 2

A man runs for 33 minutes with average speed 12 km/h. How far does he run?

1. The speed is in km/h, so convert the time into hours.

2. Substitute the speed and time into the formula.

3. The speed is in km/h, so the distance will be in km.

$33 \text{ minutes} = 33 \div 60 = 0.55 \text{ hours}$

$\text{Distance} = \text{Speed} \times \text{Time}$

$= 12 \times 0.55 = \textbf{6.6 km}$

Example 3

A car travels 85 miles at an average speed of 34 mph. How many minutes does the journey take?

1. Substitute the distance and speed into the formula. $\text{Time} = \dfrac{\text{Distance}}{\text{Speed}} = \dfrac{85}{34} = 2.5$ hours

2. Convert your answer into minutes. 2.5 hours $= 2.5 \times 60$ minutes
$$= \textbf{150 minutes}$$

Exercise 2

1   For each of the following, use the speed and time given to calculate the distance travelled.
   a) speed = 98 km/h, time = 3.5 hours
   b) speed = 25 mph, time = 2.7 hours
   c) speed = 8 m/s, time = 49.6 seconds
   d) speed = 3.2 km/h, time = 0.04 hours
   e) speed = 15 m/s, time = 9 minutes
   f) speed = 72 mph, time = 171 minutes

2   For each of the following, use the speed and distance given to calculate the time taken.
   a) speed = 2.5 km/h, distance = 4 km
   b) speed = 5 m/s, distance = 9.3 m
   c) speed = 15 mph, distance = 55.2 miles
   d) speed = 4 m/s, distance = 0.05 m
   e) speed = 9 m/s, distance = 61.2 km
   f) speed = 8 cm/s, distance = 1.96 m

3   A dart is thrown with speed 15 m/s.
It hits a dartboard 2.4 m away.
How long is the dart in the air?

6   A train travels at 78 km/h for 5.6 km.
How long does the journey take?
Give your answer to the nearest minute.

4   A flight to Spain takes 2 hours and 15 minutes.
The plane travels at an average speed of 480 mph.
How far does the plane travel?

7   A leopard runs 0.25 miles at an average
speed of 40 mph. How many seconds
does this take the leopard?

5   A girl skates at an average speed of 7.5 mph.
How far does she skate in 75 minutes?

8   A snail slides 14.8 cm in 1 minute 25 seconds.
Find the snail's average speed in m/s.
Give your answer to two significant figures.

Density

Density is a compound measure — it is a measure of **mass** per unit **volume**.
Density, mass and volume
are connected by this formula: $\textbf{Density} = \dfrac{\textbf{Mass}}{\textbf{Volume}}$

You can rearrange the formula
to find mass and volume. $\textbf{Volume} = \dfrac{\textbf{Mass}}{\textbf{Density}}$ $\textbf{Mass} = \textbf{Volume} \times \textbf{Density}$

Example 4

A 1840 kg concrete block has a volume of 0.8 m³. Calculate the density of the concrete block.

1. Substitute the mass and volume into the formula. $\text{Density} = \dfrac{\text{Mass}}{\text{Volume}}$

2. The units of density are a combination of the units
of mass (kg) and volume (m³). $= \dfrac{1840}{0.8} = \textbf{2300 kg/m}^3$

Exercise 3

1 For each of the following, use the mass and volume to calculate the density.
  a) mass = 200 kg, volume = 540 m³   **b)** mass = 23 kg, volume = 0.5 m³
  c) mass = 1088 kg, volume = 1.6 m³   **d)** mass = 2498 kg, volume = 0.25 m³
  e) mass = 642 kg, volume = 0.05 m³   **f)** mass = 0.06 kg, volume = 0.025 m³

2 **a)** Write down the formula to calculate volume from density and mass.
  b) Use your answer to calculate the volume for each of the following.
    (i) density = 8 kg/m³, mass = 1 kg   **(ii)** density = 1510 kg/m³, mass = 3926 kg
    (iii) density = 1.25 kg/m³, mass = 4 kg   **(iv)** density = 240 kg/m³, mass = 14.4 kg

3 A limestone statue has a volume of 0.4 m³. Limestone has a density of 2610 kg/m³.
  a) Write down the formula to calculate a mass from a volume and a density.
  b) Calculate the mass of the statue.

4 A paperweight has a volume of 8 cm³ and a density of 11 500 kg/m³.
  Calculate the mass of the paperweight.

Pressure

Pressure is a compound measure — it is the **force** of an object per unit **area**.

Pressure, force and area are
connected by these formulas:
$$\textbf{Pressure} = \frac{\textbf{Force}}{\textbf{Area}} \qquad \textbf{Area} = \frac{\textbf{Force}}{\textbf{Pressure}} \qquad \textbf{Force} = \textbf{Pressure} \times \textbf{Area}$$

Pressure is usually measured in **N/m²** (also known as pascals — **Pa**) or **N/cm²**.

Example 5

An object is resting with its base on horizontal ground. The area of the object's base is 20 cm²
and the object weighs 60 N. What pressure is the object exerting on the ground?

1. Substitute the force and area into the formula. $\text{Pressure} = \dfrac{\text{Force}}{\text{Area}} = \dfrac{60}{20}$
2. The units of pressure are a combination
    of the units of force (N) and area (cm²). $= \textbf{3 N/cm}^2$

Exercise 4

1 For each of the following, calculate the missing measure.
  a) Pressure = ?, Area = 4 m², Force = 4800 N   **b)** Pressure = ?, Area = 80 cm², Force = 640 N
  c) Pressure = 180 N/m², Area = ?, Force = 540 N   **d)** Pressure = 36 N/cm², Area = 30 cm², Force = ?

2 A square-based pyramid is resting with its square face on horizontal ground.
  The pyramid has a weight of 45 N and its square face has a side length of 3 cm.
  What pressure is the pyramid exerting on the ground? Give your answer in: **a)** N/cm²   **b)** N/m²

3 A cube of metal with a volume of 512 cm³ is resting with one of its faces on horizontal ground.
  The cube has a weight of 1792 N. What pressure is the cube exerting on the ground?

4 A cylinder with a height of 80 cm is resting with one of its circular faces on horizontal ground.
  The weight of the cylinder is 560 N and it exerts a pressure of 70 000 N/m² on the ground.
  What is the volume of the cylinder in cm³?

25.2   Distance-Time Graphs

A **distance-time** graph shows how far an object has travelled in a particular time.

The **gradient** of a distance-time graph shows the **speed** of the object.
The **steeper** the graph, the **faster** the object is moving.

A **straight** line shows the object is moving at a **constant speed**.
A **horizontal** line means the object is **stationary**.

A **curved graph** shows the **speed** of the object is **changing** — it is **accelerating** or **decelerating**.

Example 1

This graph represents a bus journey.

a) How far had the bus travelled before it stopped?

b) Describe the motion of the bus
    during the journey.

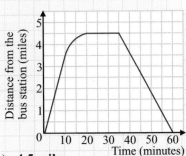

1. The bus is stationary where the
    graph is a horizontal line.

2. At first the graph is a straight line, so
    the bus moves at a constant speed.

3. As the graph curves, the gradient decreases
    — the bus must be slowing down.

4. The graph is a straight line again, and the distance
    from the bus station decreases — so the bus
    must be travelling in the opposite direction.

a) **4.5 miles**

b) Between 0 and 10 minutes the
    bus was travelling at a **constant speed**.

Between 10 and 20 minutes the bus was
decelerating (slowing down).

Between 20 and 35 minutes the bus was **stationary**.

Between 35 and 60 minutes the bus travels at a
constant speed in the opposite direction to before.

Exercise 1

1   This graph shows a family's car journey.
    The family left home at 8:00 am.
    a) (i)   How long did the family travel for before stopping?
        (ii)   How far had they travelled when they stopped?
    b) How long did the family stay at their
        destination before setting off home?
    c) (i)   What time did they start back home?
        (ii)   How long did the journey home take?
    d) Without doing any calculations, state whether the family travelled at a greater speed
        on the way to their destination or on the way back. Explain your answer.

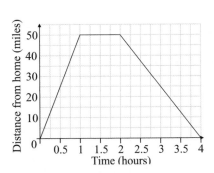

2   Harry walks 3 km in 50 minutes at a constant speed to his friend's house. He stays there for 1 hour.
    He then walks at a constant speed back towards home for 30 minutes until he gets to the shop,
    1 km from home. He stays at the shop for 10 minutes before walking home at a constant speed,
    which takes a further 15 minutes.

    Draw a graph to represent Harry's journey.

3 Describe the journey represented by each of these distance-time graphs.

a)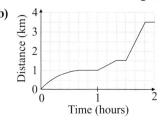

b)

c)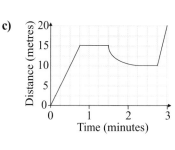

Finding Speed from a Distance-Time Graph

Example 2

The graph on the right represents a train journey from Clumpton Station to Hillybrook Station.

a) Find the speed of the train (in kilometres per hour) at 9:15.

b) Find the average speed of the train for this journey.

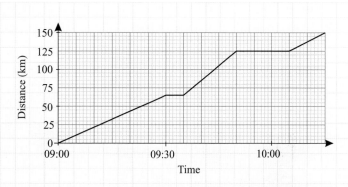

1. The speed is constant from 9:00 until 9:30.

2. Use the formula 'speed = distance $(d) \div$ time (t)'.

3. You can find the average speed by dividing the total distance travelled by the total time taken.

a) Distance = 65 km, Time = 0.5 hours

Speed = 65 ÷ 0.5 = **130 km/h**

b) Speed = total distance ÷ total time
= 150 km ÷ 1.25 hours = **120 km/h**

Exercise 2

1 This graph shows a commuter's journey to work. His journey consists of two stages of travelling, separated by a break of 30 minutes.

a) What was his speed (in km/h) during the first stage of his journey?

b) What was his speed (in km/h) during the second stage of his journey?

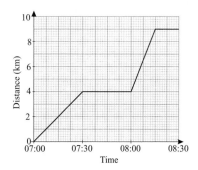

2 Find the speed of the object represented by each of the following distance-time graphs.

a)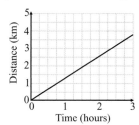

b)

c)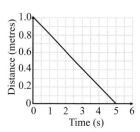

3 The graph on the right shows two cyclists' journeys.

a) Which cyclist had the highest maximum speed?

b) Find the difference in the speeds of the cyclists during the first 15 minutes of their journeys.

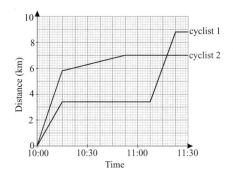

4 Chay travels to Clapham by taking a bus and a train. His journey is shown by the graph below.

a) Find the average speed Chay travelled:
   (i) by bus   (ii) by train

b) Chay spends 30 minutes in Clapham before he returns home by taxi at an average speed of 60 km/h.
   (i) Copy the graph and extend the line to show Chay's 30 minutes in Clapham.
   (ii) Find the time it took Chay to travel home by taxi.
   (iii) Show Chay's taxi ride home on the graph.

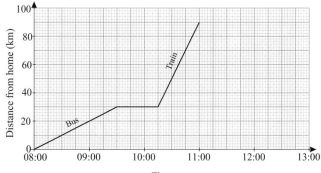

5 Draw distance-time graphs to show the following journeys.

a) Ash catches a train at 10:00, then travels for 280 miles at a constant speed of 80 mph.

b) Corey sets off from home at 09:00 and drives 90 miles at a constant speed of 60 mph. After 45 minutes at his destination, he drives back home at a constant speed of 40 mph.

6 Estimate the speed of the object represented by each of these distance-time graphs when time = 1 hour.

a)
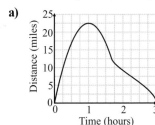

b)
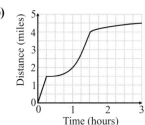

c)
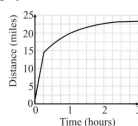

25.3 Velocity-Time Graphs

A **velocity-time** graph shows the **speed** and **direction** of an object during a particular period of time.
E.g. objects with velocities of **5 m/s** and **−5 m/s** are travelling at the **same speed** but in **opposite directions**.

Calculating Acceleration from a Velocity-Time Graph

Acceleration is the **rate of change** of **velocity** over time.
The **units** of acceleration are a combination of the units for velocity and time e.g. m/s^2.

The **gradient** of a velocity-time graph shows the **acceleration (or deceleration)** of an object.

The **steeper** the graph, the **greater the acceleration** of the object is.

A **straight** line shows that the object has a **constant acceleration**.
A **horizontal** line means the object is moving at a **constant velocity**.

Example 1

The graph shows the velocity of a taxi during a journey.

Calculate the acceleration of the taxi

a) 6 seconds into the journey,

b) 10 seconds into the journey.

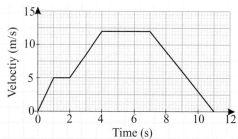

1. The graph is horizontal, so the velocity is constant and there is no acceleration. Make sure you remember the units — m/s².

a) **0 m/s²**

2. Calculate the gradient using acceleration = change in velocity ÷ change in time. The gradient is negative so the acceleration will be negative — the taxi is decelerating.

b) Change in velocity = 0 – 12 m/s = –12 m/s

Change in time = 11 – 7 = 4 s

Acceleration = $\frac{-12}{4}$ = **–3 m/s²**

Exercise 1

1 Calculate the acceleration shown by each of the graphs below.

a)
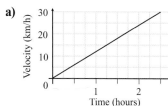

b)
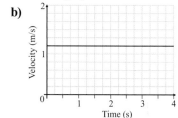

c)
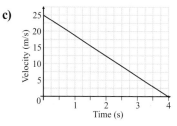

2 The diagram shows the velocity of a train travelling between two stations.

a) What is the maximum velocity of the train during the journey?

b) Calculate the initial acceleration of the train.

c) Calculate the deceleration of the train at the end of its journey.

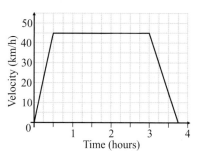

Example 2

Look at the velocity-time graph for a tram on the right.

a) Describe the velocity of the tram in the first second of the journey.

b) Describe the acceleration of the tram in the first second of the journey.

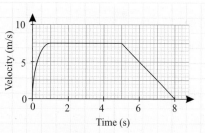

The gradient starts off steep and then decreases. This means the tram's acceleration also decreases.

a) The tram's velocity increases from 0 to 7.5 m/s.

b) The acceleration of the tram decreases over time.

Exercise 2

1 Look at the velocity-time graph on the right.

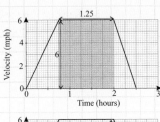

  a) Describe the velocity of the object between points

    (i) A and B   **(ii)** D and E   **(iii)** G and H.

  b) Describe the acceleration of the object between points

    (i) A and B   **(ii)** D and E   **(iii)** G and H.

  c) Calculate the acceleration between points

    (i) C and D   **(ii)** E and F.

  d) Estimate the acceleration of the object after   **(i)** 1 hour   **(ii)** 11 hours

Calculating Distance from a Velocity-Time Graph

The **area** underneath a velocity-time graph is equal to the **distance** travelled.

Example 3

The graph shows the velocity of a runner.

a) Calculate the distance run at a constant velocity.

b) Calculate the distance travelled in
the last half hour of the run.

1. Calculate the area of
the rectangle under the
flat part of the graph.

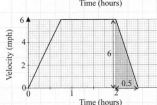

  a) Distance = 6 mph × 1.25 h

            = **7.5 miles**

2. Calculate the area
of the triangle under
the part of the graph
representing the last
half hour.

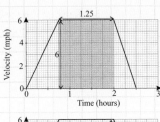

  b) Distance = $\frac{1}{2}$(6 mph × 0.5 h)

            = **1.5 miles**

Exercise 3

1 Calculate the distance travelled for each of the following graphs.

  a) 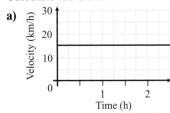   **b)**    **c)**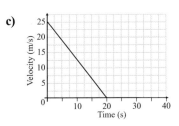

2 The diagram shows the velocity of a train for
the first 60 seconds of a journey.

  a) Calculate the total distance travelled
during this part of the train's journey.

  b) Calculate the average
velocity of the train.

3 A car accelerates for 8 seconds, causing its velocity to increase from 0 m/s to 48 m/s. The car travels at a constant velocity of 48 m/s for 20 seconds, before decelerating for 5 seconds. The final velocity of the car is 23 m/s.

    a) Draw a velocity-time graph to show the car's velocity during this part of the journey.

    b) Calculate both the acceleration and deceleration of the car.

    c) Calculate the distance travelled by the car.

4 The diagram shows the velocity of an object over 60 seconds. It has been split up into 20 second intervals.

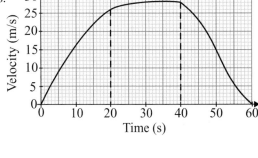

    a) Estimate the distance travelled during the first 20 seconds of the journey.

    b) Estimate the distance travelled during the last 20 seconds of the journey.

    c) By splitting the middle 20 seconds into two intervals estimate the total distance the object travelled.

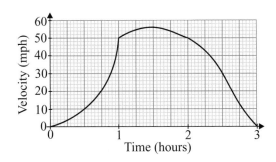

5 The graph on the left shows the velocity of an object during a 3 hour journey.

    a) Estimate the total distance travelled by the object.

    b) Estimate the average velocity of the object over the 3 hour journey.

Exercise 4 — Mixed Exercise

1 The graph shows the velocity of a car as it travels between two sets of traffic lights.

    a) Calculate the deceleration of the car as it approaches the second set of lights.

    b) Work out the total distance the car moves between the traffic lights.

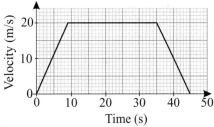

2 The graph below shows 120 seconds of a coach journey.

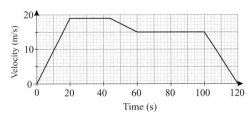

    a) Describe fully how the velocity and acceleration of the coach changed during the 120 second journey.

    b) How far did the coach travel in this 120 second time period?

3 The velocity-time graph shows the velocity of two ostriches.

    a) How far did each ostrich run?

    b) Calculate the average velocity of Bert.

    c) Work out the initial acceleration of Ernie.

    d) Without any further calculation, state which ostrich had the greatest initial acceleration. Explain your answer.

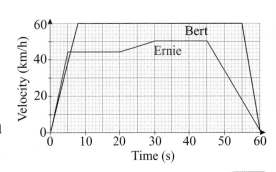

Section 26 — Constructions

26.1   Scale Drawings

A **scale** tells you the relationship between distances on a map or plan and distances in real life.

E.g. a map scale of 1 cm : 100 m means that 1 cm on the map represents an actual distance of 100 m.
A scale without units (e.g. 1 : 100) means you can use any units. For example, 1 cm : 100 cm or 1 mm : 100 mm.

Example 1

A plan of a garden is drawn to a scale of 1 cm : 5 m.

a)   The distance between two trees marked on the plan is
     3 cm. What is the actual distance between the trees?

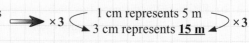

b)   The actual distance between the garden
     shed and the pond is measured as 2.5 m.
     What would the distance between the
     shed and the pond be on the plan?

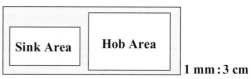

Exercise 1

1   The scale on a map of Europe is 1 cm : 50 km. Find the distance used on the map to represent:

   a) 150 km   **b)** 600 km   **c)** 1000 km   **d)** 25 km   **e)** 10 km   **f)** 15 km

2   The floor plan of a house is drawn to a scale of 1 cm : 2 m.
    Find the actual dimensions of the rooms if they are shown on the plan as:

   a) 2.7 cm by 1.5 cm   **b)** 3.2 cm by 2.2 cm   **c)** 1.85 cm by 1.4 cm   **d)** 0.9 cm by 1.35 cm

3   A bridge of length 0.8 km is to be drawn on a
    map with scale 1 cm : 0.5 km. What length will
    the bridge appear on the map?

4   A set of toy furniture is made to a scale of 1 : 40.
    Find the dimensions of the actual furniture when
    the toys have the following measurements.

   a) Width of bed: 3.5 cm

   b) Length of table: 3.2 cm

   c) Height of chair: 2.4 cm

5   A road of length 6.7 km is to be drawn on a map.
    The scale of the map is 1 : 250 000.
    How long will the road be on the map?

6   A model railway uses a scale of 1 : 500.
    Use the actual measurements given below
    to find measurements for the model.

   a) Length of footbridge: 100 m

   b) Height of signal box: 6 m

7   Below is the plan for a kitchen surface.

Sink Area	**Hob Area**

   1 mm : 3 cm

   Use the plan to find the actual dimensions of:
   a) The sink area   **b)** The hob area

Example 2

A plan of the grounds of a palace has a scale of 1 : 40 000. Represent this scale in the form 1 cm : *n* m.

1.   Write the scale down using centimetres   1 cm : 40 000 cm
     to match the left-hand side of 1 cm : *n* m.

2.   Convert the right-hand side to metres by   1 cm : (40 000 ÷ 100) m
     dividing by 100.
                                                        1 cm : 400 m

8 A path of length 4.5 km is shown on a map as a line of length 3 cm. Express the scale in the form 1 cm : n km.

9 The plan for a school has a scale of 1 : 1500.

   a) Express this scale in the form 1 cm : n m.

   b) The school playground is 60 m in length. Find the corresponding length on the plan.

10 On the plans for a house, 3 cm represents the length of a garden with actual length 18 m.

   a) Find the map scale in the form 1 : n.

   b) On the plan, the width of the garden is 1.2 cm. What is its actual width in metres?

   c) The lounge has a length of 4.5 m. What is the corresponding length on the plan?

11 The map below shows tourist attractions in a city.

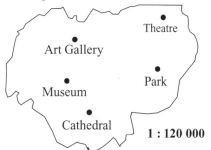

1 : 120 000

Find the actual distances between:

   a) the museum and the cathedral

   b) the art gallery and the theatre

   c) the cathedral and the theatre

Example 3

The diagram shows a rough sketch of a garden.
Use the scale 1 : 400 to draw an accurate plan of the garden.

1. Write down the scale in cm.   1 cm : 400 cm

2. Change the right-hand side to metres.   1 cm : 4 m

3. Use the scale to work out the lengths for the plan, then use these lengths to draw your plan.

   4 m is shown as 1 cm, so:
   12 m is shown as 3 cm
   8 m is shown as 2 cm

   2 m is shown as 0.5 cm
   3 m is shown as 0.75 cm

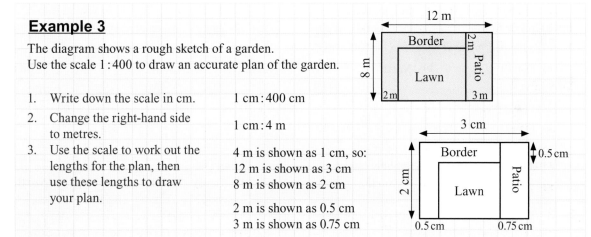

Exercise 2

1 Using a scale of 1 : 20, draw an accurate plan of the kitchen shown below.

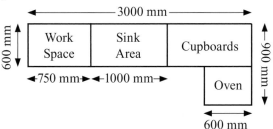

2 Use the scale 1 : 25 to draw a scale drawing for the house extension shown in the rough sketch below.

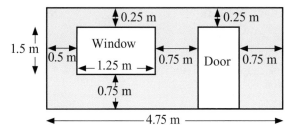

3 Below is a sketch of a park lake.

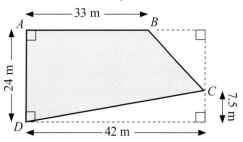

   a) Draw an accurate plan of the lake using the scale 1 cm : 3 m.

   b) There is a duck house at the intersection of *AC* and *BD*. Find the actual distance from the duck house to point *B*.

26.2 Bearings

A **bearing** tells you the direction of one point from another.
Bearings are given as **three-figure angles**, measured **clockwise** from **north**.

Example 1

a) Find the bearing of B from A.

b) Find the bearing of C from A.

Find the clockwise angle from north, then give the bearing as three figures.

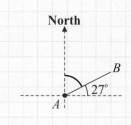

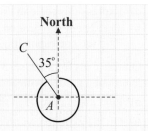

a) $90° - 27° = 63°$, so the bearing of B from A is **063°**.

b) $360° - 35° = 325°$, so the bearing of C from A is **325°**.

Exercise 1

1 Find the bearing of B from A in the following.

a) **North**

b) **North**

c) **North**

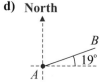
d) **North**

e) **North**

2 Find the angle θ in each of the following using the information given.

a) **North**

b) **North**

c) **North**

d) **North**

e) **North**

Bearing of D from C is 111°

Bearing of D from C is 203°

Bearing of D from C is 285°

Bearing of D from C is 135°

Bearing of D from C is 222°

3 Liverchester is 100 km south of Manpool.
King's Hill is 100 km east of Liverchester.

a) Sketch the layout of the three locations.

b) Find the bearing of King's Hill from Liverchester.

c) Find the bearings from King's Hill of:

   (i) Liverchester   (ii) Manpool

4 Mark a point O and draw in a north line.
Use a protractor to help you draw the points
a) to f) with the following bearings from O.

a) 040°   b) 079°   c) 321°

d) 163°   e) 007°   f) 283°

Example 2

The bearing of X from Y is 244°. Find the bearing of Y from X.

1. Draw a diagram showing what you know.

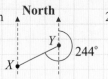

2. Find the **alternate angle** to the one you're looking for.

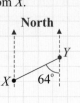

3. Use angle properties to find the bearing.

So the bearing of Y from X is **064°**.

Exercise 2

1 Find the bearing of *A* from *B* in the following diagrams.

a)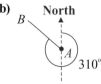

North

A •) 125°

B

b) North

B

A 310°

2 The bearing of *H* from *G* is 023°. Find the bearing of *G* from *H*.

3 The bearing of *K* from *J* is 101°. Find the bearing of *J* from *K*.

4 Find the bearing of *N* from *M* given that the bearing of *M* from *N* is:

a) 200°   **b)** 310°   **c)** 080°

d) 117°   **e)** 015°   **f)** 099°

5 **a)** Measure the angle *θ* in the diagram on the right.

b) Write down the bearing of *R* from *S*.

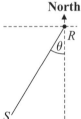

North

R

θ

S

6 The point *Q* lies due west of point *P*.

a) Write down the bearing of *Q* from *P*.

b) Write down the bearing of *P* from *Q*.

7 The point *Z* lies southeast of the point *Y*.

a) Write down the bearing of *Z* from *Y*.

b) Find the bearing of *Y* from *Z*.

8 North

U 68°

V

a) Find the bearing of *V* from *U*.

b) Find the bearing of *U* from *V*.

9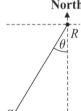

North

E

34° 55° *B*

A 88°

D 101°

C

Find the bearing of:

a) *B* from *A*   **b)** *C* from *A*

c) *D* from *A*   **d)** *E* from *A*

e) *A* from *B*   **f)** *A* from *C*

g) *A* from *D*   **h)** *A* from *E*

Example 3

The points *P* and *Q* are 75 km apart. *Q* lies on a bearing of 055° from *P*. Use the scale 1 cm : 25 km to draw an accurate scale diagram of *P* and *Q*.

1. Draw *P* and measure the required bearing.

North

055°

P

2. Use the scale to work out the distance between the two points.

25 km is shown by 1 cm, so 75 km is shown by 3 cm.

3. Draw *Q* the correct distance and direction from *P*.

North

Q

3 cm

P

Exercise 3

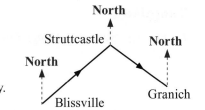

1   A pilot flies from Blissville to Struttcastle, then on to Granich.
    This journey is shown by the scale diagram on the right,
    which is drawn using a scale of 1 cm : 100 km.
    a) Find the distance and bearings of the following stages of the journey.
        (i) Blissville to Struttcastle **(ii)** Struttcastle to Granich
    b) The pilot returns directly from Granich to Blissville. Find the actual distance travelled in this stage.

2   Paul's house is 150 km from Tirana, on a bearing of 048°.
    Draw an accurate scale diagram of Paul's house and Tirana using the scale 1 cm : 30 km.

3   Paradise City lies 540 km from Pretty Grimville, on a bearing of 125°.
    Draw an accurate scale diagram of the two locations using the scale 1 cm : 90 km.

4   A pilot flies 2000 km from Budarid to Madpest, on a bearing of 242°.
    Draw an accurate scale diagram of the journey using the scale 1 : 100 000 000.

5   Use the scale 1 : 22 000 000 to draw an accurate scale diagram
    of an 880 km journey from Budarid to Blissville, on a bearing of 263°.

6   The scale drawing on the right shows three cities.
    The scale of the diagram is 1 : 10 000 000.
    a) Use the diagram to find the following actual distances.
        (i) *PQ*   **(ii)** *QR*   **(iii)** *PR*
    b) Use a protractor to find the following bearings.
        (i) *Q* from *P*   **(ii)** *R* from *Q*   **(iii)** *P* from *R*

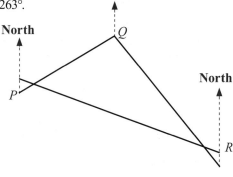

26.3   Constructions

You should be able to do constructions just using a **pencil**, a **ruler** and **compasses**. Remember to **always** leave
compass arcs and other construction lines on finished drawings to show you've used the right method.

Constructing Triangles

Example 1

Draw triangle *ABC*, where *AB* is 3 cm, *BC* is 2.5 cm and *AC* is 2 cm.

1. Draw and label side *AB*.

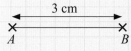

2. Set your compasses to 2.5 cm.   3. Now set your compasses to 2 cm.   4. *C* is where your
    Draw an arc 2.5 cm from *B*.   Draw an arc 2 cm from *A*.   arcs cross.

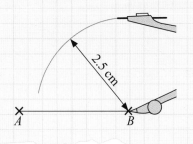   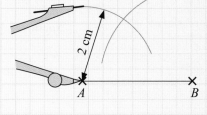   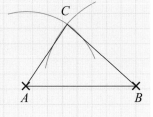

Exercise 1

1 Draw the following triangles accurately.

a)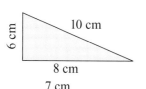

b)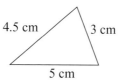

c)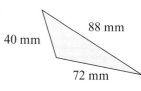

d)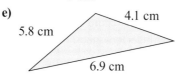

e)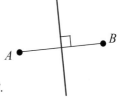

f)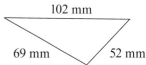

2 Draw each of the triangles ABC described below.

  a) AB is 5 cm, BC is 6 cm, AC is 7 cm.
  b) AB is 4 cm, BC is 7 cm, AC is 9 cm.
  c) AB is 8 cm, BC is 8 cm, AC is 4 cm.
  d) AB is 4.6 cm, BC is 5.4 cm, AC is 8.4 cm.

3 Draw an isosceles triangle with two sides of length 5 cm and a side of length 7 cm.

4 Using a scale of 1 cm : 10 miles, draw a map showing the relative positions of the three places described on the right. (All distances are 'as the crow flies'.)

- High Cross is 54 miles due west of Low Cross.
- Very Cross is 47 miles from Low Cross and 27 miles from High Cross
- Very Cross lies to the south of High Cross and Low Cross.

Constructing a Perpendicular Bisector

The **perpendicular bisector** of a line between points A and B
- is at right angles to the line AB
- cuts the line AB in half.

All points on the perpendicular bisector are equally far from both A and B.

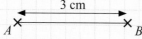

Example 2

Draw a line AB which is 3 cm long. Construct its perpendicular bisector.

1. Draw AB.

2. Place the compass point at A, with the radius set at more than half of the length AB. Draw two arcs as shown.

3. Keep the radius the same and put the compass point at B. Draw two more arcs.

4. Use a ruler to draw a straight line through the points where the arcs meet. This is the perpendicular bisector.

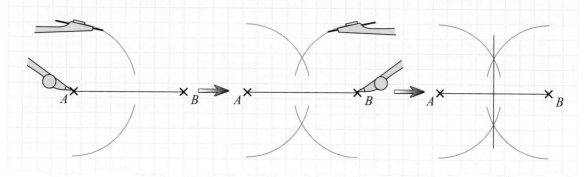

Exercise 2

1 Draw the following lines and construct their perpendicular bisectors using only a ruler and compasses.
  a) A horizontal line PQ 5 cm long.   **b)** A vertical line XY 9 cm long.   **c)** A line AB 7 cm long.

2 **a)** Draw a line AB 6 cm long. Construct the perpendicular bisector of AB.
  b) Draw the rhombus $ACBD$ with diagonals 6 cm and 8 cm.

3 **a)** Draw a circle with radius 5 cm, and draw <u>any</u> two chords. Label your chords AB and CD.
  b) Construct the perpendicular bisector of chord AB.
  c) Construct the perpendicular bisector of chord CD.
  d) Where do the two perpendicular bisectors meet?

Constructing an Angle Bisector

An **angle bisector** cuts an angle in half.

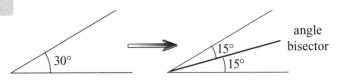

Example 3

Draw an angle of 60° using a protractor. Construct the angle bisector using only a ruler and compasses.

  1. Place the point of the compasses on the angle...

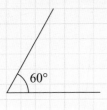

  2. ...and draw arcs crossing both lines...

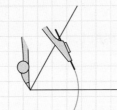

  3. ...using the same radius.

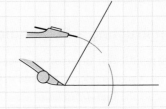

  4. Now place the point of the compasses where your arcs cross the lines, and draw two more arcs — using the same radius.

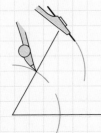
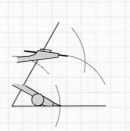

  5. Draw the angle bisector through the point where the arcs cross.

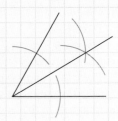

Exercise 3

1 Draw each angle using a protractor, then construct its angle bisector using a ruler and compasses.
  a) 100°   **b)** 140°   **c)** 96°   **d)** 44°
  e) 50°   **f)** 70°   **g)** 20°   **h)** 65°

2 Draw a triangle and construct the bisectors of each of the angles. What do you notice about these bisectors?

3 **a)** Draw an angle ABC of 110°, with $AB = BC = 5$ cm. Construct the bisector of angle ABC.
  b) Mark point D on your drawing, where D is the point on the angle bisector with $BD = 8$ cm.
    What kind of quadrilateral is $ABCD$?

Constructing a Perpendicular from a Point to a Line

The **perpendicular** from a point to a line
- passes through the point, and
- meets the line at 90°.

perpendicular from the point X to the line AB ⟹

Example 4

Construct the perpendicular from the point X to the line AB using only a ruler and compasses.

X

A ——————— B

1. Draw an arc centred on X cutting the line twice. (You may need to extend the line.)

2. Draw an arc centred on one of the points where your arc meets the line.

3. Do the same for the other point, keeping the radius the same.

4. Draw the perpendicular to where the arcs cross.

Exercise 4

1   Use a ruler to draw any triangle. Label the corners of the triangle X, Y and Z. Construct the perpendicular from X to the line YZ.

2   Draw three points that do not lie on a straight line. Label your points P, Q and R.
    Draw a straight line passing through points P and Q.
    Construct the perpendicular from R to this line.

3   **a)** On squared paper draw axes with x-values from 1 to 10 and y-values from 1 to 10.
    b) Plot the points $A(1, 2)$, $B(9, 1)$ and $C(6, 8)$.
    c) Construct the perpendicular from point C to the line AB.

4   Draw any triangle. Construct a perpendicular from each of the triangle's corners to the opposite side. What do you notice about these lines?

5   **a)** Construct triangle DEF, where $DE = 5$ cm, $DF = 6$ cm and angle $FDE = 55°$.
    b) Construct the perpendicular from F to DE.
        Label the point where the perpendicular meets DE as point G.
    c) Measure the length FG. Use your result to work out the area of the triangle to 1 decimal place.

Constructing 60° and 30° Angles

You'd need to construct an angle of 60° to draw an accurate equilateral triangle.

You can construct an angle of 30° by bisecting an angle of 60°.

 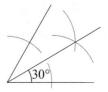

Example 5

Draw a line *AB* and construct an angle of 60° at *A*.

1. Place the compass point on *A* and draw a long arc that crosses the line *AB*.

2. Place the compass point where the arc meets the line, and draw another arc of the same radius.

3. Draw a straight line through *A* and the point where your arcs cross. The angle will be 60°.

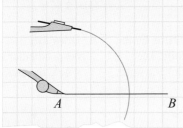 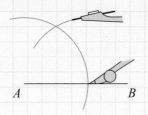 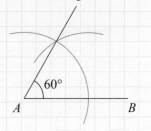

Exercise 5

1 Draw a line *AB* measuring 5 cm. Construct an angle of 60° at *A*.

2 Draw an equilateral triangle with sides measuring 6 cm.

3 Draw a line *AB* measuring 6 cm. Construct an angle of 30° at *A*.

4 Construct the triangle *ABC* where *AB* = 7 cm, angle *CAB* = 60° and angle *CBA* = 30°.

5 Construct an isosceles triangle *PQR* where *PQ* = 8 cm and the angles *RPQ* and *RQP* are both 30°.

Constructing 90° and 45° Angles

You can construct a right angle (90°) using compasses and a ruler.

You can construct an angle of 45° by bisecting an angle of 90°.

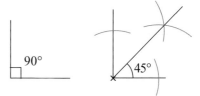

Example 6

Construct an angle of 90° using compasses and a ruler.

1. Draw a straight line, and mark the point where you want to form the right angle.

2. Draw arcs of the same radius on either side of your point.

3. Increase the radius of your compasses, and draw two arcs of the same radius — one arc centred on each of the intersections.

4. Draw a straight line to complete the right angle.

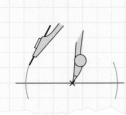 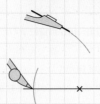 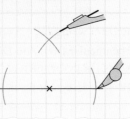 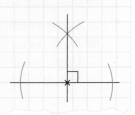

Exercise 6

1 **a)** Draw a straight line, and mark a point roughly halfway along it. Label the point X.
  b) Construct a right angle at X using only a ruler and compasses.

2 Using ruler and compasses only, construct a rectangle with sides of length 5 cm and 7 cm.

3 **a)** Draw a straight line, and mark a point roughly halfway along it. Label the point X.
  b) Construct an angle of 45° at X using only a ruler and compasses.

4 Construct an isosceles triangle ABC where $AB = 8$ cm and the angles CAB and CBA are both 45°.

Constructing Parallel Lines

You can construct parallel lines by making two angles of 90°.

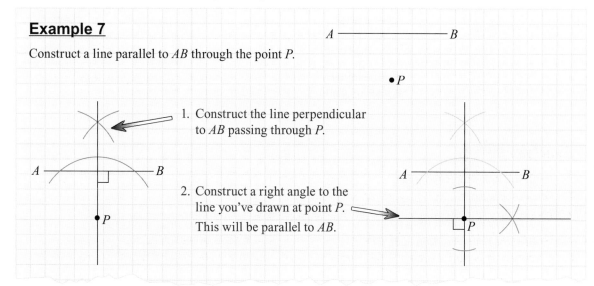

Example 7

Construct a line parallel to AB through the point P.

1. Construct the line perpendicular to AB passing through P.

2. Construct a right angle to the line you've drawn at point P. This will be parallel to AB.

Exercise 7

1 Draw a horizontal line AB, and mark a point P approximately 4 cm from your line. Construct a line parallel to AB through the point P.

2 Draw two straight lines that cross each other at a single point. By adding two parallel lines, construct a parallelogram.

3 Use a ruler and compasses to construct the quadrilateral $ABCD$ such that:
  (i) $AB = 10$ cm   **(ii)** angle $ABC = 60°$ and $BC = 3$ cm
  (iii) angle $BAD = 30°$ **(iv)** AB and CD are parallel

Exercise 8 — Mixed Exercise

1 Draw a line AB 8 cm long.
  a) Construct an angle of 60° at A.
  b) Complete a construction of a rhombus $ABCD$ with sides of length 8 cm.

2 **a)** Construct an equilateral triangle DEF with sides of 5.8 cm.
  b) Construct a line that is parallel to side DE and passes through point F.

3 **a)** Construct the triangle ABC with $AB = 7.4$ cm, angle $CAB = 60°$ and angle $ABC = 45°$.
  b) Calculate the size of angle ACB.

4 Construct an angle of 15° using a ruler and compasses only.

26.4 Loci

A **locus** is a set of points which satisfy a particular condition.

The locus of points 1 cm from a point P is a **circle** with radius 1 cm centred on P.

The locus of points 1 cm from a line AB is a 'sausage shape'.

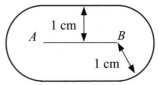

The locus of points **equidistant** (the same distance) from points A and B is the **perpendicular bisector** of AB.

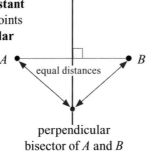

perpendicular bisector of A and B

The locus of points equidistant from two lines is their **angle bisector**.

Example 1

Construct the locus of points that satisfy all the following conditions:

(i)   inside rectangle $ABCD$,

(ii) more than 2 cm from point A,

(iii) less than 1 cm from side CD.

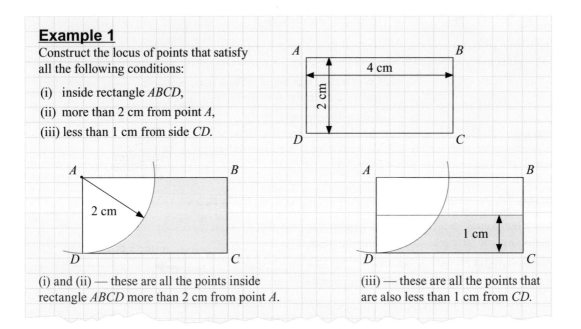

(i) and (ii) — these are all the points inside rectangle $ABCD$ more than 2 cm from point A.

(iii) — these are all the points that are also less than 1 cm from CD.

Exercise 1

1   Draw a 7 cm long line AB. Construct the locus of all the points 2 cm from the line.

2   **a)** Mark a point X on your page. Draw the locus of all points which are 3 cm from X.

   b) Shade the locus of all the points on the page that are less than 3 cm from X.

3   Mark two points A and B that are 6 cm apart.
   Construct the locus of all points on the page which are equidistant from A and B.

4   Draw two lines that meet at an angle of 50°.
   Construct the locus of all points on the page which are equidistant from the two lines.

5   Draw a line AB 6 cm long. Draw the locus of all points which are 3 cm from AB.

6 a) Draw axes on squared paper with *x*- and *y*-values from 0 to 10.
Plot the points *P*(2, 7) and *Q*(10, 3).

   b) Construct the locus of points which are equidistant from *P* and *Q*.

7 a) Mark points *P* and *Q* that are 5 cm apart.

   b) Draw the locus of points which are 3 cm from *P*.

   c) Draw the locus of points which are 4 cm from *Q*.

   d) Show clearly which points are both 3 cm from *P* and 4 cm from *Q*.

8 Draw a line *RS* which is 5 cm long. Construct the locus equidistant from *R* and *S* and less than 4 cm from *R*.

9 a) Construct a triangle with sides 4 cm, 5 cm and 6 cm.

   b) Draw the locus of all points which are exactly 1 cm from any of the triangle's sides.

10 a) Construct an isosceles triangle *DEF* with *DE* = *EF* = 5 cm and *DF* = 3 cm.

   b) Draw the locus of points which are equidistant from *D* and *F* and less than 2 cm from *E*.

11 Lines *AB* and *CD* are both 6 cm long. *AB* and *CD* are perpendicular
to each other and cross at the midpoint of each line, *M*.

   a) Construct lines *AB* and *CD*.

   b) Draw the locus of points which are less than 2 cm from *AB* and *CD*.

Exercise 2

1 A ship sails so that it is always the same distance from a port *P*
and a lighthouse *L*. The lighthouse and the port are 3 km apart.

   a) Draw a scale diagram showing the port and lighthouse. Use a scale of 1 cm:1 km.

   b) Show the path of the ship on your diagram.

2 Some students are doing a treasure hunt. They know the treasure is
- located in a square region *ABCD*, which measures 10 m × 10 m
- the same distance from *AB* as from *AD*
- 7 m from corner *C*.

Draw a scale diagram to show the location of the treasure. Use a scale of 1 cm : 1 m.

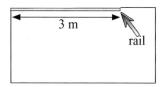

3 Two walls of a field meet at an angle of 80°.
A bonfire has to be the same distance from each wall
and 3 m from the corner. Copy and complete the
diagram on the right to show the position of the fire.

80°   Scale 1 cm : 1 m

4 Two camels set off at the same time from towns
A and *B*, located 50 miles apart in the desert.

   a) Draw a scale diagram showing towns *A* and *B*. Use a scale of 1 cm : 10 miles.

   b) If a camel can walk up to 40 miles in a day, show on your diagram the region
where the camels could possibly meet each other after walking for one day.

5 A walled rectangular yard has length 4 m and width 2 m.
A dog is secured by a lead of length 1 m to a post in a corner of the yard.

   a) Show on an accurate scale drawing the area in
which the dog can move. Use the scale 1 cm : 1 m.

   b) The post is replaced with a 3 m rail mounted horizontally
along one of the long walls, with one end in the corner.

      If the end of the lead attached to the rail is free to slide,
show the area in which the dog can move.

3 m

rail

Section 27 — Pythagoras and Trigonometry

27.1 Pythagoras' Theorem

In a **right-angled triangle**, the lengths of the sides are connected by Pythagoras' theorem:

$$h^2 = a^2 + b^2$$

h is the **hypotenuse** — the longest side, opposite the right angle.
a and b are the shorter sides.

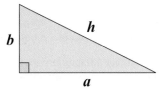

Example 1

Find the exact length x on the triangle shown.

1. Substitute the values from the diagram into the formula.

2. 'Exact length' means you should give your answer as a surd — simplified if possible.

$$h^2 = a^2 + b^2$$
$$x^2 = 6^2 + 4^2$$
$$x^2 = 36 + 16 = 52$$
$$x = \sqrt{52}$$
$$= 2\sqrt{13} \text{ cm}$$

4 cm   6 cm

Exercise 1

1 Find the exact length of the hypotenuse in each of the triangles below.

a) x, 3 cm, 4 cm

b) 12 mm, 5 mm, z

c) q, 18 cm, 24 cm

d) r, 52 m, 52 m

2 Find the length of the hypotenuse in each of the triangles below.
Give your answers correct to 2 decimal places where appropriate.

a) 2.4 m, 0.7 m, s

b) u, 5.12 km, 3.78 km

c) 11.5 mm, 7.2 mm, v

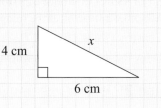

d) 1.3 m, 0.5 m, w

3 Find the exact lengths of the missing sides in these triangles.

a) 13 cm, l, 12 cm

b) 26 cm, 10 cm, p

c) 7 mm, n, 11 mm

d) 37 mm, i, 45 mm

4 Find the lengths of the missing sides in these triangles. Give your answers correct to 2 decimal places.

a) k, 15.9 km, 21.7 km

b) 2.4 mm, g, 1.65 mm

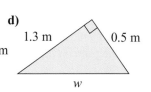

c) 9.54 m, 3.17 m, b

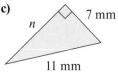

d) 1.7 cm, c, 3.2 cm

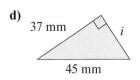

Exercise 2

Unless told otherwise, round your answers to these questions correct to 2 decimal places where appropriate.

1 Find the length of the longest side of a right-angled triangle if the other sides are 8.7 cm and 6.1 cm in length.

2 A rectangular field is 20 m long and 15 m wide. What is the distance diagonally across the field?

3 The triangle *JKL* is drawn inside a circle centred on *O*, as shown. *JK* and *KL* have lengths 4.9 cm and 6.8 cm respectively.

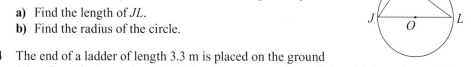

    a) Find the length of *JL*.
    b) Find the radius of the circle.

4 The end of a ladder of length 3.3 m is placed on the ground 0.8 m from the base of a wall. When leant against the wall, how high up the wall does the ladder reach?

5 A kite gets stuck at the top of a tree. The kite's 15 m string is taut, and its other end is held on the ground, 8.5 m from the base of the tree. Find the height of the tree.

6 Newtown is 88 km northwest of Oldtown. Bigton is 142 km from Newtown, and lies northeast of Oldtown. What is the distance from Bigton to Oldtown, to the nearest kilometre?

7 My favourite twig is 41 cm long. Will it fit on a tray 35 cm long and 25 cm wide?

8 A swimming pool measures 50 m by 25 m. How many whole 6 cm-long goldfish could float nose-to-tail across the diagonal of the pool?

9 A boat is rowed 200 m east and then 150 m south. If it had been rowed to the same point in a straight line instead, how much shorter would the journey have been?

10 A delivery company charges extra if a letter has a diagonal length greater than 25 cm. I want to send a letter that measures 205 mm by 155 mm. Will I have to pay extra?

11 An equilateral triangle has sides of length 10 cm. Find the triangle's vertical height.

12 Find the following exact lengths.
    a) *AB*
    b) *BC*
    c) *AC*

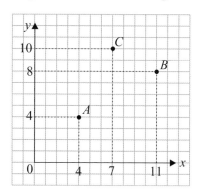

13 Find the exact distance between points *P* and *Q* with coordinates (11, 1) and (17, 19) respectively.

14 Kevin wants to set up a 20 m death-slide from the top of his 5.95 metre-high tower.

    a) How far from the base of the tower should Kevin anchor the slide?

    b) A safety inspector shortens the slide and anchors it 1.5 m closer to the tower. What is the new length of the slide?

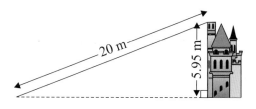

Look for **right-angled triangles** and use **Pythagoras** to find distances in three dimensions.

Example 1

Find the exact length AG in the cuboid shown.

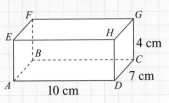

1. Use Pythagoras on the triangle ACD to find the length AC.

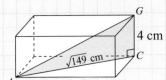

$AC^2 = 10^2 + 7^2 = 149$

$AC = \sqrt{149}$ cm

2. Use Pythagoras on the triangle AGC to find the length AG.

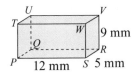

$AG^2 = (\sqrt{149})^2 + 4^2$
$= 149 + 16 = 165$

3. Give your answer in surd form, simplifying if possible.

$AG = \sqrt{165}$ **cm**

Exercise 1

1   The cuboid $ABCDEFGH$ is shown on the right.

   a) By considering the triangle ABD, find the exact length BD.

   b) By considering the triangle BFD, find the exact length FD.

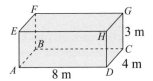

2   The cuboid $PQRSTUVW$ is shown on the right.

   a) Find the exact length PR.

   b) Find the exact length RT.

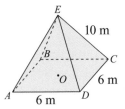

3   The square-based pyramid $ABCDE$ is shown on the right.
   O is the centre of the square base, directly below E.

   a) (i)   By considering the triangle ACD, find the exact length AC.
      (ii) Hence find the exact length AO.

   b) By considering the triangle AEO, find the exact length OE, the pyramid's vertical height.

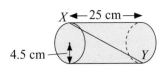

4   A cylinder of length 25 cm and radius 4.5 cm is shown on the right. X and Y are points on opposite edges of the cylinder, such that XY is as long as possible. Find the length XY to 3 significant figures.

5   A cuboid measures 2.5 m × 3.8 m × 9.4 m. Find the length of the diagonal of the cuboid to 2 d.p.

In Questions 6-11, give all answers to 3 significant figures.

6 The triangular prism *PQRSTU* is shown on the right.

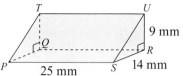

  a) Find the length *QS*.

  b) Find the length *ST*.

7 Find the length of the diagonal of a cube of side 5 m.

8 A pencil case is in the shape of a cuboid. The pencil case is 16.5 cm long, 4.8 cm wide and 2 cm deep.
What is the length of the longest pencil that will fit in the case? Ignore the thickness of the pencil.

9 A spaghetti jar is in the shape of a cylinder. The jar has radius 6 cm and height 28 cm.
What is the length of the longest stick of dried spaghetti that will fit inside the jar?

10 A square-based pyramid has a base of side 4.8 cm and sloped edges of length 11.2 cm.
Find the vertical height of the pyramid.

11 A square-based pyramid has a base of side 3.2 m and a vertical height of 9.2 m.
Find the length of the sloped edges of the pyramid.

12 The diagram on the right shows a shape made up of the
square-based pyramid *EFGHI* and the cuboid *ABCDEFGH*.
P is the centre of the square *EFGH* and *O* is the centre of
ABCD. *P* lies on the vertical line *OI*.

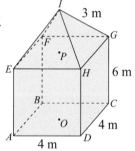

  a) (i) Find the length *PH* to 3 s.f.
    (ii) Find the length *PI*.
    (iii) Hence find the length *OI*.

  b) (i) Find the length *OA* to 3 s.f.
    (ii) Find the length *AI* to 3 s.f.

13 The square-based pyramid *JKLMN* is shown on the right.
O is the centre of the square base, directly below *N*.
P is the midpoint of *LM*.

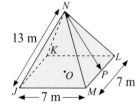

  a) Find the exact length *NP*.

  b) Find the exact length *OJ*.

  c) Find the exact length *ON*, the pyramid's vertical height.

14 The square-based pyramid *VWXYZ* is shown on the right.
Point *O*, the centre of the square *VWXY*, is directly below *Z*.

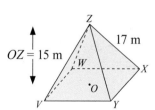

  a) Find the length *VX*.

  b) Hence find the area of the square *VWXY*.

15 A fly is tied to one end of a piece of string. The other end of the
string is attached to point *O* on a flat, horizontal surface.
The string becomes taut when the fly is 19 cm from *O* in the *x*-direction,
13 cm from *O* in the *y*-direction, and 9 cm from *O* in the *z*-direction.

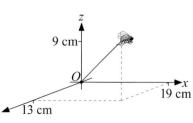

Find the length of the piece of string to 3 s.f.

27.3 Trigonometry — Sin, Cos and Tan

The Three Formulas

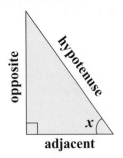

In a right-angled triangle, the side opposite the right angle is called the **hypotenuse**, the side opposite an angle is called the **opposite** and the side next to an angle is called the **adjacent**.

The three sides are linked by the following formulas:

$$\sin x = \frac{\text{opp}}{\text{hyp}}, \quad \cos x = \frac{\text{adj}}{\text{hyp}}, \quad \tan x = \frac{\text{opp}}{\text{adj}}$$

Example 1

Find the length of side y.
Give your answer correct to 3 significant figures.

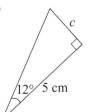

You are given the hypotenuse and asked to find the adjacent, so use the formula for $\cos x$.

$\cos 29° = \dfrac{y}{4}$

$4\cos 29° = y$

$y = \underline{\textbf{3.50 cm}}$ (to 3 s.f.)

Exercise 1

1 Find the lengths of the missing sides marked with letters. Give your answers to 3 significant figures.

a)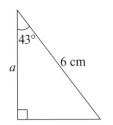

b)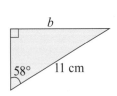

c)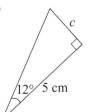

d)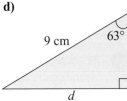

e)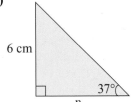

f)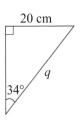

g)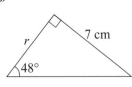

h)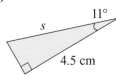

2 Find the missing length m (to 3 s.f.).

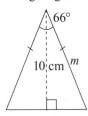

3 Find the missing length n (to 3 s.f.).

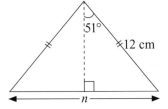

Example 2

Liz and Phil are putting up decorations for a street party. Liz is at the window of her house, holding one end of a 7 m paper chain, which is taut. Phil is standing in the garden below holding the other end of the paper chain. Phil's end of the paper chain is 6 m below Liz's end.

Find the size of the angle of depression from Liz to Phil.

1. Use the information to draw a right-angled triangle — the 'angle of depression' is the angle below the horizontal.

2. You are given the hypotenuse and the opposite, so use the formula for $\sin x$.

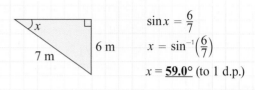

$$\sin x = \frac{6}{7}$$
$$x = \sin^{-1}\left(\frac{6}{7}\right)$$
$$x = \underline{\mathbf{59.0°}} \text{ (to 1 d.p.)}$$

Exercise 2

1 Find the sizes of the missing angles marked with letters. Give your answers to 1 decimal place.

a)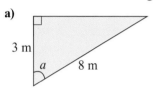

b)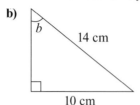

c)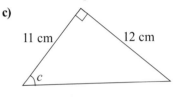

d)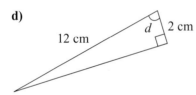

e)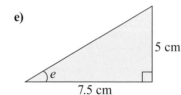

f)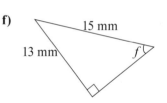

2 Melissa is building a slide for an adventure playground.

a) The first slide she builds has an 8 m high vertical ladder and a slide of 24 m. She wants to work out if the slide is too steep, so she stands at the bottom of the slide and looks up. Find m, the slide's angle of elevation, to 1 d.p.

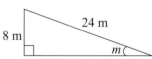

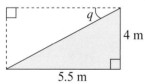

b) The second slide in the park has a 4 m ladder, and the base of the slide reaches the ground 5.5 m from the base of the ladder as shown. Find q, the angle of depression at the top of the second slide, to 1 d.p.

3 Find the missing angle z. Give your answer correct to 1 d.p.

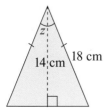

4 Find the missing angles marked with letters. Give all answers correct to 1 d.p.

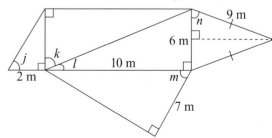

Common Trig Values

The sin, cos and tan of some angles have **exact values** shown in this table:

$\sin 0° = 0$	$\sin 30° = \dfrac{1}{2}$	$\sin 45° = \dfrac{1}{\sqrt{2}}$	$\sin 60° = \dfrac{\sqrt{3}}{2}$	$\sin 90° = 1$
$\cos 0° = 1$	$\cos 30° = \dfrac{\sqrt{3}}{2}$	$\cos 45° = \dfrac{1}{\sqrt{2}}$	$\cos 60° = \dfrac{1}{2}$	$\cos 90° = 0$
$\tan 0° = 0$	$\tan 30° = \dfrac{1}{\sqrt{3}}$	$\tan 45° = 1$	$\tan 60° = \sqrt{3}$	

Exercise 3

1 Without using your calculator, find the size of the angles marked with letters.

a)
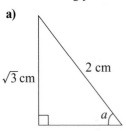

b)
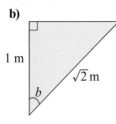

c)
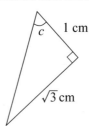

d)
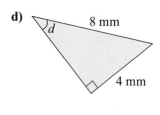

2 Find the exact length of the sides marked with letters.

a)
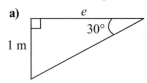

b)
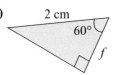

c)

d)
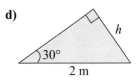

3 Show that:

a) $\tan 45° + \sin 60° = \dfrac{2 + \sqrt{3}}{2}$ b) $\sin 45° + \cos 45° = \sqrt{2}$ c) $\tan 30° + \tan 60° = \dfrac{4\sqrt{3}}{3}$

4 Triangle ABC is isosceles. $AC = 7\sqrt{2}$ cm and angle $ABC = 90°$.
What is the exact length of side AB?

5 Triangle DEF is an equilateral triangle with a vertical height of 4 mm.
What is the exact side length of the triangle? Give your answer in its simplest form.

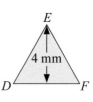

Exercise 4 — Mixed Exercise

1 Find the values of the letters in each of the following. Give your answers to 3 significant figures.

a)
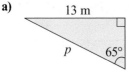

b)
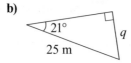

c)
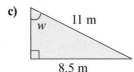

d)
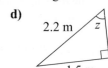

e)
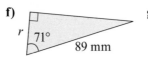

f)

g)
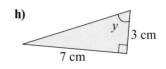

h)

2 The shape shown on the right is made up of two right-angled triangles.

   a) Show that $a = 8\sin 40°$.

   b) Hence find the value of x, correct to 1 decimal place.

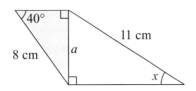

3 Find the values of the letters in each of the following. Give your answers to 3 significant figures.

   a)

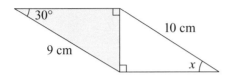

   b)

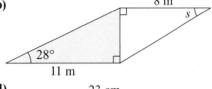

   c)

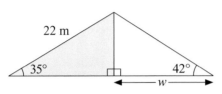

   d)

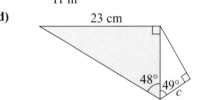

4 Find the exact values of the letters in each of the following.

   a)

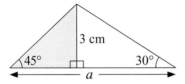

   b)

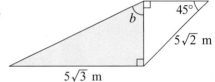

5 Hugh starts at point A and walks 6 km north then 5 km east to point B. If he had walked directly from A to B, on what bearing would he have been walking (to the nearest degree)?

7 A ladder is leaning against the side of a tower. It reaches a window 20 m above the ground. The base of the ladder is placed 8 m away from the bottom of the tower. What is the angle of elevation? Give your answer correct to 1 decimal place.

6 Bernard is looking at a boat out at sea, as shown. Find the angle of depression, correct to 1 d.p.

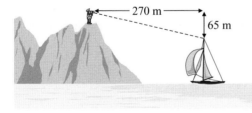

8 Town W is 25 km due south of Town X. Town Y is 42 km due east of Town W. Find the bearing of Town Y from Town X, to 1 d.p.

9 A kite with taut string of length 5.8 m is flying in the air. The vertical distance from the kite to the other end of the string is 4.1 m. Find the kite's angle of elevation, to 1 d.p.

10 The points P and R have coordinates $P(1, 3)$ and $R(7, 8)$. Find the bearing of R from P, correct to 1 d.p.

11 A zip line of length 45 m goes between platforms A and B. Platform A is 80 m above the ground, and platform B is 65 m above the ground, as shown. Find x, the angle the wire forms with the vertical at platform A. Give your answer correct to 1 d.p.

The Sine Rule

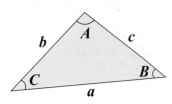

For **any triangle:** $\dfrac{a}{\sin A} = \dfrac{b}{\sin B} = \dfrac{c}{\sin C}$

where angle A is opposite side a, angle B is opposite side b and angle C is opposite side c.

This can also be written as: $\dfrac{\sin A}{a} = \dfrac{\sin B}{b} = \dfrac{\sin C}{c}$

Use the sine rule when there are **two angles and one side** given, or **one angle, the opposite side and one adjacent side**.

Example 1

a) Find the length of side x.

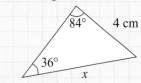

Using the sine rule, $\dfrac{4}{\sin 36°} = \dfrac{x}{\sin 84°}$

So $x = \dfrac{4 \sin 84°}{\sin 36°} = \mathbf{\underline{6.77\ cm}}$ (to 2 d.p.)

b) Find the size of angle y.

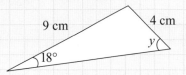

Using the sine rule, $\dfrac{\sin y}{9} = \dfrac{\sin 18°}{4}$

So $y = \sin^{-1}\left(\dfrac{9 \sin 18°}{4}\right) = \mathbf{\underline{44.1°}}$ (to 1 d.p.)

Exercise 1

1 Find the lengths of the missing sides marked with letters. Give your answers to 3 significant figures.

a)
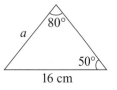

b)
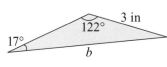

c)

2 Find the lengths of the missing sides marked with letters. Give your answers to 3 significant figures.

a)
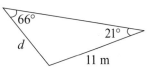

b)
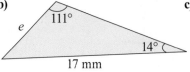

c)
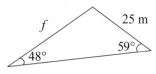

3 For each triangle, find the missing angle marked with a letter. Give your answers to 1 decimal place.

a)
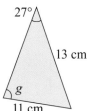

b)
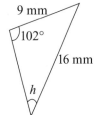

c)
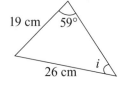

4 Find the missing angle marked with a letter in each of these triangles. Give your answers to 1 decimal place.

a)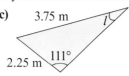

b)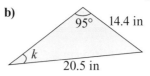

c)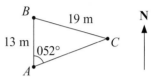

5 The triangle XYZ is such that angle $YXZ = 55°$, angle $XYZ = 40°$ and length $YZ = 83$ m. Find:

a) the length XZ, to 3 s.f. **b)** the length XY, to 3 s.f.

6 A triangular piece of metal PQR is such that angle $RPQ = 61°$, length $QR = 13.1$ mm and length $PQ = 7.2$ mm. Find the size of the angle PQR, correct to 1 decimal place.

7 Point B is 13 m north of point A. Point C lies 19 m from point B, on a bearing of 052° from A.
Find the bearing of C from B, to the nearest degree.

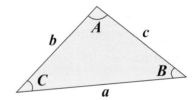

The Cosine Rule

For **any triangle**, $a^2 = b^2 + c^2 - 2bc \cos A$

This can be rearranged as:

$$\cos A = \frac{b^2 + c^2 - a^2}{2bc}$$

Use the cosine rule to find **one side** when you know the other **two sides and the angle between them**, or to find **an angle** when you know **all three sides**.

Example 2

a) Find the length of the missing side.

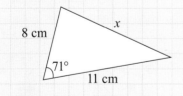

Using the cosine rule:

$x^2 = 8^2 + 11^2 - (2 \times 8 \times 11)\cos 71°$

$= 127.70...$

$x = \sqrt{127.70...} = \underline{\textbf{11.30 cm}}$ (to 2 d.p.)

b) Find the size of the angle y.

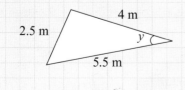

Using the cosine rule,

$\cos y = \dfrac{5.5^2 + 4^2 - 2.5^2}{2 \times 5.5 \times 4} = 0.909...$

$y = \cos^{-1}(0.909...) = \underline{\textbf{24.6°}}$ (to 1 d.p.)

Exercise 2

1 Use the cosine rule to find the lengths of the missing sides. Give your answers to 3 significant figures.

a)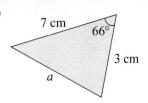

7 cm
66°
3 cm
a

b)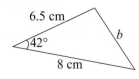

6.5 cm
b
42°
8 cm

c)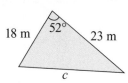

18 m
52°
23 m
c

d)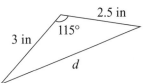

2.5 in
115°
3 in
d

e)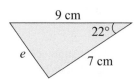

9 cm
22°
e
7 cm

f)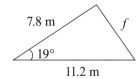

7.8 m
f
19°
11.2 m

2 Use the cosine rule to find the sizes of the missing angles marked with letters. Give your answers to 1 d.p.

a)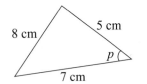

8 cm
5 cm
p
7 cm

b)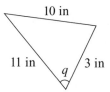

10 in
11 in
3 in
q

c)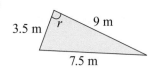

3.5 m
r
9 m
7.5 m

d)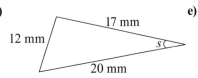

17 mm
12 mm
s
20 mm

e)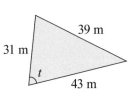

39 m
31 m
t
43 m

f)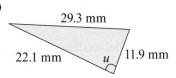

29.3 mm
22.1 mm
u
11.9 mm

3 A triangular sign *XYZ* is such that *XY* = 67 cm, *YZ* = 78 cm and *XZ* = 99 cm.
Find the size of the angle *XYZ*, correct to 3 s.f.

4 Find the exact values of the letters in each of these triangles, without using a calculator.

a)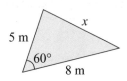

x
5 m
60°
8 m

b)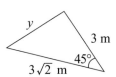

y
3 m
45°
$3\sqrt{2}$ m

c)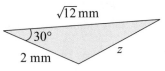

$\sqrt{12}$ mm
30°
2 mm
z

5 Village *B* is 12 miles north of village *A*.
Village *C* is 37 miles north-east of village *A*.
Find the direct distance between village *B* and village *C*,
correct to 3 s.f.

B
C
N
12 miles
37 miles
A

6 Two ramblers set off walking from point *P*.
The first rambler walks for 2 km on a bearing of 025° to point *A*.
The second rambler walks for 3 km on a bearing of 108° to point *B*.
Find the direct distance between *A* and *B*, correct to 3 s.f.

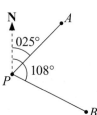

N
025°
A
108°
P
B

Area

To find the area of a triangle, use the formula: $Area = \frac{1}{2}ab \sin C$

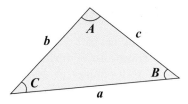

Use this formula when you know **two sides** and the **angle between them**.

Example 3

Find the area of this triangle.

$$Area = (\tfrac{1}{2} \times 7 \times 8)\sin 65°$$
$$= \underline{\textbf{25.38 cm}^2} \text{ (to 2 d.p.)}$$

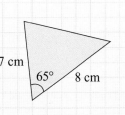

Exercise 3

1 Find the area of each triangle. Give your answers to 2 decimal places.

a)

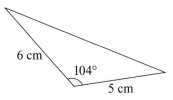

b)

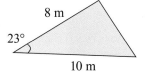

c)

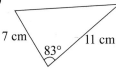

d)

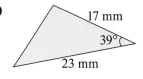

e)

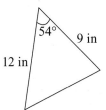

f)

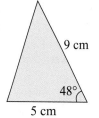

In Questions 2–7, give all answers to 3 significant figures.

2 Find the area of the triangle shown.

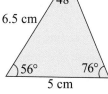

5 A field in the shape of an equilateral triangle has sides of length 32 m. Find the area of the field.

6

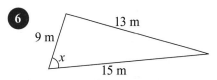

a) Use the cosine rule to calculate x.
b) Find the area of the triangle.

3 Find the area of the triangle shown.

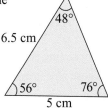

4 A triangular piece of paper has a side of length 4.5 cm and a side of length 7.1 cm. The angle between these two sides is 67°. Find the area of the piece of paper.

7

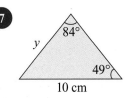

a) Use the sine rule to calculate y.
b) Find the area of the triangle.

27.5　Sin, Cos and Tan of Larger Angles

Sin, cos and tan are really useful for working out acute angles (angles between 0° and 90°).
They can also be used to find **obtuse angles** (angles between 90° and 180°)
and **reflex angles** (angles between 180° and 360°).

Sin of Obtuse and Reflex angles

The graph shows $y = \sin x$ for $-180° \leq x \leq 360°$.

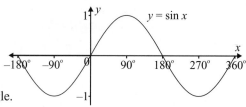

For each value of y (except $y = 1$, $y = -1$ and $y = 0$)
there are **two positive values** of x between 0° and 360°.

For $0 < y \leq 1$, putting $\sin^{-1}y$ into a calculator gives the acute angle.
To find the obtuse angle, **subtract** the acute angle from 180°.

For $-1 \leq y < 0$, putting $\sin^{-1}y$ into a calculator gives a negative angle.
To find the two reflex angles, **subtract** the **negative** angle from 180° or **add** it to 360°.

Example 1

Find the two values of x in the range $0° \leq x \leq 180°$ for which $\sin x = 0.85$.

1. Putting $\sin^{-1}(0.85)$ into a calculator gives the acute angle.　$\sin^{-1}(0.85) = \underline{\textbf{58.2°}}$ (to 1 d.p.)

2. Subtract the acute angle from 180° to get the obtuse angle.　$180° - 58.2° = \underline{\textbf{121.8°}}$ (to 1 d.p.)

Exercise 1

1　Find both values of x in the range $0° \leq x \leq 180°$ that satisfy the following equations.
Give your answers correct to 1 decimal place where appropriate.

a)　$\sin x = 0.24$ 　　　　　b)　$\sin x = 0.49$ 　　　　　c)　$\sin x = 0.64$

d)　$\sin x = 0.13$ 　　　　　e)　$\sin x = 0.5$ 　　　　　f)　$\sin x = 0.05$

2　Find both values of x in the range $180° \leq x \leq 360°$ that satisfy the following equations.
Give your answers correct to 1 decimal place where appropriate.

a)　$\sin x = -0.36$ 　　　　b)　$\sin x = -0.55$ 　　　　c)　$\sin x = -0.89$

d)　$\sin x = -0.5$ 　　　　　e)　$\sin x = -0.27$ 　　　　f)　$\sin x = -0.07$

3　a)　$\sin 23° = 0.39$ (to 2 d.p.).　Write down the integer obtuse angle whose sine is equal to 0.39 to 2 d.p.

b)　$\sin 131° = 0.75$ (to 2 d.p.).　Write down the integer acute angle whose sine is equal to 0.75 to 2 d.p.

c)　$\sin 222° = -0.67$ (to 2 d.p.).　Write down the other integer reflex angle whose sine is equal to −0.67 to 2 d.p.

4　In each of the following, use the sine rule to find the size of the obtuse angle correct to 1 d.p.

a)

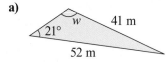

b)

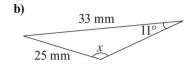

c)

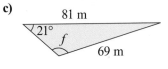

d)

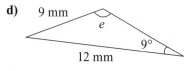

e)

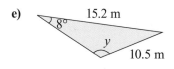

f)

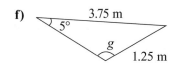

Cos of Obtuse and Reflex angles

The graph shows $y = \cos x$ for $0° \leq x \leq 360°$.

For each value of y (except $y = -1$) there are **two** possible values of x.

Putting $\cos^{-1} y$ into your calculator gives the acute or obtuse angle. To find the reflex angle, **subtract** the acute or obtuse angle from $360°$.

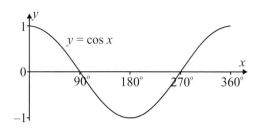

Example 2

Find the reflex angle x for which $\cos x = -0.26$.

1. Putting $\cos^{-1}(-0.26)$ into a calculator gives the obtuse angle. $\cos^{-1}(-0.26) = 105.070...°$

2. Subtract the obtuse angle from $360°$ to get the reflex angle. $360° - 105.070...° = \underline{\mathbf{254.9°}}$ (to 1 d.p.)

Exercise 2

1 Find the obtuse angle x that satisfies each of the following equations. Give your answers to 1 d.p.

a) $\cos x = -0.75$ b) $\cos x = -0.62$ c) $\cos x = -0.91$

d) $\cos x = -0.36$ e) $\cos x = -0.42$ f) $\cos x = -0.01$

2 Find the reflex angle x that satisfies each of the following equations. Give your answers to 1 d.p.

a) $\cos x = 0.26$ b) $\cos x = -0.84$ c) $\cos x = 0.33$

d) $\cos x = -0.19$ e) $\cos x = 0.56$ f) $\cos x = -0.74$

3 a) $\cos 68° = 0.37$ (to 2 d.p.). Write down the integer reflex angle whose cosine is equal to 0.37 to 2 d.p.

  b) $\cos 199° = -0.95$ (to 2 d.p.). Write down the integer obtuse angle whose cosine is equal to -0.95 to 2 d.p.

  c) $\cos 281° = 0.19$ (to 2 d.p.). Write down the integer acute angle whose cosine is equal to 0.19 to 2 d.p.

4 In each of the following, use the cosine rule to find the size of the obtuse angle correct to 1 d.p.

a)
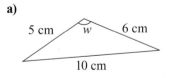

b)
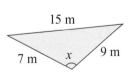

c)
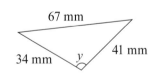

d)
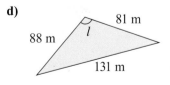

e)
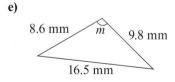

f)
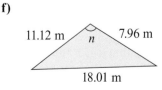

5 Find the exact value of the following, without using your calculator.

a) $\cos 330°$ b) $\cos 300°$ c) $\cos 315°$

Tan of Obtuse and Reflex Angles

The graph shows $y = \tan x$ for $-90° \leq x \leq 360°$. The values of $\tan x$ for obtuse angles are negative, but putting $\tan^{-1} y$ into a calculator gives a negative x-value. To find the obtuse angle, add on $180°$.
To find the reflex angle from an acute or obtuse angle, add on $180°$.

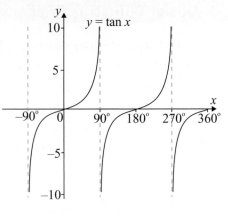

Example 3

Find the obtuse angle x for which $\tan x = -10$.

$$\tan^{-1}(-10) = -84.29° \text{ (to 2 d.p.)}$$
For the obtuse angle, $x = -84.29° + 180° = \underline{\textbf{95.7°}}$ (to 1 d.p.)

Exercise 3

1 Find the acute and reflex angles that satisfy each of the following equations.
   Give your answers to 1 d.p. where appropriate.
   a) $\tan x = 6.4$ b) $\tan x = 3.6$ c) $\tan x = 1$ d) $\tan x = 2.1$

2 Find the three values in the range $-90° \leq x \leq 360°$ that satisfy each of the following equations.
   Give your answers to 1 d.p. where appropriate.
   a) $\tan x = -2.7$ b) $\tan x = -10.5$ c) $\tan x = -1$ d) $\tan x = -7.1$

Exercise 4 — Mixed Exercise

Unless told otherwise, round your answers to these questions to 1 d.p. where appropriate.

1 In each of the following, find the size of the obtuse angle x.

a)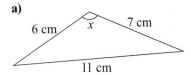

b)
24 mm   19°
x
10 mm

c)
28 cm
18 cm x
16 cm

2 a) Find the obtuse angle x for which $\tan x = -6.4$
   b) Find angles x and y in the range $0° \leq x < y \leq 180°$ such that $\sin x = \sin y = 0.72$
   c) Find the obtuse angle x for which $\cos x = -0.57$
   d) Find the obtuse angle x for which $\tan x = -0.2$
   e) Find the obtuse angle x for which $\cos x = -0.5$
   f) Find the two values of x in the range $0° \leq x \leq 180°$ for which $\sin x = 0.82$

3 The triangle PQR is such that $PQ = 12.3$ cm, $QR = 11.1$ cm and $PR = 22.0$ cm.
   Find the obtuse angle PQR.

4 Two joggers set off running from point O.
   The first jogger runs 5.2 km on a bearing of 109° to point X.
   The second jogger runs 7.5 km to point Y.
   The direct distance between X and Y is 11.8 km.
   Find the bearing of Y from O, correct to the nearest degree.

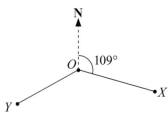

5 Find the exact value of each of the following, without using a calculator.
   a) $\sin 150°$ b) $\tan 240°$ c) $\sin 135°$ d) $\tan 225°$

Look for right-angled triangles and use **Pythagoras** and the **trigonometric formulas** to find **angles** and **areas in 3D**.

Example 1

Find the angle *BDF* in the cuboid shown. Give your answer correct to 1 d.p.

1. Use Pythagoras on the triangle *ABD* to find the length *BD*.

$$BD^2 = 6^2 + 7^2 = 85$$

$$BD = \sqrt{85} \text{ cm}$$

2. *BDF* is a right-angled triangle and you know the lengths opposite and adjacent to *x*, so use $\tan x = \dfrac{\text{opp.}}{\text{adj.}}$

$$\tan x = \frac{4}{\sqrt{85}}$$

$$x = \tan^{-1}\left(\frac{4}{\sqrt{85}}\right)$$

3. You could also have found the length of *DF* first, then used the formula for sin *x*.

$$\angle BDF = \underline{\mathbf{23.5°}} \text{ (to 1 d.p.)}$$

Exercise 1

1 For the cube shown with sides of length 3 m, find:
a) the exact length *AF*
b) the exact length *FC*
c) the angle *AHC*, to 1 d.p.

2 For the square-based pyramid shown, find:
a) the exact vertical height
b) the angle *BCE*, to 1 d.p.
c) the angle *AEB*, to 1 d.p.

3 For the triangular prism shown, find:
a) the exact length *BC*
b) the angle *EDF*, to 1 d.p.
c) the exact length *DC*

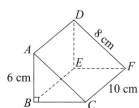

4

For the cuboid shown, find:
a) the exact length *AH*
b) the angle *EDG*, to 1 d.p.

5

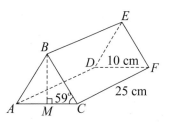

For the triangular prism shown, where *M* is the midpoint of *AC*, find:
a) the perpendicular height, *BM*, to 3 s.f.
b) the length *EM*, to 3 s.f.

Exercise 2

1 The diagram shows the triangular prism *IJKLMN*.

a) Use the cosine rule to find the size of angle *JIK*, correct to 1 d.p.

b) Hence find the area of triangle *IJK*, correct to 1 d.p.

c) Hence find the volume of the triangular prism *IJKLMN*, to the nearest m³.

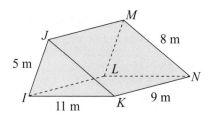

2 The diagram shows the triangle *CEH* drawn inside the cuboid *ABCDEFGH*.

a) Find the exact length *CE*.

b) Find the exact length *CH*.

c) Find the exact length *EH*.

d) Hence use the cosine rule to find the size of angle *ECH*, correct to 1 d.p.

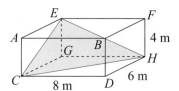

3 The diagram shows the cuboid *PQRSTUVW*.

a) Use Pythagoras and the cosine rule to find the size of angle *PSU*, correct to 1 d.p.

b) Hence find the area of triangle *PSU*, correct to 1 d.p.

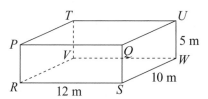

27.7 Pythagoras and Trigonometry Problems

Exercise 1

1 Find the value of the letter in each of the following. Give your answers to 3 s.f.

a)

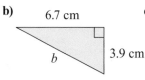

b)

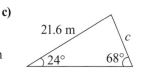

6.7 cm · 3.9 cm · *b*

c)

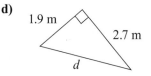

21.6 m · 24° · 68° · *c*

d)

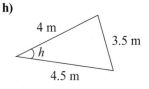

1.9 m · 2.7 m · *d*

e)

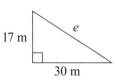

17 m · 30 m · *e*

f)

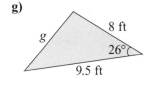

32° · 28 cm · *f*

g)

8 ft · *g* · 26° · 9.5 ft

h)

4 m · *h* · 3.5 m · 4.5 m

i)

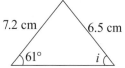

7.2 cm · 6.5 cm · 61° · *i*

j)

12 ft · 15 ft · *j*

k)

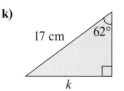

17 cm · 62° · *k*

l)

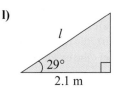

l · 29° · 2.1 m

2 Find the size of the missing obtuse angle q, to 1 d.p.

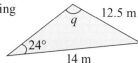

3 The square $PQRS$ is drawn inside the square $ABCD$. Find the side length of $ABCD$, to 3 s.f.

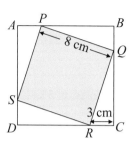

4 Find the side lengths of the rhombus shown, to 3 s.f.

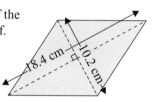

5 a) Find the length of corrugated iron needed to make the roof of my bike shed, to 3 s.f.

b) Find the angle of elevation of the roof of my bike shed, to 1 d.p.

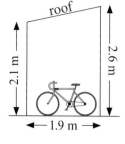

6 Using the sine and/or cosine rules, find the angles x, y and z in the triangle shown, correct to 1 d.p.

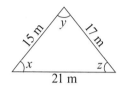

7 The shape shown is made up of two right-angled triangles. Find the value of x.

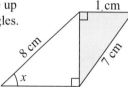

8 Find the value of the letter in each of the following. Give your answers to 1 d.p.

a)

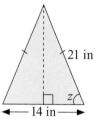

b)

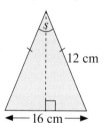

c)

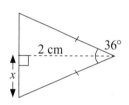

9 I want to put a gold ribbon around the edges of my kite. Ribbon is sold in lengths of 10 cm. What length of ribbon should I buy?

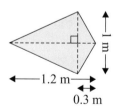

10 A bird is flying in the sky. Point P is on flat, horizontal ground. The horizontal distance between the bird and point P is 37.5 m. The angle of elevation between point P and the bird is 61°. Find the vertical height of the bird above the ground, to the nearest metre.

11 Logan cycles 6 miles due north from P to Q, then 8.5 miles from Q to R. Find the bearing of R from Q (to the nearest degree), given that the direct distance from P to R is 11 miles.

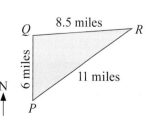

12 A pilot flies 950 km from Rambleside to Alverston, on a bearing of 030°.
He then flies a further 950 km to Marrow on a bearing of 120°.
Find the direct return distance from Marrow to Rambleside to the nearest kilometre.

13 Leo has a triangular piece of fabric with dimensions as shown.
   a) Find the size of the missing angle p, to 3 s.f.
   b) Hence find the area of the fabric, to 3 s.f.

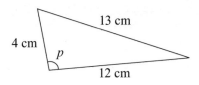

14 Find the vertical heights of the following symmetrical houses, to 3 s.f.

a)

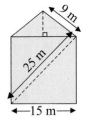

b)

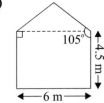

15 Find the exact areas of the following triangles, without using a calculator.

a)

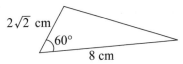

b)

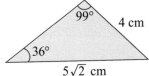

16 Gabrielle has a wooden crate in the shape
of a cuboid, as shown.
   a) Find: **(i)** the exact length ED
   (ii) the angle FDH, to 1 d.p.
   (iii) the angle CHD, to 1 d.p.
   b) Gabrielle wants to pack a 10 ft metal
   pole in the crate. Will it fit?

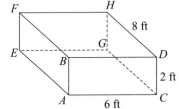

17 Points P, Q and R are plotted on a grid of 1 cm squares.
P has coordinates $(1, 3)$, Q has coordinates $(5, 4)$ and R has coordinates $(7, 1)$.

   a) **(i)** Find the exact distance PQ.
   (ii) Find the exact distance PR.
   b) **(i)** Find the bearing of Q from P, to 2 d.p.
   (ii) Find the bearing of R from P, to 2 d.p.
   c) Find the area of the triangle PQR.

18 The diagram on the right shows a shape made up of the
square-based pyramid $EFGHI$ and the cuboid $ABCDEFGH$.
P is the centre of the square $EFGH$ and O is the centre of
$ABCD$. P lies on the vertical line OI.

   a) **(i)** Find the length AI, to 2 d.p.
   (ii) Find the angle OAI, to 1 d.p.
   b) Find the angle OAP, to 1 d.p.

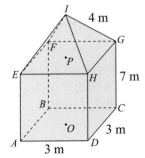

Section 28 — Vectors

28.1 Vectors and Scalars

A **vector** has **magnitude** (size) and **direction**.

A vector can be written as a **column vector** or drawn as an **arrow**.

Column vector:

$$\vec{AB} = \mathbf{a} = \begin{pmatrix} 3 \\ 2 \end{pmatrix}$$

⟸ *x*-component: 3 units right

⟸ *y*-component: 2 units up

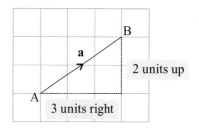

2 units up

3 units right

Example 1

Draw the vector $\mathbf{m} = \begin{pmatrix} -3 \\ 2 \end{pmatrix}$.

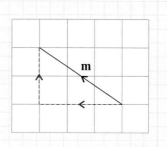

The positive and negative directions in column vectors are the same as they are for coordinates.

So –3 in the *x*-component means '3 units left', and 2 in the *y*-component means '2 units up'.

Exercise 1

1 Draw arrows to represent the following vectors.

a) $\begin{pmatrix} 1 \\ 4 \end{pmatrix}$
b) $\begin{pmatrix} 3 \\ 5 \end{pmatrix}$
c) $\begin{pmatrix} -2 \\ 4 \end{pmatrix}$
d) $\begin{pmatrix} 0 \\ 5 \end{pmatrix}$

e) $\begin{pmatrix} -3 \\ -5 \end{pmatrix}$
f) $\begin{pmatrix} 3 \\ 0 \end{pmatrix}$
g) $\begin{pmatrix} -3 \\ -3 \end{pmatrix}$
h) $\begin{pmatrix} 2.5 \\ 4 \end{pmatrix}$

i) $\begin{pmatrix} 0 \\ -3 \end{pmatrix}$
j) $\begin{pmatrix} 1.5 \\ -2 \end{pmatrix}$
k) $\begin{pmatrix} 7 \\ 1 \end{pmatrix}$
l) $\begin{pmatrix} -3.5 \\ 3.5 \end{pmatrix}$

2 Write down the column vectors represented by these arrows:

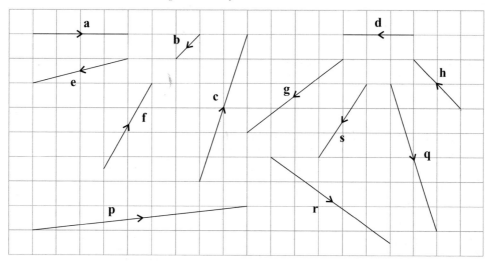

A **scalar** is just a number — scalars have size, but **not** direction.
A vector can be **multiplied** by a scalar to give another vector.

The resulting vector is **parallel** to the original vector.
If the scalar is **negative**, the direction of the vector is **reversed**.

Example 2

If $\mathbf{p} = \begin{pmatrix} 2 \\ -3 \end{pmatrix}$, write the following as column vectors: a) $2\mathbf{p}$ b) $\frac{1}{2}\mathbf{p}$ c) $-\mathbf{p}$

Multiply a vector by a scalar by multiplying the x-component and the y-component separately.

a) $2\mathbf{p} = \begin{pmatrix} 2 \times 2 \\ 2 \times -3 \end{pmatrix} = \begin{pmatrix} 4 \\ -6 \end{pmatrix}$ b) $\frac{1}{2}\mathbf{p} = \begin{pmatrix} \frac{1}{2} \times 2 \\ \frac{1}{2} \times -3 \end{pmatrix} = \begin{pmatrix} 1 \\ -1.5 \end{pmatrix}$ c) $-\mathbf{p} = \begin{pmatrix} -1 \times 2 \\ -1 \times -3 \end{pmatrix} = \begin{pmatrix} -2 \\ 3 \end{pmatrix}$

3   If $\mathbf{q} = \begin{pmatrix} -1 \\ 3 \end{pmatrix}$, find and draw the following vectors.

   a) $3\mathbf{q}$ b) $5\mathbf{q}$ c) $\frac{3}{2}\mathbf{q}$ d) $-2\mathbf{q}$

4

$\mathbf{a} = \begin{pmatrix} 4 \\ -2 \end{pmatrix}$ $\mathbf{b} = \begin{pmatrix} -1 \\ 4 \end{pmatrix}$ $\mathbf{c} = \begin{pmatrix} 3 \\ 12 \end{pmatrix}$ $\mathbf{d} = \begin{pmatrix} 8 \\ -4 \end{pmatrix}$ $\mathbf{e} = \begin{pmatrix} 1 \\ 4 \end{pmatrix}$ $\mathbf{f} = \begin{pmatrix} 0 \\ 3 \end{pmatrix}$ $\mathbf{g} = \begin{pmatrix} 3 \\ -12 \end{pmatrix}$ $\mathbf{h} = \begin{pmatrix} 6 \\ 0 \end{pmatrix}$

From the list of vectors above:
   a) Which vector is equal to $2\mathbf{a}$?   **b)** Which vector is equal to $-3\mathbf{b}$?
   c) Which vector is parallel to $\mathbf{e}$?   **d)** Which two vectors are perpendicular?

Adding and Subtracting Vectors

To **add** or **subtract** vectors, add or subtract the x-components and y-components separately.
The sum of two vectors is called the **resultant vector**.

Vectors can also be added by drawing them in a chain, nose-to-tail.
The resultant vector goes in a straight line from the start to the end of the chain of vectors.

Example 3

$\mathbf{p} = \begin{pmatrix} 3 \\ 1 \end{pmatrix}$ $\mathbf{q} = \begin{pmatrix} -2 \\ 0 \end{pmatrix}$ $\mathbf{r} = \begin{pmatrix} 1 \\ -3 \end{pmatrix}$

Work out the following and draw the resultant vectors:
a) $\mathbf{p} + \mathbf{q}$ b) $\mathbf{r} - \mathbf{q}$ c) $2\mathbf{q} + \mathbf{p} - \mathbf{r}$

$= \begin{pmatrix} 3 + (-2) \\ 1 + 0 \end{pmatrix} = \begin{pmatrix} 1 \\ 1 \end{pmatrix}$ $= \begin{pmatrix} 1 - (-2) \\ -3 - 0 \end{pmatrix} = \begin{pmatrix} 3 \\ -3 \end{pmatrix}$ $= \begin{pmatrix} 2 \times (-2) + 3 - 1 \\ 2 \times 0 + 1 - (-3) \end{pmatrix} = \begin{pmatrix} -2 \\ 4 \end{pmatrix}$

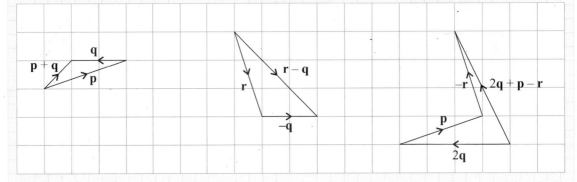

Exercise 2

1 Write the answers to the following calculations as column vectors.
For each expression, draw arrows to represent the two given vectors and the resultant vector.

a) $\begin{pmatrix} 5 \\ 2 \end{pmatrix} + \begin{pmatrix} 3 \\ 4 \end{pmatrix}$
b) $\begin{pmatrix} 4 \\ -1 \end{pmatrix} + \begin{pmatrix} 1 \\ 6 \end{pmatrix}$
c) $\begin{pmatrix} 0 \\ 5 \end{pmatrix} + \begin{pmatrix} -3 \\ 4 \end{pmatrix}$
d) $\begin{pmatrix} -2 \\ 6 \end{pmatrix} + \begin{pmatrix} -3 \\ 1 \end{pmatrix}$

e) $\begin{pmatrix} 7 \\ 6 \end{pmatrix} - \begin{pmatrix} 3 \\ 4 \end{pmatrix}$
f) $\begin{pmatrix} 5 \\ -1 \end{pmatrix} - \begin{pmatrix} 1 \\ 3 \end{pmatrix}$
g) $\begin{pmatrix} 2 \\ -1 \end{pmatrix} - \begin{pmatrix} -2 \\ 2 \end{pmatrix}$
h) $\begin{pmatrix} -3 \\ 0 \end{pmatrix} - \begin{pmatrix} 6 \\ 2 \end{pmatrix}$

2 If $\mathbf{a} = \begin{pmatrix} 2 \\ 3 \end{pmatrix}$, $\mathbf{b} = \begin{pmatrix} 0 \\ -2 \end{pmatrix}$ and $\mathbf{c} = \begin{pmatrix} -1 \\ 4 \end{pmatrix}$, work out:

a) $\mathbf{b} + \mathbf{c}$
b) $\mathbf{c} - \mathbf{a}$
c) $2\mathbf{c} + \mathbf{a}$
d) $3\mathbf{a} + \mathbf{b}$

e) $\mathbf{a} - 2\mathbf{c}$
f) $\mathbf{a} + \mathbf{b} - \mathbf{c}$
g) $5\mathbf{b} + 4\mathbf{c}$
h) $4\mathbf{a} - \mathbf{b} + 3\mathbf{c}$

3 If $\mathbf{p} = \begin{pmatrix} 5 \\ 0 \end{pmatrix}$, $\mathbf{q} = \begin{pmatrix} -3 \\ -1 \end{pmatrix}$ and $\mathbf{r} = \begin{pmatrix} 2 \\ 7 \end{pmatrix}$, work out:

a) $\mathbf{p} + \mathbf{r}$
b) $\mathbf{p} - \mathbf{q}$
c) $3\mathbf{q} + \mathbf{r}$
d) $4\mathbf{r} - 2\mathbf{q}$

e) $3\mathbf{p} + 2\mathbf{r}$
f) $\mathbf{p} + \mathbf{r} - \mathbf{q}$
g) $6\mathbf{r} - 3\mathbf{q}$
h) $2\mathbf{p} - 3\mathbf{q} + \mathbf{r}$

4 $\mathbf{u} = \begin{pmatrix} 6 \\ -2 \end{pmatrix}$, $\mathbf{v} = \begin{pmatrix} -2 \\ 3 \end{pmatrix}$ and $\mathbf{w} = \begin{pmatrix} 1 \\ 2 \end{pmatrix}$

a) Work out $\mathbf{u} + 2\mathbf{v}$
b) Draw the vectors $\mathbf{u} + 2\mathbf{v}$ and $\mathbf{w}$
c) What do you notice about the directions of the vectors $\mathbf{u} + 2\mathbf{v}$ and $\mathbf{w}$?

Example 4

Describe the following vectors in terms of **a** and **b**.
a) $\vec{RS}$ b) $\vec{TU}$

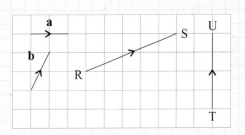

1. Find a route from R to S using just vectors **a** and **b**.

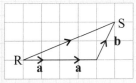

2. From the diagram, $\vec{RS} = \begin{pmatrix} 5 \\ 2 \end{pmatrix}$, $\mathbf{a} = \begin{pmatrix} 2 \\ 0 \end{pmatrix}$ and $\mathbf{b} = \begin{pmatrix} 1 \\ 2 \end{pmatrix}$.
You can check the answer by doing the vector addition.

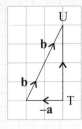

a) $\vec{RS} = 2\mathbf{a} + \mathbf{b}$

Check:

$2\mathbf{a} + \mathbf{b} = 2\begin{pmatrix} 2 \\ 0 \end{pmatrix} + \begin{pmatrix} 1 \\ 2 \end{pmatrix}$

$= \begin{pmatrix} 4 \\ 0 \end{pmatrix} + \begin{pmatrix} 1 \\ 2 \end{pmatrix} = \begin{pmatrix} 5 \\ 2 \end{pmatrix} = \vec{RS}$

b) $\vec{TU} = -\mathbf{a} + 2\mathbf{b}$

Check:

$-\mathbf{a} + 2\mathbf{b} = -\begin{pmatrix} 2 \\ 0 \end{pmatrix} + 2\begin{pmatrix} 1 \\ 2 \end{pmatrix}$

$= \begin{pmatrix} -2 \\ 0 \end{pmatrix} + \begin{pmatrix} 2 \\ 4 \end{pmatrix} = \begin{pmatrix} 0 \\ 4 \end{pmatrix} = \vec{TU}$

Exercise 3

1

		C	D	E	F	G	H
	a	I	J	K	L	M	N
		O	P	Q	R	S	T
	b	U	V	W	X	Y	Z

Write the following vectors in terms of **a** and **b**.

a) $\overrightarrow{WH}$ **b)** $\overrightarrow{ZH}$ **c)** $\overrightarrow{HR}$ **d)** $\overrightarrow{FX}$ **e)** $\overrightarrow{UD}$

f) $\overrightarrow{DU}$ **g)** $\overrightarrow{EM}$ **h)** $\overrightarrow{TP}$ **i)** $\overrightarrow{YJ}$ **j)** $\overrightarrow{CF}$

k) $\overrightarrow{FZ}$ **l)** $\overrightarrow{CZ}$ **m)** $\overrightarrow{KC}$ **n)** $\overrightarrow{DW}$ **o)** $\overrightarrow{OZ}$

28.2   Magnitude of Vectors

The **magnitude** of a vector is just its length. The magnitude of vector **p** is written as |**p**| or p.

If $\mathbf{p} = \begin{pmatrix} x \\ y \end{pmatrix}$ then |**p**| is the hypotenuse of a right-angled triangle with sides x and y.

So by Pythagoras' theorem, $|\mathbf{p}|^2 = x^2 + y^2$, and $|\mathbf{p}| = \sqrt{x^2 + y^2}$.

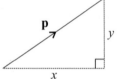

Example 1

$\mathbf{q} = \begin{pmatrix} 3 \\ -4 \end{pmatrix}$. Find the magnitude of: a) **q**   b) 3**q**   c) −**q**

a) $|\mathbf{q}| = \sqrt{3^2 + (-4)^2} = \sqrt{9 + 16} = \sqrt{25} = \underline{5}$

3**q** is three times the length of **q**.

b) $|3\mathbf{q}| = 3|\mathbf{q}| = 3 \times 5 = \underline{15}$

−**q** is the same length as **q** — the direction is the only thing that's different.

c) $|-\mathbf{q}| = |\mathbf{q}| = \underline{5}$

Exercise 1

1 Find the magnitude of the following vectors. Give your answers to 1 decimal place where appropriate.

a) $\begin{pmatrix} 6 \\ 8 \end{pmatrix}$ **b)** $\begin{pmatrix} 3 \\ 2 \end{pmatrix}$ **c)** $\begin{pmatrix} 5 \\ 12 \end{pmatrix}$ **d)** $\begin{pmatrix} -4 \\ 3 \end{pmatrix}$

e) $\begin{pmatrix} 6 \\ -2 \end{pmatrix}$ **f)** $\begin{pmatrix} -1 \\ 4 \end{pmatrix}$ **g)** $\begin{pmatrix} -2 \\ -3 \end{pmatrix}$ **h)** $\begin{pmatrix} -8 \\ 3 \end{pmatrix}$

i) $\begin{pmatrix} 7 \\ -3 \end{pmatrix}$ **j)** $\begin{pmatrix} 2.5 \\ -1 \end{pmatrix}$ **k)** $\begin{pmatrix} 6 \\ 0 \end{pmatrix}$ **l)** $\begin{pmatrix} 4.5 \\ -6 \end{pmatrix}$

2 $\mathbf{p} = \begin{pmatrix} 9 \\ 12 \end{pmatrix}$

   a) Show that $|\mathbf{p}| = 15$

   b) Use your answer from **(a)** to write down the magnitudes of:

     (i) $\begin{pmatrix} -9 \\ 12 \end{pmatrix}$ **(ii)** $\begin{pmatrix} 12 \\ 9 \end{pmatrix}$ **(iii)** $\begin{pmatrix} 18 \\ 24 \end{pmatrix}$ **(iv)** $\begin{pmatrix} 27 \\ -36 \end{pmatrix}$ **(v)** $\begin{pmatrix} 4.5 \\ 6 \end{pmatrix}$ **(vi)** $\begin{pmatrix} 90 \\ 120 \end{pmatrix}$

3 If $\mathbf{a} = \begin{pmatrix} 2 \\ 1 \end{pmatrix}$, $\mathbf{b} = \begin{pmatrix} -4 \\ 0 \end{pmatrix}$ and $\mathbf{c} = \begin{pmatrix} -3 \\ 7 \end{pmatrix}$, find the magnitude, to 1 d.p., of:

   a) $2\mathbf{a}$ **b)** $\mathbf{a} + \mathbf{b}$ **c)** $\mathbf{c} - 3\mathbf{a}$ **d)** $\mathbf{a} + \mathbf{b} + \mathbf{c}$

4 Write down three vectors with the same magnitude as:

   a) $\begin{pmatrix} 6 \\ -5 \end{pmatrix}$ **b)** $\begin{pmatrix} 1 \\ 7 \end{pmatrix}$ **c)** $\begin{pmatrix} -3 \\ -8 \end{pmatrix}$ **d)** $\begin{pmatrix} a \\ b \end{pmatrix}$

Example 2

A plane flies from point A 120 km due north to point B. It then flies 80 km due east to point C.

   a) Draw a diagram to show the plane's journey.

   b) Write the journey from A to C as the sum of two column vectors, and find the resultant vector $\overrightarrow{AC}$.

   c) Find $|\overrightarrow{AC}|$, the direct distance of the plane from its starting point, to the nearest km.

a)
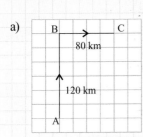

b) $\overrightarrow{AB} = \begin{pmatrix} 0 \\ 120 \end{pmatrix}$ and $\overrightarrow{BC} = \begin{pmatrix} 80 \\ 0 \end{pmatrix}$, so $\overrightarrow{AC} = \begin{pmatrix} 0 \\ 120 \end{pmatrix} + \begin{pmatrix} 80 \\ 0 \end{pmatrix} = \begin{pmatrix} \mathbf{80} \\ \mathbf{120} \end{pmatrix}$

c) $|\overrightarrow{AC}| = \sqrt{120^2 + 80^2}$

$= \sqrt{14400 + 6400}$

$= \sqrt{20800} = 144.222 = \underline{\mathbf{144\ km}}$ to the nearest km

---

Exercise 2

1 Abraham went hiking last Saturday. From the car park, he walked 4 km due north, then 2.5 km due west before stopping to eat his picnic.

   a) Draw a diagram to show his journey.

   b) Write down the journey as the sum of two column vectors.

   c) After his picnic, Abraham walked in a straight line back to the car park. How far did he walk to get back?

2 A ship sails from a port due south for 24 km and then due east for 34 km, before changing course and sailing directly back to port.

   a) Draw a diagram to show the ship's journey.

   b) Write down the column vector of the last stage of the ship's journey as it returns to port.

   c) Find the distance the ship sails in the last part of its journey, to 3 significant figures.

Exercise 1

1   a) Match the following column vectors to the correct vectors in the diagram below.

$\begin{pmatrix} 1 \\ 4 \end{pmatrix}$ $\begin{pmatrix} -2 \\ -4 \end{pmatrix}$

$\begin{pmatrix} -4 \\ -1 \end{pmatrix}$ $\begin{pmatrix} 4 \\ -2 \end{pmatrix}$

$\begin{pmatrix} 0 \\ -5 \end{pmatrix}$ $\begin{pmatrix} 3 \\ 4 \end{pmatrix}$

$\begin{pmatrix} 4 \\ -1 \end{pmatrix}$ $\begin{pmatrix} 1 \\ -4 \end{pmatrix}$

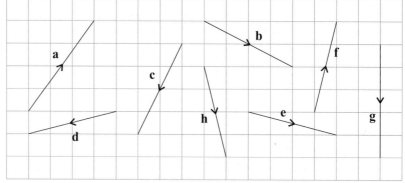

b) Which vector has the same magnitude as **c**?

c) Which vector has the same magnitude as **a**?

d) Four of the vectors have the same magnitude. Find the magnitude of these vectors to 1 d.p.

2 If $\mathbf{p} = \begin{pmatrix} 4 \\ -3 \end{pmatrix}$, $\mathbf{q} = \begin{pmatrix} 0 \\ 2 \end{pmatrix}$ and $\mathbf{r} = \begin{pmatrix} -1 \\ 5 \end{pmatrix}$, find: **a)** $3\mathbf{p}$ **b)** $2\mathbf{q} + \mathbf{r}$ **c)** $\mathbf{r} - 2\mathbf{p}$ **d)** $\mathbf{p} + 5\mathbf{r} - 3\mathbf{q}$

3 $\mathbf{a} = \begin{pmatrix} 6 \\ -4 \end{pmatrix}$ $\mathbf{b} = \begin{pmatrix} -2 \\ 3 \end{pmatrix}$ $\mathbf{c} = \begin{pmatrix} 1 \\ 2 \end{pmatrix}$ $\mathbf{d} = \begin{pmatrix} 4 \\ -2 \end{pmatrix}$ $\mathbf{e} = \begin{pmatrix} 3 \\ 6 \end{pmatrix}$ $\mathbf{f} = \begin{pmatrix} 4 \\ -6 \end{pmatrix}$

a) Draw the vector **a** + **b** and write down the resultant vector as a column vector.

b) Draw the vector **e** – **d** and write down the resultant vector as a column vector.

c) Which two vectors above give the resultant vector $\begin{pmatrix} 10 \\ -10 \end{pmatrix}$ when they are added together?

d) Which two vectors above can be added to give the resultant vector $\begin{pmatrix} 1 \\ 9 \end{pmatrix}$?

e) Which vector above is parallel to **c**?

f) Which vector above is parallel to **b**?

4 $\mathbf{s} = \begin{pmatrix} -5 \\ 12 \end{pmatrix}$ **a)** Find the magnitude of **s**.

b) Use your answer to **(a)** to write down the magnitude of: **(i)** $-\mathbf{s}$ **(ii)** $3\mathbf{s}$ **(iii)** $\frac{1}{2}\mathbf{s}$

5 **a** and **b** are two vectors such that $|\mathbf{a}| = 3$ and $|\mathbf{b}| = 5$.

a) Which of these vectors could be equal to **b**? $\begin{pmatrix} 2 \\ 3 \end{pmatrix}$ $\begin{pmatrix} 5 \\ 0 \end{pmatrix}$ $\begin{pmatrix} -3 \\ 8 \end{pmatrix}$ $\begin{pmatrix} 0 \\ -5 \end{pmatrix}$ $\begin{pmatrix} 3 \\ 4 \end{pmatrix}$

b) Mark says, "The magnitude of **a** + **b** must be equal to 8 because 3 + 5 = 8".
Give an example to show that Mark is wrong.

6 A plane takes off from Wrighton Airport and flies 50 km due east to Braidford,
before changing direction and flying 75 km due south to Ronanburgh.

a) Write down the two parts of the journey as vectors and find the resultant vector.

b) The pilot flies directly back from Ronanburgh to Wrighton Airport.
Write down the vector of the return journey.

c) As the plane sets off back towards Wrighton Airport, it has enough fuel to fly exactly 100 km.
Is there enough fuel to complete the journey back to the airport?

7 In Gridsville, streets run east to west and north to south. All the blocks are the same length and width.
The journey from one end of a block to the other, travelling east, is represented by the vector **a**.
The journey from one end of a block to the other, travelling north, is represented by the vector **b**.

a) If $|\mathbf{a}| = x$ and $|\mathbf{b}| = y$, write **a** and **b** as column vectors.

b) Jo drives 5 blocks east, then 8 blocks south from her house to the
library. Write down the journey from Jo's house to the library:
  (i) in terms of **a** and **b**,   (ii) as a column vector.

c) Jo then drives 2 blocks south and 9 blocks west to the cinema.
Write down the journey from the library to the cinema:
  (i) in terms of **a** and **b**,   (ii) as a column vector.

d) Describe Jo's journey home from the cinema:
  (i) in terms of **a** and **b**,   (ii) as a column vector.

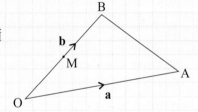

e) If $x = 100$ m and $y = 80$ m,
  (i) what would be the length, to the nearest m, of a straight line from Jo's house to the cinema?
  (ii) how far does Jo actually travel as she drives home?

Vector Geometry

Example 1

In triangle OAB, $\overrightarrow{OA} = \mathbf{a}$ and $\overrightarrow{OB} = \mathbf{b}$. M is the midpoint of OB.

Write down, in terms of **a** and **b**,   a) $\overrightarrow{AO}$ b) $\overrightarrow{OM}$ c) $\overrightarrow{AM}$

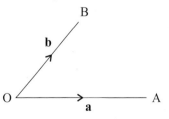

To get from A to O, you go
backwards along the vector **a**.   a) $\overrightarrow{AO} = -\mathbf{a}$

To get from O to M, you go
halfway along the vector **b**.   b) $\overrightarrow{OM} = \frac{1}{2}\mathbf{b}$

To get from A to M, go from
A to O, then from O to M.   c) $\overrightarrow{AM} = \overrightarrow{AO} + \overrightarrow{OM} = -\mathbf{a} + \frac{1}{2}\mathbf{b}$

Exercise 2

1 ABCD is a trapezium.
$\overrightarrow{AB} = 4\mathbf{p}$, $\overrightarrow{AD} = \mathbf{q}$ and $\overrightarrow{DC} = \mathbf{p}$.

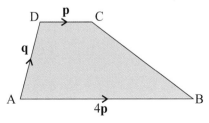

Write down, in terms of **p** and **q**:
a) $\overrightarrow{CA}$ b) $\overrightarrow{CB}$ c) $\overrightarrow{BD}$

2 In the diagram below, $\overrightarrow{OA} = \mathbf{a}$ and $\overrightarrow{OB} = \mathbf{b}$.

Point C is added such that $\overrightarrow{OC} = \mathbf{a} + \mathbf{b}$.
a) What type of shape is OACB?
b) Write down, in terms of **a** and **b**:
  (i) $\overrightarrow{CO}$ (ii) $\overrightarrow{AB}$

3 In the triangle OBD, $\overrightarrow{OA} = \mathbf{a}$ is $\frac{1}{4}$ of the length of $\overrightarrow{OB}$,
$\overrightarrow{OC} = \mathbf{c}$ is $\frac{1}{3}$ of the length of $\overrightarrow{OD}$ and E is the midpoint of BD.

Write down, in terms of $\mathbf{a}$ and $\mathbf{c}$:

a) $\overrightarrow{OB}$ **b)** $\overrightarrow{OD}$ **c)** $\overrightarrow{AB}$ **d)** $\overrightarrow{CD}$ **e)** $\overrightarrow{BA}$
f) $\overrightarrow{AC}$ **g)** $\overrightarrow{AD}$ **h)** $\overrightarrow{BD}$ **i)** $\overrightarrow{OE}$ **j)** $\overrightarrow{CE}$

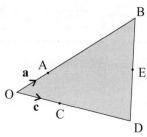

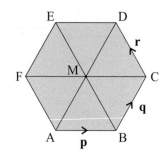

4 ABCDEF is a regular hexagon. M is the centre of the hexagon.
$\overrightarrow{AB} = \mathbf{p}$ and $\overrightarrow{BC} = \mathbf{q}$ and $\overrightarrow{CD} = \mathbf{r}$.

a) Write down, in terms of $\mathbf{p}$, $\mathbf{q}$ and $\mathbf{r}$:
   (i) $\overrightarrow{DE}$ **(ii)** $\overrightarrow{AC}$ **(iii)** $\overrightarrow{FA}$ **(iv)** $\overrightarrow{AE}$

b) Using vectors, show that $\overrightarrow{FD} = \overrightarrow{AC}$.

c) Write down, in terms of $\mathbf{q}$ and $\mathbf{r}$:   **(i)** $\overrightarrow{AM}$ **(ii)** $\overrightarrow{MB}$

d) Write $\mathbf{p}$ in terms of $\mathbf{q}$ and $\mathbf{r}$.

5 WXYZ is a parallelogram.
$\overrightarrow{WX} = \mathbf{u}$ and $\overrightarrow{WZ} = \mathbf{v}$. M is the midpoint of WY.

a) Write down, in terms of $\mathbf{u}$ and $\mathbf{v}$:
   (i) $\overrightarrow{WY}$ **(ii)** $\overrightarrow{WM}$ **(iii)** $\overrightarrow{XW}$ **(iv)** $\overrightarrow{XZ}$

b) Show using vectors that M is the midpoint of XZ.

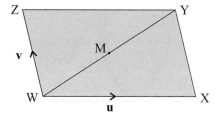

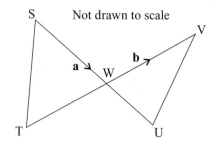

6 In the diagram, $\overrightarrow{SU} = \mathbf{a}$, $\overrightarrow{TV} = \mathbf{b}$, $\overrightarrow{SW} = 2\overrightarrow{WU}$ and $3\overrightarrow{TW} = 2\overrightarrow{WV}$

a) Write: **(i)** $\overrightarrow{WU}$ in terms of $\overrightarrow{SW}$
   (ii) $\overrightarrow{SU}$ in terms of $\overrightarrow{SW}$
   (iii) $\overrightarrow{SW}$ in terms of $\mathbf{a}$

b) Write: **(i)** $\overrightarrow{WV}$ in terms of $\overrightarrow{TW}$
   (ii) $\overrightarrow{TV}$ in terms of $\overrightarrow{WV}$
   (iii) $\overrightarrow{VW}$ in terms of $\mathbf{b}$

c) Write, in terms of $\mathbf{a}$ and $\mathbf{b}$:   **(i)** $\overrightarrow{ST}$ **(ii)** $\overrightarrow{UV}$

7 $\overrightarrow{GE} = \mathbf{m}$, $\overrightarrow{GF} = \mathbf{n}$, $\overrightarrow{GA} = 5\overrightarrow{GE}$ and $\overrightarrow{GB} = 3\overrightarrow{GF}$.
B is the midpoint of AD, and C is the midpoint of BD.

a) Write down, in terms of $\mathbf{m}$ and $\mathbf{n}$:
   (i) $\overrightarrow{GA}$ **(ii)** $\overrightarrow{GB}$ **(iii)** $\overrightarrow{FB}$ **(iv)** $\overrightarrow{AB}$ **(v)** $\overrightarrow{BC}$

If E, F and C were on a straight line, $\overrightarrow{EF}$ and $\overrightarrow{FC}$ would be parallel.

b) Find $\overrightarrow{EF}$ and $\overrightarrow{FC}$ in terms of $\mathbf{m}$ and $\mathbf{n}$, and use your answers to
show that E, F and C do not lie on a straight line.

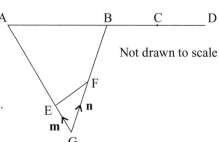

Section 29 — Perimeter and Area

29.1 Triangles and Quadrilaterals

Perimeter (P) is the distance around the outside of a shape.

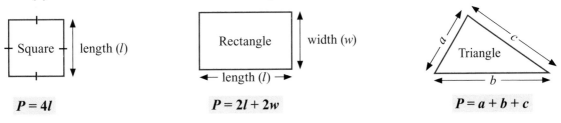

$P = 4l$ $P = 2l + 2w$ $P = a + b + c$

Area (A) is the amount of space inside a shape.

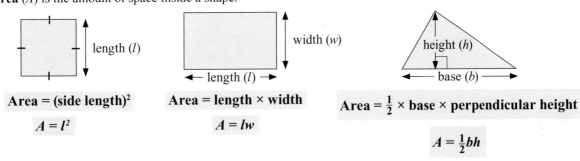

Area = (side length)^2   **Area = length × width**   **Area = $\frac{1}{2}$ × base × perpendicular height**

$A = l^2$ $A = lw$ $A = \frac{1}{2}bh$

Exercise 1

1 For each shape below, find: **(i)** its perimeter, **(ii)** its area.

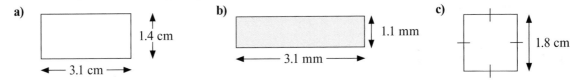

a) 1.4 cm, 3.1 cm   b) 1.1 mm, 3.1 mm   c) 1.8 cm

2 For each shape described below, find: **(i)** its perimeter, **(ii)** its area.
   a) a square with sides of length 4 cm.
   b) a rectangle of width 6 m and length 8 m.
   c) a rectangle 23 mm long and 15 mm wide.
   d) a square with 17 m sides.
   e) a rectangle 22.2 m long and 4.3 m wide.
   f) a rectangle of length 9 mm and width 2.4 mm.

3 For each of the triangles below, find: **(i)** its perimeter, **(ii)** its area.

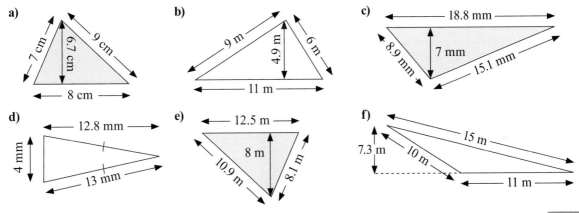

Example 1

Find this shape's: a) perimeter,   b) area.

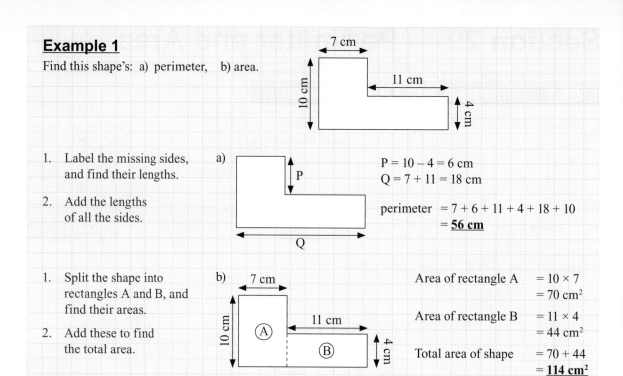

1. Label the missing sides, and find their lengths.

2. Add the lengths of all the sides.

a)

$P = 10 - 4 = 6$ cm
$Q = 7 + 11 = 18$ cm

perimeter $= 7 + 6 + 11 + 4 + 18 + 10$
$= \textbf{56 cm}$

1. Split the shape into rectangles A and B, and find their areas.

2. Add these to find the total area.

b)

Area of rectangle A $= 10 \times 7$
$= 70$ cm^2

Area of rectangle B $= 11 \times 4$
$= 44$ cm^2

Total area of shape $= 70 + 44$
$= \textbf{114 cm}^2$

Exercise 2

1 For each shape below, find: **(i)** its perimeter,   **(ii)** its area.

a)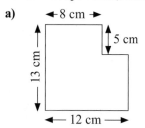

b)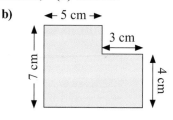

c)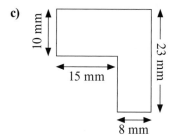

2 Find the area of each shape below.

a)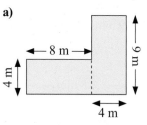

b)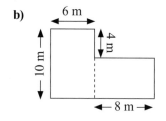

c)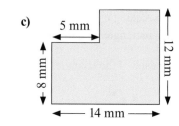

3 Find the areas of the shapes below.

a)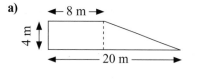

b)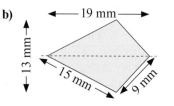

c)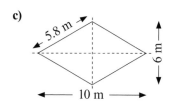

Parallelograms and Trapeziums

The **area** of a **parallelogram** is given by the formula: $A = bh$

Here, h is the perpendicular height —
it's measured at right angles to the base.

The **area** of a **trapezium** is given by the formula: $A = \frac{1}{2}(a + b) \times h$

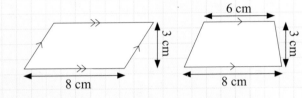

Example 2
Find the area of:
a) the parallelogram   b) the trapezium.

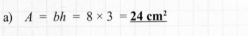

a) $A = bh = 8 \times 3 = \underline{\textbf{24 cm}^2}$

b) $A = \frac{1}{2}(a + b) \times h = \frac{1}{2}(6 + 8) \times 3 = \frac{1}{2} \times 14 \times 3 = \underline{\textbf{21 cm}^2}$

Exercise 3

1 Find the area of each shape below.

a)
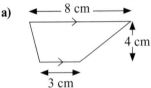

b)
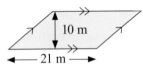

c)
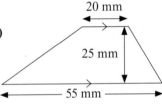

d)
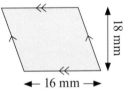

e)
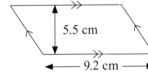

f)
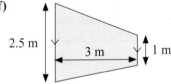

Example 3
For the composite shape on the right, find:
a) its area,
b) its perimeter.

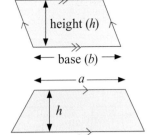

8 cm

A   3 cm

B   4 cm

1. Find the areas of
parallelograms A and B.

2. Add these areas to find
the total area.

Opposite sides of a parallelogram are the same length.

a) Area of A = $bh = 8 \times 3 = 24$ cm^2
Area of B = $bh = 8 \times 4 = 32$ cm^2

Total area = $24 + 32 = \underline{\textbf{56 cm}^2}$

b) $P = 8 + 3.3 + 4.4 + 8 + 4.4 + 3.3$
 $= \underline{\textbf{31.4 cm}}$

Exercise 4

1 Find each shaded area below.

a)

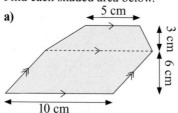

b)

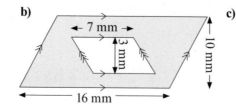

c)

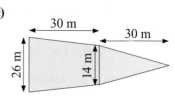

2 For each shape below, find: **(i)** the area, **(ii)** the perimeter. The dotted lines show lines of symmetry.

a)

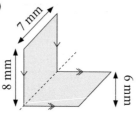

b)

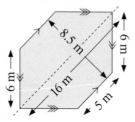

c)

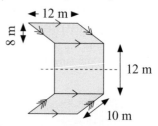

3 The picture below shows part of a tiled wall. All the tiles are parallelograms.

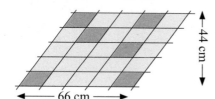

Find the area of one tile.

4 The flag below is in the shape of a trapezium. The coloured strips along the top and bottom edges are parallelograms.

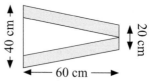

a) Find the total area of the flag.

b) Find the total area of the coloured strips.

29.2 Circles and Sectors

Circumference of a Circle

The **circumference** (C) of a circle is given by the formula: $C = \pi d$

The **diameter** (d) of a circle is twice as long as the **radius** (r): $d = 2r$

So, the circumference of a circle is also given by the formula: $C = 2\pi r$

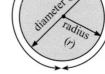

Example 1

Find the circumference of a circle which has radius 6 m. Give your answer to 1 decimal place.

$C = 2\pi r = 2 \times \pi \times 6 = \underline{\textbf{37.7 m}}$ (to 1 d.p.)

Exercise 1

1 Find the circumference of each circle. Give your answers to 1 decimal place.

a)

6 cm

b)

6 m

c)

2 cm

d)

15 mm

2 Find the circumference of the circles with the diameter (*d*) or radius (*r*) given below.
Give your answers to 1 decimal place.

a) $d = 4$ cm
b) $d = 8$ mm
c) $r = 11$ m
d) $r = 22$ cm
e) $r = 14$ km
f) $r = 35$ mm
g) $r = 0.1$ km
h) $d = 6.3$ mm

Example 2

The shape on the right consists of a semicircle on top of a rectangle.
Find the perimeter of the shape.

1. Find the curved length.
   This is half the circumference of a circle with diameter 6 cm.

   Curved length = $\pi d \div 2$
   $= \pi \times 6 \div 2$
   $= 9.42$ cm (to 2 d.p.)

2. Find the total length of the straight sides and add the two parts.

   Total of straight sides $= 4 + 6 + 4 = 14$ cm

   Total length = curved length + straight length
   $= 9.42 + 14 = \underline{\textbf{23.4 cm}}$ (to 1 d.p.)

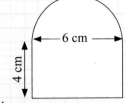

Exercise 2

1 Find the perimeter of each shape below. Give your answers to 1 decimal place.

a)
 4 cm

b)
 2 m

c)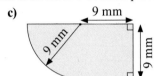
 9 mm, 9 mm, 9 mm

d)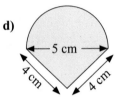
 5 cm, 4 cm, 4 cm

Area of a Circle

The area (*A*) of a circle is given by the formula: $A = \pi r^2$

Example 3

Find the area of the circle below. Give your answer to 1 decimal place.

 3 cm

$A = \pi r^2 = \pi \times 3 \times 3 = 28.274...$
$= \underline{\textbf{28.3 cm}^2}$ (to 1 d.p.)

Exercise 3

In the following questions, give your answers to 1 decimal place unless told otherwise.

1 Find the area of each circle.

a) 2 cm
b) 10 mm
c) 8 m
d) 30 mm
Also: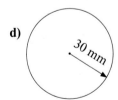

2 Find the areas of the circles with the diameter (*d*) or radius (*r*) given below.

a) $r = 6$ mm
b) $r = 5$ cm
c) $r = 4$ m
d) $r = 6.5$ cm
e) $d = 8.5$ mm
f) $d = 3.5$ m
g) $d = 1.2$ mm
h) $r = 1.05$ m

3 Find the area of each shape below.

a)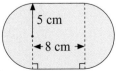
 5 cm, 8 cm

b)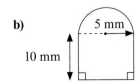
 5 mm, 10 mm

c)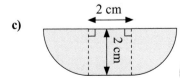
 2 cm, 2 cm

4 What is the area of a circular rug whose radius is 3.5 m? Give your answer in terms of π.

5 Find the coloured area in the diagram below.

6 **a)** A 2p coin has a radius of 1.3 cm.
        What is the area of one face of a 2p coin?

  b) A 5p coin has a diameter of 1.8 cm.
        Which is greater, the area of one face of a 2p coin or the total area of both faces of a 5p coin?

7 Which of these shapes has the greater area?

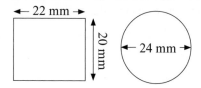

8 Find the areas of the shapes below.

Arcs and Sectors of Circles

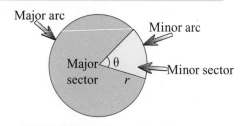

Length of arc = $\dfrac{\theta}{360}$ × circumference of circle = $\dfrac{\theta}{360}$ × 2πr

Area of sector = $\dfrac{\theta}{360}$ × area of circle = $\dfrac{\theta}{360}$ × πr²

Example 4

For the circle below, calculate the exact area of the minor sector and the exact length of the minor arc.

For exact solutions, leave the answers in terms of π.

Area of sector = $\dfrac{60}{360}$ × π × 3² = $\dfrac{1}{6}$ × 9π = $\dfrac{3}{2}$π cm²

Length of arc = $\dfrac{60}{360}$ × (2 × π × 3) = $\dfrac{1}{6}$ × 6π = **π cm**

Exercise 4

1 For each of the circles below, find the exact minor arc length and exact minor sector area.

a)   **b)**   **c)**   **d)**

2 Find the exact major arc length and major sector area for the following circles.

a)   **b)**   **c)**   **d)**

3 For the circles below, find the major sector area and major arc length to 2 decimal places.

a)   **b)**   **c)**   **d)**

4 Find the arc length and sector area for a circle with diameter 18 cm and sector angle 12°.
Give your answers to 2 d.p.

5 Find the major arc length and major sector area for a circle with radius 13 cm and minor sector angle 14°.
Give your answers to 2 d.p.

6 Find the exact minor arc length and sector area for a circle with diameter 10 m and major sector angle 320°.

29.3 Perimeter and Area Problems

Exercise 1

1 Barbie has a rectangular lawn 23.5 m long by 17.3 m wide. She is going to mow the lawn and then put edging around the outside.

   a) What area will Barbie have to mow (to the nearest m²)?

   b) How much lawn edging will she need?

2 The police need to cordon off and then search a square crime scene of area 4.84 m². What is the perimeter of the crime scene?

3 Timi made an apron from a rectangle of material 50 cm wide and 80 cm high. She cut out a quarter circle of radius 15 cm from each corner.
Calculate the area of the finished apron, to 1 d.p.

4 A rectangular garden 24 m long and 5.4 m wide is to be re-turfed. Turf is bought in rolls that are 60 cm wide and 8 m long. How many rolls of turf are needed to cover the garden?

5 A rectangular floor measures 9 m by 7.5 m. It is to be tiled using square tiles with sides of length 0.5 m.

   a) What is the area of the floor?

   b) What is the area of one of the tiles?

   c) How many tiles are needed to cover the floor?

6 Ali bakes the cake shown below.

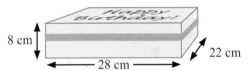

   a) What length of ribbon is needed to go around the outside of the cake?

   b) If the top and the four sides are to be iced, what area of icing will be needed?

Exercise 2

In the following questions, give your answers to 1 decimal place unless the question tells you otherwise.

1 What is the circumference of a circular flower bed with a diameter of 3 m?

2 Find the circumference of this circular cake.

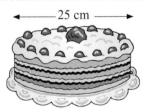

   25 cm

3 An archaeologist plans to excavate a circular burial mound with circumference 144 m.
What is the radius of the mound?

4 A circular volcanic crater has a radius of 5.7 km. Kate and William walked all the way around the outside. How far did they walk?

5 Measure the diameter of the circle below, and then calculate its circumference to the nearest mm.

6 A flower bed is in the shape of a semicircle of area 19.6 m. What is the length of its straight edge?

7 A church window is in the shape of a rectangle 1 m wide and 2 m high, with a semicircle on top. What is its area?

8 Find the area of the sports field below.

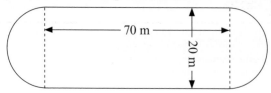

9 Dave makes a circular table with a radius of 55 cm.

    a) What is the circumference of the table?

    b) A customer orders a smaller circular
        table with a diameter only half as big.
        Find the circumference of the smaller table.

10 A window consists of a rectangle 1.5 m wide and
2.1 m high below a semicircle of the same width.
Calculate the perimeter and area of the window.

11 Alec used wooden fencing to build a semicircular
sheep pen, with a wall forming the straight side.
If the radius of the semicircle is 16 m, how many
metres of fencing did Alec have to use?

12 A circular pond of diameter 4 m is surrounded
by a path 1 m wide, as shown below.
What is the area of the path?

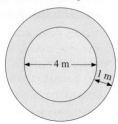

Exercise 3

1 Find the coloured area in
the diagram on the right.
Give your answer to
2 decimal places.

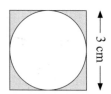

2 Tyler makes some circular soap, and cuts it into 10
segments wrapped in ribbon, as shown below.
What length of ribbon is needed to
wrap once around one segment?
Give your answer to 1 decimal place.

3 Find the area of each coloured shape below. Round your answers to 1 decimal place where appropriate.

a)

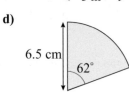

b)

c)

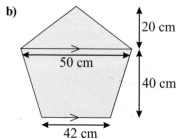

d)

e)

f)

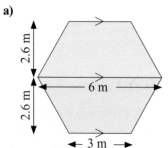

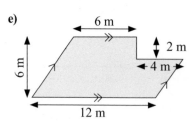

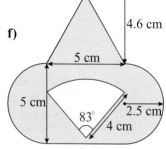

4 What can you say about the areas of these two
shapes? Explain your answer.

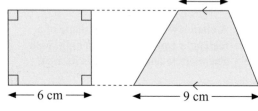

5 Calculate the total coloured area in the shape below.
Give your answer to 1 decimal place.

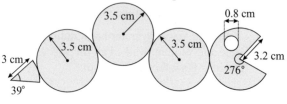

Section 30 — 3D Shapes

30.1 Plans, Elevations and Isometric Drawings

Plans and Elevations

Plans and elevations are 2D pictures of 3D objects, viewed from particular directions.
The view looking vertically downwards from above is the **plan**.
The views looking horizontally from the front and side are the **front** and **side elevations**.

Example 1

Draw the plan and elevations of this cuboid.
Label the plan and elevations with their dimensions.

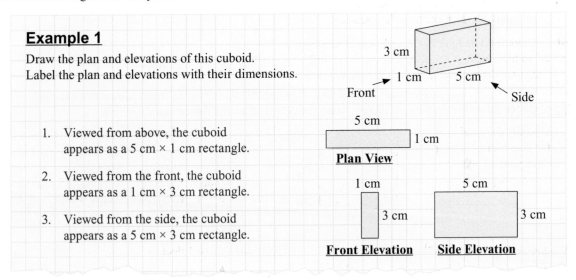

1. Viewed from above, the cuboid appears as a 5 cm × 1 cm rectangle.

2. Viewed from the front, the cuboid appears as a 1 cm × 3 cm rectangle.

3. Viewed from the side, the cuboid appears as a 5 cm × 3 cm rectangle.

Exercise 1

1 For each of the following, draw: (i) the plan view,
   (ii) the front and side elevations, using the directions shown in **a)**.

a) 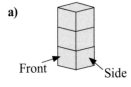 b) 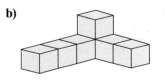 c) 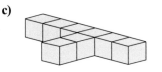 d)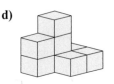

2 For each of the following, draw the plan, front elevation and side elevation from the directions indicated in part **a)**. Label the plan and elevations with their dimensions.

a) 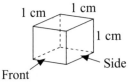 b) 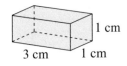 c)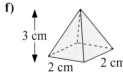

d) 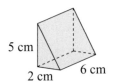 e)   f)

3 Draw the plan, front elevation and side elevation for each of the following.
Label the plan and elevations with their dimensions.
  a) a cube of side 2 cm
  b) a 2 cm × 1 cm × 5 cm cuboid
  c) a cylinder of radius 3 cm and height 4 cm
  d) a cone of height 4 cm and base radius 1 cm
  e) a 4 cm long prism whose cross-section is an isosceles triangle of height 5 cm and base 3 cm
  f) a pyramid of height 5 cm whose base is a square of side 3 cm

Isometric Drawings

Isometric drawings are drawn on a grid of dots or lines arranged in a pattern of equilateral triangles.

Example 2

Draw this triangular prism on isometric paper.

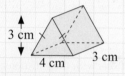

1. Vertical lines stay vertical on isometric drawings, while horizontal lines appear at an angle.
2. Build up the drawing as shown, using the dots to draw the dimensions accurately.

Exercise 2

1 Draw the following 3D objects on isometric paper.

a)   **b)**   **c)**   **d)**

2 Draw the following 3D objects on isometric paper.
  a) a cube with 2 cm edges
  b) a 2 cm × 2 cm × 3 cm cuboid
  c) a prism of length 3 cm whose triangular cross-section has base 3 cm and vertical height 2 cm
  d) a prism of length 2 cm whose triangular cross-section has base 4 cm and vertical height 4 cm

Example 3

The diagram shows the plan and front and side elevations of a 3D object.
Draw the prism on isometric paper.

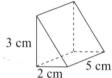

1. Draw the front elevation, using the dots for the dimensions.

2. Use the side elevation and plan view to complete the drawing.

   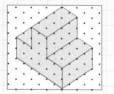

Exercise 3

1   The following diagrams show the plan and front and side elevations of different 3D objects.
    Draw each object on isometric paper.

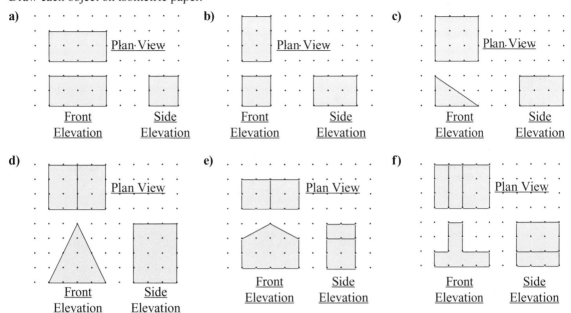

a)   Plan View
     Front Elevation   Side Elevation

b)   Plan View
     Front Elevation   Side Elevation

c)   Plan View
     Front Elevation   Side Elevation

d)   Plan View
     Front Elevation   Side Elevation

e)   Plan View
     Front Elevation   Side Elevation

f)   Plan View
     Front Elevation   Side Elevation

30.2   Volume

Volume of a Cuboid

The volume of a cuboid is given by the following formula.

$$\textbf{\textit{Volume = Length} × \textit{Width} × \textit{Height}}$$

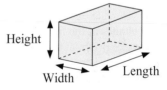

Height
Width   Length

Remember, volume is measured in cubic units, e.g. cm³, m³.

Exercise 1

1   Find the volumes of the following cuboids.

a)   4 m
     4 m   4 m

b)   9 cm   1.5 cm   2 cm

c)   6 mm   2 mm   7 mm

2   Find the volume of a cube whose edges are 3.2 mm long.

3   Will 3.5 m³ of sand fit in a cuboid-shaped box with dimensions 1.7 m × 1.8 m × 0.9 m?

4   A matchbox is 5 cm long and 3 cm wide. The volume of the matchbox is 18 cm³. What is its height?

5   A cuboid has a height of 9.2 mm and a width of 11.5 mm. Its volume is 793.5 mm³. What is its length?

6   A bath can be modelled as a cuboid with dimensions 1.5 m × 0.5 m × 0.6 m.
    a) What is the maximum volume of water that the bath will hold?
    b) Find the volume of water needed to fill the bath to a height of 0.3 m.
    c) Find the height of the water in the bath if the volume of water in the bath is 0.3 m³.

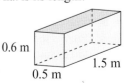

0.6 m
0.5 m   1.5 m

Volume of a Prism

A **prism** is a 3D shape which has a **constant cross-section**.
The volume of a prism is given by the following formula.

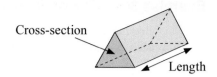
Cross-section
Length

$$Volume = Area\ of\ Cross\text{-}Section \times Length$$

Example 1

Find the volume of each of the shapes shown.

a)
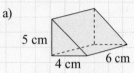
5 cm
4 cm   6 cm

Area of Cross-section $= \frac{1}{2} \times$ base $\times$ height $= \frac{1}{2} \times 4 \times 5 = 10$ cm²

Volume = Area of Cross-section $\times$ Length $= 10 \times 6 = $ **60 cm³**

b)
2 cm   7 cm

Area of Cross-section $= \pi r^2 = \pi \times 2^2 = 4\pi$ cm²

Volume = Area of Cross-section $\times$ Length $= 4\pi \times 7 = $ **88.0 cm³** (to 1 d.p.)

Exercise 2

1 Find the volumes of the following prisms.

a)
4 cm
2 cm   7 cm

b)
3 cm
4 cm   5 cm

c)
6 cm
5 cm   1.5 cm

d)
5 cm
1 cm

2 Find the volumes of the following prisms.
   a) a triangular prism of base 13 cm, vertical height 12 cm and length 8 cm
   b) a triangular prism of base 4.2 m, vertical height 1.3 m and length 3.1 m
   c) a cylinder of radius 4 m and length 18 m
   d) a cylinder of radius 6 mm and length 2.5 mm
   e) a prism with parallelogram cross-section of base 3 m and vertical height 4.2 m, and length 1.5 m

3 By first calculating their cross-sectional areas, find the volumes of the following prisms.

a)

3.6 m
1.2 m
1.2 m
2.4 m   2.5 m

b)
6 cm
2 cm
4 cm   5 cm

c)
2 mm
2 mm
4 mm   5.5 mm

d)
1 m
1.5 m
1 m   1 m   1 m
3 m   2 m

4 The triangular prism shown has a volume of 936 cm³.
   Find x, the length of the prism.

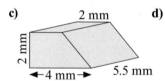
9 cm
8 cm x

5 The cylinder shown has a volume of 589 cm³.
   Find y, the length of the cylinder.
   Give your answer correct to 1 d.p.

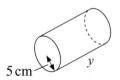
5 cm y

6 Find the values of the missing letters in the following prisms.

a)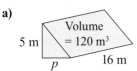
5 m Volume = 120 m³ 16 m p

b)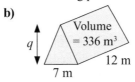
q Volume = 336 m³ 12 m 7 m

c)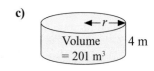
r Volume = 201 m³ 4 m

Exercise 3

Use the conversion 1 litre = 1000 cm³ to answer these questions.

1 A cylindrical tank of radius 28 cm and height 110 cm is half-full of water.
Find the volume of water in the tank. Give your answer in litres, correct to 1 d.p.

2 A cube-shaped box with edges of length 15 cm is filled with water from a glass.
The glass has a capacity of 0.125 litres. How many glasses of water will it take to fill the box?

3 A tank is in the shape of a cuboid of length 140 cm and width 85 cm.
It is filled with water to a depth of 65 cm. There is room for another 297.5 litres of water in the tank.
What is the height of the tank?

4 9 litres of rain falls into a cylindrical paddling pool, filling it to a depth of 3.5 cm.
Find the radius of the paddling pool.

30.3 Nets and Surface Area

Nets

A **net** of a 3D object is a 2D shape that can be folded to make the 3D object.

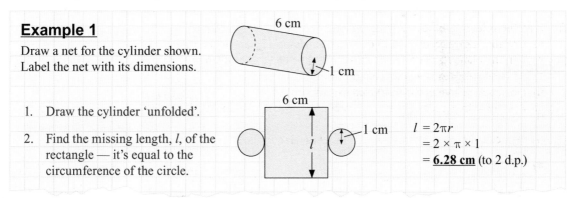

Example 1

Draw a net for the cylinder shown.
Label the net with its dimensions.

6 cm 1 cm

1. Draw the cylinder 'unfolded'.

2. Find the missing length, l, of the rectangle — it's equal to the circumference of the circle.

6 cm 1 cm l

$l = 2\pi r$
$= 2 \times \pi \times 1$
$= \textbf{6.28 cm}$ (to 2 d.p.)

Exercise 1

1 Draw a net of each of the following objects. Label each net with its dimensions.

a)
1 cm 1 cm 1 cm

b)
1.5 cm 3 cm 1 cm

c)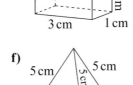
1.5 cm 1.5 cm 1.5 cm 3.5 cm

d)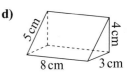
5 cm 8 cm 3 cm 4 cm

e)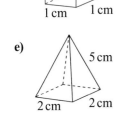
5 cm 2 cm 2 cm

f)
5 cm 5 cm 5 cm 5 cm 5 cm

g)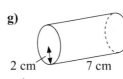
2 cm 7 cm

h)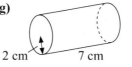
6 cm 3 cm

2 Draw a net of each of the following objects. Label each net with its dimensions.

   a) a cube with 2 cm edges

   b) a 1.5 cm × 2 cm × 2.5 cm cuboid

   c) a tetrahedron with 3.5 cm edges

   d) a cylinder of length 4 cm and radius 2.5 cm

   e) a prism of length 3 cm whose cross-section is an equilateral triangle of side 2 cm

   f) a pyramid with square base of side 5 cm and slanted edge of length 4 cm

3 Which of the nets *A*, *B* or *C* is the net of the triangular prism shown below?

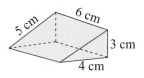 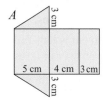 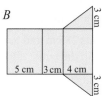 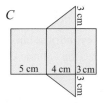

Surface Area

Find the surface area of a 3D shape by **adding** together the **areas** of all its **faces**.

Example 2

Find the surface area of the cuboid shown.

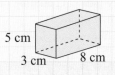

5 cm   3 cm   8 cm

  1. Find the area of each face of the shape.

       2 faces of area 8 × 5 = 40 cm²

       2 faces of area 8 × 3 = 24 cm²

       2 faces of area 5 × 3 = 15 cm²

  2. Add together the individual areas of each face.

       Total surface area is

       (2 × 40) + (2 × 24) + (2 × 15) = 80 + 48 + 30

       = **158 cm²**

Exercise 2

1 Find the surface area of the following prisms.

  a)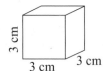

  b)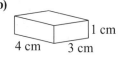

  c)

  d)

  e)

  f)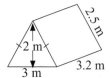

  g)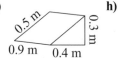

  h)

2 Find the surface area of the following prisms.

  a) a cube with edges of length 5 m

  b) a cube with edges of length 6 mm

  c) a 1.5 m × 2 m × 6 m cuboid

  d) a 7.5 m × 0.5 m × 8 m cuboid

  e) an isosceles triangular prism of height 4 m, slant edge 5m, base 6 m and length 2.5 m

Example 3

By considering its net, find the surface area of a cylinder of radius 2 cm and length 8 cm.

1. Draw the net of the cylinder.

2. Find the length, l, of the rectangle — it's equal to the circumference of the circle.

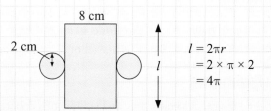

$l = 2\pi r$
$= 2 \times \pi \times 2$
$= 4\pi$

3. Find the area of each face.

Area of circle $= \pi r^2 = \pi \times 2^2 = 4\pi = 12.566$ cm²
Area of rectangle $= 8 \times 4\pi = 100.531$ cm²

4. Add together the individual areas.

Total surface area $= (2 \times 12.566) + 100.531$
$= \mathbf{125.7}$ **cm²** (to 1 d.p.)

Exercise 3

1 Find the surface area of the following cylinders. Give your answers correct to 2 d.p.

a)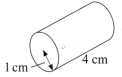

b)

c)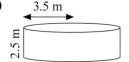

d)

2 Find the surface area of the cylinders with the following dimensions. Give your answers correct to 2 d.p.
a) radius = 2 m, length = 7 m
b) radius = 7.5 mm, length = 2.5 mm
c) radius = 12.2 cm, length = 9.9 cm
d) diameter = 22.1 m, length = 11.1 m

3 A cylindrical metal pipe has radius 2.2 m and length 7.1 m. The ends of the pipe are open.
a) Find the curved surface area of the outside of the pipe.
b) A system of pipes consists of 9 of the pipes described above. What area of metal is required to build the system of pipes? Give your answer correct to 1 decimal place.

4 Ian is painting all the outside surfaces of his cylindrical gas tank. The tank has radius 0.8 m and length 3 m. 1 litre of Ian's paint will cover an area of 14 m². To 2 decimal places, how many litres of paint will Ian need?

Exercise 4

1 The shape shown on the right is made up of a triangular prism and a cube. The bottom face of the prism coincides with the top face of the cube. Find the surface area of the shape.

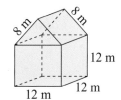

2 By splitting the shape on the right into two cuboids, find its surface area.

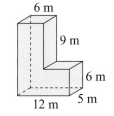

3 The shape on the right is made up of two cylinders. Find its surface area.

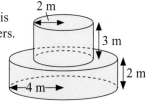

30.4 Spheres, Cones and Pyramids

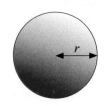

Spheres

For a sphere of radius r: **Surface area** $= 4\pi r^2$ **Volume** $= \frac{4}{3}\pi r^3$

Example 1

Find the exact surface area and volume of a sphere with radius 6 cm.

'Exact' means you should leave your answer in terms of π.

Surface area $= 4 \times \pi \times 6^2 = \mathbf{144\pi\ cm^2}$

Volume $= \frac{4}{3} \times \pi \times 6^3 = \mathbf{288\pi\ cm^3}$

Exercise 1

1 For each of the following, find **(i)** the exact surface area, and **(ii)** the exact volume of the sphere with the given radius, r.
   a) $r = 5$ cm   b) $r = 4$ cm   c) $r = 2.5$ m   d) $r = 10$ mm   e) $r = 12$ m

2 Find the radius of the sphere with surface area 265.9 cm². Give your answer correct to 1 d.p.

3 Find the radius of the sphere with volume 24 429 cm³. Give your answer correct to 1 d.p.

4 The surface area of a sphere is 2463 mm². Find the volume of the sphere, correct to 1 d.p.

5 The volume of a sphere is 6044 m³. Find the surface area of the sphere, correct to 1 d.p.

6 The 3D object shown on the right is a hemisphere (half a sphere).
   a) Find the volume of the hemisphere.
   b) **(i)** Find the area of the curved surface of the hemisphere.
      (ii) Hence find the total surface area of the hemisphere.

7 The value of the surface area of a sphere (in m²) is equal to the value of the volume of the sphere (in m³). What is the sphere's radius?

Cones

For a cone with base radius r, perpendicular height h and slant height l:

Surface area $= \pi r l + \pi r^2$ **Volume** $= \frac{1}{3}\pi r^2 h$

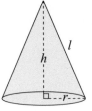

Example 2

Find the exact surface area and volume of the cone shown.

Surface area $= (\pi \times 3 \times 5) + (\pi \times 3^2) = 15\pi + 9\pi$

$\qquad\qquad = \mathbf{24\pi\ cm^2}$

Volume $= \frac{1}{3} \times \pi \times 3^2 \times 4 = \mathbf{12\pi\ cm^3}$

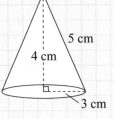

Exercise 2

1 Find **(i)** the exact surface area, and **(ii)** the exact volume of the cones with the given properties.
  a) $r = 5$ m, $h = 12$ m, $l = 13$ m
  b) $r = 7$ cm, $h = 24$ cm, $l = 25$ cm
  c) $r = 15$ m, $h = 8$ m, $l = 17$ m
  d) $r = 30$ mm, $h = 5.5$ mm, $l = 30.5$ mm

2 a) Find the exact surface area of the cone shown.

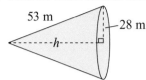

  b) (i) Use Pythagoras' theorem to find h, the perpendicular height of the cone.
  (ii) Find the exact volume of the cone.

3 A cone has base radius 56 cm and perpendicular height 33 cm.
  a) Find the exact volume of the cone.
  b) (i) Use Pythagoras' theorem to find the slant height of the cone.
  (ii) Find the exact surface area of the cone.

4 A cone has perpendicular height 6 mm and volume 39.27 mm³.
  a) Find the base radius of the cone, to 1 d.p.
  b) (i) Use your answer to part (a) to find the slant height, l, of the cone.
  (ii) Find the surface area of the cone, to 1 d.p.

5 A cone has vertical height 20 cm, slant height 29 cm and volume 9236.28 cm³.
  a) Find the base radius of the cone, to 1 d.p.
  b) Find the surface area of the cone, to 1 d.p.

6 A cone of perpendicular height 4 cm is removed from a cone of perpendicular height 16 cm and base radius 12 cm, as shown in the sketch below.

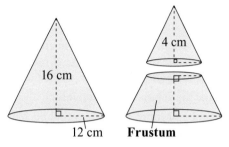

The 3D object which remains is a frustum.
  a) By considering the ratio of the heights of the cones, find the base radius of the smaller cone.
  b) Find the exact volume of the larger cone.
  c) Find the exact volume of the smaller cone.
  d) Hence find the exact volume of the frustum.

7 Find the exact volume of the frustum shown.

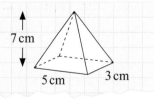

Pyramids

Find the surface area of a pyramid by calculating the area of each face and adding them together.
Find the volume of a pyramid using the formula:

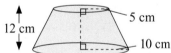

$$Volume = \frac{1}{3} \times base\ area \times height$$

Example 3

Find the volume of the rectangular-based pyramid shown.

Volume $= \frac{1}{3} \times (5 \times 3) \times 7 = \textbf{35 cm}^3$

7 cm

5 cm   3 cm

Example 4

Find the surface area of the regular tetrahedron shown. Give your answer correct to 3 s.f.

1. Each face is an equilateral triangle of side 5 cm.
2. Use 'area $= \frac{1}{2}ab\sin C$' to find the area of each face.

5 cm

Area of one face =
$\frac{1}{2} \times 5 \times 5 \times \sin 60° = 10.825...$

Total surface area $= 4 \times 10.825...$
$= \textbf{43.3 cm}^2$ (to 3 s.f.)

Exercise 3

1   A hexagon-based pyramid is 15 cm tall. The area of its base is 18 cm². Calculate its volume.

2   Just to be controversial, Pharaoh Tim has decided he wants a pentagon-based pyramid.
    The area of the pentagon is 27 m² and the perpendicular height of the pyramid is 12 m.
    What is the volume of Tim's pyramid?

3   Find the volume of a pyramid of height 10 cm with rectangular base with dimensions 4 cm × 7 cm.

4   Find the surface area of a regular tetrahedron of side 12 mm.

5   A square-based pyramid has height 11.5 cm and volume 736 cm³. Find the side length of its base.

6   The diagram on the right shows the square-based pyramid *ABCDE*.
    The side length of the base is 96 m and the pyramid's height is 55 m.
    O is the centre of the square base, directly below *E*.
    M is the midpoint of *AD*.

    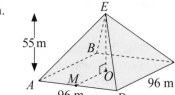

    a) Find the volume of the pyramid.

    b) Use Pythagoras' theorem to find the length *EM*.

    c) Hence find **(i)** the area of triangle *ADE*,
                   (ii) the surface area of the pyramid.

30.5   Rates of Flow

Rates of flow are measured as a **volume** per unit of **time** (e.g. litres per minute or cm³ per second).

Example 1

Water flows into this cuboid tank at a rate of 150 cm³ per second.
How long does it take to fill the tank?

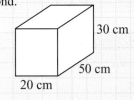

1.   Calculate the volume of the cuboid.
     Volume of cuboid = 20 × 30 × 50 = 30 000 cm³

2.   Divide volume by rate of flow to get the time taken.
     Time to fill the tank = 30 000 ÷ 150 = **200 seconds**

Exercise 1

1   Work out the average rates of flow when tanks with these volumes are completely filled in the given time:
    a) Volume = 600 cm³, Time = 15 seconds   b) Volume = 7200 litres, Time = 40 minutes
    c) Volume = 385 m³, Time = 5 minutes   d) Volume = 150 litres, Time = 8 hours

2   A stream is flowing at a rate of 3 litres per second. Convert this rate of flow into:
    a) cm³ per second   b) cm³ per minute   c) m³ per minute
    d) m³ per hour   e) m³ per day   f) litres per day

3   A fish tank is in the shape of a cuboid and has side lengths of 0.3 m, 1.2 m and 2 m.
    It is being filled with water at a rate of 0.09 m³ per minute.
    How long will it take to completely fill the fish tank?

4   A cube with a side length of 30 cm is filled with sand at a rate of 15 cm³ per second.
    How many minutes does it take to fill the cube?

5 Water flows into a container at a rate of 90 cm³ per second. It takes 8 minutes to fill the container. What is the capacity of the container?

6 A 4.5 litre bucket is completely full of water.
It has a leak and loses 2.5 cm³ of water every second.
How many minutes does it take for the bucket to completely empty?

7 Grain is being poured into the empty cylindrical silo shown on the right. The grain is flowing at a rate of 12 m³ every minute.

How long will it take to half fill the silo?
Give your answer to the nearest minute.

8 Concrete is being poured into a spherical mould, shown on the left, in order to make concrete balls.
Concrete is flowing into the mould at a rate of 2π litres every second.

How long does it take to completely fill the mould?

30.6   Symmetry of 3D Shapes

A **plane of symmetry** cuts a solid into **two identical halves**.

The number of planes of symmetry of a **prism** is always **one greater** than the number of lines of symmetry of its cross-section. The only exception is a cube, which has nine planes of symmetry.

Example 1
How many planes of symmetry does an isosceles triangular prism have?

 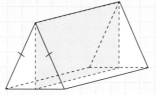 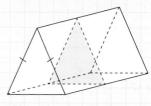

An isosceles triangle has 1 line of symmetry, so an isosceles triangular prism has **2** planes of symmetry.

Exercise 1

1 Write down the number of planes of symmetry of the prisms with the following cross-sections.
   a) regular pentagon
   b) regular octagon
   c) scalene triangle

2 Draw the planes of symmetry of the prisms with the following cross-sections.
   a) equilateral triangle
   b) rectangle
   c) regular hexagon

3 Draw all the planes of symmetry of a cube.

4 Draw a prism with 5 planes of symmetry.

The number of planes of symmetry of a **pyramid** is equal to the number of lines of symmetry of its base. The only exception is a regular tetrahedron, which has 6 planes of symmetry.

Example 2

How many planes of symmetry does a rectangle-based pyramid have?

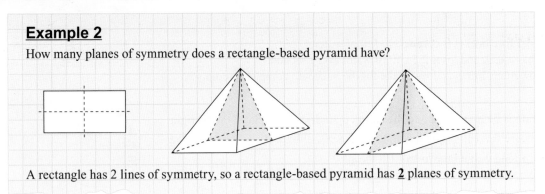

A rectangle has 2 lines of symmetry, so a rectangle-based pyramid has **2** planes of symmetry.

Exercise 2

1   Write down the number of planes of symmetry of the pyramids with the following bases.
    a) regular pentagon   b) regular octagon

2   Draw the planes of symmetry of the pyramids with the following bases.
    a) square   b) regular hexagon

3   Draw all the planes of symmetry of a regular tetrahedron.

30.7   3D Shapes Problems

Exercise 1

Where appropriate, give your answers to these questions to 2 decimal places.

1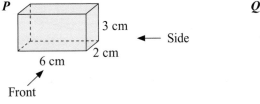

    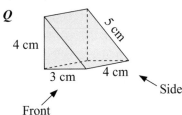

    For each of the shapes **P** and **Q** above, complete the following.
    a) Draw a net of the shape.
    b) Draw the plan, and front and side elevations of the shape from the directions indicated.
    c) Draw the shape on isometric paper.
    d) Calculate the shape's volume.
    e) Calculate how long it would take to fill the shape with water flowing at a rate of 2 cm³ per second.
    f) Calculate the shape's surface area.
    g) Write down the number of planes of symmetry of the shape.

2   A cylindrical disc has a radius of 4 cm and height of 0.5 cm.
    a) Find the surface area of the disc.
    b) Find the surface area of a stack of 10 discs,
        assuming there are no gaps between each disc.
    c) Find the volume of the stack of 10 discs.

3 Draw the following prisms on isometric paper.

a)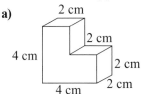

b)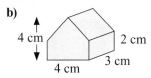

c)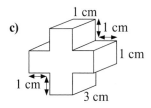

4 A cube has a total surface area of 54 cm².
  a) Find the area of one face of the cube.
  b) Find the length of the edges of the cube.
  c) Find the cube's volume.

5 Beans are sold in cylindrical tins of diameter 7.4 cm and height 11 cm.
  a) Find the volume of one tin.

  The tins are stored in boxes which hold 12 tins in three rows of 4, as shown.
  b) Find the dimensions of the box.
  c) Find the volume of the box.
  d) Calculate the volume of the box that is not taken up by tins when it is fully packed.

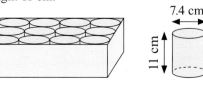

6 Toilet paper is sold in cylindrical rolls of diameter 12 cm and height 11 cm. The card tube at the centre of the roll is 5 cm in diameter.
  a) Find the total volume of one roll of toilet paper, including the card tube.
  b) Find the volume of the card tube.
  c) Hence find the volume of the paper.

  Each rectangular sheet of paper measures 11 cm × 13 cm and is 0.03 cm thick.
  d) Find the volume of one sheet of paper.
  e) Hence find the number of sheets of paper in one roll, to the nearest sheet.

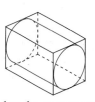

7 A cylinder of diameter 25 mm has volume 7854 mm³.
  a) Find the length of the cylinder to the nearest mm.
  b) Find the surface area of the cylinder to the nearest mm².

  The cylinder is enclosed in a cuboid, as shown.
  c) Find the volume of the cuboid to the nearest mm³.
  d) Find the volume of the empty space between the cylinder and the cuboid to the nearest mm³.

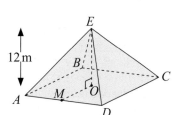

8 The diagram on the right shows the square-based pyramid *ABCDE*. The pyramid's vertical height is 12 m and its volume is 400 m³. *O* is the centre of the square base, directly below *E*. *M* is the midpoint of *AD*.
  a) Find the side length of the square base.
  b) Find the length *EM*.
  c) Find the surface area of the pyramid.

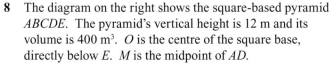

9 A giant novelty pencil is made up of a cone, a cylinder and a hemisphere, as shown.
  a) Find the exact volume of the pencil.
  b) (i) Find the exact slant height of the cone.
     (ii) Hence find the exact surface area of the pencil.

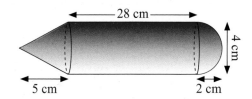

Section 31 — Transformations

31.1 Reflections

When an object is **reflected** in a line, its size, shape and distance from the mirror line all stay the same.

Example 1

a) Copy the axes shown, then reflect the shape *ABCDE* in the *y*-axis.

b) Label the image points A_1, B_1, C_1, D_1 and E_1 with their coordinates.

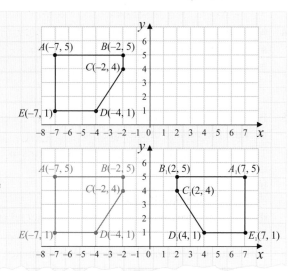

1. Reflect the shape — one point at a time.

2. Each image point should be the same distance from the *y*-axis as the original point.

3. Write down the coordinates of each of the image points.

Exercise 1

1 a) Copy the diagram shown, and reflect the shape in the *y*-axis.

   b) Label the image points A_1, B_1, C_1, D_1 and E_1 with their coordinates.

   c) Describe a rule connecting the coordinates of *A*, *B*, *C*, *D* and *E* and the coordinates of A_1, B_1, C_1, D_1 and E_1.

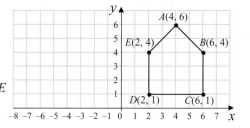

2 Copy each of the diagrams below, and reflect the shapes in the *y*-axis.

a)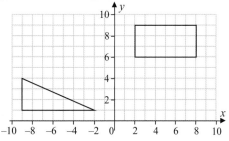

b)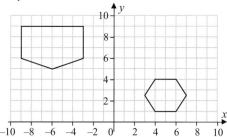

3 a) Copy each of the diagrams below, and reflect the shapes in the *x*-axis.

(i)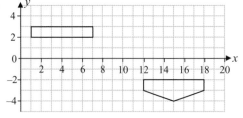

(ii)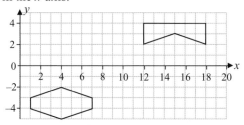

b) Describe a rule connecting the coordinates of a point and its reflection in the *x*-axis.

4 The following points are reflected in the *x*-axis. Find the coordinates of the image points.

    a) (1, 2)   **b)** (3, 0)   **c)** (–2, 4)   **d)** (–1, –3)   **e)** (–2, –2)

5 The following points are reflected in the *y*-axis. Find the coordinates of the image points.

    a) (4, 5)   **b)** (7, 2)   **c)** (–1, 3)   **d)** (–3, –1)   **e)** (–4, –8)

6 Copy the diagram shown on the right.

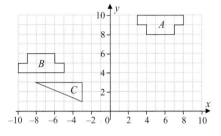

    a) Reflect shape *A* in the line $x = 2$. Label the image A_1.

    b) Reflect shape *B* in the line $x = -1$. Label the image B_1.

    c) Reflect shape *C* in the line $x = 1$. Label the image C_1.

    d) Shape B_1 is the reflection of shape *A* in which mirror line?

7 Copy the diagram shown on the right.

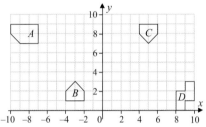

    a) Reflect shape *A* in the line $y = 6$. Label the image A_1.

    b) Reflect shape *B* in the line $y = 4$. Label the image B_1.

    c) Reflect shape *C* in the line $y = 5$. Label the image C_1.

    d) Reflect shape *D* in the line $y = 3$. Label the image D_1.

    e) Shape C_1 is the reflection of shape *B* in which mirror line?

    f) Reflect shape *B* in the line $y = 2$ and circle any points of invariance.

Example 2

Copy the diagram below, then reflect the shape in the line $y = x$.

1.   Reflect the shape one point at a time.

2.   The image points should be the same distance from the line $y = x$ as the originals.

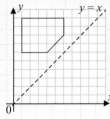 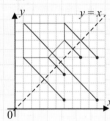 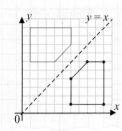

8 Copy each of the diagrams below, and reflect the shapes in the line $y = x$.

    a)

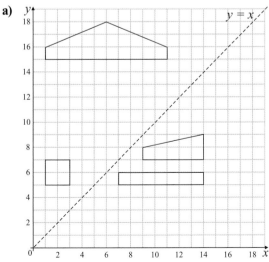

    b)

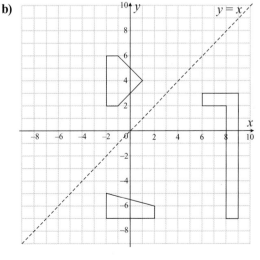

9 The points with the following coordinates are reflected in the line $y = x$.
Find the coordinates of the reflections.

   a) (1, 2)   **b)** (3, 0)   **c)** (−2, 4)   **d)** (−1, −3)   **e)** (−2, −2)

10 Find the equation of the mirror line
for the following reflections.

   a) Shape A onto shape B.

   b) Shape C onto shape A.

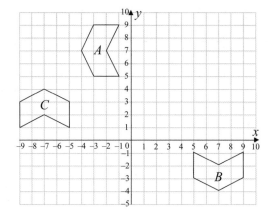

31.2   Rotations

When an object is **rotated** about a point, its size, shape and distance from the centre of rotation all stay the same.
You need three pieces of information to describe a rotation:

   (i) the **centre** of rotation   (ii) the **direction** of rotation   (iii) the **angle** of rotation

(But a rotation of 180° is the same in both directions, so you don't need the direction in that case.)

Example 1

Copy the first diagram below, then rotate the shape 90° clockwise about point P.

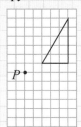   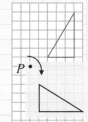   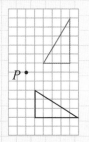

1. Draw the shape on a
    piece of tracing paper.
    (Or imagine a drawing of it.)

2. Rotate the tracing paper 90°
    clockwise about P.
    ('About P' means P doesn't move.)

3. Draw the image in
    its new position.

Exercise 1

1 Copy the diagrams below, then rotate the shapes
180° about P.

   a) 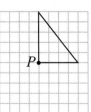   **b)**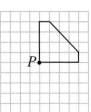

2 Copy the diagrams below, then rotate the shapes
90° clockwise about P.

   a) 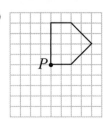   **b)**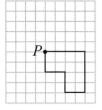

3

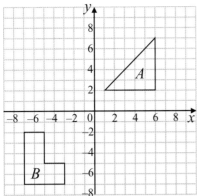

Copy the diagram, then complete the following.
a) Rotate A 90° clockwise about the origin.
b) Rotate B 270° anticlockwise about the origin.

4

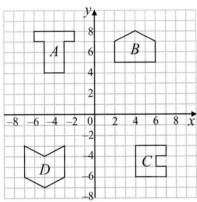

Copy the diagram, then complete the following.
a) Rotate A 90° clockwise about (−8, 5).
b) Rotate B 90° clockwise about (1, 4).
c) Rotate C 90° clockwise about (8, −4).
d) Rotate D 180° about (−2, −5).

5

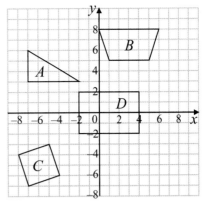

Copy the diagram, then complete the following.
a) Rotate A 180° about (−5, 6).
b) Rotate B 90° anticlockwise about (5, 9).
c) Rotate C 180° about (−3, −5).
d) Rotate D 180° about (3, −1).

6 The triangle ABC has vertices $A(-2, 1)$, $B(-2, 6)$ and $C(4, 1)$.

a) Draw the triangle on a pair of axes.
b) Rotate the triangle 90° clockwise about (5, 4). Label the image $A_1B_1C_1$.
c) Write down the coordinates of A_1, B_1 and C_1.

7 The triangle DEF has coordinates $D(-2, -2)$, $E(-2, 5)$ and $F(3, 5)$. DEF is rotated 180° about (2, 0) to create the image $D_1E_1F_1$. Find the coordinates of D_1, E_1 and F_1.

Example 2

Describe fully the rotation that transforms shape A to shape B.

1. The shape looks like it has been rotated clockwise by 90°.

2. Rotate the shape 90° clockwise about different points until you get the correct image — tracing paper will help if you have some.

3. Write down the centre, direction and angle of rotation.

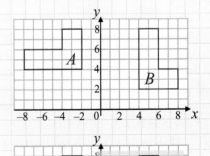

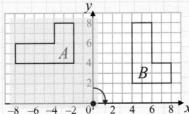
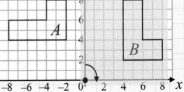

So A is transformed to B by a rotation of **90° clockwise** (or **270° anticlockwise**) about **the origin**.

Exercise 2

1

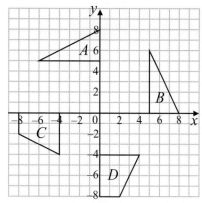

a) Describe fully the rotation that transforms shape *A* to shape *B*.

b) Describe fully the rotation that transforms shape *C* to shape *D*.

3

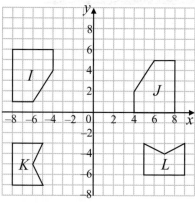

a) Describe fully the rotation that transforms shape *I* to shape *J*.

b) Describe fully the rotation that transforms shape *K* to shape *L*.

2

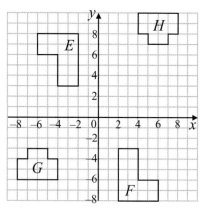

a) Describe fully the rotation that transforms shape *E* to shape *F*.

b) Describe fully the rotation that transforms shape *G* to shape *H*.

4

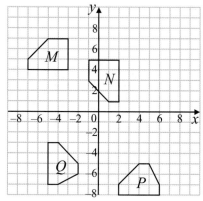

a) Describe fully the rotation that transforms shape *M* to shape *N*.

b) Describe fully the rotation that transforms shape *P* to shape *Q*.

5 a) Describe fully the rotation that transforms shape *R* to shape *S*.

b) Describe fully the rotation that transforms shape *R* to shape *T*.

c) Describe fully the rotation that transforms shape *S* to shape *T*.

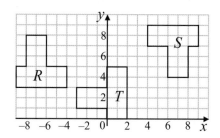

6 The triangle *UVW* has vertices *U*(1, 1), *V*(3, 5) and *W*(–1, 3).
The triangle *XYZ* has vertices *X*(–2, 4), *Y*(–6, 6) and *Z*(–4, 2).

a) Draw the two triangles on a pair of axes.

b) Describe fully the rotation that transforms *UVW* to *XYZ*.

When an object is **translated**, its size and shape stay the same, but its position changes.

A translation can be described by the vector $\begin{pmatrix} a \\ b \end{pmatrix}$ — where the shape moves a units right and b units up.

Example 1

Copy the diagram below, then translate the shape by the vector $\begin{pmatrix} 5 \\ -3 \end{pmatrix}$.

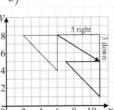

$\begin{pmatrix} 5 \\ -3 \end{pmatrix}$ is a translation of:

(i)   5 units to the right,

(ii) 3 units down (which is the same as –3 units up).

Exercise 1

1   Copy the diagrams below, then translate each shape by the vector written next to it.

a)

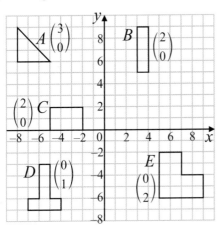

b)

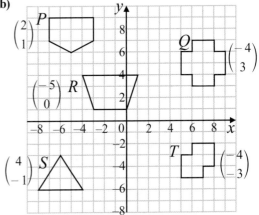

2   **a)** Copy the diagram on the right, then translate the triangle ABC by the vector $\begin{pmatrix} -10 \\ -1 \end{pmatrix}$.

Label the image $A_1B_1C_1$.

b) Label A_1, B_1 and C_1 with their coordinates.

c) Describe a rule connecting the coordinates of A, B and C and the coordinates of A_1, B_1 and C_1.

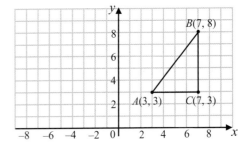

3   The triangle DEF has corners $D(1, 1)$, $E(3, -2)$ and $F(4, 0)$. After the translation $\begin{pmatrix} -2 \\ 2 \end{pmatrix}$, the image of DEF is $D_1E_1F_1$. Find the coordinates of D_1, E_1 and F_1.

4   The quadrilateral $PQRS$ has corners $P(0, 0)$, $Q(4, 1)$, $R(2, 3)$ and $S(-1, 2)$. After the translation $\begin{pmatrix} -3 \\ -4 \end{pmatrix}$, the image of $PQRS$ is $P_1Q_1R_1S_1$. Find the coordinates of P_1, Q_1, R_1 and S_1.

Example 2

Give the vector that describes
the translation of A onto B.

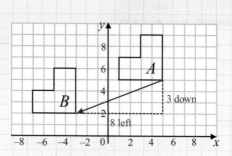

1. Count how many units horizontally
   and vertically the shape has moved.

2. Write the translation as a vector.

The image is 8 units to the left and 3 units down,

so the translation is described by the vector $\begin{pmatrix} -8 \\ -3 \end{pmatrix}$.

Exercise 2

1

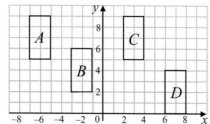

Give the vector that describes each of the
following translations.

a) A onto B   **b)** A onto C   **c)** C onto B

d) C onto D   **e)** D onto A   **f)** D onto B

2

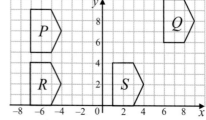

Give the vector that describes each of the
following translations.

a) P onto R   **b)** R onto S   **c)** P onto Q

d) S onto R   **e)** Q onto R   **f)** S onto P

3 The triangle DEF has vertices D(–3, –2), E(1, –1) and F(0, 2). The triangle GHI has vertices
G(0, 2), H(4, 3) and I(3, 6). Give the vector that describes the translation that maps DEF onto GHI.

4 The triangle JKL has vertices J(1, 0), K(–2, 4) and L(–4, 7).
The triangle MNP has vertices M(0, 2), N(–3, 6) and P(–5, 9).

a) Give the vector that describes the translation that maps JKL onto MNP.

b) Give the vector that describes the translation that maps MNP onto JKL.

5 This question is about the diagram on the right.

a) Give the vector that describes the translation that maps X onto Y.

b) Give the vector that describes the translation that maps Y onto X.

c) What do you notice about your answers to **a)** and **b)**?

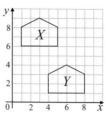

6 Shape W is the image of shape Z after the translation $\begin{pmatrix} 1 \\ -4 \end{pmatrix}$.
Write as a vector the translation that maps W onto Z.

7 The triangle PQR has vertices P(–1, 0), Q(–4, 4) and R(3, 2). PQR is the image of
the triangle DEF after the translation $\begin{pmatrix} -1 \\ 4 \end{pmatrix}$. Find the coordinates of D, E and F.

When an object is **enlarged**, its shape stays the same, but its size changes.
The **scale factor** of an enlargement tells you how much the size changes, and the
centre of enlargement tells you where the enlargement is measured from.

Example 1

Copy the first diagram below, then enlarge the shape by
scale factor 2 with centre of enlargement (2, 2).

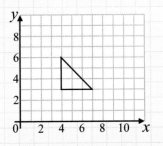
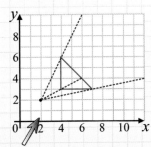
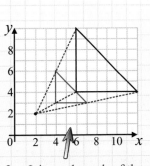

1. Draw a line from (2, 2) through each vertex of the shape.
    All the distances are multiplied by the scale factor, so
    continue each line until it is twice as far away from (2, 2)
    as the original vertex.

2. Join up the ends of the
    lines to create the image.

Exercise 1

1   Copy the diagrams below, then enlarge each shape by scale factor 2 with centre of enlargement (0, 0).

a)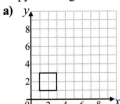
b)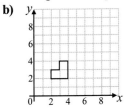
c)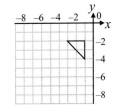
d)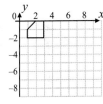

2   Copy the diagram on the right.

a) Enlarge A by scale factor 2 with centre of enlargement (−8, 9).

b) Enlarge B by scale factor 2 with centre of enlargement (9, 9).

c) Enlarge C by scale factor 3 with centre of enlargement (9, −8).

d) Enlarge D by scale factor 4 with centre of enlargement (−8, −8).

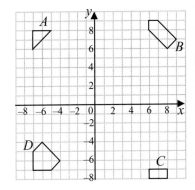

3   The triangle PQR has corners at P(1, 1), Q(1, 4) and R(4, 2).

a) Draw PQR on a pair of axes.

b) Enlarge PQR by scale factor 2 with centre of enlargement (−1, 1).

4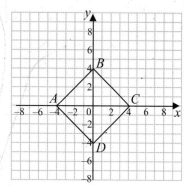

The square $ABCD$ is shown on the left. $A_1B_1C_1D_1$ is the image of $ABCD$ after it has been enlarged by scale factor 2 with centre of enlargement (0, 0).

a) Find the distance of each of the following corners from (0, 0).
  (i) A **(ii)** B **(iii)** C **(iv)** D

b) What will the distance of the following corners be from (0, 0)?
  (i) A_1 **(ii)** B_1 **(iii)** C_1 **(iv)** D_1

c) Copy the diagram. Draw a line from (0, 0) through each corner of $ABCD$. Mark the points A_1, B_1, C_1 and D_1 on these lines. Join up the points A_1, B_1, C_1 and D_1 to draw $A_1B_1C_1D_1$.

5 Copy the diagram below, then enlarge each shape by scale factor 2, using the centre of enlargement marked inside the shape.

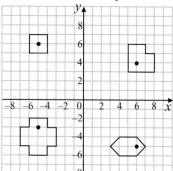

7 Copy the diagram below, then enlarge each shape by scale factor 2, using the centre of enlargement marked on the shape's corner.

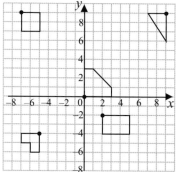

6 The shape $WXYZ$ has corners at $W(0, 0)$, $X(1, 3)$, $Y(3, 3)$ and $Z(4, 0)$.

a) Draw $WXYZ$ on a pair of axes.

b) Enlarge $WXYZ$ by scale factor 3 with centre of enlargement (2, 2).

8 The shape $KLMN$ has corners at $K(3, 4)$, $L(3, 6)$, $M(5, 6)$ and $N(5, 5)$.

a) Draw $KLMN$ on a pair of axes.

b) Enlarge $KLMN$ by scale factor 3 with centre of enlargement (3, 6). Label the shape $K_1L_1M_1N_1$.

c) Enlarge $KLMN$ by scale factor 2 with centre of enlargement (5, 6). Label the shape $K_2L_2M_2N_2$.

Example 2

Copy the first diagram below, then enlarge the shape by scale factor $\frac{1}{2}$ with centre of enlargement (2, 7).

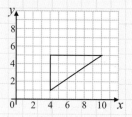 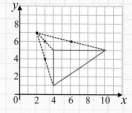 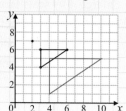

1. An enlargement where the magnitude of the scale factor is less than 1 gives a smaller image.
2. Draw lines from (2, 7) to each corner. The image points will lie half as far from the centre of enlargement as the original corners.

Exercise 2

1

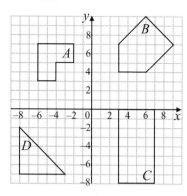

Copy the diagram on the left.

a) Enlarge A by scale factor $\frac{1}{2}$ with centre of enlargement (–8, 9).

b) Enlarge B by scale factor $\frac{1}{3}$ with centre of enlargement (0, 1).

c) Enlarge C by scale factor $\frac{1}{4}$ with centre of enlargement (–1, –8).

d) Enlarge D by scale factor $\frac{1}{5}$ with centre of enlargement (2, 3).

2 Copy the diagram on the right.

a) Enlarge A by scale factor $\frac{1}{2}$ with centre of enlargement (–4, 5).

b) Enlarge B by scale factor $\frac{1}{3}$ with centre of enlargement (7, 7).

c) Enlarge C by scale factor $\frac{1}{4}$ with centre of enlargement (6, –4).

d) Enlarge D by scale factor $\frac{1}{5}$ with centre of enlargement (–3, –2).

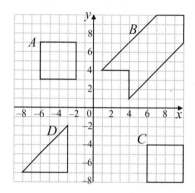

Example 3

Copy the first diagram below, then enlarge the shape by scale factor –2 with centre of enlargement (8, 7).

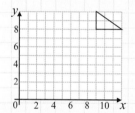 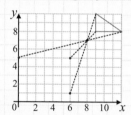 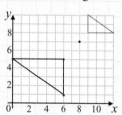

1. A negative scale factor means the image will be on the opposite side of the centre of enlargement to the original object, and will be 'upside down'.

2. Draw lines from each corner through (8, 7). The image points will lie twice as far from the centre of enlargement as the original corner, but in the opposite direction.

Exercise 3

1 Copy the diagram on the right.

a) Enlarge A by scale factor –2 with centre of enlargement (–6, 7).

b) Enlarge B by scale factor –3 with centre of enlargement (7, 7).

c) Enlarge C by scale factor –2 with centre of enlargement (–2, –4).

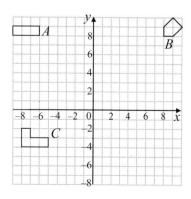

2 Copy the diagram on the right.

a) Enlarge *A* by scale factor $-\frac{1}{2}$ with centre of enlargement (−4, 4).

b) Enlarge *B* by scale factor $-\frac{1}{3}$ with centre of enlargement (6, 4).

c) Enlarge *C* by scale factor $-\frac{1}{2}$ with centre of enlargement (4, −4).

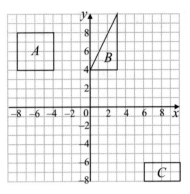

Example 4

Describe the enlargement that maps shape *X* onto shape *Y*.

1. Pick any side of the shape, and see how many times bigger this side is on the image than the original. This is the scale factor.

2. Draw a line from each corner on the image through the corresponding corner on the original shape. The point where these lines meet is the centre of enlargement.

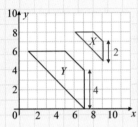

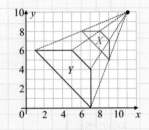

An enlargement by scale factor **2**, centre **(11, 10)**.

Exercise 4

1 For each of the following, describe the enlargement that maps shape *A* onto shape *B*.

a)
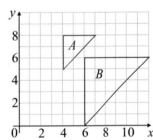

b)
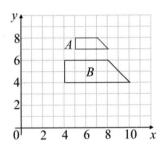

c)
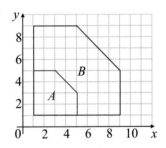

2 For each of the following, describe the enlargement that maps shape *A* onto shape *B*.

a)
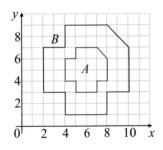

b)
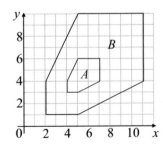

c)
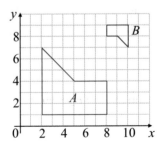

Example 1

Draw triangle ABC, which has its vertices at $A(2, 2)$, $B(6, 5)$ and $C(6, 2)$.

a) Rotate ABC 180° about the point (1, 1), then translate the image by $\begin{pmatrix} -2 \\ -2 \end{pmatrix}$. Label the image $A_1B_1C_1$.

b) Find a **single** rotation that transforms triangle ABC onto the image $A_1B_1C_1$.

a)

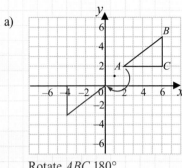

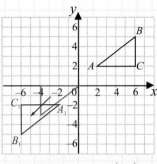

b)

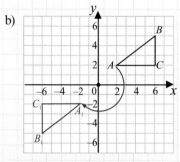

Rotate ABC 180°
about (1, 1)...

... then translate by $\begin{pmatrix} -2 \\ -2 \end{pmatrix}$.

A rotation of 180° about the
origin maps ABC onto $A_1B_1C_1$.

Exercise 1

1 Copy the diagram below.

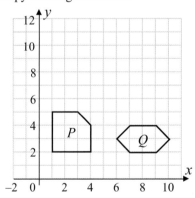

a) (i) Rotate shape P 180° about (4, 5).

(ii) Translate the image by $\begin{pmatrix} 2 \\ 2 \end{pmatrix}$. Label the final image P_1.

b) Rotate shape P 180° about (5, 6). Label the final image P_2.

c) (i) Rotate shape Q 180° about (4, 5).

(ii) Translate the image by $\begin{pmatrix} 2 \\ 2 \end{pmatrix}$. Label the final image Q_1.

d) Rotate shape Q 180° about (5, 6). Label the final image Q_2.

e) What do you notice about images P_1 and P_2
and about images Q_1 and Q_2?

2 Triangle ABC has its corners at $A(2, 1)$, $B(6, 4)$ and $C(6, 1)$.

a) Draw triangle ABC on a pair of axes, where both the x- and y-axes are labelled from –6 to 6.

b) Reflect ABC in the y-axis. Label the image $A_1B_1C_1$.

c) Reflect the image $A_1B_1C_1$ in the x-axis. Label the image $A_2B_2C_2$.

d) Find a single rotation that transforms triangle ABC onto the image $A_2B_2C_2$.

3 Draw triangle PQR with corners at $P(2, 3)$, $Q(4, 3)$ and $R(4, 4)$.

a) Rotate PQR 90° clockwise about the point (2, 3). Label the image $P_1Q_1R_1$.

b) Translate $P_1Q_1R_1$ by $\begin{pmatrix} 1 \\ -5 \end{pmatrix}$. Label the new image $P_2Q_2R_2$.

c) Describe a single transformation that maps triangle PQR onto the image $P_2Q_2R_2$.

4 Triangle *WXY* has its corners at *W*(–5, –5), *X*(–4, –2) and *Y*(–2, –4).

    a) Draw triangle *WXY* on a pair of axes, where both the *x*- and *y*-axes are labelled from –6 to 6.

    b) Reflect *WXY* in the line *y* = *x*. Label the image $W_1X_1Y_1$.

    c) Reflect the image $W_1X_1Y_1$ in the *y*-axis. Label the image $W_2X_2Y_2$.

    d) Find a single transformation that maps *WXY* onto the image $W_2X_2Y_2$.

5 Copy the diagram on the right.

    a) Reflect triangle *DEF* in the line *x* = 5. Label the image $D_1E_1F_1$.

    b) Reflect the image $D_1E_1F_1$ in the line *x* = 3. Label the image $D_2E_2F_2$.

    c) Find a single transformation that maps *DEF* onto $D_2E_2F_2$.

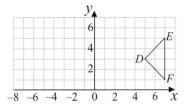

6 Copy the diagram on the right.

    a) Translate shape *ABCDE* by $\begin{pmatrix} -2 \\ -1 \end{pmatrix}$. Label the image $A_1B_1C_1D_1E_1$.

    b) Enlarge the image $A_1B_1C_1D_1E_1$ by scale factor 2 with centre of enlargement (2, 1). Label the image $A_2B_2C_2D_2E_2$.

    c) Find a single transformation that maps *ABCDE* onto $A_2B_2C_2D_2E_2$.

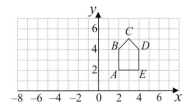

7 Shape *WXYZ* has its corners at *W*(–6, 2), *X*(–3, 3), *Y*(–2, 6) and *Z*(–2, 2).

    a) Draw *WXYZ* on a pair of axes, where both the *x*- and *y*-axes are labelled from –6 to 6.

    b) Reflect *WXYZ* in the *y*-axis. Label the image $W_1X_1Y_1Z_1$.

    c) Rotate the image $W_1X_1Y_1Z_1$ 90° clockwise about (0, 0). Label the image $W_2X_2Y_2Z_2$.

    d) Find a single transformation that maps *WXYZ* onto the image $W_2X_2Y_2Z_2$.

8 By considering triangle *XYZ* with corners at *X*(2, 2), *Y*(4, 4) and *Z*(6, 2), find the single transformation equivalent to a reflection in the line *y* = 2, followed by a reflection in the line *x* = 2.

9 By considering triangle *STU* with corners at *S*(1, 1), *T*(3, 1) and *U*(1, 2), find the single transformation equivalent to a rotation of 180° about the origin, followed by a translation by $\begin{pmatrix} 6 \\ 2 \end{pmatrix}$.

10 Copy the diagram on the right.

    a) Rotate triangle *ABC* 180° about (0, 0). Label the image $A_1B_1C_1$.

    b) Enlarge the image $A_1B_1C_1$ by scale factor $\frac{1}{2}$ with centre of enlargement (0, 0). Label the image $A_2B_2C_2$.

    c) Find a single transformation that maps triangle *ABC* onto the image $A_2B_2C_2$.

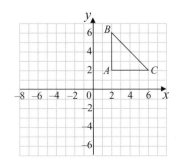

11 By considering shape *PQRS* with corners at *P*(2, –2), *Q*(4, –2), *R*(5, –5) and *S*(2, –4), find the single transformation equivalent to a rotation of 90° anticlockwise about (2, –2), followed by a reflection in the *y*-axis, followed by a translation by $\begin{pmatrix} 0 \\ 4 \end{pmatrix}$.

Shapes on a grid can be represented by a **matrix**.
Each **column** of the matrix gives the **coordinates** of a point.

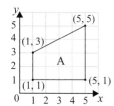

E.g. shape **A** is given by the matrix $\begin{pmatrix} 1 & 1 & 5 & 5 \\ 1 & 3 & 5 & 1 \end{pmatrix}$.

Transformations can also be given by matrices —
multiplying the transformation matrix and the shape
matrix gives a matrix which represents the image.

Example 1

The shape **A** $\begin{pmatrix} 1 & 3 & 6 & 6 \\ 1 & 4 & 3 & 1 \end{pmatrix}$ is transformed by the matrix **M** $\begin{pmatrix} 1 & 0 \\ 0 & -1 \end{pmatrix}$.

Find the matrix representing the transformed shape **B**, draw shapes **A** and **B**
on the same grid and describe the transformation given by **M**.

1. Multiply the transformation
   matrix and shape matrix to find
   the matrix of the image.

2. Plot the coordinates from this
   matrix to draw the image.

3. Use your diagram to describe
   the transformation.

MA = B:

$$\begin{pmatrix} 1 & 0 \\ 0 & -1 \end{pmatrix}\begin{pmatrix} 1 & 3 & 6 & 6 \\ 1 & 4 & 3 & 1 \end{pmatrix} = \begin{pmatrix} 1 & 3 & 6 & 6 \\ -1 & -4 & -3 & -1 \end{pmatrix}$$

So matrix **M** represents a
reflection in the x-axis.

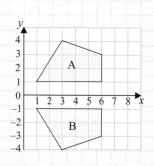

Exercise 1

1 Give the matrices that represent shapes
A, B, C and D, shown below.

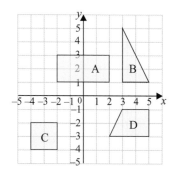

2 **A** $\begin{pmatrix} 1 & 1 & 3 & 3 \\ 1 & 4 & 4 & 1 \end{pmatrix}$ is transformed by matrix **E** $\begin{pmatrix} 2 & 0 \\ 0 & 2 \end{pmatrix}$.

  a) Find **B**, the matrix of the transformed shape.

  b) Draw the shapes **A** and **B**.

  c) Describe the transformation given by **E**.

3 **P** $\begin{pmatrix} 1 & 1 & 3 \\ 0 & 2 & 2 \end{pmatrix}$ is transformed by matrix **R** $\begin{pmatrix} 0 & -1 \\ 1 & 0 \end{pmatrix}$.

  a) Find the matrix of the transformed shape **Q**.

  b) Draw the shapes **P** and **Q**.

  c) Describe the transformation given by **R**.

4 **C** $\begin{pmatrix} 2 & 4 & 4 \\ 4 & 4 & 2 \end{pmatrix}$ is transformed by matrix **E** $\begin{pmatrix} \frac{1}{2} & 0 \\ 0 & \frac{1}{2} \end{pmatrix}$.

  a) Draw the shape **C** and the transformed shape **D**.

  b) Describe the transformation given by **E**.

5 **V** $\begin{pmatrix} 1 & 1 & 3 & 3 \\ -1 & 2 & 1 & 0 \end{pmatrix}$ is transformed by matrix **R** $\begin{pmatrix} 0 & 1 \\ -1 & 0 \end{pmatrix}$.

  a) Find the matrix of the transformed shape **W**.

  b) Draw **V** and **W**.

  c) Describe the transformation **R**.

Example 2

Find the transformation matrix, **M**, that maps shape **A** onto shape **B**, as shown.

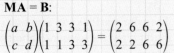

1. Write down matrices **A** and **B**.
   The corresponding columns of the two matrices must represent the corresponding vertices of the two shapes.

$$\mathbf{A}\begin{pmatrix} 1 & 3 & 3 & 1 \\ 1 & 1 & 3 & 3 \end{pmatrix} \qquad \mathbf{B}\begin{pmatrix} 2 & 6 & 6 & 2 \\ 2 & 2 & 6 & 6 \end{pmatrix}$$

MA = B:

2. Multiplying the transformation matrix by the original shape matrix gives the matrix of the image.

$$\begin{pmatrix} a & b \\ c & d \end{pmatrix}\begin{pmatrix} 1 & 3 & 3 & 1 \\ 1 & 1 & 3 & 3 \end{pmatrix} = \begin{pmatrix} 2 & 6 & 6 & 2 \\ 2 & 2 & 6 & 6 \end{pmatrix}$$

$$\begin{pmatrix} a+b & 3a+b & 3a+3b & a+3b \\ c+d & 3c+d & 3c+3d & c+3d \end{pmatrix} = \begin{pmatrix} 2 & 6 & 6 & 2 \\ 2 & 2 & 6 & 6 \end{pmatrix}$$

3. Put the corresponding entries equal to each other and solve the equations simultaneously to find the unknowns.

$$\begin{aligned} 3a+b &= 6 \\ -\ \ a+b &= 2 \\ \hline 2a &= 4 \\ a = 2 \text{ and } b &= 0 \end{aligned} \qquad \begin{aligned} 3c+d &= 2 \\ -\ \ c+d &= 2 \\ \hline 2c &= 0 \\ c = 0 \text{ and } d &= 2 \end{aligned}$$

$$\text{So } \mathbf{M} = \begin{pmatrix} 2 & 0 \\ 0 & 2 \end{pmatrix}$$

Exercise 2

1 For each of the following, find the transformation matrix that maps **A** onto **B**.

a)
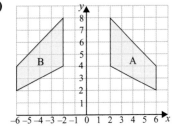

b)
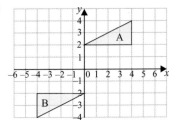

c)
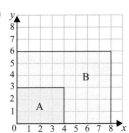

d)
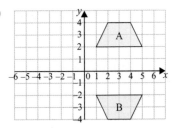

e)
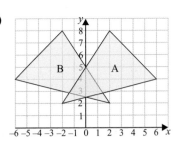

f)
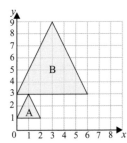

g)
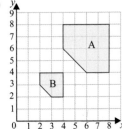

h)
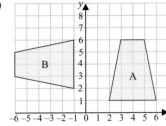

i)
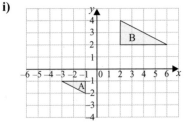

Example 3

Shape **A**, given by the matrix **A** $\begin{pmatrix} 1 & 1 & 3 & 3 \\ 1 & 2 & 2 & 1 \end{pmatrix}$, is transformed by **M** $\begin{pmatrix} 1 & 0 \\ 0 & -1 \end{pmatrix}$ then by **E** $\begin{pmatrix} 2 & 0 \\ 0 & 2 \end{pmatrix}$ into shape **B**. Draw shapes **A** and **B**.

1. Put the matrices in the right order. The first transformation goes to the left of **A**, and the second to the left of that. So **EMA = B**.

2. Multiply the matrices to find **B**. (You could find **MA** first, and multiply the result by **E**, but here it's easier to find **EM** first, then multiply by **A**.)

3. Use matrices **A** and **B** to draw the shapes.

$$\mathbf{B} = \begin{pmatrix} 2 & 0 \\ 0 & 2 \end{pmatrix}\begin{pmatrix} 1 & 0 \\ 0 & -1 \end{pmatrix}\begin{pmatrix} 1 & 1 & 3 & 3 \\ 1 & 2 & 2 & 1 \end{pmatrix}$$

$$= \begin{pmatrix} 2 & 0 \\ 0 & -2 \end{pmatrix}\begin{pmatrix} 1 & 1 & 3 & 3 \\ 1 & 2 & 2 & 1 \end{pmatrix}$$

$$= \begin{pmatrix} 2 & 2 & 6 & 6 \\ -2 & -4 & -4 & -2 \end{pmatrix}$$

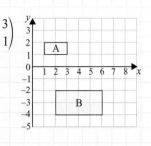

Exercise 3

1. For each of the following, **(i)** find the matrix **B**, and **(ii)** draw shapes **A** and **B**.

   a) Shape **A** $\begin{pmatrix} 1 & 2 & 0 \\ 1 & 3 & 4 \end{pmatrix}$ is transformed by the matrix **L** $\begin{pmatrix} 0 & 1 \\ -1 & 0 \end{pmatrix}$, then by the matrix **M** $\begin{pmatrix} 1 & 0 \\ 0 & -1 \end{pmatrix}$ into shape **B**.

   b) Shape **A** $\begin{pmatrix} 0 & 2 & 4 \\ 0 & 2 & 0 \end{pmatrix}$ is transformed by the matrix **L** $\begin{pmatrix} 2 & 0 \\ 0 & 2 \end{pmatrix}$, then by the matrix **M** $\begin{pmatrix} -1 & 0 \\ 0 & 1 \end{pmatrix}$ into shape **B**.

2. Shape **A**, shown here, is transformed by the matrix **P** $\begin{pmatrix} 1 & 0 \\ 0 & -1 \end{pmatrix}$ to give shape **B**.

   B is then transformed by **Q** $\begin{pmatrix} 3 & 0 \\ 0 & 3 \end{pmatrix}$ to give shape **C**.

   a) Copy the diagram shown and draw shape **B**.
   b) Draw shape **C**.
   c) **(i)** Find the matrix **R** that maps **A** directly onto **C**.
      (ii) Describe the two consecutive transformations that **R** represents.

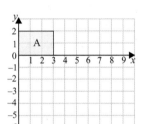

3. Shape **A**, shown, is transformed by the matrix **X** $\begin{pmatrix} -1 & 0 \\ 0 & 1 \end{pmatrix}$ to give shape **B**.

   B is then transformed by **Y** $\begin{pmatrix} \frac{1}{3} & 0 \\ 0 & \frac{1}{3} \end{pmatrix}$ to give shape **C**.

   a) Copy the diagram shown and draw shape **B**.
   b) Draw shape **C**.
   c) **(i)** Find the matrix **Z** that maps **A** directly onto **C**.
      (ii) Describe the two consecutive transformations that **Z** represents.

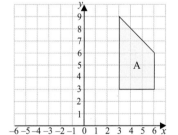

4. Shape **A** $\begin{pmatrix} 1 & 2 & 4 & 4 \\ 2 & 3 & 3 & 1 \end{pmatrix}$ is transformed by the matrix **M** $\begin{pmatrix} 1 & 0 \\ 0 & -1 \end{pmatrix}$, then by matrix **N** $\begin{pmatrix} -1 & 0 \\ 0 & 1 \end{pmatrix}$ into shape **C**.

   a) Draw shapes **A** and **C**.
   b) Find the matrix, **L**, that maps shape **A** directly onto shape **C**.
   c) Describe the single transformation that matrix **L** represents.

5. a) Find the matrix, **T**, that maps shape **A** onto shape **B**, shown.
   b) Find the matrix, **U**, that maps shape **B** onto shape **C**.
   c) Hence find the matrix, **V**, that maps shape **A** directly onto shape **C**.
   d) Describe the two consecutive transformations that **V** represents.

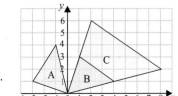

Section 32 — Congruence and Similarity

32.1 Congruence and Similarity

Congruent shapes are exactly the **same shape** and **size**. The images of **rotated** and **reflected** shapes are congruent to the original shapes.

Similar shapes are exactly the **same shape** but **different sizes**. Similar shapes can be in different orientations. The image of a shape after it has been **enlarged** is similar to the original shape.

Congruent Triangles

Two triangles are congruent if they satisfy any of the following '**congruence conditions**'.

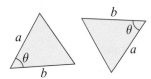

Side, Angle, Side:
Two sides and the angle between on one triangle are the same as two sides and the angle between on the other triangle.

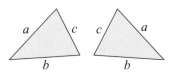

Side, Side, Side:
The three sides on one triangle are the same as the three sides on the other triangle.

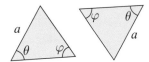

Angle, Angle, Side:
Two angles and a side on one triangle are the same as two angles and the corresponding side on the other triangle.

Right angle, Hypotenuse, Side:
Both triangles have a right angle, both triangles have the same hypotenuse and one other side is the same.

Example 1

Are these two triangles congruent? Give a reason for your answer.

Two of the sides and the angle between them are the same on both triangles.
So the triangles **are congruent**.

Exercise 1

1 The following pairs of triangles are congruent. Find the value of the angles and sides marked with letters.

a)

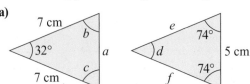

b)

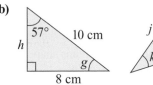

2 For each of the following, decide whether the two triangles are congruent.
In each case explain either how you know they are congruent, or why they must not be.

a)
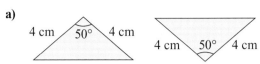

b)
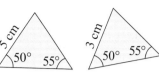

c)
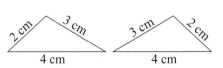

d)
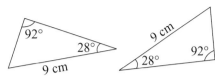

e)
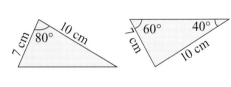

f)
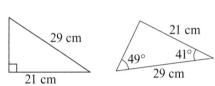

g)
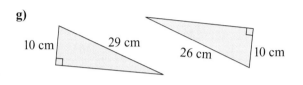

h)
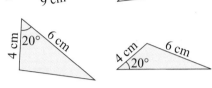

Exercise 2

1 Show that the two triangles below are congruent.

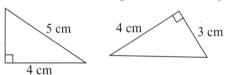

2 *ABCD* is a parallelogram. Prove that triangles *ABC* and *ADC* are congruent.

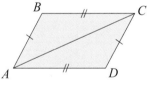

3 *ABCDE* is a regular pentagon. Prove that triangles *ABC* and *CDE* are congruent.

4 *ABCD* is a kite and *O* is the point where the diagonals of the kite intersect.
Prove that *BOC* and *DOC* are congruent triangles.

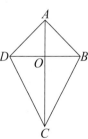

Similar Triangles

Two triangles are similar if they satisfy **any one** of the following conditions.
If two triangles are similar, then **all** of the conditions are true.

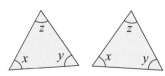
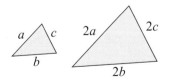
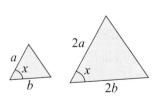

All the angles on one triangle are the same as the angles on the other triangle.

All the sides on one triangle are in the same ratio as the corresponding sides on the other triangle.

Two sides on one triangle are in the same ratio as the corresponding sides on the other triangle, and the angle between is the same on both triangles.

Example 2

Are these two triangles similar?
Give a reason for your answer.

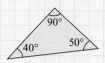
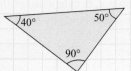

All the angles in one triangle are the same as the angles in the other triangle.
So the triangles **are similar**.

Exercise 3

1 For each of the following, decide whether the two triangles are similar.
In each case explain either how you know they are similar, or why they must not be.

a)
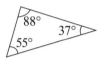
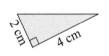

b)

c)
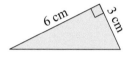

d)
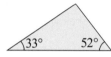

e)
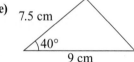
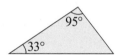

f)
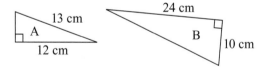

Exercise 4

1 Show that triangles A and B are similar.

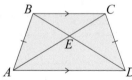

2 *ABCD* is an isosceles trapezium.

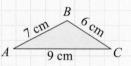

Prove that triangles *BEC* and *AED* are similar.

3 *ABC* is an isosceles triangle.

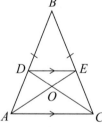

a) Prove that triangles *ABC* and *DBE* are similar.
b) Find another pair of triangles that are similar but not congruent. Explain your answer.

Example 3

Triangles *ABC* and *DEF* are similar.
Find the lengths *DE* and *DF*.

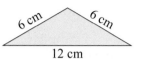
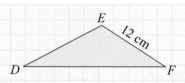

1. The side lengths of the triangles are in the same ratio from one triangle to the other.
2. Use this ratio to find the missing side lengths.

$EF = 2BC$

So $DE = 2AB = 2 \times 7 = \underline{\textbf{14 cm}}$
and $DF = 2AC = 2 \times 9 = \underline{\textbf{18 cm}}$

Example 4

Triangles *PQR* and *UVW* are
similar. Find angle *x*.

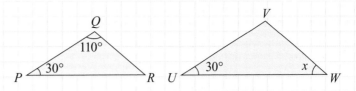

1. Use properties of similar triangles to find
    the corresponding angle in *PQR*.

    x = angle *QRP*, as corresponding
    angles in similar triangles are equal.

2. Calculate the size of this angle.

    Angle *QRP* = 180° − 110° − 30° = 40°
    So **_x_ = 40°**

Exercise 5

1 Triangles *PQR* and *XYZ* are similar.
   a) Find the ratio of the length *XY*
       to the length *PQ*.
   b) Find the length *YZ*.

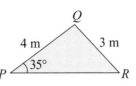

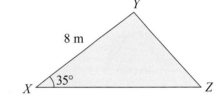

2 The diagram shows two similar triangles, *ABC* and *ADE*.
   a) Find the ratio of the length *AB* to the length *AD*.
   b) Find the length *AE*.
   c) Find the length *BC*.

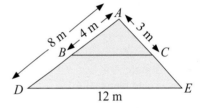

3 The diagram below shows two similar triangles,
   QRU and *QST*. Find the following lengths.
   a) *ST*   **b)** *QT*   **c)** *UT*

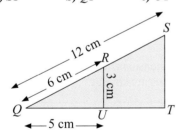

4 The diagram below shows two similar triangles,
   JKN and *JLM*. Find the following lengths.
   a) *JL*   **b)** *JN*   **c)** *NM*

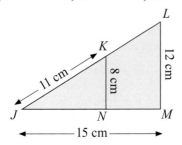

5 The diagram below shows two similar triangles,
   STW and *SUV*. Find the following lengths.
   a) *TW*   **b)** *SU*   **c)** *TU*

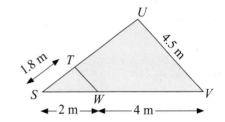

6 The triangles shown below are similar. Find *y*.

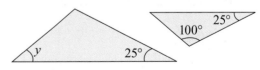

7 The triangles shown below are similar. Find *z*.

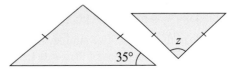

32.2 Areas of Similar Shapes

For two similar shapes, where one has sides that are twice as long as the sides of the other, the area of the larger shape will be four times (i.e. 2^2 times) the area of the smaller shape.

In general, for an enlargement of **scale factor n**, the area of the larger shape will be n^2 **times** the area of the smaller shape.

If the ratio of sides is $a : b$, the ratio of the areas is $a^2 : b^2$.

Example 1

Triangles A and B are similar. The area of triangle A is 10 cm^2 and the area of triangle B is 250 cm^2. What is the scale factor of enlargement?

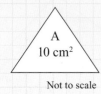

A
10 cm^2

B
250 cm^2

Not to scale

$250 = 10n^2$
so $n^2 = 250 \div 10 = 25$
$n = 5$

The scale factor is **5**.

Exercise 1

1 Work out the area of the square formed when square A is enlarged by a scale factor of 4.

A
10 cm

2 Triangles A and B are similar. Calculate the area of B.

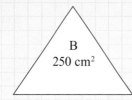

Not to scale

A
5 cm^2
3 cm

B
9 cm

3 The shapes below are similar. Work out the base length of shape Q.

Not to scale

P
25 cm^2
4 cm

Q
400 cm^2

4 The rectangles below are similar. Calculate the area of shape A.

Not to scale

2 cm   A

B
125 cm^2 5 cm

5 A triangle has perimeter 12 cm and area 6 cm^2. It is enlarged by a scale factor of 3 to produce a similar triangle. What is the perimeter and area of the new triangle?

6 Find the dimensions of rectangle B, given that the rectangles are similar.

Not to scale

3 cm
A
15 cm^2
5 cm

B
540 cm^2

Exercise 2

1 Squares A and B have side lengths given by the ratio $2 : 3$. Square A has sides of length 8 cm.

  a) Find the side length of B.

  b) Find the area of B.

  c) Find the ratio of the area of A to the area of B.

2 The ratio of the areas of two similar shapes is $2.25 : 6.25$. Find the ratios of their side lengths.

3 The ratio of the sides of two similar shapes is $4 : 5$. The area of the smaller shape is 20 cm^2. Find the area of the larger shape.

4 Stuart is drawing a scale model of his workshop. He uses a scale of 1 cm : 50 cm. The area of the bench on his drawing is 3 cm^2. What is the area of his bench in real life?

The rules about enlargements and areas of 2D shapes also apply to **surface areas** of **3D shapes**.

Example 2

Shapes A and B on the right are similar.
Find the surface area of shape B.

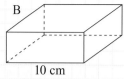

1. Find the surface area of A.
2. Compare corresponding side lengths to find the scale factor of enlargement.
3. Use these to find the surface area of B.

Surface area of A $= 2[(2 \times 4) + (4 \times 10) + (2 \times 10)]$
$= 2(8 + 40 + 20) = 136 \text{ cm}^2$
$10 \text{ cm} \div 4 \text{ cm} = 2.5$, so the scale factor is 2.5
Surface area of B $= 136 \times 2.5^2 = 136 \times 6.25 = \underline{\textbf{850 cm}^2}$

Exercise 3

1 A and B are similar prisms. B has a surface area of 1440 in². Calculate the surface area of A.

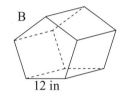

2 A sphere has surface area 400π mm².
What is the surface area of a similar sphere with a diameter three times as large?

3 The 3D solid P has a surface area of 60 cm².
Q, a similar 3D solid, has a surface area of 1500 cm². If one side of shape P measures 3 cm, how long is the corresponding side of shape Q?

4 Cylinder A has surface area 63π cm².
Find the surface area of the similar cylinder B.

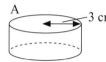

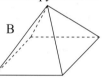

5 The vertical height of pyramid A is 5 cm.
Find the vertical height of similar pyramid B.

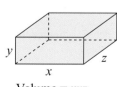

Surface area = 32 cm²   Surface area = 72 cm²

6 Similar shapes P, Q and R have surface areas in the ratio $4 : 9 : 12.25$. Find the ratio of their sides.

32.3   Volumes of Similar Shapes

For two similar 3D shapes, when the side lengths are doubled, the volume is multiplied by a factor of 8 ($= 2^3$).

In general, if the sides increase by a scale factor of n, the volume increases by a scale factor of n^3.

For two similar shapes with sides in the ratio $a : b$, their volumes will be in the ratio $a^3 : b^3$.

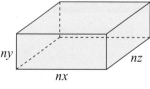

Volume $= xyz$ Volume $= nx \times ny \times nz$
$= n^3xyz$

Example 1

Triangular prisms A and B are similar.
Find the volume of B.

$15 \div 5 = 3$, so B is 3 times bigger than A.

Volume of B $= 3^3 \times$ volume of A
$= 27 \times 80 = \underline{\textbf{2160 cm}^3}$

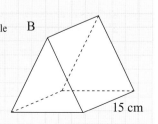

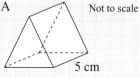

Volume = 80 cm³

Exercise 1

1 Rectangular prisms A and B are similar.
Find the dimensions of B.

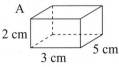
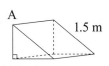
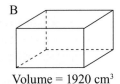

Volume = 30 cm³   Volume = 1920 cm³

2 A 3D solid of volume 18 m³ is enlarged by scale factor 5. What is the volume of the new solid?

3 A and B are similar. Find the volume of A.

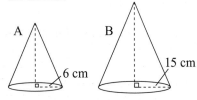

Volume = 84 cm³

4 A cube has sides of length 3 cm.
Find the side length of a similar cube whose volume is 3.375 times as big.

5 Cone A below has a volume of 60π cm³.
Find the volume of cone B, given that the shapes are similar.

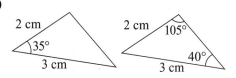

6 Two similar solids have side lengths in the ratio 2 : 5.
 a) What is the ratio of their volumes?
 b) The smaller shape has a volume of 100 mm³. What is the volume of the larger shape?

7 A pyramid has volume 32 cm³ and vertical height 8 cm. A similar pyramid has volume 16 384 cm³. What is its vertical height?

8 Two similar solids have volumes of 20 m³ and 1280 m³. James says that the sides of the larger solid are 4 times as long as the sides of the smaller solid. Claire says that the sides are 8 times longer. Who is correct?

9 The radius of the planet Uranus is approximately 4 times the size of the radius of Earth. What does this tell you about the volumes of these planets?

10 The rectangular prisms below are similar. Calculate the volume of shape A.

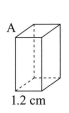
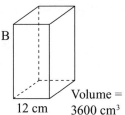

1.2 cm   12 cm   Volume = 3600 cm³

32.4   Congruence and Similarity Problems

Exercise 1

1 For each of the following, decide whether the two triangles are congruent, similar or neither.
In each case, explain your answer.

a)

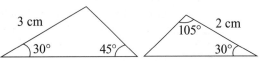

b)

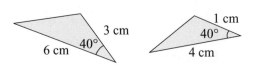

c)

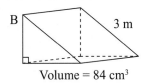

d)

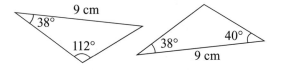

2 *JKN* and *JLM* are two similar triangles.
   a) Find length *KN*.
   b) Find length *KL*.

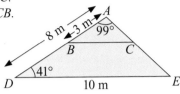

3 *ABC* and *ADE* are two similar triangles.
   a) Find length *BC*.
   b) Find angle *ACB*.

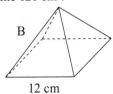

4 The triangles shown are similar. Find *y*.

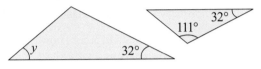

5 The square-based pyramid A, below, has surface area 132 cm² and volume 120 cm³.

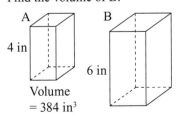

   a) Find the surface area of the similar pyramid B.
   b) Find the volume of B.

6 Two similar solids have side lengths in the ratio 3:5.
   a) Find the ratios of their surface areas.
   b) Find the ratios of their volumes.

7 Josephine is making cakes. One cake is cylindrical, with diameter 16 cm and height 6 cm. The other cake is a similar cylinder, and the area of the top of this cake is 1600π cm². Calculate the diameter and volume of the larger cake.

8 A and B are similar rectangular prism-shaped tins. Find the volume of B.

9 The cross-section of a hexagonal prism has an area of 18 cm². A similar prism has a cross-sectional area of 162 cm². If the volume of the first prism is 270 cm³, what is the volume of the second prism?

10 Two similar solids have surface areas in the ratio 49:81. Find the ratios of:
   a) their side lengths   **b)** their volumes

11 Spherical balls of bird food come in two different sizes: one with radius 3 cm and one with radius 6 cm. The larger ball costs twice as much as the smaller ball. Is this better value for money?

12 Vicky has two similar jewellery boxes in the shape of rectangular prisms shown below. The larger box has a volume of 1620 in³ and the smaller box has a volume of 60 in³. Find the dimensions of the smaller box.

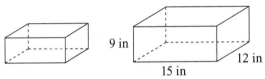

13 A solid has surface area 22 cm² and volume 18 cm³. A similar solid has sides that are 1.5 times as long.
   a) Calculate its surface area.
   b) Calculate its volume.

14 Mike has an unfortunate habit of falling down wells. The well he usually falls down has a volume of 1.25π m³. His friends need a ladder that's at least 5 m long to rescue him. One day he falls down a similar well with a volume of 10π m³. How long does the ladder need to be this time?

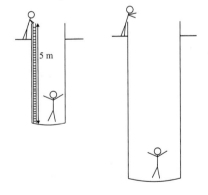

15 An octagonal prism has a surface area of 50 mm² and a volume of 88 mm³. Another octagonal prism has a surface area of 450 mm² and a volume of 792 mm³. Are these two shapes similar? Explain your answer.

Section 33 — Collecting Data

33.1 Using Different Types of Data

To test a hypothesis, you need to first decide **what data** you need to collect and **how** you're going to get it. Once you've collected your data, you need to **process** and **interpret** your results.

This often allows you to improve your hypothesis, which you may then want to test by collecting, processing and interpreting more data. This is known as the **data-handling cycle**.

Primary data is data you **collect yourself**, e.g. by doing a survey or experiment.

Secondary data is data that has been **collected by someone else**. You can get secondary data from things like newspapers or the internet.

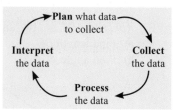

Example 1

Jon wants to test whether a six-sided dice has an equal chance of landing on each of its sides. Explain how he could collect data for the test. Will his data be primary or secondary data?

1. Jon needs to do an experiment.   He could roll the dice lots of times and record how many times it lands on each side using a tally chart.

2. He collects the data himself, so...   His data will be **primary** data.

Exercise 1

For each investigation below: **a)** Describe what data is needed and give a suitable method for collecting it.
b) Say whether the data will be primary or secondary data.

1   Nikita wants to know what the girls in her class think about school dinners.

2   Dan wants to find the most common colour of car passing his house in a 30-minute interval.

3   Anne wants to compare the daily rainfall in London and Manchester last August.

4   Rohan wants to test his theory that the boys in his class can throw a ball further than the girls.

5   Jim wants to find out how the temperature in his garden at 10 a.m. each morning compares with the temperature recorded by the Met Office for his local area.

Discrete and Continuous Data

Data can be **qualitative** (in the form of **words**) or **quantitative (numbers)**.

Quantitative data can be **discrete** or **continuous**. **Discrete data** can only take certain values.
Continuous data can take any value in a range — it's always measured, e.g. the height or weight of something.

Example 2

Say whether the following data is qualitative, discrete quantitative or continuous quantitative.

a)   The hometowns of 100 people.
This data is in the form of words, so...   It's **qualitative** data.

b)   The weights of the bags of potatoes on sale in a greengrocer's.
This data is numerical and isn't restricted to certain specific values.   It's **continuous quantitative** data.

Exercise 2

1 Say whether the following data is qualitative, discrete quantitative or continuous quantitative.

   a) The number of words in your favourite song.
   b) The time it takes Matt to walk to school.
   c) Your favourite food.
   d) The nationalities of the people in a park.
   e) The numbers of pets in 20 households.
   f) The lengths of 30 worms.
   g) The sizes of the crowds at 10 rugby matches.
   h) The distances of planets from the Sun.
   i) The heights of 100 tomato plants.
   j) The hair colours of 50 people.

2 Gemma thinks there is a link between the average number of chocolate bars eaten each week by pupils in her class and how fast they can run 100 metres.

   a) Describe two sets of data Gemma should collect to investigate this link.
   b) Describe suitable methods for collecting the data.
   c) Say whether each set of data is qualitative, discrete quantitative or continuous quantitative.
   d) Say whether each set of data is primary data or secondary data.

3 Blair wants to find out what 12 people think about his favourite TV show, 'The One Direction is Cumbria'.

He first asks 6 people, "How much do you like 'The One Direction is Cumbria'?", and notes down their responses. He then asks another 6 people the same question, and asks them to give their response as a mark out of 10. His results are shown on the right.

   a) (i) Does his first set of results consist of qualitative, discrete quantitative or continuous quantitative data?

      (ii) Does his second set of results consist of qualitative, discrete quantitative or continuous quantitative data?

   b) Suggest one advantage and one disadvantage of collecting qualitative data instead of quantitative data.

> 'It's alright.'   'It's brilliant!'
>
> 'OMG, I love it! Cuthbert's so hot!'
>
> 'It's really annoying, I hate it.'
>
> 'I shouldn't like it, but I do.'
>
> 'I liked the first episode, but after that it all just seemed really fake. I don't like it any more.'

| 2 | 4 | 10 | 8 | 7 | 9 |

33.2   Data-Collection Sheets and Questionnaires

Data-Collection Sheets

Tally charts are a really useful way of recording data. If there's a **large range** of data values, you need to **group** them into classes. If **two variables** are being recorded, you can use a **two-way table**.

Example 1

An assault course is designed to take about 10 minutes to complete.
Design a tally chart that could be used to record the times taken by 100 people.

1. The data is continuous, so write the classes using inequalities.

2. Make sure there are no gaps between classes and that classes don't overlap.

3. Leave the last class open-ended to make sure all possible times are covered.

Time (t mins)	Tally	Frequency
$0 < t \le 5$		
$5 < t \le 10$		
$10 < t \le 15$		
$15 < t \le 20$		
$20 < t$		

Tally column with plenty of space to record the marks

Frequency column for adding up the tally marks

Exercise 1

1 Design a tally chart that could be used to record the answers to each of these questions.

    a) How many siblings do you have?
    b) What transport do you use to get to work?
    c) What's your favourite type of fruit?
    d) How many days were there in the month you were born?

2 Here are the ages of 48 guests at a christening.

    a) Copy and complete this grouped frequency table, using groups of 10 years for the rest of the table.

Age (years)	Tally	Frequency
1-9		
10-19		
20-29		

30	56	4	18	19	35	65	79
54	54	45	32	36	39	26	27
1	3	51	56	19	23	9	11
23	45	41	48	23	32	39	43
54	5	77	61	62	78	39	47
52	56	1	2	80	21	48	54

    b) Use your table to find which of these age groups is the most common.

3 Give two things that are wrong with each of these tally charts, and design an improved version of each.

    a) Chart for recording the number of times people went to the cinema last year.

No. of cinema trips	Tally	Frequency
1 – 10		
10 – 20		
20 – 30		
30 – 40		
40 or more		

    b) Chart for recording the number of people watching a band play at each venue on their tour (max. venue capacity = 25 000).

No. of people	Tally	Frequency
0 – 5000		
6000 – 10 000		
11 000 – 15 000		
16 000 – 20 000		

    c) Chart for recording the length of time people can hop on one leg for.

Time (t mins)	Tally	Frequency
$t \leq 5$		
$t \geq 5$		

    d) Chart for recording weights of pumpkins.

Weight (w kg)	Tally	Frequency
$w < 3$		
$3 < w < 3.5$		
$3.5 < w < 4$		

4 Write down five classes that could form a tally chart for recording each set of data below.

    a) The number of quiz questions, out of a total of 20, answered correctly by some quiz teams.
    b) The weights of 30 bags of apples, where each bag should weigh roughly 200 g.
    c) The volumes of tea in 50 cups of tea as they're served in a cafe. Each cup can hold 300 ml.

5 A mathematics test is marked out of 100.
The marks for 50 students are in the box on the right.

    a) Draw and complete a grouped frequency table to show the students' marks. Split the data into groups of 10 marks, starting with the group '20–29'.

    b) The pass mark for this test was 60 out of 100. Use your table to say how many students passed the test.

    c) Could you use your table to find out how many students would have passed the test if the pass mark had been reduced to 55 out of 100? Explain your answer.

20	90	64	35	44	62	29	30	68	69
73	88	80	45	55	61	39	29	47	91
38	65	66	42	81	92	99	33	81	88
45	56	65	65	78	91	95	36	56	27
65	98	39	79	81	82	31	31	98	92

6 Design a tally chart that could be used to record the following data.

   a) The numbers of pairs of socks owned by 50 students.

   b) The hand spans of 20 people.

   c) The distances that 30 people travel to get to work and back each day.

Two-Way Tables

Example 2

Raymond is investigating how fast the players at a tennis club can serve.
He's interested in whether being right-handed or left-handed has any effect on average speed.

Design a two-way table he could use to record the data he needs.

One variable goes down the side and the other goes across the top

Use inequalities for continuous data

Make sure there are no gaps and classes don't overlap

	Serve average speed (s mph)				
	$s < 40$	$40 \leq s < 50$	$50 \leq s < 60$	$60 \leq s < 70$	$70 \leq s$
Right-handed					
Left-handed					

Rows and columns should cover every possible answer

Space for tally marks

Exercise 2

1 This table has been designed to record the hair colour and age (in whole years) of 100 adults.

   a) Give three criticisms of the table.

   b) Design an improved version of the table.

	Age in whole years					
	0 – 15	15 – 30	30 – 45	45 – 60	60 – 75	75 or older
Blonde						
Light brown						
Dark brown						

2 For each of the following, design a two-way table that could be used to record the data described.

   a) The type of music adults and children prefer listening to out of pop, classical and rock.

   b) The average length of time spent doing homework each evening by pupils in each of the school years 7-11. Assume no one spends more than an average of 4 hours an evening on homework.

3 For each investigation below, design a two-way table for recording the data.

   a) Hoi Wan is going to ask 50 adults if they prefer cats or dogs.
      She wants to find out if it's true that men prefer dogs and women prefer cats.

   b) Nathan wants to find out whether children watch more TV on average each day than adults.

   c) Chloe is going to ask people how tall they are and how many portions of fruit they eat on average each week.

Exercise 3 — Mixed Exercise

For each investigation below, design a data-collection sheet to record the data.

1 Camilla plans to count the number of people in each of 50 cars driving into a car park.

2 Theo is going to ask 100 people to rate his new hairstyle from 1 to 5.
He's interested in whether children give him higher scores than adults.

3 Greg is investigating how much pocket money everyone in his class gets.

4 Simran wants to test her theory that people who play a lot of sport don't watch much TV.

Questionnaires

Questionnaires need to be **easy to use** — e.g. the questions should be clear and easy to answer accurately. It's also important to design the questions so that the answers will be **easy to analyse** and will give relevant and unbiased information.

Example 3 The following questions are from a questionnaire. Criticise each question.

a) **How many hours of TV do you watch?** 0–1 ☐ 1–2 ☐ 2–3 ☐ 3–4 ☐

   1. Look at how easy the questions are to answer.
      The question is hard to answer because you've not been given a **specific time span**.

   2. Look closely at the tick boxes.
      The **tick boxes overlap**, e.g. if you watch 1 hour of TV, you don't know whether to tick the first or second box. And the **boxes don't cover all possible options**.

b) **How old are you?**

   Think about the people answering the question.
   This is a **sensitive question**, so it would be better to have a range of options to tick.

c) **Do you agree that it's important to watch the news?**

   Think about whether the question is fair or biased.
   This is a **leading question**.
   It encourages people to give a certain opinion, so the results might be **biased**.

Exercise 4

1 Here are questions from Amber and Jay's questionnaires about how much sport people play. Say whose question is better and give two reasons why.

Amber: How much sport do you play?

Jay: How many times a week do you play sport on average? Tick one box.
     None ☐ Once ☐ Twice ☐ Three ☐ More than three ☐

2 Write an improved version of each question below.

  a) How much time do you spend reading each week on average?
    0–1 hours ☐ 1–2 hours ☐ 2 to 3 hours ☐ 3 to 4 hours ☐ 4 or more hours ☐

  b) What's your favourite type of TV programme? Tick one box.
    Comedy ☐ Soap ☐ Reality ☐ Sport ☐

  c) Which type of film do you prefer — horror or thriller?   Horror ☐   Thriller ☐

  d) Do you agree that the gym should open a new tennis court rather than a new squash court?

  e) How much credit card debt do you have?

3 Write a question to find out each of the following pieces of information. Use suitable tick boxes.

   a) The main method people use to travel to school.

   b) How often the members of a gym use the facilities.

   c) Which days of the week people usually shop at the supermarket (allow more than one day).

   d) What the people who attend a dance class think of the length of the class.

33.3 Sampling and Bias

The group of people or things you want to find out about is called the **population**. Usually, it's quicker, cheaper and more practical to collect data on a **sample** of the population, rather than the whole thing.

Different samples will give different results, but the **bigger** the sample, the more reliable they should be.

Example 1

Michael and Tina have written questionnaires to find out what students at their college think about public transport. Michael gives the questionnaire to 10 students, and Tina gives the questionnaire to 50 students. Michael concludes that 50% of students are happy with public transport, and Tina concludes that 30% are happy.

   a) Suggest two reasons why Michael and Tina only gave the questionnaire to some of the students.

   Think about the advantages of sampling, for example...

   There are fewer copies to print, so **print costs will be lower**.
   Also, it will take them **much less time** to collect and analyse the results.

   b) Whose results are likely to be more reliable? Explain your answer.

   Think about the size of the sample...

   Tina's results are likely to be more reliable because she has used a **bigger sample**.

Exercise 1

1 Jenny wants to know how long it takes the pupils in Year 7 to type out a poem. She plans to time a sample of 30 out of the 216 Year 7 pupils. Give two advantages for Jenny of using a sample.

2 A supermarket chain wants to know what people in a town think of their plan to build a new supermarket there. They've hired a team of researchers to interview a sample of 500 people. Give one reason why they wouldn't want to interview everyone in the town.

3 Alfie and Lisa want to find out what people's favourite flavour of ice cream is. Alfie asks 30 people and gets the answer 'chocolate'. Lisa asks 15 people and finds that it's 'strawberry'. Based on this information, what would you say is the favourite flavour?

4 Jack, Nikhil and Daisy bake a batch of 200 cupcakes to sell on their market stall. Jack thinks they should taste one cake to check the quality is OK. Nikhil thinks they should taste 10 cakes and Daisy thinks they should taste 50 cakes. Say who you agree with and explain why.

5 Melissa and Karen are doing an experiment to see if a coin is fair. They each toss the coin 100 times and record the number of heads. 52% of Melissa's tosses are heads and 47% of Karen's tosses are heads. Whose result is more reliable? Explain your answer.

Random Sampling

When you're choosing a sample, it's important to make sure that it **fairly represents** the **population**.

To **avoid bias**, you need to think carefully about how to choose
the sample, including when and where you're going to select it.

If you select a sample at **random**, every member of the population has an equal chance of being selected.

Example 2

Adam wants to choose 20 of the 89 members of his choir to fill in a questionnaire.
Explain how he could select a random sample.

Everyone should have the same chance of being chosen,
so he needs to start with a list of everyone in the population...

1. First, he should make a list of all the people in the choir and assign everyone a number.
2. Then he could use a calculator or computer to generate 20 random numbers.
3. Finally, he needs to match these numbers to the people on the list to create the sample.

Exercise 2

1   Explain why the following methods of selecting a sample will each result in a biased sample.

   a) A library needs to reduce its opening hours. The librarian asks 20 people
      on a Monday morning whether the library should close on a Monday or a Friday.

   b) At a large company, 72% of the employees are women and 28% are men.
      The manager wants to know what employees think about changing the uniform,
      so he surveys 20 women and 20 men.

   c) A market research company wants to find out about people's working hours.
      They select 100 home telephone numbers and call them at 2 pm one afternoon.

2   The manager of a health club wants to survey a random sample of 40 female members.
   Explain how she could do this.

3   George and Stuart want to find out which football team is most popular at
   their school. George asks a random selection of 30 pupils and Stuart asks
   the first 5 pupils he sees at lunchtime. Give two reasons why George's
   sample is likely to be more representative of the whole school.

4   Seema wants to find out about the religious beliefs of people in her street, so she stands outside
   her house on a Sunday morning and interviews the first 20 people she sees. Explain all the reasons
   why her sample is likely to be biased and suggest a better method for selecting her sample.

5   A company has 5 branches across the country. Describe how the management team could select a
   representative sample of 100 employees to question about pay and working conditions.

6   A factory makes hundreds of the same component each day. Describe how a representative sample
   of 50 components could be tested each day to make sure the machinery is working properly.

Stratified Sampling

To select a **stratified sample**, you divide the population you want to sample into categories.
The **proportion** of things from each category is the **same** in the sample and the population. The sample taken from each category is selected at **random**. This makes the sample more representative of the population.

Example 3

A teacher wants to take a stratified sample of 60 pupils in the school. The table shows the number of pupils in each year group.

Calculate how many people from each year group should be in the sample.

Year Group	No. of pupils
7	250
8	150
9	216
10	204
11	180

1. Calculate the total number of pupils.

Total number of pupils $= 250 + 150 + 216 + 204 + 180 = 1000$

2. The number of pupils that need to be picked from each year group is the proportion of the total number of pupils that the year group makes up, multiplied by the sample size.

$$\text{Number of students to be picked} = \frac{\text{no. of pupils in year group}}{\text{total no. of pupils}} \times \text{sample size}$$

$$\text{Year 7} = \frac{250}{1000} \times 60 = \mathbf{15}$$

$$\text{Year 8} = \frac{150}{1000} \times 60 = \mathbf{9}$$

3. You can only have whole numbers of pupils, so round any decimal answers to the nearest number.

$$\text{Year 9} = \frac{216}{1000} \times 60 = 12.96 \approx \mathbf{13}$$

$$\text{Year 10} = \frac{204}{1000} \times 60 = 12.24 \approx \mathbf{12}$$

$$\text{Year 11} = \frac{180}{1000} \times 60 = 10.8 \approx \mathbf{11}$$

4. Double-check that your rounded answers give the correct sample size.

$(15 + 9 + 13 + 12 + 11 = 60 \checkmark)$

Exercise 3

1 A rowing club has 105 male and 45 female club members. The club wants to survey a stratified sample made up of 20 club members. Work out how many male and female club members should be in the sample.

2 A sixth form has 54 boys and 36 girls in Year 12 and 45 boys and 45 girls in Year 13. 25 pupils are to be selected using a stratified sample. Work out how many of each sex and year group should be selected.

3 The table shows the number of members of a gym in different age groups. The gym wants to survey a stratified sample of 100 of their members.

   a) Use the table to work out how many members of each age group should be selected to be in the sample.

   b) Suggest how the members in the sample could be picked.

Age (a) in years	No. of members
$a < 15$	40
$15 \leq a < 25$	580
$25 \leq a < 35$	740
$35 \leq a < 50$	460
50+	180

4 A school wants to survey a stratified sample of 50 pupils.

   a) Explain why there shouldn't be an equal number of pupils from Year 7 and Year 8 in the sample.

   b) Use the information in the table to work out how many boys and girls from each year group should be in the sample.

Year group	No. of boys	No. of girls
Year 7	100	95
Year 8	76	67
Year 9	144	136
Year 10	98	108
Year 11	112	114

Systematic Sampling

When your population is **large** you can generate your sample using systematic sampling.

Choose a **random starting point** and take a sample at **regular intervals**
— e.g. every 10th member of the population.

Example 4

A telephone directory consist of 80 000 names listed in alphabetical order.
Stacey wants to take a random sample of 500 people from the telephone directory.

Explain how she could select the sample using systematic sampling.

You need to make sure there are 500 people in your sample and that your sample is random.

1. The names are already ordered so just number them 1-80 000.
2. 80 000 ÷ 500 = 160 — use a calculator or computer to
    randomly generate a number between 1 and 160.
3. Use that number as your starting point and add every 160th name after it to the sample —
    e.g. the names in her sample might be 78th (starting point), 238th, 398th, 558th, ... , 79 918th.
4. This would give her a sample of 500 names.

Exercise 4

1 A list of 100 cars are each given a number from 1-100.

  a) Alan wants to take a systematic sample of 5 cars, starting with the 8th car.
  What are the numbers of the other 4 cars that should be in his sample?

  b) John takes a systematic sample of 4 cars. The 34th, 59th and 84th cars are each in the sample.
  Which other car should be in John's sample?

2 Give one reason why systematic sampling might result in a biased sample in each of these cases.

  a) The number of people standing at a bus stop was recorded every minute for a whole day.
  A bus company analyses how busy the bus stop is by systematically sampling
  the number of people standing at the bus stop every 12 minutes.

  b) Quality control is done on the weight of ball bearings produced by a machine.
  Every 100th ball bearing is sampled and its weight is checked.

  c) An energy company wants to check the energy usage of houses on a street.
  There are 380 terraced houses on the street and they systematically sample every 6th house.

3 A journalist wants to interview a random sample of 50 out of 650 politicians.
Explain how he could do this using systematic sampling.

4 A water company wants to assess the condition of its underground water pipes along
a 200 m stretch of pipe. They decide to take 10 random samples of 1 m sections of the pipe.
Explain why it might be better to use systematic sampling rather than random sampling.

5 The town council wants to know people's opinions on some new wind turbines.
It decides to take a random sample of 200 of the 6000 residents.
Explain why the council might choose to use a systematic sample rather than a stratified sample.

Section 34 — Averages and Range

34.1 Averages and Range

An **average** is a way of representing a whole set of data using just one number.
The **mode**, **median** and **mean** are three different types of average.

> **mode** (or **modal value**) = the **most common** value
>
> **median** = the **middle value** once the items have been put **in size order**
>
> **mean** = the **total** of all the values ÷ the **number** of values

The **range** tells you how spread out your values are: **range** = **largest** value – **smallest** value

Example 1

20 customers each gave a restaurant a mark out of 10. Their marks are shown below.

Find   a) the modal mark,
        b) the median mark,
        c) the mean mark,
        d) the range.

| 3 | 7 | 4 | 8 | 3 | 7 | 5 | 2 | 8 | 9 |
| 9 | 6 | 1 | 3 | 4 | 5 | 6 | 5 | 7 | 7 |

1. Put the numbers in order first.

   From smallest to largest, the numbers are:
   1, 2, 3, 3, 3, 4, 4, 5, 5, 5, 6, 6, 7, 7, 7, 7, 8, 8, 9, 9

2. The mode is the most common number.

   a) The mode is <u>7</u>.

3. If there's an even number of values, the median will be halfway between the two middle numbers.

   b) There are 20 values, so the median will be between the 10th and 11th values.

   10th mark = 5, 11th mark = 6, median = $\frac{5+6}{2}$ = **5.5**

4. Divide the total of the values by the number of values to find the mean.

   c) Total = $1 + 2 + 3 + 3 + 3 + 4 + 4 + 5 + 5 + 5$
   $+ 6 + 6 + 7 + 7 + 7 + 7 + 8 + 8 + 9 + 9 = 109$

   Mean = $\frac{109}{20}$ = **5.45**

5. Subtract the lowest value from the highest.

   d) Range = 9 – 1 = **8**

Exercise 1

1 For the following sets of data: **(i)** Find the mode.   **(ii)** Find the range.

  a) 6, 9, 2, 7, 7, 6, 5, 9, 6   **b)** 16, 8, 12, 13, 13, 8, 8, 17   **c)** 8.2, 8.1, 8.1, 8.2, 8.1, 8.2, 8.2

2 Find the median of the following sets of data.

  a) 3, 3, 3, 3, 3, 3, 4, 4, 4, 4, 4   **b)** 2, 4, 7, 1, 5, 9, 2, 7, 8, 0   **c)** 5.85, 6.96, 2.04, 7.45, 6.9, 7.8

3 The times (to the nearest second) of athletes running the 400 m hurdles are: 78 78 84 81 90 79 84 78 95

  a) Find the range of times taken to run the 400 m hurdles.   **b)** Find the median time.

4 Nine students score the following marks on a test: 34   67   86   58   51   52   71   65   58
Find the mean score.

5 Abdul counts the number of crisps in 28 packets. His results are shown below.

| 12 20 21 15 18 20 21 20 15 9 22 16 18 19 |
| 20 18 13 15 18 20 17 16 15 16 16 18 21 20 |

a) Find the modal number of crisps in a packet.

b) Calculate:
   (i) the range of the data,
   (ii) the median number of crisps in a packet,
   (iii) the mean number of crisps in a packet.

6 Look at this data set: 6, 5, 8, 8, 5, **?**

a) If the range of this data set is 6, what are the two possible values for the missing number?

b) If the mean of the set is 7, find the missing value.

7 The heights (in metres) of a class of students are given below. Which is greater — the mean or the median height of the students?

1.68 1.45 1.70 1.30 1.72 1.80 1.29 1.40 1.42
1.60 1.65 1.75 1.67 1.69 1.72 1.72 1.63 1.63
1.78 1.70 1.50 1.65 1.40 1.36 1.69

Example 2

This frequency table shows the number of mobile phones owned by a group of people.

Number of mobile phones	0	1	2	3	4
Frequency	4	8	5	2	1

a) How many people were in the group surveyed?
   Find the total frequency.

   Total number of people = 4 + 8 + 5 + 2 + 1 = **20**

b) Find the modal number of mobile phones owned.
   This is the number with the highest frequency.

   Modal number of phones owned = **1**

c) What is the median number of mobile phones owned?
   Total frequency = 20.
   So the median is halfway between the 10th and the 11th values in the table.

   $$\text{Median} = \frac{10\text{th value} + 11\text{th value}}{2} = \frac{1+1}{2} = \mathbf{1}$$

d) Find the range for this data.

   Range $= 4 - 0 = \mathbf{4}$

e) What is the total number of mobile phones owned by this group of people?

   First multiply the number of mobile phones by its frequency, then add the results together.

Number of mobile phones	0	1	2	3	4
Frequency	4	8	5	2	1
Phones × frequency	0	8	10	6	4

   Total no. of mobile phones = 0 + 8 + 10 + 6 + 4 = **28**

f) Find the mean number of mobile phones owned by a person.

   $$\text{Mean no. of mobile phones owned} = \frac{\text{Total number of mobile phones}}{\text{Total number of people}} = \frac{28}{20} = \mathbf{1.4 \text{ mobile phones}}$$

Exercise 2

1 The table shows the number of people living in each of 30 houses.

Number of people	1	2	3	4	5
Frequency	4	5	8	10	3

a) Write down the modal number of people per house.

b) Find the median number of people per house.

c) Calculate the mean number of people per house.

d) Work out the range of the data.

2 This table shows the number of goals scored one week by 18 teams in the premier division.

a) Write down the modal number of goals.

b) Find the mean number of goals.
Give your answer to one decimal place.

Number of goals	0	1	2	3	4	5
Number of teams	1	3	4	5	3	2

c) The mean number of goals scored in the same week last year was 2.4. How do these results compare?

3 A student wrote down the temperature in his garden in Aberdeen every day at noon during the summer. His results are shown in the table.

a) Find the median noon temperature.

b) Find the mean temperature.

c) The mean midday temperature during the summer in the UK is approximately 18.5 °C. What does this suggest about the temperature in the student's garden?

Temperature (°C)	Frequency
16	18
17	27
18	7
19	15
20	12
21	11

4 Use the data in the table to calculate the mean number of eggs laid by a hen on a farm in a month. Give your answer to two decimal places.

No. of eggs laid	24	25	26	27	28	29	30	31
Frequency	7	23	45	109	541	1894	3561	2670

5 A survey asked 200 people, 'How many televisions do you own?'. The results are shown in this table.

No. of Televisions	1	2	3	4	5
Frequency	77	p	q	11	3

a) Show that $p + q = 109$.

b) The mean number of televisions is 1.88. Show that $2p + 3q = 240$.

c) Use your answers to **a)** and **b)** to find the number of people who own: **(i)** 2 televisions, **(ii)** 3 televisions.

Moving Averages

Sometimes data will be affected by the **time** it is collected, e.g. a shop will sell more wellies in winter than summer. It can be sensible to calculate a **moving average** to remove this effect so that you can compare data.

To work out how many data points you should average over, look at how many points make up a **repeating pattern**. E.g. the number of wellies sold will change each season, so it would be sensible to do a 4-point moving average (i.e. average over 4 points, one for each season).

Example 3

The table shows the number of people that signed up to tango lessons each term over the past two years.

a) The dance school want to use the data to predict how many people will sign up for tango lessons next year. Explain why it would be appropriate to use a 3-point moving average.

	Year 1			Year 2		
Term	Term 1	Term 2	Term 3	Term 1	Term 2	Term 3
No. of people	150	142	64	167	135	49

b) Calculate the last 3-point moving average for the data.

1. Look at the data and see if there's a pattern in the data.

2. Calculate the mean of the last 3 terms.

a) There are three terms in each year. Which term it is may affect the number signing up, e.g. the number signing up in term 1 is larger than the number in term 3 in both years.

b) $\dfrac{167 + 135 + 49}{3} = \underline{\mathbf{117}}$

Exercise 3

1 The table shows the number of scarves sold by a shop over 2 years.
The shop wants to use the data to estimate
how many scarves they should stock next year.

  a) Explain why it would be appropriate
  to use a 2-point moving average.

  b) Calculate the three 2-point moving averages for the data shown.

Season	Year 1		Year 2	
	spring / summer	autumn / winter	spring / summer	autumn / winter
No. of people	82	784	100	987

34.2 Averages for Grouped Data

If your data is grouped, then you can only **estimate** the mean using the **midpoint** of each group.
For the median, you can only say **which group** it lies in — not the exact value.
And instead of a mode, you can only find a **modal group**.

Example 1

The table shows a summary of the times taken by 20 people to eat three crackers without having a drink.

Time (t) in s	$50 \le t < 60$	$60 \le t < 70$	$70 \le t < 80$	$80 \le t < 90$	$90 \le t < 100$	$100 \le t < 120$
Frequency	2	3	6	4	4	1

a) Write down the modal group.
  The modal group is the one with the highest frequency.   Modal group is **$70 \le t < 80$**.

b) Which group contains the median?
  Both the 10th and 11th values are in the   There are 20 values, so the median lies
  group for $70 \le t < 80$ marks. So the   halfway between the 10th and 11th values.
  median must lie in that group too.   This means the median is in the group **$70 \le t < 80$**.

c) Find an estimate for the mean.
  Find the midpoint for each group — add together the highest and lowest values then divide by 2.

Time (t) in s	$50 \le t < 60$	$60 \le t < 70$	$70 \le t < 80$	$80 \le t < 90$	$90 \le t < 100$	$100 \le t < 120$
Frequency	2	3	6	4	4	1
Midpoint of group	$\frac{50+60}{2}=55$	$\frac{60+70}{2}=65$	$\frac{70+80}{2}=75$	$\frac{80+90}{2}=85$	$\frac{90+100}{2}=95$	$\frac{100+120}{2}=110$

  Now find the mean as before, using the midpoints instead of the actual data values.

Midpoint × frequency	$2 \times 55 = 110$	$3 \times 65 = 195$	$6 \times 75 = 450$	$4 \times 85 = 340$	$4 \times 95 = 380$	$1 \times 110 = 110$

$$\text{Estimated mean} = \frac{110 + 195 + 450 + 340 + 380 + 110}{2 + 3 + 6 + 4 + 4 + 1} = \frac{1585}{20} = \underline{\textbf{79.25}}$$

Exercise 1

1 The table on the right shows some
information about the weights of some
tangerines in a supermarket. Find an
estimate for the mean tangerine weight.

Weight (w) in grams	Frequency
$0 \le w < 20$	1
$20 \le w < 40$	6
$40 \le w < 60$	9
$60 \le w < 80$	24

2 Troy collected some information about the number
of hours students spent watching television over a week.
His results are shown in the table

  a) Write down the modal group.

  b) Which group contains the median?

  c) Find an estimate for the mean to 1 decimal place.

Time (t) in hours	Frequency
$0 \le t < 5$	3
$5 \le t < 10$	8
$10 \le t < 15$	11
$15 \le t < 20$	4

3 This table shows information about the heights of 200 people.
   a) Write down the modal group.
   b) Which group contains the median?
   c) Find an estimate for the mean.

Height (*h*) in metres	Frequency
$1.50 \leq h < 1.60$	27
$1.60 \leq h < 1.70$	92
$1.70 \leq h < 1.80$	63
$1.80 \leq h < 1.90$	18

4 The table below shows the times taken to deliver pizzas in one week.

Time (*t*) in minutes	$0 \leq t < 5$	$5 \leq t < 10$	$10 \leq t < 15$	$15 \leq t < 20$	$20 \leq t < 25$	$25 \leq t < 30$
Frequency	40	64	89	82	34	18

   a) Which group contains the median time taken to deliver a pizza?

   b) Estimate the mean time taken to deliver a pizza.

   c) The pizza company guarantee to deliver your pizza in less than 15 minutes or
      your pizza is free. What percentage of the pizzas delivered that week were free?

34.3   Interpreting Data Sets

Choosing the Right Average

Averages are a good way to summarise and represent data, but using the wrong average can be **misleading**.
The mode, median and mean averages all have different advantages and disadvantages.

	Advantages	Disadvantages
Mode	1. It's easy to find. 2. It's always a data set value.	1. It doesn't always exist, or there are several modes. 2. Not always a good representation of the data — it doesn't use all the data values.
Median	1. Easy to find for ungrouped data. 2. It doesn't get distorted by extreme data points.	1. Not always a good representation of the data — it doesn't use all the data values. 2. It isn't always a data set value.
Mean	It is usually the most representative average — it uses all the data set values.	1. It can be distorted by extreme data points. 2. It isn't always a data set value.

Exercise 1

1   The clothes sizes of 20 women are shown on the left.

18	4	10	10	16
12	14	14	6	18
14	12	12	8	16
14	12	12	14	14

   a) (i)   Find the mode.
      (ii) Find the median clothes size.
      (iii) Calculate the mean clothes size.

   b) Suggest why you might choose to use the mode
      instead of the median or mean to represent this data.

2   The ages of the 30 audience members at
        a McBeetle concert are shown on the right.

   a) (i)   Find the modal age.
      (ii) Work out the median age.
      (iii) Calculate the mean age.

60	12	17	60	14	16	29	15	12	17
60	60	16	17	16	14	13	14	10	16
14	17	19	17	18	19	60	16	19	16

   b) A slightly embarrassed 29-year-old says, 'The mean age is the most representative
      of the ages of the people at the concert.' Do you agree? Explain your answer.

3 A company asked 190 women to test their latest wrinkle cream and give it a mark out of 10. The table shows their results.

a) Find the mode, median and mean for the data.

Mark	1	2	3	4	5	6	7	8	9	10
Frequency	31	34	35	34	4	6	36	7	2	1

b) **(i)** The company claims, 'On average, women gave our product 7 out of 10'. Which average has it used in its claim?

(ii) Do you think this average represents the data well? Explain your answer.

Measures of Spread — Interquartile Range

The **upper quartile**, the **median** and the lower **quartile** are values that divide a data set into four equal groups.

For a data set in ascending order with n values, you can work out the position of the quartiles using these formulas: The quartiles are 25%, 50% and 75% through the data.

The **interquartile range** is the difference between the upper quartile (Q_3) and the lower quartile (Q_1). It is a measure of how spread out data is.

> lower quartile $Q_1 = (n + 1) \div 4$
>
> median $Q_2 = (n + 1) \div 2$
>
> upper quartile $Q_3 = 3(n + 1) \div 4$

Example 1

The data on the right shows the goals scored by Team A at each hockey game in a season.

Game	1	2	3	4	5	6	7	8	9
Goals scored	2	4	0	3	4	2	2	3	2

a) Calculate the interquartile range for this data.

1. Put the data in ascending order, then find the positions of Q_1 and Q_3.

   0 2 2 2 2 3 3 4 4

   Q_1 position $= (9 + 1) \div 4 = 2.5$
   Q_3 position $= 3(9 + 1) \div 4 = 7.5$

2. The positions are midway between data values. Find the halfway point between the two numbers on either side of these positions.

   0 2 2 2 2 3 3 4 4

   $Q_1 = 2$ $Q_3 = (3 + 4) \div 2 = 3.5$

   Interquartile range $= Q_3 - Q_1 = 3.5 - 2 = \underline{\mathbf{1.5}}$

b) Team B scores the same total number of goals as Team A, but their scores have an interquartile range of 0.5. Which team scored the most consistent number of goals per game?

The lower the interquartile range, the less spread out the data values are.

Team B — their interquartile range is much lower than for Team A.

Exercise 2

1 Calculate the interquartile range for each of the following data sets.

a) 8 9 9 9 10 10 12 15 16 17 19

b) 1.5 1.5 1.3 1.4 1.6 1.8 1.2

c) 80 70 34 21 21 56 75 89 84 20 17 45 87

d) 1 9 3 9 3 4 5 6 9 0 1 9 9 5 9 2 5

2 The table shows the number of spots on 79 ladybirds.

No. of Spots	2	3	4	5	6	7	8	9	10
Frequency	3	16	9	18	9	6	9	7	2

Find the interquartile range for the data.

3 Look at the data on the right.

    a) (i) Calculate the range for the data.

       (ii) Calculate the interquartile range.

13	28	893	192	89	98	67	45	78	90	34	56	78	20	783
60	33	45	12	67	54	58	101	56	89	708	9	82	76	90
55	89	347	104	43	76	38	13	27	51	92	18	44	87	71

    b) Which of the ranges you calculated in part **a)** do you think represents the data best? Explain your answer.

4 The list on the right shows the exam results for the students in class 3A.

    a) Only students with a mark in the upper quartile of the class results passed the exam. What was the pass mark for this exam?

    b) Calculate how many people passed the exam.

    c) (i) Find the interquartile range for this data.

30	36	89	92	76	20	57	89	23
55	56	56	98	35	20	86	38	25
13	90	54	67	67	34	78	72	53
88	24	40	76	20	24			

       (ii) Class 3B's results for the same exam have an interquartile range of 20.
       Comment on how the spread of the exam results for the two classes differs.

Measures of Spread — Percentiles

Percentiles P_1 to P_{99} divide data into 100 equal groups. $P_a = a(n + 1) \div 100$

Example 2

The data on the right shows 24 student's scores on a test. Calculate the 80th percentile.

19 23 26 28 32 33 44 47 56 56 57 60
62 63 63 66 67 67 71 ⑦⑥ 82 90 91 96

Find the position of P_{80} using $P_a = a(n + 1) \div 100$

There are 24 values, so the position of $P_{80} = 80 \times (24 + 1) \div 100 = 20$. So $P_{80} = \underline{\textbf{76}}$

$n = 20$

Exercise 3

1 **a)** Calculate the 20th percentile of this data set: 3 3 3 5 8 9 20 42 50

    b) Calculate the 80th percentile of this data set: 450 95 102 120 210 220 80 240 26 280 290 30 320 46

    c) Calculate the 92nd percentile of this data set:
       1.2 1.4 1.8 1.6 1.8 1.9 1.0 1.0 2.5 4.5 2.1 0.3 2.5 4.6 2.1 4.3 5.0 1.8 3.4 1.1 3.2 3.3 4.1 0.2

Exercise 4 — Mixed Exercise

1 A company asks 40 people to taste 'Peanut Better' peanut butter and give it a mark out of 10. Their results are shown in the box.

    a) (i) Find the modal score.

       (ii) Calculate the median score.

      (iii) Calculate the mean score.

Scores for Peanut Better:
5 2 8 9 5 5 7 8 1 2 3 4 6 8 1 5 3 2 4 5
7 7 8 6 2 7 2 8 9 2 5 7 8 9 8 5 7 8 2 6

    b) The company want to quote an average score in their next advertising campaign. Which average best represents the data? Explain your answer.

    c) Give one reason why the company may choose to use a different average.

2 A group of 17 pantomime horses were timed as they ran 100 m. The finishing times for the pantomime horses (in seconds) are shown on the right.

15.3 18.9 40.2 20.5 14.0 17.3 17.8 30.5 60.2
56.0 32.1 34.2 22.7 36.2 19.2 41.1 26.4

17 kittens ran the same course. The mean time it took a kitten to run 100 m was 24.6 seconds.
The interquartile range of the kittens' times was 48.6 seconds.
Use this data to investigate the hypothesis 'Pantomime horses run faster than kittens'.

Section 35 — Displaying Data

35.1 Tables and Charts

Two-Way Tables

A **two-way table** shows frequencies for two different variables.

Example 1

This table shows how students in a class travel to school.

	Walk	Bus	Car	Total
Boys	8	7		19
Girls	6		2	
Total		12		

a) Complete the table.
   Add entries to find row/column totals.
   Subtract from row/column totals to find other entries.

	Walk	Bus	Car	Total
Boys	8	7	$19 - 8 - 7 = \underline{4}$	19
Girls	6	$12 - 7 = \underline{5}$	2	$6 + 5 + 2 = \underline{13}$
Total	$8 + 6 = \underline{14}$	12	$4 + 2 = \underline{6}$	$19 + 13 = \underline{32}$

b) How many girls take the bus to school?   **5**

c) What percentage of students take the bus to school?
   Divide the total of the Bus column by the overall total. $\frac{12}{32} = 0.375 = \underline{\textbf{37.5\%}}$

Exercise 1

1 This two-way table gives information about the colours of the vehicles in a car park.

   a) Copy and complete the table.
   b) How many motorbikes were blue?
   c) How many vans were there?
   d) What percentage of vehicles were:
      (i) cars?   **(ii)** vans?   **(iii)** red?

	Red	Black	Blue	White	Total
Cars	8	7	4		22
Vans		2	1	10	
Motorbikes	2	1		2	
Total	12		6		

2 A group of schoolchildren were asked if they have been ice skating before. Copy the two-way table below, then use the following information to complete it.

   - 20 girls were asked.
   - Half as many boys as girls were asked.
   - 18 of the children have been ice skating.
   - One fifth of the girls haven't been ice skating.

	Have been ice skating	Haven't been ice skating	Total
Boys			
Girls			
Total			

3 This two-way table shows the heights in centimetres of 50 people.

	$h < 160$	$160 \leq h < 170$	$170 \leq h < 180$	$180 \leq h < 190$	$190 \leq h$	Total
Women	4		11		0	24
Men		2	6		5	
Total	4	9				50

   a) Copy and complete the table.
   b) How many of the people are smaller than 170 cm?
   c) What fraction of the women are at least 180 cm tall?
   d) Comment on the difference between the heights of the men and the women.

Bar Charts

Bar charts are used to display **discrete data**. They show the number (or frequency) of items in different categories.

To show the categories for two different people or groups, you can draw a **dual bar chart**, which has two bars per category — one for each person or group.
Or you can draw a **composite bar chart**, which has single bars split into different sections.

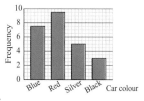

Example 2

Manpreet and Jack recorded how many TV programmes they watched each day for a week. Their results are shown in this table.

Day	Mon	Tues	Wed	Thur	Fri	Sat	Sun
No. watched by Manpreet	1	2	4	2	3	7	4
No. watched by Jack	2	1	0	2	3	4	0

a) Draw a dual bar chart to display this information.
  1. Each day should have two bars
     — one for Manpreet and one for Jack.
  2. Use different colours for Manpreet and Jack's bars
     — and include a key to show which is which.

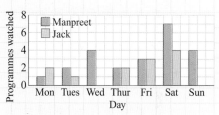

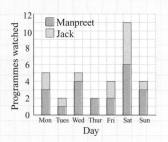

b) The composite bar chart on the left shows the number of TV programmes that Manpreet and Jack watched in a different week. Use the chart to draw a frequency table to show the data.

The frequencies are shown by the heights of the sections of the bars.

Day	Mon	Tues	Wed	Thur	Fri	Sat	Sun
No. watched by Manpreet	3	1	4	2	2	6	3
No. watched by Jack	2	1	1	0	2	5	1

Exercise 2

1 The eye colour of 50 students is shown in the table opposite.

Eye colour	Blue	Brown	Green	Other
No. of males	8	7	5	4
No. of females	7	12	5	2

  a) Draw a dual bar chart to display the data.

  b) Draw a composite bar chart to display the data.

2 A group of children and adults were asked to rate a music magazine on a scale from 1 to 5. This dual bar chart shows the results.

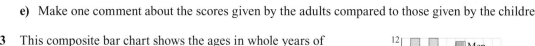

  a) How many children gave the magazine a score of 1?

  b) How many adults rated the magazine?

  c) Which score did no children give?

  d) Which score was given by twice as many children as adults?

  e) Make one comment about the scores given by the adults compared to those given by the children.

3 This composite bar chart shows the ages in whole years of the members of a small gym.

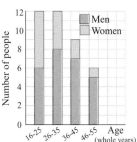

  a) How many members are in the age range 26-35 years?

  b) How many members does the gym have in total?

  c) What is the modal age range for the female members?

  d) Which age range has the greatest difference in numbers of men and women?

Pie Charts

Like bar charts, **pie charts** show how data is divided into categories, but they show the **proportion** in each category, rather than the actual frequency. The sizes of the **angles** of the sectors **represent** the **frequencies**, so you can compare the frequencies of categories in the same chart by comparing their angles.

Example 3

Jake asked everyone in his class to name their favourite colour. The frequency table on the right shows his results.

Draw a pie chart to show his results.

Colour	Red	Green	Blue	Pink
Frequency	12	7	5	6

1. Calculate the total frequency — the total number of people in Jake's class.

   Total frequency = 12 + 7 + 5 + 6 = 30

2. Divide 360° by the total frequency to find the number of degrees needed to represent each person.

   Each person represented by 360° ÷ 30 = 12°

3. Multiply each frequency by the number of degrees for one person to get the angle.
   (Check that the angles add up to 360°.)

Colour	Red	Green	Blue	Pink
Frequency	12	7	5	6
Angle	144°	84°	60°	72°

4. Draw the pie chart — using the angles you've just calculated to mark out the sectors.

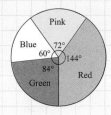

Exercise 3

1   Daisy asked a group of people where they went on holiday last year. Her results are shown in the table.

Destination	UK	Europe	USA	Other	Nowhere
Frequency	22	31	8	11	18

   a) Calculate the angle needed to represent each place on a pie chart.

   b) Draw a pie chart to show Daisy's data.

2   Vicky asked people entering a sports centre what activity they were going to do.
   - 33 were going to play squash
   - 21 were going swimming
   - 52 were going to use the gym
   - 14 had come to play table tennis.

   a) Calculate the angle needed to represent each activity on a pie chart.
   b) Draw a pie chart to show the data.

3   Peter surveyed his friends to find out how they travel to school. The table opposite shows his results.

   Draw a pie chart to represent Peter's data.

Method of transport	Walking	Bus	Car	Bike
Frequency	36	16	12	16

4   Basil used a questionnaire to find out which subject pupils at his school enjoyed the most. His data is shown in the frequency table below. Show this data in a pie chart.

Subject	Maths	Art	PE	English	Science	Other
Frequency	348	297	195	87	108	45

Example 4

A head teacher carries out a survey to find out how pupils travel to school.
The pie chart on the right shows the results of the survey.

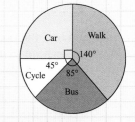

a) What is the most popular way to travel to school?
This is the sector with the largest angle. **Walking**

b) Which method of transport is twice as common as cycling?
Cycling is represented by a sector with an angle of 45°.
Travelling by car is represented by a sector with an angle of 90°. **Travelling by car**

c) 280 pupils said they walk to school. How many pupils took part in the survey altogether?

1. The 280 pupils who walk are represented by an angle of 140°.

2. Use this to work out how many pupils the whole pie chart represents.

140° represents 280 pupils

So 1° represents 280 ÷ 140 = 2 pupils.

This means 360° represents 360 × 2 = **720 pupils**

Exercise 4

1 Jennifer asked pupils in her school to name their favourite type of pizza.
The pie chart on the right shows the results.

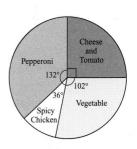

a) Which was the most popular type of pizza?

b) What fraction of the pupils said cheese and tomato was their favourite?

c) Jennifer asked 60 pupils altogether.
Calculate the number of pupils who said vegetable was their favourite.

2 Andy and Beth record the number of homework tasks they are
set in their Maths, English and Science lessons during one term.
Their data is displayed in the pie charts on the right.

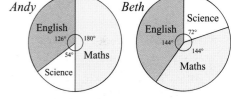

a) Andy says: "Half of all the homework tasks I was given
from these three subjects were in Maths." Is he correct?

b) Beth says: "I was given the same number of Maths tasks and English tasks." Is she correct?

c) Do the pie charts tell you who spent more time on their English homework? Explain your answer.

3 A librarian carried out a survey of the ages of people using the library. Chart **A** below shows the results.

a) There were 18 people aged 17-29 who took part in the survey.
How many people took part in the survey altogether?

b) Use your answer to part **a)** to calculate the number of people surveyed who were:

(i) Under 11   (ii) 11-16   (iii) 30-49   (iv) 50+

Leaflets were handed out to persuade more young people to use the library.
Another survey was then carried out to find the ages of library users.
The results are shown in chart **B** on the right.

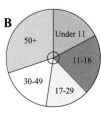

c) What fraction of the people who took part in the second survey were aged 11-16?

d) Compare the fraction of people aged 11-16 in the second survey with the fraction
of people aged 11-16 in the first survey.

e) Do these pie charts show that there were more people aged 11-16 in the second
survey than in the first survey? Explain your answer.

35.2 Stem and Leaf Diagrams

Stem and leaf diagrams are a bit like bar charts, but the bars are made out of the actual data.
Displaying data in an **ordered** stem and leaf diagram makes it easy to find the mode and the median.
And you can quickly work out the range and interquartile range for the data.

Example 1

The marks scored by pupils in a class test are shown here.

| 56, 52, 82, 65, 76, 82, 57, 63, 69, 73, |
| 58, 81, 73, 52, 73, 71, 67, 59, 63 |

a) Use this data to draw an ordered stem and leaf diagram.

1. Write down the 'stems'
   — here use the first
   digit of the marks.

5	6 2 7 8 2 9
6	5 3 9 7 3
7	6 3 3 3 1
8	2 2 1

2. Make a 'leaf' for each data value by adding the second digit to the correct stem.

3. Put the leaves in each row in order — from lowest to highest.

5	2 2 6 7 8 9
6	3 3 5 7 9
7	1 3 3 3 6
8	1 2 2

4. And remember to include a key. ⟹ Key: 5 | 2 means 52

b) Use your stem and leaf diagram to find the mode, median and range of the data.

1. Find the mode by looking for the 'leaf' that repeats most often in one of the rows — here, there are three 3's in the third row.   Mode = **73**
2. There are 19 data values, so the median is the 10th value.   Median = **67**
3. Find the range by subtracting the first number from the last.   Range = 82 − 52 = **30**

Exercise 1

1 Use the data sets below to draw ordered stem and leaf diagrams.

   a) 41, 48, 51, 54, 59, 65, 65, 69, 74, 80, 86, 89   **b)** 12, 15, 26, 15, 39, 24, 41, 41, 27, 17, 36, 31

   c) 3.1, 4.0, 4.4, 5.3, 5.7, 5.9, 6.0, 7.7, 3.4, 4.9, 5.4   **d)** 203, 205, 221, 232, 203, 234, 240, 207, 225, 236, 221
   Use the key: 3 | 1 means 3.1   Use the key: 20 | 3 means 203

2 The amount of rainfall in cm over Morecambe Bay was recorded every week for 16 weeks.
   The measurements are shown below. Use this data to draw an ordered stem and leaf diagram.

   | 0.0 | 3.8 | 3.6 | 0.1 | 2.7 | 0.6 | 0.3 | 1.1 |
   | 2.0 | 1.3 | 0.0 | 1.6 | 4.1 | 0.0 | 2.5 | 3.1 |

3 Use this diagram showing 12 pupils' test marks to find:
   a) the modal mark
   b) the median mark
   c) the number of marks above 60
   d) the number of marks between 53 and 63
   e) the range of marks

5	2 5 5 7 8
6	1 1 8 9
7	1 7 7

   Key: 2 | 1 means 21

4 The times (in seconds) that 15 people took to run a 100 m race are shown in the box.
   a) Use these times to create an ordered stem and leaf diagram.
   b) Find the mode of the times.
   c) Find the median time.
   d) Find the lower and upper quartiles of the data
   and calculate the interquartile range.

10.2	13.1	13.9	14.2	17.3
11.7	11.4	12.9	15.4	13.6
13.9	10.6	12.8	12.4	13.3

Back-to-Back Stem and Leaf Diagrams

Back-to-back stem and leaf diagrams can be used to compare two sets of data alongside each other.
One set of data is read as usual, while the other is read "backwards".

Example 2

14 girls and 14 boys completed a puzzle. The time in seconds it took each pupil to finish was recorded.

This ordered back-to-back stem and leaf diagram shows the results.

Key: 1 | 2 for girls means 21
     1 | 2 for boys means 12

```
         girls  |   | boys
                | 1 | 4  4  7  9
9 8 8 5 5 3     | 2 | 7  9
    8 7 4 2 1   | 3 | 2  3  8
          4 2 2 | 4 | 5  6  6  7  9
```

a) Find the median times for the girls and the boys.

There are 14 data values for each set of data, so the median is between the 7th and 8th values.

Median for girls $= \frac{31 + 32}{2} = $ **31.5 seconds**

Median for boys $= \frac{32 + 33}{2} = $ **32.5 seconds**

b) Find the range of times for the girls and the boys.

Subtract the first number from the last.

Range for girls $= 44 - 23 = $ **21 seconds**

Range for boys $= 49 - 14 = $ **35 seconds**

c) Use your answers to parts a) and b) to make two comparisons between the times for the girls and boys.

Compare the median and the range and interpret what the numbers show about the times.

The median for the boys is slightly higher than for the girls, which suggests that on average the boys took slightly longer to complete the puzzle. The range for the girls is much smaller than for the boys, which shows that the girls' times were a lot more consistent.

Exercise 2

1 Use these two data sets to draw an ordered back-to-back stem and leaf diagram.

Set 1: | 12, 18, 29, 24, 28, 33, 38, 37, 32, 41, 48 | *Set 2:* | 13, 19, 13, 15, 18, 23, 22, 25, 27, 22, 32 |

2 Babatunde measured the heart rates in beats per minute (bpm) of 15 people at rest, and then again after they'd exercised. His results are shown in the diagram.
   a) Find the median of each set of data.
   b) Calculate the interquartile range of each set of data.
   c) What conclusions can you draw from your answers to parts **a)** and **b)**?

```
  heart rate at rest |   | heart rate after exercise
8 7 6 4 3 2 2        | 6 | 5  8  8  9
  9 8 6 3 2 2        | 7 | 4  5  7  7  8
            4 1      | 8 | 5  6  7
                     | 9 | 1  3  7
```

Key: 7 | 6 at rest means 67
     7 | 6 after exercise means 76

3 The data on the right shows daily temperatures (in °C) in Dundee and in London during the same period.
   a) Draw a back-to-back stem and leaf diagram to show the data.
   b) By calculating the median and range for each set of data, compare the temperatures in the two places.

Dundee	12	19	6	7	23	4
	3	1	15	5	2	3

London	4	9	18	7	24	12
	13	12	15	21	11	16

35.3 Frequency Polygons

Frequency polygons are used to show **continuous** data, so they have a continuous scale on the horizontal axis. Each frequency is plotted at the midpoint of the class and the points are joined with straight lines.

You can compare two distributions by drawing a frequency polygon for each and comparing their shapes.

Example 1

Amin recorded the speeds of the cars that passed outside his house one day.
The results are shown in the grouped frequency table below.
Draw a frequency polygon to represent this information.

Speed (s) in mph	Frequency
$25 \leq s < 30$	1
$30 \leq s < 35$	5
$35 \leq s < 40$	12
$40 \leq s < 45$	16
$45 \leq s < 50$	9
$50 \leq s < 55$	2

1. Find the midpoint of each class by adding the endpoints, and dividing by 2.

2. For each class, plot the frequency at the midpoint.

3. Join your points with straight lines.

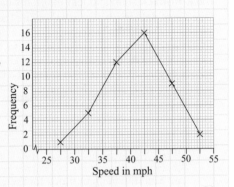

Exercise 1

1 Some students recorded the total floor area of local supermarkets for a project.
Their results are shown in the table.

Draw a frequency polygon to show this information.

Floor area (a) in thousands of square feet	Frequency
$9 \leq a < 13$	3
$13 \leq a < 14$	7
$14 \leq a < 15$	5
$15 \leq a < 16$	2

2 An airline recorded the delay in minutes of all of its flights one day, using class intervals 5 minutes wide. Their results are shown in this frequency polygon.

a) How many flights had a delay that was 40 minutes or longer?

b) What is the modal class for this data?

c) The airline gets fined if 8 or more of its flights on a day are delayed by more than 20 minutes. Should the airline have been fined that day? Explain your answer.

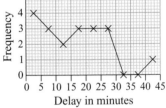

3 Emma recorded the number of hours (h) of sunshine each day in February and July.
She used classes with a width of 1 hour, starting with $0 \leq h < 1$, $1 \leq h < 2$, $2 \leq h < 3$, and so on.
The frequency polygons on the right show her results.

a) How many days with 4 or more hours of sunshine were there in February?

b) How many days were there in February?

c) What is the modal class for February?

d) What is the modal class for July?

e) Use your answers to parts c) and d) to compare the daily hours of sunshine in February and July, and compare the spread of the data for the two months.

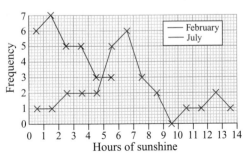

Histograms are a bit like bar charts, but they're used to show **continuous** data. Instead of plotting frequency on the vertical axis, you plot **frequency density**, which is calculated using the formula:

$$\text{Frequency density} = \frac{\text{Frequency}}{\text{Class width}}$$

So the **frequency** of data values in each class is shown by the **area** of each bar, not the height.

Example 1

This frequency table shows some information about the heights of 30 adults.
Draw a histogram to represent this information.

1. Add a 'frequency density' column to the table and use the formula to work out the value for each class.

2. Draw axes with a continuous scale for height along the bottom and frequency density up the side.

Height (h) in cm	Frequency	Frequency Density
$155 \leq h < 165$	4	$4 \div 10 = 0.4$
$165 \leq h < 170$	3	$3 \div 5 = 0.6$
$170 \leq h < 175$	4	$4 \div 5 = 0.8$
$175 \leq h < 180$	9	$9 \div 5 = 1.8$
$180 \leq h < 185$	7	$7 \div 5 = 1.4$
$185 \leq h < 200$	3	$3 \div 15 = 0.2$

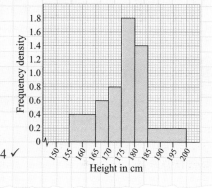

3. Draw a bar for each class and check that the area equals the frequency.
   E.g. the area of the first bar = $10 \times 0.4 = 4$ ✓

Exercise 1

1 The grouped frequency tables below show data on the heights of some plants. Copy and complete each table.

a)

Height (h) in cm	Frequency	Frequency Density
$0 < h \leq 5$	4	
$5 < h \leq 10$	6	
$10 < h \leq 15$	3	
$15 < h \leq 20$	2	

b)

Height (h) in cm	Frequency	Frequency Density
$10 < h \leq 20$	5	
$20 < h \leq 25$	15	
$25 < h \leq 30$	12	
$30 < h \leq 40$	8	

2 Each grouped frequency table below shows some information about the volume of tea drunk each day by a group of people. Copy and complete each table and use it to draw a histogram to represent the information.

a)

Volume (v) in ml	Frequency	Frequency Density
$0 \leq v < 500$	50	
$500 \leq v < 1000$	75	
$1000 \leq v < 1500$	70	
$1500 \leq v < 2000$	55	

b)

Volume (v) in ml	Frequency	Frequency Density
$0 \leq v < 300$	30	
$300 \leq v < 600$	15	
$600 \leq v < 900$	24	
$900 \leq v < 1500$	42	
$1500 \leq v < 2100$	12	

3 The table on the right shows some information about the weights (w) in kg of 22 pigs on a farm. Draw a histogram to represent this information.

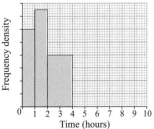

Weight (w) in kg	Frequency
$10 \le w < 20$	5
$20 \le w < 30$	7
$30 \le w < 50$	10

Time (t) in seconds	Frequency
$0 \le t < 4$	18
$4 \le t < 8$	12
$8 \le t < 12$	6
$12 \le t < 20$	4
$20 \le t < 30$	1

4 Participants in a circus skills workshop were asked to juggle three balls for as long as possible without dropping them. The table on the left shows some information about how long they were able to do this for.

Draw a histogram to represent this information.

5 This incomplete table and histogram show information about the length of time (in hours) that some people spend watching the TV programme 'Celebrity Ironing Challenge' each week.

Time (t) in hours	Frequency
$0 \le t < 1$	
$1 \le t < 2$	
$2 \le t < 4$	16
$4 \le t < 6$	14
$6 \le t < 10$	12

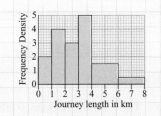

a) Copy the histogram and use the information given to label the vertical axis.

b) Copy the table and use the information in the histogram to fill in the gaps.

c) Use the table to add the missing bars to your histogram.

Interpreting Histograms

You can use histograms to estimate things about the data they represent. For example, the number of data values that are in a particular interval, or values for the mean or median.

Example 2

Some students were asked the length of their journey to university. The histogram opposite shows the information.

a) Estimate the number of students with a journey of 1.5 km or less.

   1. Work out the number of journeys between 0 and 1 km by finding the area of the first bar.

      $1 \times 2 = 2$ journeys between 0 and 1 km

   2. Estimate how many are between 1 and 1.5 km by finding the area of the second bar up to 1.5 km.

      $0.5 \times 4 = 2$ journeys between 1 and 1.5 km

   3. Add the two values you've calculated together.

      $2 + 2 = \underline{\textbf{4 students}}$

b) Estimate the mean journey length for the students.

   1. Draw a grouped frequency table using the classes shown on the histogram.

      Work out the frequency and midpoint for each class, then add a column to multiply them together.

Journey (j) in km	Frequency (class width × frequency density)	Midpoint	Midpoint × frequency
$0 < j \le 1$	2	0.5	1
$1 < j \le 2$	4	1.5	6
$2 < j \le 3$	3	2.5	7.5
$3 < j \le 4$	5	3.5	17.5
$4 < j \le 6$	3	5	15
$6 < j \le 8$	1	7	7
Totals	18		54

   2. Estimate the mean in the usual way — total the 'midpoint × frequency' column and divide by the total frequency.

      Estimated mean $= \dfrac{54}{18} = \underline{\textbf{3 km}}$

Exercise 2

1 For each of the histograms below, work out the frequency represented by each bar.

a)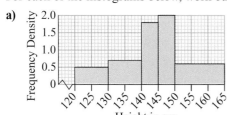

b)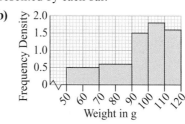

2 Use the histogram on the right to estimate the number of data values in the following intervals.

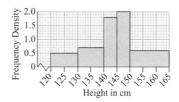

a) 150–155 cm
b) 150–160 cm
c) 145–160 cm
d) 120–126 cm

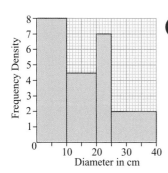

3 The histogram on the left represents the diameters in centimetres of all the cakes made at a bakery one day.

a) Estimate the number of cakes with a diameter of less than 16 cm.
b) Estimate the number of cakes with a diameter in the range 20–30 cm.
c) Work out the total number of cakes made.
d) Calculate an estimate of the mean diameter of the cakes.

4 The histogram on the right represents the heights in centimetres of all the penguins at a wildlife park.

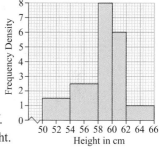

a) Estimate the number of penguins with a height of less than 56 cm.
b) Work out the total number of penguins at the wildlife park.
c) 24 of the penguins have a height of less than H cm. Estimate the value of H.
d) Use your answers to **b)** and **c)** to write down an estimate of the median height.

Exercise 3 — Mixed Exercise

1 The grouped frequency table opposite shows the distances that 260 people in the same city live from their nearest supermarket.

a) Draw a histogram to show the data.
b) Estimate the number of people who live within 2800 metres of a supermarket.
c) Estimate, to 3 s.f., the mean distance that these people live from a supermarket.

Distance (d) in metres	Frequency
$0 < d \leq 1000$	60
$1000 < d \leq 1500$	40
$1500 < d \leq 2000$	45
$2000 < d \leq 2500$	35
$2500 < d \leq 3500$	80

2 100 people take part in a 'guess the weight of the Shetland pony' competition. This grouped frequency table shows information about the weights they guessed.

a) Draw a histogram to represent the data.
b) Write down the interval containing the median weight guessed. Then use your histogram to estimate the median weight guessed.
c) Thirteen people guessed a weight that was heavier than the actual weight, W. Use this information and your histogram to estimate the actual weight W.

Weight (w) in kg	Frequency
$100 \leq w < 140$	20
$140 \leq w < 160$	40
$160 \leq w < 170$	18
$170 \leq w < 180$	18
$180 \leq w < 200$	4

35.5 Cumulative Frequency Diagrams

Cumulative frequency is the **running total** of frequencies for a set of data. You can use a cumulative frequency table to draw a **cumulative frequency diagram**, which you can use to find the **median** and **interquartile range**. (If the data is grouped, you can only estimate the median and interquartile range.)

There are two types of cumulative frequency diagram:
- a cumulative frequency curve — the points are joined with a smooth curve.
- a cumulative frequency polygon — the points are joined with straight lines instead of a curve.

Example 1

The table below shows the heights of a set of plants, measured to the nearest cm.

a) Complete the cumulative frequency column for the table.

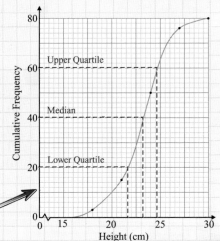

Height, h (cm)	Frequency	Cumulative Frequency
$15 < h \leq 18$	3	**3**
$18 < h \leq 21$	12	$3 + 12 =$ **15**
$21 < h \leq 24$	35	$15 + 35 =$ **50**
$24 < h \leq 27$	26	$50 + 26 =$ **76**
$27 < h \leq 30$	4	$76 + 4 =$ **80**

b) (i) Draw a cumulative frequency diagram for the data. Always put the cumulative frequency on the vertical axis. For grouped data, plot the frequency for each group using the highest value in the group.

(ii) Estimate the median and interquartile range for the data.
1. Median — read off the plant height that corresponds to a cumulative frequency of 40 (half of 80).

Median = **23.25 cm**

2. Interquartile range (IQR) — read off the plant height that corresponds to 60 (= ¾ of 80) for the upper quartile and 20 (= ¼ of 80) for the lower quartile. Then find the difference. IQR = 24.75 – 21.75 = **3 cm**

Exercise 1

1 The cumulative frequency graph on the right shows the monthly earnings for a group of 16-year-olds.

a) How many 16-year-olds took part in the survey?

b) Estimate how many earned less than £20.

c) Estimate how many earned less than £80.

d) Estimate how many earned between £40 and £100.

e) Estimate the median earnings for a 16-year-old.

f) Estimate the lower quartile, the upper quartile and the interquartile range for this data.

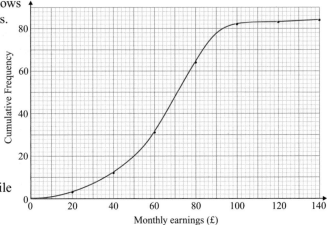

2 This table shows Year 11 marks in a Maths test.

a) Copy the table and complete
   the cumulative frequency column.

b) Draw a cumulative frequency curve for the marks.

c) Estimate the median mark.

d) Estimate the upper and lower quartiles
   and interquartile range for the data.

e) Pupils who achieved less than 45 marks have to
   resit the test. Estimate how many pupils will resit.

f) Pupils who achieved more than 55 marks will
   sit the higher tier exam. Estimate how many
   will be entered for the higher tier.

Marks, m	Frequency	Cumulative Frequency
$0 < m \le 10$	0	
$10 < m \le 20$	2	
$20 < m \le 30$	4	
$30 < m \le 40$	5	
$40 < m \le 50$	19	
$50 < m \le 60$	33	
$60 < m \le 70$	43	
$70 < m \le 80$	10	
$80 < m \le 90$	3	
$90 < m \le 100$	1	

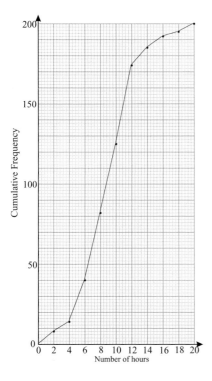

3 This cumulative frequency diagram
shows the number of hours of television
watched in a week by a group of 200
girls. The table shows the number of
hours of TV watched by 200 boys.

a) Use the cumulative frequency diagram
   to estimate how many girls watched:
   (i) less than 9 hours a week,
   (ii) more than 11 hours a week.

b) Estimate the median, upper and
   lower quartiles and interquartile
   range for the girls' data.

c) Copy the girls' cumulative frequency
   diagram and the boys' frequency table.
   (i) Add and complete a cumulative frequency
   column for the boys' data table.
   (ii) Plot a cumulative frequency diagram for the boys' data
   on the same axes as the girls' cumulative frequency diagram.

d) Estimate the median and interquartile range for the boys' data.

e) Compare the amounts of television
   watched by the groups of boys and girls.

No. of hours, h	Frequency
$h < 2$	35
$2 \le h < 4$	76
$4 \le h < 6$	51
$6 \le h < 8$	34
$8 \le h < 10$	3
$10 \le h < 12$	0
$12 \le h < 14$	1
$14 \le h < 16$	0
$16 \le h < 18$	0
$18 \le h < 20$	0

4 Some students are asked to pour out a sample of sand that
they estimate will have a mass of 25 g. The table shows a
summary of the masses of their samples.

a) Draw a cumulative frequency curve for this data.

b) Use your diagram to:
   (i) estimate the median and interquartile range,
   (ii) estimate the 70th percentile.

c) Estimate how many students' samples were within 10 g of the median.

d) Comment on the accuracy of the students' estimates.

Mass, m, in g	Frequency
$m \le 5$	2
$5 < m \le 10$	3
$10 < m \le 15$	4
$15 < m \le 20$	7
$20 < m \le 25$	25
$25 < m \le 30$	51
$30 < m \le 35$	31
$35 < m \le 40$	9
$40 < m \le 45$	5
$45 < m \le 50$	3

Box Plots

A box plot can be used to summarise the distribution of data in a data set.

If the data is grouped, the highest and lowest data values are unknown. In this case, the highest and lowest possible values are used.

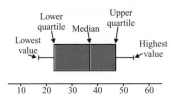

Example 2

The box plots below show the distribution of time it took to answer calls to a call centre over two weeks. The call centre manager says, 'The data shows the times taken to answer calls in Week 1 were greater but more consistent than those in Week 2'. Do you agree? Use the data to explain your answer.

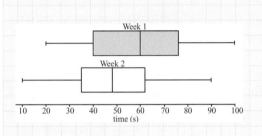

Compare the medians, quartiles, interquartile ranges, minimum and maximum values of the data sets. E.g.

The median, the quartiles and the minimum and maximum times are greater for Week 1 than Week 2, so the data supports the first part of the manager's statement. However, the interquartile range for Week 2 is smaller than for Week 1, so the times taken to answer calls were more consistent during Week 2.

Exercise 2

1 For each of the following box plots, find:
 (i) the median, (ii) the upper quartile,
 (iii) the lower quartile, (iv) the interquartile range,
 (v) the lowest value, (vi) the highest value.

a)

b)

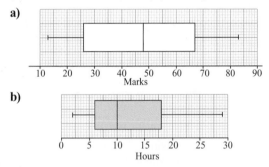

2 The box plots below show the distributions of the times a group of busybodies and a group of chatterboxes were able to stay silent.

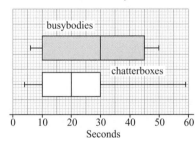

A busybody says, 'The busybodies were definitely better at staying silent than the chatterboxes'. Do you agree? Use the data to support your answer.

Exercise 3 — Mixed Exercise

1 The table shows the battery life for two types of battery. 200 of each type of battery were tested.

Hours of use, h	$h < 5000$	$5000 \leq h < 6000$	$6000 \leq h < 7000$	$7000 \leq h < 8000$	$8000 \leq h < 9000$	$9000 \leq h < 10\,000$	$10\,000 \leq h < 11\,000$	$11\,000 \leq h < 12\,000$
Type A	25	15	23	17	50	41	24	5
Type B	13	13	18	21	36	72	19	8

a) Copy the table. Add rows to your table to show the cumulative frequencies for each type of battery.
b) Draw a cumulative frequency curve for each battery type.
c) Estimate the median and interquartile range for each type of battery.
d) Draw a box plot to summarise the data for each type of battery.
e) Use your box plots to compare the battery lives of the two types of battery.

2 A store manager is analysing the sales figures of two assistants.
Their weekly figures for last year are shown in the table below.

Sales, £s 000	< 100	100 ≤ s < 200	200 ≤ s < 300	300 ≤ s < 400	400 ≤ s < 500
Sean	0	5	29	15	3
Maria	4	17	21	10	0

a) Construct cumulative frequency diagrams for both sets of sales figures on the same axes.

b) Estimate the median and interquartile range for each assistant.

c) Sean's lowest weekly figure was £160 000 and his highest was £490 000. Maria's lowest was £95 000 and her highest was £360 000. Draw box plots to illustrate each assistant's sales figures.

d) Sean and Maria are currently both paid the same salary.
Who would you suggest deserves a pay rise, Sean or Maria? Use the data to support your answer.

35.6   Time Series

A **time series** is a set of data collected at regular intervals over a period of time.
Time series are usually shown as a line graph. You can use time series graphs to find **trends** in the data.

Example 1

The graph on the right shows the midday temperatures in Athens every day during the first week of July. The table below gives the corresponding temperatures for Oslo on the same days.

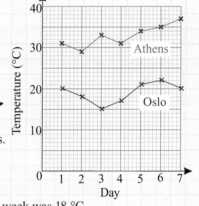

Date	1st	2nd	3rd	4th	5th	6th	7th
Temperature (°C)	20	18	15	17	21	22	20

a) Draw the time series for Oslo on the same axes.

b) Use your graph to comment on the temperatures in the two cities.
    Some comments you could make on the graph:

    • The recorded temperature in Oslo was always at least
      10 °C lower than that in Athens.
    • The greatest difference in recorded temperatures during the week was 18 °C.

Exercise 1

1 The graph shows the average rainfall in London.
The average rainfall for Glasgow is shown below.

Month	Jan	Feb	Mar	Apr	May	Jun
Rainfall (mm)	111	85	69	67	63	70

Month	Jul	Aug	Sep	Oct	Nov	Dec
Rainfall (mm)	97	93	102	119	106	127

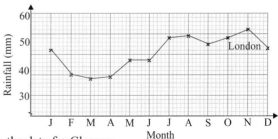

a) Copy the time series graph for London and draw on the data for Glasgow.

b) Write two sentences to compare the rainfall in the two cities.

c) Find the range of each set of data.

2 A shop records its sales (in £) of two different brands over an 8-week period in the table on the right.

a) Draw a comparative time series graph of this data.

b) Comment on the sales of the two brands.

Week	1	2	3	4	5	6	7	8
Impact	520	365	815	960	985	1245	1505	1820
On Trend	840	795	830	925	960	875	905	965

3 The graph shows how the value of £1 sterling in US dollars varied during 2010.
The conversion rates for the previous year are given in the table below.

Month (09)	Jan	Feb	Mar	Apr	May	Jun	Jul	Aug	Sep	Oct	Nov	Dec
US dollars ($)	1.45	1.44	1.42	1.47	1.54	1.63	1.64	1.65	1.63	1.62	1.66	1.62

a) Copy the original graph, and add a line showing the data from the table.

b) What was the highest value of £1 in dollars in 2010?

c) What was the highest value of £1 in dollars in 2009? When did it occur?

d) Work out the mean value of £1 in dollars for both periods shown on the graph.

e) A businesswoman always travels to New York in June. She changes £500 into dollars each time. How much less is it worth in dollars in June 2010 than in June 2009?

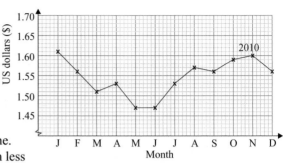

Moving Averages

Calculating **moving averages** can make it easier to see **trends** in data sets. You can make predictions from moving averages by drawing a **trend line** — a line of best fit through the moving average points.

The number of data points the average is calculated over depends on how many points make a **repeating pattern**.

Example 2

The graph on the right shows the profits made in the summer (S) and winter (W) sales of a clothes company over three years. The 2-point moving averages are also plotted (×).

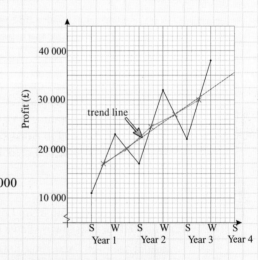

a) (i) Show how the last moving average has been calculated.

It's a 2-point moving average, so find the mean of the last two points.

Year 3 S profit = £22 000, Year 3 W profit = £38 000
Average = $(22\,000 + 38\,000) \div 2 = £30\,000$

(ii) Use the moving averages shown on the graph to describe the trend shown by the data.

Drawing a trend line can help you clearly see any trends in the data.

The profit per year has **increased**.

b) By predicting the next moving average, estimate the amount of profit the company will make in the Year 4 summer sale.

1. Read off the profit shown by the trend line from the graph at the point halfway between Year 3 W and Year 4 S. This is a prediction for the next moving average.

   The trend line suggests the moving average will probably be around £34 000.

   x = estimate of the profit for Summer of Year 4.
   $34\,000 = (38\,000 + x) \div 2$

2. Write an equation for your predicted moving average. Solve this equation to estimate the profit.

   $68\,000 = 38\,000 + x$
   $x = \mathbf{£30\,000}$

Exercise 2

1 a) Use the moving averages plotted (●) to describe the general trend in the data shown by each graph.

(i)

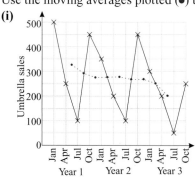

(ii)

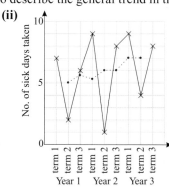

(iii)

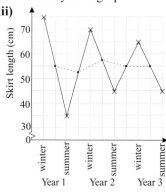

b) Explain what causes the pattern in the data points shown in graph **(i)**.

2 A museum has recorded the number of visitors for the past three years. The data for the first two and a half years is shown on the graph on the right. The 4-point moving averages are also plotted (●).

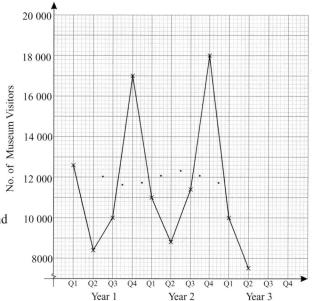

a) The table below shows the number of visitors to the museum in the last year. Calculate the next two 4-point moving averages.

	Year 3			
Quarter	Q1	Q2	Q3	Q4
No. of visitors	10 000	7500	10 500	18 800

b) Copy and complete the graph shown on the right to include all the visitor data for Year 3 and the moving averages you calculated in part **a)**.

c) Use the moving average data to describe the trend in the number of visitors to the museum over the last three years.

3 A college runs a cake decorating course each term. The graph shows the number of entrants that registered for the course each term for the past two years.

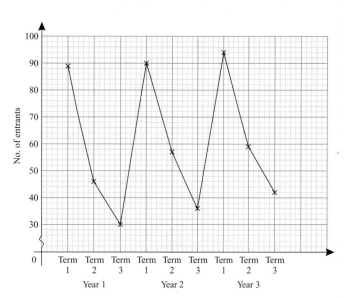

a) (i) Copy the graph on the right. Calculate each of the 3-point moving averages for this data and plot them on your graph.

(ii) Explain why it's appropriate to use a 3-point moving average.

b) The college only wants to run the course next year if they can expect at least 200 students to take the course. Should they run the course next year? Show how you worked out your answer.

35.7   Scatter Graphs

Correlation

A **scatter graph** shows two variables plotted against each other.

Two variables are **correlated** if they are related to each other.
- **Positive correlation** means that the variables increase and decrease together.
- **Negative correlation** means that as one variable increases, the other decreases.

Example 1

Describe the relationship shown by each of the graphs.

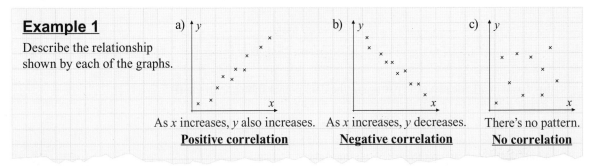

As *x* increases, *y* also increases.
Positive correlation

As *x* increases, *y* decreases.
Negative correlation

There's no pattern.
No correlation

Exercise 1

1   State whether each of the scatter graphs on the right show positive correlation, negative correlation or no correlation.

a)   b)   c)

2   The outside temperature and the number of ice creams sold in a cafe were recorded for six days. The results are shown in the table on the right.

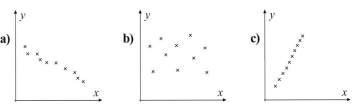

Temp (°C)	28	25	26	21	23	29
Ice creams sold	30	22	27	5	13	33

   a)   Use the data from the table to plot a scatter graph.

   b)   Is there a correlation between the outside temperature and the number of ice creams sold? If so, describe the type of correlation.

3   Ten children of different ages were asked how many baby teeth they still had.

Age (years)	5	6	8	7	9	7	10	6	8	9
Baby teeth	20	17	11	15	7	17	5	19	13	8

   a)   Use the results in the table to plot a scatter graph.

   b)   Describe the relationship between the age of the children and the number of baby teeth they have.

Example 2

Describe the strength and type of correlation shown by each scatter graph.

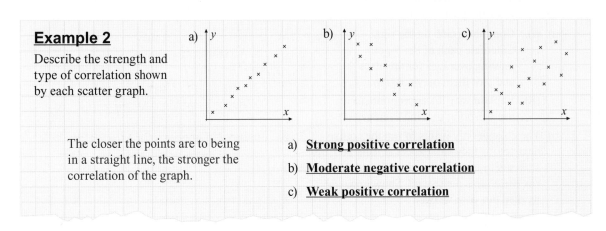

a)   b)   c)

The closer the points are to being in a straight line, the stronger the correlation of the graph.

   a)   **Strong positive correlation**

   b)   **Moderate negative correlation**

   c)   **Weak positive correlation**

4 Describe the strength and type of correlation shown by each of the scatter graphs shown on the right.

a)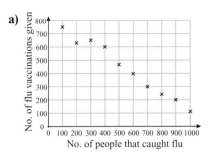

b)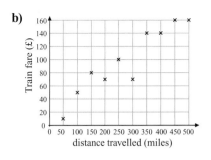

5 Jeremy measured the height and shoe size of 10 people.

Height (cm)	165	159	173	186	176	172	181	169	179	194
Shoe size	6	5	8	9	8.5	7	8	6	8	11

a) Use his results in the table to plot a scatter graph of shoe size against height in cm.

b) Is there evidence to show that height and shoe size are correlated? Explain your answer.

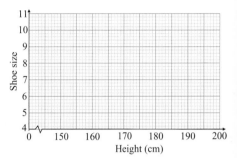

Lines of Best Fit

If two variables are correlated, then you can draw a **line of best fit** on their scatter graph.

Example 3

The scatter graph shows the marks for a class of pupils in a Maths test plotted against the marks they got in an English test.

a) Draw a line of best fit on the graph.

b) Jimmy was ill on the day of the Maths test. If he scored 75 in his English test, predict what his Maths mark would have been.

c) Elena was ill on the day of the English test. If she scored 35 on her Maths test, predict what her English result would have been.

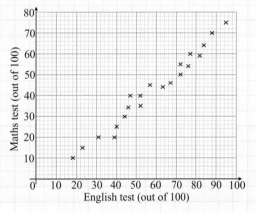

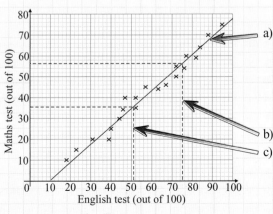

a) 1. Draw a line of best fit — there should be about the same number of points on either side of the line.

2. Use the line of best fit to predict Jimmy's and Elena's results.

b) Predicted Maths mark for Jimmy = **56**

c) Predicted English mark for Elena = **51**

Exercise 2

1 The graph on the right shows the height of a number of trees plotted against the width of their trunks.

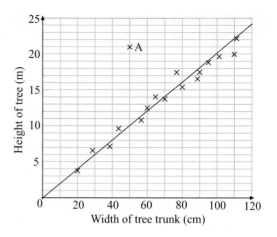

a) Describe the strength and type of correlation between the width of the trunks and the height of the trees.

b) Point A does not fit the correlation pattern shown by the rest of the data. Suggest a reason for this.

c) Use the graph to predict the width of a tree's trunk if it is 13 m tall.

d) A tree has grown into power lines, meaning that measuring its height would be dangerous. If the trunk is 100 cm wide, predict the tree's height.

2 Anton wants to buy a particular model of car. The table below shows the cost of several of these cars that are for sale, as well as their mileage.

Mileage	5000	20 000	10 000	12 000	5000	25 000	27 000
Cost (£)	3500	2000	3000	2500	3900	1000	500

a) Draw a scatter graph to show this data.

b) Draw a line of best fit through your points.

c) Thelma has seen a car of this model with a mileage of 15 000 miles. Predict the cost of this car.

3 The outside temperature and the number of drinks sold by two vending machines were recorded over a 10-day period. The results are shown in these tables.

Temperature (°C)	14	29	23	19	22	31	33	18	27	21
Drinks sold from Machine 1	6	24	16	13	15	28	31	13	22	14

Temperature (°C)	14	29	23	19	22	31	33	18	27	21
Drinks sold from Machine 2	7	25	18	15	17	32	35	14	24	17

For each machine:

a) Draw a scatter graph to represent the data. Draw a line of best fit for the data.

b) Predict the number of drinks that would be sold if the outside temperature was 25 °C.

c) Explain why it might not be appropriate to use your lines of best fit to estimate the number of drinks sold from each machine if the outside temperature was 3 °C.

d) Lucas says, "An increase in temperature causes more vending machine drinks to be sold." Do you agree with Lucas's statement? Explain your answer.

4 Craig measures the leg length of 10 members of a running club. He then times how long it takes each member to run 100 m. His results are shown below.

Club member	1	2	3	4	5	6	7	8	9	10
Leg length (in cm)	60.0	65	75	90	80	69	96	76.5	85	66
Time taken to run 100 m (in s)	16.90	12.80	15.60	13.50	14.30	15.40	13.0	14.80	14.40	16.30

a) Plot a scatter graph of this data.

b) Describe the relationship shown by the scatter graph.

c) Circle any outlier data points and draw a line of best fit for the data.

d) Use your graph to predict how long it would take for a running club member with a leg length of 87 cm to run 100 m.

e) **(i)** Estimate how long it would take a running club member with a leg length of 100 cm to run 100 m.

   (ii) Is your answer to part **(i)** a reliable estimate? Explain your answer.

Exercise 1

1   The children at a youth club were asked to name their favourite flavour of ice cream.
The dual bar chart opposite shows the results.

   a) How many girls were asked altogether?

   b) How many boys were asked altogether?

   c) How many more boys than girls chose chocolate?

   d) Which three answers were given by twice as many girls as boys?

   e) Which flavour did no boys choose?

   f) What is the modal flavour for the girls?

The pie chart below shows the data for the girls.

   g) Work out the number of degrees used to represent one girl.

   h) Draw a pie chart to show the data for the boys.

   i) Rocky road was chosen by the same number of girls and boys.
Explain why the sectors representing rocky road
in each pie chart are different sizes.

2   The data on the right shows the ages of people
queuing in a post office at 10 am and 3 pm.

> *10 am*:   65, 48, 51, 27, 29, 35, 58, 51, 54, 60, 59
>
> *3 pm*:   15, 23, 32, 31, 35, 22, 23, 18, 27

   a) Draw a back-to-back stem and leaf diagram to show the data.

   b) Find the modal age of the people queuing at each time.

   c) By calculating measures of average and spread, compare the ages of the people queuing at 10 am and 3 pm.

3   Ten people competed in a quiz. Their scores for the
first two rounds are shown in the table opposite.

Player	A	B	C	D	E	F	G	H	I	J
Round 1	12	19	6	11	16	15	18	13	12	8
Round 2	9	16	1	8	15	11	13	10	7	4

   a) Copy the two-way table below and use the scores to fill in the missing frequencies.

	0–3 points	4–7 points	8–11 points	12–15 points	16–20 points	Total
Round 1	0					
Round 2	1					
Total	1					

   b) What percentage of people scored 12 or more in round 1?

   c) How many of the 20 scores were less than 8?

   d) The questions in one of the rounds were easier than in the other round.
Use your two-way table to suggest which round was easier and explain your answer.

   e) Draw a scatter graph showing the scores for round 1 against the scores for round 2.

   f) Describe the relationship between the scores people got in round 1 and the scores they got in round 2.

4 The table opposite shows the number of components made by a machine each hour for 10 hours.

Hour	1	2	3	4	5	6	7	8	9	10
Number of components	148	151	150	150	149	150	147	142	136	131

a) Draw a time series graph to show this data.

b) The machine is designed to produce 150 components per hour.
Draw a line on your graph to show the target number of components for each hour.

c) A factory worker thinks the machine should be checked for faults.
Do you agree? Use the data to explain your answer.

5 The histogram below shows information about the heights of all the members of a netball club.

a) Copy this grouped frequency table and use the histogram to fill in the frequencies.

Height (h) in cm	Frequency
$155 \leq h < 160$	
$160 \leq h < 165$	
$165 \leq h < 170$	
$170 \leq h < 175$	
$175 \leq h < 180$	
$180 \leq h < 185$	

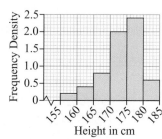

b) Estimate the number of netball players who are taller than 172 cm.

The frequency polygon below shows information on the heights of all the members of a gymnastics club.

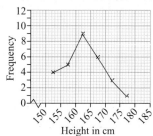

c) What is the modal class for the gymnasts' heights?

d) How many gymnasts are there in the club?

e) Copy the frequency polygon for the gymnasts and draw a frequency polygon for the heights of the netball players on the same axes.

f) Use the frequency polygons to compare the heights of the netball players and the gymnasts.

6 The cumulative frequency graph on the right shows the distances that 100 school children travel to school.

a) Use the graph to estimate the median distance travelled.

b) Use the graph to estimate the interquartile range.

c) Children who live more than 4 km away get the school bus.
How many children get the school bus?

The box plot below shows the distribution of the distances that 100 children at a second school travel to school.

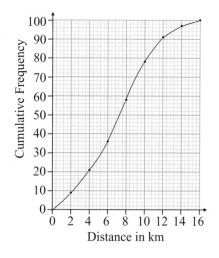

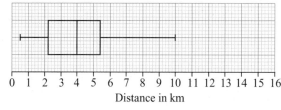

d) How many of the children at the second school travel less than 4 km to school?

e) Copy the box plot for the second school and draw a box plot for the first school above it.
Use 1 km as the shortest distance travelled and 15.5 km as the longest distance travelled.

f) Use your box plots to compare the distances travelled by the children at the two schools.

Exercise 1

1 This box plot shows information about the temperature inside a fridge, measured at hourly intervals during a day.

a) Explain why the range might not be a good representation of the spread of temperatures inside the fridge.

b) Do you think the mean would be a better or worse average to use than the median for this data? Explain your answer.

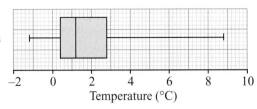

2 The grouped frequency table and histogram below show the scores hit per dart by a darts player during a match.

Score (s)	Frequency
$0 < s \leq 20$	13
$20 < s \leq 30$	35
$30 < s \leq 40$	15
$40 < s \leq 50$	3
$50 < s \leq 55$	20
$55 < s \leq 60$	35

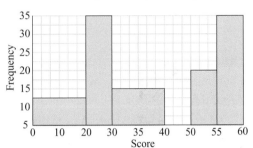

a) Give four criticisms of the histogram. Draw a more appropriate histogram.

b) Would a pie chart be a good way to represent this data? Explain your answer.

3 The histograms below show information about the weights of employees at company A and company B.

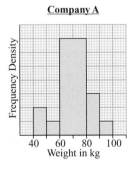

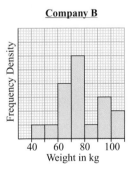

a) Petra says, "More people in company A were between 60 kg and 80 kg than in company B." Is Petra's statement correct? Explain your answer.

b) Gary claims that the range of weights of employees in company B is exactly 10 kg more than the weights of employees in company A. Is Gary likely to be correct? Explain your answer.

c) In which company is the median weight of the employees the greatest? Explain your answer.

4 The scatter graphs below show how the scores on a maths test relate to both the score on an IQ test and the percentage of maths lesson attended.

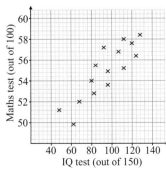

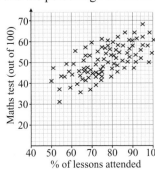

a) Describe the correlation shown by each of the scatter graphs.

b) Jenny says, "Maths test scores are more closely correlated with IQ test scores than with percentage of lessons attended." Do the scatter graphs support her claim? Explain your answer.

Section 36 — Probability

36.1 Calculating Probabilities

All probabilities are between **0 and 1**. An event that's **impossible** has a probability of **0** and an event that's **certain** to happen has a probability of **1**. You can write probabilities as fractions, decimals or percentages.

The different things that could possibly happen are called **outcomes**. When **all** the possible outcomes are **equally likely**, you can work out probabilities of events using this formula:

$$\text{Probability of event} = \frac{\text{number of ways the event can happen}}{\text{total number of possible outcomes}}$$

The probability of an event can be written as P(event).

Example 1

A box contains 20 counters, numbered 1 to 20. If one counter is selected at random, work out the probability that the number is less than 12.

1. All the possible outcomes are equally likely, so use the formula.
   The total number of possible outcomes is the number of counters.   Total possible outcomes = 20

2. Count the number of outcomes that are less than 12.   11 ways of getting less than 12

3. Put the numbers into the formula. $P(\text{less than 12}) = \frac{11}{20}$

Exercise 1

1 Calculate the probability of rolling a fair, six-sided dice and getting each of the following.
   a) 6
   b) 2
   c) 7
   d) 4 or 5
   e) a multiple of 3
   f) a factor of 6

2 A standard pack of 52 playing cards is shuffled and one card is selected at random.
   Find the probability of selecting each of the following.
   a) a club
   b) an ace
   c) a red card
   d) the two of hearts
   e) not a spade
   f) a 4 or a 5

3 A bag contains some coloured balls — 2 black, 4 blue, 2 green, 3 red, 2 yellow, 1 orange, 1 brown and 1 purple. If one ball is selected at random, find the probabilities of getting the following colours.
   a) green
   b) red
   c) orange
   d) black
   e) blue or green
   f) red, green or brown
   g) not purple
   h) white

4 For each of these questions, draw a copy of this spinner and number the sections in a way that fits the given rule.

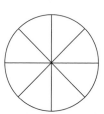

   a) The probability of getting 2 is $\frac{3}{8}$.

   b) The probability of getting 3 is $\frac{1}{2}$.

   c) The probability of getting 5 and the probability of getting 6 are both $\frac{1}{4}$.

5 Diane has 20 pairs of socks and each pair is different. She picks one sock at random. If she then picks another sock at random from the remaining socks, what is the probability that the 2 socks make a pair?

6 A box of identically wrapped chocolates contains 8 caramels, 6 truffles and 4 pralines. Half of each type of chocolate are coated in milk chocolate and half are coated in white chocolate. Chelsea selects a chocolate at random. She doesn't like pralines or white chocolate, but she likes all the others.
  a) What is the probability that she gets a white chocolate coated praline?
  b) What is the probability that she gets a chocolate she likes?

7 This table shows information about the books Harry owns.
If one of Harry's books is selected at random, find the probability it's:
  a) a paperback fiction book
  b) a non-fiction book

	Paperback	Hardback
Fiction	14	6
Non-fiction	2	8

Probabilities That Add Up to 1

Events that **can't happen at the same time** are called **mutually exclusive**.
For example, rolling a 1 and rolling a 3 in one dice roll are mutually exclusive events.

The probabilities of **mutually exclusive events** that cover **all possible outcomes** always **add up to 1**.

For any event there are only two possibilities — it either happens or it doesn't happen.

So: The **probability** an event **doesn't happen** is equal to **1 minus the probability it does happen**.

Example 2

The probability that Kamui's train is late is 0.05. Work out the probability that his train is not late.

The train is either late or not late.   P(train is not late) = 1 – P(train is late)
So P(late) + P(not late) = 1. $= 1 - 0.05 = \underline{\textbf{0.95}}$

Example 3

A bag contains red, green, blue and white counters. This table shows the probabilities of randomly selecting a red, green or white counter from the bag.
Work out the probability of selecting a blue counter.

Colour	Red	Green	Blue	White
Probability	0.2	0.1		0.5

The probabilities of the 4 colours add up to 1. So the   P(blue) = 1 – (0.2 + 0.1 + 0.5)
probability of blue is 1 minus the other 3 probabilities. $= 1 - 0.8 = \underline{\textbf{0.2}}$

Exercise 2

1 The probability that it will snow in a particular Canadian town on a particular day is $\frac{5}{8}$.
What is the probability that it won't snow there on that day?

2 The probability that Clara wins a raffle prize is 25%. Find the probability that she doesn't win a prize.

3 If the probability that Jed doesn't finish a crossword is 0.74, what's the probability he does finish it?

4 The probability that Gary wins a tennis match is twice the probability that he loses it.
Work out the probability that he wins a tennis match.

5 Everyone taking part in a certain lucky dip wins a prize.
The table below shows the probabilities of winning the four possible prizes.

   a) Find the missing probability.

   b) What's the probability of winning a prize that's not a pen?

Prize	Lollipop	Pen	Cuddly toy	Gift voucher
Probability	0.4	0.1		0.2

6 When two football teams play each other the probability that Team A wins is 0.4 and the probability that Team B wins is 0.15. What is the probability that the match is a draw?

7 One counter is selected at random from a box containing blue, green and red counters.
The probability that it's a blue counter is 0.5 and the probability that it's a green counter is 0.4.
If there are four red counters in the box, how many counters are there altogether?

8 A spinner has three sections, coloured pink, blue and green. The probability it lands on pink is 0.1.
If the probability it lands on blue is half the probability it lands on green,
find the probability that it lands on green.

36.2 Listing Outcomes

When **two things** are happening at once, for example a coin toss and a dice roll,
it's much easier to work out probabilities if you **list all the possible outcomes** in a logical way.

It's often a good idea to use a **sample space diagram** (also called a **possibility diagram**),
which can be in the form of a two-way table or grid.

Example 1

Anne has three tickets for a theme park. She chooses two friends at random to go with her.
She chooses one girl from Belinda, Claire and Dee, and one boy from Fred and Greg.
What is the probability that Anne chooses Claire and Fred to go with her?

Girls	Boys
Belinda	Fred
Belinda	Greg
Claire	Fred
Claire	Greg
Dee	Fred
Dee	Greg

1. Use a simple two-column table to list the outcomes.
    Write in each girl in turn and fill in all the possibilities for the boys.
    Each row of the table is a possible outcome.

2. Count the number of rows that Claire
and Fred both appear in. Then divide
by the total number of rows.

    There's 1 outcome that includes both Claire and Fred,
and 6 outcomes in total. So P(Claire and Fred) = $\frac{1}{6}$

Exercise 1

1 A burger bar offers the meal deal shown on the right.
Jana picks one combination of burger and drink at random.

   a) What is the probability she chooses a veggie burger and cola?

   b) What is the probability she chooses at least one of
      cheeseburger and coffee?

> ***Choose 1 burger and 1 drink***
> | *Burgers* | *Drinks* |
> |---|---|
> | Hamburger | Cola |
> | Cheeseburger | Lemonade |
> | Veggie burger | Coffee |

2 The fair spinner shown opposite is spun twice.

   a) What is the probability of spinning 1 on both spins?

   b) What is the probability of getting less than 3 on both spins?

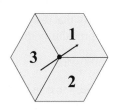

3 A fair coin is tossed three times. Work out the probability of getting:

   a) three tails   **b)** no tails   **c)** one head and two tails

Example 2

Two fair, four-sided dice, one white and one blue, are rolled together. Both are numbered 1-4.

a) List all the possible total scores.

1. Draw a two-way table with the outcomes for one dice across the top and those for the other dice down the side.

2. Fill in each square with the score for the row plus the score for the column.

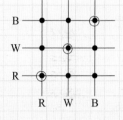

b) What is the probability of scoring a total of 4?

Count how many times a total of 4 appears in the table. Then divide by the total number of outcomes.

3 of the outcomes are 4 and there are 16 outcomes in total. So P(total of 4) = $\frac{3}{16}$

Example 3

A spinner with three equal sections — red, white and blue, is spun twice. Find the probability of spinning the same colour both times.

1. Draw a two-way table or grid to show all the possible outcomes.

2. Count the number of ways of spinning the same colour both times, then divide by the total number of outcomes.

There are 3 ways of spinning the same colour and there are 9 outcomes in total. So P(same colour) = $\frac{3}{9}$ or $\frac{1}{3}$

Exercise 2

1 Two fair six-sided dice are rolled.

a) Copy and complete this table to show all the possible total scores.

b) Find the probability of each of the following total scores.

	1	2	3	4	5	6
1						
2						
3						
4						
5						
6						

    (i) 6   **(ii)** 12   **(iii)** 1

    (iv) less than 8   **(v)** more than 8   **(vi)** an even number

2 Craig likes to eat curries, but he always finds it difficult to choose what type of rice to have. He is equally happy to eat boiled, lemon, pilau or vegetable rice. He decides that from now on, he's going to select his rice at random from those four options.

a) Draw a diagram to show all the possible combinations of rice he could eat with his next two curries.

b) Find the probability that he eats the following types of rice with his next two curries:

    (i) pilau rice both times   **(ii)** the same type both times   **(iii)** lemon rice at least once

3 Tom rolls a fair six-sided dice and spins a spinner with four equal sections labelled A, B, C and D. Find the probability that Tom gets each of the following.

    a) 6 and A   **b)** B and less than 3   **c)** C and an even number

4 Hayley and Asha are playing a game. In each round they both spin a spinner with five equal sections labelled 1 to 5, and whoever gets the higher score wins the round. If the winner spins a 5, she scores 2 points, and if the winner spins less than 5, she scores 1 point. If both players spin the same number, no one wins a point.

a) What is the probability that Hayley wins 1 point in the first round?

b) What is the probability that Hayley wins 2 points in the first round?

Product Rule for Counting Outcomes

Example 4 How many different six-digit numbers are there
that only include the digits 1, 2 and 3?

For each digit in the six-digit number
there are three choices (1, 2 or 3). $3 \times 3 \times 3 \times 3 \times 3 \times 3 = \underline{\underline{729}}$

Exercise 3

1 On a menu in a restaurant there are 4 starters, 8 main courses and 3 desserts to choose from.
   a) How many different three-course meals could you have?
   b) In a two-course meal one of the meals has to be a main course.
      How many different two-course meals could you have?

2 A combination lock has five rotating wheels which can each be set to one of the numbers 0-6.
   a) How many different combinations could you set for the lock?
   b) How many different combinations could you set that only include odd numbers?
   c) If you randomly choose a combination, what is the probability that all wheels are set to odd numbers?

3 A vending machine contains 6 different flavours of fruit juice. Trish buys 4 cans of fruit juice from
   the vending machine. She says, "There are 1296 different combinations of fruit juice I could get."
   Is Trish correct? Explain your answer.

36.3   Probability from Experiments

Relative Frequency

You can **estimate** probabilities using the results of an experiment or what you know has already happened.
Your estimate is the **relative frequency** (also called the **experimental probability**), which you work out
using this formula:

$$\text{Relative frequency} = \frac{\text{Number of times the result happens}}{\text{Number of times the experiment is done}}$$

The **more times** you do the experiment, the **more accurate** the estimate should be.

Example 1

A biased dice is rolled 100 times. Here are the results.
Estimate the probability of rolling a 1 with this dice.

Score	1	2	3	4	5	6
Frequency	11	14	27	15	17	16

Divide the number of times 1 was rolled
by the total number of rolls.

1 was rolled 11 times.
So $P(1) = \frac{11}{100}$

Exercise 1

1 A spinner with four sections is spun 100 times. The results are shown in the table below.
   a) Estimate the probability of spinning each colour.
   b) How could the estimates be made more accurate?

Colour	Red	Green	Yellow	Blue
Frequency	49	34	8	9

2 Stacy rolls a six-sided dice 50 times and 2 comes up 13 times.
   Jason rolls the same dice 100 times and 2 comes up 18 times.
   a) Use Stacy's results to estimate the probability of rolling a 2 on this dice.
   b) Use Jason's results to estimate the probability of rolling a 2 on this dice.
   c) Explain whose estimate should be more accurate.

3 Jamal records the colours of the cars passing his school. Estimate the probability, as a decimal, that the next car passing Jamal's school will be:

Colour	Silver	Black	Red	Blue	Other
Frequency	452	124	237	98	89

    a) silver   **b)** red   **c)** not silver, black, red or blue

4 Jack and his dad have played golf against each other 15 times. Jack has won 8 times.

    a) Estimate the probability that Jack will win the next time they play.

    b) Estimate the probability that Jack's dad will win the next time they play.

5 Describe how Lilia could estimate the probability that the football team she supports will win a match.

Expected Frequency

You can **estimate** the **number of times** an event will happen by working out its **expected frequency**.

> **Expected frequency** = number of times the experiment is done × probability of the event happening

> **Example 2** The probability that a biased dice lands on 1 is 0.2.
> How many times would you expect to roll a 1 if you roll the dice 50 times?
>
> Multiply the number of rolls by the probability of rolling a 1.   50 × 0.2 = **10 times**

Exercise 2

1 The probability that a biased dice lands on 4 is 0.75. How many times would you expect to roll 4 in:

    a) 20 rolls?   **b)** 60 rolls?   **c)** 100 rolls?   **d)** 1000 rolls?

2 The spinner on the right has three equal sections. How many times would you expect to spin 'penguin' in:

    a) 60 spins?   **b)** 300 spins?   **c)** 480 spins?

3 A fair, six-sided dice is rolled 120 times. How many times would you expect to roll:

    a) a 5?   **b)** a 6?   **c)** an even number?   **d)** higher than 1?

Frequency Trees

When an experiment has two or more steps, you can record your results in a **frequency tree**.

> **Example 3** James asks 200 people of various ages to roll a dice.
> There were 120 people under the age of 20 and 16 of them rolled a six.
> Of the people aged 20 and over, 18 rolled a six.
> Fill in the frequency tree below to show this information.
>
> Fill in the bits of the tree given in the question first — the total number of people goes in this box.
>
> The numbers at the end of a set of branches should always add up to the number at the start of the branches.
>
>   200 – 120 = 80 people are aged 20 and over
>   120 – 16 = 104 people under 20 didn't roll a six
>   80 – 18 = 62 people aged 20 and over didn't roll a six
>
> Under 20?   Rolled a six?
>
> 200 — Yes — 120 — Yes — **16**
>   No — **104**
>   No — 80 — Yes — **18**
>   No — **62**

Exercise 3

1   720 truck drivers were asked to do an eye test. 640 said their vision was fine.
    180 of the drivers who said their vision was fine failed the eye test.
    30 of the drivers who said their vision wasn't fine passed the eye test.
    Draw and complete a frequency tree to represent this information.

2   Information on 800 UK residents' hair and eye colour was collected.
    The data was recorded in the two-way table shown on the right.

		Has brown hair?	
		Yes	No
Has brown eyes?	Yes	220	105
	No	335	140

   a) Show the information from this
       two-way table on a frequency tree.

   b) Find the relative frequency of someone having brown hair and brown eyes.

   c) If you collected the same data on another group of 2000 UK residents,
       how many would you estimate won't have brown eyes or brown hair?

Fair or Biased?

Things like dice and spinners are **fair** if they have the same chance of landing on each side or section.
To decide whether something is fair or biased, you need to do an **experiment**. Then you can compare the
experimental results with what you would expect in theory.

For example, if you roll a six-sided dice, you expect it to land on 6 about $\frac{1}{6}$ of the time. So if you rolled it 120 times,
you'd expect about 20 sixes. If 60 of the rolls were 6 (relative frequency of $6 = \frac{1}{2}$), you'd say the dice was **biased**.

Example 4

Here are the results of 60 dice rolls.

Score	1	2	3	4	5	6
Frequency	12	3	9	10	14	12

   a) Work out the relative frequencies of each score.

   1. Work out frequency ÷ 60 for each score.

   $1 = \frac{12}{60} = \underline{\textbf{0.2}}$ $2 = \frac{3}{60} = \underline{\textbf{0.05}}$ $3 = \frac{9}{60} = \underline{\textbf{0.15}}$

   2. Write the probabilities as decimals so
       they're easier to compare.

   $4 = \frac{10}{60} = \underline{\textbf{0.17}}$ $5 = \frac{14}{60} = \underline{\textbf{0.23}}$ $6 = \frac{12}{60} = \underline{\textbf{0.2}}$

   b) Do you think the dice is fair or biased? Explain your answer.
       Compare the relative frequencies to the theoretical probability of $\frac{1}{6} = 0.17$.

       The relative frequency of a score of 2 is very different from the theoretical probability,
       so the experiment suggests that the dice is **biased**.

Exercise 4

1   A spinner has four sections coloured blue, green, white and pink. This table shows the results of 100 spins.

   a) Work out the relative frequencies of the four colours.

   b) Explain whether you think the spinner is fair or biased.

Colour	Blue	Green	White	Pink
Frequency	22	21	18	39

2   A six-sided dice is rolled 120 times and 4 comes up 32 times.

   a) How many times would you expect 4 to come up on a fair dice in 120 rolls?

   b) Use your answer to part **a)** to explain whether you think the dice is fair or biased.

3   Three friends each toss a coin and record the number of heads they get. This table shows their results.

   a) Copy and complete the table.

   b) Explain whose results are the most reliable.

   c) Explain whether you think the coin is fair or biased.

	Amy	Steve	Hal
No. of tosses	20	60	100
No. of heads	12	33	49
Relative frequency			

36.4   The AND Rule for Independent Events

Two events are **independent** if one of them happening has **no effect** on the probability that the other happens.

If A and B are independent events: **P(A and B) = P(A) × P(B)**

Example 1

A biased dice has a probability of 0.2 of landing on 6. The dice is rolled twice.

a) What is the probability that two sixes are rolled?

The first roll has no effect on the second roll, so the events '6 on first roll' and '6 on second roll' are independent.

$$P(\text{6 on 1st roll and 6 on 2nd roll}) = P(\text{6 on 1st}) \times P(\text{6 on 2nd})$$
$$= 0.2 \times 0.2$$
$$= \underline{\mathbf{0.04}}$$

b) What is the probability that neither roll is a 6?

1. On any roll, either a 6 is rolled or a 6 isn't rolled, so P(6) + P(not 6) = 1.
2. The events 'not 6 on first roll' and 'not 6 on second roll' are independent.

$$P(\text{not 6}) = 1 - P(6) = 1 - 0.2 = 0.8$$
$$P(\text{neither roll is a 6}) = P(\text{not 6 on 1st}) \times P(\text{not 6 on 2nd})$$
$$= 0.8 \times 0.8$$
$$= \underline{\mathbf{0.64}}$$

Exercise 1

1   Say whether each of these pairs of events are independent or not.

   a) Tossing a coin and getting heads, then tossing the coin again and getting tails.

   b) Selecting a coffee-flavoured chocolate at random from a box of chocolates. Then, after eating the first chocolate, randomly selecting another coffee-flavoured chocolate from the same box.

   c) Rolling a 6 on a dice and randomly selecting a king from a pack of cards.

2   A fair coin is tossed and a fair, six-sided dice is rolled. Find the probability that the results are:

   a) a head and a 6   **b)** a head and an odd number   **c)** a tail and a square number

   d) a tail and a prime number   **e)** a head and a multiple of 3   **f)** a tail and a factor of 5

3   10% of the pupils in a school are left-handed and 15% wear glasses. Assuming that the hand they write with and glasses wearing are independent, find the probability that a pupil picked at random:

   a) is right-handed   **b)** doesn't wear glasses

   c) wears glasses and is left-handed   **d)** doesn't wear glasses and is right-handed

4   A bag contains ten coloured balls. Five of them are red and three of them are blue. A ball is taken from the bag at random, then replaced. A second ball is then selected at random. Find the probability that:

   a) both balls are red   **b)** neither ball is red   **c)** the first ball is red and the second ball is blue

5   The probability of Selvi passing some exams is shown in the table.
Assuming that her passing any subject is independent of her passing any of the other subjects, find the probability that she:

Subject	Maths	English	Geography	Science
Probability	0.8	0.6	0.3	0.4

   a) passes English and Maths   **b)** passes Maths and Geography   **c)** passes Maths and fails Science

6   The probability of randomly selecting an ace from a pack of cards is $\frac{4}{52}$. Len says the probability of randomly selecting an ace, then randomly selecting another ace (without replacing the first ace) is $\frac{4}{52} \times \frac{4}{52} = \frac{1}{169}$.
Say whether you agree with Len and explain why.

36.5 The OR Rule

The OR Rule for Mutually Exclusive Events

Two events are **mutually exclusive** if they **can't both happen** at the same time — they have no common outcomes.

If A and B are mutually exclusive events: **P(A or B) = P(A) + P(B)**

Example 1

A bag contains red, yellow and blue counters. The probabilities of randomly selecting each colour are shown in the table opposite.

Red	Yellow	Blue
0.3	0.5	0.2

Find the probability that a randomly selected counter is red or blue.

The counter can't be both red and blue, so the events 'counter is red' and 'counter is blue' are mutually exclusive.

P(red or blue) = P(red) + P(blue)
$$= 0.3 + 0.2$$
$$= \textbf{0.5}$$

Exercise 1

1 A fair spinner has eight sections labelled 1 to 8. Say whether these pairs of events are mutually exclusive or not.

   a) The spinner landing on 6 and the spinner landing on 3.

   b) The spinner landing on 2 and the spinner landing on a factor of 6.

   c) The spinner landing on a number less than 4 and the spinner landing on a number greater than 3.

2 A bag contains some coloured balls. The probability of randomly selecting a pink ball is 0.5, a red ball is 0.4 and an orange ball is 0.1. Find the probability that a ball picked out at random will be:

   a) pink or orange   **b)** pink or red   **c)** red or orange

3 Chocolates in a box are wrapped in four different colours of foil — gold, silver, red and blue. The table shows the probabilities of randomly picking a chocolate wrapped in each colour.

Colour	Gold	Silver	Red	Blue
Probability	0.4	0.26	0.14	0.2

   Find the probability of picking a chocolate wrapped in:

   a) red or gold foil   **b)** silver or red foil   **c)** gold or blue foil   **d)** silver or gold foil

4 On sports day, pupils are split into three equal teams — the Eagles, the Falcons and the Ospreys. What is the probability that a pupil picked at random belongs to:

   a) the Eagles?   **b)** the Eagles or the Falcons?   **c)** the Falcons or the Ospreys?

5 Jane is told that in a class of 30 pupils, 4 wear glasses and 10 have blonde hair. She says that the probability that a pupil picked at random from the class will have blonde hair or wear glasses is $\frac{10}{30} + \frac{4}{30} = \frac{14}{30}$.
Say whether you agree with Jane and explain why.

6 The owner of a cafe records the sandwich fillings chosen by customers who buy a sandwich one lunchtime. The table shows the probabilities that a randomly chosen sandwich buyer chose each of five fillings. Customers can choose any combination of fillings, apart from pickle and mayonnaise together.

   a) Find the probability that a randomly selected customer chose pickle or mayonnaise.

Cheese	Tuna	Salad	Pickle	Mayo
0.54	0.5	0.26	0.22	0.28

   b) Explain why the probabilities add up to more than 1.

The General OR Rule

When two events are **not mutually exclusive** (i.e. they **can both happen** at the same time):

$$P(A \text{ or } B) = P(A) + P(B) - P(A \text{ and } B)$$

Example 2 The fair spinner shown is spun once.
What is the probability that it lands on a 2 or a shaded sector?

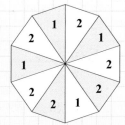

The spinner can land on both 2 and a shaded sector at the same time.

P(2 or shaded) = P(2) + P(shaded) − P(2 and shaded)

$$= \frac{6}{10} + \frac{5}{10} - \frac{2}{10} = \frac{9}{10} = \underline{\textbf{0.9}}$$

Exercise 2

1 A fair 20-sided dice is rolled. What is the probability that it lands on:

  a) a multiple of 3 or an odd number?   **b)** a factor of 20 or a multiple of 4?

2 A card is randomly chosen from a standard pack of 52 playing cards.

  a) What's the probability that it's a red suit or a queen?

  b) What's the probability that it's a club or a picture card?

3 The table shows the number of boys and girls in each year group at a school.
What is the probability that a randomly chosen pupil is:

  a) in Year 11 or a girl?

  b) a boy or not in Year 9?

	Boys	Girls
Year 9	240	310
Year 10	305	287
Year 11	212	146

4 Sumi organises some elements into two sets, A and B.
$n(A) = 28$, $n(B) = 34$, $n(A \cap B) = 12$, $n(\xi) = 100$.
Calculate the probability that a randomly chosen element is in set A or set B.

5 The frequency tree shows some information about scores achieved by girls and boys on a maths test.

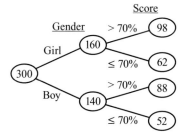

Use the frequency tree to find the probability
that a randomly chosen student is:

  a) a girl or scored $\leq 70\%$ on the maths test.

  b) a boy or scored $> 70\%$ on the maths test.

  c) a boy who scored $\leq 70\%$ or a girl who scored $> 70\%$.

6 The Venn diagram on the right shows three events A, B and C.
A and B are not mutually exclusive.
A and C are mutually exclusive.
B and C are mutually exclusive.

Use the Venn diagram to derive an expression for $P(A \cup B \cup C)$.

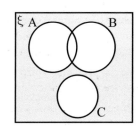

You can work out trickier probability questions by breaking them down into smaller chunks.

Example 1

A biased dice lands on each number with the probabilities shown in the table opposite. The dice is rolled twice.

Find the probability of rolling one 2 and one 3.

1	2	3	4	5	6
0.1	0.15	0.2	0.2	0.3	0.05

1. There are two options for rolling one 2 and one 3.

2. Find the probability of getting 2 on the first roll and 3 on the second roll. These events are independent, so you can multiply the probabilities.

$$P(2, \text{ then } 3) = P(2) \times P(3)$$
$$= 0.15 \times 0.2$$
$$= 0.03$$

3. Find the probability of getting 3 on the first roll and 2 on the second roll.

$$P(3, \text{ then } 2) = P(3) \times P(2)$$
$$= 0.2 \times 0.15$$
$$= 0.03$$

4. Find the probability of getting the first option or the second option. These events are mutually exclusive, so you can add the probabilities.

$$P(2 \text{ then } 3 \text{ or } 3 \text{ then } 2) = 0.03 + 0.03$$
$$= \underline{\mathbf{0.06}}$$

Exercise 1

1   A fair coin is tossed twice. Work out the probability of getting:

a) 2 heads

b) 2 tails

c) both tosses the same

2   All of Justin's shirts are either white or black and all his trousers are either black or grey. The probability that he chooses a white shirt on any day is 0.8. The probability he chooses black trousers is 0.55. His choice of shirt colour is independent of his choice of trousers colour.

On any given day, find the probability that Justin chooses:

a) a white shirt and black trousers

b) a black shirt and black trousers

c) a black shirt and grey trousers

d) either a black shirt or black trousers, but not both

3   A spinner has four sections labelled A, B, C and D.
The probabilities of landing on each section are shown in the table.

If the spinner is spun twice, find the probability of spinning:

A	B	C	D
0.5	0.15	0.05	0.3

a) A both times

b) B both times

c) not C on either spin

d) C, then not C

e) not C, then C

f) C on exactly one spin

4   This table shows how a class of pupils travel to school.
One boy and one girl from the class are picked at random.

Find the probability that:

	Car	Bus	Walk	Cycle
Girls	5	6	3	1
Boys	2	7	2	4

a) both travel by bus

b) the girl walks and the boy travels by car

c) exactly one of them cycles

d) at least one of them cycles

36.7 Tree Diagrams

Tree diagrams show all the possible results for a series of experiments or situations.
They're really useful for working out probabilities of combinations of events.

Example 1

Two fair coins are tossed.

a) Draw a tree diagram showing all the possible results for the two tosses.

1. Draw a set of branches for the first toss.
   You need 1 branch for each of the 2 results.

2. Draw a set of branches for the second toss.
   Again, there are two possible results.

3. Write on the probability for each branch.

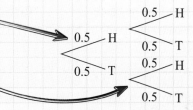

b) Find the probability of getting 2 Heads.
   Multiply along the branches for Heads and Heads.   P(H and H) = 0.5 × 0.5 = **0.25**

c) Find the probability of getting heads and tails in any order.

1. Multiply along the branches for Heads and Tails.   P(H and T) = 0.5 × 0.5 = 0.25
2. Multiply along the branches for Tails and Heads.   P(T and H) = 0.5 × 0.5 = 0.25
3. Both these results give H and T, so add the probabilities.   P(1H and 1T) = 0.25 + 0.25 = **0.5**

Exercise 1

1 Copy and complete the following tree diagrams.

a) A fair spinner has five equal sections
— three are red and two are blue.
The spinner is spun twice.

1st   2nd

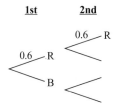

b) A bag contains ten coloured balls — five red,
three blue and two green. A ball is selected
at random and replaced, then a second ball is
selected.

1st   2nd

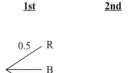

2 For each of these questions, draw a tree diagram showing all the possible results.
Write the probability on each branch.

a) A biased coin lands on heads with a probability
of 0.65. The coin is tossed twice.

b) A spinner with pink and blue sections is spun
twice. The probability it lands on pink is 0.3.

c) A fair six-sided spinner has two sections
labelled 1, two labelled 2 and two labelled 3.
The spinner is spun twice.

d) The probability a football team wins is 0.7,
draws is 0.1 and loses is 0.2. The team plays
three matches.

3 The probability that Freddie beats James at snooker is 0.8. They play two games of snooker.

  a) Draw a tree diagram to show all the possible results for the two games.

  b) Find the probability that Freddie wins both games.

  c) Find the probability that Freddie wins exactly one of the games.

4 Clayton has two fair spinners. Spinner A has six equal sections — five red and one black.
  Spinner B has five equal sections — three red and two black. He spins spinner A, then spinner B.

  a) Draw a tree diagram to show all the possible results of the two spins.

  b) Find the probability that:

   (i) both land on black   **(ii)** both land on red   **(iii)** exactly one lands on red

   (iv) exactly one lands on black   **(v)** both land on the same colour   **(vi)** at least one lands on black

5 On any Saturday, the probability that Alex goes to the cinema is 0.7. Use a tree diagram to work
  out the probability that Alex either goes to the cinema on all three of the next three Saturdays,
  or doesn't go to the cinema on any of the next three Saturdays.

6 Layla rolls a fair six-sided dice three times. Use a tree diagram to find the probability that she rolls:

  a) 'less than 3' on all three rolls   **b)** 'less than 3' once and '3 or more' twice

---

Example 2

Two bags each contain red, green and white balls. This tree diagram shows
all the possible results when one ball is picked at random from each bag.

Find the probability that the two balls picked are different colours.

1. The quickest way to do this is to work out the probability that
    they're the same colour, then subtract this from 1.

2. There are 3 combinations which give the
    same colour — (R,R), (G,G) and (W,W).   P(same) = (0.4 × 0.2) + (0.4 × 0.1) + (0.2 × 0.7) = 0.26

3. P(different colours) = 1 − P(same colour)   P(different colours) = 1 − 0.26 = **0.74**

1st bag	2nd bag

0.4 R   0.2 R
          0.1 G
          0.7 W
0.4 G   0.2 R
          0.1 G
          0.7 W
0.2 W   0.2 R
          0.1 G
          0.7 W

Exercise 2

1 Sally owns 12 DVDs, four of which are comedies, and Jesse owns 20 DVDs, eight of which are comedies.
  They each select one of their DVDs at random to watch over the weekend.

  a) Draw a tree diagram showing the probabilities of each choice being 'comedy' or 'not a comedy'.

  b) Find the probability that neither of them chooses a comedy.

  c) Find the probability that at least one of them chooses a comedy.

2 A fair spinner has six equal sections — three red, two blue and one yellow. It is spun twice.
  Use a tree diagram to find the probability of spinning:

  a) red then red   **b)** blue then red   **c)** yellow then blue

  d) red once and blue once   **e)** the same colour twice   **f)** two different colours

  g) red at least once   **h)** blue at least once   **i)** not yellow then not yellow

36.8 Conditional Probability

The AND Rule for Dependent Events

When probabilities **depend** on what's already happened, they're called **conditional**.

Conditional probabilities often come up in situations where objects are selected **without replacement**. The probabilities for the second selection **depend** on what happened in the first selection.

If **A** and **B** are **dependent** events: **P(A and B) = P(A) × P(B given A)**

Example 1

A box of chocolates contains 10 white chocolates and 10 milk chocolates.

a) Jane picks a chocolate at random. Find the probability that it's a white chocolate.

Use the formula for equally likely outcomes.   20 possible outcomes and 10 are white chocolates

So P(white choc) = $\frac{10}{20}$ or $\frac{1}{2}$

b) Given that Jane has taken a white chocolate, what's the probability that Geoff randomly selects a white chocolate?

This probability is conditional — there are now 19 chocolates left and 9 are white.

19 possible outcomes and 9 are white chocolates

So P(white choc given white choc taken) = $\frac{9}{19}$

c) Use a tree diagram to find the probability that both Jane and Geoff select a white chocolate.

Use the probabilities you've worked out to label the branches. Then multiply along the branches for white and white.

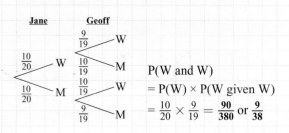

P(W and W)
= P(W) × P(W given W)
= $\frac{10}{20} \times \frac{9}{19} = \frac{90}{380}$ or $\frac{9}{38}$

Exercise 1

1   A bag contains ten balls numbered 1 to 10. Ball 8 is selected at random and not replaced.
Find the probability that the next ball selected at random is ball 7.

2   In a Year 11 class there are 16 boys and 14 girls. Two names are picked at random.
Given that the first student picked is a girl, what is the probability that the second student picked is:
a) a girl?   **b)** a boy?

3   The members of a drama group are choosing their characters for a pantomime. There are nine left to choose — four wizards, three elves and two toadstools. Nobody wants to play the toadstools, so the names of the nine characters are put into a bag so they can be selected at random. John is going to pick first, followed by Kerry.
a) If John picks an elf, what is the probability that Kerry also picks an elf?
b) If John picks an elf, what is the probability that Kerry picks a wizard?
c) If John picks an elf, what is the probability that Kerry picks a toadstool?
d) If John picks a toadstool, what is the probability that Kerry also picks a toadstool?

4 A standard pack of 52 cards contains 13 cards of each of the four suits — hearts, diamonds, clubs and spades. A club is drawn at random from the pack and not replaced. Find the probability that the next card drawn at random:

a) is a club
b) is not a club
c) is a diamond

d) is a black card
e) is a red card
f) has the same value as the 1st card

5 The probability of rolling a 4 on an unfair dice is 0.1.
The probability that in two rolls you score a total of 10, given that a 4 is rolled first, is 0.4.
What is the probability of rolling a 4 on your first roll and having a total score of 10 after two rolls?

6 The probability that Shaun has a stressful day at work is 0.6.
Given that Shaun doesn't have a stressful day at work, the probability he eats ice cream in the evening is 0.2.
What is the probability that Shaun doesn't have a stressful day and eats ice cream?

Exercise 2

1 A school quiz team is chosen by randomly selecting two students from each class.
In class A there are 12 boys and 8 girls.

a) If the first student chosen from class A is a girl, find the probability that the second one chosen is a girl.

b) If the first student chosen from class A is a boy, find the probability that the second one chosen is a girl.

c) Draw a tree diagram showing all the possible results for the two choices from class A.

d) Find the probability that two girls are chosen from class A.

e) Find the probability that two boys are chosen from class A.

2 Two balls are chosen at random from a bag containing five red balls and three blue balls.

a) Draw a tree diagram showing all the possible results for the two choices.

b) Find the probability that both balls are red.

c) Find the probability that both balls are the same colour.

3 The probability that a school bus is late is 0.6 if it was late the day before, but 0.3 if it was not late the day before. Given that the bus is late today:

a) Draw a tree diagram showing all the possible results for the next two days.

b) Find the probability that the bus will be late on both of the next two days.

c) Find the probability that the bus will be late on one of the days, but not late on the other day.

4 A drawer contains 12 socks — 8 blue and 4 grey. Two socks are picked at random.
Use a tree diagram to work out the following probabilities.

a) both socks are blue
b) at least one of the socks is blue
c) both socks are the same colour

5 Latifah has three classical music CDs, four jazz CDs and three pop CDs. She chooses two of these CDs at random to listen to in the car. Use a tree diagram to work out the following probabilities.

a) both CDs are classical
b) one CD is jazz and one CD is pop
c) at least one of the CDs is jazz

d) both CDs are the same style
e) the CDs are different styles
f) neither CD is pop

6 Three children are chosen at random from a class of 15 boys and 12 girls. Find the probability that:

a) no girls are chosen
b) two girls and one boy are chosen

7 Three cards are selected at random from ten cards labelled 1 to 10. Find the probability that:

a) all three cards are even numbers

b) one card is odd and the other two are even

8 When Tom goes to his favourite Italian restaurant he always orders pizza or pasta. The probability that he orders pizza is 0.5 if he ate pizza last time, but 0.9 if he ate pasta last time. Given that he ate pizza last time, find the probability that:

a) He orders pizza on each of the next three times he eats there.

b) He orders pizza on two of the next three times he eats there.

c) He doesn't order pizza on any of the next three times he eats there.

Conditional Probability using Venn Diagrams

Example 2

The Venn diagram shows the number of males (M) and the number of people who are drinking coffee (C) at a cafe.

What is the probability that a randomly selected person at the cafe is male given that they are drinking coffee?

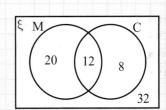

Divide the number of males drinking coffee by the total number of people drinking coffee.

$$P(M \text{ given } C) = \frac{n(M \text{ and } C)}{n(C)} = \frac{12}{12 + 8} = \frac{12}{20} = \mathbf{\underline{0.6}}$$

Exercise 3

1 A survey was taken at a hotel in a ski resort which asked people if they could ski and if they could snowboard. The results are shown in the Venn diagram on the right.

What is the probability that a randomly chosen hotel guest:

a) can ski?   **b)** can snowboard?

c) can ski and can snowboard?

d) can ski given that they can snowboard?

e) can't snowboard given that they can't ski?

2 The Venn diagram below shows the number of members in a drama group who can act (A), dance (D) and sing (S).

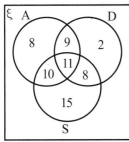

What is the probability that a randomly chosen member:

a) can act given that they can dance?

b) can sing given that they can't dance?

c) can't dance given that they can act?

d) can't act given that they can't sing?

e) can act and dance given that they can sing?

f) can sing and act given that they can't dance?

g) can act or dance given that they can't sing?

36.9　Probability Problems

Exercise 1

1　280 pupils have to choose whether to study history or geography. The numbers choosing each subject are shown in the table opposite.

One pupil is chosen at random. Find the probability that the pupil is:

	History	Geography
Girls	77	56
Boys	63	84

a) a girl studying geography　　**b)** a boy studying geography　　**c)** a girl

d) a boy　　**e)** studying history　　**f)** not studying history

2　Amy's CD collection is organised into four categories — groups, male vocal, female vocal and compilations. The table shows the probability that she randomly selects a CD of each category.

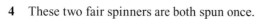

Category	Groups	Male vocal	Female vocal	Compilations
Probability	0.45	0.15	0.1	

a) Find the missing probability from the table.

b) Amy selects one CD at random. What is the probability that it isn't a male vocal CD?

c) Given that Amy has 80 CDs in total, how many female vocal CDs does she have?

3　There is a 0.002 probability that a particular component produced in a factory is faulty.

a) What is the probability that the component is not faulty?

b) 60 000 of these components are produced in a week.

　　(i)　How many of the components would you expect to be faulty?

　　(ii)　How many of the components would you expect not to be faulty?

4　These two fair spinners are both spun once.

a) Show all the possible outcomes using a sample space diagram.

b) Find the probabilities of spinning the following:

　　(i)　double 4　　**(ii)** a 2 and a 3　　**(iii)** both numbers the same

　　(iv) two different numbers　　**(v)** at least one 5　　**(vi)** no fives

c) If the five-sided spinner above is spun 100 times, how many times would you expect to spin 3?

5　One fair spinner has five equal sections numbered from 1 to 5 and a second fair spinner has eight equal sections numbered from 1 to 8. The spinners are both spun once and the (non-negative) difference between the two scores is found.

a) Draw a two-way table to show all the possible outcomes.

b) Find the probability of getting each of the following differences.

　　(i)　0　　**(ii)** 2　　**(iii)** 5　　**(iv)**　6

　　(v)　3　　**(vi)** 1　　**(vii)** 4　　**(viii)** 7

　　(ix) less than 2　　**(x)** 2 or more　　**(xi)**　4 or more　　**(xii)**　less than 4

6　At a fast food restaurant there are two options for side dishes — fries or salad. The side dish choices of 200 customers are recorded in this Venn diagram.

What is the probability that a randomly chosen customer:

a) only had salad?　　　　**b)** only had fries?

c) didn't have a side?　　　**d)** had fries and salad?

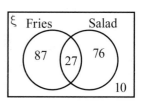

7 Kate and Sarah are members of a snail-racing club. Their snails have raced each other 30 times. Kate's snail has won 17 of the races, Sarah's snail has won 12 of the races and one memorable race was a tie.

a) Estimate the probability that:

(i) Kate's snail will win their next race   (ii) the snails will tie their next race

b) How many of their next ten races would you expect Sarah's snail to win?

8 The results of rolling a four-sided dice 200 times are shown in the table.

a) Work out the relative frequencies of the dice scores.

Score	1	2	3	4
Frequency	56	34	54	56

b) Explain whether these results suggest that the dice is fair or biased.

c) Estimate the probability or rolling a 1 or a 2 with this dice.

d) Salim rolls this dice and tosses a fair coin. Estimate the probability that he gets a 2 and heads.

9 The probability that Colin wins any game of chess is 0.8. Work out the following probabilities.

a) He wins both of his next two games.   b) He wins neither of his next two games.

c) He wins his next game but loses the one after.   d) He wins one of his next two games.

10 A box contains ten coloured marbles — five blue, four white and one red. Two marbles are picked at random.

a) Draw a tree diagram showing all the possible results.

b) Work out the following probabilities.

(i) Both are blue   (ii) Neither is blue   (iii) Exactly one is blue

(iv) At least one is blue   (v) One is red and one is white   (vi) They are different colours

11 A board game has four categories of question, each split into two difficulty levels. The table shows the probability of randomly selecting a question card of each type.

	Easy	Challenge
TV	0.20	0.10
Music	0.15	0.07
Sport	0.12	0.08
Literature	0.15	

a) Find the missing probability from the table.

b) Which of the four categories has the most easy questions?

c) Mark randomly selects one card from all the question cards. What is the probability that he selects:

(i) a music question?   (ii) a sport question?   (iii) a music or a sport question?

(iv) a music question or a challenging question?   (v) an easy question or a sport question?

d) Dahlia plays two games of the board game. Each game starts with the first question card being randomly selected from all the cards. Find the probability that the two starting cards are:

(i) both challenge music questions   (ii) both easy literature questions

12 Eight friends have to pick three from the group to represent them at a meeting. Five of the friends are in Year 10 and three are in Year 11. If they pick the three representatives at random, find the probability that:

a) all three are in Year 10   b) all three are in Year 11

c) two are in Year 10 and one is in Year 11   d) two are in Year 11 and one is in Year 10

Answers

and

Index

Answers

.1 Calculations

Page 2 Exercise 1

1 a) 8   b) 1   c) 16   d) 8   e) 9
   f) 33   g) 28   h) 15   i) 10   j) 7
   k) 25   l) 11   m)17   n) 26   o) 3
   p) 5   q) 14   r) 3   s) 2   t) 13

2 a) 2   b) 2   c) 4   d) $4\frac{1}{2}$
   e) $\frac{3}{5}$ f) $\frac{2}{3}$ g) 3   h) 1

Page 2 Exercise 2

1 a) −1   b) −5   c) 3   d) −11
   e) 6   f) −4   g) −10   h) 0
   i) 12   j) 26   k) −60   l) 90

Page 3 Exercise 3

1 a) −12   b) 5   c) −3   d) −16
   e) 12   f) −7   g) 48   h) 9
   i) 39   j) −42   k) −5   l) −68

2 a) 1   b) −1   c) 45   d) −90
   e) −49   f) 40   g) 50   h) 72

3 a) 2   b) 7   c) −4   d) 10
   e) 3   f) −6   g) −12   h) −77

Page 3 Exercise 4

1 a) 3.8   b) 0.9   c) 19.74   d) 4.409
   e) 6.9   f) 11.7   g) 3.5   h) 0.77
   i) 18.23 j) 1.829 k) 92.192 l) 7.394
   m)63.19   n) 11.14 o) 6.441   p) 0.876

2 a) 7.61 + 0.60 = 8.21   b) 5.98 + 0.42 = 6.40
   c) 6.75 + 2.48 = 9.23   d) 5.43 − 2.12 = 3.31

3 6.9 km   4 £50.49
5 1.45 m   6 £51.24

Page 4 Exercise 5

1 a) 3141.6   b) 31.416
   c) 0.31416   d) 0.031416

2 a) 9.2   b) 141   c) 72 500 d) 133.6
   e) 187.2   f) 206.4 g) 124   h) 420
   i) 0.18   j) 0.002 k) 0.04   l) 0.0008
   m)1.26   n) 4.05   o) 1.08   p) 0.064
   q) 0.366   r) 0.468 s) 13.23   t) 3.22
   u) 4.32   v) 32.37 w) 0.528   x) 0.2688

3 8.8 pints   4 5.6 km
5 £12.42   6 £2.95

Page 4 Exercise 6

1 a) 2.59   b) 2.13   c) 0.535   d) 1.724
   e) 2.85   f) 0.009 g) 7.05   h) 1.5075

2 a) 32   b) 7.8   c) 2.08   d) 44
   e) 8.85   f) 9.435 g) 11.5   h) 0.55
   i) 752   j) 821   k) 5.14   l) 13.5
   m)255.5   n) 0.65   o) 150   p) 720
   q) 30   r) 355   s) 700   t) 270
   u) 220   v) 40.03 w) 2880   x) 1.2

3 £137.62   4 £3.95
5 34   6 £1.98

Page 5 Exercise 7

1 −1 °C   2 −3.75
3 £83.21   4 14.85 s
5 £6.33   6 £13.65
7 £0.86

1.2 Multiples and Factors

Page 6 Exercise 1

1 a) 9, 18, 27, 36, 45   b) 13,26, 39, 52, 65
   c) 16, 32, 48, 64, 80

2 a) 16   b) 24, 36. 48. 60, 72, 84, 96
   c) 28, 42, 56, 70, 84

3 a) 10, 20, 30, 40, 50, 60, 70, 80, 90, 100
   b) 15, 30, 45, 60, 75, 90, 105
   c) 30, 60, 90

4 a) 21, 24, 27, 30, 33
   b) 20, 24, 28, 32   c) 24

5 30   6 None
7 None   8 18, 36, 54, 72, 90

Page 6 Exercise 2

1 a) 1, 2, 5, 10   b) 1, 2, 4
   c) 1, 13   d) 1, 2, 4, 5, 10, 20
   e) 1, 5, 25   f) 1, 2, 3, 4, 6, 8, 12, 24
   g) 1, 5, 7, 35   h) 1, 2, 4, 8, 16, 32
   i) 1, 2, 4, 5, 8, 10, 20, 40
   j) 1, 2, 5, 10, 25, 50
   k) 1, 3, 9   l) 1, 3, 5, 15
   m)1, 2, 3, 4, 6, 9, 12, 18, 36   n) 1, 7, 49
   o) 1, 2, 3, 4, 6, 8, 12, 16, 24, 48

2 a) 1   b) 1, 2   c) 1, 5   d) 1, 2, 5, 10
3 6 — 1 × 12, 2 × 6, 3 × 4, 4 × 3, 6 × 2, 12 × 1
4 9 — 1 × 100, 2 × 50, 4 × 25, 5 × 20, 10 × 10,
   20 × 5, 25 × 4, 50 × 2, 100 × 1
5 a) (i) 1, 3, 5, 15   (ii)   1, 3, 7, 21
   b) 1, 3
6 a) 1, 5   b) 1, 3
   c) 1, 3, 5, 15   d) 1, 2, 5, 10
   e) 1, 5, 25   f) 1, 2, 4, 8
   g) 1, 2, 3, 4, 6, 12   h) 1, 2, 4, 8, 16
   i) 1, 3, 9   j) 1, 2, 3, 4, 6, 12
7 a) 1, 5   b) 1, 2   c) 1, 5
   d) 1   e) 1, 2, 4   f) 1, 3, 9
   g) 1, 2, 3, 4, 6, 8, 12, 24   h) 1, 11

1.3 Prime Numbers and Prime Factors

Page 7 Exercise 1

1 a) 15   b) 3, 5
2 a) 33, 35, 39
   b) 33 = 3 × 11, 35 = 5 × 7, 39 = 3 × 13
3 5, 47, 59
4 a) 2, 3, 5, 7   b) 23, 29, 31, 37, 41, 43, 47
5 a) (i) 2   (ii) 2, 7   (iii) 2, 17   (iv) 2, 37
   b) Numbers ending in 4 are even, so they are
      divisible by 2.
6 E.g. They all end in zero, and are therefore
   divisible by 10.

Page 8 Exercise 2

1 a) 2 × 7   b) 3 × 11   c) 2 × 5   d) 5 × 5
   e) 5 × 11   f) 3 × 5   g) 3 × 7   h) 2 × 11
   i) 5 × 7   j) 3 × 13   k) 7 × 11   l) 11 × 11

2 a) (i)

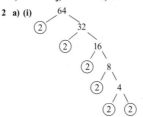

2 (ii)

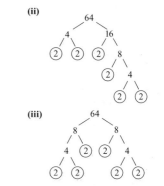

(iii)

64
8   8
4 2 2 4
2 2   2 2

b) 2^6
All the factor trees give the same answer,
however you break the number down.

3 a) 2 × 3   b) 2 × 3 × 5
   c) 2 × 3 × 7   d) 2 × 3 × 11
   e) 2 × 5 × 7   f) 2 × 23
   g) 2 × 5 × 11   h) 2 × 3 × 13
   i) 2 × 5 × 19   j) 2 × 3 × 5 × 7
   k) 2 × 3 × 23   l) 3 × 5 × 17

4 a) 2^3 b) $2^2 \times 11$ c) $2^3 \times 3$
   d) 2^4 e) $2^4 \times 3$ f) $2^3 \times 3^2$
   g) $2 \times 3^2 \times 5$ h) 2×3^2 i) 2×5^2
   j) $2^2 \times 7$ k) 3^3 l) $2^2 \times 3 \times 5$
   m)2×7^2 n) $2^2 \times 3^2$ o) $2 \times 3 \times 5^2$
   p) $2^2 \times 3 \times 11$ q) $2^3 \times 3 \times 7$ r) $3^2 \times 5^2$
   s) $5^2 \times 13$ t) $2^3 \times 5^3$

5 a) 3×5^2
   b) 3 — This way it would be $(3 \times 5)^2 = 15^2$.
6 a) 5   b) 10   c) 26   d) 21   e) 15

1.4 LCM and HCF

Page 9 Exercise 1

1 a) 12   b) 15   c) 24   d) 10
   e) 42   f) 36   g) 30   h) 60

2 a) 24   b) 30   c) 30
   d) 36   e) 70   f) 90

3 a) 8, 16, 24, 32, 40, 48, 56, 64, 72, 80
   b) 12, 24, 36, 48, 60, 72, 84, 96, 108, 120
   c) After 24 minutes.

4 20   5 150
6 280   7 35

Page 10 Exercise 2

1 a) 1, 2, 4   b) 4
2 a) 4   b) 8   c) 6   d) 12
   e) 1   f) 12   g) 7   h) 7
3 a) 2   b) 3   c) 6
   d) 18   e) 12   f) 25
4 19
5 a) 9   b) 13
6 20

Page 11 Exercise 3

1 a) $2 \times 3 \times 5^2$, 2×5^3 b) 50
2 a) $2^3 \times 3 \times 5$, 5×31 b) 5
3 a) $2^2 \times 19$, $2^3 \times 11$ b) 1672
4 a) $2 \times 3 \times 5 \times 7$, $2^2 \times 5^2 \times 7$ b) 2100
5 a) (i) 12   (ii) 144
   b) (i) 15   (ii) 300
   c) (i) 6   (ii) 864
   d) (i) 36   (ii) 432
   e) (i) 40   (ii) 1200
   f) (i) 28   (ii) 1176
   g) (i) 14   (ii) 4620
   h) (i) 30   (ii) 900
6 31   7 32 232

8 156 **9** 105
10 10 152
11 a) 30 = 2 × 3 × 5
 140 = 2^2 × 5 × 7
 210 = 2 × 3 × 5 × 7
b) 10
12 a) 121 = 11^2
 280 = 2^3 × 5 × 7
 550 = 2 × 5^2 × 11
b) 169 400
13 a) (i) 1 **(ii)** 15 015
b) (i) 63 **(ii)** 3969
c) (i) 35 **(ii)** 1225
d) (i) 3 **(ii)** 154 350
e) (i) 2 **(ii)** 728 728
f) (i) 17 **(ii)** 235 620
g) (i) 385 **(ii)** 20 020
h) (i) 11 **(ii)** 2 166 021
14 a) 12, 120 or 24, 60
b) 20, 300 or 60, 100

Section 2 — Approximations

2.1 Rounding

Page 12 Exercise 1
1 a) (i) 10 **(ii)** 8 **(iii)** 12
  (iv) 46 **(v)** 11
b) (i) 30 **(ii)** 30 **(iii)** 50
  (iv) 660 **(v)** 187 520
c) (i) 200 **(ii)** 600 **(iii)** 4700
  (iv) 2400 **(v)** 12 300
d) (i) 3000 **(ii)** 9000 **(iii)** 0
  (iv) 10 000 **(v)** 57 000
2 301 000 km²
3 391 000 000 miles

Page 12 Exercise 2
1 a) (i) 2.7 **(ii)** 2.689
b) (i) 0 **(ii)** 0.032
c) (i) 5.6 **(ii)** 5.602
d) (i) 0 **(ii)** 0.043
e) (i) 6.3 **(ii)** 6.257
f) (i) 0.4 **(ii)** 0.353
g) (i) 0.1 **(ii)** 0.080
h) (i) 1.0 **(ii)** 0.967
i) (i) 0.3 **(ii)** 0.255
j) (i) 2.4 **(ii)** 2.437
k) (i) 6.5 **(ii)** 6.533
l) (i) 0 **(ii)** 0.009
2 0.04 kg   **3** 1.2 m

Page 13 Exercise 3
1 a) 500 **b)** 30 **c)** 7000
d) 900 **e)** 4000 **f)** 80 000
g) 100 000 **h)** 1000 **i)** 0.07
j) 0.3 **k)** 0.0006 **l)** 0.02
m) 0.5 **n)** 0.0008 **o)** 0.1
2 a) 740 **b)** 6600 **c)** 7100
d) 2600 **e)** 12 **f)** 670
g) 140 000 **h)** 970 **i)** 0.0038
j) 0.026 **k)** 0.00018 **l)** 0.087
m) 3600 **n)** 0.56 **o)** 0.00070
3 a) 4760 **b)** 46.9 **c)** 5070
d) 595 **e)** 35 700 **f)** 694 000
g) 80.6 **h)** 925 000 **i)** 0.579
j) 0.0852 **k)** 0.107 **l)** 0.000418
m) 147 **n)** 34.7 **o)** 0.00845
4 1200 km/h
5 121 000 km
6 0.09 kg/m³

7

Mammal	Mass (kg)
Common Vole	0.028
Badger	9.1
Meerkat	0.78
Red Squirrel	0.20
Shrew	0.0061
Hare	3.7

Page 13 Exercise 4
1 a) 400 **b)** 2400 **c)** 40
d) 1000 **e)** 50 **f)** 0.8
g) 100 **h)** 25 **i)** 5
j) 32 **k)** 1000 **l)** 4
2 a) 5252 **b)** 47.04 **c)** 1115.52
d) 1259.50 **e)** 3.04 **f)** 47.42
g) 0.255 **h)** 95.55
3 a) 50 **b)** 1.8 **c)** 0.3
d) 3 **e)** 20 **f)** 7.5
g) 200 **h)** $\frac{1}{9}$

Page 14 Exercise 5
1 a) 4 **b)** 8 **c)** 7
d) 9 **e)** 11
2 a) 3.3 **b)** 5.5 **c)** 4.5
d) 6.1 **e)** 6.7

2.2 Upper and Lower Bounds

Page 14 Exercise 1
1 a) 9.5, 10.5 **b)** 14.5, 15.5
c) 33.5, 34.5 **d)** 25.5, 26.5
e) 75.5, 76.5 **f)** 101.5, 102.5
g) 98.5, 99.5 **h)** 998.5, 999.5
i) 248.5, 249.5 **j)** 2499.5, 2500.5
2 a) 644.5 kg, 645.5 kg **b)** 254.5 l, 255.5 l
c) 164.5 g, 165.5 g **d)** 750 g, 850 g
e) 154.5 cm, 155.5 cm **f)** 129.5 km, 130.5 km
3 a) £14.50, £15.50 **b)** £315, £325
c) £76.65, £76.75 **d)** £575, £625

Page 15 Exercise 2
1 a) maximum 24 cm, minimum 20 cm
b) maximum 18 m, minimum 14 m
c) maximum 22.5 cm, minimum 19.5 cm
d) maximum 36.4 cm, minimum 36 cm
e) maximum 62.75 cm, minimum 62.25 cm
2 a) 675 sweets **b)** 665 sweets
3 12.02 m
4 tallest 1.405 m, shortest 1.295 m
5 0.395

Page 15 Exercise 3
1 a) (i) 1.5 m **(ii)** 15.5 m, 12.5 m
  (iii) 14 m **(iv)** 54.5 m
b) 49.5 m
2 maximum 16.15 m, minimum 15.65 m
3 max. 22.93 m³, min. 22.67 m³ (both to 2 d.p.)
4 a) maximum 35.75 cm², minimum 24.75 cm²
b) max. 274.625 cm³, min. 166.375 cm³
c) maximum 89.26 cm³, minimum 83.29 cm³
5 68.25 m
6 max. 5.80 m/s, min. 5.74 m/s (both to 2 d.p.)
7 0.187 cm/s (to 3 d.p.)
8 1.64 litres (to 2 d.p.)

Page 16 Exercise 4
1 a) 1.3 **b)** 19.1 **c)** 55.7
d) 103.6 **e)** 85.9
2 a) 2738.29 **b)** 1.24 **c)** 3.38
d) 17.16 **e)** 100.09

Page 16 Exercise 5
1 a) 7.55 ≤ m < 7.65 **b)** 15.15 ≤ n < 15.25
c) 37.05 ≤ p < 37.15 **d)** 109.85 ≤ q < 109.95
e) 69.95 ≤ r < 70.05

2 a) 6.57 ≤ s < 6.58 **b)** 25.71 ≤ t < 25.72
c) 33.47 ≤ u < 33.48 **d)** 99.99 ≤ v < 100
e) 51.00 ≤ w < 51.01
3 9.95 km ≤ d < 10.05 km
4 14.635 ≤ 2x + y < 14.845

Section 3 — Fractions

3.1 Equivalent Fractions

Page 17 Exercise 1
1 a) 2 **b)** 3 **c)** 12 **d)** 3
e) 25 **f)** 18 **g)** 60 **h)** 90
i) 3 **j)** 5 **k)** 2 **l)** 3
m) 5 **n)** 27 **o)** 16 **p)** 11
2 Dev

Page 18 Exercise 2
1 a) $\frac{1}{5}$ **b)** $\frac{5}{12}$ **c)** $\frac{3}{4}$ **d)** $\frac{4}{5}$ **e)** $\frac{3}{5}$
f) $\frac{3}{8}$ **g)** $\frac{4}{9}$ **h)** $\frac{3}{11}$ **i)** $\frac{2}{7}$ **j)** $\frac{5}{13}$
2 a) $\frac{5}{20}$ $\left(\frac{6}{18} = \frac{1}{3}, \frac{5}{20} = \frac{1}{4}, \frac{9}{27} = \frac{1}{3}\right)$
b) $\frac{6}{8}$ $\left(\frac{6}{8} = \frac{3}{4}, \frac{9}{15} = \frac{3}{5}, \frac{15}{25} = \frac{3}{5}\right)$
c) $\frac{6}{33}$ $\left(\frac{4}{18} = \frac{2}{9}, \frac{6}{33} = \frac{2}{11}, \frac{9}{27} = \frac{2}{9}\right)$
d) $\frac{24}{40}$ $\left(\frac{18}{24} = \frac{3}{4}, \frac{60}{80} = \frac{3}{4}, \frac{24}{40} = \frac{3}{5}\right)$
3 a) $\frac{7}{10}$ **b)** $\frac{35}{46}$ **c)** $\frac{17}{29}$ **d)** $\frac{49}{166}$

3.2 Mixed Numbers

Page 18 Exercise 1
1 a) 4 **b)** 9 **c)** 5 **d)** 25
2 a) $\frac{9}{5}$ **b)** $\frac{17}{12}$ **c)** $\frac{29}{10}$ **d)** $\frac{53}{10}$
e) $\frac{19}{4}$ **f)** $\frac{59}{6}$ **g)** $\frac{62}{5}$ **h)** $\frac{110}{7}$
i) $\frac{41}{6}$ **j)** $\frac{28}{9}$ **k)** $\frac{103}{10}$ **l)** $\frac{23}{3}$

Page 19 Exercise 2
1 a) $1\frac{2}{3}$ **b)** $1\frac{4}{5}$ **c)** $1\frac{7}{10}$ **d)** $1\frac{5}{7}$ **e)** $1\frac{2}{11}$
f) $2\frac{1}{4}$ **g)** $2\frac{1}{6}$ **h)** $3\frac{1}{5}$ **i)** $2\frac{2}{9}$ **j)** $3\frac{2}{3}$
2 a) $\frac{13}{2}$ **b)** $6\frac{1}{2}$
3 a) $1\frac{1}{2}$ **b)** $2\frac{1}{2}$ **c)** $3\frac{1}{3}$ **d)** $4\frac{1}{2}$ **e)** $1\frac{1}{3}$
f) $1\frac{2}{3}$ **g)** $2\frac{1}{4}$ **h)** $4\frac{1}{4}$ **i)** $5\frac{2}{3}$ **j)** $12\frac{1}{4}$
4 a) $\frac{5}{2}$ **b)** $3\frac{1}{2}$ **c)** $\frac{15}{4}$ **d)** $\frac{11}{3}$

3.3 Ordering Fractions

Page 20 Exercise 1
1 a) E.g. $\frac{2}{9}, \frac{3}{9}$ **b)** E.g. $\frac{8}{12}, \frac{9}{12}$
c) E.g. $\frac{35}{42}, \frac{6}{42}$ **d)** E.g. $\frac{4}{18}, \frac{9}{18}$
e) E.g. $\frac{15}{40}, \frac{32}{40}$ **f)** E.g. $\frac{10}{12}, \frac{7}{12}$
g) E.g. $\frac{35}{40}, \frac{12}{40}$ **h)** E.g. $\frac{18}{45}, \frac{20}{45}$
2 a) E.g. $\frac{18}{24}, \frac{15}{24}, \frac{14}{24}$ **b)** E.g. $\frac{4}{20}, \frac{14}{20}, \frac{9}{20}$
c) E.g. $\frac{6}{42}, \frac{8}{42}, \frac{15}{42}$ **d)** E.g. $\frac{12}{24}, \frac{9}{24}, \frac{16}{24}$
e) E.g. $\frac{24}{60}, \frac{25}{60}, \frac{22}{60}$ **f)** E.g. $\frac{5}{40}, \frac{14}{40}, \frac{24}{40}$
g) E.g. $\frac{28}{42}, \frac{30}{42}, \frac{35}{42}$ **h)** E.g. $\frac{100}{360}, \frac{105}{360},$

1 a) $\frac{5}{8}$ b) $\frac{7}{10}$ c) $\frac{9}{14}$ d) $\frac{2}{3}$

e) $\frac{5}{6}$ f) $\frac{2}{3}$ g) $\frac{3}{4}$ h) $\frac{3}{4}$

2 a) $\frac{7}{16}, \frac{1}{2}, \frac{5}{8}$ b) $\frac{3}{10}, \frac{7}{20}, \frac{2}{5}$

c) $\frac{7}{12}, \frac{5}{8}, \frac{3}{4}$ d) $\frac{19}{24}, \frac{5}{6}, \frac{11}{12}$

3 a) $\frac{5}{12}, \frac{4}{9}, \frac{2}{3}$ b) $\frac{4}{5}, \frac{9}{10}, \frac{11}{12}$

c) $\frac{5}{22}, \frac{1}{4}, \frac{3}{11}$ d) $\frac{7}{9}, \frac{4}{5}, \frac{13}{15}$

e) $\frac{13}{16}, \frac{5}{6}, \frac{7}{8}$ f) $\frac{3}{15}, \frac{7}{27}, \frac{12}{45}$

g) $\frac{5}{16}, \frac{7}{20}, \frac{9}{25}$ h) $\frac{4}{15}, \frac{11}{36}, \frac{9}{24}$

4 Charlene

4 Adding and Subtracting Fractions

1 a) $\frac{5}{12}$ b) $\frac{22}{15} = 1\frac{7}{15}$

c) $\frac{26}{15} = 1\frac{11}{15}$ d) $\frac{33}{28} = 1\frac{5}{28}$

e) $\frac{131}{99} = 1\frac{32}{99}$ f) $\frac{92}{63} = 1\frac{29}{63}$

g) $\frac{51}{35} = 1\frac{16}{35}$ h) $\frac{123}{80} = 1\frac{43}{80}$

2 a) $\frac{23}{18} = 1\frac{5}{18}$ b) $\frac{11}{20}$ c) $\frac{7}{16}$ d) $\frac{3}{7}$

e) $\frac{7}{4} = 1\frac{3}{4}$ f) $\frac{11}{15}$ g) $\frac{19}{60}$

h) $\frac{65}{42} = 1\frac{23}{42}$

1 $\frac{3}{10}$ **2** $\frac{19}{56}$ **3** $\frac{1}{3}$ **4** $\frac{89}{180}$

1 a) $1\frac{5}{8}$ b) $1\frac{7}{12}$ c) $2\frac{5}{14}$ d) $5\frac{17}{18}$

2 a) $2\frac{7}{20}$ b) $3\frac{7}{24}$ c) $5\frac{22}{35}$ d) $5\frac{19}{30}$

e) $3\frac{1}{28}$ f) $1\frac{28}{45}$ g) $\frac{11}{28}$ h) $6\frac{4}{33}$

i) $8\frac{59}{60}$ j) $3\frac{11}{72}$ k) $5\frac{8}{63}$ l) $3\frac{17}{30}$

3 $67\frac{41}{72}$

5 Multiplying and Dividing Fractions

1 a) $13\frac{5}{9}$ b) $4\frac{1}{2}$ c) $21\frac{1}{3}$ d) $27\frac{1}{5}$

e) $17\frac{7}{9}$ f) $18\frac{3}{4}$ g) $19\frac{7}{11}$ h) $38\frac{3}{4}$

2 a) 21 b) $7\frac{1}{9}$ c) 18 d) 25

e) 20 f) 12 g) $22\frac{1}{2}$ h) $57\frac{1}{6}$

1 a) $\frac{1}{10}$ b) $\frac{1}{9}$ c) $\frac{5}{16}$ d) $\frac{3}{4}$ e) $\frac{1}{4}$

2 a) $\frac{11}{9} = 1\frac{2}{9}$ b) $\frac{3}{2} = 1\frac{1}{2}$ c) $\frac{10}{21}$

d) $\frac{23}{48}$ e) $\frac{92}{25} = 3\frac{17}{25}$ f) $\frac{11}{12}$

g) $\frac{323}{42} = 7\frac{29}{42}$ h) $\frac{155}{24} = 6\frac{11}{24}$

1 a) $\frac{4}{3} = 1\frac{1}{3}$ b) $\frac{10}{11}$ c) $\frac{2}{15}$ d) $\frac{1}{14}$

2 a) $\frac{12}{23}$ b) $\frac{4}{11}$ c) $\frac{3}{17}$ d) $\frac{7}{30}$

3 a) $\frac{15}{2} = 7\frac{1}{2}$ b) $\frac{14}{3} = 4\frac{2}{3}$

c) $\frac{17}{21}$ d) $\frac{20}{27}$ e) $\frac{10}{51}$

---

f) $\frac{21}{116}$ g) $\frac{36}{217}$ h) $\frac{40}{549}$

i) $\frac{25}{24} = 1\frac{1}{24}$ j) $\frac{32}{15} = 2\frac{2}{15}$

k) $\frac{29}{14} = 2\frac{1}{14}$ l) $\frac{110}{63} = 1\frac{47}{63}$

m) $\frac{57}{14} = 4\frac{1}{14}$ n) $\frac{64}{23} = 2\frac{18}{23}$

o) $\frac{20}{7} = 2\frac{6}{7}$ p) $\frac{77}{50} = 1\frac{27}{50}$

3.6   Fractions and Decimals

Page 24   Exercise 1

1 a) 0.658 b) 0.7578125 c) 2.125
   d) 6.35 e) 2.37 f) 4.719
   g) 7.34375 h) 8.4375

2 a) $0.8\dot{3}$ b) $0.\dot{4}$ c) $0.\dot{6}0\dot{3}$ d) $0.123\dot{4}$
   e) $0.2\dot{6}$ f) $0.\dot{1}23\dot{4}$ g) $29.\dot{3}$ h) $3.\dot{7}073\dot{1}$

3 a) $\frac{87}{160}, \frac{196}{360}, \frac{167}{287}$ b) $\frac{5}{6}, \frac{16}{17}, \frac{96}{99}$

   c) $\frac{13}{9}, \frac{77}{52}, \frac{963}{650}$

Page 25   Exercise 2

1 a) 65 b) 0.65

2 a) 0.46 b) 0.492 c) 0.3 d) 0.6
   e) 0.34 f) 0.88 g) 0.86 h) 0.32
   i) 0.002 j) 0.132 k) 0.515 l) 0.102
   m) 0.4 n) 0.48 o) 0.666 p) 0.48
   q) 0.09 r) 0.62 s) 0.35 t) 0.615

3 a) 0.02 b) 0.025 c) 0.45 d) 0.0625
   e) 0.875 f) 0.175 g) 0.008 h) 0.1625
   i) 0.09375 j) 0.65625

Page 26   Exercise 3

1 a) $0.\dot{4}$ b) $0.1\dot{6}$ c) $0.0\dot{9}$ d) $0.\dot{6}$
   e) $0.3\dot{6}$ f) $0.4\dot{6}$ g) $0.8\dot{3}$ h) $0.\dot{7}$
   i) $0.3\dot{6}$ j) $0.6\dot{2}$ k) $0.5\dot{2}$ l) $0.2\dot{4}\dot{5}$

2 a) (i) $0.\dot{1}42857$ (ii) $0.\dot{2}85714$
   (iii) $0.\dot{4}2857\dot{1}$ (iv) $0.\dot{5}71428$
   (v) $0.\dot{7}14285$
   b) In each case it is the same pattern
   with a different start point.
   c) $0.\dot{8}5714\dot{2}$

Page 27   Exercise 4

1 a) $\frac{3}{25}$ b) $\frac{59}{250}$ c) $\frac{21}{250}$

   d) $\frac{3}{8}$ e) $\frac{7654321}{10000000}$

2 a) $\frac{2}{11}$ b) $\frac{1}{99}$ c) $\frac{23}{111}$ d) $\frac{800}{1111}$ e) $\frac{1}{7}$

3 a) $\frac{1}{9}$ b) $\frac{34}{99}$ c) $\frac{863}{999}$ d) $\frac{5}{66}$ e) $\frac{48}{55}$

3.7   Fractions Problems

Page 27   Exercise 1

1 $\frac{2}{3}, \frac{11}{16}, \frac{3}{4}, \frac{5}{6} = \frac{32}{48}, \frac{33}{48}, \frac{36}{48}, \frac{40}{48}$

2 a) $0.39, 0.35, 0.32, 0.3$

   b) $\frac{3}{10}, \frac{8}{25}, \frac{7}{20}, \frac{39}{100}$

3
```
0 ├┬┬┬┬┬┬┬┬┬┬┬┬┬┬┬┤ 1
   a) 1/3  c) 5/12  b) 5/8  d) 5/6
```

4 a) $\frac{29}{21} = 1\frac{8}{21}$ b) $\frac{11}{72}$

c) $\frac{11}{10} = 1\frac{1}{10}$ d) $\frac{11}{40}$

5 a) $\frac{7}{22}$ b) $\frac{9}{7} = 1\frac{2}{7}$ c) $\frac{3}{7}$ d) $\frac{8}{9}$

6 a) $\frac{221}{40} = 5\frac{21}{40}$ b) $\frac{17}{40}$

c) $\frac{153}{20} = 7\frac{13}{20}$ d) $\frac{17}{8} = 2\frac{1}{8}$

---

7 a) $\frac{49}{18} = 2\frac{13}{18}$ b) $\frac{5}{2} = 2\frac{1}{2}$

c) $\frac{385}{16} = 24\frac{1}{16}$ d) $\frac{22}{5} = 4\frac{2}{5}$

8 $4\frac{13}{16}$ inches

9 a) $\frac{7}{12}$ b) $\frac{23}{30}$ c) $\frac{3}{5}$

d) $-\frac{3}{16}$ e) $\frac{9}{5} = 1\frac{4}{5}$ f) $\frac{27}{20} = 1\frac{7}{20}$

g) $\frac{23}{36}$ h) $\frac{159}{56} = 2\frac{47}{56}$

10 $\frac{5}{6}$ and $\frac{2}{9}$ **11** a) $10\frac{9}{20}$ cm   b) $5\frac{17}{20}$ cm²

12 10 ($9\frac{1}{3}$ tins are needed.)

13 16 **14** $\frac{11}{15}$

15 a) $\frac{4}{5}$ b) 80 c) 112

16 a) $\frac{5}{12}$ b) $\frac{41}{42}$ c) $\frac{3}{4}$

17 a) $\frac{4}{15}$ b) 20 red, 24 blue, 16 yellow

18 a) $\frac{24}{112} = \frac{8 \times 3}{8 \times 14} = \frac{3}{14} \neq \frac{3}{8}$

b) $\frac{1}{3} \times \frac{1}{15} = \frac{1}{45} \neq \frac{1}{5}$

c) $\frac{1}{2} + \frac{1}{5} = \frac{5}{10} + \frac{2}{10} = \frac{7}{10}$

$\frac{7}{10} \div 2 = \frac{7}{20}$

so $\frac{7}{20}$ is halfway between $\frac{1}{2}$ and $\frac{1}{5}$.

$\frac{1}{4} = \frac{5}{20} \neq \frac{7}{20}$

so $\frac{1}{4}$ is not halfway between $\frac{1}{2}$ and $\frac{1}{5}$.

d) $\frac{8}{9} = 0.\dot{8} > 0.8\dot{7}$

19 a) $\frac{8}{16}, 0.5\dot{4}, \frac{6}{11}, \frac{5}{9}$ b) $\frac{51}{110}, 0.4\dot{6}, \frac{116}{232}, \frac{8}{15}$

20 Jess and Eric.

Section 4 — Ratio and Proportion

4.1   Ratios

Page 29   Exercise 1

1 a) $1:3$ b) $1:3$ c) $4:1$ d) $2:3$ e) $4:1$
   f) $5:2$ g) $1:4$ h) $5:3$ i) $4:3$ j) $25:3$
   k) $4:3$ l) $1:4$ m) $5:2$ n) $3:7$ o) $11:3$

2 a) $3:1:2$ b) $5:4:1$ c) $2:3:10$
   d) $3:7:6$ e) $3:8:4$

3 $6:5$

4 $13:8$

Page 29   Exercise 2

1 a) $1:10$ b) $1:2$ c) $1:100$ d) $2:1$
   e) $2:5$ f) $3:20$ g) $3:10$ h) $2:7$
   i) $20:3$ j) $1:10$ k) $4:55$ l) $3:100$
   m) $15:2$ n) $5:3$ o) $1:24$ p) $5:2$

2 $1:9$

3 $2:5$

Page 30   Exercise 3

1 a) $1:3$ b) $1:5$ c) $1:4$ d) $1:4$
   e) $1:3.5$ f) $1:6.5$ g) $1:3.25$ h) $1:0.5$
   i) $1:0.3$ j) $1:3.5$ k) $1:0.625$ l) $1:1.8$

2 a) $1:5$ b) $1:50$ c) $1:4$ d) $1:40$
   e) $1:80$ f) $1:40$ g) $1:12.5$ h) $1:0.2$

3 $1:40\,000$

4 20 ml

Page 30   Exercise 4

1 50 g   **2** 189 **3** 18 years

4 199.2 cm   **5** £110.50 **6** 1500 ml

7 9 slices of courgette and 12 slices of goat's cheese.

8 459 cm

9 Max has been waiting 30 minutes, Maisie has been waiting 20 minutes.

10 7 adults **11** 12 over-30s

12 4 aubergines **13** 9 minutes

Page 31 Exercise 5

1 $\frac{1}{3}$ **2** $\frac{9}{13}$ **3** $\frac{7}{20}$

4 $\frac{1}{2}$ **5** $\frac{1}{10}$ **6** $\frac{1}{7}$

7 a) $\frac{1}{2}$ **b)** $\frac{3}{10}$

8 a) $\frac{1}{2}$ **b)** $\frac{3}{22}$ **c)** $\frac{7}{11}$

Page 32 Exercise 6

1 $1:2$ **2** $3:7$ **3** $1:5:2$

4 $3:1$ **5** $7:1$

6 $3:4:1$ **7** $2:3$

8 a) $5:2$ **b)** 18

9 $5:7$

4.2 Dividing in a Given Ratio

Page 32 Exercise 1

1 a) £32 and £16 **b)** £12 and £36
c) £40 and £8 **d)** £28 and £20

2 a) 24 cm, 36 cm and 12 cm
b) 16 cm, 16 cm and 40 cm
c) 30 cm, 18 cm and 24 cm
d) 28 cm, 24 cm and 20 cm

3 a) £15, £60 and £75 **b)** £45, £15 and £90
c) £60, £70 and £20 **d)** £65, £55 and £30

4 a) £10 **b)** 198 g **c)** 10 kg **d)** 500 ml

5 a) £22.50 **b)** 21.6 g
c) 75 kg **d)** 15 000 ml

Page 33 Exercise 2

1 12 and 20

2 Kat gets 18 cupcakes and Lindsay gets 12.

3 72 men and 40 women

4 Lauren gets £640 and Cara gets £560.

5 24 litres of yellow paint and 18 litres of red paint

6 525 **7** £3420 **8** 20 passengers

9 Length = 30 cm, width = 6 cm.

Page 33 Exercise 3

1 Gemma is 155 cm, Alisha is 160 cm and Omar is 175 cm.

2 £25 **3** 40 **4** 14

5 150 g of raspberries, 75 g of redcurrants and 225 g of strawberries.

6 Nicky gets 10 sweets, Jacinta gets 20 sweets and Charlie gets 5 sweets.

7 The angles are 60°, 30° and 90°.

8 The angles are 30°, 150°, 60° and 120°.

9 11 cm **10** £5000 **11** 80 tomatoes

12 Ali gets £100, Max gets £75 and Tim gets £25.

13 Stan gets £11.57 and Jan gets £15.43

4.3 More Ratio Problems

Page 34 Exercise 1

1 a) $\frac{3}{8}$ **b)** $3:5$

2 $4:3$ **3** $15:17$ **4** $46:99$

Page 35 Exercise 2

1 a) 18 **b)** $1:2$

2 $8:3$ **3** $13:14$

4 72 **5** 8

4.4 Proportion

Page 35 Exercise 1

1 £54 **2** 3 kg **3** 3.75 l

4 £12.96 **5** 982.5 Japanese yen

6 a) £13.50 **b)** £63 **c)** £59.40

7 £80 **8** £13.86

Page 36 Exercise 2

1 a) £8.77 **b)** £87.72 **c)** £219.30

2 3.75 kg **3** 4 DVDs

4 13 builders **5** £6.16

Page 36 Exercise 3

1 a) 52 min **b)** 20 km

2 a) 357 km **b)** 56 l

3 a) 19 g **b)** 26.4 g (accept 26.3 g)

4 a) 73.5 Swiss francs **b)** £20

Page 37 Exercise 4

1 20 hotdogs **2** 4675 coins

3 198 bulbs **4** 42 toy soldiers

Page 37 Exercise 5

1 1 hour, 12 min **2** 1 hour, 40 min

3 16 min **4** 1 hour, 30 min

5 a) 155 days **b)** 8 builders

Page 38 Exercise 6

1 1 hour **2** 9 days **3** 128 min

4 1 hour, 15 min **5** 20 people

6 a) 6 weeks **b)** 23 workers

4.5 Ratio and Proportion Problems

Page 38 Exercise 1

1 a) $2:5$ **b)** $1:2.5$ **c)** $0.4:1$ **d)** $2:7$

2 a) $2:5$ **b)** $\frac{2}{7}$

3 a) $12:35$ **b)** 62 mm

4 a) $\frac{1}{4}$ **b)** 24

5 a) $\frac{6}{11}$ **b)** 82 g

6 a) Luiz gets £288, Seth gets £480, Fran gets £537.60 and Ali gets £134.40.
b) $28:25$

7 Caroline's squash is stronger.

8 36 **9** 30 cm

10 a) £96 **b)** 18.75 l

11 a) 5200 rand **b)** £122.45

12 a) 80 g **b)** 392 g **c)** 6

13 2

14 a) 12 trees **b)** 4 hours **c)** 12 trees

15 15 min **16** 22 min, 51 sec

17 5.5 days

Section 5 — Percentages

5.1 Percentages

Page 40 Exercise 1

1 48% **2** 15%

3 a) 44% **b)** 66% **c)** 15% **d)** 80%
e) 25% **f)** 89% **g)** 150% **h)** 60%
i) 84% **j)** 125% **k)** 40% **l)** 30%

4 a) 75% **b)** 25%

5 40%

Page 40 Exercise 2

1 a) 62.5% **b)** 85% **c)** 132.2% **d)** 41%
e) 68.8% **f)** 28% **g)** 38% **h)** 120.4%

2 60% **3** 95%

4 a) 55% **b)** 32.5% **c)** 12.5% **d)** 108%
e) 37.5% **f)** 182.5% **g)** 32.4% **h)** 3.5%

5 18.5% **6** 30%

Page 41 Exercise 3

1 a) 12 **b)** 9 **c)** 9 **d)** 27
e) 15 **f)** 7 **g)** 105 **h)** 225

2 a) 9 **b)** 13 **c)** 117 **d)** 60
e) 77 **f)** 126 **g)** 33 **h)** 78

3 4.95 m

Page 41 Exercise 4

1 a) 34 **b)** 11.99 **c)** 217.6 **d)** 817.7
e) 485.85 **f)** 584.73 **g)** 699.79 **h)** 874.5

2 8.16 kg **3** 119.35 km

4 46% of £28 is larger by 34p.

5 1.584 litres

5.2 Percentages, Fractions and Decimals

Page 42 Exercise 1

1 a) $\frac{15}{100}$ **b) (i)** 15% **(ii)** 0.15

2 a) $0.4\dot{5}$ **b)** 45.45% (to 2 d.p.)

3 a) (i) 0.75 **(ii)** $\frac{3}{4}$ **b) (i)** 1.3 **(ii)** $\frac{13}{10}$

c) (i) 0.4 **(ii)** $\frac{2}{5}$ **d) (i)** 0.65 **(ii)** $\frac{13}{20}$

e) (i) 0.95 **(ii)** $\frac{19}{20}$ **f) (i)** 0.34 **(ii)** $\frac{17}{50}$

g) (i) 0.48 **(ii)** $\frac{12}{25}$ **h) (i)** 2.05 **(ii)** $\frac{41}{20}$

i) (i) 0.02 **(ii)** $\frac{1}{50}$ **j) (i)** 0.06 **(ii)** $\frac{3}{50}$

4 a) (i) 0.3 **(ii)** 30%
b) (i) 0.2 **(ii)** 20%
c) (i) 0.875 **(ii)** 87.5%
d) (i) $0.\dot{3}$ **(ii)** 33.3% (to 1 d.p.)
e) (i) $0.\dot{1}$ **(ii)** 11.1% (to 1 d.p.)
f) (i) $0.1\dot{3}$ **(ii)** 13.3% (to 1 d.p.)
g) (i) $0.6\dot{3}$ **(ii)** 63.6% (to 1 d.p.)
h) (i) $0.1\dot{6}$ **(ii)** 16.2% (to 1 d.p.)
i) (i) 0.4375 **(ii)** 43.75%
j) (i) $0.\dot{7}$ **(ii)** 77.8% (to 1 d.p.)

5 a) (i) 35% **(ii)** $\frac{7}{20}$ **b) (i)** 170% **(ii)** $\frac{17}{10}$

c) (i) 52% **(ii)** $\frac{13}{25}$ **d) (i)** 60% **(ii)** $\frac{3}{5}$

e) (i) 48% **(ii)** $\frac{12}{25}$ **f) (i)** 72% **(ii)** $\frac{18}{25}$

g) (i) 40% **(ii)** $\frac{2}{5}$ **h) (i)** 1% **(ii)** $\frac{1}{100}$

i) (i) 268% **(ii)** $\frac{67}{25}$ **j) (i)** 14% **(ii)** $\frac{7}{50}$

6 86% **7** 0.08 **8** 60%

9 $\frac{9}{25}$ **10** 68%

Page 43 Exercise 2

1 a) 0.35 **b)** 68% **c)** 0.4 **d)** 90%
e) $\frac{21}{100}$ **f)** $\frac{7}{10}$ **g)** $\frac{3}{4}$ **h)** $\frac{3}{5}$

2 a) 25%, $\frac{2}{5}$, 0.42 **b)** 45%, $\frac{1}{2}$, 0.505
c) 0.37, $\frac{3}{8}$, 38% **d)** 0.2, 22%, $\frac{2}{9}$
e) 12.5%, 0.13, $\frac{3}{20}$ **f)** $\frac{9}{40}$, 23%, 0.25
g) 2.5%, $\frac{1}{25}$, 0.4 **h)** 0.06%, 0.006, $\frac{3}{50}$

3 No **4** Team X **5** Oliver

Page 43 Exercise 3

1 30% **2** 33% **3** 21%

4 20% **5** 40% **6** 25%

7 21.5%

Page 44   Exercise 1

1 a) 99　　b) 75　　c) 140　　d) 324
 e) 176　　f) 1032　　g) 203　　h) 285

2 a) 49.5　　b) 12　　c) 17.5　　d) 48
 e) 75　　f) 3.3　　g) 67.5　　h) 442

3 247 acres　　4 2040　　5 £582

Page 44   Exercise 2

1 a) 543.9　b) 117.16　c) 130.35　d) 143.29
 e) 177.92　f) 996.84　g) 1614.06　h) 1346.97

2 a) 70.84　b) 28.44　c) 71.34　d) 57.57
 e) 117.18　f) 118.94　g) 199.95　h) 75.87

3 60 inches　　4 £31 291.40

5 £400　　6 £20

7 480 frogs, 540 newts

Page 45   Exercise 3

1 Mary earns more by £5.

2 Raj has more money by £250.

3 University A has 465 more students.

4 Meristock has a larger population by 24 265
 (accept 24 264).

5 a) £262.50　　b) £803.70　　c) 7.16%

Page 46   Exercise 4

1 a) 20%　　b) 160%

2 a) 20%　　b) 12%

3 60%　　4 25%　　5 15%

6 8%　　7 40%

Page 46   Exercise 1

1 a) £7.50　　b) £4.17　　c) £6.09
 d) £91.35　　e) £11.30　　f) £57.34

2 a) £3822.09　　b) £4361.64

Page 47   Exercise 2

1 a) £41　　　　b) £119.46
 c) £22.73　　d) £25.30

2 a) £1246.18　　b) £760.95

3 £750.59

4 67 820 565 (accept 67 820 564)

5 £88.97　　6 36 people (accept 35)

7 £755.27　　8 319 ants

9 108.6 cm　　10 150 cats

Page 48   Exercise 3

1 a) £48.03　　b) £105.70
 c) £4437.05　　d) £3796.88

2 £26 726.72　　3 93.6 kg (to 1 d.p.)

4 £77 287.80　　5 £3476.51

6 646.3 Bq (to 1 d.p.)　　7 £46 511.72

8 £3253.25　　9 £1037.66

Page 48   Exercise 4

1 14 years　　　　2 15 days

3 4 years　　　　4 5 hours

Page 49   Exercise 1

1 a) 26%　　b) 67.5%　　c) 80%
 d) 33.3% (to 1 d.p.)　　e) 60%
 f) 70%　　g) 40%　　h) 20%

2 a) 40%　b) 20%　c) 1.25%　d) $\frac{4}{9}$
 e) 8%　f) 0.615　g) 0.22　h) $\frac{4}{24}$

3 40%　　　　4 39 games

5 40%　　　　6 300 pupils

7 607.5 g　　8 10%, 0.11, $\frac{1}{8}$

---

9 $\frac{3}{5}$　　　　10 £104

11 3.36 kg　　12 There is no difference.

Page 49   Exercise 2

1 a) 6.3　　　b) 73.8
 c) 340.91　　d) 40.5
 e) 420.67　　f) 674.86
 g) 1.8　　　h) 6.02

2 40.83% (to 2 d.p.)　　3 15

4 47.46% (to 2 d.p.)　　5 16.14 m (to 2 d.p.)

6 6%　　　7 £259.88　　8 Kelly

9 6%, $\frac{2}{33}$, 0.061　　10 £9.50

11 Shop B has the lower price by £16.10.

12 71.9%

13 a) 76.5%　　b) 294 525

14 2%

15 a) 32%　　b) 50%

16 12%　　　17 £706.55

18 56.25%

Page 50   Exercise 3

1 £3526.25

2 a) 14 580　　b) 18 367 (accept 18 366)

3 a) £714.32　　b) £887.40

4 £39 030.69　　5 £2518.56

6 5 years　　7 £1003.53

8 2 years　　9 7 years

10 6 hours　　11 10 months

12 No

Section 6 — Expressions

6.1   Simplifying Expressions

Page 51   Exercise 1

1 a) $3c + 2d$　b) $a + 2b$　c) $3x + y$
 d) $4m + 2n$　e) $8x + 2y$　f) $11a + 7b$
 g) $7p + 4q$　h) $3a + 7b$　i) $3b + 3c$

2 a) $5x + y + 12$　　b) $-4a + 3b - 8$
 c) $7x + 6y - 3$　　d) $5m + 2n + 4$
 e) $8x - 3$　　f) $21a + 7b + 7$

3 a) $14p + q - 4$　　b) $4a + 13b + 3$
 c) $8b + 3c + 7$　　d) $-13x + 13y + 2z - 5$
 e) $-11m - 5n - 1$　　f) $4p + 4q - 20r - 9$

4 a) $x^2 + 5x + 5$　　b) $x^2 + 7x - 2$
 c) $2x^2 + 6x + 4$　　d) $3x^2 + x$
 e) $3p^2 - 2p$　　f) $7p^2 + 2q$
 g) $7p^2 + pq + 3$　　h) $p^2 - pq + 4p - 2q$
 i) $2b^2 + 12b + 7$

5 a) $2x^2 + 2xy + 4ab - cd$
 b) $p^2 + q^2 + 2pq$　c) $b^2 + 4ab + 3b$
 d) $b^2 + 6abc + 2ab - 3bc + 5b$

Page 52   Exercise 2

1 a) a^3　b) $6a^2$　c) $16pq$　d) $21a^2$
 e) $15xy$　f) m^4　g) $48ab$　h) $48p^2$

2 a) a^2b　b) $20a^3$　c) $14pq^2$
 d) $8a^2b^2$　e) x^3y　f) $24i^2j^3$
 g) $3m$　h) $63x^2yz$　i) $20st^2$
 j) $3a$　k) $8pq$　l) $30a^3b^4c^5$

3 a) $4y^2$　b) a^4　c) $27c^3$　d) $8z^6$
 e) $4ab^2$　f) $5q^4$　g) x^2y^2　h) $i j^2k^2$

6.2   Expanding Brackets

Page 52   Exercise 1

1 a) $2a + 10$　b) $4b + 12$　c) $5d + 35$
 d) $3p + 12$　e) $4x + 32$　f) $30 - 6r$
 g) $4b - 16$　h) $15 - 5y$　i) $8y - 40$
 j) $3x + 3y$　k) $9d - 81$　l) $4x + 28$

---

m) $3x + 36$　n) $12t - 12r$　o) $7x - 7y$
p) $44 - 11b$

2 a) $6n - 18m$　b) $20u + 40v$　c) $35n - 42m$
 d) $3u + 24v$　e) $16x - 28y$　f) $6p - 33q$
 g) $16s - 96t$　h) $24x + 30y$

3 a) $xy + 5x$　b) $pq + 2p$　c) $ab + 4a$
 d) $mp + 8m$　e) $x^2 - 2x$　f) $8p - pq$
 g) $8x - x^2$　h) $ab - 12a$　i) $ab + 12a$
 j) $xy + 7x$　k) $pq + 3p$　l) $xy + 6x$
 m) $3pq - 8p$　n) $5r - rs$　o) $14t - t^2$
 p) $2ab - 4a$

4 a) $-q - 2$　b) $-x - 7$　c) $-h - 3$
 d) $-g - 3$　e) $-m - 3$　f) $-n + 11$
 g) $-p - 4$　h) $-q + 7$　i) $-v^2 - 4v$
 j) $-v^2 + 5v$　k) $-12x + x^2$　l) $-4y - y^2$

5 a) $-30g + 18$　b) $-28v - 56$　c) $-10 - 8m$
 d) $-50 + 40v$　e) $-10 - 15n$　f) $-32z + 8z^2$
 g) $-12b + 6$　h) $-8y^2 - 24y$　i) $-4pu + 28p$
 j) $-24 + 2v$　k) $-56 + 8w$　l) $-25y + 5xy$

Page 53   Exercise 2

1 a) $6z + 14$　b) $8c + 38$　c) $12u + 64$
 d) $5c + 19$　e) $9v + 57$　f) $10w + 26$
 g) $8a + 25$　h) $3z - 9$　i) $4x + 3$
 j) $10b + 15$　k) $9y + 69$　l) $41b - 22$

2 a) $4p - 21$　b) $c - 17$　c) $4q - 16$
 d) $j - 7$　e) $4y - 18$　f) $14c - 27$
 g) $4f - 21$　h) $13d - 93$　i) $54x - 35$

3 a) $8q + 29$　b) $-2c - 48$　c) $18q - 8$
 d) $-a - 14$　e) $17z$　f) $2q + 2$
 g) $-9y + 96$　h) $27x - 27$　i) $6g - 68$

4 a) $12p^2 + 17p - 3$　b) $14m^2 + 45m + 30$
 c) $-7k^2 + 3k + 4$　d) $42b^2 + 69b$
 e) $-56t^2 + 81t + 4$　f) $-19h^2 + 24h$
 g) $36x^2 + 28x$　h) $-40u^2 - 10u - 8$
 i) $15b^2 + 140b$

Page 54   Exercise 3

1 a) $ab + 3a + 2b + 6$　b) $jk - 5j + 4k - 20$
 c) $xy - x - 4y + 4$　d) $xy + 2x + 6y + 12$
 e) $16 + 2y + 8x + xy$　f) $9b - 27 - ab + 3a$
 g) $st + 3t - 5s - 15$　h) $yz - 3y + 12z - 36$

2 a) $2ap + 12a + 2p + 12$
 b) $5xy - 35x + 15y - 105$
 c) $3jk + 12j - 6k - 24$
 d) $8gh + 72g + 40h + 360$
 e) $2wz - 16w - 12z + 96$
 f) $6xy - 12x - 30y + 60$
 g) $27x - 9xy + 108 - 36y$
 h) $7ab - 56a - 49b + 392$

3 a) $x^2 + 11x + 24$　b) $b^2 - 2b - 8$
 c) $a^2 + a - 2$　d) $d^2 + 13d + 42$
 e) $-c^2 - 2c + 15$　f) $-y^2 + 14y - 48$
 g) $2x^2 + 6x + 4$　h) $z^2 - 2z - 108$
 i) $-3y^2 + 3y + 18$　j) $4b^2 - 4b - 24$
 k) $6x^2 - 36x + 48$　l) $12a^2 + 12a - 864$

4 a) $x^2 + 2x + 1$　b) $x^2 + 8x + 16$
 c) $x^2 + 10x + 25$　d) $x^2 - 4x + 4$
 e) $x^2 - 6x + 9$　f) $x^2 - 12x + 36$
 g) $4x^2 + 8x + 4$　h) $2x^2 + 20x + 50$
 i) $3x^2 - 12x + 12$　j) $2x^2 + 24x + 72$
 k) $5x^2 - 30x + 45$　l) $2x^2 - 16x + 32$

Page 55   Exercise 4

1 a) $abc + 2ab + ac + 2a + bc + 2b + c + 2$
 b) $def + 2de + 3df + 6d - 2ef - 4e - 6f - 12$
 c) $4hi - 12h + 8i - 24 + ghi - 3gh + 2gi - 6g$
 d) $jkl + 3jk - 5jl - 15j - 2kl - 6k + 10l + 30$
 e) $mnp - 3mn - mp + 3m - 5np + 15n + 5p - 15$
 f) $2rs - 12r + 8s - 48 - qrs + 6qr - 4qs + 24q$
 g) $12t + 3tv + 12tu + 3tuv + 8 + 2v + 8u + 2uv$
 h) $2wxy - 4wx + 14wy - 28w + 2xy - 4x + 14y - 28$
 i) $-15b - 45 + 6ab + 18a$
　　　$+ 5bz + 15z - 2abz - 6az$

2 a) $x^2y + 2x^2 + 4xy + 8x + 3y + 6$
b) $p^2q + p^2 + 2pq + 2p - 8q - 8$
c) $s^2t - 3s^2 + 3st - 9s - 10t + 30$
d) $r^3 - 10r^2 + 31r - 30$
e) $y^3 - 13y^2 + 54y - 72$
f) $3q^3 + 20q^2 + 27q + 10$
g) $2u^3 + 6u^2 - 20u - 48$
h) $-v^3 + v^2 + 4v - 4$
i) $-3z^3 - 5z^2 + 47z - 15$

3 a) $2z^3 + 12z^2 + 22z + 12$
b) $5u^3 + 45u^2 + 120u + 100$
c) $6c^3 + 18c^2 - 24c - 72$
d) $3v^3 - 3v^2 - 42v + 72$
e) $4w^3 - 44w^2 + 152w - 160$
f) $-x^3 + x^2 + 37x + 35$
g) $-8s^3 + 36s^2 - 28s - 24$
h) $-6y^3 - 15y^2 + 12y + 9$
i) $-18q^3 + 45q^2 + 9q - 54$

4 a) $x^3 + 9x^2 + 27x + 27$
b) $x^3 + 6x^2 + 12x + 8$
c) $x^3 - 6x^2 + 12x - 8$
d) $x^3 + 12x^2 + 48x + 64$
e) $-x^3 + 9x^2 - 27x + 27$
f) $-x^3 + 15x^2 - 75x + 125$
g) $3x^3 - 9x^2 + 9x - 3$
h) $2x^3 + 30x^2 + 150x + 250$
i) $24x^3 + 72x^2 + 72x + 24$
j) $8x^3 - 60x^2 + 150x - 125$
k) $108x^3 - 324x^2 + 324x - 108$
l) $2x^3 + 12x^2 + 24x + 16$

Page 56   Exercise 1

1 a) $2(a + 5)$ **b)** $3(b + 4)$ **c)** $3(5 + y)$
d) $7(4 + v)$ **e)** $5(a + 3b)$ **f)** $3(3c - 4d)$
g) $3(x + 4y)$ **h)** $7(3u - v)$ **i)** $4(a^2 - 3b)$
j) $3(c + 5d^2)$ **k)** $5(c^2 - 5f)$ **l)** $6(x - 2y^2)$

2 a) x **b)** $2y$ **c)** $8p$ **d)** $5n$
e) $5d$ **f)** $8m$ **g)** $6a$ **h)** $2b$

3 a) $a(3a + 7)$ **b)** $b(4b + 19)$
c) $x(2x + 9)$ **d)** $x(4x - 9)$
e) $q(21q - 16)$ **f)** $y(15 - 7y)$
g) $y(7 + 15y)$ **h)** $z(27z + 11)$
i) $d(10d^2 + 27)$ **j)** $y^2(4y - 13)$
k) $y^3(11 + 3y)$ **l)** $w(22 - 5w^3)$

4 a) $5a(3 + 2b)$ **b)** $3b(4 + 3c)$ **c)** $4y(4x - 1)$
d) $3x(7 + y)$ **e)** $7a(2 + b)$ **f)** $3c(5 - 4d)$
g) $3x(1 - 5y)$ **h)** $6v(4u + 1)$

5 a) $5p(2p + 3q)$ **b)** $4y(3x + 2y)$
c) $5a(3b - 4a)$ **d)** $6q(2q - 3p)$
e) $5ab(6b + 5)$ **f)** $14x(x - 2y^2)$
g) $4xy(3y + 2x)$ **h)** $2ab(4b + 5a)$
i) $3a^2(2 + 3b)$ **j)** $4p(3q - 2p^2)$
k) $2a^2(4 + 3a^2b^2)$ **l)** $8x^2(3xy - 2)$

Page 57   Exercise 2

1 a) 4 **b)** y^2
c) x **d)** $4xy^2(x^2 + 2y^2)$

2 a) $x^4(x^2 + 1 - x)$ **b)** $a^2(8 + 17a^4)$
c) $5x^2(x - 3)$ **d)** $6y^4(2y^2 + 1)$
e) $8c(3b^2c^2 - 1)$ **f)** $6q^2(4 - 3q^3)$
g) $2x^3(1 - 2x^2)$ **h)** $z^2(25 + 13z^4)$
i) $3p^2(4 + 5p^3q^3)$ **j)** $9ab(a^3 + 3b^2)$
k) $3(5b^4 - 7a^2 + 6ab)$ **l)** $11pq^2(2 - p^2q)$
m) $x^2y(y^2 + x + x^3 + y^5)$ **n)** $2xy(8x - 4y + x^2y^2)$
o) $4x^2y^2(9x^5 + 2y^7)$ **p)** $x^3(5x + 3y^4 - 25y)$

3 a) $x^2y^2(13 + 22x^4y + 20x^3y)$
b) $ab^3(16a^4b^2 - a^3b^2 - 1)$
c) $7pq(3p^5q - 2q + p^2)$
d) $xy^3(14y + 13x^4 - 5x^5y)$
e) $y^2(7x + 4y^4 + 17x^5)$

f) $2c^3(8c^3d^5 - 7 + 4d^6)$
g) $8a^4b^2(2a^2b^2 + 1)$
h) $3jk(6 + 7j^2k^5 - 5jk^2)$
i) $18xy^3(2xy - 4x^4y^4 + 1)$
j) $a^3b^4(20ab + 4 - 5a^3b^{11})$
k) $11xy^2(xy + x^2 + 6y^3)$
l) $jk(2 - 9j^3 - 12jk^2)$

Page 57   Exercise 1

1 a) $(x + 3)(x + 2)$ **b)** $(a + 3)(a + 4)$
c) $(x + 7)(x + 1)$ **d)** $(z + 6)(z + 2)$
e) $(x + 4)(x + 1)$ **f)** $(v + 3)^2$

2 a) $(x + 3)(x + 1)$ **b)** $(x - 4)(x - 2)$
c) $(x - 5)(x - 2)$ **d)** $(x - 4)(x - 1)$
e) $(x + 5)(x - 2)$ **f)** $(x + 4)(x - 2)$
g) $(s + 6)(s - 3)$ **h)** $(x + 3)(x - 5)$
i) $(t + 2)(t - 6)$

Page 58   Exercise 2

1 a) $(2x + 1)(x + 1)$ **b)** $(3x - 1)(x - 5)$
c) $(5x - 2)(x - 3)$ **d)** $(2t + 3)(t - 4)$
e) $(2x - 1)(x - 6)$ **f)** $(3b + 2)(b - 3)$
g) $(5x - 3)(x + 3)$ **h)** $(2x - 1)(x - 1)$
i) $(7a - 2)(a + 3)$ **j)** $(11x + 4)(x - 6)$
k) $(7z + 3)(z + 5)$ **l)** $(3y - 2)(y - 8)$

2 a) $(3x + 1)(2x + 1)$ **b)** $(3x - 2)(2x - 3)$
c) $(5x - 2)(3x + 1)$ **d)** $(5x - 2)(2x - 3)$
e) $(5a + 4)(5a + 9)$ **f)** $(3x - 1)(4x - 5)$
g) $(3u + 3)(4u - 2)$ **h)** $(7w + 9)(2w + 1)$

Page 59   Exercise 3

1 a) $(x + 5)(x - 5)$ **b)** $(x + 3)(x - 3)$
c) $(x + 6)(x - 6)$ **d)** $(x + 9)(x - 9)$

2 a) $4x$ **b)** $(4x)^2 - 3^2$
c) $(4x + 3)(4x - 3)$

3 a) $(2x + 7)(2x - 7)$ **b)** $(x + 8)(x - 8)$
c) $(6x + 2)(6x - 2)$ **d)** $(3x + 10)(3x - 10)$
e) $(b + 11)(b - 11)$ **f)** $(4z + 1)(4z - 1)$
g) $(5x + 4)(5x - 4)$ **h)** $3(3t + 2)(3t - 2)$

Page 59   Exercise 4

1 a) $(x + 1)(x - 5)$ **b)** $(t - 4)^2$
c) $(x + 6)(x - 6)$ **d)** $(y - 5)(y + 4)$
e) $(x - 4)(x + 3)$ **f)** $(y + 6)(y + 2)$
g) $(x + 6)(x - 1)$ **h)** $(x - 9)(x + 5)$
i) $(s - 8)(s - 2)$ **j)** $(x + 8)(x + 4)$
k) $(b - 2)(b + 3)$ **l)** $(t - 7)(t - 2)$

2 a) $(4a + 5)(4a - 5)$ **b)** $(b - 9)(b + 2)$
c) $(10x + 8)(10x - 8)$ **d)** $(y + 7)(y + 12)$
e) $(z + 1)(z - 1)$ **f)** $(6x + 13)(6x - 13)$
g) $(5x + 2)(x - 1)$ **h)** $(9t + 11)(9t - 11)$
i) $(2c + 14)(2c - 14)$ **j)** $(a + 12)(a - 3)$
k) $(z - 7)(z - 8)$ **l)** $(12y + 15)(12y - 15)$
m) $(2z + 5)(z + 8)$ **n)** $(3x + 4)(x - 7)$
o) $(x - 1)^2$ **p)** $(7t - 8)(t + 2)$
q) $(4y + 2)(y - 1)$ **r)** $(6z - 3)(z - 4)$
s) $(8x + 3)(x + 2)$ **t)** $(2x - 7)(x - 3)$

Page 59   Exercise 1

1 a) $\dfrac{2}{x}$ **b)** $\dfrac{7}{2x}$ **c)** $\dfrac{3x}{y}$ **d)** $5s^2t$ **e)** $\dfrac{a^2c^3}{2b^2}$

2 a) $\dfrac{7}{5 - x}$ **b)** $\dfrac{3(8 - t)}{4s^2}$ **c)** $\dfrac{3d}{2(4 + 3c)}$
d) $\dfrac{x - 2}{4y}$ **e)** $\dfrac{3}{a^2b^3(1 + 2a^5b^6)}$

3 a) $\dfrac{s}{2t}$ **b)** $\dfrac{2}{5}$ **c)** $\dfrac{3(x + 1)}{5y(x - 1)}$
d) $2x$ **e)** $\dfrac{3a + 5b}{7b^2}$

4 a) $\dfrac{2}{x - 1}$ **b)** $-\dfrac{3}{5}$ **c)** $\dfrac{x + 2}{x - 3}$

d) $\dfrac{x - 3}{x + 2}$ **e)** $\dfrac{x}{x + 3}$ **f)** $\dfrac{t + 5}{2t + 9}$

Page 60   Exercise 2

1 a) $\dfrac{9x}{20}$ **b)** $\dfrac{x}{6}$ **c)** $\dfrac{19b}{42}$ **d)** $\dfrac{7z}{18}$

2 a) $\dfrac{8x - 1}{15}$ **b)** $\dfrac{10t - 1}{12}$
c) $\dfrac{13x - 1}{12}$ **d)** $\dfrac{3c + 5}{2c}$

3 a) $\dfrac{3x - 5}{(x + 1)(x - 3)}$ **b)** $-\dfrac{3}{(x - 1)(x + 2)}$
c) $\dfrac{5a^2 + 11a - 5}{(a + 2)(a + 3)}$ **d)** $\dfrac{5x^2 - 6x + 8}{(3x - 2)(2x + 1)}$
e) $\dfrac{6s^2 - 2s - 5}{(3s - 1)(3s + 2)}$ **f)** $\dfrac{3x^2 - x + 5}{15x}$
g) $\dfrac{3y + 7}{(y + 1)(y + 3)}$ **h)** $-\dfrac{x^2 + 7x + 5}{(x + 2)(x + 1)}$
i) $\dfrac{x^2 + 15x + 1}{(x - 2)(x + 3)}$

Page 61   Exercise 3

1 a) $\dfrac{6x + 3}{(x - 3)(x + 1)}$ **b)** $\dfrac{4x + 1}{(x + 1)(x + 2)}$
c) $\dfrac{5}{(x + 4)(x + 3)}$

2 a) $\dfrac{11z + 20}{(z + 1)(z + 2)}$ **b)** $\dfrac{2x^2 + 7x - 3}{(x - 2)(x + 3)}$
c) $\dfrac{4x - 3}{x(x + 4)}$ **d)** $\dfrac{6}{(a - 3)(a + 3)}$

3 a) $\dfrac{t^2 + t + 1}{t(t + 3)(t + 1)}$ **b)** $\dfrac{2x^2 + 3x + 6}{(x + 3)(x - 3)(x - 2)}$
c) $\dfrac{4x^2 - 15x}{(x - 3)(x - 1)(x - 4)}$
d) $\dfrac{y^2 - 5y + 2}{(y - 1)(y - 2)(y - 3)}$

Page 62   Exercise 4

1 a) $\dfrac{3}{xy}$ **b)** $\dfrac{5}{2a^2b}$ **c)** $2st$ **d)** $\dfrac{4x^2}{3}$

2 a) $\dfrac{3x}{(x + 4)(x + 2)}$ **b)** $\dfrac{a(6a + b)}{4(b + 1)}$
c) $\dfrac{3z}{(2z + 5)(z - 1)}$ **d)** $\dfrac{t^3(t^2 + 5)}{3(1 - t)}$

3 a) $\dfrac{x - 4}{x + 2}$ **b)** $\dfrac{x + 1}{2(x + 2)}$
c) $\dfrac{(x + 1)(x + 2)}{(x + 3)}$ **d)** $\dfrac{(z + 5)^2}{z + 3}$

4 a) $8y^2$ **b)** $\dfrac{60}{b}$ **c)** $\dfrac{21y^3}{x^3}$ **d)** $\dfrac{b^3}{3a}$

5 a) $\dfrac{4y^4}{3y + 2}$ **b)** $\dfrac{6(2c + 1)}{cd^3}$
c) $\dfrac{1 - x^3y^5}{5x^2y}$ **d)** $\dfrac{2t^3}{2 + t^2}$

6 a) $\dfrac{(x - 1)(x + 3)}{(x + 2)(x + 5)}$ **b)** $\dfrac{3(x - 2)}{2(x + 1)}$
c) $\dfrac{3(y - 3)}{(y + 5)}$ **d)** $\dfrac{(x - 2)(x - 3)}{(x + 5)^2}$
e) $\dfrac{(x + 1)(x + 2)}{(x - 1)(x + 3)}$ **f)** $\dfrac{(t - 3)(t + 7)}{(t + 2)(t + 3)}$

Page 63   Exercise 1

1 a) $5x$ **b)** $8y$
c) $-6a$ **d)** $-x + 7y$
e) $4x + 2y$ **f)** $6s - 2t + 6$
g) $12p + 7q - 12$ **h)** $5x^2 + 2x - 3$
i) $x^2 + 3x + 11$

2 a) $8x - 7$ **b)** $9x + 6$
c) $2a + 8$ **d)** $2p + 22$
e) $-2x + 3$ **f)** $22x - 13$
g) $-b + 12$ **h)** $x^2 + 5x - 2$
i) $4x^2 + 9x - 12$

3 $(6x + 5)$ cm

4 a) $(4x + 6)$ cm   **b)** $(x^2 + 3x - 10)$ cm²

5 a) $(12x - 8)$ cm   **b)** $(9x^2 - 12x + 4)$ cm²

6 $£(18x - 7)$

7 $(8x + 40)$ miles

8 $(11x + 6)$ pence

9 a) $(8x - 4)$ m   **b)** $(4x^2 - 4x - 15)$ m²

10 $(36y - 100x)$ pence

11 a) $(4x^2 + 2x - 12)$ m³
b) $(4000x^2 + 2000x - 12000)$ litres

12 $(13x + 35)$ cm

13 a) $x^2 + 4x + 3$ **b)** $s^2 + 7s + 10$
c) $x^2 + x - 12$ **d)** $y^2 - 4y - 12$
e) $x^2 - 9x + 20$ **f)** $t^2 - 5t - 6$

14 a) $2x^2 - 3x - 9$ **b)** $6x^2 + 17x + 5$
c) $6t^2 - t - 2$ **d)** $6a^2 - 19a + 10$
e) $4x^2 + 13x + 3$ **f)** $4y^2 - 4y - 3$
g) $x^2 - 25$ **h)** $4z^2 - 9$
i) $4x^2 + 4x + 1$ **j)** $b^2 + 10b + 25$
k) $9x^2 - 12x + 4$ **l)** $9x^2 + 24x + 16$
m) $x^3 + 2x^2 - 5x - 6$ **n)** $y^3 - 6y^2 - y + 30$
o) $-t^3 + 8t^2 + t - 8$ **p)** $3z^3 + 9z^2 - 30z - 72$

Page 64   Exercise 2
1 a) $4(x - 2)$ **b)** $3(2a + 1)$
c) $5(t - 2)$ **d)** $3x(1 + 2y)$
e) $3(2x - 5y + 4)$ **f)** $4(2a + 3b - 4)$

2 a) $5x(3 - 2x)$ **b)** $4x(2y - 3x)$
c) $y(y + 4x)$ **d)** $3xy(2 + 3xy)$
e) $pq(q - p)$ **f)** $ab(a - 2 + b)$
g) $3c(2cd - 3d^2 + 4c^2)$
h) $4x(4x + 3xy - 2y^2)$
i) $jk^2(k - 2j)$

3 a) $5x^2y(x^2 + 5y^5)$
b) $2p^2q^3(2p^5 - 1)$
c) $2ab^2(3b - 2b^2 + 4)$
d) $3c^2(3d - 3c^3d^2 + 5c)$
e) $7x(2x^2 + xy - y^4)$
f) $2j^5k^4(4j^4k^4 - 3)$

4 a) $(a + 4)(a + 2)$ **b)** $(x + 3)(x + 1)$
c) $(z - 3)(z - 2)$ **d)** $(x + 6)(x - 3)$
e) $(x - 5)(x - 3)$ **f)** $(x + 5)(x + 4)$
g) $(x + 6)(x - 4)$ **h)** $(x - 5)(x + 2)$

5 a) $(t + 7)(t - 2)$ **b)** $(x + 5)(x - 4)$
c) $(a - 5)(a + 1)$ **d)** $(m + 5)(m + 2)$
e) $(x + 7)(x - 3)$ **f)** $(x + 10)(x - 10)$
g) $(r - 6)(r + 3)$ **h)** $(x - 9)(x - 3)$

6 a) $(2x + 1)(x + 2)$ **b)** $(3m - 2)(m - 2)$
c) $(3x + 1)(x - 2)$ **d)** $(2g + 1)^2$
e) $(3n + 2)(2n + 3)$ **f)** $(4k + 3)(4k - 3)$
g) $(5x - 3)(x + 1)$ **h)** $(5z - 2)(2z + 3)$

Page 64   Exercise 3
1 a) $\dfrac{3a}{8}$ **b)** $\dfrac{2x}{63}$ **c)** $\dfrac{7p}{6}$

d) $\dfrac{8x}{21}$ **e)** $\dfrac{5y - 1}{6}$ **f)** $\dfrac{19x - 7}{20}$

g) $-\dfrac{t + 18}{12}$ **h)** $\dfrac{6x + 10}{(x + 3)(x - 1)}$

i) $\dfrac{2z + 9}{(z + 2)(z + 3)}$

2 a) $\dfrac{2z^2 + 4z - 1}{(z + 3)(z - 2)}$ **b)** $\dfrac{5x - 4}{(x + 3)(x + 1)(x - 2)}$

c) $\dfrac{t - 9}{t(t + 3)^2}$ **d)** $\dfrac{2x^2 + x - 8}{(x + 4)(x - 4)(x - 1)}$

e) $\dfrac{3p^3 - 2p^2 + 8p - 8}{p^2(p - 2)}$ **f)** $\dfrac{3(x + 2)}{2(x - 1)}$

3 a) $\dfrac{x - 4}{x + 2}$ **b)** $\dfrac{x(x - 3)}{3(x - 2)}$

c) $\dfrac{(a - 2)(a - 1)}{(a + 2)^2}$ **d)** $\dfrac{4x}{3}$

e) $\dfrac{3(y - 1)}{2(x + 1)}$ **f)** $\dfrac{s + 3}{s - 4}$

g) $\dfrac{3(b + 2)}{2(b + 5)}$ **h)** $\dfrac{(x + 5)(x + 2)}{(x - 2)(x + 1)}$

Section 7 — Powers and Roots

7.1   Squares, Cubes and Roots

Page 65   Exercise 1
1 a) 25   **b)** 49   **c)** 10 000   **d)** 400
e) 4   **f)** 25   **g)** 121   **h)** 900
i) 0.01   **j)** 0.25

2 a) 8   **b)** 125   **c)** −1000   **d)** 216
e) −512   **f)** −1   **g)** 729   **h)** 8000
i) −27 000 000   **j)** −0.001

3 a) 9   **b)** 27   **c)** −27   **d)** 9
e) 64   **f)** 144   **g)** −125   **h)** −1000
i) 64   **j)** 64

Page 65   Exercise 2
1 a) 6   **b)** 100   **c)** −4   **d)** 9
e) 11   **f)** 13   **g)** −12   **h)** 20
i) 7 and −7   **j)** 3000 and −3000

2 a) 2   **b)** 3   **c)** 10   **d)** −1
e) −5   **f)** 8   **g)** 6   **h)** −2

Page 66   Exercise 3
1 a) 17   **b)** 25   **c)** 113   **d)** 125
e) 4   **f)** 5   **g)** 12   **h)** 3
i) 6   **j)** 20   **k)** 4   **l)** 6

2 a) 1.44   **b)** 11.56   **c)** 39.06   **d)** 20.98
e) 585.64   **f)** 18.55   **g)** 9.46   **h)** 3.16
i) 5.66   **j)** 39.30   **k)** 636.06   **l)** 5.24
m) 3.38   **n)** 4.33   **o)** 592.70

7.2   Indices and Index Laws

Page 66   Exercise 1
1 a) 3^7 **b)** 2^5 **c)** 7^7
d) 9^8 **e)** 12^4 **f)** 17^3

2 a) h^4 **b)** t^5 **c)** s^7
d) a^2b^3 **e)** f^3k^5 **f)** m^4n^2

3 a) 10^3 **b)** 10^7 **c)** 10^4 **d)** 10^5 **e)** 10^8

Page 67   Exercise 2
1 a) 81   **b)** 256   **c)** 7776
d) 512   **e)** 256   **f)** 371 293
g) 30 000 000 000   **h)** 59 049
i) 768   **j)** 5000   **k)** 40
l) 69   **m)** 100 128   **n)** 2592
o) 20 903   **p)** 512   **q)** 10 000 000
r) 64   **s)** 537 289   **t)** 0.1296

Page 67   Exercise 3
1 a) $\dfrac{1}{4}$ **b)** $\dfrac{1}{8}$ **c)** $\dfrac{1}{16}$ **d)** $\dfrac{4}{9}$

e) $\dfrac{9}{100}$ **f)** $\dfrac{27}{8}$ **g)** $\dfrac{625}{81}$ **h)** $\dfrac{16}{25}$

i) $\dfrac{64}{27}$ **j)** $\dfrac{216}{343}$

Page 68   Exercise 4
1 a) 3^8 **b)** 10^4 **c)** a^{10} **d)** 4^{11}
e) 4^9 **f)** 6^3 **g)** 7^7 **h)** 8
i) c^{20} **j)** b^3 **k)** 11^{10} **l)** 2^{13}
m) f^{50} **n)** 20^{12} **o)** g^{88} **p)** e^{15}
q) 100^{69} **r)** 17^{444} **s)** 34^{364} **t)** 147^{7d}

2 a) 9   **b)** 5   **c)** 2   **d)** 40
e) 9   **f)** 4   **g)** 3   **h)** 6
i) 13   **j)** 7   **k)** 6   **l)** 7
m) 7   **n)** 5   **o)** 5   **p)** 8

3 a) 3^{14} **b)** 5^{13} **c)** p^{17} **d)** 9^{35}
e) 7^2 **f)** 8   **g)** 12^{12} **h)** q^{14}

4 a) 3^3 **b)** r^3 **c)** 8^4 **d)** 6^{15}
e) s^3 **f)** 2^4 **g)** 4   **h)** 7^4
i) 5^5 **j)** 10^5 **k)** t^7 **l)** 8^7

5 a) (i) 2^2 (ii) 2^{10} (iii) 2^{13}
b) (i) 3^5 (ii) 5^6 (iii) 4^5
c) (i) 64   (ii) 1 000 000 000   (iii) 216

Page 68   Exercise 5
1 a) $\dfrac{1}{4}$ **b)** $\dfrac{1}{7}$ **c)** $\dfrac{1}{2^2}\left(= \dfrac{1}{4}\right)$

d) $\dfrac{1}{5^3}\left(= \dfrac{1}{125}\right)$ **e)** $\dfrac{2}{3}$

2 a) 5^{-1} **b)** 11^{-1} **c)** 3^{-2}
d) 2^{-7} **e)** 5×7^{-2}

3 a) 2   **b)** $\dfrac{3}{2}$ **c)** 9
d) $\dfrac{8}{125}$ **e)** $\dfrac{100}{49}$

4 a) 5^2 **b)** 8^{-3} **c)** g^{12} **d)** 3^{-16}
e) h^5 **f)** 2^{20} **g)** 17^6 **h)** 7^{-10}
i) p^{-20} **j)** k^4 **k)** 4^2 **l)** l^{33}
m) 12^{18} **n)** 6^8 **o)** 3^{-6} **p)** m^{21}
q) 7^3 **r)** n^{15} **s)** 10^{45} **t)** 13^{-15}

5 a) (i) $\dfrac{1}{100}$ (ii) $\dfrac{1}{10^2}$ (iii) 10^{-2}
b) (i) 10^{-1} (ii) 10^{-8} (iii) 10^{-4} (iv) 10^0

6 a) $\dfrac{1}{3}$ **b)** $\dfrac{1}{9}$ **c)** $\dfrac{9}{25}$ **d)** $\dfrac{7}{8}$

e) $\dfrac{4}{9}$ **f)** $\dfrac{1}{36}$ **g)** $-\dfrac{81}{125}$ **h)** $\dfrac{27}{64}$

i) $\dfrac{1}{10\ 000\ 000}$ **j)** $\dfrac{16}{81}$

k) $\dfrac{36}{1000}\left(= \dfrac{9}{250}\right)$ **l)** $\dfrac{1}{6}$

Page 70   Exercise 6
1 a) $\sqrt[5]{a}$ **b)** $\sqrt[8]{a}$ **c)** $(\sqrt[5]{a})^3$
d) $(\sqrt[5]{a})^2$ **e)** $(\sqrt[2]{a})^5$

2 a) 8   **b)** 12   **c)** 4
d) 2   **e)** 1000   **f)** 10

3 a) 25   **b)** 27   **c)** 8000
d) 100 000   **e)** 8   **f)** 160 000

4 a) 2.65   **b)** 20.59   **c)** 0.14   **d)** 2.22
e) 5.85   **f)** −2.29   **g)** 20.68   **h)** 2.39
i) −1.43   **j)** 0.48

Page 70   Exercise 7
1 a) 7^{15} **b)** d^{-10} **c)** $4^{24}(= 2^{48})$
d) $14^{\frac{5}{2}}$ **e)** $p^1 = p$ **f)** $9^{-\frac{7}{4}}(= 3^{-\frac{7}{2}})$
g) $23^{-\frac{5}{3}}$ **h)** c^2 **i)** $q^{-\frac{1}{4}}$ **j)** $12^{\frac{4}{3}}$
k) $99^{-\frac{4}{3}}$ **l)** $r^{\frac{4}{5}}$ **m)** $21^{-\frac{3}{2}}$ **n)** $2^{\frac{19}{6}}$
o) $s^{-\frac{6}{5}}$ **p)** $t^{\frac{1}{6}}$

2 a) $3m^{\frac{1}{3}}$ **b)** $\dfrac{n^{\frac{15}{2}}}{1000}$ **c)** $y^{-3}z^{-\frac{9}{4}}$ **d)** $\dfrac{b^6}{16c^2}$

e) $\dfrac{s^{\frac{11}{2}}}{2}$ **f)** $3t^{\frac{7}{2}}$ **g)** $\dfrac{1}{4u^{\frac{3}{2}}}$ **h)** $\dfrac{2v^{\frac{3}{4}}}{5}$

3 a) 2^3 **b)** $2^{\frac{1}{2}}$ **c)** $2^{\frac{7}{2}}$ **d)** $2^{-\frac{7}{2}}$

4 a) $3^{\frac{4}{3}}$ **b)** $4^{\frac{5}{2}}$ **c)** $25^{\frac{1}{2}}$
d) $8^{\frac{1}{3}}$ **e)** $10^{-\frac{5}{2}}$ **f)** $3^{\frac{10}{3}}$

7.3   Standard Form

Page 71   Exercise 1
1 a) 2.5×10^2 **b)** 1.1×10^3
c) 3.3×10^2 **d)** 4.8×10^4
e) 5.9×10^6 **f)** 2.75×10^6
g) 8.56×10^3 **h)** 7.34×10^3
i) 8.0808×10^5 **j)** 7.45×10^3
k) 2.7×10^3 **l)** 1.40014×10^6
m) 9.30078×10^5 **n)** 5.4×10^{10}
o) 2.9007×10^5

2 a) 2.5×10^{-3} **b)** 6.7×10^{-3}
c) 3.03×10^{-2} **d)** 4.8×10^{-4}
e) 5.6×10^{-5} **f)** 3.75×10^{-1}
g) 7.8×10^{-5} **h)** 7.07×10^{-2}
i) 2.1×10^{-10} **j)** 5.002×10^{-4}

Page 71   Exercise 2

1 a) 3 000 000   b) 400
   c) 94 000   d) 880 000
   e) 4090   f) 198 900 000
   g) 66.9   h) 7.2
   i) 0.00000356   j) 0.0423
   k) 0.000945   l) 0.0000888
   m) 0.000000019   n) 0.669
   o) 0.00000705

Page 72   Exercise 3

1 a) 3.4×10^2 b) 5.67×10^6
   c) 5.05×10^1 d) 9.07×10^7
   e) 9.532×10^3 f) 3.4×10^{-6}
   g) 5.05×10^{-5} h) 5.67×10^{-3}
   i) 9.07×10^{-3} j) 2.63×10^{-5}
   k) 8.45×10^2 l) 6.13×10^{-7}

2 a) 1.53×10^4 b) 2.53×10^6
   c) 1.422×10^8 d) 9.52×10^{-2}
   e) 2.958×10^1 f) 6.36×10^{10}
   g) 1.08×10^{-10} h) 4.32×10^{10}
   i) 2.178×10^{-8}

3 a) 3×10^3 b) 1.2×10^{-4}
   c) 1.5×10^{-12} d) 4×10^5
   e) 9×10^1 f) 1.1×10^2

Page 72   Exercise 4

1 a) 5.3×10^3 b) 7.2×10^2
   c) 1.832×10^5 d) 9.955×10^8
   e) 5.52×10^{-1} f) 7.28×10^{-4}
   g) 1.47×10^0 h) 1.005×10^5
   i) 6.05×10^8

2 a) 4.87×10^4 b) 7.05×10^{-3}
   c) 2.66×10^7 d) -3.29935×10^2
   e) 2.68×10^4 f) 8.337×10^2
   g) 8.317×10^4 h) 2.747×10^0
   i) 2.078×10^4

Page 73   Exercise 5

1 1.178×10^{-3} m   2 2.56×10^8
3 1.5×10^0 g   4 1.6×10^3 people
5 1.99×10^{30} kg   6 5×10^4 ants
7 5.51×10^{-3} %

7.4   Surds

Page 74   Exercise 1

1 a) $2\sqrt{3}$ b) $2\sqrt{5}$ c) $2\sqrt{6}$ d) $5\sqrt{2}$
   e) $3\sqrt{3}$ f) $4\sqrt{2}$ g) $6\sqrt{3}$ h) $10\sqrt{3}$
   i) $7\sqrt{2}$ j) $8\sqrt{3}$

2 a) $4\sqrt{3}$ b) 6 c) $6\sqrt{2}$ d) $2\sqrt{5}$
   e) $3\sqrt{5}$ f) $4\sqrt{5}$ g) $6\sqrt{5}$ h) $7\sqrt{5}$
   i) $10\sqrt{5}$ j) $8\sqrt{3}$

Page 74   Exercise 2

1 a) 3 b) 6 c) 5 d) 9
   e) 7 f) $2\sqrt{2}$ g) $2\sqrt{3}$ h) $2\sqrt{15}$
   i) $2\sqrt{5}$ j) 4 k) $5\sqrt{7}$ l) $6\sqrt{2}$

2 a) $\frac{1}{3}$ b) $\frac{2}{5}$ c) $\frac{3}{2}$ d) $\frac{7}{11}$
   e) $\frac{5}{4}$ f) $\frac{3}{10}$ g) $\frac{\sqrt{2}}{5}$ h) $\frac{6}{7}$
   i) $\frac{3\sqrt{3}}{8}$ j) $\frac{7\sqrt{2}}{11}$

Page 75   Exercise 3

1 a) $5\sqrt{3}$ b) $4\sqrt{7}$ c) $4\sqrt{5}$
   d) $2\sqrt{3} + 3\sqrt{7}$ e) $-\sqrt{7}$ f) $11\sqrt{2}$
   g) $3\sqrt{3}$ h) $3\sqrt{6}$ i) $11\sqrt{7}$
   j) $-2\sqrt{5}$ k) $26\sqrt{3}$ l) $17\sqrt{6}$

Page 75   Exercise 4

1 a) $\sqrt{2}$ b) $2 + \sqrt{3} + 2\sqrt{2} + \sqrt{6}$
   c) $16 - 6\sqrt{7}$ d) $12 - 2\sqrt{3}$
   e) $20 - 5\sqrt{7} - 4\sqrt{2} + \sqrt{14}$
   f) $7 + 7\sqrt{5} + \sqrt{2} + \sqrt{10}$
   g) $15 - 12\sqrt{2}$
   h) $8 + 4\sqrt{5} + 4\sqrt{2} + 2\sqrt{10}$
   i) $10 - 15\sqrt{3} - 6\sqrt{2} + 9\sqrt{6}$
   j) 41
   k) $8 - 2\sqrt{3} + 4\sqrt{6} - 3\sqrt{2}$
   l) $6 - \sqrt{15} - 12\sqrt{10} + 10\sqrt{6}$

Page 76   Exercise 5

1 a) $\sqrt{6}$ b) $2\sqrt{2}$ c) $\sqrt{5}$ d) $\frac{\sqrt{3}}{3}$
   e) $\frac{\sqrt{7}}{7}$ f) $3\sqrt{5}$ g) $3\sqrt{3}$ h) $\frac{7\sqrt{5}}{5}$
   i) $2\sqrt{6}$ j) $4\sqrt{2}$

2 a) $\frac{\sqrt{5}}{25}$ b) $\frac{\sqrt{3}}{9}$ c) $\frac{\sqrt{7}}{21}$ d) $\frac{3\sqrt{2}}{16}$
   e) $\frac{3\sqrt{5}}{10}$ f) $\frac{2\sqrt{3}}{21}$ g) $\frac{5\sqrt{2}}{4}$ h) $\frac{\sqrt{3}}{36}$
   i) $\frac{2\sqrt{5}}{7}$ j) $\frac{\sqrt{10}}{18}$

3 a) $\frac{2 - \sqrt{2}}{2}$ b) $-\left(\frac{5 + 5\sqrt{7}}{6}\right)$
   c) $\frac{12 - 3\sqrt{2}}{14}$ d) $-\left(\frac{3 + \sqrt{13}}{2}\right)$
   e) $\frac{25 - 5\sqrt{11}}{7}$ f) $\frac{16 - 4\sqrt{3}}{13}$
   g) $\frac{4\sqrt{5} - 2}{19}$ h) $-12 - 3\sqrt{17}$
   i) $\frac{3 - \sqrt{2}}{7}$ j) $\frac{5\sqrt{7} + 2\sqrt{14}}{17}$

4 a) $-3 - 2\sqrt{2}$ b) $\frac{-5 - 3\sqrt{3}}{2}$ c) $3 + \sqrt{5}$
   d) $-2 - \sqrt{5}$ e) $4 + 2\sqrt{5} + 2\sqrt{2} + \sqrt{10}$
   f) $\frac{-9 - 4\sqrt{2}}{7}$ g) $\frac{1 + 13\sqrt{3}}{22}$
   h) $\frac{14 + 4\sqrt{5} - 7\sqrt{3} - 2\sqrt{15}}{3}$
   i) $\frac{-89 - 41\sqrt{2}}{47}$ j) $\frac{-17 + 37\sqrt{2}}{31}$

5 $\dfrac{1}{1 - \frac{1}{\sqrt{2}}} = \dfrac{\sqrt{2}}{\sqrt{2} - 1}$ 6 $\dfrac{1}{1 + \frac{1}{\sqrt{3}}} = \dfrac{\sqrt{3}}{\sqrt{3} + 1}$

$= \dfrac{\sqrt{2}(\sqrt{2} + 1)}{(\sqrt{2} - 1)(\sqrt{2} + 1)}$ $= \dfrac{\sqrt{3}(\sqrt{3} - 1)}{(\sqrt{3} + 1)(\sqrt{3} - 1)}$

$= 2 + \sqrt{2}$ $= \dfrac{3 - \sqrt{3}}{2}$

Section 8 — Formulas

8.1   Writing Formulas

Page 77   Exercise 1

1 a) $2f$ b) $3f$ c) $3f - 6$
2 $F = 3b + 5$ 3 $l = c - 25$
4 $M = 18 + 8h$ 5 $t = 50n + 25$
6 $C = tp + 25$ 7 $C = 3 + 0.08g$
8 a) $m = \frac{5k}{8}$ b) $k = \frac{8m}{5}$
9 a) $c = \frac{f - 32}{1.8}$ b) $f = 1.8c + 32$
10 $M = 3(n - 1) + 4 = 3n + 1$

8.2   Substituting into a Formula

Page 78   Exercise 1

1 a) $z = 6$ b) $z = 2$ c) $z = 7$ d) $z = -1$
   e) $z = 8$ f) $z = 9$ g) $z = 7$ h) $z = 21$

2 a) $l = 10$ b) $l = 25$ c) $l = 1$ d) $l = 5$
   e) $l = 15$ f) $l = 6$ g) $l = 0.4$ h) $l = 20$

3 a) $c = -8$ b) $c = -7$ c) $c = -12$ d) $c = -14$
   e) $c = -27$ f) $c = -1.5$ g) $c = -29$ h) $c = 90$

4 a) $r = 1.9$ b) $r = 8$ c) $r = -12.8$
   d) $r = 31.68$ e) $r = -32.768$ f) $r = -0.4$
   g) $r = 25.6$ h) $r = 137.472$

5 a) $q = 3$ b) $q = \frac{2}{3}$ c) $q = -\frac{1}{4}$
   d) $q = -\frac{4}{9}$ e) $q = \frac{5}{12}$ f) $q = 1\frac{1}{12}$
   g) $q = 2\frac{2}{3}$ h) $q = \frac{1}{2}$

6 a) $u = 38$ b) $u = 267$ c) $u = 16.24$
   d) $u = 48.32$ e) $u = -53$ f) $u = -120.65$

Page 76   Exercise 5 *(right column top)*

7 a) $s = 44$ b) $s = 1241.5$
   c) $s = 585.47$ d) $s = 5866.48$
   e) $s = -864.26$ f) $s = 780.38$

8 a) $w = 18$ b) $w = 285.25$ c) $w = -20$.
   d) $w = 6.63$ e) $w = -3457.56$ f) $w = -12$.
   g) $w = -11$ h) $w = 12.28$

Page 79   Exercise 2

1 a) 7.27 m/s   b) 28.57 m/s
   c) 16.67 m/s   d) 177.78 m/s
   e) 8000 m/s

2 a) 100 °C   b) 20 °C
   c) −40 °C   d) 37 °C

3 a) $y = 10$ b) $y = 42$
   c) $y = 154$ d) $y = 192$

4 a) $S = 55$ b) $S = 5050$
   c) $S = 500500$

5 a) $T = 1.99$ s   b) $T = 1.4$ s
   c) $T = 0.99$ s   d) $T = 7.95$ s

6 a) $V = 226.19$ cm^3 b) $V = 1900.66$ cm
7 a) $V = 25.13$ cm^3 b) $V = 302.78$ cm

8.3   Rearranging Formulas

Page 80   Exercise 1

1 a) $x = y - 2$ b) $x = b + 5$
   c) $x = 2z - 3r$ d) $x = \frac{y}{4}$
   e) $x = \frac{c - 1}{2}$ f) $x = \frac{k - 2}{4}$
   g) $x = \frac{3v + 6}{2}$ h) $x = \frac{2u - 1}{5}$
   i) $x = 3y + 4$

2 a) $x = 1 - z$ b) $x = \frac{2 - p}{7}$
   c) $x = \frac{1.8 - 3r}{4.2}$ d) $x = \frac{1 - u}{2}$
   e) $x = 3 - 3t$ f) $x = \frac{6 - uv}{9}$
   g) $x = 4 - 3y$ h) $x = \frac{1 - 5w}{2}$
   i) $x = \frac{8 - 7z}{4}$

3 a) $w(1 + y) = 1$ b) $y = \frac{1 - w}{w}$

4 a) $y = \frac{1}{a}$ b) $y = \frac{3}{2w}$
   c) $y = \frac{1 - 2b}{2b}$ d) $y = 1 - \frac{2}{z + 2} = \frac{z}{z + 2}$
   e) $y = \frac{2}{3(k - 1)}$ f) $y = \frac{1}{c - b}$
   g) $y = \frac{1}{2} - \frac{1}{2uv} = \frac{uv - 1}{2uv}$
   h) $y = \frac{4}{3} - \frac{2}{3(a + b)} = \frac{4(a + b) - 2}{3(a + b)}$
   i) $y = -\frac{2}{3(z - 10)} = \frac{2}{30 - 3z}$

5 a) $\sqrt{w - 2} = 12 - 2k$
   b) $w = (12 - 2k)^2 + 2 = 146 - 48k + 4k^2$

6 a) $w = a^2$ b) $w = (x - 1)^2$
   c) $w = y^2 + 2$ d) $w = (a - y - 2)^2$
   e) $w = \left(\frac{f - 3}{2}\right)^2$ f) $w = \frac{1 - a^2}{2}$
   g) $w = \frac{j^2 - 3}{4}$ h) $w = \frac{4e - e^2}{12}$
   i) $w = -2$

7 a) $(z + 1)^2 = \frac{1 - t}{3}$ b) $z = \sqrt{\frac{1 - t}{3}} - 1$

8 a) $z = \sqrt{x - 1}$ b) $z = \sqrt{3 - 2t}$
   c) $z = \sqrt{u} - 2$ d) $z = \frac{\sqrt{1 - xy}}{2}$
   e) $z = \sqrt{\frac{t + 2}{3}} + 2$ f) $z = \frac{\sqrt{b - 2} - 3}{2}$

g) $z = \dfrac{\sqrt{4-g}-3}{2}$ h) $z = 1 - \sqrt{\dfrac{1-k}{6}}$

i) $z = \dfrac{5 - \sqrt{\dfrac{4-r}{2}}}{3}$

9 a) $a = \dfrac{bx+1}{1-x}$ b) $a = \dfrac{1}{1-b}$

c) $a = \dfrac{c-x}{d-b} = \dfrac{x-c}{b-d}$

d) $a = \dfrac{11}{23}$ e) $a = \dfrac{4b+11}{5}$

f) $a = \dfrac{3}{2}$ g) $a = \dfrac{c-1}{1+2c}$

h) $a = \dfrac{2}{2e-3}$ i) $a = \dfrac{by}{y-1}$

.4 Formulas Problems

Page 81 Exercise 1

1 a) $m = \dfrac{j}{2}$ b) $m = 12$

2 a) $C = 30 + 1.25n$ b) $C = 70$

3 a) 31   b) $h = \dfrac{m-1}{5}$ c) 7

4 a) $h = \dfrac{5}{8}(g - 17)$

   b) (i) $h = 30.625$ (ii) $h = 121.875$

     (iii) $h = -35.625$ (iv) $h = 40$

5 a) $C = 5 + 1.7h$ b) £13.50

   c) $h = \dfrac{C-5}{1.7}$ d) 3 hours

6 a) $d = \sqrt{\dfrac{A}{21.5}}$ b) $d = 1.6$

7 a) 77 min 30 sec   b) $w = \dfrac{T-25}{35}$

   c) 5.2 kg   d) 5.8 kg

8 a) £7.50   b) 6p   c) £53.10

   d) $n = \dfrac{C-7.5}{0.06}$ e) 550 units

9 a) (i) $x = 4 - \dfrac{3}{-2+y} = \dfrac{11-4y}{2-y}$ (ii) $x = 5$

   b) (i) $x = 1 - \dfrac{1}{y^2}$ (ii) $x = 0$

   c) (i) $x = \dfrac{2-3y}{y+2}$ (ii) $x = 5$

   d) (i) $x = \dfrac{2-y}{2y+3}$ (ii) $x = 3$

   e) (i) $x = \dfrac{1}{(8-y)^2}$ (ii) $x = \dfrac{1}{81}$

   f) (i) $x = 2 - \left(\dfrac{2y-1}{3}\right)^2$ (ii) $x = 1$

10 a) $s = 8$ b) $t = 2.2$ c) $u = -5.5$ d) $v = 1$

11 a) $v = \pm\sqrt{12} = \pm2\sqrt{3}$ b) $a = 10$ c) $u = \pm5$

12 a) $x = 1$ b) $z = 4$

13 a) $x = -2$ b) $y = -4, y = 6$

ection 9 — Equations

.1 Solving Equations

Page 83 Exercise 1

1 a) $x = 3$ b) $x = 8.9$ c) $x = 1$

   d) $x = 3$ e) $x = 6$ f) $x = -10$

   g) $x = -0.6$ h) $x = -0.8$ i) $x = 6$

   j) $x = 6.4$ k) $x = -0.64$ l) $x = 15$

2 a) $x = 7$ b) $x = 10$ c) $x = 8$

   d) $x = 4$ e) $x = -14$ f) $x = -30$

   g) $x = -20$ h) $x = -10$ i) $x = 1$

   j) $x = 4$ k) $x = -2$ l) $x = -9$

   m) $x = 6$ n) $x = -15$ o) $x = -1.5$

   p) $x = -\dfrac{5}{9}$

3 a) $x = 5$ b) $x = 7$ c) $x = 9$

   d) $x = 2$ e) $x = -2$ f) $x = -3$

   g) $x = -5$ h) $x = -7$ i) $x = 8$

   j) $x = 6$ k) $x = 12$ l) $x = 13$

   m) $x = -12$ n) $x = -7$ o) $x = -9$

   p) $x = -30$

4 a) $1 = 3(x - 2)$ b) $x = 2\frac{1}{3}$

5 a) $x = \frac{1}{2}$ b) $x = \frac{2}{5}$

   c) $x = 5$ d) $x = -\frac{1}{4}$

Page 84 Exercise 2

1 a) $x = 5$ b) $x = 1$ c) $x = 3$

   d) $x = 2$ e) $x = 7$ f) $x = 10$

   g) $x = 0.5$ h) $x = 2.1$ i) $x = -0.6$

2 a) $x = 4$ b) $x = 14$ c) $x = 12$

   d) $x = 10$ e) $x = 3$ f) $x = 14$

   g) $x = -1$ h) $x = -2$ i) $x = 10$

   j) $x = \frac{2}{7}$ k) $x = 2.2$ l) $x = -1.6$

Page 84 Exercise 3

1 a) $x = 0.8$ b) $x = 6$ c) $x = 5$

   d) $x = 6$ e) $x = 8$ f) $x = -10$

2 a) $x = 8$ b) $x = -1$ c) $x = 5$

   d) $x = 11$ e) $x = 8$ f) $x = 21$

   g) $x = 10$ h) $x = 6$ i) $x = 4$

Page 85 Exercise 4

1 a) $x = 7$ b) $x = 19$

   c) $x = 2\frac{7}{16}$ d) $x = -9$

2 a) $x = 6$ b) $x = -16$

   c) $x = 94\frac{1}{2}$ d) $x = 12$

3 a) $x = -8\frac{2}{3}$ b) $x = -18$ c) $x = -10\frac{1}{7}$

   d) $x = -\frac{1}{2}$ e) $x = -1\frac{2}{7}$ f) $x = -36\frac{1}{2}$

4 a) $x = 9$ b) $x = -5$ c) $x = -15\frac{3}{5}$

   d) $x = -22$ e) $x = -9$ f) $x = 89$

9.2 Writing Equations

Page 85 Exercise 1

1 a) $2x + 3 = 19$ b) $x = 8$

2 27

3 9, 10, 11, 12   **4** 8, 10, 12

5 Anna — 20, Bill — 23, Christie — 40

6 Deb — £16.50, Eduardo — £22.50, Fiz — £67.50

7 Macy — 8, Stacey — 11, Tracy — 22

Page 86 Exercise 2

1 a) (i) $3x + 5x + 20 = 180$ (ii) $x = 20°$

   b) (i) $3x + 4x + 110 = 180$ (ii) $x = 10°$

   c) (i) $7x + 23x + 30x = 180$ (ii) $x = 3°$

   d) (i) $6x + 10x + 3x - 10 = 180$ (ii) $x = 10°$

   e) (i) $5x + 3x + 2x + 40 = 180$ (ii) $x = 14°$

   f) (i) $5x + 3x - 5 + 5x - 10 = 180$ (ii) $x = 15°$

2 $x = 55°$

3 a) (i) $x = 13$ (ii) 1092 cm²

   b) (i) $x = 40$ (ii) 2150 cm²

4 4.48 cm²   **5** 26 cm and 30 cm

9.3 Iterative Methods

Page 87 Exercise 1

1 a) -1.25 b) greater than

   c) (i) greater than   (ii) greater than

     (iii) less than

   d) $x = 2.7$

2 $x = 4.6$

3 a) $x = 5.3$ b) $x = 5.6$

4 $x = 4.3$

5 $x = 5.44$

6 a) $x = 4.32$ b) $x = 3.24$

   c) $x = 5.76$ d) $x = 7.09$

7 $x = 6.446$ **8** $x = 2.281$

9 a) $x^2 + 7x = 100$ b) $x = 7.1$

   c) 14.1 cm and 7.1 cm

10 a) 2.3   b) 5.5   c) 17.7

Page 89 Exercise 2

1 $x = 1.8$

2 $x = 0.47$

3 $x = 2.345$

4 a) $2x^3 + 2x - 7 = 0$

     $2x^3 + 2x = 7$

     $2x^3 = 7 - 2x$

     $x^3 = \dfrac{7-2x}{2}$

     $x = \sqrt[3]{\dfrac{7-2x}{2}}$

   b) $x = 1.300$

9.4 Equations Problems

Page 89 Exercise 1

1 a) $x = 4$ b) $x = 35$ c) $x = 23.5$

   d) $x = 15$ e) $x = 9$ f) $x = -12$

   g) $x = -3$ h) $x = -6$ i) $x = -63$

   j) $x = -32$ k) $x = 5$ l) $x = -11$

2 a) $x = 4$ b) $x = \frac{3}{4}$ c) $x = 0$

   d) $x = 9$ e) $x = -16$ f) $x = -31$

   g) $x = 4\frac{11}{13}$ h) $x = 15$ i) $x = 1$

3 a) $x = 6\frac{3}{8}$ b) $x = 4\frac{2}{11}$ c) $x = 4\frac{5}{19}$

   d) $x = 3\frac{2}{11}$ e) $x = -6\frac{2}{21}$ f) $x = 7\frac{1}{2}$

4 a) $\dfrac{x-4}{5} = 15$ b) $x = 79$

5 a) $x = 30°$ b) $x = 28\frac{5}{6}°$ c) $x = 30$

6 16 cm   **7** 849.5 cm²

8 a) $x = 2.8$ b) $x = 8.2$ c) $x = 14.8$

   d) $x = 6.2$ e) $x = 1.8$ f) $x = 1.6$

9 a) $x = 2$ b) 6 cm²   c) $y = 1.4$

10 a) 2.46   b) 8.54

11 a) $x + x^2 + 30 = 128$

   b) Lol — 9.41 m, Norm — 30 m, Maddie — 88.55 m

12 a) 9.6°   b) 1.1

9.5 Identities

Page 91 Exercise 1

1 a) No   b) No   c) No   d) No

   e) Yes   f) No   g) Yes   h) Yes

   i) Yes   j) No

2 a) $a = 9$ b) $a = 4$ c) $a = 4$ d) $a = 2$

   e) $a = 3$ f) $a = 4$ g) $a = \frac{1}{2}$ h) $a = 1$

   i) $a = 2$ j) $a = -2$

3 $(x+5)^2 + 3(x-1)^2$

   $\equiv x^2 + 10x + 25 + 3x^2 - 6x + 3$

   $\equiv 4x^2 + 4x + 28$

   $\equiv 4(x^2 + x + 7)$

4 $3(x+2)^2 - (x-4)^2$

   $\equiv 3x^2 + 12x + 12 - x^2 + 8x - 16$

   $\equiv 2x^2 + 20x - 4$

   $\equiv 2(x^2 + 10x - 2)$

Section 10 — Direct and Inverse Proportion

10.1 Direct Proportion

Page 92 Exercise 1

1 a)

x	22	33
y	2	3

b)

x	24	32
y	18	24

c)

x	7	2	10	21	24
y	10.5	3	15	31.5	36

d)

x	-4	0	6	12
y	-14	0	21	42

e)

x	10.67	8
y	12	9

f)

x	-27	78	204	735
y	-36	104	272	980

2 120   **3** 11.25
4 14.5   **5** 22.5
6 a) 38   **b)** 382.5
7 a) 159.75   **b)** 22.56 (to 2 d.p.)
8 a) C   **b)** 0.5

Page 93   Exercise 2
1 a) 400   **b)** ±11 **c)** 555.56 (2 d.p.)
2 a) 375   **b)** 2   **c)** -3.75
3 a) 87.5   **b)** 2.94 (2 d.p.)
4

x	2	8	10	12.386
y	4	256	500	950

5

x	1	9	16	400
y	28	84	112	560

6

x	2	3	3.430	4.5
y	34	76.5	100	172.125

7 a) 75.645   **b)** $10\sqrt{7}$
8 1.990 secs
9 a) $k = \frac{4}{3}\pi$, $V = \frac{4}{3}\pi r^3$ **b)** $12\,348\pi$ cm³
c) 6.2 cm (1 d.p.)

10.2   Inverse Proportion

Page 94   Exercise 1
1 a)

x	12	15
y	15	12

b)

x	11	22
y	4	2

c)

x	1	3	6	20	1/3
y	90	30	15	4.5	270

d)

x	2.5	7
y	25.2	9

Page 95   Exercise 2
1 0.5   **2** 12
3 0.16   **4** 1.67
5 a) 1.33   **b)** 2.67
c)

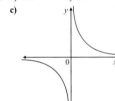

6 a) 2.4 **b)** z is halved   **c)** w is divided by 3
Page 96   Exercise 3
1 a)

x	2	5	±4	0.4
y	8	1.28	2	200

b)

x	16	9	100	5184
y	6	8	2.4	1/3

c)

x	2	8	5.894	0.4
y	256	4	10	32 000

2 a) $m = \frac{8}{\sqrt{t}}$ **b)** 16
3 0.8   **4** ±3
5 a) y is inversely proportional to the cube of x
b) $y = \frac{120}{x^3}$ **c)** 7.68   **d)** 1.063 (3 d.p.)
6 a) 8.89 units (2 d.p.)
b) $\frac{10\sqrt{6}}{3} = 8.165$ mm (3 d.p.)

7 $b = c = 4$
8 a) (i) false **(ii)** true   **(iii)** false **(iv)** true
b) At least three of:
$v = 1$, $u = 30$; $v = 4$, $u = 15$; $v = 9$, $u = 10$;
$v = 25$, $u = 6$; $v = 36$, $u = 5$; $v = 100$, $u = 3$;
$v = 225$, $u = 2$; $v = 900$, $u = 1$

10.3   Direct and Inverse Proportion Problems
Page 96   Exercise 1
1 a) (i)

x	2	3	9	37.5
y	5.33	8	24	100

(ii)

x	2	3	9	0.24
y	12	8	2.67	100

b) In direct proportion, as x increases, y increases, whereas in inverse proportion, as x increases, y decreases.

2 a) 3.644   **b)** 1.310
3 2.384 (to 3 d.p.)
4 $r \propto h$; $r = 1.3h$; reach $= 2.275$ m
Based on the data, you would expect a person who is 1.75 m tall to have a reach of 2.275 m, so it is not likely that they would be able to reach to a height of 2.5 m.

5 Statement A with table L and graph T
Statement B with table M and graph S
Statement C with table K and graph R
Statement D with table N and graph Q.

6 a) (i)

x	-6	-4	-2	2	4	6
y	-2	-3	-6	6	3	2

(ii)

x	-6	-4	-2	2	4	6
y	0.67	1.5	6	6	1.5	0.67

(iii)

x	-6	-4	-2	2	4	6
y	-0.22	-0.75	-6	6	0.75	0.22

(iv)

x	-6	-4	-2	2	4	6
y	no real solutions			6	4.24	3.46

b) (In all cases, both axes should be marked as asymptotes.)
(i)

(ii)

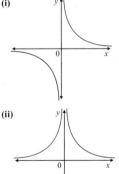

(iii)

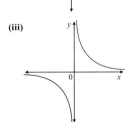

(iv)

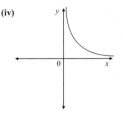

7 a) k = the distance travelled
b) k = the percentage rate of VAT
c) k = the area of the rectangle
d) k = the scale factor of the enlargement
e) k = the volume of the cylinder
8 140 625 units

Section 11 — Quadratic Equations

11.1   Solving Quadratics by Factorising

Page 98   Exercise 1
1 a) $x = 0$, $x = -8$ **b)** $x = 5$, $x = 1$
c) $x = -2$, $x = -6$ **d)** $x = 9$, $x = -7$
2 a) (i) $x(x + 6)$ **(ii)** $(x + 2)(x - 1)$
(iii) $(x + 1)(x - 2)$ **(iv)** $(x + 6)(x - 4)$
(v) $(x + 4)(x + 9)$
b) (i) $x = 0$, $x = -6$ **(ii)** $x = -2$, $x = 1$
(iii) $x = -1$, $x = 2$ **(iv)** $x = -6$, $x = 4$
(v) $x = -9$, $x = -4$
3 a) $x = 0$, $x = 3$ **b)** $x = -5$, $x = 0$
c) $x = 0$, $x = 1$ **d)** $x = 0$, $x = -12$
e) $x = -2$, $x = -1$ **f)** $x = 1$, $x = 2$
g) $x = -2$ **h)** $x = 2$
i) $x = -4$, $x = 1$ **j)** $x = -1$, $x = 4$
k) $x = -4$, $x = -1$ **l)** $x = 1$, $x = 4$
m) $x = -1$, $x = 5$ **n)** $x = 2$, $x = 3$
o) $x = 1$, $x = 6$ **p)** $x = -3$, $x = 4$
q) $x = -6$, $x = -2$ **r)** $x = -4$, $x = 6$
s) $x = 3$, $x = 12$ **t)** $x = -18$, $x = 2$

Page 99   Exercise 2
1 a) $x = 0$, $x = 1.5$ **b)** $x = 2$, $x = \frac{1}{3}$
c) $x = -\frac{4}{3}$, $x = -2.5$ **d)** $x = 1.75$, $x = -0.4$
2 a) (i) $(2x + 5)(x + 1)$ **(ii)** $(3x + 2)(x + 1$
(iii) $(2x - 3)(2x + 5)$ **(iv)** $(4x + 3)(x + 2$
(v) $(6x - 5)(x + 2)$ **(vi)** $3(4x + 1)(x -$
b) (i) $x = -2.5$, $x = -1$ **(ii)** $x = -\frac{2}{3}$, $x = -1$
(iii) $x = 1.5$, $x = -2.5$ **(iv)** $x = -0.75$, $x =$
(v) $x = \frac{5}{6}$, $x = -2$ **(vi)** $x = -0.25$, $x =$
3 a) $x = 0$, $x = -\frac{5}{3}$ **b)** $x = -1.5$, $x = 1$
c) $x = -1$, $x = -\frac{7}{3}$ **d)** $x = 0.4$, $x = -1$
e) $x = \frac{2}{3}$, $x = 3$ **f)** $x = \frac{1}{3}$, $x = 1.5$
g) $x = -4$, $x = -0.25$ **h)** $x = 1.5$, $x = 2.5$
i) $x = -3$, $x = 1.75$ **j)** $x = -2$, $x = \frac{11}{6}$
k) $x = -1.5$, $x = -0.8$ **l)** $x = -0.25$, $x =$
m) $x = -\frac{5}{6}$, $x = 0.5$ **n)** $x = \frac{2}{3}$, $x = \frac{4}{3}$
o) $x = -0.5$, $x = \frac{4}{9}$ **p)** $x = -\frac{7}{18}$, $x = 2$

Page 99   Exercise 3
1 a) $x = 0$, $x = 1$ **b)** $x = -3$, $x = 1$
c) $x = -2$, $x = 5$ **d)** $x = 3$, $x = 7$
e) $x = 2$, $x = 4$ **f)** $x = -3$, $x = 7$
g) $x = 2$, $x = 6$ **h)** $x = -1$, $x = 3$
i) $x = -11$, $x = 0.5$ **j)** $x = -1.5$, $x = 0.5$

k) $x = -0.5, x = \frac{1}{3}$ **l)** $x = 0.5, x = \frac{2}{3}$

m) $x = 1, x = -\frac{2}{3}$ **n)** $x = 0.5$

o) $x = -0.5, x = \frac{7}{3}$ **p)** $x = \frac{5}{3}$

2 a) $x = -2, x = 4$ **b)** $x = -7, x = 5$
c) $x = -8, x = 9$ **d)** $x = -6$
e) $x = 7$ **f)** $x = -2, x = 2$
g) $x = -7, x = -0.5$ **h)** $x = -\frac{4}{3}, x = 1$
i) $x = \frac{1}{3}, x = 3$ **j)** $x = -1, x = \frac{1}{12}$
k) $x = 0.25, x = 0.5$ **l)** $x = -\frac{2}{3}, x = -\frac{1}{6}$

3 a) $x = -3, x = 2$ **b)** $x = -2, x = 3$
c) $x = -6, x = 5$ **d)** $x = 1.5, x = 2$
e) $x = -1, x = \frac{5}{6}$ **f)** $x = -0.5, x = \frac{5}{12}$

1.2 Completing the Square

Page 100   Exercise 1
1 a) 1   **b)** –10   **c)** –2   **d)** 3
e) 2   **f)** –13   **g)** 39   **h)** –60
i) –8   **j)** 400

2 a) $(x + 1)^2 + 5$ **b)** $(x - 1)^2 + 3$
c) $(x - 1)^2 - 11$ **d)** $(x - 2)^2 + 6$
e) $(x + 2)^2 + 16$ **f)** $(x + 3)^2 - 8$
g) $(x + 4)^2 + 44$ **h)** $(x + 4)^2 + 65$
i) $(x + 5)^2 - 27$ **j)** $(x - 6)^2 + 64$
k) $(x + 6)^2 + 8$ **l)** $(x + 7)^2 - 49$
m) $(x - 7)^2 + 47$ **n)** $(x - 10)^2 - 300$
o) $(x + 10)^2 - 250$

3 a) $\left(x + \frac{3}{2}\right)^2 - \frac{5}{4}$ **b)** $\left(x + \frac{3}{2}\right)^2 - \frac{13}{4}$
c) $\left(x - \frac{3}{2}\right)^2 - \frac{5}{4}$ **d)** $\left(x + \frac{5}{2}\right)^2 + \frac{23}{4}$
e) $\left(x + \frac{5}{2}\right)^2 - \frac{13}{4}$ **f)** $\left(x - \frac{5}{2}\right)^2 + \frac{55}{4}$
g) $\left(x + \frac{7}{2}\right)^2 - \frac{9}{4}$ **h)** $\left(x - \frac{7}{2}\right)^2 - \frac{53}{4}$
i) $\left(x - \frac{9}{2}\right)^2 - \frac{121}{4}$ **j)** $\left(x + \frac{11}{2}\right)^2 - \frac{21}{4}$
k) $\left(x + \frac{19}{2}\right)^2 - \frac{1}{4}$ **l)** $\left(x + \frac{13}{2}\right)^2 - \frac{9}{4}$
m) $\left(x - \frac{13}{2}\right)^2 - \frac{173}{4}$ **n)** $\left(x - \frac{15}{2}\right)^2 - \frac{725}{4}$
o) $\left(x - \frac{21}{2}\right)^2 - \frac{1}{4}$

Page 101   Exercise 2
1 a) $x = -2$ **b)** $x = 3$
c) $x = 1 \pm \sqrt{5}$ **d)** $x = -3, x = -1$
e) $x = -3 \pm \sqrt{13}$ **f)** $x = -4 \pm 2\sqrt{3}$
g) $x = -4 \pm \sqrt{11}$ **h)** $x = \frac{1}{2} \pm \frac{\sqrt{5}}{2}$
i) $x = 1, x = 4$ **j)** $x = \frac{7}{2} \pm \frac{\sqrt{13}}{2}$
k) $x = -8, x = -1$ **l)** $x = \frac{11}{2} \pm \frac{\sqrt{21}}{2}$

2 a) $x = -5.24, x = -0.76$
b) $x = 1.44, x = 5.56$
c) $x = -1.45, x = 3.45$
d) $x = -3.73, x = -0.27$
e) $x = -6.46, x = 0.46$
f) $x = -6.83, x = -1.17$
g) $x = 0.35, x = 5.65$
h) $x = -2.70, x = 3.70$
i) $x = 0.70, x = 4.30$
j) $x = 0.30, x = 6.70$
k) $x = -7.70, x = -1.30$
l) $x = 2.30, x = 8.70$

3 a) $x = -\frac{1}{3} \pm \frac{\sqrt{7}}{3}$ **b)** $x = -\frac{1}{5} \pm \frac{\sqrt{51}}{5}$
c) $x = \frac{3}{4} \pm \frac{\sqrt{13}}{4}$ **d)** $x = 3 \pm \sqrt{\frac{13}{2}}$
e) $x = 4 \pm \sqrt{\frac{39}{2}}$ **f)** $x = -\frac{3}{8} \pm \frac{\sqrt{73}}{8}$
g) $x = -\frac{5}{6} \pm \frac{\sqrt{145}}{6}$ **h)** $x = -\frac{7}{20} \pm \frac{\sqrt{89}}{20}$

4 a) $x = -1.82, x = 0.82$
b) $x = -1.90, x = 1.23$
c) $x = -2.94, x = 0.94$
d) $x = 1.78, x = 4.22$
e) $x = -1.05, x = 9.05$
f) $x = -0.73, x = 0.23$
g) $x = -2.79, x = 0.79$
h) $x = -3.64, x = 0.64$

11.3 The Quadratic Formula

Page 102   Exercise 1
1 a) $x = -2.62, x = -0.38$
b) $x = -2.73, x = 0.73$
c) $x = -0.79, x = 3.79$
d) $x = -1.45, x = 3.45$
e) $x = -5.70, x = 0.70$
f) $x = 1.76, x = 6.24$
g) $x = -0.77, x = 7.77$
h) $x = -6.32, x = 0.32$
i) $x = 0.24, x = -4.24$
j) $x = -6.41, x = 1.41$
k) $x = -6.45, x = -1.55$
l) $x = -1.32, x = 8.32$

2 a) $x = \frac{3 \pm \sqrt{5}}{2}$ **b)** $x = 1 \pm \sqrt{13}$
c) $x = \frac{3 \pm \sqrt{41}}{2}$ **d)** $x = 1 \pm \sqrt{5}$
e) $x = \frac{-5 \pm \sqrt{29}}{2}$ **f)** $x = 4 \pm \sqrt{21}$
g) $x = \frac{7 \pm \sqrt{41}}{2}$ **h)** $x = -3 \pm \sqrt{14}$
i) $x = -2 \pm \sqrt{10}$ **j)** $x = \frac{5 \pm \sqrt{37}}{2}$
k) $x = -4 \pm \sqrt{3}$ **l)** $x = \frac{7 \pm \sqrt{37}}{2}$

3 a) $x = -4.37, x = 1.37$
b) $x = -1.54, x = 4.54$
c) $x = 0.27, x = 3.73$
d) $x = 1.44, x = 5.56$
e) $x = 1.21, x = 5.79$
f) $x = -4.46, x = 2.46$
g) $x = -1.83, x = 3.83$
h) $x = -4.19, x = 1.19$

4 a) $x = \frac{-3 \pm \sqrt{13}}{2}$ **b)** $x = \frac{3 \pm 3\sqrt{5}}{2}$
c) $x = 2 \pm \sqrt{2}$ **d)** $x = \frac{7 \pm \sqrt{61}}{2}$
e) $x = 3 \pm \sqrt{5}$ **f)** $x = -1 \pm \sqrt{7}$
g) $x = 1 \pm \sqrt{14}$ **h)** $x = \frac{-3 \pm \sqrt{53}}{2}$

5 a) $x = -0.43, x = 0.77$
b) $x = -0.82, x = 1.82$
c) no real solution
d) $x = -0.28, x = 1.78$
e) $x = -1.85, x = 1.35$
f) no real solution
g) $x = -0.10, x = 2.60$
h) $x = -3.31, x = 1.81$
i) $x = -0.39, x = 1.72$
j) $x = 0.55, x = 1.45$
k) $x = -1.26, x = 0.26$
l) $x = -0.57, x = 0.17$
m) $x = -0.18, x = 1.85$
n) $x = -0.39, x = 3.89$
o) no real solution
p) $x = -2.76, x = -0.24$

6 a) no real solution   **b)** $x = -0.78, x = 1.28$
c) no real solution   **d)** $x = 1.72, x = 3.78$
e) no real solution   **f)** $x = 0.36, x = 1.39$
g) $x = -2.33, x = 1.08$ **h)** no real solution
i) no real solution

7 a) $x = \frac{-5 \pm \sqrt{37}}{2}$ **b)** $x = -2 \pm \sqrt{11}$
c) $x = 4 \pm \sqrt{30}$ **d)** $x = \frac{-5 \pm \sqrt{129}}{4}$
e) no real solution   **f)** $x = \frac{7 \pm \sqrt{33}}{2}$
g) no real solution   **h)** $x = \frac{-9 \pm \sqrt{101}}{2}$

i) $x = \frac{-5 \pm \sqrt{43}}{3}$ **j)** $x = \frac{-3 \pm \sqrt{69}}{2}$
k) $x = 3 \pm \sqrt{6}$ **l)** $x = \frac{5 \pm \sqrt{57}}{4}$
m) $x = \frac{1 \pm \sqrt{73}}{12}$ **n)** $x = \frac{-3 \pm \sqrt{137}}{8}$
o) $x = \frac{3 \pm \sqrt{61}}{6}$ **p)** $x = \frac{1 \pm \sqrt{17}}{2}$
q) $x = 1 \pm \sqrt{2}$ **r)** $x = \frac{1 \pm \sqrt{13}}{2}$
s) $x = \frac{-1 \pm \sqrt{5}}{2}$ **t)** $x = \frac{-11 \pm \sqrt{291}}{10}$

11.4 Quadratic Equations Problems

Page 104   Exercise 1
1 a) $x = -2, x = 10$
b) $x = -5, x = 4$
c) $x = 1.38, x = 19.62$
d) $x = -0.17, x = 18.17$
e) $x = -5, x = 10$
f) $x = -9.06, x = 7.06$
g) $x = -8, x = 6$
h) $x = -\frac{5}{3}, x = 3$
i) $x = -2.76, x = 3.26$
j) $x = -0.74, x = 1.57$
k) $x = -2.5, x = 0.25$
l) No real solution
m) $x = \pm 9$
n) $x = -0.60, x = 9.10$
o) $x = -1.39, x = 0.48$
p) No real solution
q) $x = -1$
r) $x = -2.30, x = 1.30$
s) $x = -0.81, x = 2.21$
t) $x = 0.57, x = 1.23$

Page 104   Exercise 2
1 $(x + 1)^2 = 9, x = -4, x = 2$
2 $x^2 + 3 = 147, x = \pm 12$
3 $x^2 - x = 30, x = -5, x = 6$
4 $x^2 + x = 22, x = -5.22, x = 4.22$ (to 2 d.p.)
5 $25 - x^2 = 9, x = \pm 4$
6 $x^2 + 5x = 24, x = -8, x = 3$
7 $4x^2 = 36, x = \pm 3$
8 $2x^2 - 4 = x, x = -1.19, x = 1.69$ (to 2 d.p.)
9 $(x + 5)^2 = 100, x = -15, x = 5$
10 $(2x - 1)^2 = 64, x = -3.5, x = 4.5$

Page 104   Exercise 3
1 a) $x = 4$ **b)** $x = 3$
c) $x = 6.39$ (to 2 d.p.)   **d)** $x = 8$
2 a) total length of fence used = $2x + y = 20$
So $y = 20 - 2x$
b) Area = length × width, so $A = xy$
From part a), $y = 20 - 2x$.
So if $A = 50$, $x(20 - 2x) = 50$
c) The dimensions of the rectangle are 5 m × 10 m.
3 0.69 m × 11.62 m or 5.81 m × 1.38 m
4 50 m × 100 m
5 17.34 m × 115.34 m or 57.66 m × 34.69 m
6 a) $x^2 - 12x + 32 = 0$; $x = 4$ or $x = 8$
b) $x^2 - 15x + 56 = 0$; $x = 7$ or $x = 8$
c) $x^2 - 50x + 600 = 0$; $x = 20$ or $x = 30$
d) $2x^2 - 17x + 16 = 0$;
$x = 1.08$ or $x = 7.42$ (to 2 d.p.)

Page 105   Exercise 4
1 $x = 15$ **2** $x = 15.95$
3 $x = 1.37$ **4** $x = 10.73$
5 $x = 0.27$ **6** $x = 3.56$
7 $x = 4.87$ **8** $x = 7.20$

Section 12 — Simultaneous Equations

12.1 Simultaneous Equations

Page 106 Exercise 1

1 a) $x = 7, y = 2$ **b)** $x = 5, y = 3$
c) $x = -2, y = 4$ **d)** $x = 6, y = 1$
e) $x = 3, y = -5$ **f)** $x = 8, y = 0$
g) $x = \frac{1}{2}, y = 3$ **h)** $x = \frac{1}{3}, y = 10$
i) $e = 0.6, f = 3.2$ **j)** $g = \frac{2}{5}, h = 4$
k) $z = 27, u = 12$ **l)** $i = -5, j = -\frac{1}{2}$

2 a) $x = 2, y = 5$ **b)** $x = 1, y = 4$
c) $x = 6, y = 2$ **d)** $x = 3, y = 1$
e) $x = 5, y = 0$ **f)** $x = 3, y = 2$
g) $x = \frac{1}{2}, y = 6$ **h)** $x = 4, y = -3$
i) $y = 1.25, d = 5$ **j)** $e = -1, r = -4$
k) $p = -\frac{1}{7}, m = 0$ **l)** $c = 126, v = 82$

3 a) $x = 4, y = 2$ **b)** $p = 5, q = -1$
c) $u = 2, v = 1$ **d)** $k = -1, l = 3$
e) $c = 8, d = \frac{1}{2}$ **f)** $r = -2, s = 4$
g) $m = 3, n = 1$ **h)** $e = 2, f = -\frac{1}{2}$
i) $w = \frac{4}{7}, z = \frac{1}{7}$ **j)** $g = 72, h = 18$
k) $i = -0.2, j = 1.6$ **l)** $a = -4, b = -\frac{1}{3}$

Page 107 Exercise 2

1 $x = 40, y = 18$

2 Sherbet dip $= 35$p, Supa-Choc bar $= 17$p

3 1 kg apples $=$ £3.60, 1 kg pears $=$ £4.50

4 a) An exercise book weighs 0.15 kg or 150 g, the textbook weighs 1.2 kg
   b) Yes (4.95 kg)   **c)** 17

5 83 points   **6** £4206.64   **7** 15 cm

12.2 More Simultaneous Equations

Page 108 Exercise 1

1 a) $x = 2, y = 4$ and $x = 4, y = 8$
b) $x = -3, y = 11$ and $x = 1, y = -1$
c) $x = -3, y = -7$ and $x = 10, y = 32$
d) $x = 1, y = 2$ and $x = -5, y = 8$
e) $x = 2, y = -2$ and $x = 4, y = 2$
f) $x = -2, y = 5$ and $x = 7, y = 32$
g) $x = -2, y = 1$ and $x = 5, y = 15$
h) $x = 1, y = 5$ and $x = 4, y = 8$
i) $x = \frac{1}{2}, y = -1$ and $x = 3, y = 19$
j) $x = -1.5, y = 21$ and $x = -7, y = 65$
k) $x = 1, y = 1$ and $x = \frac{3}{4}, y = \frac{1}{2}$
l) $x = -\frac{1}{7}, y = \frac{6}{7}$ and $x = 3, y = 26$

2 a) (i) $(1, 0)$ **(ii)** $(1, 3.6)$
   b) Line A represents all the points where $y = 2x - 2$, and line B represents all the points where $5y = 20 - 2x$, so the point where the lines cross is the only point where $y = 2x - 2$ and $5y = 20 - 2x$ at the same time.
   c) $(2.5, 3)$

3 $M = (-1, 1)$ and $N = (3.5, 3.25)$

4 $(-2.5, 11.5)$ and $(\frac{1}{3}, 3)$

5 $(1, 5)$
The line only touches the curve at one point. / The line is a tangent to the curve.

6 $x = 0.4, y = -0.4$ and $x = 2, y = 0$

7 a) $x = -0.5, y = 7.5$ and $x = 4, y = 3$
b) $x = 6, y = -1$ and $x = 8, y = -3$
c) $x = 1, y = 1$ and $x = 3, y = -3$
d) $x = 2, y = -2$ and $x = -3, y = -7$
e) $x = 4, y = -8$ and $x = 8, y = -20$
f) $x = -2, y = 3$ and $x = 16, y = -1.5$
g) $x = -0.5, y = 4$ and $x = 2, y = 9$

h) $x = 3, y = \frac{1}{3}$ and $x = 16, y = -4$
i) $x = -5, y = -1$ and $x = 0.25, y = 0.75$
j) $x = 0.4, y = 0.2$ and $x = -1, y = 3$
k) $x = -16, y = -3.5$ and $x = 22, y = 6$
l) $x = 0, y = 0$ and $x = -0.25, y = 0.25$

8 a) The points where the circle and line cross are the points where both equations are true. Combine the two equations using the substitution method:
Rearrange $3y - 2x = -1$ to get x on its own:
$x = \frac{3y + 1}{2}$.
Substitute for x in the equation of the circle: $\left(\frac{3y + 1}{2}\right)^2 + y^2 = 1$
$\frac{9y^2 + 6y + 1}{4} + y^2 = 1$
$9y^2 + 6y + 1 + 4y^2 = 4$
$13y^2 + 6y - 3 = 0$
b) $y = \frac{-3 \pm 4\sqrt{3}}{13}$
c) $\left(\frac{2 + 6\sqrt{3}}{13}, \frac{-3 + 4\sqrt{3}}{13}\right)$
and $\left(\frac{2 - 6\sqrt{3}}{13}, \frac{-3 - 4\sqrt{3}}{13}\right)$

9 a) $x = 0.68, y = 3.38$ and $x = -0.88, y = -2.08$
b) $x = 4.70, y = -1.70$ and $x = -1.70, y = 4.70$

10 a) $x = -5, y = -3$ and $x = 5.8, y = 0.6$
b) $x = \frac{1 + \sqrt{7}}{4}, y = \frac{1 - \sqrt{7}}{4}$
and $x = \frac{1 - \sqrt{7}}{4}, y = \frac{1 + \sqrt{7}}{4}$
c) $x = -6, y = 0$ and $x = 4, y = 2\sqrt{5}$

Section 13 — Inequalities

13.1 Inequalities

Page 110 Exercise 1

1 a) $x > 5$
b) $x \le 9$
c) $x \ge 16$
d) $x < 26$
e) $x > 16$
f) $x \ge 16$
g) $x < 18$
h) $x \le 1$

2 a) $x \ge 3$
b) $x < 5$
c) $x > 4$
d) $x \le 3$
e) $x < -4$
f) $x > -8$
g) $x \le 3$
h) $x < 22.5$

3 a) $x \ge 6$
b) $x < 10$
c) $x < 24$
d) $x \le 35$

e) $x < -8$
f) $x \le 3$
g) $x \ge 11$
h) $x < -0.64$

4 a) $x \le -12$ **b)** $x \le 8$
   c) $x > 84$ **d)** $x \le -77$

5 a) $x < 3$ **b)** $x \le 8$ **c)** $x \le -2$
   d) $x > 11$ **e)** $x \ge -12$ **f)** $x < -1$
   g) $x < 2.1$ **h)** $x \ge -6.5$

6 a) $x < 1$ **b)** $x \ge 6$ **c)** $x > 22$
   d) $x \le 10$ **e)** $x \ge 14$ **f)** $x > -3.5$
   g) $x < -4.9$ **h)** $x \ge -11.84$

7 a) $x < -2$ **b)** $x \le -0.5$ **c)** $x \ge 1$
   d) $x > 1$ **e)** $x \ge 8$ **f)** $x > -0.2$
   g) $x > -2.5$ **h)** $x \le -1$

Page 111 Exercise 2

1 a) $4 < x \le 12$
b) $6 \le x \le 16$
c) $-6 \le x \le -1$
d) $37 \le x \le 60$

2 a) $4 < x < 7$ **b)** $16 < x \le 21$
   c) $6 < x \le 16$ **d)** $-3 \le x < 4$

3 a) $2 < x < 4$ **b)** $4 < x \le 10$
   c) $-7 < x \le 12$ **d)** $-3.3 \le x < -2.1$
   e) $5\frac{2}{3} < x \le 9$ **f)** $-2.5 < x < 1$

4 a) $-7.2 < x \le -2.6$ **b)** $-19.7 < x < -1.2$
   c) $-5 \le x < 3$ **d)** $-8.4 \le x < -5.6$
   e) $-7 \le x < 6$ **f)** $-2 \le x < 0$

13.2 Quadratic Inequalities

Page 112 Exercise 1

1 a) $x^2 - 16 > 0$
   b) (i) $f(x) = (x + 4)(x - 4)$
     (ii) $x = -4$ and $x = 4$
   c) $x < -4$ and $x > 4$

2 a) $x < -4$ and $x > 4$
   b) $-3 \le x \le 3$
   c) $x < -5$ and $x > 5$
   d) $x \le -6$ and $x \ge 6$
   e) $-1 < x < 1$
   f) $-7 \le x \le 7$
   g) $x < -8$ and $x > 8$
   h) $-10 < x < 10$

3 a) $-\frac{1}{2} < x < \frac{1}{2}$
   b) $x \le -\frac{1}{5}$ and $x \ge \frac{1}{5}$

Answers   395

c) $-\frac{1}{11} \le x \le \frac{1}{11}$

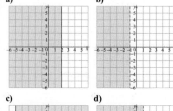

d) $x < -\frac{1}{6}$ and $x > \frac{1}{6}$

e) $-\frac{2}{3} < x < \frac{2}{3}$

f) $x \le -\frac{5}{7}$ and $x \ge \frac{5}{7}$

g) $-\frac{3}{4} \le x \le \frac{3}{4}$

h) $-\frac{4}{13} < x < \frac{4}{13}$

4 a) $-3 < x < 3$

b) $x \le -5$ and $x \ge 5$

c) $-4 < x < 4$

d) $x \le -7$ and $x \ge 7$

5 a) $x^2 + 4x - 12 \le 0$
b) (i) $g(x) = (x + 6)(x - 2)$
   (ii) $x = -6$ and $x = 2$
c) $-6 \le x \le 2$

6 a) $-2 < x < 1$ b) $-1 \le x \le 2$
c) $x < 3$ and $x > 5$ d) $-5 \le x \le -1$
e) $x \le -3$ and $x \ge 4$ f) $-1 < x < 7$
g) $3 \le x \le 4$ h) $x \le -6$ and $x \ge -4$
i) $-2 < x < 8$ j) $-5 < x < 3$
k) $-1 \le x \le 11$ l) $-9 < x < -2$

7 a) $x < -6$ and $x > 8$ b) $-2 \le x \le 5$
c) $4 < x < 5$ d) $3 \le x \le 6$
e) $x \le -9$ and $x \ge 4$ f) $-2 < x < 11$
g) $-3 < x < 9$ h) $4 < x < 8$

8 a) $x < 0$ and $x > 4$ b) $-3 \le x \le 0$
c) $0 < x < 5$ d) $x \le -8$ and $x \ge 0$
e) $x < 0$ and $x > 12$ f) $0 \le x \le 2$
g) $x \le 0$ and $x \ge 9$ h) $-3 \le x \le 0$

3.3 Graphing Inequalities

Page 113 Exercise 1

1 a) b)

c) d)

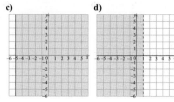

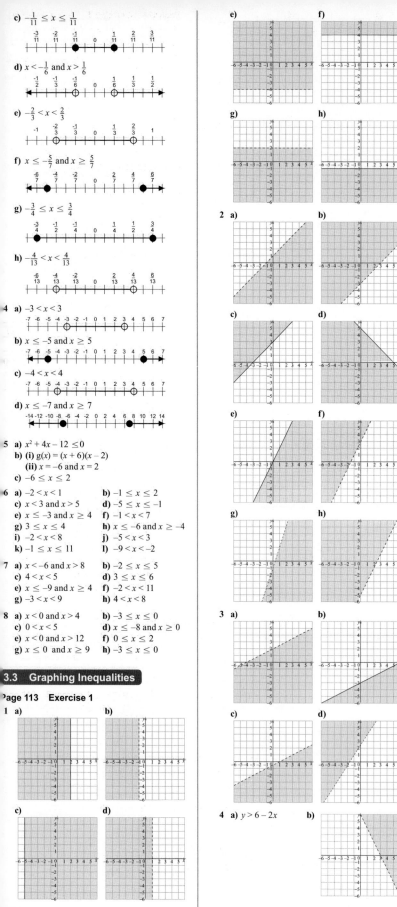

e) f)

g) h)

2 a) b)

c) d)

e) f)

g) h)

3 a) b)

c) d)

4 a) $y > 6 - 2x$ b)

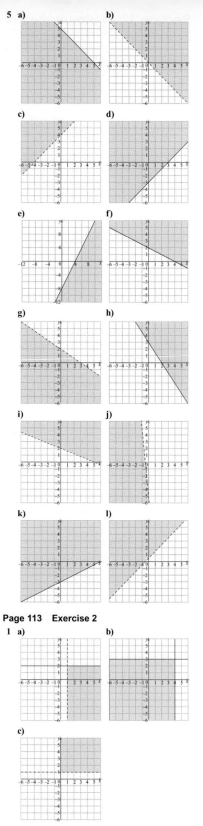

5 a) b)

c) d)

e) f)

g) h)

i) j)

k) l)

Page 113 Exercise 2

1 a) b)

c)

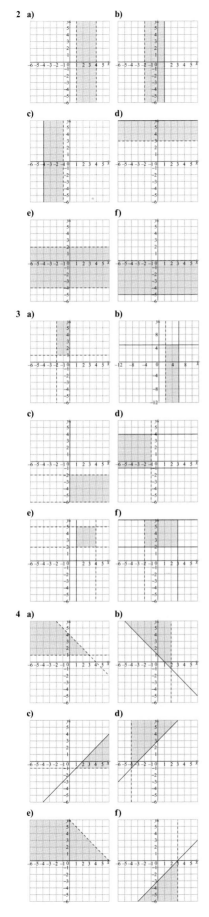

2 a) b) c) d) e) f)

3 a) b) c) d) e) f)

4 a) b) c) d) e) f)

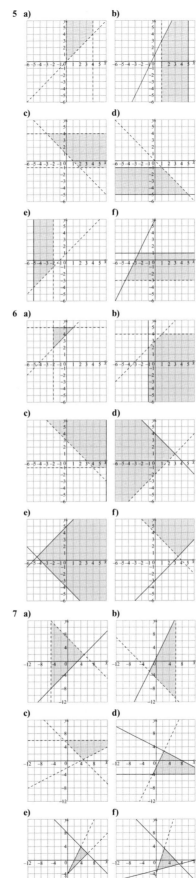

5 a) b) c) d) e) f)

6 a) b) c) d) e) f)

7 a) b) c) d) e) f)

Page 114   Exercise 3

1 a) $x > 3$ b) $y \leq 4$ c) $y < x$

2 a) $y \leq 4 - x$ b) $y \geq x + 1$ c) $y < 4 - 2x$

3 a) $-1 < x < 2$ b) $x < -1$, $y \geq -1$
c) $1 \leq x < 4$, $2 < y \leq 3$

4 a) $y \geq 3$, $x \geq -1$, $y > x + 1$
b) $x > -1$, $y \geq 1$, $y \leq -x$
c) $2 \leq x < 3$, $y \geq 1$, $y < 2x$

5 a) $y > x$, $y \leq x + 2$
b) $y \geq -1$, $y > x - 2$, $3y \leq x + 3$
c) $3y > 2x - 3$, $y \geq -x$, $2y \leq 4 - x$

13.4   Linear Programming

Page 116   Exercise 1

1 a)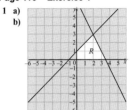
b)

c)

(x, y)	$(0, 0)$	$(0, 1)$	$(2, 3)$	$(3.5, 0)$
$3x + y$	0	1	9	10.5

d) Maximum value 10.5, when $x = 3.5$, $y = 0$

2 a)

b) $x - 2y = 5$ at $(1, -2)$

3 a)

b) $3x + 2y = 16$ at $(5, 0.5)$
c) $2x - 3y = -2$ at $(2, 2)$

4 14 (at $(2\frac{1}{2}, 1\frac{1}{2})$)

Page 117   Exercise 2

1 a) $x \geq 1$ b) $y \geq 3$ c) $8x + 5y \leq 50$

2 a) (i) $y \geq 2x$ (ii) $x + y \leq 14$
b) $x \geq 0$ and $y \geq 0$ — The baker cannot make a negative number of cakes.

3 a) $x \geq 4$, $y \geq x$, $x + 2y \leq 18$
b)

c)

Undercoat	4	4	4	4	5	5	6
Emulsion	4	5	6	7	5	6	6

4 a) $x + y \leq 50$, $x + 3y \geq 60$, $x \geq 15$, $y \geq 0$

b)

c) 5 **d)** £3000 — 15 regular and 35 Gold

5 a) $2x + y \leq 24$, $y \leq x$, $x \geq 0$, $y \geq 0$

b) 12 **c)** £200 — 8 cups, 8 saucers

6 a) $x + 2y \leq 10$, $x + y \geq 7$, $y \geq 1$, $x \geq 0$

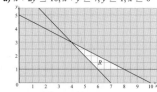

b) 4 motorbikes and 3 vans,
5 motorbikes and 2 vans,
6 motorbikes and 2 vans,
6 motorbikes and 1 van,
7 motorbikes and 1 van,
8 motorbikes and 1 van.
c) 6 motorbikes and 1 van — £5750

ection 14 — Sequences

4.1 Term to Term Rules

Page 118 Exercise 1

1 a) 14, 55, 219, 875, 3499
b) 11, −21, 43, −85, 171

2 a) 2 **b)** 48, 96, 192

3 a) (i) Add 2 to the previous term.
(ii) 11, 13, 15
b) (i) Multiply the previous term by 2.
(ii) 16, 32, 64
c) (i) Multiply the previous term by 3.
(ii) 324, 972, 2916
d) (i) Add 3 to the previous term.
(ii) 16, 19, 22
e) (i) Subtract 2 from the previous term.
(ii) −3, −5, −7
f) (i) Add 0.5 to the previous term.
(ii) 3, 3.5, 4
g) (i) Multiply the previous term by 10.
(ii) 100, 1000, 10 000
h) (i) Divide the previous term by 2.
(ii) 12, 6, 3

4 a) (i) Subtract 4 from the previous term.
(ii) −16, −20, −24
b) (i) Divide the previous term by 2.
(ii) 1, 0.5, 0.25
c) (i) Multiply the previous term by 3.
(ii) −162, −486, −1458
d) (i) Multiply the previous term by −2.
(ii) 16, −32, 64

5 a) Multiply the previous term by 3.
b) (i) 81 **(ii)** 729 **(iii)** 6561

6 a) 7, 13, 19, 25, 31, 37
b) 9, 5, 1, −3, −7, −11
c) −1, −4, −16, −36, −256, −1024

d) −72, −36, −18, −9, −4.5, −2.25
e) 0.2, 0.8, 3.2, 12.8, 51.2, 204.8
f) −63, −55, −47, −39, −31, −23

7 a) Add 3 to the previous term.
b) (i) 7 **(ii)** 22
c) 154

Page 119 Exercise 2

1 a) (i) +1, +2, +3, +4 **(ii)** 22, 28, 35
b) (i) +1, +2, +3, +4 **(ii)** 18, 24, 31
c) (i) +2, +4, +6, +8 **(ii)** 35, 47, 61
d) (i) −2, −3, −4, −5 **(ii)** 0, −7, −15
e) (i) +2, +4, +6, +8 **(ii)** 33, 45, 59
f) (i) +1, −2, +3, −4 **(ii)** 4, −2, 5

2 8, 13, 21

3 a) 1, 2, 3, 4 **b)** 120, 720

Page 119 Exercise 3

1 a) $b = 1$ **b)** $b = 1$ **c)** $b = 6$
d) $b = 3$ **e)** $b = 3$

Page 120 Exercise 4

1 a) 28 **b)** −15 **c)** 486
d) 189 **e)** 4 **f)** 15.75
2 a) 22 **b)** 70 **c)** 52
d) 2 **e)** 1320

Page 120 Exercise 5

1 a) (i) E.g. Add 2 matches to the right hand side to form another equilateral triangle.
(ii)
(iii) 13
b) (i) Add 3 matches to form another square to the right of the top right square and 3 matches to form another square below the bottom left square.
(ii)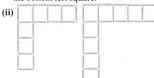
(iii) 34
c) (i) E.g. Add three matches to the left hand side to form a new square.
(ii)
(iii) 18

2 a) (i)
(ii) E.g. Add 2 circles to the right of the previous pattern.
(iii) 13 **(iv)** 19
b) (i)
(ii) E.g. Add 2 circles to the right of the previous pattern.
(iii) 14 **(iv)** 20
c) (i)

(ii) E.g. Add a row of circles to the bottom of the triangle, with one more circle in the new row than in the bottom row of the previous shape in the pattern.
(iii) 28 **(iv)** 55
d) (i)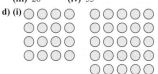

(ii) E.g. Add an extra row and column of circles to the right and bottom of the shape so that a new 'square' is formed that is wider and taller than the previous square by 1 circle.
(iii) 49 **(iv)** 100

14.2 Using the nth Term

Page 121 Exercise 1

1 a) 6, 7, 8, 9, 10
b) 5, 8, 11, 14, 17
c) 2, 6, 10, 14, 18
d) 4, 9, 14, 19, 24
e) 9, 8, 7, 6, 5
f) −1, −5, −9, −13, −17
g) 2, 12, 22, 32, 42
h) −10, −13, −16, −19, −22

2 a) 2, 5, 10, 17, 26
b) 3, 9, 19, 33, 51
c) 2, 11, 26, 47, 74
d) 0, 2, 6, 12, 20

3 a) 30 **b)** 40 **c)** 60 **d)** 220
4 a) 91 **b)** 70 **c)** 10 **d)** −20
5 a) 40 **b)** 60 **c)** 85 **d)** 135
e) 535

6 a) (i) 16 **(ii)** 21 **(iii)** 111
b) (i) 13 **(ii)** 23 **(iii)** 203
c) (i) 29 **(ii)** 59 **(iii)** 599
d) (i) 32 **(ii)** 52 **(iii)** 412
e) (i) 95 **(ii)** 90 **(iii)** 0
f) (i) 15 **(ii)** 0 **(iii)** −270
g) (i) 492 **(ii)** 992 **(iii)** 9992
h) (i) −10 **(ii)** 0 **(iii)** 180

7 a) (i) 36 **(ii)** 84 **(iii)** 164
b) (i) 430 **(ii)** 400 **(iii)** 350
c) (i) 32 **(ii)** 35 **(iii)** 40
d) (i) 48 **(ii)** 300 **(iii)** 1200
e) (i) 40 **(ii)** 208 **(iii)** 808
f) (i) 20 **(ii)** 110 **(iii)** 420
g) (i) 270 **(ii)** 4950 **(iii)** 39 950
h) (i) 96 **(ii)** 30 **(iii)** −240

8 a) (i) 8 **(ii)** 50 **(iii)** 800
b) (i) 11 **(ii)** 53 **(iii)** 803
c) (i) 11 **(ii)** 95 **(iii)** 1595
d) (i) 18 **(ii)** 81 **(iii)** 1206
e) (i) 22 **(ii)** 32.5 **(iii)** 220
f) (i) 6 **(ii)** 30 **(iii)** 420
g) (i) 396 **(ii)** 375 **(iii)** 0
h) (i) 10 **(ii)** 127 **(iii)** 8002

Page 122 Exercise 2

1 a) 7th **b)** 9th **c)** 6th **d)** 8th
2 a) 4th **b)** 10th
3 a) 8th **b)** 4th **c)** 9th **d)** 12th
4 a) 3rd **b)** 10th
5 a) 2nd **b)** 5th **c)** 7th **d)** 9th

6 16th

7 a) (i) 13   **(ii)** 201
  b) (i) 25   **(ii)** 401

8 a) 21st   **b)** 9th

9 a) 21   **b)** 1711   **c)** 20th

10 a) 15th   **b) (i)** 8th   **(ii)** 5th

11 a) 6th   **b)** 4th

14.3   **Finding the nth Term**

Page 124   Exercise 1

1 a) $6n + 1$ **b)** $7n - 4$ **c)** $4n$
  d) $10n - 4$ **e)** $5n$ **f)** $20n - 13$
  g) $40n + 1$ **h)** $8n - 5$

2 a) $2n - 3$ **b)** $3n - 5$
  c) $4n - 13$ **d)** $19n - 64$

3 a) (i) $12 - 2n$ **(ii)** -128
  b) (i) $43 - 3n$ **(ii)** -167
  c) (i) $80 - 10n$ **(ii)** -620
  d) (i) $87 - 9n$ **(ii)** -543
  e) (i) $65 - 5n$ **(ii)** -285
  f) (i) $108 - 8n$ **(ii)** -452
  g) (i) $9 - 3n$ **(ii)** -201
  h) (i) $5 - 15n$ **(ii)** -1045

4 a) $1 + 3n$ **b)** $2 + 3n$
  c) (i) Each term is 1 greater than in A.
  (ii) They differ only in the constant.

5 a) $17 - 4n$ **b)** $15 - 4n$

6 a) (i) $4n$ **(ii)** $2n - 1$ units^2
  (iii) 92 dots, area of 45 units^2
  b) (i) $n^2 + 2n - 1$
  (ii) $n^2 - 1$ units^2
  (iii) 574 dots, area of 528 units^2

Page 124   Exercise 2

1 $3n - 1 = 80$, $n = 27$, so 80 is a term.

2 $21 - 2n = -1$, $n = 11$, so -1 is a term.

3 a) $6 + 6n$
  b) $6 + 6n = 34$, $n = 4.6...$ so 34 is not a term.

4 a) No   **b)** Yes   **c)** No
  d) Yes   **e)** No

5 a) Yes $(n = 13)$ **b)** Yes $(n = 20)$
  c) No   **d)** No   **e)** Yes $(n = 222)$

Page 125   Exercise 3

1 a) $\dfrac{1}{2n}$ **b)** $\dfrac{1}{3n}$ **c)** $\dfrac{n+4}{n+1}$

  d) $\dfrac{3n-2}{5n}$ **e)** $\dfrac{6-n}{5-n}$ **f)** $\dfrac{2+3n}{10-n}$

  g) $\dfrac{20n-4}{4n-1}$ **h)** $\dfrac{3-2n}{20+10n}$

Page 126   Exercise 4

1 a) (i) $a = 3$, $d = 2$
  (ii) nth term $= 2n + 1$
  b) (i) $a = 9$, $d = 4$
  (ii) nth term $= 4n + 5$
  c) (i) $a = 1$, $d = 4$
  (ii) nth term $= 4n - 3$
  d) (i) $a = 2$, $d = -1$
  (ii) nth term $= 3 - n$
  e) (i) $a = -5$, $d = -5$
  (ii) nth term $= -5n$
  f) (i) $a = -38$, $d = 10$
  (ii) nth term $= 10n - 48$

2 a) (i) $a = 5$, $d = 5$
  (ii) nth term $= 5n$
  b) (i) $a = 5$, $d = 7$
  (ii) nth term $= 7n - 2$
  c) (i) $a = 1$, $d = 8$
  (ii) nth term $= 8n - 7$
  d) (i) $a = 18$, $d = -5$
  (ii) nth term $= 23 - 5n$
  e) (i) $a = -21$, $d = 9$
  (ii) nth term $= 9n - 30$
  f) (i) $a = 1$, $d = 12$
  (ii) nth term $= 12n - 11$

---

3 a) $a = -10$, $d = 3$ **b)** $3n - 13$

4 a) $a = \dfrac{14}{3}$, $d = -\dfrac{1}{3}$ **b)** $-\dfrac{1}{3}n + 5$

5 Yes, 42 is in the sequence $(n = 5)$.

Page 127   Exercise 5

1 a) (i) 256   **(ii)** 4^{n-1}
  b) (i) 32   **(ii)** 2^{n-1}
  c) (i) 3125   **(ii)** 5^n
  d) (i) 243   **(ii)** 3^n
  e) (i) 162   **(ii)** $2 \times 3^{n-1}$
  f) (i) $9\sqrt{3}$ **(ii)** $\sqrt{3}^n$
  g) (i) 96   **(ii)** $6 \times 2^{n-1}$ or 3×2^n
  h) (i) $12\sqrt{2}$ **(ii)** $3 \times \sqrt{2}^{n-1}$

2 a) $\dfrac{5 \times 3^{n-1}}{2 \times 7^{n-1}}$ **b)** $\dfrac{2^n}{9 \times 3^{n-1}} = \dfrac{2^n}{3^{n+1}}$

Page 127   Exercise 6

1 a) (i) $n^2 + n - 1$ **(ii)** 109
  b) (i) $n^2 + 4n$ **(ii)** 140
  c) (i) $2n^2 + n + 2$ **(ii)** 212
  d) (i) $3n^2 + 4n$ **(ii)** 340
  e) (i) $5n^2 + 3n - 2$ **(ii)** 528
  f) (i) $4n^2 + n + 5$ **(ii)** 415

Page 128   Exercise 7

1 a) (i) $n^3 + 8$ **(ii)** 520
  b) (i) $n^3 + 6n + 1$ **(ii)** 561
  c) (i) $2n^3 + n^2$ **(ii)** 1088
  d) (i) $n^3 + 2n^2 + 3$ **(ii)** 643

14.4   **Arithmetic Series**

Page 129   Exercise 1

1 a) $S_{20} = 120$ **b)** $S_{20} = 650$
  c) $S_{20} = 120$ **d)** $S_{20} = -300$

2 a) $S_5 = 75$, $S_{10} = 275$, $S_{50} = 6375$
  b) $S_5 = 55$, $S_{10} = 210$, $S_{50} = 5050$
  c) $S_5 = 15$, $S_{10} = 230$, $S_{50} = 9150$
  d) $S_5 = 185$, $S_{10} = 220$, $S_{50} = -4900$

3 8625

Page 129   Exercise 2

1 $S_{20} = 1340$

2 $S_{12} = 108$

3 $S_{25} = 1325$

4 $S_{50} = 2000$

5 $S_{101} = -28\,583$

Section 15 — Straight-Line Graphs

15.1   **Straight-Line Graphs**

Page 130   Exercise 1

1 A $x = -5$ B $x = -2$ C $y = 2$
  D $x = 5$ E $y = -3$

2 a)

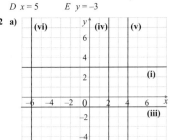

  b) 0   **c)** $y = 0$

3 $x = 0$

4 a) $y = 8$ **b)** $x = -2$ **c)** $x = 1$ **d)** $y = 6$

---

5 a) $(8, -11)$ **b)** $(-5, -13)$
  c) $(0.7, 80)$ **d)** $\left(-\dfrac{6}{11}, -500\right)$

Page 131   Exercise 2

1 a)

x	-2	-1	0	1	2
y	-4	-2	0	2	4
Coords.	$(-2, -4)$	$(-1, -2)$	$(0, 0)$	$(1, 2)$	$(2, 4$

  b), c), d) – See below

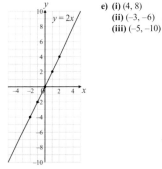

  e) (i) $(4, 8)$
  (ii) $(-3, -6)$
  (iii) $(-5, -10)$

2 a)

x	0	1	2	3	4
y	8	7	6	5	4
Coords.	$(0, 8)$	$(1, 7)$	$(2, 6)$	$(3, 5)$	$(4,$

  b, c)

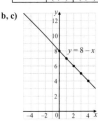

3 a)

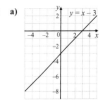

  b)

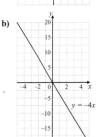

  c)

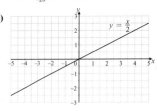

  d)

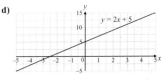

---

e)

$y = 4 - x$

f)

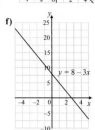

$y = 8 - 3x$

g)

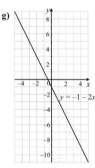

$y = -1 - 2x$

h)

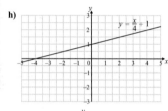

$y = \frac{x}{4} + 1$

4 a)

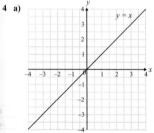

$y = x$

b)

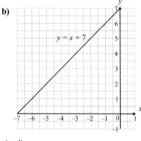

$y = x + 7$

c)

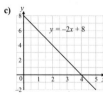

$y = -2x + 8$

d)

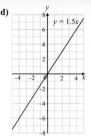

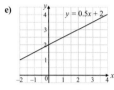

$y = 1.5x$

e)

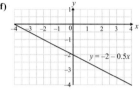

$y = 0.5x + 2$

f)

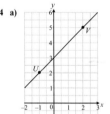

$y = -2 - 0.5x$

15.2 Gradients

Page 132 Exercise 1

1 a) Negative b) -4 c) 5 d) $-\frac{4}{5}$

2 a) $-\frac{2}{5}$ b) $-\frac{1}{2}$ c) $\frac{2}{3}$

3 a) (i) $G = (2, -5), H = (6, 6)$ (ii) $\frac{11}{4} = 2.75$
  b) (i) $I = (-10, 5), J = (30, -25)$ (ii) $-\frac{3}{4}$
  c) (i) $K = (-8, -25), L = (8, 35)$
    $M = (-4, 30), N = (6, -15)$
    (ii) Line 1 gradient $= \frac{15}{4} = 3.75$,
    Line 2 gradient $= -\frac{9}{2} = -4.5$

4 a) b) 1

5 a) 3 b) 6 c) $\frac{1}{2}$

6 a) 3 b) 2 c) $\frac{2}{3}$
  d) $-\frac{3}{4}$ e) $-\frac{3}{4}$ f) $\frac{3}{4}$

7 a) 5 b) $\frac{1}{4}$ c) $-\frac{2}{3}$ d) 20

15.3 Equations of Straight-Line Graphs

Page 134 Exercise 1

1 a) $2, (0, -4)$ b) $5, (0, -11)$
  c) $-3, (0, 7)$ d) $4, (0, 0)$
  e) $\frac{1}{2}, (0, -1)$ f) $-1, (0, -\frac{1}{2})$
  g) $-1, (0, 3)$ h) $0, (0, 3)$

2 A $y = -\frac{1}{3}x + 4$ B $y = 3x$
  C $y = \frac{1}{3}x + 2$ D $y = \frac{7}{3}x - 1$
  E $y = x + 2$ F $y = -x + 6$

3 a) $2, (0, 4)$ b) $1, (0, 3)$
  c) $-1, (0, 3)$ d) $7, (0, 5)$
  e) $-1, (0, 8)$ f) $3, (0, 12)$
  g) $\frac{1}{2}, (0, -3)$ h) $-3, (0, 1)$
  i) $2, (0, 5)$ j) $2, (0, -\frac{5}{2})$
  k) $-\frac{2}{3}, (0, 3)$ l) $\frac{4}{5}, (0, 1)$
  m) $6, (0, -7)$ n) $4, (0, -7)$
  o) $-\frac{9}{2}, (0, \frac{11}{2})$ p) $-\frac{5}{4}, (0, -\frac{3}{4})$
  q) $-2, (0, 3)$ r) $2, (0, -\frac{2}{3})$
  s) $-3, (0, 2)$ t) $\frac{3}{2}, (0, -2)$
  u) $1, (0, -\frac{2}{5})$ v) $2, (0, \frac{1}{3})$
  w) $-2, (0, -\frac{1}{4})$ x) $-\frac{5}{6}, (0, 0)$

Page 135 Exercise 2

1 a) $y = 8x + 2$ b) $y = -x + 7$
  c) $y = 11x - 5$ d) $y = -6x - 1$
  e) $y = 3x + 7$ f) $y = \frac{1}{2}x - 7$
  g) $y = -7x + 10$ h) $y = 6x + 8$
  i) $y = 5x + 8$ j) $y = -4x - 9$

2 a) $y = 2x + 1$ b) $y = 5x - 1$
  c) $y = 2x - 9$ d) $y = x - 3$
  e) $y = 2x + 5$ f) $y = 3x + 2$
  g) $y = 3x + 11$ h) $y = \frac{1}{2}x + 3$
  i) $y = -x + 1$ j) $y = -4x + 7$
  k) $y = 3x + 13$ l) $y = \frac{3}{2}x - \frac{1}{2}$

3 A $y = 2 - x$ B $y = 5x$
  C $y = x - 1$ D $y = -3$
  E $y = -\frac{1}{2}x + 2$ F $y = \frac{2}{5}x + 1$
  G $y = \frac{2}{5}x - 4$ H $y = \frac{3}{2}x - \frac{5}{2}$
  I $y = -\frac{2}{3}x - \frac{10}{3}$ J $y = 4x + 16$
  K $y = -\frac{7}{3}x + \frac{38}{3}$ L $y = \frac{1}{3}x + \frac{8}{3}$

4 A $y = x + 0.7$ B $y = 0.1x + 2$
  C $y = -\frac{5}{4}x - \frac{5}{8}$

15.4 Parallel and Perpendicular Lines

Page 137 Exercise 1

1 a) E.g. $y = 5x + 1$, $y = 5x + 2$, $y = 5x + 3$
  b) E.g. $x + y = 6$, $x + y = 5$, $x + y = 4$

2 (i) a), c) and g) (ii) e), h) and i)

3 b), e) and f)

4 a) $y = 5x + 3$ b) $y = 2x + 7$
  c) $y = \frac{1}{2}x - 10$ d) $y = 4x - 15$
  e) $y = 8x + 19$ f) $y = x - 12$
  g) $y = 3x + 13$ h) $y = -9x - 2$
  i) $y = -x + 16$ j) $y = -2x - 8$
  k) $y = 3x - 7$ l) $y = -\frac{1}{3}x + 6$

Page 138 Exercise 2

1 a) $-\frac{1}{6}$ b) $\frac{1}{3}$ c) -2 d) 1
  e) 4 f) $-\frac{1}{12}$ g) $\frac{1}{7}$ h) $-\frac{3}{2}$
  i) $\frac{1}{2}$ j) -1 k) $-\frac{2}{3}$ l) $-\frac{10}{3}$
  m) $\frac{2}{9}$ n) $\frac{3}{4}$ o) $\frac{5}{6}$ p) $-\frac{2}{7}$

2 a) E.g. $y = -\frac{1}{2}x + 3$ b) E.g. $y = \frac{1}{3}x + 5$
  c) E.g. $y = \frac{1}{6}x + 5$ d) E.g. $y = -\frac{1}{9}x + 1$
  e) E.g. $y = -\frac{2}{5}x + 1$ f) E.g. $y = x + 2$
  g) E.g. $y = \frac{3}{2}x + 5$ h) E.g. $y = -2x + 8$

3 a and c, b and g, d and l,
  e and j, f and k, h and i

4 a) $y = \frac{1}{3}x + 5$ b) $y = -2x + 2$
  c) $y = -4x - 5$ d) $y = -\frac{1}{6}x + 4$
  e) $y = -\frac{3}{4}x + 8$ f) $y = \frac{2}{5}x - 4$

g) $y = x - 3$ **h)** $y = -\frac{1}{3}x - 1$
i) $y = \frac{3}{8}x + 4$ **j)** $y = 2x + 7$
k) $y = -5x - 2$ **l)** $y = -\frac{1}{4}x + \frac{3}{2}$

15.5 Line Segments

Page 139 Exercise 1

1 a) (6, 3) **b)** (4, 1) **c)** (2, 4)
d) (1, –3) **e)** (3, –1) **f)** (–5, 2)
g) (–1, –2) **h)** (1.5, –8) **i)** (–3.75, 1)
j) $(0, \frac{1}{2})$ **k)** $(4p, 4q)$ **l)** $(5p, 8q)$

2 a) Midpoint of AB is (–0.5, 1)
Midpoint of BC is (3, 1)
Midpoint of CA is (0.5, –2)
b) Midpoint of DE is (–1, 0)
Midpoint of EF is (1.5, 1)
Midpoint of FD is (0.5, –2)

3 (9, –2) **4** (–2, 5)

5 a) (0, 5) **b)** (–3.5, 4) **c)** (3.5, 3)
d) (–0.5, –2.5) **e)** (0.5, 1) **f)** (0.5, 0.5)

Page 140 Exercise 2

1 a) 5 **b)** 6.40 **c)** 3.16 **d)** 7
e) 15.6 **f)** 18.9 **g)** 8.06 **h)** 10.0
i) 10.8 **j)** 8.54 **k)** 9.85 **l)** 15.8

2 $AB = 6.08$ $BC = 5.10$ $CD = 3.61$
$DA = 4.47$ $EF = 5$ $FG = 6.40$
$GH = 2.24$ $HE = 6.71$

Page 140 Exercise 3

1 a) (2, 0) **b)** (4, 0) **c)** (6, 2)
d) (4, 2) **e)** (–8, –5)

2 a) 1 : 2 **b)** 4 : 1 **c)** 2 : 3
d) 4 : 3 **e)** 1 : 2 **f)** 1 : 3

3 a) (4, 9) **b)** (16, –8)
c) (34, 23) **d)** (43, –21)

Page 141 Exercise 4

1 a) (6, 0.5) **b)** 17

2 a) Midpoint of A is (0, –1.5)
Midpoint of B is (–3, 2.5)
Midpoint of C is (0.5, –0.5)
b) Length of A is 8.1
Length of B is 3.6
Length of C is 7.6

3 a) Length = 5.66, midpoint = (3, 5)
b) Length = 6.71, midpoint = (5.5, 8)
c) Length = 10.6, midpoint = (2, 4.5)
d) Length = 13.4, midpoint = (1, 3)
e) Length = 15.6, midpoint = (1, –7)
f) Length = 8.25, midpoint = (–7, –3)

4 a) (2, 2) **b)** 13.4

5 a) (2, 7) **b)** 17.9

15.6 Straight-Line Graphs Problems

Page 141 Exercise 1

1 a)

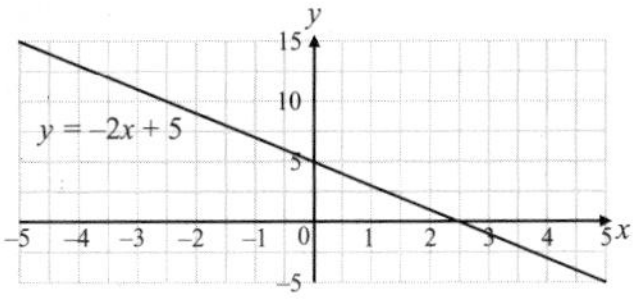

b)

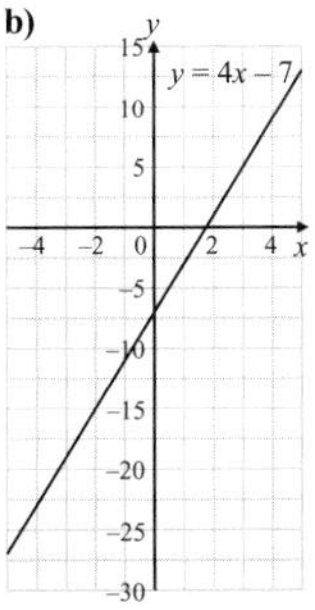

c)

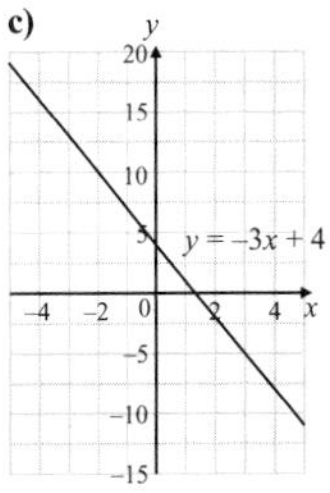

d)

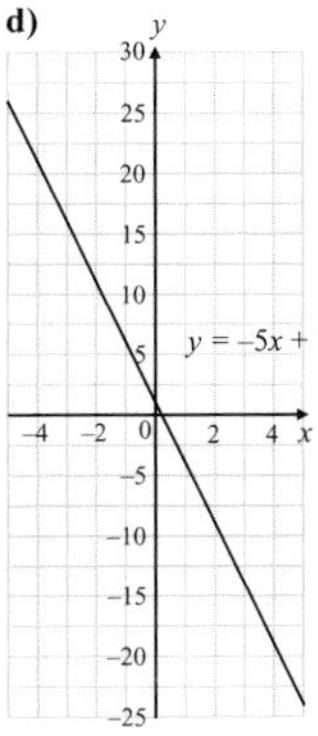

e)

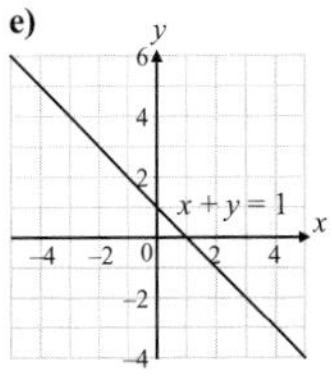

f)

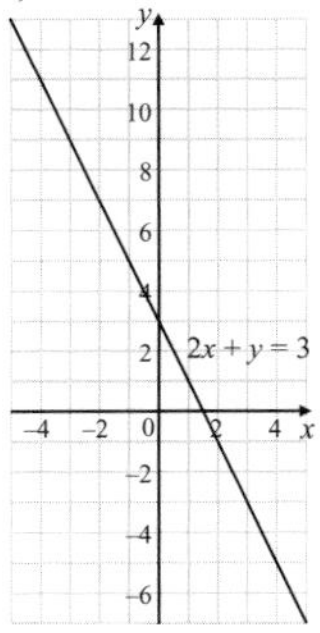

g)

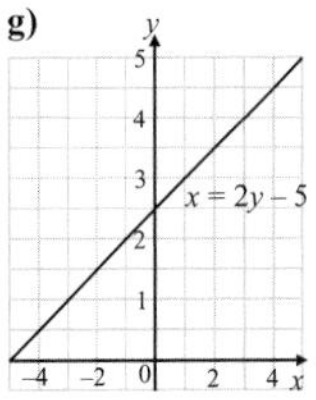

h)

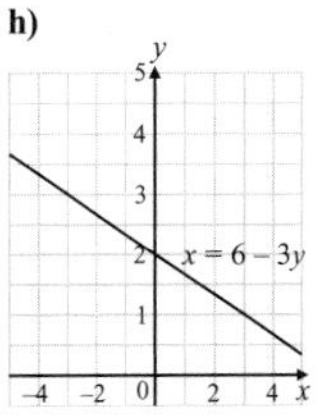

2 a) 2 **b)** 4 **c)** –1 **d)** $-\frac{1}{2}$ **e)** $\frac{3}{2}$
f) –3 **g)** $-\frac{2}{3}$ **h)** $\frac{1}{2}$ **i)** $-\frac{1}{4}$ **j)** $\frac{9}{8}$

3 A $y + x = 0$ B $y = -0.5x$
C $2y = x$ D $y - x = 0$
E $y = 2x$

4 a) $a = 19$ **b)** $b = 5$

5 a) 5, (0, –9) **b)** 7, (0, 3)
c) –2, (0, 11) **d)** 3, (0, –8)
e) –5, (0, 12) **f)** $-\frac{2}{3}$, (0, 2)
g) $\frac{1}{4}$, $(0, \frac{7}{4})$ **h)** 4, $(0, -\frac{9}{2})$

6 A $x = -4y$ B $4x + y + 4 = 0$
C $x + 2y = 6$ D $y = 4(x - 1)$
E $y = 2x - 6$

7 a) $y = -4x + 6$ **b)** $y = 2x - 9$
c) $2y = x + 6$ **d)** $y = -3x + 7$
e) $y = -2x - 5$ **f)** $4y = x - 2$

8 a) Perpendicular **b)** Parallel
c) Neither **d)** Parallel
e) Neither **f)** Neither
g) Parallel **h)** Perpendicular

9 a) $p = -2, q = 0$ **b)** 4.5 **c)** 1.1

10 AB: Gradient = $\frac{3}{4}$, length = 5, midpoint = (–1, 1.5)
BC: Gradient = –3, length = 6.32, midpoint = (2, 0)
CA: Gradient = $-\frac{1}{2}$, length = 6.71, midpoint = (0, –1.5)
DE: Gradient = $\frac{5}{3}$, length = 5.83, midpoint = (–2.5, 0.5)
EF: Gradient = $-\frac{1}{5}$, length = 5.10, midpoint = (1.5, 2.5)
FG: Gradient = $\frac{3}{2}$, length = 7.21, midpoint = (2, –1)
GD: Gradient = $-\frac{1}{2}$, length = 4.47, midpoint = (–2, –3)

11 Perimeter of ABC = 20.7
Perimeter of $DEFG$ = 21.3

12 A $y = -3x - 6$ B $y = 0.75x - 1$
C $y = -\frac{2}{3}x + 2$ D $y = 3x - 8$

13 a) $y = 3x - 6$ **b)** $y = -7x + 18$
c) $y = 9x - 34$ **d)** $y = -x + 7$
e) $y = -1.5x + 17$ **f)** $y = \frac{1}{3}x - 5$

14 a) $y = -0.25x + 12$ **b)** $y = 0.5x + 1$
c) $y = -\frac{1}{3}x - 3$ **d)** $y = 3x + 14$
e) $y = \frac{2}{3}x - 7$ **f)** $y = -5x - 8$

Section 16 — Other Types of Graph

16.1 Quadratic Graphs

Page 143 Exercise 1

1 a)

x	–4	–3	–2	–1	0	1	2	3	4
x^2	16	9	4	1	0	1	4	9	16

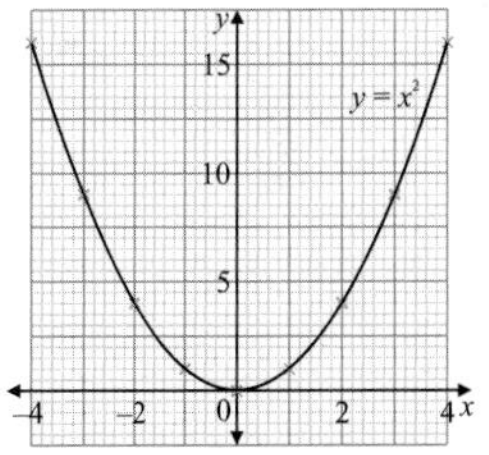

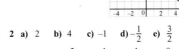

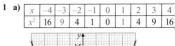

b)

x	–4	–3	–2	–1	0	1	2	3	4
x^2	16	9	4	1	0	1	4	9	1
$x^2 + 2$	18	11	6	3	2	3	6	11	1

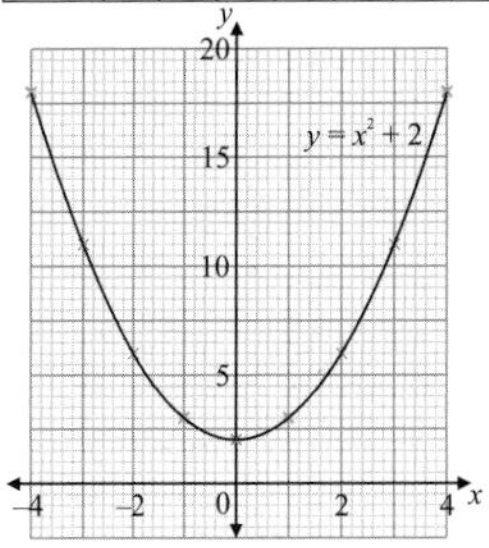

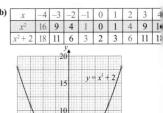

c)

x	-4	-3	-2	-1	0	1	2	3	4
x^2	16	9	4	1	0	1	4	9	16
$2x^2$	32	18	8	2	0	2	8	18	32

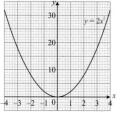

d)

x	-4	-3	-2	-1	0	1	2	3	4
x^2	16	9	4	1	0	1	4	9	16
$6-x^2$	-10	-3	2	5	6	5	2	-3	-10

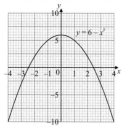

2

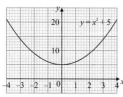

a) (i) $y = 11.3$ (to 1 d.p — accept 11.2 to 11.3)
(ii) $y = 5.3$ (to 1 d.p — accept 5.2 to 5.3)
b) (i) $x = 1.2$ and $x = -1.2$
(ii) $x = 2.2$ and $x = -2.2$

3

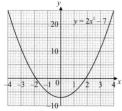

a) (i) $y = -2.5$ **(ii)** $y = 17.5$
b) (i) $x = 2.4$ and $x = -2.4$ (both to 1 d.p — accept 2.4 to 2.5, -2.5 to -2.4)
(ii) $x = 3.7$ and $x = -3.7$ (both to 1 d.p.)

4

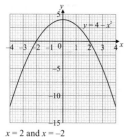

$x = 2$ and $x = -2$

5

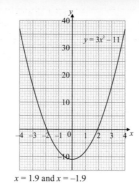

$x = 1.9$ and $x = -1.9$

Page 144   Exercise 2

1 a)

x	-4	-3	-2	-1	0	1	2	3	4
x^2	16	9	4	1	0	1	4	9	16
$+2x$	-8	-6	-4	-2	0	2	4	6	8
$+3$	3	3	3	3	3	3	3	3	3
x^2+2x+3	11	6	3	2	3	6	11	18	27

b)

x	-4	-3	-2	-1	0	1	2	3	4
x^2	16	9	4	1	0	1	4	9	16
$-4x$	16	12	8	4	0	-4	-8	-12	-16
-1	-1	-1	-1	-1	-1	-1	-1	-1	-1
x^2-4x-1	31	20	11	4	-1	-4	-5	-4	-1

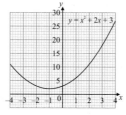

c)

x	-4	-3	-2	-1	0	1	2	3	4
4	4	4	4	4	4	4	4	4	4
$+2x$	-8	-6	-4	-2	0	2	4	6	8
$-x^2$	-16	-9	-4	-1	0	-1	-4	-9	-16
$4+2x-x^2$	-20	-11	-4	1	4	5	4	1	-4

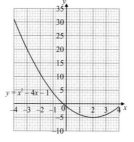

d)

x	-4	-3	-2	-1	0	1	2	3	4
$2x^2$	32	18	8	2	0	2	8	18	32
$+3x$	-12	-9	-6	-3	0	3	6	9	12
-7	-7	-7	-7	-7	-7	-7	-7	-7	-7
$2x^2+3x-7$	13	2	-5	-8	-7	-2	7	20	37

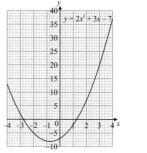

2

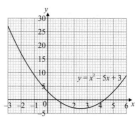

a) (i) $y = 12.8$ (to 1 d.p — accept 12.7 to 12.8)
(ii) $y = -2.3$ (to 1 d.p — accept -2.3 to -2.2)
b) (i) $x = -0.9$ and $x = 5.9$ (both to 1 d.p — accept -0.9 to -0.8, 5.8 to 5.9)
(ii) $x = 1.4$ and $x = 3.6$ (both to 1 d.p)

3

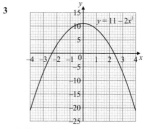

a) (i) $y = -1.5$
(ii) $y = 7.9$ (to 1 d.p — accept 7.8 to 7.9)
b) (i) $x = -2.3$ and $x = 2.3$ (both to 1 d.p — accept -2.4 to -2.3, 2.3 to 2.4)
(ii) $x = 0$

4 a) $x^2 + x - 6$
b)

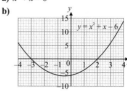

c) $(2, 0)$ and $(-3, 0)$
d) The x-coordinates are the solutions of the equation.

Page 146   Exercise 1

1 a)

x	-3	-2	-1	0	1	2	3
x^3	-27	-8	-1	0	1	8	27

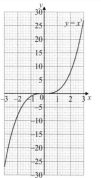

b)

x	-3	-2	-1	0	1	2	3
x^3	-27	-8	-1	0	1	8	27
$x^3 + 5$	-22	-3	4	5	6	13	32

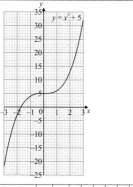

c)

x	-4	-3	-2	-1	0	1	2	3	4
x^3	-64	-27	-8	-1	0	1	8	27	64
$-3x$	12	9	6	3	0	-3	-6	-9	-12
$+7$	7	7	7	7	7	7	7	7	7
$x^3 - 3x + 7$	-45	-11	5	9	7	5	9	25	59

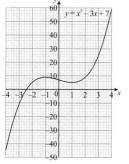

d)

x	-3	-2	-1	0	1	2	3	4
x^3	-27	-8	-1	0	1	8	27	64
$-3x^2$	-27	-12	-3	0	-3	-12	-27	-48
$-x$	3	2	1	0	-1	-2	-3	-4
$+3$	3	3	3	3	3	3	3	3
$x^3 - 3x^2 - x + 3$	-48	-15	0	3	0	-3	0	15

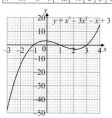

e)

x	-3	-2	-1	0	1	2	3
$2x^3$	-54	-16	-2	0	2	16	54
$-2x^2$	-18	-8	-2	0	-2	-8	-18
$-3x$	9	6	3	0	-3	-6	-9
$+5$	5	5	5	5	5	5	5
$2x^3 - 2x^2 - 3x + 5$	-58	-13	4	5	2	7	32

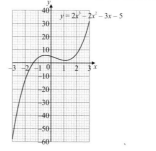

f)

x	-3	-2	-1	0	1	2	3
5	5	5	5	5	5	5	5
$-x^3$	27	8	1	0	-1	-8	-27
$5 - x^3$	32	13	6	5	4	-3	-22

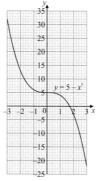

g)

x	-3	-2	-1	0	1	2	3
$3x^3$	-81	-24	-3	0	3	24	81
$-4x^2$	-36	-16	-4	0	-4	-16	-36
$+2x$	-6	-4	-2	0	2	4	6
-8	-8	-8	-8	-8	-8	-8	-8
$3x^3 - 4x^2 + 2x - 8$	-131	-52	-17	-8	-7	4	43

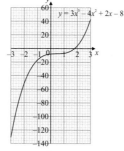

2

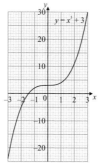

When $x = -2.5$, $y = -12.6$ (to 1 d.p.)
(Accept y-values from -12.4 to -12.8)

3

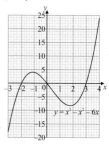

The graph crosses the x-axis at $x = 0.6$ (to 1 d.p.)
(Accept x-values from 0.5 to 0.6)

4

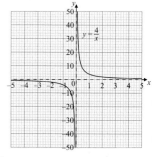

a) When $y = 10$, $x = 3.5$ (to 1 d.p.)
(Accept x-values from 3.4 to 3.6)
b) When $y = -15$, $x = -2.9$ (to 1 d.p.)
(Accept x-values from -3.0 to -2.8)

Page 147   Exercise 1

1 a)

x	-5	-4	-3	-2	-1	-0.5	-0.1
$\frac{4}{x}$	-0.8	-1	-1.33	-2	-4	-8	-40

x	0.1	0.5	1	2	3	4	5
$\frac{4}{x}$	40	8	4	2	1.33	1	0.8

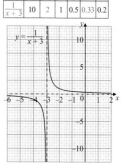

b)

x	-6	-5	-4	-3.5	-3.1
$x + 3$	-3	-2	-1	-0.5	-0.1
$\frac{1}{x+3}$	-0.33	-0.5	-1	-2	-10

x	-2.9	-2.5	-2	-1	0	2
$x + 3$	0.1	0.5	1	2	3	5
$\frac{1}{x+3}$	10	2	1	0.5	0.33	0.2

c)

x	-5	-4	-3	-2	-1	-0.5	-0.1
$\frac{1}{x}$	-0.2	-0.25	-0.33	-0.5	-1	-2	-10
+3	3	3	3	3	3	3	3
$\frac{1}{x}+3$	2.8	2.75	2.67	2.5	2	1	-7

x	0.1	0.5	1	2	3	4	5
$\frac{1}{x}$	10	2	1	0.5	0.33	0.25	0.2
+3	3	3	3	3	3	3	3
$\frac{1}{x}+3$	13	5	4	3.5	3.33	3.25	3.2

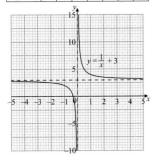

$y=\frac{1}{x}+3$

d)

x	-5	-4	-3	-2	-1	-0.5	-0.1
$-\frac{1}{x}$	0.2	0.25	0.33	0.5	1	2	10

x	0.1	0.5	1	2	3	4	5
$-\frac{1}{x}$	-10	-2	-1	-0.5	-0.33	-0.25	-0.2

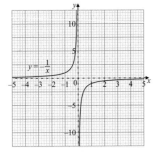

$y=-\frac{1}{x}$

e)

x	-5	-4	-3	-2	-1	-0.5	-0.1
5	5	5	5	5	5	5	5
$-\frac{1}{x}$	0.2	0.25	0.33	0.5	1	2	10
$5-\frac{1}{x}$	5.2	5.25	5.33	5.5	6	7	15

x	0.1	0.5	1	2	3	4	5
5	5	5	5	5	5	5	5
$-\frac{1}{x}$	-10	-2	-1	-0.5	-0.33	-0.25	-0.2
$5-\frac{1}{x}$	-5	3	4	4.5	4.67	4.75	4.8

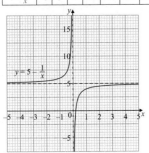

$y=5-\frac{1}{x}$

2 a) $x = 2$

b) As x increases, $\frac{1}{x-2}$ gets closer to zero.

c) $x = 2$ and $y = 0$

3 a) $x = 0$ and $y = 0$ **b)** $x = 0$ and $y = 4$

c) $x = -5$ and $y = 0$ **d)** $x = 0$ and $y = -1$

e) $x = 3$ and $y = 10$ **f)** $x = 0.4$ and $y = 8$

16.4 More Reciprocal Graphs

Page 149 Exercise 1

1 a)

x	-4	-3	-2	-1	-0.5	0.5	1	2	3	4
x^2	16	9	4	1	0.25	0.25	1	4	9	16
$\frac{2}{x^2}$	0.125	0.22	0.5	2	8	8	2	0.5	0.22	0.125

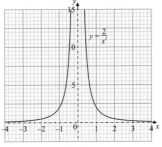

$y=\frac{2}{x^2}$

b)

x	-5	-4	-3	-2	-1.5
$x+1$	-4	-3	-2	-1	-0.5
$(x+1)^2$	16	9	4	1	0.25
$\frac{1}{(x+1)^2}$	0.06	0.11	0.25	1	4

x	-0.5	0	1	2	3
$x+1$	0.5	1	2	3	4
$(x+1)^2$	0.25	1	4	9	16
$\frac{1}{(x+1)^2}$	4	1	0.25	0.11	0.06

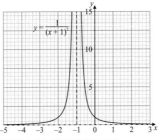

$y=\frac{1}{(x+1)^2}$

c)

x	-2	-1	0	1	1.5
$x-2$	-4	-3	-2	-1	-0.5
$(x-2)^2$	16	9	4	1	0.25
$\frac{1}{(x-2)^2}$	0.06	0.11	0.25	1	4

x	2.5	3	4	5	6
$x-2$	0.5	1	2	3	4
$(x-2)^2$	0.25	1	4	9	16
$\frac{1}{(x-2)^2}$	4	1	0.25	0.11	0.06

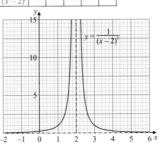

$y=\frac{1}{(x-2)^2}$

---

d)

x	-4	-3	-2	-1	-0.5
x^2	16	9	4	1	0.25
$\frac{1}{x^2}$	0.06	0.11	0.25	1	4
$\frac{1}{x^2}-5$	-4.94	-4.89	-4.75	-4	-1

x	0.5	1	2	3	4
x^2	0.25	1	4	9	16
$\frac{1}{x^2}$	4	1	0.25	0.11	0.06
$\frac{1}{x^2}-5$	-1	-4	-4.75	-4.89	-4.94

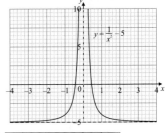

$y=\frac{1}{x^2}-5$

e)

x	-4	-3	-2	-1	-0.5
x^2	16	9	4	1	0.25
$-\frac{1}{x^2}$	-0.06	-0.11	-0.25	-1	-4

x	0.5	1	2	3	4
x^2	0.25	1	4	9	16
$-\frac{1}{x^2}$	-4	-1	-0.25	-0.11	-0.06

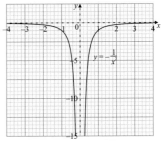

$y=-\frac{1}{x^2}$

f)

x	-4	-3	-2	-1	-0.5
x^2	16	9	4	1	0.25
$\frac{1}{x^2}$	0.06	0.11	0.25	1	4
$4-\frac{1}{x^2}$	3.94	3.89	3.75	3	0

x	0.5	1	2	3	4
x^2	0.25	1	4	9	16
$\frac{1}{x^2}$	4	1	0.25	0.11	0.06
$4-\frac{1}{x^2}$	0	3	3.75	3.89	3.94

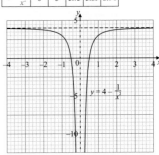

$y=4-\frac{1}{x^2}$

2 a) $x = 0,\ y = 0$

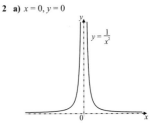

$y=\frac{1}{x^2}$

b) $x = 1$, $y = 0$

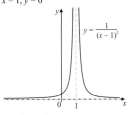
$y = \dfrac{1}{(x-1)^2}$

c) $x = -8$, $y = 0$

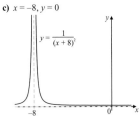
$y = \dfrac{1}{(x+8)^2}$

d) $x = -1$, $y = 0$

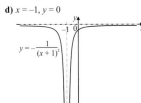
$y = -\dfrac{1}{(x+1)^2}$

e) $x = 0$, $y = 6$

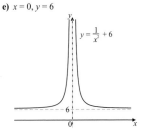
$y = \dfrac{1}{x^2} + 6$

f) $x = -4$, $y = 3$

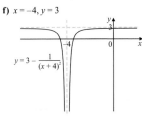
$y = 3 - \dfrac{1}{(x+4)^2}$

16.5 Exponential Graphs

Page 150   Exercise 1

1 a)

x	-3	-2	-1	0	1	2	3
3^x	0.04	0.11	0.33	1	3	9	27

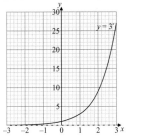
$y = 3^x$

b)

x	-3	-2	-1	0	1	2	3
0.25^x	64	16	4	1	0.25	0.06	0.02

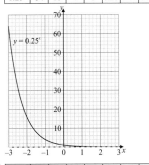
$y = 0.25^x$

c)

x	-3	-2	-1	0	1	2	3
4^x	0.02	0.06	0.25	1	4	16	64
$+3$	3	3	3	3	3	3	3
$4^x + 3$	3.02	3.06	3.25	4	7	19	67

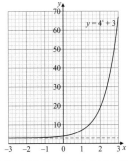
$y = 4^x + 3$

d)

x	-3	-2	-1	0	1	2	3
2^{-x}	8	4	2	1	0.5	0.25	0.13

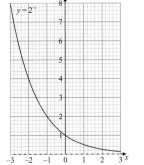
$y = 2^{-x}$

2 a) Asymptote is $y = 0$,
graph crosses y-axis at $y = 1$

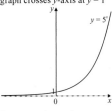
$y = 5^x$

b) Asymptote is $y = -1$,
graph crosses y-axis at $y = 0$

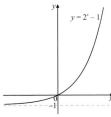
$y = 2^x - 1$

c) Asymptote is $y = 10$,
graph crosses y-axis at $y = 9$

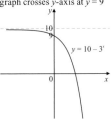
$y = 10 - 3^x$

d) Asymptote is $y = 0$,
graph crosses y-axis at $y = 1$

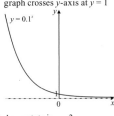
$y = 0.1^x$

e) Asymptote is $y = 3$,
graph crosses y-axis at $y = 4$

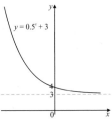
$y = 0.5^x + 3$

f) Asymptote is $y = 0$,
graph crosses y-axis at $y = 1$

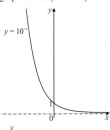
$y = 10^{-x}$

3

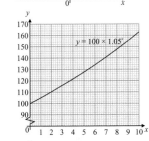
$y = 100 \times 1.05^x$

4 a)

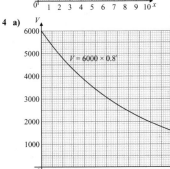
$V = 6000 \times 0.8^t$

b) £2750 (to the nearest £50)
Accept answers in the range £2700-£28●

Page 151 Exercise 1

1 **a)** Centre (0, 0), radius 5 units
 b) Centre (0, 0), radius 1 unit
 c) Centre (1, 2), radius 2 units
 d) Centre (5, 3), radius 9 units
 e) Centre (–2, 1), radius 3 units
 f) Centre (2, –2), radius 8 units
 g) Centre (–1, –3), radius 7 units
 h) Centre (0, 0), radius 2.5 units
 i) Centre (0, 5), radius 3.5 units

2 **a)** $x^2 + y^2 = 9$ **b)** $x^2 + y^2 = 2.25$
 c) $(x - 3)^2 + (y - 1)^2 = 9$
 d) $(x + 1)^2 + (y - 1)^2 = 4$ **e)** $(x - 1)^2 + y^2 = 1$
 f) $(x - 4)^2 + (y + 3)^2 = 25$

3 **a)**
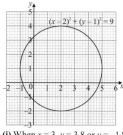

b) (i) When $x = 3$, $y = 3.8$ or $y = -1.8$ (to 1 d.p.)
 (ii) When $y = -1$, $x = -0.2$ or
 $x = 4.2$ (to 1 d.p.)

4
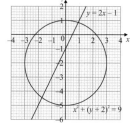

Points of intersection at (0.9, 0.9) and
(–1.7, –4.4) to 1 d.p.
(Accept (0.9, 0.8) and (–1.7, –4.5).)

5 **a)** $(x - 1)^2 = x^2 - x - x + (-1)^2 = x^2 - 2x + 1$
 b) $(y + 2)^2 = y^2 + 4y + 4$
 c) If $x^2 - 2x + y^2 + 4y = 11$
 then $(x - 1)^2 - 1 + (y + 2)^2 - 4 = 11$
 $(x - 1)^2 + (y + 2)^2 = 16$

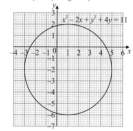

6
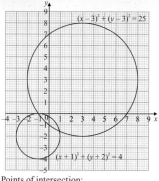

Points of intersection:
(–1, 0) and (0.95, –1.56) (to 2 d.p.)

16.7 Trigonometric Graphs

Page 153 Exercise 1

1 **a)**

x	0°	30°	45°	60°	90°	120°	135°	150°	180°
$\cos x$	1	0.87	0.71	0.5	0	–0.5	–0.71	–0.87	–1

x	210°	225°	240°	270°	300°	315°	330°	360°
$\cos x$	–0.87	–0.71	–0.5	0	0.5	0.71	0.87	1

b) (i) 66° and 294° (accept 67°, 293°)
 (ii) 139° and 221° (accept 138°, 222°)

2 **a)**

x	0°	30°	45°	60°	90°	120°	135°	150°	180°
$\sin x$	0	0.5	0.71	0.87	1	0.87	0.71	0.5	0
$2\sin x$	0	1	1.41	1.73	2	1.73	1.41	1	0

x	210°	225°	240°	270°	300°	315°	330°	360°
$\sin x$	–0.5	–0.71	–0.87	–1	–0.87	–0.71	–0.5	0
$2\sin x$	–1	–1.41	–1.73	–2	–1.73	–1.41	–1	0

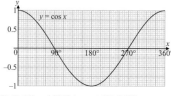

b) (i) 37° and 143°
 (ii) 204° and 336° (accept 203°, 337°)

3

x	0°	30°	45°	60°	90°	120°	135°	150°	180°
$\cos x$	1	0.87	0.71	0.5	0	–0.5	–0.71	–0.87	–1
$2 + \cos x$	3	2.87	2.71	2.5	2	1.5	1.29	1.13	1

x	210°	225°	240°	270°	300°	315°	330°	360°
$\cos x$	–0.87	–0.71	–0.5	0	0.5	0.71	0.87	1
$2 + \cos x$	1.13	1.29	1.5	2	2.5	2.71	2.87	3

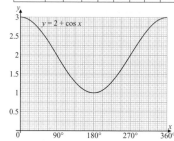

4

x	0°	30°	45°	60°	80°	85°	95°
$\tan x$	0	0.58	1	1.73	5.67	11.43	–11.43

x	100°	120°	150°	180°	210°	240°	260°
$\tan x$	–5.67	–1.73	–0.58	0	0.58	1.73	5.67

x	265°	275°	280°	300°	330°	360°
$\tan x$	11.43	–11.43	–5.67	–1.73	–0.58	0

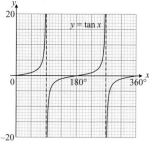

5 **a)**

x	0°	30°	45°	60°	90°	120°	135°	150°	180°
$2x$	0°	60°	90°	120°	180°	240°	270°	300°	360°
$\sin 2x$	0	0.87	1	0.87	0	–0.87	–1	–0.87	0

x	210°	225°	240°	270°	300°	315°	330°	360°
$2x$	420°	450°	480°	540°	600°	630°	660°	720°
$\sin 2x$	0.87	1	0.87	0	–0.87	–1	–0.87	0

b) E.g. The graphs of $y = \sin x$ and $y = \sin 2x$
 have the same shape, but $y = \sin 2x$ repeats
 twice as often as $y = \sin x$.

6 **a)**

x	0°	30°	45°	60°	90°	120°
$x - 90°$	–90°	–60°	–45°	–30°	0°	30°
$\cos (x - 90°)$	0	0.5	0.71	0.87	1	0.87

x	135°	150°	180°	210°	225°	240°
$x - 90°$	45°	60°	90°	120°	135°	150°
$\cos (x - 90°)$	0.71	0.5	0	–0.5	–0.71	–0.87

x	270°	300°	315°	330°	360°
$x - 90°$	180°	210°	225°	240°	270°
$\cos (x - 90°)$	–1	–0.87	–0.71	–0.5	0

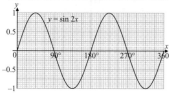

b) The graph of $y = \cos (x - 90°)$ is the
 same as the graph of $y = \sin x$.

16.8 Transforming Graphs

Page 154 Exercise 1

1 **a)** 3 units up **b)** 1 unit right
 c) 2 units left **d)** 6 units down
 e) 7 units right **f)** 5 units right, 6 units up
 g) 6 units left, 4 units down
 h) 3 units right, 2 units up

2 a) Translation 1 unit up.

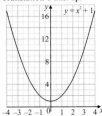

$y = x^2 + 1$

b) Translation 5 units up.

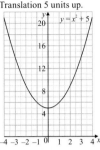

$y = x^2 + 5$

c) Translation 2 units down.

$y = x^2 - 2$

d) Translation 4 units right.

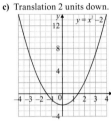

$y = (x - 4)^2$

e) Translation 1 unit left.

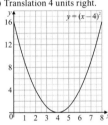

$y = (x + 1)^2$

f) Translation 3 units left and 2 units down.

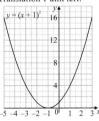

$y = (x + 3)^2 - 2$

g) Translation 2 units right and 2 units down.

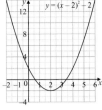

$y = (x - 2)^2 + 2$

h) Translation 5 units right and 3 units up.

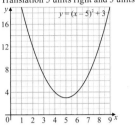

$y = (x - 5)^2 + 3$

3 a) Translation 1 unit left.

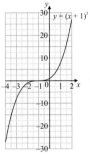

$y = (x + 1)^3$

b) Translation 4 units up.

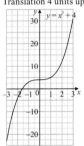

$y = x^3 + 4$

c) Translation 5 units down.

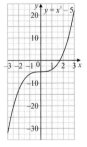

$y = x^3 - 5$

d) Translation 3 units right and 2 units up.

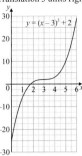

$y = (x - 3)^3 + 2$

e) Translation 5 units right and 4 units up.

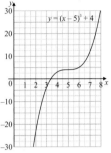

$y = (x - 5)^3 + 4$

f) Translation 2 units left and 3 units down

$y = (x + 2)^3 - 3$

g) Translation 4 units right and 6.5 units up

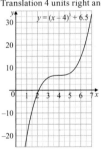

$y = (x - 4)^3 + 6.5$

h) Translation 2.5 units left and 3 units down

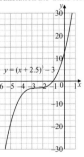

$y = (x + 2.5)^3 - 3$

4 a) $y = x^2 + 4$ **b)** $y = (x-3)^2$
c) $y = x^2 - 1$ **d)** $y = (x-1)^2$
e) $y = (x+2)^2 + 1$ **f)** $y = (x-1)^2 + 3$
g) $y = (x-4)^2 - 2$ **h)** $y = (x-2)^2 - 5$

5 a) Translation 1 unit up.

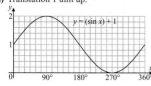

b) Translation 2 units down.

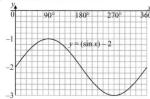

c) Translation 60° left.

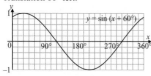

d) Translation 90° right.

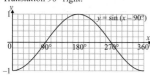

e) Translation 180° left.

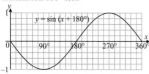

f) Translation 360° right.

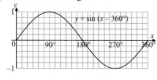

g) Translation 30° right and 1 unit up.

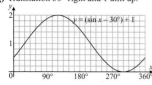

h) Translation 90° left and 2 units up.

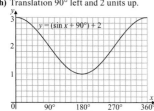

6 a) E.g. $y = \tan(x + 180°)$
b) E.g. $y = \cos(x - 180°)$
c) E.g. $y = \sin(x + 405°)$

Page 156   Exercise 2

1 a) Reflection in the y-axis.

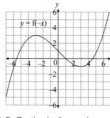

b) Reflection in the x-axis.

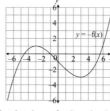

2 Sketches drawn for Question 2 may vary from those given here if different ranges of x-values have been used.

a)

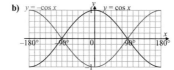

b)

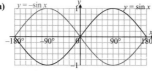

c)

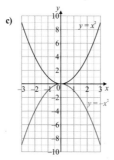

d)

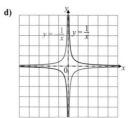

e)

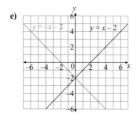

f)

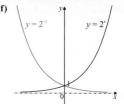

3

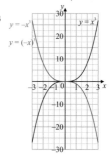

$(-x)^3 = -(x^3)$, so the graphs of $y = (-x)^3$ and $y = -x^3$ are the same.

Page 157   Exercise 3

1 a) Stretch of scale factor $\frac{1}{3}$ in the x-direction.

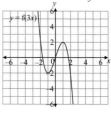

b) Stretch of scale factor $\frac{1}{5}$ in the x-direction.

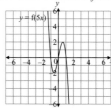

c) Stretch of scale factor 2 in the x-direction.

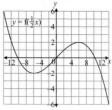

d) Stretch of scale factor 4 in the x-direction.

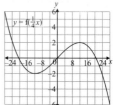

e) Stretch of scale factor 3 in the y-direction.

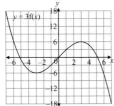

f) Stretch of scale factor 1.5 in the y-direction.

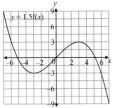

g) Stretch of scale factor $\frac{1}{3}$ in the y-direction.

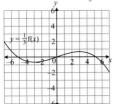

h) Stretch of scale factor $\frac{1}{10}$ in the y-direction.

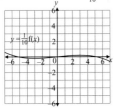

2 a) $y = \sin 4x$ **b)** $y = \sin \frac{1}{3}x$

c) $y = 5\sin x$ **d)** $y = \sin \frac{1}{5}x$

e) $y = 10\sin x$ **f)** $y = \frac{1}{4}\sin x$

g) $y = 2\sin 3x$ **h)** $y = 4\sin \frac{1}{2}x$

i) $y = \frac{1}{4}\sin 4x$

Page 158   Exercise 4

1 a), b), c)

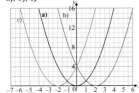

---

2 Sketches drawn for Question 2 may vary from those given here if different ranges of x-values have been used.

  a) Translation 1 unit right and reflection in the x-axis.

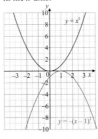

  b) Translation 3 units right and reflection in the y-axis.

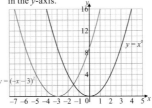

  c) Translation 90° left and reflection in the x-axis.

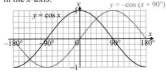

  d) Translation 1 unit up and reflection in the y-axis.

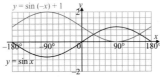

3 a) $y = (x+5)^2 - 4$ **b)** $y = -[(x+4)^2 + 5]$

c) $y = 3\cos(x - 60°)$ **d)** $y = 4\sin 2x$

e) $y = 3x^2 - 2$ **f)** $y = \frac{1}{2}(x+1)^2$

16.9   Graphs Problems

Page 159   Exercise 1

1 (i) D   **(ii)** E   **(iii)** B   **(iv)** A

  (v) F   **(vi)** G   **(vii)** H   **(viii)** C

2 (i) A   **(ii)** F   **(iii)** C

  (iv) B   **(v)** D   **(vi)** E

3 a) (i) The transformation increases the value of all y-coordinates by 3.

    (ii) $(0, 3)$

  b) (i) $(1, 0)$ **(ii)** $(-3, -2)$

4 a)

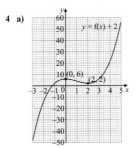

---

b)

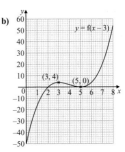

c)

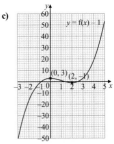

d)

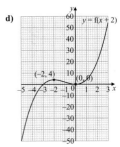

e)

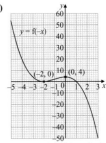

f)

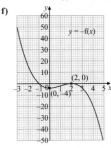

g)

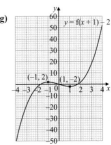

h)

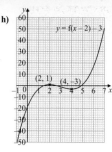
$y = f(x - 2) - 3$
(2, 1)   (4, −3)

i)

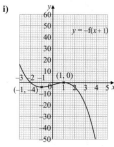
$y = -f(x + 1)$
(1, 0)
(−1, −4)

j)

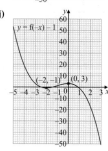
$y = f(-x) - 1$
(−2, −1)   (0, 3)

5 a)

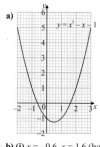
$y = x^2 - x - 1$

b) (i) $x = -0.6$, $x = 1.6$ (both to 1 d.p.)
(ii) $x = -1.6$, $x = 2.6$
(both to 1 d.p. — accept −1.5, 2.5)

6 a)

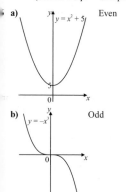
$y = x^2 + 5$ Even

b)
$y = -x^3$ Odd

c)

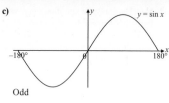
$y = \sin x$
−180°   0   180°
Odd

d)

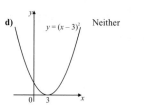
$y = (x - 3)^2$ Neither
0   3

e)

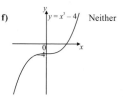
$y = \cos x$
−360°   0   360°
Even

f)
$y = x^3 - 4$ Neither
0
−4

g)

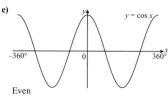
$y = \tan x$
−360°   0   360°
Odd

h)
$y = \dfrac{1}{x}$ Odd
0

7 a)

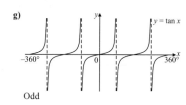
$y = \cos x$
−360°   −180°   0   180°   360°

b) (i) $x = -284°$, $x = -76°$, $x = 76°$, $x = 284°$
(accept −285°, −75°, 75°, 285°)
(ii) $x = -256°$, $x = -104°$, $x = 104°$, $x = 256°$
(accept −255°, −105°, 105°, 255°)
c) (i) $x = -310°$, $x = -50°$, $x = 50°$, $x = 310°$
(ii) $x = -230°$, $x = -130°$, $x = 130°$, $x = 230°$

8 a) 500 represents the initial amount borrowed.
1.03 represents the increase per month due
to interest.

b)

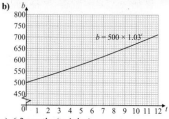
$b = 500 \times 1.03^t$

c) 6.2 months (to 1 d.p.)

9 a)

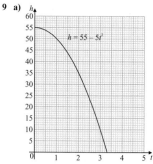
$h = 55 - 5t^2$

b) 3.3 seconds (to 1 d.p.)

10 a) 5 units   **b)** $x^2 + y^2 = 25$
c) $(x - 5)^2 + (y - 4)^2 = 4$

11 a) $x^2 + 8x + y^2 - 2y + 17$
b)

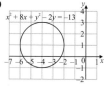
$x^2 + 8x + y^2 - 2y = -13$

12 a) (i) 25 g   **b)**
(ii) 2 g

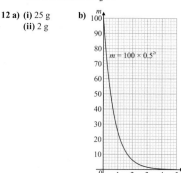
$m = 100 \times 0.5^{2t}$

c) Accept 1.6-1.7 hours (96-102 minutes)

Section 17 — Using Graphs

17.1   Interpreting Real-Life Graphs

Page 162   Exercise 1

1 a) 24 mph   **b) (i)** 40 km/h   **(ii)** 120 km/h
2 2.5 mph
3 Spain, by 8 km/h (or by 5 mph).
4 a) L   **b)** N   **c)** M   **d)** K
5 a) Oven 1   **b)** Oven 2
c) 18.5 minutes (accept 18-19 minutes)
d) Accept 28-30 °C/minute
e) (i) 630 seconds   **(ii)** 150 °C
6 a) The water got deeper for about an hour,
then shallower for about 6 hours.
Finally it got deeper for about 5 hours.
b) 09:20 (accept 09:15-09:30)
c) 1.2 m   **d)** 12:55 (accept 13:00) and 17:45
e) Accept 2h 10m - 2h 15m (130-135 minutes).

7 a) The water gets steadily deeper for 15 seconds, then steadily deeper at a slower rate for a further 15 seconds.
b) 12.5 seconds **c)** A

Page 164 Exercise 1

1 a)

Weight (kg)	1	2	3	4	5
Time (minutes)	60	95	130	165	200

b)
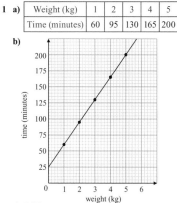

c) 2.4 kg

2 a)
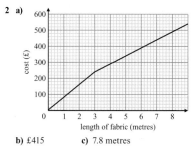

b) £415 **c)** 7.8 metres

3 a)
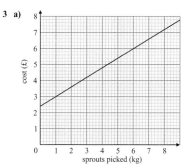

b) £5.10 **c)** 7 kg

4 a)
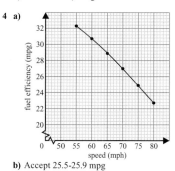

b) Accept 25.5-25.9 mpg

5 a)
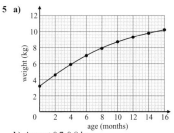

b) Accept 0.7-0.8 kg

6 a)
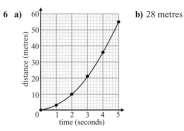
b) 28 metres

7 E.g.
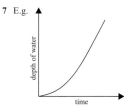

8 a)

d	0	1	2	3	4
N	5000	6000	7200	8640	10 368

b)
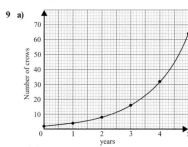

c) 3.2 days

9 a)

b) 3.9 years

Page 166 Exercise 1

1 $x = 4$ and $y = 6$

2 a), b)
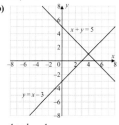

c) $x = 4$ and $y = 1$

3 a)
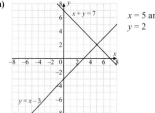
$x = 5$ an
$y = 2$

b)
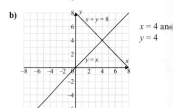
$x = 4$ an
$y = 4$

c)
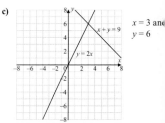
$x = 3$ an
$y = 6$

d)
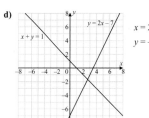
$x = 2\frac{2}{3}$ a
$y = -1\frac{2}{3}$

e)
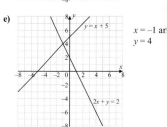
$x = -1$ ar
$y = 4$

f) 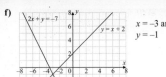 $x = -3$ and $y = -1$

g) 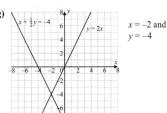 $x = -2$ and $y = -4$

h) 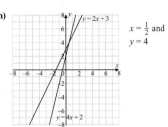 $x = \frac{1}{2}$ and $y = 4$

i) 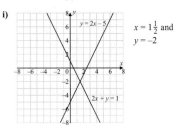 $x = 1\frac{1}{2}$ and $y = -2$

j) 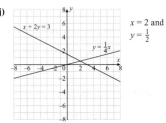 $x = 2$ and $y = \frac{1}{2}$

k) 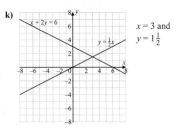 $x = 3$ and $y = 1\frac{1}{2}$

l) 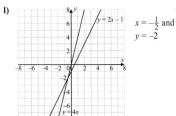 $x = -\frac{1}{2}$ and $y = -2$

m) 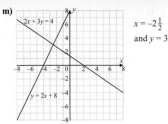 $x = -2\frac{1}{2}$ and $y = 3$

n) 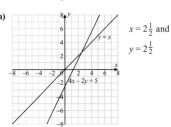 $x = 2\frac{1}{2}$ and $y = 2\frac{1}{2}$

o) 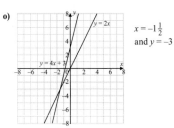 $x = -1\frac{1}{2}$ and $y = -3$

4 a)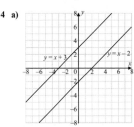

b) The lines are parallel and so do not intersect. This means there are no points where both the x and the y values are the same for both lines, and so there are no solutions.

Page 167   Exercise 2

1 a) $x = 0$ and $y = 0$, $x = 2$ and $y = 4$

b) $x = 0$ and $y = 4$

c) There are no solutions.

2 a) (i)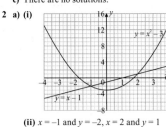

(ii) $x = -1$ and $y = -2$, $x = 2$ and $y = 1$

b) (i)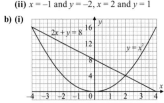

(ii) $x = -4$ and $y = 16$, $x = 2$ and $y = 4$

c) (i)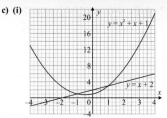

(ii) $x = -1$ and $y = 1$, $x = 1$ and $y = 3$

d) (i)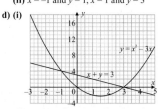

(ii) $x = -1$ and $y = 4$, $x = 3$ and $y = 0$

e) (i)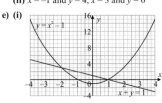

(ii) $x = -2$ and $y = 3$, $x = 1$ and $y = 0$

f) (i)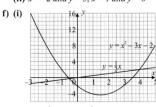

(ii) $x = -\frac{1}{2}$ and $y = -\frac{1}{4}$, $x = 4$ and $y = 2$

g) (i)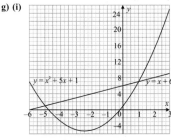

(ii) $x = -5$ and $y = 1$, $x = 1$ and $y = 7$

h) (i)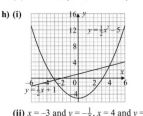

(ii) $x = -3$ and $y = -\frac{1}{2}$, $x = 4$ and $y = 3$

Page 168 Exercise 1

1 a)
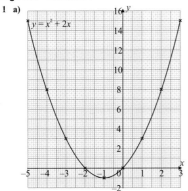

b) (i) $x = -2$ and $x = 0$
(ii) $x = -4.3$ and $x = 2.3$ (to 1 d.p.)
(iii) $x = -3.8$ and $x = 1.8$ (to 1 d.p.)

2 a)
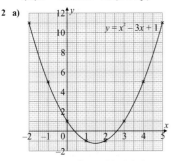

b) (i) $x = 0.4$ and $x = 2.6$ (to 1 d.p.)
(ii) $x = -0.56$ and $x = 3.56$ (to 2 d.p.), accept $x = -0.6$ to -0.5, $x = 3.5$ to 3.6.
(iii) $x = 0.63$ and $x = 2.37$ (to 2 d.p.), accept $x = 0.6$ to 0.7, $x = 2.3$ to 2.4.

3 a) (i) $x^2 + 4x - 10 = 0$
(ii) $x^2 + 4x - 3 = 0$
(iii) $x^2 + 4x + 2 = 0$
b)
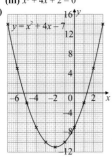

c) (i) $x = -5.3$ and $x = 1.3$ (to 1 d.p.)
(ii) $x = -5.7$ and $x = 1.7$ (to 1 d.p.)
(iii) $x = -4.6$ and $x = 0.6$ (to 1 d.p.)
(iv) $x = -3.4$ and $x = -0.6$ (to 1 d.p.)

4 a)
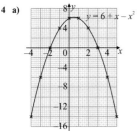

b) (i) $x = -1.8$ and $x = 2.8$ (to 1 d.p.)
(ii) $x = -3.53$ and $x = 4.53$ (to 2 d.p.), accept $x = -3.6$ to -3.5, $x = 4.5$ to 4.6
(iii) $x = -1.3$ and $x = 2.3$ (to 1 d.p.)
(iv) $x = -2.7$ and $x = 3.7$ (to 1 d.p.)

5 a)
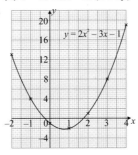

b) (i) $x = -0.3$ and $x = 1.8$ (to 1 d.p.)
(ii) $x = -1$ and $x = 2.5$
(iii) $x = -1.6$ and $x = 3.1$ (to 1 d.p.)
(iv) $x = 0$ and $x = 1.5$

Page 169 Exercise 2

1 a) (i)
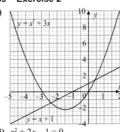

(ii) $x^2 + 2x - 1 = 0$
(iii) The intersection points (to 1 d.p.) are $(-2.4, -1.4)$ and $(0.4, 1.4)$.
Substitute the x-values into $x^2 + 2x - 1$:
$(-2.4)^2 + (2 \times -2.4) - 1 = -0.04 \approx 0$
$(0.4)^2 + (2 \times 0.4) - 1 = -0.04 \approx 0$

b) (i)
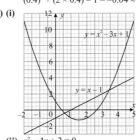

(ii) $x^2 - 4x + 2 = 0$
(iii) The intersection points (to 1 d.p.) are $(0.6, -0.4)$ and $(3.4, 2.4)$.
Substitute the x-values into $x^2 - 4x + 2$:
$(0.6)^2 - (4 \times 0.6) + 2 = -0.04 \approx 0$
$(3.4)^2 - (4 \times 3.4) + 2 = -0.04 \approx 0$

c) (i)
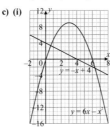

(ii) $x^2 - 7x + 4 = 0$
(iii) The intersection points (to 1 d.p.) are $(0.6, 3.4)$ and $(6.4, -2.4)$.
Substitute the x-values into $x^2 - 7x + 4$:
$(0.6)^2 - (7 \times 0.6) + 4 = 0.16 \approx 0$
$(6.4)^2 - (7 \times 6.4) + 4 = 0.16 \approx 0$

d) (i)
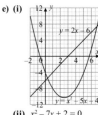

(ii) $x^2 + 3x - 5 = 0$
(iii) The intersection points (to 1 d.p.) are $(-4.2, 6.2)$ and $(1.2, 0.8)$.
Substitute the x-values into $x^2 + 3x -$
$(-4.2)^2 + (3 \times -4.2) - 5 = 0.04 \approx 0$
$(1.2)^2 + (3 \times 1.2) - 5 = 0.04 \approx 0$

e) (i)
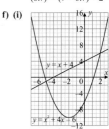

(ii) $x^2 - 7x + 2 = 0$
(iii) The intersection points (to 1 d.p.) are $(0.3, -5.4)$ and $(6.7, 7.4)$.
Substitute the x-values into $x^2 - 7x +$
$(0.3)^2 - (7 \times 0.3) + 2 = -0.01 \approx 0$
$(6.7)^2 - (7 \times 6.7) + 2 = -0.01 \approx 0$

f) (i)
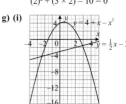

(ii) $x^2 + 3x - 10 = 0$
(iii) The intersection points (to 1 d.p.) are $(-5, -1)$ and $(2, 6)$.
Substitute x-values into $x^2 + 3x - 10$:
$(-5)^2 + (3 \times -5) - 10 = 0$
$(2)^2 + (3 \times 2) - 10 = 0$

g) (i)

(ii) $x^2 - \frac{1}{2}x - 7 = 0$
(iii) The intersection points (to 1 d.p.) are $(-2.4, -4.2)$ and $(2.9, -1.5)$.
Substitute x-values into $x^2 - \frac{1}{2}x - 7$:
$(-2.4)^2 - \frac{1}{2} \times (-2.4) - 7 = -0.04 \approx 0$
$(2.9)^2 - \frac{1}{2} \times (2.9) - 7 = -0.04 \approx 0$

h) (i)

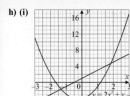

(ii) $2x^2 - x - 5 = 0$

(iii) The intersection points (to 2 d.p.) are (−1.35, −1.70) and (1.85, 4.70).
Substitute x-values into $2x^2 - x - 5$:
$2 \times (-1.35)^2 - (-1.35) - 5 = -0.005 \approx 0$
$2 \times (1.85)^2 - (1.85) - 5 = -0.005 \approx 0$

i) (i)

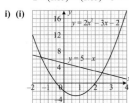

(ii) $2x^2 - 2x - 7 = 0$

(iii) The intersection points (to 2 d.p.) are (−1.44 , 6.44) and (2.44, 2.56).
Substitute x-values into $2x^2 - 2x - 7$:
$2(-1.44)^2 - 2(-1.44) - 7 = 0.0272 \approx 0$
$2(2.44)^2 - 2(2.44) - 7 = 0.0272 \approx 0$

j) (i)

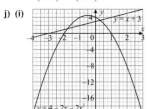

(ii) $2x^2 + 3x - 1 = 0$

(iii) The intersection points (to 2 d.p.) are (−1.78, 1.22) and (0.28, 3.28).
Substitute x-values into $2x^2 + 3x - 1$:
$2(-1.78)^2 + 3(-1.78) - 1 = -0.0032 \approx 0$
$2(0.28)^2 + 3(0.28) - 1 = -0.0032 \approx 0$

2 a) — See below   **b)** $x^2 - 2x = 2x + 1$

c)

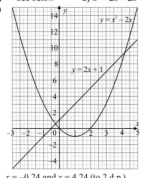

$x = -0.24$ and $x = 4.24$ (to 2 d.p.)

3 a), b)

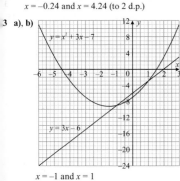

$x = -1$ and $x = 1$

4 a), b)

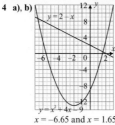

$x = -6.65$ and $x = 1.65$ (to 2 d.p.)

5 a), b)

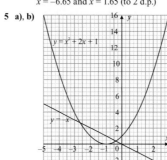

$x = -2.62$ and $x = -0.38$ (to 2 d.p.)

6 a), b)

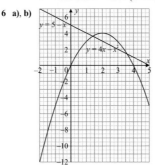

$x = 1.38$ and $x = 3.62$ (to 2 d.p.)

17.5 Sketching Quadratic Graphs

Page 170   Exercise 1

1 a) (i) (−1, 0) and (1, 0)   **(ii)** (0, −1)
  b) (i) (−7, 0) and (−1, 0)   **(ii)** (−4, −9)
  c) (i) (−10, 0) and (−6, 0)   **(ii)** (−8, −4)

2 a)

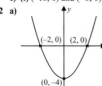

b)

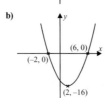

c)

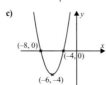

d)

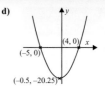

e)

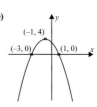

f)

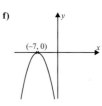

g)

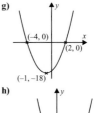

h)

i)

Page 171   Exercise 2

1 a) (i) (−8, 0) and (−2, 0)
   (ii) (0, 16)   **(iii)** (−5, −9)
  b) (i) $(3 - \sqrt{30}, 0)$ and $(3 + \sqrt{30}, 0)$
   (ii) (0, −21)   **(iii)** (3, −30)
  c) (i) $(4 - \sqrt{13}, 0)$ and $(4 + \sqrt{13}, 0)$
   (ii) (0, 3)   **(iii)** (4, −13)

2 a)

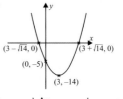

b)

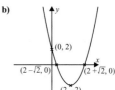

c)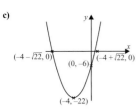
$(-4 - \sqrt{22}, 0)$ $(0, -6)$ $(-4 + \sqrt{22}, 0)$
$(-4, -22)$

d)
$(0, 8)$
$(-1, 7)$

e)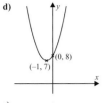
$(0, 10)$
$(0.5, 9.75)$

f)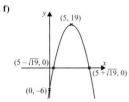
$(5, 19)$
$(5 - \sqrt{19}, 0)$
$(5 + \sqrt{19}, 0)$
$(0, -6)$

17.6 Gradients of Curves

Page 171 Exercise 1

1 a)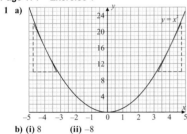
$y = x^2$

b) (i) 8   **(ii)** −8
c) They are the same apart from their sign.

2 a)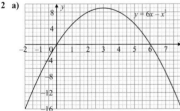
$y = 6x - x^2$

b) 0

3 a)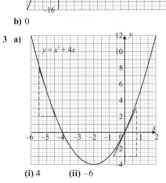
$y = x^2 + 4x$

(i) 4   **(ii)** −6

---

b)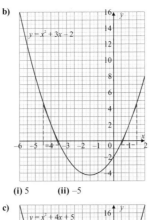
$y = x^2 + 3x - 2$

(i) 5   **(ii)** −5

c)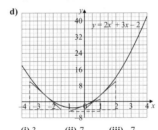
$y = x^2 + 4x + 5$

(i) −2   **(ii)** 5

d)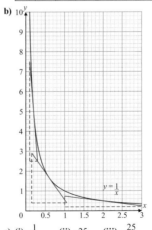
$y = 2x^2 + 3x - 2$

(i) 3   **(ii)** 7   **(iii)** −7

4 a)

x	0.1	0.2	0.5	1	1.5	2	3
y	10	5	2	1	$\frac{2}{3}$	$\frac{1}{2}$	$\frac{1}{3}$

b)
$y = \frac{1}{x}$

c) (i) $-\frac{1}{4}$ **(ii)** −25   **(iii)** $-\frac{25}{9}$

5 a)

x	−0.9	−0.8	−0.5	0	0.5	1	2
y	10	5	2	1	$\frac{2}{3}$	$\frac{1}{2}$	$\frac{1}{3}$

---

b)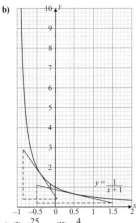
$y = \frac{1}{x + 1}$

c) (i) $-\frac{25}{9}$ **(ii)** $-\frac{4}{9}$

6 a)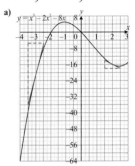
$y = x^3 - 2x^2 - 8x$

b) (i) 31   **(ii)** −4

7 a)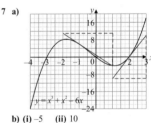
$y = x^3 + x^2 - 6x$

b) (i) −5   **(ii)** 10
c) −1.8 (to 1 d.p.) and 1.1 (to 1 d.p.)

Page 172 Exercise 2

1 a)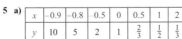
$x^2 + y^2 = 100$

b) (i) $y = -\frac{3}{4}x + \frac{25}{2}$ **(ii)** $y = -\frac{4}{3}x + \frac{50}{3}$

(iii) $y = -\frac{4}{3}x - \frac{50}{3}$ **(iv)** $y = \frac{3}{4}x + \frac{25}{2}$

2 a)
$x^2 + y^2 = 625$

b) (i) $y = -\frac{3}{4}x + \frac{125}{4}$ **(ii)** $y = \frac{7}{24}x + \frac{625}{24}$

(iii) $y = -\frac{3}{4}x - \frac{125}{4}$ **(iv)** $y = \frac{24}{7}x - \frac{625}{7}$

3 a) $y = x + 4\sqrt{2}$ **b)** $y = x - 4\sqrt{2}$
c) E.g. The two tangents have the same gradient so they are parallel.

4 $\left(0, \frac{25}{3}\right)$

Section 18 — Functions

18.1 Functions

Page 173 Exercise 1

1 a) (i) 6   **(ii)** 31   **(iii)** −1
b) (i) 0   **(ii)** 28   **(iii)** 6
c) (i) 4   **(ii)** 7   **(iii)** −2
d) (i) 8   **(ii)** 23   **(iii)** −12
e) (i) −2   **(ii)** −17   **(iii)** 9
f) (i) 5   **(ii)** 0   **(iii)** 21

2 a) (i) 36   **(ii)** 36   **(iii)** ¼
b) (i) 21   **(ii)** 21   **(iii)** −3.75
c) (i) 8   **(ii)** −7   **(iii)** 17
d) (i) 49   **(ii)** 14   **(iii)** 124
e) (i) 25   **(ii)** 9   **(iii)** 0

3 a) (i) 2   **(ii)** 16   **(iii)** −40
b) (i) 3   **(ii)** 5   **(iii)** ½
c) (i) 9   **(ii)** 3   **(iii)** 1
d) (i) −½   **(ii)** 1   **(iii)** 13
e) (i) 15   **(ii)** 6   **(iii)** 18.75
f) (i) 0   **(ii)** $\frac{1}{2}$ **(iii)** $\frac{4}{7}$
g) (i) 0   **(ii)** 1   **(iii)** $-\frac{3}{4}$
h) (i) $5\frac{1}{2}$ **(ii)** −7   **(iii)** $15\frac{1}{8}$

4 a) (i) $2k + 1$ **(ii)** $4m + 1$ **(iii)** $6w - 1$
b) (i) $2u^2 + 3u$ **(ii)** $18a^2 + 9a$
(iii) $2t^4 + 3t^2$
c) (i) $\frac{4t - 1}{t + 4}$ **(ii)** $\frac{-4x - 1}{-x + 4}$ **(iii)** $\frac{8x - 1}{2x + 4}$
d) (i) $\sqrt{5w - 1}$ **(ii)** $\sqrt{15x - 1}$
(iii) $\sqrt{4 - 10x}$
e) (i) $4h^2 - 5h + 1$ **(ii)** $16x^2 + 10x + 1$
(iii) $\frac{4}{x^2} - \frac{5}{x} + 1$

Page 174 Exercise 2

1 a) {5, 6, 7, 8, 9}   **b)** {−6, −3, 0, 3, 6}
c) {5, 7, 9, 11, 13, 15}   **d)** {1, 7, 13, 19}
e) {11, 14, 17, 20, 23}   **f)** {0, 1, 4}
g) {1, 1.2, 1.5, 2, 3, 6}   **h)** {−1, 0, 2, 9, 20}
i) {1, 9, 25}   **j)** {6, 10, 30}

2 a) $2 \le f(x) \le 5$ **b)** $2 \le f(x) \le 3$
c) $0 \le f(x) \le 4$ **d)** $-1 < f(x) \le 2$
e) $1 \le f(x) \le 10$ **f)** $5 \le f(x) \le 15$
g) $1 \le f(x) < 13$ **h)** $-12 < f(x) \le 13$
i) $7 \le f(x) \le 19$ **j)** $3 < g(x) < 9$
k) $7 \le g(x) \le 14$

3 a) $8 \le f(x) \le 50$ **b)** $3 \le f(x) < 8$
c) $-1 \le f(x) \le 8$ **d)** $5 \le f(x) \le 23$

Page 175 Exercise 3

1 a) $x = 0$ **b)** $x = -\frac{1}{2}$ **c)** $x = -2$
d) $x = \pm 5$ **e)** $x < 0$ **f)** $x < 1$
g) $x > \frac{3}{4}$ **h)** $x < -\frac{3}{10}$

2 a) $x = -2$ **b)** $x < 2$
c) No values are excluded   **d)** $t = 0$
e) $x > 3$ **f)** $x = 0, \quad x = 4$
g) $x < -21$ **h)** $-3 < x < 3$

---

3 a) Domain: $x \ne -\frac{3}{5}$, range: $f(x) \ne 0$
b) Domain: all real numbers, range: $g(x) \le 10$
c) Domain: $x \ge 5$, range: $f(x) \ge 0$
d) Domain: $x \ne 0$, range: $f(x) \ne 2$

18.2 Composite Functions

Page 176 Exercise 1

1 a) 3   **b)** 6   **c)** 8   **d)** 7
2 a) 3   **b)** 6   **c)** 6   **d)** 8
3 a) (i) 23   **(ii)** 12   **(iii)** $4x - 20$
b) (i) −2   **(ii)** 13   **(iii)** $6x + 1$
c) (i) 9   **(ii)** 2   **(iii)** $\frac{x + 5}{2}$
d) (i) 15   **(ii)** 12   **(iii)** $9 - 3x$
e) (i) 1   **(ii)** 4   **(iii)** $\frac{5x - 4}{4}$
f) (i) −10   **(ii)** 19   **(iii)** $2 - 6x$
g) (i) 63   **(ii)** 47   **(iii)** $20x + 15$
h) (i) 4   **(ii)** 4   **(iii)** $23 - 2x$
i) (i) $\frac{1}{2}$ **(ii)** $\frac{1}{3x - 7}$ **(iii)** $\frac{3}{x} - 7$

4 a) (i) 4   **(ii)** 2   **(iii)** $(10 - x)^2$
b) (i) 2   **(ii)** 9   **(iii)** $2\sqrt{x} + 1$
c) (i) 14   **(ii)** $3x^2 + 11$ **(iii)** $9x - 16$
d) (i) −25   **(ii)** $7 - 2x^2$ **(iii)** x
e) (i) 2   **(ii)** $4x - 12$ **(iii)** $\sqrt{37 - 6x}$

5 a) (i) 49   **(ii)** $\frac{1}{6x - 13}$ **(iii)** $\frac{1}{(3x + 2)^2}$
b) (i) 64   **(ii)** $2x - 4$ **(iii)** $(10 - 2x)^3$
c) (i) 14   **(ii)** 4.8   **(iii)** $\frac{1}{\sqrt{6x + 13}}$
d) (i) 156   **(ii)** $\frac{1}{3}$ **(iii)** $\frac{1}{2x^2 + 2x + 3}$

18.3 Inverse Functions

Page 177 Exercise 1

1 a) $f^{-1}(x) = x - 4$ **b)** $f^{-1}(x) = x + 3$
c) $f^{-1}(x) = x + 7$ **d)** $f^{-1}(x) = x - 1$
e) $f^{-1}(x) = \frac{x}{8}$ **f)** $g^{-1}(x) = \frac{x}{2}$
g) $g^{-1}(x) = 3x$ **h)** $f^{-1}(x) = 6x$

2 a) $f^{-1}(x) = \frac{x - 3}{4}$ **b)** $f^{-1}(t) = \frac{t + 9}{2}$
c) $g^{-1}(x) = \frac{x + 5}{3}$ **d)** $f^{-1}(x) = \frac{x - 11}{8}$
e) $f^{-1}(x) = 5(x + 7)$ **f)** $g^{-1}(x) = 8(x - 1)$
g) $f^{-1}(t) = 2t + 3$ **h)** $h^{-1}(x) = 4x - 15$

3 a) $f^{-1}(x) = \frac{5x - 6}{2}$ **b)** $g^{-1}(x) = \frac{4x + 1}{3}$
c) $f^{-1}(x) = \sqrt{x + 3}$ **d)** $g^{-1}(x) = \frac{\sqrt{x} - 7}{2}$

4 a) $f^{-1}(x) = 5(x + 8)$ **b)** $f^{-1}(x) = 4x + 6$
c) $f^{-1}(x) = \frac{5x - 1}{3}$ **d)** $g^{-1}(x) = \frac{5(x + 7)}{2}$

5 a) $f^{-1}(x) = \frac{7 - x}{3}$ **b)** $g^{-1}(x) = \frac{11 - x}{3}$
c) $f^{-1}(x) = \frac{9 - 4x}{7}$ **d)** $h^{-1}(x) = \frac{1 - 9x}{6}$

6 a) $f^{-1}(x) = \sqrt{x + 5}$ **b)** $g^{-1}(x) = \sqrt{\frac{x - 1}{4}}$
c) $g^{-1}(x) = \frac{\sqrt{x} + 1}{3}$ **d)** $h^{-1}(x) = \frac{1 - \sqrt{5x}}{2}$

7 a) $f^{-1}(x) = (x + 8)^2$ **b)** $f^{-1}(x) = \left(\frac{x - 1}{6}\right)^2$
c) $g^{-1}(x) = \frac{19 - x}{2}$ **d)** $f^{-1}(x) = \left(\frac{25 - x}{4}\right)^2$

8 a) $h^{-1}(x) = 1 + \frac{8}{x}$ **b)** $f^{-1}(x) = \frac{4}{x + 7}$
c) $g^{-1}(x) = \left(\frac{2}{8 - x}\right)^2$ **d)** $f^{-1}(x) = \frac{2}{x^2} + 1$

9 a) If $x = \frac{1 - 2y}{3y + 5}$,
then $x(3y + 5) = 1 - 2y$
$3xy + 5x = 1 - 2y$
$3xy + 2y = 1 - 5x$

---

b) $3xy + 2y = y(3x + 2)$
So if $3xy + 2y = y(3x + 2) = 1 - 5x$,
then $g^{-1}(x) = y = \frac{1 - 5x}{3x + 2}$

10 a) $f^{-1}(x) = \frac{2x + 2}{x - 3}$ **b)** $g^{-1}(x) = \frac{1 + 7x}{2x - 4}$
c) $f^{-1}(x) = \frac{2x}{1 - 3x}$

18.4 Functions Problems

Page 179 Exercise 1

1 a) $f(8) = 33$ **b)** $fg(1) = 28$
c) $x = 4$ **d)** $g^{-1}(x) = \frac{x - 5}{2}$
2 a) $x = 6$ **b)** $fg(x) = 8x + 21$
c) $f^{-1}(x) = \frac{x - 1}{4}$
3 a) $g(11) = 7$ **b)** $gf(x) = 3x + 4$
c) $g^{-1}(x) = 2x - 3$
4 a) $-1 \le f(x) \le 23$ **b)** $x = 3.5$
5 a) Exclude $x < -1$ **b)** $gf(x) = 4\sqrt{x + 1}$
c) $f^{-1}(x) = x^2 - 1$
6 a) $x = 4$ **b)** $f^{-1}(x) = \frac{x + 3}{2}$
c) $x = 3$ **d)** $ff(x) = 4x - 9$
7 a) $x = 4.2$ **b)** $gf(x) = 27 - 6x$
c) $g^{-1}(x) = \frac{18 - x}{3}$
8 a) $g(-3) = 0.5$
b) $fg(x) = x$. f and g are inverses of each other.
9 a) $x = 3$ **b)** $x = 7$
c) $fg(x) = \frac{4}{10\sqrt{x} - 15}$.
Exclude $x < 0$ and $x = 2.25$.
10 a) Range of f: $f(x) \ge 5$
Range of g: $g(x)$ can be any real number
b) $gg(4) = 32$
c) $g^{-1}(x) = \frac{x + 1}{3}$. $x = 14, -16$
11 a) $f(5) = 2.5$ **b)** $f^{-1}(x) = \frac{3x}{x - 1}$
c) $fg(x) = \frac{x^2 + 3}{x^2} = 1 + \frac{3}{x^2}$
12 a) $f(4) = 80$ m   **b)** $t = 1.6$ s
13 a) $f(20) = 68$ °F   **b)** $t = 16$ °C
c) $f^{-1}(t) = \frac{5(t - 32)}{9}$
d) a) 20 °C is equivalent to 68 °F.
b) 60.8 °F is equivalent to 16 °C.
c) The inverse function converts temperatures from degrees Fahrenheit to degrees Celsius.
14 a) $f(4) = 46$ °F   **b)** $f(7) = 35.5$ °F
c) $f^{-1}(32) = 8$.
At 8000 feet, the temperature is 32 °F.

Section 19 — Differentiation

19.1 Differentiating Powers of x

Page 180 Exercise 1

1 a) $5x^4$ **b)** $7x^6$
c) $4x^3$ **d)** $9x^8$
e) $3x^2 + 2x$ **f)** $6x^5 - 5x^4 + 4x^3$
g) $4x^3 + 2x$ **h)** $12x^3$
i) $24x^2$ **j)** $30x^4$
k) $14x$ **l)** $24x^5$
m) $6x + 2$ **n)** $15x^2 - 16x + 3$
o) $4 - 4x$ **p)** $8x^3 + 22x$
q) $x^2 - 1$ **r)** $3x^2 - x + 6$
s) $4x^5 + 10x^3 - 24x^2$ **t)** $3x^3 - \frac{x^2}{2} + 2x$

2 a) $-\frac{4}{x^5}$ **b)** $-\frac{3}{x^4} - \frac{1}{x^2} - 2x$

c) $-\dfrac{2}{x^3} - \dfrac{8}{x^2}$ d) $-\dfrac{12}{x^4} + \dfrac{12}{x^3}$

e) $-\dfrac{8}{x^3} - 10x$ f) $\dfrac{3}{x^2}$

3 a) $2x + 5$ b) $6x - 12$
c) $6x^2 - 6x$ d) $32x^3 + 6x^2$
e) $2x + 6$ f) $2x - 2$
g) $2x$ h) $4x + 7$
i) $12x - 1$ j) $2x - 4$
k) $8x + 4$ l) $-\dfrac{10}{x^3} - \dfrac{3}{x^2}$
m) $-\dfrac{6}{x^2} - 1$ n) $-\dfrac{12}{x^3} - \dfrac{6}{x^4}$
o) $-\dfrac{4}{x^3} - \dfrac{1}{x^2}$

4 a) $\dfrac{da}{db} = -8 - 4b$ b) $\dfrac{dy}{dt} = 6 - 10t$
c) $\dfrac{dx}{dt} = 15t^2 + 8t - 2$ d) $\dfrac{dx}{du} = 2u^2 + 3u - 1$
e) $\dfrac{dy}{dz} = 6z^3 - \dfrac{5}{2}z^2 + 7z$
f) $\dfrac{dm}{dn} = n^3 - \dfrac{3}{2}n^2 + \dfrac{1}{2}n$ g) $\dfrac{dr}{ds} = -s$
h) $\dfrac{ds}{dt} = 1 - \dfrac{4}{t^2}$ i) $\dfrac{dx}{dt} = t - 4$

19.2 Finding Gradients

Page 182 Exercise 1

1 a) (i) 10 (ii) -4   b) (i) -3 (ii) -3
c) (i) 1 (ii) 1   d) (i) 7 (ii) -3
e) (i) -4 (ii) 3   f) (i) 19 (ii) -3.5
g) (i) 11 (ii) $-5\frac{2}{3}$ h) (i) 6 (ii) 3.75
i) (i) -6 (ii) 27   j) (i) 1 (ii) 0

2 a) (i) -7 (ii) 5   b) (i) 7 (ii) -17
c) (i) -16 (ii) 0   d) (i) 11 (ii) -1
e) (i) 5 (ii) 2

3 a) 1   b) $x = 4$
4 a) 10   b) $x = -1$
5 a) 3   b) $x = -2$
6 a) 2.75   b) $x = 1$ or $x = -1$
7 a) 13   b) $x = -\frac{1}{3}$ or $x = 3$
8 a) $x = 0.5$ or $x = 3$ b) $x = 1.5$ or $x = 2$
9 (2, 0) and (-2, 16)
10 $(2, -9\frac{1}{3})$ and $(-4, 26\frac{2}{3})$
11 a) $y = -1$ b) 1
c) The tangent is a straight line, so has an equation of the form $y = mx + c$.
The tangent's gradient is 1, so $y = x + c$.
Point (2, -1) lies on the tangent,
so $-1 = 2 + c$
   $c = -3$
So the equation of the tangent is $y = x - 3$.
12   $y = 2x + 8$

19.3 Maximum and Minimum Points

Page 184 Exercise 1

1 a) (3, 2)   b) (1, 4)
c) (-1, -1)   d) (-1, -16)
e) (3, -13)   f) (0, 6)
g) (-8, -194)   h) (7, -17.5)
i) (1.5, 30.75)

2 a) (2, 19)   b) (1.5, 7.25)
c) (4.5, 6.25)   d) (-2.5, 30.25)
e) (-2, 17)   f) (0.5, 13.25)
g) (4, 52)   h) (-2, 17)   i) (0.5, -0.5)

3 a) $3x^2 - 6x$
b) At the turning points, $\dfrac{dy}{dx} = 0$,
so $3x^2 - 6x = 3x(x - 2) = 0$
So $x = 0$ or $x = 2$.
When $x = 0$, $y = 0^3 - 3(0)^2 + 7 = 7$
When $x = 2$,
$y = 2^3 - 3(2)^2 + 7 = 8 - 12 + 7 = 3$
So the turning points are (0, 7) and (2, 3).

c) (i) $\dfrac{dy}{dx} = 3.75$.
The graph slopes up from left to right.
(ii) $\dfrac{dy}{dx} = -2.25$.
The graph slopes down from left to right.
(iii) $\dfrac{dy}{dx} = -2.25$.
The graph slopes down from left to right.
(iv) $\dfrac{dy}{dx} = 3.75$.
The graph slopes up from left to right.
d) The graph is increasing just before the point (0, 7) and decreasing just after it, so (0, 7) is a maximum.
The graph is decreasing just before the point (2, 3) and increasing just after it, so (2, 3) is a minimum.

4 a) maximum at (-1, 14)
b) minimum at (0.5, 2.75)
c) minimum at (2, -12)
d) minimum at $\left(1\frac{1}{3}, -3\frac{1}{3}\right)$

5 minimum at (1, 18)
6 a) minimum at (0, -10); maximum at (4, 22)
b) maximum at (-1, 15); minimum at (5, -93)
c) minimum at (2, -20); maximum at (4, -16)
d) maximum at (-1, 9); minimum at (3, -23)
e) minimum at (-2, -39); maximum at (2, 25)
f) maximum at (-2, 3); minimum at $\left(0, \frac{5}{3}\right)$
g) minimum at (-4, -304);
maximum at (5, 425)
h) maximum at (-4, -42);
minimum at (-2, -50)
7 minimum at (1, -2); maximum at (-1, 2)

19.4 Using Differentiation

Page 185 Exercise 1

1 a) $v = 40$
b) (i) $t = -1.12$ or $t = 7.12$
(ii) The point where the share value dropped to zero.
(iii) The negative solution relates to a time before the shares were first traded, so it isn't relevant.
c) $\dfrac{dv}{dt} = -10t + 30$
d) $t = 3$ — this is the point at which the share value had stopped rising and was about to start falling.
e)
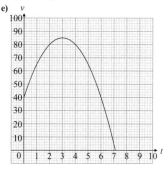

2 a) $\dfrac{ds}{dt} = 4 - 10t$ b) 2.8 metres
3 a) $\dfrac{dy}{dx} = 3x^2 - 10x + 10$ b) 3 kg/year
4 a) 93 °C   b) 3 °C/minute

Page 186 Exercise 2

1 a) $\dfrac{ds}{dt} = 10 - 2t$ b) 6 m/s
c) 5 seconds
2 a) 10 m   b) $\dfrac{ds}{dt} = 8 + 6t - 3t^2$ c) 8 m/s

3 a) $v = 12t - 3t^2$
b) At $t = 2.5$, $v = 11.25$ m/s, and at $t = 3$, $v = 9$ m/s.
So the object has greater velocity at $t = 2$
c) 4 seconds
4 a) $v = 7 - 4t$ b) 3 m/s
c) -9 m/s   d) $a = -4$ m/s²

Page 187 Exercise 3

1 a) 6 m/s   b) $\dfrac{dv}{dt} = 3 - 2t$
c) $a = 1$ m/s² The acceleration is positive, so the object is speeding up.
2 a) 2.4 m/s   b) $\dfrac{dv}{dt} = 8 - 10t$
c) 0.8 seconds
3 a) $\dfrac{dy}{dx} = -\frac{1}{2}x + 75$ b) 150 kg
4 a) $a = 8t - 6$ b) 0.75 seconds
5 a) 45 metres   b) 3 seconds
c) $\dfrac{ds}{dt} = -10t$ d) 30 m/s
6 a) 10 m/s   b) $a = 2 - \dfrac{8}{t^2}$
7 a) $\dfrac{dP}{dx} = -300x^2 + 300x + 600$ b) £2
8 a) 17 m²   b) $3\frac{1}{3}$ m²/month

Section 20 — Matrices

20.1 Matrix Addition and Subtractio[n]

Page 188 Exercise 1

1 a) $\begin{pmatrix} 7 & 5 \\ 9 & 8 \end{pmatrix}$ b) $\begin{pmatrix} -1 & 6 \\ -1 & -5 \end{pmatrix}$ c) $\begin{pmatrix} 15 & 22 \\ 25 & 22 \end{pmatrix}$
d) $\begin{pmatrix} 10.8 & 11.3 \\ 12.6 & 13.5 \end{pmatrix}$ e) $\begin{pmatrix} 15 & 26 \\ 32 & 12 \end{pmatrix}$ f) $\begin{pmatrix} -2 & -6 \\ 15 & 8 \end{pmatrix}$
g) $\begin{pmatrix} 40 & 4 \\ -8 & 4 \end{pmatrix}$ h) $\begin{pmatrix} 63 & 44 \\ 63 & 69 \end{pmatrix}$ i) $\begin{pmatrix} 3 & 2 \\ 20 & 17 \end{pmatrix}$

2 a) $\begin{pmatrix} 7 & 15 \\ 21 & 3 \\ 13 & 13 \end{pmatrix}$ b) $\begin{pmatrix} -9 & 11 & 6 \\ 3 & -5 & 4 \end{pmatrix}$
c) $\begin{pmatrix} 10 & 30 & 5 \\ 10 & -14 & 25 \\ 16 & 17 & 5 \end{pmatrix}$ d) $\begin{pmatrix} 14 & 16 \\ 10 & 23 \end{pmatrix}$

3 a) $a = -5$, $b = 11$
b) $p = 9$, $q = -5$, $r = 6$
c) $j = 17$, $k = -18$, $m = 7$
d) $a = -12$, $b = 16$, $c = 5$, $d = 15$

4 a) $\begin{pmatrix} 12 & 44 \\ 0 & 27 \\ 28 & 2 \end{pmatrix}$ b) $\begin{pmatrix} -1 & 49 & 40 \\ 18 & -2 & -6 \end{pmatrix}$
c) $\begin{pmatrix} 10 & 40 \\ 0 & 11 \\ 14 & -2 \end{pmatrix}$ d) $\begin{pmatrix} 1 & -53 & -46 \\ -14 & 4 & 6 \end{pmatrix}$
e) $\begin{pmatrix} -1 & 53 & 46 \\ 14 & -4 & -6 \end{pmatrix}$ f) $\begin{pmatrix} 2 & -1 & 3 \\ 6 & 5 & 2 \\ 0 & -8 & 0 \end{pmatrix}$
g) $\begin{pmatrix} 0 & 1 & -3 \\ -6 & -3 & -2 \\ 0 & 8 & 2 \end{pmatrix}$ h) $\begin{pmatrix} 13 & 46 \\ 0 & 35 \\ 35 & 4 \end{pmatrix}$

Page 189 Exercise 1

1 a) $\begin{pmatrix} 6 & 2 \\ 2 & 0 \end{pmatrix}$ b) $\begin{pmatrix} 60 & 48 \\ 96 & 33.6 \end{pmatrix}$

c) $\begin{pmatrix} -7 & 63 \\ 21 & -14 \end{pmatrix}$ d) $\begin{pmatrix} -99 & 165 \\ -143 & 198 \end{pmatrix}$

e) $\begin{pmatrix} -30 & -60 \\ 38 & -58 \end{pmatrix}$ f) $\begin{pmatrix} 9 & -32 \\ 13 & 51 \end{pmatrix}$

2 a) $\begin{pmatrix} 1 & 3 \\ 0 & 2 \\ 4 & 0 \end{pmatrix}$ b) $\begin{pmatrix} -5 & 9 & -2 \\ 0 & -6 & 1 \end{pmatrix}$

c) $\begin{pmatrix} -1 & 0 & -15 \\ -4 & 2 & -11 \\ \frac{1}{2} & -\frac{5}{2} & 0 \end{pmatrix}$

3 a) $\begin{pmatrix} 21a \\ -81a \end{pmatrix}$ b) $\begin{pmatrix} 12b & -21b & 48b \\ 0 & 12b & -51b \end{pmatrix}$

c) $(6c \quad -c \quad 11c \quad -18c)$

4 a) $a = 6,\ b = 9,\ c = -2$
b) $m = 6,\ n = -174$
c) $e = -5,\ f = 7,\ g = -14,\ h = -40,\ i = 105$

5 a) $\begin{pmatrix} 11 & 1 \\ 2 & -2 \end{pmatrix}$ b) $\begin{pmatrix} 10 \\ 26 \\ 8 \end{pmatrix}$ c) $\begin{pmatrix} -35 & 1 & 35 \\ 38 & -6 & -8 \end{pmatrix}$

6 a) $\begin{pmatrix} 0 & 24 & 36 \\ -24 & -12 & 0 \end{pmatrix}$ b) $\begin{pmatrix} 2 & -42 & -63 \\ 12 & 23 & 0 \end{pmatrix}$

c) $\begin{pmatrix} -1 & 14 & 21 \\ 1 & -8 & 0 \end{pmatrix}$ d) $\begin{pmatrix} -90 & -44 & 18 \\ 36 & -4 & -12 \end{pmatrix}$

e) $\begin{pmatrix} 3 & -82 & -123 \\ 37 & 44 & 0 \end{pmatrix}$ f) $\begin{pmatrix} -47 & 14 & 63 \\ 12 & -22 & -6 \end{pmatrix}$

Page 190 Exercise 2

1 a) Row 1: $(2 \times 4) + (4 \times 0),\ (2 \times 5) + (4 \times 1)$
Row 2: $(1 \times 4) + (3 \times 0),\ (1 \times 5) + (3 \times 1)$
Final matrix: $\begin{pmatrix} 8 & 14 \\ 4 & 8 \end{pmatrix}$

b) Row 1: $(1 \times 3) + (0 \times 2),\ (1 \times 1) + (0 \times 0),$
$(1 \times -1) + (0 \times -2)$
Row 2: $(2 \times 3) + (5 \times 2),\ (2 \times 1) + (5 \times 0),$
$(2 \times -1) + (5 \times -2)$
Row 3: $(4 \times 3) + (1 \times 2),\ (4 \times 1) + (1 \times 0),$
$(4 \times -1) + (1 \times -2)$
Final matrix: $\begin{pmatrix} 3 & 1 & -1 \\ 16 & 2 & -12 \\ 14 & 4 & -6 \end{pmatrix}$

2 a) $\begin{pmatrix} a + 3c & b + 3d \\ 4a + 2c & 4b + 2d \end{pmatrix}$

b) $\begin{pmatrix} -p + 2r & -q + 2s \\ -4r & -4s \end{pmatrix}$

c) $\begin{pmatrix} 11w + 13y & 11x + 13z \\ -12w + 21y & -12x + 21z \end{pmatrix}$

3 a) $\begin{pmatrix} 14 & 18 \\ 6 & 12 \end{pmatrix}$ b) $\begin{pmatrix} -65 & -14 \\ 167 & 182 \end{pmatrix}$

c) $\begin{pmatrix} -161 & -136 \\ -90 & -95 \end{pmatrix}$ d) $\begin{pmatrix} 0 & 0 \\ 0 & 0 \end{pmatrix}$ e) $\begin{pmatrix} -5 & 2 \\ -4 & -1 \end{pmatrix}$

f) $\begin{pmatrix} -9 & 8 \\ -5 & 4 \end{pmatrix}$ g) $\begin{pmatrix} -166 & -50 \\ -178 & -50 \end{pmatrix}$

h) $\begin{pmatrix} 515 & 1235 \\ 670 & 1625 \end{pmatrix}$ i) $\begin{pmatrix} -1759 & 2334 \\ 3208 & -3416 \end{pmatrix}$

4 a) $\begin{pmatrix} -2 & 40 & 32 \\ 16 & 37 & 38 \\ 21 & 39 & 42 \end{pmatrix}$ b) $\begin{pmatrix} 77 & 17 & -100 \\ 105 & 21 & -210 \\ -73 & -21 & -70 \end{pmatrix}$

c) $\begin{pmatrix} 157 & 175 \\ 66 & 48 \end{pmatrix}$ d) $\begin{pmatrix} 2 & -213 \\ -93 & 79 \end{pmatrix}$

---

e) $\begin{pmatrix} 60 & -36 \\ -180 & 108 \end{pmatrix}$ f) (68)

g) $\begin{pmatrix} 19 & -27 & 41 \\ -52 & 36 & 61 \\ 24 & -11 & -16 \end{pmatrix}$ h) $\begin{pmatrix} 0 & 3 & 2 \\ 0 & -32 & 31 \\ 0 & 3 & 1 \end{pmatrix}$

i) $\begin{pmatrix} 20 & 12 & 50 \\ 38 & 12 & 75 \\ -14 & 33 & 56 \end{pmatrix}$

5 a) 2×2 b) 2×2 c) 3×3
d) 2×3 e) 2×2 f) 1×1

6 a) (i) $\mathbf{BI} = \begin{pmatrix} 0 & 4 \\ 1 & -6 \end{pmatrix}\begin{pmatrix} 1 & 0 \\ 0 & 1 \end{pmatrix}$

$= \begin{pmatrix} (0 \times 1) + (4 \times 0) & (0 \times 0) + (4 \times 1) \\ (1 \times 1) + (-6 \times 0) & (1 \times 0) + (-6 \times 1) \end{pmatrix}$

$= \begin{pmatrix} 0 & 4 \\ 1 & -6 \end{pmatrix} = \mathbf{B}$

(ii) $\mathbf{AB} = \begin{pmatrix} 1 & -2 \\ 5 & 3 \end{pmatrix}\begin{pmatrix} 0 & 4 \\ 1 & -6 \end{pmatrix}$

$= \begin{pmatrix} (1 \times 0) + (-2 \times 1) & (1 \times 4) + (-2 \times -6) \\ (5 \times 0) + (3 \times 1) & (5 \times 4) + (3 \times -6) \end{pmatrix}$

$= \begin{pmatrix} -2 & 16 \\ 3 & 2 \end{pmatrix} = \mathbf{C}$

(iii) $\mathbf{AC} = \begin{pmatrix} 1 & -2 \\ 5 & 3 \end{pmatrix}\begin{pmatrix} -2 & 16 \\ 3 & 2 \end{pmatrix}$

$= \begin{pmatrix} (1 \times -2) + (-2 \times 3) & (1 \times 16) + (-2 \times 2) \\ (5 \times -2) + (3 \times 3) & (5 \times 16) + (3 \times 2) \end{pmatrix}$

$= \begin{pmatrix} -8 & 12 \\ -1 & 86 \end{pmatrix}$

$\mathbf{CA} = \begin{pmatrix} -2 & 16 \\ 3 & 2 \end{pmatrix}\begin{pmatrix} 1 & -2 \\ 5 & 3 \end{pmatrix}$

$= \begin{pmatrix} (-2 \times 1) + (16 \times 5) & (-2 \times -2) + (16 \times 3) \\ (3 \times 1) + (2 \times 5) & (3 \times -2) + (2 \times 3) \end{pmatrix}$

$= \begin{pmatrix} 78 & 52 \\ 13 & 0 \end{pmatrix} \neq \mathbf{AC}$

b) $\mathbf{A}^2 = \begin{pmatrix} -9 & -8 \\ 20 & -1 \end{pmatrix}$

c) (i) $\mathbf{BC} = \begin{pmatrix} 12 & 8 \\ -20 & 4 \end{pmatrix}$ (ii) $\mathbf{CA} = \begin{pmatrix} 78 & 52 \\ 13 & 0 \end{pmatrix}$

(iii) $(\mathbf{BC})\mathbf{A} = \begin{pmatrix} 12 & 8 \\ -20 & 4 \end{pmatrix}\begin{pmatrix} 1 & -2 \\ 5 & 3 \end{pmatrix} = \begin{pmatrix} 52 & 0 \\ 0 & 52 \end{pmatrix}$

$\mathbf{B}(\mathbf{CA}) = \begin{pmatrix} 0 & 4 \\ 1 & -6 \end{pmatrix}\begin{pmatrix} 78 & 52 \\ 13 & 0 \end{pmatrix} = \begin{pmatrix} 52 & 0 \\ 0 & 52 \end{pmatrix}$

d) $\mathbf{CAB} = (\mathbf{CA})\mathbf{B} = \begin{pmatrix} 78 & 52 \\ 13 & 0 \end{pmatrix}\begin{pmatrix} 0 & 4 \\ 1 & -6 \end{pmatrix}$

$= \begin{pmatrix} 52 & 0 \\ 0 & 52 \end{pmatrix} = (\mathbf{BC})\mathbf{A}$

e) The number of columns in D is 3 and the number of rows in A is 2. Since $2 \neq 3$ these matrices cannot be multiplied.

f) 2×5

7 a) $a = 1,\ b = -2$ b) $p = 11$
c) $w = 38,\ x = -8,\ y = 56$
d) $l = 10,\ m = 8,\ n = -36$

8 a) $a = 2,\ b = -1,\ c = 4,\ d = 3$
b) $a = -2,\ b = 3,\ c = 0,\ d = -3$
c) $a = 3,\ b = 2,\ c = 1,\ d = 5$

20.3 Inverse Matrices and Determinants

Page 192 Exercise 1

1 a) 7 b) 1 c) −6
d) 108 e) −116 f) 3
g) −38 h) −188 i) $a - 5b$
j) $52 - 2p$ k) $kl - mn$ l) $p^2 - 1$
m) $-7c$ n) $4f + 14g$ o) $2w^2 - 3xy$
p) $2s^2 - 2t$

---

2 a) 0 b) 864 c) −2450 d) −64 e) −328
f) −6 g) 296 h) 3904 i) 4558

Page 193 Exercise 2

1 a) $\left| \begin{pmatrix} 4 & 8 \\ 2 & 4 \end{pmatrix} \right| = (4 \times 4) - (8 \times 2) = 16 - 16 = 0$

b) $\left| \begin{pmatrix} 1 & -2 \\ 3 & -6 \end{pmatrix} \right| = (1 \times -6) - (-2 \times 3)$
$= -6 + 6 = 0$

c) $\left| \begin{pmatrix} 25 & -5 \\ -15 & 3 \end{pmatrix} \right| = (25 \times 3) - (-5 \times -15)$
$= 75 - 75 = 0$

d) $\left| \begin{pmatrix} -6 & -28 \\ -3 & -14 \end{pmatrix} \right| = (-6 \times -14) - (-28 \times -3)$
$= 84 - 84 = 0$

2 E.g. $\begin{pmatrix} 2 & -5 \\ 3 & -8 \end{pmatrix}\begin{pmatrix} 8 & -5 \\ 3 & -2 \end{pmatrix}$

$= \begin{pmatrix} (2 \times 8) + (-5 \times 3) & (2 \times -5) + (-5 \times -2) \\ (3 \times 8) + (-8 \times 3) & (3 \times -5) + (-8 \times -2) \end{pmatrix}$

$= \begin{pmatrix} 1 & 0 \\ 0 & 1 \end{pmatrix}$

3 E.g. $-\frac{1}{6}\begin{pmatrix} 9 & -8 \\ -12 & 10 \end{pmatrix}\begin{pmatrix} 10 & 8 \\ 12 & 9 \end{pmatrix}$

$= -\frac{1}{6}\begin{pmatrix} (9 \times 10) + (-8 \times 12) & (9 \times 8) + (-8 \times 9) \\ (-12 \times 10) + (10 \times 12) & (-12 \times 8) + (10 \times 9) \end{pmatrix}$

$= -\frac{1}{6}\begin{pmatrix} -6 & 0 \\ 0 & -6 \end{pmatrix} = \begin{pmatrix} 1 & 0 \\ 0 & 1 \end{pmatrix}$

4 a) $\frac{1}{2}\begin{pmatrix} 4 & -6 \\ -3 & 5 \end{pmatrix}$ b) $-\frac{1}{2}\begin{pmatrix} 6 & -8 \\ -4 & 5 \end{pmatrix}$

c) $\frac{1}{4}\begin{pmatrix} 8 & -10 \\ -2 & 3 \end{pmatrix}$ d) $\frac{1}{5}\begin{pmatrix} 2 & -3 \\ -3 & 7 \end{pmatrix}$

e) $\frac{1}{7}\begin{pmatrix} 7 & -7 \\ -5 & 6 \end{pmatrix}$

f) Singular $\left| \begin{pmatrix} 6 & 3 \\ 8 & 4 \end{pmatrix} \right| = (6 \times 4) - (3 \times 8)$
$= 24 - 24 = 0$

g) Singular $\left| \begin{pmatrix} 12 & 9 \\ 4 & 3 \end{pmatrix} \right| = (12 \times 3) - (9 \times 4)$
$= 36 - 36 = 0$

h) Singular $\left| \begin{pmatrix} 14 & 6 \\ 7 & 3 \end{pmatrix} \right| = (14 \times 3) - (6 \times 7)$
$= 42 - 42 = 0$

i) $\frac{1}{7}\begin{pmatrix} 1 & 2 \\ -2 & 3 \end{pmatrix}$

j) Singular $\left| \begin{pmatrix} 4 & -2 \\ -8 & 4 \end{pmatrix} \right| = (4 \times 4) - (-2 \times -8)$
$= 16 - 16 = 0$

k) Singular $\left| \begin{pmatrix} -4 & 12 \\ -5 & 15 \end{pmatrix} \right| = (-4 \times 15) - (12 \times -5)$
$= -60 + 60 = 0$

l) $-\frac{1}{30}\begin{pmatrix} 4 & -13 \\ -2 & -1 \end{pmatrix}$ m) $\frac{1}{18}\begin{pmatrix} 4 & 3 \\ -22 & -12 \end{pmatrix}$

n) Singular
$\left| \begin{pmatrix} -14 & 21 \\ -8 & 12 \end{pmatrix} \right| = (-14 \times 12) - (21 \times -8)$
$= -168 + 168 = 0$

o) $-\frac{1}{3}\begin{pmatrix} -18 & 21 \\ 7 & -8 \end{pmatrix}$ p) $-\frac{1}{1183}\begin{pmatrix} 17 & 16 \\ 41 & -31 \end{pmatrix}$

5 a) (i) $x = 24$ (ii) $\frac{1}{x - 24}\begin{pmatrix} 1 & -12 \\ -2 & x \end{pmatrix}$

b) (i) $x = 0$ (ii) $\frac{1}{x}\begin{pmatrix} 4 & -3 \\ -x & x \end{pmatrix}$

c) (i) $x = 0$ (ii) $\frac{1}{x^2}\begin{pmatrix} x & 11 \\ 0 & x \end{pmatrix}$

d) (i) $x = 0$ or $x = -\frac{1}{2}$ (ii) $\frac{1}{2x^2 + x}\begin{pmatrix} x & -1 \\ x & 2x \end{pmatrix}$

6 a) $\frac{1}{3456}\begin{pmatrix} -24 & -90 \\ 72 & 126 \end{pmatrix} = \frac{1}{576}\begin{pmatrix} -4 & -15 \\ 12 & 21 \end{pmatrix}$

b) $\frac{1}{88}\begin{pmatrix} 26 & 24 \\ -21 & -16 \end{pmatrix}$

c) $-\frac{1}{396}\begin{pmatrix} -38 & -4 \\ -156 & -6 \end{pmatrix} = \frac{1}{198}\begin{pmatrix} 19 & 2 \\ 78 & 3 \end{pmatrix}$

7 a) $X^{-1} = \begin{pmatrix} 6 & 31 \\ 5 & 26 \end{pmatrix}$

b) $XX^{-1} = \begin{pmatrix} 26 & -31 \\ -5 & 6 \end{pmatrix}\begin{pmatrix} 6 & 31 \\ 5 & 26 \end{pmatrix} = \begin{pmatrix} 1 & 0 \\ 0 & 1 \end{pmatrix}$

$X^{-1}X = \begin{pmatrix} 6 & 31 \\ 5 & 26 \end{pmatrix}\begin{pmatrix} 26 & -31 \\ -5 & 6 \end{pmatrix} = \begin{pmatrix} 1 & 0 \\ 0 & 1 \end{pmatrix} = XX^{-1}$

8 $|Y| = (-38 \times -7) - (53 \times 5) = 266 - 265 = 1$

$Y^{-1} = \begin{pmatrix} -7 & -53 \\ -5 & -38 \end{pmatrix}$

$|Y^{-1}| = (-7 \times -38) - (-53 \times -5) = 266 - 265 = 1$

$(Y^{-1})^{-1} = \begin{pmatrix} -38 & 53 \\ 5 & -7 \end{pmatrix} = Y$

9 Work out $(PQ)^{-1}$:

$PQ = \begin{pmatrix} -7 & 11 \\ -3 & 4 \end{pmatrix}\begin{pmatrix} 1 & 0 \\ 5 & -4 \end{pmatrix} = \begin{pmatrix} 48 & -44 \\ 17 & -16 \end{pmatrix}$

$|PQ| = (48 \times -16) - (-44 \times 17)$
$= -768 + 748 = -20$

$(PQ)^{-1} = -\frac{1}{20}\begin{pmatrix} -16 & 44 \\ -17 & 48 \end{pmatrix}$

Work out $Q^{-1}P^{-1}$:

$|Q| = -4 \qquad Q^{-1} = -\frac{1}{4}\begin{pmatrix} -4 & 0 \\ -5 & 1 \end{pmatrix}$

$|P| = 5 \qquad P^{-1} = \frac{1}{5}\begin{pmatrix} 4 & -11 \\ 3 & -7 \end{pmatrix}$

$Q^{-1}P^{-1} = -\frac{1}{4}\begin{pmatrix} -4 & 0 \\ -5 & 1 \end{pmatrix}\frac{1}{5}\begin{pmatrix} 4 & -11 \\ 3 & -7 \end{pmatrix} = -\frac{1}{20}\begin{pmatrix} -16 & 44 \\ -17 & 48 \end{pmatrix}$

So $(PQ)^{-1} = Q^{-1}P^{-1}$

Page 194   Exercise 3

1 a) $N = \begin{pmatrix} -3 & 9 \\ -2 & 7 \end{pmatrix}$ **b)** $Q = \begin{pmatrix} -3 & -6 \\ 0 & 1 \end{pmatrix}$

2 a) $E = \begin{pmatrix} 2 & 3 \\ -1 & 4 \end{pmatrix}$ **b)** $K = \begin{pmatrix} -12 & 1 \\ -22 & -1 \end{pmatrix}$

3 a) $AB = X$
$A^{-1}AB = A^{-1}X$ multiply on left by A^{-1}
$IB = A^{-1}X$ use $A^{-1}A = I$
$B = A^{-1}X$ use $IB = B$

b) $AB = X$
$ABB^{-1} = XB^{-1}$ multiply on right by B^{-1}
$AI = XB^{-1}$ use $BB^{-1} = I$
$A = XB^{-1}$ use $AI = A$

Section 21 — Sets

21.1 Sets

Page 195   Exercise 1

1 a) {February, April, June, September, November}
b) {May}
c) {January, February, March, April, May, August}

2 a) {12, 14, 16, 18, 20, 22, 24}
b) {2, 3, 5, 7, 11, 13, 17, 19, 23, 29}
c) {1, 4, 9, 16, 25, 36, 49, 64, 81, 100, 121, 144, 169, 196}
d) {1, 2, 3, 5, 6, 10, 15, 30}
e) {35, 42, 49, 56}

Page 196   Exercise 2

1 a) (i) {1, 3, 5, 7, 9} **(ii)** {1, 2, 4, 8}
(iii) {1, 4, 9} **(iv)** {1, 2, 3, 5, 6, 10}
b) (i) {21, 23, 25, 27, 29}
(ii) {20, 22, 24, 26, 28, 30}
(iii) {23, 29}
(iv) {21, 24, 27, 30}

2 a) $A = \{2, 3, 5, 7, 11, 13, 17, 19, 23, 29\}$
$B = \{1, 4, 9, 16, 25\}$
$C = \{1, 8, 27\}$
$D = \{4, 8, 12, 16, 20, 24, 28\}$

b) (i) 10 **(ii)** 5 **(iii)** 3 **(iv)** 7
c) (i) 0 **(ii)** 2 **(iii)** 3 **(iv)** 8

3 a) {16, 25, 36}
b) {11, 13, 17, 19, 23, 29, 31, 37}
c) {15, 30}
d) {15, 21, 28, 36}
e) {11, 12, 13, 14}

4 a) (i) {0, 1, 2, 3, 4} **(ii)** {1, 3}
(iii) {0, −1, −2, −3}
b) (i) {(1, 0), (1, 2), (2, 0), (2, 2), (3, 0), (4, 0)}
(ii) {(2, 4), (3, 4), (4, 2), (4, 4)}

21.2 Venn Diagrams

Page 197   Exercise 1

1 a)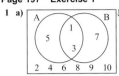

b)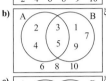

c)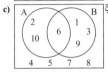

d)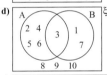

e)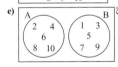

2 a) (i)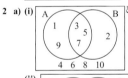

(ii)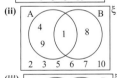

(iii)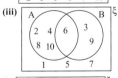

b) (i)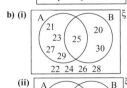

(ii)

(iii)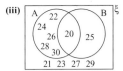

3 a) {1, 3, 5, 7, 9} **b)** 5, 7 and 9 **c)** 4
d) {3} **e)** 7, 8 and 9 **f)** {2, 8, 10}

4 a)

b)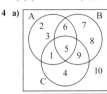

c)

d)

5 a)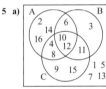

b)

c)

d)

e)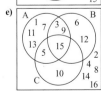

1 a) (i) $x = 8$ **(ii)** 32
b) (i) $x = 5$ **(ii)** 12 **(iii)** 19
c) (i) $x = 3$ **(ii)** 36 **(iii)** 44
d) (i) $x = 36, y = 14$ **(ii)** 58 **(iii)** 54

2 a) 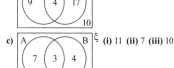 **(i)** 18 **(ii)** 48

b) 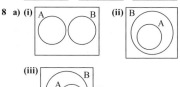 **(i)** 27 **(ii)** 19

c) 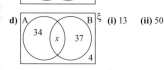 **(i)** 11 **(ii)** 7 **(iii)** 10

d) 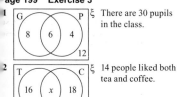 **(i)** 13 **(ii)** 50

1 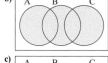 There are 30 pupils in the class.

2 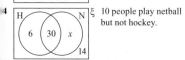 14 people liked both tea and coffee.

3 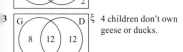 4 children don't own geese or ducks.

4 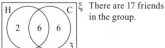 10 people play netball but not hockey.

5 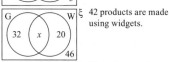 There are 17 friends in the group.

6 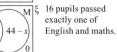 42 products are made using widgets.

7 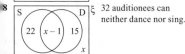 16 pupils passed exactly one of English and maths.

8 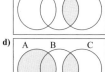 32 auditionees can neither dance nor sing.

1.3   Unions and Intersections

1 a) (i) {5, 6, 7}
(ii) {1, 2, 3, 4, 5, 6, 7, 8, 9, 10, 11, 12}
b) (i) {P, O, R} **(ii)** {T, S, P, O, R, E, D, L}
c) (i) {6, 12} **(ii)** {2, 3, 4, 6, 8, 9, 10, 12}
d) (i) {O, U} **(ii)** {A, E, I, O, U, C, S}

2 a) {blue four-wheel-drive cars}
b) {children's names}
c) {seaside towns in France}

---

d) {countries of the world}
e) {right-handed people with fair hair}

3 a) (i) {2, 4, 6, 8, 10, 12, 14, 16, 18}
(ii) {1, 2, 3, 4, 5, 6, 7, 8, 9, 10, 11, 12, 13, 14, 15, 16, 17, 18, 19}
b) (i) ∅
(ii) {1, 2, 3, 4, 5, 6, 7, 8, 9, 10, 11, 12, 13, 14, 15, 16, 17, 18, 19}
c) (i) {1, 64}
(ii) {1, 4, 8, 9, 16, 25, 27, 36, 49, 64}
d) (i) {3} **(ii)** {2, 3, 5, 6, 7, 9}

4 a) $\{x : 30 < x < 50\}$ **b)** {30} **c)** $\{x : x \le 50\}$
d) ∅ **e)** $\{x : 20 < x \le 150\}$

1 a) 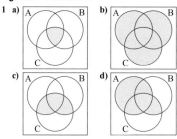 **b)**

c) **d)**

2 a)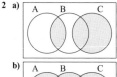

b)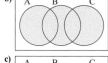

c)

d)

3 a) {6, 7, 8, 9} **b)** {4, 5, 8, 9}
c) {8, 9} **d)** {8, 9, 13, 14}
e) {6, 7, 8, 9, 13, 14}

4 a) {3, 4, 5, 6} **b)** {1, 2, 3, 4, 5, 6, 7, 8}
c) {5, 6, 7, 8} **d)** {5, 6}
e) {3, 4, 5, 6, 7, 8}

5 a) (i) Class members wearing hats but not gloves or scarves.
(ii) Class members wearing none of hats, gloves, scarves
(iii) Class members wearing all of hats, gloves, scarves

b) (i) 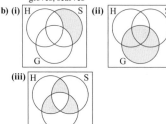 **(ii)**

(iii)

6 a) 20 **b)** 8 **c)** 31 **d)** 12 **e)** 22

---

7 a) (i) 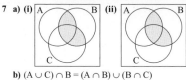 **(ii)**

b) $(A \cup C) \cap B = (A \cap B) \cup (B \cap C)$
c)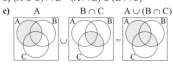
A   B ∩ C   A ∪ (B ∩ C)

A ∪ B   A ∪ C   (A ∪ B) ∩ (A ∪ C)

8 a) (i) 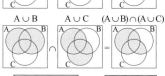 **(ii)**

(iii)

b) If $A \cap B = A \cup B$, then $A = B$.

21.4   Complement of a Set

1 a) A' = {triangles} **b)** A' = ∅
c) A' = {1, 3, 9}
d) A' = {books in the library which aren't paperbacks}
e) A' = {cars which don't have an automatic gearbox}

2 a) B' = {1, 3, 5, 7, 9} **b)** B' = {2}
c) B' = {6, 8, 12, 14, 16, 18, 22, 24, 26, 28, 30}
d) B' = {20, 24, 30, 40, 60, 120}

3 a) $A \cup B$ = {3, 4, 6, 8, 9, 12, 15, 16, 18, 20}
b) $(A \cup B)'$ = {1, 2, 5, 7, 10, 11, 13, 14, 17, 19}

4 a) (i)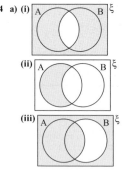
(ii)
(iii)

b) (i) B' **(ii)** $(A \cup B)'$ **(iii)** $A' \cap B$

5 a) People who didn't like Apricot Fringits
b) People who didn't like either biscuit
c) People who didn't like only Chocolate Jamborees.

6 a) {13, 14, 15, 16, 17} **b)** ∅
c) {1, 2, 3, 4, 5, 15, 16, 17} **d)** {6, 7}
e) {1, 2, 3}

7 a) $C \cap A'$ **b)** $(A \cup B \cup C)'$ **c)** $(B \cup C)'$

8 a) 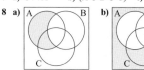 **b)**

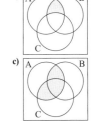

c) 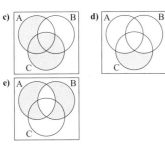 d) A B C

e) A B C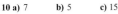

9 a) 6 **b)** 27

10 a) 7 **b)** 5 **c)** 15

11 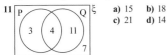 P Q ξ 3 4 11 7
  a) 15 **b)** 18
  c) 21 **d)** 14

12 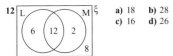 L M ξ 6 12 2 8
  a) 18 **b)** 28
  c) 16 **d)** 26

13 A B C
20 11 19 16 14 24 13 12 21 22 17 15 23 18 C
  a) {13, 19, 22}
  b) {20}
  c) {11, 13, 19, 22}
  d) {13, 14, 15, 16, 20, 21, 22, 23, 24}

14 A B
2 4 8 14 10 5 16 22 20 25 1 26 6 30 7 28 12 11 18 24 15 13 3 9 21 27 17 19 23 29 C
  a) {1, 2, 3, 4, 6, 7, 8, 9, 11, 12, 13, 14, 16, 17, 18, 19, 21, 22, 23, 24, 26, 27, 28, 29, 30}
  b) {3, 9, 21, 27}
  c) {1, 5, 7, 10, 11, 13, 15, 17, 19, 20, 23, 25, 29, 30}

21.5 Subsets

Page 205 Exercise 1

1 a) {cats} $\not\subset$ {fish}
  b) {Monday} $\subset$ {days of the week}
  c) {Spring, Summer, Autumn, Winter} $\subseteq$ {seasons of the year}
  d) {Fred, George} $\subset$ {boys' names}
  e) {red, yellow, brown} $\not\subset$ {colours in a rainbow}
  f) {tennis, squash, football} $\not\subset$ {racquet sports}

2 B $\subset$ K, C $\subset$ G, D $\subset$ E, I $\subset$ F, J $\subset$ L

3 a) 4
  b) (i) {1, 2}, {1, 3}, {1, 4}, {2, 3}, {2, 4}, {3, 4}
  (ii) {1, 2, 3}, {1, 2, 4}, {1, 3, 4} {2, 3, 4}
  c) 16

4 a) ∅, {a}, {b}, {c}, {a, b}, {a, c}, {b, c}, {a, b, c}
  b) ∅, {2}, {3}, {5}, {7}, {2, 3}, {2, 5}, {2, 7}, {3, 5}, {3, 7}, {5, 7}, {2, 3, 5}, {2, 3, 7}, {2, 5, 7}, {3, 5, 7}, {2, 3, 5, 7}
  c) ∅, {9}, {S}, {dormouse}, {spoon}, {9, S}, {9, dormouse}, {9, spoon}, {S, dormouse}, {S, spoon}, {dormouse, spoon}, {9, S, dormouse}, {9, S, spoon}, {9, dormouse, spoon}, {S, dormouse, spoon}, {9, S, dormouse, spoon}

5 a) (i) True **(ii)** False **(iii)** True **(iv)** False
  (v) True **(vi)** False **(vii)** False **(viii)** True
  b) (i) A $\not\subset$ (A ∩ B) **(ii)** (B ∩ C) $\not\subset$ (A ∩ C)
  (iii) A' $\not\subset$ B' **(iv)** C $\subset$ (A ∪ C)
  (v) B $\subset$ D' **(vi)** A' $\subset$ D'

6 a) (i) 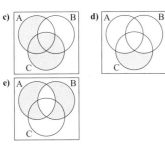 P Q **(ii)** P Q
  b) (i) X Y W **(ii)** X W Y
  (iii) X W Y

7 a) False **b)** False **c)** False **d)** True
  e) True **f)** False **g)** True **h)** False

21.6 Sets Problems

Page 206 Exercise 1

1 a) (i) False, n(A) = 8 **(ii)** True
  (iii) False, n(B') = 11 **(iv)** True
  (v) True **(vi)** False, C ∩ B' = {8, 9, 10, 11}
  (vii) True
  (viii) False, (A ∪ B)' ∩ A' = {9, 10, 11, 17, 18, 19, 20}
  b) (i) {6, 7, 8} **(ii)** {4, 5, 6, 7}
  (iii) {6, 7} **(iv)** {6, 7, 12}
  (v) {6, 7, 8, 12} **(vi)** {9, 10, 11, 12}
  (vii) {9, 10, 11, 17, 18, 19, 20}
  (viii) {8, 9, 10, 11, 12}

2 a) T F ξ 2 4 6 8 5 12 14 10 15 16 18 1 3 7 9 11 13 17 19
  (i) 1
  (ii) 8
  b) 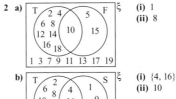 T S ξ 2 6 4 1 10 12 16 9 14 18 3 5 7 11 13 15 17 19
  (i) {4, 16}
  (ii) 10

3 a) {equilateral triangles} **b)** ∅

4 a) {11, 13, 17, 19} **b)** {3, 6, 9} **c)** {3}
  d) {1, 2, 4, 5, 7, 8, 10} **e)** 4

5 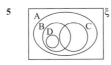 A ξ B D C

6 a) B' **b)** A ∩ B **c)** A' ∩ B
  d) (A' ∩ B) ∪ (A ∩ B') OR (A ∪ B) ∩ (A ∩ B)'

7 a) A B
  b) A B
  c) A B

8 a) (A ∩ B) ∪ (B ∩ C) OR B ∩ (A ∪ C)
  b) A ∩ C' **c)** C ∪ (A ∩ B)
  d) (A ∩ B ∩ C)' OR A' ∪ B' ∪ C'

9 a) A B C 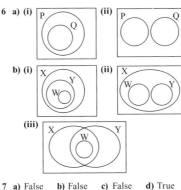 **b)** A B C

c) A B C

10 a) Let G = {families with girls},
  B = {families with boys}
  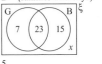 G B ξ 7 23 15 x
  b) 5

11 a) Let K = {students studying Adv. Knittir
  M = {students studying Motorcycle Main
   K M ξ 15 13 5 x
  b) 3

12 a) False **b)** True **c)** False **d)** False
  e) True **f)** False **g)** True **h)** False
  i) False **j)** False

13 a) Let K = {people with keys},
  C = {people with crayons},
  R = {people with magic rings}
  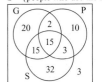 K C 3 2 5 8 72 6 3 1 R
  b) (i) 1 **(ii)** 16

14 a) Let G = {people who use the gym},
  P = {people who use the pool},
  S = {people who use the sauna}
  G P 20 2 10 15 15 3 32 3 S
  b) (i) 3 **(ii)** 62 **(iii)** 35

Section 22 — Angles and 2D Shapes

22.1 Angles and Lines

Page 208 Exercise 1

1 $a = 127°$ $b = 28°$ $c = 113°$ $d = 62°$
  $e = 107°$ $f = 33°$ $g = 45°$ $h = 72°$
  $i = 53°$ $j = 30°$ $k = 50°$ $l = 90°$
  $m = 55°$ $n = 100°$

2 Angle $AOB = 59° + 65° + 58° = 182°$, not 180°. So AB cannot be a straight line.

3 $m = 220°$

Page 209 Exercise 2

1 $a = 75°$ $b = 105°$ $c = 90°$
  $d = 90°$ $e = 90°$ $f = 82°$
  $g = 98°$ $h = 45°$ $i = 30°$

a = 81°   b = 49°   c = 60°
d = 63°   e = 47°   f = 70°
g = 12°   h = 3°

3   w = 64°   x = 64°   y = 52°   z = 76°

4   a = 65°   b = 65°   c = 50°   d = 116°
e = 52°   f = 64°   g = 116°

Page 210   Exercise 3

1   a = 108°   b = 72°   c = 39°   d = 39°
e = 141°   f = 75°   g = 105°   h = 75°
i = 75°   j = 105°   k = 75°   l = 21°
r = 78°   s = 4°   t = 17°   u = 78°
v = 102°   w = 78°   x = 102°

2   y = 81°

3   a = 65°   b = 115°   c = 65°   d = 115°
e = 69°   f = 69°   g = 111°   h = 111°
i = 69°   j = 114°   k = 66°   l = 24°

Page 211   Exercise 4

1   c = 37°   e.g. corresponding angle to 37°
d = 143°   e.g. angles on a straight line = 180°
e = 143°   e.g. angles on a straight line = 180°
f = 143°   e.g. vertically opposite angle to e
g = 143°   e.g. corresponding angle to f
h = 37°   e.g. vertically opposite angle to 37°
i = 37°   e.g. corresponding angle to h
m = 55°   e.g. corresponding angle to 55°
n = 125°   e.g. angles on a straight line = 180°
o = 65°   e.g. corresponding angle to 65°
p = 40°   e.g. alternate angle to 40°
q = 75°   e.g. angles on a straight line = 180°
r = 115°   e.g. corresponding angle to 115°
s = 105°   e.g. s + 10 is the corresponding angle to 115°
u = 40°   e.g. the unmarked angle in the lower triangle is a corresponding angle to 30° in the upper triangle. The sum of the interior angles of a triangle is 180°, therefore u = 180° − 110° − 30° = 40°.
v = 52°   e.g. sum of interior angles of a triangle = 180°. The triangle is isosceles so the missing angle must also be v. Therefore v + v + 76° = 180°, v = 104° ÷ 2 = 52°.
w = 52°   e.g. alternate angle to v

2   w = 48°   e.g. vertically opposite angle to 48°
x = 48°   e.g. corresponding angle to w
y = 84°   e.g. The triangle made by the scaffolding is isosceles, so the unmarked angle in the triangle must equal 48°. Sum of interior angles of a triangle = 180°, therefore y + 48° + 48° = 180°, y = 180° − 96° = 84°.
z = 84°   e.g. vertically opposite angle to y

22.2   Triangles

Page 212   Exercise 1

1   a = 53°   b = 22°   c = 15°   d = 16°

2   e = 73°   f = 41°   g = 52°   h = 49°
i = 131°

3   a = 20°   b = 10°   c = 60°   d = 60°

4   a = 30°   b = 120°   c = 70°   d = 45°
e = 36°   f = 66°   g = 114°

5   x = 60°   y = 120°

6   a) p = 5°   b) q = 110°

7   a = 44°   b = 64°   c = 72°

8   Alternate angles are equal, so the angles between b and the straight line are a and c. The angles on a straight line equal 180°. Therefore a + b + c = 180°.

22.3   Quadrilaterals

Page 213   Exercise 1

1   a = 112°   b = 92°   c = 30°   d = 71°
e = 101.5°

2   a = 90°   b = 122°   c = 72°   d = 108°
e = 125°   f = 10.2°   g = 6°

3   a = 113°   b = 111°   c = 90°   d = 10°
e = 98°

4   a = 120°   b = 120°   c = 60°   d = 64°
e = 123°   f = 14°

Page 215   Exercise 2

1   a) square, rhombus
b) square, rectangle
c) square, rhombus, rectangle, parallelogram, kite
d) square, rectangle, parallelogram, rhombus
e) square, rectangle, parallelogram, rhombus, trapezium
f) trapezium

2   a = 128°   b = 116°   c = 82°   d = 60°
e = 120°   f = 114°   g = 230°   h = 130°
i = 57°   j = 118°   k = 31°   l = 54°
m = 13.5°   n = 51°   x = 77°   y = 108°
z = 7°

3   138°   4   80°   5   127°   6   110°

22.4   Polygons

Page 216   Exercise 1

1   a) 720°   b) 1440°   c) 1800°   d) 3240°

2   a) (i) 360°   (ii) 118°
b) (i) 720°   (ii) 247°
c) (i) 1260°   (ii) 210°

3   a) 135°   b) 140°   c) 144°

4   a) 100°   b) No, the interior angles are not all the same size.

5   a) 3 sides   b) 12 sides

6   E.g.

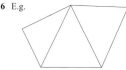

A pentagon can be split into 3 triangles. The sum of the interior angles of a triangle = 180°. Therefore the sum of the interior angles of a pentagon = 3 × 180° = 540°.

Page 217   Exercise 2

1   a) 45°   b) 40°   c) 51.4° (to 1 d.p.)

2   a = 54°   b = 56°   c = 74°   d = 135°

3   a) 53°   b) 40°   c) 35°   d) 40°

4   a) 8 sides — an octagon.
b) E.g.

c) 135°   d) 1080°

5   a) (i) 9 sides   (ii) 140°   (iii) 1260°
b) (i) 3 sides   (ii) 60°   (iii) 180°
c) (i) 36 sides   (ii) 170°   (iii) 6120°
d) (i) 40 sides   (ii) 171°   (iii) 6840°
e) (i) 60 sides   (ii) 174°   (iii) 10 440°
f) (i) 72 sides   (ii) 175°   (iii) 12 600°
g) (i) 90 sides   (ii) 176°   (iii) 15 840°
h) (i) 120 sides   (ii) 177°   (iii) 21 240°
i) (i) 75 sides   (ii) 175.2°   (iii) 13 140°

6   u = 20°   v = 10°   w = 15°
x = 30°   y = 100°   z = 20°

7   Sum of interior angles = (6 − 2) × 180° = 720°
Interior angle = 180° − exterior angle
(180° − a) + (180° − b) + (180° − c) + (180° − d) + (180° − e) + (180° − f) = 720°
1080° − a − b − c − d − e − f = 720°
a + b + c + d + e + f = 1080° − 720° = 360°

22.5   Symmetry

Page 218   Exercise 1

1   a) (i) 4 (ii) 4   b) (i) 1 (ii) 1
c) (i) 4 (ii) 4   d) (i) 5 (ii) 5
e) (i) 1 (ii) 1   f) (i) 0 (ii) 2
g) (i) 1 (ii) 1   h) (i) 10 (ii) 10

2   3

22.6   Angles and 2D Shapes Problems

Page 219   Exercise 1

1   u = 62°   v = 28°   w = 71°   x = 95°
y = 92°   p = 56°   q = 118°   r = 103°

2   a = 58°   b = 70°   c = 66°   d = 284°
e = 66°   f = 33°   g = 111°   h = 114°

3   a = 61°   b = 119°   c = 43°
d = 43°   e = 98°   f = 24.5°
g = 91°   h = 91°   i = 22.25°
j = 78°   k = 78°   l = 97°
m = 25.5°   n = 250°   o = 55°
p = 35°   q = 7°   r = 30°

4

	equilateral triangle	parallelogram
No. of sides	3	4
Lines of symmetry	3	0
Order of rotational symmetry	3	2
Sum of interior angles	180°	360°

	isosceles trapezium	regular nonagon
No. of sides	4	9
Lines of symmetry	1	9
Order of rotational symmetry	1	9
Sum of interior angles	360°	1260°

5   a) 36°   b) 30°   c) 24°   d) 14.4°

6   No, angle BAC + angle ACD = 178°, not 180°.

7   a) 540°   b) w = 110°

8   p = 34°

9   x = 30°   y = 25°   z = 100°

10   a) a = 105°   b) b = 165°   c = 146°

11   a) x = 60°   b) y = 120°

12   x = 45°   y = 90°

13   x = 45°

14   260°

15   From vertically opposite and alternate angles, the missing angle in triangle ABC must be a.

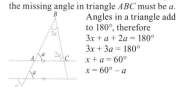

Angles in a triangle add to 180°, therefore
3x + a + 2a = 180°
3x + 3a = 180°
x + a = 60°
x = 60° − a

Label the top two interior angles a and b.
From allied angles, the bottom two interior
angles must be $180° - a$ and $180° - b$. So the
sum of interior angles in a trapezium is
$a + b + 180° - a + 180° - b$
$= 180° + 180° = 360°$

Section 23 — Circle Geometry

23.1   Circle Theorems 1

Page 221   Exercise 1
1   $a = 90°$
2   $e = 54°$
3   $m = 47°, n = 20°$
4   $p = 21°$
5   $k = 42°$
6   $x = 30°$
7   $i = 18°$
8   $v = 38°, w = 52°$

Page 222   Exercise 2
1   $c = 53°$
2   $p = 63°, q = 27°$
3   $z = 73°$
4   $a = 76°, b = 132°, c = 70°$
5   A, B and E must all be isosceles, as they each
    have two sides which are radii.
6   d is a right angle, because it's the angle in a
    semicircle.
    e is a right angle, because the diameter is a
    perpendicular chord bisector.
    i is a right angle, because a tangent and radius
    meet at a right angle.

23.2   Circle Theorems 2

Page 223   Exercise 1
1   $a = 64°$
2   $b = 198°$
3   $c = 318°$
4   $d = 112°$
5   $e = 37°$
6   $f = 40°$
7   $g = 133°$
8   $h = 39°$
9   AO and BO are radii, so $\angle ABO = \angle BAO = 60°$.
    So $\angle AOB = 180 - 60 - 60 = 60°$.
    Angle at the centre is twice the angle at the
    circumference, so $\angle ACB = 60 \div 2 = 30°$.
    So $\angle ACD = 62 - 30 = 32°$, so using angle at
    centre rule again $\angle AOD = 2 \times 32 = 64°$
10 $m = 14°, n = 28°$ 11 $x = 75°$

Page 224   Exercise 2
1   $k = l = 54°$
2   $m = 74°, n = 106°$
3   $v = 31°, w = 61°$
4   $c = 14°$
5   $t = 64°$
6   $p = 25°, q = 107°$
7   $a = 114°, b = 70°$
8   $u = 44°, v = 27°, w = 27°$
9   $x = 38°, y = 30°, z = 55°$
10 $r = 68°, s = 24°$

Page 225   Exercise 3
1   $a = 86°, b = 95°$
2   $m = 108°, n = 112°$
3   $e = f = 78°$
4   $u = 109°$
5   $x = y = 90°, z = 83°$
6   $p = 131°, q = 49°, r = 91°, s = 55°$
7   $a = 59°, b = 101°, c = 72°$
8   $k = 60°, l = 36°$

23.3   Circle Theorems 3

Page 225   Exercise 1
1   $x = 117°$
2   $g = 28°$
3   $a = 40°$
4   $k = 63°$
5   $p = 59°, q = 31°, r = 59°$
6   $m = 114°$

Page 226   Exercise 2
1   a) d b) g
2   $a = 67°, b = 49°$
3   $x = 59°, y = 34°, z = 34°$
4   $p = 70°, q = 34°$
5   $a = 90°, b = 45°, c = 45°$
6   $u = 45°, v = 70°$
7   $l = 61°, m = 59°, n = 31°$
8   $i = 47°, j = 35°$
9   $p = 70°, q = 56°$

Page 227   Exercise 3
1   $a = 21$
2   $d = 3.47$
3   a) $j = 20$ b) PO = 17 cm
4   $h = 7.39$
5   $c = 3.74$
6   $b = 10.3$
7   $e = 12$
8   $f = 3$

23.4   Circle Geometry Problems

Page 228   Exercise 1
1   A triangle formed by two radii is isosceles,
    so $a = (180 - 122) \div 2 = 29°$.
    Using the alternate segment theorem,
    $b = 29 + 19 = 48°$.
2   Angles in a semicircle are always 90°, so both
    triangles shown are right-angled triangles.
    So $c = 180 - 90 - 28 = 62°$.
    Opposite angles in a cyclic quadrilateral sum
    to 180°, so $28° + d + 3d = 180°$
    $4d = 152°$
    $d = 38°$
3   Two radii make an isosceles triangle, so the
    angle at the centre is $180 - 2 \times 36 = 108°$.
    The angle at the centre is twice the angle at
    the circumference, so $e = 108 \div 2 = 54°$.
4   A diameter which bisects a chord meets it at a
    right angle, so $f = 180 - 17 - 90 = 73°$.
    Two radii make an isosceles triangle, so
    $g + 17 = (180 - 73) \div 2 = 53.5$
    $g = 36.5°$
5   Two radii make an isosceles triangle,
    so $h = 31°$, and the other angle in that triangle
    is $180 - 2 \times 31 = 118°$.
    Angles on a straight line add up to 180°,
    so $i = 180 - 118 = 62°$.
    Tangents and radii form right angles,
    and angles in a quadrilateral sum to 360°,
    so $j = 360 - 2 \times 90 - 62 = 118°$.
6   Tangent and radius make a right angle,
    so $k = 90 - 23 = 67°$.
    Angle in alternate segment to k is also 67°,
    and angles on a straight line sum to 180°,
    so $l = 180 - 67 = 113°$.
7   Angles on a straight line sum to 180°, and
    angles subtended by an arc in the same
    segment are equal, so $m = 180 - 104 = 76°$.
    Opposite angles in a cyclic quadrilateral sum
    to 180°, so $n = 180 - 76 = 104°$.
8   Tangent and radius make a right angle,
    so $\angle OPQ = 90°$.
    So $\angle OPM = 90 - 69 = 21°$.
    Two radii make an isosceles triangle,
    so $\angle OMP = \angle OPM = 21°$.
    Angle at centre is double the angle at the
    circumference, so $\angle NMP = 102 \div 2 = 51°$.
    So $\angle NMO = 51 - 21 = 30°$.
9   a) By the alternate segment theorem,
       $\angle BDE = 83°$.

b) $\angle BDE = 83°$, so $\angle ADE$ must be
   less than 83°.
   A tangent always makes a right angle w
   a radius or diameter, so as $\angle ADE \neq 90°$
   AD cannot be a diameter.
10 a) If N is the centre of the circle, then the
      tangent KL and the radius NL meet at a
      right angle, so $\angle KLN = 90°$.
      So $\angle MLN = 90 - 35 = 55°$.
   b) (i) If N is the centre, then MN and LN a
         both radii, so they must be the same
         length.
      (ii) If MN = LN, then triangle LMN is
         isosceles, so $\angle LMN = 55°$ and
         $\angle MNL = 180 - 2 \times 55 = 70°$.
   c) (i) If N is the centre, then JN and LN are
         both radii, so they form congruent ri
         angled triangles with tangents from
         same point.
      (ii) Triangles KJN and KLN are congru
         and $\angle JNK = \angle KNL = 70°$.
         So $\angle JNL = 70 + 70 = 140°$.
   d) Angles in a quadrilateral sum to 360°, s
      $\angle JNL = 140°$ and $\angle KJN = \angle KLN = 90$
      then $\angle JKL = 360° - 140 - 90 - 90 = 40$

Section 24 — Units, Measuring and Estimating

24.1   Converting Metric Units — Length, Mass and Volume

Page 229   Exercise 1
1   a) 3 tonnes   b) 0.4 g
    c) 0.123 litres   d) 0.05116 kg
    e) 0.0126 tonnes   f) 2.7165 m
    g) 0.15 litres   h) 0.001532 tonnes
    i) 0.01005 km   j) 0.003023 kg
2   4 pizzas
3   7 bottles
4   a) 500 laps   b) 200 km
5   Yes. The total mass = 0.2292 tonnes.
6   14.75 km
7   200 cm^3
8   267 days
9   a) 1.6025 kg   b) 8 people

24.2   Converting Metric Units — Area and Volume

Page 230   Exercise 1
1   a) 0.84 cm^2 b) 0.175 m^2
    c) 290 cm^2 d) 1 000 000 m^3
    e) 15 000 mm^3 f) 200 000 cm^3
    g) 3.15 km^2 h) 85 cm^2
    i) 0.17 m^2 j) 435 000 000 m^3
    k) 6 700 000 000 m^3 l) 0.045 mm^3
2   33.24 m^2
3   a) 40   b) 525 cm^3
4   a) 1 125 000 000 cm^3
    b) 1 125 000 litres
5   a) 0.0022785 m^3 b) 197 970 mm^2
6   a) 1 200 000 mm^2
    b) 10 000 000 cm^2
    c) 50 m^2
    d) 0.0673 km^2
    e) 5 000 000 mm^2
    f) 0.0605 m^2
    g) 0.000000000003 km^3
    h) 600 000 mm^3
    i) 0.000000000000999 km^3

j) 0.00001744 m³

k) 0.000019 m³

l) 3 450 000 000 000 000 mm³

4.3 Metric and Imperial Units

Page 231   Exercise 1

Some answers given in this Exercise may vary depending on which conversion factor is used.

1 a) 4 pounds 4 ounces
b) 1 pound 14 ounces
c) 6 pounds
d) 10 pounds 15 ounces
e) 2 pounds 3 ounces

2 a) 6 feet 8 inches
b) 1 foot 9 inches
c) 5000 feet
d) 2 feet 6 inches
e) 2 inches

3 a) 3.5 m   **b)** 7 kg
c) 10 miles   **d)** 9 litres
e) 1.5 kg   **f)** 5 stone
g) 160 stone   **h)** 10 litres

4 No, only Lily is tall enough to go on the ride. (Maddie ≈ 132.5 cm, Lily ≈ 142.5 cm)

5 4 laps

6 No. (They need about 784 g.)

7 a) 5 jugs   **b)** 0.15 litres

8 56 mph

Page 231   Exercise 2

Some answers given in this Exercise may vary depending on which conversion factor is used.

1 a) 18 m   **b)** 51 km   **c)** 11 kg
d) 730 cm   **e)** 5800 ml   **f)** 720 cm

2 2 litres   **3** 550 miles

4 No. (Their combined mass is about 735 kg.)

4.4 Estimating in Real Life

Page 232   Exercise 1

1 a) centimetres (or millimetres)   **b)** grams
c) millimetres (or centimetres)   **d)** tonnes
e) kilometres

2 a) probably between 2 m and 3 m
b) between 3.5 m and 5 m
c) around 2.5 m
d) between 1.5 m and 2 m
e) between 20 cm and 25 cm
f) between 300 l and 500 l

3 length between 10 m and 12 m
height between 3.2 m and 3.5 m

4 The dinosaur is about 3 times as tall as the chicken and 7 times as long. So if you reckon the height and length of an average chicken are around 30 cm, the dinosaur will be around 0.9 m tall and 2.1 m long.

Section 25 — Compound Measures

25.1 Compound Measures

Page 233   Exercise 1

1 a) 400 mph   **b)** 1.25 m/s
c) 21.25 km/h   **d)** 0.625 m/s

2 a) 12 km/h   **b)** 3 km/h
c) 2.5 km/h   **d)** 14 km/h

3 17 000 mph   **4** 576 km/h

5 22 m/s   **6** 0.002 m/s

Page 234   Exercise 2

1 a) 343 km   **b)** 67.5 miles **c)** 396.8 m
d) 0.128 km   **e)** 8100 m   **f)** 205.2 miles

2 a) 1.6 hours   **b)** 1.86 s   **c)** 3.68 hours
d) 0.0125 s   **e)** 6800 s   **f)** 24.5 s

3 0.16 s   **4** 1080 miles

5 9.375 miles   **6** 4 minutes

7 22.5 s   **8** 0.0017 m/s

Page 235   Exercise 3

1 a) 0.37 kg/m³   **b)** 46 kg/m³
c) 680 kg/m³   **d)** 9992 kg/m³
e) 12 840 kg/m³   **f)** 2.4 kg/m³

2 a) Volume = $\dfrac{\text{Mass}}{\text{Density}}$

b) (i) 0.125 m³   **(ii)** 2.6 m³
(iii) 3.2 m³   **(iv)** 0.06 m³

3 a) Mass = Volume × Density   **b)** 1044 kg

4 0.092 kg

Page 235   Exercise 4

1 a) 1200 N/m²   **b)** 8 N/cm²
c) 3 m²   **d)** 1080 N

2 a) 5 N/cm²   **b)** 50 000 N/m²

3 28 N/cm²

4 6400 cm³

25.2 Distance-Time Graphs

Page 236   Exercise 1

1 a) (i) 1 hour   **(ii)** 50 miles
b) 1 hour
c) (i) 10:00 am   **(ii)** 2 hours
d) The family travelled at a greater speed on the way to their destination, because e.g. the graph for this journey is steeper than for the journey home.

2

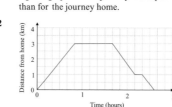

3 a) Between 0 and 1 hours the object travelled 2.5 km at a constant speed. Between 1 and 1.5 hours the object was stationary. Between 1.5 and 2 hours the object travelled 1.5 km at a constant speed. Between 2 and 2.25 hours the object was stationary. Between 2.25 and 3 hours the object travelled 4 km in the opposite direction at a constant speed.

b) For the first 40 minutes the object travelled 1 km while decelerating. Between 40 minutes and 1 hour the object was stationary. Between 1 hour and 1 hour 20 mins, the object travelled 0.5 km at constant speed. Between 1 hour 20 mins and 1 hour 30 minutes the object was stationary. Between 1 hour 30 mins and 1 hour 50 mins the object travelled 2 km at constant speed. Between 1 hour 50 mins and 2 hours the object was stationary.

c) In the first 45 seconds the object travelled 15 m at a constant speed. Between 45 seconds and 1 minute 30 seconds the object was stationary. Between 1 minute 30 seconds and 2 minutes 15 seconds the object travelled 10 m in the opposite direction while decelerating. Between 2 minutes 15 seconds and 2 minutes 45 second the object was stationary. In the last 15 seconds the object travelled 10 m at a constant speed.

Page 237   Exercise 2

1 a) 8 km/h   **b)** 20 km/h

2 a) 11.25 mph   **b)** 1.25 km/h   **c)** 0.2 m/s

3 a) Cyclist 2   **b)** 9.6 km/h

4 a) (i) 20 km/h   **(ii)** 80 km/h
b) (i) See below   **(ii)** 1.5 hours
(iii) See below

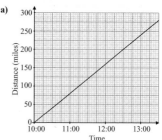

5 a)

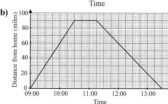

b)

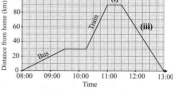

6 a) 0 mph
b) 2 mph (accept 1.8 mph - 2.2 mph)
c) 5 mph (accept 4.8 mph - 5.2 mph)

25.3 Velocity-Time Graphs

Page 239   Exercise 1

1 a) 12 km/h²   **b)** 0 m/s²   **c)** −6.25 m/s²

2 a) 45 km/h   **b)** 90 km/h²
c) Decelerating at 60 km/h²

Page 240   Exercise 2

1 a) (i) The velocity increases from 0 to 5 km/h.
(ii) The velocity is constant at 11.5 km/h.
(iii) The velocity decreases from 7.5 to 0 km/h.
b) (i) The object is accelerating, and the rate of acceleration is decreasing.
(ii) No acceleration.
(iii) The object is decelerating, and the rate of deceleration is increasing.
c) (i) 2.71 km/h²   **(ii)** −2 km/h²
d) (i) 2.0 km/h² (accept 1.8 km/h² - 2.2 km/h²)
(ii) 1.7 km/h² (accept 1.5 km/h² - 1.9 km/h²)

Page 240   Exercise 3

1 a) 37.5 km   **b)** 80 miles   **c)** 250 metres

2 a) 1125 m   **b)** 18.75 m/s

3 a)

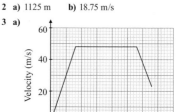

b) Acceleration = 6 m/s²,
   deceleration = 5 m/s²
   (or acceleration = –5 m/s²)
c) 1214.5 m

4 a) 260 m   **b)** 280 m   **c)** 1090 m

5 Your answers may be different depending
  on how you've split the graph up:
  a) 98 miles   **b)** 32.67 mph (2 d.p.)

Page 241   Exercise 4

1 a) 2 m/s² (acceleration of –2 m/s²)
  b) 710 m

2 a) In the first 20 seconds, the coach was
   accelerating constantly at 0.95 m/s² to a
   velocity of 19 m/s. Between 20 and 44 s
   the coach travelled at a constant velocity of
   19 m/s. Between 44 s and 60 s the coach
   decelerated at 0.25 m/s² to a velocity of
   15 m/s. Between 60 and 100 s the coach
   travelled at a constant 15 m/s. In the last
   20 s the coach decelerated to 0 m/s at a
   constant deceleration of 0.75 m/s².
  b) 1668 m

3 a) Bert ran 0.9 km, Ernie ran 0.7 km.
  b) 54 km/h
  c) 31 680 km/h²
  d) Ernie had the greatest initial acceleration
   since his velocity-time graph is steeper.

Section 26 — Constructions

Page 242   Exercise 1

1 a) 3 cm   **b)** 12 cm   **c)** 20 cm
  d) 0.5 cm   **e)** 0.2 cm   **f)** 0.3 cm

2 a) 5.4 m by 3 m   **b)** 6.4 m by 4.4 m
  c) 3.7 m by 2.8 m   **d)** 1.8 m by 2.7 m

3 1.6 cm

4 a) 140 cm   **b)** 128 cm   **c)** 96 cm

5 2.68 cm

6 a) 20 cm   **b)** 1.2 cm

7 a) 57 cm by 30 cm   **b)** 66 cm by 45 cm

8 1 cm : 1.5 km

9 a) 1 cm : 15 m   **b)** 4 cm

10 a) 1 : 600   **b)** 7.2 m   **c)** 0.75 cm

11 a) 1.2 km (accept 1.08 km - 1.32 km)
  b) 3 km (accept 2.76 km - 3 km)
  c) 3.84 km (accept 3.72 - 3.84 km)

Page 243   Exercise 2

For this exercise use a ruler to check that your
drawings have the measurements shown.

1
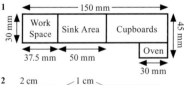

2
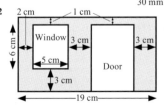

3 a)
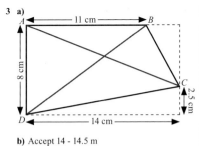

b) Accept 14 - 14.5 m

Page 244   Exercise 1

1 a) 062° **b)** 130° **c)** 227° **d)** 071° **e)** 288°

2 a) θ = 21°   **b)** θ = 23°   **c)** θ = 75°
  d) θ = 45°   **e)** θ = 48°

3 a)

b) 090°   **c) (i)** 270°   **(ii)** 315°

4 a)   **b)**

Page 245   Exercise 2

1 a) 305°   **b)** 130°

2 203°   **3** 281°

4 a) 020°   **b)** 130°   **c)** 260°
  d) 297°   **e)** 195°   **f)** 279°

5 a) 32°   **b)** 032°

6 a) 270°   **b)** 090°

7 a) 135°   **b)** 315°

8 a) 112°   **b)** 292°

9 a) 055°   **b)** 143°   **c)** 244°   **d)** 326°
  e) 235°   **f)** 323°   **g)** 064°   **h)** 146°

Page 246   Exercise 3

1 a) (i) 240 km, 050°   **(ii)** 190 km, 125°
  b) 340 km

For **Questions 2 - 5** use a ruler and a protractor
to check that your diagram has the measurements
shown.

2

3

4

5
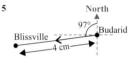

6 a) (i) 300 km   **(ii)** 450 km   **(iii)** 580 km
  b) (i) 060°   **(ii)** 140°   **(iii)** 290°

Page 247   Exercise 1

1 Measure all 3 sides of your triangles and
  check the lengths are correct.

2 Measure all 3 sides of your triangles and
  check the lengths are correct.

3 Measure all 3 sides of your triangle and check
  the lengths are correct.

4 Use a ruler to check your diagram has the
  measurements shown.

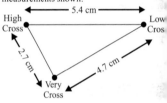

Page 248   Exercise 2

1 a)   **b)**

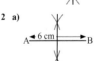

c)

2 a)

b) Use part a) to get:

3 a)

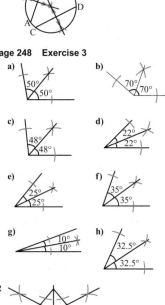

b)

c)

d) In the centre of the circle.

1 a)

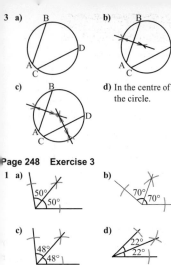

50°
50°

b)

70°
70°

c)

48°
48°

d)

22°
22°

e)

25°
25°

f)

35°
35°

g)

10°
10°

h)

32.5°
32.5°

2

They intersect at a single point.

3 a)

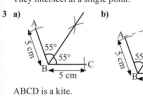

5 cm
55°
55°
B   5 cm   C

b)

5 cm
55°
55°
B   5 cm   C

ABCD is a kite.

1 E.g.

X
Y   Z

2

or

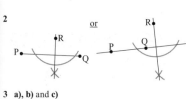

•R
P•   •Q

R•
P•   Q

3 a), b) and c)

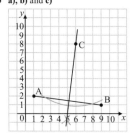

---

4 E.g.

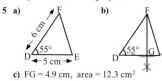

They intersect at a single point.

5 a)

6 cm
55°
D 5 cm E

b)

F
55°
D   G   E

c) FG = 4.9 cm, area = 12.3 cm²

1 Measure the length of AB and the size of the angle in your diagram to check they are correct.

2 Measure the 3 sides and angles in your triangle to check they are correct.

6 cm   60°   6 cm
60°   60°
6 cm

3 Measure the length of AB and the size of the angle in your diagram to check they are correct.

4 Measure the length of AB and the sizes of the 3 angles in your triangle to check they are correct.

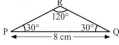

C
60°   30°
A   7 cm   B

5 Measure the sides and angles in your triangle to check they are correct.

R
120°
P 30°   30° Q
8 cm

1 Measure your angle to check that it is a right angle.

2 Measure the sides of your rectangle and check the lengths and angles are correct.

3 Measure your angle to check that it is 45°.

4 Measure the length AB and the angles in your triangle to check they are correct.

C
45°   45°
A   8 cm   B

1

A ——— B
P

2

First parallel line

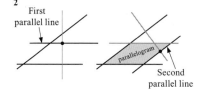

parallelogram

Second parallel line

3

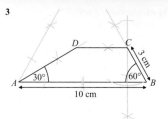

D   C
3 cm
30°   60°
A   B
10 cm

1 a)

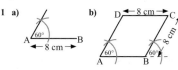

60°
A ——— B
8 cm

b)

D ← 8 cm → C
8 cm
60°   60°
A   B

2 a)

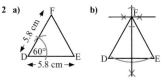

5.8 cm
F
60°
D 5.8 cm E

b)

F
D   E

3 a)

C
60°   45°
A   B
7.4 cm

b) 75°

4

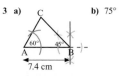

15°

Construct an angle of 60°. Then bisect that angle to get an angle of 30°. Then bisect this angle of 30° to construct an angle of 15°.

26.4   Loci

For this exercise use a ruler to check that your drawings have the measurements shown.

1

← 7 cm →
A ———————— B
2 cm

2 a)

3 cm
•X

b)

3 cm
•X

3

A   6 cm   B

4

25°
25°

5

← 6 cm →
A ——————— B
3 cm

6 a), b)

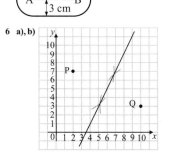

7 a)-d)

3 cm P 5 cm Q 4 cm

The points marked with crosses are both 3 cm from P and 4 cm from Q.

8 Locus shown by the black line.

R 4 cm G S 5 cm

9 a)   4 cm 5 cm 6 cm   **b)** 1 cm 1 cm

10 a) 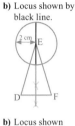 E D F 5 cm 5 cm 3 cm   **b)** Locus shown by black line. 2 cm E D F

11 a) 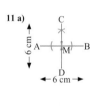 C A M B D 6 cm 6 cm   **b)** Locus shown by shaded area.   C 2 cm A M B 2 cm D

Page 253   Exercise 2

1 a), b) 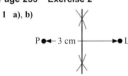 P 3 cm L

2 Location of treasure marked by the dot.   10 cm A B 7 cm D C 10 cm

3 Location of bonfire marked by the dot.   3 cm 40°

4 a), b) 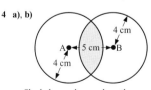 A 5 cm B 4 cm 4 cm

Shaded area shows where they could meet.

---

5 Shaded regions show where the dog can move.

a) 1 cm 2 cm 4 cm

b) 3 cm 2 cm 4 cm

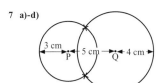

Section 27 — Pythagoras and Trigonometry

27.1 Pythagoras' Theorem

Page 254   Exercise 1

1 a) $x = 5$ cm **b)** $z = 13$ mm
c) $q = 30$ cm **d)** $r = 52\sqrt{2}$ m

2 a) $s = 2.5$ m **b)** $u = 6.36$ km
c) $v = 13.6$ mm **d)** $w = 1.39$ m

3 a) $l = 5$ cm **b)** $p = 24$ cm
c) $n = 6\sqrt{2}$ mm **d)** $i = 4\sqrt{41}$ m

4 a) $k = 14.77$ km **b)** $g = 1.74$ mm
c) $b = 9.00$ m **d)** $c = 2.71$ cm

Page 255   Exercise 2

1 10.63 cm **2** 25 m
3 a) 8.38 cm **b)** 4.19 cm **4** 3.20 m
5 12.36 m **6** 111 km
7 Yes, the tray is 43.01 cm corner to corner
8 931 fish **9** 100 m
10 Yes, letter has diagonal length of 25.7 cm
11 8.66 cm
12 a) $AB = \sqrt{65}$ **b)** $BC = 2\sqrt{5}$
c) $AC = 3\sqrt{5}$
13 $PQ = 6\sqrt{10}$
14 a) 19.09 m **b)** 18.57 m

27.2 Pythagoras' Theorem in 3D

Page 256   Exercise 1

1 a) $BD = 4\sqrt{5}$ m **b)** $FD = \sqrt{89}$ m
2 a) $PR = 13$ mm **b)** $RT = 5\sqrt{10}$ mm
3 a) (i) $AC = 6\sqrt{2}$ m **(ii)** $AO = 3\sqrt{2}$ m
b) $OE = \sqrt{82}$ m
4 $XY = 26.6$ cm **5** 10.44 m
6 a) $QS = 28.7$ mm **b)** $ST = 30.0$ mm
7 8.66 m **8** 17.3 cm **9** 30.5 cm
10 10.7 cm **11** 9.47 m
12 a) (i) $PH = 2.83$ m **(ii)** $PI = 1$ m
(iii) $OI = 7$ m
b) (i) $OA = 2.83$ m **(ii)** $AI = 7.55$ m
13 a) $NP = \dfrac{\sqrt{627}}{2}$ m **b)** $OJ = \dfrac{7\sqrt{2}}{2}$ m
c) $ON = \sqrt{\dfrac{289}{2}} = \dfrac{17\sqrt{2}}{2}$ m
14 a) $VX = 16$ m **b)** 128 m²
15 24.7 cm

27.3 Trigonometry — Sin, Cos and Tan

Page 258   Exercise 1

1 a) $a = 4.39$ cm **b)** $b = 9.33$ cm
c) $c = 1.06$ cm **d)** $d = 8.02$ cm
e) $p = 7.96$ cm **f)** $q = 35.8$ cm
g) $r = 6.30$ cm **h)** $s = 4.58$ cm

2 $m = 11.9$ cm **3** $n = 18.7$ cm

Page 259   Exercise 2

1 a) $a = 68.0°$ **b)** $b = 45.6°$ **c)** $c = 47.5°$
d) $d = 80.4°$ **e)** $e = 33.7°$ **f)** $f = 60.1°$

2 a) $m = 19.5°$ **b)** $q = 36.0°$

3 $z = 77.9°$

4 $j = 71.6°$, $k = 59.0°$, $l = 31.0°$, $m = 45.6°$, $n = 70.5°$

Page 260   Exercise 3

1 a) 60° **b)** 45° **c)** 60° **d)** 30
2 a) $\sqrt{3}$ m **b)** 1 cm **c)** 8 mm **d)** 1 r

3 a) $\tan 45° + \sin 60° = 1 + \dfrac{\sqrt{3}}{2} = \dfrac{2}{2} + \dfrac{\sqrt{3}}{2}$
$$= \dfrac{2 + \sqrt{3}}{2}$$

b) $\sin 45° + \cos 45° = \dfrac{1}{\sqrt{2}} + \dfrac{1}{\sqrt{2}} = \dfrac{2}{\sqrt{2}}$
$$= \dfrac{2\sqrt{2}}{2} = \sqrt{2}$$

c) $\tan 30° + \tan 60° = \dfrac{1}{\sqrt{3}} + \sqrt{3}$
$$= \dfrac{1}{\sqrt{3}} + \dfrac{3}{\sqrt{3}}$$
$$= \dfrac{4}{\sqrt{3}} = \dfrac{4\sqrt{3}}{3}$$

4 7 cm **5** $\dfrac{8\sqrt{3}}{3}$ mm

Page 260   Exercise 4

1 a) $p = 14.3$ m **b)** $q = 8.96$ m
c) $w = 50.6°$ **d)** $z = 43.0°$
e) $x = 62.5°$ **f)** $r = 29.0$ mm
g) $s = 2.33$ m **h)** $y = 66.8°$

2 a) $\sin 40° = \frac{a}{8}$ therefore $a = 8 \sin 40°$
b) $x = 27.9°$

3 a) $x = 26.7°$ **b)** $s = 36.2°$
c) $w = 14.0$ m **d)** $c = 13.6$ cm

4 a) $a = 3 + 3\sqrt{3}$ cm **b)** $b = 60°$

5 040° **6** 13.5°
7 68.2° **8** 120.8°
9 45.0° **10** 050.2°
11 $x = 70.5°$

27.4 The Sine and Cosine Rules

Page 262   Exercise 1

1 a) $a = 12.4$ cm **b)** $b = 8.70$ in
c) $c = 5.59$ mm

2 a) $d = 4.32$ m **b)** $e = 4.41$ mm
c) $f = 28.8$ m

3 a) $g = 32.4°$ **b)** $h = 33.4°$
c) $i = 38.8°$

4 a) $j = 67.0°$ **b)** $k = 44.4°$
c) $l = 34.1°$

5 a) $XZ = 65.1$ m **b)** $XY = 101$ m

6 $PQR = 90.3°$ **7** 085°

Page 264   Exercise 2

1 a) $a = 6.40$ cm **b)** $b = 5.38$ cm
c) $c = 18.5$ m **d)** $d = 4.65$ in
e) $e = 3.63$ cm **f)** $f = 4.59$ m

2 a) $p = 81.8°$ **b)** $q = 63.0°$
c) $r = 54.0°$ **d)** $s = 36.7°$
e) $t = 61.1°$ **f)** $u = 115.7°$

3 $XYZ = 85.8°$

4 a) $x = 7$ m   **b)** $y = 3$ m
c) $z = 2$ mm

5 29.8 miles   **6** 3.4 km

Page 265   Exercise 3

1 a) 14.55 cm²   **b)** 15.63 m²
c) 38.21 cm²   **d)** 123.03 mm²
e) 43.69 in²   **f)** 16.72 cm²

2 13.5 cm²   **3** 6.47 in²

4 14.7 cm²   **5** 443 m²

6 a) $x = 59.5°$ **b)** 58.2 m²

7 a) $y = 7.59$ cm   **b)** 27.7 cm²

7.5   Sin, Cos and Tan of Larger Angles

Page 266   Exercise 1

1 a) $x = 13.9°, 166.1°$ **b)** $x = 29.3°, 150.7°$
c) $x = 39.8°, 140.2°$ **d)** $x = 7.5°, 172.5°$
e) $x = 30°, 150°$ **f)** $x = 2.9°, 177.1°$

2 a) $x = 201.1°, 338.9°$ **b)** $x = 213.4°, 326.6°$
c) $x = 242.9°, 297.1°$ **d)** $x = 210°, 330°$
e) $x = 195.7°, 344.3°$ **f)** $x = 184.0°, 356.0°$

3 a) 157°   **b)** 49°   **c)** 318°

4 a) $w = 153.0°$ **b)** $x = 165.4°$
c) $f = 155.1°$ **d)** $e = 168.0°$
e) $y = 168.4°$ **f)** $g = 164.8°$

Page 267   Exercise 2

1 a) $x = 138.6°$ **b)** $x = 128.3°$
c) $x = 155.5°$ **d)** $x = 111.1°$
e) $x = 114.8°$ **f)** $x = 90.6°$

2 a) $x = 285.1°$ **b)** $x = 212.9°$
c) $x = 289.3°$ **d)** $x = 259.0°$
e) $x = 304.1°$ **f)** $x = 222.3°$

3 a) 292°   **b)** 161°   **c)** 79°

4 a) $w = 130.5°$ **b)** $x = 138.9°$
c) $y = 126.3°$ **d)** $l = 101.6°$
e) $m = 127.3°$ **f)** $n = 140.9°$

5 a) $\frac{\sqrt{3}}{2}$ **b)** $\frac{1}{2}$ **c)** $\frac{1}{\sqrt{2}} \left(\text{or } \frac{\sqrt{2}}{2} \right)$

Page 268   Exercise 3

1 a) $x = 81.1°, 261.1°$ **b)** $x = 74.5°, 254.5°$
c) $x = 45°, 225°$ **d)** $x = 64.5°, 244.5°$

2 a) $x = -69.7°, 110.3°, 290.3°$
b) $x = -84.6°, 95.4°, 275.4°$
c) $x = -45°, 135°, 315°$
d) $x = -82.0°, 98.0°, 278.0°$

Page 268   Exercise 4

1 a) $x = 115.4°$ **b)** $x = 128.6°$
c) $x = 110.7°$

2 a) $x = 98.9°$ **b)** $x = 46.1°, y = 133.9°$
c) $x = 124.8°$ **d)** $x = 168.7°$
e) $x = 120°$ **f)** $x = 55.1°, 124.9°$

3 140.1°   **4** 245°

5 a) $\frac{1}{2}$ **b)** $\sqrt{3}$ **c)** $\frac{1}{\sqrt{2}}$ **d)** 1

7.6   Trigonometry in 3D

Page 269   Exercise 1

1 a) $AF = 3\sqrt{2}$ m   **b)** $FC = 3\sqrt{3}$ m
c) $AHC = 35.3°$

2 a) $\sqrt{41}$ m   **b)** $BCE = 73.4°$
c) $AEB = 33.2°$

3 a) $BC = 2\sqrt{7}$ cm   **b)** $EDF = 41.4°$
c) $DC = 2\sqrt{41}$ cm

---

4 a) $AH = 7\sqrt{2}$ in   **b)** $EDG = 17.6°$

5 a) $BM = 8.32$ cm   **b)** $EM = 26.3$ cm

Page 270   Exercise 2

1 a) $JIK = 41.8°$ **b)** 18.3 m²
c) 165 m³

2 a) $CE = 2\sqrt{13}$ m   **b)** $CH = 10$ m
c) $EH = 4\sqrt{5}$ m   **d)** $ECH = 60.1°$

3 a) $PSU = 80.1°$ **b)** 71.6 m²

27.7   Pythagoras and Trigonometry Problems

Page 270   Exercise 1

1 a) $a = 5.83$ cm   **b)** $b = 7.75$ cm
c) $c = 9.48$ m   **d)** $d = 3.30$ m
e) $e = 34.5$ m   **f)** $f = 17.5$ cm
g) $g = 4.20$ ft   **h)** $h = 48.2°$
i) $i = 75.7°$ **j)** $j = 36.9°$
k) $k = 15.0$ cm   **l)** $l = 2.40$ m

2 $q = 152.9°$ **3** 10.4 cm

4 10.5 cm   **5 a)** 1.96 m   **b)** 14.7°

6 $x = 53.2°, y = 81.8°, z = 45.0°$

7 $x = 60°$

8 a) $z = 70.5°$ **b)** $s = 83.6°$
c) $x = 0.6$ cm

9 Perimeter is 3.23 m, so buy 330 cm of ribbon.

10 68 m   **11** 083°   **12** 1344 km

13 a) $p = 95.4°$ **b)** 23.9 cm²

14 a) 25.0 m   **b)** 5.30 m

15 a) $4\sqrt{6}$ cm²   **b)** 10 cm²

16 a) (i) $ED = 2\sqrt{26}$ ft   **(ii)** $FDH = 36.9°$
     (iii) $CHD = 14.0°$
b) Yes, the diagonal of the crate is 10.2 feet

17 a) (i) $PQ = \sqrt{17}$ cm   **(ii)** $PR = 2\sqrt{10}$ cm
b) (i) 075.96°   **(ii)** 108.43°
c) 7 cm²

18 a) (i) $AI = 10.61$ m   **(ii)** $OAI = 78.5°$
b) $OAP = 73.1°$

Section 28 — Vectors

28.1   Vectors and Scalars

Page 273   Exercise 1

1

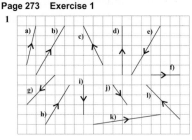

2 $\mathbf{a} = \begin{pmatrix} 4 \\ 0 \end{pmatrix}$ $\mathbf{b} = \begin{pmatrix} -1 \\ -1 \end{pmatrix}$ $\mathbf{c} = \begin{pmatrix} 2 \\ 6 \end{pmatrix}$ $\mathbf{d} = \begin{pmatrix} -3 \\ 0 \end{pmatrix}$

$\mathbf{e} = \begin{pmatrix} -4 \\ -1 \end{pmatrix}$ $\mathbf{f} = \begin{pmatrix} 2 \\ 3.5 \end{pmatrix}$ $\mathbf{g} = \begin{pmatrix} -4 \\ -3 \end{pmatrix}$ $\mathbf{h} = \begin{pmatrix} -2 \\ 2 \end{pmatrix}$

$\mathbf{p} = \begin{pmatrix} 9 \\ 1 \end{pmatrix}$ $\mathbf{q} = \begin{pmatrix} 2 \\ -6 \end{pmatrix}$ $\mathbf{r} = \begin{pmatrix} 5 \\ -3.5 \end{pmatrix}$ $\mathbf{s} = \begin{pmatrix} -2 \\ -3 \end{pmatrix}$

---

3 a) $\begin{pmatrix} -3 \\ 9 \end{pmatrix}$ **b)** $\begin{pmatrix} -5 \\ 15 \end{pmatrix}$ **c)** $\begin{pmatrix} -1.5 \\ 4.5 \end{pmatrix}$ **d)** $\begin{pmatrix} 2 \\ -6 \end{pmatrix}$

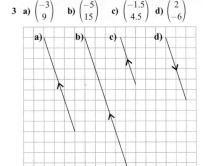

4 a) d   **b)** g   **c)** c   **d)** f and h

Page 275   Exercise 2

1 a) $\begin{pmatrix} 8 \\ 6 \end{pmatrix}$ **b)** $\begin{pmatrix} 5 \\ 5 \end{pmatrix}$

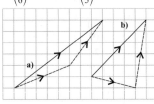

c) $\begin{pmatrix} -3 \\ 9 \end{pmatrix}$ **d)** $\begin{pmatrix} -5 \\ 7 \end{pmatrix}$

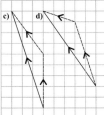

e) $\begin{pmatrix} 4 \\ 2 \end{pmatrix}$ **f)** $\begin{pmatrix} 4 \\ -4 \end{pmatrix}$

g) $\begin{pmatrix} 4 \\ -3 \end{pmatrix}$ **h)** $\begin{pmatrix} -9 \\ -2 \end{pmatrix}$

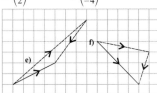

2 a) $\begin{pmatrix} -1 \\ 2 \end{pmatrix}$ **b)** $\begin{pmatrix} -3 \\ 1 \end{pmatrix}$ **c)** $\begin{pmatrix} 0 \\ 11 \end{pmatrix}$ **d)** $\begin{pmatrix} 6 \\ 7 \end{pmatrix}$

e) $\begin{pmatrix} 4 \\ -5 \end{pmatrix}$ **f)** $\begin{pmatrix} 3 \\ -3 \end{pmatrix}$ **g)** $\begin{pmatrix} -4 \\ 6 \end{pmatrix}$ **h)** $\begin{pmatrix} 5 \\ 26 \end{pmatrix}$

3 a) $\begin{pmatrix} 7 \\ 7 \end{pmatrix}$ **b)** $\begin{pmatrix} 8 \\ 1 \end{pmatrix}$ **c)** $\begin{pmatrix} -7 \\ 4 \end{pmatrix}$ **d)** $\begin{pmatrix} 14 \\ 30 \end{pmatrix}$

e) $\begin{pmatrix} 19 \\ 14 \end{pmatrix}$ **f)** $\begin{pmatrix} 10 \\ 8 \end{pmatrix}$ **g)** $\begin{pmatrix} 21 \\ 45 \end{pmatrix}$ **h)** $\begin{pmatrix} 21 \\ 10 \end{pmatrix}$

4 a) $\begin{pmatrix} 2 \\ 4 \end{pmatrix}$ **b)**

c) The vectors are parallel because $\mathbf{u} + 2\mathbf{v} = 2\mathbf{w}$

Page 276 Exercise 3

1 a) 3a   **b)** 3b   **c)** −2a
d) −3b   **e)** a + 2b   **f)** −a − 2b
g) 2a − 3b   **h)** −4a + 4b   **i)** −3a + 5b
j) 3a − 3b   **k)** 2a − 5b   **l)** 5a − 8b
m) −2a + 3b   **n)** a − 4b   **o)** 5a − 6b

28.2 Magnitude of Vectors

Page 276 Exercise 1

1 a) 10   **b)** 3.6   **c)** 13   **d)** 5
e) 6.3   **f)** 4.1   **g)** 3.6   **h)** 8.5
i) 7.6   **j)** 2.7   **k)** 6   **l)** 7.5

2 a) $9^2 + 12^2 = 81 + 144 = 225$,
so $|\mathbf{p}| = \sqrt{225} = 15$
b) (i) 15   **(ii)** 15   **(iii)** 30
(iv) 45   **(v)** 7.5   **(vi)** 150

3 a) 4.5   **b)** 2.2   **c)** 9.8   **d)** 9.4

4 a) E.g. $\begin{pmatrix} 6 \\ 5 \end{pmatrix}, \begin{pmatrix} -6 \\ 5 \end{pmatrix}, \begin{pmatrix} -6 \\ -5 \end{pmatrix}$

b) E.g. $\begin{pmatrix} -1 \\ 7 \end{pmatrix}, \begin{pmatrix} 1 \\ -7 \end{pmatrix}, \begin{pmatrix} -1 \\ -7 \end{pmatrix}$

c) E.g. $\begin{pmatrix} 3 \\ 8 \end{pmatrix}, \begin{pmatrix} -3 \\ 8 \end{pmatrix}, \begin{pmatrix} 3 \\ -8 \end{pmatrix}$

d) E.g. $\begin{pmatrix} -a \\ b \end{pmatrix}, \begin{pmatrix} a \\ -b \end{pmatrix}, \begin{pmatrix} -a \\ -b \end{pmatrix}$

Page 277 Exercise 2

1 a)

2.5 km
4 km

b) $\begin{pmatrix} 0 \\ 4 \end{pmatrix} + \begin{pmatrix} -2.5 \\ 0 \end{pmatrix} = \begin{pmatrix} -2.5 \\ 4 \end{pmatrix}$
c) 4.72 km (to 2 d.p.)

2 a)

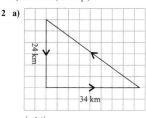

24 km
34 km

b) $\begin{pmatrix} -34 \\ 24 \end{pmatrix}$ **c)** 41.6 km

28.3 Vectors Problems

Page 278 Exercise 1

1 a) $\mathbf{a} = \begin{pmatrix} 3 \\ 4 \end{pmatrix}$ $\mathbf{b} = \begin{pmatrix} 4 \\ -2 \end{pmatrix}$ $\mathbf{c} = \begin{pmatrix} -2 \\ -4 \end{pmatrix}$

$\mathbf{d} = \begin{pmatrix} -4 \\ -1 \end{pmatrix}$ $\mathbf{e} = \begin{pmatrix} 4 \\ -1 \end{pmatrix}$ $\mathbf{f} = \begin{pmatrix} 1 \\ 4 \end{pmatrix}$

$\mathbf{g} = \begin{pmatrix} 0 \\ -5 \end{pmatrix}$ $\mathbf{h} = \begin{pmatrix} 1 \\ -4 \end{pmatrix}$

b) b   **c)** g   **d)** 4.1

2 a) $\begin{pmatrix} 12 \\ -9 \end{pmatrix}$ **b)** $\begin{pmatrix} -1 \\ 9 \end{pmatrix}$ **c)** $\begin{pmatrix} -9 \\ 11 \end{pmatrix}$ **d)** $\begin{pmatrix} -1 \\ 16 \end{pmatrix}$

---

3 a)

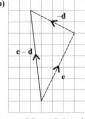

$\mathbf{a} + \mathbf{b} = \begin{pmatrix} 4 \\ -1 \end{pmatrix}$

b)

$\mathbf{e} - \mathbf{d} = \begin{pmatrix} -1 \\ 8 \end{pmatrix}$

c) a and f   **d)** b and e   **e)** e   **f)** f

4 a) 13   **b) (i)** 13   **(ii)** 39   **(iii)** 6.5

5 a) $\begin{pmatrix} 5 \\ 0 \end{pmatrix}, \begin{pmatrix} 0 \\ -5 \end{pmatrix}$ or $\begin{pmatrix} 3 \\ 4 \end{pmatrix}$

b) E.g. If $\mathbf{a} = \begin{pmatrix} 3 \\ 0 \end{pmatrix}$ and $\mathbf{b} = \begin{pmatrix} -5 \\ 0 \end{pmatrix}$,
then $|\mathbf{a}| = 3$ and $|\mathbf{b}| = 5$,
but $\mathbf{a} + \mathbf{b} = \begin{pmatrix} -2 \\ 0 \end{pmatrix}$ so $|\mathbf{a} + \mathbf{b}| = 2$.

6 a) $\begin{pmatrix} 50 \\ 0 \end{pmatrix} + \begin{pmatrix} 0 \\ -75 \end{pmatrix} = \begin{pmatrix} 50 \\ -75 \end{pmatrix}$ **b)** $\begin{pmatrix} -50 \\ 75 \end{pmatrix}$

c) Magnitude of the resultant vector is 90 km (to the nearest km) so there is enough fuel.

7 a) $\mathbf{a} = \begin{pmatrix} x \\ 0 \end{pmatrix}$, $\mathbf{b} = \begin{pmatrix} 0 \\ y \end{pmatrix}$

b) (i) 5a − 8b   **(ii)** $\begin{pmatrix} 5x \\ -8y \end{pmatrix}$

c) (i) −9a − 2b   **(ii)** $\begin{pmatrix} -9x \\ -2y \end{pmatrix}$

d) (i) 4a + 10b   **(ii)** $\begin{pmatrix} 4x \\ 10y \end{pmatrix}$

e) (i) 894 m   **(ii)** 1200 m

Page 279 Exercise 2

1 a) −p − q   **b)** 3p − q   **c)** −4p + q
2 a) parallelogram   **b) (i)** −a − b   **(ii)** −a + b
3 a) 4a   **b)** 3c   **c)** 3a   **d)** 2c
e) −3a   **f)** −a + c   **g)** −a + 3c
h) −4a + 3c   **i)** 2a + 1.5c   **j)** 2a + 0.5c
4 a) (i) −p   **(ii)** p + q   **(iii)** −r   **(iv)** q + r
b) $\overrightarrow{FD} = \mathbf{q} + \mathbf{p}$ and $\overrightarrow{AC} = \mathbf{p} + \mathbf{q}$
c) (i) q   **(ii)** −r
d) p = q − r
5 a) (i) u + v   **(ii)** $\frac{1}{2}\mathbf{u} + \frac{1}{2}\mathbf{v}$
(iii) −u   **(iv)** −u + v
b) If M is the midpoint of $\overrightarrow{XZ}$,
then $\frac{1}{2}\overrightarrow{XZ} = \overrightarrow{XM}$
$\frac{1}{2}\overrightarrow{XZ} = \frac{1}{2}(-\mathbf{u} + \mathbf{v}) = -\frac{1}{2}\mathbf{u} + \frac{1}{2}\mathbf{v}$
$\overrightarrow{XM} = \overrightarrow{XW} + \overrightarrow{WM} = -\mathbf{u} + \frac{1}{2}\mathbf{u} + \frac{1}{2}\mathbf{v}$
$= -\frac{1}{2}\mathbf{u} + \frac{1}{2}\mathbf{v}$
So $\frac{1}{2}\overrightarrow{XZ}$ and $\overrightarrow{XM}$ are equal,
so M is the midpoint of $\overrightarrow{XZ}$.

6 a) (i) $\overrightarrow{WU} = \frac{1}{2}\overrightarrow{SW}$ **(ii)** $\overrightarrow{SU} = \frac{3}{2}\overrightarrow{SW}$
(iii) $\overrightarrow{SW} = \frac{2}{3}\mathbf{a}$
b) (i) $\overrightarrow{WV} = \frac{3}{2}\overrightarrow{TW}$ **(ii)** $\overrightarrow{TV} = \frac{5}{3}\overrightarrow{WV}$
(iii) $\overrightarrow{VW} = -\frac{3}{5}\mathbf{b}$
c) (i) $\frac{2}{3}\mathbf{a} - \frac{2}{5}\mathbf{b}$ **(ii)** $-\frac{1}{3}\mathbf{a} + \frac{3}{5}\mathbf{b}$

---

7 a) (i) 5m   **(ii)** 3n   **(iii)** 2n
(iv) −5m + 3n   **(v)** −2.5m + 1.5n
b) $\overrightarrow{EF} = -\mathbf{m} + \mathbf{n}$
$\overrightarrow{FC} = -2.5\mathbf{m} + 3.5\mathbf{n}$
There's no number a such that $\overrightarrow{FC} = a\,\overrightarrow{EF}$
so $\overrightarrow{EF}$ and $\overrightarrow{FC}$ are not parallel.
So E, F and C don't all lie on a straight line.

Section 29 — Perimeter and Area

29.1 Triangles and Quadrilaterals

Page 281 Exercise 1

1 a) (i) 9 cm   **(ii)** 4.34 cm²
b) (i) 8.4 mm   **(ii)** 3.41 mm²
c) (i) 7.2 cm   **(ii)** 3.24 cm²

2 a) (i) 16 cm   **(ii)** 16 cm²
b) (i) 28 m   **(ii)** 48 m²
c) (i) 76 mm   **(ii)** 345 mm²
d) (i) 68 m   **(ii)** 289 m²
e) (i) 53 m   **(ii)** 95.46 m²
f) (i) 22.8 mm   **(ii)** 21.6 mm²

3 a) (i) 24 cm   **(ii)** 26.8 cm²
b) (i) 26 m   **(ii)** 26.95 m²
c) (i) 42.8 mm   **(ii)** 65.8 mm²
d) (i) 30 mm   **(ii)** 25.6 mm²
e) (i) 31.5 m   **(ii)** 50 m²
f) (i) 36 m   **(ii)** 40.15 m²

Page 282 Exercise 2

1 a) (i) 50 cm   **(ii)** 136 cm²
b) (i) 30 cm   **(ii)** 47 cm²
c) (i) 92 mm   **(ii)** 334 mm²

2 a) 68 m²   **b)** 108 m²   **c)** 148 mm²

3 a) 56 m²   **b)** 123.5 mm²   **c)** 30 m²

Page 283 Exercise 3

1 a) 22 cm²   **b)** 210 m²   **c)** 937.5 mm²
d) 288 mm²   **e)** 50.6 cm²   **f)** 5.25 m²

Page 284 Exercise 4

1 a) 82.5 cm²   **b)** 139 mm²   **c)** 810 m²

2 a) (i) 96 mm²   **(ii)** 46 mm
b) (i) 89.25 m²   **(ii)** 34 m
c) (i) 336 m²   **(ii)** 88 m

3 116.16 cm²

4 a) 1800 cm²   **b)** 1200 cm²

29.2 Circles and Sectors

Page 284 Exercise 1

1 a) 18.8 cm   **b)** 37.7 m
c) 6.3 cm   **d)** 94.2 mm

2 a) 12.6 cm   **b)** 25.1 mm
c) 69.1 m   **d)** 138.2 cm
e) 88.0 km   **f)** 219.9 mm
g) 0.6 km   **h)** 19.8 mm

Page 285 Exercise 2

1 a) 10.3 cm   **b)** 10.3 m
c) 50.1 mm   **d)** 15.9 cm

Page 285 Exercise 3

1 a) 12.6 cm²   **b)** 78.5 mm²
c) 201.1 m²   **d)** 2827.4 mm²

2 a) 113.1 mm²   **b)** 78.5 cm²
c) 50.3 m²   **d)** 132.7 cm²
e) 56.7 mm²   **f)** 9.6 m²
g) 1.1 mm²   **h)** 3.5 m²

3 a) 158.5 cm²   **b)** 139.3 mm²
c) 10.3 cm²

4 $\frac{49\pi}{4}$ m²   **5** 21.2 cm²

6 a) 5.3 cm²
   b) Two faces of a 5p coin have a total area of 5.1 cm², so one face of a 2p coin has the greater area.

7 The area of the rectangle is 440 mm² and the area of the circle is 452 mm², so the circle has a greater area.

8 39.3 cm², 3.1 cm²

Page 286   Exercise 4

1 a) arc length $\frac{\pi}{4}$ cm, sector area $\frac{3\pi}{8}$ cm²
   b) arc length $\frac{20\pi}{9}$ cm, sector area $\frac{40\pi}{9}$ cm²
   c) arc length $\frac{5\pi}{2}$ cm, sector area $\frac{25\pi}{2}$ cm²
   d) arc length $\frac{10\pi}{3}$ cm, sector area $\frac{25\pi}{3}$ cm²

2 a) arc length $\frac{21\pi}{2}$ cm, sector area $\frac{147\pi}{4}$ cm²
   b) arc length $\frac{80\pi}{9}$ in, sector area $\frac{320\pi}{9}$ in²
   c) arc length $\frac{33\pi}{2}$ mm, sector area $\frac{297\pi}{4}$ mm²
   d) arc length $\frac{31\pi}{2}$ cm, sector area $\frac{465\pi}{4}$ cm²

3 a) sector area 403.38 in², arc length 67.23 in
   b) sector area 82.10 cm², arc length 29.85 cm
   c) sector area 69.32 m², arc length 21.33 m
   d) sector area 198.20 in², arc length 37.75 in

4 arc length 1.88 cm, sector area 8.48 cm²

5 arc length 78.50 cm, sector area 510.28 cm²

6 arc length $\frac{10\pi}{9}$ m, sector area $\frac{25\pi}{9}$ m²

29.3   Perimeter and Area Problems

Page 287   Exercise 1

1 a) 407 m²   **b)** 81.6 m
2 8.8 m
3 3293.1 cm²
4 27 rolls
5 a) 67.5 m²   **b)** 0.25 m²   **c)** 270 tiles
6 a) 100 cm   **b)** 1416 cm²

Page 287   Exercise 2

1 9.4 m   **2** 78.5 cm
3 22.9 m   **4** 35.8 km
5 110 mm   **6** 7.1 m
7 2.4 m²   **8** 1714.2 m²
9 a) 345.6 cm   **b)** 172.8 cm
10 perimeter = 8.1 m, area = 4.0 m²
11 50.3 m   **12** 15.7 m²

Page 288   Exercise 3

1 1.93 cm²
2 18.4 cm
3 a) 23.4 m²   **b)** 2340 cm²
   c) 125.7 cm² **d)** 22.9 cm²
   e) 62 m²   **f)** 44.5 cm²

4 Both have the same area.
   Call the vertical height of the shapes h, then the rectangle has area $6 \times h = 6h$ cm², and the trapezium has area $0.5 \times (9 + 3) \times h = 6h$ cm².

5 142.7 cm²

Section 30 — 3D Shapes

30.1   Plans, Elevations and Isometric Drawings

Page 289   Exercise 1

1 a) (i) □
   Plan
   (ii)
   Front   Side

b) (i)
   Plan
   (ii)
   Front   Side

c) (i)
   Plan
   (ii)
   Front   Side

d) (i)
   Plan
   (ii)
   Front   Side

2 a) 1 cm
   Plan
   1 cm   1 cm
   Front   Side

b) 3 cm
   Plan
   3 cm   1 cm
   Front   Side

c) 1 cm
   Plan
   3 cm   3 cm
   Front   Side

d) 2 cm
   Plan
   5 cm   5 cm
   Front   Side

e) 3 cm
   Plan
   6 cm   6 cm
   Front   Side

f) 2 cm
   Plan
   3 cm   3 cm
   2 cm   2 cm
   Front   Side

3 a) 2 cm
   Plan
   2 cm   2 cm
   Front   Side

b) E.g. 2 cm
   Plan
   5 cm   5 cm
   2 cm   1 cm
   Front   Side

c) 3 cm
   Plan
   6 cm   6 cm
   Front   Side

d) 1 cm
   Plan
   4 cm   4 cm
   2 cm   2 cm
   Front   Side

e) 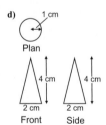 3 cm
   Plan
   5 cm   5 cm
   3 cm   4 cm
   Front   Side

f)

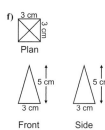

Plan

Front   Side

Page 290   Exercise 2

1 a) 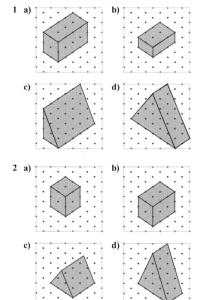 **b)**

c) **d)**

2 a) **b)**

c) **d)**

Page 291   Exercise 3

1 a) 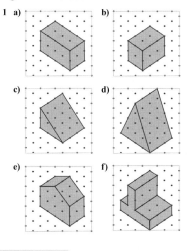 **b)**

c) **d)**

e) **f)**

30.2   Volume

Page 291   Exercise 1

1 a) 64 m³ **b)** 27 cm³ **c)** 84 mm³
2 32.768 mm³
3 No. Volume of box is only 2.754 m³
4 1.2 cm
5 7.5 mm
6 a) 0.45 m³ **b)** 0.225 m³ **c)** 0.4 m

Page 292   Exercise 2

1 a) 28 cm³ **b)** 30 cm³ **c)** 22.5 cm³
d) 15.7 cm³ (to 1 d.p.)

---

2 a) 624 cm³ **b)** 8.463 m³
c) 904.8 m³ (to 1 d.p.)
d) 282.7 mm³ (to 1 d.p.) **e)** 18.9 m³
3 a) 14.4 m³ **b)** 80 cm³ **c)** 33 mm³
d) 9 m³
4 x = 26 cm
5 y = 7.5 cm
6 a) p = 3 m **b)** q = 8 m
c) r = 4.0 m (to 1 d.p.)

Page 293   Exercise 3

1 135.5 l
2 27 glasses
3 90 cm
4 28.6 cm (to 1 d.p.)

30.3   Nets and Surface Area

Page 293   Exercise 1

1 a) E.g.

b) E.g.

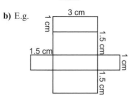

c) E.g.

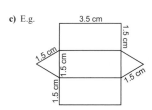

d) E.g.

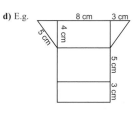

e) E.g.

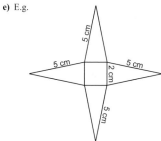

f) E.g.

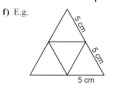

---

g) E.g.

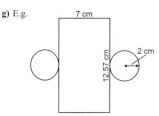

h) E.g.

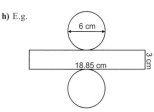

2 a)

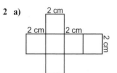

b)

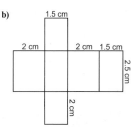

c)

d)

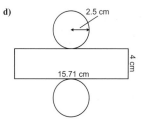

e)

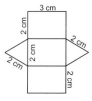

f)

3 C

Answers   **431**

1 a) 54 cm² **b)** 38 cm²
c) 23 m² **d)** 57.5 m²
e) 390 mm² **f)** 31.6 m²
g) 1.2 m² **h)** 140 m²

2 a) 150 m² **b)** 216 mm²
c) 48 m² **d)** 135.5 m²
e) 64 m²

1 a) 31.42 cm² **b)** 276.46 mm²
c) 131.95 m² **d)** 12.82 m²

2 a) 113.10 m² **b)** 471.24 mm²
c) 1694.07 cm² **d)** 1537.86 m²

3 a) 98.14 m² (to 2 d.p.) **b)** 883.3 m²

4 1.36 litres

1 976 m²

2 522 m²

3 188.50 m² (to 2 d.p.)

30.4　Spheres, Cones and Pyramids

1 a) (i) 100π cm² **(ii)** $\frac{500\pi}{3}$ cm³

b) (i) 64π cm² **(ii)** $\frac{256\pi}{3}$ cm³

c) (i) 25π m² **(ii)** $\frac{125\pi}{6}$ m³

d) (i) 400π mm² **(ii)** $\frac{4000\pi}{3}$ mm³

e) (i) 576π m² **(ii)** 2304π m³

2 4.6 cm

3 18.0 cm

4 11 494.0 mm³

5 1604.6 m²

6 a) 3619.1 m³ (to 1 d.p.)
　b) (i) 904.8 m² (to 1 d.p.)
　　(ii) 1357.2 m² (to 1 d.p.)

7 3 m

1 a) (i) 90π m² **(ii)** 100π m³
　b) (i) 224π cm² **(ii)** 392π cm³
　c) (i) 480π m² **(ii)** 600π m³
　d) (i) 1815π mm² **(ii)** 1650π mm³

2 a) 2268π m²
　b) (i) $h = 45$ m **(ii)** 11760π m³

3 a) $34\,496\pi$ cm³
　b) (i) $l = 65$ cm **(ii)** 6776π cm²

4 a) 2.5 mm
　b) (i) $l = 6.5$ mm **(ii)** 70.7 mm²

5 a) 21.0 cm **b)** 3298.7 cm²

6 a) 3 cm **b)** 768π cm³
　c) 12π cm³ **d)** 756π cm³

7 700π cm³

1 90 cm³

2 108 m³

3 93.33 cm³ (to 2 d.p.)

4 249.4 mm² (to 1 d.p.)

5 13.86 cm (to 2 d.p.)

6 a) 168 960 m³ **b)** 73 m
　c) (i) 3504 m² **(ii)** 23 232 m²

30.5　Rates of Flow

1 a) 40 cm³/s **b)** 180 litres/min
　c) 77 m³/min **d)** 18.75 litres/h

2 a) 3000 cm³/s **b)** 180 000 cm³/min
　c) 0.18 m³/min **d)** 10.8 m³/h
　e) 259.2 m³/day **f)** 259 200 litres/day

3 8 minutes **4** 30 minutes

5 43 200 cm³ **6** 30 minutes

7 53 minutes (to the nearest minute)

8 144 seconds

30.6　Symmetry of 3D Shapes

1 a) 6 **b)** 9 **c)** 1

2 a)

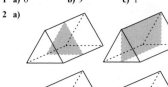

b)

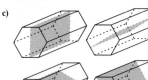

c)

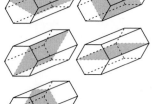

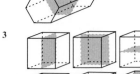

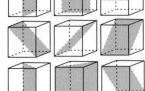

3

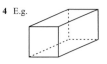

4 E.g.

30.7　3D Shapes Problems

1 a)

P

6 cm
3 cm
3 cm
3 cm
2 cm
2 cm

Q

4 cm
4 cm
5 cm
5 cm
3 cm
5 cm
4 cm

b) P

6 cm
2 cm
Plan

6 cm
3 cm
Front

2 cm
3 cm
Side

Q

3 cm
4 cm
Plan

5 cm
3 cm
Front

4 cm
4 cm
Side

1 a) 5 **b)** 8

2 a)

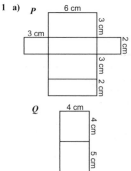

b)

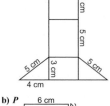

3

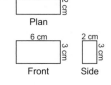

c)

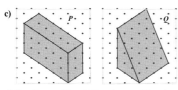

d) P: volume = 36 cm³, Q: volume = 24 cm³
e) P: 18 seconds, Q: 12 seconds
f) P: area = 72 cm², Q: area = 60 cm²
g) P: 3 planes, Q: 1 plane

2 a) 113.10 cm²   **b)** 226.19 cm² **c)** 251.33 cm³

3 a)
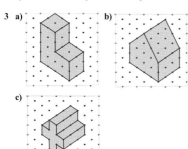

c)
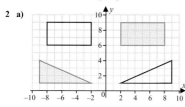

4 a) 9 cm²   **b)** 3 cm   **c)** 27 cm³

5 a) 473.09 cm³
b) 29.6 cm × 11 cm × 22.2 cm
c) 7228.32 cm³   **d)** 1551.21 cm³

6 a) 1244.07 cm³   **b)** 215.98 cm³
c) 1028.09 cm³   **d)** 4.29 cm³
e) 240 sheets

7 a) 16 mm   **b)** 2238 mm²
c) 10000 mm³   **d)** 2146 mm³

8 a) 10 m   **b)** 13 m   **c)** 360 m²

9 a) 124π cm³
b) (i) $\sqrt{29}$ cm   **(ii)** $2\pi\left(60 + \sqrt{29}\right)$ cm²

Section 31 —
Transformations

31.1 Reflections

Page 302   Exercise 1

1 a), b)

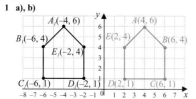

c) The y-coordinates stay the same, the x-coordinates change sign

2 a)

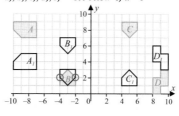

b)

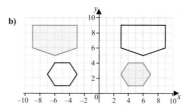

3 a) (i)

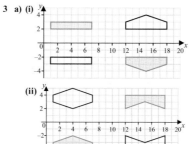

(ii)

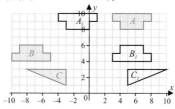

b) The x-coordinates stay the same, the y-coordinates change sign

4 a) (1, –2)   **b)** (3, 0)   **c)** (–2, –4)
   d) (–1, 3)   **e)** (–2, 2)

5 a) (–4, 5)   **b)** (–7, 2)   **c)** (1, 3)
   d) (3, –1)   **e)** (4, –8)

6 a), b), c) — see below   **d)** $y = 7$

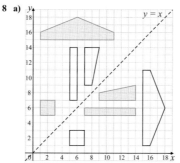

7 a), b), c), d), f) — see below   **e)** $x = 1$

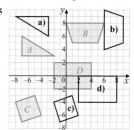

8 a)

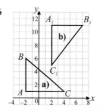

b)

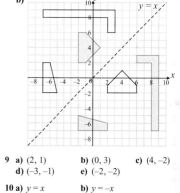

9 a) (2, 1)   **b)** (0, 3)   **c)** (4, –2)
   d) (–3, –1)   **e)** (–2, –2)

10 a) $y = x$ **b)** $y = -x$

31.2 Rotations

Page 304   Exercise 1

1 a)   **b)**

2 a)   **b)**

3

4
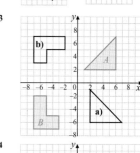

5
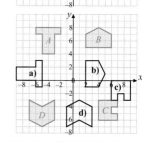

6

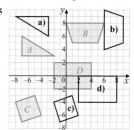

c) A_1 (2, 11) B_1 (7, 11) C_1 (2, 5)
7 D_1 (6, 2) E_1 (6, –5) F_1 (1, –5)

Page 306 Exercise 2

1 a) Rotation, 90° clockwise about (0, 0)
  b) Rotation, 90° anticlockwise about (0, 0)

2 a) Rotation, 180° about (0, 0)
  b) Rotation, 180° about (0, 2)

3 a) Rotation, 180° about (0, 3)
  b) Rotation, 90° anticlockwise about (0, 2)

4 a) Rotation, 90° anticlockwise about (−1, 7)
  b) Rotation, 90° clockwise about (1, −2)

5 a) Rotation, 180° about (0, 6)
  b) Rotation, 90° anticlockwise about (−2, 7)
  c) Rotation, 90° clockwise about (1, 8)

6 a)

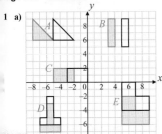

  b) Rotation, 90° anticlockwise about (−2, 1)

1.3 Translations

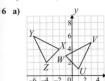

Page 307 Exercise 1

1 a)

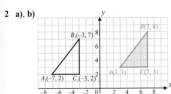

  b)

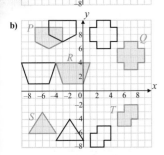

2 a), b)

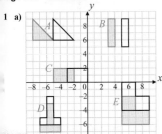

  c) To get from the original point to its image, subtract 10 from the *x*-coordinate, and subtract 1 from the *y*-coordinate.

3 D_1 (−1, 3) E_1 (1, 0) F_1 (2, 2)

4 P_1 (−3, −4) Q_1 (1, −3) R_1 (−1, −1)
  S_1 (−4, −2)

Page 308 Exercise 2

1 a) $\begin{pmatrix} 4 \\ -3 \end{pmatrix}$ **b)** $\begin{pmatrix} 9 \\ 0 \end{pmatrix}$ **c)** $\begin{pmatrix} -5 \\ -3 \end{pmatrix}$

  d) $\begin{pmatrix} 4 \\ -5 \end{pmatrix}$ **e)** $\begin{pmatrix} -13 \\ 5 \end{pmatrix}$ **f)** $\begin{pmatrix} -9 \\ 2 \end{pmatrix}$

2 a) $\begin{pmatrix} 0 \\ -5 \end{pmatrix}$ **b)** $\begin{pmatrix} 8 \\ 0 \end{pmatrix}$ **c)** $\begin{pmatrix} 13 \\ 1 \end{pmatrix}$

  d) $\begin{pmatrix} -8 \\ 0 \end{pmatrix}$ **e)** $\begin{pmatrix} -13 \\ -6 \end{pmatrix}$ **f)** $\begin{pmatrix} -8 \\ 5 \end{pmatrix}$

3 $\begin{pmatrix} 3 \\ 4 \end{pmatrix}$

4 a) $\begin{pmatrix} -1 \\ 2 \end{pmatrix}$ **b)** $\begin{pmatrix} 1 \\ -2 \end{pmatrix}$

5 a) $\begin{pmatrix} 3 \\ -5 \end{pmatrix}$ **b)** $\begin{pmatrix} -3 \\ 5 \end{pmatrix}$

  c) Each vector is equal to the other multiplied by −1.

6 $\begin{pmatrix} -1 \\ 4 \end{pmatrix}$ **7** $D(0, -4)$, $E(-3, 0)$, $F(4, -2)$

31.4 Enlargements

Page 309 Exercise 1

1 a) 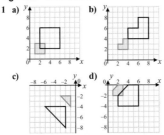 **b)**

  c) 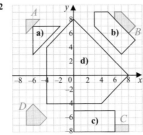 **d)**

2

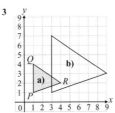

3

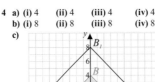

4 a) (i) 4 **(ii)** 4 **(iii)** 4 **(iv)** 4
  b) (i) 8 **(ii)** 8 **(iii)** 8 **(iv)** 8
  c)

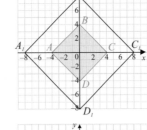

5

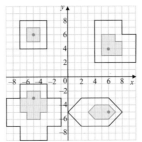

6

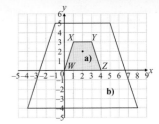

7

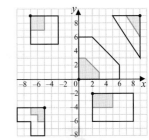

8

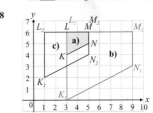

Page 311 Exercise 2

1

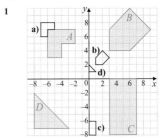

2

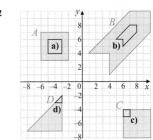

Page 311 Exercise 3

1

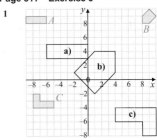

434 *Answers*

2

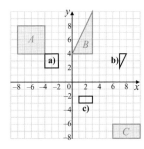

1 a) Enlargement, scale factor 2, centre (2, 10)
   b) Enlargement, scale factor 2, centre (6, 10)
   c) Enlargement, scale factor 2, centre (1, 1)

2 a) Enlargement, scale factor 2, centre (6, 5)
   b) Enlargement, scale factor 3, centre (5, 4)
   c) Enlargement, scale factor $-\frac{1}{3}$, centre (8, 7)

31.5 Combinations of Transformations

Page 313 Exercise 1

1 a)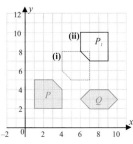

b)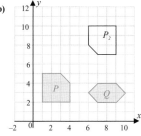

c)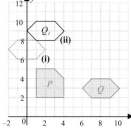

d)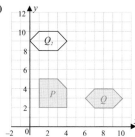

e) P_1 and P_2, and Q_1 and Q_2, are identical.

2

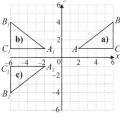

d) Rotation, 180° about (0, 0)

3

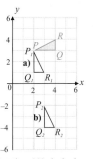

c) Rotation, 90° clockwise around (0, 0)

4 a)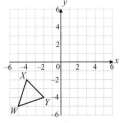

b)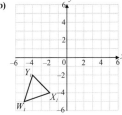

c)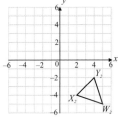

d) Rotation, 90° anticlockwise about (0, 0)

5 a)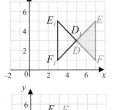

b)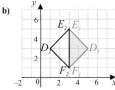

c) Translation, $\begin{pmatrix} -4 \\ 0 \end{pmatrix}$

6 a)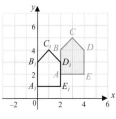

b)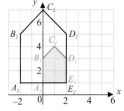

c) Enlargement, scale factor 2, centre (6, 3)

7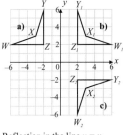

d) Reflection in the line $y = x$

8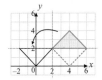

Rotation, 180° about (2, 2)

9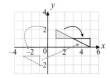

Rotation, 180° about (3, 1)

10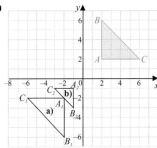

c) Enlargement, scale factor $-\frac{1}{2}$, centre (0, 0

11

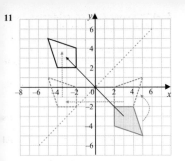

Reflection in the line $y = x$

Page 315   Exercise 1

1 (For each of **A-D** below, accept matrices with
 the same columns in any other order.)

$$A = \begin{pmatrix} -2 & 2 & 2 & -2 \\ 3 & 3 & 1 & 1 \end{pmatrix} \qquad B = \begin{pmatrix} 3 & 5 & 3 \\ 1 & 1 & 5 \end{pmatrix}$$

$$C = \begin{pmatrix} -2 & -2 & -4 & -4 \\ -2 & -4 & -4 & -2 \end{pmatrix} \quad D = \begin{pmatrix} 5 & 5 & 2 & 3 \\ -1 & -3 & -3 & -1 \end{pmatrix}$$

2 a) $B = \begin{pmatrix} 2 & 2 & 6 & 6 \\ 2 & 8 & 8 & 2 \end{pmatrix}$

 b)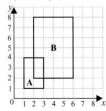

 c) Enlargement, scale factor 2, centre (0, 0)

3 a) $Q = \begin{pmatrix} 0 & -2 & -2 \\ 1 & 1 & 3 \end{pmatrix}$ b)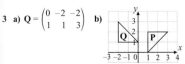

 c) Rotation, 90° anticlockwise about (0, 0)

4 a)

 b) Enlargement, scale factor $\frac{1}{2}$, centre (0, 0)

5 a) $W = \begin{pmatrix} -1 & 2 & 1 & 0 \\ -1 & -1 & -3 & -3 \end{pmatrix}$

 b)

 c) Rotation, 90° clockwise about (0, 0)

Page 316   Exercise 2

1 a) $\begin{pmatrix} -1 & 0 \\ 0 & 1 \end{pmatrix}$ b) $\begin{pmatrix} -1 & 0 \\ 0 & -1 \end{pmatrix}$ c) $\begin{pmatrix} 2 & 0 \\ 0 & 2 \end{pmatrix}$

 d) $\begin{pmatrix} 1 & 0 \\ 0 & -1 \end{pmatrix}$ e) $\begin{pmatrix} -1 & 0 \\ 0 & 1 \end{pmatrix}$ f) $\begin{pmatrix} 3 & 0 \\ 0 & 3 \end{pmatrix}$

 g) $\begin{pmatrix} \frac{1}{2} & 0 \\ 0 & \frac{1}{2} \end{pmatrix}$ h) $\begin{pmatrix} 0 & -1 \\ 1 & 0 \end{pmatrix}$ i) $\begin{pmatrix} -2 & 0 \\ 0 & -2 \end{pmatrix}$

Page 317   Exercise 3

1 a) (i) $B = \begin{pmatrix} 1 & 3 & 4 \\ 1 & 2 & 0 \end{pmatrix}$ (ii)

 b) (i) $B = \begin{pmatrix} 0 & -4 & -8 \\ 0 & 4 & 0 \end{pmatrix}$

 (ii)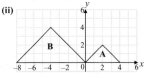

2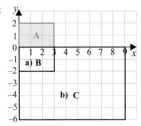

 c) (i) $R = \begin{pmatrix} 3 & 0 \\ 0 & -3 \end{pmatrix}$

 (ii) Reflection in the x-axis, then an
 enlargement by scale factor 3
 about (0, 0).

3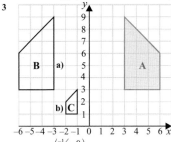

 c) (i) $Z = \begin{pmatrix} -\frac{1}{3} & 0 \\ 0 & \frac{1}{3} \end{pmatrix}$

 (ii) Reflection in the y-axis, then an
 enlargement by scale factor $\frac{1}{3}$
 about (0,0).

4 a)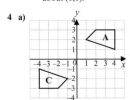

 b) $L = \begin{pmatrix} -1 & 0 \\ 0 & -1 \end{pmatrix}$

 c) Rotation, 180° around (0, 0)

5 a) $T = \begin{pmatrix} 0 & 1 \\ -1 & 0 \end{pmatrix}$ b) $U = \begin{pmatrix} 2 & 0 \\ 0 & 2 \end{pmatrix}$

 c) $V = \begin{pmatrix} 0 & 2 \\ -2 & 0 \end{pmatrix}$

 d) Rotation, 90° clockwise about (0, 0), then
 enlargement, scale factor 2, centre (0, 0)

Section 32 — Congruence and Similarity

32.1   Congruence and Similarity

Page 318   Exercise 1

1 a) $a = 5$ cm, $b = 74°$, $c = 74°$, $d = 32°$,
  $e = 7$ cm, $f = 7$ cm

 b) $g = 33°$, $h = 6$ cm, $i = 10$ cm, $j = 8$ cm,
  $k = 33°$, $l = 57°$

2 a) Yes. Two sides and the angle between on
  one triangle are the same as two sides and
  the angle between on the other triangle.

 b) No. The two angles shown are the same,
  but the corresponding sides are not equal.

 c) Yes. Two sides and the angle between on
  one triangle are the same as two sides and
  the angle between on the other triangle.

 d) Yes. Two angles and a side on one
  triangle are the same as two angles and the
  corresponding side on the other triangle.

 e) Yes. The three sides on one triangle are
  the same as the three sides on the other
  triangle.

 f) No. They could only be congruent if they
  had two 20° angles. This would make
  the angle opposite the 4 cm side 140°,
  which is impossible as the side opposite an
  obtuse angle is always longer than the
  other sides.

 g) No. The hypotenuse of the triangles is
  different so they cannot be congruent.

 h) Yes. The they are both right-angled
  triangles (180° − 41° − 49° = 90°), they
  have the same hypotenuse and one other
  side is the same.

Page 319   Exercise 2

1 Using Pythagoras' theorem the hypotenuse
 of the triangle on the right is 5 cm. Both
 triangles have a right angle, the same
 hypotenuse and another side the same, so they
 are congruent.

2 E.g. Opposite sides and angles in a
 parallelogram are equal so $AB = CD$, $AD = BC$
 and side AC is common to both triangles.
 Three sides are the same in both triangles so
 they are congruent.

3 E.g. All sides and angles in a regular pentagon
 are equal. Angle CDE = angle ABC and
 $CD = DE = BC = AB$. Two sides and the angle
 between them are the same in both triangles
 so they are congruent.

4 E.g. Angle BOC = angle DOC = 90° because
 the diagonals of a kite cross at right angles.
 $BC = DC$ because a kite has two pairs of
 equal sides. The triangles share side CO.
 Both triangles have a right angle, the same
 hypotenuse and another side the same, so they
 are congruent.

Page 320   Exercise 3

1 a) No. The angles are not all the same size.

 b) Yes. All the sides on one triangle are in the
  same ratio as the corresponding sides on
  the other triangle.

 c) Yes. Two sides on one triangle are in the
  same ratio as the corresponding sides on
  the other triangle, and the angle between is
  the same on both triangles.

 d) No. The side lengths can't be in the same
  ratio as two sides of the first triangle are
  equal, but the sides in the second triangle
  are all different.

 e) Yes. Two sides on one triangle are in the
  same ratio as the corresponding sides on
  the other triangle, and the angle between is
  the same on both triangles.

f) Yes. All the angles on one triangle are the same as the angles on the other triangle.

Page 320 Exercise 4

1 E.g. Using Pythagoras' theorem the missing side of triangle A is 5 cm.
The 10 cm and 24 cm sides of triangle B are in the same ratio as the 5 cm and 12 cm sides of triangle A. The angle between these sides is 90° in both triangles. So they are similar.

2 E.g. Angle BEC = angle AED (vertically opposite angles).
Angle ADE = angle CBE (alternate angles).
Angle DAE = angle BCE (alternate angles).
The 3 angles in BEC are the same as the 3 angles in AED so the triangles are similar.

3 a) E.g. Angle ABC = angle DBE as it is a common angle to both triangles.
$AB = BC$ as the triangle is isosceles.
$DB = BE$ as DE is parallel to AC.
So AB and BC are in the same ratio as DB and BE. Therefore triangles ABC and DBE are similar.
b) AOC and EOD.
Angle AOC = angle EOD (vertically opposite angles).
Angle ACO = angle EDO (alternate angles).
Angle CAO = angle DEO (alternate angles).
The 3 angles in AOC are the same as the 3 angles in EOD so they are similar.
AC and DE are corresponding sides but $AC \neq DE$ so the triangles aren't congruent.

Page 321 Exercise 5

1 a) 2 : 1   **b)** 6 m
2 a) 1 : 2   **b)** 6 m   **c)** 6 m
3 a) 6 cm   **b)** 10 cm   **c)** 5 cm
4 a) 16.5 cm   **b)** 10 cm   **c)** 5 cm
5 a) 1.5 m   **b)** 5.4 m   **c)** 3.6 m
6 $y = 55°$ **7** $z = 110°$

32.2 Areas of Similar Shapes

Page 322 Exercise 1

1 1600 cm²   **2** 45 cm²
3 16 cm   **4** 20 cm²
5 Perimeter 36 cm, area 54 cm²
6 18 cm × 30 cm

Page 322 Exercise 2

1 a) 12 cm   **b)** 144 cm²   **c)** 4 : 9
2 3 : 5   **3** 31.25 cm²
4 7500 cm² (or 0.75 m³)

Page 323 Exercise 3

1 360 in²   **2** 3600π mm²
3 15 cm   **4** 28π cm²
5 7.5 cm   **6** 2 : 3 : 3.5 (= 4 : 6 : 7)

32.3 Volumes of Similar Shapes

Page 324 Exercise 1

1 8 cm × 12 cm × 20 cm
2 2250 m³   **3** 10.5 cm³
4 4.5 cm   **5** 937.5π
6 a) 8 : 125   **b)** 1562.5 mm³
7 64 cm   **8** James is correct
9 Uranus is approximately 64 times the volume of the Earth
10 3.6 cm³

Page 324 Exercise 1

1 a) Congruent. Two sides and the angle between on one triangle are the same as two sides and the angle between on the other triangle.
b) Neither. The two sides with the 40° angle in between on one triangle are not in the same ratio as the corresponding sides on the other triangle.
c) Similar. All the angles on one triangle are the same as the angles on the other triangle, but they are not the same size.
d) Neither. The angles in one triangle are not all the same as the angles in the other triangle.

2 a) $KN = 10$ cm   **b)** $KL = 12$ cm
3 a) $BC = 3.75$ m   **b)** Angle $ACB = 40°$
4 $y = 37°$
5 a) 528 cm²   **b)** 960 cm³
6 a) 9 : 25   **b)** 27 : 125
7 Diameter = 80 cm, volume = 48 000π cm³
8 1296 in³   **9** 7290 cm³
10 a) 7 : 9   **b)** 343 : 729
11 Yes. The larger ball is 8 times the volume of the smaller ball, for only twice the price.
12 3 in × 5 in × 4 in
13 a) 49.5 cm²   **b)** 60.75 cm³
14 10 m
15 No. The ratio of their surface areas is 1 : 9 and the ratio of their volumes is 1 : 9.
If they were similar, the ratio of their volumes would be 1 : 27.

Section 33 — Collecting Data

33.1 Using Different Types of Data

Page 326 Exercise 1

1 a) Data needed — girls' answers to some questions about school dinners.
Method of collecting — e.g. Nikita could ask all the girls in her class to fill in a questionnaire.
b) Primary data

2 a) Data needed — colours of cars passing Dan's house in the 30-minute interval.
Method of collecting — e.g. Dan could observe cars passing his house and note the colour of each car in a tally chart.
b) Primary data

3 a) Data needed — daily rainfall figures for London and Manchester last August.
Method of collecting — e.g. Anne could look for rainfall figures on the internet.
b) Secondary data

4 a) Data needed — the distance an identical ball can be thrown by the boys and girls in his class.
Method of collecting — e.g. Rohan could ask everyone in the class to throw the same ball as far as they can. He could measure the distances and record them in a table, along with whether each thrower was male or female.
b) Primary data

---

5 a) Data needed — one set of data consists of the temperature readings in Jim's garden taken at 10 am each day. The other set consists of the Met Office's temperatures recorded for Jim's area at the same time.
Method of collecting — e.g. Jim could collect the data from his garden by taking readings from a thermometer. He can get the Met Office temperatures from their website. He should record both temperatures for each day in a table.
b) Data collected in Jim's garden is primary data. The Met Office data is secondary data.

Page 327 Exercise 2

1 a) discrete quantitative
b) continuous quantitative
c) qualitative
d) qualitative
e) discrete quantitative
f) continuous quantitative
g) discrete quantitative
h) continuous quantitative
i) continuous quantitative
j) qualitative

2 a) One set of data consists of the average number of chocolate bars eaten each week by each pupil. The other set consists of the times it takes these pupils to run 100 metres.
b) Gemma could ask each pupil how many chocolate bars they eat on average each week. She could time how long it takes each pupil to run 100 m and record the data in a table, along with the chocolate bar data.
c) The chocolate data is discrete quantitative data, and the running times data is continuous quantitative data.
d) Both sets of data are primary data.

3 a) (i) qualitative
(ii) discrete quantitative
b) E.g. Advantages — you can collect a lot more information / the information collected is more detailed.
Disadvantages — It takes more time to collect / the data is harder to analyse.

33.2 Data-Collection Sheets and Questionnaires

Page 328 Exercise 1

1 a) E.g.

Brothers/Sisters	Tally	Frequency
0		
1		
2		
3		
More than 3		

b) E.g.

Transport	Tally	Frequency
Walking		
Car		
Train		
Bus		
Bicycle		
Other		

---

c) E.g.

Fruit	Tally	Frequency
Apple		
Orange		
Banana		
Peach		
Other		

d) E.g.

Days	Tally	Frequency
28		
29		
30		
31		

a)

Age (years)	Tally	Frequency
0-9	⊥⊥⊥⊥ II	7
10-19	IIII	4
20-29	⊥⊥⊥⊥ I	6
30-39	⊥⊥⊥⊥ III	8
40-49	⊥⊥⊥⊥ II	7
50-59	⊥⊥⊥⊥ IIII	9
60-69	III	3
70-79	III	3
80-89	I	1

b) The 50-59 age group is the most common.

a) E.g. There is no row for someone who went to the cinema 0 times — the lowest possible answer is 1. The classes are overlapping.

No. of trips	Tally	Frequency
0-10		
11-20		
21-30		
31-40		
41 or more		

b) E.g. There are gaps between data classes. The classes do not cover all possible results.

No. of people	Tally	Frequency
0 - 5000		
5001 - 10 000		
10 001 - 15 000		
15 001 - 20 000		
20 001 - 25 000		

c) E.g. The classes are overlapping. There are not enough classes.

Time (t mins)	Tally	Frequency
$0 < t \leq 1$		
$1 < t \leq 2$		
$2 < t \leq 3$		
$3 < t \leq 4$		
$4 < t$		

d) E.g. There are gaps between classes. The classes don't cover all possible results.

Weight (w kg)	Tally	Frequency
$0 < w \leq 3$		
$3 < w \leq 3.5$		
$3.5 < w \leq 4$		
$4 < w$		

4 a) E.g. 0-4, 5-8, 9-12, 13-16, 17-20
b) E.g. $w \leq 180$, $180 < w \leq 190$ $190 < w \leq 200$, $200 < w \leq 210$, $w > 210$
c) E.g. $v \leq 260$, $260 < v \leq 270$ $270 < v \leq 280$, $280 < v \leq 290$, $290 < v \leq 300$

5 a)

Mark	Tally	Frequency
20-29	IIII	4
30-39	⊥⊥⊥⊥ IIII	9
40-49	⊥⊥⊥⊥	5
50-59	III	3
60-69	⊥⊥⊥⊥ ⊥⊥⊥⊥	10
70-79	III	3
80-89	⊥⊥⊥⊥ II	7
90-100	⊥⊥⊥⊥ IIII	9

b) 29
c) No, because the grouping used means the table doesn't show how many students in the 50-59 group scored less than 55 (and so failed), and how many scored 55 or over (and so passed).

6 a) E.g.

No. of pairs	Tally	Frequency
0 - 4		
5 - 8		
9 - 12		
13 - 16		
17 or more		

b) E.g.

Length (s cm)	Tally	Frequency
$0 < s \leq 15$		
$15 < s \leq 20$		
$20 < s \leq 25$		
$25 < s \leq 30$		
$30 < s$		

c) E.g.

Distance (d km)	Tally	Frequency
$0 < d \leq 5$		
$5 < d \leq 10$		
$10 < d \leq 20$		
$20 < d \leq 40$		
$40 < d$		

Page 329   Exercise 2

1 a) There are not enough hair colour data classes. The age classes overlap. The data is for adults and so does not need a data class for 0-15 years.

b) E.g.

Hair Colour	Age in whole years				
	18-30	31-45	46-60	61-75	76+
Blonde					
Light brown					
Dark brown					
Ginger					
Grey					
Other					

2 a) E.g.

Music	Age Group	
	Adult	Child
Pop		
Classical		
Rock		

b) E.g.

Time spent (t hours)	School Year				
	7	8	9	10	11
$0 < t \leq 1$					
$1 < t \leq 2$					
$2 < t \leq 3$					
$3 < t \leq 4$					

3 a) E.g.

Cats or dogs	Male or female	
	Male	Female
Cats		
Dogs		

b) E.g.

TV time (t hours)	Age Group	
	Adult	Child
$0 < t \leq 1$		
$1 < t \leq 2$		
$2 < t \leq 3$		
$3 < t \leq 4$		
$4 < t$		

c) E.g.

Height (h cm)	No. of fruit portions eaten				
	0-2	3-4	5-6	7-10	11+
$h \leq 120$					
$120 < h \leq 140$					
$140 < h \leq 160$					
$160 < h \leq 180$					
$180 < h$					

Page 329   Exercise 3

1 E.g.

No. of people	Tally	Frequency
1		
2		
3		
4		
5 or more		

2 E.g.

Hair rating	Age Group	
	Adult	Child
1		
2		
3		
4		
5		

3 E.g.

Pocket Money	Tally	Frequency
0 - £2.00		
£2.01 - £4.00		
£4.01 - £6.00		
£6.01 - £8.00		
£8.01 or more		

4 E.g.

TV time (t hours)	Sport time (s hours)			
	$0 < s \leq 5$	$5 < s \leq 10$	$10 < s \leq 20$	$20 < s$
$0 < t \leq 5$				
$5 < t \leq 10$				
$10 < t \leq 20$				
$20 < t$				

Page 330   Exercise 4

1 Jay's question is better. E.g. two from: Amber's question is too vague because people will have different ideas about how to answer (e.g. "1 hour", "a lot") / Amber's question has no time span / Amber's data could be difficult to analyse because there are no options to limit the answers / Jay's question is clearer because it has a time span / Jay's data will be easier to analyse since there are only 5 options to choose from.

2 a) The tick boxes should be changed so they don't overlap. E.g. *How much time do you spend reading each week on average?*

1 hour or less ☐

More than 1 hour, but no more than 2 hours ☐

More than 2 hours, but no more than 3 hours ☐

More than 3 hours, but no more than 4 hours ☐

4 hours or more ☐

b) There should be a tick box added for "other", and possibly more options e.g. "Documentary" or "News".
E.g. *What's your favourite type of TV programme? Tick one box.*

Comedy ☐   Soap ☐
Reality ☐   Sport ☐
Documentary ☐   News ☐
Other ☐

c) A box for "Neither" or "Don't Care" could be added. E.g. *Which type of film do you prefer — horror or thriller?*
Horror ☐   Thriller ☐   Neither ☐

d) Reword the question so it is not a leading question. E.g. *Do you think the gym should open a squash court or a tennis court?*

e) This is a sensitive question, change the question so it has a range of options for you to tick. E.g. *How much credit card debt do you have?*

£0 ☐
£0 < d ≤ £500 ☐
£500 < d ≤ £1000 ☐
£1000 < d ≤ £3000 ☐
£3000 < d ☐

3 a) Provide options for the different modes of transport, including "other", and make it clear that one answer only is to be selected.
E.g. *"What is your main means of transport to school? Please tick one box only."*
You could include boxes such as "Car", "Bus", "Walking", "Train", "Bicycle" and "Other".

b) Include a time span and tick boxes which cover all possible answers and do not overlap.
E.g. *"How many times, on average, do you use the gym each week?"*
You could include boxes such as "I don't use the gym", "Less than once a week", "1-2 times", and "More than 2 times".

c) Include a tick box for each day of the week, and make it clear that more than one can be selected.
E.g. *"On which day(s) of the week do you usually shop at the supermarket? You may tick more than one box."*

d) Include tick boxes to cover all possible opinions. E.g. *"What do you think about the length of the dance class?"* You could include boxes such as "Much too short", "A bit too short", "About right", "A bit too long", and "Much too long".

33.3 Sampling and Bias

Page 331   Exercise 1

1 E.g. It would take far too long to time all 216 pupils, and a smaller sample would create less disruption in the school routine.

2 E.g. It would be highly impractical and time-consuming to interview everyone in the town.

3 Alfie's sample was bigger and would be expected to be more accurate — therefore, "chocolate" is more likely to be the most popular flavour.

4 E.g. Nikhil's idea is best, as only tasting one cake would not be accurate, and tasting 50 out of the 200 would take too long and use up a quarter of their cakes.

5 Both Melissa and Karen have the same number of coin tosses in their sample (and use the same coin), so their results are equally reliable.

Page 332   Exercise 2

1 a) People using the library on a Monday are unlikely to want it to close on a Monday, so the sample will be biased away from a Monday closure.

b) The proportions of men and women in the sample are different to the proportions of men and women that work for the company.

c) People at work probably won't be able to answer the phone in the afternoon, so the only replies they will get will be from people who don't work, home workers, people with unusual working hours and people with the day off.

2 E.g. The manager could assign each of the female members on her database a number, generate 40 random numbers with a computer or calculator, and match the numbers to the members to create the sample.

3 George's sample will be a much higher percentage of the total number of pupils, and Stuart's sample is not random. For example, it could be a group of friends who may all support the same football team.

4 E.g. Seema's sample, being taken on a Sunday morning, may include a lower than usual percentage of churchgoers (if they are at church at the time) or a higher than usual percentage (if they are going to/from church). It would be better to conduct the survey on a weekday evening when far fewer people will be at work or at (or going to/from) a place of worship. Also, people chosen at random in the street may not even live in that street. So instead, Seema could pick 20 house numbers from her street at random and knock on the doors, asking one person from each house.

5 E.g. The management could select 20 employees from each branch by assigning each employee at the branch a number, generating 20 random numbers using a computer or calculator, and matching those numbers to the numbered employees.

6 E.g. If the factory runs for 24 hours a day, test one freshly made component roughly every 30 minutes (or at 50 random times throughout the day).

Page 333   Exercise 3

1 14 male, 6 female club members.

2 Year 12: 8 boys (rounded from 7.5), 5 girls
Year 13: 6 boys and 6 girls (rounded from 6.25)

3 a)

Age (*a*) in years	No. in sample
a < 15	2
15 ≤ *a* < 25	29
25 ≤ *a* < 35	37
35 ≤ *a* < 50	23
50+	9

b) E.g. They could select members by assigning a set of numbers to the members in each age group. They could then use a calculator or a computer to generate the required number of random numbers matching the members in each group.

4 a) There are many more students in Year 7 than in Year 8, and a sample containing the same number of students from each year would be unrepresentative of the school population.

---

b)

Year group	No. of boys in sample	No. of girls in sample
Year 7	5 (4.76)	5 (4.52)
Year 8	4 (3.62)	3 (3.19)
Year 9	7 (6.86)	6 (6.48)
Year 10	5 (4.67)	5 (5.14)
Year 11	5 (5.33)	5 (5.43)

Page 334   Exercise 4

1 a) 28th, 48th, 68th, 88th
b) 9th

2 a) E.g. A bus might come every 12 minutes, so the times you are sampling could all be just after the bus has picked everyone up or just before.

b) E.g. There could be a pattern to the faulty ball bearings. If every 10th ball bearing the machine produces is faulty, then you either get a sample containing all faulty ball bearings or no faulty ball bearings depending on your starting point.

c) E.g. The houses could be in rows of 6 so every 6th house could be on the end of a row, which could affect energy efficiency.

3 E.g. He could list the politicians in alphabetical order and number them 1 to 650. Then he could add every 650 ÷ 50 = 13th name to the sample starting with a random number from 1 to 13.

4 E.g. If you use systematic sampling you'll be guaranteed to get samples from regular intervals all the way along the pipe, whereas if you use random sampling you could get samples that are all from one part of the pipe.

5 E.g. It might be difficult to separate the residents into groups in order to take a stratified sample. They could make groups by age/ethnicity/gender, but they are not guaranteed to have this information.
A systematic sample could be carried out quickly and at a low cost, potentially by a machine.

Section 34 — Averages and Range

34.1 Averages and Range

Page 335   Exercise 1

1 a) (i) 6   **(ii)** 7   **b) (i)** 8   **(ii)** 9
c) (i) 8.2   **(ii)** 0.1

2 a) 3   **b)** 4.5   **c)** 6.93

3 a) 17 seconds **b)** 81 seconds

4 60.2 (to 1 d.p.)

5 a) 20
b) (i) 13   **(ii)** 18   **(iii)** 17.5 (to 1 d.p.)

6 a) 2 and 11   **b)** 10

7 Median (Median = 1.65 m, Mean = 1.596 m)

Page 336   Exercise 2

1 a) 4   **b)** 3   **c)** 3.1   **d)** 4

2 a) 3   **b)** 2.7
c) The mean number of goals scored this year is higher than last year.

3 a) 17.5 °C   **b)** 18.1 °C
c) The student's garden has a pretty average temperature.

4 29.89 eggs

a) 200 people were surveyed, so the total
frequency = 200. Therefore
$77 + p + q + 11 + 3 = 200$
$p + q = 200 - 77 - 11 - 3$
$p + q = 109$

b) Mean $= \dfrac{77 + 2p + 3q + 44 + 15}{200} = 1.88$
$2p + 3q + 136 = 376$
$2p + 3q = 240$

c) (i) 87 **(ii)** 22

age 338   Exercise 3

a) There are two fashion seasons. Which
season it is seems to affect the number
of scarves sold (more seem to be sold in
autumn/winter than spring/summer).

b) Year 1 spring/summer to autumn/winter:
433 scarves
Year 1 autumn/winter to Year 2 spring/
summer: 442 scarves
Year 2 spring/summer to autumn/winter:
543.5 scarves

4.2   Averages for Grouped Data

age 338   Exercise 1

1 58 g
2 **a)** $10 \le t < 15$ **b)** $10 \le t < 15$
c) 10.6 hours
3 **a)** 1.60 m $\le h < 1.70$ m
b) 1.60 m $\le h < 1.70$ m
c) 1.69 m (to 2 d.p.)
4 **a)** 10 min $\le t < 15$ min
b) 13.4 minutes (to 1 d.p.)
c) 41% (to the nearest per cent)

4.3   Interpreting Data Sets

age 339   Exercise 1

1 **a) (i)** 14 **(ii)** 13 **(iii)** 12.5
b) E.g. The mode is a data value, but the mean
and the median are not (12.5 and 13 are not
dress sizes).
2 **a) (i)** 16   **(ii)** 16.5   **(iii)** 23.4 (to 1 d.p.)
b) E.g. No — the majority of people were
under 20. The mean is affected by the five
60-year-olds present. This average doesn't
fairly represent the data.
3 **a)** Mode = 7
Median = 3
Mean = 3.85 (to 2 d.p.)
b) (i) mode
(ii) E.g. No — the majority of marks given
are between 1 and 4 marks, so this
average doesn't represent the data well.

age 340   Exercise 2

1 **a)** 7   **b)** 0.3   **c)** 61   **d)** 6.5
2 3 spots
3 **a) (i)** 884   **(ii)** 49
b) E.g. The interquartile range — it isn't
affected by the extreme data values and so
reflects the spread of the majority of the
data better than the range.
4 **a)** 77   **b)** 8 students
c) (i) 49.5
(ii) E.g. Class 3A's results are much more
spread out than class 3B's.

Page 341   Exercise 3

1 **a)** 3 **b)** 290 **c)** 4.6

Page 341   Exercise 4

1 **a) (i)** 8   **(ii)** 5.5   **(iii)** 5.4
b) E.g. The mean — it takes all data points
into account.

---

c) E.g. The mean has a very low value, so
using the mean won't make the product
sound as good. They're more likely to use
the mode which has a much higher value.

2 For the pantomime horses:
Mean time = 29.6 s (to 1 d.p.)
Median time = 26.4 s
IQR = 19.85 s
E.g. The mean time it took a kitten to run
100 m is less than the mean time it took a
pantomime horse to run the course. However
the interquartile range for the pantomime
horses is smaller than that for the kittens.
This means that the horses ran at a more
consistent pace than the kittens. The fastest
kitten ran faster than the fastest horse.

Section 35 —
Displaying Data

35.1   Tables and Charts

Page 342   Exercise 1

1 **a)**

	Red	Black	Blue	White	Total
Cars	8	7	4	3	22
Vans	2	2	1	10	15
Motorbikes	2	1	1	2	6
Total	12	10	6	15	43

b) 1   **c)** 15
d) (i) 51.2% (to 1 d.p.) **(ii)** 34.9% (to 1 d.p.)
(iii) 27.9% (to 1 d.p.)

2

	Have been ice skating	Haven't been ice skating	Total
Boys	2	8	10
Girls	16	4	20
Total	18	12	30

3 **a)**

	$h < 160$	$160 \le h < 170$	$170 \le h < 180$	$180 \le h < 190$	$190 \le h$	Total
Women	4	7	11	2	0	24
Men	0	2	6	13	5	26
Total	4	9	17	15	5	50

b) 13   **c)** $\dfrac{2}{24}$ or $\dfrac{1}{12}$
d) More of the men's heights are in the taller
height intervals, so this suggests that, in
general, the men are taller than the women.

Page 343   Exercise 2

1 **a)**
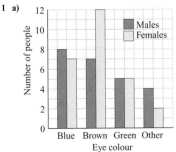
b)
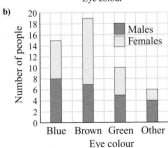

---

2 a) 2   **b)** 29   **c)** 2   **d)** 3
e) The scores given by the adults were
generally lower than the scores given by
the children.

3 **a)** 12   **b)** 39   **c)** 16-25 yrs   **d)** 36-45 yrs

Page 344   Exercise 3

1 **a)**

Destination	UK	Europe	USA	Other	Nowhere
Frequency	22	31	8	11	18
Angle	88°	124°	32°	44°	72°

b)
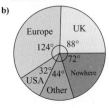

2 **a)**

Activity	Squash	Swimming	Gym	Table tennis
Angle	99°	63°	156°	42°

b)
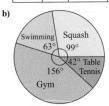

3
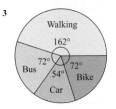

4
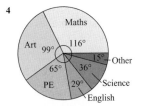

Page 345   Exercise 4

1 **a)** Pepperoni   **b)** $\dfrac{1}{4}$ **c)** 17

2 **a)** Yes   **b)** Yes
c) No. The pie charts do not represent times,
just the proportion of homework tasks set
for each subject.

3 **a)** 120 **b) (i)** 24   **(ii)** 12   **(iii)** 24   **(iv)** 42
c) $\dfrac{1}{5}$
d) The fraction of people aged 11-16 in
the second survey is twice as big as the
fraction aged 11-16 in the first survey.
e) No, they only show that a bigger proportion
of the people in the second survey were
aged 11-16. You don't know whether there
were more people without knowing how
many people were surveyed.

Page 346 Exercise 1

1 a)
```
4 | 1 8
5 | 1 4 9
6 | 5 5 9
7 | 4
8 | 0 6 9
```
Key: 4|1 means 41

b)
```
1 | 2 5 5 7
2 | 4 6 7
3 | 1 6 9
4 | 1 1
```
Key: 1|2 means 12

c)
```
3 | 1 4
4 | 0 4 9
5 | 3 4 7 9
6 | 0
7 | 7
```
Key: 3 | 1 means 3.1

d)
```
20 | 3 3 5 7
21 |
22 | 1 1 5
23 | 2 4 6
24 | 0
```
Key: 20 | 3 means 203

2
```
0 | 0 0 0 1 3 6
1 | 1 3 6
2 | 0 5 7
3 | 1 6 8
4 | 1
```
Key: 0|1 means 0.1 cm

3 a) There are 3 modes — 55, 61 and 77.
b) 61 c) 7 d) 6 e) 25

4 a)
```
10 | 2 6
11 | 4 7
12 | 4 8 9
13 | 1 3 6 9 9
14 | 2
15 | 4
16 |
17 | 3
```
Key: 10 | 1 means 10.1 seconds

b) 13.9 s c) 13.1 s
d) Q_1 = 11.7 s Q_3 = 13.9 s IQR = 2.2 s

Page 347 Exercise 2

1 E.g.
```
      Set 2 | | Set 1
9 8 5 3 3 | 1 | 2 8
7 5 3 2 2 | 2 | 4 8 9
          2 | 3 | 2 3 7 8
            | 4 | 1 8
```
Key: 1|2 for Set 1 means 12
1|2 for Set 2 means 21

2 a) Median for 'at rest' data = 72
Median for 'after exercise' data = 77
b) IQR for 'at rest' data = 14
IQR for 'after exercise' data = 18

c) The higher median for the 'after exercise' data suggests that, on average, people's heart rate was faster after they'd exercised. The greater IQR for the 'after exercise' data shows that there was more variety in the heart rates after exercise, than at rest.

3 a) E.g.
```
      London | | Dundee
       9 7 4 | 0 | 1 2 3 3 4 5 6 7
8 6 5 3 2 2 1 | 1 | 2 5 9
         4 1 | 2 | 3
```
Key: 1|2 for London means 21 °C
1|2 for Dundee means 12 °C

b) The median temperature for London was 12.5 °C and the median for Dundee was 5.5 °C. This suggests that the temperatures in London were generally higher than the temperatures in Dundee. The range for London was 20 °C and the range for Dundee was 22 °C. This shows that the spread of temperatures was slightly greater in Dundee.

Page 348 Exercise 1

1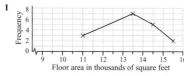

2 a) 1 b) 0-5 minutes
c) The airline should not have been fined because only 7 of its flights were delayed by 20 minutes or more.

3 a) 6 b) 29 c) 1-2 hours d) 6-7 hours
e) The modal classes suggest that there were generally more daily hours of sunshine in July than in February. The graphs show that the range of daily hours of sunshine was much greater in July than in February.

Page 349 Exercise 1

1 a)

Height (h) in cm	Frequency	Frequency Density
$0 < h \leq 5$	4	0.8
$5 < h \leq 10$	6	1.2
$10 < h \leq 15$	3	0.6
$15 < h \leq 20$	2	0.4

b)

Height (h) in cm	Frequency	Frequency Density
$10 < h \leq 20$	5	0.5
$20 < h \leq 25$	15	3
$25 < h \leq 30$	12	2.4
$30 < h \leq 40$	8	0.8

2 a)

Volume (v) in ml	Frequency	Frequency Density
$0 \leq v < 500$	50	0.1
$500 \leq v < 1000$	75	0.15
$1000 \leq v < 1500$	70	0.14
$1500 \leq v < 2000$	55	0.11

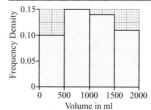

b)

Volume (v) in ml	Frequency	Frequency Densi
$0 \leq v < 300$	30	0.1
$300 \leq v < 600$	15	0.05
$600 \leq v < 900$	24	0.08
$900 \leq v < 1500$	42	0.07
$1500 \leq v < 2100$	12	0.02

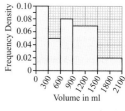

3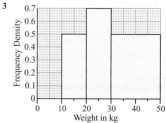

4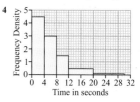

5 a), c)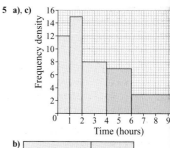

b)

Time (t) in hours	Frequency
$0 \leq t < 1$	12
$1 \leq t < 2$	15
$2 \leq t < 4$	16
$4 \leq t < 6$	14
$6 \leq t < 10$	12

Page 351 Exercise 2

1 a) The frequencies are: 5, 7, 9, 10, 9.
b) The frequencies are: 10, 12, 15, 18, 16.
2 a) 3 b) 6 c) 16 d) 3
3 a) 107 b) 45 c) 190 d) 14.9 cm (1 d.p
4 a) 11 b) 48 c) 59 d) 59 cm

Page 351 Exercise 3

1 a)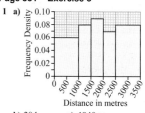
b) 204 c) 1840 m

a)

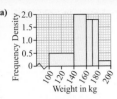

b) $140 \le w < 160$ kg, 155 kg   **c)** 175 kg

5.5   Cumulative Frequency Diagrams

age 352   Exercise 1

a) 84   **b)** 3   **c)** 64   **d)** 70
e) Median = £67 (accept £66 – £67)
f) Lower quartile = £52 (accept £51 – £52)
upper quartile = £79 (accept £79 – £80)
IQR = £27 (accept £27 – £29)

a)

Cumulative Frequency
0
2
6
11
30
63
106
116
119
120

b)

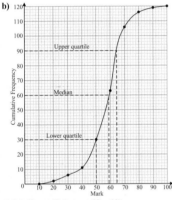

c) Median = 59 (accept 58 – 60)
d) upper quartile = 64 (accept 63 – 65)
lower quartile = 50
IQR = 14 (accept 13 – 15)
e) 18 (accept 16 – 20)
f) 76 (accept 74 – 78)

a) (i) 104   **(ii)** 50
b) Median = 8.8 h, lower quartile = 6.5 h,
upper quartile = 11 h, IQR = 4.5 h

c) (i)

Cumulative Frequency
35
111
162
196
199
199
200
200
200
200

(ii)

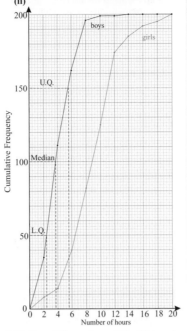

d) Median = 3.7 hours (accept 3.6 – 3.8 hours)
IQR = 3.2 hours (accept 3.0 – 3.4 hours)
e) E.g. the boys generally watched less
TV than the girls as their median is much
smaller. Also there is less variation in the
number of hours watched by the boys as
their IQR is smaller.

4 a)

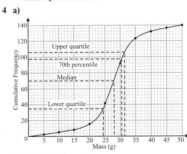

b) (i)   Median = 28 g
(accept 27.5 g – 28.5 g)
IQR = 7 g (accept 6 g – 8 g)
(ii)   70th percentile = 30.5 g
(accept 30 g – 31 g)
c) 118   (accept 114 – 122)
d) E.g. Students' estimates were quite good,
but tended to be a little high.

Page 354   Exercise 2

1 a) (i)   Median = 48 marks
(ii)   Upper quartile = 67 marks
(iii)   Lower quartile = 26 marks
(iv)   IQR = 41 marks
(v)   Lowest mark = 13
(vi)   Highest mark = 83
b) (i)   Median = 10 hours
(ii)   Upper quartile = 18 hours
(iii)   Lower quartile = 6 hours
(iv)   IQR = 12 hours
(v)   Lowest value = 2 hours
(vi)   Higher value = 29 hours

2   Busybodies   Chatterboxes
Median = 30   Median = 20
Upper quartile = 45   Upper quartile = 30
Lower quartile = 10   Lower quartile = 10
IQR = 35   IQR = 20
Lowest time = 6   Lowest time = 4
Highest time = 50   Highest time = 59
E.g. The median and upper quartile times
for the busybodies are greater than those
for the chatterboxes, so a greater number of
busybodies stayed quieter for longer than the
chatterboxes. However the maximum time a
chatterbox was able to stay silent was greater
than the maximum time a busybody managed
to stay silent.

Page 354   Exercise 3

1 a)

Hours of use, h	$h < 5000$	$5000 \le h < 6000$	$6000 \le h < 7000$	$7000 \le h < 8000$
Type A	25	15	23	17
C.F.	25	40	63	80
Type B	13	13	18	21
C.F.	13	26	44	65

Hours of use, h	$8000 \le h < 9000$	$9000 \le h < 10\,000$	$10\,000 \le h < 11\,000$	$11\,000 \le h < 12\,000$
Type A	50	41	24	5
C.F.	130	171	195	200
Type B	36	72	19	8
C.F.	101	173	192	200

b)

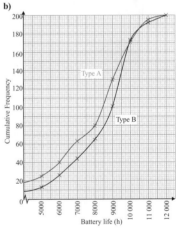

c) Type A: Median = 8450 h
(accept 8400h – 8500h)
IQR = 3050 h
(accept 2950 h – 3150 h)
Type B: Median = 8970 h
(accept 8900 h – 8990 h)
IQR = 2350 h
(accept 2250 h – 2450 h)

d)

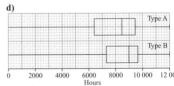

e) E.g. Type B has a longer life on average
as the median is higher, and has a more
consistent life span (the IQR is smaller).

2 a)

Sales, £s 000	$s < 100$	$100 \le s < 200$	$200 \le s < 300$	$300 \le s < 400$	$400 \le s < 500$
Sean	0	5	29	15	3
C.F.	0	5	34	49	52
Maria	4	17	21	10	0
C.F.	4	21	42	52	52

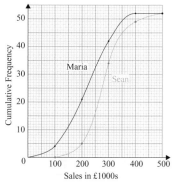

b) Sean: Median = £280 000
(accept £275 000 – £285 000)
IQR = £75 000
(accept £65 000 – £85 000)
Maria: Median = £225 000,
(accept £220 000 – £230 000)
IQR = £120 000
(accept £110 000 – £130 000)

c)

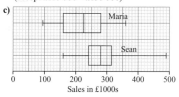

d) E.g. Sean — his median is higher and his lowest and highest sales figures are both greater than Maria's. The interquartile range for his data is also smaller than for Maria's, which shows his sales figures are more consistent than Maria's.

35.6 Time Series

Page 355 Exercise 1

1 a)

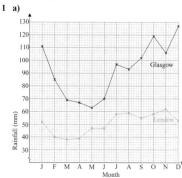

b) E.g. The average rainfall in Glasgow is higher than the average rainfall in London for every month of the year. Glasgow's average rainfall has a greater range.

c) London = 24 mm, Glasgow = 64 mm

---

2 a)

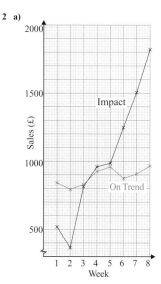

b) E.g. On Trend had fairly consistent sales over the 8-week period. Sales of Impact started off much lower, but increased rapidly, overtaking On Trend in the fourth week and selling almost twice as much by week 8.

3 a)

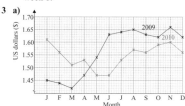

b) $1.61   **c)** $1.66 in November
d) 2009 = $1.56, 2010 = $1.55   **e)** $80

Page 357 Exercise 2

1 a) (i) There is a slight downward trend in the sales of umbrellas over the three years shown on the graph.
(ii) There is a slight upward trend in the number of sick days taken over the three years shown on the graph.
(iii) The average skirt length has stayed roughly the same over the three years shown by the graph.
b) Seasonality — different seasons cause a repeating pattern in the data.

2 a) Moving average 1
$$= \frac{18\,000 + 10\,000 + 7500 + 10\,500}{4}$$
$$= 11\,500$$
Moving average 2
$$= \frac{10\,000 + 7500 + 10\,500 + 18\,800}{4}$$
$$= 11\,700$$
b)

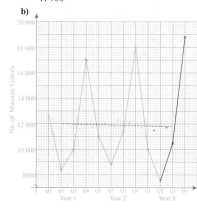

---

c) There is a slight downward trend in the data.

3 a) (i)

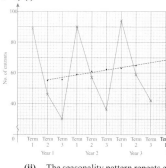

(ii) The seasonality pattern repeats ev three terms.

b) Use the trend line to estimate the movi average for Year 4, terms 1, 2 and 3. Moving average = estimated no. of students per term in Year 4 = 70. So the estimated number of students fo Year 4 = 70 × 3 = 210. So yes, the colle should run the course next year.

35.7 Scatter Graphs

Page 358 Exercise 1

1 a) Negative correlation.
b) No correlation.
c) Positive correlation.

2 a)

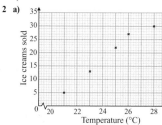

b) Yes — positive correlation.

3 a)

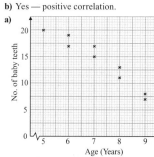

b) Negative correlation

4 a) Strong negative correlation
b) Moderate positive correlation

5 a)

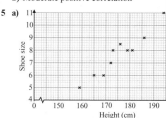

b) The graph shows moderate positive correlation (i.e. as height increases so d shoe size) so there is evidence that they correlated.

a) Strong positive correlation

b) E.g. The tree wasn't measured correctly.

c) 65 cm   d) 20 m (accept 20 m – 20.3 m)

a), b)

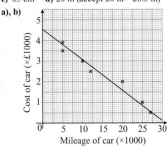

c) About £2300.
(Allow answers in the range £2200-£2400)

a)

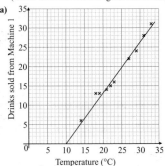

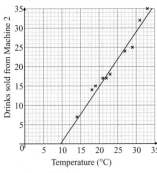

b) Machine 1: 20 drinks.
Machine 2: 22 drinks.

c) 3 °C is well below the temperature range
for this data, so the relationship shown
by this data may not apply at such a low
temperature.

d) E.g. No — just because the two things are
correlated does not mean that one thing
causes the other. They both could be
influenced by a third variable.

a), c)

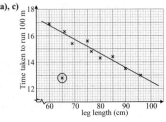

b) Strong negative correlation

d) 13.9 s (accept 13.6 s – 14.2 s)

e) (i) 12.5 s (accept 12.2 s – 12.8 s)
   (ii) E.g. 100 cm is outside the range of the
   data so you need to extrapolate.
   This can lead to unreliable estimates.

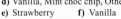

35.8 Displaying Data Problems

Page 361 Exercise 1

1 a) 30   b) 20   c) 3
  d) Vanilla, Mint choc chip, Other
  e) Strawberry   f) Vanilla   g) 12°
  h)

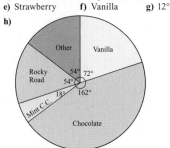

  i) There are fewer boys than girls, so the
  angle that represents one boy is larger than
  the angle that represents one girl.

2 a)

	10 am		3 pm	
		1	5 8	
9 7		2	2 3 3 7	
5		3	1 2 5	
8		4		
9 8 4 1		5		
5 0		6		

Key: 1 | 2 for 10 am means 21
      1 | 2 for 3 pm means 12

  b) Modal age at 10 am = 51
  Modal age at 3 pm = 23

  c) At 10 am: Median age = 51
            Mean age = 49 (to 2 s.f.)
            Lower quartile = 35
            Upper quartile = 59
            IQR = 24
   At 3 pm: Median age = 23
            Mean age = 25 (to 2 s.f.)
            Lower quartile = 20
            Upper quartile = 31.5
            IQR = 11.5
   E.g. The average age of the people in the
   queue at 3 pm was much younger than at
   10 am. There was a greater spread of ages
   at 10 am than at 3 pm — the interquartile
   range is larger. The maximum age of a
   person in the queue was greater at 10 am
   than at 3 pm. The minimum age was smaller
   at 3 pm than 10 am.

3 a)

	0–3 points	4–7 points	8–11 points	12–15 points	16–20 points	Tot.
Rnd 1	0	1	2	4	3	10
Rnd 2	1	2	4	2	1	10
Total	1	3	6	6	4	20

  b) 70%   c) 4

  d) E.g. The data suggests that round 1 was
  easier — 70% of people got a score of 12 or
  more, compared to only 50% in round 2.

  e)

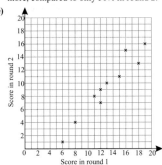

---

f) There is a strong positive correlation
between the scores in round 1 and round
2.

4 a), b)

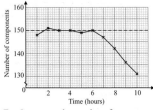

c) E.g. I agree — the number of
components produced has dropped
significantly from the target amount
over the last 4 hours shown by the data.

5 a)

Height (h) in cm	Frequency
$155 \leq h < 160$	1
$160 \leq h < 165$	2
$165 \leq h < 170$	4
$170 \leq h < 175$	10
$175 \leq h < 180$	12
$180 \leq h < 185$	3

b) 21 players

c) 160 cm - 165 cm

d) 28

e)

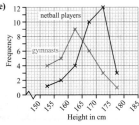

f) E.g. The ranges of the heights of
the netball players and gymnasts are
roughly the same. The modal height
of the netball players is larger than the
modal height of the gymnasts.

6 a) 7.2 km

b) Lower quartile ≈ 4.6 km
   Upper quartile ≈ 9.6 km
   IQR ≈ 9.6 – 4.6 = 5 km

c) 79   d) 50

e)

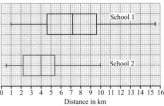

f) E.g. The maximum distance a child
travels is greater for students at school 1
than school 2. The interquartile range
is larger for school 1 than school 2, so
there is a greater spread of distances
travelled by children attending school
1 than school 2. The median distance
travelled to school 1 is also greater than
the median distance travelled to school
2, so on average children travel further
to get to school 1 than to school 2. The
shortest distance travelled by a child
to school is shorter for school 2 than
school 1.

Page 363 Exercise 1

1 a) E.g. The range is quite large compared to the interquartile range. This is evidence that there could be an outlier in the data — perhaps the fridge door was left open for a while and the temperature rose.

b) E.g. If there really is an outlier in the data, then the mean value would be more affected than the median value. So the mean may be a worse estimate of the average.

2 a) E.g.
1. Frequency is plotted instead of frequency density.
2. The frequency for the $0 < s \leq 20$ group is plotted as 12.5 instead of 13.
3. The scale is inconsistent on the x-axis.
4. The scale starts at 5 on the y-axis so the frequency for $40 < s \leq 50$ is too low to be plotted.

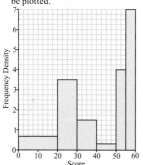

b) E.g. A pie chart would not be a good way to represent this data. It would not be as easy to interpret as a histogram. Some of the sectors would stand for different sized intervals and it wouldn't be immediately obvious what the chart was showing.

3 a) E.g. There is no scale on the y-axis so you can't tell how many people are in each company. You therefore can't tell whether Petra's statement is correct or not.

b) E.g. Gary is unlikely to be correct. You can only estimate the range is 10 kg more for company B — you cannot say for certain.

c) E.g. You cannot tell. In company A the median would appear in the 60-80 kg group and in company B the median would appear in the 70-80 kg group. As you have no information about how people are distributed within each group you cannot tell which group has the greater median.

4 a) The first graph shows moderate positive correlation and the second graph shows weak positive correlation.

b) E.g. The scatter graphs are misleading due to the scales on the y-axis. The y-axis scale on the first graph only shows marks between 50 and 60 which could be skewing the data into looking more positively correlated than it actually is. The second graph shows a bigger range of maths test marks and therefore the correlation shown is much more reliable. You'd need to see a zoomed-out version of the first scatter graph to be able to fully assess her claim.

Section 36 — Probability

Page 364 Exercise 1

1 a) $\frac{1}{6}$ b) $\frac{1}{6}$ c) 0

d) $\frac{2}{6} = \frac{1}{3}$ e) $\frac{2}{6} = \frac{1}{3}$ f) $\frac{4}{6} = \frac{2}{3}$

2 a) $\frac{13}{52} = \frac{1}{4}$ b) $\frac{4}{52} = \frac{1}{13}$ c) $\frac{26}{52} = \frac{1}{2}$

d) $\frac{1}{52}$ e) $\frac{39}{52} = \frac{3}{4}$ f) $\frac{8}{52} = \frac{2}{13}$

3 a) $\frac{2}{16} = \frac{1}{8}$ b) $\frac{3}{16}$ c) $\frac{1}{16}$ d) $\frac{2}{16} = \frac{1}{8}$

e) $\frac{6}{16} = \frac{3}{8}$ f) $\frac{6}{16} = \frac{3}{8}$ g) $\frac{15}{16}$ h) 0

4 a) Any spinner with exactly 3 sections labelled with '2'.

b) Any spinner with exactly 4 sections labelled with '3'.

c) Any spinner with exactly 2 sections labelled with '5' and exactly 2 sections labelled with '6'.

5 $\frac{1}{39}$

6 a) $\frac{2}{18} = \frac{1}{9}$ b) $\frac{7}{18}$

7 a) $\frac{14}{30} = \frac{7}{15}$ b) $\frac{10}{30} = \frac{1}{3}$

Page 365 Exercise 2

1 $\frac{3}{8}$ 2 75%

3 0.26   4 $\frac{2}{3}$

5 a) 0.3 b) 0.9   6 0.45

7 40   8 0.6

Page 366 Exercise 1

1 a) $\frac{1}{9}$ b) $\frac{5}{9}$

2 a) $\frac{1}{9}$ b) $\frac{4}{9}$

3 a) $\frac{1}{8}$ b) $\frac{1}{8}$ c) $\frac{3}{8}$

Page 367 Exercise 2

1 a)

	1	2	3	4	5	6
1	2	3	4	5	6	7
2	3	4	5	6	7	8
3	4	5	6	7	8	9
4	5	6	7	8	9	10
5	6	7	8	9	10	11
6	7	8	9	10	11	12

b) (i) $\frac{5}{36}$ (ii) $\frac{1}{36}$ (iii) 0 (iv) $\frac{21}{36} = \frac{7}{12}$

(v) $\frac{10}{36} = \frac{5}{18}$ (vi) $\frac{18}{36} = \frac{1}{2}$

2 a) E.g.

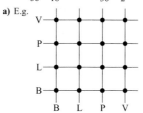

b) (i) $\frac{1}{16}$ (ii) $\frac{4}{16} = \frac{1}{4}$ (iii) $\frac{7}{16}$

3 a) $\frac{1}{24}$ b) $\frac{2}{24} = \frac{1}{12}$ c) $\frac{3}{24} = \frac{1}{8}$

4 a) $\frac{6}{25}$ b) $\frac{4}{25}$

Page 368 Exercise 3

1 a) 96 b) 56

2 a) 16 807 b) 243 c) $\frac{243}{16\,807}$

3 She is not correct. E.g. $6 \times 6 \times 6 \times 6 = 1296$, but if the different flavours of fruit juice are A, B, C, D, E, F then the combination A, A, A, B is the same as the combination A, A, B, A. So there will be far fewer than 1296 different combinations.

Page 368 Exercise 1

1 a) P(Red) = 0.49, P(Green) = 0.34, P(Yellow) = 0.08, P(Blue) = 0.09

b) The estimates should be more accurate if the spinner is spun a greater number of times.

2 a) $\frac{13}{50} = 0.26$ b) $\frac{18}{100} = \frac{9}{50} = 0.18$

c) Jason's estimate should be more accurate as he repeated the experiment more times.

3 a) 0.452 b) 0.237 c) 0.089

4 a) $\frac{8}{15}$ b) $\frac{7}{15}$

5 E.g. Lilia could examine the records of her team's recent matches against a similar level of opposition, count the number of wins and divide it by the total number of matches in those records.

Page 369 Exercise 2

1 a) 15 b) 45 c) 75 d) 750
2 a) 20 b) 100 c) 160
3 a) 20 b) 20 c) 60 d) 100

Page 370 Exercise 3

1 E.g.

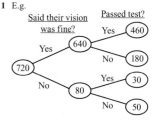

2 a) E.g.

b) $\frac{11}{40} = 0.275$ c) 350

Page 370 Exercise 4

1 a) P(Blue) = 0.22, P(Green) = 0.21, P(White) = 0.18, P(Pink) = 0.39

b) If the spinner was fair, you would expect the relative frequencies of all the colours to be about the same (roughly 0.25). The relative frequency of pink is around twice the size of the others. This suggests that the spinner is biased.

2 a) 20

b) 4 came up a lot more times than you would expect on a fair dice, which suggests the dice may be biased.

3 a)

	Amy	Steve	Hal
No. of tosses	20	60	100
No. of heads	12	33	49
Relative frequency	0.6	0.55	0.49

b) Hal's results are the most reliable as he repeated the experiment the most times.

c) The results suggest the coin is fair, as the relative frequency from Hal's results was very close to 0.5, the result you would expect from a fair coin.

36.4 The AND Rule for Independent Events

Page 371 Exercise 1

1 a) Independent
b) Not independent
c) Independent

2 a) $\frac{1}{12}$ **b)** $\frac{1}{4}$ **c)** $\frac{1}{6}$
d) $\frac{1}{4}$ **e)** $\frac{1}{6}$ **f)** $\frac{1}{6}$

3 a) 90% or 0.9 **b)** 85% or 0.85
c) 1.5% or 0.015 **d)** 76.5% or 0.765

4 a) $\frac{1}{4} = 0.25$ **b)** $\frac{1}{4} = 0.25$ **c)** $\frac{3}{20} = 0.15$

5 a) 0.48 **b)** 0.24 **c)** 0.48

6 Len is wrong.
When one ace has been removed, there are 3 aces remaining out of 51 cards, so the probability is $\frac{4}{52} \times \frac{3}{51} = \frac{1}{221}$

36.5 The OR Rule

Page 372 Exercise 1

1 a) Mutually exclusive
b) Not mutually exclusive
c) Mutually exclusive

2 a) 0.6 **b)** 0.9 **c)** 0.5

3 a) 0.54 **b)** 0.4 **c)** 0.6 **d)** 0.66

4 a) $\frac{1}{3}$ **b)** $\frac{2}{3}$ **c)** $\frac{2}{3}$

5 No, having glasses and having blonde hair are not mutually exclusive (some people could have both) so you can't add the probabilities unless you know that none of the pupils both wear glasses and have blonde hair.

6 a) 0.5
b) The probabilities add up to more than 1 because some people chose more than one sandwich filling.

Page 373 Exercise 2

1 a) $\frac{13}{20}$ **b)** $\frac{9}{20}$

2 a) $\frac{28}{52} = \frac{7}{13}$ **b)** $\frac{22}{52} = \frac{11}{26}$

3 a) $\frac{955}{1500} = \frac{191}{300}$ **b)** $\frac{1190}{1500} = \frac{119}{150}$

4 $\frac{1}{2}$

5 a) $\frac{212}{300} = \frac{53}{75}$ **b)** $\frac{238}{300} = \frac{119}{150}$ **c)** $\frac{1}{2}$

6 $P(A \cup B \cup C)$
$= P(A) + P(B) - P(A \cap B) + P(C)$

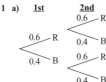

36.6 Using the AND / OR Rules

Page 374 Exercise 1

1 a) 0.25 **b)** 0.25 **c)** 0.5

2 a) 0.44 **b)** 0.11 **c)** 0.09 **d)** 0.53

3 a) 0.25 **b)** 0.0225 **c)** 0.9025
d) 0.0475 **e)** 0.0475 **f)** 0.095

4 a) $\frac{14}{75}$ **b)** $\frac{2}{75}$ **c)** $\frac{67}{225}$ **d)** $\frac{71}{225}$

36.7 Tree Diagrams

Page 375 Exercise 1

1 a)

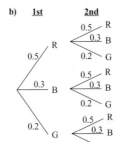

b)

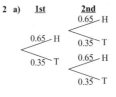

2 a)

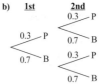

b)

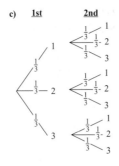

c)

---

d)

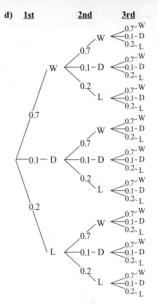

3 a)

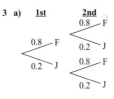

b) 0.64 **c)** 0.32

4 a)

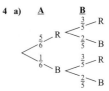

b) (i) $\frac{1}{15}$ **(ii)** $\frac{1}{2}$ **(iii)** $\frac{13}{30}$
(iv) $\frac{13}{30}$ **(v)** $\frac{17}{30}$ **(vi)** $\frac{1}{2}$

5 C = Goes to cinema,
NC = Does not go to cinema:

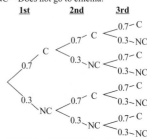

P(C,C,C or NC,NC,NC) = 0.37

6

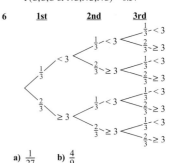

a) $\frac{1}{27}$ **b)** $\frac{4}{9}$

Page 376 Exercise 2

1 a)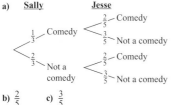
Sally   Jesse

$\frac{1}{3}$ Comedy
$\frac{2}{5}$ Comedy
$\frac{3}{5}$ Not a comedy
$\frac{2}{3}$ Not a comedy
$\frac{2}{5}$ Comedy
$\frac{3}{5}$ Not a comedy

b) $\frac{2}{5}$ c) $\frac{3}{5}$

2   1st   2nd

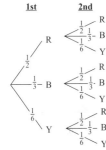

a) $\frac{1}{4}$ b) $\frac{1}{6}$ c) $\frac{1}{18}$
d) $\frac{1}{3}$ e) $\frac{7}{18}$ f) $\frac{11}{18}$
g) $\frac{3}{4}$ h) $\frac{5}{9}$ i) $\frac{25}{36}$

36.8 Conditional Probability

Page 377 Exercise 1

1 $\frac{1}{9}$

2 a) $\frac{13}{29}$ b) $\frac{16}{29}$

3 a) $\frac{1}{4}$ b) $\frac{1}{2}$ c) $\frac{1}{4}$ d) $\frac{1}{8}$

4 a) $\frac{12}{51}$ b) $\frac{39}{51} = \frac{13}{17}$ c) $\frac{13}{51}$
d) $\frac{25}{51}$ e) $\frac{26}{51}$ f) $\frac{3}{51} = \frac{1}{17}$

5 0.04

6 0.08

Page 378 Exercise 2

1 a) $\frac{7}{19}$ b) $\frac{8}{19}$

c)   1st   2nd   d) $\frac{14}{95}$ e) $\frac{33}{95}$

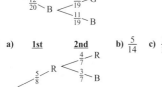
$\frac{8}{20}$ G
$\frac{7}{19}$ G
$\frac{12}{19}$ B
$\frac{12}{20}$ B
$\frac{8}{19}$ G
$\frac{11}{19}$ B

2 a)   1st   2nd   b) $\frac{5}{14}$ c) $\frac{13}{28}$
$\frac{5}{8}$ R
$\frac{4}{7}$ R
$\frac{3}{7}$ B
$\frac{3}{8}$ B
$\frac{5}{7}$ R
$\frac{2}{7}$ B

3 a)   1st   2nd

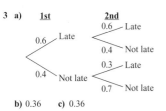
0.6 Late
0.6 Late
0.4 Not late
0.4 Not late
0.3 Late
0.7 Not late

b) 0.36   c) 0.36

4   1st   2nd

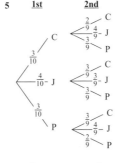
$\frac{8}{12}$ B
$\frac{7}{11}$ B
$\frac{4}{11}$ G
$\frac{4}{12}$ G
$\frac{8}{11}$ B
$\frac{3}{11}$ G

a) $\frac{14}{33}$ b) $\frac{10}{11}$ c) $\frac{17}{33}$

5   1st   2nd

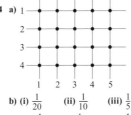
$\frac{3}{10}$ C
$\frac{2}{9}$ C
$\frac{4}{9}$ J
$\frac{3}{9}$ P
$\frac{4}{10}$ J
$\frac{3}{9}$ C
$\frac{3}{9}$ J
$\frac{3}{9}$ P
$\frac{3}{10}$ P
$\frac{3}{9}$ C
$\frac{4}{9}$ J
$\frac{2}{9}$ P

a) $\frac{1}{15}$ b) $\frac{4}{15}$ c) $\frac{2}{3}$
d) $\frac{4}{15}$ e) $\frac{11}{15}$ f) $\frac{7}{15}$

6 a) $\frac{7}{45}$ b) $\frac{22}{65}$

7 a) $\frac{1}{12}$ b) $\frac{5}{12}$

8 a) 0.125   b) 0.575   c) 0.005

Page 379 Exercise 3

1 a) $\frac{75}{137}$ b) $\frac{60}{137}$ c) $\frac{16}{137}$
d) $\frac{4}{15}$ e) $\frac{36}{124} = \frac{9}{31}$

2 a) $\frac{2}{3}$ b) $\frac{25}{33}$ c) $\frac{9}{19}$
d) $\frac{2}{19}$ e) $\frac{1}{4}$ f) $\frac{10}{33}$
g) 1

36.9 Probability Problems

Page 380 Exercise 1

1 a) $\frac{1}{5}$ b) $\frac{3}{10}$ c) $\frac{19}{40}$
d) $\frac{21}{40}$ e) $\frac{1}{2}$ f) $\frac{1}{2}$

2 a) 0.3   b) 0.85   c) 8

3 a) 0.998   b) (i) 120   (ii) 59 880

4 a)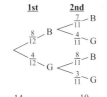

b) (i) $\frac{1}{20}$ (ii) $\frac{1}{10}$ (iii) $\frac{1}{5}$
(iv) $\frac{4}{5}$ (v) $\frac{1}{5}$ (vi) $\frac{4}{5}$
c) 20

5 a)

	1	2	3	4	5	6	7	8
1	0	1	2	3	4	5	6	7
2	1	0	1	2	3	4	5	6
3	2	1	0	1	2	3	4	5
4	3	2	1	0	1	2	3	4
5	4	3	2	1	0	1	2	3

b) (i) $\frac{1}{8}$ (ii) $\frac{1}{5}$ (iii) $\frac{3}{40}$
(iv) $\frac{1}{20}$ (v) $\frac{7}{40}$ (vi) $\frac{9}{40}$
(vii) $\frac{1}{8}$ (viii) $\frac{1}{40}$ (ix) $\frac{7}{20}$
(x) $\frac{13}{20}$ (xi) $\frac{11}{40}$ (xii) $\frac{29}{40}$

6 a) $\frac{19}{50}$ b) $\frac{87}{200}$ c) $\frac{1}{20}$ d) $\frac{27}{200}$

7 a) (i) $\frac{17}{30}$ (ii) $\frac{1}{30}$ b) 4

8 a) P(1) = 0.28, P(2) = 0.17,
P(3) = 0.27, P(4) = 0.28

b) If the dice was fair, you would expect all
the relative frequencies to be about the
same. The relative frequency of 2 is much
lower than the others, which suggests the
dice is biased.

c) 0.45   d) 0.085

9 a) 0.64   b) 0.04   c) 0.16   d) 0.32

10 a)   1st   2nd

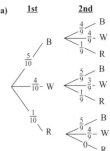
$\frac{5}{10}$ B
$\frac{4}{9}$ B
$\frac{4}{9}$ W
$\frac{1}{9}$ R
$\frac{4}{10}$ W
$\frac{5}{9}$ B
$\frac{3}{9}$ W
$\frac{1}{9}$ R
$\frac{1}{10}$ R
$\frac{5}{9}$ B
$\frac{4}{9}$ W
0 R

b) (i) $\frac{2}{9}$ (ii) $\frac{2}{9}$ (iii) $\frac{5}{9}$
(iv) $\frac{7}{9}$ (v) $\frac{4}{45}$ (vi) $\frac{29}{45}$

11 a) 0.13   b) TV
c) (i) 0.22   (ii) 0.2   (iii) 0.42
(iv) 0.53   (v) 0.7
d) (i) 0.0049   (ii) 0.0225

12 a) $\frac{5}{28}$ b) $\frac{1}{56}$ c) $\frac{15}{28}$ d) $\frac{15}{56}$

Index

Shira Glassman

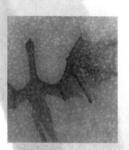

The Second Mango

Shira Glassman

The Second Mango

This is a work of fiction. Names, characters, places, and incidents either are the product of the author's imagination or are used fictitiously. While this novel is inspired by historical events, it is a fictionalized portrayal, and the author created all characters, events and storylines in the pursuit of literary fiction, not historical accuracy.

The Second Mango
PRIZM
An imprint of Torquere Press, Inc.
PO Box 2545
Round Rock, TX 78680
Copyright 2013 © by Shira Glassman
Cover illustration by BSClay
Published with permission
ISBN: 978-1-61040-526-3
www.prizmbooks.com
www.torquerepress.com

Psalms 23:1-2, as translated by Dr. Alana M. Vincent, Lecturer in Jewish Studies, Department of Theology & Religious Studies, University of Chester, UK, Esther 7:3 as translated by Dr. Alana M. Vincent, Lecturer in Jewish Studies, Department of Theology & Religious Studies, University of Chester, UK

All quoted literature sourced from the public domain.

First Prizm Printing: August 2013
Printed in the USA

prizm
there's room under the rainbow
www.prizmbooks.com

The Second Mango

Shira Glassman

The Second Mango

Dedication

Dedicated to my good friend Anastasia "Ducky" Bower, and in memory of my father.

The Second Mango

Chapter 1: The Northerner

Once upon a time, in a lush tropical land of agricultural riches and shining white buildings, there was a young queen who spent the night tied up in a tent, panicking.

Apparently, a visit to a bawdy house got you kidnapped.

That wasn't entirely accurate. Queen Shulamit was sure that plenty of men went in and out of such places every night without so much as losing a hair on their heads. But a skinny woman of barely twenty—even one who had been queen of Perach for two whole months—well, that was a different story. Especially if that young queen had ditched her bodyguards and snuck out by herself.

It didn't feel real. Shulamit had the same numb feeling she had gotten two months earlier, when they'd first told her that her father was going to die. *But can't I go back to yesterday?* She visualized herself turning a page backward in a book, undoing her part in the events of the previous evening.

She wondered if her bodyguards were close to finding her. She knew they were looking—the queen's safety was their entire career. They were probably very frustrated with her right now, and she couldn't blame them. That is, if they even knew where she was. The only sign they had of where she'd gone was her frantic scream—"I'm the queen! Tell the palace! *Get help!*"—to two of the so-called "willing women" as she was carried away wrapped

in a bolt of cloth.

Eventually, she knew from eavesdropping, someone from the court would have to ransom her if she wasn't rescued. How long would that take? She'd been tied up in the tent like this for hours, long enough that fear and shame had been joined by boredom and hunger. Her stomach gnawed at itself, but she was worried that even if her kidnappers gave her something to eat, she'd throw up or—or worse.

One comfort was that she was still wearing all of her clothes, and, blissfully, the men guarding her were ignoring her at the moment. She felt thankful for her average looks. If the men had gone anywhere near her *like that—*

She was roused from her self-absorbed stupor by noises outside the brigands' tent. Maybe they were fighting over whether or not to rape her after all, instead of just worrying about money. *Please, Aba, no, no. Please send someone to rescue me.* Or maybe there was a mutiny in the ranks! That sounded much better.

Or maybe the commotion was caused by the big blond warrior wearing a cloth mask over the bottom half of his face who now burst into the tent, scattering sleepy guards with a fist and a gigantic sword.

"I hope you're on my side," Shulamit found herself saying, frightened anew by his foreignness. Like all of her people, her skin was medium brown, but this man's was much lighter, and his body was taller and bulkier than even most of her guards. Where had he come from?

"*Malka?* Queen?"

"No, I'm the head kidnapper," Shulamit snapped. "How do you like my Queen Shulamit costume? I'm practicing for my singing debut." Was this stranger out for his own ends, stealing from thieves and kidnapping from kidnappers? That would make it even harder for her

bodyguards to track her down.

"Very funny. No, I'm not one of the bad guys. I'm your hired help." The warrior was already untying her bonds, tugging at ropes and slicing them with a dagger in places where the brigands had gotten virtuosic with their knots. "Are you unharmed?"

"For the most part." Shulamit studied the warrior. "Who are you?" His brown leather tunic was sleeveless, leaving plenty of room for the powerful muscles of his upper arms. Hair exploded in a messy tangle of several yellows from the base of his helmet down past his shoulders. His thick, sleek eyebrows were darker than his hair, and his speech was accented—although the northern folk used the same alphabet, their language was different.

"I'm Riv." There was a respectful pause, and a bow from the neck. "Mercenary and bounty hunter. I travel, I fight—I do what needs doing. Your bodyguards are out looking for you, but since they wanted you back before anyone else knew you'd been taken, they also hired *me*. Lucky for them!"

"Lucky for me," added Shulamit. "You're... from the north?"

"You can tell?" Riv smirked. "I think I got all the knots. Let's go!"

Shulamit barely had time to brace herself nervously for such intimate contact with the body of a strange man before Riv scooped her up into his mighty arms and flung her over his shoulder. He carried her out of the tent, pausing here and there to launch powerful kicks at the surprised brigands, but mostly running all the way. The next thing Shulamit knew, she had been plunked down roughly onto the back of an enormous horse, bigger than any she'd ever seen, and Riv had leapt up behind her. The horse immediately broke into a run.

But the men who had kidnapped her had horses too.

"They're gaining on us," Shulamit pointed out.

"No, they're not."

The horse reared on its back legs, sending Shulamit backward into Riv's torso. Then they were suddenly rising away from the ground, and the horse had turned green. A robust and powerful wave of muscle on each side pushed them farther into the air. Shulamit hadn't expected the horse to fly, and she certainly hadn't expected green wings either—

"But this was a *horse*!"

"And now she's a dragon. And you're a freed prisoner. Congratulations." Riv looked self-satisfied and patted the dragon's side. As a dragon, the beast was even larger; certainly big enough to carry the two of them, and maybe even a third person. Her scales were a deep, dark green, and textured, like a jeweled avocado rind, and they covered most of her, except the short, stubby horns on her head, which were a dull gold, like dirty jewelry. Two enormous wings, angular and with pointed tips like a bat's, stuck out from her sides and propelled them through the air. Beyond Riv at the back of the dragon, the queen caught glimpses of a powerfully muscled tail.

Shulamit was entranced—she'd never seen a dragon this close before. In fact, she hadn't seen a dragon since her father's fiftieth birthday celebration several years ago, when lots of exotic and exciting things were brought to the palace for the general amusement of its residents. She had liked it then and had wanted a closer look, but her father was concerned for her safety and wouldn't permit her to observe it from anywhere except the dais from which they watched the aerial performance. How ironic, considering the great man had never thought elephants unsafe as long as you weren't underfoot. Shulamit hadn't had any reason to disagree until the day her father fell off the one he was riding during his return from a diplomatic

visit. She had a horror of elephants now. But she still loved dragons, and this one was first-rate.

She peered around the countryside, where the first rays of sun glittered over the palm trees. "Wow, they really took me a long way outside the city."

"Did your captors give you any food?" Riv asked.

"I haven't eaten all night."

"There's a pita in my bag."

"Thanks, but I can't," said the queen sadly.

"Can't?"

Shulamit didn't answer. If her own servants didn't believe her about her food problems, what hope had she with a stranger? After her ordeal, she certainly didn't have the energy to argue.

The beast swerved upward slightly, shifting against the wind, and Shulamit once again slid backward against Riv's chest. What she thought she felt the first time she'd crashed into Riv upon liftoff was definitely there, confirming her suspicions. "Your dragon's not the only one of you who's hiding things."

There was only silence behind her as Riv waited for her to continue—apparently, too seasoned to finish Shulamit's thoughts for her, in case the little queen was bluffing.

"You're a woman."

"What if I am?"

"You're a woman dressed as a man." Shulamit's mind was racing, and she whirled her head around to face her rescuer. "Does that mean you seek women for love... like I do?" The words tumbled out impulsively, the child of a night without affection and a morning without breakfast. From beneath her thick, dark brows she gazed into Riv's undeniably foreign gray-blue eyes and tried to look as alluring as an underslept hungry person could possibly manage.

Riv laughed, her face relaxing, probably relieved that she wasn't having her reputation or skill challenged. "No, it does not," said Riv. "Except as friends, of course, and I think maybe we're already friends."

"Oh." Shulamit was still too tired and her stomach too empty—or possibly, she was too much a monarch—to be anything but blunt. "I mean, yes—yes, we can be friends."

"Careful—your sadness is bringing down the dragon," said Riv. It took Shulamit a moment to realize Riv was only teasing. "By the way, I'm really Rivka. But don't let anyone else hear that, Your Majesty."

"You're a very good fighter," said Shulamit, still feeling rather awkward as she turned back around to face forward, her neck hurting from craning around for so long. She was riding pressed very close to the chest of this person and confused over whether or not it was okay to enjoy herself, now that she knew definitely that Rivka was not interested.

"Thank you! I know, as a paid mercenary, it's probably none of my business, but as a new friend... that wonderful retinue of bodyguards you keep—how did you manage to get stolen from under their noses?"

Shulamit sighed. "I wasn't under their noses. I snuck out." If only her bodyguards would stop acting like baby-sitters and had agreed to go with her. How aggravating it was that they hadn't allowed her to go—especially since it would have meant an excuse to venture inside themselves under the pretext of chaste employment. Any man would welcome that! Well, most men, anyway.

Shulamit reasoned that if there were women like her who sought other women—and she'd had a sweetheart once, so she knew she wasn't the only one, even if Rivka wasn't one of them—there must be men who sought other men. Once she was out of her current predicament, she wondered if she shouldn't fire all her bodyguards and find

some of that sort. Surely, *they* would understand and not go around constantly trying to protect her from herself.

Rivka's jaw dropped. "All this trouble—"

"I know, I know! And I'm sorry." Shulamit sighed, apologizing silently once again to her dead father. This was not how she was supposed to be ruling from his throne. "I just—I wanted—" She paused for a moment, knowing she probably shouldn't be talking about her indiscretions. On the other hand, Rivka was the first real ally she'd had since Aviva's disappearance, and besides, she held Rivka's secret herself, so it was likely Rivka wouldn't talk. "I went to a bawdy house. I don't have a sweetheart—"

"You know what you do have? You have a hole in the head," said Rivka, trying to sound cross but with a strong feeling of indulgent pity coming through anyway. "Pardon my directness, Your Majesty, but why not just ask for a woman to be brought in—if a young queen really has to pay for love to begin with?"

"My bodyguards are still loyal to my father, may he rest, and not to me. They wouldn't bring a woman in, or escort me there themselves, either. I loved my father, but I don't agree with all of his rules."

Rivka took so long to respond that for a moment, Shulamit was nervous that she'd said something wrong. Then, finally, Rivka snorted, almost to herself, "To get between a young lady and her first kiss."

"I have had that," Shulamit pointed out. "That, and more." She tensed up, half in defiance, half in fear, waiting for Rivka to disapprove.

"I don't condemn you, Your Majesty," said Rivka. "I've never even kissed a man, but I've lived it all in my heart."

"If you've never—I—how do you know you like men at all?" Shulamit asked, hope creeping back into her face.

"He's dead."

"Oh. I'm sorry." Shulamit looked down. "Mine ran away. I mean—the woman I loved."

Rivka patted her gently on the head. "Begging your pardon for my familiarity, of course, Your Majesty."

"I'd really like to find a new love," said Shulamit. "But I don't know how to find someone else who's different like I am. That first time was a happy accident. So I brought gold to a bawdy house to buy a woman's favors. The only favor I got was about five seconds of looking at her bare bosom. Then I was carried off."

Rivka exhaled loudly through her nose.

"Do you think there are many women like me?"

"I have no idea," said Rivka. "This is the first time I ever really sat down and talked with someone like you."

Shulamit was silent for a long while, knitting up an idea in her mind. Several moments were punctuated only with the sound of the dragon's flapping wings.

Then, the queen broke the silence. "Do you want to be a warrior forever?"

Rivka answered right away. "Combat is my passion. Doing good is my mission. And feeding my face and keeping the horse in grain, of course."

Shulamit's voice changed. Suddenly, she was *Malka Shulamit bat Noach*, Queen of Perach. "In that case, I have a mission for you—if you accept. I'll find a way to make you Captain of my Guard if you'll find me a woman to cherish, and who'd cherish me in return."

Chapter 2: The Agreement

The sun had crept high and was melting its way back down the brilliant blue sky when Rivka crossed the palace green to the queen's private garden. She was still in her male disguise, despite the way the cloth made her sweat in these tropical climates far from home.

The queen was seated on velvet cushions beside the spiky-leaved pandanus trees that hung over the river. Several of her ladies-in-waiting lounged around her, but not too close, gossiping quietly. Shulamit herself was not speaking to anyone, but instead stared intently at a book in her lap as she picked at a bowl of fruit resting beside her in the grass.

The ladies-in-waiting all stared at Rivka and whispered to each other as she stalked up between them. "Your Majesty," said Rivka, bowing deeply. "One of your guards said you sent for me."

"Friends," Shulamit announced in her royal voice. "This is the man who rescued me last night. I'm grateful for his skill."

Rivka knew that despite Shulamit's obvious lack of discretion with these ladies about her own activities, the queen had kept *her* secret. "I'm glad to see you looking well, Your Majesty."

"Have my bodyguards rewarded you—generously?"

"They've been more than generous," said Rivka, whose heart was as light as her purse was now full.

"Good," said Shulamit. "Come closer. We have plans to make."

Rivka approached her. "What are you reading?"

She was expecting to hear the name of some traditional love story, or perhaps one of the more exciting, newer tales, and was taken aback when the queen answered, "*Canon of Counterfeits*."

"What?"

"It's about how to tell the difference between counterfeits and real art—gold or something adulterated with another metal—or if someone's forged an artifact of antiquity. Oh, you can sit down."

Rivka plopped down onto the grass. She had no cushion and didn't need one.

Shulamit's voice dropped so that only Rivka could hear her. "Have you thought about my proposal?"

"I have, Majesty. It would be an honor and a thrill to win that position. I'll give your quest my all, if you hold to your promise."

"I will, absolutely. I swear it. Besides, I like you." An eager expression, half-sheepish, half-seductive, slipped across her face for a moment.

"As I told you, little Queenling, *Malkeleh*, nothing happens to me when we're close. I don't feel that way about women, and I'm not the one you seek."

"*We* seek," Shulamit corrected. She held out her hand, and Rivka, still acting the male, kissed it ceremoniously and without emotion. "You win. I'll be good."

"Are none of your ladies-in-waiting interested in other women?" Rivka asked, wondering if they'd had to fight off the queen's advances too.

"Oh, *no*," said Shulamit, shaking her head slowly. "I don't even think they all understand it, entirely. I know a couple of them think that if they could just find me a prince beautiful enough, I'd stop being so strange."

"Yes, a prince with breasts," said Rivka in a low, throaty chuckle.

"If I think about having to touch a man that way, I feel like I'm trying to run away with my legs stuck on backwards. When I think about women it feels so natural and right and correct. I can't explain it, other than to tell you this must be how men feel. But I know I'm not a man. Despite having the smallest breasts in court, I still feel very womanly." Shulamit looked down at her spindly body, then back up at Rivka with a more businesslike expression. "Do you have any ideas about where we can find me a partner?"

"Well," Rivka began, "I gossiped with some of your bodyguards as they were waiting for you to wake up, and apparently one of them saw a show in a bawdy house where the women—"

"But that was for money," Shulamit interrupted. "That doesn't mean they like it when they're not being paid."

"And of course there are women who dress as men because they prefer to live as men, and not because it eases their career as a traveling warrior," Rivka continued glibly.

"They sound delightful! But how would I know if someone was hiding a secret like that?" Shulamit's brow furrowed. "The only reason I—it's not like I can bump into everyone's chest by mistake." She grimaced at her near slip.

"Maybe if you issued a proclamation for all the women in the land who could love the queen to come visit the palace—"

"No, no," said Shulamit, shaking her head in a tiny, frantic motion. "Think of all the ways that could go wrong. They could be men wearing dresses just to sneak into the competition; they could be women pretending to be like me but only to get at the power of the throne

and not really *love* me. And my bodyguards!" She looked sick. "They'd be scandalized and nagging me constantly."

"You could order them not to," Rivka pointed out, noting not for the first time since their meeting that the queen was still so very young, and acted even younger. Perhaps this is what came of a pampered and sheltered upbringing.

"Yeah, because *that's* been working out so far."

"You have to believe in your own authority if you want anyone else to," Rivka commented.

"I have another idea," said the queen, rather conspicuously changing the subject. "What if a woman didn't want to marry a man—ever—but didn't have as much freedom as I do?" Seeing a blank look in Rivka's eyes, she continued. "She could join one of the holy houses. Sure, there's the vow of poverty, a life of service... but if it were my only choice, it might almost be worth it."

"What are you talking about?"

"The celibate sisters in the temples."

"Our temples don't have celibate attendants up north, just rabbis," Rivka explained in a tense voice. Both countries celebrated the same holidays and worshipped the same One God, but naturally, the customs deviated. "Celibacy isn't part of our worship. That's for wizards..." She relaxed the fists she had unconsciously clenched.

"We have rabbis too," Shulamit explained, "but since the reign of my father's grandfather there are also temples where women can go and live by themselves."

"Huh."

"They dress very plainly—usually just a simple old robe dyed yellow with turmeric."

"Oh, yes, yes," said Rivka. "I think maybe I saw some of them without knowing what the clothing meant."

"Anyway, I'm sure among all the holy houses in Perach

there's got to be at least one woman who's only in there so she won't have to lie down with a man against her nature."

"Didn't you say something about a celibacy vow?" Rivka slipped one hand beneath her cloth mask to wipe off a layer of sweat that had suddenly become intolerable.

"Maybe she only took the vow because she thought she didn't have any other choice," Shulamit pointed out enthusiastically. "There are at least three holy houses a few days' ride of Home City. Will you take me there, Riv? It's the best idea I've got."

Rivka thought it a fairly simplistic idea, and was concerned that Shulamit might discover nothing more than a number of women who didn't wish to be disturbed. But she could see the restless loneliness in the little queen, and it called on deeply buried needs to be asked to protect her. And neither did she have a better idea. How *should* a young woman with such... different... tastes find another like her? Rivka certainly had no idea. "You're coming with me?"

"I have to love her, don't I? Anyhow, I can't leave a decision as important as this to someone who loves only men."

"You make a good argument."

"I'll announce that I need some time in a holy house to meditate. The individual ministers of each bureau can oversee the kingdom while I'm gone—and then you and I can go searching for likely candidates for a woman to rescue!"

"If she wants rescuing," added Rivka.

"My bodyguards will probably jump for joy that I'm being so spiritual, especially after last night," said Shulamit. "They'll love the idea of you as my protection, since you've already proven that you're more than competent in keeping me out of trouble."

"I hope I can keep it up!"

"And your dragon as well," Shulamit added. "Can we ride her the whole way, or will she wear out?"

"She can't remain a dragon for the entire journey, but she'll be able to carry us as a mare as long as she's well treated. You're small."

Shulamit grinned weakly, more of a grimace than a smile. "I know. Sometimes when I look down at my wrists I'm shocked at how thin they are. Like I could snap in half like a stick."

"I won't let anyone snap you in half."

"Hurray, I've got hired muscle!" Now the grin was self-conscious, but happier.

The sky was darkening, and the ladies-in-waiting were picking up their cushions and brushing off the dust from the ground. "Come, Majesty," one of them called. "Come inside before the rain."

Rivka watched them flutter back toward the palace, each carrying a cushion except for the queen, who had given hers to one of the other women. She grinned and shook her head.

"Queenling," Rivka said in her own language to the droplets of rain that were beginning to fall, "There aren't any velvet cushions out there."

Chapter 3: Dawn and the Beginning of a Journey

The two women set out the following morning at dawn's first light so they could achieve a considerable distance before they were overtaken by the heat of the afternoon. Shulamit had been unable to sleep all night, her head filled with anticipation and dreams about both the journey and the woman she hoped she would meet upon it. It was therefore natural that within a few minutes of Dragon the Horse breaking into her gentle lope, the queen nodded off completely.

Rivka easily shielded her with the bulk of her body. The people of Perach were smaller in every dimension than those of the far cold north, and to the mercenary, Shulamit's body almost felt like a child's. She rode into the damp dawn air, holding back from her usual one-sided conversation with Dragon so she wouldn't disturb her sleeping passenger, and instead kept her own counsel.

Shulamit woke when Rivka let Dragon rest in the afternoon, during the worst heat of the day. They'd stopped beside a stream flanked by coconut palms and pandanus trees. Under the uneven shade of their sword-shaped leaves, she dipped her hands in the water and wiped the dust from her eyes. "How far have we gone?"

"We're halfway to Ir Ilan," said Rivka. "We'll stay the

night there, and by the next night, if we push ourselves, we should come to the first of the temples. I know it's at least a full day's ride from any settlements."

"You know your way around Perach," Shulamit remarked. She peered into the stream curiously to check if the twisted knots of braided hair at the base of her neck had survived her horseback nap intact.

"I've been among your people long enough. Two years it's been since I left..." Rivka's voice sounded as though she had been about to say more to complete the thought, like "my people" or "home," or even just "the north," but then she just stopped. Behind her, the horse grazed peacefully on the bank of the stream.

There was so much Shulamit wanted to ask her that it was hard to choose where to begin. "Did you always know you wanted to be a warrior?"

Rivka smiled broadly. "As far back as I can remember. I used to pick up sticks in the courtyard of my uncle's castle and embarrass him by trying to swordfight with his guards." A sparkle like broken glass shone from her eyes, proudly defiant.

"Castle? Are you... are you of noble birth?"

"I don't know how to answer that," said Rivka. "My mother is the younger sister of the baron of our valley. My father, he was a farmhand who worked at the castle growing vegetables. She was a lot younger than you are now when they ran him out of town. You've been around palaces and the politics of reputation and decorum all your life—you can probably imagine how ashamed my uncle was that I dared to exist at all." She looked away at the horse, then back at the queen.

"It sounds so painful—but yet you're so calm when you talk about it."

"It was years ago," said Rivka, "and I have my own life and my own accomplishments to be proud of now.

Believe me, I have my grievances with my uncle, and our relationship's basically beyond repair, but I found a way to forgive him on Yom Kippur. If I let my losses conquer me, I can't fight, nor smile, nor live."

"Your mother must have been a little bit like me," said Shulamit. "I had a sweetheart once, from the palace staff too. She was our palace's second cook. I love her—loved her so much sometimes I felt like I could burst open just from looking at her." Thoughts of a bosomy beauty with a goofy smile, her hair piled up on her head with a couple of sticks through it and some of it coming down around her ears unevenly, brought a tugging hunger to the queen's heart. "She was the first person to cook me food that didn't make me sick. We figured it out together, and became friends... and then... but then she acted distant and cranky, and I didn't know why, and then one day she was gone. There was a note saying that she was leaving and that I shouldn't ever try to find her or contact her. I went looking for her at her parents' house anyway, but her father said she had decided to go work as a cook somewhere else—somewhere far away. I figured if I kept looking for her after that I'd be crossing a line."

"I'm sorry that was her choice," said Rivka, "but I'm sure we'll find someone out there for you. What was that bit about food making you sick?"

Shulamit looked at her a little timidly, used to the reactions of everyone else in her life. *Oh, Princess Shulamit, her father's precious little darling, can't bear the thought of food unless it's made of solid gold and served by holy women. She pretends to be ill to look delicate.* "It started a couple of years ago. Nobody could explain it, and eventually they just decided I was shamming. Aviva—the cook I was telling you about—she fed me very pure foods one at a time until we figured out the foods my body rejects."

"Rejects?"

"Do you really want details?" Shulamit grinned hideously, frightened inside. There was a part of her that had always wondered if Aviva had left because she was unable to contain her disgust anymore. Chicken was worse than wheat—all bread did was knock her out with stomach cramps and indigestion, but chicken and other fowl—she cringed with self-loathing, thinking of the mess.

"How about no. So what can't you eat?"

"The short version—fowl and wheat."

"No *wheat*?" Rivka's eyes widened. "No—no pita, no... and wait, no chicken soup when you're sick?!"

Shulamit nodded. "Tell me about it. So I make do. I've learned little tricks—when I eat flesh, or cooked vegetables, for that matter, I have to make sure the cooking surface hasn't seen a fowl, or has been cleaned recently."

"Sounds complicated. How can you tell what's making you sick? Are you sure you're not being poisoned? The king of Imbrio—"

Shulamit shook her head. "No, that was the first thing they tested, when my father was still alive. I was the only person who got sick—nothing was wrong with the food. Then he hired a magician, because he thought it might be a curse. But the magician said I wasn't under any spells, and after that, nobody believed me anymore. The whole court decided it was all in my mind and gave up on solving it. The head cook even tried to trick me into eating the things that were making me sick—she was convinced that if I didn't know it was there, the symptoms would go away."

"I'm guessing it didn't work."

"Then finally, after days of pain and not being able to keep anything down, Aviva came to me with nothing

but a glass of water. She said that's where we were going to start, and we'd try adding back foods one at a time, prepared simply, until something made me sick. Then we'd know for sure what it was."

What Aviva had actually said was, *We'll add one new food or ingredient each day until we've found all the eggs the chickens have hidden in the grass.* Her colorful speech complemented the rainbow of food stains across her clothing, mostly the brilliant orange-gold of turmeric.

"So what are you going to do about food when we get to Ir Ilan?" Rivka's brow furrowed. "I doubt the local inns want you nosing around in the kitchen inspecting the pans, and you won't be able to control stray wheat flour."

"I know. I've been dreading their reaction all morning. People never believe me, and then they lie and say they've done what I asked them to do when they haven't, and I have no way to tell until—" She waved her hand around helplessly.

"What about the public market? With the open stalls, you can watch the food cook and then just pick the ones who are doing it your way. Then you won't have to convince anyone of anything."

"That would be much better." Shulamit sighed with relief. "Hopefully I'll find someone selling lamb or vegetables."

"We'd better get back on the road, then, or most of the vendors will pack up for the night before we get there."

They passed the rest of their riding time that day singing, sometimes teaching each other new songs, sometimes singing ones they both knew in two-part harmony. Shulamit's voice was a pretty soprano, but she couldn't project very well; Rivka had a bellowing alto that was startling compared with her gruff, throaty "Riv" voice intended to imitate a male.

The women were still singing when they reached the

gates to the town. Rivka pulled on the reins of the horse to pause her so she could tie the cloth mask around her face again. "Queenling, you should probably also be disguised. We attract less trouble if we attract less attention."

"I guess you know best," said Shulamit. She removed the filmy, decorative scarf from her neck and repositioned it as a head covering, wrapping it back around her neck when her black braids were hidden and her face in shadow.

The marketplace was a colorful paradise of food, flowers, and useful household objects. Brightly colored fruits and vegetables spilled out of woven baskets, and in one stall shoppers could buy a different kind of olive for every day of the week. There were also people selling honey or cheese, and a boy talking to everyone who would listen about the scarves his very pregnant mother, sitting in the shade at the back of the stall fanning herself and drinking out of a coconut, had hand-painted in hues of sunset and dusk.

A young man with bushy hair hovered at one of the stalls, examining several different piles of vegetables. He was carrying a large basket, and Shulamit watched him work out some sort of deal with the farmer behind the table. He walked away with the basket filled to the brim with stalks of kohl sprouts. From the quantity, Shulamit guessed it must be for a restaurant, and her mind drifted to a conversation she'd had ages ago, with Aviva.

"You went to the market yourself?" Shulamit had arrived at Aviva's kitchen house to find the buxom cook unpacking a basket full of unusual delicacies. "Why didn't you just send one of the kitchen servants like the head cook does?"

"What, with some list I got out of my head?" Aviva retrieved a strange vegetable from her basket. "How

*would I ever know what was new, or fresh, or get any
ideas? Same old clothes is not what I'm good at."*

*"What is that?" Shulamit studied the unfamiliar item.
It looked like a fluorescent-green cauliflower, but instead
of florets, each section rose into perfectly mathematical
spiraling peaks. She was transfixed by its beauty and stood
there staring, almost in disbelief that such a thing had
grown naturally instead of sculpted by human hands—let
alone intended for eating!*

*"I don't know, but we'd never have the chance to find
out if I wasn't the type to go to market on my own."*

The memory was so vivid that for a moment she
almost felt as though Aviva was there with her, but the
feeling faded quickly. Swallowing her loneliness, Shulamit
hopped from stall to stall, peering inside at the cooks
preparing their victuals. Of course, the most convenient
takeaway food would have been anything in a pita, but
that door was closed forever—or opened into a night of
indigestion. She eventually found enough to eat, because
the man selling lamb kabobs didn't have meat other than
lamb, and the woman selling rice balls was wrapping
them in banana leaves. She also picked up a mango, and
then, after thinking about it for a moment, bought a
second as well.

Meanwhile, Rivka kept one eye on Shulamit and the
other eye on a display of daggers. Should she buy one for
the young queen? Or would it just be a liability, because a
weapon in the hands of an untrained innocent can easily
be used against her? She realized it would probably be a
good idea to start teaching Shulamit weaponless martial
arts the next time they were out in the open.

They took a room in the Cross-Eyed Tiger, a wholesome-

looking inn near the marketplace. An advertisement on the door bragged about the food, and the rates were reasonable. The story they gave the proprietor was simply that a woman had hired protection for her trip to the holy house, which wasn't untrue.

Rivka put their things in the room and then stopped at the cook's stewpot for a plate of something that looked like overcooked chicken and smelled mediocre at best. She could also tell by looking at it that it was going to be too spicy, so she heaped yogurt onto it until the cook glared at her. As if she cared.

Shulamit was sitting and eating her lamb kabobs and other finds from the market, when Rivka appeared with a loaded plate. "I should have done that," Rivka commented. "Look at this." She glared at her food.

"I bought you a mango," said Shulamit brightly, handing her the second mango. Until that moment, she hadn't been entirely sure whether it was Rivka's dessert or her own midnight snack. To her surprise, she was genuinely happy that she had decided to give it to Rivka.

"Thank you, Shula!" Rivka began to attack her plate of strangeness with gusto.

Shulamit's face froze slightly, so Rivka reminded her in a whisper, "I can't call you Queenling here. Too risky."

As if to illustrate her point, a group of drunk men at a nearby table had noticed them and began to heckle. "Hey! How come she's got better food than the rest of us?" shouted one.

"They've got mangoes!"

"What is this swill?"

"I want some of that lamb."

One of the men approached the women's table. "That's

not fair. Why did he give you better food than everyone else?"

Shulamit looked up from her plate of food with an expression of deep anger, almost like a threatened animal, but before she could say anything, Rivka leapt to her defense. "She bought it in the market. Fowl makes her ill."

"Yeah, well, this food would make anyone ill. Hand it over."

Rivka stood up to her full height, towering over him. "You really don't want to mess with me," she growled at him, fingering the hilt of her sword. "Or I might have to buy you a drink with this steel."

The man's eyes opened into wide circles, and he backed away, stumbling. "My apologies, sir." He went back to his table, and nobody bothered them again.

"A traveling comedian he's expecting, not a warrior," Rivka muttered, going back to her food. Shulamit was looking at her with an expression warm like the firelight that lit the room.

"Riv—thank you."

"Oh, that was nothing! Aren't I your—what did you say—hired muscle?"

"No, I mean—thank you for believing me." She paused. "Back at home, I'm a queen. I used to be a princess. So many people think I made up my food problems to get attention, or that I'm just lying to get everyone to take my preferences more seriously."

"Hey," said Riv through a mouthful of chicken curry, "never underestimate your right to the things you like. You have a right to eat mangoes if you want to. Or chase women."

"I guess you're right," said Shulamit, smiling with half her mouth. She appreciated Rivka's support, but "chase" had made her feel awkward. There was a strong

physical component to her longings, true, but she hoped Rivka knew that it went beyond that. She was looking for a woman to love, for the sweet mutual understanding of hearts that share each other's secrets—not just a concubine. "But anyway, I really do get sick if I eat the wrong things, or even the right things prepared the wrong way—near the wrong things, I mean. And I'll get sick whether people believe me or not. Aviva was the first person to believe me—and sometimes I feel like she's the only person. Even though I've finally gotten the palace cooks to serve me food that I can eat safely, they all just think I'm being finicky."

"No wonder you fell in love with her," Rivka observed.

"So why did *you* believe me?"

Rivka smiled thoughtfully. "Because you talk to me like a human being," she said, "and not like I'm just part of the peasant crowd beneath your feet. Because you're not the type of person to play the game you just described. You're interested in me and in my story—I know there are questions you're dying to ask and just haven't worked up the nerve. I see it in your face. It means you see me as a person."

They continued eating in peace, their friendship growing by the firelight like a sprouting plant under the rays of the sun.

Chapter 4: Boots

Shulamit lay in bed, wide awake because she had spent the morning sleeping, her brains slowly cooking from being up and down at the wrong times. She wasn't comfortable in the tiny bed, and moonlight poured in through curtains that were pretty, but too sheer to be of much use. Rivka, surely worn out from riding all day, had fallen asleep within seconds of flopping down onto the other bed, so the queen was all alone in her reveries. She thought of Aviva and ached. She thought of her father and wept a little. She thought of how helpless she had felt earlier when the drunk man had challenged her in the dining area, and she wondered how the inn could possibly have the "most inviting kitchen in all of Ir Ilan" as the sign outside had claimed, if the food was really as bad as he and Rivka both seemed to think.

Wonder, wonder, wonder. Too much light. Too much awake. Nervous energy set in. She peered over at Rivka to make sure she was really sound asleep, but then chided herself—any companion, even a sleeping one, would make it impolite to pet herself to wear herself out. Not that it would work in her current mood. Most likely, she would sob and miss Aviva instead of tiring happily.

If only she could fall asleep.

It seemed as if hours had gone by when she realized there were noises in the hallway. She listened to them for

a few minutes, trying to entertain herself and take her mind off *Aviva... Aba... Helpless...* by imagining possible scenarios to cause the noises. Perhaps a party of guests had shown up late. But then why were there noises for a moment, and then nothing, and then more noises, and then nothing again?

In fact, the sound appeared and disappeared with regularity.

Since she wasn't sleeping anyway, she slid out of bed. Wrapping her scarf around her shoulders, more out of modest instinct than cold, she padded quietly to the door and lowered herself to the light pouring from its base. It was set high off the floor, the hallway was illuminated for safety, so with her head against the floor, she could peer out into the hall.

Someone wearing a pair of boots walked out of one of the rooms at the far side of the hallway and shut the door. The boots stood in the hallway for a moment, then hurried to the next room. The door opened. As the person slipped inside the room, Shulamit's heart started pounding heavily, filling her with nauseating dread as when she had first heard of her father's accident. A few minutes later, Boots appeared again, and the behavior repeated.

Shulamit hurried over to Rivka's bed and shook her by the shoulder. "Rivka! Wake up—I think someone's robbing the rooms."

Rivka's chest heaved deeply in the breaths of sleep. She did not wake.

"Riv!" Shulamit hissed, right into her ear. Rivka had an interesting, unfamiliar scent, possibly from running around in armor all day. Then, because nothing else had worked, the queen took Rivka's face in both her hands and shook her head slightly but urgently.

Rivka's eyes remained closed, and her body was still languid. The word "Isaac," escaped from her lips like a

piece of ash falling on a campsite after the fire was out.

Shulamit could hear the noises getting closer. She smacked Rivka hard in the chest. "Wake! Up!" *She isn't waking up. And he's going to come in here and—*

Whipping her head around quickly, she scanned the room for ideas. At the edge of the room, there was a heavy wooden box where the proprietors of the inn kept extra bedding.

Gritting her teeth in aggravation, she stomped across the room toward the box and tried to lift it. Yeah, right.

She scurried back to the crack under the door and looked across. The intruder was five doors down. Okay. No more time to waste.

Still on the floor, Shulamit slid herself to the far side of the wooden box. With all her might, with all her righteous anger and all her fear, she pushed, pushed, *pushed* until the box began to slide. Muscles burning, she didn't allow herself to pause until the box completely blocked her door.

The door beside hers opened and closed.

She collapsed on top of the box, racking with silent sobs. *Aba! Aba, protect me.*

Someone tried the door.

It remained shut.

My God is my shepherd; I do not lack. In lush vegetation He does cause me to recline...

Eventually, the intruder gave up and went on to the next room over.

Shulamit was still.

She woke up the next morning at the sun's first light, cramped and sore, after only a few hours of sleep on top of the wooden box. She tried once again to rouse Rivka,

but the warrior was still deeply asleep. There was a lot of chatter outside in the hallway, so she felt safe removing the box from the door once she had dressed so that she could venture outside. It took twice as long because she had calmed down, but since there was no immediate threat this time that didn't matter.

The guests of the inn were milling about like ants out of a kicked pile of sand, and many of them looked angry or sad. Here and there she caught phrases:

"Ten thousand it was worth! And never mind that, it was a gift from my late husband! My *late* husband!"

"—*Never* be able to find another like it."

"How will we pay our bill?"

"He took my earrings!"

"I'm missing fifty. What about you?"

"We should have stayed in that other—"

"I didn't hear a thing!"

"To think I should finally sleep soundly, only to wake up to this."

"I wonder why he left my necklace?"

"Maybe it's not real."

As Shulamit feared, the hotel had been robbed. Nobody had been cleaned out entirely, but the man with the boots had been in and out of every room. Or woman. Ever since meeting Rivka she had been unsure if everyone was the sex they dressed to be.

She scratched her head thoughtfully, concentrating.

Rivka finally appeared in the common area carrying both women's bags, where everyone had gathered to discuss the crime, when the sun was bright in the sky. "I can't understand what happened," she told Shulamit. "I wake up at dawn. We won't be able to make it to the temple by nightfall. I'm not like this. I don't understand."

"I think I do," the young queen said under her breath. "You remember how spicy dinner was yesterday?"

"Dinner was awful."

"This inn bragged about its food. But what I got from the street vendor was much better."

"Maybe they've got a substitute cook."

"I don't think so," said Shulamit. "I think the cook's the one who robbed everyone. I think the spice in the food was covering up the taste of a sleeping drug."

Rivka's eyes narrowed into angry little slits, and her hands curled. "That *shtik drek*." More northern invective followed.

Shulamit swallowed uncomfortably, not recognizing any of the words, but the tone was unmistakable; Rivka's radiating rage was unsettling her nerves even more. "I had my own food, so I was awake. I saw him creeping around from under the door. Well, I saw a pair of boots, anyway."

"You were *awake*? When he came in our room? What did he take? Were you pretending to be asleep?"

Shulamit blinked. "Actually, I blocked the door with that big wooden box."

Rivka lifted an eyebrow, clearly impressed.

"You wouldn't wake up! I was scared!"

"If he came in the room and found you awake he might have killed you," Rivka observed. "Everyone else in the inn was asleep, and cooks have knives. Plus, you don't know how to defend yourself. I was going to talk to you about fixing that."

"You there! Stop talking." The innkeeper called out to them. They quickly straightened up and ended the conversation. "We're going to search everyone," he informed the grumpy guests, "because I locked the door last night and only just unlocked it this morning to receive the milk delivery from the goat girl."

"You could have stolen everything yourself and given it to the goat girl! She's your accomplice!" called out one of the guests.

"No, I saw the transaction," said another guest. "He gave her two coins, and she gave him two bottles."

"I saw too."

"I hope we've settled *that*," growled the innkeeper. "The search begins now."

"They're going to find your breasts," said Shulamit under her breath.

"Shut up," Rivka barked.

It turned out that too many bulky things had been stolen for a search that thorough, but both women still breathed a sigh of relief when they had passed the innkeeper's seal of approval. They watched intently while the cook was searched, but nothing was found on him either.

"Are you done yet?" the cook bellyached. "I have to get back to breakfast. Some of us have *honest* work to do around here, you know.

Shulamit's eyes flew open wide. "Rivka!" she whispered furiously to her companion, forgetting to use the male name in her excitement. "He hid everything at the bottom of the cauldron. It's a perfect hiding place for metal goods!"

Without another thought, Rivka stomped across the room to the enormous stewpot and crashed its contents across the floor. Guests fled from the wave of boiling water and undercooked couscous.

And necklaces and earrings and coins bearing pictures of Shulamit's father.

"Yes, *some* of us have honest work," the innkeeper observed with a lifted eyebrow. Two of the guests seized hold of the cook on either side.

"We are *so* done here," growled Rivka. She threw a handful of coins onto the table in front of the innkeeper and stormed off toward the door. Shulamit scurried after her, stifling nervous laughter.

Rivka didn't speak until they were already on the horse and moving again. "We won't make it there by nightfall thanks to that *nudnik*. I can't believe he drugged me. We'll have to camp."

"That's okay," said Shulamit. "What about breakfast?"

"There's dried goat and dried apricots in my bag. Will that work?"

"Probably," said Shulamit. Then she started to giggle. "You were fantastic back there! I'll never forget the sight of that tidal wave of couscous."

"You were pretty fantastic yourself, Queenling," said Rivka, calming down maybe five percent. "The way you worked out what had happened—you're like a little detective!"

Shulamit grinned. She felt her father would be proud of her that day.

Then her eyes widened again and blinked rapidly. "Rivka, if the robber *had* come into the room and found me awake and killed me, I bet I'd have been in the couscous too!"

"Talk about wheat intolerance."

Even the horse seemed to laugh at that one.

Chapter 5: The Temple

S orry today's been a bit of a failure."

"Please," asserted Shulamit, leaning all the way back in the water to submerge her head down to the hairline. "We caught a criminal this morning, didn't get killed, put a few miles behind us, and now we're bathing in this beautiful creek. If this is a failure, I'm looking forward to more of them."

Rivka scrubbed her face vigorously with both hands. "*You* caught a criminal. I overslept because I got drugged by some *putzveytig* who made us late. And now what does the sun do? Shines hotter than usual, and we're stuck here, getting even later."

"But can't we just ride the dragon? Flying is faster than walking, isn't it?" Shulamit felt awkward around a naked Rivka and was keeping to herself near the trees at the shoreline.

"We were already supposed to be flying," Rivka admitted. "That's why I let her rest yesterday, when all we did was walk. Oh, well."

"It's okay," Shulamit reassured her. "We'll still get there tomorrow." She squeezed the water out of her long, thick black hair. "Is her ability to turn into a dragon the reason she's so big?"

"I guess so," said Rivka. "And it's a good thing, too, or else she wouldn't be able to carry both of us."

"Are there many dragon-horses in the north? I've

read about your country and heard stories, but I don't remember anything like that."

"Neither had I," said Rivka. "I don't know who bred her. To be honest, I stole her. She belonged to my enemies. But she's been steadfastly loyal to me, so maybe they mistreated her."

Shulamit gazed out onto the bank of the creek, where Dragon was grazing peacefully underneath a date palm. She was a large, beautiful, muscled creature, with no signs of her hidden powers save for her size. Somehow, her enormity felt appropriate because her mistress was herself so much larger than Shulamit and her people, so the queen hadn't even questioned it. "So you won her in battle?"

"It's a little more complicated than that." Rivka dunked her entire head in the creek, then whipped it out again, her wet yellow hair flinging water everywhere wildly. "My family's always been at war with another family for control of our little valley. They attacked us, and we—despite what my uncle wanted we should believe—attacked them. I took Dragon from them one night as they tried to storm our castle. Without her help I probably wouldn't have lived."

Still shy of beholding Rivka's apparently unselfconscious nudity, Shulamit looked away, wondering about the granite tone that had come into Rivka's voice. "That sounds terrifying."

"It was the worst night of my life," said Rivka. "And I'm done talking about it right now." Her voice had gone grave.

"Sorry," Shulamit said hastily, mentally groping around for another topic. The name Isaac flashed into her mind, a remnant of the previous night's horrors, and she wondered if he—or his death—had anything to do with the painful topic. She was too scared of upsetting Rivka

to ask. "How long have you been a warrior on the road?"

"Two years," said Rivka, "during which I fought in three wars, rescued some people, captured some criminals, and served as temporary bodyguard where need be."

"Where did you learn to fight?"

"I spent a year as the gatekeeper in a bawdy house, if you can believe it," said Rivka with a smirk. "Every time a warrior passed through its doors, I paid him to teach me a new skill, or give me sparring practice."

Shulamit giggled in evidence of her young years. "I don't know whether to wish I was you or not!"

"We're about to introduce you to a whole temple full of women, so how about not," said Rivka. "Although while we're on the subject, you could stand to learn to defend yourself. One never knows. And think of last night."

"But I'm small."

"That doesn't mean anything. There are fighting techniques, used for defense, where agility and a clear head mean more than brute strength. I'll teach you, if you let me."

Shulamit froze. Rivka was still naked, and she would not—*not!*—let herself peek. "You don't mean right now, do you?"

"Of course not. It's far too hot. Unless you want a demonstration here in the water—"

"*No!* I mean—oh, dear." She fidgeted. "Thank you for offering. Maybe at the campsite tonight?"

"It's a deal."

Despite their best intentions, further aggravations plagued their journey that day. Deep into the afternoon, thunder opened up the sky and turned the ground into a sea of mud. The women huddled together atop the horse under the pelting rain. "It's not the safest way, but we have to fly," Rivka told her. "It's the only chance we have

of reaching dry ground by nightfall."

"Whatever you think is best!"

The horse transformed and carried the women into the splashing sky. The deep-green wings beat valiantly against the wind, and both Rivka and Shulamit cheered her each time she refused to let the powerful gusts carry her off course. Twice, lightning split the sky and Shulamit yelped after each.

The most terrifying moment, however, was when the dragon's strength began to flag. "She's flying lower!" Shulamit cried frantically.

"Come on, Dragon," Rivka urged. "See that rocky ground over there? That's all. That's all. Good girl." She petted the deep green-black scales.

With renewed energy, Dragon gave it a final push. As soon as they reached solid ground, she landed and almost instantly turned—no, *collapsed*—back into her horse form. "Good girl," Rivka repeated. "Come on, let's get down and let her rest."

After a good long rest, during which the rain thankfully died down, Rivka and Shulamit walked beside the horse down a rocky path. They were still some distance from the temple, but there was no reason they couldn't keep walking until nightfall. Besides, Rivka had mentioned they might find an area where it hadn't rained, so they they'd have firewood for their camp.

That night, as promised, Rivka showed Shulamit a few self-defense basics. In the glow of the campfire they eventually succeeded in lighting, Shulamit practiced throwing Rivka's closed fists off her wrists by twisting her arms in a spiral. "Another thing you need to remember," said Rivka, "is not to let your feelings about your attacker interfere with your defense."

"You mean, if I like the person, and he tries to hurt me, I might not defend myself as well?"

Rivka nodded. "Not only that—another thing that could happen is that you hate him so much that it takes your focus away from your performance."

"Oh, okay, good point."

The lesson was a hard workout, and between its vigors and the trials of the day, both women were ready for sleep before long. Shulamit's mind was as full of reveries as her belly was full of dried meat and dried fruit, and she lay there imagining the future.

After all, tomorrow they would meet the holy women. Though there was no guarantee that any of them would be the husband-fleeing lover of her own sex who Shulamit sought, she still anticipated with great relish the idea of being around such virtuous and mysterious women for a few days. She thought lots of different types of women were beautiful, but it was a *good* woman she sought above all other concerns. Aviva was fragrant and adventurous and made her laugh with her odd pronouncements, but at the core, it was her warmth and kindness Shulamit missed most. Sometimes the ladies-in-waiting treated her as if she were a curiosity, their friendship singed with amusement. Aviva never laughed at her unless Shulamit was already laughing at herself, and she had seemed genuinely interested in what she was talking about instead of listening politely because she was royal.

Shulamit was sure a diverse flock of personalities would inhabit the temple, but beneath their differences, all the women there must have that same inner goodness. Nobody could make their kind of sacrifice without it. She imagined a beautiful sea of mango-colored robes, dyed with turmeric, cloaking delicate, graceful movements and crowned with smiling faces. Maybe they would welcome her with flowers. She had brought a donation for the temple, at any rate. She might be there on extremely frivolous business, but she was still their queen and

wanted to do the right thing.

She glanced over at Rivka and noticed the muscles in her face were twitching in her sleep. The last thought Shulamit remembered before succumbing to slumber was to remember the name she'd heard Rivka murmur the night before, and she wondered if Rivka was once again dreaming about her past.

The morning to which they awoke was white and silent. The sky was bleached of all color like forgotten bones, and there was no wind to rustle the leaves around them. Rivka packed up the camp without speaking, while Shulamit fussed obsessively over the braided knots at the back of her head, undoing them and redoing them one after the other several times. Finally, they headed off down the road toward the temple, Shulamit growing more nervous with each footfall of the horse beneath them. She really, *really* wanted to make a good impression.

When they got to the temple, they hopped down from the horse, and Shulamit turned to her companion. "How do I look?"

Rivka smiled. "You look great. Don't be nervous. Confidence is attractive."

Shulamit grinned. "In that case, onward!"

They led the horse inside the temple gates.

Under the white sky, Shulamit beheld the stillness of the courtyard. A dragonfly landing on a small pool of water on the ground attracted their attention simply because it was the only moving thing in sight. The rest of the courtyard was dominated by somewhere between a dozen and two dozen life-sized statues of women in the simple robes of holy women.

Rivka and Shulamit left the horse by the entrance and walked down the central path, looking at the statues. There was something terrifying about them—they were incredibly realistic, and were completely free of dirt,

dust, or animal leavings, as if they had just been installed before the women's arrival. Each one was different, and they seemed to be placed haphazardly around the yard.

"Why are their faces so..." Shulamit asked in a hushed voice.

"This one looks like she's had the life scared out of her. What a thing to carve," Rivka commented.

"This one looks angry. I'm scared of *her*!"

"Their poses look so natural, so—lifelike." Rivka furrowed her brow. "I don't understand. I thought you said there's no art in holy houses."

"Something like this would distract from their meditation and simplicity," agreed Shulamit. "And no holy house could afford statuary this well-crafted."

"Don't you dare tell me the holy women carved these," said Rivka. "I won't believe it. Not with expressions like these."

For every single stone face was wracked with pain. In some, it was the pain of anger, of rage, and one statue even looked as if it were ready to attack any observer. In some, it was terror, and in some, merely sadness. Some of the faces were older, and some more youthful.

Shulamit had paused beside a younger face that was shaped in an expression of sad resignation. "She's so beautiful," she murmured, reaching out to gently caress the stone shoulder.

"I don't like it," said Rivka, turning away. "Ho! Who's there?"

An aged woman had appeared from inside the temple, her yellow-orange robe hanging from her frail, bony body as if it had blown into a tree branch during the previous afternoon's storm. "Peace, my son. Peace, my daughter."

"Peace to you," said Rivka and Shulamit together, and bowed their heads in respect.

"I've prayed for your arrival for many months," said

the woman. "I'm all alone here and couldn't go for help."

"Help? Why? What's happened here?" Rivka's hand flew to her sword hilt instinctively.

"Please, sit down and have tea with me, my son," she replied. "I'll explain everything. You *must* help us. We have nobody, and we have no money. But you have been sent by God." She turned around and led them inside the temple with faltering steps.

"I hope this isn't a trap," Shulamit whispered as they followed.

"Shhh." Rivka nodded toward her waist, indicating her sword. Shulamit knew that even if it was a trap, Rivka had everything under control.

They sat on simple cushions facing the old woman and let her serve them tea, and then listened as they drank.

"My name is Tamar. I'm the oldest woman here. That is why I'm the only one who wasn't turned to stone when the sorcerer came to steal a wife."

Rivka spewed tea and rocked forward. "*What?!*"

Shulamit covered her face with her hands. "Oh, dear Lord."

"How long ago was this?" Rivka asked.

"I've lost the days, my son," said Tamar sadly. "I'm old and brittle, and I do what I can, but it's not much, not anymore. Each day I tend my sisters. I brush the dirt from their bodies, and sing to them, and tell them I love them. I clean away anything the animals have left, and I pray to God that someone will come and deliver us before age takes me and they're left untended and stone forever."

"You said there was a sorcerer?"

"Yes, my son. He came to us in the guise of a rabbi, but once he was inside, he tried to seduce my sisters. When he realized that none of us would break our vow of celibacy, he got very angry and regained his true form. In the courtyard during our morning prayers he asked us one

47

by one, one last time, if we'd be the woman who would come to him, and we all refused. His anger has been our curse these many days. I alone was spared, because he had no interest in one so old. I thank God for my age, for it has kept me safe to see to their care."

"That sounds absolutely terrifying," said Shulamit. "Those poor women!"

The old woman took her by the hands. "And that's why you must help us, my child. That's why you're here."

"How can we right this wrong?" Rivka's brow was deeply furrowed, her stare intense.

"Go to the sorcerer," said Sister Tamar. "Go to him, and fight him, and win the elixir that blights all curses. I'll show you the way on the map. Only then will my sisters be free, and safe, for I'm failing... my son, I'm failing."

Rivka looked down at her tea thoughtfully. "I'm in the hire of the queen. I can't make my own decisions while on her coin."

"But we have no time," Tamar pleaded. "I have few days. I don't know how many, but once I'm gone, they'll be forgotten and lost and uncared for. We're isolated, and nobody comes here by accident—they'll never be found. Surely she'll have compassion if you were to undertake this task and then beg her forgiveness afterwards. She'll understand."

"Ask her yourself."

"Ask her?

Rivka turned toward Shulamit, who nodded slightly.

Tamar's eyes grew wide. "Your Majesty! I didn't know! Forgive me for offering only my humble tea, but it's all I have."

"Then it's all I need," Shulamit reassured her. "Riv, can't we rescue the holy women?"

"It's your decision, Your Majesty," said Rivka, growing more formal since they were now around another person

who knew Shulamit's rank.

"But how could we leave them?!"

"It'll be dangerous. It won't be anything like traveling around visiting temples," said Rivka. "You'll get a taste of my real life, which doesn't usually include queens and pretty lilac scarves made of silk."

Shulamit also understood the words she wasn't saying, which was *This part of the adventure is probably not going to include finding you a sweetheart.* "I know. We don't have a choice. We came here, and now we're the only ones who can fix this mess."

Rivka smiled so broadly it was obvious even though the lower half of her face was covered in cloth. She held out her hand to Tamar. "Then we have ourselves a pledge. We'll start right away."

Chapter 6: Preparations

S tarting right away" meant from that moment forward they would be in the service of Sister Tamar, not that they finished their tea and immediately hopped onboard Dragon. Rivka had lots of questions to ask about the sorcerer before they set out. She followed Tamar as the old woman toddled around the garden, meticulously polishing each of her stone sisters with a cloth.

Shulamit followed them outside and heard her asking about the sorcerer's appearance, about his manner of speaking and his behavior, about his seduction techniques, about whether he raised his voice or became very quiet when angered, and anything else that came up. "I have to know everything you can tell me about him before I meet him in combat," Rivka explained.

"Of course, my son," said Tamar.

Rivka took one of the cloths from Tamar's bucket of water and helped her polish the statues as she listened to the old woman's stories. Altogether, they made a shocking tale of a group of kind, trusting souls betrayed by a manipulative liar. He had tried a different approach with each woman, waiting until he had gotten to know the diverse personalities of the cloister and then tailoring his words and behavior to the occasion. He'd started with the most vulnerable—the youngest and those who still felt some ambivalence about their vows.

"With some of us," said Tamar, shaking her finger

knowingly and pausing in her work, "he thought we might already have talked about him. He started right off the mark with a little fiction about how he was a hunted man for a reputation he didn't deserve. He wanted to make sure that if any of us told the others what he had tried, that she wouldn't be believed."

"Such a *mensch*, he's not," said Rivka dryly.

"We were very unfortunate," Tamar agreed. "Excuse me, my son. I have to go have a little private moment. I'll return."

"You're so thorough," Shulamit observed once they were alone. "I'm impressed!"

"Well, I do need to know all of this," said Rivka, "and later on we need to go look at some maps so we'll know how to get to the sorcerer's hold in the mountains. But I'm also hanging around because I wanted to help her, and doing it while we talk saves her dignity."

By the time Tamar had come back, Shulamit had found a third cloth and was vigorously cleaning statues too.

She came to the beautiful, sad-faced novice she'd noted earlier. Tenderly she wiped swaths of water across the statue's feet and wondered if the woman trapped inside could feel it, or sense her in any other way. "I don't know who you are," she whispered, "but if there's any way I can bring you comfort in there, I'll try."

Shulamit's hands were slower and gentler on this one than on the others, and she couldn't help wondering what the woman was like. Had she come here out of deep religious conviction and a desire to serve her fellow humans? Or was she living within these walls in order to hide from the outside world? Did she like to read, and if so, did she prefer stories or lessons? With a rush of heat to her cheeks, Shulamit realized she couldn't bring herself to polish the woman's entire body—not her bosom. She knew she would enjoy it and couldn't live with the guilt

of reveling in such a moment at someone else's expense. Especially if the woman was awake inside the stone. "Riv?"

"Your Majesty?"

"We're switching."

Rivka lifted an eyebrow, and the corner of her mouth twitched up knowingly. Shulamit crossed the garden and began to work on another statue.

Later on, they pored over maps together. "Up there—in those mountains." Tamar pointed on the parchment.

Rivka squinted. The map was blurry and old. "How can you know that for sure? He was a liar, and you couldn't believe anything else that he said."

"Oh, once we all knew what he was doing, we finally figured out who he was. He's quite notorious around here ever since he first showed up from who knows where, two or three years ago... or was it... Anyway, they call him the bird-master. He raises birds, but his real hobby is causing trouble with women. We didn't know that's who the rabbi was. You see, he had changed his hairstyle and put on the right clothing... And he brought no birds with him, so how were we to know?"

She left to fetch a candle, for the sun was departing.

"Will Dragon be able to fly up all that way?"

"I hope so—she should be," said Rivka. "I've let her rest nearly all of today, and that makes a lot of difference. She'll have more than just flying up to the mountains to worry about. The ground on the way there is far too rocky and uneven for a horse. And in between us and the mountain are this lake"—she pointed to the map—"this waterfall"—moving her hand again—"and this other... rock... thing. I'm not taking a horse in that. We fly."

"I'm looking forward to flying when it's not pouring rain!"

Rivka grinned. "I'll show you some tricks while we're on our way. We have work to do, though. I'm not tossing you into this without more self-defense training."

"I'm grateful for it."

When the old woman came back, an issue arose over where they would sleep. She refused to let "Riv" sleep in the temple—for no man, even a holy man, was permitted to sleep there. The sorcerer posing as a rabbi had even camped in the courtyard where his victims now stood in breathless sleep. And Shulamit refused to sleep in the temple without Rivka's protection.

"There's always the garden, I suppose," suggested Tamar.

A pebble landed on the ground beside them, and all three women looked up into the dusk. Dragon was standing on the roof, in her horse form, and had kicked it down.

"We could sleep up there," Shulamit suggested. "Then we wouldn't be disturbing all the holy women."

"An excellent solution," said Tamar. "Come, I'll show you the way to the staircase and bring you bedding."

The roof of the temple was a flat surface dominated in the front by a large shallow basin. "Holy water," Tamar indicated.

"Rainwater pools here," Shulamit explained under her breath, no doubt noting Rivka's confused expression, "and the sisters come and bless it. It's a cache that protects the temple."

"Don't drink from it," Tamar warned them. "Now, good night, my son, Your Majesty." She nodded to both of them and walked slowly and carefully back down the staircase to her cell.

"Why didn't she ask how the horse got up on the roof?"

Rivka shrugged. "Age? Or maybe she's so enlightened that she's learned that the world is a much stranger place than most of us realize."

She unpacked some of their bedding, then noticed Dragon had transformed into her reptilian form. "You know what, Shula? You can use as much of the bedding as you want. I'm going to sleep against Dragon."

"Really? That doesn't look very comfortable."

"It's what I'm used to when fighting's on the agenda. It'll help me to wake up as a warrior."

Shulamit nodded. "But won't staying a dragon sap her strength?"

"It's the flying that does that," said Rivka, "not the form. Sometimes I think she prefers this form, but we attract too much attention with a grounded dragon, and she doesn't like that."

"How can you tell what she's thinking?"

Rivka smiled sadly from one side of her mouth. "When you spend three years with one single creature as your only constant friend, you pick up on things."

Shulamit lay on the bedding and wrapped her silk wrap around her shoulders as she gazed up at the stars. She was just about to lose herself in reverie, possibly about the young woman down there in the courtyard, when she heard Rivka singing. Her strong voice was now gentle, and she sent the melody placidly out into the night. "Jeweled stars, pearl stars, silver coins in olive jars... glittering deep within the dark, see them flicker, see them spark..."

Blood rushed into the queen's cheeks. She joined in, tears spilling down her face. Her voice was choked and sounded like hell, but she sang anyway.

They made it through three verses in duet, during which Shulamit held herself together. Then the earthquakes of sobbing began, the type of crying during which nobody is beautiful. She hugged herself and curled up.

"Aba sang that to me to put me to sleep when I was a child," she whispered into her silk wrap, which was now slimy with tears and saliva.

"May his memory be blessed," said Rivka very quietly.

"I still can't believe it, even though I'm queen and there's a shrine and it's been months. It doesn't feel real. He was supposed to get old. His old nursemaid—she was the one who told me he'd fallen off the elephant. I went to him, and he barely woke; they had him under such strong elixirs to ease his pain. But I knew he could sense me, and when I sang that song back to him, I could see tears in his eyes."

Rivka took Shulamit into her arms and folded the little queen's tear-sodden face against the muscled curve of her shoulder.

Shulamit continued. "The sun was so bright that last day—just completely *pouring* into the room. The servants tried putting up curtains because he was too hot, but they wouldn't stay up. It just glowed whiter and whiter until we had to squint to see, even though we were inside. The light got stronger, and he got weaker—almost like he was becoming part of the sun."

The queen was silent, reliving the moment after the incredible glaring whiteness relaxed its grip on the room, and everyone could see distinct shapes again. Curled up in a tight knot on the floor beside her father's bed, her arms clasped firmly around her knees, she felt someone put a crown on her head. She tipped her head forward and let it slide down into her lap, where she hugged it while sobbing.

Rivka's voice brought her back to the present. "You're

a smart young woman. He would be proud of you. I'm sure he was proud of you in life too."

The corners of Shulamit's mouth turned up in a heartbroken little smile. "Yeah, he was... he used to tease me about all the books I was reading and facts I'd rattle off from my lessons, but he meant it in a good way. He'd call me his little Princess Brainy."

"That's cute!" said Rivka. "What was he like? I never met him in person, only saw him from a distance."

"He was so full of energy," said Shulamit, pepping up a little as she went back to a happier past. "So many interests. Did you know he knew how to climb up the side of a sheer rock face?"

"No, I didn't," said Rivka, wide-eyed. "I'm impressed."

"And he could speak four languages, and he'd been everywhere," Shulamit continued. "He didn't sleep as much as the rest of us. Sometimes he'd be busy late at night working on laws or listening to arguments in court cases, and have an entire meal in the middle of the night. If I was still up, I'd keep him company."

"It's good that you could spend so much time together."

Shulamit nodded, shifting positions within Rivka's embrace so she could wipe her face clean. "Everyone around me, when they were mourning him, it was so wonderful to be surrounded by people who were sad about the same thing I was because I wasn't alone, but it was also jarring because they were all talking about him as king, not as a father. When we put his kippah into the museum, everyone was talking about how much money it was worth and the embroidery by some famous artist and how it was a national relic, and all this—but I was just thinking of Shabbat, and seders, and—and it didn't mean any of those things to me. It meant lighting candles. It meant he'd hid the afikomen in the palace for me and joking with his advisors as he waited around for

me to find it so he could give me a new book. National treasure? I—" She blinked away new tears, but this time the look on her face was one of indignation.

"Do you have anything of his that you carry around as a memento?" Rivka's hand fidgeted with something beneath her helmet.

Shulamit grinned, that bizarre grin of hers that looked more like a grimace than a real smile. "Well, myself! I look like him. Everybody says so. Especially my eyebrows."

"That's perfect. I know you'll carry on his legacy."

Shulamit leaned her head back down against Rivka's chest. "It hurts *so much*. When does this get better?"

"I wish it did," said Rivka. "Instead, we get used to it. We live around it." She paused. "The olive song's special to me too. The man I loved is with me again when I sing it. Thoughts of him still bring me joy, even though they hurt too. I know that if I'm to live my life with a man at my side, it won't be him. I've met many men as I fought in battles and guarded the rich—valiant men, smart men, good, kind men. But I just never looked on them as a woman looks at a man—I mean, as an ordinary woman who likes men—even though I could see their good qualities. I don't think I'm the type who falls in love very often. A man can be a good match, but that's not enough to make him special to me that way..."

"I know the feeling you're talking about," said Shulamit, her face crinkling as she thought about the way Aviva had filled her with exhilaration just by being in the room. "He must have been wonderful, for a woman as amazing as you to have cared for him so deeply." She pulled away from their hug and stretched her arms.

Rivka nestled against the dragon's thick hide and closed her eyes. "We have a long way to go tomorrow. Maybe I'll tell you all about him."

Nearby, Shulamit pulled her lilac wrap more tightly

around herself, sliding a small patch of the slippery fabric back and forth between her thumb and fingers. The repetitive motion comforted her, and she forced herself to concentrate on something other than the people she missed. The first thing that came to mind was Dragon, so she pretended that she was an artist and quantified each interesting feature, from her clawed and grasping hands to the horns on top of her head. Once distracted from her grief, she fell asleep quickly, for she was genuinely very tired.

The next morning, after eating breakfast and bidding Sister Tamar goodbye, the two women set out for the sorcerer's hold. Dragon, who had been waiting outside the temple gates still in her reptile form, soared into a brilliant blue sky that promised better weather than their last day of travels. They sailed over the tropical landscape, banana thickets and palm trees clustered together, bathed in early sunlight.

"Want to try something fun?" Rivka asked.

"Okay," said Shulamit, a little hesitantly.

"Trust me." Rivka, confident in her strength and years of practice, tightened her thighs around the dragon's torso and let go of her with her hands. She grabbed Shulamit's hips, holding her firmly down to the animal's backbone. "Hold your hands out into the air while we fly."

Shulamit let out a raucous peal of pure joy. "It feels like it's me who's flying—my arms are wings!" They passed by a noisy white waterfall, and its mist lightly kissed their cheeks in greeting. "*Woooooo!*"

Eventually, Shulamit put her arms down, and they relaxed into a more conventional riding posture. "Thank you so much. I don't think I've ever been this awake." She

craned her head around slightly to look at Rivka, and her grin was broad and sparkling under the bright sun.

"Would you like to hear about the man I loved?" Rivka's voice was gentle and intimate. She was pleased with herself for having made Shulamit so happy after last night's tears. Empathy for their shared affliction had opened up her heart, and she had realized just before going to sleep that Shulamit was the first person in three years with whom she felt the impulse to share her story.

"Yes, I would."

And as they sailed over the rocks and the trees, Rivka unfolded her life before her friend.

Chapter 7: The Brat from the Beet-garden

In a valley of the northern lands, there lived a baron who spent half his time wishing he wasn't at war with the family who ruled over Apple Valley, to their immediate west, and the other half of his time cooking up new ways to start trouble with them. He never noticed the hypocrisy of this because he was the least self-aware person in the valley over which he held title. Or *they* held title—depending on whose side you were on.

Rivka was on his side, although she had little choice in the matter because she had been born there. She wouldn't have been *his* first choice either—her very existence was an embarrassment and a burden. Even had she been conventionally beautiful, delicate and demure, and talented in all the noblewomanly tasks of listening and textile art, she still would remain a living, breathing reminder that his foolish younger sister had allowed herself to be, well, *harvested* by one of the workers who grew the castle's beets and potatoes.

Of course, once the pregnancy was discovered, the worker was quickly dismissed from his position and sent away. The other choice was almost certainly death, for the baron valued nothing so much as his reputation, and if he couldn't keep the women in his own *family* safe, well, then the Apple Valley folks would attack at once, thinking him weak!

He wanted the people in his valley to respect him

too, so having the daughter of a nobody running around the castle was already embarrassing enough. On top of that, though, she was also nothing like his own sweet daughters. She was a large and ungraceful thing, rough in her manners, too obviously the child of a field hand, but, unfortunately, also too obviously the child of his sister. She was an inconvenience and a source of aggravation. Her childhood efforts to mimic the soldiers, whose presence was a constant at the castle, filled him with dread of what she would be like as an adult.

Marrying her off became his private obsession, with what little brain he had left over after plotting the demise of the Apple Valley ruling house once and for all. Then she would be gone, and perhaps her shallow, uninteresting mother with her, if he could deftly manage it.

But none of the men who would have been appropriate for a relation of his house ever showed interest in his tall, outspoken, physical niece. And certainly he would have rather hidden her away in a tower forever than let her run off with *somebody else*. Too much damage had been done already by his dolt of a sister, Miriam—known by her intimate family as Mitzi.

Not to mention the Apple Valley ruling house and their persistent raids! True, he sent his own men into their valley on occasion, to show them he still had the might to defend his keep. And yet, they sent wave after wave of troublemakers, determined to ruin the peace.

It was so difficult to be the baron of the valley.

One year, after a particularly bloody set of squabbles between the two valleys, a group of wizards who lived in the surrounding mountains decided to take matters into their own hands. Between their magic and the level of respect their Order commanded with everyone in the nation, they were much more powerful than either the baron or the heads of the other family. They were able

to use that power to place one of their own in the court of each valley, to oversee matters there and attempt to subdue the feud at its source. They were not an unwarlike brotherhood, but it insulted their very dignity to see wars being fought over a dispute as old and petty as this one. Let each valley to itself in peace, they thought, and if there were wars to be fought, let them be heroic ones.

Rivka, at this point alarmingly too old to have no marriage prospects, was sitting with her mother in the Great Hall watching the newly arrived wizard verbally spar with her uncle. It was rare for anyone else in the castle to contradict the baron, but even without him opening his mouth, his appearance set him apart and marked him a definite outsider. In a household where the men's hair was grown long and usually tied back, his was cropped short. Their beards were full; his beard and mustache were trimmed down nearly to the point where they looked as if they'd been inked with a brush onto his unusually round face. And, most outlandish of all, he wore a black cassock embroidered with strange dark-green-and-purple designs. The wizard was in his late thirties, close to Rivka's mother's age but certainly younger than her uncle—which did him no favors earning the baron's respect.

"This is never going to work," Mitzi observed under her breath. She was knitting on a piece of fancywork, but her eyes never left the two men arguing in the center of the room. "He already hates being told what to do."

"No man could ever win a battle that way!" the baron exclaimed, slamming his fist upon a nearby table.

"Clearly you don't read," said the wizard, sounding more irritated and insulted than angry. "Some already have, in this century *and* the last."

The calmer the wizard's tone, the more the baron turned red. "I have no use for your folktales. Why should

I believe something just because it's been inked onto a parchment by some fool in a cassock? Over what my *vast* experience can tell me? I've been fighting these wars since I was ten years old. You were drinking your mother's milk when I first held a sword!"

"I've held a sword as well, in case nobody told you," said the wizard in a quiet, steely tone. He pushed back the right sleeve of his cassock to show the grisly, twisted snake of a scar that slashed across his palm and curled up the length of his forearm. "When the Marantz blade fell, I didn't stop fighting—I learned to brandish my sword in my left hand. So don't assume wizards know nothing of fighting—or of bravery."

"He also hates wizards," Rivka murmured to her mother. "A wizard telling him what to do—"

"Well, it's just that he disagrees with so many things about them," Mitzi explained indulgently, her tone making it clear that she sympathized with her older brother. "He thinks their devotion to histories and parchments, and their vows of celibacy and service, are all unnatural and self-important. He always says the service makes them look weak, and I agree with him that the celibacy's a bit self-centered—like he says, any woman wooed by a wizard would fall asleep of sheer boredom or die of exasperation."

Rivka had heard these words come out of her uncle's mouth before and indeed was mimicking them along as her mother spoke. "He just doesn't like the fact that their power is so much greater than his," she pointed out.

"Can you blame him?" Her mother was not a complicated creature; she liked living in a castle and having someone else clean her room and feed her, and since it was her brother's power that kept her there, she didn't mind his power-hungry stance at all.

Rivka sighed. "He's going to be exceptionally hard on

me while he gets used to this, isn't he?"

"Oh, Rivkeleh! He just wants what's going to make you a happy woman someday. He doesn't want you to end up like your old mammeh, hanging around being useless and having even the lowest scullery maid in the castle know her most intimate business." Mitzi smiled sadly.

"Don't worry, Mammeh, I won't embarrass you that way." Rivka smiled. "If I must marry, I'll marry a warrior, so I can go off and fight at his side."

"Rivka, you can't run around holding sticks as swords anymore. You're a grown woman, and it's going to scare away husbands, not attract them."

"We're at war. We're always at war. Why can't I help fight it?"

"Because it's unwomanly, and you wouldn't be any good at it. Here. Work on this." Her mother stood up and placed the unfinished piece of lace in her daughter's lap. "It'll help calm your mind and drive away those unsettling thoughts. Don't worry about defending the hold. The men have it under control."

"—*never* let one of you wizards command my men! Are you *crazy*? Wait, why am I even asking that? Of course you're crazy. You've been inhaling parchment fumes and your—"

"—too many of your own men, your tenants and your most loyal soldiers, die every—"

"—never had a woman, not even allowed to *touch* a woman! I bet when you joined up they even cut—"

"—fought under three kings *after* my vows, so don't you accuse me of—"

Rivka looked at her mother and deadpanned, "Yes, the men have it under control." She picked up the knitting and fiddled with it, making three mistakes without even trying on her first row.

She didn't know how she felt about having the wizard around. She didn't disagree with his ideas, but she *was* a member of the family, even if pretty much all of them were completely alien to her; she felt threatened, like an animal whose burrow had been breached.

On the other hand, he had parchments, and some of them were about military strategy or the history of warfare. She yearned to read them. Here, at last, she would find the information for which she had been so thirsty all her life. Caught between her sex and her uncle's distaste for written histories, it had been dry pickings. She had listened intently every time a soldier told a tale, but they presented only the narrowest view, and she knew she needed more.

The idea came into her head that she might get her hands on these parchments in secret and read them quickly, replacing each one before he might miss it. What a delicious prank!

She plotted this for days before actually beginning the project. Already practicing her strategizing, she took note of any times the wizard could predictably be found in the Great Hall (and nearly as predictably, arguing with her uncle over any topic from whether the sky was blue to the treatment of the guard's dogs.) After a while it became apparent that he always lingered after luncheon, usually by falling prey to verbal taunts given out by the baron between the soup and the rest of the meal.

This, then, would be her time of opportunity. She ate her food quickly and unobtrusively, and then, as the baron's voice grew louder and louder in an attempt to drown out the wizard's gentle basso, she slipped out of the Great Hall into the dark passageways.

The wizard had been given a room high in a tower, at the end of two flights of rickety stone stairs. It was actually the room where Mitzi had stayed during the final

few months of her pregnancy, hidden away in her shame from curious eyes, and so it was lavishly furnished and relatively clean. But it was as inconvenient a room as the baron could muster, and he was doing everything he could to make it clear that he resented everything about the wizards stepping in and mucking around with his business.

Rivka scurried up the stairs as quickly as was prudent on their uncertain surface and then pushed open the door in one sweeping gesture—better to find out right away if there was some kind of spell put on the room, trapping her or informing the wizard of her intrusion.

Nothing happened.

She looked around the room. It was as she had always known it from her childhood wanderings, save for a few spare cassocks and several trunks, all of which belonged to the wizard. Two of the trunks were open, both containing piles of bound parchments. She stared for a moment, breathing heavily over the sudden wealth at her fingertips. Where to start?

Stepping over to the first trunk and peering in, she read the title of the book on the top. *A Complete History of King Pampas IV's Battles—His Victories and Defeats.* She had no idea who King Pampas was, let alone his three ancestors before him, but she figured this was as good a place to start as any.

Her hand darted out and snatched the book off the pile.

The ceiling did not collapse, and neither did the spare cassocks hanging across the back of the chair get up and block her way. Everything was as it was before. "That's right... He thinks we don't read," she said out loud to herself. *He'd be mostly right*, she added internally.

She was back in her room reading the brittle old book before she let herself relax—not that she could relax

completely. Her heart was pounding pretty strongly as a result of her little pilfering adventure. The book in her hands was a connection to all her dreams for the future, and it was a few minutes before she could focus on its words instead of the importance of the moment.

The king in the book had been a great general who lived in another land several hundred years ago. During his reign he protected his people from numerous invasions and also won a civil war when another member of the royal family grew strong against him. She could tell there were plenty of things in the book that could help her uncle, whose situation was always on her mind because it was on his. But she knew he'd never want to hear about anything that had happened to people so irrelevant to his life.

That was okay. She'd find a way to defend his keep even over his own objections.

When she had finished the book several days later, she waited until the daily lunchtime battle and then snuck back into the tower to switch it out for the next one. So did Rivka bat Miriam slowly make her way through the books in the trunk. Her hungry mind soaked up all the new information. She didn't dare take notes for fear they'd be found, so while she ran around in the garden feeling the sun's warmth battle the crispness of the air, or during bad weather when she was trapped inside mangling yet another piece of fancywork, she repeated the important points to herself over and over until they were nearly as automatic as *Bless you, O Lord, King of the Universe...*

One day, she had taken one of the books into the garden because she knew a place in a tree where she wouldn't easily be seen and could hide there to read in peace. She opened the book, and to her breathless horror she beheld an unfamiliar scrawl—

If you're going to borrow my parchments, why not ask permission?

Chapter 8: The Wizard

Rivka's first reaction to the note was, naturally, to panic about being caught, but then the warrior's heart that could not be squashed within her neither by motherly concern nor avuncular edict woke up and wrote back her response.

Only to have you say no?

She didn't give the wizard any especial look of deference that evening, nor did she return the book until she was good and finished with it. Then, and no sooner, she returned to the tower and exchanged it for the next one in the pile.

His reply was waiting for her two books later. *And have me say yes. Anyone in this dank monument to human ignorance who finds value in these histories would be a welcome friend.*

After that, she felt as though they had a secret inside joke. She supposed that eventually the joke would be on her, because he never guessed that she was female. She was sure this was why he let her write about her dreams of becoming a great warrior and helping to defend the keep, and encouraged her instead of trying to silence her like everybody else. If he ever found out, she presumed, he'd probably gently but firmly admonish her for her presumptuous plans.

How are you with a sword?

I look forward to my opportunity to find out.

If you're able, I'll give you instruction. I would find it a welcome respite from what I endure in the Great Hall, wrote the wizard back in brazen disrespect of the baron. He surely knew full well that a book in the bottom of an old trunk would never find its way into the baron's hands even by accident. Especially not the *middle* of a book.

Rivka wished he could give her lessons via notes scribbled in books, but that was probably impossible. Besides, she had no sword. Not even a broken remnant from a heroic father lost in battle. Instead, he had left for her the nickname Rivka bat Beet-greens, daughter of the vegetable garden, as if Mitzi had gone out walking one night and been defiled by the crop itself.

I would gladly learn if I could, she wrote back into the book, *but if I can't, what are the first things I should know?*

When she was finished with lunch, she tried to leave to return the book, but her mother kept her a few minutes just outside the Great Hall asking if she thought this or that new piece of jewelry more fine upon her ears. She picked one at random, eager to get the book back to the wizard's room before his daily argument with the baron was concluded. No danger of its being over any time soon, she thought—even this far from the Great Hall she could hear her uncle bellowing. Would it hurt him to just *shut up* even for only a few minutes?

Gladly moving away from the sound of his voice, she rushed up to the tower and into the wizard's room. She picked up the next book in the pile, placing the previous one on the stack in its place.

"What's that there?"

Rivka froze.

She turned around to face the wizard, who had been sitting in a chair in the corner of the room. She hadn't seen him in the shadow, and nobody had ever been in the

room before when she had come up.

"How are you here? The baron—"

"Is abusing someone else today, blissfully enough for me." He stood up. "You're not what I was expecting. A soldier's page, perhaps, or a stableboy."

"Not the baron's bastard niece?" She faced him without fear, daring him to send her away with steady eyes and even breathing—even though her heart was pounding heavily.

The wizard opened one of the trunks that had always been closed and locked during her visits and took from it a long flashing thing of silver steel. He straightened up and approached her, offering her the hilt. "Do you have the next hour free?"

Far across the fields, there stood an abandoned shell of a barn, four stone walls with nothing but sky overhead. Together, without speaking much, they cleared away the remains of what had been the roof. When there was enough space for them to move, the wizard showed her the basics of swordsmanship. She entered the practice with a lot of zeal and strength, the natural outcomes of her lifelong interest and her athletic temperament, but she was also gravely unpracticed at telling her body what to do.

"We'll work on the swords," he said, after watching her for a time, "but I think I should also show you some exercises to bring you in touch with your movements, and in control of your body."

Rivka concentrated on her lesson and committed everything he told her to memory. At the end of the session, she thanked him profusely and tried to give him back the sword he had lent her.

He held up his hand. "Keep it for now. Someday you'll have your own, but that one's only an extra, a token of appreciation from one of the kings under whom I fought—you can read about it on the inscription—and I barely even use the one I truly consider mine." He held up his own blade, the one in his left hand. "I fight with the wrong hand," he explained. "Had to learn to write with this one too."

"I saw your scar," said Rivka.

"Oh, in the Great Hall? Your uncle certainly brings out the warrior in my *tongue*, that's for sure, even if my hands are often idle." He drew back from her. "I think I know where I can find some old rakes nobody will miss. Take off the heads and they'll make good safety weapons. I know you'll practice before then, but you'll have an easier time of it if you start with that."

Rivka nodded enthusiastically. "Yes, of course! I'm so grateful... Wizard...?"

"My name's Isaac," he said.

"Rivka," she said. "But surely you knew that."

"Even if I did, it's new to me now," said the wizard with a smile. "Before today, I knew you, and I knew my strange friend who was stealing my books and returning them after reading them. Now that I know who you are, I meet the name anew."

"I won't let you down," Rivka assured him.

"Let me down? No, Rivka, I don't do this for my own glory. I'm teaching you as an excuse to interact with the one other soul in this cave who values learning and knowledge."

"What book should I read next?"

"Since we've broken out the swords, I'll lend you Face's Treatise on sword craftsmanship. You'll learn about words like 'tang' and start thinking about angles of swing."

"I'm ready for anything."

"I can see that already."

Rivka had never felt better in her life as she did when she smuggled the sword back to her bedroom and spent all evening after dinner practicing with it. She also remembered to dutifully repeat the weaponless exercises that Isaac thought she needed, and she was pleased to discover that they caused a marked improvement in her carriage and movements over the next few weeks. The slight change in her made her catch the baron's attention, and reminded him of his search to find her a suitably honorable husband.

Rivka and Isaac met whenever they could within the forgotten stone walls. They fought with the wooden rake-handles until she was ready to graduate to full-time sword work. Sometimes he talked about his history in battle, using his own adventures to illustrate lessons in combat. Rivka eagerly soaked up every story, determined to have her own someday.

Of course, it wasn't all easy. Learning how to fall safely meant collecting a full spectrum of bruises before she mastered the technique. Luckily, she already had a reputation for "unladylike" behavior, so the few that showed up in places her dresses didn't cover generated nothing beyond the unbridled disdain of her married cousin, Frayda, the baron's eldest daughter, who was visiting to show off her new baby.

The hardest part came when she had mastered parrying and thrusting, and now faced the step where she must decide which order in which to put them, to keep an enemy on his guard. Rivka, whose brain wasn't wired to constantly plan attacks complex enough to surprise an

opponent, practiced incessantly until varying her choice of blow became instinct.

One day, as Rivka and Isaac were sparring in the rain, she realized to her heady surprise that she was besting him in blow after blow, and that all her months of practicing had grown her skill to where she outshone Isaac's uninjured but non-dominant left hand. She continued wielding, not quite understanding the placid, yet slightly impish expression on his round face. What would she do for practice if she could now easily beat any sword he could hold?

His answer came in the form of swirling ribbons of light that suddenly appeared from his right hand. They surprised her and surrounded her sword, but then she roused herself and slashed back at them heavily. Then she put her sword down by her side, blinking raindrops from her eyelashes. "What was that?!"

"I can't close these fingers around the hilt of a sword anymore," Isaac explained, "but I can still do magic." He was usually fairly tight-lipped on exactly what wizard training entailed and didn't reveal more than was necessary.

Rivka didn't move, squinting at his hands critically as she studied the winding silver whips.

"They won't hurt you," Isaac reassured her, sheathing his sword. "You won't even feel them, not in the beginning."

"And then what?"

"An irritating buzz. Enough to sharpen the game. Rivka, mind your sword!" The whips jetted out of both of his hands with no other warning, and she quickly raised her steel to meet them.

His magical abilities were a perfect grindstone for her skill, because he could improve both the stakes and the complexity of their sparring matches almost infinitely. Over the year that followed, she grew to be a formidable warrior, all under her uncle's nose. Every day when the maid was cleaning her room, Rivka took the sword out from under her bed and hid it behind a suit of armor that stood as decoration in the passageway. It was a terrible hiding place, but it was only there for an hour each day. Thankfully for Rivka, the maid was like clockwork, and this was not difficult—only annoying.

The wedding of Cousin Bina, the baron's middle child, was approaching, and as soon as Rivka heard that the great General Zusmann was on the guest list as a good friend of the groom's, she remembered her plan to marry a warrior and follow him into battle. She showed uncharacteristic interest in her frock and jewelry for the event, filling her mother's face with smiles and her cousins' with mocking eye-rolls. When they had finished with her, she looked passably pretty in dark brown, even though she towered over her cousins. The vegetable gardener had been a tall man, and from that, one could not escape.

She studied her reflection in the glass. Would the general find her appealing? She was greatly interested in anything he had to say about his adventures, or his ideas on various bits and pieces of military theory. She had reread a couple of Isaac's books on strategy before the wedding so she could make sure to follow the general's conversation and show by her replies that she was a worthy wife.

The baron must have had similar ideas about his lowborn niece and the single, respectable general, for he engineered a partnering of the two during one of the row dances in the Great Hall after the wedding ceremony was completed. Rivka did her best to lead his conversation

to the field, and he gladly followed her there to relive his past exploits. But when she said, "Certainly a fitting wife for you would be she who could hold her own in battle," his reply dashed her hopes.

"My wife? What an idea!" The general laughed. "My wife needs to stay at home and show the world evidence of that which produces my strength on the field, by breeding my sons."

Rivka couldn't suppress a face of disgust. She got through the rest of the dance somehow, but then fate added to her distemper by pairing her with her uncle for the next dance. "How did you scare him off, you foolish girl?"

"I didn't scare him off. He scared *me* off."

"In what way have you found him wanting? He is honorable, powerful, and wealthy."

"He wouldn't let me fight for him, just as you refuse to let me fight for you." Rivka's patience with enduring her uncle's mindset was wearing thin of late, in direct proportion to her confidence as she gained skill at the blade.

"What would the family of Apple Valley think if they saw a woman defending my keep?" The baron snorted derisively. "They'd see a weak old man so desperate and confused he'd send out his own womenfolk in front of him as a shield! They'd attack *tomorrow*, and you wouldn't know what to do. Imagine a woman fighting one of *them*. Huh." He made a noise that reminded her of a barking dog. "You wouldn't know the first thing about fighting."

"I'm done." Ripping through an absolutely unbreakable rule of etiquette, she dropped out of the dance and stormed across the Great Hall to an uninteresting corner in shadow.

The dance continued smoothly as an older woman who had not been dancing rose swiftly to the occasion

and filled in the place Rivka had vacated.

Isaac appeared by her side. "Theatrics?"

"He's insufferable," she grumbled.

"Which one?"

"Yes."

"We could spar after the ball."

"Please. I don't think I could sleep very easily after this."

"I'll be there."

"I'll try not to cut off your hands."

Making no comment about the strange things her frustration and rage were making her say, Isaac floated away into the crowd. Rivka's mind was moving a mile a minute, and the ballroom had become an oppressive distraction as she struggled to keep up with her own thoughts. She needed to get someplace quiet, where she could think without being disturbed.

She slipped outside into the crisp night air. Without too much thought about how it would stain or rend her dress, she crawled into the little cavern made by the low-hanging branches of the tree where she had first read Isaac's handwriting in the book.

The general's disdain for her dreams had horrified her. What entrapment he offered her! What an infinitely tall tower of imprisonment! After spending several years naïvely assuming that a man with a sword would want a woman who matched him, she had discovered in one moment how very different that woman was who he expected—the woman into whom he would have tried to change her.

Speaking with Isaac after such an insult had felt like eating the roast chicken after the stale bread. This was the way she wanted a man to talk to her—to be concerned for her feelings, to invite her to spar, to be unafraid of her aggressive moods. Far from being a wet blanket

upon her fiery nature—instead, he was a sturdy hearth that nurtured that fire and gave it a safe place to flourish. She was happiest when she was around him and looked forward to their next meeting when they were apart. Often, she wished for his company in unlikely moments.

A frisson of fear rippled through her body. She forbade herself even to think the words. But the idea itself, wordless, bubbled forth from her heart and could not be contained. Try as she did, she couldn't suppress a sudden thought of the thick solidity of his body—tall, strong, and a little stout but sturdy—and his impish, placid expression and pointed eyebrows that suddenly made her think of a cat smiling at you with its eyes closed. She saw them with new eyes and clenched her fists at her sides.

Feeling as if her very blood had been replaced by a substance both unfamiliar and intoxicating, she went to her room to collect her sword, ready to meet him at the battlefield of her heart.

Chapter 9: Press the Night, Collect the Sun

Rivka darted around within the stone walls, each stroke of her sword falling silently on one or two of Isaac's spiraling whips of light. She hated the startling buzz they made if they touched her, and they made a strong but ultimately harmless incentive for her to be on her toes with her technique. After her heart had burst like a ripe grape, exposing unseen parts to her conscious mind, she had been filled with a relentless manic energy, and tonight, she fought off the whips with extra vigor.

The whips didn't catch her at all, and she thought her technique was flawless. But in one swift moment, Isaac once again changed the game. Moving his hands down to his sides, he suddenly looked into her eyes. "You are distracted."

In an echo of her courage in his room in the tower on the first day of their sparring, she faced him without flinching or denying anything. "It's of no consequence," she retorted. "It wouldn't be a factor with any adversary I would meet in battle."

She knew there was so much he was trying to say with his eyes, and with the rest of that impish face, but all he said was, "Ah, but what if you hate him as much as you…" He stopped.

Rivka knew why he was silent. The celibacy vow of the Wizard Order was held in place by a number of strange

and terrifying spells, the price of each wizard's entry into the secret magic they taught. If he touched a woman, if he spoke about love to a woman, or even moved his hands in the shape of the letters to write them—she had known this from the beginning. Fool that her heart was, it didn't care.

But she didn't want to scare him away. "I ask nothing of you but the friendship you already give," she blurted out. She could endure her feelings, but what if he found them threatening? Or even insulting?

"I'm not scared of you, Rivka," he said quietly. Then, after a moment of consideration, he lifted his right hand and blasted light at a halved log in the corner. She stood in place, puzzled, until he motioned with his head for her to go look.

She had to bend down and bring the log close to her eyes to read the words that he had branded there in the most beautiful script she had ever seen,

I can give only my heart, but it is absolutely yours.

Her mind stopped, halted in that moment of discovery, and she might have even forgotten to breathe.

"Rivka, mind your sword!" And the next thing she knew she was fumbling to block his attacks again. He aimed one of his hands at the log as they continued to spar, and it burst into flames, destroying the evidence— everywhere but within her breast.

They spoke no more that night of what Rivka now knew to be a mutual love, but now that the egg had been cracked there was no putting it back into the shell. Rivka tossed and turned in her bed, longing to be with him, exploring thoughts she had never before considered. She ran her hand down her body, imagining it was his touch she felt. At the very idea, she cried out into the night.

Sleep would not come. She could think only of him. And so she arose, wrapped her dressing gown around her

body, and crept into the passageways.

There was a knock at the wizard's locked door.

"Who disturbs my sleep?" growled a familiar bass voice, the low tones resonating more powerfully and more harshly than usual through the door.

"Please let me in."

"What happened to not asking more of me?"

"I'm sorry—I'm weak—" She pressed herself against his door, yearning for the impossible, wanting him to hold her and turn whatever felt like a heart beating between her legs into an oasis of sweet relief.

"No, you're strong because you know what you want and you're not afraid to ask for it."

"Open the door, I beg of you."

"You know my vows."

"I promise not to shame you. I won't even look at you. I just want to be near you." She banged on the door once with both fists. "I'll stay out here if I have to."

"Heed, Rivka." He was close to the door now, and even this intimacy shot ribbons of feeling through her body. "Go back to your room and close your door, and if you promise not to open it during the night, *I* promise that I will follow you and stay with you on the outside as you sleep."

"Why my door, and not yours?"

"Because I would rather the risk of being caught in the passageway fall to me. Let this be something I can give you."

Breaking, Rivka whispered, "I promise!" and made for her room as quickly as she could.

Shutting the door behind her, she remained right beside it, eventually sitting on the floor with her back against the door as she waited. Finally, she heard his voice. "Rivka."

"Isaac," she replied, her face spreading into a grin. "I'm sorry—"

"You have no reason to apologize," he said. "My vows are mine alone to keep—my burden and my responsibility—not yours. Cherish your feelings, and don't be ashamed of them. Enjoy them as I cannot."

"Then I love you, and in my mind you're holding me."

He began to sing in another language. It was the speech of Perach, to the south, just as in their prayers, but the text was one she'd never heard before.

Jeweled stars, pearl stars
Silver coins in olive jars
Glittering deep within the dark
See them flicker, see them spark
Press the olives, pool the oil
Golden sunlight, golden royal
Press so olive oil will run
Press the night, collect the sun...

She leaned into the door and let his deep voice resonate through her body, caressing her with sound. As he sang, delight flooded her brain and drove out all thought.

For several hours they shared hearts, talking of their childhoods and of his adventures out on the battlefield. As sleep finally overtook the frustrated but soothed maiden, she said to him, "I hope that I dream that we're fighting side by side." It wasn't all she was hoping to dream, but what she'd said out loud had a reasonable chance of coming true—at least, in the alternate reality where the baron would let her fight and would respect Isaac enough to take his advice. And she didn't want to make him feel guilty for holding true to his vows, which he couldn't break even if he wanted to without serious wizard consequences.

"I hope your dreams bring you comfort," was his heavy-laden reply.

She hugged herself and felt his love in it. He sang again until she slept.

***

Two days later, the maid was sick. Somebody else cleaned Rivka's room and came at a different time, and before Rivka knew anything about it, the alternate maid had found her sword and shown it to enough people that it was too late to try to bribe anyone to be silent. She rushed toward the Great Hall, hoping to intercept her uncle before someone else told him about the sword. She knew he'd take the secrecy just as badly as the disregard of his wishes.

"Uncle!" She dashed into the room in a hot flurry of skirts. Then she clapped her hands to her face and shrieked.

Isaac was standing in the center of the room, grimacing, with Rivka's sword pointed fixedly at his throat—courtesy of the baron.

Chapter 10: The Blood-Streaked Flower

D eceit. Deceit, and shame, and insult." With each percussive word, the hand that held the sword twitched slightly, as if the baron were trying very hard not to simply kill the wizard there and then. "You invade my castle with your useless ideas and two-faced words of peace, and then embarrass me before my enemies. Was that your game all along, wizard? Show them that our forces are so pathetic that a bastard wench must raise a sword in our defense? Whose side are you on?"

"She has talent." Isaac's voice was quiet, grim, and resolute.

"A woman *cannot* wield a sword!" the baron bellowed. "You defile my house with your insolent ideas. Hersch!" He gestured to an attendant page. "Fetch a messenger. Then go to my private weapons room and bring me the black box that sits in the southeast corner."

Rivka studied him, looking for an opening, but he had been a lifelong warrior and the hand that held her blade showed no sign of weakness. Instead, she said simply, "Uncle, I *can* fight for you. You and I both know it's useless for me to add that I wish it wasn't true, but the Apple Valley troops are always a danger. I promise that I can help you repel the next attack."

"Useless—your *promise* is *useless!*" screamed the baron, close enough to Isaac's face to cause the stoic, stony mask of anger to momentarily flinch. "You would

collapse at what I've seen in one half-minute of ordinary battle."

"Uncle—"

He put up his other hand. "Save your breath. Guards, hold my niece."

Before Rivka could dart out of the way, four strong men appeared from the shadowed corners and grabbed her arms and legs. She wriggled with all her might, but none of her heavy, muscled pushes could break her free. There were simply too many guards.

"Wizard, you have interfered with the supervision of my valley, you have interfered with the peace of my home, and now you have interfered with my family—especially this fatherless girl whose upbringing has been my burden these many years." The baron sounded like a judge passing down a verdict. "Of course her weak woman's mind would believe whatever twaddle you told her about dead kings and theoretical battle plans based on dreams."

"You would dig in a gold mine and see only potatoes," Isaac growled. "And you would swallow them whole, bitterly regretting your misfortune while filling your stomach with countless riches."

"Why, you—"

"I hope you choke on them."

"I have a sword to your throat! Your words mean nothing."

But to Rivka, bound and struggling, they meant everything, especially as one who had been called Daughter of Beet-greens. She knew in her heart, with a certainty as real as the air in her lungs, that Isaac valued her as nobody else had. Beets and potatoes come up from the earth and taste of earth. Gold comes out of the dirt but shines like sunlight.

The messenger entered, followed by the page and his cargo. "Sire, you sent for me?"

"Yes. Report this message to the Wizard Order in the mountains," said the baron officiously. "I've found their wizard representative completely unacceptable and demand his removal immediately. If they insist on replacing him—if they *must* nursemaid me—tell them to send me someone who isn't so insufferably *smug*"— he glared at Isaac—"and who doesn't constantly quote ancient histories, and who won't disobey my rules in my own castle! You never should have even spoken to the girl, fool wizard."

The messenger cleared his throat. "Sire, was that all?"

"What? Oh, yes. Yes. Just tell them to get here as soon as possible to collect him."

"Collect him?" Rivka's heart pounded in her ears.

The baron's response was to gesture at his page for the black box.

Rivka's glance met Isaac's. In that moment of terror she memorized his eyes. For a moment, she was able to forget the room, the sword, the baron, the four strong men holding her, and the nightmare she was sure would follow.

The baron's free hand emerged from the black box holding a small vial of liquid. "Wizard, I don't believe for a moment you would actually leave if I banished you awake. You're a sneaky, slithering, treacherous, interfering—"

"What is that?" Rivka demanded.

"Shut up, girl! It's sleep... sleep in a bottle." He held it up for her. "He's going to drink it, and then he won't be able to cause any more trouble until the other wizards come to get him and *take him far away.*"

Isaac pursed his lips and glanced up at the baron defiantly. He lifted one of his pointed eyebrows and closed his lips tightly.

Rivka noticed his hands at his side, slowly tensing into

action. She silently prayed that his magical whips of light would be swift and effective. Could he use them to free himself and get out of the room before the baron could swing his sword?

"Guards, knives," said the baron, unexpectedly.

In one confusing moment, light flared from Isaac's fingers, and the guards holding Rivka suddenly held daggers to her flesh. "You would harm your own blood?" he growled at the baron in horror.

"Of course I wouldn't kill her," explained the baron. "But there are things those men can do with their daggers that I know you don't want them to do to her." He grabbed the wizard's right arm and pulled back his sleeve roughly to expose the scar across his wrist and forearm.

"You monster," Isaac growled. Rivka had never seen him so bitterly angry, almost as if he were buried under an avalanche of his own rage.

"Drink the cordial like a good little irritating meddler," said the baron, "and Rivka won't be harmed."

"*No!*" Her voice was like a hawk's scream.

"Shut *up*, girl!"

"Get those things away from me!" Rivka hissed at the guards. They were trying to be extra threatening by showing her how sharp the daggers were, shaving off bits of hair on her arms. Her fists clenched, and she longed for an army.

"Isaac—"

The wizard looked at her straight on, ignoring the baron completely for a moment. "I believe in you."

Then he tilted his head slightly and opened his lips.

Without taking his eyes off Rivka, he let the baron's rough hands tip the contents of the vial into his mouth.

"No!" Rivka's jaw shook. Everything shook. "I'll find you."

The wizard's blue eyes closed, beholding last an image

of tall, blonde Rivka, trembling pridefully in the grasp of her captors. He fell limp into the arms of more guards who had turned up at the baron's gesture.

"No, you won't," said the baron calmly. "Guards, get her into her room and lock the door from the outside. Make sure she gets regular meals."

Stuffing the frantic, fighting Rivka into her room was like trying to bail out a boat that was leaking in fourteen places, but the guards managed it somehow and then bundled themselves off to dinner. She wore herself out banging on the door and then collapsed onto the floor with her hands once again clenched into fists.

She rushed to her window. It was too high to make a practical escape, despite the deep pond just beneath. Studying the landscape just outside the castle, her eye caught movement on the ground. What was that, if not the guards carrying the unconscious wizard into one of the wooden towers that had been built as storage for last year's exceptionally bountiful crops? She stared at the strange, horrifying procession, torturing herself with every moment of beholding Isaac in such a state. He was beautiful in repose—that repose should be with *her*, not as punishment for her friendship!

The guards disappeared with their prisoner into the tower, and before long she saw them in the topmost window, two or three stories up, fussing around in the room. Probably making room for him amid the sacks of beets.

Realizing she wasn't going to be able to watch him anymore—they must have lain him down on the floor—she looked around the room and tried to plan an escape.

Unfortunately, the guards burst in a little while later with her food, interrupting her knotted bedsheet rope scheme. She wasn't quick enough to hide it under the bed in time, and they took it away with them. They left

part of a chicken and overcooked kasha varnishkes in its place, but it was a poor trade.

She ate for strength, not pleasure.

"Rivkeleh."

"Mammeh, isn't there any way you can soften his heart and get me out of here?"

Mitzi sighed through the door. "He's right—you can't keep getting involved in these dangerous things that you don't understand."

"I do understand."

"You say you want to fight. You could get killed out there."

"Has it occurred to you that I might be good enough that I would actually survive a battle?"

"Your uncle has tried to give you all that a woman needs in life—a nice bed to sleep in, good food, pretty clothing, social position—which, need I remind you, you and I are not naturally blessed with, thanks to my behavior at your age."

She still thinks I'm fifteen. "I'm not you, Mammeh. Those are all the things *you* need."

Several hours later, Rivka had taken up position at the window to gaze out at the tower through the cool night air. There was nothing to watch, but she felt closer to Isaac if she could at least see his prison. So deep was she in her thoughts—of his voice, his unspoken love, his sacrifice—that it was several minutes before she noticed the men on horseback riding into the grounds. She squinted into the inky night, trying to see—

Someone else raised the alarm, and then she realized what was going on. Their enemies from the other valley. What timing! Was her whole life to collapse like a poorly constructed model house of sticks in one climactically awful night?

If only she could get out of the room and help fight. Not that she had her sword anymore, of course. Her uncle had awarded it to Lev, one of the guards who had been shaving the hairs off her arm with his dagger. *Her* sword—that had Isaac's name on it.

Women were rushing around in the passageway screaming, and she heard the heavy clomp of men's boots as they prepared for battle. "Let me out! Let me fight!" she screamed at nobody, and nobody answered.

Hastening back to the window, she saw that a group of attackers holding torches were spreading flames across the land. Reaching her hands out the window at them as if she could hold them back with sheer will, she tried to pray them away from the tower where Isaac lay. "Please," she cried uselessly into the night. "He's asleep. He can't escape. Oh, please!"

It was unlikely the men downstairs had any idea that they were destroying anything beyond resources. The inexorable torches moved toward the tower and kissed it with flame. The structure was constructed out of wood, and caught easily.

"*No!*" Rivka grabbed the sides of the window with both hands and wriggled through, then launched herself from its height into the pond below. She had no room in her heart to fear the fall. All her fear was for that dearest heart trapped high in the burning tower.

She hit the water with a violent splash. When she lifted her head above the surface and wiped the droplets and dripping hair from her face, what she saw by firelight turned her blood to a frozen poison.

The tower...

Rudimentary remainders of the first story were still standing, as black sticks amidst a forest of orange flame. But the upper stories were completely gone. Ash was everywhere. Men ran and horses galloped back and forth, thundering over the quiet rumble-crackle of the fire.

Rivka walked out of the pond, her wet dress not the only shackle weighing her down. She kept her eyes on the ruined tower, unable to ask—

The ash-laden wind whipped up, chilling her and plastering her face with a cloth rag with singed edges that had flown about on its eddies. She pulled it away from her face only to shudder in fright.

It was a piece of Isaac's cassock.

She gasped as if she were breaking, her legs weak and shaky and barely holding her up, and then screamed. A horrible feeling devoured her stomach and threatened to rip the breath from her throat.

Before she had time to think, a warrior wearing the Apple Valley crest approached her on horseback. He made as if to draw his sword, but his unusually large horse, most likely spooked by the fire, suddenly reared and threw him off. With one quick look back at the surprised invader, lying on his backside in the mud, she leapt onto the horse's back. It didn't occur to her that a spooked horse might not like her either.

Once on the horse, she wrapped the cassock fragment around her hair and knotted it. She could shatter into a thousand pieces later for all she cared, but right now, without a way to defend herself, her first idea was to get out of the fray and back into the castle.

She rode away from the confusion at the burning crop towers and toward the castle entrance. The battle had been here already and moved on, and the last few steps of the horse were in between corpses—those of her own

family's guards, but also those of invaders from the other valley. They lay here and there all mixed together, all human in death.

The main entrance was still a confusion of swords and shouting, and since she still had no sword, she guided the horse into the relative safety of the shadow made by a side doorway. There, she took a deep breath and looked around her.

A glint of metal on the mud caught her eye.

Lev lay faceup and lifeless, and beside him was Rivka's sword.

Without another thought, she hopped off the horse and grabbed it. For a moment she could do nothing but clutch its hilt with both hands, and then suddenly she broke into bone-quaking sobs. *Isaac.* Never to spar with him again—never to see his face again, hear his voice, all lost—

Focus.

She looked back down at Lev's corpse. His battle armor of leather and metal looked relatively undamaged by the fate that had felled him. After placing the sword against the corner of the doorway for safekeeping, she dragged the body into the shadows and quickly removed every useful bit of battle-kit.

Caring nothing for modesty in that strange night, she cast off her dress and donned the pants, the tunic, and the helmet.

The sword felt perfect in the scabbard she now wore across her waist.

Jumping back onto the back of the enormous mare, she raised her sword and dashed into the thick of the battle.

It wasn't long before she found the baron. He was bravely holding the doorway against three men at once—despite being an awful person he was indeed a good

fighter. But eventually a fourth invader fought his way through the lesser guards and tipped the balance.

The baron gritted his teeth and plowed into them, surely knowing that he risked his life.

"Hyahhh!" Rivka shouted, galloping forward on her horse. She helped her uncle to drive back the four men, then fought at his side for the rest of the battle. At one point, she even sliced off an arm that was about to stab the baron in the kidneys. She didn't know whose arm it was, and she didn't have time to care. The warrior spirit Isaac had brought out in her was fully born, and there was no putting the flower back into the bud, that flower that was now streaked deep red with the blood of her enemies.

Nobody had any idea who she was.

When the thing was done, and their enemies had been driven away for the time being, she stalked into the Great Hall where the baron was feeding the survivors thick, awful coffee and an impromptu breakfast of boiled potatoes. "Uncle," she said, breathlessly, removing her helmet. "So you see, I can fight."

The baron's weary but satisfied face twisted into a fiery scowl. "What—that was *you* out there?"

"I saved your life, Uncle." Her smile fled, and the face of an adult woman began to replace it. "You saw—"

"I certainly hope none of the surviving Apple Valley fighters saw! How could you betray me like that?"

"Betray you?" She glared at him. "I kept an enemy sword from stabbing you in the back! I wouldn't let those men overpower you. Do you value your own life so little—"

"Come on, girl, I know what you're really upset about. Don't pretend."

"No, Uncle, this is not about what happened to Isaac." Several of the warriors eating around the room

had stopped mid-bite and were watching the show. Rivka had always been headstrong, but never had she displayed such deadly calm and resolve in her outbursts. "He died because you imprisoned him, and yet I stayed to fight for you, to defend this keep, because this has been my home and I am part of this family, whether you like it or not. He died because of you and yet I *defended you*. And for that, you reject me?" The baron moved his mouth as if he wanted to interject, but she kept talking, her words fueled by the stinging nettles in her heart. "I reject *you*, Uncle. Thank you for my childhood. You don't deserve my talents. And you certainly do not deserve my respect. I. Am. Done. Here. Go shit in the sea."

Mitzi dashed out at her from a corner, a look of desperate pain across her face. "Rivka!"

"Mammeh, I'll send word. I love you, and some day if I settle down to guard one keep—which is what I've *always wanted*"—she glared at the baron—"I will send for you. And you'll still have a warm bed and good food, without his disdain."

There was one moment, during which nobody in the room—Rivka, Mitzi, the baron, the soldiers, the servants—moved at all. Then, with a final nod at her mother, Rivka turned around and stalked out, her sword at her side.

She lifted herself onto the huge mare and rode away. To her surprise, the mare reared suddenly and sprang up into the sky. The next thing she knew, she was riding a Dragon...

Chapter 11: Lighting the Candles

Rivka hadn't spoken much since trailing off at the end of her story, and the final hour of the ride was mostly silent. Shulamit felt an awkwardness that was practically tangible; it was likely Rivka was withdrawing after spending most of the day speaking about her past. She remembered her own parallel incidents—for example, those moments when she first told her ladies-in-waiting of her attraction toward other women—when she was shy after revealing her heart and found it clumsy to return to ordinary discourse. So she tried not to take it personally.

But it made for a tense afternoon. She was awed at the painful events she had heard, but had little of value to say in response. Fortunately, at least the weather and the dragon's stamina were both cooperating, and they arrived at a safe place to sleep without too much physical hardship.

"It's still light," said Rivka abruptly as she bustled around the rocks setting up their makeshift camp. "We should work on some of those self-defense techniques—if you're not fatigued from traveling." She didn't meet the queen's eyes.

"No, I'm ready. Like this?" Shulamit took a stance on the rock as Rivka had shown her.

She tried her best to concentrate on the movements, and managed about a half an hour of work before she

realized she had pushed herself beyond where her muscles wanted to go. "Rivka, I'm sorry. I need to stop and eat."

"I'll send Dragon to go hunt us some food," said Rivka. "I saw some wild goats beyond the lake. That should give both of us more strength."

"How will she know not to catch birds first? Aviva taught me that even cooking my meat in the same pan as fowl can contaminate my food and cause... problems... and I see ducks in the water, in the reeds."

Rivka sighed, biting her lip. "I suppose I could ride with her and keep her to the goats. Do you feel safe waiting here for a few minutes by yourself?"

Shulamit weighed her options. After all she had been through, she still feared the assaults of unknown strangers. But she also had vivid, horrifying, humiliating memories of what would happen to her body if she ate anything tainted by the duck meat. Since it was something she'd experienced again and again, it rose up and took precedence. "I'll wait here. I think I see mint growing by the lake; I'll go collect some to season the goat."

"Good idea. I noticed wild tangerines growing over that way too." Rivka pointed.

Shulamit's face brightened at the idea of unexpected fresh fruit. She hurried off toward the lake as Rivka hopped onboard her dragon's back and leapt into the air.

Kneeling beside the lake gathering the choicest leaves from the wild mint plants into her lilac scarf brought back memories... scenes stored away close to her heart, wrapped in silk and scented with rose water.

With each new food Aviva's experiments had cleared for Shulamit's safe consumption, the princess grew stronger and healthier. No more was she racked by daily

digestive calamities; she had the energy to frolic in the palace gardens and enjoy life again. During the process, the two girls had become constant companions, and as Shulamit perked up, Aviva began teaching her more about food preparation so that she could take charge of her own health more easily.

Aviva took her to the palace herb garden to teach her what all the herbs looked like. She plucked a handful of rippled green leaves and crushed them beneath Shulamit's nose. The cold, fresh scent flowed forth. "Is it singing to you?"

"It's mint!"

Aviva smiled in affirmation. "She smells cool because she keeps a secret part of herself always hidden away from the sun. She's strong enough to remain cold even in the hottest weather. She has principles and she sticks to 'em."

Shulamit giggled. "You always talk in poetry. Do you ever write anything down?"

A warm but slightly self-conscious smile spread over the cook's face. "I never thought of it as poetry—it just happens on its own when I talk. I get in a hurry to say what I'm feeling, and before I know it, I've said something goofy."

"I'm never bored around you," Shulamit observed. "Aviva—" Shulamit suddenly turned to face her and took one of her hands in both her own. She felt strength beneath the softness and warmth. "Why did you believe me? About being sick, I mean. When everyone else thinks it was in my head, or a ruse to look... well... princessy?"

"My mother's been sickly most of my life, so I know about illness and helping those who are ailing," Aviva explained. "When I was younger, I tended to her while my father moved mountains and reversed rivers all by

himself. But now that I'm old enough I left home to go work, so I could replace the money she earned when she was a washerwoman. Aba's a tailor, and even though he'd rather be out in the marketplace selling his creations or visiting clients, if he stays home to take care of Ima, he can still take in mending and receive customers there. It's better for us all this way. Maybe someday we'll even be able to afford surgery so she can walk again."

It awed Shulamit that this young woman, not two years older than herself, was financially contributing to her family in such a significant way. Especially since she, as the crown princess, was living a completely antithetical life. She felt undeserving and grateful that someone as incredible as Aviva even wanted to talk to her.

Shulamit crushed the mint in her fingers, thinking about the relieving coolness who refused to compromise her ideas even in the face of something as powerful as the sun. She inhaled, and saw Aviva's dark, smiling face, her friendly eyes, the luscious curves of her body radiating femininity from beneath her sleeveless tunic and loose-fitting trousers. She could even hear that quirky, peasant-accented voice spouting its outlandish poetry.

With a sigh, she quickly gathered up the rest of the mint they needed and brought it back to the campsite. Rivka had left a pouch for her to use to collect tangerines both for tonight and for the rest of their journey, so she brought that back with her as she walked along the lakeshore to the wild grove.

But her heart wasn't finished replaying Aviva-infused memories. Her eyes were looking at fruit, picking the ones that were the most colorful and unblemished, but what

she was in truth seeing was a scene from many months ago, when she had stolen away to Aviva's kitchen late at night.

So much of that day was taken up by tutors, in their attempt to make up for time lost to digestive illness, that she had her fill neither of food nor of Aviva's company. It was several hours past moonrise by the time she finally tripped lightly down the path to the small building where all her meals were now prepared. It was a fowl-free, wheat-free, and most importantly, judgment- and doubt-free little paradise where all the food was edible and Shulamit was always believed.

It was far later than she had ever appeared there, so she knew Aviva wouldn't be expecting her. But what she herself wasn't expecting was the sight that greeted her eyes when she slipped unnoticed through the doorway.

Aviva was busily preparing a meal, most likely a trial run of some new experiment for Shulamit. But she didn't do so silently, and she wasn't merely cooking.

Instead, she was singing at the top of her lungs, a vivacious working-class dance tune. She was also using the handles of her knives, spoons, and other implements as drumsticks, beating them against the stone tables in time with her song. She twirled around the room, all hips and elbows, as she grabbed ingredients, chopped them up, and even tossed them into the dish in time to her dancing. She didn't know all the words, either—sometimes she just sang nonsense syllables.

Finally, she noticed the princess standing there watching her. She stopped dancing, put her hands on her hips, and said, "So what?"

Shulamit just giggled.

"Okay, so you see I've hidden a whole plague of frogs in my kitchen. Sometimes they do the work for me while they chirp." She paused to scoop up a handful of chopped herbs and toss it into the pot. "Well?"

"Well, what?"

"Now you know something embarrassing about me. So you should tell me something embarrassing about yourself. That way we're even."

"I like women the way men do," Shulamit blurted out, before she knew what she was doing. Heat crept into her face.

Aviva studied her from across the room for a moment, her head cocked like a bird's. Then she opened her mouth and began to sing again, and her feet began once again their dance. Only, this time, she held both of her hands out to Shulamit.

She didn't say anything about what Shulamit had admitted, but as she drew the princess close into their dance, it was clear that she was anything but scared away.

A cast-iron pot boiled over and interrupted their first kiss. Aviva rushed over to attend to it while Shulamit stood still, memorizing every detail—Aviva's soft mouth that tasted of fennel seeds, her full bosom pressed against Shulamit's own, those hands that made her feel so safe and well cared for. "Does the food agree with you?" asked Aviva, looking up from the stove with a wink.

Shulamit squeaked and then decided to nod instead of speaking. Embracing Aviva was like holding a huge bouquet of flowers in your arms, soft and glorious, with the scent overtaking you and pollen leaving yellow speckles across your nose.

"In my kitchen, there's always more for you to sample..."

And then another, from months later:

Shulamit darted through the palace, slipping as silently as she could between rooms and courtyards. With nervous eyes she checked her path to make sure nobody was paying attention to her as she made her way toward Aviva's kitchen house for their prearranged tryst. Her jaws worked away at the fennel seeds she was chewing to make sure she wouldn't be repaying top-notch kisses with stale breath. Aviva kept saying she didn't care too much about Shulamit's ornaments, but the little princess didn't care and had bedecked herself in the clothing she thought prettiest: delicate fabrics of pastel-pink and lilac.

She rounded a corner, and her heart leapt; Aviva was rushing to meet her. The two women met in the corridor and joined hands. "We can't go back to my kitchen," Aviva explained. "The head chef is in there hiding from her flock—she was like a bag of tigers this morning and now she's too embarrassed to go back in there."

"But what's she doing?"

"Baking," said Aviva. "I know—I'll have to clean it all out again. I promise I'll be thorough."

"I wish there was a way to convince her I'm not just being picky!" Shulamit huffed. "Maybe I can help you clean when she finally leaves."

"It'll be like cleaning up for Passover."

Noises at both ends of the corridor made Shulamit tense up and whip her head in both directions, flinging her braids over her shoulders. "Someone's coming!"

"Quick! Come on!" Aviva grabbed her hand. There was a small door in the wall, leading into a cupboard, and Aviva pulled it open. Inside was a haphazard collection of rolled-up rugs, to be used in some of the palace hallways when the other rugs were dirty or a different color was required. The two girls could just fit inside if they folded their limbs, and Aviva pulled the door shut just as several

courtiers entered the hallway.

They sounded as though they were arguing, but the door was thick and Shulamit couldn't make out any words. She was too busy kissing Aviva, and moving as best she could in the cramped space to get her arms around her. It was easy to be overwhelmed by the sensation of Aviva's lush body against her own, with her fleshy upper arms, large bosom, and generous hips.

Soon they were touching each other more intimately, and Shulamit moaned into the tender place on Aviva's neck where she rested her head. Her left hand was full of one of Aviva's breasts, the feel of which sent her brain spiraling into pinwheels of delight. "I tried looking in books to see why these make me so happy," she commented. "Nobody knew."

Aviva giggled at her. "You would." Moans overtook her ability to speak as she ground herself harder against Shulamit's other hand.

"It wasn't a complete waste of time—I did find some pretty interesting reading on how our bodies work."

Aviva clenched her teeth, clearly trying to muffle herself, but the next groan escaped anyway, even stronger. "Is that why you're—Ahhh! Okay, you studied for sex. You are truly amazing."

"The book said if I—" Shulamit altered the movement of her fingers slightly.

Aviva let out a noise like wind rustling through palm fronds before a storm. "Smart book. Good book. Gonna make... halvah... for the... book...ohh..."

Then Shulamit felt like a magician, the same way she did every time she'd achieved the seemingly miraculous feat of making Aviva climax. She made sure to continue what she'd been doing until Aviva calmed down, and then concentrated on the sensations of her own body until she followed her.

"*We're gonna have such backaches after being in here,*" *she commented, snuggling into Aviva's warmth.*

"*We still have to work it off cleaning out my kitchen after we've got it back to ourselves!*"

"*Mmmm.*" *Shulamit inhaled deeply. The inside of the little cupboard smelled of woman, and she felt dizzyingly content.*

Shulamit was so lost in the heat of these passionate memories that she gathered far more tangerines than she had intended. Not wanting to waste them, she carried them all back to the campsite and began juicing them into one of the drinking vessels.

It was getting darker, and the sun had started to paint the sky brilliant colors with its departure, so she was relieved to see her companion returning. Dragon clutched a slain goat in the claws of her back legs like an eagle holding a rabbit. "This will feed us for several days," said Rivka. She was acting like herself again.

"What about Dragon? Or—wait, she feeds as a horse. I'm confused."

"I let her feed first."

"That makes sense. I picked too many tangerines, so I've been juicing them. And here's the mint."

Rivka butchered the goat and set it up over the fire to cook. Then she stood up and gazed out over the lake at the sunset.

"It's Shabbat," Shulamit suddenly realized out loud.

Rivka muttered quietly in her own language in a cadence Shulamit took for counting out the days. "So it is. There's our Shabbas candle..."

"Where?" Shulamit felt smart for noticing Rivka's usage of the northern version of the word.

Rivka pointed at the sunset, a pink-and-gold marvel that spread across the far shore of the lake. "And the lake can be the wine."

"We can say the wine blessing over the tangerine juice," Shulamit suggested.

Rivka grinned. "That's the idea." Then a look of horror spread across her face. "You can't eat challah!"

"I know. I miss it."

"Never mind, I don't know why I said that." Rivka shook her head at her own bluntness.

Shulamit shrugged. "I miss sufganiyot more, especially at Chanukah when everyone has them at once. But Aviva used to fry me sweet plantains instead. I like the bits that get a little burnt the best."

"What are sufganiyot?"

"Fried dough with sugar on top."

"We fry potato pancakes for Chanukah."

"That sounds good. I can eat potato," said Shulamit. "We'd better start before the colors start fading. They're so... they go away so quickly. Sometimes the prettiest part only lasts a minute."

The two women sat down and covered their eyes to say a blessing, and then looked out over the beautiful sunset.

As they waited for the goat to cook, their talk turned to business. "What do you think it's going to be like when we get to the sorcerer's keep?" Shulamit asked.

"From what Tamar told me, it sounded like he's actually a pretty big coward," said Rivka, peeling a tangerine with her thumbs. "All the sleazy behavior toward women—he tends to keep that in check when men are around. He was singing to one of them, once, and stopped right in the middle and refused to continue because a man showed up to deliver rice. And did you hear what she said about how paranoid he was? He even told some of the holy

women bad things about himself so that he could 'expose' the truth as a lie—preemptively, since it turned out that nobody had warned anyone at all."

"I remember her saying that," said Shulamit. "I bet someone cowardly, paranoid, and skilled in magic would protect himself with plenty of enchantments."

Rivka nodded. "Exactly. So you've been thinking about it too."

Shulamit nodded. "It's keeping my mind off Aviva. The smell of the mint brought back... things."

"I'm sorry about that," said Rivka. "But thinking is good. I like the way your mind works. Back there in the inn, you really impressed me with the way you solved that crime."

Shulamit smiled and pulled her knees up to her chest, hugging them. "That felt amazing," she admitted, "once I knew I wasn't going to die, of course!"

"Nobody said you can't be a queen and solve crimes at the same time," Rivka pointed out. "Wisdom and justice are traits that will earn the respect and trust of your people."

"I wanted to solve a mystery back home once," said Shulamit. "Money was stolen from my father's treasury. Only a few people had keys, but he trusted them all. He wouldn't let me ask questions, and he never did find out what happened."

Rivka studied her with darkened eyes. "Does that have anything to do with the elephant?"

Shulamit shook her head quickly. "No, that was just a freak accident. He was pushing himself too hard—not enough sleep—working all day and then trying to spend time with me *and* his lady friends *and* hobbies, athletics... he was trying to do everything." She sighed heavily. "Maybe he got all his living done fast, and if he'd have lived slower, he'd have lived longer."

"Maybe," said Rivka. "Or maybe a *howdah* is just a terrible place for an exhausted man of any age."

"I feel safer on Dragon than up on an elephant now."

"She's a good girl." Rivka smiled and patted the beast. "Oh, hey, the goat's ready."

They fed themselves as quickly as the hot meat would allow them. "Can we go back to practicing after dinner?" Rivka asked.

"On Shabbat?"

Rivka just raised one eyebrow.

"I guess you're right."

"Tomorrow afternoon we face our enemy," Rivka reminded her. "I don't want you should get killed."

"I'll concentrate twice as hard," Shulamit announced proudly.

Chapter 12: The Honey Trap

The next morning, they set out for the sorcerer's mountain stronghold. Dragon's flight took them over areas of rocky ground and deep chasms that no horse and definitely no pair of humans could have made on foot, and Shulamit was nervously thankful that she had enough energy to get off the ground.

Finally, in the afternoon, they reached the keep. A proud, high sun illuminated a tower of stone carved straight into the mountainside. Leading up to the tower was a gravel walkway edged with larger stones and planted with olive trees. Dragon landed at the edge of the walkway and morphed into her horse form. After Rivka and Shulamit dismounted, she swept her sensitive muzzle over the rocks, devouring any blade of grass she could find.

"She's tiring," Rivka observed. Then she turned to Shulamit. "You should remove that."

"What?"

Rivka fingered the lilac scarf around Shulamit's neck. "Very pretty, but look." She grabbed the scarf and jerked it suddenly.

Shulamit froze up in panic and nearly burst into tears even though it was only a mock attack. After producing an embarrassing gasping noise, she nodded, eyeing Rivka as if she were not entirely certain her demonstration had been in good taste.

"Hey, I'm sorry." Rivka offered her arm. "*Nu*, did I make my point?"

Shulamit fell into the comforting hug and then quickly put the scarf away in her bag.

Rivka swept her fingers over her sword hilt. "Well? Let's go see what there is to see." She led her queen and her steed down the gravel path. Pebbles crunched beneath their feet. "He really likes stone, doesn't he?" Shulamit observed. "He lives in stone, with little stones leading up to it, and he turned the holy women into stone." She paused for a moment, working on an idea.

Rivka took another step.

The larger stones at the side of the path began to spit spherical golden blobs at them. "What?!" Shulamit shrieked.

Rivka tried to dodge the assault, but it was coming from so many directions that it was impossible. Before long, both women and even the horse were covered in—

"*Honey?*" Rivka lifted her eyebrow. "I don't underst—"

Then the stones firing honey balls rotated ninety degrees and switched ammunition. Tiny, hard particles spewed out at the travelers from all angles. Rivka batted at the storm with both hands, trying to protect her face. "I'm glad I took off my scarf!" Shulamit wailed, looking down at her clothing.

"*These* are his enchantments to keep out invaders?" bellowed Rivka. "What is this, *grain*? Shula, make sure it doesn't get in your mou—"

"Your eyes! Cover your eyes!" Shulamit suddenly screamed.

"*Nu?*" And then Rivka stopped asking questions, because a flock of crazed birds was descending all around them. Drawn by the seeds spat out by their master's magical rocks, the cloud of brightly colored flapping

hellions closed in on the warrior and the queen. Shulamit shrank to the ground and pulled her body into as tiny a ball as she could manage, whereas Rivka unsheathed her sword with one hand while covering her eyes with the elbow of the other.

Then they heard a familiar, welcome sound—the much louder, deeper flap of the dragon's wings. It only took a few mighty blows for her to drive away the birds. Rivka uncovered her eyes and watched Dragon dispatch the last few birds, scaring away the quick and munching on the slower. "Good girl," she said with a relieved smile, and patted the beast's scaly avocado-rind hide. "You deserve that little nosh. I hope it's tasty."

Shulamit was still sitting on the ground, trying to clean herself off. "I'm disgusting. Wait, did the two things I can't eat just *attack* me?"

"Just be careful, so it won't get in your mouth." Then Rivka let out an uncharacteristic giggle, because Dragon had transformed back into a horse and was licking some of the foul honey-birdseed mixture off her face. "*Oy.* Don't even talk to me about disgusting."

"I see water up there." Shulamit sprang up and made a beeline for the large stone fountain near the entrance of the fortress.

Rivka and the horse followed her. "If it's even water," Rivka muttered, "and not borscht, at this rate."

The horse sneezed. "You're right," Rivka added, as if the horse's sneeze had meant something. "We're too far south for borscht."

Shulamit reached the fountain but then hesitated. "Riv! What if it's *not* water?"

"I was joking."

"I know, but—he's a sorcerer. What if it's poison or acid or something?"

Rivka lifted one eyebrow. "Good thinking. Only one

way to find out!" She plunged one hand into the water. "Seems safe to me."

Shulamit's mouth dropped open. Sometimes Rivka's bravery scared her. She smiled, but it was a horrified smile.

"I should taste it just to double-check," Rivka mused. But the horse had ambled up beside her and was drinking out of the fountain herself with no ill effects.

The two women began to scrub off the honey and birdseed. As they washed, a young woman ran out of the fortress. She was exceedingly lovely, and her hands were bound. Her feet had been bound too, but the rope was cut roughly, as if against a stone. Barely a wisp of clothing hid a dark, luxurious landscape of a body. Her hair had been pinned up behind each ear but the pins were coming down as if she hadn't been able to tend to it in a while. "At last! Finally, someone will rescue me!"

Rivka quickly secured her cloth face-mask and turned to face her. "Rescue you? You're a prisoner here?"

The woman nodded. "Yes. I'm Ori. The bird-master took me from my people and tried to make me his wife. Again and again, I refused, but he won't let me go. I heard movement on the path and managed to cut some of my bindings, in hopes that you would take me away with you. I can't leave this place by myself—not on foot. The surrounding lands are too rocky, and I couldn't run away. But now that you've come, I'll be saved!" She exhaled happily, her bosom rising and falling and her hardened nipples visible through the sheer fabric of her dress.

Shulamit was entranced. Moving closer, she undid the rope around Ori's wrists and then took one hand in both of hers. "Of course we'll save you." The beautiful captive smelled of flowers, and her hand was soft and warm. Shulamit suddenly wanted to kiss her very badly, and she was astonished to see Ori gazing at her as if she were thinking the same thing.

Rivka stayed back, studying the scene critically. "We can't leave right away—we're here for a purpose. We have... business with the sorcerer."

"I'll show you the way into the keep. Come! Quickly!" Ori ran toward the door.

Shulamit made as if to follow, but Rivka caught her by one hand. The queen turned around in confusion, but Rivka gave her a hard look. "Don't follow her."

"What? Why not? Rivka, she could be the one! Maybe the reason God got me mixed up in this rescue mission instead of just sending you by yourself was because she's the woman I'm out here looking for."

"Put your tongue back in your head, Queenling. She's no good."

"What are you talking about? She's just another one of his victims."

"I don't think so. She feels wrong." Rivka was speaking very quietly so Ori couldn't hear.

"Come, warriors!" called Ori from the doorway.

Rivka picked up one of the pebbles from the path and chucked it through the door. It was a good three seconds before they heard a tiny *tock* noise—a noise that clearly came from much farther away.

"See? No floor." Rivka was still holding Shulamit's wrist and dragged the queen behind her as she stalked around the fortress entrance. "That's not the real way in."

"But what about Ori?"

"She's there to lure intruders to fall to their deaths," Rivka explained. "See, she has no effect on me—I bet it never occurred to that *schmendrick* that women would ever try to break in. He just thinks of women as prizes, not people."

"She wouldn't catch a man if he were like me, either," observed the queen with a somber face. "But he probably

isn't too worried about them."

"I wouldn't be surprised if she were just an illusion," Rivka added. "She's not coming after us. Follow me this way while I look for a real entrance."

Both human and horse obeyed. Shulamit glanced back down the rocky path at Ori, who was still looking after them with big sad eyes—but, as Rivka said, without any attempt to call them back. She felt foolish.

But she quickly redeemed herself. "Hey! There!"

Rivka studied the spot where Shulamit was pointing. It appeared to be just more solid rock face, with the type of texture that happens when a slice of rock sheers off and falls to the ground—but its solidness was an illusion. Part of the rock was actually *behind* the section of rock beside it, and it was possible to slip between the two and venture inside. "Good work, Queenling!"

Shulamit smiled with half her face.

The women and the horse stepped inside and found themselves in a dark hall of stone, lit only by skylights. There was nowhere to walk except forward, so they proceeded down the hallway. Their footsteps echoed in the cold, dark-gray world. It was cooler in here than outside, and silent, and felt terrifyingly timeless. By the time they reached the door at the end of the passageway, several minutes had gone by and they could no longer even see any light from the entrance through which they had come—only the feeble light from above.

Rivka put a firm grip on the door handle and pulled it forward.

The next room was better lit, and decorated with all manner of military artifacts. "Wow," Rivka exclaimed breathily. "These aren't just from Perach—those over there are from Imbrio, and Zembluss, and some of the other little countries to the north. I remember meeting them in battle."

111

"There are so many different types." Shulamit peered around at the abundance and disarray.

"Look over there." Rivka pointed to the far side of the room, a wistful note in her voice. "Those armor and weapons are from my homeland. And *those*—I've never even seen those in person. I just recognize them from Isaac's history books." She paused. "I bet he could identify every single thing in this room. *Oy vey iz mir*, Queenling, do I miss him..."

Shulamit didn't say anything, because she couldn't find the right words to comfort her. But into the silence there suddenly came a horrible noise, a rough clang like metal falling into metal. Then two of the suits of armor began to pace forward from the wall, toward the women. Rivka stepped out in front of Shulamit and unsheathed her sword. She held it at the ready, eyes narrowed.

Chapter 13: The Sorcerer's Arsenal

Both soulless suits of armor picked up a sword and brandished it. Shulamit's eyes went from one to the other. They looked identical. Rivka stood at the ready, head held high, clearly waiting for one of them to do something.

"You protect a worthless child!" rasped the one on the right, glaring at Rivka. "A spoiled princess is no queen."

Shulamit, cowering behind Rivka, gritted her teeth. "Don't listen to them!" hissed Rivka. "I don't know what they're up to."

"What right have you to seek a woman for your sweetheart, when those women who work hard for their living may never be able to follow their true nature?" continued the disembodied male voice from the armor on the right. "You are an undeserving fool."

"I'm not a fool!" Shulamit shouted. "I may be pampered, but at least my brain works. A brain that you don't even *have*, you overgrown tin drinking vessel!" But her face was hot, and her heart was pounding.

Then the armor on the left lifted his sword against Rivka. She blocked the blow and began to fight him, leaving Shulamit unprotected from the other suit of armor. It stomped around the fighting pair to face Shulamit. "No sword? Do you expect to escape me with the pathetic bits of self-defense this harpy has been teaching you?"

"No, not really!" Shulamit darted across the room

and climbed into a small alcove behind a display cabinet full of daggers. The suit of armor followed, swinging its sword. She was trapped, but at least she was so far inside her hiding place that its reach was too short to injure her.

"What right have you to jeopardize your father's kingdom by not marrying to produce an heir? Perach should never have been trusted to a freak like you."

Shulamit narrowed her eyes and gritted her teeth. "I don't have to think about that yet." But she knew it was right, at least about the heir.

"You think you're so smart, but look how distracted you were when Ori's nipples were pointing at you outside! You could be so easily manipulated." The suit of armor crashed its sword against the display cabinet, shattering its glass.

Shulamit pulled herself tighter into a ball and shut her eyes to protect herself from the flying shards. She was still ashamed about Ori. Wasn't this whole trip unfair to the kingdom in some way? If she died here, in this castle, because she'd gone off looking for feminine companionship, it would just prove she'd been too broken to rule from the start. She'd worried about that from the beginning, especially because liking women wasn't the only surprise her body had thrown at her.

"One day, your subjects will see you sick from your food, and, oh, will they be disgusted!" shouted the suit of armor. "How could anybody touch such a body with love, a body that spews filth without control?"

Shulamit covered her face at the images its words were putting into her head.

"Useless daughter of indolence!" it shouted at her. "It's no surprise your lover lost patience with you!"

Shulamit burst into tears.

"Of course she stayed for a while, your slutty cook, but she likes men too—you had to have known you wouldn't

be able to keep her forever. Why would she stay with you when she could go off and have a real family with a husband to satisfy her properly?" The suit of armor stomped on the floor angrily, then began trying to rip the display cabinet off the wall so it could get at Shulamit. One entire shelf of the cabinet broke off in its mighty grip, and this it tossed inside the alcove. She ducked and squished her body farther against the corner.

This was it. Rivka was busy fighting the other suit of armor and couldn't rescue her, and she was going to die. Desperately, she whimpered, "Aba..." hoping that he would at least come down and get her and make it not hurt so much.

Then she noticed that the suit of armor was having trouble ripping up the cabinet. It couldn't muster the strength to tear off another shelf the way it had the first one. "Heartless walking fork," said Shulamit bitterly, wiping away a tear that was dripping off her nose. "If you feed on negative thoughts, why don't you just go for the mother lode? I lost my father. That should make you strong enough to knock down the wall—the whole castle!"

The suit of armor stumbled in confusion. Shulamit was confused too. The more overwhelmed by filial grief she felt, the less effective against her were its attacks. "Okay," she mumbled to herself. "It's not feeding on negative emotion. It's feeding on insecurity. Well, then, *I am completely amazing.*" She walked out of the alcove, head held high, her arms folded across her chest. "I'm smart. I may not have grown up working hard, but I'm not afraid to do it when I have to. Maybe Aviva did run away because she got tired of me, but *I like myself.* And I swear on my father's grave *I will never let my people down just because I'm different.*"

The suit of armor was standing completely motionless,

but it still held its gleaming sword. Trembling, Shulamit reached out and took the weapon away from it.

She had no idea what to do with it once she had it, but now the suit was unarmed, and that was the important thing.

She scurried back to Rivka and was shocked to discover that the warrior maiden wasn't doing so well. There was nothing flawed in her swordplay, but the suit of armor was stronger than she was, and had a skill beyond any that she had ever encountered.

Shulamit listened to what it was saying. "—act without thinking, leading to *death*! You've always known that had you been more careful, Isaac would never have died," rasped the armor in a flat, unemotional drone. "On long, lonely nights you've thought about how you should have gone straight up to his room once you discovered your sword was no longer secret. If you had gone to his room instead *and taken his sword*, you would have been armed when confronting your uncle. Those men couldn't have held you, and he would have had no sway over Isaac. Together, the two of you could have fought your way out of the room and run away together. What have you cheated yourself out of, Rivka bat Beet-Greens? Think of the years together you've lost. Think of his voice, his eyes—"

"Don't listen to it, Rivka! It feeds on insecurity," Shulamit shrieked.

"I don't care!" Rivka screamed back in agony. "It's right!" She kept on fighting, but her breath heaved with fatigue.

"Instead, you jumped in—" the armor continued.

"I acted quickly out of bravery," Rivka insisted.

"Every brave act you have ever committed is tainted with what loss that bravery has wrought! Every time you rode, fearless, into battle, was disgraced by how your

impetuousness cost you your wizard."

Shulamit, heady at her own victory over the armor, thought quickly. "No, Rivka! Remember? Remember how, as soon as your uncle had the sword, he sent the four guards to capture you? You didn't even know they'd found the sword. Four guards showed up at your room, and burst in—"

"What are you—?"

Shulamit watched a change come over Rivka's face and hoped she was beginning to understand—she needed to picture the events as Shulamit described them, not as they were. "Remember how horrible it felt to have Lev's hands on your body? Remember his terrible breath? Remember the feel of the daggers poking against your skin?" The memories were from the Great Hall, when the baron had commanded his guards to clap hold of her, but Rivka had to imagine them taking place in her room instead—or else they were lost.

"You had no choice, no opportunity to make a decision," Shulamit continued.

Rivka concentrated on the lie. Soon, the suit of armor was more manageable, and eventually, she defeated it. Kicking it over with a loud yell, she grabbed its sword and tossed it into a corner. "Come on! The door!"

They ran toward the door on the other side of the room, the horse following soon after. As soon as they were through, they banged it shut and leaned back against it.

Rivka turned to look at Shulamit. "None of that was true."

"No, but I needed to save our lives," Shulamit pointed out.

"Thank you," said Rivka. She was silent for a moment. "I can't run away from that, though. I was impulsive and stupid and didn't think, and now Isaac is gone. If I could do it over..."

Shulamit didn't know what to say, so she looked around the new room instead. "Is that a crystal ball?"

The new room was full of dusty books and lit by sunlight pouring in through several open windows, but the table in the center of the room held a crystal ball. "It looks like it," said Rivka. She approached the table. "Maybe I should ask it where the antidote is. Then we won't even have to fight the sorcerer." She held out her hand—

Then the horse suddenly broke into a gallop, indoors though they were, and kicked the entire table over so hard the crystal ball was shot clear through one of the windows. Rivka and Shulamit ran to the window, but it was too late to catch it. One of the bird-master's birds was flying past the window, and the unfortunate creature was right in the trajectory. Upon touching it, the ball exploded into an orange fireball. The smoke rushed toward the women, and they quickly drew back from the window, coughing and rubbing their pained eyes.

"That could have been me," Rivka said in shock. She put her arms around Dragon's neck and rested her head against her mane for a moment.

"How on earth—?" Shulamit looked at the horse, then at the table. Then she followed Rivka into the next room.

Except for the intruders, this room was empty. It was a plain but somehow proportionally pleasant room, with plenty of sunlight and pretty much nothing else. "I don't get it," said Rivka, crankily. "What's going to explode this time?"

Shulamit pondered. "The bird attack was supposed to get rid of, well, most people trying to get in. Then there was Ori, the suits of armor, and the exploding ball. So, anyone who made it in here isn't that interested in women, doesn't have strong insecurities, and has no inclination to look into the future. I'm getting an image in my mind

of a very holy man—someone completely enlightened. You know what? I bet the idea is that an enlightened man would enter this room and then never leave. This room's too perfect. He'd just sit here forever, pondering the universe."

"Too enlightened to have a sex drive, insecurities, or curiosity," grumbled Rivka. "The two of us, that's not! *Oy gevalt*."

"Yes, but if we had brought Sister Tamar along with us, we'd be carrying her away over our shoulders." Shulamit grinned mischievously.

"How *do* we get out of here?" Rivka wondered aloud, peering around. "The only way out, besides the windows, seems to be..."

"Up there?"

The ceiling of the room rose far higher on the far side than where they stood, and if they squinted they could make out a second level to the room, almost approximating a loft. "*Nu*, Dragon?"

The horse walked up to them and transformed, but when they climbed onto her back, her wings flapped uselessly without lifting anyone into the air. "What's the matter?"

"She needs rest," Rivka pointed out.

They sat there on her back for a few more minutes until she was finally able to push, push, *push* herself upward. With a few last flaps of her wings, she landed safely on the loft and then abruptly curled up, breathing heavily. Her wings drooped uselessly at her sides like wilted beet greens.

From atop the dragon's back, the women surveyed the scene before them. This had apparently been one of the sorcerer's living quarters, but it was in utter disarray. All across the room lay upturned and broken furniture, and smaller objects like books and goblets were scattered here

and there at random.

And there, in the center of the chamber before them on a large rug of intricate geometric design, existed two unexpected sights.

One of them was a man of indeterminate age, dark-skinned like Shulamit's people but with hair in a foreign style, and wearing dark-blue robes, sprawled out on the rug. His face was contorted in agony, and the open-eyed stare over his jowly cheeks proclaimed him dead as dumplings. In his fist he clutched a crystal vial with a gold rim; only a few drops of the blue liquid inside remained in the very bottom corners.

The other sight was a voluptuous young woman, collapsed on the rug with her eyes closed, her clothing torn open and her limbs sticking out at odd angles. It was Aviva, and she wasn't moving.

Chapter 14: Bittersweet Discoveries

Shulamit scrambled down off the dragon's back so fast she lost her bearing. She landed hard on one unprepared arm and yowled in pain as her wrist protested the abuse. Rivka deftly dismounted and rushed to her side.

"I'm okay. I'm okay." Shulamit gasped, holding her arm close to her body. "Rivka, that's Aviva." No more words could she utter in her stunned amazement.

She tried to move toward the fallen girl, but Rivka intercepted her. "Can you move it?"

Shulamit experimented, and yelped at the result. "Ow-oww!"

Rivka felt up and down the afflicted limb. "I think you just sprained it. Just... take it easy for now. Or—wait. Where's that silk scarf?"

"Here." Shulamit took it out of her bag with her good hand, and Rivka quickly wrapped it around the sprain.

As soon as she was free of Rivka's protective grasp, she dashed to Aviva's side, ignoring the gnawing, twisted pain in her own arm. She put her good hand to Aviva's shoulder and drew back in horror when she felt something cold and hard instead of the warm, pliant flesh she was expecting. Not dead!—But, no, not dead, for now that she was close enough she could hear that Aviva still breathed.

Timidly but steadily, she brought her hand to Aviva's cheek and touched two fingers to her temple. The skin

of her face was warm and human. Shulamit's fingers slid down the side of her cheek down to her jawline.

A weak sound came from the other girl's throat, from behind closed lips. Then, finally, her lips parted. "Wa…"

"She needs water," shouted Rivka, bounding over from across the room where she'd been studying the corpse of what was most likely the sorcerer. "Here." She thrust one of the drinking vessels at Shulamit, who held it to Aviva's mouth.

Tangerine juice dribbled out onto Aviva's parched lips. Shulamit held the vessel carefully, and then slid her injured arm around Aviva's head to cradle her face upward slightly. She forced herself to ignore the pain and just concentrate on making sure most of the juice went into Aviva's mouth instead of running down her chin.

Finally, Aviva's lips began to move, helping the juice along, and then her eyes slowly opened. When she tried to speak it was in an unintelligible mumble, but Shulamit caught the word 'dream.' "I'm not a dream," said the queen. "It's really me."

Aviva couldn't say anything more, but a radiant look lit her gaunt face.

"We need to get more into her. She looks like she hasn't eaten for days." Rivka, in her exploration of the room, had found a side entrance that led into a small galley-style kitchen. She was opening cabinet doors and peering inside jars, looking for anything suitable.

"Riv—" Shulamit studied the body of her runaway sweetheart with a growing sense of understanding. "I think—it's like the holy women. Part of her—*most* of her's been turned to stone, but her head and this bit of her neck are still awake." She lifted one of Aviva's hands from the rug, and it came up much more easily than she had anticipated. "And where she's stone, it's not heavy like real stone. It's as light as if she were hollow."

"I found broth. Here. She'll need it to get strong again." Rivka brought over a drinking vessel she had found in the kitchen, filled with a broth that, from the smell of it, had been made from lamb or goat. "It's not hot, but that's not important."

Shulamit kept feeding her the nourishing liquid. "If that's the sorcerer over there, and she's been mostly turned to stone, I bet he cursed her before he died, but then died before the curse was complete."

"That makes sense." Rivka kept looking all around the room. "I hope there's another bottle of that curse blight Tamar kept talking about. The one he's holding is nearly empty, and I don't know how we're going to turn that entire courtyard of women *plus* your stone girlfriend over there back into regular human beings, with barely a full drop left."

"There's got to be another one somewhere around here."

"Why?"

"Because... bah." Shulamit had nearly said something as inane as *Because I'm the queen.* She was frantic with worry over Aviva, and since she still didn't know why Aviva had left in the first place, she was also filled with anxiety about whether or not Aviva wanted anything to do with her once she had nursed her back to health.

She tried to reassure herself by thinking of the happy look in Aviva's eyes when she had recognized Shulamit and realized she was real, but hey, maybe she was just happy to be rescued. Right now that was more important, anyway. Even if she didn't want to talk to her after she was safe, there was no way Shulamit would ever just leave her there.

They remained there for quite some time—Shulamit feeding Aviva meat broth or tangerine juice or water from Rivka's canteen, then letting her rest; Rivka stalking

about the room, poring over old books and peeping in every cubbyhole she could find; and Dragon resting in the corner of the room.

Then, weakly, from Aviva's mouth, came, "Thank you."

Sun rose on Shulamit's face. "Aviva! I—"

"I can't move," said Aviva.

"I think the sorcerer turned you to stone," said Shulamit. "I mean—that man over there—the dead one. Was he the sorcerer?"

"Yes, that was the bird man," said Aviva. "He's dead because he went hunting in the wrong forest, and the trees... rose up and swallowed him whole."

"I missed hearing you do that. But I still don't understand."

Aviva glanced down at her torn clothing, then back up at Shulamit—who had been trying to ignore the flesh exposed by the tears, especially since it was now disturbingly stone. "I came here as his hired cook and chambermaid. But he was an awful man, always looking for the next woman to pester. I knew that someday he'd try to force himself on me. So every morning after I bathed, I ground a fatal herb and spread it across my bosom. I knew that's where he'd start. Everyone seems to start there, with me... I guess it's only natural, with their size."

Shulamit flushed and wanted to cover her face with her hands because she fit neatly into that category herself, but she suppressed the impulse. "So, he ripped open your clothes, and...?"

"Got a mouthful of poison for his trouble," said Aviva. "He screamed at me that I was a witch, and drank the whole bottle of curse blight trying to save himself. But I'm not a witch, and herbs aren't magic. It wasn't a curse. It was just a poisonous plant. The curse blight did

nothing. So he cursed me, but he had his final seizure and died before the curse finished. And then I must have fallen asleep because I couldn't move, and I've had nothing to eat or drink in days. Oh, Lord, I'm so weak!"

Shulamit quickly fed her more broth, then began peeling a tangerine for her. "Aviva, I'm a terrible person for not waiting to ask this, but I'm going to explode if I don't know. Why did you leave the palace? What did I do?"

Aviva closed her eyes, and her face contorted with painful memory. "It had nothing to do with you. Nathan said he'd pay for my mother to have surgery that would make her nearly well again if I left the palace and never spoke to you again. I'm so sorry! That's why I was such a cactus those last few days. I had to do it. She's my *mother*."

"Nathan? The captain of Aba's guard?"

Aviva nodded. "He thought I was too lowborn to be seen... amusing you." She looked as if she wanted to crawl into a hole.

"He's a fool. And where did he get the money to pay for that surgery, anyway? He has seven children!"

"I don't know anything about that," said Aviva. "I just know it was a bag of old coins with a picture of your great-grandfather on them."

Shulamit's mouth dropped open. For several seconds she was unable to speak. Then she squeaked out, "I can't believe it. Rivka! Hey, Riv!" For a moment, she had forgotten to keep Rivka's identity private, but then she recovered.

Rivka bounded over, the curse-blight bottle in her hand. "*Nu?*"

"Remember that money I was telling you about? The money stolen from my father's treasury? Apparently, the captain of the guard took it, and used it to—What

insolence! What betrayal! Aviva—"

"I didn't know!" Aviva protested.

"Not *you*," Shulamit reassured her hastily. "You did what you had to."

"Well, I certainly reject my promise to him, now that I know the money wasn't his to give."

"*Good*, because I'm taking you back! I mean—will you—I know I—"

"Mint is cold and can resist the sun's heat by the strength of her convictions," said Aviva, "but mint is a plant, and plants wither and die without the sun." She looked up at Shulamit lovingly. "I hated it. I had to, but I hated it. I always wanted to stay with you."

"If Nathan were here right now, I'd fire him right on the spot! I want Riv to take his place anyway, but even though I'm queen, it's still hard to stand up to those guards sometimes! This will give me a good reason. Oh," she suddenly realized. "Aviva, this is Riv, the new captain of my royal guard."

"Hello," said Aviva. "I'm a cook, made of stone. Nice to meet you."

"Charmed," said Rivka, bowing.

"I'm sorry to call you Your Majesty," said Aviva, her face suddenly growing solemn.

"Then don't," urged Shulamit, taking one stone hand in hers, even though she knew Aviva probably couldn't feel it. "I'm always just your Shulamit."

"I'm grateful for that—that you can still say that after the way I left."

"You left because you were too good a person to let your mother go on in anguish and your father in a lifetime of service simply so you could be happy. How am I supposed to not love you *more* for being that kind of person?"

Aviva smiled briefly, and then her face grew cloudy

again. "But, Shulamit, that's not what I meant. I'm sorry to call you Your Majesty instead of Your Highness."

Shulamit's face fell. "Oh."

"I cried for you. While all of Perach mourned our king, I mourned Shulamit's father. I'm so sorry."

"Maybe your mother and father would come to the palace to live with us," Shulamit suggested. "My parents are both gone. In fact, I have very few people in the word that I like right now. You, and Riv, and sometimes my ladies-in-waiting when they aren't being tiresome."

"I hope you'll like them," said Aviva, smiling at the idea.

Then Aviva wanted to know how Shulamit and Rivka had come to the fortress, so they told her about the holy women who had been turned to stone. "I don't know what we're going to do if we can't find another bottle of curse blight," said Rivka.

"That's the only one," Aviva affirmed sadly. "And if he'd had more, he would have drained them too. He shouldn't have touched me..."

Shulamit was thinking again. "Aviva, is the magic in that bottle very strong?"

"The strongest," said Aviva. "It hardly takes any."

"But how would we get it spread across eighteen or nineteen grown women? Not to mention you there?" Rivka put her hands on her hips and sighed.

"There's that basin of holy water on the roof," suggested the queen. "If the magic is powerful enough, we could put the bottle at the bottom of the basin, and then... if Sister Tamar lets us... we could knock down the front of the basin. The water would spill down into the courtyard, and—"

"—soak all the women at once. I think it could work!" said Rivka.

"Can you smash the basin?"

The warrior shrugged. "Probably. I don't know. I'll try. If it doesn't work, we'll have to carry it down the stairs in buckets one at a time."

"At least we have a place to start."

"Now that we have a plan, are we ready to get out of here?" Rivka put the crystal vial deep inside her clothing where it would be safe.

Dragon made a show of flapping her wings, to show that they weren't strong enough yet.

"Flying can't be the only way in or out of this room," said Rivka. "Unless these two have wings I don't see." She was pointing at the dead body and the mostly stone woman.

"Oh, there are stairs back down into the rest of the fortress," said Aviva. "They come out of the rock on his command. All the stones of this place obey him."

"That explains the rock walkway shooting honey and birdseed at us on the way in," said Shulamit.

"That doesn't do us any good. He can't command anymore." Rivka paced the room.

"It wasn't so much a command," Aviva explained, "as him putting his hand on the wall in the right place."

"He's still got hands," Shulamit remarked.

Rivka took a hold of the sorcerer's lifeless wrist and dragged him over to the wall. "Where?"

"Higher."

Rivka hoisted him up, while Shulamit marveled at her ability to play with a dead body without flinching. "Here?"

"Right where that crack is, between the two smaller rocks."

Rivka pressed the dead man's fist against the spot.

There was a low rumble. Far away, there was the sound of something crashing to the ground. Then the floor began to vibrate disconcertingly.

"That's not supposed to happen," said Aviva.

"The stone!" Shulamit cried with alarm. "It obeys his command, but now it can tell he's dead."

Rivka steadied herself as the room started to shake. "It didn't know before?"

"No, he died on the rug so his dead body hadn't touched the stone." Shulamit dragged Aviva out of the way of a falling piece of rocky ceiling. "All those enchantments and traps—"

Rivka's eyes flared in horror. "I bet he set this whole place to collapse if something happened to him!"

Chapter 15: Is It Here That I Learn Fear?

Hurry, Shula! Dragon!" Rivka ran over to Aviva and hefted the poor girl over her shoulder, then followed the queen to the beast. With the three of them on her back, the dragon scrabbled around the room on foot, trying her best to dodge falling rocks. Her wings flapped at her sides, trying to gain elevation.

"It's not working!" Shulamit burst into tears.

"Why is your dragon broken?" Aviva asked calmly.

"Dragon," Rivka muttered with her eyes closed. "You might just have to jump out the window and hope your wings figure it out before we hit the ground."

And a minute later, she had to, because the walls began to crash down around them. As Dragon burst through the open window just before the room was reduced to rubble, all four pairs of eyes—the beast's included—were screwed shut. But they stopped falling, and close to the ground the dragon's wings found a little strength. It was just enough to cushion their landing. Quickly, she transformed back into a horse and galloped away from the exploding pile of debris. Shulamit felt the oddly light bulk of Aviva behind her and leaned back slightly, keeping her safe between her own body and Rivka's. She could feel Rivka's knuckles digging into her back from where she had her arms around Aviva, but it was easier to endure that than think about what would happen if they let Aviva fall.

The horse couldn't go far on the rocky ground, but they

managed to make it far enough away that the sorcerer's magic no longer touched the rocks. With her hooves precariously pawing at the uneven ground, she stood in place as Shulamit and Rivka craned their necks around to watch the final destruction of the sorcerer's fortress.

"So that's that," said Rivka flatly, still holding Aviva tightly in both arms since she couldn't very well straddle a horse securely in her condition. "I hope what magic we found will work, because it's all we've got, for now."

"If she can't fly, does that mean we're stuck here?" asked Shulamit.

Rivka nodded. "But I think it's safe to camp. I'm used to the wild, and this is just like any other wild place, with that *schreckliches chazzer* gone." She looked over Aviva with wide eyes and a slowly nodding head. "To think of such a thing—"

"I had to do *something*," said Aviva firmly. "God made many plants and many creatures that taste of death. I merely copied a good defense."

"Like a lantana," Shulamit said, smiling flirtatiously as she played lovingly with Aviva's hair.

Rivka hopped down from the horse. "Come on. Let's set up camp."

Dragon transformed again, and Shulamit and Rivka placed the paralyzed Aviva against the curves of her cool, scaly flesh. "I know you're stone right now, but I'm afraid you'd chip if we set you up against those rocks," Rivka explained.

"Thank you, my lady."

"Please," said Rivka. "I'm no noble. And who said anything about lady?"

"Shulamit called you Rivka."

Rivka huffed. "Okay, fine. But keep it to yourself. I'm Riv." She wandered off suddenly into the distant rocks, her boots crunching on gravel.

"Your new captain is made of thunder," said Aviva. "Now she's going away to rain by herself. She doesn't want to get us wet."

"She has a lot to thunder about," explained Shulamit. "And I don't think she's trying to protect us from what's on her mind. There's something she's ashamed about, and she probably doesn't want to talk about it with anyone." Shulamit was thinking about the things the empty suit of armor said to Rivka back in the fortress, about how her impetuous, almost mindless bravery could have cost her the man to whom she had given her heart.

"How did you meet her?"

Shulamit covered her face with her hand. "There are things *I'm* ashamed about. Oh, Lord, Aviva... the things you missed. Never mind. Your mother's doing better, then?"

"Mostly," said Aviva. "She can walk now—can you believe it? We got her a cane and she can get around everywhere—the fields, the forests, or over to the neighbors' houses to tutor their children. You should have seen her face when we went out to the lake and she was picking ripe sea grapes to eat off the trees, just like in the old days. She can even go to the marketplace with Aba. He's so happy that he can go out and sell his clothing at the market again."

They continued talking until Aviva—who was still recuperating from nearly starving to death—was tired, and Shulamit held her until she fell asleep. Then the queen carefully extricated herself from the tangle of stone woman and scaly dragon flesh and went to find Rivka.

Shulamit walked with quiet steps down the rocks to where Rivka was standing, staring out over the cliff face at a magnificent landscape illuminated by the liquid gold of another sunset. She was careful to announce her presence when she was still a safe distance away, so that

Rivka, ever the warrior, wouldn't hear her footfalls and unsheathe her sword in alarm.

Rivka turned to meet her."*Nu*? Is Aviva unwell?"

"She's asleep." Shulamit stepped up beside her to gaze out across the trees in the valley below. "I'm sorry. I know you probably want to be alone right now."

Rivka nodded. "I'm just trying to figure it all out."

"I wish I could be as brave as you are."

"Is it really bravery, though? Or just stupidity? Maybe I'm just too foolish to think of what could go wrong."

"Too much thinking of what could go wrong is what keeps me cowardly," said Shulamit.

"Remember when the crystal ball exploded? There I was, about to put my hands on it. What if it killed us?"

"Remember when Dragon jumped out the window? We all could have died, but it was our only choice. If she had held back and thought about crash-landing, our deaths would have been certain." Shulamit paused.

"The fortress never would have collapsed if I hadn't put the dead man's hand to the wall."

"You didn't know it would do anything bad," Shulamit pointed out. "Don't blame yourself for not thinking of things you had no way of knowing. It's the same with what happened to you up north. You didn't know Isaac was anywhere near your uncle."

"You may be right, little Queenling. How does one as young as you speak such logic?"

"I don't really know anything," said Shulamit, "not really. I just badly need you back, the way you were. You're the strong, confident, brave woman I'm not, and I have so few people to turn to right now."

Rivka's expression softened, and she blinked several times, making the idea flash into Shulamit's mind that she might be holding back tears. "I guess... even if I'm partially to blame for Isaac... and then I couldn't save

him... I can only try to make up for it. I can't change it, and I can't stand still in this one spot forever."

"There've been at least two or three Yom Kippurs since all that happened. Haven't you atoned enough?"

"I've forgiven the invaders because they didn't know they were killing an unarmed man. I've forgiven my uncle because he never intended for Isaac to die. But... I've... never even thought about asking for forgiveness for myself. Probably because keeping that guilt helps me hold on to his memory."

"You'll still have all the love you both felt for each other."

"I'd feel like I was disrespecting him."

"He wouldn't want you to feel this way. And he wouldn't want you to have stayed alone so long for his sake."

Rivka's face wrinkled into a cranky scowl. "I'm not saving myself for a memory! I just don't fall in love every five minutes like a lady-in-waiting in some bard's tale."

"I'm sorry. I wasn't thinking." Shulamit looked down. "I know it's not *love*, but I notice women so easily. Even when I was missing Aviva with all my heart, there were the willing women, the statue, the—the make-believe trick woman back there...." *And I approached you, too, that way at least three times*, she added inwardly, glad they were past that.

"That's not how my mind works," said Rivka. "And you know, *Malkeleh*, yes, you're a little girl-crazy, but I can see it's different with Aviva. Now that you're around her, that serious mouth of yours smiles just a little bit more—your eyes open a little wider—you just seem more alive."

"I'm so glad we found her in time!" Then Shulamit instantly felt guilty, because Rivka was still alone.

Rivka must have read the frantic expression on her face

because she rubbed the queen's shoulder affectionately and replied, "Be happy—don't worry about me. Remember, there are plenty of real men who are career warriors and remain single. It's only on a woman that being unmarried looks odd. Like those men, I've got plenty of other things to do." She smiled slightly. "Not many can brag of triumphs and adventures like mine."

Shulamit took her hand and squeezed it comfortingly. "He would be *so* proud of you."

The warrior sighed heavily. "It's dark. We should go back to Aviva."

As Rivka followed the queen back to the sleeping dragon, she was surprised to realize that she actually did feel a little bit better. Maybe it was just allowing herself to think of Isaac that had lightened her mood. Even all these years later, picturing his face or imagining his voice made her feel as if she were full of bubbles. They might be bubbles of searing hot pain at this point, but they still filled her and made her whole.

There was also a beautiful new feeling growing within her as she slowly realized that for the first time in her life, a young person looked up to her and depended on her. So she vowed to honor her dead by being the strong woman Isaac would have been proud to see, and honor her living by being the strong woman Shulamit needed.

The next day, Shulamit awoke to find Rivka doing physical exercises around the rocks. "You're full of energy this morning."

"I had a great dream," said Rivka, and she turned a cartwheel.

Shulamit's eyebrows lifted. "Must have been some dream. I've never been able to move around like that."

"I dreamed about marrying Isaac," Rivka told her, practically bouncing off the rocks.

"When I wake up from good dreams I'm sad," Aviva observed. "Often as a child I'd dream that Ima was well again, and then when I woke up and realized she was still in bed, it would crush me."

"It's different when someone dies," Shulamit explained. "I'm happy to dream of my father, because I miss him and that way I get to see him again."

"What was the wedding like?" Aviva asked.

"I was wearing a fancy dress from my people, and he was in his cassock. We were standing in the empty room back there in the fortress—the room we figured was intended to trap the enlightened? Anyway, you performed the ceremony"—she pointed at Shulamit—"and my mother was there, and she didn't think my dress had enough jewels on it. And I kept worrying about whether or not I had bathed." She let out a ribald chuckle, flushing.

Dragon flapped her wings. A powerful wind swirled up around the three women.

"She can fly again!" Shulamit clapped her hands and jumped up and down. "To the holy house!"

"I'm thinking two days. We can leave now, if you're willing to eat breakfast while we ride."

Dragon lifted the three of them into the air as they passed old goat meat and tangerines between themselves.

They spent the next two days in flight, and Aviva entertained them with colorful renditions of the folktales of the region. When she had exhausted her supply, Shulamit picked up the conversational reins with memories of her

father, and Rivka talked of her years in battle fighting in this or that war for this or that king. When they camped again by the lake, they gathered more tangerines for the rest of the journey.

It was nightfall on the second day when they finally reached the holy house. Tamar was standing in the doorway reciting her evening prayer at the moon when the three women, followed by Dragon in her horse form, entered the garden. "Good evening," Rivka called out.

"You've returned, my son! I hope you are well, Your Majesty. Have you been victorious? And who is this?" The old woman hobbled toward them with her arms outstretched in welcome.

Rivka removed the crystal vial from where she had hidden it in her clothing. "Is this the curse blight?"

"Yes!" Tamar beamed. But then she squinted at the bottle. "But, my son, the bottle is empty!"

Rivka bit her lip. "Well, yes. But we have an idea. Actually, it was the queen's idea." She held out her hand toward Shulamit.

"If we put the vial deep into the holy water, and then Riv here breaks the front of the vessel, the water will flow down into the courtyard and free everyone at once." Shulamit's eyes were fixed with nervous intensity on Tamar, and Rivka hoped along with her that her suggestion would go over well.

"But... the holy water..."

"Needs to be put to practical use," Shulamit pointed out. She took Tamar's hands in hers. "We must save lives, Sister."

Tamar nodded solemnly. "Yes, we must." Then she noticed Aviva again. "This woman is stone, and yet not all stone!"

"He died before he could finish the curse," Aviva explained.

Tamar's eyes widened. "Then the sorcerer is dead?"

They explained how the sorcerer died, and how his death and the drought within the bottle were part of the same tale.

"It's too dark to do this work now," said Tamar. "I was just about to prepare myself for sleep. Do you wish to sleep upon the roof again?"

"Your Majesty, why don't you and Aviva take a room inside the temple for tonight," Rivka suggested. It had occurred to her that the lovers hadn't been alone, not *truly*, since their reunion, and she wanted to engineer an opportunity to give them privacy—even if Aviva was still made out of stone. With any luck, she'd be transformed tomorrow, and then they'd spend another night with the same sleeping arrangements without attracting undue attention. "Now that you have company, and that the sorcerer's no longer a threat, I hope you feel safer without me guarding you."

To be honest, she also relished the idea of a night to herself. When Tamar and the girls had finally gone to bed, she curled up against Dragon's comforting muscles and fell asleep as if blown out like a candle.

"Answering, Esther said: if I find favor in your eyes, if the king judges it to be good, then grant to me my soul and my people, in answer to my plea," Shulamit read, her voice rising dramatically. The only thing she'd found in the temple to read were religious stories, which didn't surprise her, but that was okay. Even in the mass of male-centered, violent tales, she could still find something that resonated with her.

Aviva listened intently from her position of forced repose on the bed in the modest cell Tamar had given

them for the duration of their stay. Her head was propped up against what cushions Shulamit had managed to scrounge, and now a loose lock of hair had floated into her face. She attempted unsuccessfully to blow it away. "My hair sticks are gone, aren't they?"

Shulamit looked up from the book and grimaced. "Yeah, sorry—I think you were wearing them when we found you, but then the fortress collapsed and Dragon was flying sideways—" She reached out a trembling hand and brushed Aviva's hair back out of her face. Heat coursed through her body at the intimate contact, but she mentally slapped herself because the sensation felt like taking advantage, given Aviva's condition.

"Shulamit?" Aviva was looking up at her with large, questioning eyes.

"Hmm?"

"If the power of that moon-juice died with the sorcerer," Aviva said in a heartfelt voice, "or if the magic runs out and there isn't enough for me—"

Shulamit instinctively tried to take Aviva's hands in hers, but then jolted at the feeling of cold stone against her palms. She looked into her eyes. "I'll still take you back to the palace and keep reading to you. Although you'll probably have to put up with things like *Kefir the Younger's Observations on Stalagmites* until I can find some good fiction for you. You know what kinds of things I usually read!"

"I've always admired that about you—that you want to know *everything* about your kingdom, even the rocks and plants." Aviva's eyes glittered. "That wasn't what I was going to ask, but I'll gladly come along. I was going to offer to teach. Even if I can't hatch out of my egg, I can instruct others. I just need a little help building the trellis—I can grow my own vine."

Shulamit exhaled. "Sometimes I can't even fathom your generosity."

"Then stop fathoming and get back to reading!" Aviva stuck her tongue out at her.

"You just want me to say the bad guy's name again so you can go back to making silly noises to drown it out."

"And *you* only picked this story because you have honey in your heart for Queen Esther."

"I guess I have high standards, then," Shulamit shot back, and returned to squinting at the book in the flickering lantern light.

The sun arose on the morning of the magic and bathed the temple in radiance. Shulamit brought breakfast up to Rivka and Dragon on the roof. "I carried Aviva out into the garden so she can be healed with everybody else. I can't believe how light she is, even though she's made of rock."

"Already in a week you're stronger—now you can carry a grown woman!" Rivka chuckled.

"A grown woman made of pumice," Shulamit amended. "I think that's what they call very light rocks. I read about it in a book on gems. At least she didn't get turned to gold!"

Rivka, munching on rice, looked out over the courtyard. "Where's Tamar?"

"Down there." Shulamit pointed. "She wants to be ready to greet her afflicted sisters when they return to life."

"Beautiful day for them to wake up to. Hey! Where're you going?" For Dragon had flapped her wings and lifted off the roof. She landed in the courtyard and returned to her horse form. Rivka soon had her answer as the mare began to graze heartily. "Breakfast time for everyone."

"I hope Tamar made enough food for the rest of her

flock. If not, if any of them are hungry when they come back to life, we'll have to work fast!"

Rivka took out the nearly empty crystal vial and placed it deep within the center of the calm still pool of holy water.

Shulamit stared down after it, sunlight glinting painfully into her eyes. Impulsively, she dipped one hand into the basin and then cooled her face with the water.

Rivka gave her a sharp glance. "What are you doing?"

Shulamit turned to look at her. "I know I'm not cursed. But if I didn't *try*, I'd feel silly later. Just in case." What would it be like to be able to eat challah again? Or enjoy the savory tanginess of chicken roasted with lemon and herbs?

"Poor Queenling!" Then a change came over Rivka's face. For a moment, she stood still, staring at the edge of the basin and centering her physical strength. Next, she unsheathed her sword.

Shulamit watched her in impressed awe as the warrior held her sword in both hands, pointed in the air. Rivka was breathing deeply. She might even have been praying.

Shulamit prayed too. The fingers of each hand, down at her side, separated into the hand position that looked like her initial, shin. *Shehkina*, feminine of God. *Female strength, do not fail us today.*

Rivka raised her sword.

Far away in the courtyard, Tamar looked up at her expectantly.

Down came the blade with a dull *bang*.

The clay chipped.

Rivka hacked away at the edge of the basin nearest the roof's edge, until finally a fissure formed. "You're doing it! It's working!" Shulamit exclaimed, her eyes sparkling.

Again and again Rivka brought her sword down upon the basin, until finally, a chunk came free. Water began to

flow. But it wasn't enough. "Faster!"

Rivka hammered away, until finally—

Splash went the water, carrying away pieces of broken basin with it. The holy water poured down from the roof, draining the broken basin entirely. It flowed into the courtyard, soaking each and every statue, including Aviva—not to mention Tamar and the horse.

Shulamit watched as color returned to the flesh of the statues. No more were they cold gray; a rich, healthy golden-brown flooded each woman from head to toe. Their simple robes returned to the brilliant mango color of the turmeric that had dyed them, and their hair was once more soft and black. It was incredible. She beheld Aviva stand up of her own accord, and she held out her arms to her beloved. "Aviva!"

Aviva came tripping up the center path toward the temple. "Shulamit! Oh..."

"Don't hurt yourself," Shulamit admonished her.

Tamar was toddling around between the women, greeting them with tearful, smiling hugs.

Then Shulamit noticed something she hadn't anticipated. Something was happening to the horse. She had been standing somewhere at the side of the courtyard, but she, too, was transforming—and not in a way they'd ever seen before.

"Rivka? Look at Dragon—she's—the curse blight is working on her too! She's not really a horse!" And as Shulamit kept watching, she could barely believe her eyes. The horse's body was rapidly shrinking into that of a human's—and—"She's not really a *she*!"

The queen clapped her hands to her face as the man crouching on the ground where the horse had been straightened his posture and stood to face the roof. He was stocky, tall, and lighter-skinned, like Rivka, with a broad chest and shoulders, muscular arms, and a bit of

a stomach. His dark-blond hair was cropped short, and his impish eyes looked up at them from beneath pointed eyebrows on a round face.

Shulamit wheeled around to face the warrior beside her. "Rivka?"

"*Isaac?!*"

Chapter 16: Has the Dragon a Heart?

One by one, the nuns began to notice the naked man in their midst. Some drew back in fright; others giggled, or hid their faces. Others merely pointed and murmured to those nearest. A few of them, the braver ones who had stood up to the sorcerer, charged toward him with their hand clasped into fists.

"*Do not harm him!*" Rivka shouted down from the roof. She stood there, as still as a statue herself holding her sword at her side. Finally, the impulsive warrior had encountered a moment that required her to wait and see before acting.

Shulamit, ever the intellectual, couldn't help peering down at the unclothed wizard. Since she had most recently known him as a female horse, she was relieved—for Rivka's sake, of course—to discover that no damage remained from the years without his own body. He may have been a mare, but now he was—well, an ordinary human male, with all the usual parts restored.

The visibility of those parts was causing a commotion amid the celibate holy women. Finally, one of them removed the headscarf that covered her hair and handed it to him.

He nodded to her in thanks. As she withdrew from him, he knotted it around his waist. Then he held his arms up to the sky.

"Hail this luminous day!" he bellowed, his northern

accent a bit stronger than Rivka's. His piercing blue gaze was fixed directly on Rivka, who watched him from the roof, breathing heavily but otherwise still. "And the hero who awakened me?"

Slowly, Rivka raised the arm that held her sword. The steel glinted in the sunlight.

"Mighty Riv," Isaac began, his voice this time slightly more cajoling, even slithering, "may I beg of you the fragment of cloth that you wear beneath your helmet? I'm unclothed and I don't want these good women should turn back to stone if they look upon me." A mischievous smile followed his words.

"It's only—" Well, of *course* he knew what it was! He'd been there the whole time! Without another word, Rivka took off her helmet and unpeeled the charred cassock fragment from her unruly blonde hair. She threw it down into the courtyard, where Aviva caught it and carried it over to the wizard.

He accepted it and manipulated it a few times, tossing it around and around as if trying to find something. With each turn, the fabric grew in his hands until soon it had become a full-sized cassock again. He wrapped it around himself and fastened all the closures, until he stood before Rivka just as he once had, far away in their northern homeland.

Then he lifted his head and spoke once more to the stunned woman on the rooftop.

"Mighty One," he began. "Three years ago my Wizard Order cursed me into the form of a mare, and I thank you for freeing me from that curse. It was a punishment intended to shame me. Thinking that I had already broken my vows, they declared them forfeit and cast me from the Order. They thought I devised new enchantments to obscure my activities with a certain lady, when they were mistaken and I never broke my vows at all. Now that

I'm free of both the curse and of my vows, I ask of you now—"

Rivka listened, obviously entranced and trembling slightly—

"Do you know where I might find that lady, and if she still feels as she did when she spoke intimately with her queen about me? Because, while I'd be perfectly content to ride with you and fight alongside you until the day I *truly* die, if that lady is willing, now that I'm free, I would beg of her the privilege of becoming her husband."

Rivka's voice rang out loud and clear down from the temple roof. "I know that lady, and she still loves you. She thought you were dead, but she never met a man worthy of succeeding you. She will *absolutely* marry you. There are things that fire cannot destroy." Rivka paused. "Speaking of which, how are you alive?! I'm so glad to see you, but I'm completely *fartumult*!"

"I will show you. Behold—" And Isaac, raising his arms in the air, transformed back into the dragon form. The holy sisters scattered in awe and pointed and stared as he flew up to the rooftop to join his warrior bride.

As soon as he was safely on the roof, he returned to human form—still in the cassock, Shulamit noted. She had to crane her head upward to look at him—he was even taller than Rivka, even if by only a few inches, and his broadness and height were startling and majestic like a baobab tree. "So..." She put her finger to her jawline and tapped it a few times thoughtfully. "The dragon form is one of your magical abilities, and not part of the curse?"

"Exactly, Your Majesty. The curse robbed me of most of my abilities and even my humanity. The power to transform into a dragon was the only thing I had left—and even that, they managed to weaken. You will find that my flight won't tire now as it once did—at least, not as easily."

"Oh, Isaac," was all Rivka could say, her breathing both deep and rapid.

"Why did they leave you with that?" asked Shulamit curiously.

"They'd nearly finished the curse when the attack began," the wizard explained. "My Order—my *ex*-Order, that is—they didn't want to get tangled up in the middle of the baron's feuding. Leaving me as I was, they fled for the mountains. They, uh, had *better* things to do."

"Just like Aviva!"

"So you flew out of the building before the second floor exploded?" Rivka's eyes were moving back and forth, as if she were putting the pieces together.

"I saw you jump out the window," said Isaac. "My intention was to fly over and join you, but after being drugged by the baron, my wings failed nearly instantly. I was a horse again before you came up for air, and then one of those *paskudnyaks* from Apple Valley was on my back."

"The other wizards really thought you'd—that you and I had—" Rivka flushed, and she wiped sweat from her face underneath the mask.

"The messenger mentioned you being there when he was taking down the baron's words," Isaac explained. "That was all it took, because honestly, they wouldn't believe that the baron's anger had nothing to do with anyone being seduced and deflowered. They knew what happened to your mother, and how it irritated the baron. When they woke me to berate me and cast me out, I protested that I never laid with you—I never laid with anybody in my life—and if we did anything against their arbitrary rules, they would have seen it, with all the enchantments watching over me. All they did was laugh and say I came up with a way to hide it from them. They stripped me, beat me up..."

147

"Horrible. I wish I'd known you were with me all along..."

"I had no way of telling you," said Isaac sadly. "A real dragon's mind can't understand written language, so I couldn't scratch it into the dirt with my claws, and when I was a mare, as part of the curse, I had a mare's mind, which was even worse. Yet, somehow, even as a mare, I still knew that I loved you... I just didn't know who you were, or what that meant." Then he turned to face Shulamit. "Your Majesty, you are, without a doubt, one of the most intelligent young women I've ever been lucky enough to meet. You read encyclopedias for fun. Surely your great brain can think of a reason not to be up here right now?"

It has been said that sometimes the intellect and the common sense do not necessarily occupy the same skull at the same time. Shulamit grinned with shame, then nodded. "I'm sorry. I'll go down to Aviva. Um," she added as she started for the stairs, "nice to meet you."

Rivka carefully sheathed her sword, unable to tear her eyes from the man before her. There were so many more questions she wanted to ask him; confidences to tell him; shared adventures to discuss. Three years of conversations they might have had burst forth from her mind at once, vying for fruition like dogs scrambling to be first on a bone. She gazed over those features she remembered so well. He was a ghost made real, a cherished memory now flesh that rose and fell with every breath, with eyes that blinked in the glare of the tropical sun and lips that twitched up subtly at the edges to smile at her, just as she'd remembered.

Now he was talking to her just as in her dreams, instead

of his heavily accented Perachi. "I'm sorry I eavesdropped on your private conversations with the queen," Isaac told Rivka in their native language. "Of course, it's not as if I had a choice."

"I need no privacy from you, Isaac," said Rivka, her eyes growing heavy-lidded and her voice confident. "I want *less* privacy from you."

Isaac smirked. "I should remind you that I've seen you bathing."

"I saw *you* down in the courtyard." Rivka was still digesting the fact that she'd gone from living in a reality where he had died years ago to seeing him naked within the span of forty-five seconds. Her body tingled, and the daylight felt even hotter than usual. "I never knew you could turn into a dragon."

Isaac nodded. "Dragons and other general serpent-type creatures. I'll explain it all later. The night the door stood between us, that's how I was able to get through the passageways unmolested. Didn't you wonder why you heard no footsteps as I approached? It was a lizard who wooed you that night. I stood on the door itself."

"A lizard!" She pictured what he must have looked like, his red dewlap pushing in and out, and shook her head with the sheer unexpectedness of it all. "It's still strange to hear you talk openly of wooing."

"Would it be strange if I touched you?" His voice had turned to chocolate.

"Very strange. And very delicious."

One of his hands took one of hers. Despite sleeping against him almost every night, this was the first time she had knowingly touched him. Her fingers grabbed at him hungrily, and she drew closer, eager for more.

"Mind yourself, *Riv*. You don't want to shatter the carefully constructed conceit I concocted down there."

"I'm glad you said those things," said Rivka. "Not

just to keep my secret, but also because I knew instantly that you were no mind-reading trick like the suits of armor in the sorcerer's keep. Absolutely nothing in my own mind would have produced such sly cleverness. I'm far too straightforward for that."

"You always have been. It's one of the reasons I love you." He moved closer, then quickly stopped and glanced down into the courtyard at the holy women. With a growl, he added, "Would that I had you alone."

His tone was so unexpected that Rivka moaned out loud before she realized what she was doing. Then she turned her head quickly. "There's the stairwell. The women are all occupied downstairs."

"And if they come upon us?"

"We're both warriors. We'll know if anyone approaches."

Bustling each other into the stairwell with the excitement of frolicking kittens, the warrior and the wizard disappeared from view.

From the moment his lips touched hers, her blood turned to wine and the wine into liquid fire. Both his hands were clasped firmly on her biceps, holding her body close to his. She wrapped every available limb around him, exploring wonderful unfamiliar territory with curious fingers. Now she was pressed against the wall, and he broke away from the kiss to nuzzle a trail with his mouth across her throat. Pushing aside leather armor, he tasted the side of her neck.

In between gasps of pleasure, she murmured throatily, "Isaac... mind your sword!"

"Why, do you mind it?"

"Hardly."

"That's two of those. You said you weren't—ahhh!—sly and clever. Maybe my sense of humor is rubbing off on you."

Rivka gasped again, craving him with an intensity bordering on pain. "I'm sorry. I don't have any more. You win."

"What do I win?"

"Many adventure stories begin with a dragon who carries off a virgin."

"Those same stories end with the dragon being conquered by a warrior."

"Oh, if we're not married soon I shall gnaw off my own head!"

"Marry me now." He took both her hands in his. "Can't Queen Shulamit help us?"

"What, really? Like in my dream?"

"In some countries the monarch has that power."

"I'm going to go ask her." Rivka broke away from him, but he pulled her back by one hand.

"One more kiss."

"Oh...."

Eventually, Rivka managed to get downstairs and into the courtyard. Isaac followed her, so the holy women wouldn't get nervous about having two strange men in the temple by themselves.

She found Shulamit seated next to Aviva, who was lying down on the ground being examined by the very woman whom Shulamit had first admired in statue form. "Riv! Guess what? It turns out that Keren is trained in healing arts. She's going to take care of Aviva while we're here and make sure she gets her strength back."

Rivka smiled. "I know we just banished you," she said in a low murmur, "but could you come back up to the roof for a moment? Isaac thinks you have... a certain privilege, as a head of state."

Shulamit understood instantly, and one hand flew to her mouth with happy surprise. "Oh! I—I don't know the words yet."

"Do they matter?"

"I guess not." She took Aviva's hand. "I'll be back. Queen stuff."

Aviva smiled back at her and then returned to answering Keren's questions about how each part of her body felt from the period of starvation and dehydration.

Shulamit and Rivka joined Isaac, who was waiting for them at the door to the temple. "She'll do it," said Rivka, "but she doesn't know the words."

"I won't hold it against her. She's got plenty of time to learn them later for other people."

The three of them clambered back up the stairs to the roof.

"Wait! I know one thing!" Shulamit bent down and reached into the wreckage of the holy water basin to pluck out the now completely empty crystal vial that had held the curse blight. "For him to step on."

She put it on the ground between herself and the impatient lovers, then stood straight up and blinked a few times. "Isaac of the Wizards and Rivka bat Beet-greens... oh, I'm so sorry, you should never have told me that. It stuck in my head, and now it came out because I'm flustered."

"Forget it," said Rivka, laughing. "I'm about to marry Isaac. Do you really think I care?"

Shulamit smiled with relief.

"It should be 'daughter of *Bitter*-greens', anyway," Isaac suggested. "Isn't your mother called Miriam?"

"Riv Maror," Rivka mused. She lifted one eyebrow. "I like it!"

"I like it too—I think it's really clever," Shulamit agreed. "If I had to think of a food that was bold and assertive like you are, horseradish is a good one! Anyway: Isaac and Rivka—may God bless you both with a lifetime of shared love, and may He forgive me for improvising.

Wait—don't we need a ketubah?"

"I promise to keep saving your life," said Isaac directly to Rivka.

"I promise to keep giving you reasons to want to," said Rivka back to him. They were both beaming.

"Since I can't remember what else to say—you're married now. Have a good life together. Oh, and the glass!"

With one stomp of her boot, Rivka smashed the thing to powder.

Isaac lifted his pointed eyebrows and smiled his impish smile, and Shulamit burst into giggles.

"What's going on up there?" called a voice from the courtyard. One of the sisters was looking up at them curiously.

"Your Majesty, please send the warrior down so that we may thank him!" called another. "He's too shy. We must have a feast!"

"Though our fare is humble, we're indeed grateful and wish to repay you both," spoke a third. "We thought he was coming down to receive his honors, but then you both went back up to the roof."

Isaac transformed back into a dragon and gave the two women a lift straight into the midst of the crowd.

Chapter 17: Sharing the Treasure

There was a great celebration, and the holy women played instruments and sang and danced for the four of them. When they knew the songs and dances, they joined in. Eventually, everybody wore themselves out and sat down on the ground to feast. Some of the women carried low, wooden tables out to the courtyard and spread the meal out across them. The food was simple, but there was enough to go around.

The two northerners spoke quietly in their own language while they ate. "The night when we were together and you were a lizard," Rivka asked, "you still spoke as a man. Sang to me, even. When you were a dragon these past three years, couldn't you speak and identify yourself?"

Isaac shook his head. "I was under too many curses. Sometimes it was hard to remember human language at all. That's why my first words to you today were in their language." He cocked his head toward the bevy of Perachis. "It's all I've been hearing lately."

"I wish you'd told me about your serpent powers," said Rivka, "so I had a chance of guessing it was you all along."

"I made a lot of decisions based on what I thought was best. One of them was not telling anyone more than I thought they needed to know—even you. I'm so sorry about that." He gazed deeply into her eyes. "Even

befriending you was a decision made from arrogance—I thought, with the celibacy vow, it wouldn't matter if I was friends with a woman, because—woman, man, everyone is the same if you're chaste and not supposed to love any of them. And maybe it would have worked out that way—if the woman had been anyone but you, Mighty One." At these last words, his eyebrows reached for her and Rivka had to wipe sweat off her face beneath her cloth mask. She wanted to touch him so badly it made her rib cage ache, but she looked away and ate another mouthful of rice instead.

When everyone was finished with the main meal, some of the holy women produced mangoes and litchis. As they peeled fruit and relaxed in the shade of the palm trees, the women listened to Isaac and Riv's stories of adventure and combat. They heard the story of the injury to Isaac's right hand (during which Isaac managed to accidentally start a rumor that Riv's cloth mask hid an even more grisly and disfiguring scar), and of their joint capture of the famous twin brothers who had robbed so many travelers in the lands just north of them. So raptly did the warriors' tales hold their attention that nobody noticed when the sky grew silver and the air alive with dead leaves.

And so the rain started up too quickly to avoid, and many of them were drenched as they scurried about clearing away dishes and tables and gathering up the piles of pits and peels to throw away. By the time everyone had bustled everything safely inside the temple, a gloriously heavy shower was pelting the courtyard.

Tamar toddled toward Isaac and Rivka, holding a lit lamp. "My sons, you'll be more comfortable drying off in our private meditation room. Come." She led them down the hall, and Rivka shot a shocked look at Isaac, barely able to believe their luck.

"I'm sure she's trying to keep our male eyes away from

her holy women's clinging wet robes," Isaac murmured in barely audible northern tongue. Rivka smirked.

Tamar opened a big, heavy door at the end of a hallway and showed them inside a room decorated with simple curtains designed to induce inner peace. "You'll need this lamp—there are no windows." She set the lamp down on the floor and stepped back into the hallway. "Come out when you've dried off your clothes, and we'll be waiting in the main hall. Thank you for all your stories. We enjoyed that so much!"

"And thank you for the food," said Rivka.

"Don't be alarmed if you hear heavy footsteps or thumping," Isaac piped up. "We may spar to pass the time."

Rivka stifled a laugh.

"Enjoy yourselves, my sons!" Tamar turned and started her slow walk back down the hallway.

Rivka closed the big wooden door and carefully made sure it was latched as sturdily as possible. Then she turned around, and burst into laughter as she beheld not Isaac the man, but a large python, as big around as her thigh in some places, slithering toward her. Its scales were a mottled yellow-and-cream color like rich pasture-fed butter, and its tongue flickered in and out of its mouth as it sniffed for her. Of course, at this point, she knew who he was.

She could also see Isaac's wet cassock on the other side of the room draped over a stone bench.

The snake glided across the floor and then began to climb up her left leg. As its squeezing muscles wrapped around her, she couldn't help quivering with pleasure, her back thrown against the door. "Stop showing off," she commanded. "I know I married a traveling menagerie, but right now I want my husband as a human."

"At once," said Isaac's voice from *somewhere*, and

then the snake dropped in a coil on the floor in front of her. He rose up again in human form and seized her in his arms. She caressed the massive bulk of his back and shoulders, kissing him, lifting her chin as he breathed fire across her throat like the dragon he was. His good hand was underneath her soaked tunic fumbling at the cord between the legs of her trousers, opening them to the air, and then his fingers brushed her skin directly.

Once more, Rivka had her back to a door and was moaning over love and desire for Isaac the wizard, but this time he was on the right side of that door—pinning her to its surface, holding her, and now joining with her. She stood with her legs wide and her arms around him, clutching at him and pressing him closer. Like a river overflowing its banks, ardor and relief poured from her heart and made her feel as if she were floating. Isaac was in her arms at last.

When the room stopped spinning, a panting, somewhat sweaty man rested his head in the soft place between her neck and her shoulder, his nose buried in her skin. "Who is this brave woman," he said softly between gasps, "who has pierced my heart?"

Rivka smiled, at peace, and held him.

She was still wearing her sword.

When Rivka and Isaac's clothing had dried enough to wear comfortably they emerged from their chrysalis, taking the lamp with them. They found the rest of the holy women scattered throughout the temple, mostly reading peacefully, but some cleaning or praying or working at various crafts. Aviva sat against the wall on a cushion made from something coarse and green, with her hands massaging Shulamit's head, which lay in her lap.

There was something suspicious about the position of Shulamit's body, and Rivka quickened her pace as she approached them. "Is everything okay?"

"Everyone else bites pita, but with my darling, the pita bites back," said Aviva.

Rivka lifted an eyebrow. "Shula, what did you—"

"I just wanted to see if the curse antidote had cured me."

"She just ate a bite or two, so it's only stomach cramps, thank God," Aviva explained. "But I couldn't even get her to a bed."

"Sorry." Rivka poked the queen's shoulder affectionately. "I can carry you somewhere more comfortable."

"I'll be all right," Shulamit said weakly. "I'm used to this." She drew her knees up closer to her chest. "Aviva didn't want to let me, but if I didn't try, I'd never know."

"Do you need anything?"

"Water might help," Shulamit mumbled.

Rivka and Isaac ran off in search.

"I'm so happy you're here to take care of me again," said Shulamit, burying her face in Aviva's lap. "Losing you hurt worse than these cramps."

"I hurt myself too," Aviva reminded her. "I just couldn't think of anything but how I owe my mother my life, and..." She hugged the girl in her lap.

"But we could have figured out a way to make *everybody* happy—maybe not honestly, but Nathan was a wicked criminal and he deserved to be tricked." Shulamit winced with pain, and when the wave of squeezing in her gut had subsided, she continued. "What's more, I want you in my life, by my side, forever, but now I'm scared

that the next time you're in trouble you'll run away again and I won't know anything about it. My brain runs and runs around in circles and keeps thinking of all these perfectly logical reasons that you wouldn't want to be around me, except they're really probably silly—"

"What do you want?"

"I—"

"I want you to feel safe. I'm sorry about the way I did things before, and I want to make sure I do better."

"Now I feel ashamed. What you did for your mother was wonderful. I don't think I have that kind of strength."

"I need to know what will make you feel safe."

"Just please—promise me that you'll tell me things from now on. If you need money, if someone threatens your family, anything. Owww..." Shulamit breathed heavily for a few seconds. "Whatever it is, we can—tackle it together.

"I promise."

"In any case, my father's money paid for your mother's operation, so I'm glad at least to know the money went somewhere good."

Isaac and Rivka returned with the water, and Shulamit drank deeply and rested.

That night before dinner, Keren examined the queen and determined that it was safe for her to eat again, and even that her wrist sprain was healing up quickly. She also declared that Aviva had recovered fully from her ordeal back at the fortress. The two ate heartily and then prepared for bed in the room in which they had slept the night before.

Only, this time there would be no Book of Esther, only their own version of the Song of Songs. Tonight would be a sanctified reunion of hands and bodies and dreams and sighs. This night would be the warmhearted self-satisfaction of knowing that you had brought her

pleasure, and the sweet gratefulness of your own pleasure under her touches.

They eventually dozed off, but as appealing as it sounds to fall asleep tangled up with another person without any clothes on, sometimes your arm falls asleep or they breathe on you funny and the situation may be more comfortable in the heart than it is on the limbs. Shulamit woke up again while it was still dark. She felt sticky and stale from falling asleep sweaty. In her effort to extricate the arm that had fallen asleep from beneath Aviva's body, she inadvertently woke her up. "Mmm," Aviva mumbled. "Your face smells of flowers."

She wasn't talking about the ones that grew on trees.

Shulamit grinned awkwardly. "Yours too. We should probably go out to the creek in the back of the temple and clean up before we present ourselves to anybody."

"Good idea," said Aviva, still groggy. The only movement she made was to plant a hand on each of Shulamit's hips and pull her back on top of her.

"Well, since we haven't bathed *yet*..." Shulamit murmured, and slithered down in between Aviva's legs.

When, as Aviva phrased it, "the soft little kittens had finished meowing," the girls put their clothing back on and made their way to the back of the temple as best they could without being seen. They dodged two women who were on breakfast duty and a third who was doing the cleaning, holding themselves flat against the wall and moving in shadows, all while trying their hardest not to giggle. Finally they were outside, in a quiet gray world of predawn mist. Birdcalls rang from distant trees, preparing the way for the inevitable sunrise.

Rivka was already in the water, scrubbing away her own trophies. "She's glowing," Aviva whispered, giggling. "I bet she can even understand the birds." Then she raised her voice. "Good morning, Riv! What are the

birds singing about today?"

The warrior raised her eyebrows in amusement and waved to them. "They're saying it's good you two are up. We can get an early start. We'll stay in Ir Ilan tonight, but we'll have to make it to the marketplace in time to get Shulamit her dinner."

"Where's Isaac?" asked Shulamit.

Rivka cocked her head upward. "He went back to sleep."

Shulamit and Aviva looked up and saw the snoozing dragon on the rooftop. "So, we can fly on his back the whole time on the way home?" Shulamit asked as they removed their clothing and entered the water.

Rivka nodded. "His stamina will be much better now that we've lifted the curse."

"But you won't have a horse anymore."

Rivka smirked at her. "Guess I'll only have a dragon!"

"And a husband," Shulamit pointed out. "We should be home by tomorrow night. Then I can send Nathan away and put you in his place. His crime doesn't fit his position."

"Will the rest of the guards resent me if I displace him so suddenly?" Rivka asked.

"There's something neither of you know," said Aviva. "Each time King Noach gave him more money to increase the wages of the guards, Nathan told himself it would be permissible, just this once, to keep it for himself—because of his growing family."

Shulamit's eyes were once again saucers. "How did you find out?"

"He sent his older sons with the money in the bag to pay the surgeons directly, when they treated Ima," said Aviva. "I was thrown together with them a bit during the ordeal. They liked me a little too much, and it was hard to get away from them. Remember what I said about

my bosom. Anyway, I encouraged them to flirt with the Lady Wine instead of me, and they told her many secrets that I had the benefit of overhearing. Lady Wine knows everyone's secrets."

"When I'm drunk, I just sing louder," Rivka muttered. "So if I pay them the wages they deserve—"

"Besides, they've already heard of your reputation," Shulamit pointed out. "They hired you to rescue me from the kidnappers."

"Some of my captures—as a bounty hunter—are a bit well-known, to those in the trade," Rivka acceded.

"How did you get the job at the bawdy house, before you had all your war experience?" Shulamit asked. "I mean, I know Isaac had taught you how to swordfight, and you'd been in the one battle back home, but you weren't, you know, *the mighty Riv* yet."

"I was staying there as a guest—it was also an inn— mostly just keeping to myself so I could practice with my sword, except when I was looking for odd jobs to earn money. And one night, one of the customers tried to attack one of the willing women. Seems he was, uh, having some trouble."

"His leaves had wilted," Aviva supplied helpfully.

"Exactly. Anyway, he blamed Raizel for his own deficiencies, and things got violent. I heard the commotion and the screaming and grabbed my sword. He ended up tossed out the window into a pile of rotting kitchen scrapings. I threw his luggage out after him, after taking out Raizel's fee."

"I wish I could have seen that," said Shulamit admiringly.

"The rest of the willing women were clustered in the hallway at that point, and they'd all seen what happened. They pretty much demanded that I stay on as their guard. Shayna—the madam—her lover had walked out on her

and he'd been the guard before me. That's why they didn't have anyone to protect them that night. So I agreed to stay on. Of course, a few of them found it necessary to insist that I understand their rule against the guard making free with their services. You've known me for only a week or two but you've already seen how direct I am—and this was the middle of the night, only weeks after I thought I'd lost Isaac and left the only home I'd ever known. I simply opened my shirt, and said that I had a pair of my own and wasn't interested, so they didn't have to worry."

Shulamit wilted.

"I'm sorry, Queenling," Rivka added. "I wasn't really thinking about women like you two. To be honest I'm not sure I knew it existed at that point."

Shulamit's expression softened, and then broke into a smile. "And then, despite all your talk of loving only men, you spent three years loving a soul imprisoned inside a female body."

"I knew you weren't going to let that alone." Rivka splashed her in the face, then quickly got out of the water and started pulling on her clothing. "Better get dressed before the holy women see all this and bust up my cover."

Shulamit grinned. "Right before I met you, I was thinking that I wanted to fire all my guards and replace them with men who were like Aviva and me. Now, with you and Isaac around, that's what you're going to look like."

"*Feh*," Rivka said with a shrug. "I've got Isaac back, and I'm about to start my dream job. Plus, I'm good at what I do! So the rest doesn't matter."

Rivka walked away a little distance into the trees, giving the girls some privacy. Gazing back at the temple,

Rivka could see the black-green of her husband still asleep in dragon form on the roof. She felt overwhelmed by joy, and clasped a paper to her breast.

In the golden light of sunrise, she reread the words to which she'd awoken.

My beloved, my wife, my Mighty One—

You've fallen asleep (and no wonder, considering our exertions!) but I can't sleep just yet—I'm still getting used to being myself again, and my mind is too active. So I snuck downstairs to find paper and ink and now I'm writing to you, with my clumsy left hand just as I did all those years ago when you were borrowing my books.

The morning you left your uncle's castle, I carried you away in a mix of sorrow and joy—I had lost most of my human faculties, but I was also filled with elation that we were together, fighting as we'd dreamed. You wept for me, and told me things about myself without knowing to whom you spoke. I was flattered and it felt good to hear it, but I quickly worked out a plan to reveal myself to you.

As soon as we'd gotten beyond the forest, you told me to land so you could bathe in the river. That was exactly what I'd wanted. But when I reached my claws to the mud, I realized to my mind-numbing horror that I'd forgotten how to write. I was devastated, and panicked. Do you remember how I scraped around, frantically, hoping physical rote memory would take over for my poor, feebled, curse-riddled mind? I think I even rolled in the mud, frustration shutting out all other thought.

Oh, Rivka, Rivka! To have you so close and not be able to tell you!

Then I had another idea, and used my left hand to point to my right hand, hoping you'd recognize the position of my scar. You were kind to me, but I think you said something like, "What's the matter, girl? Did your

paw get hurt in the battle?"

Once my mare form had put the idea into your head, it never occurred to you that I was anything but female. Dragons' anatomy is confusing for a beginner, I admit!

I was filled with despair, but then, the very next thing you did was peel off all your clothing to bathe, and I was so overcome that I lost control and turned back into a horse.

Do you remember saying kaddish *for me that night? As a dragon, I curled around you and held you, breaking that you were in such pain, but reveling in the straightforwardness and strength of your love.*

Writing this has calmed me down enough to sleep. I'm leaving this for you to find when you wake up—please let me sleep a little longer so I have enough stamina to carry you and the girls all day.

I love you, and I can't wait to spend the rest of my life with you—NOT AS A HORSE.

Your husband,
Isaac

Chapter 18: The Queen of Perach

The troupe joined the holy women inside the temple for breakfast, and after everyone had eaten, they said their farewells to the sisterhood. Then they were off once more on the dragon's back.

"Thank you for carrying us around this whole time," said the queen, who was riding in front because she was the smallest. "I'm a little bit embarrassed that we work you so hard, now that I know who you are!"

"She rode me into battle for two years," the dragon responded in a booming voice. "I'm used to hard work."

"Your voice sounds different when you're a dragon!" Shulamit tried to quantify the difference—the low tones were louder, somehow, and some of the beauty had fallen away, leaving behind a sort of raw, naked power.

"His voice comes from inside a great cavern now," Aviva observed.

"*Ay yay yay*, I've just figured out that you were in your dragon form when I first came to your door that night in my uncle's castle!" Rivka's head was thrown back in laughter.

"That only took you a whole day," quipped Isaac.

"I'm amazed that you could fit inside in this form!" Rivka exclaimed. "You must have been cramped."

"I was, but I think maybe I found it comforting at the time."

"But then why weren't you squeaky when you were

serenading me as a lizard?"

"I used extra magic to be able to use my human voice. Would you have been as impressed with me if I'd spent that whole night with you talking like a lizard?"

"You'd impress me even if you never spoke again," said Rivka, "but I do love listening to your voice."

"You have a wonderful voice," piped up the queen. "I'm not going to make you sing to us when you're already doing so much work to get us home, but I'm looking forward to hearing what that sounds like."

It was very late in the afternoon by the time the travelers reached Ir Ilan, but luckily for Shulamit, most of the stalls in the marketplace were still open. The northerners went off to buy Isaac some new clothes so he wouldn't be stuck wearing a black cassock under the tropical sun, leaving the two younger women on their own. "I got lamb over there last time." Shulamit pointed to the left. "It was pretty good, and I didn't get sick."

"Sounds good to me," said Aviva. "If Riv will let me use one of his smaller knives, I can make a salad for you from those vegetables over there." In public, they were already using all male words for Rivka.

"I'm sure he will—and I'd really like that."

"I'll come with you to get the lamb, first, and then we can pick out our crunchy friends." Aviva followed Shulamit over to the kabob stall, which both scrutinized for any trace of fowl before happily forking over coins with King Noach's picture on them.

"You'll be on the money soon, won't you," Aviva whispered as they left.

"I will! Isn't it weird?"

"Ooh, look at these lovely cucumbers." They were about five inches long and dappled dark green. Aviva began collecting them, while Shulamit swept her gaze over the rest of the vegetables on the table.

"What about onions?" asked the queen.

"Those onions are sweet," the farmer announced proudly.

"Oh, then definitely," said Aviva. "And lemons? Were they able to come to the party today?"

"I don't know what you mean, but I don't have any lemons. You can buy them two stalls down, from the man with the mustache. He's also got lemonade, and mint lemonade too."

They paid the man for the cucumbers and onions and hurried off to the lemon grower. "I'm so glad to be back to this market with you," said Shulamit. "When I was here last week, you kept popping into my head. I thought about how you always liked to shop for your own ingredients to get ideas, and I wished I was here with you."

"That's some wishing power," said Aviva, nuzzling her cheek against Shulamit's since she had too many thing to carry to take her hand.

Shulamit, feeling bold, turned her head and kissed Aviva on the cheek.

"Would you mind not doing that right in front of my shop?" called an unfriendly voice.

Both women started, and looked for the source of the complaint. It was the man with the mustache, the one whose lemons they'd been about to buy. Shulamit felt her face grow hot, and her heartbeat quickened.

"Excuse me?" Aviva asked politely.

"You two. You're disgusting. If everyone was like you, the human race would go extinct."

A poisonous sea began to boil in Shulamit's stomach, and she felt tears of anger spring forth from her eyes. But then she heard familiar voices behind her, one very deep, and both murmuring in the northern tongue—and she knew she was not alone. Still afraid but ignoring it, she

took a deep breath, lifted her head, and said haughtily, "Nobody's like me, and you can bet nobody's *ever* been like her—we're pretty amazing!"

"And we don't need lemons that badly if they're going to be as sour as you," Aviva added over her shoulder as they turned around.

Of course, Isaac and Rivka had been right there. Rivka's mask was secure, but it was still easy to tell that she was grinning heartily. "That's the spirit, *Malkeleh*!"

"I'm proud of you," said Isaac, smiling warmly. He had changed into a simple white tunic and trousers, newly purchased at one of the stalls.

"That wasn't fun," said Shulamit, trembling. "But I felt like I could do it because I knew you were there."

"That's what we're here for," said Rivka.

"May God always allow us to be there for you," added Isaac.

Aviva was peering around the marketplace quizzically. "Is anyone else selling lemons?"

They spent the night at a different inn with a reputation for reliability, and then one more day of traveling put the four of them within the palace walls. It was dark when Isaac finally landed in the garden before the great entrance, but people were still bustling about in the space between dinnertime and sleep. One of the guards, a tall, fit older man with shoulder-length hair, rushed up to greet them.

"Tivon!" Shulamit called out, hopping off Isaac's back and rushing toward him.

"Your Majesty! It's good to see you safe and home. I have news—" Then he broke off, noticing Aviva. "Aviva? Aviva the cook? Wherever did you find her?"

169

Shulamit waved away the question. "Never mind that for now. Where's Nathan? I have to see him, immediately."

"That's what I was trying to tell you," said Tivon. "He's gone off."

"What?"

"Left early one morning with only a bag of clothing and a sword," said Tivon to the astonished young queen. "His wife woke up and found herself alone. We were all eating breakfast in the courtyard when she came storming in, a babe at her breast, frantic to find him. It was all I could do to comfort her, poor thing."

Shulamit clapped her hands to her face. "The treasury! We have to get to the treasury." She rushed past Tivon into the palace.

Tivon hurried to catch up with her, with Rivka, Aviva, and Isaac in his human form following after. "Your Majesty! What is it?"

"She thinks Nathan stole from her before he left," Rivka called out.

Tivon whipped his head backward. "Stole? Not possible. Others were guarding it that night. Why would you think that?"

"He had already stolen from it once before," said Aviva, "to pay for my mother's surgery. That's how he bribed me to leave the palace."

"I remember him talking about some fool scheme like that," mused the guard. "He knew His Majesty King Noach, may he rest, disapproved of your—er, begging your pardon, Majesty—and thought he would get rewarded for sending you away. He was rewarded with words, not coin, poor wretch. I did wonder where he'd gotten the money from. He was already up to his ears in debt. That's why he left town—to escape the debtors."

"They'll come to scratch at his wife and children, won't they?" asked Aviva.

"I suppose we have to do something for them," said Shulamit, who had stopped rushing around at Tivon's reassurance that the treasury had not been under Nathan's responsibility during the time of his departure. "Oh! My mind is racing from traveling all day and then coming home to such excitement. I've forgotten my manners. Tivon, you've met Riv already, he whom you hired to retrieve me from the kidnappers."

"Yes. I enjoyed his company last week before you left for the temple. Good to see you, sir."

Rivka nodded. "Likewise."

"This is Isaac, his..." Shulamit dithered helplessly.

Sensing Shulamit's panic, Aviva faked a very loud sneeze.

"Isaac's a wizard," Shulamit added. "He'll be added on to the guard as auxiliary."

"Your Majesty, about the guard—" Tivon stopped, his eyes a bit uneasy.

"Yes? You were second-in-command under Nathan," Shulamit pointed out, girding her emotional loins for a conflict. "I suppose you're asking about the captaincy."

"Actually, I am. Your Majesty, I'm set in my ways and don't wish to change my role. I wish to continue serving you and doing my duty, but I don't want the responsibility of heading up the company. I don't want to let you down, but I need to be realistic."

Shulamit relaxed. "This works perfectly—Riv's going to be your new captain."

"Splendid!" Tivon clapped his hands together. "I'll find rooms for you both in the guards' quarters."

"We only need one room," Isaac piped up.

Shulamit and Aviva exchanged pleased looks. For an ordinary man to commit willingly to spending the rest of his life being mistaken for one of them was to win their admiration.

Tivon shrugged. "Fine by me."

Shulamit seized the opportunity to ask, "Tivon, are there any others in the guard who will be unhappy to see Aviva return, now that Nathan's damage has been... patched up?"

Tivon shook his head. "May I speak freely, Your Majesty?" When Shulamit nodded, he continued, "We'd rather your companion be someone we trust, and a resident of the palace. You're our queen and we've sworn to protect you with our lives; however, you have to meet us halfway. Anyone can pose as a willing woman. You simply can't put yourself in a position of that much vulnerability with a stranger. You owe it to your people not to make it that much harder for us to do our jobs."

Shulamit smiled. "I understand now. But I—well, never mind. Aviva's back."

"Will she be rejoining the crew in the kitchen?"

"I'd like to," said Aviva.

"Speaking of kitchens," said Isaac, "I'd like a meal, if that's possible. I should remind you all that I wasn't riding back there with the rest of you." He bestowed upon them a graceful, subtle smirk.

"Hurray! I can be useful again!" cried Aviva with joy. She grabbed his hand and pulled him toward the cooking houses.

Shulamit and Rivka watched them go, Rivka laughing softly to herself.

"Riv?" Tivon's voice broke into their reverie. "Let me show you where to put your things. Then you can go and join your companion in the kitchen."

As Rivka and Shulamit walked back from the guard quarters to the kitchens, they realized they were alone again for the first time in days. "Riv—" said Shulamit, turning toward her on the moonlit path, "thank you. Thank you for everything. I'm so blessed and lucky to

have found you—and not just because you brought Aviva back to me. Before our adventure, I felt like an overgrown princess. Now, I know that I can be a proper queen."

"I have to thank you as well," said Rivka gravely. "It makes me sick to think that if I hadn't taken you up on your offer, I'd have grieved for Isaac forever—with him right there under my nose."

"And under your rear," Shulamit quipped.

"See what good comes of helping people?" Rivka pointed out. "Think if you hadn't agreed to help turn the holy women back from stone. And if Aviva hadn't put her mother before herself, you'd never know who stole from your father."

"I'm so glad I gave you that second mango," said Shulamit, grinning. "You remember, back in the Cross-Eyed Tiger? When I bought it I couldn't make up my mind if it was an extra for me, or if it was for you."

"So, *nu*, Queenling—I know this is none of my business, but it will be eventually—have you thought about what you're going to do about producing an heir?"

"A bit," said Shulamit. "Someone in my position can't afford to ignore the question forever. I know it seems like this is my solution for everything, but I was pondering the existence of a young man with my own preferences. He could be Prince Consort, with his own companion, and then I can fulfill my duty to my country."

"How do you propose seeking such a man?"

A sheepish grin spread over Shulamit's face. "I hear there's a mercenary called Riv who's particularly experienced at such things?"

"Oh, you! Well, you'd still have to lie with your prince without pleasure, so you might want to reconsider that plan."

"I did have one other idea," said Shulamit. "You and Isaac might have a baby someday—"

"Never mind, never mind! I think I've heard enough ideas for one night."

Laughing, Rivka followed Shulamit back to the lights of the kitchen house, where both their sweethearts were waiting for them.

Acknowledgements:

Infinite thanks for the following golden souls:

My spouse, for putting up with having these characters move into our apartment with us, and invaluable revising help and advice. Not easy on me, but easy on my spirit.

My mother for introducing me to things like Judaism, Wagner, and feminism, all of which went into the crock-pot, and for always making sure I had enough to eat growing up.

My family, for encouragement, Yiddish consulting, and the connection with my heritage.

My amazing cheerleading in-laws, especially Kat.

Katharine "Kate the Great" Thomas O'Gara, for being the kindest, most patient critique buddy I could ever ask for, and Dr. Tof Eklund, for always being there to answer random questions even when hir schedule was eating hir like a rabid three-headed rhino.

Jane, Erika, Rachel, and Mina for their artistic enthusiasm.

Sarah, Rania, Erin, Lorena, Rosie, Beverly, Louise, Dr. Tony Offerle, and Dr. Alana M. Vincent for varied and assorted help.

Bonnie, for believing in my ability to write a novel since before puberty.

Two German musicians, Richard Wagner and René Pape, who inspired me to fly beyond my boundaries.

And finally, Jessica, my stalwart editor; Allison and Jo who helped proofread; and everyone else on the Prizm team!